Themes and Writers Series

G. Robert Carlsen

General Editor

FOCUS
Themes in Literature

PERCEPTION
Themes in Literature

INSIGHTS
Themes in Literature

ENCOUNTERS
Themes in Literature

AMERICAN LITERATURE
Themes and Writers

BRITISH AND
WESTERN LITERATURE
Themes and Writers

About the Editors of the Themes and Writers Series

G. Robert Carlsen, Professor of English and Professor of Education at the University of Iowa, has taught English in the public schools of Minneapolis and at the Universities of Minnesota, Colorado, Texas, Hawaii, and Iowa. He has served as a consultant in curriculum revision to a number of school systems in Texas, Iowa, Colorado, California, Oklahoma, and Virginia. For many years he was the book review editor of young people's books for the *English Journal* and was a coauthor of an edition of *Books for You.* Dr. Carlsen is a past president of the National Council of Teachers of English. He has written some seventy articles for professional journals and is coauthor of *The Brown-Carlsen Test of Listening Comprehension* and of the National Council of Social Studies' publication entitled *Social Understanding Through Literature.* He is also the author of *Books and the Teen-Age Reader.*

Ruth Christoffer Carlsen is a coauthor with Dr. Carlsen of several anthologies for young readers. She has also written successful juvenile books. Her research was of particular value in the development of the anthology series. As a coauthor with her husband she works on the development of anthology materials, in particular, for the texts *Perception* and *Encounters.*

Anthony Tovatt is Professor of English in Burris Laboratory School, Ball State University. He has been the director of an extended research study on the teaching of composition under the Program for English of the United States Office of Education. For eighteen years he edited the column "This World of English," which appeared regularly in *The English Journal.* Active over the years in the National Council of Teachers of English, he has made many contributions to materials that the NCTE has published and made available to classroom teachers. His articles have appeared in professional journals and his poetry has appeared in magazines and newspapers. Dr. Tovatt's colorful career began in a rural, one-room high school near a western Indian reservation where teachers before him had been intimidated by the students and beaten off before the school year ended. His stories of four happy years there read like some of Jesse Stuart's accounts of his early teaching experience.

Patricia O. Tovatt has taught English at both high school and junior high school levels in Colorado and Indiana. She works as a coauthor with her husband on the development of anthology materials, in particular for the texts *Focus* and *Insights.*

Edgar H. Schuster, Language Arts Coordinator for the Allentown (Pa.) School District, has taught English in both urban and suburban high schools in the Philadelphia area. He has also taught at the college level. He has written articles for many professional journals, including the *Clearing House,* the *English Journal,* and *Educational Leadership.* Dr. Schuster has been a Master Teacher at Harvard University and is a recipient of a Lindback Foundation Award for Distinguished Teaching. He is a coauthor of McGraw-Hill's *American English Today.*

Miriam Gilbert, Associate Professor of English at the University of Iowa, has taught English and American Literature at Iowa since 1969. Her primary work, both as a teacher and a director, has been with Shakespeare's plays. She has presented papers and led discussions on the teaching of Shakespeare, including two workshops for teachers at the Institute of Renaissance Students in Ashland, Oregon. At Iowa she has been a frequent teacher in the Literature Semester, a team-taught intensive survey course. Dr. Gilbert currently serves as Director of Undergraduate Studies in English at the University of Iowa.

AMERICAN LITERATURE

Third Edition
THEMES AND WRITERS

G. Robert Carlsen / Edgar H. Schuster / Anthony Tovatt

Webster Division, McGraw-Hill Book Company
New York, St. Louis, San Francisco, Dallas, Atlanta

Special Acknowledgment

The Editors and the Publisher wish to thank Mr. Lee Davis, English and Humanities Teacher, Sleepy Hollow High School, Tarrytown, New York, for his work on the Galleries of Fine Art and on the development of related gallery and humanities activities for the program.

Editorial Development: John A. Rothermich, Hester Eggert
Editing and Styling: Linda Richmond
Design: James Darby
Production: Suzanne Cox

Permissions: Karen Sekiguchi
Photo Editor: Suzanne Volkman
Cover Photo: Nicholas Foster/The Image Bank

Library of Congress Cataloging in Publication Data

Carlsen, G   Robert, date   comp.
    American literature.

(Themes and writers series)
Includes index.
SUMMARY: A thematically arranged anthology of poems, short stories, plays, novellas, and excerpts from longer works by American authors for the eleventh-grade reader.
    1. American literature.   [1. American literature—Collections]   I. Schuster, Edgar Howard, date joint author.   II. Tovatt, Anthony, joint comp.
III. Title.
PS507.C342   1979   810'.8   77-28400
ISBN 0-07-009867-0

Copyright © 1979, 1973, 1967 by McGraw-Hill, Inc. All Rights Reserved. Printed in the United States of America. No part of this publication may be reproduced, stored in a retrieval system, or transmitted, in any form or by any means, electronic, mechanical, photocopying, recording, or otherwise, without the prior written permission of the publisher.

Contents

Independent Spirit

The Comic Imagination

The Struggle for Justice

The Search for Values

DREAM AND PROMISE

America was always promises.
From the first voyage and the first ship there were promises. . . .
From "America Was Promises" by Archibald MacLeish

KAUTERSKILL FALLS
S. R. Gifford
Metropolitan Museum of Art, New York
Bequest of Maria DeWitt Jessup, 1915

To the oppressed peoples of the Old World the dream of finding freedom, of gaining wealth, and of building a heritage for their children in America was made doubly real. The dream was made real not only by the promise in the vast expanse of the rich and fertile land, but it was made real also by the promise enunciated in the assertions of our earliest writers and thinkers.

1

When John Smith, whom some have called the first true American, returned to England in 1609 from the ill-fated colony at Jamestown, he professed such a love for the new land of Virginia that he devoted himself to writing glowing tracts that would inspire his readers and listeners to dream the golden dream. If a person has both virtue and courage, Smith asked, "what to such a mind can be more pleasant than planting and building a foundation for his posterity, got from the rude earth, by God's blessing and his own industry? What so truly suits with honor and honesty as discovering things unknown? Erecting towns, peopling countries, informing the ignorant, reforming things unjust, teaching virtue. . . ? Then who would live at home idly, or think himself of any worth if he live only to eat, drink, and sleep, and so to die?"

Thus our beginnings were dedicated to the proposition that we do not merely exist but that we exist to be free. And it was this issue of freedom, freedom from British injustices, that sparked our war for independence and soon after gave impetus to the restless surge of people westward across the continent. From the Old World, too, came the teeming hordes of immigrants, sustained by the dream and the promise of this new land.

As you read the selections in this unit, ask yourself if the DREAM AND PROMISE of America are still forces in our lives and in our literature. Are traits and values like independence, courage, integrity, and equality still vital aspects of American society?

More than a century after Columbus's voyage. the dream
of going to the New World touched increasing numbers of Europeans.
What kinds of people came to this new land, and why did they risk its
uncertainties rather than remain in the country of their birth?
In the following excerpt from *Western Star,* a long narrative poem,
Stephen Vincent Benét must have been troubled by the same question. He
must have asked, "What was it like on the voyage and at the landing of those
sent by the East India Company to Virginia in the early 1600s?"

FROM

Western Star

STEPHEN VINCENT BENÉT

There was a wind over England, and it blew.
(Have you heard the news of Virginia?)
A west wind blowing, the wind of a western star,
To gather men's lives like pollen and cast them forth,
Blowing in hedge and highway and seaport town,   5
Whirling dead leaf and living, but always blowing,
A salt wind, a sea wind, a wind from the world's end,
From the coasts that have new, wild names, from the huge unknown. . . .

Gather them up, the bright and drowning stars,
And with them gather, too,   10
The clay, the iron, and the knotted rope,
The disinherited, the dispossessed,
The hinds[1] of the midland, eaten by the squire's sheep,
The outcast yeoman, driven to tramp the roads,
The sturdy beggars, roving from town to town,   15
Workless, hopeless, harried by law and State,
The men who lived on nettles[2] in Merry England,
The men of the blackened years
When dog's meat was a dainty in Lincolnshire,
(Have you heard the news from Virginia?)   20
The poor, the restless, the striving, the broken knights,
The cast-off soldiers, bitter as their own scars,
The younger sons without office or hope of land,

"Western Star" by Stephen Vincent Benét. Holt, Rinehart &
Winston, Inc. Copyright 1943 by Rosemary Carr Benét.
Copyright renewed © 1971 by Rachel Benét Lewis, Thomas
C. Benét and Stephanie Benét Mahin.

1. **hinds,** hired farm laborers.
2. **nettles,** herbs with minute hairs that sting.

3

"James Fort"
under construction
in spring of 1607.

Glover and cooper, mercer and cordwainer,[3]
("Have you heard the news from Virginia? Have you heard?   25
Wat swears he'll go, for the gold lies heaped on the ground
And Ralph, the hatter, is ready as any man.
I keep my shop but my shop doth not keep me.
Shall I give such chances the go-by and walk the roads?
I am no hind to scratch in the earth for bread.   30
Nay, a stocking-weaver I, and of good repute
Though lately dogged by mischances. They'll need such men.
Have you heard the news from Virginia?")
Gather the waifs of the London parishes,
The half-starved boys, the sparrows of London streets,   35
The ones we caught before they could cut a purse,
And bind them out and send them across the sea.
("They will live or die but at least we are rid of them.
We'll pick the likeliest ones. Boy, what's your name?
Good lad. You sail in *The Fortune*. The fool looks mazed.   40
Well, give him a wash and see he is fitted out.
We'll settle his master later.")
                          Oh, spread the news,
The news of golden Virginia across the sea,
And let it sink in the hearts of the strange, plain men   45
Already at odds with government and church,
The men who read their Bibles late in the night,
Dissenter and nonconformist and Puritan,
Let it go to Scrooby[4] and stop at the pesthouse[5] there,

---

3. **cooper**\ˈkü·pər\ maker of wooden casks; **mercer,** dealer in textile fabrics; **cordwainer**
\kɔr ˈdwā·nər\ shoemaker.
4. **Scrooby**\ˈskrü·bĭ\ The Separatists, those who advocated withdrawal from the Church
of England, formed a group in Scrooby, England; then the group fled to Holland in
1608, to America on the *Mayflower* in 1620.
5. **pesthouse,** a public hospital for patients suffering from plague or infectious diseases.

Let it go to the little meeting at Austerfield.   50
(We must worship God as we choose. We must worship God
Though King and law and bishop stand in the way.
It is far, in the North, and they will not touch us here,
Yet I hear they mean to harry the sheep of God
And His elect[6] must be steadfast. I hear a sound   55
Like the first, faint roll of thunder, but it is far.
It is very far away.
Have you heard the news of Virginia?
                              Friend, I have heard
The burning news of the elections of God,   60
The comfortable word, the clear promise sealed,
My heart is shaken with grace to my heart's root.
I have prayed and wrestled and drunk at the living fount
And God walks with me, guiding me with His hand.
What matter your little news and your tinsel world?)   65

Have you heard the news of Virginia? Have you heard
The news, the news of Virginia? . . .

There were a hundred and forty-four, all told,
In the three small ships.[7] You can read the names, if you like,
In various spellings. They are English names,   70
William Tankard, Jeremy Alicock,
Jonas Profit, the sailor, James Read, the blacksmith,
Love, the tailor, and Nicholas Scot, the drum.
One laborer is put down with a mere "Ould Edward",
Although, no doubt, they knew his name at the time,   75
But, looking back and remembering, it is hard
To recollect every name. . . .

—It is so they perish, the cast grains of corn,
The blown, chance pollen, lost in the wilderness—
And we have done well to remember so many names,   80
Crofts and Tavin and Johnson, Clovell and Dixon,
And even the four boys, come with the gentlemen,
In a voyage somewhat topheavy with gentlemen,
As John Smith[8] found.
                              A hundred and forty-four   85
Men, on a five months' voyage to settle Mars.
And a hundred and five men landed on the strange shore. . . .

---

6. **elect,** belief that certain persons are favored, chosen by God for salvation.
7. **three·small ships,** *Sarah Constant* under Captain Christopher Newport who was given complete command of the group; the *Goodspeed* under Bartholomew Gosnold; the *Discovery* under John Ratcliffe.
8. **John Smith** became head of government in September, 1608.

And yet, a good voyage,
And others would fare worse in other ships,
Bad water, crowded quarters, stinking beef, 90
And, at the end, the hurricane and death.
Though this voyage carried a locked Pandora's box,[9]
Sure to make trouble, sealed orders from the Company,
Naming a council of seven to rule the colony
But not to be opened till they reached their goal. 95
It was the way of the East India Company[10]
But it worked badly here—on a four months' voyage,
With fifty-five gentlemen scattered in three ships
And each one thinking himself as good as the rest.
There were plots and gossiping, wranglings and suspicions, 100
"Have you heard what So-and-so planneth? Nay, bend closer.
My fellow heard him roaring in the great cabin,
Swears, when he's of the Council,[11] he'll have thy head.
But we'll pull him down from his perch."

                    The idle, human 105
Gossip of hot-blooded, quarrelsome men,
Cooped up together too long through the itching weeks
When you get to hate a man for the way he walks
Or snores at night or dips his hand in the dish,
But, most of all, because you keep seeing him 110
And cannot help but see him, day after day,
And yet, working harm, for when land rose out of the West,
The council-to-be was already badly jangled
And Smith, accused of mutiny, under arrest.[12]

And so, at dawn, on the twenty-sixth day of April, 115
Just over four months from London,
They sailed between Cape Henry[13] and Cape Charles[14]
And saw the broad Chesapeake,[15] and the wished-for shore.
We shall not see it as they, for no men shall
Till the end and the ruin have come upon America, 120

---

9. **Pandora's box** contained all human ills. Pandora, in Greek mythology, was the first woman sent to earth, as punishment for the world. She opened the lid of the box, allowing all the ills to escape, leaving only hope at the bottom of the box.
10. **East India Company** (1600–1858), chartered by English Parliament for trade with the Eastern Hemisphere.
11. **Council,** Council of Seven established by the Virginia Company to govern the colony.
12. **John Smith,** elected as president of the colony, became unpopular and was somewhat of a dictator. He was charged with inciting the Indians, starving the company, and planning to marry Pocahontas and make himself king.
13. **Cape Henry,** named for King James's elder son.
14. **Cape Charles,** named for the King's younger son, later Charles I.
15. **Chesapeake**\ˈchĕ·sə·pēk\ inlet of the Atlantic Ocean with its lower section in Virginia and upper in Maryland.

The murmuring green forest, the huge god,
Smiling, cruel, lying at ease in the sun,
And neither smiling nor cruel, but uncaring,
The vastness where no road ran but the Indian trail
And the little clearings of man were small in the forest,   125
The little dirt of man soon washed away,
The riches of man white shells and opossum skins,
The scalp of a foe, the ritual of the clan,
Squash-vine and pumpkin-seed and the deer's sinew
And the yellow, life-giving corn.   130
We shall not see the birds in their multitudes,
The thundercloud of pigeons, blotting the sun,
The fish that had never struck at an iron hook,
The beaver, breeding faster than men could kill,
The green god, with the leaves at his fingertips   135
And a wreath of oak and maple twining his brows,
Smiling, cruel, majestic and uncaring,
As he lies beside bright waters under the sun,
Whose blood is the Spring sap and the running streams,
Whose witchery is the fever of the marsh,   140
Whose bounty is sun and shadow and life and death,
The huge, wild god with the deerhorns and the green leaf.
We shall not see their Americas as they saw them
And this was what they saw.
Now we must follow them, into the wood.   145

They landed and explored.
It was the first flood of Virginia Spring,
White with new dogwood, smelling of wild strawberries,
Warm and soft-voiced, cornflower-skied and kind.
And they were ravished with it, after the sea,   150
And half-forgot their toils, half-forgot the gold,
As they went poking and prying a little way
In childish wonderment.
A handful of men in hot, heavy, English gear,
With clumsy muskets, sweating but light at heart,   155
Staring about them, dubiously but ravished,
As a flying-squirrel leapt from a swaying branch
And a gray opossum squeaked and scuttled away.
Oh, the fair meadows, the goodly trees and tall,
The fresh streams running in silver through the woods!   160
'Twas a land, a land!

"'TWAS A LAND, A LAND!"

Fired by dreams of gold, trade, and land when they had sailed from England, the ill-equipped and quarreling company that stepped ashore on the wooded island they later named Jamestown faced incredible hardship and danger. At first amazed and delighted by the sights and sounds of the bountiful land, they soon became afraid of the hostile Indians and the fatal fever and at once set about building a stockade and planting a few crops unsuited both to the climate and to the time of year. Woefully ignorant in the ways of establishing a self-sufficient settlement, they nevertheless looked about them in "childish wonderment" and exulted in the promise of "the fair meadows, the goodly trees," "the fresh streams running silver through the woods!"

"'Twas a land, a land!" Virginia, indeed, was an earthly paradise!

1. At that time in England what were conditions that prompted people to come to the New World?

2. What was the "Pandora's box" the company carried?

3. In line 86, Benét suggests that the men were "on a five months' journey to settle Mars." This comparison—a *metaphor*, to use the technical term—likens the voyage sponsored by the East India Company to a comparable undertaking today. As with any good metaphor, the comparison is not between two things that are totally similar. The voyage to Virginia does not compare in every respect with a trip today to Mars, but the comparison is rich in suggestive power. Note how effectively and briefly the metaphor makes the event take on meaning for the modern reader.

Metaphor is one of the resources used by writers to achieve intensity. Unless readers understand the implications of metaphorical language, they can hardly hope to appreciate literature fully.

Study the following metaphors and be prepared to say what the implied comparisons are. For example, in "a five months' voyage to settle Mars," the poet compares a voyage to settle that planet to a voyage to settle Virginia.

1. It is so they perish, *the cast grains of corn.* (line 78)

2. *The green god,* with the leaves at *his fingertips.* (line 135)

3. It was the first flood of Virginia Spring. . . Warm and *soft-voiced.* (lines 147–149)

In the hot early summer of 1776, the members of the Second Continental Congress sweltered in Philadelphia. Up and down the land the colonists seethed with the spirit of rebellion. Revolution was in the air. On June 11, the Congress voted to name a committee of five to draft a declaration of independence from Great Britain. John Adams and Benjamin Franklin, committee members themselves, made certain that young Thomas Jefferson of Virginia was named to the group. For, as Adams related, Jefferson had "a happy talent for composition. Writings of his were handed about remarkable for the peculiar felicity of expression."

The committee repaired to a muggy, horsefly-infested room over a stable, where Jefferson was urged, and reluctantly agreed, to write the first draft of the declaration. From his pen came the world-shaking document that is at once a clear-cut articulation of the American dream and the affirmation of its promise.

Declaration of Independence
July 4, 1776
The unanimous Declaration of the thirteen United States of America

THOMAS JEFFERSON

When in the course of human events, it becomes necessary for one people to dissolve the political bands which have connected them with another, and to assume among the powers of the earth the separate and equal station to which the Laws of Nature and of Nature's God entitle them, a decent respect to the opinions of mankind requires that they should declare the causes which impel them to the separation.

We hold these truths to be self-evident, that all men are created equal, that they are endowed by their Creator with certain unalienable rights, that among these are life, liberty, and the pursuit of happiness. That to secure these rights, governments are instituted among men, deriving their just powers from the consent of the governed. That whenever any form of government becomes destructive of these ends, it is the right of the people to alter or to abolish it, and to institute new government, laying its foundation on such principles and organizing its powers in such form, as to them shall seem most likely to effect their safety and happiness. Prudence, indeed, will dictate that governments long established should not be changed for light and transient causes; and accordingly all experience hath shown, that mankind are more disposed to suffer, while evils are sufferable, than to right themselves by abolishing the forms to which they are accustomed. But when a long train of abuses and usurpations,[1] pursuing invariably the same object evinces a design to reduce them under absolute despotism, it is their right, it is their duty, to throw off such government, and to provide new guards for their future security. Such has been the patient sufferance of these Colonies; and such is now the necessity which

---

1. **usurpations** \ˈyo͞o·sər·pā·shənz\ illegal encroachment upon or exercise of authority or privilege belonging to another.

constrains them to alter their former systems of government. The history of the present King of Great Britain is a history of repeated injuries and usurpations, all having in direct object the establishment of an absolute tyranny over these States. To prove this, let facts be submitted to a candid world.

He has refused his assent to laws, the most wholesome and necessary for the public good.

He has forbidden his Governors to pass laws of immediate and pressing importance, unless suspended in their operation till his assent should be obtained; and when so suspended, he has utterly neglected to attend to them.

He has refused to pass other laws for the accommodation of large districts of people, unless those people would relinquish the right of representation in the legislature, a right inestimable to them and formidable to tyrants only.

He has called together legislative bodies at places unusual, uncomfortable, and distant from the depository of their public records, for the sole purpose of fatiguing them into compliance with his measures.

He has dissolved representative houses repeatedly, for opposing with manly firmness his invasions on the rights of the people.

He has refused for a long time, after such dissolutions, to cause others to be elected; whereby the legislative powers, incapable of annihilation, have returned to the people at large for their exercise; the State remaining in the meantime exposed to all the dangers of invasion from without and convulsions within.

He has endeavored to prevent the population of these States; for that purpose obstructing the laws for naturalization of foreigners; refusing to pass others to encourage their migration hither, and raising the conditions of new appropriations of lands.

He has obstructed the administration of justice, by refusing his assent to laws for establishing judiciary powers.

He has made judges dependent on his will alone, for the tenure of their offices, and the amount and payment of their salaries.

He has erected a multitude of new offices, and sent hither swarms of officers to harass our people, and eat out their substance.

He has kept among us, in times of peace, standing armies without the consent of our legislatures.

He has affected to render the military independent of and superior to the civil power.

He has combined with others to subject us to a jurisdiction foreign to our constitution, and unacknowledged by our laws; giving his assent to their acts of pretended legislation:

For quartering large bodies of armed troops among us:

For protecting them, by a mock trial, from punishment for any murders which they should commit on the inhabitants of these States:

For cutting off our trade with all parts of the world:

For imposing taxes on us without our consent:

For depriving us in many cases of the benefits of trial by jury:

For transporting us beyond seas to be tried for pretended offences:

For abolishing the free system of English laws in a neighbouring Province,[2] establishing therein an arbitrary government, and enlarging its boundaries so as to render it at once an example and fit instrument for introducing the same absolute rule into these Colonies:

For taking away our Charters, abolishing our most valuable laws, and altering fundamentally the forms of our governments:

For suspending our own Legislatures, and declaring themselves invested with power to legislate for us in all cases whatsoever.

He has abdicated government here, by declaring us out of his protection and waging war against us.

He has plundered our seas, ravaged our coasts, burnt our towns, and destroyed the lives of our people.

---

2. **neighbouring Province,** Reference here is to Quebec, acquired by Britain in the French and Indian War and enlarged to include much of the land between the Ohio and Mississippi Rivers.

He is at this time transporting large armies of foreign mercenaries to compleat the works of death, desolation, and tyranny, already begun with circumstances of cruelty and perfidy scarcely paralleled in the most barbarous ages, and totally unworthy the head of a civilized nation.

He has constrained our fellow citizens taken captive on the high seas to bear arms against their country, to become the executioners of their friends and brethren, or to fall themselves by their hands.

He has excited domestic insurrections amongst us, and has endeavoured to bring on the inhabitants of our frontiers the merciless Indian savages, whose known rule of warfare is an undistinguished destruction of all ages, sexes, and conditions.

In every stage of these oppressions we have petitioned for redress in the most humble terms: our repeated petitions have been answered only by repeated injury. A prince whose character is thus marked by every act which may define a tyrant, is unfit to be the ruler of a free people.

Nor have we been wanting in attention to our British brethren. We have warned them from time to time of attempts by their Legislature to extend an unwarrantable jurisdiction over us. We have reminded them of the circumstances of our emigration and settlement here. We have appealed to their native justice and magnanimity, and we have conjured[3] them by the ties of our common kindred to disavow these usurpations, which would inevitably interrupt our connections and correspondence. They too have been deaf to the voice of justice and of consanguinity.[4] We must, therefore, acquiesce in the necessity, which denounces[5] our separation, and hold them, as we hold the rest of mankind, enemies in war, in peace friends.

We, therefore, the Representatives of the United States of America, in General Congress assembled, appealing to the Supreme Judge of the world for the rectitude of our intentions, do, in the name, and by authority of the good people of these Colonies, solemnly publish and declare, That these United Colonies are, and of right ought to be Free and Independent States; that they are absolved from all allegiance to the British Crown, and that all political connection between them and the State of Great Britain is and ought to be totally dissolved; and that as Free and Independent States they have full power to levy war, conclude peace, contract alliances, establish commerce, and to do all other acts and things which independent States may of right do. And for the support of this declaration, with a firm reliance on the protection of Divine Providence, we mutually pledge to each other our lives, our fortunes and our sacred honor.

"WE HOLD THESE TRUTHS . . ."

In addition to being an accomplished writer, Thomas Jefferson was a political leader, lawyer, planter, inventor, architect, and tireless reader of the humanitarian thinkers of the seventeenth and eighteenth centuries. From the latter he drew many of the ideas on human rights and liberty that he incorporated into the Declaration of Independence. All people, he believed, had rights—not only those who claimed rank or privilege. Everyone should be free to think, to speak, to establish a free press, to earn a living, and to seek happiness. The purpose of government was to benefit the people, not to exploit them. These ideals are the heady stuff of the American dream, but the promise of that dream could be realized only through our becoming an independent nation.

1. According to the Declaration, where does a government get its powers?

2. Compare the attitude expressed in the Declaration toward the British people with that toward King George III.

3. What pledge did the signers of the Declaration make to each other?

---

3. **conjured** \ˈkŏn·jərd\ called upon solemnly.
4. **consanguinity** \ˈkŏn·săngˈgwĭn·ə·tē\ blood relationship.
5. **denounces,** proclaims.

As the first settlements along the Atlantic seaboard were
fighting to become the thirteen states, ever-increasing numbers of intrepid
settlers pushed westward, at first over the Appalachian Mountains,
then across the Great Plains, heading toward the Pacific Ocean as they
sought the good soil, the good life. But with the cry of "Gold!"
at Sutter's Mill in California in 1848, adventurers from all over the world
went off to "Californy" with their wash pans on their knees.
They came, not to settle, but to dig and sluice and hammer. Here
was the promise of riches beyond their wildest dreams!

All Gold Canyon

JACK LONDON

It was the green heart of the canyon, where the walls swerved back from the rigid plan and relieved their harshness of line by making a little sheltered nook and filling it to the brim with sweetness and roundness and softness. Here all things rested. Even the narrow stream ceased its turbulent downrush long enough to form a quiet pool. Knee-deep in the water, with drooping head and half-shut eyes, drowsed a red-coated, many-antlered buck.

On one side, beginning at the very lip of the pool, was a tiny meadow, a cool, resilient surface of green that extended to the base of the frowning wall. Beyond the pool a gentle slope of earth ran up and up to meet the opposing wall. Fine grass covered the slope—grass that was spangled with flowers, with here and there patches of color, orange and purple and golden. Below, the canyon was shut in. There was no view. The walls leaned together abruptly and the canyon ended in a chaos of rocks, moss-covered and hidden by a green screen of vines and creepers and boughs of trees. Up the canyon rose far hills and peaks, the big foothills, pine-covered and remote. And far beyond, like clouds upon the border of the sky, towered minarets of white, where the Sierra's eternal snows flashed austerely the blazes of the sun.

There was no dust in the canyon. The leaves and flowers were clean and virginal. The grass was young velvet. Over the pool three cottonwoods sent their snowy fluffs fluttering down the quiet air. On the slope the blossoms of the wine-wooded manzanita[1] filled the air with springtime odors, while the leaves, wise with experience, were already beginning their vertical twist against the coming aridity of summer. In the open spaces on the slope, beyond the farthest shadow-reach of the manzanita, poised the mariposa lilies,[2] like so many flights of jeweled moths suddenly arrested and on the verge of trembling into flight again. Here and there that woods harlequin,[3] the madroña,[4] permitting itself to be caught in the act of changing its pea-green trunk to madder red, breathed its fragrance into the air from great clusters of waxen bells. Creamy white were these bells, shaped like lilies of the valley, with

---

1. **manzanita**\\'man·zə ▲nē·da\\ a variety of several evergreen shrubs of the western United States.
2. **mariposa lilies**\\ma·rə·▲pō·sə\\ plants of the lily family whose flowers of white, red, yellow, or violet are somewhat turban, or tulip, shaped.
3. **harlequin**\\▲här·lə 'kwĭn\\ a comic character dressed in multicolored tights, usually carrying a wooden wand or sword.
4. **madroña**\\ma ▲drō·nya\\ an evergreen tree or shrub with smooth bark, large shiny leaves, and edible red berries.

Reprinted by permission of Mr. Irving Milo Shepard, executor.

the sweetness of perfume that is of the spring-time.

There was not a sigh of wind. The air was drowsy with its weight of perfume. It was a sweetness that would have been cloying had the air been heavy and humid. But the air was sharp and thin. It was as starlight transmuted into atmosphere, shot through and warmed by sunshine, and flower-drenched with sweetness.

An occasional butterfly drifted in and out through the patches of light and shade. And from all about rose the low and sleepy hum of mountain bees—feasting sybarites[5] that jostled one another good-naturedly at the board, nor found time for rough discourtesy. So quietly did the little stream drip and ripple its way through the canyon that it spoke only in faint and occasional gurgles. The voice of the stream was as a drowsy whisper, ever interrupted by dozings and silences, ever lifted again in the awakenings.

The motion of all things was a drifting in the heart of the canyon. Sunshine and butterflies drifted in and out among the trees. The hum of the bees and the whisper of the stream were a drifting of sound. And the drifting sound and drifting color seemed to weave together in the making of a delicate and intangible fabric which was the spirit of the place. It was a spirit of peace that was not of death, but of smooth-pulsing life, of quietude that was not silence, of movement that was not action, of repose that was quick with existence without being violent with struggle and travail. The spirit of the place was the spirit of the peace of the living, somnolent with the easement and content of prosperity, and undisturbed by rumors of far wars.

The red-coated, many-antlered buck acknowledged the lordship of the spirit of the place and dozed knee-deep in the cool, shaded pool. There seemed no flies to vex him and he was languid with rest. Sometimes his ears moved when the stream awoke and whispered; but they moved lazily, with foreknowledge that it was merely the stream grown garrulous at discovery that it had slept.

The "well-dressed" miner in 1857.

But there came a time when the buck's ears lifted and tensed with swift eagerness for sound. His head was turned down the canyon. His sensitive, quivering nostrils scented the air. His eyes could not pierce the green screen through which the stream rippled away, but to his ears came the voice of a man. It was a steady, monotonous, singsong voice. Once the buck heard the harsh clash of metal upon rock. At the sound he snorted with a sudden start that jerked him through the air from water to meadow, and his feet sank into the young velvet, while he pricked his ears and again scented

5. **sybarites**\ˈsibə ˌrīts\ inhabitants of the ancient city of Sybaris, a city noted for its love of luxury and pleasure.

the air. Then he stole across the tiny meadow, pausing once and again to listen, and faded away out of the canyon like a wraith,[6] soft-footed and without sound.

The clash of steel-shod soles against the rocks began to be heard, and the man's voice grew louder. It was raised in a sort of chant and became distinct with nearness, so that the words could be heard:

> *"Tu'n around an' tu'n yo' face*
> *Untoe them sweet hills of grace.*
> *(D' pow'rs of sin yo' am scornin'!)*
> *Look about an' look aroun',*
> *Fling yo' sin pack on d' groun'.*
> *(Yo' will meet wid d' Lord in d' mornin'!)"*

A sound of scrambling accompanied the song, and the spirit of the place fled away on the heels of the red-coated buck. The green screen was burst asunder, and a man peered out at the meadow and the pool and the sloping sidehill. He was a deliberate sort of man. He took in the scene with one embracing glance, then ran his eyes over the details to verify the general impression. Then, and not until then, did he open his mouth in vivid and solemn approval:

"Smoke of life an' snakes of purgatory! Will you just look at that! Wood an' water an' grass an' a sidehill! A pocket hunter's[7] delight an' a cayuse's[8] paradise! Cool green for tired eyes! Pink pills for pale people ain't in it. A secret pasture for prospectors and a resting place for tired burros by hang!"

He was a sandy-complexioned man in whose face geniality and humor seemed the salient characteristics. It was a mobile face, quick-changing to inward mood and thought. Thinking was in him a visible process. Ideas chased across his face like windflaws across the surface of a lake. His hair, sparse and unkempt of growth, was as indeterminate and colorless as his complexion. It would seem that all the color of his frame had gone into his eyes, for they were startlingly blue. Also they were laughing and merry eyes, within them much of the naïveté and wonder of the child; and yet, in an

unassertive way, they contained much of calm self-reliance and strength of purpose founded upon self-experience and experience of the world.

From out the screen of vines and creepers he flung ahead of him a miner's pick and shovel and gold pan. Then he crawled out himself into the open. He was clad in faded overalls and black cotton shirt, with hobnailed brogans[9] on his feet, and on his head a hat whose shapelessness and stains advertised the rough usage of wind and rain and sun and camp smoke. He stood erect, seeing wide-eyed the secrecy of the scene and sensuously inhaling the warm, sweet breath of the canyon garden through nostrils that dilated and quivered with delight. His eyes narrowed to laughing slits of blue, his face wreathed itself in joy, and his mouth curled in a smile as he cried aloud:

"Jumping dandelions and happy hollyhocks, but that smells good to me! Talk about your attar o' roses[10] an' cologne factories! They ain't in it!"

He had the habit of soliloquy. His quick-changing facial expressions might tell every thought and mood, but the tongue, perforce, ran hard after, repeating, like a second Boswell.[11]

The man lay down on the lip of the pool and drank long and deep of its water. "Tastes good to me," he murmured, lifting his head and gazing across the pool at the sidehill, while he wiped his mouth with the back of his hand. The sidehill attracted his attention. Still lying on his stomach, he studied the hill formation long and

---

6. **wraith**\rāth\ a ghost, figure of living person supposedly seen just before or after death.
7. **pocket-hunter**, someone who hunts a small cavity containing gold.
8. **cayuse**\'kai▲ūs\ a native range horse, an Indian pony.
9. **hobnailed brogans**, coarse shoes of untanned leather with broad-headed nails on the soles to prevent wear or slipping.
10. **attar o' roses**, a fragrant oil made from the petals of roses.
11. **James Boswell** (1740–1795), famed biographer of Samuel Johnson who took meticulous notes of Johnson's conversations.

carefully. It was a practiced eye that traveled up the slope to the crumbling canyon wall and back and down again to the edge of the pool. He scrambled to his feet and favored the sidehill with a second survey.

"Looks good to me," he concluded, picking up his pick and shovel and gold pan.

He crossed the stream below the pool, stepping agilely from stone to stone. Where the sidehill touched the water he dug up a shovelful of dirt and put it into the gold pan. He squatted down, holding the pan in his two hands, and partly immersing it in the stream. Then he imparted to the pan a deft circular motion that sent the water sluicing in and out through the dirt and gravel. The larger and the lighter particles worked to the surface, and these, by a skillful dipping movement of the pan, he spilled out and over the edge. Occasionally, to expedite matters, he rested the pan and with his fingers raked out the large pebbles and pieces of rock.

The contents of the pan diminished rapidly until only fine dirt and the smallest bits of gravel remained. At this stage he began to work very deliberately and carefully. It was fine washing, and he washed fine and finer, with a keen scrutiny and delicate and fastidious touch. At last the pan seemed empty of everything but water; but with a quick semicircular flirt[12] that sent the water flying over the shallow rim into the stream he disclosed a layer of black sand on the bottom of the pan. So thin was this layer that it was like a streak of paint. He examined it closely. In the midst of it was a tiny golden speck. He dribbled a little water in over the depressed edge of the pan. With a quick flirt he sent the water sluicing across the bottom, turning the grains of black sand over and over. A second tiny golden speck rewarded his effort.

The washing had now become very fine— fine beyond all need of ordinary placer mining.[13] He worked the black sand, a small portion at a time, up the shallow rim of the pan. Each small portion he examined sharply, so that his eyes saw every grain of it before he allowed it to slide over the edge and away. Jeal-

ously, bit by bit, he let the black sand slip away. A golden speck, no larger than a pin point, appeared on the rim, and by his manipulation of the water it returned to the bottom of the pan. And in such fashion another speck was disclosed, and another. Great was his care of them. Like a shepherd he herded his flock of golden specks so that not one should be lost. At last, of the pan of dirt nothing remained but his golden herd. He counted it, and then, after all his labor, sent it flying out of the pan with one final swirl of water.

But his blue eyes were shining with desire as he rose to his feet. "Seven," he muttered aloud, asserting the sum of the specks for which he had toiled so hard and which he had so wantonly thrown away. "Seven," he repeated, with the emphasis of one trying to impress a number on his memory.

He stood still a long while, surveying the hillside. In his eyes was a curiosity, new-aroused and burning. There was an exultance about his bearing and a keenness like that of a hunting animal catching the fresh scent of game.

He moved down the stream a few steps and took a second panful of dirt.

Again came the careful washing, the jealous herding of the golden specks, and the wantonness with which he sent them flying into the stream when he had counted their number. "Five," he muttered, and repeated, "five."

He could not forbear another survey of the hill before filling the pan farther down the stream. His golden herds diminished. "Four, three, two, two, one," were his memory tabulations as he moved down the stream. When but one speck of gold rewarded his washing he stopped and built a fire of dry twigs. Into this he thrust the gold pan and burned it till it was blue-black. He held up the pan and examined it critically. Then he nodded approbation. Against such a color background he could defy the tiniest yellow speck to elude him.

---

12. **flirt,** a rapid, jerky movement.
13. **placer** \ˈplă·sĕr\ **mining,** the process of extracting gold by washing away sand and gravel.

This old print shows the many different methods used to mine gold in California.

Still moving down the stream, he panned again. A single speck was his reward. A third pan contained no gold at all. Not satisfied with this, he panned three times again, taking his shovels of dirt within a foot of one another. Each pan proved empty of gold, and the fact, instead of discouraging him, seemed to give him satisfaction. His elation increased with each barren washing, until he arose, exclaiming jubilantly:

"If it ain't the real thing, may God knock off my head with sour apples!"

Returning to where he had started operations, he began to pan up the stream. At first his golden herds increased—increased prodigiously. "Fourteen, eighteen, twenty-one, twenty-six," ran his memory tabulations. Just above the pool he struck his richest pan—thirty-five colors.

"Almost enough to save," he remarked regretfully as he allowed the water to sweep them away.

The sun climbed to the top of the sky. The man worked on. Pan by pan he went up the stream, the tally of results steadily decreasing.

"It's just boo-ful, the way it peters out," he exulted when a shovelful of dirt contained no more than a single speck of gold.

And when no specks at all were found in several pans he straightened up and favored the hillside with a confident glance.

"Aha! Mr. Pocket!" he cried out as though to an auditor hidden somewhere above him beneath the surface of the slope. "Aha! Mr. Pocket! I'm a-comin', I'm a-comin', an' I'm shorely gwine to get yer! You heah me, Mr. Pocket? I'm gwine to get yer as shore as punkins ain't cauliflowers!"

He turned and flung a measuring glance at the sun poised above him in the azure of the cloudless sky. Then he went down the canyon, following the line of shovel holes he had made in filling the pans. He crossed the stream below the pool and disappeared through the green screen. There was little opportunity for the spirit of the place to return with its quietude and repose, for the man's voice, raised in rag-time song, still dominated the canyon with possession.

After a time, with a greater clashing of steel-shod feet on rock, he returned. The green screen was tremendously agitated. It surged back and forth in the throes of a struggle. There was a loud grating and clanging of metal. The man's voice leaped to a higher pitch and was sharp with imperativeness. A large body plunged and panted. There was a snapping and ripping and rending, and amid a shower of falling leaves a horse burst through the screen. On its back was a pack, and from this trailed broken vines and torn creepers. The animal gazed with astonished eyes at the scene into which it had been precipitated, then dropped its head to the grass and began contentedly to graze. A second horse scrambled into view, slipping once on the mossy rocks and regaining equilibrium when its hoofs sank into the yielding surface of the meadow. It was riderless, though on its back was a high-horned Mexican saddle, scarred and discolored by long usage.

The man brought up the rear. He threw off pack and saddle, with an eye to camp location, and gave the animals their freedom to graze. He unpacked his food and got out frying pan and coffeepot. He gathered an armful of dry wood, and with a few stones made a place for his fire.

"My," he said, "but I've got an appetite! I could scoff iron filings an' horseshoe nails an' thank you kindly, ma'am, for a second helpin'."

He straightened up, and while he reached for matches in the pocket of his overalls his eyes traveled across the pool to the sidehill. His fingers had clutched the matchbox, but they relaxed their hold and the hand came out empty. The man wavered perceptibly. He looked at his preparations for cooking and he looked at the hill.

"Guess I'll take another whack at her," he concluded, starting to cross the stream.

"They ain't no sense in it, I know," he mumbled apologetically. "But keepin' grub back an hour ain't goin' to hurt none, I reckon."

A few feet back from his first line of test pans he started a second line. The sun dropped down the western sky, the shadows lengthened, but the man worked on. He began a third line of test pans. He was crosscutting the hillside, line by line, as he ascended. The center of each line produced the richest pans, while the ends came where no colors showed in the pan. And as he ascended the hillside the lines grew perceptibly shorter. The regularity with which their length diminished served to indicate that somewhere up the slope the last line would be so short as to have scarcely length at all, and that beyond could come only a point. The design was growing into an inverted V. The converging sides of this V marked the boundaries of the gold-bearing dirt.

The apex of the V was evidently the man's goal. Often he ran his eye along the converging sides and on up the hill, trying to divine the apex, the point where the gold-bearing dirt must cease. Here resided "Mr. Pocket"—for so the man familiarly addressed the imaginary point above him on the slope, crying out:

"Come down, out o' that, Mr. Pocket. Be right smart an' agreeable, an' come down!"

"All right," he would add later, in a voice resigned to determination. "All right, Mr. Pocket. It's plain to me I got to come right up an' snatch you out bald-headed. An' I'll do it! I'll do it!" he would threaten still later.

Each pan he carried down to the water to wash, and as he went higher up the hill the pans grew richer, until he began to save the gold in an empty baking-powder can which he carried carelessly in his lap pocket. So engrossed was he in his toil that he did not notice the long twilight of oncoming night. It was not until he tried vainly to see the gold colors in the bottom of the pan that he realized the passage of time. He straightened up abruptly. An expression of whimsical wonderment and awe overspread his face as he drawled:

"Gosh darn my buttons, if I didn't plumb forget dinner!"

He stumbled across the stream in the darkness and lighted his long-delayed fire. Flapjacks and bacon and warmed-over beans constituted his supper. Then he smoked a pipe by the smoldering coals, listening to the night noises and watching the moonlight stream through the canyon. After that he unrolled his bed, took off his heavy shoes, and pulled the blankets up to his chin. His face showed white in the moonlight, like the face of a corpse. But it was a corpse that knew its resurrection, for the man rose suddenly on one elbow and gazed across at his hillside.

"Good night, Mr. Pocket," he called sleepily. "Good night."

He slept through the early gray of morning until the direct rays of the sun smote his closed eyelids, when he awoke with a start and looked about him until he had established the continuity of his existence and identified his present self with the days previously lived.

To dress, he had merely to buckle on his shoes. He glanced at his fireplace and at his hillside, wavered, but fought down the temptation and started the fire.

"Keep yer shirt on, Bill; keep yer shirt on," he admonished himself. "What's the good of rushin'? No use in gettin' all het up an' sweaty. Mr. Pocket'll wait for you. He ain't a runnin' away before you can get yer breakfast. Now what you want, Bill, is something fresh in yer bill o' fare. So it's up to you to go an' get it."

He cut a short pole at the water's edge and drew from one of his pockets a bit of line and a draggled fly that had once been a royal coachman.

"Mebbe they'll bite in the early morning," he muttered as he made his first cast into the pool. And a moment later he was gleefully crying: "What'd I tell you, eh? What'd I tell you?"

He had no reel nor any inclination to waste time, and by main strength, and swiftly, he drew out of the water a flashing ten-inch trout. Three more, caught in rapid succession, furnished his breakfast. When he came to the steppingstones on his way to his hillside, he was struck by a sudden thought, and paused.

"I'd just better take a hike downstream a ways," he said. "There's no tellin' what cuss may be snoopin' around."

But he crossed over on the stones, and with a "I really oughter take that hike" the need of the precaution passed out of his mind and he fell to work.

At nightfall he straightened up. The small of his back was stiff from stooping toil, and as he put his hand behind him to soothe the protesting muscles he said:

"Now what d'ye think of that, by gum? I clean forgot my dinner again! If I don't watch out I'll sure be degeneratin' into a two-meal-a-day crank."

"Pockets is the darndest things I ever see for makin' a man absentminded," he communed that night as he crawled into his blankets. Nor did he forget to call up the hillside, "Good night, Mr. Pocket! Good night!"

Rising with the sun, and snatching a hasty breakfast, he was early at work. A fever seemed to be growing in him, nor did the increasing richness of the test pans allay this fever. There was a flush in his cheek other than that made by the heat of the sun, and he was oblivious to fatigue and the passage of time. When he filled a pan with dirt he ran down the hill to wash it; nor could he forbear running up the hill again, panting and stumbling profanely, to refill the pan.

He was now a hundred yards from the water, and the inverted V was assuming definite proportions. The width of the pay dirt steadily decreased, and the man extended in his mind's eye the sides of the V to their meeting place far up the hill. This was his goal, the apex of the V, and he panned many times to locate it.

"Just about two yards above the manzanita bush an' a yard to the right," he finally concluded.

Then the temptation seized him. "As plain as the nose on your face," he said as he abandoned his laborious crosscutting and climbed to the indicated apex. He filled a pan and carried it down the hill to wash. It contained no trace of gold. He dug deep, and he dug shallow, filling and washing a dozen pans, and was unrewarded even by the tiniest golden speck. He was enraged at having yielded to the temptation, and cursed himself blasphemously and pridelessly. Then he went down the hill and took up the crosscutting.

"Slow an' certain, Bill; slow an' certain," he crooned. "Short cuts to fortune ain't in your line, an' it's about time you know it. Get wise, Bill; get wise. Slow an' certain's the only hand you can play; so go to it, an' keep to it, too."

As the crosscuts decreased, showing that the sides of the V were converging, the depth of the V increased. The gold trace was dipping into the hill. It was only at thirty inches beneath the surface that he could get colors in his pan. The dirt he found at twenty-five inches from the surface, and at thirty-five inches, yielded barren pans. At the base of the V, by the water's edge, he had found the gold colors at the grass roots. The higher he went up the hill, the deeper the gold dipped. To dig a hole three feet deep in order to get one test pan was a task of no mean magnitude; while between the man and the apex intervened an untold number of such holes to be dug. "An' there's no tellin' how much deeper it'll pitch,"[14] he sighed in a moment's pause, while his fingers soothed his aching back.

Feverish with desire, with aching back and stiffening muscles, with pick and shovel gouging and mauling the soft brown earth, the man toiled up the hill. Before him was the smooth slope, spangled with flowers and made sweet with their breath. Behind him was devastation. It looked like some terrible eruption breaking out on the smooth skin of the hill. His slow progress was like that of a slug, befouling beauty with a monstrous trail.

Though the dipping gold trace increased the man's work, he found consolation in the increasing richness of the pans. Twenty cents, thirty cents, fifty cents, sixty cents, were the values of the gold found in the pans, and at nightfall he washed his banner pan, which gave him a dollar's worth of gold dust from a shovelful of dirt.

"I'll just bet it's my luck to have some inquisitive cuss come buttin' in here on my pasture," he mumbled sleepily that night as he pulled the blankets up to his chin.

Suddenly he sat upright. "Bill!" he called sharply. "Now listen to me, Bill; d'ye hear! It's up to you, tomorrow mornin', to mosey round an' see what you can see. Understand? Tomorrow morning, an' don't you forget it!"

He yawned and glanced across at his sidehill. "Good night, Mr. Pocket," he called.

In the morning he stole a march on the sun, for he had finished breakfast when its first rays caught him, and he was climbing the wall of the canyon where it crumbled away and gave footing. From the outlook at the top he found himself in the midst of loneliness. As far as he could see, chain after chain of mountains heaved themselves into his vision. To the east his eyes, leaping the miles between range and range and between many ranges, brought up at last against the white-peaked Sierras—the main crest, where the backbone of the Western world reared itself against the sky. To the north and south he could see more distinctly the cross systems that broke through the main trend of the sea of mountains. To the west the ranges fell away, one behind the other, diminishing and fading into the gentle foothills that, in turn, descended into the great valley which he could not see.

And in all that mighty sweep of earth he saw no sign of man nor of the handiwork of man— save only the torn bosom of the hillside at his feet. The man looked long and carefully. Once, far down his own canyon, he thought he saw in the air a faint hint of smoke. He looked again and decided that it was the purple haze of the hills made dark by a convolution of the canyon wall at its back.

"Hey, you, Mr. Pocket!" he called down into the canyon. "Stand out from under! I'm a-comin', Mr. Pocket! I'm a-comin'!"

The heavy brogans on the man's feet made him appear clumsy-footed, but he swung down

_____
14. **pitch,** refers to the downward slant of a vein.

from the giddy height as lightly and airily as a mountain goat. A rock, turning under his foot on the edge of the precipice, did not disconcert him. He seemed to know the precise time required for the turn to culminate in disaster, and in the meantime he utilized the false footing itself for the momentary earth contact necessary to carry him on into safety. Where the earth sloped so steeply that it was impossible to stand for a second upright, the man did not hesitate. His foot pressed the impossible surface for but a fraction of the fatal second and gave him the bound that carried him onward. Again, where even the fraction of a second's footing was out of the question, he would swing his body past by a moment's handgrip on a jutting knob of rock, a crevice, or a precariously rooted shrub. At last, with a wild leap and yell, he exchanged the face of the wall for an earth slide and finished the descent in the midst of several tons of sliding earth and gravel.

His first pan of the morning washed out over two dollars in coarse gold. It was from the center of the V. To either side the diminution in the values of the pans was swift. His lines of crosscutting holes were growing very short. The converging sides of the inverted V were only a few yards apart. Their meeting point was only a few yards above him. But the pay streak was dipping deeper and deeper into the earth. By early afternoon he was sinking the test holes five feet before the pans could show the gold trace.

For that matter the gold trace had become something more than a trace; it was a placer mine in itself, and the man resolved to come back after he had found the pocket and work over the ground. But the increasing richness of the pans began to worry him. By late afternoon the worth of the pans had grown to three and four dollars. The man scratched his head perplexedly and looked a few feet up the hill at the manzanita bush that marked approximately the apex of the V. He nodded his head and said oracularly:

"It's one o' two things, Bill; one o' two things. Either Mr. Pocket's spilled himself all out an' down the hill, or else Mr. Pocket's that rich you maybe won't be able to carry him all away with you. And that'd be awful wouldn't it, now?" He chuckled at contemplation of so pleasant a dilemma.

Nightfall found him by the edge of the stream, his eyes wrestling with the gathering darkness over the washing of a five-dollar pan.

"Wisht I had a good light to go on working," he said.

He found sleep difficult that night. Many times he composed himself and closed his eyes for slumber to overtake him; but his blood pounded with too strong desire, and as many times his eyes opened and he murmured wearily, "Wisht it was sunup."

Sleep came to him in the end, but his eyes were open with the first paling of the stars, and the gray of dawn caught him with breakfast finished and climbing the hillside in the direction of the secret abiding place of Mr. Pocket.

The first crosscut the man made, there was space for only three holes, so narrow had become the pay streak and so close was he to the fountainhead of the golden stream he had been following for four days.

"Be ca'm, Bill; be ca'm," he admonished himself as he broke ground for the final hole where the sides of the V had at last come together in a point.

"I've got the almighty cinch on you, Mr. Pocket, an' you can't lose me," he said many times as he sank the hole deeper and deeper.

Four feet, five feet, six feet, he dug his way down into the earth. The digging grew harder. His pick grated on broken rock. He examined the rock. "Rotten quartz," was his conclusion as, with the shovel, he cleared the bottom of the hole of loose dirt. He attacked the crumbling quartz with the pick, bursting the disintegrating rock asunder with every stroke.

He thrust his shovel into the loose mass. His eye caught a gleam of yellow. He dropped the shovel and squatted suddenly on his heels. As a farmer rubs the clinging earth from fresh-dug potatoes, so the man, a piece of rotten quartz held in both hands, rubbed the dirt away.

"Sufferin' Sardanopolis!"[15] he cried. "Lumps an' chunks of it! Lumps an' chunks of it!"

It was only half rock he held in his hand. The other half was virgin gold. He dropped it into his pan and examined another piece. Little yellow was to be seen, but with his strong fingers he crumbled the rotten quartz away till both hands were filled with glowing yellow. He rubbed the dirt away from fragment after fragment, tossing them into the gold pan. It was a treasure hole. So much had the quartz rotted away that there was less of it than there was of gold. Now and again he found a piece to which no rock clung—a piece that was all gold. A chunk, where the pick had laid open the heart of the gold, glittered like a handful of yellow jewels, and he cocked his head at it and slowly turned it around and over to observe the rich play of the light upon it.

"Talk about yer Too Much Gold diggin's!" the man snorted contemptuously. "Why, this diggin'd make it look like thirty cents. This diggin' is all gold. An' right here an' now I name this yere canyon 'All Gold Canyon,' b' gosh!"

Still squatting on his heels, he continued examining the fragments and tossing them into the pan. Suddenly there came to him a premonition of danger. It seemed a shadow had fallen upon him. But there was no shadow. His heart had given a great jump up into his throat and was choking him. Then his blood slowly chilled and he felt the sweat of his shirt cold against his flesh.

He did not spring up nor look around. He did not move. He was considering the nature of the premonition he had received, trying to locate the source of the mysterious force that had warned him, striving to sense the imperative presence of the unseen thing that threatened him. There is an aura of things hostile, made manifest by messengers too refined for the senses to know; and this aura he felt, but knew not how he felt it. His was the feeling as when a cloud passes over the sun. It seemed that between him and life had passed something dark and smothering and menacing; a

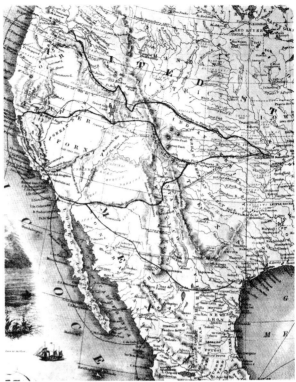

Map of Western United States, 1849, showing land and sea routes to the west coast.

gloom, as it were, that swallowed up life and made for death—his death.

Every force of his being impelled him to spring up and confront the unseen danger, but his soul dominated the panic, and he remained squatting on his heels, in his hands a chunk of gold. He did not dare to look around, but he knew by now that there was something behind him and above him. He made believe to be interested in the gold in his hand. He examined it critically, turned it over and over, and rubbed the dirt from it. And all the time he knew that something behind him was looking at the gold over his shoulder.

Still feigning interest in the chunk of gold in his hand, he listened intently and he heard the

---

15. **Sardanopolis**\ˈsar·də·nă ˈpŏ·ləs\ probably a reference to Sardanapalus, a weak, corrupt ruler of Assyria (*c.* 822 B.C.) who supposedly burned himself, his queen, and his treasures when threatened with capture.

breathing of the thing behind him. His eyes searched the ground in front of him for a weapon, but they saw only the uprooted gold, worthless to him now in his extremity. There was his pick, a handy weapon on occasion; but this was not such an occasion. The man realized his predicament. He was in a narrow hole that was seven feet deep. His head did not come to the surface of the ground. He was in a trap.

He remained squatting on his heels. He was quite cool and collected; but his mind, considering every factor, showed him only his helplessness. He continued rubbing the dirt from the quartz fragments and throwing the gold into the pan. There was nothing else for him to do. Yet he knew that he would have to rise up, sooner or later, and face the danger that breathed at his back. The minutes passed, and with the passage of each minute he knew that by so much he was nearer the time when he must stand up or else—and his wet shirt went cold against his flesh again at the thought—or else he might receive death as he stooped there over his treasure.

Still he squatted on his heels, rubbing dirt from gold and debating in just what manner he should rise up. He might rise up with a rush and claw his way out of the hole to meet whatever threatened on the even footing above-ground. Or he might rise up slowly and carelessly, and feign casually to discover the thing that breathed at his back. His instinct and every fighting fiber of his body favored the mad, clawing rush to the surface. His intellect, and the craft thereof, favored the slow and cautious meeting with the thing that menaced and which he could not see. And while he debated, a loud, crashing noise burst on his ear. At the same instant he received a stunning blow on the left side of the back, and from the point of impact felt a rush of flame through his flesh. He sprang up in the air, but halfway to his feet collapsed. His body crumpled in like a leaf withered in sudden heat, and he came down, his chest across his pan of gold, his face in the dirt and rock, his legs tangled and twisted because of the restricted space at the bottom of

the hole. His legs twitched convulsively several times. His body was shaken as with a mighty ague. There was a slow expansion of the lungs, accompanied by a deep sigh. Then the air was slowly, very slowly, exhaled, and his body as slowly flattened itself down into inertness.

Above, revolver in hand, a man was peering down over the edge of the hole. He peered for a long time at the prone and motionless body beneath him. After a while the stranger sat down on the edge of the hole so that he could see into it, and rested the revolver on his knee. Reaching his hand into a pocket, he drew out a wisp of brown paper. Into this he dropped a few crumbs of tobacco. The combination became a cigarette, brown and squat, with the ends turned in. Not once did he take his eyes from the body at the bottom of the hole. He lighted the cigarette and drew its smoke into his lungs with a caressing intake of the breath. He smoked slowly. Once the cigarette went out and he relighted it. And all the while he studied the body beneath him.

In the end he tossed the cigarette stub away and rose to his feet. He moved to the edge of the hole. Spanning it, a hand resting on each edge, and with the revolver still in the right hand, he muscled his body down into the hole. While his feet were yet a yard from the bottom he released his hands and dropped down.

At the instant his feet struck bottom he saw the pocket miner's arm leap out, and his own legs knew a swift, jerking grip that overthrew him. In the nature of the jump his revolver hand was above his head. Swiftly as the grip had flashed about his legs, just as swiftly he brought the revolver down. He was still in the air, his fall in process of completion, when he pulled the trigger. The explosion was deafening in the confined space. The smoke filled the hole so that he could see nothing. He struck the bottom on his back, and like a cat's the pocket miner's body was on top of him. Even as the miner's body passed on top, the stranger crooked in his right arm to fire; and even in that instant the miner, with a quick thrust of elbow, struck his wrist. The muzzle was thrown up and the bullet thudded into the dirt of the side of the hole.

The next instant the stranger felt the miner's hand grip his wrist. The struggle was now for the revolver. Each man strove to turn it against the other's body. The smoke in the hole was clearing. The stranger, lying on his back, was beginning to see dimly. But suddenly he was blinded by a handful of dirt deliberately flung into his eyes by his antagonist. In that moment of shock his grip on the revolver was broken. In the next moment he felt a smashing darkness descend upon his brain, and in the midst of the darkness even the darkness ceased.

But the pocket miner fired again and again, until the revolver was empty. Then he tossed it from him and, breathing heavily, sat down on the dead man's legs.

The miner was sobbing and struggling for breath. "Measly skunk!" he panted; "a-campin' on my trail an' lettin' me do the work, an' then shootin' me in the back!"

He was half crying from anger and exhaustion. He peered at the face of the dead man. It was sprinkled with loose dirt and gravel, and it was difficult to distinguish the features.

"Never laid eyes on him before," the miner concluded his scrutiny. "Just a common an' ordinary thief! An' he shot me in the back! He shot me in the back!"

He opened his shirt and felt himself, front and back, on his left side.

"Went clean through, and no harm done!" he cried jubilantly. "I'll bet he aimed all right, all right; but he drew the gun over when he pulled the trigger—the cuss! But I fixed 'm! Oh, I fixed 'm!"

His fingers were investigating the bullet hole in his side, and a shade of regret passed over his face. "It's goin' to be stiffer'n tarnation! An' it's up to me to get mended an' get out o' here."

He crawled out of the hole and went down the hill to his camp. Half an hour later he returned, leading his pack horse. His open shirt disclosed the rude bandages with which he had dressed his wound. He was slow and awkward with his left-hand movements, but that did not prevent his using the arm.

The bight of the pack rope under the dead man's shoulders enabled him to heave the body out of the hole. Then he set to work gathering up his gold. He worked steadily for several hours, pausing often to rest his stiffening shoulder and to exclaim:

"He shot me in the back, the measly skunk! He shot me in the back!"

When his treasure was quite cleaned up and wrapped securely into a number of blanket-covered parcels, he made an estimate of its value.

"Four hundred pounds or I'm a Hottentot,"[16] he concluded. "Say two hundred in quartz an' dirt—that leaves two hundred pounds of gold. Bill! Wake up! Two hundred pounds of gold! Forty thousand dollars! An' it's yourn—all yourn!"

He scratched his head delightedly and his fingers blundered into an unfamiliar groove. They quested along it for several inches. It was a crease through his scalp where the second bullet had plowed.

He walked angrily over to the dead man.

"You would, would you?" he bullied. "You would, eh? Well, I fixed you good an' plenty, an' I'll give you decent burial, too. That's more'n you'd have done for me."

He dragged the body to the edge of the hole and toppled it in. It struck the bottom with a dull crash, on its side, the face twisted up to the light. The miner peered down at it.

"An' you shot me in the back!" he said accusingly.

With pick and shovel he filled the hole. Then he loaded the gold on his horse. It was too great a load for the animal, and when he had gained his camp he transferred part of it to his saddle horse. Even so, he was compelled to abandon a portion of his outfit—pick and shovel and gold pan, extra food and cooking utensils, and divers odds and ends.

16. **Hottentot** \ˈhȯt ən ˌtȯt\ a member of the black race living in South Africa.

The sun was at the zenith when the man forced the horses at the screen of vines and creepers. To climb the huge boulders the animals were compelled to uprear and struggle blindly through the tangled mass of vegetation. Once the saddle horse fell heavily and the man removed the pack to get the animal on its feet. After it started on its way again the man thrust his head out from among the leaves and peered up at the hillside.

"The measly skunk!" he said, and disappeared.

There was a ripping and tearing of vines and boughs. The trees surged back and forth, marking the passage of the animals through the midst of them. There was a clashing of steel-shod hoofs on stone, and now and again an oath or a sharp cry of command. Then the voice of the man was raised in song:

"*Tu'n around an' tu'n yo' face*
Untoe them sweet hills of grace.
  (D' pow'rs of sin yo' am scornin'!)
Look about an' look aroun',
Fling yo' sin pack on d' groun'.
  (Yo' will meet wid d' Lord in d' mornin'!)"

The song grew faint and fainter, and through the silence crept back the spirit of the place. The stream once more drowsed and whispered; the hum of the mountain bees rose sleepily. Down through the perfume-weighted air fluttered the snowy fluffs of the cottonwoods. The butterflies drifted in and out among the trees, and over all blazed the quiet sunshine. Only remained the hoofmarks in the meadow and the torn hillside to mark the boisterous trail of the life that had broken the peace of the place and passed on.

I

THE DREAM-SEEKERS
AND DESPOILERS

Many of those who came to California seeking gold were impatient adventurers who had walked 2000 miles overland to reach the goldfields. They had no interest in the land and looked upon it as an infernal nuisance that stood between them and

riches. Land was something to be plundered.

In this story, the miner coming into the "green heart" of the canyon seems to appreciate the beauties of nature around him. Nevertheless, he soon sets about plundering the land of the wealth he discovers there. How do you think Jack London feels about the miner's intrusion into the canyon paradise?

1. What excites Bill when he begins to pan the canyon stream? How does he locate the pocket of gold?

2. How is he careless as he gets closer to his rich find? What strategies does he use to overcome his assailant? Why does he feel such indignation against him?

3. What is the value of Bill's find? What is similar about the descriptions of his coming to and leaving the canyon?

II

IMPLICATIONS

Reading should always be a pleasure. Whether a piece of literature is light or serious, readers will enjoy it more and understand it better if they let it stimulate their own thinking. After most of the selections in this anthology, you will find general questions or statements, called *implications*, like the ones below. Their purpose is to encourage you to evaluate in your own terms what you have read. These implications may be used for class discussion or as topics for brief written essays or for formal debates. And as these activities help you to clarify and organize your reactions to a selection, they will also sharpen your ability to express your own opinions accurately.

The object of these implications, however, is not to provide an outlet for the expression of prejudices. If you really think about the selections you read and the implications you are asked to consider, you should at the very least find some of your present ideas modified.

Consider each of the following statements in the light of your understanding of the selection, your own experience, and other reading you may have done. Remember that, in the interaction of discussion, an open mind that permits you to consider the other person's viewpoint also permits you to grow intellectually.

1. In humankind there is a greed, selfishness, and destructiveness not found in other forms of life.

2. Human beings will never dominate nature.

3. As the stranger would have victimized Bill, so Bill victimized nature.

III
TECHNIQUES

The Greek word for art is *technikos,* a word from which we get our word *technique.* (Our word *art* comes from the Latin, *ars.*) Technique is as important in literature as it is in music, painting, and sculpture. Good writers are distinguished from poor ones by their skill in handling words—their artistic medium.

In this section of the study notes, the techniques by which writers establish *setting* and *characterization* will be emphasized. In subsequent units other aspects of technique will be taken up. In addition, throughout the anthology these sections will focus attention upon the matter of how authors develop their themes.

Setting

In the broadest sense, *setting* includes the elements of *place, time,* and *atmosphere.* The relative importance of each of these elements depends upon the writers' purpose and the type of writing they are doing. In historical fiction, for example, authors usually are expected to give the reader a solid feeling of both place and time. In mystery or "ghost" stories, it is important for writers to create an appropriate atmosphere or mood. On the other hand, in certain types of writing, such as some forms of the essay, setting is not a consideration at all.

In "All Gold Canyon" the setting is of primary importance. It is not merely a backdrop against which the characters move but rather an essential part of the theme, overshadowing the characters in lasting significance. Jack London's minute description of place, the sheltered nook that is the locale for the action in "All Gold Canyon," covers seven rather lengthy paragraphs. What are some of the details that describe its beauty?

Atmosphere is usually more difficult to describe than place and time. It may be defined as the mood the reader feels throughout a literary work and is almost always established, at least in part, by the way an author describes place and time. Mood or atmosphere may shift as a story develops.

Everything in nature is in such perfect harmony in London's opening description that he communicates an atmosphere of sweetness and tranquillity. This mood changes, though, when the miner appears and then shifts back to tranquillity when he leaves. Pick out some of those details that create a tranquil atmosphere as the story opens, and then contrast them with the details given when the miner invades the canyon.

Characterization

Writers of fiction and nonfiction have at their disposal a number of ways to reveal the character of persons about whom they are writing. Perhaps the most important method is through what they have the characters themselves do and say. This is an especially good way of developing character because it allows readers to make their own estimates of the character of persons they read about.

In addition to this method, authors may describe characters directly in expository passages. Or they may reveal what characters are like by telling the way other characters react to them. Finally, authors may make comparisons between one character and another or others.

The way the reader is introduced to the miner, Bill, indirectly reveals London's attitude toward him. With his harsh noises, the '49er clashes with the perfection of the setting, but what he has to say is lively and colorful.

In the paragraphs that follow, London uses direct exposition to tell what the miner looks like: "He was a sandy-complexioned man in whose face geniality and humor seemed a salient characteristic. It was a mobile face, quick-changing to inner mood and thought . . . . His hair, sparse and unkempt of growth, was as indeterminate and colorless as his complexion. It would seem that all the color of his frame had gone into his eyes, for they were startlingly blue." The direct exposition is interspersed with description that tells what the miner says and does: "The man lay down on the lip of the pool and drank long and deep of its water. 'Tastes good to me,' he murmured, lifting his head and gazing across the the pool at the sidehill, while he wiped his mouth with the back of his hand."

What is the line the author uses to describe the man's thinking as a visible process? Why do you think London gave the man the habit of soliloquy? How does London's description of the miner's actions make him less attractive as he gets closer to finding the gold?

As Americans moved West they found two aspects of nature
unlike anything they had known in Europe: the vast forests of towering trees
and the broad, empty, hilly seas of grass we call prairies.
Both of these natural phenomena emphasized the smallness of the settler
and the difficulty of the pioneer's task. It was probably for these reasons
that they excited the imaginations of writers. Among the writers impressed
by the grandeur of the prairies was William Cullen Bryant,
who is often considered America's first great poet. Bryant composed
the following lyric poem after his visit to the Midwest
early in the nineteenth century.

The Prairies

WILLIAM CULLEN BRYANT

These are the Gardens of the Desert, these
The unshorn fields, boundless and beautiful,
For which the speech of England has no name—
The Prairies. I behold them for the first,
And my heart swells, while the dilated sight   5
Takes in the encircling vastness. Lo! they stretch
In airy undulations, far away,
As if the Ocean, in his gentlest swell,
Stood still, with all his rounded billows fixed,
And motionless forever.—Motionless?—   10
No—they are all unchained again. The clouds
Sweep over with their shadows, and, beneath,
The surface rolls and fluctuates to the eye;
Dark hollows seem to glide along and chase
The sunny ridges. Breezes of the South!   15
Who toss the golden and the flame-like flowers,
And pass the prairie-hawk that, poised on high,
Flaps his broad wings, yet moves not—ye have played
Among the palms of Mexico and vines
Of Texas, and have crisped the limpid brooks   20
That from the fountains of Sonora[1] glide
Into the calm Pacific—have ye fanned
A nobler or a lovelier scene than this?
Man hath no part in all this glorious work:
The hand that built the firmament hath heaved   25

---

1. **Sonora**\sō ⁴nō•rə\ a state in northwest Mexico.

And smoothed these verdant[2] swells, and sown their slopes
With herbage, planted them with island groves,
And hedged them round with forests. Fitting floor
For this magnificent temple of the sky—
With flowers whose glory and whose multitude   30
Rival the constellations! The great heavens
Seem to stoop down upon the scene in love,—
A nearer vault, and of a tenderer blue,
Than that which bends above our eastern hills.

    As o'er the verdant waste I guide my steed,   35
Among the high rank grass that sweeps his sides
The hollow beating of his footstep seems
A sacrilegious sound. I think of those
Upon whose rest he tramples. Are they here—
The dead of other days?—and did the dust   40
Of these fair solitudes once stir with life
And burn with passion? Let the mighty mounds
That overlook the rivers, or that rise
In the dim forest crowded with old oaks,
Answer. A race, that long has passed away,   45
Built them;—a disciplined and populous race
Heaped, with long toil, the earth, while yet the Greek
Was hewing the Pentelicus[3] to forms
Of symmetry, and rearing on its rock
The glittering Parthenon.[4] These ample fields   50
Nourished their harvests, here their herds were fed,
When haply by their stalls the bison lowed,
And bowed his manèd shoulder to the yoke.
All day this desert murmured with their toils,
Till twilight blushed, and lovers walked, and wooed   55
In a forgotten language, and old tunes,
From instruments of unremembered form,
Gave the soft winds a voice. The red man came—
The roaming hunter tribes, warlike and fierce,
And the mound-builders vanished from the earth.   60
The solitude of centuries untold
Has settled where they dwelt. The prairie-wolf
Hunts in their meadows, and his fresh-dug den
Yawns by my path. The gopher mines the ground
Where stood their swarming cities. All is gone;   65

---

2. **verdant**\vər·dənt\ green, covered with growing vegetation.
3. **Pentelicus**\pĕn ▲tĕ·lĭ·kəs\ (Greek: Pentelikon\pĕn ▲tĕ·lĭ·kɔn\) a mountain famous for its marble, located northwest of Athens, Greece.
4. **Parthenon**\▲par·thə·nŏn\ temple of Athena on the Acropolis at Athens; one of the finest examples of Doric architecture.

All—save the piles of earth that hold their bones,
The platforms where they worshipped unknown gods,
The barriers which they builded from the soil
To keep the foe at bay—till o'er the walls
The wild beleaguerers broke, and, one by one,   70
The strongholds of the plain were forced, and heaped
With corpses. The brown vultures of the wood
Flocked to those vast uncovered sepulchres,
And sat unscared and silent at their feast.
Haply some solitary fugitive,   75
Lurking in marsh and forest, till the sense
Of desolation and of fear became
Bitterer than death, yielded himself to die.
Man's better nature triumphed then. Kind words
Welcomed and soothed him; the rude conquerors   80
Seated the captive with their chiefs; he chose
A bride among their maidens, and at length
Seemed to forget—yet ne'er forgot—the wife
Of his first love, and her sweet little ones,
Butchered, amid their shrieks, with all his race.   85

    Thus change the forms of being. Thus arise
Races of living things, glorious in strength,
And perish, as the quickening breath of God
Fills them, or is withdrawn. The red man, too—
Has left the blooming wilds he ranged so long,   90
And, nearer to the Rocky Mountains, sought
A wilder hunting-ground. The beaver builds
No longer by these streams, but far away,
On waters whose blue surface ne'er gave back
The white man's face—among Missouri's springs,   95
And pools whose issues swell the Oregon,
He rears his little Venice.[5] In these plains
The bison feeds no more. Twice twenty leagues
Beyond remotest smoke of hunter's camp,
Roams the majestic brute, in herds that shake   100
The earth with thundering steps—yet here I meet
His ancient footprints stamped beside the pool.

    Still this great solitude is quick with life.
Myriads of insects, gaudy as the flowers
They flutter over, gentle quadrupeds,[6]   105
And birds, that scarce have learned the fear of man,

---

5. **Venice,** a seaport in Italy consisting of many small islands separated by
small canals crossed by approximately 380 bridges.
6. **quadrupeds**\ˈkwɔd ˈrū·pədz\ animals having four feet.

And here, the sliding reptiles of the ground,
Startlingly beautiful. The graceful deer
Bounds to the wood at my approach. The bee,
A more adventurous colonist than man,   110
With whom he came across the eastern deep,
Fills the savannas[7] with his murmurings,
And hides his sweets, as in the golden age,
Within the hollow oak. I listen long
To his domestic hum, and think I hear   115
The sound of that advancing multitude
Which soon shall fill these deserts. From the ground
Comes up the laugh of children, the soft voice
Of maidens, and the sweet and solemn hymn
Of Sabbath worshippers. The low of herds   120
Blends with the rustling of the heavy grain
Over the dark-brown furrows. All at once
A fresher wind sweeps by, and breaks my dream,
And I am in the wilderness alone.

---

7. savannas\sə ▲văn•əz\ open, level regions containing scattered shrubs
and subjected to heavy rains followed by dry periods.

I
A ROMANTIC DREAM

"The Prairies" is not a very realistic poem. For one thing, Bryant exaggerates and personifies often, notably when he imagines the heavens stooping to the prairies "in love." For another, the author ignores the dangers and hardships of frontier life. For example, he calls attention to "reptiles" that are "startlingly beautiful" but says nothing about "snakes" that are "full of deadly poison."

Poems—like "The Prairies"—in which the individual, personal (subjective) point of view and experience is stressed and in which imagination prevails over the factual and even sometimes over the rational, are often called *romantic*.

1. According to Bryant what natural phenomenon makes the prairies appear to move in ocean waves? (lines 6–15)

2. Would you say that Benét's poem, *Western Star*, (pp. 3–8) is more or less subjective than "The Prairies"?

II
IMPLICATIONS

Discuss the following in the light of the poem.

1. A visitor's brief view of a place is likely to be more romantic than the view of those living there.

2. The objective (realistic) view is to be preferred to the subjective (personal) view.

3. Bryant's description of the prairies would inspire pioneers to dream of settling on them.

III
TECHNIQUES

Setting

Although we have defined *setting* broadly as the place, time, and atmosphere of a work of literature, the third of these is sometimes distinguished from the other two. *Atmosphere* may be defined as the mood of a literary work or as its emotional aura. It is the general, overall feeling aroused in the reader by the handling of the work as a whole. Thus the place and time—as well as such elements as character and theme—may all contribute to the establishment of atmosphere.

Which of the following words would you use to describe the atmosphere of "The Prairies": gloomy, cheerful, chilly, brooding, peaceful, foreboding, melancholic, charming?

After the burning fever for California gold had abated, a new dream fired the minds of those moving west—free land. Passage of the Homestead Act in 1862 made it possible for anyone to have 160 acres simply by agreeing to work the land and produce a crop on it within five years.

In the novel *Let the Hurricane Roar*, Charles, eighteen, and Caroline, sixteen, marry and set out for a homestead in the Dakota Territory. That first year, their son is born in the dugout that Charles had scooped from a creek bank, and they have great hopes for the wheat crop Charles had planted. But a plague of grasshoppers destroys the crop, and the year's hopes and labors are lost. Unable to find a job nearby, in desperation the young husband goes off to a town in Iowa but breaks his leg and is immobilized. Caroline, rather than leave the homestead, decides that she and the baby must spend the winter in their isolated dugout. The following excerpt from the novel is a moving account of her struggles.

The Lonely Winter

ROSE WILDER LANE

That week she wrote Charles a long letter, which she meant to ask Mr. Gray[1] to take to the post office in town. She would not worry Charles by telling him that the Svensons[2] had gone. With a pen she was more articulate than with words; she wrote him that she loved him. She wrote about the baby's tooth and Mr. Svenson's cutting the hay on shares. The money he had sent was ample; she and the baby were in the best of health and wanted for nothing. Mr. and Mrs. Svenson were kindness itself, and all was snug for the winter. And carefully, in her delicate writing, every letter precisely slanted, she wrote,

We are having hard times now, but we should not dwell upon them but think of the future. It has never been easy to build up a country, but how much easier it is for us, with such great comforts and conveniences, kerosene, cookstoves, and even rail-

roads and fast posts, than it was for our forefathers. I trust that, like our own parents, we may live to see times more prosperous than they have ever been in the past, and we will then reflect with satisfaction that these hard times were not in vain.

This letter, carefully folded, sealed and addressed, was never mailed. It lay all winter between the pages of the Bible, for the weather changed suddenly. Saturday morning was mild as May; Saturday afternoon a dark cloud rose from the northwest. It hung across the sky for a time, with an ominous feathery undercloud. Then, like a solid white wall, the blizzard advanced. With the snow came the winds, howling.

Three days and nights the winds did not cease to howl, and when Caroline opened the door she could not see the door ledge through

---

"The Lonely Winter" from *Young Pioneers* by Rose Wilder Lane. Copyright 1961 by Roger Lea MacBride; reprinted by permission.

1. Mr. Gray had hauled winter supplies from town for her.
2. **The Svensons**, Caroline's nearest neighbors.

swirling snow. How cold it was she could not guess. At sight of the cloud she had hurriedly begun cramming every spare inch of the dugout with hay. Twisted hard, it burned with a brief, hot flame. Her palms were soon raw and bleeding from handling the sharp, harsh stuff, but she kept on twisting it; she kept the dugout warm.

In the long dark hours—for she was frugal with kerosene; a wavering light came from the drafts and the broken lid of the stove—she began to fight a vague and monstrous dread. It lay beneath her thoughts; she could not grasp it as a whole; she was always aware of it and never able to defeat it. It lay shapeless and black in the depths of her. From time to time it flung up a question:

What if the baby gets sick?

"He won't be sick!" she retorted. "He's a strong, healthy baby. If he's sick, I'll take care of him. I'd take care of him anyway; there's no doctor in town."

Suppose something has happened to Charles? Suppose he never comes back?

"Be still! I won't listen."

That was like a wolf's howl in the wind. Wolves?

"Nonsense, I have the gun. How could a wolf get through the door?"

When you go out—— If a wolf sprang suddenly—— What of the baby, alone in the dugout?

"Why am I scaring myself with horrible fancies? Nothing like that will happen."

She could never conquer the shapeless, nameless dread itself. Silenced, it did not leave her. It would begin again.

What if the baby gets sick?

"Oh, stop, stop! I can't stand this!" her spirit cried out in anguish. And she asked herself angrily, "What is the matter with you? Brace up and show a little decent spunk! It's only a storm; there'll be lots of them before spring." She tried to conquer the shapeless, dark thing by ignoring it.

The wind howled, gray darkness pressed against the paper pane;[3] a little hard snow, dry as sand, was forced through the crack beneath the door.

On the fourth morning Caroline was awakened by an immense, profound silence. The frosty air stung her nostrils; the blanket was edged with rime from her breath. Snug in the hollow of her body the baby slept cozily. The window was a vague gray in the dark. She lighted the lamp and started a fire in the cold stove.

She was not perturbed until she tried to open the door. Something outside held it against her confident push. And suddenly wild terror possessed her. She felt a Thing outside, pressed against the door.

It was only snow. She said to herself that it was only snow. There was no danger; the ledge was narrow. She flung all her strength and weight against the door. The stout planks quivered; they pressed against a crunching and a squeaking, and from top to bottom of them ran a sound like a derisive scratch of claws. Then snow fell down the abrupt slope below the ledge, and sunlight pierced Caroline's eyes.

Taking the shovel, she forced her body through the narrow aperture she had gained. For an instant the pain in her eyes blinded her. Then she saw the immensity of whiteness and dazzling blue. She confronted space.

Under the immeasurably vast sky, a limitless expanse of snow refracted the cold glitter of the sun. Nothing stirred, nothing breathed; there was no other movement than the ceaseless interplay of innumerable and unthinkably tiny rays of light. Air and sun and snow were the whole visible world—a world neither alive nor dead, and terrible because it was alien to life and death, and ignorant of them.

In that instant she knew the infinite smallness, weakness, of life in the lifeless universe. She felt the vast, insensate forces against which life itself is a rebellion. Infinitely small and weak was the spark of warmth in a living heart.

———
3. **paper pane,** Since glass was both scarce and costly, heavy brown paper was tacked over a window frame and rubbed with grease to increase its resistance to wind and rain.

Yet valiantly the tiny heart continued to beat. Tired, weak, burdened by its own fears and sorrows, still it persisted, indomitably it continued to exist, and in bare existence itself, without assurance of victory, even without hope, in its indomitable existence among vast, incalculable, lifeless forces, it was invincible.

Caroline was never able to say, even in her own thoughts, what she knew when she first came out of the dugout after the October blizzard. It was a moment of inexpressible terror, courage and pride. She was aware of human dignity. She felt that she was alive, and that God was with life. She thought: "The gates of hell shall not prevail against me." She could feel what Charles felt, singing: "Let the hurricane roar! We'll weather the blast."

She drew a deep breath, and with her shovel she attacked the snow. The winds had packed it hard as ice against the door and the creek bank. The path was buried under a slanting drift. Inch by inch, pounding, digging, scraping, lifting, she made a way on which she could safely walk, and that scratch on the illimitable waste of trackless snow was a triumph.

A blizzard of such severity so early in October seemed to predict an unusually hard winter. She could not know when the next storm might strike, and her first care was fuel. She dug into the snow-covered stacks by the barn, and tying a rope around big bundles of hay, she dragged them one by one down the path and into the dugout.

When she threw out the water in which she washed her hands, she noticed that its drops tinkled on the ice crust. They had frozen in the air. Startled, she looked into the mirror. Her nose and ears were white, and she had to rub them with snow till they painfully thawed.

Then for three weeks the weather was mild, the snow was melting. There were days when the door stood open and the air was like spring. From above the dugout she could see the town; she could, indeed, see fifty miles beyond it. But her letter remained unmailed. Mr. Gray and his Ada did not come; perhaps he had no sleigh, perhaps they dared not venture so far

from shelter, lest another blizzard catch them.

In early November the winter settled down. Blizzard followed blizzard out of the northwest. Sometimes there was a clear day between them, sometimes only a few hours. As soon as the winds ceased their howling and the snow thinned so that she could see, she went out with the shovel.

The wind would be steadily blowing, driving a low scud of snow before it. She worked sometimes waist deep in blown snow so thick that she could not see her feet. The whole world seemed covered with white spray flying under the cold sunshine. Her eyes were bloodshot and her skin burned red and blistered, and she never came into the dugout without looking to see if face and ears were frozen.

On the dark days of the blizzards she twisted hay; she lighted the lamp for cleaning and cooking and washing. And she played with the baby.

He was older now; he watched the gleams of firelight and clapped his hands, and his soft little palms hardly ever missed each other. His blue eyes looked into Caroline's, his firm little body had a will of its own. He could hold up his own head proudly; he could straighten his backbone; all by himself he could sit up, and he could crawl. Kicking and crowing, he burbled sounds almost like words. "Mama," she could hear him say.

"Papa," she urged him. "Say it, baby dumpling! Say 'papa.'"

"Blablub!" he replied triumphantly, giving her a roguish glance that melted her heart. Kneeling by the bunk, she squeezed his wriggling body between her raw hands, she rolled and tumbled him and buried her rough face in his softness, in the warm perfume of his baby body. His fist tugged painfully at her hair and she laughed, teasing his nose with the loosened ends. She had begun to be almost as cheerful as Charles. She wondered, "Is Charles cheerful because he's frightened, because he has to be brave?"

There was always the ache of incompleteness without him. The shapeless dread might at any moment stab her with a question. But day by day the baby and she survived, and in the dugout the howling winds, the cold and snow and dark could not touch them. Her light spirit was a defiance.

Then came the seven days' blizzard. There had been only a few hours of clear weather, but Caroline had worked desperately; she had enough hay for three days and she had never known a blizzard to last longer. On the third day she burned the hay sparingly, but she was not alarmed. On the fourth day she broke up and burned a box, keeping the stove barely warm. On the fifth day she burned the remaining box. The heavy benches and table were left, and the cradle; in her folly she had left the ax in the barn.

She sat wrapped in blankets on the edge of the bunk. When the fire went out there was no light at all. The window was obscurely gray, a dim and unnaturally square eye, looking in upon her. The stout door shook to the pounding and prying of yelling winds. And time was lost, so that she did not know whether this were day or night, nor how long those winds had possessed all space. She had so long hoped to hear their energy exhausted that it seemed to her inexhaustible. The tiny pocket of still air in the dugout was increasingly cold.

If she and the baby lay close together under blankets, they could exist for some time in the warmth of their own bodies. If this were to go on forever—— It could not, of course. Feebly she gave up the problem of the heavy benches, which she could not break up with her hands. It must be the cradle. But she feared to burn it so soon.

During the seventh day she smashed and frugally burned the cradle. The birds that Charles had carved helped to boil tea and potatoes. She mashed a potato in a little hot water and fed it with a spoon to the baby. Then she put out the lamp and lay down with him under all the bedding.

A change in the sound of the wind awakened her. She did not know whether it was night or day, but when she forced the door open she saw a whiteness of driven snow. A fierce north wind was driving the flakes steadily before it, and Caroline's relief was like a shout of joy. The snow was not swirling; the blizzard was over!

When next she opened the door, the storm had diminished so that she could see vaguely into it. She was able to clear the path, and when she reached its top she could see dim shapes of barn and haystacks. The wind almost took her off her feet, and when she had a bundle of hay and was dragging it through the soft drifts, she had to fight it as though it were a live thing struggling to get away.

After she had filled the dugout with hay, she stretched a rope from the barn to the top of the path, so that she could fetch fuel, if necessary, during a blizzard.

Vaguely through the storm she seemed to see a dark patch on the opposite bank of the creek. It troubled her, for she could not imagine what it might be; perhaps an illusion of eyes weeping in the wind, perhaps some danger against which she should defend herself. She shut the door against it hurriedly and gave herself to the marvel of warmth and rest.

In the morning, in the dazzling glitter of sun on snow, she saw across the creek a herd of cattle. Huddled together, heads toward the south and noses drooping to their knees, they stood patiently enduring the cold. In terror she thought of the haystacks. The creek bank hid them from the cattle now, but if the herd moved southeast, across the slough, and saw that food, would all the strength of the wind prevent them from turning and destroying her fuel?

She put on her wraps and took the pistol. Not with pitchfork or ax, she knew, could she keep starving cattle from food. Nor did she dare risk facing the stampede. She could only try to turn it with shots, and, failing, take refuge in the barn. If the fuel were lost——

The cattle did not move. It came to her, while she watched, that for a long time they had not moved. Yesterday she had seen the herd, huddled motionless in the storm. This prodigy, this incredible fact of cattle not mov-

33

ing before a storm, chilled her thought. She stared at them—gaunt sides and ridged backbones, dropped necks and lax tails, motionless as if carved. Were they dead—frozen? No; breath came white from their nostrils.

The thought that they might be dead had brought a vision of meat.

Her courage quailed. There was something monstrous, something that gave her an unreasoning terror, like a breath of the supernatural, in this herd of motionless cattle. Her jaw clenched against the cold, she went slowly, knee-deep in drifts, down the bank and across the frozen creek. Was this too great a risk? Leaving the baby in the dugout and venturing into she knew not what? The cattle did not move. She went within ten yards of them, five, two. They did not even lift their heads.

Over their eyes—thick over their eyes and hollowed temples—were cakes of ice. When she saw this, she understood. Their own breath, steaming upward while they plodded before the storm, had frozen and blinded them.

In a rage of pity, an outbursting cry against the universal cruelty, she plunged through the snow to the nearest patiently dying creature; she wrenched the ice from its eyes. The steer snorted; he flung up his head in terror, and ran, staggering. The herd quivered. A few yards away, the steer stopped, hesitated in fear of the loneliness around him, and turned back uncertainly toward the herd. A long bawl of misery came from his throat. Then he, too, let his head droop.

Caroline knew what she must do. She thought of the baby, drawing his strength from hers. She held all thought, all feeling, firmly to the baby, and walking to the nearest young steer, she put the pistol to his temple, shut her eyes and fired. The report crashed through her.

She felt the shudder of all the beasts. When she opened her eyes they had not moved. The steer lay dead, only a little blood trickling, freezing, from the wound. And perhaps it had been merciful to kill him.

Then, like an inspiration, a revival of all hope, she thought of a cow. The cow! Why not? In the herd there were many cows. Alas, they belonged to somebody. To whom? She did not know; that might never be known; impossible to guess how many miles—hundreds, perhaps—they had been driven by the storm. But they were branded. She could not steal. Yet, if she did not take one of these cows, would it not die? The whole blinded herd was helpless and dying. To kill for food was permissible, but to steal? Was she a cattle thief? But a cow—to have a cow! Milk for the baby. To surprise Charles, when he came home, with a cow!

She thought that perhaps there was a yearling that was not branded.

In her excitement she was almost laughing. Clumsy in boots and coat and shawls, she pushed into the harmless herd. The heifers, she knew, would be in the center. The old bull grumbled in his throat, shaking his blind head, but he did not move; he did not even paw the snow. There was a young heifer, unbranded, almost plump, a clear red all over. Caroline marked it for her own, for their own cow.

This incredible marvel of good fortune filled her with laughing joy. What a triumph, what a joke—to take a cow from the blizzard, to take it from the very midst of a dangerous herd! And to have a cow—after so many calamities, in spite of calamities, to have a cow—this was a vindication of all confidence and hope.

She struggled through the drifts, across the creek, up the bank, to the dugout. She fed the stove with hay, she nursed the baby, dressed him warmly, wrapped him in blankets like a cocoon. Then she went to the barn for a rope.

The short winter day gave her not too much time. The sun was overhead before she had succeeded in prodding and tugging the terrified, wild, blinded heifer out of the herd. It clung with desperation to the safety of the herd, and she had still to get it across the creek, up the bank and into the barn. Its strength—greater than hers—wore her out. In one frantic plunge and leap it undid the work of half an hour. Its blindness was her only help and she thanked God for the continued bitter cold. But often she stopped to rub face and ears with snow, and beating her numb hands on her chest did not keep the feeling in them.

It was near sunset before she got the heifer into the barn. She put hay into the manger and tore the ice from the heifer's eyes. With the rope and ax she went back to the herd. She cut the best parts of meat from the half-frozen carcass, and tied the pieces together. Then, trembling in her weariness, she went from animal to animal, tearing off the blinding ice. The cattle snorted and plunged; each one ran staggering a little way and waited, bawling. Slowly the herd drifted before the wind. The sun sank in coldness, the glow faded from the snow, and in the dusk she released the old bull. He lifted his head, bellowed weakly, and plunged staggering after the herd.

In the dark they would not see her hay. The wind was blowing toward the town site; let the townspeople deal with the survivors who reached it. Caroline had given the cattle a chance for their lives, and she felt she had earned her cow.

The blizzard that came that night lasted only a day. Caroline lay cozily in bed. The baby gurgled and kicked in exuberance of spirits; a great beef stew simmered on the stove, filling the air with its fragrance. The snowy hay in the manger would suffice the heifer for both food and water. The howling of the blizzard did not disturb Caroline; she felt the braggart joy of Samson, hugging in secret his triumph. "A lion stood in the way; but out of the eater I have taken meat; out of the strong I have taken sweetness."

If only Charles could know that they had a cow! But now she was confident that Charles would come home strong and well; this winter would end, they would be together in the spring. And how good to lie on a soft hay tick, under warm blankets; how good to feel the heartening strength of meat stealing drowsily all through one's body; how good to be warm

and to rest. She felt she had never been thankful enough for all her blessings.

Two haunches of the beef she had left outside the door, to freeze on the snow. The blizzard had buried them, and she did not touch that drift when she dug the path again. Snow was still falling thickly enough to fill the air as with a mist, through which she saw the barn and haystacks.

The heifer was still safely tied to the manger. It snorted and plunged, wild-eyed, while she brought in hay and set two pails of snow within its reach. She spoke to it soothingly, but did not touch it. In time it would learn her kindness and be gentle. It had all the marks of a good milch cow.

She closed the barn door and snapped the padlock, feeling a proud sense of property to be taken care of. There was no wind, and all around her she could hear the soft rustle of the falling snow. With the shovel and rope, she went toward the haystack. Afterward she always said she did not know what made her stop and turn around. By the corner of the barn stood a wolf.

If you went out——— If a wolf sprang ——— What would become of the baby, alone in the dugout? *It's come,* her frozen heart knew.

She had only the shovel.

The wolf's haunches quivered, not quite crouching. The hair stood rough along its back. Fangs showed beneath the curling lip. It was a gaunt, big timber wolf. Its mate could not be far away. Its mate was perhaps creeping up behind her.

She dared not turn lest this one spring. Its eyes shone green in the half light. The snow sifted downward, a moving, transparent screen between her and those eyes. Snowflakes settled on the wolf's shaggy neck. His mouth opened in a soundless pant; the red tongue flicked hungrily over the pointed muzzle.

He shifted a paw. Caroline did not move. Swiftly the wolf turned and vanished, a shadow, in the falling snow. The snow at once became a menace, hiding the lurking danger.

Caroline walked steadily through the white blindness toward the dugout. She did not run; she knew that if she ran, her inmost self would yield to shattering terror. As long as the wolf could not be seen anywhere, she was safe; the wolf would not spring unless he could see her. But while she was going down the path in the creek bank, he might spring on her from above. She knew he was following her.

She reached the path and ran. There was no measure in time for the length of that distance from the edge of the prairie to the door's slamming behind her. A long wolf howl rose from the ceiling above her head. Another answered it from the frozen creek below.

Several times that day she faintly heard the heifer's desperate bawling. The barn door was solid; the walls were thick, and the roof, too, was of sod. Whether the wolves could scratch their way through it, she did not know. They were hungry; she had seen the fur hollowed between the ribs.

That evening she heard snarling and crunching at the door. The wolves had found the fresh meat. They must have been following the cattle, and the carcass of the steer she had killed had kept them near her. She heard a snuffling along the threshold, a scratch of claws on the door.

She kept the lamp lighted and sat all night watching the paper pane. The window space was too small to let a wolf through easily. If paw or head appeared, she was ready to shoot. The ax was in the dugout, and she decided, rather than go out in the snowstorm again, to chop up table and benches, and burn them. But she made the hay last two days, and then a sliver of brightness above the snow piled against the window told her that the sun was shining.

Little by little she forced the door open. The pistol was in her hand. She could not see the wolves. This did not mean that they might not be waiting beyond the edge of the bank above. But she could not survive all winter without fuel. Some dangers must be faced.

She found no trace of the wolves anywhere, and in the barn the heifer was safe. After that she often heard wolves howling, and found their tracks at the door and around the barn. She never left the dugout without the pistol. She made a belt in which to carry it, so that it was always ready to her hand while she was clearing the path or struggling with the bundles of hay.

The reality of the wolves constantly reminded her of Charles' warning. Wolves, he had written—and outlaws. When she stirred the fire she thought of the smoke ascending from the chimney. For seventy miles around, on clear days, it could be seen that the dugout was inhabited. Claim jumpers[4] would probably not come. But outlaws?

She felt within herself a certainty that at any human threat of danger she would kill. She said to herself that no stranger should enter that dugout—not under any circumstances, not with any fair words. This she determined upon, sure of herself. But she did not yet know herself.

Blizzard followed blizzard, with clear hours or days between. She had lost reckoning of time and was not quite sure whether December had ended and January begun. But each day brought nearer the end of this winter. The baby was healthy, the heifer was safe in the barn, and she was holding out pretty well. More and more often she dreamed of springtime and Charles, beyond her reach, and she too confused or too weak to reach them, or to make Charles hear her calling to him. But in the daytime she knew she had only to hold on; Charles would come, spring would come; she did not need to go toward them.

February had come, though she did not know it. Three clear days of terrible cold were ending, near nightfall, in the rising of the blizzard winds. That day Caroline had filled half the barn with hay; the heifer was now so gentle that she could turn it loose with that abundance of feed, and the washtub full of

---

4. **claim jumpers**, those who, by violence or fraud, take over another's claim, improvements, and equipment.

water provided for it if this blizzard lasted a week. The baby slept. The box was full of twisted hay, the supper dishes washed, and by the faint light of the dying fire Caroline combed her hair for the night.

A blow struck the door, and all at once the forces of the air gave tongue. Caroline thought how like demon riders they sounded, racing and circling overhead with unearthly, inhuman shriek and scream and wild halloo. A little snow, fine and hard as sand, was driven through the crack beneath the door. She shook her hair back and put up her hands to braid it, and in the gleam of light from the broken stove lid she saw a joint of the stovepipe suddenly bend. The two ends of pipe slid upon each other, a crack opened between them. Petrified, she heard a human cry, a groaned exclamation.

A man was on top of the dugout. Blind in the storm, he had stumbled against the chimney.

No honest man, no lost homesteader. Not for miles around was there an undeserted homestead. All afternoon the blizzard had been threatening; no honest man would have gone far from shelter. Only a rider out of the northwest might have fled before the storm. Out of the northwestern refuges of the outlaws. "Wolves and outlaws will be moving back to settled country."

He had struck the chimney on the eastern side; he was going toward the creek. Only a few steps and he would fall down the creek bank, down into the deep drifts below. He would be gone, lost, buried somewhere by the storm. Only his bones would be found after the snow melted in the spring. "Keep still!" she said. "Don't move. It isn't your business. Don't let him in. Who knows what he is, what he would do? Think of the baby. *What are you doing?*"

Her mouth close to the stovepipe, she

shouted, "Stand still! Don't move!" The soot dislodged from the open joint of the pipe fell on her face, so quickly had she acted. "You hear me?" she called.

A vague shout replied. He seemed to have fallen or to have wandered a step or two toward the creek. She knew how the winds were swirling, beating and tugging at him from every side, how the sandlike snow was flaying his face; she saw him blinded, deafened, lost. An outlaw, but human, fighting the storm.

"Lie down! Crawl!" she shouted. "Creek bank ahead! Follow it to the right! The right! Find a rope! You hear?"

His shout was dull through the shriller winds. Then she hesitated. But the barn was padlocked. "There is a path!" she called. "Path! Down! To the left!"

If he shouted again, she did not hear him. She twisted her hair and thrust pins into it, buttoned her basque and lighted the lamp. She got her pistol and made sure it was loaded. Some instinct, hardly reasonable—for who would harm a baby?—made her lift Charles John, wrap him in a blanket and lay him on the hay in the wood box. She felt better with the baby behind her. Then she lifted the bar on the door, and retreating behind the table, she waited.

She had time to regret what she had done, and to know that she could not have done otherwise.

The wind suddenly tore open the door. Snow whirled in, and cold. The lamp flared smokily, and as she started forward, the man appeared in the white blizzard. He was tall and shapeless in fur coat and cap and ear muffs caked with snow; he was muffled to reddened slits of eyes and snow-matted eyebrows; it was an instant before she knew him and screamed. The wild scream was dizzily circling in her head when his arms closed around her, hard and cold as ice.

"Oh, how—how—how did you get here?" she gasped after a while, unable still to believe it. Her hands kept clutching, clutching up and down the snowy fur, as if her hands were separate things, frantic too, to make sure this was Charles.

"Gosh, I'm freezing you to death! I got to shut the door," he said. And at these homely words, because Charles was shutting the door, she burst into tears.

"H-h-have you—had any supper?" she wept. "Hang supper!" he sang out joyously.

Later he teased her a little. "What's so surprising? Didn't I tell you I'd get here quick as I could?" He scolded her seriously: "Caroline, God only knows what I went through when they told me in town that Svensons had quit and you were out here alone. Don't you ever do another fool trick like that. Do you suppose I care a rap for anything in the world compared to you?"

He asked, "How's the little shaver?" and she said, "Oh, Charles, he's wonderful! He's got two teeth! Just————" But then he hugged her, and there was so much to ask, to tell.

They had warned him in town that he couldn't beat the blizzard, but he thought he could make it. He had almost reached the slough when the storm struck. He must have been confused and gone the wrong way; he was looking for the well in the slough when he struck the chimney. "I thought from the well I could make the barn, and then the creek bank. But I thought I was going north. Then, when I hit the chimney, I didn't know where I was. I couldn't make out what it was. It just hit me, and then I couldn't find it again. That was what I was doing—looking for it—when I heard you!"

"Oh," she told him, "and we've got a cow!"

"A—not our own cow?"

"Well, a heifer. A good, gentle, red heifer. She'll make a fine milker."

"But how did you ever———— Look," he said, "I've got forty dollars. I want to tell you Roslyn's the best man in twenty counties.[5] I didn't expect to have a penny left, but————"

"Oh, Charles, how's your leg?"

"Well, I have to favor it a little—you notice

----
5. **Roslyn's . . . counties,** Charles's employer in Iowa.

I've got you on the other knee. But it stood the walk pretty well; it'll be fine as ever for spring plowing."

"And you walked ten miles! Oh, Charles!"

"What did you think I'd do, and you out here?"

It didn't matter, really, what they said. They were together; everything was all right. She heard the clamor of the storm, all the demons shrieking; simply a blizzard, simply the winter weather on their farm.

A little sound made her turn; there was the baby! There was little Charles John, wide-awake, lifting himself up with his tiny fingers on the edge of the wood box. A spear of hay clung to his wave-curl of hair. He bounced once, and then, clearly, triumphantly, he spoke.

"Blablub!" he said. A dimple quivered in his cheek; then his mouth spread in Charles' wide grin, and there were the two white teeth.

"Look, Charles, look! Oh, did you hear him call you papa?"

Somehow, without quite thinking it, she felt that a light from the future was shining in the baby's face. The big white house was waiting for him, and the acres of wheat fields, the fast driving teams and swift buggies. If he remembered at all this life in the dugout, he would think of it only as a brief prelude to more spacious times.

I
SHE SAVED THEIR DREAM

In the letter to Charles that was never mailed, Caroline wrote: "We are having hard times now, but we should not dwell upon them but think of the future." Her attitude was one often reflected by thousands of homesteaders who slaved, scrimped, and suffered, but who stayed on the land. It was the homesteaders—rather than the lone trappers, the roving gold-seekers, or the rambling cowhands—who peopled the plains and put down enduring family roots. As one of these brave pioneers, Caroline conquered her nagging doubts, her sudden terrors, and the numbing loneliness to ensure that her family, too, would reap the promise of the land.

1. How did Caroline keep the baby and herself from freezing to death during the week-long blizzard?

2. Why does she search for an unbranded heifer in the herd?

3. Although she had promised herself not to allow a stranger to enter the dugout, why does she shout instructions to whoever is stumbling on the roof?

II
IMPLICATIONS

Discuss the following as they apply to the story.

1. Human beings are more resourceful than they know.

2. There is nothing more fearful than fear itself.

3. Hunger does not justify theft.

III
TECHNIQUES

Setting

The writer paints the harsh wintry setting quickly. The dugout, the meager furnishings, the few tools, the barn, the creek, and the white unbroken landscape serve to establish scene and season.

To build atmosphere she uses colors, sounds, and Caroline's moods and thoughts. The atmosphere is shifting, much like undulating layers of light, gray, and black smoke. It is now hopeful, now somber, now threatening, and finally joyous at the story's end.

1. Explain what makes for a hopeful atmosphere in the first two paragraphs.

2. What colors and sounds in paragraphs two, three, and four make for a shift to an ominous atmosphere?

3. Caroline debates with herself in paragraph five. What mood is thus created and how?

Characterization

Since Caroline's character is drawn clearly in the first part of the novel, in this excerpt her character is depicted principally through her thoughts and actions. Explain what the following quotations from the story reveal about her character:

1. In a rage of pity, an outbursting cry against the universal cruelty, she plunged through the snow to the nearest patiently dying creature. (p. 34)

2. She did not run; she knew that if she ran, her inmost self would yield to shattering terror. (p. 36)

DREAM AND PROMISE

The dream and promise of America forever lie before us. Repeatedly,
we find that each dream realized opens a new horizon, a new promise for the daring
and the imaginative.

This gallery of paintings records the dreams Americans have cherished over
the years, since the time they abandoned the European culture of
their past and surged through thousands of miles of wilderness to create one of the
freest and wealthiest societies the world has yet seen—vast cities, new technologies, and
a view of the future that opens on the universe itself. Though widely
different in subject matter, these paintings all extol the rich promise of the
American land and the American people.

DANIEL BOONE ESCORTING A BAND OF PIONEERS INTO THE WESTERN COUNTRY
George Caleb Bingham

The renowned pioneer Daniel Boone
not only blazed the Wilderness Road
over the Cumberland Mountains
from Tennessee to Kentucky
but also spent many years leading settlers
to new territory. After building
Fort Boonesboro near the end
of the Wilderness Road, Boone brought
his courageous wife Rebecca and their daughter
Jemima to the new settlement. This view
of Boone and his party may record the first
time that white women saw the promise
of the Kentucky wilderness.

   Though he was only nine years old
when Boone died, the famous portrait painter
Bingham created a treasure trove of realistic
works celebrating the westward movement.

IN SEARCH OF THE LAND
OF MILK AND HONEY
Harvey Dunn

Farther west and nearly one hundred years later,
dauntless Americans continued to search for
the "Land of Milk and Honey," the fair country
where they could carve out a new and abundant life.
A tribute to the pioneers, this painting hangs
in the Library of DeSmet, South Dakota.

Once the land had been found, the resourceful settlers began the working
of it, inspired in their toil by dreams of
strong barns, cozy farmhouses, and food aplenty.
The Kansas-bred artist Curry realized his own dream by pioneering
in the American regional style of painting.

HOMESTEADERS
John Steuart Curry

APPROACHING
BUFFALO—
BATISTE BEYOND
AND I
George Catlin

The American dream of adventure is captured in Catlin's painting of his guide and himself approaching a winding herd of buffalo. This self-taught artist of the last century lived among many different tribes of Native Americans, recording a way of life that was rapidly disappearing—yielding to the advance of homesteads and railways, "talking wires" and the miner's shovel.

SONG OF THE TALKING WIRE
Henry Farny

Despite the still lonely prairie, the promise of an open frontier was dying for this solitary brave trying to decode with a hunter's ear the strange song of the "talking wires." Throughout history, a dream of a new and better life has often spelled the end of ancient cultures from the past.

Uniting the frontier with small towns and Eastern cities, America's first train traveled west in 1864 on Union Pacific rails. Implicit in this popular Currier and Ives print is the dream of linking America together, from coast to coast, through the power of the mighty "iron horse."

ACROSS THE CONTINENT
Currier and Ives

A devoted painter of the American scene, Burchfield has given us a strong watercolor statement about early industrial life. From BLACK IRON can you imagine how he felt? In a sense his meaning may be basically the same as that of the SONG OF THE TALKING WIRE. What dream is dying here?

BLACK IRON
Charles Burchfield

43

The sea, as well
as the land, incited
the imagination
of hardy Americans,
especially around the
middle of the last century.
As WHALEMAN suggests,
there are those who prefer
the excitement of danger
to a life without
dreams or challenges.
Again, the secondary
theme within a theme:
a people's dream
can spell death to those
who stand in
the way of progress.

WHALEMAN
Ben Stahl

A dream is fulfilled, and yet stretching out
beyond is the almost limitless promise
of electric power to be explored and mastered.
Notice the detailed and amusing portraits
included in this painting of a historic moment
in the laboratory of Thomas Edison.

EDISON AND HIS WORKERS IN THE PROCESS OF TESTING
THE FIRST PRACTICAL INCANDESCENT LAMP
Dean Cornwell

Thomas Price's laboratory was
in San Francisco. He was
California State Mineralogist
and Chemist. America owes a debt
of thanks to the dreams and hard work of
such dedicated scientists as Thomas Price.

THE LABORATORY
OF THOMAS PRICE
Henry Alexander

Centered on the soaring cables of a suspension bridge, this painting by Joseph Stella speaks of America's dream for the future.

THE BRIDGE
Joseph Stella
Collection of the
Newark Museum

On November 19, 1863, the military cemetery on the site of the Battle of Gettysburg was dedicated. Edward Everett, popular orator and political leader, delivered the principal address. President Lincoln had been invited to offer "a few appropriate remarks." He spoke for two minutes, and his words reaffirmed the American dream and promise in a time of tragic civil strife.

Gettysburg Address

ABRAHAM LINCOLN

Four score and seven years ago our fathers brought forth on this continent a new nation, conceived in liberty, and dedicated to the proposition that all men are created equal.

Now we are engaged in a great civil war, testing whether that nation, or any nation so conceived and so dedicated, can long endure. We are met on a great battlefield of that war. We have come to dedicate a portion of that field as a final resting place for those who here gave their lives that that nation might live. It is altogether fitting and proper that we should do this.

But in a larger sense we cannot dedicate, we cannot consecrate, we cannot hallow this ground. The brave men, living and dead, who struggled here, have consecrated it far above our poor power to add or detract. The world will little note nor long remember what we say here, but it can never forget what they did here. It is for us, the living, rather, to be dedicated here to the unfinished work which they who fought here have thus far so nobly advanced. It is rather for us to be here dedicated to the great task remaining before us—that from these honored dead we take increased devotion to that cause for which they gave the last full measure of devotion; that we here highly resolve that these dead shall not have died in vain; that this nation, under God, shall have a new birth of freedom; and that government of the people, by the people, for the people, shall not perish from the earth.

"A NEW BIRTH OF FREEDOM"

The address that Abraham Lincoln gave at Gettysburg has been variously praised as "beautifully and simply phrased" and as "one of the great American poems." Generations of students have committed the speech to memory, and it has been translated into almost every language.

In the opening sentence Lincoln reminded his listeners once again of the lofty ideals enunciated in the Declaration of Independence. In his final sentence he articulated the promise that this nation "shall have a new birth of freedom."

1. What was this "new birth of freedom"?

2. In what way does the address show Lincoln's humility?

To many persons living in the newly opened West, a solid home, a growing family, and a prosperous farm meant the realization of the American dream. To a few individuals, though, these things meant a dream ended. In this story, John Steinbeck, winner of the Nobel Prize for Literature in 1962, shows three generations of the same family. Each generation has different thoughts about "westering." Try to determine what "westering" means, and see if you agree with any of the characters about its significance.

The Leader of the People

JOHN STEINBECK

On Saturday afternoon Billy Buck, the ranch-hand, raked together the last of the old year's haystack and pitched small forkfuls over the wire fence to a few mildly interested cattle. High in the air small clouds like puffs of cannon smoke were driven eastward by the March wind. The wind could be heard whishing in the brush on the ridge crests, but no breath of it penetrated down into the ranch-cup.[1]

The little boy, Jody, emerged from the house eating a thick piece of buttered bread. He saw Billy working on the last of the haystack. Jody tramped down scuffling his shoes in a way he had been told was destructive to good shoe-leather. A flock of white pigeons flew out of the black cypress tree as Jody passed, and circled the tree and landed again. A half-grown tortoiseshell cat[2] leaped from the bunkhouse[3] porch, galloped on stiff legs across the road, whirled and galloped back again. Jody picked up a stone to help the game along, but he was too late, for the cat was under the porch before the stone could be discharged. He threw the stone into the cypress tree and started the white pigeons on another whirling flight.

Arriving at the used-up haystack, the boy leaned against the barbed wire fence. "Will that be all of it, do you think?" he asked.

The middle-aged ranch-hand stopped his careful raking and stuck his fork into the ground. He took off his black hat and smoothed down his hair. "Nothing left of it that isn't soggy from ground moisture," he said. He replaced his hat and rubbed his dry leathery hands together.

"Ought to be plenty mice," Jody suggested.

"Lousy with them," said Billy. "Just crawling with mice."

"Well, maybe, when you get all through, I could call the dogs and hunt the mice."

"Sure, I guess you could," said Billy Buck. He lifted a forkful of the damp ground-hay and threw it into the air. Instantly three mice leaped out and burrowed frantically under the hay again.

Jody sighed with satisfaction. Those plump, sleek, arrogant mice were doomed. For eight months they had lived and multiplied in the haystack. They had been immune from cats, from traps, from poison and from Jody. They had grown smug in their security, overbearing and fat. Now the time of disaster had come; they would not survive another day.

Billy looked up at the top of the hills that surrounded the ranch. "Maybe you better ask your father before you do it," he suggested.

---

1. **ranch-cup,** low area in the land.
2. **tortoiseshell cat,** cat with patches of yellow and brown.
3. **bunkhouse,** sleeping quarters for ranch hands.

From *The Red Pony* by John Steinbeck. Copyright 1938, © 1966 by John Steinbeck. Reprinted by permission of The Viking Press.

"Well, where is he? I'll ask him now."

"He rode up to the ridge ranch[4] after dinner. He'll be back pretty soon."

Jody slumped against the fence post. "I don't think he'd care."

As Billy went back to his work he said ominously, "You'd better ask him anyway. You know how he is."

Jody did know. His father, Carl Tiflin, insisted upon giving permission for anything that was done on the ranch, whether it was important or not. Jody sagged farther against the post until he was sitting on the ground. He looked up at the little puffs of wind-driven cloud. "Is it like to rain, Billy?"

"It might. The wind's good for it, but not strong enough."

"Well, I hope it don't rain until after I kill those damn mice." He looked over his shoulder to see whether Billy had noticed the mature profanity. Billy worked on without comment.

Jody turned back and looked at the side-hill where the road from the outside world came down. The hill was washed with lean March sunshine. Silver thistles, blue lupins[5] and a few poppies bloomed among the sagebushes. Halfway up the hill Jody could see Doubletree Mutt, the black dog, digging in a squirrel hole. He paddled for a while and then paused to kick bursts of dirt out between his hind legs, and he dug with an earnestness which belied the knowledge he must have had that no dog had ever caught a squirrel by digging in a hole.

Suddenly, while Jody watched, the black dog stiffened, and backed out of the hole and looked up the hill toward the cleft in the ridge where the road came through. Jody looked up too. For a moment Carl Tiflin on horseback stood out against the pale sky and then he moved down the road toward the house. He carried something white in his hand.

The boy started to his feet. "He's got a letter," Jody cried. He trotted away toward the ranch house, for the letter would probably be read aloud and he wanted to be there. He reached the house before his father did, and ran in. He heard Carl dismount from his creaking saddle and slap the horse on the side to send it to the barn where Billy would unsaddle it and turn it out.

Jody ran into the kitchen. "We got a letter!" he cried.

His mother looked up from a pan of beans. "Who has?"

"Father has. I saw it in his hand."

Carl strode into the kitchen then, and Jody's mother asked, "Who's the letter from, Carl?"

He frowned quickly. "How did you know there was a letter?"

She nodded her head in the boy's direction. "Big-Britches Jody told me."

Jody was embarrassed.

His father looked down at him contemptuously. "He *is* getting to be a Big-Britches," Carl said. "He's minding everybody's business but his own. Got his big nose into everything."

Mrs. Tiflin relented a little. "Well, he hasn't enough to keep him busy. Who's the letter from?"

Carl still frowned on Jody. "I'll keep him busy if he isn't careful." He held out a sealed letter. "I guess it's from your father."

Mrs. Tiflin took a hairpin from her head and slit open the flap. Her lips pursed judiciously. Jody saw her eyes snap back and forth over the lines. "He says," she translated, "he says he's going to drive out Saturday to stay for a little while. Why, this is Saturday. The letter must have been delayed." She looked at the postmark. "This was mailed day before yesterday. It should have been here yesterday." She looked up questioningly at her husband, and then her face darkened angrily. "Now what have you got that look on you for? He doesn't come often."

Carl turned his eyes away from her anger. He could be stern with her most of the time, but when occasionally her temper arose, he could not combat it.

---

4. **ridge ranch,** building on hills between two valleys used when checking cattle grazing in the mountains.
5. **blue lupins**\ˈlüˑpənz\ also spelled **lupine**\ˈlüˑpən\ a wild plant of pale blue, common in the sandy soil of both eastern and western United States.

"What's the matter with you?" she demanded again.

In his explanation there was a tone of apology Jody himself might have used. "It's just that he talks," Carl said lamely. "Just talks."

"Well, what of it? You talk yourself."

"Sure I do. But your father only talks about one thing."

"Indians!" Jody broke in excitedly. "Indians and crossing the plains!"

Carl turned fiercely on him. "You get out, Mr. Big-Britches! Go on, now! Get out!"

Jody went miserably out the back door and closed the screen with elaborate quietness. Under the kitchen window his shamed, downcast eyes fell upon a curiously shaped stone, a stone of such fascination that he squatted down and picked it up and turned it over in his hands.

The voices came clearly to him through the open kitchen window. "Jody's right," he heard his father say. "Just Indians and crossing the plains. I've heard that story about how the horses got driven off about a thousand times. He just goes on and on, and he never changes a word in the things he tells."

When Mrs. Tiflin answered her tone was so changed that Jody, outside the window, looked up from his study of the stone. Her voice had become soft and explanatory. Jody knew how her face would have changed to match the tone. She said quietly, "Look at it this way, Carl. That was the big thing in my father's life. He led a wagon train clear across the plains to the coast, and when it was finished, his life was done. It was a big thing to do, but it didn't last long enough. Look!" she continued, "it's as though he was born to do that, and after he finished it, there wasn't anything more for him to do but think about it and talk about it. If there'd been any farther west to go, he'd have gone. He's told me so himself. But at last there was the ocean. He lives right by the ocean where he had to stop."

She had caught Carl, caught him and entangled him in her soft tone.

"I've seen him," he agreed quietly. "He goes down and stares off west over the ocean." His voice sharpened a little. "And then he goes up to the Horseshoe Club in Pacific Grove,[6] and he tells people how the Indians drove off the horses."

She tried to catch him again. "Well, it's everything to him. You might be patient with him and pretend to listen."

Carl turned impatiently away. "Well, if it gets too bad, I can always go down to the bunkhouse and sit with Billy," he said irritably. He walked through the house and slammed the front door after him.

Jody ran to his chores. He dumped the grain to the chickens without chasing any of them. He gathered the eggs from the nests. He trotted into the house with the wood and interlaced it so carefully in the wood-box that two armloads seemed to fill it to overflowing.

His mother had finished the beans by now. She stirred up the fire and brushed off the stove-top with a turkey wing. Jody peered cautiously at her to see whether any rancor toward him remained. "Is he coming today?" Jody asked.

"That's what his letter said."

"Maybe I better walk up the road to meet him."

Mrs. Tiflin clanged the stove-lid shut. "That would be nice," she said. "He'd probably like to be met."

"I guess I'll just do it then."

Outside, Jody whistled shrilly to the dogs. "Come on up the hill," he commanded. The two dogs waved their tails and ran ahead. Along the roadside the sage had tender new tips. Jody tore off some pieces and rubbed them on his hands until the air was filled with the sharp wild smell. With a rush the dogs leaped from the road and yapped into the brush after a rabbit. That was the last Jody saw of them, for when they failed to catch the rabbit, they went back home.

Jody plodded on up the hill toward the ridge top. When he reached the little cleft where the road came through, the afternoon wind struck

---

6. **Pacific Grove,** a residential and resort city at the south end of Monterey Bay, California.

him and blew up his hair and ruffled his shirt. He looked down on the little hills and ridges below and then out at the huge green Salinas Valley. He could see the white town of Salinas[7] far out in the flat and the flash of its windows under the waning sun. Directly below him, in an oak tree, a crow congress had convened. The tree was black with crows all cawing at once. Then Jody's eyes followed the wagon road down from the ridge where he stood, and lost it behind a hill, and picked it up again on the other side. On that distant stretch he saw a cart slowly pulled by a bay horse. It disappeared behind the hill. Jody sat down on the ground and watched the place where the cart would reappear again. The wind sang on the hilltops and the puff-ball clouds hurried eastward.

Then the cart came into sight and stopped. A man dressed in black dismounted from the seat and walked to the horse's head. Although it was so far away, Jody knew he had unhooked the check-rein, for the horse's head dropped forward. The horse moved on, and the man walked slowly up the hill beside it. Jody gave a glad cry and ran down the road toward them. The squirrels bumped along off the road, and a road-runner[8] flirted its tail and raced over the edge of the hill and sailed out like a glider.

Jody tried to leap into the middle of his shadow at every step. A stone rolled under his foot and he went down. Around a little bend he raced, and there, a short distance ahead, were his grandfather and the cart. The boy dropped from his unseemly running and approached at a dignified walk.

The horse plodded stumble-footedly up the hill and the old man walked beside it. In the lowering sun their giant shadows flickered darkly behind them. The grandfather was dressed in a black broadcloth suit and he wore kid congress gaiters[9] and a black tie on a short, hard collar. He carried his black slouch hat in his hand. His white beard was cropped close and his white eyebrows overhung his eyes like mustaches. The blue eyes were sternly merry. About the whole face and figure there was a granite dignity, so that every motion seemed an impossible thing. Once at rest, it seemed the old man would be stone, would never move again. His steps were slow and certain. Once made, no step could ever be retraced; once headed in a direction, the path would never bend nor the pace increase nor slow.

When Jody appeared around the bend, Grandfather waved his hat slowly in welcome, and he called, "Why, Jody! Come down to meet me, have you?"

Jody sidled near and turned and matched his step to the old man's step and stiffened his body and dragged his heels a little. "Yes, sir," he said. "We got your letter only today."

"Should have been here yesterday," said Grandfather. "It certainly should. How are all the folks?"

"They're fine, sir." He hesitated and then suggested shyly, "Would you like to come on a mouse hunt tomorrow, sir?"

"Mouse hunt, Jody?" Grandfather chuckled. "Have the people of this generation come down to hunting mice? They aren't very strong, the new people, but I hardly thought mice would be game for them."

"No, sir. It's just play. The haystack's gone. I'm going to drive out the mice to the dogs. And you can watch, or even beat the hay a little."

The stern, merry eyes turned down on him. "I see. You don't eat them then. You haven't come to that yet."

Jody explained. "The dogs eat them, sir. It wouldn't be much like hunting Indians, I guess."

"No, not much—but then later, when the troops were hunting Indians and shooting children and burning teepees, it wasn't much different from your mouse hunt."

They topped the rise and started down into the ranch-cup, and they lost the sun from their

---

7. **Salinas**\sə ˈlē·nəs\ city in Monterey County, west California; birthplace of Steinbeck.

8. **road-runner**, a long-tailed bird that resembles the cuckoo and is noted for running at great speeds.

9. **congress gaiters**\ˈkŏn·grəs ˈgā·tərz\ ankle-high shoes with elastic inserts in the upper portion to provide for expansion; formerly popular with members of Congress.

shoulders. "You've grown," Grandfather said. "Nearly an inch, I should say."

"More," Jody boasted. "Where they mark me on the door, I'm up more than an inch since Thanksgiving even."

Grandfather's rich throaty voice said, "Maybe you're getting too much water and turning to pith and stalk. Wait until you head out, and then we'll see."

Jody looked quickly into the old man's face to see whether his feelings should be hurt, but there was no will to injure, no punishing nor putting-in-your-place light in the keen blue eyes. "We might kill a pig," Jody suggested.

"Oh, no! I couldn't let you do that. You're just humoring me. It isn't the time and you know it."

"You know Riley, the big boar, sir?"

"Yes. I remember Riley well."

"Well, Riley ate a hole into that same haystack, and it fell down on him and smothered him."

"Pigs do that when they can," said Grandfather.

"Riley was a nice pig, for a boar, sir. I rode him sometimes, and he didn't mind."

A door slammed at the house below them, and they saw Jody's mother standing on the porch waving her apron in welcome. And they saw Carl Tiflin walking up from the barn to be at the house for the arrival.

The sun had disappeared from the hills by now. The blue smoke from the house chimney hung in flat layers in the purpling ranch-cup. The puff-ball clouds, dropped by the falling wind, hung listlessly in the sky.

Billy Buck came out of the bunkhouse and flung a wash basin of soapy water on the ground. He had been shaving in mid-week, for Billy held Grandfather in reverence, and Grandfather said that Billy was one of the few men of the new generation who had not gone soft. Although Billy was in middle age, Grandfather considered him a boy. Now Billy was hurrying toward the house too.

When Jody and Grandfather arrived, the three were waiting for them in front of the yard gate.

Carl said, "Hello, sir. We've been looking for you."

Mrs. Tiflin kissed Grandfather on the side of his beard, and stood still while his big hand patted her shoulder. Billy shook hands solemnly, grinning under his straw mustache. "I'll put up your horse," said Billy, and he led the rig away.

Grandfather watched him go, and then, turning back to the group, he said as he had said a hundred times before, "There's a good boy. I knew his father, old Mule-tail Buck. I never knew why they called him Mule-tail except he packed mules."

Mrs. Tiflin turned and led the way into the house. "How long are you going to stay, Father? Your letter didn't say."

"Well, I don't know. I thought I'd stay about two weeks. But I never stay as long as I think I'm going to."

In a short while they were sitting at the white oilcloth table eating their supper. The lamp with the tin reflector hung over the table. Outside the dining-room windows the big moths battered softly against the glass.

Grandfather cut his steak into tiny pieces and chewed slowly. "I'm hungry," he said. "Driving out here got my appetite up. It's like when we were crossing. We all got so hungry every night we could hardly wait to let the meat get done. I could eat about five pounds of buffalo meat every night."

"It's moving around does it," said Billy. "My father was a government packer.[10] I helped him when I was a kid. Just the two of us could about clean up a deer's ham."

"I knew your father, Billy," said Grandfather. "A fine man he was. They called him Mule-tail Buck. I don't know why except he packed mules."

"That was it," Billy agreed. "He packed mules."

Grandfather put down his knife and fork and looked around the table. "I remember one time

_____

10. **government packer,** official chosen to supervise packing of marketable items, as beef, pork, tobacco.

On the right, one group is headed north to Oregon; on the left, another group heads west to California.

we ran out of meat—" His voice dropped to a curious low sing-song, dropped into a tonal groove the story had worn for itself. "There was no buffalo, no antelope, not even rabbits. The hunters couldn't even shoot a coyote. That was the time for the leader to be on the watch. I was the leader, and I kept my eyes open. Know why? Well, just the minute the people began to get hungry they'd start slaughtering the team oxen. Do you believe that? I've heard of parties that just ate up their draft cattle.[11] Started from the middle and worked towards the ends. Finally they'd eat the lead pair,[12] and then the

wheelers.[13] The leader of a party had to keep them from doing that."

In some manner a big moth got into the room and circled the hanging kerosene lamp. Billy got up and tried to clap it between his hands. Carl struck with a cupped palm and caught the moth and broke it. He walked to the window and dropped it out.

"As I was saying," Grandfather began again, but Carl interrupted him. "You'd better eat

11. **draft cattle,** cattle suitable for drawing heavy loads.
12. **lead pair,** oxen fastened to vehicle in front of all others in the same team.
13. **wheelers,** oxen harnessed nearest the wheels.

some more meat. All the rest of us are ready for our pudding."

Jody saw a flash of anger in his mother's eyes. Grandfather picked up his knife and fork. "I'm pretty hungry, all right," he said. "I'll tell you about that later."

When supper was over, when the family and Billy Buck sat in front of the fireplace in the other room, Jody anxiously watched Grandfather. He saw the signs he knew. The bearded head leaned forward; the eyes lost their sternness and looked wonderingly into the fire; the big lean fingers laced themselves on the black knees.

"I wonder," he began, "I just wonder whether I ever told you how those thieving Piutes[14] drove off thirty-five of our horses."

"I think you did," Carl interrupted. "Wasn't it just before you went up into the Tahoe[15] country?"

Grandfather turned quickly toward his son-in-law. "That's right. I guess I must have told you that story."

"Lots of times," Carl said cruelly, and he avoided his wife's eyes. But he felt the angry eyes on him, and he said, "'Course I'd like to hear it again."

Grandfather looked back at the fire. His fingers unlaced and laced again. Jody knew how he felt, how his insides were collapsed and empty. Hadn't Jody been called a Big-Britches that very afternoon? He arose to heroism and opened himself to the term Big-Britches again. "Tell about Indians," he said softly.

Grandfather's eyes grew stern again. "Boys always want to hear about Indians. It was a job for men, but boys want to hear about it. Well, let's see. Did I ever tell you how I wanted each wagon to carry a long iron plate?"

Everyone but Jody remained silent. Jody said, "No. You didn't."

"Well, when the Indians attacked, we always put the wagons in a circle and fought from between the wheels. I thought that if every wagon carried a long plate with rifle holes, the men could stand the plates on the outside of the wheels when the wagons were in the circle and

they would be protected. It would save lives and that would make up for the extra weight of the iron. But of course the party wouldn't do it. No party had done it before and they couldn't see why they should go to the expense. They lived to regret it, too."

Jody looked at his mother, and knew from her expression that she was not listening at all. Carl picked at a callus on his thumb and Billy Buck watched a spider crawling up the wall.

Grandfather's tone dropped into its narrative groove again. Jody knew in advance exactly what words would fall. The story droned on, speeded up for the attack, grew sad over the wounds, struck a dirge at the burials on the great plains. Jody sat quietly watching Grandfather. The stern blue eyes were detached. He looked as though he were not very interested in the story himself.

When it was finished, when the pause had been politely respected as the frontier of the story, Billy Buck stood up and stretched and hitched his trousers. "I guess I'll turn in," he said. Then he faced Grandfather. "I've got an old powder horn and a cap and ball pistol down to the bunkhouse. Did I ever show them to you?"

Grandfather nodded slowly. "Yes, I think you did, Billy. Reminds me of a pistol I had when I was leading the people across." Billy stood politely until the little story was done, and then he said, "Good night," and went out of the house.

Carl Tiflin tried to turn the conversation then. "How's the country between here and Monterey?[16] I've heard it's pretty dry."

"It is dry," said Grandfather. "There's not a drop of water in the Laguna Seca.[17] But it's a long pull from '87. The whole country was

---

14. **Piutes**\ˈpaɪ·ūt\ variation of Paiute\ˈpaɪ·ūt\ Indian people of Western Utah, northwestern Arizona, southeastern Nevada, and southeastern California.
15. **Tahoe**\ˈta ˈhō\ country, area around California-Nevada boundary.
16. **Monterey,** city in west California, south end of Monterey Bay.
17. **Laguna Seca**\la ˈgū·nə ˈsē·kə\ meaning "dry lake."

powder then, and in '61 I believe all the coyotes starved to death. We had fifteen inches of rain this year."

"Yes, but it all came too early. We could do with some now." Carl's eye fell on Jody. "Hadn't you better be getting to bed?"

Jody stood up obediently. "Can I kill the mice in the old haystack, sir?"

"Mice? Oh! Sure, kill them all off. Billy said there isn't any good hay left."

Jody exchanged a secret and satisfying look with Grandfather. "I'll kill every one tomorrow," he promised.

Jody lay in his bed and thought of the impossible world of Indians and buffaloes, a world that had ceased to be forever. He wished he could have been living in the heroic time, but he knew he was not of heroic timber. No one living now, save possibly Billy Buck, was worthy to do the things that had been done. A race of giants had lived then, fearless men, men of a staunchness unknown in this day. Jody thought of the wide plains and of the wagons moving across like centipedes. He thought of Grandfather on a huge white horse, marshaling the people. Across his mind marched the great phantoms, and they marched off the earth and they were gone.

He came back to the ranch for a moment, then. He heard the dull rushing sound that space and silence make. He heard one of the dogs, out in the doghouse, scratching a flea and bumping his elbow against the floor with every stroke. Then the wind arose again and the black cypress groaned and Jody went to sleep.

He was up half an hour before the triangle[18] sounded for breakfast. His mother was rattling the stove to make the flames roar when Jody went through the kitchen. "You're up early," she said. "Where are you going?"

"Out to get a good stick. We're going to kill the mice today."

"Who is 'we'?"

"Why, Grandfather and I."

"So you've got him in it. You always like to have some one in with you in case there's blame to share."

"I'll be right back," said Jody. "I just want to have a good stick ready for after breakfast."

He closed the screen door after him and went out into the cool blue morning. The birds were noisy in the dawn and the ranch cats came down from the hill like blunt snakes. They had been hunting gophers in the dark, and although the four cats were full of gopher meat, they sat in a semi-circle at the back door and mewed piteously for milk. Doubletree Mutt and Smasher moved sniffing along the edge of the brush, performing the duty with rigid ceremony, but when Jody whistled, their heads jerked up and their tails waved. They plunged down to him, wriggling their skins and yawning. Jody patted their heads seriously, and moved on to the weathered scrap pile. He selected an old broom handle and a short piece of inch-square scrap wood. From his pocket he took a shoelace and tied the ends of the sticks loosely together to make a flail.[19] He whistled his new weapon through the air and struck the ground experimentally, while the dogs leaped aside and whined with apprehension.

Jody turned and started down past the house toward the old haystack ground to look over the field of slaughter, but Billy Buck, sitting patiently on the back steps, called to him, "You better come back. It's only a couple of minutes till breakfast."

Jody changed his course and moved toward the house. He leaned his flail against the steps. "That's to drive the mice out," he said. "I'll bet they're fat. I'll bet they don't know what's going to happen to them today."

"No, nor you either," Billy remarked philosophically, "nor me, nor anyone."

Jody was staggered by this thought. He knew it was true. His imagination twitched away from the mouse hunt. Then his mother came out on the back porch and struck the triangle, and all thoughts fell in a heap.

---

18. **triangle,** a steel rod bent into the shape of a triangle, sounded by striking with a metal rod; used for calling ranch hands to eat.

19. **flail** \flāl\ an instrument for threshing grain.

Grandfather hadn't appeared at the table when they sat down. Billy nodded at his empty chair. "He's all right? He isn't sick?"

"He takes a long time to dress," said Mrs. Tiflin. "He combs his whiskers and rubs up his shoes and brushes his clothes."

Carl scattered sugar on his mush. "A man that's led a wagon train across the plains has got to be pretty careful how he dresses."

Mrs. Tiflin turned on him. "Don't do that, Carl! Please don't!" There was more of threat than of request in her tone. And the threat irritated Carl.

"Well, how many times do I have to listen to the story of the iron plates, and the thirty-five horses? That time's done. Why can't he forget it, now it's done?" He grew angrier while he talked, and his voice rose. "Why does he have to tell them over and over? He came across the plains. All right! Now it's finished. Nobody wants to hear about it over and over."

The door into the kitchen closed softly. The four at the table sat frozen. Carl laid his mush spoon[20] on the table and touched his chin with his fingers.

Then the kitchen door opened and Grandfather walked in. His mouth smiled tightly and his eyes were squinted. "Good morning," he said, and he sat down and looked at his mush dish.

Carl could not leave it there. "Did—did you hear what I said?"

Grandfather jerked a little nod.

"I don't know what got into me, sir. I didn't mean it. I was just being funny."

Jody glanced in shame at his mother, and he saw that she was looking at Carl, and that she wasn't breathing. It was an awful thing that he was doing. He was tearing himself to pieces to talk like that. It was a terrible thing to him to retract a word, but to retract it in shame was infinitely worse.

Grandfather looked sidewise. "I'm trying to get right side up," he said gently. "I'm not being mad. I don't mind what you said, but it might be true, and I would mind that."

"It isn't true," said Carl. "I'm not feeling well this morning. I'm sorry I said it."

"Don't be sorry, Carl. An old man doesn't see things sometimes. Maybe you're right. The crossing is finished. Maybe it should be forgotten, now it's done."

Carl got up from the table. "I've had enough to eat. I'm going to work. Take your time, Billy!" He walked quickly out of the dining-room. Billy gulped the rest of his food and followed soon after. But Jody could not leave his chair.

"Won't you tell any more stories?" Jody asked.

"Why, sure I'll tell them, but only when—I'm sure people want to hear them."

"I like to hear them, sir."

"Oh! Of course you do, but you're a little boy. It was a job for men, but only little boys like to hear about it."

Jody got up from his place. "I'll wait outside for you, sir. I've got a good stick for those mice."

He waited by the gate until the old man came out on the porch. "Let's go down and kill the mice now," Jody called.

"I think I'll just sit in the sun, Jody. You go kill the mice."

"You can use my stick if you like."

"No, I'll just sit here a while."

Jody turned disconsolately away, and walked down toward the old haystack. He tried to whip up his enthusiasm with thoughts of the fat juicy mice. He beat the ground with his flail. The dogs coaxed and whined about him, but he could not go. Back at the house he could see Grandfather sitting on the porch, looking small and thin and black.

Jody gave up and went to sit on the steps at the old man's feet.

"Back already? Did you kill the mice?"

"No, sir. I'll kill them some other day."

The morning flies buzzed close to the ground and the ants dashed about in front of the steps.

---

20. **mush spoon,** a utensil for eating mush, a porridge of thick consistency made from cornmeal.

The heavy smell of sage slipped down the hill. The porch boards grew warm in the sunshine.

Jody hardly knew when Grandfather started to talk. "I shouldn't stay here, feeling the way I do." He examined his strong old hands. "I feel as though the crossing wasn't worth doing." His eyes moved up the side-hill and stopped on a motionless hawk perched on a dead limb. "I tell those old stories, but they're not what I want to tell. I only know how I want people to feel when I tell them.

"It wasn't Indians that were important, nor adventures, nor even getting out here. It was a whole bunch of people made into one big crawling beast. And I was the head. It was westering and westering. Every man wanted something for himself, but the big beast that was all of them wanted only westering. I was the leader, but if I hadn't been there, someone else would have been the head. The thing had to have a head.

"Under the little bushes the shadows were black at white noonday. When we saw the mountains at last, we cried—all of us. But it wasn't getting here that mattered, it was movement and westering.

"We carried life out here and set it down the way those ants carry eggs. And I was the leader. The westering was as big as God, and the slow steps that made the movement piled up and piled up until the continent was crossed.

"Then we came down to the sea, and it was done." He stopped and wiped his eyes until the rims were red. "That's what I should be telling instead of stories."

When Jody spoke, Grandfather started and looked down at him. "Maybe I could lead the people some day," Jody said.

The old man smiled. "There's no place to go. There's the ocean to stop you. There's a line of old men along the shore hating the ocean because it stopped them."

"In boats I might, sir."

"No place to go, Jody. Every place is taken. But that's not the worst—no, not the worst. Westering has died out of the people. Westering isn't a hunger any more. It's all done. Your

father is right. It is finished." He laced his fingers on his knee and looked at them.

Jody felt very sad. "If you'd like a glass of lemonade I could make it for you."

Grandfather was about to refuse, and then he saw Jody's face. "That would be nice," he said. "Yes, it would be nice to drink a lemonade."

Jody ran into the kitchen where his mother was wiping the last of the breakfast dishes. "Can I have a lemon to make a lemonade for Grandfather?"

His mother mimicked—"And another lemon to make a lemonade for you."

"No, ma'am. I don't want one."

"Jody! You're sick!" Then she stopped suddenly. "Take a lemon out of the cooler," she said softly. "Here, I'll reach the squeezer down to you."

I

A DREAM FINISHED

In fiction, particularly, titles are often of great importance; they give the reader cues on what to look for in the pages that follow. Sometimes a title tells the reader that the work of fiction is going to center on a certain character or a certain action; at other times a title may give the reader some indication of the author's theme.

On the basis of the title of this story, the reader knows that the author attaches great significance to the fact that Grandfather had been the leader of a "whole bunch of people made into one big crawling beast" that was part of the westering movement. According to Grandfather, when did the dream and excitement of westering vanish? Why, in his opinion, is there no chance for Jody to be a leader? Do you agree that the "westering" spirit is dead in America? Why or why not?

II

IMPLICATIONS

Consider and discuss the following:

1. Generations view events from different perspectives, and this often leads to antagonism between generations.

2. Viewed through the rosy glow of retrospection, events of the past are surrounded by romance.

3. All persons are potential leaders. All they need are the right circumstances to bring out the leadership qualities they possess.

4. The desire to push to new frontiers is a dead dream for the American people.

III
TECHNIQUES

Setting

In "The Leader of the People," the place setting is a farm in the Salinas Valley of California. Steinbeck makes the reader aware of this setting in various ways. The haystack, for example, which stands as a kind of shorthand symbol of farm life, is mentioned throughout the story. Steinbeck also continually reminds his reader that the story is taking place in the Far West, "right by the ocean."

Specific details are particularly helpful in visualizing a locality. What are some of the trees, wild flowers, shrub growth, and small animals mentioned that help give you an idea of the farm landscape? What specific place-names are given to identify this area of California?

The time setting is less specifically realized than the place setting. We are never told that the story occurs in such and such a year. But we are still kept quite conscious of a special aspect of time— we know that the story takes place two generations after the frontier has been reached. And this, of course, is what matters to the theme of Steinbeck's story.

Steinbeck, like most good short-story writers, subtly begins to build the atmosphere through specific details early in the story. At the end of the first paragraph we read, "The wind could be heard whishing in the brush on the ridge crests, but no breath of it penetrated down into the ranch-cup." A moment later we find Billy *looking up* at the top of the hills, and shortly after Jody *looks up* at "the little puffs of wind-driven cloud." It seems clear from these details that the ranch is a settled place where the westering spirit is hardly likely to grow.

The atmosphere associated with the ranch is in direct contrast with the spirit of Grandfather and with Jody's hunger for frontiers to explore. Steinbeck points up this contrast by having Jody leave the "ranch-cup" just as he is about to meet the old man for the first time in the story. Wind—a natural symbol for creativity, change, and the westering urge—does not touch Carl, but when Grandfather arrives, we read, "The wind sang on the hilltops and the puff-balls of clouds hurried eastward."

Details like these are not accidental. Whether or not the reader consciously takes note of them is perhaps not of great importance; but they are there, doing their work of creating an atmosphere, a mood that the author hopes the reader will *feel*.

To appreciate the techniques a writer uses to create atmosphere, it would be worthwhile for you to reread this story. As you do, make a list of the various phrases and sentences that help to communicate the feeling that the Tiffin ranch is "sealed off," removed from outside influences and thus from the westering spirit that endlessly sought new frontiers to explore.

Characterization

The reader learns about Grandfather, the central figure in "The Leader of the People," (1) from what Grandfather says and does: "I tell these old stories, but they're not what I want to tell. I only know how I want people to feel when I tell them"; (2) from the author's description: "The blue eyes were sternly merry. About the whole face and figure there was a granite dignity, so that every motion seemed an impossible thing"; (3) from what others say: "Well, how many times do I have to listen to the story of the iron plates, and the thirty-five horses? That time's done. Why can't he forget it, now it's done?"; and (4) from the implicit comparison between Grandfather and Carl, which runs throughout the story.

When authors want to impress a character on the reader's mind, they often repeat a detail or a series of related details about that character. Grandfather, for example, is described as possessing "granite dignity"; the adjective "stern" is used several times to describe him; and of course he dresses sternly, with "granite dignity," all in black.

Steinbeck's characters in this story are obviously of greater importance than the plot. There is a climax in the story—Grandfather's overhearing his son-in-law's insulting remarks—but it is hardly more than a brief episode in a series. The characters, however, loom large in importance. By what methods does Steinbeck reveal the character of Jody, of his mother, of his father, and of the ranchhand, Billy? Can you find any particular repetition of adjectives or phrases used to describe any of these characters?

Give me your tired, your poor,
Your huddled masses yearning to breathe
   free,
The wretched refuse of your teeming shore.
Send these, the homeless, tempest-tost
   to me,
I lift my lamp beside the golden door."

FROM "THE NEW COLOSSUS"
BY EMMA LAZARUS

Graven on the base of the Statue of Liberty, these words have long promised
a loving welcome to the immigrant coming to America. Think about this
promise when you read the following account, part truth and part fiction, of
an immigrant girl's search for fulfillment of that American pledge.

How I Found America

ANZIA YEZIERSKA

Every breath I drew was a breath of fear, every shadow a stifling shock, every footfall struck on my heart like the heavy boot of the Cossack.[1]

On a low stool in the middle of the only room in our mud hut sat my father, his red beard falling over the Book of Isaiah open before him. On the tile stove, on the benches that were our beds, even on the earthen floor, sat the neighbors' children, learning from him the ancient poetry of the Hebrew race.

As he chanted, the children repeated:

The voice of him that crieth in the wilderness,
Prepare ye the way of the Lord.
Make straight in the desert a highway for our God.

Every valley shall be exalted,
And every mountain and hill shall be made low,
And the crooked shall be made straight,
And the rough places plain.

And the glory of the Lord shall be revealed,
And all flesh shall see it together.

Undisturbed by the swaying and chanting of teacher and pupils, old Kakah, our speckled hen, with her brood of chicks, strutted and pecked at the potato-peelings which fell from my mother's lap, as she prepared our noon meal.

I stood at the window watching the road, lest the Cossack come upon us unawares to enforce the ukaz[2] of the Czar, which would tear the bread from our mouths: "No Chadir [Hebrew school] shall be held in a room used for cooking and sleeping."

With one eye I watched ravenously my mother cutting chunks of black bread. At last the potatoes were ready. She poured them out of the iron pot into a wooden bowl and placed them in the center of the table.

"How I Found America" by Anzia Yezierska from *Hungry Hearts* by Anzia Yezierska. Reprinted by Arno Press, 1975. Copyright 1948. By permission of Louise Levitas Henriksen.

1. **Cossack** \▲kŏs•ăk\ One of a people of southern Russia, noted as horse soldiers.
2. **ukaz** \yo͞o▲kȧz\ an order. The English spelling is *ukase*.

Instantly the swaying and chanting ceased, the children rushed forward. The fear of the Cossacks was swept away from my heart by the fear that the children would get my potato.

I deserted my post. With a shout of joy I seized my portion and bit a huge mouthful of mealy delight.

At that moment the door was driven open by the blow of an iron heel. The Cossack's whip swished through the air. Screaming, we scattered.

The children ran out—our livelihood gone with them.

"Oi weh," wailed my mother, clutching her breast, "is there a God over us and sees all this?"

With grief-glazed eyes my father muttered a broken prayer as the Cossack thundered the ukaz: "A thousand rubles[3] fine or a year in prison if you are ever found again teaching children where you're eating and sleeping."

"Gottuniu!" pleaded my mother, "would you tear the last skin from our bones? Where else can we be eating and sleeping? Or should we keep chadir in the middle of the road? Have we houses with separate rooms like the Czar?"

Ignoring my mother's entreaties, the Cossack strode out of the hut. My father sank into a chair, his head bowed in the silent grief of the helpless.

"God from the world," my mother wrung her hands, "is there no end to our troubles? When will the earth cover me and my woes?"

I watched the Cossack disappear down the road. All at once I saw the whole village running toward us. I dragged my mother to the window to see the approaching crowd.

"Gewalt! What more is falling over our heads?" she cried in alarm.

Masheh Mindel, the water-carrier's wife, headed a wild procession. The baker, the butcher, the shoemaker, the tailor, the goatherd, the workers of the fields, with their wives and children, pressed toward us through a cloud of dust.

Masheh Mindel, almost fainting, fell in front of the doorway. "A letter from America!" she gasped.

"A letter from America!" echoed the crowd, as they snatched the letter from her and thrust it into my father's hands.

"Read! Read!" they shouted tumultuously.

My father looked through the letter, his lips uttering no sound. In breathless suspense the crowd gazed at him. Their eyes shone with wonder and reverence for the only man in the village who could read.

Masheh Mindel crouched at his feet, her neck stretched toward him to catch each precious word of the letter.

"To my worthy wife, Masheh Mindel, and to my loving son, Susha Feifel, and to my precious darling daughter, the apple of my eye, the pride of my life, Tzipkeleh!

"Long years and good luck on you! May the blessings from heaven fall over your beloved heads and save you from all harm!

"First I come to tell you that I am well and in good health. May I hear the same from you.

"Secondly, I am telling you that my sun is beginning to shine in America. I am becoming a person, a business man.

"I have for myself a stand in the most crowded part of America, where people are as thick as flies and every day is like market-day by a fair. My business is from bananas and apples. The day begins with my pushcart full of fruit, and the day never ends before I count up at least $2.00 profit. That means four rubles. Stand before your eyes, I, Gedalyeh Mindel, four rubles a day, twenty-four rubles a week!"

"Gedalyeh Mindel, the water-carrier, twenty-four rubles a week . . ." The words leaped like fire in the air.

We gazed at his wife, Masheh Mindel, a dried-out bone of a woman.

"Masheh Mindel, with a husband in America, Masheh Mindel, the wife of a man earning twenty-four rubles a week!"

We looked at her with new reverence. Already she was a being from another world. The

---

3. **rubles** \ˈroo·bəlz\ the basic Russian monetary unit.

dead, sunken eyes became alive with light. The worry for bread that had tightened the skin of her cheek-bones was gone. The sudden surge of happiness filled out her features, flushing her face as with wine. The two starved children clinging to her skirts, dazed with excitement, only dimly realized their good fortune by the envious glances of the others.

"Thirdly, I come to tell you," the letter went on, "white bread and meat I eat every day just like the millionaires.

"Fourthly, I have to tell you that I am no more Gedalyeh Mindel. *Mister* Mindel they call me in America.

"Fifthly, Masheh Mindel and my dear children, in America there are no mud huts where cows and chickens and people live all together. I have for myself a separate room with a closed door, and before any one can come to me, I can give a say, 'Come in,' or 'Stay out,' like a king in a palace.

"Lastly, my darling family and people of the Village of Sukovoly, there is no Czar in America."

My father paused; the hush was stifling. No Czar—no Czar in America! Even the little babies repeated the chant: "No Czar in America!"

"In America they ask everybody who should be the President, and I, Gedalyeh Mindel, when I take out my Citizens papers, will have as much to say who shall be the next President in America, as Mr. Rockefeller the greatest millionaire.

"Fifty rubles I am sending you for your ship-ticket to America. And may all Jews who suffer in Goluth from ukazes and pogroms[4] live yet to lift up their heads like me, Gedalyeh Mindel, in America."

Fifty rubles! A ship-ticket to America! That so much good luck should fall on one head! Savage envy bit us. Gloomy darts from narrowed eyes stabbed Masheh Mindel. Why should not we too have a chance to get away from this dark land? Has not every heart the same hunger for America, the same longing to live and laugh and breathe like a free human being? America is for all. Why should only Masheh Mindel and her children have a chance to the new world?

Murmuring and gesticulating the crowd dispersed. Each one knew every one else's thought: How to get to America. What could they pawn? From where could they borrow for a ship-ticket?

Silently we followed my father back into the hut from which the Cossack had driven us a while before.

We children looked from mother to father and from father to mother.

"Gottuniu! The Czar himself is pushing us to America by this last ukaz." My mother's face lighted up the hut like a lamp.

"Meshugeneh Yidini!" admonished my father. "Always your head in the air. What—where—America? With what money? Can dead people lift themselves up to dance?"

"Dance?" The samovar[5] and the brass pots rang and reëchoed with my mother's laughter. "I could dance myself over the waves of the ocean to America."

In amazed delight at my mother's joy, we children rippled and chuckled with her. My father paced the room, his face dark with dread for the morrow.

"Empty hands, empty pockets; yet it dreams itself in you—America."

"Who is poor who has hopes on America?" flaunted my mother.

"Sell my red quilted petticoat that grandmother left for my dowry," I urged in excitement.

"Sell the feather beds, sell the samovar," chorused the children.

"Sure we can sell everything—the goat and all the winter things," added my mother. "It must be always summer in America."

---

4. **pogroms** \ˈpoˌgrəmz\ an organized massacre or persecution of a minority group.

5. **samovar** \ˈsămˌəˈvär\ metal urn with spigot, used to boil water for tea.

I flung my arms around my brother and he seized Bessie by the curls, and we danced about the room crazy with joy.

"Beggars!" laughed my mother, "why are you so happy with yourselves? How will you go to America without a shirt on your back, without shoes on your feet?"

But we ran out into the road, shouting and singing: "We'll sell everything we got; we'll go to America."

"White bread and meat we'll eat every day in America! In America!"

That very evening we fetched Berel Zalman, the usurer, and showed him all our treasures, piled up in the middle of the hut.

"Look, all these fine feather beds, Berel Zalman!" urged my mother. "This grand fur coat came from Nijny itself. My grandfather bought it at the fair."

I held up my red quilted petticoat, the supreme sacrifice of my young life.

Even my father shyly pushed forward the samovar. "It can hold enough tea for the whole village."

"Only a hundred rubles for them all," pleaded my mother, "only enough to lift us to America! Only one hundred little rubles."

"A hundred rubles? Pfui!" sniffed the pawnbroker. "Forty is overpaid. Not even thirty is it worth."

But coaxing and cajoling my mother got a hundred rubles out of him.

Steerage,[6] dirty bundles, foul odors, seasick humanity; but I saw and heard nothing of the foulness and ugliness around me. I floated in showers of sunshine; visions upon visions of the New World opened before me.

From lip to lip flowed the golden legend of the golden country:

"In America you can say what you feel; you can voice your thoughts in the open streets without fear of a Cossack."

"In America is a home for everybody. The land is your land. Not like in Russia where you feel yourself a stranger in the village where you were born and raised, the village in which your father and grandfather lie buried."

"Everybody is with everybody alike, in America. Christians and Jews are brothers together."

"An end to the worry for bread. An end to the fear of the bosses over you. Everybody can do what he wants with his life in America."

"There are no high or low in America. Even the President holds hands with Gedalyeh Mindel."

"Plenty for all. Learning flows free like milk and honey."

"Learning flows free."

The words painted pictures in my mind. I saw before me free schools, free colleges, free libraries, where I could learn and learn and keep on learning.

In our village was a school, but only for certain children. In the schools of America I'd lift up my head and laugh and dance, a child with other children. Like a bird in the air, from sky to sky, from star to star, I'd soar and soar.

"Land! Land!" came the joyous shout.

"America! We're in America!" cried my mother, almost smothering us in her rapture.

All crowded and pushed on deck. They strained and stretched to get the first glimpse of the "golden country," lifting their children on their shoulders that they might see beyond them. Men fell on their knees to pray. Women hugged their babies and wept. Children danced. Strangers embraced and kissed like old friends. Old men and women had in their eyes a look of young people in love. Age-old visions sang themselves in me, songs of freedom of an oppressed people.

America! America!

Between buildings that loomed like mountains, we struggled with our bundles, spreading around us the smell of the steerage. Up Broadway, under the bridge, and through the swarming streets of the ghetto, we followed Gedalyeh Mindel.

---

6. **steerage,** section of a passenger ship with the cheapest travel accommodations.

I looked about the narrow streets of squeezed-in stores and houses, ragged clothes, dirty bedding oozing out of the windows, ashcans and garbage-cans cluttering the sidewalks. A vague sadness pressed down my heart, the first doubt of America.

"Where are the green fields and open spaces in America?" cried my heart. "Where is the golden country of my dreams?"

A loneliness for the fragrant silence of the woods that lay beyond our mud hut welled up in my heart, a longing for the soft, responsive earth of our village streets. All about me was the hardness of brick and stone, the stinking smells of crowded poverty.

"Here's your house with separate rooms like in a palace." Gedalyeh Mindel flung open the door of a dingy, airless flat.

"Oi weh!" my mother cried in dismay. "Where's the sunshine in America?"

She went to the window and looked out at the blank wall of the next house. "Gottuniu! Like in a grave so dark . . ."

"It ain't so dark; it's only a little shady." Gedalyeh Mindel lighted the gas. "Look only"—he pointed with pride to the dim gaslight.

"No candles, no kerosene lamps in America, you turn on a screw and put to it a match and you got it light like with sunshine."

Again the shadow fell over me, again the doubt of America!

In America were rooms without sunlight, rooms to sleep in, to eat in, to cook in, but without sunshine, and Gedalyeh Mindel was happy. Could I be satisfied with just a place to sleep and eat in, and a door to shut people out, to take the place of sunlight? Or would I always need the sunlight to be happy?

And where was there a place in America for me to play? I looked out into the alley below and saw pale-faced children scrambling in the gutter. "Where is America?" cried my heart.

My eyes were shutting themselves with sleep. Blindly, I felt for the buttons on my dress, and buttoning I sank back in sleep again—the deadweight sleep of utter exhaustion.

"Heart of mine!" my mother's voice moaned above me. "Father is already gone an hour. You know how they'll squeeze from you a nickel for every minute you're late. Quick only!"

I seized my bread and herring and tumbled down the stairs and out into the street. I ate running, blindly pressing through the hurrying throngs of workers, my haste and fear choking each mouthful. I felt a strangling in my throat as I neared the sweatshop[7] prison; all my nerves screwed together into iron hardness to endure the day's torture.

For an instant I hesitated as I faced the grated windows of the old dilapidated building. Dirt and decay cried out from every crumbling brick.

In the maw of the shop raged around me the roar and the clatter, the merciless grind of the pounding machines. Half maddened, half deadened, I struggled to think, to feel, to remember. What am I? Who am I? Why am I here?

I struggled in vain, bewildered and lost in a whirlpool of noise. "Where was America?" cried my heart.

The factory whistle, the slowing-down of the machines, shouted release, hailing the noon hour. I woke as from a tense nightmare, a weary waking to pain. In the dark chaos of my brain reason began to dawn. In my stifled heart feelings began to pulse. The wound of my wasted life began to throb and ache. With my childhood choked with drudgery, must my youth, too, die, unlived? Here was the odor of herring and garlic, the ravenous munching of food, laughter and loud, vulgar jokes. Was it only I who was so wretched? I looked at those around me. Were they happy or only insensible to their slavery? How could they laugh and joke? Why were they not torn with rebellion against this galling grind, the crushing, dead-

---

7. **sweatshop,** shop or factory in which workers are paid low wages to work long hours under poor conditions.

ening movements of the body, where only hands live and hearts and brains must die?

A touch on my shoulder. I looked up. It was Yetta Solomon from the machine next to mine.

"Here's your tea."

I stared at her, half hearing.

"Ain't you going to eat nothing?"

"Oi weh! Yetta! I can't stand it!" The cry broke from me. "I didn't come to America to turn into a machine. I came to America to make from myself a person. Does America want only my hands, only the strength of my body, not my heart, not my feelings, my thoughts?"

"Our heads ain't smart enough," said Yetta, practically. "We ain't been to school like the American-born."

"What for did I come to America but to go to school, to learn, to think, to make something beautiful from my life?"

"Sh-sh! Sh-sh! The boss! The boss!" came the warning whisper.

A sudden hush fell over the shop as the boss entered. He raised his hand.

Breathless silence.

The hard, red face with pig's eyes held us under its sickening spell. Again I saw the Cossack and heard him thunder the ukaz.

Prepared for disaster, the girls paled as they cast at each other sidelong, frightened glances.

"Hands," he addressed us, fingering the gold watch-chain that spread across his fat stomach, "it's slack in the other trades and I can get plenty girls begging themselves to work for half what you're getting; only I ain't a skinner. I always give my hands a show to earn their bread. From now on I'll give you fifty cents a dozen shirts instead of seventy-five, but I'll give you night-work, so you needn't lose nothing." And he was gone.

The stillness of death filled the shop. Each one felt the heart of the other bleed with her own helplessness.

A sudden sound broke the silence. A woman sobbed chokingly. It was Balah Rifkin, a widow with three children.

"Oi weh!" She tore at her scrawny neck. "The blood-sucker! The thief! How will I give them to eat, my babies, my hungry little lambs!"

"Why do we let him choke us?"

"Twenty-five cents less on a dozen—how will we be able to live?"

"He tears the last skin from our bones!"

"Why didn't nobody speak up to him?"

Something in me forced me forward. Rage at the bitter greed tore me. Our desperate helplessness drove me to strength.

"I'll go to the boss!" I cried, my nerves quivering with fierce excitement. "I'll tell him Balah Rifkin has three hungry mouths to feed."

Pale, hungry faces thrust themselves toward me; thin, knotted hands reached out; starved bodies pressed close about me.

"Long years on you!" cried Balah Rifkin, drying her eyes with a corner of her shawl.

"Tell him about my old father and me, his only bread-giver," came from Bessie Sopolsky, a gaunt-faced girl with a hacking cough.

"And I got no father or mother and four of them younger than me hanging on my neck." Jennie Feist's beautiful young face was already scarred with the gray worries of age.

America, as the oppressed of all lands have dreamed America to be, and America *as it is*, flashed before me—a banner of fire! Behind me I felt masses pressing, thousands of immigrants; thousands upon thousands crushed by injustice, lifted me as on wings.

I entered the boss's office without a shadow of fear. I was not I; the wrongs of my people burned through me till I felt the very flesh of my body a living flame of rebellion.

I faced the boss.

"We can't stand it!" I cried. "Even as it is we're hungry. Fifty cents a dozen would starve us. Can you, a Jew, tear the bread from another Jew's mouth?"

"You, fresh mouth, you! Who are you to learn me my business?"

"Weren't you yourself once a machine slave, your life in the hands of your boss?"

"You loaferin! Money for nothing you want! The minute they begin to talk English they get flies in their nose. A black year on you, trouble-maker! I'll have no smart heads in my shop! Such freshness! Out you get. Out from my shop!"

Stunned and hopeless, the wings of my courage broken, I groped my way back to them—back to the eager, waiting faces, back to the crushed hearts aching with mine.

As I opened the door, they read our defeat in my face.

"Girls!" I held out my hands. "He's fired me."

My voice died in the silence. Not a girl stirred. Their heads only bent closer over their machines.

"Here, you! Get yourself out of here!" The boss thundered at me. "Bessie Sopolsky and you, Balah Rifkin, take out her machine into the hall. I want no big-mouthed Americanerins in my shop."

Bessie Sopolsky and Balah Rifkin, their eyes black with tragedy, carried out my machine.

Not a hand was held out to me, not a face met mine. I felt them shrink from me as I passed them on my way out.

In the street I found I was crying. The new hope that had flowed in me so strongly bled out of my veins. A moment before, our togetherness had made me believe us so strong, and now I saw each alone, crushed, broken. What were they all but crawling worms, servile grubbers for bread?

And then in the very bitterness of my resentment the hardness broke in me. I saw the girls through their own eyes as if I were inside of them. What else could they have done? Was not an immediate crust of bread for Balah Rifkin's children more urgent than truth, more vital than honor?

Could it be that they ever had dreamed of America as I had dreamed? Had their faith in America wholly died in them? Could my faith be killed as theirs had been?

Gasping from running, Yetta Solomon flung her arms around me.

"You golden heart! I sneaked myself out from the shop only to tell you I'll come to see you tonight. I'd give the blood from under my nails for you, only I got to run back. I got to hold my job. My mother———"

I hardly saw or heard her, my senses stunned with my defeat. I walked on in a blind daze, feeling that any moment I would drop in the middle of the street from sheer exhaustion.

Every hope I had clung to, every human stay, every reality was torn from under me.

Was it then only a dream, a mirage of the hungry-hearted people in the desert lands of oppression, this age-old faith in America—the beloved, the prayed-for "golden country"?

Had the starved villagers of Sukovoly lifted above their sorrows a mere rainbow vision that led them—where? Where? To the stifling submission of the sweatshop or the desperation of the streets!

Again I saw the mob of dusty villagers crowding around my father as he read the letter from America, their eager faces thrust out, their eyes blazing with the same hope, the same age-old faith that drove me on.

A sudden crash against my back. Dizzy with pain I fell—then all was darkness and quiet.

I opened my eyes. A white-clad figure bent over me. Had I died? Was I in heaven?

"Soon she's all right to come back to the shop. Yes, nurse?" The voice of Yetta Solomon broke into my dreaming.

Wearily I opened my eyes. I saw I was still on earth.

Yetta's broad, generous face smiled anxiously at me. "Lucky yet the car that run you over didn't break your hands or your feet. So long you got yet good hands you'll soon be back by the machine."

"Machine?" I shuddered. "I can't go back to the shop again. I'll not be able to stand it again."

"Shah!—Shah!" soothed Yetta. "Why don't you learn yourself to take life like it is? What's got to be, got to be. In Russia, you could hope to run away from your troubles to America. But from America where can you go?"

As Yetta walked out, my mother, with the shawl over her head, rushed in and fell on my bed kissing me.

"Oi weh! Oi weh! Half my life is out from me from fright. How did all happen?"

"Don't worry yourself so. I'm nearly well already and will go back to work soon."

"Talk not work. Get only a little flesh on your bones. They say they send from the hospital people to the country. Maybe they'll send you."

"But how will you live without my wages?"

"Davy is already peddling with papers and Bessie is selling lolly-pops after school in the park. Yesterday she brought home already twenty-eight cents."

For all her efforts to be cheerful, I looked at her pinched face and wondered if she had eaten that day. . . .

I went back to the shop, to the same long hours, to the same low wages, to the same pig-eyed, fat boss. But I was no longer the same. For the first time in my life I bent to the inevitable. I accepted my defeat. But something in me, stronger than I, rose triumphant even in my surrender.

"Yes, I must submit to the shop," I thought. "But the shop shall not crush me. Only my body I must sell into slavery—not my heart—not my soul.

"To any one who sees me from without, I am only a dirt-eating worm, a grub in the ground, but I know that above this dark earth-place in which I am sunk is the green grass—and beyond the green grass, the sun and sky. Alone, unaided, I must dig my way up to the light!" I went to night school.

Lunch-hour at the factory. My book of Shelley's poems before me and I was soon millions of miles beyond the raucous voices of the hungry eaters.

"Did you already hear the last news?" Yetta tore my book from me in her excitement.

"What news?" I scowled at her for waking me from my dreams.

"We're going to have electricity by the machines. And the forelady says that the new boss will give us ten cents more on a dozen waists!"

"What! How did it happen? Electricity? Better pay?" I asked in amazement. For that was the first I had heard of improved conditions of work.

But little by little, step by step, the sanitation improved. Open windows, swept floors, clean wash-rooms, individual drinking-cups introduced a new era of factory hygiene. Our shop was caught up in the general movement for social betterment that stirred the country.

It was not all done in a day. Weary years of struggle passed before the workers emerged from the each-for-himself existence into an organized togetherness for mutual improvement.

With the shortened hours of work, I had enough vitality left that again my dream flamed. Again America beckoned. In the school there was education—air, life for my cramped-in spirit. I would learn to form the thoughts that surged formless in me. . . .

More and more the all-consuming need for a friend possessed me. In the street, in the cars, in the subways, I was always seeking, ceaselessly seeking, for eyes, a face, the flash of a smile that would be light in my darkness.

I felt sometimes that I was only burning out my heart for a shadow, an echo, a wild dream. But I couldn't help it. Nothing was real to me but my hope of finding a friend.

One day my sister Bessie came home much excited over her new high-school teacher. "Miss Latham makes it so interesting!" she exclaimed. "She stops in the middle of the lesson and tells us things. She ain't like a teacher. She's like a real person."

At supper next evening, Bessie related more wonder stories of her beloved teacher. "She's so different! She's friends with us. . . . Today, when she gave us out our composition, Mamie Cohen asked from what book we should read up and she said, 'Just take it out of your heart and say it.'"

"Just take it out of your heart and say it." The simple words lingered in my mind, stirring a whirl of hidden thoughts and feelings. It seemed as if they had been said directly to me.

A few days later Bessie ran in from school, her cheeks flushed, her eyes dancing with excitement. "Give a look at the new poem teacher gave me to learn!" It was a quotation from Kipling:

> Then only the Master shall praise us,
> And only the Master shall blame,
> And no one shall work for money,
> And no one shall work for fame;
> But each for the joy of the working,
> And each in his separate Star,
> Shall draw the thing as he sees it
> For the God of things as they are.

Only a few brief lines, but in their music the pulses of my being leaped into life. And so it was from day to day. Miss Latham's sayings kept turning themselves in my mind like a lingering melody that could not be shaken off. Something irresistible seemed to draw me to her. She beckoned to me almost as strongly as America had on the way over in the boat.

I wondered, "Should I go to see her and talk myself out from my heart to her?"

"Meshugeneh! Where—what? How come you to her? What will you say for your reason?"

"What's the difference what I'll say! I only want to give a look on her . . ."

And so I kept on restlessly debating. Should I follow my heart and go to her, or should I have a little sense?

Finally the desire to see her became so strong that I could no longer reason about it. I left the factory in the middle of the day to seek her out.

All the way to her school I prayed: "God— God! If I could only find one human soul that cared . . ."

I found her bending over her desk. Her hair was gray, but she did not look tired like the other teachers. She was correcting papers and was absorbed in her task. I watched her, not daring to interrupt. Presently she threw back her head and gave a little laugh.

Then she saw me. "Why, how do you do?" She rose. "Come and sit down."

I felt she was as glad to see me as though she had expected me.

"I feel you can help me," I groped toward her.

"I hope I can." She grasped my outstretched hands and led me to a chair which seemed to be waiting for me.

A strange gladness filled me.

"Bessie showed me the poem you told her to learn . . ." I paused bewildered.

"Yes?" Her friendly eyes urged me to speak.

"From what Bessie told me I felt I could talk myself out to you what's bothering me." I stopped again.

She leaned forward with an inviting interest. "Go on! Tell me all."

"I'm an immigrant many years already here, but I'm still seeking America. My dream America is more far from me than it was in the old country. Always something comes between the immigrant and the American," I went on blindly. "They see only his skin, his outside— not what's in his heart. They don't care if he has a heart. . . . I wanted to find some one that would look on me—myself. . . . I thought you'd know yourself on a person first off."

Abashed at my boldness I lowered my eyes to the floor.

"Do go on . . . I want to hear."

With renewed courage I continued my confessional.

"Life is too big for me. I'm lost in this each-for-himself world. I feel shut out from everything that's going on. . . . I'm always fighting, fighting with myself and everything around me. . . . I hate when I want to love and I make people hate me when I want to make them love me."

She gave me a quick nod. "I know. I know what you mean. Go on."

"I don't know what is with me the matter. I'm so choked. . . . Sundays and holidays when the other girls go out to enjoy themselves, I walk around by myself—thinking—thinking . . . . My thoughts tear in me and I can't tell them to no one! I want to do something with my life and I don't know what."

"I'm glad you came," she said. And after a pause, "You can help me."

"Help you?" I cried. It was the first time that an American suggested that I could help her.

"Yes, indeed! I have always wanted to know more of that mysterious vibrant life of the immigrant. You can help me know my girls."

The repression of centuries seemed to rush out of my heart. I told her everything—of the mud hut in Sukovoly where I was born, of the Czar's pogroms, of the constant fear of the Cossack, of Gedalyeh Mindel's letter, and of our hopes in coming to America.

After I had talked myself out, I felt suddenly ashamed for having exposed so much, and I cried out to her: "Do you think like the others that I'm all wrapped up in self?"

For some minutes she studied me, and her serenity seemed to project itself into me. And then she said, as if she too were groping, "No. No, but too intense."

"I hate to be so all the time intense. But how can I help it? Everything always drives me back in myself. How can I get myself out into the free air?"

"Don't fight yourself." Her calm, gray eyes penetrated to the very soul in me. "You are burning up too much vitality. . . .

"You know that some of us," she went on, "not many, unfortunately, have a sort of divine fire which if it does not find expression turns into smoke. This egoism and self-centeredness which troubles you is only the smoke of repression."

She put her hand over mine. "You have had no one to talk to, no one to share your thoughts."

I marveled at the simplicity with which she explained me to myself. I couldn't speak. I just looked at her.

"But now," she said, gently, "you have some one. Come to me whenever you wish."

"I have a friend," it sang itself in me. "I have a friend."

"And you are a born American?" I asked.

"Yes, indeed! My mother, like so many mothers, claims we're descendants of the Pilgrim fathers. And that one of our lineal ancestors came over in the Mayflower."

"For all your mother's pride in the Pilgrim fathers, you yourself are as plain from the heart as an immigrant."

"Weren't the Pilgrim fathers immigrants two hundred years ago?"

She took from her desk a book called "Our America," by Waldo Frank, and read to me: "We go forth all to seek America. And in the seeking we create her. In the quality of our search shall be the nature of the America that we create."

"Ach, friend! Your words are life to me! You make it light for my eyes!"

Breathlessly I felt myself drawn to her. Bonds seemed to burst. A suffusion of light filled my being. Great choirings lifted me in space.

I walked out unseeingly.

All the way home the words she read flamed before me: "We go forth all to seek America. And in the seeking we create her. In the quality of our search shall be the nature of the America that we create."

So all those lonely years of seeking and praying were not in vain! How glad I was that I had not stopped at the husk, a good job, a good living, but pressed on, through the barriers of materialism.

Through my inarticulate groping and reaching-out I had found the soul, the spirit, of America!

WE CREATE OUR AMERICA

To get to America, this Jewish family sold everything. They even pawned their warm clothing because the mother, in her anticipation of living in a land of dreams come true, said, "It must always be summer in America." Such has been the promise that America has represented to the poor and oppressed in foreign countries over the years. America—the land of continual summer where learning and gold flow free.

On landing in New York, Anzia's family faced such disillusionment that she cried, "Where is America?" It took years of searching and unhappiness before she found an answer she could accept. Discuss whether you feel satisfied with the answer she found. Is it a realistic one?

II

IMPLICATIONS

Consider and discuss.

1. When good fortune comes to people, it arouses the jealousy and envy of their friends.

2. Most people are eager to take advantage of others who are not as fortunate as they.

3. Dreams usually exceed reality.

4. Only those persons can be defeated who allow themselves to be defeated.

5. Material success is not sufficient to guarantee happiness.

III

TECHNIQUES

Setting

In "How I Found America," the setting changes more than once in time and place. The account opens in a mud hut in Sukovoly, Russia, where Anzia's father, the only man in the village who can read, is holding school. What are some of the specific details that help the reader visualize the inside of the hut? To what place does the setting then move? Discuss some of the details of this setting that make Anzia look back with longing to life in the village they had left. How does this setting gradually change with time?

Atmosphere

Although both place and time change in the setting of this story, there is little or no change in its atmosphere or mood. What words can you think of to describe the atmosphere in "How I Found America"?

Characterization

The reader learns much about the central character in this story through what she says and does. For example, she reveals her depth of feeling when she says: "Oi weh! Yetta! I can't stand it! I didn't come to America to turn into a machine. I came to make from myself a person. Does America want only my hands, only the strength of my body, not my heart, not my feelings, my thoughts?" This speech shows the frustration she feels as she searches frantically for fulfillment as a creative and intelligent human being—fulfillment she had expected to find in America.

Through the author's recording of the reaction of other characters toward Anzia and what they have to say to her, we gain insight into her personality. Discuss what is learned about her in the episodes in which she (1) confronts the sweatshop boss; (2) talks to Yetta in the hospital; and (3) goes to see her sister Bessie's teacher.

What techniques does the author use to characterize Anzia's father, her mother, and Masheh and Gedalyeh Mindel?

In the following lyrical passage from the novel *You Can't Go Home Again*, Thomas Wolfe gives any "seeker" who would understand America a panoramic view of the country and a glimpse at the strivings of some of its individuals. In the final paragraph, what does the author say is the promise of America?

The Promise of America

THOMAS WOLFE

Go, seeker, if you will, throughout the land and you will find us burning in the night.[1]

There where the hackles[2] of the Rocky Mountains blaze in the blank and naked radiance of the moon, go make your resting stool upon the highest peak. Can you not see us now? The continental wall juts sheer and flat, its huge black shadow on the plain, and the plain sweeps out against the East, two thousand miles away. The great snake that you see there is the Mississippi River.

Behold the gem-strung towns and cities of the good, green East, flung like star dust through the field of night. That spreading constellation to the north is called Chicago, and that giant wink that blazes in the moon is the pendant lake that it is built upon. Beyond, close-set and dense as a clenched fist, are all the jeweled cities of the eastern seaboard. There's Boston, ringed with the bracelet of its shining little towns, and all the lights that sparkle on the rocky indentations of New England. Here, southward and a little to the west, and yet still coasted to the sea, is our intensest ray, the splintered firmament of the towered island of Manhattan. Round about her, sown thick as grain, is the glitter of a hundred towns and cities. The long chain of lights, there, is the necklace of Long Island and the Jersey shore. Southward, and inland by a foot or two, behold the duller glare of Philadelphia. Southward further still, the twin constellations—Baltimore and Washington. Westward, but still within the borders of the good, green East, that night-time glow and smolder of hell-fire is Pittsburgh. Here, St. Louis, hot and humid in the cornfield belly of the land, and bedded on the mid-length coil and fringes of the snake. There at the snake's mouth, southward six hundred miles or so, you see the jeweled crescent of old New Orleans. Here, west and south again, you see the gemmy[3] glitter of the cities on the Texas border.

Turn now, seeker, on your resting stool atop the Rocky Mountains and look another thousand miles or so across moon-blazing fiend-worlds of the Painted Desert, and beyond Sierras' ridge. That magic congeries[4] of lights there to the west, ringed like a studded belt around the magic setting of its lovely harbor, is the fabled town of San Francisco. Below it, Los Angeles and all the cities of the California shore. A thousand miles to north and west, the sparkling towns of Oregon and Washington.

Observe the whole of it, survey it as you might survey a field. Make it your garden, seeker, or your back yard patch. Be at ease in it. It's your oyster—yours to open if you will. Don't be frightened, it's not so big now, when your footstool is the Rocky Mountains. Reach

---

1. **burning in the night,** With this phrase Wolfe suggests that individuals are burning up their energies in ceaseless striving to achieve some goal, to take advantage of the opportunities open to them in America. Often this striving carries far into the night.
2. **hackles,** scraggy hair along the neck and back of some animals and birds.

"The Promise of America" from *You Can't Go Home Again* by Thomas Wolfe. Copyright 1940 by Maxwell Perkins, as Executor; renewed 1968 by Paul Gitlin. Reprinted by permission of Harper & Row, Publishers, Inc.

3. **gemmy,** gemlike.
4. **congeries** \kən⁂jîr·ēz\ collection of things heaped together.

"Wisconsin Landscape," John Steuart Curry, Metropolitan Museum of Art, New York

out and dip a hatful of cold water from Lake Michigan. Drink it—we've tried it—you'll not find it bad. Take your shoes off and work your toes down in the river oozes of the Mississippi bottom—it's very refreshing on a hot night in the summertime. Help yourself to a bunch of Concord grapes up there in northern New York State—they're getting good now. Or raid that watermelon patch down there in Georgia. Or, if you like, you can try the Rockyfords[5] here at your elbow in Colorado. Just make yourself at home, refresh yourself, get the feel of things, adjust your sights, and get the scale. It's your pasture now and it's not so big—only three thousand miles from east to west, only two thousand miles from north to south—but all between, where ten thousand points of light prick out the cities, towns, and villages, there, seeker, you will find us burning in the night.

Here, as you pass through the brutal sprawl, the twenty miles of rails and rickets of the South Chicago slums—here in an unpainted shack is a black boy, and, seeker, he is burning in the night. Behind him is a memory of the cotton fields, the flat and mournful pineland barrens of the lost and buried South, and at the fringes of the pine another shack with mother and eleven children. Farther still behind, the slavedriver's whip, the slave ship, and, far off, the jungle dirge of Africa. And before him, what? A roped-in ring, a blaze of lights, across from him a white champion; the bell, the opening, and all around the vast sea-roaring of the crowd. Then the lightning feint and stroke, the black panther's paw—the hot, rotating presses, and the rivers of sheeted print! O seeker, where is the slave ship now?[6]

Or there, in the clay-baked piedmont[7] of the South, that lean and tan-faced boy who sprawls there in the creaking chair among admiring cronies before the open doorways of the fire department, and tells them how he pitched the team to shutout victory today. What visions burn, what dreams possess him, seeker of the night? The packed stands of the stadium, the

5. **Rockyfords,** melons that take their name from the eastern Colorado town around which they are grown —Rocky Ford.

6. Wolfe is suggesting improved conditions at that time for black people through the accomplishments of the black boxer.
7. **piedmont,** upland or foothill country.

bleachers sweltering with their unshaded hordes, the faultless velvet of the diamond, unlike the clay-baked outfields down in Georgia. The mounting roar of eighty thousand voices and Gehrig[8] coming up to bat, the boy himself upon the pitching mound, the lean face steady as a hound's; then the nod, the signal, and the windup, the rawhide arm that snaps and crackles like a whip, the small white bullet of the blazing ball, its loud report in the oiled pocket of the catcher's mitt, the umpire's thumb jerked upward, the clean strike.

Or there again, in the east-side ghetto of Manhattan, two blocks away from the East River, a block away from the gashouse district and its thuggery, there in the swarming tenement, shut in his sweltering cell, breathing the sun-baked air through open window at the fire escape, celled there away into a little semblance of privacy and solitude from all the brawling and vociferous life[9] and argument of his family and the seething hive around him, the Jewish boy sits and pores upon his book. In shirtsleeves, bent above his table to meet the hard glare of a naked bulb, he sits with gaunt, starved face, the weak eyes squinting painfully through his thick-lens glasses, his hair roached[10] back in scrolls above the slanting cage of his painful and constricted brow. And for what? For what this agony of concentration? For what this hell of effort? For what this intense withdrawal from the poverty and squalor of dirty brick and rusty fire escapes, from the raucous cries and violence and never-ending noise? For what? Because, brother, he is burning in the night. He sees the class, the lecture room, the shining apparatus of gigantic laboratories, the open field of scholarship and

pure research, certain knowledge, and the world distinction of an Einstein name.

So, then, to every man[11] his chance—to every man, regardless of his birth, his shining, golden opportunity—to every man the right to live, to work, to be himself, and to become whatever thing his manhood and his vision can combine to make him—this, seeker, is the promise of America.

I
LAND OF OPPORTUNITY

Thomas Wolfe expressed this view of the American promise in the late 1930s. Would you say that this same promise exists today? Is there still the same individual striving to take advantage of the "golden opportunity"?

II
IMPLICATIONS

1. The American spirit is one of optimism rather than pessimism.

2. The "golden opportunity" in America is equal for all.

III
TECHNIQUES

Setting

The passage falls into two parts. In the first, Wolfe takes the "seeker" on a quick, guided tour of the United States—there were 48 in the 1930s. In the second part, he concentrates on three nameless Americans in different regional settings, as each struggles to realize his own personal dream.

To establish the panoramic setting rapidly, to condense his description, and at the same time to add a lyrical quality, Wolfe relies heavily on figurative language—*metaphor*. In the second paragraph, for example, note what the use of one word, *hackles*, accomplishes in reference to the uneven and jagged heights of the Rocky Mountains. It suggests a great shadowy beast stretched slumbering in the moonlight along the western section of the continent. What metaphor does he use for the Mississippi River? Discuss the appropriateness of this figure of speech.

Characterization

The three characters in the selection are nameless, simply representatives of a particular group and locality. Each boy, however, is burning with a different dream. In what respect are all these dreams alike?

---

8. **Gehrig,** Lou Gehrig (1903–1941), famous New York Yankee first base player and hitter.
9. **vociferous** \vō**sif•ər•əs\ life, noisy and violent.
10. **roached,** brushed into a roll above the forehead.
11. At the time Wolfe wrote, the word *man* was widely used in the generic sense; that is, it referred to both men and women. In keeping with this custom, the third person singular pronoun, masculine gender (he, him, his), was generally used—unless, of course, a person was identified as female.

We have been a restless, imaginative people;
our image of America has always been an image of the future. We have never
long remained satisfied with past accomplishments; we have ever sought
new frontiers to conquer, new dreams to realize. But today,
Archibald MacLeish asks, are we at a resting place? Have we fallen back
on the past? Will we find the courage to imagine a new, dynamic America,
an America that will once again look to the future?

The Unimagined America

ARCHIBALD MacLEISH

It is a strange and curious picture of Americans. If ever a people had behind them a tradition of great purposes, tremendous dreams, the people of America have that tradition. There is not one of us, there is not a child in this Republic, who does not know the story. The whole history of our continent is a history of the imagination. Men imagined land beyond the sea and found it. Men imagined the forests, the great plains, the rivers, the mountains—and found these plains, these mountains. No force of terror, no pressure of population, drove our ancestors across this continent. They came, as the great explorers crossed the Atlantic, because of the imagination of their minds—because they imagined a better, a more beautiful, a freer, happier world; because they were men not only of courage, not only of strength and hardiness, but of warm and vivid desire; because they desired; because they had the power to desire.

And what was true of the continent was true of the Republic we created. Because our forefathers were able to conceive a freeman's government, they were able to create it. Because those who lived before us in this nation were able to imagine a new thing, a thing unheard of in the world before, a thing the skeptical

and tired men who did not trust in dreams had not been able to imagine, they erected on this continent the first free nation—the first society in which mankind was to be free at last.

The courage of the Declaration of Independence is a far greater courage than the bravery of those who risked their necks to sign it. The courage of the Declaration of Independence is the courage of the act of the imagination. Jefferson's document is not a call to revolution only. Jefferson's document is an image of a life, a plan of life, a dream—indeed a dream. And yet there were men as careful of their own respect, as hard-headed, as practical, as eager to be thought so, as any now in public life, who signed that Declaration for the world to look at.

The *truth* is that the tradition of imagination is behind us as behind no people in the history of the world. But our right to live as we imagine men should live is not a right drawn from tradition only. There are nations of the earth in which the act of the imagination would be an act *in* the imagination only—an action of escape. But not with us.

We have, and we know we have, the abundant means to bring our boldest dreams to pass —to create for ourselves whatever world we have the courage to desire. We have the metal and the men to take this country down, if we please to take it down, and to build it again as

"The Unimagined America" by Archibald MacLeish. From *A Continuing Journey*. Copyright © 1967 by Archibald MacLeish. Reprinted by permission of Houghton Mifflin Company.

we please to build it. We have the tools and the skill and the intelligence to take our cities apart and to put them together, to lead our roads and rivers where we please to lead them, to build our houses where we want our houses, to brighten the air, to clean the wind, to live as men in this Republic, free men, should be living. We have the power and the courage and the resources of good-will and decency and common understanding—a long experience of decency and common understanding—to enable us to live, not in this continent alone but in the world, as citizens in common of the world, with many others.

We have the power and the courage and the resources of experience to create a nation such as men have never seen. And, more than that, we have the moment of creation in our hands. Our forefathers, when they came to the New England valleys or the Appalachian meadows, girdled the trees and dragged the roots into fences and built themselves shelters and, so roughly sheltered, farmed the land for their necessities. Then, later, when there were means to do it, when there was time, when the occasion offered, they burned the tangled roots and rebuilt their fences and their houses—but rebuilt them with a difference: rebuilt them as villages, as neighborhoods; rebuilt them with those lovely streets, those schools, those churches which still speak of their conception of the world they wanted. When the means offered, when the time offered, men created, on the clearings of the early useful farms, the towns that made New England and the Alleghenies.

Now is the time for the re-creation, the rebuilding, not of the villages and towns but of a nation. Now is the time to consider that the trees are down, that the land has been broken, that the means are available and the continent itself must be rebuilt. Our necessities have been accomplished as men have always accomplished their necessities—with wastefulness, with ugliness, with cruelty, as well as with the food of harvests. Our necessities have been accomplished with the roots of the broken trees

along the fences, the rough shelters, the lonely lives. Now is the time to build the continent itself—to take down and to rebuild; and not the houses and the cities only, but the life itself, raising upon the ready land the brotherhood that can employ it and delight in it and use it as a people such as ours should use it.

We stand at the moment of the building of great lives. . . . But to seize the moment and the means we must agree, as men in those New England valleys were agreed, upon the world we mean to bring about. We must agree upon the image of that world. . . .

When we speak of our ideal conception of ourselves, we speak still in terms of the agricultural and sparsely settled nation Thomas Jefferson and his contemporaries had in mind. The ideal landscape of America which Jefferson painted hangs unaltered in the American imagination—a clean, small landscape with its isolated figures, its pleasant barns, its self-reliant rooftrees, its horizons clear of the smoke and the fumes of cities, its air still, its frontiers protected by month-wide oceans, year-wide wildernesses. No later hand has touched it, except Lincoln's maybe, deepening the shadow, widening the sky, broadening the acreage of the name of freedom, giving the parts a wholeness that in brighter, sharper light they lacked. For fifty years and longer it has been a landscape of a world that no man living could expect to see except behind him, a landscape no Americans could bring to being, a dream—but of the past, and not the future.

And yet we keep this image in our minds. This, and not the world beyond us, is the world we turn to: the lost, nostalgic image of a world that was the future to a generation dead a hundred years. No other image has been made to take its place. No one has dreamed a new American dream of the new America—the industrial nation of the huge machines, the limitless earth, the vast and skillful population, the mountains of copper and iron, the mile-long plants, the delicate laboratories, the tremendous dams. No one has imagined this America—what its life should be; what life it should lead with its great wealth and the tools in its hands and the men to employ them.

The plants and the factories and their products have been celebrated often enough—perhaps too often. The statistics have been added up. The camera has held its mirror to the great machines. But the central question we have never asked. What are they *for,* these plants and products, these statistics? *What are they for in terms of a nation of men*—in Jefferson's terms? What is the ideal landscape of this new America? What are we trying to become, to bring about? What is our dream of ourselves as a great people? What would we be if we could: what would our lives be? And how will we use this skill, this wealth, this power to create those lives?

What is demanded of us in this time of change, what our whole history and our present need demand of us, is that we find the answers to these questions—that we consider what we wish this new America to be. For what we wish to be we can become.

And if we cannot wish—we shall become that also.

There are men, it is true, who believe there are no answers. There are men, and among the wisest of our time, who do not believe that an image of this new America can be conceived—who do not believe in a world of plenty; do not believe in it with their hearts whatever their senses tell them; do not believe that the lives of men can be good lives in the industrialized society which alone makes plenty possible. . . .

Is the fault with the machines or with ourselves? Is it because we have automobiles to ride in, because we can purchase certain commodities easily, because our presses can turn out tons of printed paper in a day, that our fiber is soft, our will feeble, our suggestibility infantile? Or is it because we do not use these things as we should use them—because we have not made them serve our moral purpose as a people, but only contribute to our private comfort as their owners?

Is the whole question indeed not a question of ourselves instead of our devices? Is it not for us to *say* how these devices, these inventions, should be used? Does their use not rest upon the purpose of their use? And does the purpose not depend upon our power to conceive the purpose—our power as a people to conceive the purpose of the tools we use; our power as a people to conceive and to imagine?

A hundred and fifty years ago de Crèvecoeur[1] asked a famous question which has echoes now: "What then is the American, this new man?" But what then *is* he? What then is he now? A man incapable of the act of the imagination or a man to whom it is native and natural? A man to dare the dream of plenty with all its risks and dangers, or a man to hold to the old nostalgic landscape with the simple virtues safely forced upon him by the necessary self-denial?

. . . A man who has the hardihood or the courage to believe that the machines which have enslaved his fathers will make his children free—free as no human beings in the world have yet known freedom; free of the twisting miseries and hungers; free to become themselves? Or a man to reject the hope of that enfranchised freedom and to seek his independence in the ancient narrow circle of his old dependence on himself?

Which of these two men is the American? We should have said a while ago we knew. We should have said the American character was self-evident: A restless man. A great builder and maker and shaper, a man delighting in size and height and dimensions: the world's tallest; the town's biggest. A man never satisfied—never—with anything: his house or the town where his grandfather settled or his father's profession or even his own, for that matter. An inveterate voyager and changer and finder. A man naturally hopeful; a believing man, believing that things progress, that things get forwarder. A skillful man with contraptions of one kind and another—machines, engines, various devices: familiar with all of them. A man of

---

1. **de Crèvecoeur**\krĕv·kər\ born in France, became a naturalized United States citizen. Famous for his "Letters from an American Farmer."

certain unquestioned convictions—of a strong, natural attachment to certain ideas and to certain ideals. But first of all and foremost of all a restless man and a believing man, a builder and changer of things and of nations.

We should have said, a generation back, there was no possible doubt or question of the will and power of this nation to propose the kind of future for itself which would employ the means of plenty for a human purpose. We should have said the principal characteristic of the American people was a confidence in the future and themselves—confidence that the future was the thing they'd make it. I cannot think, for myself, we have so changed that we do not believe this now. I cannot believe we are so changed that we'll let ourselves go with the drag and the current of history—that we'll let the future happen to us as the future happens to chips on a river or sheep in a blizzard; that we'll let the peace make us; not us the peace. I cannot believe we have so changed that we do not believe in ourselves and the future.

And yet we have not done what must be done if we believe the future is the thing we'll make it. We have not named that future.

And the time is short.

It is many years since Matthew Arnold saw his generation standing between two worlds, one dead, the other waiting to be born.[2] Our time is still the time between these worlds; and the wars we suffer, the disasters, the uneasiness, are natural to the time we live in like the continuing and violent storms that drive the days between the seasons. We shall not have peace in truth, peace for our lives, peace for the purposes of our lives, until the world we wait for has been born. But it will not be born until we recognize it, until we shape it with our expectation and our hope. The new worlds do not bring themselves to being. Men's minds, when they are ready for them, find them. The labor and the longing must be ours.

They must be ours as men and also—and this is the truth our generation in this country must accept—as Americans. For the future is Amer-

ica's to make. It is not our future, as a few Americans have asked us to believe, to master or exploit. It is not an American future for some vast imperial enterprise, some huge dominion of the earth or sky. And yet it is our future. It is ours to shape. It is ours to shape, not because we have many planes or great numbers of ships or rich industrial resources but for a different reason: because we have the power as a people to conceive so great a future as mankind must now conceive—because we have behind us a tradition of imagination in the people.

But because we have the power we have also a responsibility to use the power. While there still is time.

I

TRACING THE LINE
OF AN ARGUMENT

Although "The Unimagined America" is a passionate, poetic essay, there is a clear line of reasoning running through it. Let us attempt to trace MacLeish's argument point by point.

The first question MacLeish asks is, "What is an American?" He answers the question historically, pointing out that our ancestors were imaginative people who looked constantly to the future. Is this a definition the critical reader can accept?

MacLeish then asserts that contemporary Americans have forsaken the tradition of the imagination and have turned from the future to the past. What evidence does he offer for this assertion? Is it true, in your opinion? What evidence can you offer for your belief?

The author next claims that it is imperative that we recover the tradition of the imagination. *Why* does he feel that this is necessary? Do you agree that it is? What is wrong with clinging to an image of America of the past?

2. From Matthew Arnold's poem "Stanzas from the Grande Chartreuse." "Wandering between two worlds, one dead, \The other powerless to be born . . ."

Finally, MacLeish says that Americans must agree upon and build a new image of America. He does not give a fully rounded description of his image, but he notes a few details in various places. What are some of these details? Assuming that you agree with him up to this point, explain why you would include or exclude the same details in your image of the future America.

II
IMPLICATIONS

Thoughtfully consider each of the following statements. Decide whether, on the whole, you would classify the statement as true or false. Be prepared to defend your opinion.

1. If the United States were to become part of a world federation, we would lose all sense of identity as Americans.

2. Americans have not used their material wealth to serve their moral purposes as a people.

3. Most persons settle into a routine of life and do not like to have that routine disturbed.

4. The fact that people are practical means that they probably are not imaginative.

5. A single individual is helpless to do anything to change the future of a country.

6. A principal quality of Americans is confidence in the future and in themselves.

7. The high standard of living in America has left us free to become ourselves and we have proved to be a passive people.

8. Today the people of America have a strong sense of identity and a clear sense of purpose.

Dream and Promise

Documents, stories, and famous characters that come from the pens of a nation's writers live on in the public mind to become models, or archetypes, for future behavior. Thus life copies literature even as literature copies life.

In the foregoing literary selections, you have seen how the dreams and promises of a new life with freedom, justice, equality—and perhaps instant riches—brought people to the Eastern seaboard of America and thence in a steady throng across the mountain ranges and sweeping plains to the western shore.

America's development was dramatically affected by the documentary writing of such leaders as Thomas Jefferson and Abraham Lincoln. The first preoccupation of the nation's imaginative writers, however, was with the settlement of the frontier. But by the beginning of the twentieth century, when there was no more land left to settle, when the last big gold rush was over, and when immigration and business expansion were causing rapid growth of the cities, American authors turned their attention to urban life and its problems.

Until this time, the literature of America had expressed the buoyancy of a new nation, its faith in the individual, and its appetite for constant change and improvement. Now, such writers as John Steinbeck began to question whether Americans had lost their ability to dream and to envision a future for the nation.

In "The Leader of the People," Grandfather expresses the idea that the America he admired was finished—that it had become a country where there was no place left to go. In her discouragement, immigrant Anzia Yezierska feels for many years that America is a land of disappointment—a land where dreams do not come true. Nevertheless, in "How I Found America," she finally reaches very much the same conclusion as Thomas Wolfe does in his poetic passage from *You Can't Go Home Again*. What is the continuing promise of America that these authors discover? What admonition does Archibald MacLeish give about the promise of the future?

Americans today are among the most economically secure people on earth. How does this affect their imaginative and pioneering spirit? What long-range effect could this have on the future of America?

What effect do you think this literary composition may have had in reminding the American people of their dreams and promises over the years?

IMPLICATIONS

Discuss the implications you find in this poem written by Katharine Lee Bates in 1895—a poem that has become unofficially but indisputably America's national hymn.

America the Beautiful

O beautiful for spacious skies,
  For amber waves of grain,
For purple mountain majesties
  Above the fruited plain!
    America! America!
God shed his grace on thee
And crown thy good with brotherhood
  from sea to shining sea!

O beautiful for pilgrim feet,
  Whose stern, impassioned stress
A thoroughfare for freedom beat
  Across the wilderness!
    America! America!
God mend thine every flaw,
Confirm thy soul in self-control,
  Thy liberty in law!

O beautiful for heroes proved
  In liberating strife,
Who more than self their country loved,
  And mercy more than life!
    America! America!
May God thy gold refine
Till all success be nobleness
And every gain divine!

O beautiful for patriot dream
  That sees beyond the years
Thine alabaster cities gleam
  Undimmed by human tears!
    America! America!
God shed his grace on thee
And crown thy good with brotherhood
  from sea to shining sea!

KATHARINE LEE BATES

From *Poems* by Katharine Lee Bates. Published by E. P. Dutton and reprinted with their permission.

TECHNIQUES

Setting

The place and time setting in which events occur may be of no significance, of relatively minor importance, or of major importance. From the following titles, select two in which place and time are of major importance and one in which they are of little or no importance. Discuss *why* setting is important or unimportant in each instance.

1. "All Gold Canyon"
2. "The Prairies"
3. "The Lonely Winter"
4. "The Leader of the People"
5. "How I Found America"
6. "The Unimagined America"
7. "The Promise of America"

Characterization

In fiction, writers reveal the character of imaginary persons. In autobiography and biography, they reveal the character of real persons. Authors use a variety of techniques to show character, and it is one of the most important aspects of nearly all literary works.

Choose three selections from those listed above in which you feel the author was particularly successful in creating character. Be prepared to discuss the techniques the author used in creating character in each.

BIOGRAPHICAL NOTES

Stephen Vincent Benét

Stephen Vincent Benét (1898–1943), born in Bethlehem, Pennsylvania, lived in many parts of the country and, as he grew older, developed a deep interest in America's past. His first writings were ballads, such as "William Sycamore," combining American folklore and humor. He then turned to the writing of epic poems, notably the Pulitzer Prize-winning *John Brown's Body*, the story of men and women in both the North and South during the Civil War, and *Western Star*, in which he captured the flavor, excitement, and color of a robust young country. Benét also wrote five novels, two one-act operas, and many short stories.

Thomas Jefferson

Thomas Jefferson (1743–1826) was born in Virginia, studied privately, attended the college of William and Mary for two years, and prepared for a career in law. He was soon drawn into public life, however, as a member of the Virginia House of Burgesses and went on to serve in the following posts: delegate to the Second Continental Congress, governor of Virginia, delegate to the Congress of the Confederation, minister to France, the first Secretary of State, Vice President, and President. He designed his home, Monticello (Italian for "little mountain"), instituted the national library (now the Library of Congress), founded the University of Virginia, and was chief architect of its first buildings. He died on the fiftieth anniversary of the signing of the Declaration of Independence.

Jack London

Sailor, oyster pirate, Alaskan gold hunter, hobo, war correspondent, adventurer, and writer, Jack London (1876–1916) was born in San Francisco. He grew up in poverty, educated by his reading in the public library and by experiences along the Oakland waterfront. When he sold several stories to the *Overland Monthly*, he settled down seriously to a writing career. His most successful works were several short stories and two novels, the dog stories *Call of the Wild* and *White Fang*. His major themes were the survival of the fittest and reversion to savagery. He wrote three autobiographical novels: *The Road, Martin Eden,* and *John Barleycorn*. He became the champion of social revolution in the early years of this century and wrote several volumes of political propaganda.

William Cullen Bryant

William Cullen Bryant (1794–1878), born in Massachusetts, had his first verses, satirizing President Jefferson, published at the age of thirteen. One of his most famous poems, "Thanatopsis," concerned with nature and death, was written at seventeen. In his long life, Bryant achieved fame as critic, editor, biographer, and civic leader. His catholic interests

and activities, ranging from his study of the American landscape to his fight for freedom of speech and the abolition of slavery, were reflected in his writings. His poetry was acclaimed in England and America, but his literary reputation is not as great today as during his own lifetime.

Rose Wilder Lane

Rose Wilder Lane (1887–1968) was born of pioneer parents on a homestead near De Smet, Dakota Territory, now South Dakota. Unable to make a living on their claim, the family moved to the Ozark Mountains. Later the author used these places as background for her novels and stories. In addition to her fiction, Lane wrote biographies of Henry Ford and Herbert Hoover. For a time she lived in Albania, the first foreign person many of the natives had ever seen. Her popular novel, *Let the Hurricane Roar*, has gone through several printings.

Abraham Lincoln

Abraham Lincoln (1809–1865), born in Hardin County, Kentucky, attended school only briefly in his youth but read and reread such books as the Bible, *Pilgrim's Progress*, and *Aesop's Fables*. The family moved first to Indiana and then to Illinois where Lincoln read and eventually practiced law. He went as a volunteer to the Black Hawk War and was elected to the state legislature where he spoke out vigorously for the abolition of slavery. Following his famous debates with Stephen Douglas, he was elected to the Presidency in 1860. He served as President through the Civil War and was assassinated a little over a month after he began his second term of office.

John Steinbeck

The sixth American to win the Nobel Prize in Literature (1962), John Steinbeck (1902–1968) was born and grew up in California. He turned from his college studies in marine biology to writing. His first novel to catch the attention of both critics and the public was *Tortilla Flat*, published in 1935. Other novels about his native Monterey are *Cannery Row* and *Sweet Thursday*. His social documentaries were to draw even greater attention; *In Dubious Battle* is the story of a strike of migratory workers in California; *Grapes of Wrath* is the powerful and moving story of the dust-bowl victims who moved to California. This novel won the Pulitzer Prize in 1940. Other widely read works include three of his novels— *Of Mice and Men*, *The Pearl*, and *East of Eden*—and "The Red Pony," a sensitive, carefully wrought short story. His last major book, *Travels with Charley*, is the story of his journey around the United States with his dog.

Emma Lazarus

Emma Lazarus (1849–1887) was born in New York City, the daughter of wealthy parents. Educated privately, she early displayed a talent for writing, and her first book, *Poems and Translations*, was praised by Ralph Waldo Emerson. In the 1880s she began to work for the relief of Jewish immigrants. Her sonnet "The New Colossus" was chosen to be engraved on the base of the Statue of Liberty, and it has become one of the best-known poems ever written. (The entire text of this poem appears in the *Teacher's Resource Guide* for *American Literature* 3/e, page 14.)

Anzia Yezierska

Anzia Yezierska (1885–   ) was born in a mud hut in Sukovoly, Russia. Along with her family, she came to New York in 1901, worked in a sweatshop, cooked for a wealthy family, found time to attend school, and eventually found work for wages that permitted her to move her family from the ghetto on the Lower East Side. In 1912 she became a naturalized citizen. Her short stories have appeared in numerous magazines, and her books include *Hungry Hearts*, from which a Hollywood film was made, *All I Could Never Be*, and *Red Ribbon on a White Horse*, her autobiography.

Thomas Wolfe

Thomas Wolfe (1900–1938) was born and reared in Asheville, North Carolina. He was educated privately and was graduated from the University of North Carolina at fifteen. After studying play writing at Harvard, he taught at New York University. His first book, the autobiographical novel, *Look Homeward, Angel*, was a critical success. His other books include *Of Time and the River*, *The Story of a Novel*, *The Web and the Rock*, *You Can't Go Home Again*, *The Hills Beyond*, and *From Death to Morning*. The last two are collections of his short stories and other pieces.

Archibald MacLeish

Archibald MacLeish, who was born in Glencoe, Illinois, in 1892, was educated at Yale and at Harvard Law School. After serving with the American Army in France during World War I, he returned to Boston to practice law. Soon, however, he gave up his practice to devote full time to traveling and to writing. His travels included retracing the route of Cortez through Mexico, which led to his writing *Conquistador*. Caught up in the country's mood of social protest in the thirties, he wrote *Frescoes for Mr. Rockefeller's City* and *America Was Promises*. Twice winner of the Pulitzer Prize for Poetry, versatile MacLeish also wrote prose, a ballet, and radio and stage plays. From 1939 to 1944 he was Librarian of Congress. In 1972 he published a book of selected poems, *The Human Season*.

Katharine Lee Bates

Katharine Lee Bates (1859–1929) was born in Falmouth, Massachusetts, was graduated from Wellesley College, and served as a professor there for forty years. Her writings include several volumes of poetry, some travel books, and many scholarly works. Perhaps her most popular piece has been the poem "America the Beautiful." Set to the music of Samuel A. Ward's "Materna," it has become our unofficial national hymn.

COLONIAL, REVOLUTIONARY, & EARLY NATIONAL PERIODS

1608-1830

COLONIAL PERIOD (1608–1765)

It is often said that the literature of a people reflects the interests and concerns of that people. By this measure, the chief concerns of colonial Americans were their land and their religion. Early Americans wrote descriptions and histories of where they lived and moralistic tracts and sermons about how to live.

"The spirit of place is a great reality" wrote D. H. Lawrence in the opening chapter of his *Studies in Classic American Literature*, and so it must indeed have seemed to such early settlers as Captain John Smith. His account of the founding of Jamestown, Virginia, entitled *A True Relation* (1608), was the first book written in America. Later, Smith published other descriptions of "the new world," such as *A Description of New England* (1616) and *A General History of Virginia* (1624). These books along with many others of the same character, as well as works like Samuel Sewall's *Diary* (1674–1729) and Sarah Knight's *Journal of a Journey* (1704), begin a long tradition of concern with our land. This concern with the spirit of place is still very much alive in America today in such works as the poetry of Robert Frost and John Steinbeck's *Grapes of Wrath* and *Travels with Charley*.

For many early Americans, of even greater concern than the spirit of place was the Spirit itself. Harvard College was founded in 1636, just 16 years after the Pilgrims landed at Plymouth, largely for the purpose of guaranteeing a literate ministry for the churches. That that ministry was indeed literate is proved by the enormous number of sermons, pamphlets, and books turned out by such Puritan divines as Increase Mather, author of over 100 tracts, and his son, Cotton,

whose output was closer to 500 titles. The Mathers —including Increase's father, Richard, who was one of the translators of the *Bay Psalm Book* (1640), a collection of church hymns and the first book printed in America—exercised an enormous influence over the writing of New England for three-quarters of a century.

Although the Mather dynasty lost some of its influence as a result of popular reaction against the Salem witchcraft executions of 1692, Puritanism shot one last comet into the sky before its influence dimmed—the fiery, brilliant, and original pastor of Northampton, Massachusetts, Jonathan Edwards. Thanks largely to him, religious revivals spread through many of the colonies, culminating in the period from 1740 to 1745 known as the Great Awakening. Edwards, also a prolific writer, made significant contributions to the field of theology.

However important it may have been in its time, most of this early writing—both historical and religious—is read today only by specialists, and rightly so; for we have more reliable and comprehensive histories than John Smith could possibly have written, and we have little interest in the subjects of most of the religious tracts, such as "Essay to Silence the Outcry . . . against Regular Singing" or "Hoop Petticoats Arraigned and Condemned by the Light of Nature and the Law of God." There is no question, however, that the deeper issues of how to live, of what values to live by, have absorbed American writers from Hawthorne to Hemingway.

Of somewhat more universal appeal was a third type of writing that appeared in the colonies: poetry. Some of the poems of our first American poet, Anne

Bradstreet, can still be read with pleasure. And the best work of Edward Taylor, a physician and minister, compares favorably with the religious "metaphysical" poetry of seventeenth-century England.

By and large, however, Puritan poets were moved to write poems by impulses far too gloomy for modern tastes. The most popular verse form of the latter half of the seventeenth century was the verse elegy, the type of poem written by Emmeline Grangerford, a character in Mark Twain's *The Adventures of Huckleberry Finn*, who "kept a scrap-book . . . and used to paste obituaries and accidents and cases of patient suffering in it . . . and write poetry after them out of her own head." Many were sorry when Emmeline died, but we are more likely to agree with Huck, who says, "I reckoned that with her disposition she was having a better time in the graveyard."

By the beginning of the eighteenth century, America was clearly not a graveyard. In an expanding and prosperous and increasingly enlightened new world, it was hard to accept the Calvinist notion that humans were born in sin and irretrievably lost but for the grace of an inscrutable God. And literature—interpreting the term broadly—performed a major role in the secularization of the colonies.

The first newspaper, the Boston *News Letter*, was established in 1704, and by 1765 there were about two dozen others. Almanacs—of which Benjamin Franklin's *Poor Richard's Almanac*, begun in 1732, was the most famous—were storehouses of information. They could be found in nearly every home. Because of the growing interest in science, there were increasing numbers of scientific writers, such as the botanist John Bartram and his son William; the physician Benjamin Rush; and of course Franklin himself—scientist, inventor, printer, philosopher, educator, author, political leader: America's first "Renaissance" man.

REVOLUTIONARY PERIOD (1765–1790)

In the revolutionary period, politics took center stage, and from the pens of Americans flowed some of the greatest political writing of all time.

Thomas Paine's *Common Sense* and his series of essays entitled "The Crisis" come first to mind because his castigation of the "summer soldier and the sunshine patriot" and his praise of those who stood by the cause helped as much as bullets to win the Revolutionary War. Similar support came from stirring speeches by Patrick Henry and George Wash-

ington. Then there were the great political documents—Thomas Jefferson's Declaration of Independence, the Constitution itself, the Bill of Rights. And finally there was the famous *Federalist* (1787–1788), a series of essays composed by Alexander Hamilton, James Madison, and John Jay. Written to win support for the new Constitution, these essays represent some of the best thinking we have on the American political system.

Other writers of the period also treated political themes. Philip Freneau, for example, who has been described as the poet of the Revolutionary War, wrote on all the major issues of the time. Phillis Wheatley, our first black poet, addressed one of her poems to "His Excellency General Washington." And Royall Tyler's *The Contrast* (1787), which was the first American comedy to be acted by professionals, compares a man of British manners unfavorably with an American.

EARLY NATIONAL OR FEDERALIST PERIOD (1790–1830)

The Federalist period began with the publication of the first American novels—William Hill Brown's *The Power of Sympathy* (1789); Susanna Rowson's best-seller, *Charlotte Temple* (1794); and Charles Brockden Brown's six melodramatic novels (published between 1798 and 1801)—none of which is read today. By the end of the period, however, Hawthorne had published his first novel, *Fanshawe* (1828), and American fiction was about to enter a golden age.

During this period, Washington Irving, William Cullen Bryant, and James Fenimore Cooper made for themselves the first great names in American literature. All three were praised not only in their own country but abroad as well. All have left work that is enjoyable reading today. But each achieved greatest success in a different genre.

Washington Irving, our first world-famous author, is discussed elsewhere in this book. Let it suffice to say here that he was the author of the first American short stories.

Poetry was Bryant's forte, although he also became a famous journalist and editor. His most famous poems include "Thanatopsis" (which he wrote when he was only 17), "To a Waterfowl," and "The Prairies." Bryant was a poet of reflection and strove for a universal note in his poems. His main theme is Nature, or rather the effect of Nature upon people. Though many of his poems lack the concreteness that characterizes most twentieth-century poetry, his best work brings to mind what Robinson Jeffers says at the end of "The Stone-Cutters":

Yet stones have stood for a thousand years, and pained thoughts found
The honey of peace in old poems.

The only early writer to rival Bryant as a conveyer of the grandeur of American forests and prairies was the novelist James Fenimore Cooper. Although Cooper wrote more than thirty novels, he is best remembered for those that comprise the Leather-stocking series, all of which deal with the mythic frontier figure, Natty Bumppo, variously called Leatherstocking, Hawkeye, Pathfinder, or Deer-slayer. The novels are *Pioneers* (1823), *Last of the Mohicans* (1826), *The Prairie* (1827), *Pathfinder* (1840), and *The Deerslayer* (1841).

Like the explorers and colonists 100 years or more before their time, Bryant, Cooper, and Irving loved the land and drew sustenance from its spirit. But unlike their Puritan ancestors, they largely side-stepped great moral dilemmas, such as the problem of good and evil. It was Nathaniel Hawthorne who first used the novel and story to probe the depths of the American conscience, the remoter mysteries of the human heart. Along with Poe and Melville, he became a mighty explorer of the "powers of black-ness" and brought American literature up to the best that the European continent had to offer.

LITERARY FIGURES

1580–1631	Captain John Smith	1737–1809	Thomas Paine
1612–1672	Anne Bradstreet	1743–1826	Thomas Jefferson
1639–1723	Increase Mather	1752–1832	Philip Freneau
1645–1729	Edward Taylor	1753–1784	Phillis Wheatley
1652–1730	Samuel Sewall	1757–1826	Royall Tyler
1663–1728	Cotton Mather	1762–1824	Susanna Haswell Rowson
1666–1727	Sarah Kemble Knight	1771–1810	Charles Brockden Brown
1703–1758	Jonathan Edwards	1783–1859	Washington Irving
1706–1790	Benjamin Franklin	1789–1851	James Fenimore Cooper
1732–1799	George Washington	1794–1878	William Cullen Bryant
1736–1799	Patrick Henry		

1607 **Time Line** 1829

Historical Events

1600

1607 Settlement at Jamestown, Virginia

1620 Pilgrims land at Plymouth, Massachusetts

1636 Founding of Harvard College

1640 First book printed in America
(*Bay Psalm Book*)

1650–1728 Mather dynasty flourishes

1692 Salem witchcraft executions

1700

1704 First American newspaper founded
(Boston *News Letter*)

1732 Ben Franklin opens first public library
(Philadelphia) and publishes first issue of
Poor Richard's Almanac

1740–1745 Religious revival—the Great Awakening

1765 Stamp Act

1770 Boston Massacre
1773 Boston Tea Party
1774 First Continental Congress
1775–1783 Revolutionary War
1776 Declaration of Independence

1781 Surrender of Cornwallis at Yorktown; Articles
of Confederation ratified

1789 Federal government established;
Washington's First Inaugural

1800

1803 Louisiana Purchase
1804–1806 Lewis and Clark expedition
1806 Noah Webster's first dictionary
1807 Fulton's steamboat
1812–1814 War with England
1815 *North American Review* established
1820 Missouri Compromise
1823 Monroe Doctrine
1829 Andrew Jackson elected President

Literary Events

1608 Captain John Smith, *A True Relation*
1616 Smith, *A Description of New England*
1624 Smith, *A General History of Virginia*

1650 Anne Bradstreet, *The Tenth Muse, Lately
Sprung Up in America*
1684 Increase Mather, *Illustrious Providences*
1693 Cotton Mather, *Wonders of the Invisible
World*

1702 Cotton Mather, *Magnalia Christi Americani*
1704 Sarah K. Knight, *Journal of a Journey*

1741 Jonathan Edwards, *Sinners in the Hands of
an Angry God*
1751 John Bartram, *Observations on American
Plants*
1754 Edwards, *Freedom of the Will*

1773 Phillis Wheatley, *Poems*
1774 Benjamin Rush, *Natural History of Medicine
among Indians of North America*
1776 Thomas Paine, *Common Sense* and
"The Crisis" (1776–1783)
Thomas Jefferson, *Declaration of
Independence*
1786 Philip Freneau, *Poems*
1787 Royall Tyler, *The Contrast* (acted)
1788 Alexander Hamilton et al., *The Federalist*

1789 William Hill Brown, *The Power of Sympathy*
George Washington, "First Inaugural"
1791 William Bartram, *Travels*
1794 Susanna H. Rowson, *Charlotte Temple*
1798 Charles Brockden Brown, *Wieland*

1809 Washington Irving, *Knickerbocker's History*
1820 Irving, *Sketch Book*
1821 William Cullen Bryant, *Poems*
James Fenimore Cooper, *The Spy*
1823 Cooper, *Pioneers*
1826 Cooper, *Last of the Mohicans*
1827 Edgar Allan Poe, *Tamerlane and Other Poems*
1828 Nathaniel Hawthorne, *Fanshawe*

WASHINGTON IRVING

1783-1859

*What James Fenimore Cooper did for
the early American novel and William
Cullen Bryant for poetry, Irving
did for* belles lettres—*witty, entertaining
essays and tales that incorporated
history, biography, legend,
and a fertile imagination. It
is not surprising that Washington
Irving's sketches and short
stories inspired Hawthorne and Poe
and many of their contemporaries.
He set high standards.*

In 1820, Sydney Smith, an English minister, asked in the pages of the *Edinburgh Review:* "In the four quarters of the globe, who reads an American book? or goes to an American play? or looks at an American picture or statue?" He did not have to wait long for his answer. Washington Irving was our first genuine author of *belles lettres,* and the British who had delighted in looking down on the American colonies were happy to welcome him to the company of Byron and Coleridge and Scott. America to be sure had produced political writers, competent historians, and even poets in the years before the Revolution; but our stylists, masters of polished prose, were few in number. That Irving came to a literary career through a side door, as it were, makes his life and his achievements all the more fascinating.

Born in New York City, the youngest of eleven children, he began reading for the law at the age of sixteen, but his heart was not in his studies. "I was always fond of visiting new scenes and observing strange characters and manners," he later recalled. "Even when a mere child I began my traveling, and made many tours of discovery into foreign parts and unknown regions of my native city, to the frequent alarm of my parents." Travel continued to entice him, first to the Hudson Valley and Canada, then to France, Italy, and Holland where he spent two years as a literary vagabond, reading whatever he pleased and endlessly observing the customs and especially the theater of Europe.

When he became a lawyer at the age of twenty-three, his family expected him to settle down. Irving preferred the literary to the legal world. He and his brother William published the *Salmagundi* papers, satirical essays and poems written to ridicule local theater, politics, and fashions. The next year, 1809, he began *A History of New York*, signing it Diedrich Knickerbocker. It was one of America's first pieces of comic literature, a burlesque of serious history that dared to satirize the persons and policies of John Adams, Madison, and Jefferson as well as the old Dutch administrator and symbol of the old aristocracy Peter Stuyvesant, "the Headstrong." One of Irving's favorite character studies in this history is still a delight today: the "golden reign of Wouter Van Twiller," governor of New Amsterdam. A "model of majesty and lordly grandeur," he was "exactly five feet six inches in height, and six feet five inches in circumference," and when he stood erect "he had not a little the appearance of a beer barrel on skids."

As Diedrich Knickerbocker, Irving established an enviable reputation. New York feted the young, witty lawyer, but again he was restless and by no means convinced that he could sustain a literary career. He worked for a while in the family hardware business, then served as a staff colonel during the War of 1812, finally sailed for Europe in 1815, little realizing that he would remain abroad for seventeen years. For business reasons he lived chiefly in England; but when the family business failed he realized that he would have to support himself by other means, and literary work seemed the most attractive. Always a collector of tales, a

keen observer, and an amateur artist, he naturally drifted into writing familiar essays and sketches. Under the pseudonym Geoffrey Crayon, Gent., they were published serially in the United States in 1819–1820. When he gathered them into a volume called *The Sketch Book* for publication in England in 1820, he was greeted with a reception such as no American author had ever received from the British public. Lord Byron declared that "Crayon is very good"; Sir Walter Scott and Thomas Moore, personal friends by now, gave him public acclaim. American literary critics were as quick to recognize his considerable achievement.

As a visitor to England, Irving had filled his journals with anecdotes, quotations, notes of his travels, and details of English life taken from close observation. *The Sketch Book* is a graceful reworking of these notes. Most of the thirty-six pieces recount the pleasures of the English countryside, typical village life, and landmarks no visitor should miss. With much genial humor, he describes Westminster Abbey, Stratford-on-Avon, the Boar's Head Tavern, an English Christmas, and more. Six of the chapters treat American subjects; not surprisingly they were the ones to achieve lasting fame, especially "Rip Van Winkle" and "The Legend of Sleepy Hollow."

Irving wrote these American narratives as though he were recounting well-known legends of colonial Dutch-American life in the lower Hudson Valley. We know now that he borrowed the tales from German folklore and simply blended the two cultures, creating the first American short stories. It is possible that not even Irving was aware of how widely his *Sketch Book* would be publicized in the next decades or how carefully he had caught the mood of romantic melancholy so popular with both English and American readers. "The truth presses home upon us as we advance in life," he wrote in his notebook, "that everything around us is transient and uncertain. . . . When I look back for a few short years, what changes of all kind have taken place, what wrecks of time and

*Sunnyside, Irving residence near
Tarrytown, New York.*

fortune are strewn around me." In these tales
and essays of time past, Irving had found his
talent, and he knew it.

Bracebridge Hall followed in 1822. Like so
many sequels, it hardly measures up to the
charms of his first success. This collection of
sketches begins in England, then moves across
the channel to France and Spain for its settings;
but only "Dolph Heyliger" and "The Storm-
Ship" are remembered. Irving's interest in
tales of the supernatural continued to grow,
however, and he crossed the Rhine to visit
Dresden and Vienna, to explore "the rich mine
of German literature." *Tales of a Traveller*
(1824) resulted, a highly uneven collection
but notable for "The Devil and Tom Walker,"

a short story far superior to the Gothic romances—tales filled with magic, mystery, and
medieval trappings—that make up most of the
volume.

During the next eight years before his return
to the United States, Irving made two diplo-
matic journeys to Spain, living for a time in
the Alhambra as attaché to the American
envoy; and he served in London as secretary
to the American legation. These were highly
productive years in terms of his reputation
abroad and of newly published volumes. A
huge life of Christopher Columbus appeared
in 1828; *The Conquest of Granada,* a mixture
of romance and history, in 1829. Both works
were the result of prodigious research, but
there is no doubt that *The Alhambra* (1832)
struck the familiar chord and more clearly reflects Irving's genuine talents. His American

public called it the "Spanish Sketch Book." They welcomed his return to the leisurely narrative, the intimate legends of barbaric Spain, the sights and sounds of an opulent era of history. In describing this Moorish palace at Granada, one of the architectural wonders of Western Europe, his purpose, he said, was "to depict its half Spanish, half Oriental character, . . . to revive the traces of grace and beauty fast fading from its walls." Irving was never happier than when he was recreating a historical personage. Here he dotes on frail Boabdil, the last Moorish king to possess the Alhambra, known to his subjects as El Rey Chico, "King Do-Nothing." He is only one of the many delights of this collection.

The United States seemed strange to Irving when he returned in 1832, and some of his American critics were quick to suggest that his long stay abroad had "Europeanized" him. Irving set out to prove the charge exaggerated. After a journey to the West, he set down his impressions in *A Tour on the Prairies* (1835). Compared with H. L. Ellsworth's account of the same trip, Irving's impressions are more quaint than accurate, more idealized than realistic. But his Eastern readers were accustomed to this aspect of his art. They were willing to accept the picturesque, even the sentimental, because Irving could hold their attention with intimate, vibrant description. What is more, they had never seen a savage Indian or a buffalo hunt. By now the professional writer, Irving sensed a market. He never again equaled the quality of his *Sketch Book* prose, but he supplied his public with what they wanted. *Astoria* (1836) is a history of John Jacob Astor's fur trade in the Northwest, written from original materials in a New York library, not from notes of personal expeditions. *The Adventures of Captain Bonneville* (1837) recounts life in the Rocky Mountains, but it too was done under Astor's patronage.

Perhaps if Irving had not achieved such acclaim as a young man, his later years would not strike us as anticlimactic. In 1836, he moved into Sunnyside, his home near Tarrytown, New York, and for the next two decades he played the country squire, the successful writer pursued by politicians and public alike. He turned down nominations for Congress and for mayor of New York; he refused President Van Buren's invitation to be Secretary of the Navy. He agreed, however, to spend four years in Spain as United States Minister, but he longed to return to Sunnyside and his nieces and this time he came home without a copiously filled notebook from which to create new work. His last volumes are rather plodding biographies of the eighteenth-century writer Oliver Goldsmith and of Mahomet and a monumental five-volume biography of George Washington, completed just before his death on the eve of the Civil War. A glimmer of the lively young Irving remains in *Wolfert's Roost and Miscellanies* (1855), a volume of sketches he published under several pseudonyms in the *Knickerbocker Magazine,* a New York journal established in his honor. The splendid urbanity of style is still there, the pleasant variety of subject (Spanish legends, colonial American history, frontier explorations), and above all Irving's stamp: personal observations couched in homely, memorable details.

For these superlative familiar essays American letters will always be in Irving's debt. For too long the colonies and the young nation had been fed on political tracts, harsh sermons, propaganda, and factual histories. What James Fenimore Cooper did for the early American novel and William Cullen Bryant for poetry, Irving did for *belles lettres*—witty, entertaining essays that incorporated history, biography, legend, and a fertile imagination. These three American writers earned international reputations at a time when American letters were in their infancy, acquainting European audiences with American regional life and establishing a respect for literary artists in a young country only beginning to discover its cultural heritage. It is not surprising that Washington Irving's sketches and short stories inspired Hawthorne and Poe and many of their contemporaries. He set high standards.

Four years after the success
of *The Sketch Book,* Irving collected
32 stories and essays, written chiefly
from notes gathered during a tour
of Germany, and published them as *Tales
of a Traveller* (1824). Though not
as well received as his earlier work,
they continued to demonstrate his mastery
of the anecdotal style—relaxed, graceful
reminiscences mixed with genial humor
and credible incident. Although the first three
sections of the book have European backgrounds,
the last section, "The Money Diggers," is set
in New York and New England and contains
five tales "found among the papers
of the late Diedrich Knickerbocker." The best
by far is this tale of the miserly Tom Walker
and his encounter with "the black woodsman."
Here again Irving blends European legend
with American folklore.

The Devil
and Tom Walker

A few miles from Boston in Massachusetts, there is a deep inlet, winding several miles into the interior of the country from Charles Bay, and terminating in a thickly-wooded swamp or morass. On one side of this inlet is a beautiful dark grove; on the opposite side the land rises abruptly from the water's edge into a high ridge, on which grow a few scattered oaks of great age and immense size. Under one of these gigantic trees, according to old stories, there was a great amount of treasure buried by Kidd[1] the pirate. The inlet allowed a facility to bring the money in a boat secretly and at night to the very foot of the hill; the elevation of the place permitted a good lookout to be kept that no one

was at hand; while the remarkable trees formed good landmarks by which the place might easily be found again. The old stories add, moreover, that the devil presided at the hiding of the money, and took it under his guardianship; but this, it is well known, he always does with buried treasure, particularly when it has been ill-gotten. Be that as it may, Kidd never returned to recover his wealth; being shortly after seized at Boston, sent out to England, and there hanged for a pirate.

About the year 1727, just at the time that earthquakes were prevalent in New England, and shook many tall sinners down upon their knees, there lived near this place a meagre, miserly fellow, of the name of Tom Walker. He had a wife as miserly as himself: they were so miserly that they even conspired to cheat each other. Whatever the woman could lay hands on, she hid away; a hen could not cackle but she was on the alert to secure the new-laid egg. Her husband was continually prying about to detect her secret hoards, and many and fierce were the conflicts that took place about what ought to have been common property. They lived in a forlorn-looking house that stood alone, and had an air of starvation. A few straggling savin-trees, emblems of sterility, grew near it; no smoke ever curled from its chimney; no traveller stopped at its door. A miserable horse, whose ribs were as articulate as the bars of a gridiron, stalked about a field, where a thin carpet of moss, scarcely covering the ragged beds of pudding-stone, tantalized and balked his hunger; and sometimes he would lean his head over the fence, look piteously at the passer-by, and seem to petition deliverance from this land of famine.

The house and its inmates had altogether a bad name. Tom's wife was a tall termagant, fierce of temper, loud of tongue, and strong of arm. Her voice was often heard in wordy warfare with her husband; and his face sometimes

---
1. **William Kidd** (1645?–1701), known as Captain Kidd, tried and convicted for murder and piracy; hanged in London, 1701.

showed signs that their conflicts were not con-fined to words. No one ventured, however, to interfere between them. The lonely wayfarer shrunk within himself at the horrid clamor and clapper-clawing; eyed the den of discord askance; and hurried on his way, rejoicing, if a bachelor, in his celibacy.

One day that Tom Walker had been to a distant part of the neighborhood, he took what he considered a short cut homeward, through the swamp. Like most short cuts, it was an ill-chosen route. The swamp was thickly grown with great gloomy pines and hemlocks, some of them ninety feet high, which made it dark at noonday, and a retreat for all the owls of the neighborhood. It was full of pits and quag-mires,[2] partly covered with weeds and mosses, where the green surface often betrayed the traveller into a gulf of black, smothering mud: there were also dark and stagnant pools, the abodes of the tadpole, the bullfrog, and the water-snake; where the trunks of pines and hemlocks lay half-drowned, half-rotting, look-ing like alligators sleeping in the mire.

Tom had long been picking his way cau-tiously through this treacherous forest; step-ping from tuft to tuft of rushes and roots, which afforded precarious footholds among deep sloughs; or pacing carefully, like a cat, along the prostrate trunks of trees; startled now and then by the sudden screaming of the bittern, or the quacking of a wild duck rising on the wing from some solitary pool. At length he ar-rived at a firm piece of ground, which ran out like a peninsula into the deep bosom of the swamp. It had been one of the strongholds of the Indians during their wars with the first colo-nists. Here they had thrown up a kind of fort, which they had looked upon as almost impreg-nable, and had used as a place of refuge for their squaws and children. Nothing remained of the old Indian fort but a few embankments, gradually sinking to the level of the surround-ing earth, and already overgrown in part by oaks and other forest trees, the foliage of which formed a contrast to the dark pines and hem-locks of the swamp.

It was late in the dusk of evening when Tom Walker reached the old fort, and he paused there awhile to rest himself. Any one but he would have felt unwilling to linger in this lonely, melancholy place, for the common peo-ple had a bad opinion of it, from the stories handed down from the time of the Indian wars; when it was asserted that the savages held in-cantations here, and made sacrifices to the evil spirit.

Tom Walker, however, was not a man to be troubled with any fears of the kind. He reposed himself for some time on the trunk of a fallen hemlock, listening to the boding cry of the tree-toad, and delving with his walking-staff into a mound of black mould at his feet. As he turned up the soil unconsciously, his staff struck against something hard. He raked it out of the vegetable mould, and lo! a cloven skull, with an Indian tomahawk buried deep in it, lay be-fore him. The rust on the weapon showed the time that had elapsed since this deathblow had been given. It was a dreary memento of the fierce struggle that had taken place in this last foothold of the Indian warriors.

"Humph!" said Tom Walker, as he gave it a kick to shake the dirt from it.

"Let that skull alone!" said a gruff voice. Tom lifted up his eyes, and beheld a great black man seated directly opposite him, on the stump of a tree. He was exceedingly surprised, having neither heard nor seen any one approach; and he was still more perplexed on observing, as well as the gathering gloom would permit, that the stranger was neither negro nor Indian. It is true he was dressed in a rude half-Indian garb, and had a red belt or sash swathed round his body; but his face was neither black nor cop-per-color, but swarthy and dingy, and be-grimed with soot, as if he had been accustomed to toil among fires and forges. He had a shock of coarse black hair, that stood out from his head in all directions, and bore an axe on his shoulder.

---

2. **quagmires**\ˈkwăg ˈmairz\ soft, wet, miry land that gives way under foot.

He scowled for a moment at Tom with a pair of great red eyes.

"What are you doing on my grounds?" said the black man, with a hoarse growling voice.

"Your grounds!" said Tom, with a sneer, "no more your grounds than mine; they belong to Deacon Peabody."

"Deacon Peabody be d——d," said the stranger, "as I flatter myself he will be, if he does not look more to his own sins and less to those of his neighbors. Look yonder, and see how Deacon Peabody is faring."

Tom looked in the direction that the stranger pointed, and beheld one of the great trees, fair and flourishing without, but rotten at the core, and saw that it had been nearly hewn through, so that the first high wind was likely to blow it down. On the bark of the tree was scored the name of Deacon Peabody, an eminent man, who had waxed wealthy by driving shrewd bargains with the Indians. He now looked around, and found most of the tall trees marked with the name of some great man of the colony, and all more or less scored by the axe. The one on which he had been seated, and which had evidently just been hewn down, bore the name of Crowninshield; and he recollected a mighty rich man of that name, who made a vulgar display of wealth, which it was whispered he had acquired by buccaneering.

"He's just ready for burning!" said the black man, with a growl of triumph. "You see I am likely to have a good stock of firewood for winter."

"But what right have you," said Tom, "to cut down Deacon Peabody's timber?"

"The right of a prior claim," said the other. "This woodland belonged to me long before one of your white-faced race put foot upon the soil."

"And pray, who are you, if I may be so bold?" said Tom.

"Oh, I go by various names. I am the wild huntsman in some countries; the black miner in others. In this neighborhood I am known by the name of the black woodsman. I am he to whom the red men consecrated this spot, and in honor of whom they now and then roasted a white man, by way of sweet-smelling sacrifice. Since the red men have been exterminated by you white savages, I amuse myself by presiding at the persecutions of Quakers and Anabaptists;[3] I am the great patron and prompter of slave-dealers, and the grand-master of the Salem witches."

"The upshot of all which is, that, if I mistake not," said Tom, sturdily, "you are he commonly called Old Scratch."

"The same, at your service!" replied the black man, with a half civil nod.

Such was the opening of this interview, according to the old story; though it has almost too familiar an air to be credited. One would think that to meet with such a singular personage, in this wild, lonely place, would have shaken any man's nerves; but Tom was a hard-minded fellow, not easily daunted, and he had lived so long with a termagant wife, that he did not even fear the devil.

It is said that after this commencement they had a long and earnest conversation together, as Tom returned homeward. The black man told him of great sums of money buried by Kidd the pirate, under the oak trees on the high ridge, not far from the morass. All these were under his command, and protected by his power, so that none could find them but such as propitiated his favor. These he offered to place within Tom Walker's reach, having conceived an especial kindess for him; but they were to be had only on certain conditions. What these conditions were may be easily surmised, though Tom never disclosed them publicly. They must have been very hard, for he required time to think of them, and he was not a man to stick at trifles when money was in view. When they had reached the edge of the swamp, the stranger paused. "What proof have I that all you have been telling me is true?" said Tom. "There's my signature," said the black man, pressing his

---

3. **Anabaptists,** religious sect, originating in Zurich, advocated return to primitive Christianity, denied necessity of infant baptism, and opposed union of church and state.

finger on Tom's forehead. So saying, he turned off among the thickets of the swamp, and seemed, as Tom said, to go down, down, down, into the earth, until nothing but his head and shoulders could be seen, and so on, until he totally disappeared.

When Tom reached home, he found the black print of a finger burnt, as it were, into his forehead, which nothing could obliterate.

The first news his wife had to tell him was the sudden death of Absalom Crowninshield, the rich buccaneer. It was announced in the papers, with the usual flourish, that "A great man had fallen in Israel."

Tom recollected the tree which his black friend had just hewn down, and which was ready for burning. "Let the freebooter roast," said Tom, "who cares!" He now felt convinced that all he had heard and seen was no illusion.

He was not prone to let his wife into his confidence; but as this was an uneasy secret, he willingly shared it with her. All her avarice was awakened at the mention of hidden gold, and she urged her husband to comply with the black man's terms, and secure what would make them wealthy for life. However Tom might have felt disposed to sell himself to the Devil, he was determined not to do so to oblige his wife; so he flatly refused, out of the mere spirit of contradiction. Many and bitter were the quarrels they had on the subject; but the more she talked, the more resolute was Tom not to be damned to please her.

At length she determined to drive the bargain on her own account, and if she succeeded, to keep all the gain to herself. Being of the same fearless temper as her husband, she set off for the old Indian fort towards the close of a summer's day. She was many hours absent. When she came back, she was reserved and sullen in her replies. She spoke something of a black man, whom she had met about twilight hewing at the root of a tall tree. He was sulky, however, and would not come to terms: she was to go again with a propitiatory offering, but what it was she forebore to say.

The next evening she set off again for the swamp, with her apron heavily laden. Tom waited and waited for her, but in vain; midnight came, but she did not make her appearance: morning, noon, night returned, but still she did not come. Tom now grew uneasy for her safety, especially as he found she had carried off in her apron the silver tea-pot and spoons, and every portable article of value. Another night elapsed, another morning came; but no wife. In a word, she was never heard of more.

What was her real fate nobody knows, in consequence of so many pretending to know. It is one of those facts which have become confounded by a variety of historians. Some asserted that she lost her way among the tangled mazes of the swamp, and sank into some pit or slough; others, more uncharitable, hinted that she had eloped with the household booty, and made off to some other province; while others surmised that the tempter had decoyed her into a dismal quagmire, on the top of which her hat was found lying. In confirmation of this, it was said a great black man, with an axe on his shoulder, was seen late that very evening coming out of the swamp, carrying a bundle tied in a check apron, with an air of surly triumph.

The most current and probable story, however, observes, that Tom Walker grew so anxious about the fate of his wife and his property, that he set out at length to seek them both at the Indian fort. During a long summer's afternoon he searched about the gloomy place, but no wife was to be seen. He called her name repeatedly, but she was nowhere to be heard. The bittern alone responded to his voice, as he flew screaming by: or the bull-frog croaked dolefully from a neighboring pool. At length, it is said, just in the brown hour of twilight, when the owls began to hoot, and the bats to flit about, his attention was attracted by the clamor of carrion crows hovering about a cypress-tree. He looked up, and beheld a bundle tied in a check apron, and hanging in the branches of the tree, with a great vulture perched hard by, as if keeping watch upon it. He leaped with joy;

for he recognized his wife's apron, and supposed it to contain the household valuables.

"Let us get hold of the property," said he, consolingly to himself, "and we will endeavor to do without the woman."

As he scrambled up the tree, the vulture spread its wide wings, and sailed off, screaming, into the deep shadows of the forest. Tom seized the checked apron, but, woeful sight! found nothing but a heart and liver tied up in it!

Such, according to this most authentic old story, was all that was to be found of Tom's wife. She had probably attempted to deal with the black man as she had been accustomed to deal with her husband; but though a female

scold is generally considered a match for the devil, yet in this instance she appears to have had the worse of it. She must have died game, however; for it is said Tom noticed many prints of cloven feet deeply stamped about the tree, and found handfuls of hair, that looked as if they had been plucked from the coarse black shock of the woodman. Tom knew his wife's prowess by experience. He shrugged his shoulders, as he looked at the signs of a fierce clapper-clawing. "Egad," said he to himself, "Old Scratch must have had a tough time of it!"

Tom consoled himself for the loss of his property, with the loss of his wife, for he was a man of fortitude. He even felt something like gratitude towards the black woodman, who, he considered, had done him a kindness. He sought, therefore, to cultivate a further acquaintance with him, but for some time without success; the old blacklegs played shy, for whatever people may think, he is not always to be had for calling for: he knows how to play his cards when pretty sure of his game.

At length, it is said, when delay had whetted Tom's eagerness to the quick, and prepared him to agree to anything rather than not gain the promised treasure, he met the black man one evening in his usual woodman's dress, with his axe on his shoulder, sauntering along the swamp, and humming a tune. He affected to receive Tom's advances with great indifference, made brief replies, and went on humming his tune.

By degrees, however, Tom brought him to business, and they began to haggle about the terms on which the former was to have the pirate's treasure. There was one condition which need not be mentioned, being generally understood in all cases where the devil grants favors; but there were others about which, though of less importance, he was inflexibly obstinate. He insisted that the money found through his means should be employed in his service. He proposed, therefore, that Tom should employ it in the black traffic; that is to say, that he should fit out a slave-ship. This, however, Tom resolutely refused: he was bad enough in all conscience; but the devil himself could not tempt him to turn slave-trader.

Finding Tom so squeamish on this point, he did not insist upon it, but proposed, instead, that he should turn usurer; the devil being extremely anxious for the increase of usurers, looking upon them as his peculiar people.

To this no objections were made, for it was just to Tom's taste.

"You shall open a broker's shop in Boston next month," said the black man.

"I'll do it to-morrow, if you wish," said Tom Walker.

"You shall lend money at two per cent a month."

"Egad, I'll charge four!" replied Tom Walker.

"You shall extort bonds, foreclose mortgages, drive the merchants to bankruptcy"——

"I'll drive them to the d——," cried Tom Walker.

"You are the usurer for my money!" said black-legs with delight. "When will you want the rhino?"[4]

"This very night."

"Done!" said the devil.

"Done!" said Tom Walker.—So they shook hands and struck a bargain.

A few days' time saw Tom Walker seated behind his desk in a counting-house in Boston.

His reputation for a ready-moneyed man, who would lend money out for a good consideration, soon spread abroad. Everybody remembers the time of Governor Belcher, when money was particularly scarce. It was a time of paper credit. The country had been deluged with government bills, the famous Land Bank had been established; there had been a rage for speculating; the people had run mad with schemes for new settlements; for building cities in the wilderness; land-jobbers went about with maps of grants, and townships, and Eldorados,[5] lying nobody knew where, but which everybody was ready to purchase. In a word, the great speculating fever which breaks out every now and then in the country, had raged to an alarming degree, and everybody was dreaming of making sudden fortunes from nothing. As usual the fever had subsided; the dream had gone off, and the imaginary fortunes with it; the patients were left in doleful plight, and the whole country resounded with the consequent cry of "hard times."

At this propitious time of public distress did Tom Walker set up as usurer in Boston. His door was soon thronged by customers. The needy and adventurous; the gambling speculator; the dreaming land-jobber; the thriftless

---

4. **rhino,** money, cash (origin of the word unknown).
5. **Eldorado,** the fabulously rich city sixteenth-century Spanish explorers vainly sought for in South America.

tradesman; the merchant with cracked credit; in short, everyone driven to raise money by desperate means and desperate sacrifices, hurried to Tom Walker.

Thus Tom was the universal friend of the needy, and acted like a "friend in need"; that is to say, he always exacted good pay and good security. In proportion to the distress of the applicant was the highness of his terms. He accumulated bonds and mortgages; gradually squeezed his customers closer and closer: and sent them at length, dry as a sponge, from his door.

In this way he made money hand over hand; became a rich and mighty man, and exalted his cocked hat upon 'Change. He built himself, as usual, a vast house, out of ostentation; but left the greater part of it unfinished and unfurnished, out of parsimony. He even set up a carriage in the fulness of his vainglory, though he nearly starved the horses which drew it; and as the ungreased wheels groaned and screeched on the axle-trees, you would have thought you heard the souls of the poor debtors he was squeezing.

As Tom waxed old, however, he grew thoughtful. Having secured the good things of this world, he began to feel anxious about those of the next. He thought with regret on the bargain he had made with his black friend, and set his wits to work to cheat him out of the conditions. He became, therefore, all of a sudden, a violent church-goer. He prayed loudly and strenuously, as if heaven were to be taken by force of lungs. Indeed, one might always tell when he had sinned most during the week, by the clamor of his Sunday devotion. The quiet Christians who had been modestly and steadfastly travelling Zionward,[6] were struck with self-reproach at seeing themselves so suddenly outstripped in their career by this new-made convert. Tom was as rigid in religious as in money matters; he was a stern supervisor and censurer of his neighbors, and seemed to think every sin entered up to their account became a credit on his own side of the page. He even talked of the expediency of reviving the perse-

cution of Quakers and Anabaptists. In a word, Tom's zeal became as notorious as his riches.

Still, in spite of all this strenuous attention to forms, Tom had a lurking dread that the devil, after all, would have his due. That he might not be taken unawares, therefore, it is said he always carried a small Bible in his coat-pocket. He had also a great folio Bible on his counting-house desk, and would frequently be found reading it when people called on business; on such occasions he would lay his green spectacles in the book, to mark the place, while he turned round to drive some usurious bargain.

Some say that Tom grew a little crack-brained in his old days, and that, fancying his end approaching, he had his horse new shod, saddled and bridled, and buried with his feet uppermost; because he supposed that at the last day the world would be turned upside down; in which case he should find his horse standing ready for mounting, and he was determined at the worst to give his old friend a run for it. This, however, is probably a mere old wives' fable. If he really did take such a precaution, it was totally superfluous; at least so says the authentic old legend; which closes his story in the following manner.

One hot summer afternoon in the dogdays, just as a terrible black thunder-gust was coming up, Tom sat in his counting-house, in his white linen cap and India silk morning-gown. He was on the point of foreclosing a mortgage, by which he would complete the ruin of an unlucky land-speculator for whom he had professed the greatest friendship. The poor land-jobber begged him to grant a few months' indulgence. Tom had grown testy and irritated, and refused another day.

"My family will be ruined, and brought upon the parish," said the land-jobber.

"Charity begins at home," replied Tom; "I must take care of myself in these hard times."

"You have made so much money out of me," said the speculator.

6. **Zionward**\ˈzai·ən·wərd\ heavenward. Zion is identified with Jerusalem, considered the earthly home of God by the Israelites and early Christians.

Tom lost his patience and his piety. "The devil take me," said he, "if I have made a farthing!"

Just then there were three loud knocks at the street-door. He stepped out to see who was there. A black man was holding a black horse, which neighed and stamped with impatience.

"Tom, you're come for," said the black fellow, gruffly. Tom shrank back, but too late. He had left his little Bible at the bottom of his coat-pocket, and his big Bible on the desk buried under the mortgage he was about to foreclose: never was sinner taken more unawares. The black man whisked him like a child into the saddle, gave the horse the lash, and away he galloped, with Tom on his back, in the midst of the thunder-storm. The clerks stuck their pens behind their ears, and stared after him from the windows. Away went Tom Walker, dashing down the streets; his white cap bobbing up and down; his morning-gown fluttering in the wind, and his steed striking fire out of the pavement at every bound. When the clerks turned to look for the black man, he had disappeared.

Tom Walker never returned to foreclose the mortgage. A countryman, who lived on the border of the swamp, reported that in the height of the thunder-gust he had heard a great clattering of hoofs and a howling along the road, and running to the window caught sight of a figure, such as I have described, on a horse that galloped like mad across the fields, over the hills, and down into the black hemlock swamp towards the old Indian fort; and that shortly after a thunder-bolt falling in that direction seemed to set the whole forest in a blaze.

The good people of Boston shook their heads and shrugged their shoulders, but had been so much accustomed to witches and goblins, and tricks of the devil, in all kinds of shapes, from the first settlement of the colony, that they were not so much horror-struck as might have been expected. Trustees were appointed to take charge of Tom's effects. There was nothing, however, to administer. On searching his coffers, all his bonds and mortgages were found reduced to cinders. In place of gold and silver, his iron chest was filled with chips and shavings; two skeletons lay in his stable instead of his half-starved horses, and the very next day his great house took fire and was burnt to the ground.

Such was the end of Tom Walker and his ill-gotten wealth. Let all griping money-brokers lay this story to heart. The truth of it is not to be doubted. The very hole under the oak-trees, whence he dug Kidd's money, is to be seen to this day; and the neighboring swamp and old Indian fort are often haunted in stormy nights by a figure on horseback, in morning-gown and white cap, which is doubtless the troubled spirit of the usurer. In fact, the story has resolved itself into a proverb, and is the origin of that popular saying, so prevalent throughout New England, of "The Devil and Tom Walker."

I
AN AMERICAN FABLE

A fable is a brief story told to point a moral. Its subject matter deals with supernatural and unusual incidents often originating in folklore. The Faust theme—the legend of humans bargaining with the devil for their souls—originating from a medieval fable, has for centuries inspired much European literature, always deadly serious—even harrowing. Although Irving's tale is more leisurely than most fables, it still has a fablelike flavor—frequent references to popular local legend, the extraordinary meetings with "Old Scratch" as well as Tom's and his wife's remarkable exits from life, criticism of human nature and institutions, and the pointing of a moral in the closing paragraph. But unlike its European ancestors, the story does not take itself seriously, for Irving won't let it. He lingers too long and fondly over rich descriptions, chuckles too genially over old folk figures and situations—shrewish wives, pretentious aristocrats, misers, marriage—and keeps the reader too emotionally distant from the characters for the reader to take the proceedings seriously. In short, for

Irving the old fable is not so much an occasion to point a moral as to tell a good story.

II
IMPLICATIONS

A. Explain what Irving is criticizing in the following statements.

1. The lonely wayfarer shrunk within himself at the horrid clamor and clapper-clawing; eyed the den of discord askance; and hurried on his way, rejoicing, if a bachelor, in his celibacy.

2. . . . Tom was the universal friend of the needy, and acted like a "friend in need"; that is to say, he always exacted good pay and good security.

3. Tom was as rigid in religious as in money matters; he was a stern supervisor and censurer of his neighbors, and seemed to think every sin entered up to their account became a credit on his own side of the page.

B. Below are opposed statements about this story. Select the statement that best expresses your own opinion.

a. The theme of Irving's story is universal; it could therefore be placed in any geographical setting.

b. The idea of selling one's soul to the devil is essentially a European theme, and Irving should have used a European setting for his story.

III
TECHNIQUES

Setting

Much of the charm of this story can be attributed to Irving's careful creation of an atmosphere foreboding mystery and evil. What specific sights, colors, sounds, and feelings contribute to this atmosphere: (1) in the swamp, (2) at the old Indian fort, (3) when Tom finds his wife's remains?

Characterization

(1) Look back to the second paragraph. How do the house, the farm, and the horse help to show the Walkers' chief character trait? (2) What new traits of each are revealed throughout the remainder of the story? (3) What details of the black woodsman's physical appearance suggest his inner nature?

In 1835, Irving published a collection of autobiographical pieces called *A Tour on the Prairies,* based on his visit three years earlier to the Indian territories on the frontier, what is now the state of Oklahoma. He visited the Pawnee, Osage, and Creek tribes, taking notes on frontier customs, living conditions, and local legends. The following excerpt describes a camp on the Arkansas River.

The Camp of the Wild Horse

We had encamped in a good neighborhood for game, as the reports of rifles in various directions speedily gave notice. One of our hunters soon returned with the meat of a doe, tied up in the skin, and slung across his shoulders. Another brought a fat buck across his horse. Two other deer were brought in, and a number of turkeys. All the game was thrown down in front of the Captain's fire, to be portioned out among the various messes. The spits and camp-kettles were soon in full employ, and throughout the evening there was a scene of hunters' feasting and profusion.

We had been disappointed this day in our hopes of meeting with buffalo, but the sight of the wild horse had been a great novelty, and gave a turn to the conversation of the camp for the evening. There were several anecdotes told of a famous gray horse, which has ranged the prairies of this neighborhood for six or seven years, setting at naught every attempt of the hunters to capture him. They say he can pace

Chapter 20 of *A Tour on the Prairies,* 1835.

and rack (or amble) faster than the fleetest horses can run. Equally marvellous accounts were given of a black horse on the Brassos, who grazed the prairies on that river's banks in the Texas. For years he outstripped all pursuit. His fame spread far and wide; offers were made for him to the amount of a thousand dollars; the boldest and most hard-riding hunters tried incessantly to make prize of him, but in vain. At length he fell a victim to his gallantry, being decoyed under a tree by a tame mare, and a noose dropped over his head by a boy perched among the branches.

The capture of the wild horse is one of the most favorite achievements of the prairie tribes; and, indeed, it is from this source that the Indian hunters chiefly supply themselves. The wild horses which range those vast grassy plains, extending from the Arkansas to the Spanish settlements, are of various forms and colors, betraying their various descents. Some resemble the common English stock, and are probably descended from horses which have escaped from our border settlements. Others are of a low but strong make, and are supposed to be of the Andalusian breed,[1] brought out by the Spanish discoverers.

Some fanciful speculatists have seen in them descendants of the Arab stock, brought into Spain from Africa, and thence transferred to this country; and have pleased themselves with the idea that their sires may have been of the pure coursers of the desert, that once bore Mahomet[2] and his warlike disciples across the sandy plains of Arabia.

The habits of the Arab seem to have come with the steed. The introduction of the horse on the boundless prairies of the Far West changed the whole mode of living of their inhabitants. It gave them that facility of rapid motion, and of sudden and distant change of place, so dear to the roving propensities of man. Instead of lurking in the depths of gloomy forests, and patiently threading the mazes of a tangled wilderness on foot, like his brethren of the north, the Indian of the West is a rover of the plain; he leads a brighter and more sun-

shiny life; almost always on horseback, on vast flowery prairies and under cloudless skies.

I was lying by the Captain's fire, late in the evening, listening to stories about those coursers of the prairies, and weaving speculations of my own, when there was a clamor of voices and a loud cheering at the other end of the camp; and word was passed that Beatte, the half-breed, had brought in a wild horse.

In an instant every fire was deserted; the whole camp crowded to see the Indian and his prize. It was a colt about two years old, well grown, finely limbed, with bright prominent eyes, and a spirited yet gentle demeanor. He gazed about him with an air of mingled stupefaction and surprise, at the men, the horses, and the camp-fires; while the Indian stood before him with folded arms, having hold of the other end of the cord which noosed his captive, and gazing on him with a most imperturbable aspect. Beatte, as I have before observed, has a greenish olive complexion, with a strongly marked countenance, not unlike the bronze casts of Napoleon; and as he stood before his captive horse, with folded arms and fixed aspect, he looked more like a statue than a man.

If the horse, however, manifested the least restiveness, Beatte would immediately worry him with the lariat, jerking him first on one side, then on the other, so as almost to throw him on the ground; when he had thus rendered him passive, he would resume his statue-like attitude and gaze at him in silence.

The whole scene was singularly wild; the tall grove, partially illumined by the flashing fires of the camp, the horses tethered here and there among the trees, the carcasses of deer hanging around, and, in the midst of all, the wild huntsman and his wild horse, with an admiring throng of rangers almost as wild.

In the eagerness of their excitement, several of the young rangers sought to get the horse

---

1. **Andalusian breed**\'an·də ^lū·zhən\ named for an old province of Southern Spain.
2. **Mahomet**\mə ^hŏm·ĭt\ Mohammed, Arabian founder of Islam whose revelations are found in the *Koran*.

by purchase or barter, and even offered extravagant terms; but Beatte declined all their offers. "You give great price now," said he; "tomorrow you be sorry, and take back, and say d—d Indian!"

The young men importuned him with questions about the mode in which he took the horse, but his answers were dry and laconic; he evidently retained some pique at having been undervalued and sneered at by them; and at the same time looked down upon them with contempt as greenhorns little versed in the noble science of woodcraft.

Afterwards, however, when he was seated by our fire, I readily drew from him an account of his exploit; for, though taciturn among strangers, and little prone to boast of his actions, yet his taciturnity, like that of all Indians, had its times of relaxation.

He informed me, that on leaving the camp, he had returned to the place where we had lost sight of the wild horse. Soon getting upon its track, he followed it to the banks of the river. Here, the prints being more distinct in the sand, he perceived that one of the hoofs was broken and defective, so he gave up the pursuit.

As he was returning to the camp, he came upon a gang of six horses, which immediately made for the river. He pursued them across the stream, left his rifle on the river-bank, and putting his horse to full speed, soon came up with the fugitives. He attempted to noose one of them, but the lariat hitched on one of his ears, and he shook it off. The horses dashed up a hill, he followed hard at their heels, when, of a sudden, he saw their tails whisking in the air, and they plunging down a precipice. It was too late to stop. He shut his eyes, held in his breath, and went over with them—neck or nothing. The descent was between twenty and thirty feet, but they all came down safe upon a sandy bottom.

He now succeeded in throwing his noose round a fine young horse. As he galloped alongside of him, the two horses passed each side of a sapling, and the end of the lariat was jerked out of his hand. He regained it, but an intervening tree obliged him again to let it go. Having once more caught it, and coming to a more open country, he was enabled to play the young horse with the line until he gradually checked and subdued him, so as to lead him to the place where he had left his rifle.

He had another formidable difficulty in getting him across the river, where both horses stuck for a time in the mire, and Beatte was nearly unseated from his saddle by the force of the current and the struggles of his captive. After much toil and trouble, however, he got across the stream, and brought his prize safe into camp.

For the remainder of the evening the camp remained in a high state of excitement; nothing was talked of but the capture of wild horses; every youngster of the troop was for this harum-scarum kind of chase; every one promised himself to return from the campaign in triumph, bestriding one of these wild coursers of the prairies. Beatte had suddenly risen to great importance; he was the prime hunter, the hero of the day. Offers were made him by the best-mounted rangers, to let him ride their horses in the chase, provided he would give them a share of the spoil. Beatte bore his honors in silence, and closed with none of the offers. Our stammering, chattering, gasconading little Frenchman, however, made up for his taciturnity by vaunting as much upon the subject as if it were he that had caught the horse. Indeed he held forth so learnedly in the matter, and boasted so much of the many horses he had taken, that he began to be considered an oracle; and some of the youngsters were inclined to doubt whether he were not superior even to the taciturn Beatte.

The excitement kept the camp awake later than usual. The hum of voices, interrupted by occasional peals of laughter, was heard from the groups around the various fires, and the night was considerably advanced before all had sunk to sleep.

With the morning dawn the excitement revived, and Beatte and his wild horse were

The Camp of the Wild Horse

again the gaze and talk of the camp. The captive had been tied all night to a tree among the other horses. He was again led forth by Beatte, by a long halter or lariat, and, on his manifesting the least restiveness, was, as before, jerked and worried into passive submission. He appeared to be gentle and docile by nature, and had a beautifully mild expression of the eye. In his strange and forlorn situation, the poor animal seemed to seek protection and companionship in the very horse which had aided to capture him.

Seeing him thus gentle and tractable, Beatte, just as we were about to march, strapped a light pack upon his back, by way of giving him the first lesson in servitude. The native pride and independence of the animal took fire at this indignity. He reared, and plunged, and kicked, and tried in every way to get rid of the degrading burden. The Indian was too potent for him. At every paroxysm[3] he renewed the discipline of the halter, until the poor animal, driven to despair, threw himself prostrate on the ground, and lay motionless, as if acknowledging himself vanquished. A stage hero, representing the despair of a captive prince, could not have played his part more dramatically. There was absolutely a moral grandeur in it.

The imperturbable Beatte folded his arms, and stood for a time, looking down in silence upon his captive; until seeing him perfectly subdued, he nodded his head slowly, screwed his mouth into a sardonic smile of triumph, and, with a jerk of the halter, ordered him to rise. He obeyed, and from that time forward offered no resistance. During that day he bore his pack patiently, and was led by the halter; but in two days he followed voluntarily at large among the supernumerary horses of the troop.

I could not but look with compassion upon this fine young animal, whose whole course of existence had been so suddenly reversed. From being a denizen of these vast pastures, ranging at will from plain to plain and mead to mead, cropping of every herb and flower, and drinking of every stream, he was suddenly reduced to perpetual and painful servitude, to pass his life under the harness and the curb, amid, perhaps, the din and dust and drudgery of cities. The transition in his lot was such as sometimes takes place in human affairs, and in the fortunes of towering individuals:—one day, a prince of the prairies—the next day, a packhorse!

I
A WILD AND NOBLE WEST

Carefully omitting the harsher aspects of camp life—stifling dust, overpowering smells of animals and crusty men, rough and often vulgar language—Irving delights his Eastern reader with vivid glimpses of noble savage and beast set against the expected, classic background of flashing camp fires, rustic feasts, and story telling before the tent. Although some may object to his avoidance of realism, Irving still captures and preserves those beautiful and dramatic flashes of color and nobility that are lost on cruder souls.

II
IMPLICATIONS

What do the following quotations reveal either about Irving, the prairies, or life in general?

1. There was absolutely a moral grandeur in it [the wild horse's fall].

2. The transition in his lot was such as sometimes takes place in human affairs, and in the fortunes of towering individuals:—one day, a prince of the prairies—the next day, a packhorse!

III
TECHNIQUES

Setting

Irving is very sparing with details about the camp, but those he chooses are quite picturesque. What specific details does he cite? Why would these broad strokes be particularly effective for readers who have never seen such a camp?

---

3. **paroxysm**\ˈpă·rĕk ˈsĭz·əm\ a sudden outburst of action or emotion, usually occurring at intervals.

99

NATHANIEL HAWTHORNE

1804-1864

NATHANIEL HAWTHORNE, *Henry Inman*

Hawthorne began his stories with an idea, then clothed that idea in reality. He was not interested, like Washington Irving, in picturesque descriptions, or, like Poe, in carefully controlled suspense. That is not to say Hawthorne was intent on writing narrative sermons. His poetic imaginations would never allow his tales to become treatises on the Origin of Evil. But they began with the idea of guilt or pride or intolerance and moved from there into complex personal relationships, into the mysteries of the human heart.

New England was in Nathaniel Hawthorne's blood, but rarely has an American writer been so consciously tied to his birthplace and his ancestry and, at the same time, so aware of his aversion to both. Born in Salem, Massachusetts, on Independence Day, 1804, he was descended from wealthy and influential citizens who, in spite of their prominence, left a blot on the family's history which Hawthorne spent a lifetime trying to atone. William Hathorne (Nathaniel changed the spelling), arriving in the American Colonies in 1630, a soldier and eventually a judge, condemned a Quaker woman to be whipped in the streets of Salem for holding to a religion the Puritans strongly opposed. "Grave, bearded, sable-cloaked and steeple-crowned," Hawthorne described him. His son, John, was also a judge; and Hawthorne could not forget that in 1692 this ancestor "made himself so conspicuous in the martyrdom of witches that their blood may be said to have left a stain upon him." Intolerance, cruelty, pride—these sins obsessed the young Hawthorne as he listened to the history of early Salem and his ancestors.

It is true that Bold Daniel Hathorne, his grandfather, belonged to that early Salem. He was a naval captain in the Revolutionary War, of such bravery that he became the hero of a popular ballad. Other ancestors fought Indians, sailed merchant ships, built up considerable fortunes in trade. But Hawthorne grew up in nineteenth-century "joyless" Salem, as he called it, in the "chilliest of social atmospheres," and he loathed it. His own father, a sea captain, died of a fever in Dutch Guiana when Hawthorne was only four, and shortly thereafter his mother was forced to move her three children first into her parents' crowded Salem home, eventually into her brother's house in Raymond, Maine. There is no reason to believe Hawthorne's childhood was abnormally disordered, but certainly the family's impoverishment, his mother's prolonged mourning and fits of seclusion, his own distaste for school, his fragile health—these aspects of his youth, coupled with his sense of inherited guilt, began to shape the young man's mind.

After four years at Bowdoin College, at his uncle's expense, he returned to Salem not to read law or to enter business, as his relatives expected, but to seclude himself in his mother's

Nathaniel Hawthorne's birthplace,
Benjamin Pickman House, Salem, Mass.

house and, quite simply, turn himself into a writer. "I do not want to be a doctor and live by men's diseases," he had written to his mother from Bowdoin, "nor a minister to live by their sins, nor a lawyer and live by their quarrels. So, I don't see that there is anything left for me but to be an author." For the next twelve years he lived physically in "the chamber under the eaves" of his mother's house, seldom going out except at twilight or to make a brief journey to another city; mentally he lived in a world of books. "I had read endlessly all sorts of good and good-for-nothing books," he recalled many years later, "and, in the dearth of other employment, had early begun to scribble sketches and stories most of which I burned." His first novel, *Fanshawe,* was published anonymously at his own expense in 1828. In anger at the lack of sales or at his own immaturity as a writer, he recalled every copy he could find and destroyed them. When a local printer delayed publishing his *Seven Tales of My Native Land,* he withdrew the manuscript and burned it "in a mood half savage, half despairing." Other stories he destroyed before publication because they were "morbid."

A weaker man would have withered under such an apprenticeship. Hawthorne only grew, in self-respect, in determination to succeed on his own terms, in patience with the world "outside." He traveled briefly to New Haven, to Swampscott, to the mountains of Vermont, always keeping a notebook in which he jotted observations of places and people, ideas for stories, phrases which pleased him. He sold tales and sketches to New England magazines; he was even persuaded to edit a Boston magazine for six months. Finally in 1837, at the age of thirty-two, he published his first collection, *Twice-Told Tales.* Longfellow, the most popular poet of the day, gave it a full, almost flattering review. New York magazine editors read it and asked for contributions to their pages. Even Salem recognized its merits. One family in particular, the Nathaniel Peabodys, so wooed the young author that within two years he was engaged to their youngest daughter, Sophia.

The "Old Manse," Concord, Mass.

Supporting a wife, Hawthorne realized, is not a task a recluse can face without qualms. He could never manage it by writing stories, so with as decisive a manner as he entered his apprenticeship he left Salem and his mother's house for a political appointment as measurer of coal and salt in the Boston customhouse. The contrast was a shock. He had hoped to discover what "reality" was like as well as earn a respectable salary, and he gave it a fair try; but after two years he resigned from this "very grievous thraldom." He had been able to write little more than notebook entries, and he found "nothing in the world that [he] thought preferable to [his] old solitude." He thought marriage might be the answer, and in one way it was. He learned to share his life.

With their moving to the Old Manse in rural Concord, Massachusetts, the Hawthornes found a happiness neither expected out of life. "Everybody that comes here," he wrote in 1843, "falls asleep; but for my own part, I feel as if, for the first time in my life, I was awake. I have found a reality, though it looks very much like some of my old dreams." Intellectually he was still content to trust his "dreams," his secret musings, his private thoughts, in spite of conversations with extraordinary neighbors who tried to draw him out of his protective shell. Henry David Thoreau (see pages 192–214) struck him as "ugly as sin, long-nosed, queer mouthed," and yet "a healthy, wholesome man to know." They had long, involved talks together. Emerson was for him "the one great original thinker," but Hawthorne looked upon him as a "poet of deep beauty" rather than a philosopher. They stimulated Hawthorne, they showed him the optimistic side of reality, but he doubted whether either of them had a theory of tragedy, whether they could ever know the dark recesses of the human heart. He produced more than twenty tales during these three years in Concord, sold them to magazines, and then collected them in *Mosses from an Old Manse*. His reputation was growing. Edgar Allan Poe, who knew intimately what made a short story memorable, called Hawthorne "*the* example, *par excellence,* in this country, of the privately admired and publicly unappreciated man of genius."

It took a return to Salem to bring him fame. A Bowdoin classmate, Franklin Pierce, found him a lucrative post as surveyor in the Salem customhouse. After three years of coping with the dullness of the work, he was not distressed to find himself dismissed for political reasons. "Now you can write your book," Sophia told him. In seven months it was finished. In April, 1850, Ticknor and Fields of Boston published *The Scarlet Letter.* Had Hawthorne not written another word than this long tale of Puritan Boston, he would still find a high place in the history of American literature. He called it "positively a hell-fired story, into which I found it almost impossible to throw any cheering light." The contemporary critics, accustomed to Hawthorne's moralizing and his fondness for somber moods, found it unforgettable, perhaps America's first tragedy. Readers of Hester Prynne's story have agreed ever since.

The last fourteen years of Hawthorne's life were such a contrast to his long struggle for recognition that it is almost as though their chronicle belongs to another man. Ambitious with the success of *The Scarlet Letter,* he enlarged his scope with plans for novels and romances. Within a year he had finished the story of the Pyncheon family of Salem and Maule's curse, *The House of the Seven Gables.* "I think it a work more characteristic of my mind," he wrote a friend, "and more proper and natural for me to write." Perhaps it was more proper, if he meant a romance with a happy ending that would charm more readers. But it was hardly characteristic of the best part of Hawthorne's mind and talent. A year later he published *The Blithedale Romance,* a satire of Brook Farm, the co-operative community in West Roxbury where he had lived briefly before his marriage. In spite of a memorable villain, the cold-hearted social reformer, Hollingsworth, the story is static and uninspired. After seven years in Europe (Hawthorne had written a campaign biography for Franklin Pierce who, after his election, rewarded him with the consulship at Liverpool), he tried an even more ambitious novel, *The Marble Faun,* set in contemporary Rome amid the splendors of that alluring city. He took as his theme nothing less than the origin of evil, the coming of sin into the world, and tried to illustrate it through two young couples, one of them a faunlike pagan Roman, called Donatello, and a mysterious American girl, Miriam. But the scope of the novel is too large; too many guidebook details of Rome interfere with our believing the mystery that is supposed to surround these people. Clearly Hawthorne had achieved his most powerful work in his early tales and in his masterpiece, *The Scarlet Letter.*

The moral nature of these early sketches and tales was, for Hawthorne, the reason for their being and the secret of their strength. He began these stories with an idea, then clothed that idea in reality. He was not interested, like Irving, in picturesque description, or, like Poe, in carefully controlled suspense. That is not to say Hawthorne was intent on writing narrative sermons. His poetic imagination would never allow his tales to become treatises on the Origin of Evil. But they began with the idea of guilt or pride or intolerance and moved from there into complex personal relationships, into the mysteries of the human heart.

From his own years of solitude, Hawthorne discovered much about the human heart, and what he discovered left him anxious about the world. His tales reflect this anxiety, particularly those in which the pride of intellect is revealed so nakedly as in "Ethan Brand," where the protagonist searches for the Unpardonable Sin only to discover it in himself, or in "Rappaccini's Daughter," where a learned scientist poisons his daughter in a mad experiment which goes beyond nature's limit. When the mind takes precedence over the heart, Hawthorne tells us, only misery, the misery of isolation from our fellows, can be the result. In his greatest novel, *The Scarlet Letter*, it is not the adulterers, Hester and the Reverend Dimmesdale, but the evil doctor, the wronged husband, Roger Chillingworth, who is most guilty. "That old man's revenge has been blacker than my sin," Dimmesdale tells Hester. "He has violated, in cold blood, the sanctity of the human heart." Once we are accustomed to the somber colors of Hawthorne's parables, we sense as clearly as he did that through them he speaks for every person.

Although the following story
is one of Hawthorne's earliest, one can find
in it much of the flavor as well as some
of the themes of the author's maturer fiction.
The story was apparently stimulated
in part by a true story about a minister
from Maine who wore a black veil nearly all
his life because he had accidentally
killed a close friend.

The Minister's Black Veil

A PARABLE

The sexton[1] stood in the porch of Milford meeting-house, pulling busily at the bell-rope. The old people of the village came stooping along the street. Children, with bright faces, tripped merrily beside their parents, or mimicked a graver gait, in the conscious dignity of their Sunday clothes. Spruce bachelors looked sidelong at the pretty maidens, and fancied that the Sabbath[2] sunshine made them prettier than on week days. When the throng had mostly streamed into the porch, the sexton began to toll the bell, keeping his eye on the Reverend Mr. Hooper's door. The first glimpse of the clergyman's figure was the signal for the bell to cease its summons.

"But what has good Parson Hooper got upon his face?" cried the sexton in astonishment.

All within hearing immediately turned about, and beheld the semblance of Mr. Hooper, pacing slowly his meditative way towards the meeting-house. With one accord they started, expressing more wonder than if some strange minister were coming to dust the cushions of Mr. Hooper's pulpit.

"Are you sure it is our parson?" inquired Goodman Gray of the sexton.

"Of a certainty it is good Mr. Hooper," replied the sexton. "He was to have exchanged pulpits with Parson Shute, of Westbury; but Parson Shute sent to excuse himself yesterday, being to preach a funeral sermon."

The cause of so much amazement may appear sufficiently slight. Mr. Hooper, a gentlemanly person, of about thirty, though still a bachelor, was dressed with due clerical neatness, as if a careful wife had starched his band, and brushed the weekly dust from his Sunday's garb. There was but one thing remarkable in his appearance. Swathed about his forehead, and hanging down over his face, so low as to be shaken by his breath, Mr. Hooper had on a black veil. On a nearer view it seemed to consist of two folds of crape,[3] which entirely concealed his features, except the mouth and chin, but probably did not intercept his sight, further than to give a darkened aspect to all living and inanimate things. With this gloomy shade before him, good Mr. Hooper walked onward, at a slow and quiet pace, stooping somewhat, and looking on the ground, as is customary with abstracted men, yet nodding kindly to those of his parishioners who still waited on the meeting-house steps. But so wonder-struck were they that his greeting hardly met with a return.

"I can't really feel as if good Mr. Hooper's face was behind that piece of crape," said the sexton.

"I don't like it," muttered an old woman, as she hobbled into the meeting-house. "He has changed himself into something awful, only by hiding his face."

"Our parson has gone mad!" cried Goodman Gray, following him across the threshold.

A rumor of some unaccountable phenomenon had preceded Mr. Hooper into the meeting-house, and set all the congregation astir.

---

1. **sexton** \ˈsĕks·tən\ person who tends a church.
2. **Sabbath** \ˈsăb·əth\ day of the week for rest and worship.
3. **crape** \krāp\ material with a crinkled surface.

Few could refrain from twisting their heads towards the door; many stood upright, and turned directly about; while several little boys clambered upon the seats, and came down again with a terrible racket. There was a general bustle, a rustling of the women's gowns and shuffling of the men's feet, greatly at variance with that hushed repose which should attend the entrance of the minister. But Mr. Hooper appeared not to notice the perturbation of his people. He entered with an almost noiseless step, bent his head mildly to the pews on each side, and bowed as he passed his oldest parishioner, a white-haired great-grandsire, who occupied an armchair in the centre of the aisle. It was strange to observe how slowly this venerable man became conscious of something singular in the appearance of his pastor. He seemed not fully to partake of the prevailing wonder, till Mr. Hooper had ascended the stairs, and showed himself in the pulpit, face to face with his congregation, except for the black veil. That mysterious emblem was never once withdrawn. It shook with his measured breath, as he gave out the psalm;[4] it threw its obscurity between him and the holy page, as he read the Scriptures; and while he prayed, the veil lay heavily on his uplifted countenance. Did he seek to hide it from the dread Being whom he was addressing?

Such was the effect of this simple piece of crape, that more than one woman of delicate nerves was forced to leave the meeting-house. Yet perhaps the pale-faced congregation was almost as fearful a sight to the minister, as his black veil to them.

Mr. Hooper had the reputation of a good preacher, but not an energetic one: he strove to win his people heavenward by mild, persuasive influences, rather than to drive them thither by the thunders of the Word. The sermon which he now delivered was marked by the same characteristics of style and manner as the general series of his pulpit oratory. But there was something, either in the sentiment of the discourse itself, or in the imagination of the auditors,[5] which made it greatly the most powerful effort that they had ever heard from their pastor's lips. It was tinged, rather more darkly than usual, with the gentle gloom of Mr. Hooper's temperament. The subject had reference to secret sin, and those sad mysteries which we hide from our nearest and dearest, and would fain conceal from our own consciousness, even forgetting that the Omniscient[6] can detect them. A subtle power was breathed into his words. Each member of the congregation, the most innocent girl, and the man of hardened breast, felt as if the preacher had crept upon them, behind his awful veil, and discovered their hoarded iniquity of deed or thought. Many spread their clasped hands on their bosoms. There was nothing terrible in what Mr. Hooper said, at least, no violence; and yet, with every tremor of his melancholy voice, the hearers quaked. An unsought pathos came hand in hand with awe. So sensible were the audience of some unwonted attribute in their minister that they longed for a breath of wind to blow aside the veil, almost believing that a stranger's visage would be discovered, though the form, gesture, and voice were those of Mr. Hooper.

At the close of the services, the people hurried out with indecorous confusion, eager to communicate their pent-up amazement, and conscious of lighter spirits the moment they lost sight of the black veil. Some gathered in little circles, huddled closely together, with their mouths all whispering in the centre; some went homeward alone, wrapt in silent meditation; some talked loudly, and profaned the Sabbath day with ostentatious laughter. A few shook their sagacious heads, intimating that they could penetrate the mystery; while one or two affirmed that there was no mystery at all, but only that Mr. Hooper's eyes were so weakened by the midnight lamp, as to require a shade. After a brief interval, forth came good Mr. Hooper also, in the rear of his flock.

---

4. **psalm**\sam\ any of 150 sacred songs in the Old Testament.
5. **auditors**\ˈɔ·de·tərs\ hearers; listeners.
6. **Omniscient**\ŏm ˈnĭsh·ənt\ all-knowing; God.

Turning his veiled face from one group to another, he paid due reverence to the hoary heads, saluted the middle aged with kind dignity as their friend and spiritual guide, greeted the young with mingled authority and love, and laid his hands on the little children's heads to bless them. Such was always his custom on the Sabbath day. Strange and bewildered looks repaid him for his courtesy. None, as on former occasions, aspired to the honor of walking by their pastor's side. Old Squire Saunders, doubtless by an accidental lapse of memory, neglected to invite Mr. Hooper to his table, where the good clergyman had been wont to bless the food almost every Sunday since his settlement. He returned, therefore, to the parsonage, and, at the moment of closing the door, was observed to look back upon the people, all of whom had their eyes fixed upon the minister. A sad smile gleamed faintly from beneath the black veil, and flickered about his mouth, glimmering as he disappeared.

"How strange," said a lady, "that a simple black veil, such as any woman might wear on her bonnet, should become such a terrible thing on Mr. Hooper's face!"

"Something must surely be amiss with Mr. Hooper's intellects," observed her husband, the physician of the village. "But the strangest part of the affair is the effect of this vagary, even on a sober-minded man like myself. The black veil, though it covers only our pastor's face, throws its influence over his whole person, and makes him ghostlike from head to foot. Do you not feel it so?"

"Truly do I," replied the lady; "and I would not be alone with him for the world. I wonder he is not afraid to be alone with himself!"

"Men sometimes are so," said her husband.

The afternoon service was attended with similar circumstances. At its conclusion, the bell tolled for the funeral of a young lady. The relatives and friends were assembled in the house, and the more distant acquaintances stood about the door, speaking of the good qualities of the deceased, when their talk was interrupted by the appearance of Mr. Hooper, still covered with his black veil. It was now an appropriate emblem. The clergyman stepped into the room where the corpse was laid, and bent over the coffin, to take a last farewell of his deceased parishioner. As he stooped, the veil hung straight down from his forehead, so that, if her eyelids had not been closed forever, the dead maiden might have seen his face. Could Mr. Hooper be fearful of her glance, that he so hastily caught back the black veil? A person who watched the interview between the dead and living scrupled[7] not to affirm, that, at the instant when the clergyman's features were disclosed, the corpse had slightly shuddered, rustling the shroud and muslin cap, though the countenance retained the composure of death. A superstitious old woman was the only witness of this prodigy. From the coffin Mr. Hooper passed into the chamber of the mourners, and thence to the head of the staircase, to make the funeral prayer. It was a tender and heart-dissolving prayer, full of sorrow, yet so imbued with celestial[8] hopes, that the music of a heavenly harp, swept by the fingers of the dead, seemed faintly to be heard among the saddest accents of the minister. The peopled trembled, though they but darkly understood him when he prayed that they, and himself, and all of mortal race, might be ready, as he trusted this young maiden had been, for the dreadful hour that should snatch the veil from their faces. The bearers went heavily forth, and the mourners followed, saddening all the street, with the dead before them, and Mr. Hooper in his black veil behind.

"Why do you look back?" said one in the procession to his partner.

"I had a fancy," replied she, "that the minister and the maiden's spirit were walking hand in hand."

"And so had I, at the same moment," said the other.

---

7. **scrupled**\ˈskrū·pəld\ hesitated.
8. **celestial**\sə ˈlĕs·chəl\ heavenly; divine.

That night, the handsomest couple in Milford village were to be joined in wedlock. Though reckoned a melancholy man, Mr. Hooper had a placid cheerfulness for such occasions, which often excited a sympathetic smile where livelier merriment would have been thrown away. There was no quality of his disposition which made him more beloved than this. The company at the wedding awaited his arrival with impatience, trusting that the strange awe, which had gathered over him throughout the day, would now be dispelled. But such was not the result. When Mr. Hooper came, the first thing that their eyes rested on was the same horrible black veil, which had added deeper gloom to the funeral, and could portend nothing but evil to the wedding. Such was its immediate effect on the guests that a cloud seemed to have rolled duskily from beneath the black crape, and dimmed the light of the candles. The bridal pair stood up before the minister. But the bride's cold fingers quivered in the tremulous hand of the bridegroom, and her deathlike paleness caused a whisper that the maiden who had been buried a few hours before was come from her grave to be married. If ever another wedding were so dismal, it was that famous one where they tolled the wedding knell. After performing the ceremony, Mr. Hooper raised a glass of wine to his lips, wishing happiness to the new-married couple in a strain of mild pleasantry that ought to have brightened the features of the guests, like a cheerful gleam from the hearth. At that instant, catching a glimpse of his figure in the looking-glass, the black veil involved his own spirit in the horror with which it overwhelmed all others. His frame shuddered, his lips grew white, he spilt the untasted wine upon the carpet, and rushed forth into the darkness. For the Earth, too, had on her Black Veil.

The next day, the whole village of Milford talked of little else than Parson Hooper's black veil. That, and the mystery concealed behind it, supplied a topic for discussion between acquaintances meeting in the street, and good women gossiping at their open windows. It was the first item of news that the tavern-keeper told to his guests. The children babbled of it on their way to school. One imitative little imp covered his face with an old black handkerchief, thereby so affrighting his playmates that the panic seized himself, and he well-nigh lost his wits by his own waggery.[9]

It was remarkable that of all the busybodies and impertinent people in the parish, not one ventured to put the plain question to Mr. Hooper, wherefore he did this thing. Hitherto, whenever there appeared the slightest call for such interference, he had never lacked advisers, nor shown himself averse to be guided by their judgment. If he erred at all, it was by so painful a degree of self-distrust, that even the mildest censure would lead him to consider an indifferent action as a crime. Yet, though so well acquainted with this amiable weakness, no individual among his parishioners chose to make the black veil a subject of friendly remonstrance. There was a feeling of dread, neither plainly confessed nor carefully concealed, which caused each to shift the responsibility upon another, till at length it was found expedient to send a deputation of the church, in order to deal with Mr. Hooper about the mystery before it should grow into a scandal. Never did an embassy so ill discharge its duties. The minister received them with friendly courtesy, but became silent, after they were seated, leaving to his visitors the whole burden of introducing their important business. The topic, it might be supposed, was obvious enough. There was the black veil swathed round Mr. Hooper's forehead, and concealing every feature above his placid mouth, on which, at times, they could perceive the glimmering of a melancholy smile. But that piece of crape, to their imagination, seemed to hang down before his heart, the symbol of a fearful secret between him and them. Were the veil but cast aside, they might

---

9. **waggery**\\ˈwāg·ə·rē\\ joking.

speak freely of it, but not till then. Thus they sat a considerable time, speechless, confused, and shrinking uneasily from Mr. Hooper's eye, which they felt to be fixed upon them with an invisible glance. Finally, the deputies returned abashed to their constituents,[10] pronouncing the matter too weighty to be handled, except by a council of the churches, if, indeed, it might not require a general synod.

But there was one person in the village unappalled by the awe with which the black veil had impressed all beside herself. When the deputies returned without an explanation, or even venturing to demand one, she, with the calm energy of her character, determined to chase away the strange cloud that appeared to be settling round Mr. Hooper, every moment more darkly than before. As his plighted wife, it should be her privilege to know what the black veil concealed. At the minister's first visit, therefore, she entered upon the subject with a direct simplicity, which made the task easier both for him and her. After he had seated himself, she fixed her eyes steadfastly upon the veil, but could discern nothing of the dreadful gloom that had so overawed the multitude: it was but a double fold of crape, hanging down from his forehead to his mouth, and slightly stirring with his breath.

"No," said she aloud, and smiling, "there is nothing terrible in this piece of crape, except that it hides a face which I am always glad to look upon. Come, good sir, let the sun shine from behind the cloud. First lay aside your black veil: then tell me why you put it on."

Mr. Hooper's smile glimmered faintly.

"There is an hour to come," said he, "when all of us shall cast aside our veils. Take it not amiss, beloved friend, if I wear this piece of crape till then."

"Your words are a mystery, too," returned the young lady. "Take away the veil from them, at least."

"Elizabeth, I will," said he, "so far as my vow may suffer me. Know, then, this veil is a type and a symbol, and I am bound to wear it ever, both in light and darkness, in solitude and before the gaze of multitudes, and as with strangers, so with my familiar friends. No mortal eye will see it withdrawn. This dismal shade must separate me from the world: even you, Elizabeth, can never come behind it!"

"What grievous affliction hath befallen you," she earnestly inquired, "that you should thus darken your eyes forever?"

"If it be a sign of mourning," replied Mr. Hooper, "I, perhaps, like most other mortals, have sorrows dark enough to be typified by a black veil."

"But what if the world will not believe that it is the type of an innocent sorrow?" urged Elizabeth. "Beloved and respected as you are, there may be whispers that you hide your face under the consciousness of secret sin. For the sake of your holy office, do away this scandal!"

The color rose into her cheeks as she intimated the nature of the rumors that were already abroad in the village. But Mr. Hooper's mildness did not forsake him. He even smiled again—that same sad smile, which always appeared like a faint glimmering of light, proceeding from the obscurity beneath the veil.

"If I hide my face for sorrow, there is cause enough," he merely replied; "and if I cover it for secret sin, what mortal might not do the same?"

And with this gentle, but unconquerable obstinacy[11] did he resist all her entreaties.[12] At length Elizabeth sat silent. For a few moments she appeared lost in thought, considering, probably, what new methods might be tried to withdraw her lover from so dark a fantasy, which, if it had no other meaning, was perhaps a symptom of mental disease. Though of a firmer character than his own, the tears rolled down her cheeks. But, in an instant, as it were, a new feeling took the place of sorrow: her eyes were fixed insensibly on the black veil, when, like a sudden twilight in

---

10. **constituents**\kən ▲stĭeh·ū·ənts\ persons who vote or appoint.
11. **obstinacy**\ŏbstə·nə·sē\ stubbornness.
12. **entreaties**\ĕn ▲trē·tēz\ earnest requests; prayers.

the air, its terrors fell around her. She arose, and stood trembling before him.

"And do you feel it then, at last?" said he mournfully.

She made no reply, but covered her eyes with her hand, and turned to leave the room. He rushed forward and caught her arm.

"Have patience with me, Elizabeth!" cried he passionately. "Do not desert me, though this veil must be between us here on earth. Be mine, and hereafter there shall be no veil over my face, no darkness between our souls! It is but a mortal veil—it is not for eternity! O! you know not how lonely I am, and how frightened, to be alone behind my black veil. Do not leave me in this miserable obscurity forever!"

"Lift the veil but once, and look me in the face," said she.

"Never! It cannot be!" replied Mr. Hooper.

"Then farewell!" said Elizabeth.

She withdrew her arm from his grasp, and slowly departed, pausing at the door, to give one long, shuddering gaze, that seemed almost to penetrate the mystery of the black veil. But, even amid his grief, Mr. Hooper smiled to think that only a material emblem had separated him from happiness, though the horrors which it shadowed forth must be drawn darkly between the fondest of lovers.

From that time no attempts were made to remove Mr. Hooper's black veil, or, by a direct appeal, to discover the secret which it was supposed to hide. By persons who claimed a superiority to popular prejudice, it was reckoned merely an eccentric whim, such as often mingles with the sober actions of men otherwise rational, and tinges them all with its own semblance of insanity. But with the multitude, good Mr. Hooper was irreparably a bugbear.[13] He could not walk the street with any peace of mind, so conscious was he that the gentle and timid would turn aside to avoid him, and that others would make it a point of hardihood to throw themselves in his way. The impertinence of the latter class compelled him to give up his customary walk at sunset to the burial ground; for when he leaned pensively over the gate, there would always be faces behind the gravestones, peeping at his black veil. A fable went the rounds that the stare of the dead people drove him thence. It grieved him, to the very depth of his kind heart, to observe how the children fled from his approach, breaking up their merriest sports, while his melancholy figure was yet afar off. Their instinctive dread caused him to feel more strongly than aught else, that a preternatural horror was interwoven with the threads of the black crape. In truth, his own antipathy[14] to the veil was known to be so great, that he never willingly passed before a mirror, nor stooped to drink at a still fountain, lest, in its peaceful bosom, he should be affrighted by himself. This was what gave plausibility to the whispers, that Mr. Hooper's conscience tortured him for some great crime too horrible to be entirely concealed, or otherwise than so obscurely intimated. Thus, from beneath the black veil, there rolled a cloud into the sunshine, an ambiguity of sin or sorrow, which enveloped the poor minister, so that love or sympathy could never reach him. It was said that ghost and fiend consorted with him there. With self-shudderings and outward terrors, he walked continually in its shadow, groping darkly within his own soul, or gazing through a medium that saddened the whole world. Even the lawless wind, it was believed, respected his dreadful secret, and never blew aside the veil. But still good Mr. Hooper sadly smiled at the pale visages of the worldly throng as he passed by.

Among all its bad influences, the black veil had the one desirable effect of making its wearer a very efficient clergyman. By the aid of his mysterious emblem—for there was no other apparent cause—he became a man of awful power over souls that were in agony for sin. His converts always regarded him with a

---

13. **bugbear**\\ˈbŭg·băr\\ thing feared without reason.
14. **antipathy**\\ăn ˈtĭp·ə·thē\\ strong dislike.

dread peculiar to themselves, affirming, though but figuratively, that, before he brought them to celestial light, they had been with him behind the black veil. Its gloom, indeed, enabled him to sympathize with all dark affections. Dying sinners cried aloud for Mr. Hooper, and would not yield their breath till he appeared; though ever, as he stooped to whisper consolation, they shuddered at the veiled face so near their own. Such were the terrors of the black veil, even when Death had bared his visage! Strangers came long distances to attend service at his church, with the mere idle purpose of gazing at his figure, because it was forbidden them to behold his face. But many were made to quake ere they departed! Once, during Governor Belcher's administration, Mr. Hooper was appointed to preach the election sermon. Covered with his black veil, he stood before the chief magistrate, the council, and the representatives, and wrought so deep an impression, that the legislative measures of that year were characterized by all the gloom and piety of our earliest ancestral sway.

In this manner Mr. Hooper spent a long life, irreproachable[15] in outward act, yet shrouded[16] in dismal suspicions; kind and loving, though unloved and dimly feared; a man apart from men, shunned in their health and joy, but ever summoned to their aid in mortal anguish. As years wore on, shedding their snows above his sable[17] veil, he acquired a name throughout the New England churches, and they called him Father Hooper. Nearly all his parishioners who were of mature age when he was settled had been borne away by many a funeral: he had one congregation in the church, and a more crowded one in the churchyard; and having wrought so late into the evening, and done his work so well, it was now good Father Hooper's turn to rest.

Several persons were visible by the shaded candle-light, in the death chamber of the old clergyman. Natural connections he had none. But there was the decorously[18] grave, though unmoved physician, seeking only to mitigate the last pangs of the patient whom he could not save. There were the deacons,[19] and other eminently pious members of his church. There, also, was the Reverend Mr. Clark, of Westbury, a young and zealous divine, who had ridden in haste to pray by the bedside of the expiring minister. There was the nurse, no hired handmaiden of death, but one whose calm affection had endured thus long in secrecy, in solitude, amid the chill of age, and would not perish, even at the dying hour. Who, but Elizabeth! And there lay the hoary head of good Father Hooper upon the death pillow, with the black veil still swathed about his brow, and reaching down over his face, so that each more difficult gasp of his faint breath caused it to stir. All through life that piece of crape had hung between him and the world: it had separated him from cheerful brotherhood and woman's love, and kept him in that saddest of all prisons, his own heart; and still it lay upon his face, as if to deepen the gloom of his darksome chamber, and shade him from the sunshine of eternity.

For some time previous, his mind had been confused, wavering doubtfully between the past and the present, and hovering forward, as it were, at intervals, into the indistinctness of the world to come. There had been feverish turns, which tossed him from side to side, and wore away what little strength he had. But in his most convulsive struggles, and in the wildest vagaries of his intellect, when no other thought retained its sober influence, he still showed an awful solicitude[20] lest the black veil should slip aside. Even if his bewildered soul could have forgotten, there was a faithful woman at his pillow, who, with averted eyes,

---

15. **irreproachable**\ˈir·ĭ ▴prō·cha·bəl\ blameless; faultless.
16. **shrouded**\shroud·ĭd\ covered; sheltered.
17. **sable**\▴sā·bəl\ black; dark.
18. **decorously**\▴děk·ər·əs·lē\ showing propriety and good taste.
19. **deacons** \▴dē·kən\ laity appointed to help the minister.
20. **solicitude** \sə▴lĭs·ə·tūd\ anxiety.

would have covered that aged face, which she had last beheld in the comeliness of manhood. At length the death-stricken old man lay quietly in the torpor of mental and bodily exhaustion, with an imperceptible pulse, and breath that grew fainter and fainter, except when a long, deep, and irregular inspiration seemed to prelude the flight of his spirit.

The minister of Westbury approached the bedside.

"Venerable Father Hooper," said he, "the moment of your release is at hand. Are you ready for the lifting of the veil that shuts in time from eternity?"

Father Hooper at first replied merely by a feeble motion of his head; then, apprehensive, perhaps, that his meaning might be doubtful, he exerted himself to speak.

"Yea," said he, in faint accents, "my soul hath a patient weariness until that veil be lifted."

"And is it fitting," resumed the Reverend Mr. Clark, "that a man so given to prayer, of such a blameless example, holy in deed and thought, so far as mortal judgment may pronounce; is it fitting that a father in the church should leave a shadow on his memory, that may seem to blacken a life so pure? I pray you, my venerable brother, let not this thing be! Suffer us to be gladdened by your triumphant aspect as you go to your reward. Before the veil of eternity be lifted, let me cast aside this black veil from your face!"

And thus speaking, the Reverend Mr. Clark bent forward to reveal the mystery of so many years. But, exerting a sudden energy, that made all the beholders stand aghast, Father Hooper snatched both his hands from beneath the bedclothes, and pressed them strongly on the black veil, resolute to struggle, if the minister of Westbury would contend with a dying man.

"Never!" cried the veiled clergyman. "On earth, never!"

"Dark old man!" exclaimed the affrighted minister, "with what horrible crime upon your soul are you now passing to the judgment?"

Father Hooper's breath heaved; it rattled in his throat; but, with a mighty effort, grasping forward with his hands, he caught hold of life, and held it back till he should speak. He even raised himself in bed; and there he sat, shivering with the arms of death around him, while the black veil hung down, awful, at that last moment, in the gathered terrors of a lifetime. And yet the faint, sad smile, so often there, now seemed to glimmer from its obscurity, and linger on Father Hooper's lips.

"Why do you tremble at me alone?" cried he, turning his veiled face round the circle of pale spectators. "Tremble also at each other! Have men avoided me, and women shown no pity, and children screamed and fled, only for my black veil? What, but the mystery which it obscurely typifies, has made this piece of crape so awful? When the friend shows his inmost heart to his friend; the lover to his best beloved; when man does not vainly shrink from the eye of his Creator, loathsomely treasuring up the secret of his sin; then deem me a monster, for the symbol beneath which I have lived, and die! I look around me, and, lo! on every visage a Black Veil!"

While his auditors shrank from one another, in mutual affright, Father Hooper fell back upon his pillow, a veiled corpse, with a faint smile lingering on the lips. Still veiled, they laid him in his coffin, and a veiled corpse they bore him to the grave. The grass of many years has sprung up and withered on that grave, the burial stone is moss-grown, and good Mr. Hooper's face is dust; but awful is still the thought that it mouldered beneath the Black Veil.

I

"ON EVERY VISAGE A BLACK VEIL"

Although the reason why the minister wears the black veil is uncertain through most of the story, Hooper himself reveals it at the end. The veil typifies the fact that *all* men and women hide their inner selves, even from those that are closest to them. They even attempt to hide themselves from God. Hawthorne is known as a writer with a tragic vision, with unusually keen perception into the darker side of human nature. Certainly the vision that he exposes in this story is dark and tragic, for it suggests that all humans are doomed to be what Father Hooper was, "a man apart from men."

II
IMPLICATIONS

Be prepared to discuss the following questions.

1. Why should one try to hide one's inner self from others? What might be the content of such knowledge that one should be so fearful of revealing it?

2. What are some of the consequences of hiding oneself from others? Do you agree or disagree that one such consequence is that love and sympathy can never reach us, as was the case with Father Hooper?

3. Hawthorne's minister is particularly afraid of being alone with himself and of seeing himself (in mirrors, for example). Is it true or not that most people are afraid of seeing themselves as they are and are afraid of being alone?

4. Argue for or against the notion that if it is true that all people are sinners, they should freely acknowledge this fact; for once the fact is acknowledged, it may stand as a universal bond of humanity.

5. Assuming that all people are sinners, is one better off to recognize this fact or to remain ignorant of it?

6. Why do you agree or disagree with the assertion that one's own heart is "the saddest of all prisons"?

7. What is your own impression of the following interpretation of the story?

There is no evidence that the Reverend Mr. Hooper had any sins to hide. His only "sin" was the wearing of the black veil itself. By wearing it, however, he ironically committed the very sin that he wished to warn others against. Thus, it is just that he should suffer the consequences of alienation, as he did.

III
TECHNIQUES
Setting

You will recall that setting includes *time, place,* and *atmosphere,* with the relative importance of each element depending on the writer's purpose and on the type of writing done.

Hawthorne soon establishes the time as long in the past. The place is a small village. Note that the author suggests this distance in time by simply referring to the character Gray as *Goodman* Gray. In England and later in early colonial times, this term was used to refer to the head of a household or a husband. It designated that the person was a farmer or laborer and not of the aristocracy. The mistress of the household was referred to as *Goodwife* or simply *Goody.*

The atmosphere or mood of the story is gloomy and mysterious. How, for example, does the black veil help create this atmosphere? Note also how the line in the second column of page 105 adds to the somber mood: "It was tinged, rather more darkly than usual, with the gentle gloom of Mr. Hooper's temperament." Other references to *dark, darkly, dismal,* and *dreadful* help sustain this mood. The atmosphere of mystery, of course, is engendered by the minister's wearing of the veil and all that this act implies.

Characterization

Mr. Hooper's character is established principally by the way his parishioners see him. In this way Hawthorne maintains the distance he wishes between his readers and his main character. In the third paragraph, the minister is observed "pacing slowly his meditative way." Four paragraphs later Hawthorne refers to Hooper as a "gentlemanly person," neat in appearance. Still later Hooper is described as a "good preacher, but not an energetic one." Later still the reader is told that the minister lived a long and irreproachable life, "kind and loving, though unloved and dimly feared."

Certainly the minister shows strong determination throughout the story. How is this demonstrated for the last time on his deathbed?

Hawthorne's first collection
of short stories, *Twice-Told Tales*,
appeared in 1837. It was a volume
of masterpieces, but few critics realized it.
Included among the stories is this fantasy
of Dr. Heidegger and his four aged friends.
Hawthorne had long been interested
in scientific experiments and had doubtless read
in many sources of the quest for perpetual
youth. The question that intrigued him most
was "What would people do if they had the
opportunity to regain their youth?"

Dr. Heidegger's Experiment

That very singular man, old Dr. Heidegger, once invited four venerable friends to meet him in his study. There were three white-bearded gentlemen, Mr. Medbourne, Colonel Killigrew, and Mr. Gascoigne,[1] and a withered gentlewoman, whose name was the Widow Wycherly. They were all melancholy old creatures, who had been unfortunate in life, and whose greatest misfortune it was that they were not long ago in their graves. Mr. Medbourne, in the vigor of his age, had been a prosperous merchant, but had lost his all by a frantic speculation, and was now little better than a mendicant. Colonel Killigrew had wasted his best years, and his health and substance, in the pursuit of sinful pleasures, which had given birth to a brood of pains, such as the gout, and divers other torments of soul and body. Mr. Gascoigne was a ruined politician, a man of evil fame, or at least had been so till time had buried him from the knowledge of the present generation, and made him obscure instead of infamous. As for the Widow Wycherly, tradition tells us that

she was a great beauty in her day; but, for a long while past, she had lived in deep seclusion, on account of certain scandalous stories which had prejudiced the gentry of the town against her. It is a circumstance worth mentioning that each of these three old gentlemen, Mr. Medbourne, Colonel Killigrew, and Mr. Gascoigne, were early lovers of the Widow Wycherly, and had once been on the point of cutting each other's throats for her sake. And, before proceeding further, I will merely hint that Dr. Heidegger and all his four guests were sometimes thought to be a little besides themselves,—as is not unfrequently the case with old people, when worried either by present troubles or woeful recollections.

"My dear old friends," said Dr. Heidegger, motioning them to be seated, "I am desirous of your assistance in one of those little experiments with which I amuse myself here in my study."

If all stories were true, Dr. Heidegger's study must have been a very curious place. It was a dim, old-fashioned chamber, festooned with cobwebs, and besprinkled with antique dust. Around the walls stood several oaken bookcases, the lower shelves of which were filled with rows of gigantic folios and black-letter quartos,[2] and the upper with little parchment-covered duodecimos.[3] Over the central bookcase was a bronze bust of Hippocrates,[4] with which, according to some authorities, Dr. Heidegger was accustomed to hold consultations in all difficult cases of his practice. In the obscurest corner of the room stood a tall and narrow oaken closet, with its door ajar, within which doubtfully appeared a skeleton. Between two

---

1. **Mr. Gascoigne**\ˈgăs ▲kɔin\.
2. **quartos,** books of pages approximately 9 x 12 inches in size.
3. **duodecimos,** books consisting of pages approximately 5 x 7½ inches.
4. **Hippocrates**\hĭ ▲pŏk·ra·tēz\ (approx. 460–377 B.C.), Greek physician known as "Father of Medicine" and credited with devising code known today as Hippocratic oath which is administered to people about to enter the medical profession.

of the bookcases hung a looking-glass, presenting its high and dusty plate within a tarnished gilt frame. Among many wonderful stories related of this mirror, it was fabled that the spirits of all the doctor's deceased patients dwelt within its verge, and would stare him in the face whenever he looked thitherward. The opposite side of the chamber was ornamented with the full-length portrait of a young lady, arrayed in the faded magnificence of silk, satin, and brocade, and with a visage as faded as her dress. Above half a century ago, Dr. Heidegger had been on the point of marriage with this young lady; but, being affected with some slight disorder, she had swallowed one of her lover's prescriptions, and died on the bridal evening. The greatest curiosity of the study remains to be mentioned; it was a ponderous folio volume, bound in black leather, with massive silver clasps. There were no letters on the back, and nobody could tell the title of the book. But it was well known to be a book of magic; and once, when a chambermaid had lifted it, merely to brush away the dust, the skeleton had rattled in its closet, the picture of the young lady had stepped one foot upon the floor, and several ghastly faces had peeped forth from the mirror; while the brazen head of Hippocrates frowned, and said,—"Forbear!"

Such was Dr. Heidegger's study. On the summer afternoon of our tale a small round table, as black as ebony, stood in the centre of the room, sustaining a cut-glass vase of beautiful form and elaborate workmanship. The sunshine came through the window, between the heavy festoons[5] of two faded damask[6] curtains, and fell directly across this vase; so that a mild splendor was reflected from it on the ashen visages of the five old people who sat around. Four champagne glasses were also on the table.

"My dear old friends," repeated Dr. Heidegger, "may I reckon on your aid in performing an exceedingly curious experiment?"

Now Dr. Heidegger was a very strange old gentleman, whose eccentricity had become the nucleus for a thousand fantastic stories. Some of these fables, to my shame be it spoken, might possibly be traced back to my own veracious self; and if any passages of the present tale should startle the reader's faith, I must be content to bear the stigma of a fiction monger.

When the doctor's four guests heard him talk of his proposed experiment, they anticipated nothing more wonderful than the murder of a mouse in an air pump, or the examination of a cobweb by the microscope, or some similar nonsense, with which he was constantly in the habit of pestering his intimates. But without waiting for a reply, Dr. Heidegger hobbled across the chamber, and returned with the same ponderous folio, bound in black leather, which common report affirmed to be a book of magic. Undoing the silver clasps, he opened the volume, and took from among its black-letter pages a rose, or what was once a rose, though now the green leaves and crimson petals had assumed one brownish hue, and the ancient flower seemed ready to crumble to dust in the doctor's hands.

"This rose," said Dr. Heidegger, with a sigh, "this same withered and crumbling flower, blossomed five and fifty years ago. It was given me by Sylvia Ward, whose portrait hangs yonder; and I meant to wear it in my bosom at our wedding. Five and fifty years it has been treasured between the leaves of this old volume. Now, would you deem it possible that this rose of half a century could ever bloom again?"

"Nonsense!" said the Widow Wycherly, with a peevish toss of her head. "You might as well ask whether an old woman's wrinkled face could ever bloom again."

"See!" answered Dr. Heidegger.

He uncovered the vase, and threw the faded rose into the water which it contained. At first, it lay lightly on the surface of the fluid, appearing to imbibe none of its moisture. Soon, however, a singular change began to be visible. The crushed and dried petals stirred, and assumed

---

5. **festoons**, ornamental carvings consisting of flowers or leaves linked together and looped between two points.
6. **damask**, a rich, reversible, elaborately patterned fabric.

a deeping tinge of crimson, as if the flower were reviving from a deathlike slumber; the slender stalk and twigs of foliage became green; and there was the rose of half a century, looking as fresh as when Sylvia Ward had first given it to her lover. It was scarcely full blown; for some of its delicate red leaves curled modestly around its moist bosom, within which two or three dewdrops were sparkling.

"That is certainly a very pretty deception," said the doctor's friends; carelessly, however, for they had witnessed greater miracles at a conjurer's show; "pray how was it effected?"

"Did you never hear of the 'Fountain of Youth,'" asked Dr. Heidegger, "which Ponce de Leon, the Spanish adventurer, went in search of two or three centuries ago?"

"But did Ponce de Leon ever find it?" said the Widow Wycherly.

"No," answered Dr. Heidegger, "for he never sought it in the right place. The famous Fountain of Youth, if I am rightly informed, is situated in the southern part of the Floridian peninsula, not far from Lake Macaco. Its source is overshadowed by several gigantic magnolias, which, though numberless centuries old, have been kept as fresh as violets by the virtues of this wonderful water. An acquaintance of mine, knowing my curiosity in such matters, has sent me what you see in the vase."

"Ahem!" said Colonel Killigrew, who believed not a word of the doctor's story; "and what may be the effect of this fluid on the human frame?"

"You shall judge for yourself, my dear colonel," replied Dr. Heidegger; "and all of you, my respected friends, are welcome to so much of this admirable fluid as may restore to you the bloom of youth. For my own part, having had much trouble in growing old, I am in no hurry to grow young again. With your permission, therefore, I will merely watch the progress of the experiment."

While he spoke, Dr. Heidegger had been filling the four champagne glasses with the water of the Fountain of Youth. It was apparently impregnated with an effervescent gas, for little

bubbles were continually ascending from the depths of the glasses, and bursting in silvery spray at the surface. As the liquor diffused a pleasant perfume, the old people doubted not that it possessed cordial[7] and comfortable properties; and though utter sceptics as to its rejuvenescent power, they were inclined to swallow it at once. But Dr. Heidegger besought them to stay a moment.

"Before you drink, my respectable old friends," said he, "it would be well that, with the experience of a lifetime to direct you, you should draw up a few general rules for your guidance, in passing a second time through the perils of youth. Think what a sin and shame it would be, if, with your peculiar advantages, you should not become patterns of virtue and wisdom to all the young people of the age!"

The doctor's four venerable friends made him no answer, except by a feeble and tremulous laugh; so very ridiculous was the idea that, knowing how closely repentance treads behind the steps of error, they should ever go astray again.

"Drink, then," said the doctor, bowing: "I rejoice that I have so well selected the subjects of my experiment."

With palsied hands, they raised the glasses to their lips. The liquor, if it really possessed such virtues as Dr. Heidegger imputed to it, could not have been bestowed on four human beings who needed it more woefully. They looked as if they had never known what youth or pleasure was, but had been the offspring of Nature's dotage, and always the gray, decrepit, sapless, miserable creatures, who now sat stooping round the doctor's table, without life enough in their souls or bodies to be animated even by the prospect of growing young again. They drank off the water, and replaced their glasses on the table.

Assuredly there was an almost immediate improvement in the aspect of the party, not unlike what might have been produced by a glass of generous wine, together with a sudden glow of

---

7. cordial\ˈkȯr·jəl\ here, meaning pleasing.

cheerful sunshine brightening over all their visages at once. There was a healthful suffusion on their cheeks, instead of the ashen hue that had made them look so corpse-like. They gazed at one another, and fancied that some magic power had really begun to smooth away the deep and sad inscriptions which Father Time had been so long engraving on their brows. The Widow Wycherly adjusted her cap, for she felt almost like a woman again.

"Give us more of this wondrous water!" cried they, eagerly. "We are younger—but we are still too old! Quick—give us more!"

"Patience, patience!" quoth Dr. Heidegger, who sat watching the experiment with philosophic coolness. "You have been a long time growing old. Surely, you might be content to grow young in half an hour! But the water is at your service."

Again he filled their glasses with the liquor of youth, enough of which still remained in the vase to turn half the old people in the city to the age of their own grandchildren. While the bubbles were yet sparkling on the brim, the doctor's four guests snatched their glasses from the table, and swallowed the contents at a single gulp. Was it delusion? even while the draught was passing down their throats, it seemed to have wrought a change on their whole systems. Their eyes grew clear and bright; a dark shade deepened among their silvery locks, they sat around the table, three gentlemen of middle age, and a woman, hardly beyond her buxom prime.

"My dear widow, you are charming!" cried Colonel Killigrew, whose eyes had been fixed upon her face, while the shadows of age were flitting from it like darkness from the crimson daybreak.

The fair widow knew, of old, that Colonel Killigrew's compliments were not always measured by sober truth; so she started up and ran to the mirror, still dreading that the ugly visage of an old woman would meet her gaze. Meanwhile, the three gentlemen behaved in such a manner as proved that the water of the Fountain of Youth possessed some intoxicating qual-

ities; unless, indeed, their exhilaration of spirits were merely a lightsome dizziness caused by the sudden removal of the weight of years. Mr. Gascoigne's mind seemed to run on political topics, but whether relating to the past, present, or future, could not easily be determined, since the same ideas and phrases have been in vogue these fifty years. Now he rattled forth full-throated sentences about patriotism, national glory, and the people's right; now he muttered some perilous stuff or other, in a sly and doubtful whisper, so cautiously that even his own conscience could scarcely catch the secret; and now, again, he spoke in measured accents, and a deeply deferential tone, as if a royal ear were listening to his well-turned periods. Colonel Killigrew all this time had been trolling forth a jolly bottle song, and ringing his glass in symphony with the chorus, while his eyes wandered toward the buxom figure of the Widow Wycherly. On the other side of the table, Mr. Medbourne was involved in a calculation of dollars and cents, with which was strangely intermingled a project for supplying the East Indies with ice, by harnessing a team of whales to the polar icebergs.

As for the Widow Wycherly, she stood before the mirror curtsying and simpering to her own image, and greeting it as the friend whom she loved better than all the world beside. She thrust her face close to the glass, to see whether some long-remembered wrinkle of crow's foot had indeed vanished. She examined whether the snow had so entirely melted from her hair that the venerable cap could be safely thrown aside. At last, turning briskly away, she came with a sort of dancing step to the table.

"My dear old doctor," cried she, "pray favor me with another glass!"

"Certainly, my dear madam, certainly!" replied the complaisant doctor; "see! I have already filled the glasses."

There, in fact, stood the four glasses, brimful of this wonderful water, the delicate spray of which, as it effervesced from the surface, resembled the tremulous glitter of diamonds. It was now so nearly sunset that the chamber had grown duskier than ever; but a mild and moonlike splendor gleamed from within the vase, and rested alike on the four guests and on the doctor's venerable figure. He sat in a high-backed, elaborately-carved, oaken arm-chair, with a gray dignity of aspect that might have well befitted that very Father Time, whose power had never been disputed, save by this fortunate company. Even while quaffing the third draught of the Fountain of Youth, they were almost awed by the expression of his mysterious visage.

But, the next moment, the exhilarating gush of young life shot through their veins. They were now in the happy prime of youth. Age, with its miserable train of cares and sorrows and diseases, was remembered only as the trouble of a dream, from which they had joyously awoke. The fresh gloss of the soul, so early lost, and without which the world's successive scenes had been but a gallery of faded pictures, again threw its enchantment over all their prospects. They felt like new-created beings in a new-created universe.

"We are young! We are young!" they cried exultingly.

Youth, like the extremity of age, had effaced the strongly-marked characteristics of middle life, and mutually assimilated them all. They were a group of merry youngsters, almost maddened with the exuberant frolicsomeness of their years. The most singular effect of their gayety was an impulse to mock the infirmity and decrepitude of which they had so lately been the victims. They laughed loudly at their old-fashioned attire, the wide-skirted coats and flapped waistcoats of the young men, and the ancient cap and gown of the blooming girl. One limped across the floor like a gouty[8] grandfather; one set a pair of spectacles astride of his nose, and pretended to pore over the black-letter pages of the book of magic; a third seated himself in an arm-chair, and strove to imitate the venerable dignity of Dr. Heidegger. Then all shouted mirthfully, and leaped about the room. The Widow Wycherly—if so fresh a damsel could be called a widow—tripped up

to the doctor's chair, with a mischievous merriment in her rosy face.

"Doctor, you dear old soul," cried she, "get up and dance with me!" And then the four young people laughed louder than ever, to think what a queer figure the poor old doctor would cut.

"Pray excuse me," answered the doctor quietly. "I am old and rheumatic, and my dancing days were over long ago. But either of these gay young gentlemen will be glad of so pretty a partner."

"Dance with me, Clara!" cried Colonel Killigrew.

"No, no, I will be her partner!" shouted Mr. Gascoigne.

"She promised me her hand, fifty years ago!" exclaimed Mr. Medbourne.

They all gathered round her. One caught both her hands in his passionate grasp—another threw his arm about her waist—the third buried his hand among the glossy curls that clustered beneath the widow's cap. Blushing, panting, struggling, chiding, laughing, her warm breath fanning each of their faces by turns, she strove to disengage herself, yet still remained in their triple embrace. Never was there a livelier picture of youthful rivalship, with bewitching beauty for the prize. Yet, by a strange deception, owing to the duskiness of the chamber, and the antique dresses which they still wore, the tall mirror is said to have reflected the figures of the three old, gray, withered grandsires, ridiculously contending for the skinny ugliness of a shrivelled grandam.

But they were young: their burning passions proved them so. Inflamed to madness by the coquetry of the girl-widow, who neither granted nor quite withheld her favors, the three rivals began to interchange threatening glances. Still keeping hold of the fair prize, they grappled fiercely at one another's throats. As they struggled to and fro, the table was overturned, and the vase dashed into a thousand

---

8. **gouty**\gau·tē\ having gout, a disease which causes swelling of the joints, especially of the feet and hands.

fragments. The precious Water of Youth flowed in a bright stream across the floor, moistening the wings of a butterfly, which, grown old in the decline of summer, had alighted there to die. The insect fluttered lightly through the chamber, and settled on the snowy head of Dr. Heidegger.

"Come, come, gentlemen!—come, Madam Wycherly," exclaimed the doctor, "I really must protest against this riot."

They stood still and shivered; for it seemed as if gray Time were calling them back from their sunny youth, far down into the chill and darksome vale of years. They looked at old Dr. Heidegger, who sat in his carved arm-chair, holding the rose of half a century, which he had rescued from among the fragments of the shattered vase. At the motion of his hand, the four rioters resumed their seats; the more readily, because their violent exertions had wearied them, youthful though they were.

"My poor Sylvia's rose!" ejaculated Dr. Heidegger, holding it in the light of the sunset clouds; "it appears to be fading again."

And so it was. Even while the party were looking at it, the flower continued to shrivel up, till it became as dry and fragile as when the doctor had first thrown it into the vase. He shook off the few drops of moisture which clung to its petals.

"I love it as well thus as in its dewy freshness," observed he, pressing the withered rose to his withered lips. While he spoke, the butterfly fluttered down from the doctor's snowy head, and fell upon the floor.

His guests shivered again. A strange chillness, whether of the body or spirit they could not tell, was creeping gradually over them all. They gazed at one another, and fancied that each fleeting moment snatched away a charm, and left a deepening furrow where none had been before. Was it an illusion? Had the changes of a lifetime been crowded into so brief a space, and were they now four aged people, sitting with their old friend, Dr. Heidegger?

"Are we grown old again, so soon?" cried they, dolefully.

In truth they had. The Water of Youth possessed merely a virtue more transient than that of wine. The delirium which it created had effervesced away. Yes! they were old again. With a shuddering impulse, that showed her a woman still, the widow clasped her skinny hands before her face, and wished that the coffin lid were over it, since it could be no longer beautiful.

"Yes, friends, ye are old again," said Dr. Heidegger, "and lo! the Water of Youth is all lavished on the ground. Well—I bemoan it not; for if the fountain gushed at my very doorstep, I would not stoop to bathe my lips in it—no, though its delirium were for years instead of moments. Such is the lesson ye have taught me!"

But the doctor's four friends had taught no such lesson to themselves. They resolved forthwith to make a pilgrimage to Florida, and quaff at morning, noon, and night, from the Fountain of Youth.

I

RELIVING THE PAST

If you compare the nonphysical characteristics of Dr. Heidegger's friends before (see p. 113) and after (see p. 117) the experiment, you will see that they have not changed one jot as a result of drinking the Water of Youth. This might suggest that Hawthorne held a rather pessimistic view of the human potential to benefit from experience. It is notable, however, that the four persons chosen for the experiment have all led rather empty lives. Suppose the Doctor had chosen four who had led fuller lives. How—if at all—might the results of the experiment have changed?

II

IMPLICATIONS

Discuss the following statements in terms of this story and of your own experience.

1. One's personality is so fixed by the time one reaches midteens that nothing short of a miracle is likely to change it.

2. "Repentance treads closely behind the steps of error."

3. The fact that people would want to relive their lives is in itself good evidence that their lives have been unsatisfactory.

4. True love or affection does not change with the passage of time.

5. History shows that humans have no significant ability to benefit from the mistakes of the past; if they had such ability, they would long ago have learned how to avoid such things as wars and depressions.

III
TECHNIQUES

Setting

The good doctor's study, Hawthorne speculates with tongue in cheek, "must have been a very curious place." The word *curious* is used here in the sense of "interesting because of novelty or rarity." What made the study curious?

The atmosphere in the story shifts. Try to trace these shifts.

Characterization

Hawthorne employs a literary device popular in his time in which a writer interrupts the story briefly to talk directly to the reader (see p. 114, bottom of the first column and top of the second). Does this admission on the writer's part help explain Dr. Heidegger's eccentricities and the strange stories connected with his past?

When the Widow Wycherly recalls (see p. 116) "that Colonel Killigrew's compliments were not always measured by sober truth," what is Hawthorne suggesting about the Colonel's character?

From his many years of reading, particularly in Cotton Mather's *The Wonders of the Invisible World*, Hawthorne was familiar with the "Witches' Sabbath," a midnight orgy which Puritan Salem dreaded even to talk about. In this famous tale, Goodman Brown (the title means "commoner," as opposed to "mister," a gentleman's title) experiences at first hand so frightful an event that critics have long called this one of Hawthorne's most powerful stories. The moral is timeless, and the evil atmosphere is as ominous as any Hawthorne ever created. It first appeared in 1835 and was later collected in *Mosses from an Old Manse* (1846).

Young Goodman Brown

Young Goodman Brown came forth at sunset into the street at Salem village; but put his head back, after crossing the threshold, to exchange a parting kiss with his young wife. And Faith, as the wife was aptly named, thrust her own pretty head into the street, letting the wind play with the pink ribbons of her cap while she called to Goodman Brown.

"Dearest heart," whispered she, softly and rather sadly, when her lips were close to his ear, "prithee put off your journey until sunrise and sleep in your own bed to-night. A lone woman is troubled with such dreams and such thoughts that she's afeard of herself sometimes. Pray tarry with me this night, dear husband, of all nights in the year."

"My love and my Faith," replied young Goodman Brown, "of all nights in the year, this one night must I tarry away from thee. My journey, as thou callest it, forth and back again, must needs be done 'twixt now and sunrise. What, my sweet, pretty wife, dost thou doubt me already, and we but three months married?"

"Then God bless you!" said Faith, with the pink ribbons; "and may you find all well when you come back."

"Amen!" cried Goodman Brown. "Say thy prayers, dear Faith, and go to bed at dusk, and no harm will come to thee."

So they parted; and the young man pursued his way until, being about to turn the corner by the meetinghouse, he looked back and saw the head of Faith still peeping after him with a melancholy air, in spite of her pink ribbons.

"Poor little Faith!" thought he, for his heart smote him. "What a wretch am I to leave her on such an errand! She talks of dreams, too. Methought[1] as she spoke there was trouble in her face, as if a dream had warned her what work is to be done to-night. But no, no; 't would kill her to think it. Well, she's a blessed angel on earth; and after this one night I'll cling to her skirts and follow her to heaven."

With this excellent resolve for the future, Goodman Brown felt himself justified in making more haste on his present evil purpose. He had taken a dreary road, darkened by all the gloomiest trees of the forest, which barely stood aside to let the narrow path creep through, and closed immediately behind. It was all as lonely as could be; and there is this peculiarity in such a solitude, that the traveller knows not who may be concealed by the innumerable trunks and the thick boughs overhead; so that with lonely footsteps he may yet be passing through an unseen multitude.

"There may be a devilish Indian behind every tree," said Goodman Brown to himself; and he glanced fearfully behind him as he added, "What if the devil himself should be at my very elbow!"

His head being turned back, he passed a crook of the road, and, looking forward again, beheld the figure of a man, in grave and decent attire, seated at the foot of an old tree. He arose at Goodman Brown's approach and walked onward side by side with him.

"You are late, Goodman Brown," said he. "The clock of the Old South[2] was striking as I came through Boston, and that is full fifteen minutes agone."[3]

"Faith kept me back a while," replied the young man, with a tremor in his voice, caused by the sudden appearance of his companion, though not wholly unexpected.

It was now deep dusk in the forest, and deepest in that part of it where these two were journeying. As nearly as could be discerned, the second traveller was about fifty years old, apparently in the same rank of life as Goodman Brown, and bearing a considerable resemblance to him, though perhaps more in expression than features. Still they might have been taken for father and son. And yet, though the elder person was as simply clad as the younger, and as simple in manner too, he had an indescribable air of one who knew the world, and who would not have felt abashed at the governor's dinner table or in King William's[4] court, were it possible that his affairs should call him thither. But the only thing about him that could be fixed upon as remarkable was his staff, which bore the likeness of a great black snake, so curiously wrought that it might almost be seen to twist and wriggle itself like a living serpent. This, of course, must have been an ocular deception, assisted by the uncertain light.

"Come, Goodman Brown," cried his fellow-traveller, "this is a dull pace for the beginning of a journey. Take my staff, if you are so soon weary."

"Friend," said the other, exchanging his slow pace for a full stop, "having kept covenant by meeting thee here, it is my purpose now to return whence I came. I have scruples touching the matter thou wot'st of."

"Sayest thou so?" replied he of the serpent, smiling apart. "Let us walk on, nevertheless,

1. **methought,** it seems to me.
2. **Old South,** Old South Church, Boston; secret meeting place of American patriots before the Revolutionary War. The church, however, was not erected until 1729 although the setting of the story seems to be earlier.
3. **agone,** archaic form of *ago.*
4. **King William III,** King of England, 1689–1702.

reasoning as we go; and if I convince thee not thou shalt turn back. We are but a little way in the forest yet."

"Too far! too far!" exclaimed the goodman, unconsciously resuming his walk. "My father never went into the woods on such an errand, nor his father before him. We have been a race of honest men and good Christians since the days of the martyrs; and shall I be the first of the name of Brown that ever took this path and kept"—

"Such company, thou wouldst say," observed the elder person, interpreting his pause. "Well said, Goodman Brown! I have been as well acquainted with your family as with ever a one among the Puritans; and that's no trifle to say. I helped your grandfather, the constable, when he lashed the Quaker woman so smartly through the streets of Salem; and it was I that brought your father a pitch-pine knot, kindled at my own hearth, to set fire to an Indian village, in King Philip's[5] war. They were my good friends, both; and many a pleasant walk have we had along this path, and returned merrily after midnight. I would fain be friends with you for their sake."

"If it be as thou sayest," replied Goodman Brown, "I marvel they never spoke of these matters; or, verily, I marvel not, seeing that the least rumor of the sort would have driven them from New England. We are a people of prayer, and good works to boot, and abide no such wickedness."

"Wickedness or not," said the traveller with the twisted staff, "I have a very general acquaintance here in New England. The deacons of many a church have drunk the communion wine with me; the selectmen of divers towns make me their chairman; and a majority of the Great and General Court are firm supporters of my interest. The governor and I, too — But these are state secrets."

"Can this be so?" cried Goodman Brown, with a stare of amazement at his undisturbed companion. "Howbeit, I have nothing to do with the governor and council; they have their own ways, and are no rule for a simple hus-

bandman[6] like me. But, were I to go on with thee, how should I meet the eye of that good old man, our minister, at Salem village? Oh, his voice would make me tremble both Sabbath day and lecture day."[7]

Thus far the elder traveller had listened with due gravity; but now burst into a fit of irrepressible mirth, shaking himself so violently that his snake-like staff actually seemed to wriggle in sympathy.

"Ha! ha! ha!" shouted he again and again; then composing himself. "Well, go on, Goodman Brown, go on; but, prithee, don't kill me with laughing."

"Well, then, to end the matter at once," said Goodman Brown, considerably nettled, "there is my wife, Faith. It would break her dear little heart; and I'd rather break my own."

"Nay, if that be the case," answered the other, "e'en go thy ways, Goodman Brown. I would not for twenty old women like the one hobbling before us that Faith should come to any harm."

As he spoke he pointed his staff at a female figure on the path, in whom Goodman Brown recognized a very pious and exemplary dame, who had taught him his catechism in youth, and was still his moral and spiritual adviser, jointly with the minister and Deacon Gookin.

"A marvel, truly, that Goody Cloyse[8] should be so far in the wilderness at nightfall," said he. "But with your leave, friend, I shall take a cut through the woods until we have left this Christian woman behind. Being a stranger to you, she might ask whom I was consorting with and whither I was going."

"Be it so," said his fellow-traveller. "Betake you the woods, and let me keep the path."

---

5. **King Philip,** name for Indian Chief, Metacomet (d. 1676), who was last leader of the Indian resistance in Southern New England.
6. **husbandman,** any man of humble station.
7. **lecture day,** day of midweek sermon, usually Thursday.
8. **Goody Cloyse,** contraction of *Goodwife* (cf. *goodman*). Goody Cloyse, Goody Cory, and Martha Carrier were sentenced in 1642 as witches by magistrates of Salem.

Accordingly the young man turned aside, but took care to watch his companion, who advanced softly along the road until he had come within a staff's length of the old dame. She, meanwhile, was making the best of her way, with singular speed for so aged a woman, and mumbling some indistinct words—a prayer, doubtless—as she went. The traveller put forth his staff and touched her withered neck with what seemed the serpent's tail.

"The devil!" screamed the pious old lady.

"Then Goody Cloyse knows her old friend?" observed the traveller, confronting her and leaning on his writhing stick.

"Ah, forsooth, and is it your worship indeed?" cried the good dame. "Yet, truly is it, and in the very image of my old gossip, Goodman Brown, the grandfather of the silly fellow that now is. But—would your worship believe it?—my broomstick hath strangely disappeared, stolen, as I suspect, by that unhanged witch, Goody Cory, and that, too, when I was all anointed with the juice of smallage, and cinquefoil, and wolf's bane"[9]—

"Mingled with fine wheat and the fat of a new-born babe," said the shape of old Goodman Brown.

"Ah, your worship knows the recipe," cried the old lady, cackling aloud. "So, as I was saying, being all ready for the meeting, and no horse to ride on, I made up my mind to foot it; for they tell me there is a nice young man to be taken into communion to-night. But now your good worship will lend me your arm, and we shall be there in a twinkling."

"That can hardly be," answered her friend. "I may not spare you my arm, Goody Cloyse; but here is my staff, if you will."

So saying, he threw it down at her feet, where, perhaps, it assumed life, being one of the rods which its owner had formerly lent to the Egyptian magi.[10] Of this fact, however, Goodman Brown could not take cognizance. He had cast up his eyes in astonishment, and, looking down again, beheld neither Goody Cloyse nor the serpentine staff, but this fellow-traveller

alone, who waited for him as calmly as if nothing had happened.

"That old woman taught me my catechism,"[11] said the young man; and there was a world of meaning in this simple comment.

They continued to walk onward, while the elder traveller exhorted his companion to make good speed and persevere in the path, discoursing so aptly that his arguments seemed rather to spring up in the bosom of his auditor than to be suggested by himself. As they went, he plucked a branch of maple to serve for a walking stick, and began to strip it of the twigs and little boughs, which were wet with evening dew. The moment his fingers touched them they became strangely withered and dried up as with a week's sunshine. Thus the pair proceeded, at a good free pace, until suddenly, in a gloomy hollow of the road, Goodman Brown sat himself down on the stump of a tree and refused to go any farther.

"Friend," said he, stubbornly, "my mind is made up. Not another step will I budge on this errand. What if a wretched old woman do choose to go to the devil when I thought she was going to heaven: is that any reason why I should quit my dear Faith and go after her?"

"You will think better of this by and by," said his acquaintance, composedly. "Sit here and rest yourself a while; and when you feel like moving again, there is my staff to help you along."

Without more words, he threw his companion the maple stick, and was as speedily out of sight as if he had vanished into the deepening gloom. The young man sat a few moments by the roadside, applauding himself greatly, and thinking with how clear a conscience he should meet the minister in his morning walk, nor shrink from the eye of good old Deacon Gookin.

---

9. **smallage**\ˈsmɔ·lij\ wild celery, credited with magic powers. **cinquefoil**\ˈsiŋk ˈfɔil\ plant of the rose family. **wolf's bane,** a poisonous plant.
10. **Egyptian magi,** member of the priestly caste believed capable of magical powers.
11. **catechism**\ˈkă·tə·kĭz·əm\ handbook of questions and answers used to teach principles of a religion.

And what calm sleep would be his that very night, which was to have been spent so wickedly, but so purely and sweetly now, in the arms of Faith! Amidst these pleasant and praiseworthy meditations, Goodman Brown heard the tramp of horses along the road, and deemed it advisable to conceal himself within the verge of the forest, conscious of the guilty purpose that had brought him thither, though now so happily turned from it.

On came the hoof tramps and the voices of the riders, two grave old voices, conversing soberly as they drew near. These mingled sounds appeared to pass along the road, within a few yards of the young man's hiding-place; but, owing doubtless to the depth of the gloom at that particular spot, neither the travellers nor their steeds were visible. Though their figures brushed the small boughs by the wayside, it could not be seen that they intercepted, even for a moment, the faint gleam from the strip of bright sky athwart which they must have passed. Goodman Brown alternately crouched and stood on tiptoe, pulling aside the branches and thrusting forth his head as far as he durst without discerning so much as a shadow. It vexed him the more, because he could have sworn, were such a thing possible, that he recognized the voices of the minister and Deacon Gookin, jogging along quietly, as they were wont to do, when bound to some ordination or ecclesiastical council. While yet within hearing, one of the riders stopped to pluck a switch.

"Of the two, reverend sir," said the voice like the deacon's, "I had rather miss an ordination dinner than to-night's meeting. They tell me that some of our community are to be here from Falmouth[12] and beyond, and others from Connecticut and Rhode Island, besides several of the Indian powwows, who, after their fashion, know almost as much deviltry as the best of us. Moreover, there is a goodly young woman to be taken into communion."

"Mighty well, Deacon Gookin!" replied the solemn old tones of the minister. "Spur up, or we shall be late. Nothing can be done, you know, until I get on the ground."

The hoofs clattered again; and the voices, talking so strangely in the empty air, passed on through the forest, where no church had ever been gathered or solitary Christian prayed. Whither, then, could these holy men be journeying so deep into the heathen wilderness? Young Goodman Brown caught hold of a tree for support, being ready to sink down on the ground, faint and overburdened with the heavy sickness of his heart. He looked up to the sky, doubting whether there really was a heaven above him. Yet there was the blue arch, and the stars brightening in it.

"With heaven above and Faith below, I will yet stand firm against the devil!" cried Goodman Brown.

While he still gazed upward into the deep arch of the firmament and had lifted his hands to pray, a cloud, though no wind was stirring, hurried across the zenith and hid the brightening stars. The blue sky was still visible, except directly overhead, where this black mass of cloud was sweeping swiftly northward. Aloft in the air, as if from the depths of the cloud, came a confused and doubtful sound of voices. Once the listener fancied that he could distinguish the accents of towns-people of his own, men and women, both pious and ungodly, many of whom he had met at the communion table, and had seen others rioting at the tavern. The next moment, so indistinct were the sounds, he doubted whether he had heard aught but the murmur of the old forest, whispering without a wind. Then came a stronger swell of those familiar tones, heard daily in the sunshine at Salem village, but never until now from a cloud of night. There was one voice, of a young woman, uttering lamentations, yet with an uncertain sorrow, and entreating for some favor, which, perhaps, it would grieve her to obtain; and all the unseen multitude, both saints and sinners, seemed to encourage her onward.

"Faith!" shouted Goodman Brown, in a voice of agony and desperation; and the echoes of

12. **Falmouth**\ˈfắl·məth\ town in southeast Massachusetts.

the forest mocked him, crying, "Faith! Faith!" as if bewildered wretches were seeking her all through the wilderness.

The cry of grief, rage, and terror was yet piercing the night, when the unhappy husband held his breath for a response. There was a scream, drowned immediately in a louder murmur of voices, fading into far-off laughter, as the dark cloud swept away, leaving the clear and silent sky above Goodman Brown. But something fluttered lightly down through the air and caught on the branch of a tree. The young man seized it, and beheld a pink ribbon.

"My Faith is gone!" cried he, after one stupefied moment. "There is no good on earth; and sin is but a name. Come, devil; for to thee is this world given."

And, maddened with despair, so that he laughed loud and long, did Goodman Brown grasp his staff and set forth again, at such a rate that he seemed to fly along the forest path rather than to walk or run. The road grew wilder and drearier and more faintly traced, and vanished at length, leaving him in the heart of the dark wilderness, still rushing onward with the instinct that guides mortal man to evil. The whole forest was peopled with frightful sounds—the creaking of the trees, the howling of wild beasts, and the yell of Indians; while sometimes the wind tolled like a distant church bell, and sometimes gave a broad roar around the traveller, as if all Nature were laughing him to scorn. But he was himself the chief horror of the scene, and shrank not from its other horrors.

"Ha! ha! ha!" roared Goodman Brown when the wind laughed at him. "Let us hear which will laugh loudest. Think not to frighten me with your deviltry. Come witch, come wizard, come Indian powwow, come devil himself, and here comes Goodman Brown. You may as well fear him as he fear you."

In truth, all through the haunted forest there could be nothing more frightful than the figure of Goodman Brown. On he flew among the black pines, brandishing his staff with frenzied gestures, now giving vent to an inspiration of horrid blasphemy, and now shouting forth such laughter as set all the echoes of the forest laughing like demons around him. The fiend in his own shape is less hideous than when he rages in the breast of man. Thus sped the demoniac on his course, until, quivering among the trees, he saw a red light before him, as when the felled trunks and branches of a clearing have been set on fire, and throw up their lurid blaze against the sky, at the hour of midnight. He paused, in a lull of the tempest that had driven him onward, and heard the swell of what seemed a hymn, rolling solemnly from a distance with the weight of many voices. He knew the tune; it was a familiar one in the choir of the village meetinghouse. The verse died heavily away, and was lengthened by a chorus, not of human voices, but of all the sounds of the benighted wilderness pealing in awful harmony together. Goodman Brown cried out, and his cry was lost to his own ear by its unison with the cry of the desert.

In the interval of silence he stole forward until the light glared full upon his eyes. At one extremity of an open space, hemmed in by the dark wall of the forest, arose a rock, bearing some rude, natural resemblance either to an altar or a pulpit, and surrounded by four blazing pines, their tops aflame, their stems untouched, like candles at an evening meeting. The mass of foliage that had overgrown the summit of the rock was all on fire, blazing high into the night and fitfully illuminating the whole field. Each pendent twig and leafy festoon was in a blaze. As the red light arose and fell, a numerous congregation alternately shone forth, then disappeared in shadow, and again grew, as it were, out of the darkness, peopling the heart of the solitary woods at once.

"A grave and dark-clad company," quoth Goodman Brown.

In truth they were such. Among them, quivering to and fro between gloom and splendor, appeared faces that would be seen next day at the council board of the province, and others which, Sabbath after Sabbath, looked devoutly heavenward, and benignantly over the crowded pews, from the holiest pulpits in the land. Some affirm that the lady of the governor was there. At least there were high dames well known to her, and wives of honored husbands and widows, a great multitude, and ancient maidens, all of excellent repute, and fair young girls, who trembled lest their mothers should espy them. Either the sudden gleams of light flashing over the obscure field bedazzled Goodman Brown, or he recognized a score of the church members of Salem village famous for their especial sanctity. Good old Deacon Gookin had arrived, and waited at the skirts of that venerable saint, his revered pastor. But, irreverently consorting with these grave, reputable, and pious people, these elders of the church, these chaste dames and dewy virgins, there were men of dissolute lives and women of spotted fame, wretches given over to all mean and filthy vice, and suspected even of horrid crimes. It was strange to see that the good shrank not from the wicked, nor were the sinners abashed by the saints. Scattered also among their pale-faced enemies were the Indian priests, or powwows, who had often scared their native forest with more hideous incantations than any known to English witchcraft.

"But where is Faith?" thought Goodman Brown; and, as hope came into his heart, he trembled.

Another verse of the hymn arose, a slow and mournful strain, such as the pious love, but joined to words which expressed all that our nature can conceive of sin, and darkly hinted at far more. Unfathomable to mere mortals is the lore of fiends. Verse after verse was sung; and still the chorus of the desert swelled between like the deepest tone of a mighty organ; and with the final peal of that dreadful anthem there came a sound, as if the roaring wind, the rushing streams, the howling beasts, and every other voice of the unconcerted wilderness were mingling and according with the voice of guilty man in homage to the prince of all. The four blazing pines threw up a loftier flame, and obscurely discovered shapes and visages of horror on the smoke wreaths above the impious assembly. At the same moment the fire on the rock shot redly forth and formed a glowing arch above its base, where now appeared a figure. With reverence be it spoken, the figure bore no slight similitude, both in garb and manner, to some grave divine of the New England churches.

"Bring forth the converts!" cried a voice that echoed through the field and rolled into the forest.

At the word, Goodman Brown stepped forth from the shadow of the trees and approached the congregation, with whom he felt a loathful brotherhood by the sympathy of all that was wicked in his heart. He could have well-nigh sworn that the shape of his own dead father beckoned him to advance, looking downward from a smoke wreath, while a woman, with dim features of despair, threw out her hand to warn him back. Was it his mother? But he had no power to retreat one step, nor to resist, even in thought, when the minister and good old Deacon Gookin seized his arms and led him to the blazing rock. Thither came also the slender form of a veiled female, led between Goody Cloyse, that pious teacher of the catechism, and Martha Carrier, who had received the devil's promise to be queen of hell. A rampant hag was she. And there stood the proselytes[13] beneath the canopy of fire.

"Welcome, my children," said the dark figure, "to the communion of your race. Ye have found thus young your nature and your destiny. My children, look behind you!"

They turned; and flashing forth, as it were, in a sheet of flame, the fiend worshippers were seen; the smile of welcome gleamed darkly on every visage.

"There," resumed the sable form, "are all whom ye have reverenced from youth. Ye deemed them holier than yourselves, and shrank from your own sin, contrasting it with their lives of righteousness and prayerful aspirations heavenward. Yet here are they all in

---

13. **proselytes**\ˈprŏ·sə ˈlaits\ persons who have been converted from one religion to another.

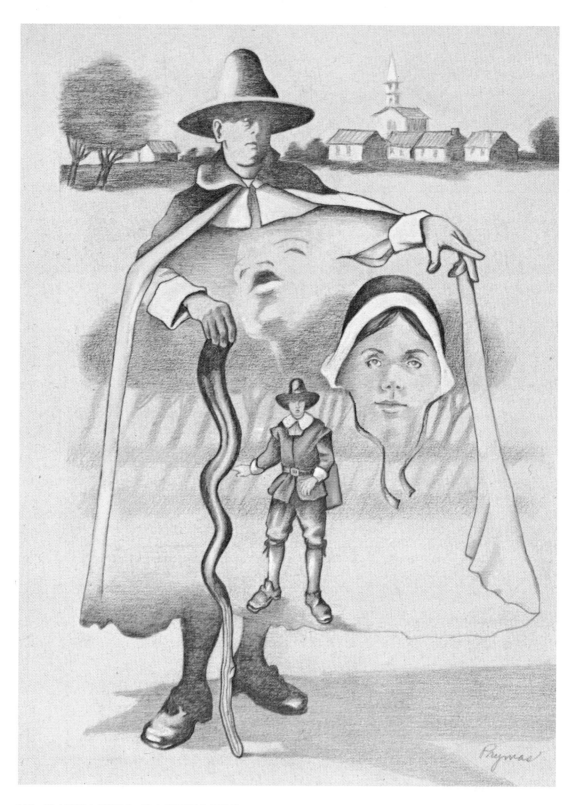

my worshipping assembly. This night it shall be granted you to know their secret deeds: how hoary-bearded elders of the church have whispered wanton words to the young maids of their households; how many a woman, eager for widows' weeds, has given her husband a drink at bedtime and let him sleep his last sleep in her bosom; how beardless youths have made haste to inherit their fathers' wealth; and how fair damsels—blush not, sweet ones—have dug little graves in the garden, and bidden me, the sole guest, to an infant's funeral. By the sympathy of your human hearts for sin ye shall scent out all the places—whether in church, bed-chamber, street, field, or forest—where crime has been committed, and shall exult to behold the whole earth one stain of guilt, one mighty blood spot. Far more than this. It shall be yours to penetrate, in every bosom, the deep mystery of sin, the fountain of all wicked arts, and which inexhaustibly supplies more evil impulses than human power—than my power at its utmost—can make manifest in deeds. And now, my children, look upon each other."

They did so; and, by the blaze of the hell-kindled torches, the wretched man beheld his Faith, and the wife her husband, trembling before that unhallowed altar.

"Lo, there ye stand, my children," said the figure, in a deep and solemn tone, almost sad with its despairing awfulness, as if his once angelic nature could yet mourn for our miserable race. "Depending upon one another's hearts, ye had still hoped that virtue were not all a dream. Now are ye undeceived. Evil is the nature of mankind. Evil must be your only happiness. Welcome again, my children, to the communion of your race."

"Welcome," repeated the fiend worshippers, in one cry of despair and triumph.

And there they stood, the only pair, as it seemed, who were yet hesitating on the verge of wickedness in this dark world. A basin was hollowed, naturally, in the rock. Did it contain water, reddened by the lurid light? or was it blood? or, perchance, a liquid flame? Herein did the shape of evil dip his hand and prepare to lay the mark of baptism upon their foreheads, that they might be partakers of the mystery of sin, more conscious of the secret guilt of others, both in deed and thought, than they could now be of their own. The husband cast one look at his pale wife, and Faith at him. What polluted wretches would the next glance show them to each other, shuddering alike at what they disclosed and what they saw.

"Faith! Faith!" cried the husband, "look up to heaven, and resist the wicked one."

Whether Faith obeyed he knew not. Hardly had he spoken when he found himself amid calm night and solitude, listening to a roar of the wind which died heavily away through the forest. He staggered against the rock, and felt it chill and damp; while a hanging twig, that had been all on fire, besprinkled his cheek with the coldest dew.

The next morning young Goodman Brown came slowly into the street of Salem village, staring around him like a bewildered man. The good old minister was taking a walk along the graveyard to get an appetite for breakfast and meditate his sermon, and bestowed a blessing, as he passed, on Goodman Brown. He shrank from the venerable saint as if to avoid an anathema. Old Deacon Gookin was at domestic worship, and the holy words of his prayer were heard through the open window. "What God doth the wizard pray to?" quoth Goodman Brown. Goody Cloyse, that excellent old Christian, stood in the early sunshine at her own lattice, catechizing a little girl who had brought her a pint of morning's milk. Goodman Brown snatched away the child as from the grasp of the fiend himself. Turning the corner by the meetinghouse, he spied the head of Faith, with the pink ribbons, gazing anxiously forth, and bursting into such joy at sight of him that she skipped along the street and almost kissed her husband before the whole village. But Goodman Brown looked sternly and sadly into her face, and passed on without a greeting.

Had Goodman Brown fallen asleep in the forest and only dreamed a wild dream of a witch-meeting?

Be it so if you will; but, alas! it was a dream of evil omen for young Goodman Brown. A stern, a sad, a darkly meditative, a distrustful, if not a desperate man did he become from the night of that fearful dream. On the Sabbath day, when the congregation were singing a holy psalm, he could not listen because an anthem of sin rushed loudly upon his ear and drowned all the blessed strain. When the minister spoke from the pulpit with power and fervid eloquence, and, with his hand on the open Bible, of the sacred truths of our religion, and of saint-like lives and triumphant deaths, and of future bliss or misery unutterable, then did Goodman Brown turn pale, dreading lest the roof thunder down upon the gray blasphemer and his hearers. Often, awaking suddenly at midnight, he shrank from the bosom of Faith; and at morning or eventide, when the family knelt down at prayer, he scowled and muttered to himself, and gazed sternly at his wife, and turned away. And when he had lived long, and was borne to his grave a hoary corpse, followed by Faith, an aged woman, and children and grandchildren, a goodly procession, besides neighbors not a few, they carved no hopeful verse upon his tombstone, for his dying hour was gloom.

I
DREAM OR REALITY?

It would seem very important for the reader to know whether Goodman Brown's experience in the forest was real or imaginary. If the experience was real, then Brown's neighbors, including his own wife and minister, are sinners. On the other hand, if the hero's forest experience was a dream, it may be that his wife and neighbors are not sinners—he may be projecting his own sense of sin onto them.

What evidence can you offer to prove that Goodman Brown's experience in the forest was either real or unreal? If you cannot find enough evidence to justify either of these conclusions, why do you think Hawthorne has left his readers in doubt?

II
IMPLICATIONS

The following statements give interpretations of the story. What are your views on each of them?

1. Hawthorne is less concerned with the causes of the loss of faith in human nature than he is with the effects.

2. The chief theme of "Young Goodman Brown" is not "sin" but "guilt."

3. The moral of this story is that once we know evil, our view of the world can never be the same as it was when we were innocent of evil.

III
TECHNIQUES
Setting and Characterization

The reader is at once plunged into an atmosphere that is dark and ominous. The major action occurs on a night that is heavy with eerie shadows and lurid lights. Fearful noises are everywhere. The fact, too, that the setting is Salem village, scene of the infamous witch trials, augers the unfolding of some evil (See Benét's "Trials at Salem," p. 495).

Characters are not what they seem in the bright light of day. Goodman Brown (a solemn color) can be led astray to sin with the wicked ones. Goody Cloyse, "a very pious and exemplary dame," seems in league with the devil. The minister and Deacon Gookin are no better. Even Brown's wife, Faith (and why has the author chosen this name for her?), allows herself to be taken to the evil exercises in the dark forest.

What effect did the night's experience have on Goodman Brown's character?

The "Device of Multiple-Choice"

The many ambiguities (multiple meanings) of "Young Goodman Brown" might lead a reader to conclude that Hawthorne lost control of his story. This, of course, is always possible in any story, but on the other hand one must not assume that ambiguity in a work of art is necessarily bad. Critics have noted that Hawthorne often purposely suggests two or more possible interpretations for the same action or event. One critic called this "the device of multiple-choice"; another critic has suggested that a good synonym for "ambiguity"—at least in certain works of art—would be "richness." Can you see how this device could lead to richness rather than to confusion of meaning?

INDEPENDENT SPIRIT

HOWL OF THE WEATHER
Frederic Remington
Remington Art Memorial
Ogdensburg, New York

The Declaration of Independence asserts, "We hold these truths to be self-evident: that all men are created equal, that they are endowed by their Creator with certain unalienable rights, that among these are life, liberty, and the pursuit of happiness." In these words our founders set forth the most fundamental American doctrine—the unalienable rights of the individual person. Later, when the Constitution defined some of these rights in the Bill of Rights, they were recognized as the civil rights of every citizen. Consequently, individual Americans were guaranteed by law the right to be different, to be uncommon, to be independent, to follow "a different drummer" as long as they respected the God-given rights of others.

The wild frontiers of the seventeenth, eighteenth, and nineteenth centuries fostered self-reliance, responsibility, and independence. American society, shorn of the rigid European class distinctions based upon inherited position, rewarded achievement and personal quality. Americans were free to pursue their own dreams—to go as far as the limits of their ambition and talent allowed.

Although the spirit of independence and self-determination cannot account for the whole of the American character, it constitutes one of the essential keys to understanding that character. At their best, Americans have been an independent breed, mistrusting tradition and established procedures. They are fond of improvising, of trying new ways, of creating innovations.

As the tension between this spirit and mass culture, "big" business, "big" labor, and "big" government mounts in our society, more and more we come to value those persons who retain their individuality and are not afraid to give leadership, even when the odds seem heavily against them. These independent spirits, recognized in almost every sector of American life, remind us of the best that is in us and in our heritage.

It is only natural that American writers have consistently celebrated the exploits of these independent spirits. Some writers have literally created such heroes out of their own imaginations; other writers have greatly strengthened the position of real life heroes through vivid portraits of their lives in fiction, nonfiction, or poetry. But whether these embodiments of the independent spirits are imagined or real, the writer guarantees their places in our national awareness. In the face of charges that Americans are conformists and organizational pawns, the writer performs a crucial role in reminding us of our national heritage, the independent spirit.

Few American heroes mean so much to us
as the heroic farmers who fought in the Revolution.
When a statue was raised in honor of these farmers,
the best-known American author, Ralph Waldo Emerson,
was asked to write a poem to celebrate the occasion.
The poem that follows Emerson's "Concord Hymn" illustrates that it is not only famous writers who have
celebrated the independent spirit. The exploits of the
folk hero, John Henry, have been passed down to us by
word of mouth from railroad workers to blues singers.

Concord Hymn

SUNG AT THE COMPLETION
OF THE BATTLE MONUMENT,
JULY 4, 1837

By the rude bridge that arched the flood,
   Their flag to April's breeze unfurled,
Here once the embattled farmers stood
   And fired the shot heard round the world.

The foe long since in silence slept;   5
   Alike the conqueror silent sleeps;
And Time the ruined bridge has swept
   Down the dark stream which seaward creeps.

On this green bank, by this soft stream,
   We set to-day a votive[1] stone;   10
That memory may their deed redeem,
   When, like our sires, our sons are gone.

Spirit, that made those heroes dare
   To die, and leave their children free,
Bid Time and Nature gently spare   15
   The shaft we raise to them and thee.

RALPH WALDO EMERSON

---

1. **votive**\ˈvō·tĭv\ dedicated in fulfillment of a vow or
in gratitude.

John Henry

John Henry was a little baby,
  Setting on his mammy's knee,
Said "The Big Bend Tunnel on the C. & O. Road
  Is gonna be the death of me,
    Lawd, gonna be the death of me."   5

One day his captain told him,
  How he had bet a man
That John Henry could beat his steam drill down,
  Cause John Henry was the best in the land,
    John Henry was the best in the land.   10

John Henry walked in the tunnel,
  His captain by his side;
The mountain so tall, John Henry so small,
  He laid down his hammer and he cried,
    Laid down his hammer and he cried.   15

John Henry kissed his hammer;
  White man turned on the steam;
Shaker held John Henry's steel;
  Was the biggest race the world had ever seen,
    Lawd, biggest race the world ever seen.   20

John Henry on the right side
  The steam drill on the left,
"Before I'll let your steam drill beat me down,
  I'll hammer my fool self to death,
    Hammer my fool self to death."   25

Captain heard a mighty rumbling,
  Said, "The mountain must be caving in."
John Henry said to the captain,
  "It's my hammer sucking de wind,
    My hammer sucking de wind."   30

John Henry said to his captain,
  "A man ain't nothin' but a man,
But before I'll let dat steam drill beat me down,
  I'll die wid my hammer in my hand,
    Lawd, die wid my hammer in my hand."   35

John Henry hammering on the mountain,
  The whistle blew for half-past two,
The last words his captain heard him say,
  "I've done hammered my insides in two,
    Lawd, I've hammered my insides in two."   40

The hammer that John Henry swung
   It weighed over twelve pound,
He broke a rib in his left-hand side
   And his intrels fell on the ground,
      Lawd, his intrels fell on the ground.   45

They took John Henry to the river,
   And buried him in the sand,
And every locomotive come a-roaring by,
   Says, "There lies that steel-drivin' man,
      Lawd, there lies that steel-drivin' man!"   50

ANONYMOUS

I

HEROIC DIVERSITY IN AMERICA

A black working man and a band of New England farmers: We see in such figures a strictly democratic tendency, a tendency to recognize and praise merit in anyone, regardless of birth or station. Freed from an aristocracy perpetuated by pomp and title, America opened its doors to diversity and individuality. And so "steel-drivin'" John Henry and the simple, common farmer became early ideals of the independent spirit.

II

IMPLICATIONS

Discuss each of the following propositions in terms of your experience and the poems above.

1. The one essential quality of all independent spirits is courage.

2. The cause that a person fights for makes little difference in our estimation of that person; that is, we can have intense admiration for someone even if we disapprove of what he or she is fighting for.

3. Being an underdog in a struggle will tend to increase rather than decrease a hero's stature.

4. A person like John Henry whose life ends tragically appeals to more people than those persons who lead generally happy lives.

5. Most American heroes tend to be nonconformists of one sort or another.

III

TECHNIQUES

Tone

You already know that in speech a **person's** *tone* is an important aspect of meaning. For example, suppose your girl friend refers to someone you do not know as "skinny." The word means "very thin," but she can say it in such a way that you know she means just the opposite, that the person is considerably overweight. Often our tone of voice also reveals how we feel about the person *to whom* we are speaking.

The meaning of what a writer says is also modified by tone. We will define this term as *the writer's attitude toward his or her subject and readers.*

You don't literally hear a writer's words. Nevertheless, it is possible to tell through a variety of means such things as whether a writer is being playful or serious about a subject and whether a writer respects or condescends to an audience. It is important that the reader grasp the writer's tone. If you think that a writer is serious when in fact that writer is being playful, you could miss the point entirely.

1. Emerson's tone could be described as one of quiet reverence. What two frequently repeated consonants help him achieve this tone?

2. "John Henry" contains a good deal of repetition. What is the function of this repetitive phrasing so far as the author's attitude is concerned?

133

Over a century and a quarter ago, Emerson set down
one of the best-known statements of a cherished American ideal—
that individuals must determine for themselves what
is the best way of life for them. Today his statement still rings true:
"Whoso would be a man, must be a nonconformist." The following passages
from "Self-Reliance" in many ways capture the essence of Emerson's thought.

FROM

Self-Reliance

RALPH WALDO EMERSON

There is a time in every man's education when he arrives at the conviction that envy is ignorance; that imitation is suicide; that he must take himself for better, for worse, as his portion; that though the wide universe is full of good, no kernel of nourishing corn can come to him but through his toil bestowed on that plot of ground which is given to him to till. The power which resides in him is new in nature, and none but he knows what that is which he can do, nor does he know until he has tried.

Trust thyself: every heart vibrates to that iron string. Accept the place the Divine Providence[1] has found for you; the society of your contemporaries, the connection of events. Great men have always done so and confided themselves childlike to the genius of their age, betraying their perception that the Eternal was stirring at their heart, working through their hands, predominating in all their being.

Society everywhere is in conspiracy against the manhood of every one of its members. The virtue in most request is conformity. Self-reliance is its aversion. It loves not realities and creators, but names and customs.

Whoso would be a man, must be a nonconformist. He who would gather immortal palms[2] must not be hindered by the name of goodness, but must explore if it be goodness. Nothing is at last sacred but the integrity of your own mind.

What I must do is all that concerns me, not what the people think. This rule, equally arduous in actual and in intellectual life, may serve for the whole distinction between greatness and meanness. It is harder because you will always find those who think they know what is your duty better than you know it. It is easy in the world to live after the world's opinion; it is easy in solitude to live after your own; but the great man is he who in the midst of the crowd keeps with perfect sweetness the independence of solitude.

For noncomformity the world whips you with its displeasure.

The other terror that scares us from self-trust is our consistency; a reverence for our past act or word because the eyes of others have no other data for computing our orbit[3] than our past acts, and we are loath to disappoint them.

But why should you keep your head over your shoulder? Why drag about this corpse of your memory, lest you contradict somewhat[4] you have stated in this or that public place? Suppose you should contradict yourself; what

---

1. **Divine Providence,** benevolent guidance of God for the future.
2. **immortal palms,** lasting victories.
3. **eyes of others . . . orbit,** that is, they don't have any basis for judging our merit other than that we have already done.
4. **somewhat,** something.

then? It seems to be a rule of wisdom never to rely on your memory alone, scarcely even in acts of pure memory, but to bring the past for judgment into the thousand-eyed present, and live ever in a new day.

A foolish consistency is the hobgoblin[5] of little minds, adored by little statesmen and philosophers and divines. With consistency a great soul has simply nothing to do. He may as well concern himself with his shadow on the wall. Speak what you think now in hard words and tomorrow speak what tomorrow thinks in hard words again, though it contradict everything you said today.—"Ah, so you shall be sure to be misunderstood."—Is it so bad then to be misunderstood? Pythagoras[6] was misunderstood, and Socrates,[7] and Jesus, and Luther,[8] and Copernicus,[9] and Galileo,[10] and Newton,[11] and every pure and wise spirit that ever took flesh. To be great is to be misunderstood.

I

HE CELEBRATED THE INDIVIDUAL

"Do not seek yourself outside yourself," wrote the Roman poet Persius.[12] Seventeen hundred years later Emerson attempted to restate this creed for his fellow Americans: "Trust thyself: every heart vibrates to that iron string," or stated more simply: individuals who heed their inner voice, their intuition, can become independent and self-sustaining.

Be ready to answer and discuss the following questions.

1. For what does "no kernel of nourishing corn" stand?

2. What virtue does Emerson say is most in demand by society? Why does society demand this?

3. Why does Emerson find conformity harmful?

II

IMPLICATIONS

Speculate on the following:

1. Self-reliance is a dream only a few can hope to achieve.

2. A nonconformist is justified in breaking the law.

3. Emerson wrote: "Hitch your wagon to a star" ("Civilization"). Is this good advice?

4. Emerson is one of the most widely quoted American writers. Consider the following quotations from his essays, select one, and discuss its relevance to your life:

a. Every man alone is sincere. At the entrance of a second person hypocrisy begins. ("Friendship")

b. A friend is a person with whom I may be sincere. Before him, I may think aloud. ("Friendship")

c. We boil at different degrees. ("Eloquence")

III

TECHNIQUES

Selection of Significant Detail

In putting words and sentences together Emerson was in revolt against the literary strictness of his age. Much of his writing was put together quickly from notes and journals. As a consequence his paragraphs are not always tightly organized, and he has the tendency to leap from paragraph to paragraph without building the kind of bridges over which most readers can go comfortably. Sometimes one has the feeling in reading Emerson that one is pushing through a kind of mishmash of sentences—with certain sentences, however, sticking out sharply like splinters of truth. These splinters Emerson sometimes embellished with significant, and often homely, detail. For example, look again at the last paragraph in the selection from "Self-Reliance." How does the inclusion of specific names add to the reader's grasp of Emerson's belief about consistency?

---

5. **hobgoblin,** a frightening apparition.
6. **Pythagoras,** Greek philosopher and mathematician.
7. **Socrates,** Athenian idealist philosopher and teacher.
8. **Luther,** Martin (1483–1546), leader of German Reformation.
9. **Copernicus,** Nicolaus (1473–1543), Polish astronomer.
10. **Galileo** (1564–1642), Italian astronomer and physicist.
11. **Newton,** Sir Isaac (1642–1727), English mathematician and philosopher.
12. **Persius,** Aulus Persius Flaccus (34–62 A.D.) wrote on the beliefs of the Stoics.

Southern mountaineers have often been
held up to ridicule and laughter. In comic strips
like "Snuffy Smith" and "Li'l Abner" they are depicted as dull clods
little removed from animals. Yet few other groups
come as close to realizing Emerson's "Self-Reliance"
as do these people. Their virtues have been extolled by
such diverse writers as William Faulkner and Edmund Wilson,
and their passing into history will leave America a little poorer.

Last of the
Rugged Individualists

WAYNE KERNODLE

That fierce individualist, the Southern mountaineer, has long been one of America's favorite characters. He has given us a whole series of folk heroes, from Andrew Jackson and Davy Crockett to Li'l Abner. His songs have become a national fad. He has inspired a considerable literature, ranging from serious fiction to the hillbilly cartoon.

And now he is about to vanish, without hope of rescue. Even if there were any practical way to save him, he wouldn't stand for it. In his aggressive—some say arrogant—tradition of independence, he would rather go under than stand beholden to any rescuer. I know, because some of the last of these rugged individualists are my friends.

As the new highways push into dozens of once-hidden coves, they are destroying that isolation which, over the course of the generations, molded the character of the Southern highlander. It is a character which the rest of the country comprehended only dimly. He was ridiculed for his insularity, and capriciously celebrated for qualities which he probably never had and doesn't have now. What he is really like is well exemplified, I think, by the McCalls of Pin Hook Gap.

Perhaps it is best not to locate the place too precisely, because there is more than one Pin Hook Gap and more McCalls than the particular family I know. It is enough to say that it lies in the westernmost end of North Carolina, close to the high, craggy spine of the Appalachians[1] that shuts the mountain country off from the coastal East. The Plott Balsams are here and Pisgah National Forest and the Blue Ridge Mountains and the Blacks. The Cherokee Indian Reservation is not far to the west. The mountains are high—the highest east of the Mississippi—but they are not peaks but domes, "balds," flat at the top and bare, or wooded with a kind of low, torn pine. Many have barely been explored, but they have names: Yellow Face, Dirty Britches, Inkem-Binkem. If you walk northwest of these ridges you come into a good thirty miles of nearly impassable balsam slicks and rhododendron thickets, briars, and dog hobble.

It is dense country. It is also beautiful country, with perhaps the most glorious displays of

---

Reprinted by permission of R. Wayne Kernodle.

1. **Appalachians**\ăp 'ə ▲lāchəns\ referring to the mountain system in the eastern United States.

ALBERT HICKS AND HIS UNCLE JIM BEARD   *Bruce Roberts*

floral vegetation of any part of the United States—dogwood and azalea and laurel and rhododendron, and about them cool pine forest and a tumble of waterfalls. This is also the land of the black bear and of the deer which once provided a main source of food for the Cherokee nation. There are frequent reports of panthers and wildcats, though few of these are actually seen these days.

Pin Hook Gap is, roughly, in between the cities of Asheville, North Carolina, and Knoxville, Tennessee. The needs of the cities have brought roads to connect them, and Pin Hook Gap has felt the glory and the sorrow of being on the route of march. But the cities have not been corruptors directly or intentionally. The boondocks themselves have conceived their own transfiguration.

The total population of Pin Hook is five McCalls plus an assortment of bears, panthers, rattlesnakes, and wild pigs.

Young John McCall, who is seventy-three years old, and his brother Charlie, who is seventy, live in a tight little cabin nestled into a cove under Devil's Courthouse. One brother and his wife live about two hundred yards away, and another brother lives by himself in a shack about a half-mile back in the thicket. Neither Young John nor Charlie has married, and only two of the McCalls have ever been more than fifty miles from Pin Hook during their entire lives. That time was almost forty years ago, when Charlie went into the Army and stayed at training camp for about three weeks before coming back home for good.

A friend of mine, Al Moore, who lives part-time in Brevard, knew a cousin of the McCalls. Through him Al got directions to Pin Hook and the proper passwords that would get us in to John and Charlie's place. It took the two of us and Al's sister, Martha Kate, the better part of the morning, in a jeep, to make it to the top of Pin Hook Ridge. Then we started to drop off into the cove at a remarkably steep angle.

Here, following instructions, we started blowing the jeep horn every minute. When we finally came in sight of the cabin, we stopped and sat on the horn until a figure appeared on the porch. Then we just sat there. It must have been thirty minutes before anything happened. The man on the porch stood in the doorway, leaning on a rifle, and we sat there in the jeep—waiting.

Then I got the feeling that someone was close to the jeep and looked around. There stood Charlie McCall. He had made no sound coming and had given no indication that he was there. Al Moore—who has hiked almost every inch of the territory in this section from Rough Butt Bald to Tennessee Bald and then some—introduced us. We nodded and followed Charlie up to the cabin. From the yard we howdy-ed Young John, but I haven't shaken hands with him to this day.

The beginning was mighty slow. Neither of the McCalls was inclined to start any conversation. They answered questions with the fewest words possible. At first some of the words were unintelligible to me, but Al and Martha Kate seemed to understand them well enough.

Everything about the place expressed the independent way of life. Their father had built the cabin when he first came to Pin Hook. The furniture was all fashioned by hand from cherry and walnut. It had the simple, true lines of great workmanship and was both comfortable and as sturdy as the rocks which surrounded the cove. All of their belongings had been made with tools they had hammered out themselves. The long rifle which stood across the entrance to the house had a barrel made by Charlie McCall.

Both men were tall—more than six feet— and thin, but they were not skinny. Their blue eyes were clear and sharp and their hearing was acute. They were confident men but not arrogant, cunning but not slick. They manifested a serenity unmatched by anything I have seen in the urban world. We talked about their life, which included some mining for precious stones, mica, and minerals.

With some prompting, Charlie told us about a long and ferocious struggle with a panther the winter before.

"This painter used that aire place up thar," he said, pointing out a promontory which jutted out from the balsam thickets about two thousand feet above the cabin. "He was driv by hungry and cold—hit ud been asnowin' fur a week a more. One night we heerd bangin' on the roof. We'suns tuk the rifles and got outside. He come aflyin' off the roof at us. We shot at him and he tuk off. But he come back later and was tearin' and clawin' at the windows and doors and all over the top of the house. Finally he tore a hole in the roof and come pilin' in. We fit him with arn bars and sticks and finally driv him outa the front door. John hit him in the hint leg and he'uns scremt and wailed like a dyin' hog. We haint saw him since. He had tore up the place baddest."

In the summer the McCalls raise a plot of corn and some other vegetables, and kill a hog or two. The hogs are put into a barrel of salt brine to keep from "spiling." In late August and early September, when the berries are plentiful, they pick for days at a time and can them for winter, using an old wood-burning stove and hand-fashioned pots for the cooking. During the long winter months they work at their mining, at making the various articles necessary to keep life and limb together. What they do and how they do it is entirely up to them. They are independent, but will share a real offer of friendship. Their wishes are simple but include the great wish not to be "a-dickertated to"—by men or panthers.

When we arrived, the McCalls were just getting ready to go do some mining, and seemed itchy to get on with it. By this time it had started to rain a bit. We noticed that they were going bareheaded and with only rough denim jackets on their backs. Martha Kate ran back to the jeep and got a couple of plastic tablecloths and held them out to the McCalls. Then for a moment we were sorry, because we feared they were insulted. After a few moments John McCall took one of the tablecloths and put it over his shoulders. Charlie turned and went into the cabin. A few minutes later he returned, and into Martha Kate's hand he placed a beautiful clear ruby. She could not refuse this gesture and still maintain his friendship, so she merely let it lie in her open palm as Charlie pulled the old plastic cloth over his shoulders and he and John McCall walked off toward the hills beyond their rough-hewn homestead. Al, Martha Kate, and I went to the jeep and began our trip back to the way of life that might some day swallow up the McCalls and the painter—if he's still alive.

For "progress" is on its way to Pin Hook Gap. Thirty miles away from the McCall cabin you come out onto a good dirt road and to a little community in the valley. The people at the country store were talking about the engineers who had been making surveys for paving the road and connecting it with the Blue Ridge Parkway at Wagon Road Gap and thence to Routes 19 and 23. This will connect with Highway 441, which is known as the "Over the Smokies Highway," the most scenic route between Brevard, Waynesville, Newfound Gap, Gatlinburg, and Knoxville.

They were excited about the future and the new life it meant for them. And if you know something about the stringencies of their life, you can't blame them for looking forward to more money and the chance to buy the city things that ease the hardships. I just hope the engineers leave enough balsam, "rhododaniel," white spruce, and briar thickets between the road and the McCalls to drown out the whir of those great instruments of change, the automobiles, as they wind around Pin Hook on their way to the scenic beauties which await them at the parking lots of Tennessee Bald.

It is evident that this way of life is already doomed. Twenty-one years ago, when I made

my first intimate contact with the people of this region, the individualistic spirit was the first thing you noticed about the people you met. They were not special people like the McCalls that you had to go out of your way to find. They were most everybody who lived there and they simply did what was to them right and natural.

It was on my first visit in 1938 that I met Turkey Plott and Sary Ellison. I was not a complete stranger to the hill country, but my previous visits had been confined to the protected atmosphere of a church-sponsored summer assembly for young people. This time I was more on my own, and I looked forward to the exploration of the vast and exciting depths of the Great Smoky Mountains, the Balsams Range, and Pisgah National Forest. My plan was to make contact with a man named Otie Moorefield, who had been described to me as knowing more about the deep woods in this area than any man alive. From him I hoped to get instructions on trails to take—or with luck even get him to take a hiking trip with me.

My search for Moorefield led indirectly to several people who later became intimate friends. For an hour after arriving, a total stranger in this small mountain community some forty miles from Asheville, I had sought my guide in vain. Two gaunt men had ignored my questions completely, and another had "never heerd of him." Finally I got a lead from a one-eyed, gimpy-legged fellow.

"I haint saw him all day," he said, "but he mought be at Turkey Plott's."

This turned out to be the hamlet's only café, across the street and down the block. Moorefield was not there, so I decided to eat something since I had had a long, cold trip from Asheville. Here in two surprising episodes, I discovered the individualism which then characterized this community—but does not now.

Sary Ellison, the daughter of Long Butt Ellison, worked as a waitress for Turkey Plott in a defiant and condescending fashion. The place was not awfully clean, and a fairly

139

rough-looking crowd was in the place. When I ordered a hot roast-beef sandwich, milk, and coffee, Sary took the order and went about getting it together rather pokily. Turkey made some remark about "was she gonna take all day." Sary squared off and blared out in front of everybody present:

"Who do you think you air—Hilter or somebody?"

She then threw a dishrag in my plate of food, took off her apron, wrapped it around Turkey's neck, and said, "If'n you'uns want hit on the table so fast—git it thar yourself." And stalked out.

Everybody in the café but Turkey guffawed. Turkey brought me some more food. One of the men said to him:

"Ain't nobody gonna boss Sary around."

Turkey nodded. I gathered that everybody, including Turkey, knew that Sary would be back in a day or two, but that she wouldn't stay long if anybody started acting like "Hilter." Turkey didn't seem to be particularly mad at her, either. As a matter of fact, he said he "guessed he'd a done the same thing if he'd been her." And it wasn't five minutes before he demonstrated that he would.

The grease on my hot roast-beef sandwich was just starting to congeal when two unshaven giants lurched into the café and plopped down on the counter stools beside me. They smelled of tobacco juice and corn whiskey.

Both men were visibly mad and it wasn't just the whiskey, though this had reduced their caution somewhat. Frank Gash, the biggest one, pounded his meat-axe fist on the counter so hard my glass of milk jumped and skidded off onto the floor. For some crazy reason it didn't break, but landed right side up and sat there sloshing up and down. Gash bellowed, "Whar's Turkey Plott? I'm agonna kill 'im."

Turkey had gone back into the kitchen to get an order, but he heard Gash. He came charging out between the swinging doors that separated the two rooms so fast he nearly tore them off the hinges. Plott was probably the biggest and strongest man in western North Carolina at that time.

"Who's agonna kill Turkey?" he shouted.

Without waiting for an answer, he grabbed the two men by their coat collars and banged their heads together with such force you could hear the bones crack. Then he dragged them over the counter one at a time, lifting them above his head, and threw them through the front glass window.

When the glass stopped breaking, there ensued a most remarkable and wonderful quiet. Everybody went back to eating, and Turkey went back to the kitchen. Gash and his friend were picked up by the sheriff and put in jail. When they had recovered and been released, they stopped by to apologize to Turkey for the trouble they had caused. I never did find out what had set them off in the first place, because nobody ever talked about it after that.

This kind of immediate, vigorous expression was typical and is explained in part by the special cultural environment in which such people lived.

The western North Carolina folk like Turkey, Sary, Frank Gash, and their kind were largely of Anglo-Saxon descent. As pioneers, their ancestors had pushed into these wilderness areas, staked out their claims, and settled in for good. Until 1920, and almost until after World War II, the strain was only slightly adulterated by the various migrations. Protected in their isolation by the mountains and by their own reluctance to mingle with strangers, these mountaineers escaped much of the change which was occurring elsewhere. Because economic opportunities were not abundant, education and "refinement" were neglected.

The result was a strange mixture of the proud and the shy, the ignorant and the astute, the wise and the uneducated. In a real sense they lived apart from the main stream of American culture and thus developed ways of doing things that emphasized the importance of self-reliance and responsibility for one's own fate. This difference has been widely misunderstood, since the peculiar or sensational aspects of these people have been focused upon in such ways as to make them appear either stupid or comical, or both.

But many thoughtful people in this region, who have themselves shared this history, are watching the present changes with regret. The great levelers which have invaded their hinterland are radio, television, movies, industry, labor unions, paved roads, parkways, and tourists. What these things have done to Turkey Plott and Sary Ellison illustrates in miniature what is happening to the customs, attitudes, and ambitions of the whole region.

While Turkey, Sary, and the other inhabitants were going their usual way, the community was being surveyed by outsiders who wanted to locate a textile mill there. They needed a wide expanse of land, pure water, and a supply of moderately cheap labor. They found the land and water in abundance at the foot of the hill about three miles from town. The first investment to build the mill amounted to more than three million dollars; later this was doubled for additions. New roads were built, workmen were brought in from the outside, and all the skilled labor in the community was put on the job. Executives and their families moved in, together with a myriad of white-collar workers and personnel experts to train the mountaineers who wanted to work in the mill.

At first this increased Turkey's business, and he added some booths "for ladies and gentlemen." He also hired two new waitresses. But a new, modern restaurant opened up near him and attracted most of the new people who wanted hygiene, soft music, tablecloths, and more courteous service. Turkey finally gave up. He sold his café, lock, stock, and swinging doors, and went to work as a construction foreman at the mill.

Sary married a young insurance salesman who later became president of a thriving firm in town. She and her husband live in a modern, ranch-style house in one of the new developments on the north side. She is president of the parent-teachers association and a charter member of the garden club. Her husband was voted "young man of the year" twice in a row and is now raising funds for a new community center, which is supposed to cut down on juvenile delinquency and rowdyism in town.

Turkey found it rough going for a while at the mill. He was a good foreman but was almost fired several times for being too demanding and for losing his temper. But he got hold of himself in time and calmed down to make a good, steady worker. For years he has been the chief of new construction and is known to be back of several plans to build better houses for the mill workers, athletic fields, and other recreational facilities. About the only time I see the fire in his eyes these days is when some die-hard native or stranger makes a crack about how the mill has taken over and ruined the place. But he talks hard now instead of hitting hard.

In varying ways such urban influences have begun to standardize the life of all mountaineers. Working hours, types of work, wages, clothes, speech, and manners that once were highly individualized are—in some places gradually, in others suddenly—becoming formalized.

There was, for example, Warrior Hull. He was a strong-minded man and able to back up what he said. You didn't have to wait a week to get his opinion, either. Warrior lived by himself in a rough-hewn cabin just outside a small mountain community near Pisgah Forest. He was an artisan in the old sense, and by experience an expert machinist. He put these talents to work at a small tannery in town, where he developed the reputation of being able to fix anything.

In time the tannery was bought by outside interests in the East, and a representative of the company made a visit to survey the investment and make suggestions for improvement.

At one point he came upon Warrior working on a piece of equipment. After a while he said, "Look here, you—you can work more efficiently if you'll get organized better." No comment from Hull. The boss shouted:

"You listen to me! I mean business—I want this done differently."

Hull turned slowly, picked up a monkey wrench, and said:

"You git yore carcass outa here and stop a-dickertatin' to me—I'll bust yore head with this here monkey wranch."

The gentleman withdrew and Hull went back to work.

There are bigger plants in Hull's town now. The population has doubled, from 3,500 to 7,000 or more, and two big mills dominate the community. Warrior Hull's type does not work for either one of them, so far as I can tell. The current residents of the town are a different breed entirely. Thirty years ago there were many Warrior Hulls, and today there are none, except those who have escaped further into the hills.

Warrior Hull is dead now. The shack he lived in, where I spent many a cold winter night sleeping in front of his open fireplace, was knocked down by a bulldozer. Over the top of Hull's way of life runs a new superhighway. . . .

The informal way of life has given way to formal organization. The social and civic activities are carried on by Rotary, Kiwanis, and Lions clubs which promote civic improvement —such as bigger and better highways into the towns and larger attractions for tourists.

Recreational activities of the old type like berry picking, mountain fox hunting, and folk dancing have also been disappearing under the onslaught of spectator sports. High-school football games on lighted fields, "huddle queen" contests, and folk festivals with imported rock-and-roll guitar players have crowded out many of the old-time street dances, informal hoedowns, and singing conventions which once were the major recreational outlets. Now kids sport Elvis Presley haircuts, talk bop slang, and dress "sharp." Their mothers belong to women's clubs.

The physical face of the communities in this region is changing, too. The kind of cabin Warrior Hull built has been replaced by rows of little white houses from Asheville to Toxaway. There is a developing sameness about everything, including the manicured camping sites for tourists, with neat piles of wood cut to the proper length for the outdoor grills. A few pure specimens like the McCalls remain. In another generation their type will disappear forever. Such men already are strangers in their own land.

I

A DISAPPEARING BREED

It is sad to realize that that fiercely independent breed, the Southern mountaineer, subject of song, cartoon, and literature throughout the years, is doomed to vanish. The mountain people's very independence will be responsible for their disappearance—for rather than be "beholden" to any source that might give them a chance to retain their independence, they are welcoming the highways, industry, and tourist trade that will eventually rob them of their uniqueness.

When anthropologist Kernodle first visited the Southern highlands in 1938, nearly all the people were extremely independent, as is evident in the actions of Sary Ellison and Turkey Plott. Some twenty years and a number of highways later though, the author found he had to seek out isolated families to find persons who still retained the true mountaineer characteristics.

Because of their isolation, the mountain people had continued to live, as the centuries went by, much the same as the early American pioneer lived. Do you think it was also characteristically "American" for them to become excited when "progress" finally began reaching them in the form of highways and industry? Discuss whether you think America has gained or lost by modernizing the mountain communities.

II

IMPLICATIONS

Discuss whether you believe the author implies all of the following:

1. Cartoon characters such as Snuffy Smith and Li'l Abner are accurate representatives of the Southern mountaineer.

2. Isolation brings serenity.

3. Being an individualist means doing what seems right and natural to you without worry about what the results might be.

4. The true mountaineer is a character to be greatly admired.

III

TECHNIQUES

Tone

Make a list of adjectives that Kernodle uses to describe the Southern mountaineer. How does this help you describe Kernodle's tone—his attitude toward his subject?

Is that attitude wholly positive? If not, what incidents, descriptions, etc., serve to modify it and make it less positive?

We have pointed out that tone also describes the writer's attitude toward the reader. Now, it is clear that Kernodle has relatively little sympathy for the life-style that is destroying the ways of the mountain people. Yet most of his readers no doubt live that way of life. In short, he is criticizing *us*; his attitude toward his readers is unfriendly.

At times, Kernodle even seems *hostile* toward some of us, as when he speaks of "Rotary, Kiwanis, and Lions clubs which promote civic improvement—such as bigger and better highways into the towns and larger attractions for tourists." How do you react toward such criticism, especially if you have a parent who belongs to a Rotary, Kiwanis, or Lions club?

What other examples can you find to show Kernodle's negative attitude toward his readers? Does he risk losing our sympathy for his positive point of view toward the mountaineer by treating us in this way? If he does not, how does he avoid doing so?

Selection of Significant Detail

Be prepared to compare and discuss with your classmates your answers to the following questions.

1. Notice that John McCall, who is seventy-three years old, is referred to by the mountain people as "*Young* John McCall." What insight does the inclusion of this detail give the reader into mountaineer character?

2. If writers are going to win readers over to their point of view, one of the things they must do is convince us that they speak about their subject with authority. Cite two or three significant incidents or details from "Last of the Rugged Individualists" that convince you that Wayne Kernodle is an authority on the Southern mountaineer.

3. Details such as Kernodle's use of mountaineer dialect lend authenticity to his portrait and also help bring his characters alive for the reader. (For an extended illustration of that dialect, see the speech on page 138, beginning, "This painter used that aire place up thar.") There is a danger, however, that some readers will consider the characters ignorant because of their strange manners of speech or pronunciation.

A good illustration would be Sary's word, "Hilter," which is "Hitler" (the dictatorial leader of Nazi Germany) with the middle consonants transposed. How does this detail affect you? If you feel that her mispronunciation does not reveal ignorance, what does it reveal?

4. The most significant position in a piece of writing is the end. Read Kernodle's last sentence again. Why would you agree or disagree that this was a good place for him to put that sentence?

5. When we skim something, we are primarily looking for main ideas; we are willing to ignore details. Someone who skimmed "Last of the Rugged Individualists" might have summed it up as follows: "The forces of modernization are destroying the last vestiges of rugged individualism in America, and this is a pity." What would such a reader have lost? In other words, what in your view is the value of significant details?

One of the most widely read books of recent years is
Harper Lee's Pulitzer Prize-winning novel, *To Kill a Mockingbird*,
from which the following selection is taken. Though there are
many reasons for the book's immense popularity, one of the main ones
is the independent spirit of the central character,
Atticus Finch.
Although our selection is Chapter 10 of the novel,
it is a self-contained story and needs little introduction.
The tale is set in Maycomb, a small Alabama town. The narrator is
Atticus's daughter, Scout (Jean Louise) Finch, who is about eight
when this episode occurs. Her brother, Jem, an important character
in this episode, is four years older. Most of the other characters
are neighbors of the Finches; Calpurnia is their maid.

FROM

To Kill a Mockingbird

HARPER LEE

CHAPTER 10

Atticus was feeble: he was nearly fifty. When Jem and I asked him why he was so old, he said he got started late, which we felt reflected upon his abilities and manliness. He was much older than the parents of our school contemporaries, and there was nothing Jem or I could say about him when our classmates said, "*My* father—"

Jem was football crazy. Atticus was never too tired to play keep-away, but when Jem wanted to tackle him Atticus would say, "I'm too old for that, son."

Our father didn't do anything. He worked in an office, not in a drugstore. Atticus did not drive a dump-truck for the county, he was not the sheriff, he did not farm, work in a garage, or do anything that could possibly arouse the admiration of anyone.

Besides that, he wore glasses. He was nearly blind in his left eye, and said left eyes were the tribal curse of the Finches. Whenever he wanted to see something well, he turned his head and looked from his right eye.

He did not do the things our schoolmates' fathers did: he never went hunting, he did not play poker or fish or drink or smoke. He sat in the livingroom and read.

With these attributes, however, he would not remain as inconspicuous as we wished him to: that year, the school buzzed with talk about him defending Tom Robinson, none of which was complimentary. After my bout with Cecil Jacobs when I committed myself to a policy of cowardice, word got around that Scout Finch wouldn't fight any more, her daddy wouldn't let her. This was not entirely correct: I wouldn't fight publicly for Atticus, but the family was private ground. I would fight anyone from a third cousin upwards tooth and nail. Francis Hancock, for example, knew that.

When he gave us our air-rifles Atticus wouldn't teach us to shoot. Uncle Jack instructed us in the rudiments thereof; he said Atticus wasn't interested in guns. Atticus said to Jem one day, "I'd rather you shot at tin cans in the back yard, but I know you'll go after birds. Shoot all the bluejays you want, if you can hit 'em, but remember it's a sin to kill a mockingbird."

From *To Kill a Mockingbird* by Harper Lee. Copyright © 1960 by Harper Lee. Published by J. B. Lippincott Company.

That was the only time I ever heard Atticus say it was a sin to do something, and I asked Miss Maudie about it.

"Your father's right," she said. "Mockingbirds don't do one thing but make music for us to enjoy. They don't eat up people's gardens, don't nest in corncribs, they don't do one thing but sing their hearts out for us. That's why it's a sin to kill a mockingbird."

"Miss Maudie, this is an old neighborhood, ain't it?"

"Been here longer than the town."

"Nome, I mean the folks on our street are all old. Jem and me's the only children around here. Mrs. Dubose is close on to a hundred and Miss Rachel's old and so are you and Atticus."

"I don't call fifty very old," said Miss Maudie tartly. "Not being wheeled around yet, am I? Neither's your father. But I must say Providence was kind enough to burn down that old mausoleum of mine, I'm too old to keep it up—maybe you're right, Jean Louise, this is a settled neighborhood. You've never been around young folks much, have you?"

"Yessum, at school."

"I mean young grown-ups. You're lucky, you know. You and Jem have the benefit of your father's age. If your father was thirty you'd find life quite different."

"I sure would. Atticus can't do anything. . . ."

"You'd be surprised," said Miss Maudie. "There's life in him yet."

"What can he do?"

"Well, he can make somebody's will so airtight can't anybody meddle with it."

"Shoot . . ."

"Well, did you know he's the best checkerplayer in this town? Why, down at the Landing when we were coming up, Atticus Finch could beat everybody on both sides of the river."

"Good heavens, Miss Maudie, Jem and me beat him all the time."

"It's about time you found out it's because he lets you. Did you know he can play a Jew's Harp?"

This modest accomplishment served to make me even more ashamed of him.

"*Well . . .*" she said.

"Well, what, Miss Maudie?"

"Well nothing. Nothing—it seems with all that you'd be proud of him. Can't everybody play a Jew's Harp. Now keep out of the way of the carpenters. You'd better go home, I'll be in my azaleas and can't watch you. Plank might hit you."

I went to the back yard and found Jem plugging away at a tin can, which seemed stupid with all the bluejays around. I returned to the front yard and busied myself for two hours erecting a complicated breastworks at the side of the porch, consisting of a tire, an orange crate, the laundry hamper, the porch chairs, and a small U.S. flag Jem gave me from a popcorn box.

When Atticus came home to dinner he found me crouched down aiming across the street. "What are you shooting at?"

"Miss Maudie's rear end."

Atticus turned and saw my generous target bending over her bushes. He pushed his hat to the back of his head and crossed the street. "Maudie," he called, "I thought I'd better warn you. You're in considerable peril."

Miss Maudie straightened up and looked toward me. She said, "Atticus, you are a devil from hell."

When Atticus returned he told me to break camp. "Don't you ever let me catch you pointing that gun at anybody again," he said.

I wished my father was a devil from hell. I sounded out Calpurnia on the subject. "Mr. Finch? Why, he can do lots of things."

"Like what?" I asked.

Calpurnia scratched her head. "Well, I don't rightly know," she said.

Jem underlined it when he asked Atticus if he was going out for the Methodists and Atticus said he'd break his neck if he did, he was just too old for that sort of thing. The Methodists were trying to pay off their church mortgage, and had challenged the Baptists to a game of touch football. Everybody in town's father was playing, it seemed, except Atticus. Jem said he didn't even want to go, but he was unable to resist football in any form, and he stood gloomily on the sidelines with Atticus and me watching Cecil Jacobs's father make touchdowns for the Baptists.

One Saturday Jem and I decided to go exploring with our air-rifles to see if we could find a rabbit or a squirrel. We had gone about five hundred yards beyond the Radley Place when I noticed Jem squinting at something down the street. He had turned his head to one side and was looking out of the corners of his eyes.

"Whatcha looking at?"

"That old dog down yonder," he said.

"That's old Tim Johnson, ain't it?"

"Yeah."

Tim Johnson was the property of Mr. Harry Johnson who drove the Mobile bus and lived on the southern edge of town. Tim was a liver-colored bird dog, the pet of Maycomb.

"What's he doing?"

"I don't know, Scout. We better go home."

"Aw Jem, it's February."

"I don't care, I'm gonna tell Cal."

We raced home and ran to the kitchen.

"Cal," said Jem, "can you come down the sidewalk a minute?"

"What for, Jem? I can't come down the sidewalk every time you want me."

"There's somethin' wrong with an old dog down yonder."

Calpurnia sighed. "I can't wrap up any dog's foot now. There's some gauze in the bathroom, go get it and do it yourself."

Jem shook his head. "He's sick, Cal. Something's wrong with him."

"What's he doin', trying to catch his tail?"

"No, he's doin' like this."

Jem gulped like a goldfish, hunched his shoulders and twitched his torso. "He's goin' like that, only not like he means to."

"Are you telling me a story, Jem Finch?" Calpurnia's voice hardened.

"No Cal, I swear I'm not."

"Was he runnin'?"

"No, he's just moseyin' along, so slow you can't hardly tell it. He's comin' this way."

Calpurnia rinsed her hands and followed Jem into the yard. "I don't see any dog," she said.

She followed us beyond the Radley Place and looked where Jem pointed. Tim Johnson was not much more than a speck in the distance, but he was closer to us. He walked erratically, as if his right legs were shorter than his left legs. He reminded me of a car stuck in a sandbed.

"He's gone lopsided," said Jem.

Calpurnia stared, then grabbed us by the shoulders and ran us home. She shut the wood door behind us, went to the telephone and shouted, "Gimme Mr. Finch's office!"

"Mr. Finch!" she shouted. "This is Cal. I swear there's a mad dog down the street a piece—he's comin' this way, yes sir, he's—Mr. Finch, I declare he is—old Tim Johnson, yes sir . . . yessir . . . yes—"

She hung up and shook her head when we tried to ask her what Atticus had said. She rattled the telephone hook and said, "Miss Eula May—now ma'am, I'm through talkin' to Mr. Finch, please don't connect me no more—listen, Miss Eula May, can you call Miss Rachel and Miss Stephanie Crawford and whoever's got a phone on this street and tell 'em a mad dog's comin'? Please ma'am!"

Calpurnia listened. "I know it's February, Miss Eula May, but I know a mad dog when I see one. Please ma'am hurry!"

Calpurnia asked Jem, "Radleys got a phone?"

Jem looked in the book and said no. "They won't come out anyway, Cal."

"I don't care, I'm gonna tell 'em."

She ran to the front porch, Jem and I at her heels. "You stay in that house!" she yelled.

Calpurnia's message had been received by the neighborhood. Every wood door within our range of vision was closed tight. We saw no trace of Tim Johnson. We watched Calpurnia running toward the Radley Place, holding her skirt and apron above her knees. She went up to the front steps and banged on the door. She got no answer, and she shouted, "Mr. Nathan,

Mr. Arthur, mad dog's comin'! Mad dog's comin'!"

"She's supposed to go around in back," I said.

Jem shook his head. "Don't make any difference now," he said.

Calpurnia pounded on the door in vain. No one acknowledged her warning; no one seemed to have heard it.

As Calpurnia sprinted to the back porch a black Ford swung into the driveway. Atticus and Mr. Heck Tate got out.

Mr. Heck Tate was the sheriff of Maycomb County. He was as tall as Atticus, but thinner. He was long-nosed, wore boots with shiny metal eye-holes, boot pants and a lumber jacket. His belt had a row of bullets sticking in it. He carried a heavy rifle. When he and Atticus reached the porch, Jem opened the door.

"Stay inside, son," said Atticus. "Where is he, Cal?"

"He oughta be here by now," said Calpurnia, pointing down the street.

"Not runnin', is he?" asked Mr. Tate.

"Naw sir, he's in the twitchin' stage, Mr. Heck."

"Should we go after him, Heck?" asked Atticus.

"We better wait, Mr. Finch. They usually go in a straight line, but you never can tell. He might follow the curve—hope he does or he'll go straight in the Radley back yard. Let's wait a minute."

"Don't think he'll get in the Radley yard," said Atticus. "Fence'll stop him. He'll probably follow the road. . . ."

I thought mad dogs foamed at the mouth, galloped, leaped and lunged at throats, and I thought they did it in August. Had Tim Johnson behaved thus, I would have been less frightened.

Nothing is more deadly than a deserted, waiting street. The trees were still, the mockingbirds were silent, the carpenters at Miss Maudie's house had vanished. I heard Mr. Tate sniff, then blow his nose. I saw him shift his gun to the crook of his arm. I saw Miss Stephanie Crawford's face framed in the glass window of her front door. Miss Maudie appeared and stood beside her. Atticus put his foot on the rung of a chair and rubbed his hand slowly down the side of his thigh.

"There he is," he said softly.

Tim Johnson came into sight, walking dazedly in the inner rim of the curve parallel to the Radley house.

"Look at him," whispered Jem. "Mr. Heck said they walked in a straight line. He can't even stay in the road."

"He looks more sick than anything," I said.

"Let anything get in front of him and he'll come straight at it."

Mr. Tate put his hand to his forehead and leaned forward. "He's got it all right, Mr. Finch."

Tim Johnson was advancing at a snail's pace, but he was not playing or sniffing at foliage: he seemed dedicated to one course and motivated by an invisible force that was inching him toward us. We could see him shiver like a horse shedding flies; his jaw opened and shut; he was alist, but he was being pulled gradually toward us.

"He's lookin' for a place to die," said Jem.

Mr. Tate turned around. "He's far from dead, Jem, he hasn't got started yet."

Tim Johnson reached the side street that ran in front of the Radley Place, and what remained of his poor mind made him pause and seem to consider which road he would take. He made a few hesitant steps and stopped in front of the Radley gate; then he tried to turn around, but was having difficulty.

Atticus said, "He's within range, Heck. You better get him before he goes down the side street—Lord knows who's around the corner. Go inside, Cal."

Calpurnia opened the screen door, latched it behind her, then unlatched it and held onto the hook. She tried to block Jem and me with her body, but we looked out from beneath her arms.

"Take him, Mr. Finch." Mr. Tate handed the rifle to Atticus; Jem and I nearly fainted.

"Don't waste time, Heck," said Atticus. "Go on."

"Mr. Finch, this is a one-shot job."

Atticus shook his head vehemently: "Don't just stand there, Heck! He won't wait all day for you—"

"For Pete's sake, Mr. Finch, look where he is! Miss and you'll go straight into the Radley house! I can't shoot that well and you know it!"

"I haven't shot a gun in thirty years—"

Mr. Tate almost threw the rifle at Atticus. "I'd feel mighty comfortable if you did now," he said.

In a fog, Jem and I watched our father take the gun and walk out into the middle of the street. He walked quickly, but I thought he moved like an underwater swimmer: time had slowed to a nauseating crawl.

When Atticus raised his glasses Calpurnia murmured, "Sweet Jesus help him," and put her hands to her cheeks.

Atticus pushed his glasses to his forehead; they slipped down, and he dropped them in the street. In the silence, I heard them crack. Atticus rubbed his eyes and chin; we saw him blink hard.

In front of the Radley gate, Tim Johnson had made up what was left of his mind. He had finally turned himself around, to pursue his original course up our street. He made two steps forward, then stopped and raised his head. We saw his body go rigid.

With movements so swift they seemed simultaneous, Atticus's hand yanked a ball-tipped lever as he brought the gun to his shoulder.

The rifle cracked. Tim Johnson leaped, flopped over and crumpled on the sidewalk in a brown-and-white heap. He didn't know what hit him.

Mr. Tate jumped off the porch and ran to the Radley Place. He stopped in front of the dog, squatted, turned around and tapped his finger on his forehead above his left eye. "You were a little to the right, Mr. Finch," he called.

"Always was," answered Atticus. "If I had my 'druthers I'd take a shotgun."

He stooped and picked up his glasses, ground the broken lenses to powder under his heel, and went to Mr. Tate and stood looking down at Tim Johnson.

Doors opened one by one, and the neighborhood slowly came alive. Miss Maudie walked down the steps with Miss Stephanie Crawford.

Jem was paralyzed. I pinched him to get him moving, but when Atticus saw us coming he called, "Stay where you are."

When Mr. Tate and Atticus returned to the yard, Mr. Tate was smiling. "I'll have Zeebo collect him," he said. "You haven't forgot much, Mr. Finch. They say it never leaves you."

Atticus was silent.

"Atticus?" said Jem.

"Yes?"

"Nothin'."

"I saw that, One-Shot Finch!"

Atticus wheeled around and faced Miss Maudie. They looked at one another without saying anything, and Atticus got into the the sheriff's car. "Come here," he said to Jem. "Don't you go near that dog, you understand? Don't go near him, he's just as dangerous dead as alive."

"Yes sir," said Jem. "Atticus—"

"What, son?"

"Nothing."

"What's the matter with you, boy, can't you talk?" said Mr. Tate, grinning at Jem. "Didn't you know your daddy's—"

"Hush, Heck," said Atticus, "let's go back to town."

When they drove away, Jem and I went to Miss Stephanie's front steps. We sat waiting for Zeebo to arrive in the garbage truck.

Jem sat in numb confusion, and Miss Stephanie said, "Uh, uh, uh, who'da thought of a mad dog in February? Maybe he wasn't mad, maybe he was just crazy. I'd hate to see Harry Johnson's face when he gets in from the Mobile run and finds Atticus Finch's shot his dog. Bet he was just full of fleas from somewhere—"

Miss Maudie said Miss Stephanie'd be singing a different tune if Tim Johnson was still coming up the street, that they'd find out soon enough, they'd send his head to Montgomery.

Jem became vaguely articulate: " 'd you see him, Scout? 'd you see him just standin' there? . . . 'n' all of a sudden he just relaxed all over, an' it looked like that gun was a part of him . . . an' he did it so quick, like . . . I hafta aim for ten minutes 'fore I can hit somethin'. . . ."

Miss Maudie grinned wickedly. "Well now, Miss Jean Louise," she said, "still think your father can't do anything? Still ashamed of him?"

"Nome," I said meekly.

"Forgot to tell you the other day that besides playing the Jew's Harp, Atticus Finch was the deadest shot in Maycomb County in his time."

"Dead shot . . ." echoed Jem.

"That's what I said, Jem Finch. Guess you'll change *your* tune now. The very idea, didn't you know his nickname was Ol' One-Shot when he was a boy? Why, down at the Landing when he was coming up, if he shot fifteen times and hit fourteen doves he'd complain about wasting ammunition."

"He never said anything about that," Jem muttered.

"Never said anything about it, did he?"

"No ma'am."

"Wonder why he never goes huntin' now," I said.

"Maybe I can tell you," said Miss Maudie. "If your father's anything, he's civilized in his heart. Marksmanship's a gift of God, a talent—oh, you have to practice to make it perfect, but shootin's different from playing the piano or the like. I think maybe he put his gun down when he realized that God had given him an unfair advantage over most living things. I guess he decided he wouldn't shoot till he had to, and he had to today."

"Looks like he'd be proud of it," I said.

"People in their right minds never take pride in their talents," said Miss Maudie.

We saw Zeebo drive up. He took a pitchfork from the back of the garbage truck and gingerly lifted Tim Johnson. He pitched the dog onto the truck, then poured something from a gallon jug on and around the spot where Tim fell. "Don't yawl come over here for a while," he called.

When we went home I told Jem we'd really have something to talk about at school on Monday. Jem turned on me.

"Don't say anything about it, Scout," he said.

"What? I certainly am. Ain't everybody's daddy the deadest shot in Maycomb County."

Jem said, "I reckon if he'd wanted us to know it, he'da told us. If he was proud of it, he'da told us."

"Maybe it just slipped his mind," I said.

"Naw, Scout, it's something you wouldn't understand. Atticus is real old, but I wouldn't care if he couldn't do anything—I wouldn't care if he couldn't do a blessed thing."

Jem picked up a rock and threw it jubilantly at the carhouse. Running after it, he called back: "Atticus is a gentleman, just like me!"

I

THE GENTLEMAN

Jem and Scout want very much to be able to think of their father as a hero. When he does perform a heroic act, the emotions of the children shift dramatically from disappointment with their father to overwhelming admiration. Yet if the need had not risen, it is doubtful that Atticus would have revealed his talent to his children even though he knew they wanted him to be like other fathers. Instead, he chose to follow his own convictions, to be true to himself. In so doing, Atticus taught Jem and Scout a far greater lesson than he could as a mere sharpshooting hero.

II

IMPLICATIONS

Discuss each of the following propositions related to this selection.

1. Youngsters want their fathers to be heroic mainly so that they will not be looked down on by other children in the school or neighborhood.

2. Atticus appeals to hero-loving readers largely because of his modesty.

3. When Jem calls his father a gentleman, he is saying, in effect, that he loves and admires him even though Atticus has no special abilities.

4. "People in their right minds never take pride in their talents."

5. The main point of this story is that youngsters want to be able to identify with their fathers.

III

TECHNIQUES

Tone

When writers use a first-person narrator, as does Lee, how can the reader discover the way the author feels about the material? Clearly, we cannot assume that Lee's judgments are identical to those of her young narrator; the author, for example, would not say, "Atticus was feeble"; nor would she agree with that opinion. Yet in spite of the fact that we have mainly to deal with Scout's words and opinions, we do feel that we also know Lee's attitude toward her characters and situations.

One reason why we can judge the author's attitude is that we know it *is* her hand that determines what Scout sees. Lee is the architect here, and we can discover how she feels about the structure she has built by inference from the structure itself. Thus, the very fact that she chose to include this chapter in her novel is evidence of the fact that she feels and wants her readers to feel that Atticus is heroic.

Selection of Significant Detail

1. In a short story, virtually every detail has to be significant, for a short-story writer is committed to brevity. In fact, Edgar Allan Poe once asserted that every *word* should count in a short story. The selection you have just read, however, is part of a novel, a literary form that generally moves at a more leisurely pace than a short story. The novelist can usually afford to include details that a story writer cannot fit in. What are some of those details in this selection?

2. Suppose you were to rewrite this chapter as a short story. What details and incidents would you choose to omit? Would any significant details have to be added?

3. Whether or not a detail is to be counted as "significant" depends largely upon the author's purposes. On the assumption that one of the main purposes of Harper Lee in this chapter is to create a suspenseful situation, discuss what the following details add to the reader's anticipation of possible action: (1) knowledge concerning who the dog is, (2) Calpurnia's conduct when told about the dog, (3) the fact that Atticus broke his glasses.

IV
WORDS

The major dialect areas of the United States reflect the movements of the settlers during the eighteenth and nineteenth centuries. After the Revolutionary War, settlers moved into Kentucky and Tennessee. These lands became crowded and the settlers moved further westward.

The completion of the Erie Canal in 1825 provided access to the midwest. What is now U.S. 40, the National Road, opened the Ohio Valley and even today is a boundary for certain dialect features. By 1840, Illinois, Indiana, Michigan, and Ohio had been settled.

The Southern expansion centered around the Mississippi delta. Defeat of the Creek and Cherokee Indians opened Alabama, Arkansas, and Georgia for further settlement. During the 1840's the West Coast was settled. Later, the railroad made possible the settlement of other areas.

From these settlement patterns emerged three dialect areas: North, South, and Midland. The Northern area includes New England, upstate New York, metropolitan New York, the Hudson Valley, and northern Pennsylvania. The Midland consists of western New Jersey, Delaware, Maryland, central and southern Pennsylvania. The South generally includes Virginia, the Carolinas, Georgia, Florida, and Louisiana. Using state boundaries oversimplifies because dialect areas do not follow state lines.

Although the dialect areas along the coast are somewhat easily identified, the westward movement resulted in overlapping distribution of features. When we compare varieties of American English we find that differences in pronunciation, grammar, and vocabulary do not always occur in combination. Widespread education and mass media of communication have tended to level dialect differences. Nevertheless, you too may be a linguistic geographer by listening to and observing language habits of those about you. Study the following list of regional names for certain common objects.

	Northern	Midland	Southern
container for water	pail	bucket	bucket
small stream	brook	run	bayou
finished siding	clapboard		weather board

Here are additional vocabulary words peculiar to certain regions. Which do you use?

paper bag: sack, poke, tote bag
praying mantis: walking stick, devil's horse
sycamore: buttonwood, cottonball, buttonball, plane tree
chimney: flue, smokestack, funnel
overall: denims, blue jeans, Levi's, overalls

Walt Whitman: Singer of Self

"I celebrate myself, and sing myself,"
so Walt Whitman begins *Leaves of Grass,* and in no other poet
can one find a more precise example of the independent
spirit. Whitman did not just write about this
cornerstone of the American character,
he also lived it. In his work *Leaves of Grass,* it is
impossible to separate the poetry from the man.

In the first of the following two poems
Whitman announces his intention to champion the individual—"The Female equally
with the Male. . . ." In the second he extols the evident
enthusiasm and self-satisfaction of a cross-section of average Americans
as they go about their daily tasks.

One's-Self I Sing

One's-self I sing, a simple separate person,
Yet utter the word Democratic, the word En-Masse.

Of physiology from top to toe I sing,
Not physiognomy[1] alone nor brain alone is worthy for the Muse.[2]
      I say the Form complete is worthier far,
The Female equally with the Male I sing.

Of Life immense in passion, pulse, and power,
Cheerful, for freest action form'd under the laws divine,
The Modern Man I sing.

---

1. **physiognomy**\'fĭ·zē ˄ŏg·nə·mē\ features that reveal character.
2. **Muse,** spirit that inspires poets.

I Hear America Singing

I hear America singing, the varied carols I hear,
Those of mechanics, each one singing his as it should be blithe and strong,
The carpenter singing his as he measures his plank or beam,
The mason singing his as he makes ready for work, or leaves off work,
The boatman singing what belongs to him in his boat, the deck hand singing on the steam-
    boat deck,   5
The shoemaker singing as he sits on his bench, the hatter singing as he stands,
The woodcutter's song, the plowboy's on his way in the morning, or at noon intermission or
    at sundown,
The delicious singing of the mother, or of the young wife at work, or of the girl sewing or
    washing,
Each singing what belongs to him or her and to none else,
The day what belongs to the day—at night the party of young fellows, robust, friendly.   10
Singing with open mouths their strong melodious songs.

In this selection from "By Blue Ontario's Shore,"
Whitman states once again that the unique, independent
individual accounts for America's greatness.

FROM

By Blue Ontario's Shore

It is not the earth, it is not America who is so great,
It is I who am great or to be great, it is you up there, or any one,
It is to walk rapidly through civilizations, governments, theories,
Through poems, pageants, shows, to form individuals.

Underneath all, individuals,   5
I swear nothing is good to me now that ignores individuals,
The American compact[1] is altogether with individuals,
The only government is that which makes minute of[2] individuals,
The whole theory of the universe is directed unerringly to one single individual—namely
    to you. . . .

---

1. **The American compact,** the tie that binds individuals in our state and national system of government.
2. **makes minute of,** takes individuals into careful consideration.

O I see flashing that this America is only you and me, 10
Its power, weapons, testimony, are you and me,
Its crimes, lies, thefts, defections, are you and me,
Its Congress is you and me, the officers, capitols, armies, ships, are you and me,
Its endless gestations of new States are you and me.
Natural and artificial are you and me, 15
Freedom, language, poems, employments, are you and me,
Past, present, future, are you and me.

I dare not shirk any part of myself,
Not any part of America good or bad,
Not to build for that which builds for mankind, 20
Not to balance ranks, complexions, creeds, and the sexes,
Not to justify science nor the march of equality,
Nor to feed the arrogant blood of the brawn beloved of time.

I am for those that have never been mastered,
For men and women whose tempers have never been mastered, 25
For those whom laws, theories, conventions, can never master.

I am for those who walk abreast with the whole earth,
Who inaugurate one to inaugurate all.

I will not be outfaced by irrational things,
I will penetrate what it is in them that is sarcastic upon me, 30
I will make cities and civilizations defer to me,
This is what I have learnt from America—it is the amount, and it I teach again.

These two brief poems are among Whitman's most popular.
They make their points directly and memorably. Written during the Civil War,
they share a religious feeling, a striving of the individual
for understanding and love. The soul, in the vast oceans of space
around it, must seek anchorage somewhere. In the first poem,
Whitman seeks the answer in the "mystical moist night-air"; in the second,
he hopes to learn from the patient spider. Both poems must be read
for what they suggest as well as what they describe.

When I Heard
the Learn'd Astronomer

When I heard the learn'd astronomer,
When the proofs, the figures, were ranged in columns before me,
When I was shown the charts and diagrams, to add, divide, and measure them,
When I sitting heard the astronomer where he lectured with much applause in
        the lecture-room,
How soon unaccountable I became tired and sick,
Till rising and gliding out I wander'd off by myself,
In the mystical moist night-air, and from time to time,
Look'd up in perfect silence at the stars.

A Noiseless Patient Spider

A noiseless patient spider,
I mark'd where on a little promontory[1] it stood isolated,
Mark'd how to explore the vacant vast surrounding,
It launch'd forth filament, filament, filament, out of itself,
Ever unreeling them, ever tirelessly speeding them.   5

And you O my soul where you stand,
Surrounded, detached, in measureless oceans of space,
Ceaselessly musing, venturing, throwing, seeking the spheres to connect them,
Till the bridge you will need be form'd, till the ductile[2] anchor hold,
Till the gossamer[3] thread you fling catch somewhere, O my soul.   10

---

1. **promontory**\ˈprŏ·mən ˈtō·rē\ high point of land projecting outward, usually into the sea.
2. **ductile**\ˈdək·təl\ capable of being drawn out or molded.
3. **gossamer**\ˈgŏ·sə·mər\ fine strands of spider's silk that float in the air or are loosely suspended from something.

IMPLICATIONS

One's-Self I Sing

1. The poet says in the opening lines that he will sing of one self and of all selves simultaneously. Explain this apparent contradiction.

2. List and discuss the other themes about which Whitman promises to sing.

I Hear America Singing

1. Explain how this poem demonstrates Whitman's interest in all kinds of people.

2. Obviously Whitman's intention in the poem is to express in condensed form the spirit of America. Discuss whether you believe he was being realistic or romantic; that is, whether all people then actually lived this happily or whether the poet is simply giving an ideal picture.

By Blue Ontario's Shore

1. What does the poet say makes for the greatness of America?

2. What does Whitman mean when he writes of balancing "ranks, complexions, creeds, and sexes"?

When I Heard the Learn'd Astronomer

1. Whitman looks in two directions in this poem and chooses one as the shorter road to an understanding of God and nature. How would you identify these two outlooks?

2. What is the cumulative effect of words like "proofs," "figures," "charts," "diagrams"?

3. What connection is there between "applause" in line 4 and "accountable" in line 5?

4. Why is the night air "mystical" and what is implied in this word? How is the implication reinforced in the "perfect silence" of the last line?

A Noiseless Patient Spider

1. As in "When I Heard the Learn'd Astronomer," Whitman divides this brief poem between two subjects, only here it is a comparison between the spider and the poet's soul, dissimilar though they may seem at first. What are the attributes he admires in the spider?

2. Does the repetition of the word "filament" help to underscore these attributes? Note that the filament comes "out of itself," meaning out of the

spider's body. Why is this important in the next stanza?

3. The soul in vast oceans of space is a familiar poetic way of speaking of the spirit "surrounded" by the body yet "living" in another element. How do the verbs "musing, venturing, throwing" connect the soul and the spider?

4. What sort of thread is a "gossamer" thread? Does the poet succeed in applying it to both the spider and the soul?

TECHNIQUES
Free Verse

When we speak of the rhythm of a line of poetry or prose, we mean the natural rise and fall of language in wavelike motion. By meter we mean carefully arranged rhythm, with the accents spaced in patterned intervals of time. Poets such as Poe, Longfellow, and Lowell used meter to limit their lines. "I lift mine eyes and all the windows blaze" is a strictly ordered five-beat line; Longfellow follows it with thirteen other five-beat lines to form a sonnet. His rhyme scheme is equally patterned, thus adding a further limit to the shape of the poem.

Whitman wished to forsake meter and rhyme. He writes what we now call *free verse;* though some poets feel free verse is not verse at all, since its only distinction from rhythmical prose is the arrangement into lines, each one usually capitalized. Whitman, however, liked the liberation of free verse. It gave him more scope, more expansiveness, and he never worried about metrical count. That is not to say he writes in paragraphs or rejects any controls that would give his stanzas unity.

You may find Whitman's verse more difficult to analyze than Longfellow's sonnets, but look closely at his poems to see if he does not use some of these devices to give his work controlling form:

a. End-stopped lines. The end of the line corresponds with the natural pause in speech. Invariably the line ends with a mark of punctuation.

b. Parallel constructions. Whole phrases or a single word are repeated at the beginning of each line. Occasionally Whitman merely repeats a grammatical form in parallel: noun-verb, or noun-verb-object.

c. Single-sentence stanzas.

d. Repetition.

e. Recurring symbols.

f. Alliteration (repetition of initial consonants) and assonance (repetition of vowel sounds).

Whitman's Song

Five poems are only a small sampling of Whitman's work but these five serve well to illustrate Whitman's main themes and various facets of his art. To the following list, a mere beginning, add your own reactions to reading Whitman, the ideas you take away from his poems. Are you willing to accept these three?

1. America is crowds at the same time it is single individuals. The poet must see and know both.

2. The poet must write for the modern world.

3. What is of most lasting worth is the individual.

Lincoln was so clearly one of the people, so clearly one of us,
that we may wonder how it was that he accomplished so much and we
so little. Baffled by his humility and simplicity, we may ask whether,
perhaps, he was one of those who have greatness thrust upon them; whether,
if it had not been for such events as the Civil War and the assassination,
he might have been just another president. To put it simply, was Lincoln
a shaper of events, or was he shaped by them? The following account
should give some basis for answering this question. It is the last chapter
of Paul Horgan's *Citizen of New Salem,* a biographical sketch which traces Lincoln's
transformation from a twenty-one-year-old flatboatman to a twenty-eight-year-old
State Assemblyman and counselor-at-law. The transformation took place
in the small frontier town of New Salem, Illinois.

Lincoln Becomes a Lawyer

PAUL HORGAN

If you are resolutely determined to make a lawyer of yourself, the thing is more than half-done already. . . .

What if there was no one at New Salem[1] to teach him the law—no one to "read with," as he said? If a man must do it alone, he could do so. The main thing was to get the necessary books and read them, and study their principal features. What did it matter if New Salem was a small town which "never had three hundred people living in it?" All that mattered were the books and his capacity for understanding them. These would be "just the same" wherever he might be. Surely his own resolution to succeed must be "more important than any other one thing?"

The stage fare from New Salem to Springfield was a dollar and a half. The assemblyman rode in a farmer's wagon or walked to Springfield to borrow law books from Attorney Stuart. He went more than once, and one day at an auction he bought a copy of Blackstone's *Commentaries on the Common Law.* Back home it was now the law books—Chitty or Blackstone[2] —which he took everywhere with him. The neighbors saw him and remembered how he studied wherever he could—"in some nook in a store," or at "the foot of a hay-stack," or "sometimes lying on his back, putting his feet up the tree. . . ." They were used to him and let him be, though to an occasional observer he was a sight. Russell Godbey, the farmer, for whom he did odd jobs, found him one day sitting barefoot at the top of a woodpile with a book. It might seem a curious thing for a farm hand to be doing, and the farmer asked,

"What are you reading?"

"I am not reading," replied the farm hand, "I am studying."

"Studying what?"

"Law, sir," said the farm hand with emphasis. Russell Godbey said it was really too much for him, as he looked at the law student, "sitting there proud as Cicero." Going on his way,

---

1. **New Salem,** village in central Illinois, now reconstructed and located on the outskirts of Springfield.
2. **Chitty or Blackstone.** Joseph Chitty, author of *Chitty on Contracts;* Sir William Blackstone, author of *Commentaries on the Laws of England,* which influenced jurisprudence in United States.

Reprinted by permission of Virginia Rice. Copyright © 1961 by Paul Horgan.

"Great Caesar's ghost!" exploded Mr. Godbey.

During the spring and summer of 1835 New Salem had its own excitements. Samuel Hill built a carder[3] and storehouse for wool. The carding machine was powered from a tread-mill walked by oxen on a tilted wooden wheel with cleats—a late marvel of the mechanic arts. A new sound—the friction of moving wood, the muffled knock of hooves on wood—entered the village day. On August seventeenth at night a tornado came tubing and screaming over the prairie and in its wake Matthew S. Marsh saw fences flat, trees uprooted, and corn beaten down. At daylight he went to put up his fence and saw to his amazement how "two great wolves walked along unconcerned within 50 yards of me." Eight days later at her father's farm northeast of New Salem, after an illness of six weeks, young Anne Rutledge died.

The law student knew her well, as he knew all her family. She was the third of nine children, and as a boarder at her father's New Salem tavern in 1833 he had surely seen her. She was vivacious and pretty, with auburn hair and blue eyes. At quilting bees she was faster than anyone with her needle, and in the other household arts she was accomplished. She would make someone a good wife.

In 1832 she became engaged to a prosperous young farmer and storekeeper who went east to arrange his affairs with a promise to return and marry Miss Rutledge. Time passed while his letters dwindled and finally ceased. She grieved. The law student saw her so, and certain neighbors wondered if he might be ready to fall in love. A few became sure for all their lives that he courted her and that she was prepared to accept him. She hesitated, but at last wrote to break her engagement. No answer came. Torn between desires, she fell ill and within a few weeks was dying of fever. One of her brothers said she kept asking for the law student and at the last she was allowed to be alone with him. A few days later she lost consciousness and on August twenty-fifth she died. They buried her in Concord graveyard.

New Salem sorrowed for Anne. Some said long afterward that the law student sorrowed more than anyone—that once again they feared for his reason. Slicky Greene reported that when the snows or rains fell, the law student was filled with "indescribable grief" at the thought of how they fell on her small resting place in the country graveyard. His inclination to occasional low spirits seemed to be increased by her death. She used to sing hymns to him. The last one she ever sang was "Vain Man, thy fond pursuits forbear." Sometimes, even where advantage lay, human pursuits seemed futile. Where of advantage there was none, depression could the more easily enter a man. "Woefully abstracted," said a friend, the law student would range along the river and into the woods. Neighbors kept an eye on him especially on "damp, stormy days, under the belief that dark and gloomy weather might produce such a depression of spirits as to induce him to take his own life."

It was one thing to be given "the hypo," as he called it, by fugitive annoyances; quite another to be lost to the whole daily world. Finally he was persuaded to stay for a few weeks with the jolly justice of the peace, Judge Bowling Green, beyond the little hills north of New Salem. Judge Green loved to laugh with all his three hundred pounds. The shape of his belly earned him the nickname of "Pot." He was good for the law student. The ordinary matters of life proceeded. The law student tended the post office, though someone complained that he neglected his duties at this time. He studied. He surveyed a ten-acre lot of timber. He wrote to the Governor of Illinois to endorse an applicant for the post of public auditor. On December seventh, 1835, he was counted present at the opening of a special session of the Assembly in Vandalia.[4] On March twenty-fourth, 1836, his name was entered on the record of the Sangamon[5] Circuit

---

3. **carder,** place for combing and cleansing wool.
4. **Vandalia**\văn ▲dā·lyə\ city in south-central Illinois; capital of Illinois 1820–36.
5. **Sangamon**\▲săŋ·gă·mən\ county in central Illinois.

Court as a man of good moral character. This was the first of three steps leading to the license to practice law. The law student was coming back to himself. Years afterward, Isaac Cogsdale, formerly of New Salem, said he heard him say of Anne Rutledge, "I loved her dearly . . ."

Throughout the spring he was active as deputy surveyor, but in May he lost his other position when the post office of New Salem was discontinued by the government. The village had ceased to grow—had even begun to decline. Families moved away. A number of them founded the town of Petersburg which the deputy surveyor had laid out in February. Perhaps the future lay elsewhere.

A daguerrotype of Lincoln taken when he was thirty-six.

In early summer an old excitement came back in the air, for it was again a campaign year, and the assemblyman announced his stand for reëlection on June thirteenth. "All," he said, should share the privileges of the government "who assist in bearing its burthens." He believed all whites who bore arms and paid taxes should vote, not excluding females—though he could not have imagined women

in the army. He declared further that he went for "distributing the proceeds of the sales of the public lands to the several states."

From July fourth, when the campaign opened at Petersburg, to the thirtieth, when it ended at Springfield two days before the election, the candidate toured the district with his rivals. They came to meetings on horseback, riding into a grove in the forenoon, when the opposing candidates took turns speaking until all were done. If a fight broke out that seemed to depart from fair play, the tall candidate from New Salem stepped in to shake the fighters apart. He spoke in groves and on farms, supporting the Whig position. On July twenty-ninth he spoke at the farm of Isaac Spear, six miles southeast of Springfield, where the campaign would wind up.

Moving on, he rode past the new house of old George Forquer, who was running against him. On top of the house—it was regarded as the finest house in Springfield—he saw, for the first time, a lightning rod.

What a contraption. He never saw the like. It led him to speculate about electrical conduction. It gave him thoughts about the owner.

George Forquer had until recently been a Whig himself, but now he was running as a Democrat, and what was more, as a new Democrat who had been given the post of register of the Land Office at a fine salary—three thousand dollars a year. No wonder he could build a new frame house with a lightning rod on top. It was enough to give a man the hypo. The New Salem candidate rode on to Springfield.

There the next day he took his turn and made his speech. He was the last. When he was done, the crowd began to go. Democratic Land Office Register George Forquer rose to detain the crowd and they turned back to listen.

He was sorry, he said, but of his opponent, who had just spoken, he must say that "the young man would have to be taken down."

The Democrat, as an elderly and prominent man, had much to say and he said it at length, and with every air of superiority. The New Salem candidate stood aside, listening intently and with growing excitement. His chance for rebuttal came, and he took the platform again, made another speech, and ended with this:

"Mr. Forquer commenced his speech by announcing that the young man would have to be taken down. It is for you, citizens, not for me to say whether I am up or down. The gentleman has seen fit to allude to my being a young man; but he forgets that I am older in years than I am in the tricks and trades of politicians. I desire to live, and I desire place and distinction; but I would rather die now, than, like the gentleman, live to see the day that I would change my politics for an office worth three thousand dollars a year, and then feel compelled to erect a lightning rod to protect a guilty conscience from an offended God."

"Wonderful," said a witness, the effect of this reply was wonderful, something he would never forget. The public was captivated by it. Two days later, on August first, the young man from New Salem—he was twenty-seven—was reëlected by the highest vote out of the field of seventeen candidates. On December fifth, then, he was present when the Tenth General Assembly of Illinois met in Vandalia.

He came there with his desired goal more clearly in sight, for on September ninth he had applied for a license to practice law in all the courts of the state, and this had been granted to him on the same day. It was the second official step which would lead him to the work he wanted. Only one more remained. But before he could take it, he must serve the Assembly in his elected duty. Because of their height, he and the other eight members of the Sangamon delegation were nicknamed the Long Nine.

In his current term, as in his previous one, the assemblyman met with a wide range of affairs in the bills proposed, the debates which resulted, the hearings which were required, and the disposals made. All these reflected the needs and aspirations, the concerns and the natures of the men and women whose lives they sought to govern for the better.

The assemblyman took part in the vote on such matters as the works of human justice and dignity which appeared in bills on the establishment of circuit courts, and on the powers of justices of the peace, and on legislative procedures, and on the delineation of voting districts and precincts. With his fellow members he voted on the election of the United States Senator. He considered as a committee member the problems inseparable from the disposition of public monies, and with scarcely a half-cent piece in his pocket, he voted on questions of taxation, of banking, and of incorporation of insurance companies and railroads. The Assembly was much occupied with the development of travel and the needs of people coming and going. He considered and helped to decide upon proposals dealing with public roads, toll bridges, canals, and river navigation. Education was public business, and the assemblyman worked on schools in general and schools for orphans. Much of the common concern had to do with the homely life of work, household and sustenance. He was on the record of legislation covering cattle marks and brands, the regulation of mills and millers, the "Little Bull Law" which meant to govern breeding of cattle but which was repealed as inequitable, the killing of wolves and the determination of bounties therefore, and—an act which reflected with intimacy and compassion the poverty, the need and the terms of the farmer's life—a bill to declare exempt from legal attachment one work horse or a yoke of oxen, so that daily work might continue. The Assembly took account of human trouble, and the assemblyman acted with his associates on bills looking to the relief of debtors, and bills against gaming, and bills regulating the penitentiary.

It was a broad experience of man and man's ways of constantly reshaping himself as a social being. In his first term the assemblyman had been "silent, observant, studious," as a contemporary said. In the new term, he was, of those his own age and length of service, "the smartest parliamentarian and cunningest 'logroller.'" These knacks of his enlivened his efforts in the second term to secure the removal of the state capital from Vandalia. Many towns were after the prize, but Springfield was the leader. The assemblyman led the fight and on the last day of February, 1837, he saw the bill he backed win the approval of the majority. On March first he saw another achievement when in the office of the clerk of the Supreme Court of Illinois his name was entered upon the roll of attorneys as a member of the State Bar. It was the third and final qualification toward which he had worked.

Before the term was over on March sixth, the assemblyman, with Dan Stone, his fellow townsman, filed dissent from a resolution adopted by the House. The House resolution went on record against the abolition of slavery. The Sangamon assemblyman and his colleague made a joint statement saying that "the institution of slavery is founded on both injustice and bad policy." In the temper of the time, however, they added that "the promulgation of abolition doctrines tends rather to increase than abate its evils." With this moral act, the assemblyman was ready for the adjournment of the House on March sixth.

During this term his self-image found words; for he told Joshua Fry Speed of Springfield that he aimed—it could only be the pinnacle of fame —he aimed at the "great distinction" of being known as "the DeWitt Clinton of Illinois." Governor Clinton of New York was dead since 1828, but he was remembered. Six feet tall, of noble proportions, he was known as "Magnus Apollo." Like the assemblyman, he had started his career in the state legislature. He had gone on to become United States senator, mayor of New York City, governor of New York State, father of the Erie Canal, and a champion of public education. Joshua Speed could be excused if he smiled kindly at the hope of anyone to equal such an illustrious record. On

March seventh and eighth the assemblyman, in his short clawhammer coat and his hiked up pantaloons, made his way home to New Salem.

He had come there the first time on the heels of a hard winter. This, of 1836–1837, was another such, when weeks of rain left puddles and snow melted to slush. Suddenly one day came a violent freeze and the countryside was fixed in ice. Chickens and geese were frozen fast to the ground. Travellers, caught by the shift of wind which brought the freeze, were endangered, and some died. Washington Crowder, riding to Springfield, was overtaken by the storm. Coming to a store he tried to dismount, but—as a local account of the marvel said—"was unable to dismount, his overcoat holding him as firmly as though it had been made of sheet iron." He called for help. Two men heard him and came out of the store. They tried to lift him down, but his clothes were frozen to the saddle. They loosened the girth and "then carried man and saddle to the fire and thawed them asunder."

Home again in New Salem, the assemblyman contained a new resolve. It would not be long until he should make it known.

New Salem had been his school, his academy, his college. There he had learned how to use language correctly and beautifully; how to speak and debate in public; how to study; how to plan towns; how to write laws by reading law; how to live amidst people and how to respect their common concerns and forgive their uncommon ones. There it was he had left the forest and the river, which had also taught him much, and had found the world. Like all others, he had to find out where to look for it, but it was there to be seen, if he would look, in a hamlet in a wood above a river. In all his young life he had worked to overcome disadvantages, and as they enlarged, so did he, in spirit, patience and strength, among his neighbors of New Salem. They had suffered him when he suffered, and laughed for him when he reached for their funny-bones, and allowed him his hopes, and voted for him when he asked them to. As he was, so had New Salem helped to make him.

On April twelfth the Springfield paper carried an announcement that the assemblyman —once a flatboatman, a store clerk, a militia captain, a candidate, a postmaster, a deputy surveyor, a law student, and now a full attorney at law—would, with J. T. Stuart, "practice conjointly in the courts of this Judicial Circuit Office No. 4 Hoffman's Row upstairs."

The resolve made, it was time to go.

On April fifteenth, 1837, he borrowed from Judge Bowling Green a small pony with a worn-out saddle. In the saddle bags he put his copy of Blackstone, a copy of the compiled laws of Illinois for 1833, three volumes of session laws, two small miscellaneous books, and some underclothes. When he mounted the pony his long legs nearly reached the ground. His fortune consisted of about seven dollars in his pocket. A friend declared that "superficially he seemed like a farm hand in search of employment." So it was he rode off to Springfield, leaving New Salem which, in two years, like the store he had once owned with William Berry, would "wink out."

Springfield numbered fewer than a thousand people but it was a lively town and promised, as the new state capital, to be livelier, after the State House was built. Business houses defined the public square, which like all the streets was dust in summer and thick with mud in winter. Street crossings consisted of slabs of wood. A few small brick buildings contained stores and offices, which were furnished with the barest conveniences. Six stores, a merchant's mill for custom work, and three country taverns completed the public buildings. Yet residents could show style. Some went richly dressed in fine carriages. Little luxuries were imported, and gave tone to literary evenings and political dinners. If the frontier was just down the street, cultivated life could be found just indoors.

The new attorney and counselor at law from New Salem rode into Springfield on April fifteenth and went to the only cabinet-maker in town to inquire for a single bedstead. He then saw the store of Joshua Speed. He tied his pony and unsaddled it and went in, hauling the saddle bags which he threw on the counter. What, he asked, would the mattress and bedding for a single bedstead cost?

Joshua Speed took his slate and pencil and worked out some figures. The total, he stated, would come to seventeen dollars.

"It is probably cheap enough," said the attorney, "but I want to say that, cheap as it is, I have not the money to pay." They looked at each other. "But," he continued, "if you will credit me until Christmas, and my experiment here as a lawyer is a success, I will pay you then." The tone of his voice, thought Speed, was so melancholy that he felt for him. The attorney said, "If I fail in that I will probably never pay you at all."

Speed looked at him and said to himself that he had never seen so gloomy and melancholy a face in his life. He said to him,

"So small a debt seems to affect you so deeply, I think I can suggest a plan by which you will be able to attain your end without incurring any debt. I have a very large room and a very large double bed in it, which you are perfectly willing to share with me if you choose."

"Where is your room?" asked the attorney.

Speed pointed to the stairs leading from the store to his room.

"Upstairs," he said.

The attorney said nothing, threw his saddlebags over his arm, went upstairs and set them on the floor, and at once returned. Speed said his face was "beaming with pleasure and smiles."

"Well, Speed," he exclaimed, "I'm moved."

The satisfaction of this youthful attainment of a momentous stage could not last.

But for now—while still lost in the inexorable future were the circuit and the Congress and the White House and Ford's Theatre and a lodging in the world's heart—it was enough for the former citizen of New Salem.

I
EVENTS AND THE INDIVIDUAL

It is possible that Lincoln would never have become quite as famous as he has without the political, social, and moral challenges with which history confronted him. On the other hand, Mr. Horgan's treatment of his formative years clearly illustrates that Lincoln was not merely a pawn in the hands of history. He was a resourceful man with a tremendous capacity for growing through experience; he possessed an unusually large measure of determination and courage; and he was selflessly devoted to causes larger than himself, to liberty and honor, justice, and truth.

All of us are shaped by events, and Lincoln was no exception. What was exceptional about him was his willingness and ability to meet the challenges of his time; he never turned his back on events or on the momentous decisions they forced him to make. He never let *them* defeat *him*.

II
IMPLICATIONS

Discuss in full the meaning of each of the following quotations; also discuss their relevance to the idea of Lincoln as a self-made individual.

1. *If you are resolutely determined . . . the thing is more than half-done already. . . .*

2. In his first term the assemblyman [Lincoln] had been "silent, observant, studious."

3. During this term [his second] his self-image found words; . . . he aimed at the "great distinction" of being known as "the DeWitt Clinton of Illinois."

4. New Salem had been his school, his academy, his college.

5. In all his young life he had worked to overcome disadvantages, and as they enlarged, so did he. . . .

III
TECHNIQUES

Tone

Discuss the vocabulary, average sentence length, and grammatical complexity of the paragraphs below, both of which were written by Horgan. On the basis of this study, compare and describe their respective tones. Is the tone in the Lincoln piece appropriate to the subject? Why or why not?

1. Ever since the eighteenth century the raising and tending of large herds of beef cattle had been practiced on the Texas river's wide, flat borderlands. All descended from animals brought to Mexico in the sixteenth century by Spaniards, there were several types of cattle on the river plains, of which the most distinctive had tremendously long horns doubled up and backward for half their length; heavy thin heads; tall legs, and narrow, powerful flanks. They were haired in various colors, with white patches. By the hundred thousand, wild cattle roved at large over the uninhabited land on both sides of the border, and constituted its prevailing form of wealth. As such they were always prizes for Indians, Mexicans and Americans who in an unbroken tradition of border violence raided the herds—preferably those already gathered into ownership by other men—and drove away thousands of animals to sell on the hoof, or to kill for their hides which were bailed and sold to traders, while the carcasses were left to carrion, and the bones to workers who gathered them up and hauled them for sale as fertilizer to Texas farming towns.

2. It was one thing to be given "the hypo," as he called it, by fugitive annoyances; quite another to be lost to the whole daily world. Finally he was persuaded to stay for a few weeks with the jolly justice of the peace, Judge Bowling Green, beyond the little hills north of New Salem. Judge Green loved to laugh with all his three hundred pounds. The shape of his belly earned him the nickname of "Pot." He was good for the law student. The ordinary matters of life proceeded. The law student tended the post office, though someone complained that he neglected his duties at this time. He studied. He surveyed a ten-acre lot of timber. He wrote to the Governor of Illinois to endorse an applicant for the post of public auditor. On December seventh, 1835, he was counted present at the opening of a special session of the Assembly in Vandalia. On March twenty-fourth, 1836, his name was entered on the record of the Sangamon Circuit Court as a man of good moral character. This was the first of three steps leading to the license to practice law. The law student was coming back to himself. Years afterward, Isaac Cogsdale, formerly of New Salem, said he heard him say of Anne Rutledge, "I loved her dearly. . . ."

IV

WORDS

A. Using what you know about context clues and word parts, determine the meaning of the italicized words. Be prepared to discuss the clues that helped you.

1. Uncle Jack instructed us in the *rudiments* thereof; he said Atticus wasn't interested in guns.

2. I . . . busied myself for two hours erecting a complicated *breastworks* at the side of the porch, . . .

3. . . . I thought he moved like an underwater swimmer: time had slowed to a *nauseating* crawl.

4. All these reflected the needs and *aspirations*, the concerns and natures of the men and women.

5. . . . while still lost in the *inexorable* future were the circuit and the Congress and the White House. . . .

6. "The gentleman has seen fit to *allude* to my being a young man. . . ."

7. The assemblyman took part in the vote. . . on the *delineation* of voting districts and precincts.

8. . . . "the *promulgation* of abolition doctrines tends rather to increase than *abate* its evils."

B. Words that have more than one meaning may also have different sets of synonyms and antonyms. The most comprehensive treatment of synonyms and antonyms may be found in *Webster's Dictionary of Synonyms*. This book contains a survey of the history of English synonymy, a discussion of the definitions of *synonym* and *antonym*, and entries for synonyms, carefully distinguishing the differences in implications, connotations, and applications. You will find this book and a collegiate-size dictionary helpful in doing the exercises that follow. Following each italicized word are several meanings of the word and an antonym

that opposes one of the meanings. Find the meaning for which the antonym is opposite.

Example: *dull* 1. gloomy 2. dusky 3. obtuse Antonym: *keen* Answer: *obtuse*

1. *obstruct* 1. block or close 2. check or impede 3. cut off sight of Antonym: *advance*

2. *prolific* 1. abundant reproduction 2. capable of reproduction Antonym: *barren*

3. *casual* 1. happening by chance 2. unconcerned 3. extemporaneous Antonym: *deliberate*

4. *confirm* 1. establish 2. ratify 3. verify Antonym: *contradict*

5. *elevation* 1. altitude 2. promotion Antonym: *degradation*

6. *copy* 1. imitate 2. model or pattern 3. subject matter Antonym: *originate*

7. *effervescent* 1. lively and high spirited 2. animated 3. brazen Antonym: *subdued*

C. It is interesting to compare two broad dialects of English, American and British. Through the years Americans have adapted English to their needs by coining new words, by finding words to label topographical features, by dropping certain features of British English, and by retaining others that were disappearing in British English.

1. Look up the etymology of *fen, moor, bluff, pond, beech, hemlock, barn, bee* (as in "spelling bee"). Which are of British origin but with new meanings in American English? Which are familiar in British English but have become obsolete in American English?

2. In *My Fair Lady*, Henry Higgins thinks about throwing the "baggage" out. Which sense of the word *baggage* does he mean?

3. What is the American word for the British *chemist, lift, bonnet, wireless, "telly"*?

4. Look up the term *Americanism*.

Gallery   INDEPENDENT SPIRIT

Moses, Achilles, Aeneas, Roland, King Arthur—you can know a people by their heroes. Over the years, Americans have come to admire those men and women whose achievements have exemplified independent spirit. Consider the small sample of independent spirits in this gallery. Beloved for different reasons and of unequal fame, the Americans in this gallery can tell you much about the variety of directions in which the independent spirit has expressed itself.

The soaring statement of upthrust girders, rooted in concrete yet reaching for the sky, is a testament and a symbol. To American artist Charles Sheeler, the Golden Gate is more than a bridge; it is a gateway, an opening, a metaphor that lifts the spirits in the same way that the spires of a cityscape thrust us skyward. Here, our independent spirit has gloriously fused loftiness and strength.

GOLDEN GATE
Charles Sheeler
Metropolitan Museum of Art, New York
George A. Hearn Fund

The elegant portrait by one of the first prominent American painters dates from 1780. This striking portrait of the obviously indomitable Mrs. Seymour Fort is the only record we have of her. But wouldn't you guess she was a dominant spirit within her own family?

The thoughtful soul often stands alone. This scene by the sea, painted by an unknown American primitive artist in the 1800s, shows this in simple, straightforward terms. In between curls of waves and grass, the meditator stands apart, an isolated figure on a barren beach.

PORTRAIT OF MRS. SEYMOUR FORT
John Singleton Copley
Wadsworth Atheneum, Hartford, Connecticut

MEDITATION BY THE SEA
Anonymous
Museum of Fine Arts, Boston
M. and M. Karolik Collection

MIDNIGHT RIDE OF PAUL REVERE
Grant Wood

One truly legendary figure
from the Revolutionary War who typified
the independent spirit of the times was Paul
Revere, whose midnight ride to give alarm
inspired works of art in both painting and verse.

This brooding woodcut is a sensitive tribute
to the German-born scientist Albert Einstein,
who opened the way for discoveries in the
fields of nuclear science and outer space.

A PORTRAIT
OF ALBERT EINSTEIN
Antonio Frasconi

After her mysterious death in 1937, a gallant woman, Amelia Earhart, joined the ranks of fabled Americans. Among many of her "firsts," she was the first woman to fly alone over the United States and the Atlantic Ocean. Her plane disappeared in the Pacific during her attempt to fly around the world.

But long before the others, a courageous woman helped open the American Frontier: the prairie wife, collective symbol of the thousands of uncelebrated independent spirits.

AMELIA EARHART
Bernard Fuchs

THE PRAIRIE WIFE
Harvey Dunn

Independent spirits exist to bless us in all fields of endeavor. The "Good Grey Poet" Whitman and the superb folk singer Odetta are vital examples. One hundred years separate the realism of the nineteenth-century painter Eakins and the color-intense stylization of the young black American Mason.

WALT WHITMAN   *Thomas Eakins*
Courtesy of the Pennsylvania Academy of Fine Arts

ODETTA   *Phillip Lindsay Mason*
Private Collection of the Rev. and Mrs.
William Black of Oakland, California

ONE HORN   *George Catlin*
Field Museum of Natural History, Chicago

Ironically, about the time the newly arrived European-Americans had virtually
eliminated their predecessors, they began to romanticize them into favorite
American symbols for independence. Paintings such as ONE HORN by George Catlin
praise the superb tracker and brave warrior.

Most of America's military heroes have been victorious, but by a curious irony the man who may well be the most beloved military hero in our history was a defeated general. Throughout the South, schools are named for him, as are towns, public parks, and children. Though he was a Confederate general, he has equally won the admiration of the North. Try to see the qualities of this man that have won the respect both of his friends and of his foes.

Lee in Battle

GAMALIEL BRADFORD, JR.

We like to imagine the master mind in a great conflict controlling everything, down to the minutest detail. But with vast modern armies this is far from being the case, even with the elaborate electrical facilities of today; and in Lee's time those facilities were much less complete. Lee himself indicated the difficulty humorously when he was remonstrated with for taking risks, and answered, "I wish someone would tell me my proper place in battle. I am always told I should not be where I am." And he expressed it with entire seriousness when he said, "During the battle my direction is of more harm than use; I must then rely on my division and brigade commanders. I think and I act with all my might to bring up my troops to the right place at the right moment; after that I have done my duty."

Some critics hold that Lee was inclined to carry the principle much too far. What impresses me in this, as in other things, is the nice balance of his gifts. Persons by nature predisposed to direct others almost always seek to direct them in everything. How wise and constant Lee's direction was, where he thought it needed, is shown by his son's remark: "We were always fully instructed as to the best way to get to Lexington, and, indeed, all the roads of life were carefully marked out for us by him." Yet the instant he reached the limit of what he felt to be his province, he drew back and left decision to others whom he knew to be, by nature or position, better qualified.

The amount of Lee's direction and influence seems to have varied greatly in different battles. At Fredericksburg[1] he adopted a central position whence he could survey the whole field. Colonel Long's remarks in describing this must have given Longstreet exquisite pleasure. "In the battle Longstreet had his headquarters at the same place, so that Lee was able to keep his hand on the rein of his 'old war horse' and to direct him where to apply his strength." At Antietam[2] critics are agreed that Lee's management of things was perfect. "He utilized every available soldier; throughout the day he controlled the Confederate operations over the whole field." On the other hand, in the Peninsular battles, owing perhaps to imperfect organization and staff arrangements, his hold on the machine was much less complete; and at Gettysburg the vast extension of his lines made immediate personal direction almost impossible, with results that were disastrous.

Pages 153–169 of Bradford's *Lee, the American.* Copyright © renewed 1940 by Helen T. Bradford. Reprinted by permission of the publisher, Houghton Mifflin Co.

1. **Fredericksburg,** a Virginia city in Spotsylvania County; site of major Confederate victory December 11–15, 1862.
2. **Antietam**\ăn ᵗē·tăm\ village in Maryland, 3 miles north of which a battle was fought at Sharpsburg, 1862.

It is at Gettysburg that we get one of the most vivid of the few pictures left us of Lee in the very midst of the crash and tumult of conflict. It is from the excellent pen of General Alexander, who says that the commander-in-chief rode up entirely alone, just after Pickett's charge, "and remained with me for a long time. He then probably first appreciated the extent of the disaster, as the disorganized stragglers made their way back past us. . . . It was certainly a momentous thing to him to see that superb attack end in such a bloody repulse. But, whatever his emotions, there was no trace of them in his calm and self-possessed bearing. I thought at that time his coming there very imprudent, and the absence of all his staff officers and couriers strange. It could only have happened by his express intention. I have since thought it possible that he came, thinking the enemy might follow in pursuit of Pickett, personally to rally stragglers about our guns and make a desperate defense. He had the instincts of a soldier within him as strongly as any man. . . . No soldier could have looked on at Pickett's charge and not burned to be in it. To have a personal part in a close and desperate fight at that moment would, I believe, have been at heart a great pleasure to General Lee, and possibly he was looking for one."

And I ask myself how much of that born soldier's lust for battle, keen enjoyment of danger and struggle and combat, Lee really had. Certainly there is little record of his speaking of any such feeling. At various times he expressed a keen sense of all the horrors of war. "You have no idea of what a horrible sight a battlefield is." And again, "What a cruel thing is war; to separate and destroy families and friends, and mar the purest joys and happiness God has granted us in this world; to fill our hearts with hatred instead of love for our neighbors, and to devastate the fair face of this beautiful world." One vivid sentence, spoken in the midst of the slaughter of Fredericksburg, lights the man's true instincts like a flash: "It is well that war is so terrible, or else we might grow too fond of it."

As to Lee's personal courage, of course the only point to be discussed is the peculiar quality of it. Judging from his character generally and from all that is recorded of him, I should not take his courage to consist in a temperamental indifference to danger, a stolid disregard of its very existence, such as we find perhaps in Grant or Wellington. Though far from being a highly nervous organization, Lee was sensitive, imaginative; and I take it that he had to accustom himself to being under fire and was always aware of any elements of peril there might be about him.

Testimony to his entire coolness in battle is of course abundant. I do not know that there is any more striking general statement than that of Cooke in reference to the second battle of Bull Run: "The writer of these pages chanced to be near the commander at this moment and was vividly impressed by the air of unmoved calmness which marked his countenance and demeanor. Nothing in the expression of his face, and no hurried movement, indicated excitement or anxiety. Here, as on many other occasions, Lee impressed the writer as an individual gifted with the most surprising faculty of remaining cool and unaffected in the midst of circumstances calculated to arouse the most phlegmatic."[3] A concrete instance of his self-possession in the midst of turmoil is narrated by a Union soldier: "A prisoner walked up to him and told him a Rebel had stolen his hat. In the midst of his orders he stopped and told the Rebel to give back the hat and saw that he done it, too."

I am not aware that Lee was wounded at any time during the war, or indeed in his life, except slightly at Chapultepec.[4] His hands were severely injured just before Antietam, but this was by the falling of his horse. He was, however, again and again under fire. At Antietam, A. P. Hill, who was close to the general, had his horse's forelegs shot off. On another occasion,

3. **phlegmatic**\flĕg ▲mă•tĭk\ apathetic, impassive.
4. **Chapultepec**\cha ▲pŭl•tə•pĕk\ a rocky hill 3 miles south of Mexico City; the site of a battle, Sept. 12–13, 1847, in war with Mexico.

LEE AND HIS GENERALS,
Charles Hoffbauer

when Lee was sitting with Stuart and his staff, "a shell fell plump in their midst, burying in the earth with itself one of General Lee's gauntlets,[5] which lay on the ground only a few feet from the general himself." In 1864 Lee was inspecting the lines below Richmond, and the number of soldiers gathered about him drew the enemy's fire rather heavily. The general ordered the men back out of range and he himself followed at his leisure; but it was observed that he stopped to pick up something. A fledgling sparrow had fallen from its nest, and he took it from the ground and tenderly replaced it, with the bullets whistling about him.

As the following incident shows, Lee was extremely solicitous about the unnecessary exposure of his men. Once, when he was watching the effect of the fire on an advanced battery, a staff officer rode up to him by the approach which was least protected. The general reprimanded him for his carelessness, and when the young man urged that he could not seek cover himself while his chief was in the open, Lee answered sharply, "It is my duty to be here. Go back the way I told you, sir." At another time Lee had placed himself in a very exposed position, to the horror of all his officers. They could not prevail upon him to come down, so finally General Gracie stepped forward and interposed himself between his commander and the enemy. "Why, Gracie," protested Lee, "you will certainly be killed." "It is better, General, that I should be killed than you. When you get down, I will." Lee smiled and got down.

When things became really critical, Lee completely threw aside all caution. In the terrific battles of the Wilderness, where at times it seemed as if Grant would succeed in breaking through, the Confederate general repeatedly (on three separate occasions, as it appears) rushed to the front to rally his men and charge, like Ney or Murat,[6] at the head of them. "Go

---

5. **gauntlets**\gŏnt·līts\ gloves with a long extension over the wrist.
6. **Ney or Murat.** Michel Ney\nā\ French soldier in the Revolutionary and Napoleonic armies; Joachim Murat, 1767–1815, French cavalry commander who aided Napoleon in a *coup d'état*\'kū·dā ▴ta\.

back, General Lee, go back!" shouted the soldiers. But he would not go back till they had promised to do as much for him as they could have done with him. And they did as much. No men could have done more.

It was this occasional fury of combativeness which made Longstreet[7] assert that the general was sometimes unbalanced, not by any personal exposure or excitement, but by critical situations affecting the army as a whole. Longstreet, defending his own conduct at Gettysburg, urges that Lee was particularly overwrought at the time of that battle. In what is, to say the least, peculiar phraseology, he writes of his commander: "That he was excited and off his balance was evident on the afternoon of the first, and that he labored under that oppression till blood enough was shed to appease him." The suggestion that Lee required blood to appease him is grotesque, and his loyal admirers ridicule the idea that at Gettysburg he was unbalanced. But there is evidence besides Longstreet's that, once in a fight, he hated to give it up and perhaps occasionally allowed his ardor to overcome his discretion. The Prussian officer Scheibert remarks that while at Chancellorsville Lee was admirably calm, at Gettysburg he was restless and uneasy. General Anderson bears witness that at Gettysburg his chief was "very much disturbed and depressed."

The most heroic picture that is left us of Lee high-wrought by the excitement of battle and determined to fight to the end is the account, received by Henderson from a reliable eyewitness, of the chief's decision to remain north of the Potomac after Antietam. General after general rode up to the commander's headquarters, all with the same tale of discouragement and counsel of retreat. Hood was quite unmanned. "My God!" cried Lee to him, with unwonted vehemence, "where is the splendid division you had this morning?" "They are lying on the field where you sent them," answered Hood. Even Jackson did not venture to suggest anything but withdrawal. There were a few moments of oppressive silence. Then Lee rose erect in his stirrups and said, "Gentlemen, we will not cross the Potomac tonight. You will go to your respective commands, strengthen your lines, send two officers from each brigade towards the ford to collect your stragglers and bring them up. Many have come in. I have had the proper steps taken to collect all the men who are in the rear. If McClellan[8] wants to fight in the morning, I will give him battle. Go!" They went, and in this case, at least, Lee's glorious audacity was justified; for he proved to all the world that McClellan did not dare attack him again.

However Lee's judgment may have been affected by the excitement of battle, it made little alteration in his bearing or manner. Fremantle tells us that the general's dress was always neat and clean, and adds, "I observed this during the three days fight at Gettysburg, when every one else looked and was extremely dirty." Stress of conflict sometimes seems to alter men's natures. Odd stories are told in the war books of officers quite saintly in common converse who in battle would swear like reprobates. Lee's politeness was always exquisite. It was only very, very rarely that some untoward incident stirred either his temper or his speech. "Probably no man ever commanded an army and, at the same time, so entirely commanded himself as Lee," says the cool-blooded Alexander. "This morning [after Chancellorsville] was almost the only occasion on which I ever saw him out of humor."

Nor was it only a question of mere politeness. Lee was as tender and sympathetic to man and beast in the fury of combat, in the chaos of defeat, as he could have been in his own domain at Arlington. After the great charge on the third day at Gettysburg, an officer rode up to him lashing an unwilling horse. "Don't whip him,

7. **Longstreet,** James, 1821–1904, Confederate brigadier general; his delay in carrying out Lee's orders to attack at Gettysburg has been said to have caused the Confederate defeat.
8. **McClellan,** George Brinton, 1826–1885, commanded U. S. Army at Antietam; defeated by Lincoln in presidential election in 1864.

Captain, don't whip him," protested the general. "I have just such another foolish beast myself, and whipping doesn't do any good." And as the tumult of disaster increased, the sympathy took larger forms of magnanimity than mere prevention of cruelty to animals. There was no faultfinding, no shifting of perhaps deserved blame to others, nothing but calmness, comfort, cheerfulness, confidence. "All will come right in the end; we'll talk of it afterwards, but in the meantime all good men must rally." "Never mind, General. All this has been my fault. It is I that have lost this fight, and you must help me out of it the best way you can."

So, with incomparable patience, tact, and energy, the great soldier held his army together after defeat and kept it in a temper and condition which went far to justify Meade's reluctance to follow up his success. Only, to complete the picture, one should turn to General Imboden's brief sketch, taken after the work was done and natural human exhaustion and despair claimed some little right over even a hero's nerve and brain. It must be remembered that this was a man fifty-six years old. Toward midnight Lee rode up to Imboden's command. "When he approached and saw us, he spoke, reined up his horse and endeavored to dismount. The effort to do so betrayed so much physical exhaustion that I stepped forward to assist him, but before I reached him, he had alighted. He threw his arm across his saddle to rest himself and fixing his eyes upon the ground, leaned in silence upon his equally weary horse; the two formed a striking group, as motionless as a statue. After some expressions as to Pickett's charge, etc., he added in a tone almost of agony, 'Too bad! Too bad! Oh, too bad!' "

With the portrait of Lee himself in the shock of battle we should put a background of his soldiers and their feeling as he came among them. We have already heard their passionate cry when he rushed to put himself at their head and charge into the thickest of the fight. "Go back, General Lee! Go back!" General Gordon, who loved to throw a high light of eloquence on all such scenes, describes this one with peculiar vividness, giving his own remonstrance, "These men are Georgians, Virginians, and Carolinians. They have never failed you on any field. They will not fail you now. Will you, boys?" and the enthusiastic answer, "No, no, no!" Those who like the quiet truth of history, even when it chills, will be interested in an eyewitness's simple comment on this picturesque narrative. "Gordon says, 'We need no such encouragement.' At this some of our soldiers called out, 'No, no!' Gordon continuing, said, 'There is not a soldier in the Confederate army who would not gladly lay down his life to save you from harm'; but the men did not respond to this last proposition."

It cannot be doubted, however, that Lee's personal influence in critical moments was immense. On one occasion, just before battle, there was heard to pass from mouth to mouth as a sort of watchword the simple comment, "Remember, General Lee is looking at us." Stuart's aide, Von Borcke, describes a scene which is immensely effective as showing how little the general relied on words, and how little he needed to. Lee was riding through the ranks before a charge. "He uttered no word. He simply removed his hat and passed bareheaded along the line. I had it from one who witnessed the act. 'It was,' said he, 'the most eloquent address ever delivered.' And a few minutes later he heard a youth, crying and reloading his musket, shout through his tears that 'any man who would not fight after what General Lee said was a coward.' "

Perhaps the most splendid battlepiece of Lee in the midst of his fighting soldiers is Colonel Marshall's account of the triumphant advance on the third day at Chancellorsville. The enemy were retiring and the troops swept forward through the tumult of battle and the smoke of woods and dwellings burning about them. Everywhere the field was strewn with the wounded and dying of both armies. "In the midst of this scene General Lee, mounted upon that horse which we all remember so well, rode to the front of his advancing battalions. His presence was the signal for one of those uncontrollable outbursts of enthusiasm which none can appreciate who have not witnessed them. The fierce soldiers, with their faces blackened with the smoke of battle, the wounded, crawling with feeble limbs from the fury of the devouring flames, all seemed possessed with a common impulse. One long unbroken cheer, in which the feeble cry of those who lay helpless on the earth blended with the strong voices of those who still fought, rose high above the roar of battle, and hailed the presence of the victorious chief. He sat in the full realization of all that soldiers dream of—triumph."

This was victory. But there came a day of defeat, when the Army of Northern Virginia, after four years of fighting and triumphing and suffering, shrunk almost to nothing, saw their great commander ride away to make his submission to a generous conqueror. Their love, their loyalty, their confidence, were no less than they had ever been. If he said further fighting was useless and inhuman, it must be so.

But this very absolute confidence increased the weight of the terrible decision. All these thousands trusted him to decide for them. He must decide rightly. What the burden was we can only imagine, never know. But under the noble serenity maintained by habitual effort, good observers detected signs of the struggle that must be taking place. "His face was still calm, but his carriage was no longer erect, as his soldiers had been used to see it. The trouble of those last days had already ploughed great furrows in his forehead. His eyes were red as if with weeping; his cheeks sunken and haggard; his face colorless. No one who looked upon him then, as he stood there in full view of the disastrous end, can ever forget the intense agony written upon his features. And yet he was calm, self-possessed, and deliberate." So great was his anguish that it wrung a wish to end it all, even from a natural self-control complete as his. "How easily I could get rid of this and be at rest. I have only to ride along the lines and all will be over. But," he quickly added, "it is our duty to live, for what will become of the

women and children of the South if we are not here to support and protect them?"

So the decision had to be made. And he made it. "Then there is nothing left me but to go and see General Grant, and I would rather die a thousand deaths." His officers protested passionately, "Oh, General, what will history say of the surrender of the army in the field?" "Yes, I know, they will say hard things of us; they will not understand how we were overwhelmed by numbers; but that is not the question, Colonel; the question is, is it right to surrender this army? If it is right, then I will take all the responsibility."

The scene that ensued has been described often: the plain farmhouse room; the officers curious, yet respectful; the formal conversation, as always painfully unequal to the huge event it covered; the short, ungainly, ill-dressed man, as dignified in his awkwardness almost as the royal, perfectly appointed figure that conferred with him. Lee bore himself nobly, say his admirers; nobly, but a little coldly, say his opponents. And who shall blame him? Then it was over. One moment he paused at the door, as he went out, waiting for his horse, and as he paused, looking far into the tragic future or the tragic past, he struck his gauntleted hands together in a gesture of immense despair, profoundly significant for so self-contained a man. Then he rode away, back to his children, back to the Army of Northern Virginia, who had seen him daily for three years and now would never see him any more.

I

THE SPREAD OF FAME

There are several reasons for the growth and spread of Lee's fame. For one thing, many Americans admire him as an underdog and as a champion of a Lost Cause. More important, Lee proved himself worthy of deep respect and admiration, for he had the courage to follow the direction of his own unique talents and temper. But in addition to these factors, some credit for the spread of Lee's fame must be given to the many writers—South and North—who have told his story. For regardless of his greatness, Lee could not have achieved national reputation and recognition unless people everywhere knew about him. Thus the writer steps into the role of spreader of fame.

II
IMPLICATIONS

Part of Lee's great fame is due to his great character. Discuss those of his character traits that are revealed in the following incidents and quotations.

1. "What a cruel thing is war; to separate and destroy families and friends, and mar the purest joys and happiness God has granted us in this world; to fill our hearts with hatred instead of love for our neighbors, and to devastate the fair face of this beautiful world."

2. Lee's replacing a fallen sparrow in its nest during the heat of battle.

3. Lee's leading army charges at the battles of the Wilderness.

4. "Never mind, General. All this has been my fault. It is I that have lost this fight, and you must help me out of it the best way you can."

5. Lee's riding bare-headed along the lines before a charge.

6. "How easily I could get rid of this and be at rest. I have only to ride along the lines and all will be over. But it is our duty to live, for what will become of the women and children of the South if we are not here to support and protect them?"

7. ". . . the question is, is it right to surrender this army? If it is right, then I will take all the responsibility."

III
TECHNIQUES

Tone

The simplest way for an author to reveal an attitude toward a subject is by direct statement. Such statements, if they are to carry weight with the reader, ought to be supported in some way by the author's reasons for holding that attitude or by evidence supporting the validity of the attitude.

In the following quotations, Bradford makes some direct statements about Lee and/or reveals his attitude toward the General. In each case what is Bradford's attitude? Also locate the quotation and determine whether or not the author backs up his statement with reasons or evidence. (The quotations are in the order of their appearance.)

1. What impresses me . . . is the nice balance of his gifts.

2. Though far from being a highly nervous organization, Lee was sensitive, imaginative. . . .

3. The suggestion that Lee required blood to appease him is grotesque, and his loyal admirers ridicule the idea that at Gettysburg he was unbalanced.

4. There was no faultfinding, no shifting of perhaps deserved blame to others, nothing but calmness, comfort, cheerfulness, confidence.

5. So, with incomparable patience, tact, and energy, the great soldier held his army together. . . .

Selection of Significant Detail

A. Bradford creates a favorable portrait of General Lee largely by selecting details that show him to be of noble character. You may have noticed, however, that some negative comments are introduced here and there. Point out two or three instances of unfavorable comments on Lee and discuss the following:

1. How the author handles them.

2. How they affect the total portrait.

3. How objective or slanted you think his essay is.

B. The paragraph with which Bradford concludes his biographical essay on Lee is so effective that it leaves the reader with a feeling of sadness and compassion that a man so gallant and courageous should be brought to defeat.

1. What small detail, included in the next to last sentence, pictures a characteristic action of Lee's and makes his departure from the farmhouse more vivid to the reader?

2. What are Lee's soldiers called in the final sentence that adds pathos to the author's conclusion?

The following selection is the story of a Navajo named Ayah, a female independent spirit. Perhaps more than any other character in this unit, Ayah demonstrates that the *spirit* may continue to be independent even in the bleakest circumstances, the starkest poverty.

Lullaby

LESLIE SILKO

The sun had gone down but the snow in the wind gave off its own light. It came in thick tufts like new wool—washed before the weaver spins it. Ayah reached out for it like her own babies had, and she smiled when she remembered how she had laughed at them. She was an old woman now, and her life had become memories. She sat down with her back against the wide cottonwood tree, feeling the rough bark on her back bones; she faced east and listened to the wind and snow sing a high-pitched Yeibechei[1] song. Out of the wind she felt warmer, and she could watch the wide fluffy snow fill in her tracks, steadily, until the direction she had come from was gone. By the light of the snow she could see the dark outline of the big arroyo a few feet away. She was sitting on the edge of Cebolleta Creek, where in the springtime the thin cows would graze on grass already chewed flat to the ground. In the wide deep creek bed where only a trickle of water flowed in the summer, the skinny cows would wander, looking for new grass along winding paths splashed with manure.

Ayah pulled the old Army blanket over her head like a shawl, Jimmie's blanket—the one he had sent to her. That was a long time ago and the green wool was faded, and it was unraveling on the edges. She did not want to think about Jimmie. So she thought about the weaving and the way her mother had done it. On the tall wooden loom set into the sand under a tamarack tree for shade. She could see it clearly. She had been only a little girl when her grandma gave her the wooden combs to pull the twigs and burrs from the raw, freshly washed wool. And while she combed the wool, her grandma sat beside her, spinning a silvery strand of yarn around the smooth cedar spindle. Her mother worked at the loom with yarns dyed bright yellow and red and gold. She watched them dye the yarn in boiling black pots full of beeweed petals, juniper berries, and sage. The blankets her mother made were soft and woven so tight that rain rolled off them like birds' feathers. Ayah remembered sleeping warm on cold windy nights, wrapped in her mother's blankets on the hogan's[2] sandy floor.

The snow drifted now, with the northwest wind hurling it in gusts. It drifted up around her black overshoes—old ones with little metal buckles. She smiled at the snow which was trying to cover her little by little. She could remember when they had no black rubber overshoes; only the high buckskin leggings that they wrapped over their elk-hide moccasins. If the snow was dry or frozen, a person could

---

1. **Yeibechei** \\ˈyā·bə'chī\\ a Navajo spirit represented by a masked dancer at traditional ceremonies.
2. **hogan** \\ˈhō'gän\\ a building usually made of logs and mud and used as a dwelling by the Navajo.

"Lullaby" by Leslie Silko, first appeared in *Chicago Review*, 26:1, © 1974 by *Chicago Review*.

walk all day and not get wet; and in the evenings the beams of the ceiling would hang with lengths of pale buckskin leggings, drying out slowly.

She felt peaceful remembering. She didn't feel cold any more. Jimmie's blanket seemed warmer than it had ever been. And she could remember the morning he was born. She could remember whispering to her mother who was sleeping on the other side of the hogan, to tell her it was time now. She did not want to wake the others. The second time she called to her, her mother stood up and pulled on her shoes; she knew. They walked to the old stone hogan together, Ayah walking a step behind her mother. She waited alone, learning the rhythms of the pains while her mother went to call the old woman to help them. The morning was already warm even before dawn and Ayah smelled the bee flowers blooming and the young willow growing at the springs. She could remember that so clearly, but his birth merged into the births of the other children and to her it became all the same birth. They named him for the summer morning and in English they called him Jimmie.

It wasn't like Jimmie died. He just never came back, and one day a dark blue sedan with white writing on its doors pulled up in front of the boxcar shack where the rancher let the Indians live. A man in a khaki uniform trimmed in gold gave them a yellow piece of paper and told them that Jimmie was dead. He said the Army would try to get the body back and then it would be shipped to them; but it wasn't likely because the helicopter had burned after it crashed. All of this was told to Chato because he could understand English. She stood inside the doorway holding the baby while Chato listened. Chato spoke English like a white man and he spoke Spanish too. He was taller than the white man and he stood straighter too. Chato didn't explain why; he just told the military man they could keep the body if they found it. The white man looked bewildered; he nodded his head and he left. Then Chato looked at her and shook his head.

He swore aloud in English, and then he told her "Jimmie isn't coming home anymore," and when he spoke, he used the words to speak of the dead. She didn't cry then, but she hurt inside with anger. And she mourned him as the years passed, when a horse fell with Chato and broke his leg, and the white rancher told them he wouldn't pay Chato until he could work again. She mourned Jimmie because he would have worked for his father then; he would have saddled the big bay horse and ridden the fence lines each day, with wire cutters and heavy gloves, fixing the breaks in the barbed wire and putting the stray cattle back inside again.

She mourned him after the white doctors came to take Danny and Ella away. She was at the shack alone that day when they came. It was back in the days before they hired Navajo women to go with them as interpreters. She recognized one of the doctors. She had seen him at the children's clinic at Cañoncito about a month ago. They were wearing khaki uniforms and they waved papers at her and a black ball point pen, trying to make her understand their English words. She was frightened by the way they looked at the children, like the lizard watches the fly. Danny was swinging on the tire swing in the elm tree behind the rancher's house, and Ella was toddling around the front door, dragging the broomstick horse Chato made for her. Ayah could see they wanted her to sign the papers, and Chato had taught her to sign her name. It was something she was proud of. She only wanted them to go, and to take their eyes away from her children.

She took the pen from the man without looking at his face and she signed the papers in three different places he pointed to. She stared at the ground by their feet and waited for them to leave. But they stood there and began to point and gesture at the children. Danny stopped swinging. Ayah could see his fear. She moved suddenly and grabbed Ella into her arms; the child squirmed, trying to get back to her toys. Ayah ran with the baby toward Danny; she screamed for him to run and then she grabbed him around his chest and carried him too. She ran south into the foothills of juniper trees and black lava rock. Behind her she heard the doctors running, but they had been taken by surprise, and as the hills became steeper and the cholla cactus were thicker, they stopped. When she reached the top of the hill, she stopped too to listen in case they were circling around her. But in a few minutes she heard a car engine start and they drove away. The children had been too surprised to cry while she ran with them. Danny was shaking and Ella's little fingers were gripping Ayah's blouse.

She stayed up in the hills for the rest of the day, sitting on a black lava boulder in the sunshine where she could see for miles all around her. The sky was light blue and cloudless, and it was warm for late April. The sun warmth relaxed her and took the fear and anger away. She lay back on the rock and watched the sky. It seemed to her that she could walk into the sky, stepping through clouds endlessly. Danny played with little pebbles and stones, pretending they were birds' eggs and then little rabbits. Ella sat at her feet and dropped fistfuls of dirt into the breeze, watching the dust and particles of sand intently. Ayah watched a hawk soar high above them, dark wings gliding; hunting or only watching, she did not know. The hawk was patient and he circled all afternoon before he disappeared around the high volcanic peak of the Mexicans call Guadalupe.

Late in the afternoon, Ayah looked down at the gray boxcar shack with the paint all peeled from the wood; the stove pipe on the roof was rusted and crooked. The fire she had built that morning in the oil drum stove had burned out. Ella was asleep in her lap now and Danny sat close to her, complaining that he was hungry; he asked when they would go to the house. "We will stay up here until your father comes," she told him, "because those white men were chasing us." The boy remembered then and he nodded at her silently.

If Jimmie had been there he could have read those papers and explained to her what they said. Ayah would have known, then, never to sign them. The doctors came back the next day and they brought a BIA[3] policeman with them. They told Chato they had her signature and that was all they needed. Except for the kids. She listened to Chato sullenly; she hated him when he told her it was the old woman who died in the winter, spitting blood; it was her old grandma who had given the children this disease. "They don't spit blood," she said coldly. "The whites lie." She held Ella and Danny close to her, ready to run to the hills again. "I want a medicine man first," she said to Chato, not looking at him. He shook his head. "It's too late now. The policeman is with them. You signed the paper." His voice was gentle.

It was worse than if they had died: to lose the children and to know that somewhere, in a place called Colorado, in a place full of sick and dying strangers, her children were without her. There had been babies that died soon after they were born, and one that died before he could walk. She had carried them herself, up to the boulders and great pieces of the cliff that long ago crashed down from Long Mesa; she laid them in the crevices of sandstone and buried them in fine brown sand with round quartz pebbles that washed down from the hills in the rain. She had endured it because they had been with her. But she could not bear this pain. She did not sleep for a long time after they took her children. She stayed on the hill where they had fled the first time, and she slept rolled up in the blanket Jimmie had sent her. She carried the pain in her belly and it was fed by everything she saw: the blue sky of their last day together and the dust and pebbles they played with; the swing in the elm tree and broomstick horse choked life from her. The pain filled her stomach and there was no room for food or for her lungs to fill with air. The air and the food would have been theirs.

---

3. **BIA**, abbreviation for Bureau of Indian Affairs.

She hated Chato, not because he let the policeman and doctors put the screaming children in the government car, but because he had taught her to sign her name. Because it was like the old ones always told her about learning their language or any of their ways: it endangered you. She slept alone on the hill until the middle of November when the first snows came. Then she made a bed for herself where the children had slept. She did not lay down beside Chato again until many years later, when he was sick and shivering and only her body could keep him warm. The illness came after the white rancher told Chato he was too old to work for him any more, and Chato and his old woman should be out of the shack by the next afternoon because the rancher had hired new people to work there. That had satisfied her. To see how the white man repaid Chato's years of loyalty and work. All of Chato's fine-sounding English talk didn't change things.

II

It snowed steadily and the luminous light from the snow gradually diminished into the darkness. Somewhere in Cebolleta a dog barked and other village dogs joined with it. Ayah looked in the direction she had come, from the bar where Chato was buying the wine. Sometimes he told her to go on ahead and wait; and then he never came. And when she finally went back looking for him, she would find him passed out at the bottom of the wooden steps to Azzie's Bar. All the wine would be gone and most of the money too, from the pale blue check that came to them once a month in a government envelope. It was then that she would look at his face and his hands, scarred by ropes and the barbed wire of all those years, and she would think 'this man is a stranger'; for 40 years she had smiled at him and cooked his food, but he remained a stranger. She stood up again, with the snow almost to her knees, and she walked back to find Chato.

It was hard to walk in the deep snow and she felt the air burn in her lungs. She stopped a short distance from the bar to rest and readjust the blanket. But this time he wasn't waiting for her on the bottom step with his old Stetson hat pulled down and his shoulders hunched up in his long wool overcoat.

She was careful not to slip on the wooden steps. When she pushed the door open, warm air and cigarette smoke hit her face. She looked around slowly and deliberately, in every corner, in every dark place that the old man might find to sleep. The bar-owner didn't like Indians in there, especially Navajos, but he let Chato come in because he could talk Spanish like he was one of them. The men at the bar stared at her, and the bartender saw that she left the door open wide. Snow flakes were flying inside like moths and melting into a puddle on the oiled wood floor. He motioned at her to close the door, but she did not see him. She held herself straight and walked across the room slowly, searching the room with every step. The snow in her hair melted and she could feel it on her forehead. At the far corner of the room, she saw red flames at the mica window of the old stove door; she looked behind the stove just to make sure. The bar got quiet except for the Spanish polka music playing on the jukebox. She stood by the stove and shook the snow from her blanket and held it near the stove to dry. The wet wool smell reminded her of new-born goats in early March, brought inside to warm near the fire. She felt calm.

In past years they would have told her to get out. But her hair was white now and her face was wrinkled. They looked at her like she was a spider crawling slowly across the room. They were afraid; she could feel the fear. She looked at their faces steadily. They reminded her of the first time the white people brought her children back to her that winter. Danny had been shy and hid behind the thin white woman who brought them. And the baby had not known her until Ayah took her into her arms, and then Ella had nuzzled close to her as she had when she was nursing. The blonde woman was nervous and kept looking at a dainty gold watch on her wrist. She sat on the bench near the small window and watched the dark snow clouds gather around the mountains; she was worrying about the unpaved road. She was frightened by what she saw inside too: the strips of venison drying on a rope across the ceiling and the children jabbering excitedly in a language she did not know. So they stayed for only a few hours. Ayah watched the government car disappear down the road and she knew they were already being weaned from these lava hills and from this sky. The last time they came was in early June, and Ella stared at her the way the men in the bar were now staring. Ayah did not try to pick her up; she smiled at her instead and spoke cheerfully to Danny. When he tried to answer her, he could not seem to remember and he spoke English words with the Navajo. But he gave her a scrap of paper that he had found somewhere and carried in his pocket; it was folded in half, and he shyly looked up at her and said it was a bird. She asked Chato if they were home for good this time. He spoke to the white woman and she shook her head. "How much longer," he asked, and she said she didn't know; but Chato saw how she stared at the boxcar shack. Ayah turned away then. She did not say goodbye.

III

She felt satisfied that the men in the bar feared her. Maybe it was her face and the way she held her mouth with teeth clenched tight, like there was nothing anyone could do to her now. She walked north down the road, searching for the old man. She did this because she had the blanket, and there would be no place for him except with her and the blanket in the old adobe barn near the arroyo. They always slept there when they came to Cebolleta. If the money and the wine were gone, she would be relieved because then they could go home again; back to the old hogan with a dirt roof and rock walls where she herself had been

born. And the next day the old man could go back to the few sheep they still had, to follow along behind them, guiding them into dry sandy arroyos where sparse grass grew. She knew he did not like walking behind old ewes when for so many years he rode big quarter horses and worked with cattle. But she wasn't sorry for him; he should have known all along what would happen.

There had not been enough rain for their garden in five years; and that was when Chato finally hitched a ride into the town, and brought back brown boxes of rice and sugar and big tin cans of welfare peaches. After that, at the first of the month they went to Cebolleta to ask the postmaster for the check; and then Chato would go to the bar and cash it. They did this as they planted the garden every May, not because anything would survive the summer dust, but because it was time to do this. And the journey passed the days that smelled silent and dry like the caves above the canyon with yellow painted buffaloes on their walls.

IV

He was walking along the pavement when she found him. He did not stop or turn around when he heard her behind him. She walked beside him and she noticed how slowly he moved now. He smelled strong of woodsmoke and urine. Lately he had been forgetting. Sometimes he called her by his sister's name and she had been gone for a long time. Once she had found him wandering on the road to the white man's ranch, and she asked him why he was going that way; he laughed at her and said "you know they can't run that ranch without me," and he walked on determined, limping on the leg that had been crushed many years before. Now he looked at her curiously, as if for the first time, but he kept shuffling along, moving slowly along the side of the highway. His gray hair had grown long and spread out on the shoulders of the long overcoat. He wore the old felt hat pulled down over his ears. His boots were worn out at the toes and he had stuffed pieces of an old red shirt in the holes. The rags made his feet look like little animals up to their ears in snow. She laughed at his feet; the snow muffled the sound of her laugh. He stopped and looked at her again. The wind had quit blowing and the snow was falling straight down; the southeast sky was beginning to clear and Ayah could see a star.

"Let's rest awhile," she said to him. They walked away from the road and up the slope to the giant boulders that had tumbled down from the red sandrock mesa throughout the centuries of rainstorms and earth tremors. In a place where the boulders shut out the wind, they sat down with their backs against the rock. She offered half of the blanket to him and they sat wrapped together.

The storm passed swiftly. The clouds moved east. They were massive and full, crowding together across the sky. She watched them with the feeling of horses—steely blue-gray horses startled across the sky. The powerful haunches pushed into the distances and the tail hairs streamed white mist behind them. The sky cleared. Ayah saw that there was nothing between her and the stars. The light was crystalline. There was no shimmer, no distortion through earth haze. She breathed the clarity of the night sky; she smelled the purity of the half moon and the stars. He was lying on his side with his knees pulled up near his belly for warmth. His eyes were closed now, and in the light from the stars and the moon, he looked young again.

She could see it descend out of the night sky: an icy stillness from the edge of the thin moon. She recognized the freezing. It came gradually, sinking snow flake by snow flake until the crust was heavy and deep. It had the strength of the stars in Orion, and its journey was endless. Ayah knew that with the wine he would sleep. He would not feel it. She tucked the blanket around him, remembering how it was when Ella had been with her; and she felt the rush so big inside her heart for the babies. And she sang the only song she knew to sing for babies. She could not remember if she had ever sung

it to her children, but she knew that her grandmother had sung it and her mother had sung it:

> The earth is your mother,
>   she holds you.
> The sky is your father,
>   he protects you.
> sleep,
> sleep,
> Rainbow is your sister,
>   she loves you.
> The winds are your brothers,
>   they sing to you.
> sleep,
> sleep,
> We are together always
> We are together always
> There never was a time
> when this
> was not so.

I
A DEEP-ROOTED INDEPENDENCE

It is of the earth and sky, the rainbow and the winds that Ayah sings—nature. It is her family, the song implies, the only family she has left; for her husband is drunk and dying, one of her children is dead, and the other two have been taken from her. But the song insists, "We are together always/There never was a time/when this/was not so."

When we realize that this lullaby has been passed down from Ayah's grandmother through her mother to her and that her husband has been transformed into a child, we see that the source of her uncommon strength is deeply rooted in her inner being, in nature, in the creative and timeless life-force of motherhood itself.

II
IMPLICATIONS

What do the following references from the story imply about the character of Ayah?

1. But she could not bear this pain (i.e., the pain of having her children taken away).

2. That had satisfied her. To see how the white man repaid Chato's years of loyalty and work.

3. Ayah turned away then. She did not say good-bye. (This occurs when her children leave after their last visit.)

4. . . . and she would think 'this man [her husband] is a stranger.'

5. She felt satisfied that the men in the bar feared her.

III
TECHNIQUES

Tone

Since this story is told largely through the point of view of Ayah, the attitudes that are revealed to us are hers. Would it be fair to assume that Silko shares these attitudes? Why or why not?

On several occasions Ayah's tone could be described as bitter. If you do not share her bitternesses—toward whites and toward males, for example—does that fact turn you away from her? Why or why not?

Selection of Significant Detail

Reread the first two and the last two paragraphs of the story. How many parallels between the two can you find? What might have been the author's purpose in using similar details at the beginning and at the end of the story?

What is the significance of the fact that at the close of the story Ayah sees that there is nothing between her and the stars? In the same paragraph in which this reference occurs, how many other references to clarity can you list? What is their purpose?

FINAL REFLECTIONS

Independent Spirit

It is nearly impossible to make generalizations about the American independent spirit. Our country was founded and built by diverse individuals, and thus it is not surprising that there is a broad diversity in the way that this spirit manifests itself in America.

We admire rugged individualists like the McCall brothers and Sary Ellison. We admire self-sacrificing and self-effacing persons such as Robert E. Lee and the fictional Atticus Finch. We admire compassionate political leaders like Abraham Lincoln. We admire strong men such as the legendary John Henry and strong women like Leslie Silko's Ayah. And we admire great writers who are not afraid to speak their minds in their own way, like Emerson and Whitman.

As we study such heroic persons, we see that all Americans are free under law to develop themselves to the limits of their ambition and talent.

IMPLICATIONS

Discuss the following propositions in terms of whatever selections from this unit may be relevant and of other pertinent reading you may have done.

1. The self-made woman or self-made man reflects the basic American belief in optimism and reinforces the idea that America is the land of opportunity.

2. Every independent person is, at some time or other, a nonconformist.

3. Americans feel a great deal of admiration for the common person.

4. Most persons are not self-reliant; we constantly rely on others.

5. The average American today is too well-off and is therefore unlikely to show any independence of spirit.

TECHNIQUES

Tone

Below you will find a list of words that may be used to describe a writer's tone. Select any five of these words and be prepared to cite a passage from one of the selections of this unit that illustrates each tone.

1. pompous	**7.** solemn
2. sarcastic	**8.** reverential
3. serious	**9.** condescending
4. playful	**10.** formal
5. ironic	**11.** intimate
6. matter-of-fact	**12.** bitter

Selection of Significant Detail

As you have seen, the writer's purpose is an important consideration in weighing the significance of any given detail. That is, the reader should always ask why the writer chose to include the detail and how it contributes to the meaning of the selection. Pick three or four of the selections in this unit, and state in a sentence or two what you think the writer's main intention was. Then discuss how several of the details chosen contribute to the overall intention.

BIOGRAPHICAL NOTES

Ralph Waldo Emerson

Lecturer, essayist, and poet, Ralph Waldo Emerson (1803–1882) was perhaps the most influential thinker in America during the nineteenth century. Born in Boston and educated at Harvard, he studied for the ministry but resigned his first pastorate because of doctrinal differences. After visiting Europe and forming lifelong friendships with Wordsworth and Carlyle, he settled in Concord, and soon drew about him a remarkable circle of friends, including A. B. Alcott, Margaret Fuller, and Thoreau. His first book, *Nature* (1836), contained the heart of his transcendental philosophy, which he soon applied to many areas of American life in lectures and essays such as "The American Scholar" and "Self-Reliance." His *Essays* (2 vol., 1841, 1844) won him an international reputation.

Wayne Kernodle

Wayne R. Kernodle (1919–   ) is currently a professor of sociology and anthropology at the College of William and Mary, Williamsburg, Virginia. In his work as a sociologist he has spent much time among the "hill people." In addition to teaching and writing, Professor Kernodle has been involved in research for the National Institute of Mental Health. Most of his writing appears in professional journals.

Harper Lee

The Pulitzer Prize in 1961 was awarded to Harper Lee (1926–   ) for *To Kill a Mockingbird*, a novel about two children who grow up in the South, learning the mores of the culture and the convictions of their lawyer father. An Alabaman, Lee seems to be the prototype of Scout Finch, the young narrator of her best-selling novel, which has been made into a motion picture and translated into many languages.

Walt Whitman

Walt Whitman (1819–1892) was born the second of nine children near Huntington, Long Island. When he was two, the family moved to Brooklyn. Before he was ten years old, Whitman quit school to work as an office clerk, then later as a typesetter and writer on a newspaper, and still later as a carpenter. In 1855 he published the first edition of his now famous book of poetry, *Leaves of Grass*, one of the first copies of which went to Ralph Waldo Emerson, whose famous essays and lectures were one of Whitman's chief inspirations. Emerson not only read the slim volume of verses but wrote at once to say he thought it "the most extraordinary that America has yet produced." Between 1855 and the year of his death, Whitman prepared nine separate editions of *Leaves of Grass*. In response to disapproval from critics—who charged him with crudities because they could not get used to his long line—and from the general reader—who was offended by his "unpoetic" language, his frankness, and his symbolic structure—Whitman wrote: "I too am not a bit tamed, I too am untranslatable, I sound my barbaric yawp over the roofs of the world." Universally Whitman is now considered one of America's great poets.

Paul Horgan

Born in Buffalo, New York, Paul Horgan (1903–   ) moved to New Mexico with his family in 1914 because of his father's health. Horgan's life was thereafter to alternate between the East, where he studied singing, and the West, where he served in various capacities at the New Mexico Military Institute. His first writing appeared in *Poetry*, and a short story was included in the 1931 O. Henry Memorial volume. His first published novel won the Harper Prize in 1933. Since then he has written many novels, plays, and short stories. In 1954 he published a two-volume history of the Rio Grande, *Great River*, which won both a Pulitzer Prize and the Bancroft Prize for History. His most recent novel is entitled *The Thin Mountain Air* (1977).

Gamaliel Bradford, Jr.

Gamaliel Bradford, Jr. (1863–1932), was a descendent of William Bradford, Governor of the Plymouth Colony. His chief vehicle was biography. He called his work *psychography*, a term he gave to his condensed psychological character sketches. Although an invalid most of his life, he wrote a great deal, seeking always a place in the literary sun. His work has probably greatest significance as an early instance of what was to become psychoanalytical criticism.

Leslie Silko

Leslie Silko (1948–   ) was born in Albuquerque, New Mexico, and grew up at Laguna Pueblo. She is of mixed-breed ancestry. In more recent years she has made her home in Ketchikan, Alaska. The 1975 volume of the *Best American Short Stories* anthology was dedicated to Ms. Silko by the editor, Martha Foley.

AMERICAN LITERATURE

THE CLASSICAL PERIOD

1830-1865

Between the years 1830 and 1865, America produced a galaxy of writers whose light shines even more brilliantly today than it did 100 years ago. At the beginning of this period, Edgar Allan Poe had already published his first poems and was turning his hand to short stories. By the end, Emily Dickinson had her extraordinary "letter to the world" well underway.

In the middle of the era, Ralph Waldo Emerson, Henry David Thoreau, Nathaniel Hawthorne, Herman Melville, and Walt Whitman wrote their greatest works—the literary classics that have given this period its name. We will focus here on most of these major figures, but it should be mentioned that many other well-known literary women and men flourished at this time. There were, for example, the Cambridge poets Henry Wadsworth Longfellow, Oliver Wendell Holmes, and James Russell Lowell, all of whom taught at Harvard. There was John Greenleaf Whittier, the author of *Snowbound*, considered America's greatest pastoral poem. There were Harriet Beecher Stowe and Louisa May Alcott, who wrote, respectively, *Uncle Tom's Cabin* (1852) and *Little Women* (1868)—two of the most popular books ever published.

How can we account for this enormous outpouring of creative energy? The explanation usually advanced is *transcendentalism*. It has been said that all, or nearly all, of the greatest American writers of the time were either directly influenced by this philosophy or were reacting against it.

EMERSON, THOREAU, AND TRANSCENDENTALISM

Many foreign writers and thinkers as well as many Americans contributed to the philosophy that goes by the name of *transcendentalism*. It is generally agreed, however, that the authors who contributed most heavily were the Americans Ralph Waldo Emerson and Henry David Thoreau. Emerson's essay "Nature" (1836) is usually considered the best and most systematic expression of the philosophy, although its premises are further elaborated in some of Emerson's other essays, in his poems, and in Thoreau's famous *Walden* (1854). Let us try to define transcendentalism.

Its root, *scandere*, means "to climb." (We find the same root in such familiar words as *ascend* and *descend*.) Its prefix, *trans-*, means "over." Thus, *to transcend* is *to climb over* or, more broadly, *to go beyond*.

"To go beyond what?" is the next question we might ask. For the transcendentalists of the middle part of the nineteenth century, the "what" was the limitations of the senses and of everyday experience. When Thoreau writes, "I have never yet met a man who was quite awake," he is commenting on these everyday limitations, saying that we do not see to the roots of things.

A next question might be, "How do we go beyond everyday experience?" The answer is, "by depending upon our intuition rather than on reason or logic." Reliance on intuition was nothing new in America. The Puritans had hoped for an intuitive revelation that they were among God's "chosen"; the Quakers tried to live by the "inner light."

Finally we may ask, "What happens when, by use of intuition, we go beyond everyday human experience?" The broadest answer, according to the transcendentalists, is that we discover higher truths and insights. For Emerson, one of the specific discoveries was "the all in each." He discovered that "the individual is the world." He placed the individual squarely at the spiritual center of the universe. This credo does not mean that the transcendentalists did not believe in God; it does mean that they did not think of God as something apart from human beings or nature. Thoreau thought God was so much a part of himself that when he was asked on his deathbed whether he had made peace with God, he answered, "I didn't know we had ever quarreled."

Transcendentalism was, then, a radically humanistic philosophy. In this respect it was opposed to the otherworldly philosophy of the Puritans. But it was similar to Puritanism in at least one respect: it was highly moralistic. Emerson and Thoreau were concerned with how human beings should live. Democracy, equality, individualism, self-reliance, integrity, optimism—these were among their key values. It is significant that one of the last and best of Emerson's works was a series of essays entitled "The Conduct of Life" (1860).

POE, HAWTHORNE, MELVILLE: THE POWER OF BLACKNESS

Certainly Poe, Hawthorne, and Melville shared many of the above-named values with Emerson and Thoreau; yet none of these great writers subscribed to transcendentalism. If they were influenced by it at all, they were negatively influenced; transcendentalism was something for them to react against.

The main reason for their rejection of the philosophy was their denial of some of Emerson's major premises and attitudes: his insistence on optimism, his belief in progress, and above all his failure to recognize fully the reality of evil. Emerson, whom we still see as more characteristically American than the other three, was full of sun and light. But Melville, who might have been speaking for Poe and Hawthorne as well, wrote of the "great power of blackness . . . from whose visitation . . . no deeply thinking mind is always and wholly free." In their concern with blackness, with evil and sin, Poe, Hawthorne, and Melville had more in common with the Puritans than they did with Emerson and Thoreau.

Edgar Allan Poe knew blackness firsthand. From the beginning, his life was a series of catastrophes (for instance, his father deserted the family, and his mother died before he was three). For most of his forty years, he struggled against poverty, in spite of the fact that his story "The Gold Bug" and his poem "The Raven" were instant successes.

Yet, undaunted by hardships, misfortunes, and acute emotional anguish, Poe achieved eminence in three fields. He was an exceptional critic (the first professional to appreciate Hawthorne), a poet, and a short-story writer of marked distinction. And although some American critics and writers have disdained Poe, he had a profound effect on literature both here and abroad. Specifically, Poe strongly influenced the French symbolist poets and thus, indirectly, such Americans as T. S. Eliot and Wallace Stevens. He also virtually invented the detective story, and some of his own works remain classics of that genre. Finally, Poe was one of the first to use fiction to explore morbid states of mind. Thus, he is an early link in a chain that runs into some of the best fiction in our own time.

Hawthorne, too, was an intrepid explorer of the darker side of human nature, and he is often given credit for founding the psychological novel. But we have discussed him elsewhere and will pass now to Herman Melville.

Melville's career began brightly enough with the successful novels *Typee* (1846) and *Omoo* (1847), which were semi-romanticized adventures about his own experiences in the South Seas; but he soon determined to follow his own genius—to tell the truth as he saw it rather than to please readers. And his pursuit of truth led him into poverty and profound despair.

Unlike the transcendentalists, who believed in a congruity between the structure of the human spirit and the structure of the universe, Melville believed that the structure of the universe was tragically flawed. He could not account for the inequities and injustices of the world, and thus he said, "No! in thunder" to that world. He used his later novels—especially *Moby Dick* (1851), *Pierre* (1852), and *The Confidence Man* (1857)—to communicate that message, but few cared to hear it during his lifetime.

Today, however, his reputation as one of our greatest writers is firmly established. *Moby Dick*, the story of Captain Ahab's maniacal pursuit of the white whale, is acknowledged to be one of the greatest novels of the world. And short works such as "Bartleby the Scrivener" (1853), "Benito Cereno" (1855), and *Billy Budd* are undisputed American classics. The last of these, incidentally, was finished just 5 days before Melville's death and was not published until 30 years later. It is a tragedy—if it had not been, it would not have been true to Melville's vision—but it also strikes an affirmative note. This

189

note is echoed in one of the last poems Melville was to write, which ends:

If sorrow come, anew we twine
The Rose-Vine round the Cross.

WALT WHITMAN: THE FULLNESS OF THE LIGHT

By 1855, when Walt Whitman personally set the type and printed the first edition of his poems, *Leaves of Grass*, there were thirty-two states in the Union, sweeping from Florida and Texas in the South, through California in the West, to Wisconsin and Michigan in the North. As we have seen, America had given more than its share of great writers to the world; but it had not yet produced a writer who in work and person could fully express the scope and grandeur of the continental United States, who could fully articulate the American dream, who could show us what it meant to be quintessentially American.

These were the achievements of Walt Whitman. The very shape and structure of his work— the fact that it was written in free verse; the long, rambling lines; the endless catalogs; its roughness and unevenness; the fact that it grew larger with each edition (and there were eight editions altogether)—suggested continental America.

As determined as Melville was to say "No! in thunder," Whitman said "Yes!" in a sunburst of optimism and energy that far surpassed his "master," Emerson. Whitman loved everything, affirmed everything, took everything in.

But most important of all was Whitman's identification with the common people. Other writers before him had expressed concern for the average citizen, and nearly all had believed deeply in the democratic ideal, but Whitman *was* a common man —a printer's devil, a reporter, a schoolteacher, a politician, a homebuilder, a volunteer nurse, a government employee. Whitman celebrated himself, to be sure, but he did so as a symbol of the "divine average," as a fellow traveler along the open road on the long journey of the American people toward freedom and self-development.

LITERARY FIGURES

1803–1882	Ralph Waldo Emerson	1812–1892	Harriet Beecher Stowe
1804–1864	Nathaniel Hawthorne	1817–1862	Henry David Thoreau
1807–1882	Henry Wadsworth Longfellow	1819–1891	James Russell Lowell
1807–1892	John Greenleaf Whittier	1819–1891	Herman Melville
1809–1849	Edgar Allan Poe	1819–1892	Walt Whitman
1809–1894	Oliver Wendell Holmes	1830–1886	Emily Dickinson
1810–1850	Margaret Fuller	1832–1888	Louisa May Alcott

1830 **Time Line** 1865

Historical Events

1830

1831 American Anti-Slavery Society founded

1836 Battle of the Alamo
 Morse invents a telegraph instrument

1840

1840 *The Dial* established; Margaret Fuller,
 first editor

1845 Texas admitted to the Union
1846–1847 War with Mexico

1848 Gold discovered at Sutter's Mill, California

1850

1850 California admitted to the Union
 Harper's Magazine established

1854 New York and Chicago connected by railroad

1857 *Atlantic Monthly* established
 Dred Scott decision
1858 Transatlantic cable completed
1859 John Brown's raid on Harper's Ferry

1860

1861 Lincoln becomes President; Outbreak of
 Civil War
1863 Emancipation Proclamation; Lincoln's
 "Gettysburg Address"
1865 End of Civil War; surrender at Appomatox
 Assassination of Lincoln

Literary Events

1831 Edgar Allan Poe, *Poems*

1836 Ralph Waldo Emerson, "Nature"
 Oliver Wendell Holmes, *Poems*
1837 Emerson, "The American Scholar"
 Nathaniel Hawthorne, *Twice-Told Tales*
 John Greenleaf Whittier, *Poems*

1840 Poe, *Tales of the Grotesque and Arabesque*
1841 Emerson, *Essays*
 Henry Wadsworth Longfellow, *Ballads and Other Poems*
1844 Margaret Fuller, *Woman in the Nineteenth Century*
1845 Poe, "The Raven"
1846 Hawthorne, *Mosses from an Old Manse*
 Herman Melville, *Typee*
1847 Emerson, *Poems*
 Longfellow, *Evangeline*
 Melville, *Omoo*
1848 James Russell Lowell, *A Fable for Critics*; *Bigelow Papers*
1849 Henry David Thoreau, *Week on the Concord and Merrimac Rivers*

1850 Hawthorne, *The Scarlet Letter*
1851 Hawthorne, *The House of the Seven Gables*
 Melville, *Moby Dick*
1852 Hawthorne, *Blithedale Romance*
 Melville, *Pierre*
 Harriet Beecher Stowe, *Uncle Tom's Cabin*
1854 Thoreau, *Walden*
1855 Longfellow, *The Song of Hiawatha*
 Walt Whitman, *Leaves of Grass*
1857 Melville, *The Confidence Man*
1858 Longfellow, *The Courtship of Miles Standish*

1860 Emerson, "The Conduct of Life"
 Hawthorne, *The Marble Faun*

1865 Whitman, *Drum-Taps*

HENRY DAVID THOREAU

1817-1862

Thoreau moved to Walden to simplify his life. "I wished to live deliberately," he wrote, "to front only the essential facts of life and see if I could not learn what it had to teach, and not, when I came to die, discover that I had not lived." But there were other reasons. He thought of himself as a philosopher and "to be a philosopher," he said, "is not merely to have subtle thoughts, nor even to found a school, but so to love wisdom as to live according to its dictates. . . . It is to solve some of the problems of life, not only theoretically but practically."

F̲ew writers in America have felt a sense of place as strongly as Henry David Thoreau. He was born in Concord, Massachusetts, lived most of his life in and around the village, died, and was buried there. Yet he was not a hermit, in spite of his resolve at the age of twenty-eight to spend more than two years alone at Walden Pond, a mile and a half south of Concord. Thoreau's neighbors knew him as a strong-minded, restless individual, a man of dry wit, frank opinions, and unquestioned integrity. Clearly he was in love with life, but less with the bustle of Concord village than with the natural world of the fields and nearby ponds. He could do without the post office and the church more easily than he could give up his walks in the woods. "If a man does not keep pace with his companions," he once wrote, "perhaps it is because he hears a different drummer. Let him step to the music which he hears, however measured or far away. It is not important that he should mature as soon as an apple tree or an oak."

The "different drummer" Thoreau stepped to set him apart from Concord even before he returned from four years at Harvard College. He questioned authority when it was unreasonable or untested; he resented traditions when they were hollow gestures to the past; above all he fought his neighbors' "desperate haste to succeed and in such desperate enterprises." On graduation he applied for a teaching position in Concord but kept it only a few weeks. When a member of the school committee insisted Thoreau must not "spare the rod" on unruly pupils, he chose six of his students at random, whipped them soundly, and then resigned. Some months later he and his brother John opened a private school in Concord which prospered for about three years in spite of its progressive theories of education. The rod was abandoned; students were encouraged to make their own observations and form their own opinions, not merely parrot what they read in books; classes were held outdoors whenever possible so that the natural world could mix with the academic. Had it not been for John Thoreau's failing health, Henry might have devoted much of his life to teaching, since it provided him with the leisure to transact what he called "private business"—the writing of poetry, keeping his journals, reading, nature study, conversation.

After his brother's premature death in 1842, he resolved that making a living should never interfere with life itself, and so he spent the next twenty years earning only the minimum he needed, never letting work become an end in itself. He helped his father in the family's pencil factory; he lived with Ralph Waldo Emerson, the famous essayist, lecturer, and poet, and his wife as caretaker of their property; he worked in Concord as a gardener, surveyor, magazine editor, and curator of the lyceum; he lectured, with only fair success, from Bangor, Maine, to Philadelphia; he tutored the children of Emerson's brother William on Staten Island until homesickness drove him back to Concord. All the while, of course, he was confiding his inward life in his journals. What passed for the world's business— "desperate enterprises," that is—little interested him.

If Thoreau had written nothing else but his journals—he began them in 1837, just a few months after graduation from Harvard, and made the last entry a few months before his death—fame might have been even slower in coming than it was. For years he had mined the journals for lecture material and for the few essays he published in *The Dial*, at Emerson's suggestion. But it was not until 1845 that he made a decision which altered his life. Making his living in town was consuming more of his time than he had bargained for. "Actually," he was to write later, "the laboring man has not leisure for a true integrity day by day; he cannot afford to sustain the manliest relations to man; his labor would be depreciated in the market. He has no time to be anything but a machine." To escape the market and the machine, Thoreau conceived of building a cabin in comparative solitude and spending uninterrupted nights and days sorting out his philosophies. He considered Flint's Pond in nearby Lincoln, but he could not convince the owner of the land that his idea was sensible. Late in 1844, Emerson purchased some wood lots on the north shore of Walden Pond, and five months later Thoreau was borrowing an ax to build his own cabin there. For "rent," he would clear the fields for gardening and leave the cabin on the edge of the pine grove after he had finished his "experiment in living." On Independence Day, 1845, he moved in. He stayed slightly more than two years and two months.

Walden; or Life in the Woods is the record of that sojourn, and much more. The writing of this book and the reasons for writing it, however, are often misunderstood. Thoreau moved to Walden to simplify his life. "I wished to live deliberately," he wrote, "to front only the essential facts of life, and see if I could not learn what it had to teach, and not, when I came to die, discover that I had not lived." But there were other reasons. He thought of himself as a philosopher and "to be a philosopher," he said, "is not merely to have subtle thoughts, nor even to found a school, but so to

WALDEN;

OR,

LIFE IN THE WOODS.

BY HENRY D. THOREAU,

AUTHOR OF "A WEEK ON THE CONCORD AND MERRIMACK RIVERS."

I do not propose to write an ode to dejection, but to brag as lustily as chanticleer in the morning, standing on his roost, if only to wake my neighbors up. — Page 92.

BOSTON:
TICKNOR AND FIELDS.
M DCCC LIV.

The original title page of Walden.

love wisdom as to live according to its dictates. . . . It is to solve some of the problems of life, not only theoretically but practically." He also wished to write a book. Not *Walden;* that was his second book. He and his brother John had made a memorable excursion in 1839 on the Concord and Merrimack Rivers, and he had delayed too long in publishing an account of the trip from the notes he had made in his journals. Possibly he had also felt the enmity of his fellow townspeople long enough. After he had refused to pay his church taxes in 1838,

he was looked upon as an extremist. Then, in 1844, when he and Edward Hoar let a cooking fire on the banks of Fairhaven Bay get out of hand and burn a hundred acres of Concord woodland, his reputation was thoroughly blackened.

His return to civilization in 1847 was dictated by equally practical considerations. Now that he had made his experiment, he had "several more lives to live, and could not spare any more time for that one." Emerson, moreover, was leaving in September for a lecture tour in England and had persuaded Thoreau once again to live in his Concord home and take care of his family. And his book was almost finished. He was eager to see it in print. Publishers in New York and Boston, alas, were not eager to accept it. It was 1849 before *A Week on the Concord and Merrimack Rivers* appeared, and then only at Thoreau's own expense. He had agreed to pay for a thousand copies. It was soon evident that the book was a total failure. The account of the voyage was vivid enough, but he bored some readers and offended others with his long digressions on history, ancient authors, philosophy, and especially religion. By 1853, the Boston publishers had sold only 219 copies. When they shipped the rest to Thoreau in October of that year he wrote in his journal: "They are something more substantial than fame, as my back knows, which has borne them up two flights of stairs to a place similar to that to which they trace their origin. . . . I have now a library of nearly nine hundred volumes, over seven hundred of which I wrote myself." Thoreau never lost his sense of humor, particularly about the eccentricities of his neighbors or about the foibles of life.

The publication of *Walden* is another story. Emerson persuaded Ticknor and Fields of Boston to print it. Before its appearance in August, 1854, excerpts appearing in the New York *Tribune* helped to spread the author's name. Even though the reviewers were not wholly satisfied, Thoreau was, with the general reception of the book and its sales. He knew he had written a masterpiece, and if it took several decades before America realized it, he was prepared for that. Surprisingly he never attempted a sequel to the book, nor did he ever cull his journals for a third volume of any kind. The last eight years of his life were concentrated on brief travels—New Jersey, the Maine woods, Brooklyn (to meet Walt Whitman), Minnesota (to regain his health)—and on social issues on which he felt compelled to speak.

As early as 1849 he had published a remarkable essay called "On the Duty of Civil Disobedience" (it became Gandhi's [1869–1948] textbook during his passive resistance campaign in India), and he frequently lectured and debated on the Abolition movement, though he never formally joined any organizations. He forever remained the staunch individualism, standing apart from, but not above, his fellows, the better to observe them and their problems. When in 1859 he rose to defend another strong-minded man, Captain John Brown, a few days after the Harper's Ferry attack, he was advised by his Concord neighbors that such a defense was ill-timed. Thoreau assured them that he was not asking for advice but calling a meeting. When the selectmen refused to toll the bell for that meeting, he pulled the rope himself. Concord should have known by that time that Henry Thoreau made most of his decisions with little thought to their popularity and much to their necessity and their rightness.

Walden is based on similar assumptions. "I do not propose to write an ode to dejection," he writes on its title page, "but to brag as lustily as Chanticleer in the morning, standing on his roost, if only to wake my neighbors up." Whether they wished to be waked or not, we might add. He is not writing for the "strong and valiant natures, who will mind their own affairs whether in heaven or hell," nor is he addressing "those who are well employed, in whatever circumstances, and [who] know whether they are well employed or not," but

"the mass of men who are discontented and idly complaining of the hardness of their lot or of the times"—to these Thoreau offers advice, inspiration, severe criticism, encouragement, even practical remedies. Modern critics see something of *Robinson Crusoe* in Thoreau's experiment in solitary life, something also of Jonathan Swift's *Gulliver's Travels* in his severe criticism of so-called civilization. Thoreau's contemporaries on reading *Walden* looked back to Emerson's essays, particularly "Self-Reliance," and to the sermons of Colonial New England preachers. But whatever comparisons are made, certain distinguishing characteristics set this book apart and give it a flavor of its own.

Thoreau first of all begins his opening sentence with the first-person pronoun and continues in that relaxed informal tone. We never lose sight of a humble citizen of Concord seeking to learn about life in observing nature and sharing his discoveries. Second, he warns us that he "would not have any one adopt [*his*] mode of living on any account." He is not advocating our leaving home to live on the edge of a pond in a timbered cabin. "I would have each one be very careful to find out and pursue *his own way*," he tells us more than once, so long as one knows where one is going and why. Finally, Thoreau's sense of humor (often missed by the hurried reader), his keen eye for the illustrative anecdote, his respect for the forces of nature, his alertness to the way language carefully shaped can reflect those forces, and above all his quality of "being," as Emerson called it, make *Walden* a unique experience. This book is not merely about nature, it *is* nature, captured. "I have travelled a good deal in Concord," he tells us with tongue in cheek early in the first chapter. We, too, can "travel" widely in Thoreau's world. Concord and Walden Pond have been reduced, in his prose, to a capsule of the human condition. He is writing not merely about life in 1840 but about us.

WALDEN

Thoreau divided his book
into eighteen chapters, the longest by far
being the first, called "Economy."
It is quite significant that he chose to begin
Walden with "Economy" and to devote more
than a quarter of the book to the chapter.
See if you can discover from the following
six excerpts some of the reasons
why economy was such a key concept
for Thoreau.

I. Economy

When I wrote the following pages, or rather the bulk of them, I lived alone, in the woods, a mile from any neighbor, in a house which I had built myself, on the shore of Walden Pond, in Concord, Massachusetts, and earned my living by the labor of my hands only. I lived there two years and two months. At present I am a sojourner in civilized life again.

I should not obtrude my affairs so much on the notice of my readers if very particular inquiries had not been made by my townsmen concerning my mode of life, which some would call impertinent, though they do not appear to me at all impertinent, but, considering the circumstances, very natural and pertinent. Some have asked what I got to eat; if I did not feel lonesome; if I was not afraid; and the like. Others have been curious to learn what portion of my income I devoted to charitable purposes; and some, who have large families, how many poor children I maintained. I will therefore ask those of my readers who feel no particular interest in me to pardon me if I undertake to answer some of these questions in this book. In most books, the *I*, or first person, is omitted; in this it will be retained; that, in respect to egotism, is the main difference. We commonly do not remember that it is, after all, always the first person that is speaking. I should not talk so much about myself if there were anybody else whom I knew as well. Unfortunately, I am confined to this theme by the narrowness of my experience. Moreover, I, on my side, require of every writer, first or last, a simple and sincere account of his own life, and not merely what he has heard of other men's lives; some such account as he would send to his kindred from a distant land; for if he has lived sincerely, it must have been in a distant land to me. Perhaps these pages are more particularly addressed to poor students. As for the rest of my readers, they will accept such portions as apply to them. I trust that none will stretch the seams in putting on the coat, for it may do good service to him whom it fits. . . .

I see young men, my townsmen, whose misfortune it is to have inherited farms, houses, barns, cattle, and farming tools; for these are more easily acquired than got rid of. Better if they had been born in the open pasture and suckled by a wolf, that they might have seen with clearer eyes what field they were called to labor in. Who made them serfs of the soil? Why should they eat their sixty acres, when man is condemned to eat only his peck of dirt? Why should they begin digging their graves as soon as they are born? They have got to live a man's life, pushing all these things before them, and get on as well as they can. How many a poor immortal soul have I met well nigh crushed and smothered under its load, creeping down the road of life, pushing before it a barn seventy-five feet by forty, its Augean

196 HENRY DAVID THOREAU

stables[1] never cleansed, and one hundred acres of land, tillage, mowing, pasture, and wood-lot! The portionless, who struggle with no such unnecessary inherited encumbrances, find it labor enough to subdue and cultivate a few cubic feet of flesh.

But men labor under a mistake. The better part of the man is soon ploughed into the soil for compost. By a seeming fate, commonly called necessity, they are employed, as it says in an old book, laying up treasures which moth and rust will corrupt and thieves break through and steal. It is a fool's life, as they will find when they get to the end of it, if not before. . . .

When I consider my neighbors, the farmers of Concord, who are at least as well off as the other classes, I find that for the most part they have been toiling twenty, thirty, or forty years, that they may become the real owners of their farms, which commonly they have inherited with encumbrances, or else bought with hired money,—and we may regard one third of that toil as the cost of their houses,—but commonly they have not paid for them yet. It is true, the encumbrances sometimes outweigh the value of the farm, so that the farm itself becomes one great encumbrance, and still a man is found to inherit it, being well acquainted with it, as he says. On applying to the assessors, I am surprised to learn that they cannot at once name a dozen in the town who own their farms free and clear. If you would know the history of these homesteads, inquire at the bank where they are mortgaged. The man who has actually paid for his farm with labor on it is so rare that every neighbor can point to him. I doubt if there are three such men in Concord. What has been said of the merchants, that a very large majority, even ninety-seven in a hundred, are sure to fail, is equally true of the farmers. With regard to the merchants, however, one of them says pertinently that a great part of their failures are not genuine pecuniary failures, but merely failures to fulfil their engagements, because it is inconvenient; that is, it is the moral character that breaks down. But this puts an infinitely worse face on the matter, and

suggests, beside, that probably not even the other three succeed in saving their souls, but are perchance bankrupt in a worse sense than they who fail honestly. Bankruptcy and repudiation are the springboards from which much of our civilization vaults and turns its somersets, but the savage stands on the unelastic plank of famine. . . .

Near the end of March, 1845, I borrowed an axe and went down to the woods by Walden Pond, nearest to where I intended to build my house, and began to cut down some tall arrowy white pines, still in their youth, for timber. It is difficult to begin without borrowing, but perhaps it is the most generous course thus to permit your fellow-men to have an interest in your enterprise. The owner of the axe, as he released his hold on it, said that it was the apple of his eye; but I returned it sharper than I received it. It was a pleasant hillside where I worked, covered with pine woods, through which I looked out on the pond, and a small open field in the woods where pines and hickories were springing up. The ice in the pond was not yet dissolved, though there were some open spaces, and it was all dark colored and saturated with water. There were some slight flurries of snow during the days that I worked there; but for the most part when I came out on to the railroad, on my way home, its yellow sand heap stretched away gleaming in the hazy atmosphere, and the rails shone in the spring sun, and I heard the lark and pewee and other birds already come to commence another year with us. They were pleasant spring days, in which the winter of man's discontent was thawing as well as the earth, and the life that had lain torpid began to stretch itself. One day, when my axe had come off and I had cut a green hickory for a wedge, driving it with a stone, and had placed the whole to soak in a pond hole in order to swell the wood, I saw a striped snake run

---

1. **Augean**\ŏ ᴬjē•ən\ **stables,** stables in which 3,000 oxen were kept, left uncleaned for 30 years; Hercules cleaned the stables in one day.

into the water, and he lay on the bottom, apparently without inconvenience, as long as I stayed there, or more than a quarter of an hour; perhaps because he had not yet fairly come out of the torpid state. It appeared to me that for a like reason men remain in their present low and primitive condition; but if they should feel the influence of the spring of springs arousing them, they would of necessity rise to a higher and more ethereal life. I had previously seen the snakes in frosty mornings in my path with portions of their bodies still numb and inflexible, waiting for the sun to thaw them. On the 1st of April it rained and melted the ice, and in the early part of the day, which was very foggy, I heard a stray goose groping about over the pond and cackling as if lost, or like the spirit of the fog.

So I went on for some days cutting and hewing timber, and also studs and rafters, all with my narrow axe, not having many communicable or scholar-like thoughts, singing to myself,—

> Men say they know many things;
> But lo! they have taken wings,—
> The arts and sciences,
> And a thousand appliances;
> The wind that blows
> Is all that anybody knows.

I hewed the main timbers six inches square, most of the studs on two sides only, and the rafters and floor timbers on one side, leaving the rest of the bark on, so that they were just as straight and much stronger than sawed ones. Each stick was carefully mortised or tenoned by its stump, for I had borrowed other tools by this time. My days in the woods were not very long ones; yet I usually carried my dinner of bread and butter, and read the newspaper in which it was wrapped, at noon, sitting amid the green pine boughs which I had cut off, and to my bread was imparted some of their fragrance, for my hands were covered with a thick coat of pitch. Before I had done I was more the friend than the foe of the pine tree, though I had cut down some of them, having become better ac-

quainted with it. Sometimes a rambler in the wood was attracted by the sound of my axe, and we chatted pleasantly over the chips which I had made.

By the middle of April, for I made no haste in my work, but rather made the most of it, my house was framed and ready for the raising. I had already bought the shanty of James Collins, an Irishman who worked on the Fitchburg Railroad, for boards. James Collins' shanty was considered an uncommonly fine one. When I called to see it he was not at home. I walked about the outside, at first unobserved from within, the window was so deep and high. It was of small dimensions, with a peaked cottage roof, and not much else to be seen, the dirt being raised five feet all around as if it were a compost heap. The roof was the soundest part, though a good deal warped and made brittle by the sun. Door-sill there was none, but a perennial passage for the hens under the door board. Mrs. C. came to the door and asked me to view it from the inside. The hens were driven in by my approach. It was dark, and had a dirt floor for the most part, dank, clammy, and aguish, only here a board and there a board which would not bear removal. She lighted a lamp to show me the inside of the roof and the walls, and also that the board floor extended under the bed, warning me not to step into the cellar, a sort of dust hole two feet deep. In her own words, they were "good boards overhead, good boards all around, and a good window,"—of two whole squares originally, only the cat had passed out that way lately. There was a stove, a bed, and a place to sit, an infant in the house where it was born, a silk parasol, gilt-framed looking-glass, and a patent new coffee-mill nailed to an oak sapling, all told. The bargain was soon concluded, for James had in the meanwhile returned. I to pay four dollars and twenty-five cents to-night, he to vacate at five to-morrow morning, selling to nobody else meanwhile: I to take possession at six. It were well, he said, to be there early, and anticipate certain indistinct but wholly unjust claims on the score of ground rent and fuel. This he assured me was the only encumbrance. At six I passed him and his family on the road. One large bundle held their all,— bed, coffee-mill, looking-glass, hens,—all but the cat; she took to the woods and became a wild cat, and, as I learned afterward, trod in a trap set for woodchucks, and so became a dead cat at last.

I took down this dwelling the same morning, drawing the nails, and removed it to the pond side by small car-loads, spreading the boards on the grass there to bleach and warp back again in the sun. One early thrush gave me a note or two as I drove along the woodland path. I was informed treacherously by a young Patrick that neighbor Seeley, an Irishman, in the intervals of the carting, transferred the still tolerable, straight, and drivable nails, staples, and spikes to his pocket, and then stood when I came back to pass the time of day, and look freshly up, unconcerned, with spring thoughts, at the devastation; there being a dearth of work, as he said. He was there to represent spectatordom, and help make this seemingly insignificant event one with the removal of the gods of Troy.[2]

I dug my cellar in the side of a hill sloping to the south, where a woodchuck had formerly dug his burrow, down through sumach[3] and blackberry roots, and the lowest stain of vegetation, six feet square by seven deep, to a fine sand where potatoes would not freeze in any winter. The sides were left shelving, and not stoned; but the sun having never shone on them, the sand still keeps its place. It was but two hours' work. I took particular pleasure in this breaking of ground, for in almost all latitudes men dig into the earth for an equable temperature. Under the most splendid house in the city is still to be found the cellar where they store their roots as of old, and long after the superstructure has disappeared posterity remark its dent in the earth. The house is still but a sort of porch at the entrance of a burrow.

At length, in the beginning of May, with the help of some of my acquaintances, rather to improve so good an occasion for neighborliness than from any necessity, I set up the frame of my house. No man was ever more honored in the character of his raisers than I. They are destined, I trust, to assist at the raising of loftier structures one day. I began to occupy my house on the 4th of July, as soon as it was boarded and roofed, for the boards were carefully feather-edged and lapped, so that it was perfectly impervious to rain, but before boarding I laid the foundation of a chimney at one end, bringing two cartloads of stones up the hill from the pond in my arms. I built the chimney after my hoeing in the fall, before a fire became necessary for warmth, doing my cooking in the mean while out of doors on the ground, early in the morning: which mode I still think is in some respects more convenient and agreeable than the usual one. When it stormed before my bread was baked, I fixed a few boards over the fire, and sat under them to watch my loaf, and passed some pleasant hours in that way. In those days, when my hands were much employed, I read but little, but the least scraps of paper which lay on the ground, my holder, or tablecloth, afforded me as much entertainment, in fact answered the same purpose as the Iliad.[4] . . .

Before winter I built a chimney, and shingled the sides of my house, which were already impervious to rain, with imperfect and sappy shingles made of the first slice of the log, whose edges I was obliged to straighten with a plane.

I have thus a tight shingled and plastered house, ten feet wide by fifteen long, and eight-feet posts, with a garret and a closet, a large window on each side, two trap doors, one door at the end, and a brick fireplace opposite. The exact cost of my house, paying the usual price for such materials as I used, but not counting the work, all of which was done by myself, was as follows; and I give the details because very

---

2. **gods of Troy**, probably an allusion to Virgil's *Aeneid*, in which the destruction of Troy is told.
3. **sumach, sumac**\ˈsū·măk\ any of a family of small trees, shrubs, and woody vines that produce small fleshy fruit and a milky juice.
4. **Iliad**\ˈĭl·ē·əd\ Greek epic composed by Homer, describing the siege of Troy and the terrible effects of Achilles' wrath.

few are able to tell exactly what their houses cost, and fewer still, if any, the separate cost of the various materials which compose them:—

Boards	$8 03½, mostly shanty boards.
Refuse shingles for roof and sides	4 00
Laths	1 25
Two second-hand windows with glass	2 43
One thousand old brick	4 00
Two casks of lime	2 40 That was high.
Hair	0 31 More than I needed.
Mantle-tree iron	0 15
Nails	3 90
Hinges and screws	0 14
Latch	0 10
Chalk	0 01
Transportation	1 40 I carried a good part on my back.
In all	$28 12½

These are all the materials excepting the timber, stones, and sand, which I claimed by squatter's right. I have also a small woodshed adjoining, made chiefly of the stuff which was left after building the house.

I intend to build me a house which will surpass any on the main street in Concord in grandeur and luxury, as soon as it pleases me as much and will cost me no more than my present one. . . .

For more than five years I maintained myself solely by the labor of my hands, and I found, that by working about six weeks in a year, I could meet all the expenses of living. The whole of my winters, as well as most of my summers, I had free and clear for study. I have thoroughly tried school-keeping, and found that my expenses were in proportion, or rather out of proportion, to my income, for I was obliged to dress and train, not to say think and believe, accordingly, and I lost my time into the bargain. As I did not teach for the good of my fellow-men, but simply for a livelihood,

this was a failure. I have tried trade; but I found that it would take ten years to get under way in that, and that then I should probably be on my way to the devil. I was actually afraid that I might by that time be doing what is called a good business. When formerly I was looking about to see what I could do for a living, some sad experience in conforming to the wishes of friends being fresh in my mind to tax my ingenuity, I thought often and seriously of picking huckleberries; that surely I could do, and its small profits might suffice,—for my greatest skill has been to want but little,—so little capital is required, so little distraction from my wonted moods, I foolishly thought. While my acquaintances went unhesitatingly into trade or the professions, I contemplated this occupation as most like theirs; ranging the hills all summer to pick the berries which came in my way, and thereafter carelessly dispose of them; so, to keep the flocks of Admetus.[5] I also dreamed that I might gather the wild herbs, or carry evergreens to such villagers as loved to be reminded of the woods, even to the city, by hay-cart loads. But I have since learned that trade curses everything it handles; and though you trade in messages from heaven, the whole curse of trade attaches to the business.

As I preferred some things to others, and especially valued my freedom, as I could fare hard and yet succeed well, I did not wish to spend my time in earning rich carpets or other fine furniture, or delicate cookery, or a house in the Grecian or the Gothic style just yet. If there are any to whom it is no interruption to acquire these things, and who know how to use them when acquired, I relinquish to them the pursuit. Some are "industrious," and appear to love labor for its own sake, or perhaps because it keeps them out of worse mischief; to such I have at present nothing to say. Those who would not know what to do with more leisure than they now enjoy, I might advise to

5. **Admetus**\ad ˈmē·təs\ husband of Alcestis, who saved the life of Admetus by dying in his place; she was brought back from Hades by Hercules.

work twice as hard as they do,—work till they pay for themselves, and get their free papers. For myself I found that the occupation of a day-laborer was the most independent of any, especially as it required only thirty or forty days in a year to support one. The laborer's day ends with the going down of the sun, and he is then free to devote himself to his chosen pursuit, independent of his labor; but his employer, who speculates from month to month, has no respite from one end of the year to the other.

In short, I am convinced, both by faith and experience, that to maintain one's self on this earth is not a hardship but a pastime, if we will live simply and wisely; as the pursuits of the simpler nations are still the sports of the more artificial. It is not necessary that a man should earn his living by the sweat of his brow, unless he sweats easier than I do. . . .

I

ECONOMY AND LIFE

"Economy" can mean either thrifty management or merely the management of affairs, especially with regard to expenses. Thoreau uses it in both senses, but when he considers "expenses" he thinks not only of financial matters but also of expenses of time and energy and spirit. That he practiced economy in the building of his house is important, but of greater importance is the fact that he practiced economy in the building of his life. He was acutely conscious that the cost of anything should be measured by the amount of life that had to be exchanged for it.

One of the great "secrets" of Thoreau's life and practice of economy is that he knew better than most of us what he wanted. In the main he wanted freedom, the leisure to "philosophize" and develop the inner self. He found freedom at Walden Pond, but he found it as well everyhere else he lived, for he was a wise economist.

II

IMPLICATIONS

Discuss what Thoreau might have said about each of the following statements. What do you say about them?

1. The more possessions one has, the more difficult it is to practice economy.

2. Most of us today are overly concerned with the future, whereas we should be primarily concerned with the present.

3. Too much of our time is spent in trying to impress others; too little is spent in trying to satisfy our own inner needs.

4. It is foolish for a person to become a doctor, say, or a teacher, for such occupations leave one with too little time for oneself.

5. Self-discipline is a necessary preliminary to spiritual growth and realization.

6. Thoreau's modern-day counterpart is the hippie.

III

TECHNIQUES

Style

In literature, *style* refers to *how* writers say whatever they say. Naturally, how someone expresses a thought—in speech as well as in writing—can tell us a good deal about that person. To put it in the famous words of the French naturalist George Buffon, "The style is the man himself."

Thoreau's style tells us much about him. One need not read very far in *Walden*, for example, to discover that its author was well acquainted with both Greek and Oriental literature. References to such things as "Augean stables" or the *Harivamsa* (p. 202) tell us that Thoreau was not simply an articulate vagabond but a well-read and well-educated man.

Thoreau is also very much a man of his time and place, and his references to his native environment far outweigh his references to antiquity. There is also much of the New England Yankee in two of the most salient characteristics of his style—its *economy* and its *concreteness*. Study the first paragraph of *Walden*, looking for these characteristics. On the basis of the economy and concreteness of his style as well as your knowledge of Thoreau himself, be prepared to discuss Buffon's statement on style.

Having used "Economy"
for his keynote, Thoreau passes on
to his equally vital second chapter,
"Where I Lived, and What I Lived For."
The following excerpts tell us clearly
in lyric prose what daily life was like
at Walden Pond and in a more reflective prose
what Thoreau feels about the way most people
live their lives. Economy remains
an important concept, and Thoreau gives
readers a one-word formula
by which they may learn to arrange
their affairs more effectively.

II. Where I Lived, and What I Lived For

When first I took up my abode in the woods, that is, began to spend my nights as well as days there, which, by accident, was on Independence day, or the fourth of July, 1845, my house was not finished for winter, but was merely a defence against the rain, without plastering or chimney, the walls being of rough weather-stained boards, with wide chinks, which made it cool at night. The upright white hewn studs and freshly planed door and window casings gave it a clean and airy look, especially in the morning, when its timbers were saturated with dew, so that I fancied that by noon some sweet gum would exude from them. To my imagination it retained throughout the day more or less of this auroral[6] character, reminding me of a certain house on a mountain which I had visited a year before. This was an airy and unplastered cabin, fit to entertain a travelling god, and where a goddess might trail

her garments. The winds which passed over my dwelling were such as sweep over the ridges of mountains, bearing the broken strains, or celestial parts only, of terrestrial music. The morning wind forever blows, the poem of creation is uninterrupted; but few are the ears that hear it. Olympus[7] is but the outside of the earth everywhere.

The only house I had been the owner of before, if I except a boat, was a tent, which I used occasionally when making excursions in the summer, and this is still rolled up in my garret;[8] but the boat, after passing from hand to hand, has gone down the stream of time. With this more substantial shelter about me, I had made some progress toward settling in the world. This frame, so slightly clad, was a sort of crystallization around me, and reacted on the builder. It was suggestive somewhat as a picture in outlines. I did not need to go out doors to take the air, for the atmosphere within had lost none of its freshness. It was not so much within doors as behind a door where I sat, even in the rainiest weather. The Harivamsa[9] says, "An abode without birds is like a meat without seasoning." Such was not my abode, for I found myself suddenly neighbor to the birds; not by having imprisoned one, but having caged myself near them. I was not only nearer to some of those which commonly frequent the garden and the orchard, but to those wilder and more thrilling songsters of the forest which never, or rarely, serenade a villager,—the wood-thrush, the veery, the scarlet tanager, the field-sparrow, the whippoorwill, and many others.

I was seated by the shore of a small pond, about a mile and a half south of the village of Concord and somewhat higher than it, in the midst of an extensive wood between that town and Lincoln, and about two miles south of that

---

6. **auroral**\ə ▲rō•rəl\pertaining to the dawn.
7. **Olympus**\ō ▲lĭm•pəs\ a mountain in Thessaly considered to be the home of the gods.
8. **garret**\▲gă•rĭt\ set of rooms in an attic.
9. **Harivamsa**\ˈha•rē ▲vam•sa\ a supplement to the great Hindu epic *Mahābhārata*.

our only field known to fame, Concord Battle Ground; but I was so low in the woods that the opposite shore, half a mile off, like the rest, covered with wood, was my most distant horizon. For the first week, whenever I looked out on the pond it impressed me like a tarn high up on the side of a mountain, its bottom far above the surface of other lakes, and, as the sun arose, I saw it throwing off its nightly clothing of mist, and here and there, by degrees, its soft ripples or its smooth reflecting surface was revealed, while the mists, like ghosts, were stealthily withdrawing in every direction into the woods, as at the breaking up of some nocturnal conventicle.[10] The very dew seemed to hang upon the trees later into the day than usual, as on the sides of mountains. . . .

Every morning was a cheerful invitation to make my life of equal simplicity, and I may say innocence, with Nature herself. I have been as sincere a worshipper of Aurora[11] as the Greeks. I got up early and bathed in the pond; that was a religious exercise, and one of the best things which I did. They say that characters were engraven on the bathing tub of king Tching-thang to this effect: "Renew thyself completely each day; do it again, and again, and forever again." I can understand that. Morning brings back the heroic ages. I was as much affected by the faint hum of a mosquito making its invisible and unimaginable tour through my apartment at earliest dawn, when I was sitting with door and windows open, as I could be by any trumpet that ever sang of fame. It was Homer's requiem; itself an Iliad and Odyssey in the air, singing its own wrath and wanderings. There was something cosmical about it; a standing advertisement, till forbidden, of the everlasting vigor and fertility of the world. The morning, which is the most memorable season of the day, is the awakening hour. Then there is least somnolence in us; and for an hour, at least, some part of us awakes which slumbers all the rest of the day and night. Little is to be expected of that day, if it can be called a day, to which we are not awakened by our Genius, but by the mechanical nudgings of some servitor, are not awakened by our own newly-acquired force and aspirations from within, accompanied by the undulations of celestial music, instead of factory bells, and a fragrance filling the air—to a higher life than we fell asleep from; and thus the darkness bear its fruit, and prove itself to be good, no less than the light. That man who does not believe that each day contains an earlier, more sacred, and auroral hour than he has yet profaned, has despaired of life, and is pursuing a descending and darkening way. After a partial cessation of his sensuous life, the soul of man, or its organs rather, are reinvigorated each day, and his Genius tries again what noble life it can make. All memorable events, I should say, transpire in morning time and in a morning atmosphere. The Vedas[12] say, "All intelligences awake with the morning." Poetry and art, and the fairest and most memorable of the actions of men, date from such an hour. All poets and heroes, like Memnon,[13] are the children of Aurora, and emit their music at sunrise. To him whose elastic and vigorous thought keeps pace with the sun, the day is a perpetual morning. It matters not what the clocks say or the attitudes and labors of men. Morning is when I am awake and there is a dawn in me. Moral reform is the effort to throw off sleep. Why is it that men give so poor an account of their day if they have not been slumbering? They are not such poor calculators. If they had not been overcome with drowsiness they would have performed something. The millions are awake enough for physical labor; but only one in a million is awake enough for effective intellectual exertion, only one in a hundred millions to a poetic or divine life. To be awake is to be alive. I have never yet met a man who was

---

10. **conventicle**\kən ▲vĕn•tĭ•kəl\ a secret religious assembly.

11. **Aurora**\ō ▲rō•rə\ the goddess of dawn.

12. **Vedas**\▲vā•dəz\ sacred literature of Hinduism written in Sanskrit.

13. **Memnon**\▲mĕm•nŏn\ a gigantic statue of an Egyptian king at Thebes, said to emit musical sound at sunrise.

quite awake. How could I have looked him in the face? . . .

I went to the woods because I wished to live deliberately, to front only the essential facts of life, and see if I could not learn what it had to teach, and not, when I came to die, discover that I had not lived. I did not wish to live what was not life, living is so dear; nor did I wish to practise resignation, unless it was quite necessary. I wanted to live deep and suck out all the marrow of life, to live so sturdily and Spartan-like as to put to rout all that was not life, to cut a broad swath and shave close, to drive life into a corner, and reduce it to its lowest terms, and, if it proved to be mean, why then to get the whole and genuine meanness of it, and publish its meanness to the world; or if it were sublime, to know it by experience, and be able to give a true account of it in my next excursion. For most men, it appears to me, are in a strange uncertainty about it, whether it is of the devil or of God, and have *somewhat hastily* concluded that it is the chief end of man here to "glorify God and enjoy him forever."

Still we live meanly, like ants; though the fable tells us that we were long ago changed into men; like pygmies we fight with cranes; it is error upon error, and clout upon clout, and our best virtue has for its occasion a superfluous and evitable wretchedness. Our life is frittered away by detail. An honest man has hardly need to count more than his ten fingers, or in extreme cases he may add his ten toes, and lump the rest. Simplicity, simplicity, simplicity! I say, let your affairs be as two or three, and not a hundred or a thousand; instead of a million count half a dozen, and keep your accounts on your thumb nail. In the midst of this chopping sea of civilized life, such are the clouds and storms and quicksands and thousand-and-one items to be allowed for, that a man has to live, if he would not founder and go to the bottom and not make his port at all, by dead reckoning, and he must be a great calculator indeed who succeeds. Simplify, simplify. Instead of three meals a day, if it be necessary eat but one; in-

stead of a hundred dishes, five; and reduce other things in proportion. Our life is like a German Confederacy, made up of petty states, with its boundary forever fluctuating, so that even a German cannot tell you how it is bounded at any moment. The nation itself, with all its so-called internal improvements, which, by the way are all external and superficial, is just such an unwieldy and overgrown establishment, cluttered with furniture and tripped up by its own traps, ruined by luxury and heedless expense, by want of calculation and a worthy aim, as the million households in the land; and the only cure for it as for them is in a rigid economy, a stern and more than Spartan simplicity of life and elevation of purpose. It lives too fast. Men think that it is essential that the *Nation* have commerce, and export ice, and talk through a telegraph, and ride thirty miles an hour, without a doubt, whether *they* do or not; but whether we should live like baboons or like men, is a little uncertain. If we do not get out sleepers, and forge rails, and devote days and nights to the work, but go to tinkering upon our *lives* to improve *them,* who will build railroads? And if railroads are not built, how shall we get to heaven in season? But if we stay at home and mind our business, who will want railroads? We do not ride on the railroad; it rides upon us. Did you ever think what those sleepers are that underlie the railroads? Each one is a man, an Irishman, or a Yankee man. The rails are laid on them, and they are covered with sand, and the cars run smoothly over them. They are sound sleepers, I assure you. And every few years a new lot is laid down and run over; so that, if some have the pleasure of riding on a rail, others have the misfortune to be ridden upon. And when they run over a man that is walking in his sleep, a supernumerary sleeper in the wrong position, and wake him up, they suddenly stop the cars, and make a hue and cry about it, as if this were an exception. I am glad to know that it takes a gang of men for every five miles to keep the sleepers down and level in their beds as it is, for this is a sign that they may sometime get up again.

Why should we live with such hurry and waste of life? We are determined to be starved before we are hungry. Men say that a stitch in time saves nine, and so they take a thousand stitches to-day to save nine to-morrow. As for *work,* we haven't any of any consequence. We have the Saint Vitus' dance,[14] and cannot possibly keep our heads still. If I should only give a few pulls at the parish bell-rope, as for a fire, that is, without setting the bell, there is hardly a man on his farm in the outskirts of Concord, notwithstanding that press of engagements which was his excuse so many times this morning, nor a boy, nor a woman, I might almost say, but would forsake all and follow that sound, not mainly to save property from the flames, but, if we will confess the truth, much more to see it burn, since burn it must, and we, be it known, did not set it on fire,—or to see it put out, and have a hand in it, if that is done as handsomely; yes, even if it were the parish church itself. Hardly a man takes a half hour's nap after dinner, but when he wakes he holds up his head and asks, "What's the news?" as if the rest of mankind had stood his sentinels. Some give directions to be waked every half hour, doubtless for no other purpose; and then, to pay for it, they tell what they have dreamed. After a night's sleep the news is as indispensable as the breakfast. "Pray tell me anything new that has happened to a man anywhere on this globe,"— and he reads it over his coffee and rolls, that a man has had his eyes gouged out this morning on the Wachito River,[15] never dreaming the while that he lives in the dark unfathomed mammoth cave of this world, and has but the rudiment of an eye himself.

For my part, I could easily do without the post-office. I think that there are very few important communications made through it. To speak critically, I never received more than one or two letters in my life—I wrote this some years ago—that were worth the postage. The penny-post is, commonly, an institution through which you seriously offer a man that penny for his thoughts which is so often safely offered in jest. And I am sure that I never read any memorable news in a newspaper. If we read of one man robbed, or murdered, or killed by accident, or one house burned, or one vessel wrecked, or one steamboat blown up, or one cow run over on the Western Railroad, or one mad dog killed, or one lot of grasshoppers in the winter,—we never need read of another. One is enough. If you are acquainted with the principle, what do you care for a myriad instances and applications? To a philosopher all *news,* as it is called, is gossip, and they who edit and read it are old women over their tea. Yet not a few are greedy after this gossip. . . .

I

THE DOCTRINE OF SIMPLICITY

Thoreau's advice to those who would live more satisfying lives is summed up in the injunction, "Simplify." He wants us to do away with what is not life, "to front only the essential facts of life." What these "essential facts" are becomes more and more clear as we read on in *Walden.* Some of the essentials, however, as well as many of the nonessentials are spelled out here.

II

IMPLICATIONS

Discuss the following statements.

1. Thoreau's advice—to simplify—applies only to those who, like him, want to live the life of a thinker.

2. It is foolish to suppose that a modern nation like ours would prosper very long if it were to adopt the kind of "rigid economy" and "Spartan simplicity" that Thoreau recommends.

3. A civilization necessarily "pays for" every technological advance it makes; in a real sense there has been no progress since the beginning of time.

4. Times have changed to such an extent that many things Thoreau considered nonessential for his time are essential for ours.

---

14. **Saint Vitus' dance,** a nervous disorder in which there is involuntary movement of the muscles.
15. **Wachito River,** apparently a phonetic spelling of Ouachita\wa ᐧchē̇·ta\ River, which rises in the Ouachita Mts. and flows southeast through southern Arkansas and northeastern Louisiana.

VI. Visitors

I think that I love society as much as most, and am ready enough to fasten myself like a bloodsucker for the time to any full-blooded man that comes in my way. I am naturally no hermit, but might possibly sit out the sturdiest frequenter of the bar-room, if my business called me thither.

I had three chairs in my house; one for solitude, two for friendship, three for society. When visitors came in larger and unexpected numbers there was but the third chair for them all, but they generally economized the room by standing up. It is surprising how many great men and women a small house will contain. I have had twenty-five or thirty souls, with their bodies, at once under my roof, and yet we often parted without being aware that we had come very near to one another. Many of our houses, both public and private, with their almost innumerable apartments, their huge halls and their cellars for the storage of wines and other munitions of peace, appear to me extravagantly large for their inhabitants. They are so vast and magnificent that the latter seem to be only vermin which infest them. I am surprised when the herald blows his summons before some Tremont or Astor or Middlesex House, to see come creeping out over the piazza for all inhabitants a ridiculous mouse, which soon again slinks into some hole in the pavement.

One inconvenience I sometimes experienced in so small a house, the difficulty of getting to a sufficient distance from my guest when we began to utter the big thoughts in big words. You want room for your thoughts to get into sailing trim and run a course or two before they make their port. The bullet of your thought must have overcome its lateral and ricochet motion and fallen into its last and steady course before it reaches the ear of the hearer, else it may plough out again through the side of his head. Also, our sentences wanted room to unfold and form their columns in the interval. Individuals, like nations, must have suitable broad and natural boundaries, even a considerable neutral ground, between them. I have found it a singular luxury to talk across the pond to a companion on the opposite side. In my house we were so near that we could not begin to hear,—we could not speak low enough to be heard; as when you throw two stones into calm water so near that they break each other's undulations. If we are merely loquacious and loud talkers, then we can afford to stand very near together, cheek by jowl, and feel each other's breath; but if we speak reservedly and thoughtfully, we want to be farther apart, that all animal heat and moisture may have a chance to evaporate. If we would enjoy the most intimate society with that in each of us which is without, or above, being spoken to, we must not only be silent, but commonly so far apart bodily that we cannot possibly hear each other's voice in any case. Referred to this standard, speech is for the convenience of those who are hard of hearing; but there are many fine things which we cannot say if we have to shout. As the conversation began to assume a loftier and grander tone, we gradually shoved our chairs farther apart till they touched the wall in opposite corners, and then commonly there was not room enough.

My "best" room, however, my withdrawing room, always ready for company, on whose carpet the sun rarely fell, was the pine wood behind my house. Thither in summer days, when distinguished guests came, I took them, and a priceless domestic swept the floor and dusted the furniture and kept the things in order. . . .

Many a traveller came out of his way to see me and the inside of my house, and, as an excuse for calling, asked for a glass of water. I told them that I drank at the pond, and pointed thither, offering to lend them a dipper. Far off as I lived, I was not exempted from that annual visitation which occurs, methinks, about the first of April, when everybody is on the move; and I had my share of good luck, though there were some curious specimens among my visitors. Half-witted men from the almshouse and elsewhere came to see me; but I endeavored to make them exercise all the wit they had, and make their confessions to me; in such cases making wit the theme of our conversation; and so was compensated. Indeed, I found some of them to be wiser than the so-called *overseers* of the poor and selectmen of the town, and thought it was time that the tables were turned. With respect to wit, I learned that there was not much difference between the half and the whole. One day, in particular, an inoffensive, simple-minded pauper, whom with others I had often seen used as fencing stuff, standing or sitting on a bushel in the fields to keep cattle and himself from straying, visited me, and expressed a wish to live as I did. He told me, with the utmost simplicity and truth, quite superior, or rather *inferior*, to anything that is called humility, that he was "deficient in intellect." These were his words. The Lord had made him so, yet he supposed the Lord cared as much for him as for another. "I have always been so," said he, "from my childhood; I never had much mind; I was not like other children; I am weak in the head. It was the Lord's will, I suppose." And there he was to prove the truth of his

words. He was a metaphysical puzzle[16] to me. I have rarely met a fellowman on such promising ground,—it was so simple and sincere and so true all that he said. And, true enough, in proportion as he appeared to humble himself was he exalted. I did not know at first but it was the result of a wise policy. It seemed that from such a basis of truth and frankness as the poor weak-headed pauper had laid, our intercourse might go forward to something better than the intercourse of sages. . . .

VIII. The Village

After hoeing, or perhaps reading and writing, in the forenoon, I usually bathed again in the pond, swimming across one of its coves for a stint, and washed the dust of labor from my person, or smoothed out the last wrinkle which study had made, and for the afternoon was absolutely free. Every day or two I strolled to the village to hear some of the gossip which is incessantly going on there, circulating either from mouth to mouth, or from newspaper to newspaper, and which, taken in homœopathic doses, was really as refreshing in its way as the rustle of leaves and the peeping of frogs. As I walked in the woods to see the birds and squirrels, so I walked in the village to see the men and boys; instead of the wind among the pines I heard the carts rattle. In one direction from my house there was a colony of musk-rats in the river meadows; under the grove of elms and button-woods in the other horizon was a village of busy men, as curious to me as if they had been prairie dogs, each sitting at the mouth of its burrow,

16. metaphysical puzzle, Thoreau means that the pauper's sincerity and simple wisdom on the one hand and his self-professed inferiority on the other are such contradictions that they cannot be explained by the accepted principles of philosophy.

or running out to a neighbor's to gossip. I went there frequently to observe their habits. The village appeared to me a great news room; and on one side, to support it, as once at Redding & Company's on State Street, they kept nuts and raisins, or salt and meal and other groceries. Some have such a vast appetite for the former commodity, that is, the news, and such sound digestive organs, that they can sit forever in public avenues without stirring, and let it simmer and whisper through them like the Etesian winds,[17] or as if inhaling ether, it only producing numbness and insensibility to pain, —otherwise it would often be painful to hear, —without affecting the consciousness. I hardly ever failed, when I rambled through the village, to see a row of such worthies, either sitting on a ladder sunning themselves, with their bodies inclined forward and their eyes glancing along the line this way and that, from time to time, with a voluptuous expression, or else leaning against a barn with their hands in their pockets, like caryatides, as if to prop it up. They, being commonly out of doors, heard whatever was in the wind. These are the coarsest mills, in which all gossip is first rudely digested or cracked up before it is emptied into finer and more delicate hoppers within doors. I observed that the vitals of the village were the grocery, the bar-room, the post-office, and the bank; and, as a necessary part of the machinery, they kept a bell, a big gun, and a fire-engine, at convenient places; and the houses were so arranged as to make the most of mankind, in lanes and fronting one another, so that every traveller had to run the gauntlet, and every man, woman, and child might get a lick at him. Of course, those who were stationed nearest to the head of the line, where they could most see and be seen, and have the first blow at him, paid the highest prices for their places; and the few straggling inhabitants in the outskirts, where long gaps in the line began to occur, and the traveller could get over walls or turn aside into cow-paths, and so escape, paid a very slight ground or window tax. Signs were hung out on all sides to allure him; some to catch him by the ap-

petite, as the tavern and victualling cellar; some by the fancy, as the dry goods store and the jeweller's; and others by the hair or the feet or the skirts, as the barber, the shoemaker, or the tailor. Besides, there was a still more terrible standing invitation to call at every one of these houses, and company expected about these times. For the most part I escaped wonderfully from these dangers, either by proceeding at once boldly and without deliberation to the goal, as is recommended to those who run the gauntlet, or by keeping my thoughts on high things, like Orpheus,[18] who, "loudly singing the praises of the gods to his lyre, drowned the voices of the Sirens,[19] and kept out of danger." Sometimes I bolted suddenly, and nobody could tell my whereabouts, for I did not stand much about gracefulness, and never hesitated at a gap in a fence. I was even accustomed to make an irruption into some houses, where I was well entertained, and after learning the kernels and very last sieve-ful of news, what had subsided, the prospects of war and peace, and whether the world was likely to hold together much longer, I was let out through the rear avenues, and so escaped to the woods again. . . .

One afternoon, near the end of the first summer, when I went to the village to get a shoe from the cobbler's, I was seized and put into jail, because, as I have elsewhere related, I did not pay a tax to, or recognize the authority of, the state which buys and sells men, women, and children, like cattle at the door of its senate-house. I had gone down to the woods for other purposes. But, wherever a man goes, men will pursue and paw him with their dirty institutions, and, if they can, constrain him to belong to their desperate odd-fellow society. It is true, I might have resisted forcibly with more or less

---

17. **Etesian winds**\ĭ ᵃtē.zhən\ northerly Mediterranean summer winds which recur annually.
18. **Orpheus**\ᵃȯr·fē·əs\ in Greek mythology, his singing charmed even beasts, rocks, and trees.
19. **Sirens**\ᵃSai·rĕnz\ mythological creatures, part beast and part woman, whose enchanting songs led sailors to shipwreck.

effect, might have run "amok" against society; but I preferred that society should run "amok" against me, it being the desperate party. However, I was released the next day, obtained my mended shoe, and returned to the woods in season to get my dinner of huckleberries on Fair Haven Hill. I was never molested by any person but those who represented the state. I had no lock nor bolt but for the desk which held my papers, not even a nail to put over my latch or windows. I never fastened my door night or day, though I was to be absent several days; not even when the next fall I spent a fortnight in the woods of Maine. And yet my house was more respected than if it had been surrounded by a file of soldiers. The tired rambler could rest and warm himself by my fire, the literary amuse himself with the few books on my table, or the curious, by opening my closet door, see what was left of my dinner, and what prospect I had of a supper. Yet, though many people of every class came this way to the pond, I suffered no serious inconvenience from these sources, and I never missed anything but one small book, a volume of Homer, which perhaps was improperly gilded, and this I trust a soldier of our camp has found by this time. I am convinced, that if all men were to live as simply as I then did, thieving and robbery would be unknown. . . .

I
A LOVER OR HATER OF HUMANKIND?

Some of Thoreau's criticism of human beings and human institutions in the foregoing selections is very strong. He speaks of people "pawing" him with their "dirty institutions," of "their desperate odd-fellow society," and of the resemblance of the villagers to prairie-dogs sitting at the mouths of their burrows. In his most famous essay, "Civil Disobedience," he calls the State "half-witted" and maintains that one "cannot without disgrace be associated with it." The town-clerk of Concord had a written statement by Thoreau which read as follows: "Know all men by these presents, that I, Henry Thoreau, do not wish to be regarded as a member of any incorporated society which I have not joined."

Such bitter criticism has led some to believe that Thoreau was essentially antisocial or even misanthropic. One of his biographers, however, defends him against such charges by saying that the truth was that Thoreau loved humanity too much to flatter it. What evidence can you find to show that Thoreau either essentially loved or essentially hated his fellow human beings?

II
IMPLICATIONS

Consider the following statements.

1. The fact that Thoreau thought one could best enjoy the most intimate society through silence and at a distance proves that he really cared very little for others.

2. A person who uncompromisingly lives a life of principle is certain to be looked upon as a "kook."

3. It is not inconsistent for those who love humanity to criticize it mercilessly if they feel it is not acting in its own best interest.

4. Those who believe that it is a disgrace to be associated with the government of their nation ought to go live elsewhere.

5. It is our *duty* as human beings and as citizens to refuse to obey a law that we know to be unjust.

6. A person who lives apart from society for a considerable period of time must be either a misfit or a misanthrope.

7. Thoreau's frequent visits to Concord prove that his Walden experiment was essentially a failure.

"Brute Neighbors,"
the twelfth chapter of *Walden*,
could easily stand by itself;
it is a delightful reminiscence of birds
and animals Thoreau came to know almost as well
as he knew his Concord neighbors.
He opens the chapter with a humorous dialogue
between a "poet" and a "hermit" and concludes
with a charming account of a loon on the pond.
Between these two episodes are
the following paragraphs.

XII. Brute Neighbors

Why do precisely these objects which we behold make a world? Why has man just these species of animals for his neighbors; as if nothing but a mouse could have filled this crevice? I suspect that Pilpay & Co. have put animals to their best use, for they are all beasts of burden, in a sense, made to carry some portion of our thoughts. . . .

The mice which haunted my house were not the common ones, which are said to have been introduced into the country, but a wild native kind not found in the village. I sent one to a distinguished naturalist, and it interested him much. When I was building, one of these had its nest underneath the house, and before I had laid the second floor, and swept out the shavings, would come out regularly at lunch time and pick up the crumbs at my feet. It probably had never seen a man before; and it soon became quite familiar, and would run over my shoes and up my clothes. It could readily ascend the sides of the room by short impulses, like a squirrel, which it resembled in its motions. At length, as I leaned with my elbow on the bench one day, it ran up my clothes, and along my sleeve, and round and round the paper which held my dinner, while I kept the latter close, and dodged and played at bo-peep with it; and when at last I held still a piece of cheese between my thumb and finger, it came and nibbled it, sitting in my hand, and afterward cleaned its face and paws, like a fly, and walked away.

A phœbe[20] soon built in my shed, and a robin for protection in a pine which grew against the house. In June the partridge (*Tetrao umbellus'*), which is so shy a bird, led her brood past my windows, from the woods in the rear to the front of my house, clucking and calling to them like a hen, and in all her behavior proving herself the hen of the woods. The young suddenly disperse on your approach, at a signal from the mother, as if a whirlwind had swept them away, and they so exactly resemble the dried leaves and twigs that many a traveller has placed his foot in the midst of a brood, and heard the whir of the old bird as she flew off, and her anxious calls and mewing, or seen her trail her wings to attract his attention, without suspecting their neighborhood. The parent will sometimes roll and spin round before you in such a dishabille,[21] that you cannot, for a few moments, detect what kind of creature it is. The young squat still and flat, often running their heads under a leaf, and mind only their mother's directions given from a distance, nor will your approach make them run again and betray themselves. You may even tread on them, or have your eyes on them for a minute, without discovering them. I have held them in my open hand at such a time, and still their only care, obedient to their mother and their instinct, was to squat there without fear or trembling. So perfect is this instinct, that once, when I had laid them on the leaves again, and one accidentally fell on its side, it was found with the rest in exactly the same position ten minutes afterward. They are not callow like the young of most birds, but more perfectly developed and precocious even than chickens.

---

20. **phœbe**\ˈfē·bē\ an American flycatcher common in eastern United States.
21. **dishabille**\ˈdĭ·sə ˈbē\ state of being carelessly dressed.

The remarkably adult yet innocent expression of their open and serene eyes is very memorable. All intelligence seems reflected in them. They suggest not merely the purity of infancy, but a wisdom clarified by experience. Such an eye was not born when the bird was, but is coeval with the sky it reflects. The woods do not yield another such a gem. The traveller does not often look into such a limpid well. The ignorant or reckless sportsman often shoots the parent at such a time, and leaves these innocents to fall a prey to some prowling beast or bird, or gradually mingle with the decaying leaves which they so much resemble. It is said that when hatched by a hen they will directly disperse on some alarm, and so are lost, for they never hear the mother's call which gathers them again. These were my hens and chickens.

It is remarkable how many creatures live wild and free though secret in the woods, and still sustain themselves in the neighborhood of towns, suspected by hunters only. How retired the otter manages to live here! He grows to be four feet long, as big as a small boy, perhaps without any human being getting a glimpse of him. I formerly saw the raccoon in the woods behind where my house is built, and probably still heard their whinnering at night. Commonly I rested an hour or two in the shade at noon, after planting, and ate my lunch, and read a little by a spring which was the source of a swamp and of a brook, oozing from under Brister's Hill, half a mile from my field. The approach to this was through a succession of descending grassy hollows, full of young pitch-pines, into a larger wood about the swamp. There, in a very secluded and shaded spot, under a spreading white-pine, there was yet a clean firm sward to sit on. I had dug out the spring and made a well of clear gray water, where I could dip up a pailful without roiling it, and thither I went for this purpose almost every day in mid-summer, when the pond was warmest. Thither too the wood-cock led her brood, to probe the mud for worms, flying but a foot above them down the bank, while they ran in a troop beneath; but at last, spying me, she would leave her young and circle round and round me, nearer and nearer till within four or five feet, pretending broken wings and legs, to attract my attention, and get off her young, who would already have taken up their march, with faint wiry peep, single file through the swamp, as she directed. Or I heard the peep of the young when I could not see the parent bird. There too the turtle-doves sat over the spring, or fluttered from bough to bough of the soft white-pines over my head; or the red squirrel, coursing down the nearest bough, was particularly familiar and inquisitive. You only need sit still long enough in some attractive spot in the woods that all its inhabitants may exhibit themselves to you by turns.

I was witness to events of a less peaceful character. One day when I went out to my wood-pile, or rather my pile of stumps, I observed two large ants, the one red, the other much larger, nearly half an inch long, and black, fiercely contending with one another. Having once got hold they never let go, but struggled and wrestled and rolled on the chips incessantly. Looking farther, I was surprised to find that the chips were covered with such combatants, that it was not a *duellum*, but a *bellum*, a war between two races of ants, the red always pitted against the black, and frequently two red ones to one black. The legions of these Myrmidons[22] covered all the hills and vales in my wood-yard, and the ground was already strewn with the dead and dying, both red and black. It was the only battle which I have ever witnessed, the only battle-field I ever trod while the battle was raging; internecine war; the red republicans on the one hand, and the black imperialists on the other. On every side they were engaged in deadly combat, yet without any noise that I could hear, and human soldiers never fought so resolutely. I watched a couple that were fast locked in each other's embraces, in a little sunny valley amid the

---

22. **Myrmidons**\ˈmȇr·mə·dŏnz\ an allusion to Homer's *Iliad;* the Greek hero Achilles led his army, the Myrmidons. They were his faithful unquestioning followers.

chips, now at noon-day prepared to fight till the sun went down, or life went out. The smaller red champion had fastened himself like a vise to his adversary's front, and through all the tumblings on that field never for an instant ceased to gnaw at one of his feelers near the root, having already caused the other to go by the board; while the stronger black one dashed him from side to side, and, as I saw on looking nearer, had already divested him of several of his members. They fought with more pertinacity than bull-dogs. Neither manifested the least disposition to retreat. It was evident that their battle-cry was Conquer or die.

In the mean while there came along a single red ant on the hillside of this valley, evidently full of excitement, who either had despatched his foe, or had not yet taken part in the battle; probably the latter, for he had lost none of his limbs; whose mother had charged him to return with his shield or upon it. Or perchance he was some Achilles, who had nourished his wrath apart, and had now come to avenge or rescue his Patroclus.[23] He saw this unequal combat from afar,—for the blacks were nearly twice the size of the red,—he drew near with rapid pace till he stood on his guard within half an inch of the combatants; then, watching his opportunity, he sprang upon the black warrior, and commenced his operations near the root of his right fore-leg, leaving the foe to select among his own members; and so there were three united for life, as if a new kind of attraction had been invented which put all other locks and cements to shame. I should not have wondered by this time to find that they had their respective musical bands stationed on some eminent chip, and playing their national airs the while, to excite the slow and cheer the dying combatants. I was myself excited somewhat even as if they had been men. The more you think of it, the less the difference. And certainly there is not the fight recorded in Concord history, at least, if in the history of America, that will bear a moment's comparison with this, whether for the numbers engaged in it, or for the patriotism and heroism displayed. For

numbers and for carnage it was an Austerlitz[24] or Dresden. Concord Fight! Two killed on the patriots' side, and Luther Blanchard wounded! Why here every ant was a Buttrick,[25] —"Fire! for God's sake fire!"—and thousands shared the fate of Davis and Hosmer. There was not one hireling there. I have no doubt that it was a principle they fought for, as much as our ancestors, and not to avoid a three-penny tax on their tea; and the results of this battle will be as important and memorable to those whom it concerns as those of the battle of Bunker Hill, at least.

I took up the chip on which the three I have particularly described were struggling, carried it into my house, and placed it under a tumbler on my window-sill, in order to see the issue. Holding a microscope to the first-mentioned red ant, I saw that, though he was assiduously gnawing at the near fore-leg of his enemy, having severed his remaining feeler, his own breast was all torn away, exposing what vitals he had there to the jaws of the black warrior, whose breastplate was apparently too thick for him to pierce; and the dark carbuncles of the sufferer's eyes shone with ferocity such as war only could excite. They struggled half an hour longer under the tumbler, and when I looked again the black soldier had severed the heads of his foes from their bodies, and the still living heads were hanging on either side of him like ghastly trophies at his saddle-bow, still apparently as firmly fastened as ever, and he was endeavoring with feeble struggles, being without feelers and with only the remnant of a leg, and I know not how many other wounds, to divest himself of them; which at length, after half an hour more, he accomplished. I raised the glass, and he went off over the window-sill in that

---

23. **Patroclus**\pə ˈtra·kləs\ in the *Iliad*, Achilles' dear friend, killed by the Trojan hero Hector.
24. **Austerlitz**\ˈös·tər·lits\ town in Czechoslovakia and site of Napoleon's victory over Austrian and Russian armies, 1805.
25. **Buttrick**, Maj. John, leader of the provincials who turned back the British advance at the North Bridge, Concord, Mass., in 1775. Blanchard, Davis, and Hosmer were casualties in the skirmish.

crippled state. Whether he finally survived that combat, and spent the remainder of his days in some Hotel des Invalides,[26] I do not know; but I thought that his industry would not be worth much thereafter. I never learned which party was victorious, nor the cause of the war; but I felt for the rest of that day as if I had had my feelings excited and harrowed by witnessing the struggle, the ferocity and carnage, of a human battle before my door. . . .

No sampling of *Walden*
could be satisfactory without these paragraphs
from Thoreau's last chapter. If we had any doubts
why he left his hut to return to civilization,
he dispels them here.

XVIII. Conclusion

I left the woods for as good a reason as I went there. Perhaps it seemed to me that I had several more lives to live, and could not spare any more time for that one. It is remarkable how easily and insensibly we fall into a particular route, and make a beaten track for ourselves. I had not lived there a week before my feet wore a path from my door to the pond-side; and though it is five or six years since I trod it, it is still quite distinct. It is true, I fear that others may have fallen into it, and so helped to keep it open. The surface of the earth is soft and impressible by the feet of men; and so with the paths which the mind travels. How worn and dusty, then, must be the highways of the world, how deep the ruts of tradition and conformity! I did not wish to take a cabin passage, but rather to go before the mast and on the deck of the world, for there I could best see the moonlight amid the mountains. I do not wish to go below now.

I learned this, at least, by my experiment; that if one advances confidently in the direction of his dreams, and endeavors to live the life which he has imagined, he will meet with a success unexpected in common hours. He will put some things behind, will pass an invisible boundary; new, universal, and more liberal laws will begin to establish themselves around and within him; or the old laws be expanded, and interpreted in his favor in a more liberal sense, and he will live with the license of a higher order of beings. In proportion as he simplifies his life, the laws of the universe will appear less complex, and solitude will not be solitude, nor poverty poverty, nor weakness weakness. If you have built castles in the air, your work need not be lost; that is where they should be. Now put the foundations under them. . . .

---

26. **Hotel des Invalides**\ō ᴧtĕl 'dā·zan·vă ᴧlēd\ in Paris, originally a hospital for veterans; now a museum containing the tomb of Napoleon.

I

"TO PASS AN INVISIBLE BOUNDARY"

The "invisible boundary" to which Thoreau refers in his "Conclusion" is that boundary that separates us from our dreams and prevents our fullest self-realization. It is the boundary of the humdrum, created by convention and laziness of spirit. It is the boundary that we can cross through the kind of self-disciplined simplicity that Henry David Thoreau practiced in his lifetime.

In "Brute Neighbors" we see some aspects of nature through the eyes of a man who has passed the invisible boundary. Thoreau gives us the subtle details that only a great observer could have noticed. And he sees his "neighbors" honestly, not sentimentally—the ant episode reminds us that brute neighbors can be as brutal as human neighbors often are.

II
IMPLICATIONS

The following quotations are gathered from all the foregoing passages. Discuss the meaning of each and the relevance of any five to your own life and experience.

1. But men labor under a mistake. The better part of the man is soon plowed into the soil for compost.

2. . . . I made no haste in my work, but rather made the most of it. . . .

3. . . . my greatest skill has been to want but little. . . .

4. . . . trade curses everything it handles; and though you trade in messages from Heaven, the whole curse of trade attaches to the business.

5. . . . I am convinced . . . that to maintain one's self on this earth is not a hardship but a pastime, if we will live simply and wisely. . . .

6. Morning is when I am awake and there is a dawn in me. Moral reform is the effort to throw off sleep.

7. I have never yet met a man who was quite awake. How could I have looked him in the face?

8. Our life is frittered away by detail.

9. . . . if railroads are not built, how shall we get to heaven in season? But if we stay home and mind our business, who will want railroads? We do not ride on the railroad; it rides upon us.

10. . . . speech is for the convenience of those who are hard of hearing. . . .

11. It is remarkable how easily and insensibly we fall into a particular route, and make a beaten track for ourselves.

III
TECHNIQUES

Tone

Sometimes, it is important to distinguish tone in the sense of the writer's attitude toward the subject from tone in the sense of the writer's attitude toward the reader. When Thoreau speaks of the "dirty institutions" of society, his tone *toward his subject* may properly be called hostile or even bitter; but he does not necessarily adopt the same tone *toward his readers*. Certainly those members of his audience who admire him do not feel that he is expressing hostility toward them; on the contrary they are far more likely to describe his tone toward his audience as friendly, honest, sincere.

Choose three or four of the quotations above—or any others from the Thoreau selections—and discuss the differences between Thoreau's attitude toward his material and his attitude toward his readers. Note especially which of the two attitudes seems to vary more and why.

EMILY DICKINSON

1830–1886

Emily Dickinson was no ordinary citizen of Amherst, Massachusetts. Born there in 1830, she lived so private a life that piecing together her biography from the letters she left behind, the reminiscences of her friends, and especially her poems has been a task that has led to a variety of conclusions. Surely she was "a strange and original genius," as the poet Conrad Aiken called her. Whether she was "the greatest woman poet who ever lived," as another critic calls her, is difficult to say. Emily Dickinson has been misrepresented, just as Poe and Whitman have been, partly through her own fault. "Biography," she said, "first convinces us of the fleeing of the biographied." But too little knowledge of the life she led in Amherst is equally as hazardous as reading intimate revelations into every line of her poetry.

In the *Atlantic Monthly* for April, 1862, Thomas Wentworth Higginson, a writer and former minister, published a "Letter to a Young Contributor," urging poets to forsake the old models and strive for new forms charged with life. Emily Dickinson wrote him at once, asking "Are you too deeply occupied to say if my verse is alive? The mind is so near itself it cannot see distinctly, and I have none to ask." She was thirty-one years old, the shy unmarried daughter of a prominent Amherst lawyer. She had published nothing. We think now that by this date she had written, privately, at least 300 poems. She sent Higginson four. He answered her promptly, urging her to send more and to tell him something about herself. Her answer is one of the most revealing letters she ever wrote; and with it began a long correspondence between a scholar and a teacher, as she chose to think of the relationship. Higginson was not the most perceptive of critics, and he tried too often to improve her unconventional style; but he offered her the friendship she needed. "You were not aware," she wrote years later, "that you saved my life." Nor was Dickinson aware that after first meeting her, Higginson wrote his wife: "I never was with anyone who drained my nerve power so much. Without touching her she drew from me. I am glad not to live near her."

Higginson not only saved her life but her poetry as well, or at least he persuaded her to go on writing. She thanked him for "the surgery," saying "it was not so painful as I supposed." Probably he had found the four poems cryptic and irregular, perhaps even jarring to his ear. If he suggested that she smooth the meters and tidy up the rhymes, he could hardly have guessed that he was dealing with a "born" poet who was assured she knew how and why she broke the rules. She would continue to write as she must write. When Higginson came to edit her poems after her death (he published three volumes beginning in 1890), he did indeed alter their roughness; but he also had the good sense to preserve the original manuscripts. To our ears, the half-rhymes, the broken syntax, the veiled meanings are intriguing rather than baffling. Even Higginson could say, following Emily Dickinson's death, "After all, when a thought takes one's breath away, a lesson on grammar seems an impertinence."

The poet's letter of 1862 had more to say. In an almost childlike hand, she wrote Higginson: "I have a brother and sister; my mother does not care for thought; and father, too busy with his briefs to notice what we do. He buys me many books, but begs me not to read them, because he fears they joggle the mind." Edward Dickinson was a successful lawyer and for years the bursar of Amherst College. His spacious house on Main Street was scarcely the center of unrestrained gaiety, since the Puritan village offered little lightheartedness to anyone, except a few rowdy college students. The church was the center of activity, morally and physically. Card games, dancing, theater, concerts were nonexistent. The main social events were Commencement Week in August and the Cattle Show in October. Of the latter, Emily Dickinson thought "The show is not the show,/ But they that go." The villagers thought otherwise.

Dickinson's mother was a nonentity; her only brother, Austin, was an image of his father. In Susan, Austin's wife, the poet found a confederate for a time, especially since Susan lived next door and enjoyed poetry. But when Susan betrayed her by sending one of her poems to the Springfield *Republican,* their friendship cooled. "Publication," Dickinson argued," is the auction of the mind." To Lavinia, her younger sister, she was always devoted, increasingly as the family diminished in size and the two unmarried sisters were left to run the big house. As the poet became more and more a recluse, Lavinia served as her only link with the outside world. It was natural that Dickinson should leave her poems in her sister's care and just as natural that Lavinia should turn to Higginson when she resolved to collect them for publication in 1890. What no one suspected was the immense number Dickinson had written: over seventeen hundred.

What companions, what education had she, Higginson must have asked, for we have the poet's answer in the 1862 letter. "You ask of my companions. Hills, sir, and the sundown, and a dog as large as myself, that father bought me. They are better than beings because they know, but do not tell." The reply is typically elusive but not wholly accurate. Though she made few trips out of Amherst—to Boston to see a physician, to Philadelphia and Washington to visit friends—she received guests in her father's house, called on new neighbors, attended local parties, and church occasionally. She had eight years of schooling, first at Amherst Academy and then at Mount Holyoke Female Seminary. By 1862, however, she was seeing less of the townspeople and more of her garden where, at dusk, she could enjoy the solitude behind hemlock hedges. She had taken to wearing only white and to communicating with the neighbors by means of hand-picked bouquets or freshly baked bread, accompanied by a poem as greeting or as cryptic note. By 1870, her seclusion was overtly admitted: "I do not cross my father's ground to any house or town." Her reasons are only hinted at: domestic chores, and they were many, ill health, natural shyness, poetic composition, psychic withdrawal. Whatever the causes, her seclusion was her own choosing. It was a hermit's existence as far as the town knew, but Emily Dickinson's private life was full of introspection and literary labor. "The soul selects her own society," she wrote, "then shuts the door."

Early biographers were quite certain that this life was emotionally frustrated to the point of despair. "I went to school," she wrote Higginson, "but in your manner of the phrase had no education. When a little girl, I had a friend who taught me Immortality; but venturing too near himself, he never returned. Soon after my tutor died, and for several years my lexicon was my own companion. Then I found one more, but he was not contented I be his scholar, so he left the land." The first "tutor" was Benjamin Newton, a young man too poor to marry who had worked in her father's law office, then moved to Worcester where he died at an early age. The second was the Reverend Charles Wadsworth of Philadelphia whom she may have met in 1854. He was considerably older than she and already married. He called on her in Amherst in 1860; of this we have record. But two years later he left for San Francisco and she did not see him again until 1880. It is extremely unlikely that Wadsworth could have encouraged her passion, if that is what she felt toward him.

The great risk in reading her poems biographically—particularly the one beginning "My life closed twice before its close"—is not the uncertainty of fact but the limitations such narrow reading imposes on the poet's lines. Dickinson's subjects are fear, frustration, death, God, friendships, love, and the natural world around her. When she speaks in the first person—"I could not live with you," one poem begins—she does not necessarily record a personal experience, though the emotions which led to creating the poem may have begun there.

Rather she is writing of universal feelings—the agony of separation, the need for love, the fear of loneliness. Like Thoreau, Dickinson traveled widely without leaving the village where she was born; we could almost say without leaving her garden and her study. She withdrew from the world in order to know it better, to contemplate the human condition, our relation to the things of this world. "To live is so startling," she wrote Higginson, "it leaves but little room for other occupations, though friends are, if possible, an event more fair." Her poems are life distilled, not the temporal happenings of Massachusetts in 1860, not even of the Civil War, but events common to all: sorrow at the loss of a friend, joy at summer noon, despair at nightfall, the first crocus in spring, the shapes the snow takes in December, walks with her dog, small-town hypocrisy, the renunciation of hope, the nature of God. To all these subjects Dickinson brings intense personal reactions, quite oblivious of fashion or acceptability. She read deeply in Keats, Emerson, the Brownings, the Bible; but her forms are her own. When Higginson suggested she wait before publishing, he was thinking of the roughness, the starkness of her meter, not the revelation of private thoughts. "I smile when you suggest I delay to 'publish,'" she replied, "that being foreign to my thought."

Possibly publication would have spoiled her genius. The rebel in Emily Dickinson had an outlet in her poetry, a release she needed partly because of her family, partly because of her self-imposed solitude. Her poems were her confidante. She labored over them with love, rewriting, reshaping her thoughts into arresting metaphors, witty observations, acute revelations of sensory experience, always with the idea that an emotion captured, a thought well expressed, were more vital to the life of a poem than a listener soothed or a critic pleased. "Is my verse alive," not "Is my poetry good poetry," she asked of Higginson. The reader who discovers her genius will answer for her. Once exposed to her frankness, to the force of her lines, one does not easily forget them.

God and Nature

Like most poets, Emily Dickinson was alert to the world
around her, particularly the natural world. In these poems she speaks
of Nature as though it were a friend, or at least a confidante.
Since she sees God's presence in all of Nature, it is not surprising, then,
to find her also thinking of God in familiar terms. Had she published
these poems during her lifetime, she very likely would have drawn censure
for her brashness. As it is they remain private thoughts
which we, at last, can "overhear."

This Is My Letter to the World

This is my letter to the world
That never wrote to me,—
The simple news that nature told,
With tender majesty.

Her message is committed
To hands I cannot see;
For love of her, sweet countrymen,
Judge tenderly of me!

Poems, 1890

The Sky Is Low, the Clouds Are Mean

The sky is low, the clouds are mean,
A travelling flake of snow
Across a barn or through a rut
Debates if it will go.

A narrow wind complains all day
How some one treated him;
Nature, like us, is sometimes caught
Without her diadem.

Poems, 1890

A Little Madness in the Spring

A little madness in the Spring
Is wholesome even for the King,
But God be with the Clown,
Who ponders this tremendous scene—
This whole experiment of green,
As if it were his own!

From *The Single Hound.* Copyright 1914, 1942 by Martha
Dickinson Bianchi. Reprinted by permission of Little, Brown
and Company.

Some Keep the Sabbath Going to Church

Some keep the Sabbath going to church;
I keep it staying at home,
With a bobolink for a chorister,
And an orchard for a dome.

Some keep the Sabbath in surplice;   5
I just wear my wings,
And instead of tolling the bell for church,
Our little sexton sings.

God preaches,—a noted clergyman,—
And the sermon is never long;   10
So instead of getting to heaven at last
I'm going all along!

Poems, 1890

Lightly Stepped a Yellow Star

Lightly stepped a yellow star
To its lofty place,
Loosed the Moon her silver hat
From her lustral face.
All of evening softly lit
As an astral hall—
"Father," I observed to Heaven,
"You are punctual."

From THE COMPLETE POEMS OF EMILY DICKINSON,
edited by Thomas H. Johnson. Copyright 1914, 1942 by Martha
Dickinson Bianchi. By permission of Little, Brown and Co.

I Never Saw a Moor

I never saw a moor,
I never saw the sea;
Yet know I how the heather looks,
And what a wave must be.

I never spoke with God,
Nor visited in heaven;
Yet certain am I of the spot
As if the chart were given.

Poems, 1890

I

PERSONAL CREEDS

These six poems reflect Emily Dickinson's deep respect for creation and the creator. No one had to teach her how to worship nor, for that matter, did she need a text. She wrote her own. With her discerning eye, she saw the evidence of God's power in the smallest creatures, the simplest gesture. In the transferring of these observations to poetry she sets forth her personal creed.

II

IMPLICATIONS

This Is My Letter to the World

Emily Dickinson says she writes a "letter" to the world to send nature's "message." Though we often use these two words interchangeably, they have distinct meanings here. Her "letter" is her poetry. What is nature's "message"?

The Sky Is Low, the Clouds Are Mean

1. Nature is personified here in the most human of terms. In what mood do we find her?

2. "Diadem" is the most vital word in the poem. What more does it suggest to you than "crown"? What would this poem lose if, instead of this last line, Dickinson had written "Yielding to every whim"?

A Little Madness in the Spring

1. What words in this poem are carefully chosen for contrast?

2. The distance from king to clown is great. Is there an equally great distance between wholesome and mad?

3. Dickinson had difficulty settling on the word "experiment" in the fifth line. She tried these lines first:
   a. This sudden legacy of green.
   b. This fair apocalypse of green.
   c. This whole apocalypse of green.
   d. This whole astonishment of green.
   e. This wild experiment of green.
Has she made the wisest choice? What does "experiment" suggest to you?

Some Keep the Sabbath Going to Church

1. How does Dickinson contrast her church with the town's church?

2. Can one be "going to heaven" every Sunday? Can this be inferred from her last lines?

Lightly Stepped a Yellow Star

1. "Lustral" is an archaic word meaning "purified" as it is used here. "Astral" suggests the starry sky. What word do they prepare for later in the poem?

2. Emily Dickinson knows the effectiveness of repeating a single vowel or consonant in a poem. What consonant is repeated in a way that ties all these lines together more surely than even rhyme could do?

I Never Saw a Moor

We are asked to make a comparison between the two halves of this poem. Why is it vital that the poet has not *seen* a moor or sea?

Observations and Comment

Society perplexed Emily Dickinson.
She seldom felt comfortable in large groups of people,
and yet she had a keen ear and eye for society's deficiencies. In these poems
her comments are terse, accurate, and perceptive. The first two deal
with social behavior. The last three are more general observations
on the nature of language, revery, and happiness.

Much Madness Is Divinest Sense

Much madness is divinest sense
To a discerning eye;
Much sense the starkest madness.
'Tis the majority
In this, as all, prevails.
Assent, and you are sane;
Demur,—you're straightway dangerous,
And handled with a chain.

Poems, 1890

Go Not Too Near a House of Rose

Go not too near a house of rose,
The depredation of a breeze
Or inundation of a dew
Alarms its walls away;
Nor try to tie the butterfly,
Nor climb the bars of ecstasy.
In insecurity to lie
Is joy's insuring quality.

Letters, 1894

To Make a Prairie It Takes a Clover and One Bee

To make a prairie it takes a clover and one bee,—
One clover, and a bee
And revery.
The revery alone will do
If bees are few.

Poems, 1896

Success Is Counted Sweetest

Success is counted sweetest
By those who ne'er succeed.
To comprehend a nectar
Requires sorest need.

Not one of all the purple host   5
Who took the flag today
Can tell the definition
So clear, of victory,

As he, defeated, dying,
On whose forbidden ear   10
The distant strains of triumph
Break, agonized and clear.

Poems, 1890

A Word Is Dead

A word is dead
When it is said,
Some say.
I say it just
Begins to live
That day.

Poems, 1896

I
SOCIETY AND THE INDIVIDUAL

As a recluse, Emily Dickinson had little contact with the citizens of Amherst other than her close friends, neighbors, and family. Yet she must have been a good listener. She had strong opinions about society's decrees, what was fashionable and not fashionable, what the world expects of us, what we ask of ourselves. She would have shared with a man like Thoreau, had she known him, a strong distrust of majority opinion and mass media.

II
IMPLICATIONS
Much Madness Is Divinest Sense

1. What is the paradox, or apparent contradiction, on which this poem is built? To appreciate it you must be certain you understand how the poet uses the words "discerning" and "demur."

2. In line 5, the poet employs a casual parenthetical phrase: "as all." What do these two seemingly unimportant words add to the major statement of the poem?

Go Not Too Near a House of Rose

1. A "house of rose" is an inspired image for the opening line of this poem. Where are sibilant *s*'s repeated in the next lines?

2. More than the sounds, the implications of "house" of rose are important. "Walls" can be connected in a literal sense. But can one "alarm" walls away literally? How has the poet chosen an oblique way of suggesting that a rose is fragile?

3. How is tying a butterfly a clear restatement of the proposition of the first line?

4. "Rose" and "butterfly" are concrete nouns. What abstract word does the poet substitute for them?

5. Explain the poet's conclusion.

Success Is Counted Sweetest

1. Here Emily Dickinson reverses her usual tack. She states a proposition in the first two lines and then illustrates it. How are "nectar" and "need" closely tied to the opening lines?

2. Lines 5–12 are one sentence. The strains of triumph are agony for the dying man to hear, yet he knows better than any of the victors what victory means. How do you make a connection between this image and "nectar/need" of the first stanza?

Portraits

Emily Dickinson might not have thought of these four poems
as "portraits," but read as a group they demonstrate her immense power
for personifying a train or a bird or even the wind. One need not share
her enthusiasm for her subject to appreciate the sharpness
of her description and the intensity of the language. She makes us *see*
common objects as clearly as she does.

A Bird Came Down the Walk

A bird came down the walk;
He did not know I saw;
He bit an angle-worm in halves
And ate the fellow, raw.

And then he drank a dew   5
From a convenient grass,
And then hopped sidewise to the wall
To let a beetle pass.

He glanced with rapid eyes
That hurried all abroad,—   10
They looked like frightened beads, I thought;
He stirred his velvet head

Like one in danger; cautious,
I offered him a crumb,
And he unrolled his feathers   15
And rowed him softer home

Than oars divide the ocean,
Too silver for a seam,
Or butterflies, off banks of noon,
Leap, plashless, as they swim.   20

Poems, 1891

A Narrow Fellow in the Grass

A narrow fellow in the grass
Occasionally rides;
You may have met him,—did you not,
His notice sudden is.

The grass divides as with a comb,   5
A spotted shaft is seen;
And then it closes at your feet
And opens further on.

He likes a boggy acre,
A floor too cool for corn.   10
Yet when a child, and barefoot,
I more than once, at morn,

Have passed, I thought, a whip-lash
Unbraiding in the sun,—
When, stooping to secure it,   15
It wrinkled, and was gone.

Several of nature's people
I know, and they know me;
I feel for them a transport
Of cordiality;   20

But never met this fellow,
Attended or alone,
Without a tighter breathing,
And zero at the bone.

Poems, 1891

The Wind Tapped Like a Tired Man

The wind tapped like a tired man,
And like a host, "Come in,"
I boldly answered; entered then
My residence within

A rapid, footless guest,   5
To offer whom a chair
Were as impossible as hand
A sofa to the air.

No bone had he to bind him,
His speech was like the push   10
Of numerous humming-birds at once
From a superior bush.

His countenance a billow,
His fingers, if he pass
Let go a music, as of tunes   15
Blown tremulous in glass.

He visited, still flitting;
Then, like a timid man,
Again he tapped—'twas flurriedly—
And I became alone.   20

Poems, 1891

To fit its sides, and crawl between,
Complaining all the while   10
In horrid, hooting stanza;
Then chase itself down hill

And neigh like Boanerges;[1]
Then, punctual as a star,
Stop—docile and omnipotent—   15
At its own stable door.

Poems, 1891

_____

1. **Boanerges**\'bō·ə 'něr·jēz\ literally, sons of thunder; name given by Jesus to sons of Zebedee; used to refer to forceful preacher.

I Like to See It Lap the Miles

I like to see it lap the miles,
And lick the valleys up,
And stop to feed itself at tanks;
And then, prodigious, step

Around a pile of mountains,   5
And, supercilious, peer
In shanties by the sides of roads;
And then a quarry pare

IMPLICATIONS

A Bird Came Down the Walk

1. Why is the kind of bird Emily Dickinson observes never made clear?

2. How do you know that the poet is more interested in the manner in which the bird flies away than in why he rejects the crumb?

A Narrow Fellow in the Grass

1. For four stanzas, this poem is chiefly description, and accurate description it is. "Spotted shaft" and "whip-lash" are not ordinary terms to describe a snake. Why are they memorable here?

2. The last stanza sets up opposition to the earlier noncommital description. What is Dickinson's feelings about the snake?

The Wind Tapped Like a Tired Man

1. The heart of this poem is movement; the wind is here and gone. Hence, what seems to be the author's main intention in this poem?

2. What similes (stated or implied) add extra dimensions to the movement and manners of the wind?

I Like to See It Lap the Miles

1. What image does Dickinson use for the train? Why is it most appropriate?

2. Considering the image used for the train, one line seems out of place: "Complaining all the while/In horrid, hooting stanza." How do you explain it?

223

Love

To be fully appreciated, these five poems
must *not* be read biographically. Emily Dickinson is talking here
of common feelings: absence, parting, arrival, life alone, life shared.
If she gives these ordinary occasions special meaning, it is more
as a responsive poet than as one particular woman in a New England town
in the mid-nineteenth century. She speaks of emotions
all of us feel and try to understand.

Elysium Is as Far as to

Elysium[1] is as far as to
The very nearest room,
If in that room a friend await
Felicity or doom.

What fortitude the soul contains,
That it can so endure
The accent of a coming foot,
The opening of a door!

Poems, 1890

---

1. **Elysium**\ĭ ˈlĭzh·ē·əm\ in Greek mythology, land of
the blessed dead.

Alter? When the Hills Do

Alter? When the hills do.
Falter? When the sun
Question if his glory
Be the perfect one.

Surfeit? When the daffodil
Doth of the dew:
Even as herself, O friend!
I will of you!

Poems, 1890

It Might Have Been Lonelier

It might have been lonelier
Without the loneliness;
I'm so accustomed to my fate
Perhaps the other—peace—

Would interrupt the dark,   5
And crowd the little room—
Too scant, by cubits, to contain
The Sacrament of Him.

I am not used to hope:
I might intrude upon   10
Its sweet parade, blaspheme the place
Ordained to suffering.

It might be easier
To fail with land in sight
Than gain my blue peninsula—   15
To perish—of delight.

From THE COMPLETE POEMS OF EMILY DICKINSON,
edited by Thomas H. Johnson. Copyright 1935 by Martha
Dickinson Bianchi, © renewed 1963 by Mary L. Hampson. By
permission of Little, Brown and Co.

We Learned
the Whole of Love

We learned the whole of love,
The alphabet, the words,
A chapter, then the mighty book—
Then revelation closed.

But in each other's eyes   5
An ignorance beheld
Diviner than the childhood's,
And each to each a child

Attempted to expound
What neither understood.   10
Alas, that wisdom is so large
And truth so manifold!

Reprinted by permission of the publishers and the Trustees of Amherst College from Thomas H. Johnson, Editor, *The Poems of Emily Dickinson,* Cambridge, Mass.: The Belknap Press of Harvard University Press, Copyright, 1951, 1955 by the President and Fellows of Harvard College.

My Life Had Stood
a Loaded Gun

My life had stood a loaded gun
In corners, till a day
The owner passed—identified,
And carried me away.

And now we roam the sov'reign woods,   5
And now we hunt the doe—
And every time I speak for him
The mountains straight reply.

And do I smile, such cordial light
Upon the valley glow—   10
It is as a Vesuvian face
Had let its pleasure through.

And when at night, our good day done,
I guard my master's head,
'Tis better than the eider duck's   15
Deep pillow to have shared.

To foe of his I'm deadly foe,
None stir the second time
On whom I lay a yellow eye
Or an emphatic thumb.   20

Though I than he may longer live,
He longer must than I,
For I have but the art to kill—
Without the power to die.

From THE COMPLETE POEMS OF EMILY DICKINSON, edited by Thomas H. Johnson. Copyright 1935 by Martha Dickinson Bianchi, © renewed 1963 by Mary L. Hampson. By permission of Little, Brown and Co.

I
BEYOND FRIENDSHIP

The more we read of Emily Dickinson's life, the more remarkable it seems to us that this impressionable but shy Amherst woman could have known as much as she did about love and friendship. Some poems seem to be written directly to or for a particular person; yet we have no clues that she ever received encouragement from male visitors, or at least not the kind that could lead her to use words like "doom" and "fate" and the "alphabet" of love. This group of poems attests clearly to the great powers of a poet's imagination.

II
IMPLICATIONS

Elysium Is as Far as to

1. What is the author's opening definition of paradise? How is it related to the word "if" in the third line?

2. What part does anticipation play in joy?

Alter? When the Hills Do

1. The pattern of the poem is familiar: three questions, three answers. Why are the comparisons apt?

2. How do the strong rhymes help to bring the poem's force to bear on the most important word: you?

It Might Have Been Lonelier

1. Show how the first two lines are the inspiration of all that follows.

2. Do you believe she really means the last stanza? Would she rather live alone in the "little room" than together on the "blue peninsula"?

We Learned the Whole of Love

1. How is this poem built on a paradox?

2. Wisdom and truth are here more spiritual than intellectual. How could the language of the eyes be as necessary to the spirit as verbal language is to reading "the mighty book"?

My Life Had Stood a Loaded Gun

1. This poem is far more complex than the others in this group. The loaded gun as a symbol for the poet's life is easy enough, but what happens after the "owner" claims the gun?

2. Do "yellow eye" and "emphatic thumb" carry out the basic metaphor of life as a gun?

3. The last stanza is tricky. Read it carefully. The gun may outlive the owner; that is credible enough. But what impasse will develop if the owner dies and the gun (that is, the poet's life) cannot expire? What irony lies in placing "kill" so close to "die" in the last stanza?

Loss and Death

Emily Dickinson tried not to sentimentalize her life.
She could become coy on occasion, but she never became maudlin,
in spite of the long years she spent in solitude. These poems speak
a brutal truth about loneliness, one she felt from her heart,
and in their forthright language they impress on the reader
the cruelty of separation and the finality of death.

They Say That "Time Assuages"

They say that "time assuages,"—
Time never did assuage;
An actual suffering strengthens,
As sinews do, with age.

Time is a test of trouble,
But not a remedy.
If such it prove, it prove too
There was no malady.

Poems, 1896

My Life Closed Twice Before Its Close

My life closed twice before its close;
It yet remains to see
If Immortality unveil
A third event to me,

So huge, so hopeless to conceive,
As these that twice befell.
Parting is all we know of heaven,
And all we need of hell.

Poems, 1896

If You Were Coming in the Fall

If you were coming in the fall,
I'd brush the summer by
With half a smile and half a spurn,
As housewives do a fly.

If I could see you in a year,   5
I'd wind the months in balls,
And put them each in separate drawers,
Until their time befalls.

If only centuries delayed,
I'd count them on my hand,   10
Subtracting till my fingers dropped
Into Van Dieman's land.[1]

If certain, when this life was out
That yours and mine should be,
I'd toss it yonder like a rind,   15
And taste eternity.

---

1. **Van Dieman's**\văn ᴧdē·mənz\ **land,** former name for
Tasmania, a state of Australia, in the poet's day considered to be extremely remote from Amherst, Mass.

But now, all ignorant of the length
Of time's uncertain wing,
It goads me, like the goblin bee,
That will not state its sting.   20

Poems, 1890

Because I Could Not Stop for Death

Because I could not stop for Death,
He kindly stopped for me;
The carriage held but just ourselves
And Immortality.

We slowly drove, he knew no haste,   5
And I had put away
My labor, and my leisure too,
For his civility.

We passed the school where children played
Their lessons scarcely done;   10
We passed the fields of gazing grain,
We passed the setting sun.

We paused before a house that seemed
A swelling in the ground;
The roof was scarcely visible,   15
The cornice but a mound.

Since then 'tis centuries; but each
Feels shorter than the day
I first surmised the horses' heads
Were toward eternity.   20

Poems, 1890

I
IMPLICATIONS
They Say That "Time Assuages"

With what commonplace saying is the poet taking issue?

My Life Closed Twice Before Its Close

Emily Dickinson may be referring in line 1 to two loves she lost during her lifetime. Does it matter that we cannot be certain?

If You Were Coming in the Fall

How does the time "build" in this poem?

Because I Could Not Stop for Death

What metaphor has Dickinson used for Death? How does she maintain it throughout the poem?

II
TECHNIQUES
Selection of Significant Details

A novelist has several hundred pages in which to build the atmosphere and setting for a narrative. A short-story writer must work faster in a relatively confined space. The poet, unless writing epics or dramas, is even more restrained and thus must make each word count. Emily Dickinson took upon herself the tightest of restrictions when she chose the four-line stanza, the two- or three-stanza poem. Her form is so miniature that she must register sharp, immediate impressions or her thought barely has a chance to expand.

Being the skillful worker she is, Dickinson developed several devices to concentrate details rather than generalities in the reader's mind. Note first the poem "Some Keep the Sabbath Going to Church." Here she wisely groups details to give the reader a clear view of *her* church: bobolink, orchard, wings, bird song implied in singing sexton, God preaching, a short sermon. Now look at "The Wind Tapped Like a Tired Man." Here she casts her details into similes: like a tired man, like a host, like the push of numerous humming-birds, his fingers as of tunes, like a timid man. Readers must help the poet by making these comparisons in their mind's eye.

If you inspect closely "I Like to See It Lap the Miles," you will notice how the details accumulate rapidly as the train rolls through the countryside:

from valleys to tanks, from a pile of mountains (not a range but a *pile*) to shanties, then on to quarries, and down hills to the stable door. Finally, turn to "If You Were Coming in the Fall." Here the poet chooses the homeliest details to describe the passage of time and uses them in unlikely, therefore arresting, ways: summer brushed away like a fly, months rolled into balls, centuries counted on fingers, life tossed away like the rind of fruit.

Choose the Dickinson poems which please you most and look at them closely, give them a second and third reading. John Crowe Ransom, a famous American poet, once said he enjoyed poetry for the logical irrelevancy of its local details. Dickinson would have understood the paradox implied in a logical irrelevancy. Her local details may, at first glance, seem strange to you. What, for example, have a rose and a butterfly to do with ecstasy, you might ask. But give the poem a chance to assert itself on its own terms—above all, on its own terms, not yours—and you will discover the joys of connotations, those meanings that cluster around words beyond the standard dictionary meanings.

Roses have petals. Houses have walls. A "house of rose" is more than a "rose," because the phrase suggests all the fragility contained within a rose *just* as walls contain a house. And when Emily Dickinson writes that dew and breeze can alarm away the walls of this house, she is implying more than she could in a simple statement that a wind will destroy the petals of a rose. But she lets you make the inference. In the same way, she wants you to move from rose to butterfly to ecstasy. And when you have connected these three details, her last two lines become crystal clear. Fragile beauty is fleeting. "Nothing gold can stay," Robert Frost says. The details vary; the implications are often the same. Without carefully wrought details, poems are skim milk.

The pleasure of discovering significant details on your own is a main part of reading poetry. Look at the following poems and consider the specific adjectives and the important nouns in their lines:

"A Bird Came Down the Walk"
"A Narrow Fellow in the Grass"
"My Life Had Stood a Loaded Gun."

A mere listing is not enough. What are the connotations of these details, the suggested meanings behind the words?

THE COMIC
IMAGINATION

Suppose at lunch one day at school you accidentally drop your lunch tray. The macaroni and cheese spills all down your legs. The milk splashes all over your shoes. You can react in two different ways. You can be terribly embarrassed, flustered,

Such Queer Fish we are, comments this lithograph of people at the aquarium. As humorists have noted, who is queer at the zoo depends on which side of the barrier is yours.

QUEER FISH, *Mabel Dwight,*
Philadelphia Museum of Art

or even angry. In other words, you can treat it as a major catastrophe: You have ruined your clothes and shoes; you'll have to use the rest of your lunch period getting back in order and won't have time to eat. Or, on the other hand, you can treat the accident as a joke. You see how funny you look with macaroni slithering down your front, with your shoes polka-dotted with milk; you can imagine the stupid expression you must have as you hold the tray limply in hand; you can imagine how unamused your math teacher will be when you give your excuse for missing class. In which direction does your imagination go as you react to the mishap—toward the serious or toward the comic?

A people and a culture also have similar alternatives. Some things society takes seriously and some humorously. What a people laughs at often reveals a good deal about the fundamental nature of that people. And often it is a country's writers who help a nation see things about itself as ridiculous that have customarily been taken seriously.

Thus, humor serves first of all as a kind of balance to keep people on an even keel. Indeed, especially in the early, hard-pressed days of our country and continuing through the awkward, hectic, and uneven periods of growth in the nineteenth century, the comic imagination helped Americans keep themselves and the world in perspective so that the grim business of living did not become too oppressive. In such stock American figures as the Yankee peddler, the well-meaning but stubborn bureaucrat, and the homespun cracker-barrel philosopher, Americans found needed comic relief.

But at the same time the comic imagination has frequently done much more than serve merely as a kind of safety valve. It has been an irreverent "balloon pricker" humorously attacking, at one time or another, almost every area of American life. Thus, beneath the "fun" and the laughter, American humor often reveals the foibles and the absurdities of American life. It has exposed and ridiculed our weaknesses, and in so doing has given us a clearer picture of ourselves. And in learning to laugh at ourselves, we have learned a healthier way of living with ourselves and the world.

The famous Canadian humorist, Stephen Leacock, once wrote that the "true humorist . . . must present the vision of a better world, if only of a lost one." We trust that all of the following selections do present the vision of a better world—or make this world a more enjoyable one in which to live.

The traveling sales agent is a peculiarly American
occupational figure. Meeting new people constantly, always on the move,
sales agents live by their wits and, sometimes, on the gullibility of those to whom they sell.
Probably the earliest example of this figure is the famous Yankee peddler,
a model used by O. Henry for Jeff Peters and Andy Tucker in the following story.
Be on your guard against these crafty peddlers, or they will take you in,
as they do the mayor of Fisher Hill.

Jeff Peters as a Personal Magnet

O. HENRY

Jeff Peters has been engaged in as many schemes for making money as there are recipes for cooking rice in Charleston, S. C.

Best of all I like to hear him tell of his earlier days when he sold liniments and cough cures on street corners, living hand to mouth, heart to heart with the people, throwing heads or tails with fortune for his last coin.

"I struck Fisher Hill, Arkansaw," said he, "in a buckskin suit, moccasins, long hair and a thirty-carat diamond ring that I got from an actor in Texarkana. I don't know what he ever did with the pocket knife I swapped him for it.

"I was Dr. Waugh-hoo, the celebrated Indian medicine man. I carried only one best bet just then, and that was Resurrection Bitters. It was made of life-giving plants and herbs accidently discovered by Ta-qua-la, the beautiful wife of the chief of the Choctaw Nation, while gathering truck to garnish a platter of boiled dog for the annual corn dance.

"Business hadn't been good at the last town, so I only had five dollars. I went to the Fisher Hill druggist and he credited me for half a gross of eight-ounce bottles and corks. I had the labels and ingredients in my valise, left over from the last town. Life began to look rosy again after I got in my hotel room with the water running from the tap, and the Resurrection Bitters lining up on the table by the dozen.

"Fake? No, sir. There was two dollars' worth of fluid extract of cinchona[1] and a dime's worth of aniline[2] in that half-gross of bitters. I've gone through towns years afterwards and had folks ask for 'em again.

"I hired a wagon that night and commenced selling the bitters on Main Street. Fisher Hill was a low, malarial town; and a compound hypothetical pneumo-cardiac anti-scorbutic tonic was just what I diagnosed the crowd as needing.[3] The bitters started off like sweetbreads[4]-on-toast at a vegetarian dinner. I had sold two dozen at fifty cents apiece when I felt somebody pull my coat tail. I knew what that meant; so I climbed down and sneaked a five dollar bill into the hand of a man with a German silver star on his lapel.

"'Constable,' says I, 'it's a fine night.'

"'Have you got a city license,' he asks, 'to sell this illegitimate essence of spooju[5] that you flatter by the name of medicine?'

"'I have not,' says I. 'I didn't know you had a city. If I can find it to-morrow I'll take one out if it's necessary.'

---

1. **cinchona**\sĭn ▲kō•nə\ probably quinine, one of the alkaloid extracts from the bark of the cinchona tree.
2. **aniline**\▲ăn•əl•ən\ colorless, oily liquid.
3. **a low, malarial town,** low elevation, subject to malaria. **pneumo-cardiac**\nū•mə ▲kar•dē•ăk\ affecting lungs and heart. **anti-scorbutic**\skər ▲byū•tĭk\ protection against scurvy.
4. **sweetbreads,** glandular tissue located near throat of young animal, especially a calf.
5. **spooju,** possibly a blend of spoon and juice.

"'I'll have to close you up till you do,' says the constable.

"I quit selling and went back to the hotel. I was talking to the landlord about it.

"'Oh, you won't stand no show in Fisher Hill,' says he. 'Dr. Hoskins, the only doctor here, is a brother-in-law of the Mayor, and they won't allow no fake doctor to practice in town.'

"'I don't practice medicine,' says I, 'I've got a State peddler's license, and I take out a city one wherever they demand it.'

"I went to the Mayor's office the next morning and they told me he hadn't showed up yet. They didn't know when he'd be down. So Doc Waugh-hoo hunches down again in a hotel chair and lights a jimpson-weed[6] regalia, and waits.

"By and by a young man in a blue necktie slips into the chair next to me and asks the time.

"'Half-past ten,' says I, 'and you are Andy Tucker. I've seen you work. Wasn't it you that put up the Great Cupid Combination package on the Southern States? Let's see, it was a Chilian diamond engagement ring, a wedding ring, a potato masher, a bottle of soothing syrup and Dorothy Vernon—all for fifty cents.'

"Andy was pleased to hear that I remembered him. He was a good street man; and he was more than that—he respected his profession, and he was satisfied with 300 per cent profit. He had plenty of offers to go into the illegitimate drug and garden seed business; but he was never to be tempted off of the straight path.

"I wanted a partner, so Andy and me agreed to go out together. I told him about the situation in Fisher Hill and how finances was low on account of the local mixture of politics and jalap.[7] Andy had just got in on the train that morning. He was pretty low himself, and was going to canvass the town for a few dollars to build a new battleship by popular subscription at Eureka Springs. So we went out and sat on the porch and talked it over.

"The next morning at eleven o'clock when I was sitting there alone, an old man shuffles into the hotel and asked for the doctor to come and see Judge Banks, who, it seems, was the Mayor and a mighty sick man.

"'I'm no doctor,' says I. 'Why don't you go and get the doctor?'

"'Boss,' says he, 'Doc Hoskins am done gone twenty miles in de country to see some sick persons. He's de only doctor in de town, and Mister Banks am powerful bad off. He sent me to ax you to please, suh, come.'

"'As man to man,' says I, 'I'll go and look him over.' So I put a bottle of Resurrection Bitters in my pocket and goes up on the hill to the Mayor's mansion, the finest house in town, with a mansard roof[8] and two cast iron dogs on the lawn.

"This Mayor Banks was in bed all but his whiskers and feet. He was making internal noises that would have had everybody in San Francisco hiking for the parks. A young man was standing by the bed holding a cup of water.

"'Doc,' says the Mayor, 'I'm awful sick. I'm about to die. Can't you do nothing for me?'

"'Mr. Mayor,' says I, 'I'm not a regular preordained disciple of S. Q. Lapius. I never took a course in a medical college,' says I. 'I've just come as a fellow man to see if I could be of assistance.'

"'I'm deeply obliged,' says he. 'Doc Waugh-hoo, this is my nephew, Mr. Biddle. He has tried to alleviate my distress, but without success. Oh, Lordy! Ow-ow-ow!!' he sings out.

"I nods at Mr. Biddle and sets down by the bed and feels the Mayor's pulse. 'Let me see your liver—your tongue, I mean,' says I. Then I turns up the lids of his eyes and looks close at the pupils of 'em.

"'How long have you been sick?' I asked.

"'I was taken down—ow-ouch—last night,' says the Mayor. 'Gimme something for it, doc, won't you?'

"'Mr. Fiddle,' says I, 'raise the window shade a bit, will you?'

---

6. **jimpson-weed**\ˈjĭm·sən\ foul-smelling plant.
7. **jalap**\ˈjă·ləp\ dried root of plant from Mexico used as purgative.
8. **mansard roof**\ˈmăn·sɔrd\ roof having two slopes with the lower slope steeper than upper one.

YANKEE PEDDLER *John Whetton Ehninger*
Collection of the Newark Museum

"'Biddle,' says the young man. 'Do you feel like you could eat some ham and eggs, Uncle James?'

"'Mr. Mayor,' says I, after laying my ear to his right shoulder blade and listening, 'you've got a bad attack of super-inflammation of the right clavicle of the harpsichord!'[9]

"'Oh no!' says he, with a groan. 'Can't you rub something on it, or set it or anything?'

"I picks up my hat and starts for the door.

"'You ain't going, doc?' says the Mayor with a howl. 'You ain't going away and leave me to die with this—superfluity of the clapboards,[10] are you?'

"'Common humanity, Dr. Whoa-ha,' says Mr. Biddle, 'ought to prevent your deserting a fellow-human in distress.'

"'Dr. Waugh-hoo, when you get through plowing,' says I. And then I walks back to the bed and throws back my long hair.

---

9. **clavicle** \\ˈklă·və·kəl\\ a bone in the body above the first rib connecting the shoulder blade and breastbone; the collarbone. **harpsichord** \\ˈhȯrp·sə'kȯrd\\ musical instrument, forerunner of piano; tone produced by key that plucks strings.
10. **clapboard,** narrow board that is thicker at one edge and used for covering outer walls.

"'Mr. Mayor,' says I, 'there is only one hope for you. Drugs will do you no good. But there is another power higher yet, although drugs are high enough,' says I.

"'And what is that?' says he.

"'Scientific demonstrations,' says I. 'The triumph of mind over sarsaparilla.[11] The belief that there is no pain and sickness except what is produced when we ain't feeling well. Declare yourself in arrears. Demonstrate.'

"'What is this paraphernalia you speak of, doc?' says the Mayor. 'You ain't a Socialist, are you?'

"'I am speaking,' says I, 'of the great doctrine of psychic financiering—of the enlightened school of long-distance, sub-conscientious treatment of fallacies and meningitis[12]—of that wonderful in-door sport known as personal magnetism.'

"'Can you work it, doc?' asks the Mayor.

"'I'm one of the Sole Sanhedrims and Ostensible Hooplas[13] of the Inner Pulpit,' says I. 'The lame talk and the blind rubber whenever I make a pass at 'em. I am a medium, a coloratura[14] hypnotist and a spirituous control. It was only through me at the recent seances at Ann Arbor that the late president of the Vinegar Bitters Company could revisit the earth to communicate with his sister Jane. You see me peddling medicine on the streets,' says I, 'to the poor. I don't practice personal magnetism on them. I do not drag it in the dust,' says I, 'because they haven't got the dust.'

"'Will you treat my case?' asks the Mayor.

"'Listen,' says I. 'I've had a good deal of trouble with medical societies everywhere I've been. I don't practice medicine. But, to save your life, I'll give you the psychic treatment if you'll agree as Mayor not to push the license question.'

"'Of course I will,' says he. 'And now get to work, doc, for them pains are coming on again.'

"'My fee will be $250.00, cure guaranteed in two treatments,' says I.

"'All right,' says the Mayor. 'I'll pay it. I guess my life's worth that much.'

"I sat down by the bed and looked him straight in the eye.

"'Now,' says I, 'get your mind off the disease. You ain't sick. You haven't got a heart or a clavicle or a funny bone or brains or anything. You haven't got any pain. Declare error. Now you feel the pain that you didn't have leaving, don't you?'

"'I do feel some little better, doc,' says the Mayor, 'darned if I don't. Now state a few lies about my not having this swelling in my left side, and I think I could be propped up and have some sausage and buckwheat cakes.'

"I made a few passes with my hands.

"'Now,' says I, 'the inflammation's gone. The right lobe of the perihelion[15] has subsided. You're getting sleepy. You can't hold your eyes open any longer. For the present the disease is checked. Now, you are asleep.'

"The Mayor shut his eyes slowly and began to snore.

"'You observe, Mr. Tiddle,' says I, 'the wonders of modern science.'

"'Biddle,' says he, 'when will you give uncle the rest of the treatment, Dr. Pooh-pooh?'

"'Waugh-hoo,' says I. 'I'll come back at eleven to-morrow. When he wakes up give him eight drops of turpentine and three pounds of steak. Good morning.'

"The next morning I went back on time. 'Well, Mr. Riddle,' says I, when he opened the bedroom door, 'and how is uncle this morning?'

"'He seems much better,' says the young man.

"The Mayor's color and pulse was fine. I gave him another treatment, and he said the last of the pain left him.

---

11. **sarsaparilla**\\'să·spə ˆrĭ·lə\\ a beverage similar to root beer with flavor from birch oil and sassafras.

12. **meningitis**\\'mĕ·nən ˆjī·dəs\\ inflammation of membranes around brain and spinal cord.

13. **Sanhedrims**\\ˆsăn·hĭ·drĭmz\\ the highest court and council of the ancient Jewish nation. **Hooplas**\\ˆhū·pləz\\ a gaudy, artificial show.

14. **coloratura**\\'kə·lər·ə ˆtū·rə\\ music which is characterized by runs and trills permitting a singer to display skill.

15. **perihelion**\\'pĕ·rə ˆhē·lĭ·ən\\ point in the path of a celestial body that is nearest the sun.

"'Now,' says I, 'you'd better stay in bed for a day or two, and you'll be all right. It's a good thing I happened to be in Fisher Hill, Mr. Mayor,' says I, 'for all the remedies in the cornucopia[16] that the regular schools of medicine use couldn't have saved you. And now that error has flew and pain proved a perjurer, let's allude to a cheerfuller subject—say the fee of $250. No checks, please, I hate to write my name on the back of a check almost as bad as I do on the front.'

"'I've got the cash here,' says the Mayor, pulling a pocket book from under his pillow.

"He counts out five fifty-dollar notes and holds 'em in his hand.

"'Bring the receipt,' he says to Biddle.

"I signed the receipt and the Mayor handed me the money. I put it in my inside pocket careful.

"'Now do your duty, officer,' says the Mayor, grinning much unlike a sick man.

"Mr. Biddle lays his hand on my arm.

"'You're under arrest, Dr. Waugh-hoo, alias Peters,' says he, 'for practising medicine without authority under the State law.'

"'Who are you?' I asks.

"'I'll tell you who he is,' says Mr. Mayor, sitting up in bed. 'He's a detective employed by the State Medical Society. He's been following you over five counties. He came to me yesterday and we fixed up this scheme to catch you. I guess you won't do any more doctoring around these parts, Mr. Fakir.[17] What was it you said I had, doc?' the Mayor laughs, 'compound—well it wasn't softening of the brain, I guess, anyway.'

"'A detective,' says I.

"'Correct,' says Biddle. 'I'll have to turn you over to the sheriff.'

"'Let's see you do it,' says I, and I grabs Biddle by the throat and half throws him out the window, but he pulls a gun and sticks it under my chin, and I stand still. Then he puts handcuffs on me, and takes the money out of my pocket.

"'I witness,' says he, 'that they're the same bills that you and I marked, Judge Banks. I'll turn them over to the sheriff when we get to his office, and he'll send you a receipt. They'll have to be used as evidence in the case.'

"'All right, Mr. Biddle,' says the Mayor. 'And now, Doc Waugh-hoo,' he goes on, 'why don't you demonstrate? Can't you pull the cork out of your magnetism with your teeth and hocus-pocus them handcuffs off?'

"'Come on, officer,' says I, dignified. 'I may as well make the best of it.' And then I turns to old Banks and rattles my chains.

"'Mr. Mayor,' says I, 'the time will come soon when you'll believe that personal magnetism is a success. And you'll be sure that it succeeded in this case, too.'

"And I guess it did.

"When we got nearly to the gate, I says: 'We might meet somebody now, Andy. I reckon you better take 'em off, and—' Hey? Why, of course it was Andy Tucker. That was his scheme; and that's how we got the capital to go into business together.'"

I

THE MYTH
OF THE YANKEE PEDDLER

One of the oldest and continuously popular characters of the American comic tradition was the so-called Yankee peddler. What he was like in real life is uncertain because his image was so early clouded by myth; the myth-figure, however, is relatively clear. He possessed the following characteristics:

1. He was a solitary person who traveled from place to place.

2. He was ingenious and quick-witted.

3. He was a master of masquerade.

4. He could sell anybody anything.

---

16. **cornucopia**\ˈkɔr·nə ˈkō·pē·ə\ the horn of plenty.
17. **Fakir**\ˈfā·kər\ faker or swindler.

O. Henry has obviously drawn both Jeff Peters and Andy Tucker from the Yankee peddler myth. The details of his portraits—for example, the odd mixture of mysticism, hypnotism, and spiritualism that makes Jeff Peters a "personal magnet"—are "modern"; but his general outlines for the two heroes clearly go all the way back to the late eighteenth or very early nineteenth century. We have here, then, a good example of a writer drawing upon literary heritage.

Point to specific details which show that Peters and Tucker are drawn from the Yankee peddler myth.

II
IMPLICATIONS

Examine the following statements about Americans. First ask yourself how the statement relates to the story; second ask whether it is true for Americans in general; and third ask whether it is a minor fault or a serious one.

1. Americans are impressed by the use of big words.

2. Americans are overly impressed by scientific terminology.

3. Americans really want to believe in magic; therefore they are susceptible to such things as "cure-alls" and Indian remedies.

4. Americans enjoy seeing an individual "put one over" on authorities.

5. Americans basically respect the sharp dealer.

6. Americans tend to believe that if buyers are stupid enough to be taken in, it's their hard luck.

III
TECHNIQUES

Comedy

O. Henry's humor in this story springs from a number of sources. From the list below select the techniques that were the source of most fun for you.

1. The mistaking of names. ("Riddle" for "Biddle," etc.)

2. The use of manufactured and misapplied words. ("super-inflammation of the right clavicle of the harpsichord," etc.)

3. Turning the tables. (On Peters, then on Mayor Banks.)

4. The double masquerade of Andy Tucker.

5. Exaggeration. (The exaggerated treatment of spiritualism and hypnotism, for example.)

6. Other factors. (You name them.)

Sympathy and Detachment

In comedy the matter of sympathy and detachment is especially important. In one way or another the author must present characters in such a way that we will sympathize with certain of them and remain detached from others. If we misplace our sympathies, the entire effect of a story may be changed. Consider the Mayor in this story: What would be the effect of the story if we sympathized strongly with Mayor Banks?

Because readers' natures vary so widely, it is probably impossible for an author to control completely the responses of all of them. The author can and does assume, however, that the majority of readers will react similarly to certain situations and characters simply because the readers belong to the same culture. Thus, O. Henry assumed that Americans of his day would naturally sympathize with the sharp dealers against the authority, Mayor Banks. Readers, however, from another culture—Native American, for example—might respond differently. An early American Puritan might have responded differently, too. Cultural factors, then, powerfully influence our responses to literature.

The chief human character in this story is Mike Flannery, an Irish shipping agent. He speaks in a dialect in which an "i" often replaces an "e" ("thim" for "them," for example) and in which "t" sometimes becomes "th" ("misther" for "mister"). Apart from this peculiarity, the story is very easy to read and is among the most hilarious tales we have ever known.

Pigs Is Pigs

ELLIS PARKER BUTLER

Mike Flannery, the Westcote agent of the Interurban Express Company, leaned over the counter of the express office and shook his fist. Mr. Morehouse, angry and red, stood on the other side of the counter, trembling with rage. The argument had been long and heated, and at last Mr. Morehouse had talked himself speechless. The cause of the trouble stood on the counter between the two men. It was a soap box across the top of which were nailed a number of strips, forming a rough but serviceable cage. In it two spotted guinea pigs were greedily eating lettuce leaves.

"Do as you like, then!" shouted Flannery, "pay for them and take them, or don't pay for them and leave them be. Rules is rules, Mister Morehouse, and Mike Flannery's not going to be called down for breaking them."

"But, you everlastingly stupid idiot!" shouted Mr. Morehouse, madly shaking a flimsy printed book beneath the agent's nose, "can't you read it here—in your own plain printed rates? 'Pets, domestic, Franklin to Westcote, if properly boxed, twenty-five cents each.'" He threw the book on the counter in disgust. "What more do you want? Aren't they pets? Aren't they domestic? Aren't they properly boxed? What?"

He turned and walked back and forth rapidly, frowning ferociously.

Suddenly he turned to Flannery and, forcing his voice to an artificial calmness, spoke slowly but with intense sarcasm.

"Pets," he said. "P-e-t-s! Twenty-five cents each. There are two of them. One! Two! Two times twenty-five are fifty! Can you understand that? I offer you fifty cents."

Flannery reached for the book. He ran his hand through the pages and stopped at page sixty-four.

"And I don't take fifty cents," he whispered in mockery. "Here's the rule for it. 'When the agent be in any doubt regarding which of two rates applies to a shipment, he shall charge the larger. The consignee may file a claim for the overcharge.' In this case, Mister Morehouse, I be in doubt. Pets them animals may be, and domestic they are, but pigs I'm blame sure they are, and my rules say plain as the nose on your face, 'Pigs, Franklin to Westcote, thirty cents each.' And, Mr. Morehouse, by my arithmetical knowledge two times thirty comes to sixty cents."

Mr. Morehouse shook his head savagely. "Nonsense!" he shouted, "confounded nonsense, I tell you! Why, you poor ignorant foreigner, that rule means common pigs, domestic pigs, not guinea pigs!"

Flannery was stubborn.

"Pigs is pigs," he declared firmly, "Guinea pigs or Irish pigs is all the same to the Interurban Express Company and to Mike Flannery. The nationality of the pig creates no differential in the rate, Mister Morehouse! It would be the same if they were Dutch pigs or Russian pigs. Mike Flannery," he added, "is here to tend to the express business and not to hold conversation with pigs in seventeen languages for to discover if they're Chinese or Tipperary[1] by birth and nativity."

Mr. Morehouse hesitated and then flung out his arms wildly.

"Very well!" he shouted, "you shall hear of

---

1. **Tipperary**, a county in south central Ireland.

this! Your president shall hear of this! It is an outrage! I have offered you fifty cents. You refuse it! Keep the pigs until you are ready to take the fifty cents, but, by George, sir, if one hair of those pigs' heads is harmed, I will have the law on you!"

He turned and stalked out, slamming the door. Flannery carefully lifted the soap box from the counter and placed it in a corner. He was not worried. He felt the peace that comes to a faithful servant who has done his duty and done it well.

Mr. Morehouse went home raging. His boy, who had been awaiting the guinea pigs, knew better than to ask him for them. He was a normal boy and therefore always had a guilty conscience when his father was angry. So the boy slipped quietly around the house. There is nothing so soothing to a guilty conscience as to be out of the path of the avenger.

Mr. Morehouse stormed into the house. "Where's the ink?" he shouted at his wife as soon as his foot was across the doorsill.

Mrs. Morehouse jumped, guiltily. She never used ink. She had not seen the ink, nor moved the ink, nor thought of the ink, but her husband's tone convicted her of the guilt of having borne and reared a boy, and she knew that whenever her husband wanted anything in a loud voice, the boy had been at it.

"I'll find Sammy," she said meekly.

When the ink was found, Mr. Morehouse wrote rapidly, and he read the completed letter and smiled a triumphant smile.

"That will settle that crazy Irishman!" he exclaimed. "When they get that letter, he will hunt another job, all right!"

A week later Mr. Morehouse received a long official envelope with the card of the Interurban Express Company in the upper left corner. He tore it open eagerly and drew out a sheet of paper. At the top it bore the number A6754. The letter was short. "Subject— Rate on guinea pigs," it said, "Dr. Sir—We are in receipt of your letter regarding rate on guinea pigs between Franklin and Westcote, addressed to the president of this company.

All claims for overcharge should be addressed to the Claims Department."

Mr. Morehouse wrote the Claims Department. He wrote six pages of choice sarcasm, vituperation, and argument, and sent them to Claims.

A few weeks later he received a reply from the Claims Department. Attached to it was his last letter.

"Dr. Sir," said the reply. "Your letter of the 16th inst., addressed to this Department, subject rate on guinea pigs from Franklin to Westcote, rec'd. We have taken up the matter with our agent at Westcote, and his reply is attached herewith. He informs us that you refused to receive the consignment or to pay the charges. You have therefore no claim against this company, and your letter regarding the proper rate on the consignment should be addressed to our Tariff Department."

Mr. Morehouse wrote to the Tariff Department. He stated his case clearly and gave his arguments in full, quoting a page or two from the encyclopedia to prove that guinea pigs were not common pigs.

With the care that characterizes corporations when they are systematically conducted, Mr. Morehouse's letter was numbered, O.K.'d, and started through the regular channels. Duplicate copies of the bill of lading, manifest, Flannery's receipt for the package, and several other pertinent papers were pinned to the letter, and they were passed to the head of the Tariff Department.

The head of the Tariff Department put his feet on his desk and yawned. He looked through the papers carelessly.

"Miss Kane," he said to his stenographer, "take this letter. 'Agent, Westcote, N.J. Please advise why consignment referred to in attached papers was refused domestic pet rates.' "

Miss Kane made a series of curves and angles on her notebook and waited with pencil poised. The department head looked at the papers again.

"Huh! guinea pigs!" he said. "Probably

starved to death by this time! Add this to that letter: 'Give condition of consignment at present.'"

He tossed the papers on the stenographer's desk, took his feet from his own desk, and went out to lunch.

When Mike Flannery received the letter he scratched his head.

"Give present condition," he repeated thoughtfully. "Now what do them clerks be wanting to know, I wonder! 'Present condition,' is it? Them pigs, praise St. Patrick, are in good health, so far as I know, but I never was no veterinary surgeon to pigs. Maybe them clerks want me to call in the pig doctor and have their pulses taken. One thing I do know, however, which is they've glorious appetites for pigs their size. Eats? They'd eat the brass padlocks off of a barn door! If the paddy pig, by the same token, ate as hearty as these pigs do, there'd be a famine in Ireland."

To assure himself that his report would be up to date, Flannery went to the rear of the office and looked into the cage. The pigs had been transferred to a larger box—a dry goods box.

"One, —two, —three, —four, —five, —six, —seven, —eight!" he counted. "Seven spotted and one all black. All well and hearty and all eating like raging hippopotamuses." He went back to his desk and wrote.

"Mr. Morgan, Head of Tariff Department," he wrote. "Why do I say guinea pigs is pigs because they is pigs and will be 'til you say they ain't which is what the rule book says stop your jollying me you know it as well as I do. As to health they are all well and hoping you are the same. P.S. There are eight now the family increased all good eaters. P.S. I paid out so far two dollars for cabbage which they like shall I put in bill for same what?"

Morgan, head of the Tariff Department, when he received this letter, laughed. He read it again and became serious. He looked up and thought it over.

"By George!" he said, "Flannery is right,

'pigs is pigs.' I'll have to get authority on this thing. Meanwhile, Miss Kane, take this letter: Agent, Westcote, N.J. Regarding shipment guinea pigs, File No. A6754. Rule 83, General Instructions to Agents, clearly states that agents shall collect from consignee all costs of provender, etc., etc., required for live stock while in transit or storage. You will proceed to collect same from consignee."

Flannery received this letter next morning, and when he read it he grinned.

"Proceed to collect," he said softly. "How them clerks do like to be talking! *Me* proceed to collect two dollars and twenty-five cents off Mister Morehouse! I wonder do them clerks *know* Mister Morehouse? I'll get it! Oh, yes! 'Mister Morehouse, two and a quarter, please.' 'Certainly, my dear friend Flannery. Delighted!' *Not!*"

Flannery drove the express wagon to Mr. Morehouse's door. Mr. Morehouse answered the bell.

"Ah, ha!" he cried as he saw it was Flannery. "So you've come to your senses at last, have you? I thought you would! Bring the box in."

"I have no box," said Flannery coldly. "I have a bill against Mister John C. Morehouse for two dollars and twenty-five cents for cabbages eaten by his pigs. Would you wish to pay it?"

"Pay—Cabbages—!" gasped Mr. Morehouse. "Do you mean to say that two little guinea pigs—"

"Eight!" said Flannery. "Papa and mamma and the six children. Eight!"

For answer Mr. Morehouse slammed the door in Flannery's face. Flannery looked at the door reproachfully.

"I take it the consignee don't want to pay for them cabbages," he said. "If I know signs of refusal, the consignee refuses to pay for one dang cabbage leaf and be hanged to me!"

Mr. Morgan, head of the Tariff Department, consulted the president of the Interurban Express Company regarding guinea pigs, as to whether they were pigs or not pigs. The president was inclined to treat the matter lightly.

"What is the rate on pigs and on pets?" he asked.

"Pigs thirty cents, pets twenty-five, said Morgan.

"Then of course guinea pigs are pigs," said the president.

"Yes," agreed Morgan, "I look at it that way, too. A thing that can come under two rates is naturally to be classed as the higher. But the guinea pigs, pigs? Aren't they rabbits?"

"Come to think of it," said the president, "I believe they are more like rabbits. Sort of halfway station between pig and rabbit. I think the question is this—are guinea pigs of the domestic pig family? I'll ask Professor Gordon. He is an authority on such things. Leave the papers with me."

The president put the papers on his desk and wrote a letter to Professor Gordon. Unfortunately the Professor was in South America collecting zoological specimens, and the letter was forwarded to him by his wife. As the Professor was in the highest Andes, where no white man had ever penetrated, the letter was many months in reaching him. The president forgot the guinea pigs, Morgan forgot them, Mr. Morehouse forgot them, but Flannery did not. One half of his time he gave to the duties of his agency; the other half was devoted to the guinea pigs. Long before Professor Gordon received the president's letter, Morgan received one from Flannery.

"About them guinea pigs," it said, "what shall I do they are great in family life, no race suicide for them, there are thirty-two now shall I sell them do you take this express office for a menagerie, answer quick."

Morgan reached for a telegraph blank and wrote:

"Agent, Westcote. Don't sell pigs."

He then wrote Flannery a letter calling his attention to the fact that the pigs were not the property of the company but were merely being held during a settlement of a dispute regarding rates. He advised Flannery to take the best possible care of them.

Flannery, letter in hand, looked at the pigs and sighed. The dry goods box cage had become too small. He boarded up twenty feet of the rear of the express office to make a large and airy home for them, and went about his business. He worked with feverish intensity when out on his rounds, for the pigs required attention and took most of his time. Some months later, in desperation, he seized a sheet of paper and wrote "160" across it and mailed it to Morgan. Morgan returned it asking for explanation. Flannery replied:

"There are now one hundred sixty of them pigs, for heavens sake let me sell off some, do you want me to go crazy, what."

"Sell no pigs," Morgan wired.

Not long after this the president of the express company received a letter from Professor Gordon. It was a long and scholarly letter, but the point was that the guinea pig was the *Cavia aparoea*[2] while the common pig was the genus *Sus* of the family *Suidae*. He remarked that they were prolific and multiplied rapidly.

"They are not pigs," said the president, decidedly, to Morgan. "The twenty-five cent rate applies."

Morgan made the proper notation on the papers that had accumulated in File A6754 and turned them over to the Audit Department. The Audit Department took some time to look the matter up and, after the usual delay, wrote Flannery that as he had on hand one hundred and sixty guinea pigs, the property of consignee, he should deliver them and collect charges at the rate of twenty-five cents each.

Flannery spent a day herding his charges through a narrow opening in their cage so that he might count them.

----

2. **Cavia aparoea**\ᵃka·vē·ə·a·pə ˈrē·ə\ the genus and species to which the guinea pig belongs.

"Audit Dept." He wrote, when he had finished the count, "you are way off there may be was one hundred and sixty guinea pigs once, but wake up don't be a back number. I've got even eight hundred, now shall I collect for eight hundred or what, how about sixty-four dollars I paid out for cabbages."

It required a great many letters back and forth before the Audit Department was able to understand why the error had been made of billing one hundred and sixty instead of eight hundred, and still more time for it to get the meaning of the "cabbages."

Flannery was crowded into a few feet at the extreme front of the office. The pigs had all the rest of the room and two boys were employed constantly attending to them. The day after Flannery had counted the guinea pigs there were eight more added to his drove, and by the time the Audit Department gave him authority to collect for eight hundred Flannery had given up all attempts to attend to the receipts of the delivery of goods. He was hastily building galleries around the express office, tier above tier. He had four thousand and sixty-four guinea pigs to care for. More were arriving daily.

Immediately following its authorization the Audit Department sent another letter, but Flannery was too busy to open it. They wrote another and then they telegraphed:

"Error in guinea pig bill. Collect for two guinea pigs, fifty cents. Deliver all to consignee."

Flannery read the telegram and cheered up. He wrote out a bill as rapidly as his pencil could travel over the paper and ran all the way to the Morehouse home. At the gate he stopped suddenly. The house stared at him with vacant eyes. The windows were bare of curtains, and he could see into the empty rooms. A sign on the porch said, "To Let." Mr. Morehouse had moved. Flannery ran all the way back to the express office. Sixty-nine guinea pigs had been born during his absence. He ran out again and made feverish inquiries in the village. Mr. Morehouse had not only

moved, but he had left Westcote. Flannery returned to the express office and found that two hundred and six guinea pigs had entered the world since he left. He wrote a telegram to the Audit Department.

"Can't collect fifty cents for two guinea pigs consignee has left town address unknown what shall I do? Flannery."

The telegram was handed to one of the clerks in the Audit Department, and as he read it he laughed.

"Flannery must be crazy. He ought to know that the thing to do is to return the consignment here," said the clerk. He telegraphed Flannery to send the pigs to the main office of the company at Franklin.

When Flannery received the telegram, he set to work. The six boys he had engaged to help him also set to work. They worked with the haste of desperate men, making cages out of soap boxes, cracker boxes, and all kinds of boxes, and as fast as the cages were completed, they filled them with guinea pigs and expressed them to Franklin. Day after day the cages of guinea pigs flowed in a steady stream from Westcote to Franklin, and still Flannery and his six helpers ripped and nailed and packed—relentlessly and feverishly. At the end of the week they had shipped two hundred and eighty cases of guinea pigs, and there were in the express office seven hundred and four more pigs than when they began packing them.

"Stop sending pigs. Warehouse full," came a telegram to Flannery. He stopped packing only long enough to wire back, "Can't stop," and kept on sending them. On the next train up from Franklin came one of the company's inspectors. He had instructions to stop the stream of guinea pigs at all hazards. As his train drew up at Westcote station, he saw a cattle car standing on the express company's siding. When he reached the express office he saw the express wagon backed up to the door. Six boys were carrying bushel baskets full of guinea pigs from the office and dumping them into the wagon. Inside the room Flannery, with his coat and vest off, was shoveling guinea pigs into bushel baskets with a coal scoop. He was winding up the guinea pig episode for once and for all.

He looked up at the inspector with a snort of anger.

"One wagonload more and I'll be quit of them, and never will you catch Flannery with no more foreign pigs on his hands. No, sir! They near was the death of me. Next time I'll know that pigs of whatever nationality is domestic pets—and go at the lowest rate."

He began shoveling again rapidly, speaking quickly between breaths.

"Rules may be rules, but you can't fool Mike Flannery twice with the same trick—when it comes to live stock, dang the rules. So long as Flannery runs this express office—pigs is pets —and cows is pets—and horses is pets—and lions and tigers and Rocky Mountain goats is pets—and the rate on them is twenty-five cents."

He paused long enough to let one of the boys put an empty basket in the place of the one he had just filled. There were only a few guinea pigs left. As he noted their limited number, his natural habit of looking on the bright side returned.

"Well, anyhow," he said cheerfully, "it's not so bad as it might be. What if them guinea pigs had been elephants!"

I

THE TALL TALE

One of the most common forms of humor on the American frontier was the tall tale. Perhaps you have read a tall tale about a traditional American hero such as Paul Bunyan, Davy Crockett, or Mike Fink. These tales are essentially simple, humorous narratives that use realistic details and everyday speech to relate the extravagantly impossible exploits of a superhuman figure.

What does "Pigs Is Pigs" have in common with the traditional tall tale? In what way or ways does it differ? Can you think of any reasons why such tales would be popular on the American frontier? Do you know any similar forms of humor that are still being published today?

II

IMPLICATIONS

Be prepared to point to specifics in the story that relate to the following human beliefs or tendencies. How do these contribute to the sense of pleasure you may have felt on reading this story?

1. The faith that everything will turn out all right in the long run.

2. The belief that as bad as things are, they could always be worse.

3. The tendency to believe that it is impossible to fight the bureaucratic system.

4. The hope that large, impersonal institutions rather than individuals will suffer.

5. The human tendency to avoid making decisions by "passing the buck."

6. The tendency to believe that the intellectual is not a practical problem solver.

III

TECHNIQUES

Comedy

One of the reasons good humorous short stories are difficult to write is that authors must not only create a basically comic situation involving a number of funny characters, but they must also provide many humorous details along the way. Select two or three details that you thought were especially funny, and be prepared to compare yours with those selected by your classmates.

Sympathy and Detachment

The "superiority theory" is sometimes advanced to explain the pleasure we get out of comedy. Essentially, the theory maintains that readers do not sympathize with characters but rather remain detached from them. We take a position above the characters and enjoy the sense of superiority we feel as a result of seeing comic characters behaving like fools.

What is your opinion of this theory, especially with respect to "Pigs Is Pigs"? Did you sympathize with any of the characters? Did you feel superior to Mike Flannery? If so, was that a main source of your enjoyment? What indications, if any, are there that the author feels superior to his chief character or would want his readers to feel that way? Does the superiority theory apply to other comedies you may have seen or read? For example, does it apply to O. Henry's "Jeff Peters as a Personal Magnet"?

Columbus, Ohio, provided the famous humorist James Thurber with more material than any writer could expect to get from a hometown. *My Life and Hard Times*, from which the following selection is taken, describes domestic disasters, local eccentrics, draft boards, family pets, and crises peculiar only to the Thurber family. "Mistaken exits and entrances," Thurber called them, autobiography as it should be written: frank, honest, and never more hilarious than in the following episode.

The Night the Ghost Got In

JAMES THURBER

JAMES THURBER, *photo by Douglas Glass*

A tall, lanky man with bushy hair, Thurber one day said, "Everyone thinks I look like the man I draw—bald and five feet one. Actually I draw the spirit of the man I am—and I'm a pussycat." His readers knew what he meant: independent, self-assured, curious, intelligent, not above purring when something pleased him, but quick to strike at irritants and intrusions. It is difficult to be neutral to his work. He engages our minds and imaginations, but above all he helps us to laugh at human behavior. And without laughter our lives would be harder to endure.

The ghost that got into our house on the night of November 17, 1915, raised such a hullabaloo of misunderstandings that I am sorry I didn't just let it keep on walking, and go to bed. Its advent caused my mother to throw a shoe through a window of the house next door and ended up with my grandfather shooting a patrolman. I am sorry, therefore, as I have said, that I ever paid any attention to the footsteps.

They began about a quarter past one o'clock in the morning, a rhythmic, quick-cadenced walking around the dining-room table. My mother was asleep in one room upstairs, my brother Herman in another; grandfather was in the attic, in the old walnut bed which, as you will remember, once fell on my father. I had just stepped out of the bathtub and was busily rubbing myself with a towel when I heard the steps. They were the steps of a man walking rapidly around the dining-room table down-

Copyright 1929, © 1961 by James Thurber. From *My Life and Hard Times*, published by Harper & Row. Originally printed in *The New Yorker*.

stairs. The light from the bathroom shone down the back steps, which dropped directly into the dining-room; I could see the faint shine of plates on the plate-rail; I couldn't see the table. The steps kept going round and round the table; at regular intervals a board creaked, when it was trod upon. I supposed at first that it was my father or my brother Roy, who had gone to Indianapolis but were expected home at any time. I suspected next that it was a burglar. It did not enter my mind until later that it was a ghost.

After the walking had gone on for perhaps three minutes, I tiptoed to Herman's room. "Psst!" I hissed, in the dark, shaking him. "Awp," he said, in the low, hopeless tone of a despondent beagle—he always half suspected that something would "get him" in the night. I told him who I was. "There's something downstairs!" I said. He got up and followed me to the head of the back staircase. We listened together. There was no sound. The steps had ceased. Herman looked at me in some alarm: I had only the bath towel around my waist. He wanted to go back to bed, but I gripped his arm. "There's something down there!" I said. Instantly the steps began again, circled the dining-room table like a man running, and started up the stairs toward us, heavily, two at a time. The light still shone palely down the stairs; we saw nothing coming; we only heard the steps. Herman rushed to his room and slammed the door. I slammed shut the door at the stairs top and held my knee against it. After a long minute, I slowly opened it again. There was nothing there. There was no sound. None of us ever heard the ghost again.

The slamming of the doors had aroused mother: she peered out of her room. "What on earth are you boys doing?" she demanded. Herman ventured out of his room. "Nothing," he said, gruffly, but he was, in color, a light green. "What was all that running around downstairs?" said mother. So she had heard the steps, too! We just looked at her. "Burglars!" she shouted intuitively. I tried to quiet her by starting lightly downstairs.

He always half suspected that something would get him.

"Come on, Herman," I said.

"I'll stay with mother," he said. "She's all excited."

I stepped back onto the landing.

"Don't either of you go a step," said mother. "We'll call the police." Since the phone was downstairs, I didn't see how we were going to call the police—nor did I want the police—but mother made one of her quick, incomparable decisions. She flung up a window of her bedroom which faced the bedroom windows of the house of a neighbor, picked up a shoe, and whammed it through a pane of glass across the narrow space that separated the two houses. Glass tinkled into the bedroom occupied by a retired engraver named Bodwell and his wife. Bodwell had been for some years in rather a bad way and was subject to mild "attacks." Most everybody we knew or lived near had *some* kind of attacks.

It was now about two o'clock of a moonless night; clouds hung black and low. Bodwell was at the window in a minute, shouting, frothing a little, shaking his fist. "We'll sell the house and go back to Peoria," we could hear Mrs. Bodwell saying. It was some time before mother "got through" to Bodwell. "Burglars!" she shouted. "Burglars in the house!" Herman and I hadn't dared to tell her that it was not burglars but ghosts, for she was even more afraid of ghosts than of burglars. Bodwell at first thought that she meant there were burglars in his house, but finally he quieted down and called the police for us over an extension phone by his bed. After he had disappeared from the window, mother suddenly made as if to throw another shoe, not because there was further need of it but, as she later explained, because the thrill of heaving a shoe through a window glass had enormously taken her fancy. I prevented her.

The police were on hand in a commendably short time: a Ford sedan full of them, two on motorcycles, and a patrol wagon with about eight in it and a few reporters. They began banging at our front door. Flashlights shot streaks of gleam up and down the walls, across the yard, down the walk between our house and Bodwell's. "Open up!" cried a hoarse voice. "We're men from Headquarters!" I wanted to go down and let them in, since there they were, but mother wouldn't hear of it. "You haven't a stitch on," she pointed out. "You'd catch your death." I wound the towel around me again. Finally the cops put their shoulders to our big heavy front door with its thick beveled glass and broke it in: I could hear a rending of wood and a splash of glass on the floor of the hall. Their lights played all over the living-room and crisscrossed nervously in the dining-room, stabbed into hallways, shot up the front stairs and finally up the back. They caught me standing in my towel at the top. A heavy policeman bounded up the steps. "Who are you?" he demanded. "I live here," I said. "Well, whattsa matta, ya hot?" he asked. I was, as a matter of fact, cold; I went to my room and pulled on some trousers. On my way out, a cop stuck a gun into my ribs. "Whatta you doin' here?" he demanded. "I live here," I said.

The officer in charge reported to mother "No sign of nobody, lady," he said. "Musta got away—whatt'd he look like?" "There were two or three of them," mother said, "whooping and carrying on and slamming doors." "Funny,"

said the cop. "All ya windows and doors was locked on the inside tight as a tick."

Downstairs, we could hear the tromping of the other police. Police were all over the place; doors were yanked open, drawers were yanked open, windows were shot up and pulled down, furniture fell with dull thumps. A half-dozen policemen emerged out of the darkness of the front hallway upstairs. They began to ransack the floor: pulled beds away from walls, tore clothes off hooks in the closets, pulled suitcases and boxes off shelves. One of them found an old zither[1] that Roy had won in a pool tournament. "Looky here, Joe," he said, strumming it with a big paw. The cop named Joe took it and turned it over. "What is it?" he asked me. "It's an old zither our guinea pig used to sleep on," I said. It was true that a pet guinea pig we once had would never sleep anywhere except on the zither, but I should never have said so. Joe and the other cop looked at me a long time. They put the zither back on a shelf.

"No sign o' nuthin'," said the cop who had first spoken to mother. "This guy," he explained to the others, jerking a thumb at me, "was nekked. The lady seems historical." They all nodded, but said nothing; just looked at me. In the small silence we all heard a creaking in the attic. Grandfather was turning over in bed. "What's 'at?" snapped Joe. Five or six cops sprang for the attic door before I could intervene or explain. I realized that it would be bad if they burst in on grandfather unannounced, or even announced. He was going through a phase in which he believed that General Meade's men, under steady hammering by Stonewell Jackson, were beginning to retreat and even desert.

When I got to the attic, things were pretty confused. Grandfather had evidently jumped to the conclusion that the police were deserters from Meade's army, trying to hide away in his attic. He bounded out of bed wearing a long

---

1. **zither,** musical instrument with 30 to 40 strings stretched over a shallow box and played with the fingers.

Police were all over the place.

flannel nightgown over long woolen underwear, a nightcap, and a leather jacket around his chest. The cops must have realized at once that the indignant white-haired old man belonged in the house, but they had no chance to say so. "Back, ye cowardly dogs!" roared grandfather. "Back t' the lines, ye yellow, lily-livered cattle!" With that, he fetched the officer who found the zither a flat-handed smack alongside his head that sent him sprawling. The others beat a retreat, but not fast enough; grandfather grabbed Zither's gun from its holster and let fly. The report seemed to crack the rafters; smoke filled the attic. A cop cursed and shot his hand to his shoulder. Somehow, we all finally got downstairs again and locked the door against the old gentleman. He fired once or twice more in the darkness and then went back to bed. "That was grandfather," I explained to Joe, out of breath. "He thinks you're deserters." "I'll say he does," said Joe.

The cops were reluctant to leave without getting their hands on somebody besides grandfather; the night had been distinctly a defeat for them. Furthermore, they obviously didn't like the "layout"; something looked—and I can see their viewpoint—phony. They began to poke into things again. A reporter, a thin-faced, wispy man, came up to me. I had put on one of

mother's blouses, not being able to find anything else. The reporter looked at me with mingled suspicion and interest. "Just what the heck is the real low down here, Bud?" he asked. I decided to be frank with him. "We had ghosts," I said. He gazed at me a long time as if I were a slot machine into which he had, without results, dropped a nickel. Then he walked away. The cops followed him, the one grandfather shot holding his now-bandaged arm, cursing and blaspheming. "I'm gonna get my gun back from that old bird," said the zither-cop. "Yeh," said Joe. "You—and who else?" I told them I would bring it to the station house the next day.

"What was the matter with that one policeman?" mother asked, after they had gone. "Grandfather shot him," I said. "What for?" she demanded. I told her he was a deserter. "Of all things!" said mother. "He was such a nice-looking young man."

Grandfather was fresh as a daisy and full of jokes at breakfast next morning. We thought at first he had forgotten all about what had happened, but he hadn't. Over his third cup of coffee, he glared at Herman and me. "What was the idee of all them cops tarryhootin' round the house last night?" he demanded. He had us there.

Some nights she threw them all.

I
THE CLASH OF TWO "WORLDS"

The main conflict in "The Night the Ghost Got In" is between groups rather than individuals, between the Thurber family on the one hand and the neighbors, police, and the reporter on the other. The latter represent the common-sense, "real" world; the former represent a zany, "unreal" world, a world in which—for one thing—ghosts really exist. One of the main sources of fun is the fact that when the two worlds clash, the zany world comes out victorious. The frustration and defeat of the common-sense world is well expressed by the "thin-faced, wispy" reporter who at the end of the episode asks, "Just what the heck is the real lowdown here, Bud?" Why is "Bud's" answer, "We had ghosts," a fitting and proper climax?

II
IMPLICATIONS

Be prepared to discuss whether you agree or disagree with the following statements and why. Be sure that you can offer specific evidence to support your own point of view.

1. It is difficult to identify with members of the Thurber family because they are such "oddballs."

2. We tend to feel superior to members of the Thurber family because we know more than they do.

3. Much of our enjoyment of Thurber stems from seeing him "put down" various "authority" figures, such as the police and the journalist in this story.

4. Still another source of our enjoyment is the fact that Thurber often lets the "underdog" triumph.

III
TECHNIQUES

Comedy

Thurber once defined humor as "a kind of emotional chaos told about calmly and quietly in retrospect." How well does this fit the selection you have just read? Would it also fit the first two stories in this unit? Explain why. If you think it does not fit them, would you say the definition applies only to Thurber himself?

Sympathy and Detachment

It has been argued that readers enjoy certain comedies because they allow them to do certain things vicariously that they would never permit themselves to do in reality. To what extent did you identify (perhaps subconsciously) with such characters as the mother and the grandfather, who—among other things—break the window of a neighbor and shoot a police officer?

Whether you call it sympathy or identification, how does Thurber get his readers on the side of zanies like the members of his family? Why don't we instead identify or sympathize with the relatively normal persons in Thurber's stories, such as the Bodwells, who live next door?

Light Verse

Richard Armour has expressed his comic imagination in both verse and prose prolifically. To appreciate his poem, "Accessories to the Fact," you might profit by recalling the nursery tale "The House That Jack Built" and the fact that "jack"—with the small "j"—is not only a playing card and something useful in fixing flats but is also slang for "money."

Accessories to the Fact

This is the bracelet that went with the ring
That went with the costume-jewelry thing
That went with the purse that went with the gloves
That went with the coat she so dearly loves
That went with the stole of mutation mink[1]   5
That went with the hat that would drive you to drink
That went with the hose that went with the shoes
That went with the buckle she couldn't refuse
That went with the buttons that went with the belt
That went with the cluster of flowers of felt   10
That went with the perfume that went with the blouse
That went with the sweet little suit for my spouse
   That my jack bought.

RICHARD ARMOUR

---

1. **mutation mink,** made of mink of a domesticated strain which differs in color from the wild type.

From *Nights with Armour* by Richard Armour. Copyright © 1958 by Richard Armour. Used with permission of McGraw-Hill Book Co.

David McCord has published more than twenty books,
including some verse for children and a well-known anthology
of light verse. He has been highly praised by many of his fellow poets,
notably Louis Untermeyer, who once said of him: "I don't know
any living writer of verse who so lightly combines simplicity
and subtlety, ingenuity and ingenuousness."

Daedalus,[1] *Stay Away from My Transom!*

The age of flight, the age of flight:
They say it hasn't come yet quite.
The atom somehow got between,
And something else may intervene
Before a man can wear his wings   5
The way he wears his socks and things,
Or jet-propel himself from here
To points beyond the stratosphere.
But still, the experts all agree,
The age of flight is what we'll see;   10
It's what we'll get, it's what we'll be.
   All right, all right:
   If flight means flee—
   That's me.

What is there in this age of flight   15
To make me hug the earth so tight?
The age of flint, the age of stone
Developed from the age of bone,
And in the prehistoric dawn
Our fathers met them axehead on.   20
The age of iron, brass, and tin
And other ages trickled in.
The age of coal, the age of steam
Were mutual, like milk and cream.
The age of coal and steam, alas,   25
Expanded to an age of gas;
And then, as if that wouldn't do,
The age of Edison came through.
So now, with this atomic age,
You think we've turned the final page?   30
Not yet, my friend: the ceiling height
Is coming with the age of flight.

I think about it day and night
   All right, all right,
   For flight means flee   35
   To me.

I do not want a pair of wings
And supersonic underthings.
I do not care to cross the street
Retracting, as I fly, my feet.   40
I do not want O'Malley's[2] gift;
I don't desire that kind of lift.
I do not long for rocket ships
And outer interstellar trips.
I'm glad they have canals on Mars: 45
I'm sorry that the moon has scars.
It's comforting to think that space
May hide the meistermaster[3] race
On some far planet, and contrast
My foolish future with their past.   50
The age of flight is food for thought:
I haven't eaten as I ought.
Out on a limb, this earthbound tree
Just suits me to a Model T—
It's plenty high enough for me   55
   All right, all right.
   And flightless me
   I'll be.

DAVID MCCORD

---

1. **Daedalus**\ˈdĕ·də·ləs\ Athenian architect who built the Cretan Labyrinth; later he escaped from Crete by use of artificial wings.
2. **O'Malley's gift,** O'Malley, once a famous comic strip character, was a little man who was invisible to all but special friends. He had the gift of flight.
3. **meister**\ˈmai·stĕr\ master.

Copyright 1951 by David McCord. From *Odds Without Ends* by David McCord, by permission of Little, Brown and Company.

Phyllis McGinley has been writing first-rate light verse—
with some serious poems mixed in—for better than thirty years.
Though she described herself in one of her poems as "sunk in content,"
we get one of her discontented views in the following poem.

Don't Shake the Bottle, Shake Your Mother-in-Law

When I was young and full of rhymes
    And all my days were salady,[1]
Almost I could enjoy the times
    I caught some current malady.
Then, cheerful, knocked upon my door   5
    The jocular[2] physician,
With tonics and with comfort for
    My innocent condition.
Then friends would fetch me flowers
    And nurses rub my back,   10
And I could talk for hours
    Concerning my attack.
But now, when vapors[3] dog me,
    What solace do I find?
My cronies can't endure me.   15
The doctors scorn to cure me,
And, though I ail, assure me
    It's all a state of mind.

It's psychosomatic,[4] now, psychosomatic.
Whatever you suffer is psychosomatic.   20
Your liver's a-quiver? You're feeling infirm?
Dispose of the notion you harbor a germ.
Angina,
    Arthritis,
        Abdominal pain—   25
They're nothing but symptoms of marital strain.

---

1. **salady,** youthful and inexperienced.
2. **jocular**\\ˈjŏk·yū·lər\\ humorous, full of fun.
3. **vapors,** depressed spirits.
4. **psychosomatic**\\ˈsī·kō·sō ˈmă·tĭk\\ physical disorder caused or aggravated by emotional processes.

From *Times Three* by Phyllis McGinley. Copyright 1948,
© 1976 by Phyllis McGinley. Reprinted by permission of The
Viking Press.

They're nothing but proof that your love life is minus.
The ego is aching
Instead of the sinus.
So face up and brace up and stifle that sneeze.   30
It's psychosomatic. And ten dollars, please.

There was a time that I recall,
    If one grew pale or thinnish,
The pundits[5] loved to lay it all
    On foods unvitaminish,   35
Or else, dogmatic, would maintain
    Infection somewhere acted.
And when they'd shorn the tonsils twain,
    They pulled the tooth impacted.
But now that orgies dental   40
    Have made a modish halt,
Your ills today are mental
    And likely all your fault.
Now specialists inform you,
    While knitting of their brows,   45
Your pain, though sharp and shooting,
Is caused, beyond disputing,
Because you hate commuting
    Or can't abide your spouse.

It's psychosomatic, now, psychosomatic.   50
You fell down the stairway? It's psychosomatic.
That sprain of the ankle while waxing the floors—
You did it on purpose to get out of chores.
Nephritis,[6]
    Neuritis,[7]   55
        A case of the ague?[8]
You're just giving in to frustrations that plague you.
You long to be coddled, beloved, acclaimed,
So you caught the sniffles.
And aren't you ashamed!   60
And maybe they're right. But I sob through my wheezes,
"They've taken the fun out of having diseases."

PHYLLIS MC GINLEY

---

5. **pundits,** persons of great learning.
6. **Nephritis**\nĕ frī·tĭs\ disease of the kidneys.
7. **Neuritis**\nū rī·tĭs\ inflammation of the nerves.
8. **ague**\ā·gū\fever marked by chills.

◆ Before reading this selection, be sure to read
Robert Frost's "Fire and Ice," on page 485. In "Frostbite,"
Conrad Aiken has a little fun at the expense of a fellow poet,
but Mr. Aiken's reputation as a great poet and short-story writer
rests on serious work.

Frostbite

Some say the world will end by Fire
And some by Frost
   By verse of ice, or vice of verser,
   (God only knows which were the worser!)
But, anyway, the world well lost.

CONRAD AIKEN

Reprinted by permission of Conrad Aiken.

I
LIGHT VERSE—WHAT IS IT?

Light verse is one of those terms that many people know the meaning of and no one can define. Probably the best way to come to understand it is to read a good deal more of the work of poets like McCord, Armour, and McGinley.

We are not going to try to define light verse rigorously, but we can say that such poetry is characterized by a light, gay, or playful manner of expression and that the poet commonly pokes fun at some human failing. Also, in light verse the rhythm is often more pronounced than it might be in "heavier" verse. Check the foregoing poems for these characteristics.

II
IMPLICATIONS

Explain what the poet is suggesting about life and the world in the following quotations.

1. This is the bracelet that went with the ring . . .
   That my jack bought.

2. . . . this earthbound tree
   Just suits me to a Model T—
   It's plenty high enough for me

3. Whatever you suffer is psychosomatic.

III
TECHNIQUES

Comedy

A. John Erskine, a writer and educator, once distinguished between humor, wit, and fun. He proposed that a literary work was funny if it was the occasion of "harmless laughter" and if it neither called for intelligence nor stimulated sympathy. A work was witty if it involved intelligence and had at least a mildly hard edge to it. Finally, he said that a work was humorous if it looked sympathetically into common human weaknesses.

How would you classify the poems in this section, using this three-part division? Does it seem to be a useful classification or not?

B. A good deal of the humorous effect of light verse comes from the use of rhyme and rhythm and word choice in unexpected ways.

1. Find examples from one or more than one poem of unexpected rhythms or rhymes used to create a humorous effect.

2. Writers of light verse enjoy playing with words. Make a brief catalog of the ways in which the foregoing poets have fun with words.

3. The surprise ending—comparable to the punch line in spoken humor—occurs in much light verse. Which of these poems have such endings?

The two following selections are a type of prose—one might say "light verse," a form of comedy relying upon pure fun or nonsense.

Ring Lardner got his start in writing as a sports reporter and later became an editor. He wrote many amusing pieces on the sports scene. In his later career he published a number of stories that are ranked by many critics as among America's best modern fiction, including the much-anthologized "Haircut" and "The Love Nest." Although he was fundamentally a satirist and has been called "a great pessimist," he was also author of a good deal of nonsense, one example of which is the following brief play.

Thompson's Vacation

PLAY IN TWO ACTS

RING LARDNER

Characters

THOMPSON, *a plain citizen*

HAINES, *another*

DILLON, *another*

Act I

August 28. The smoking car of a city-bound suburban train. THOMPSON *is sitting alone.* HAINES *comes in, recognizes him and takes the seat beside him.*

HAINES: Hello there, Thompson.
THOMPSON: Hello, Mr. Haines.
HAINES: What's the good word?

THOMPSON: Well—
HAINES: How's business?
THOMPSON: I don't know. I've been on a vacation for two weeks.
HAINES: Where was you?
THOMPSON: Atlantic City.
HAINES: Where did you stop?
THOMPSON: At the Edgar.
HAINES: The Edgar! Who steered you to that joint?
THOMPSON: I liked it all right.
HAINES: Why didn't you go to the Wallace? Same prices and everything up to date. How did you happen to pick out a dirty old joint like the Edgar?
THOMPSON: I thought it was all right.
HAINES: What did you do to kill time down there?
THOMPSON: Oh, I swam and went to a couple of shows and laid around.
HAINES: Didn't you go up in the air?
THOMPSON: No.

Reprinted with the permission of Charles Scribner's Sons from *First and Last*, pp. 329-332, by Ring Lardner. Copyright 1934 Ellisa Lardner; renewal copyright © 1962 Ring Lardner, Jr.

253

HAINES: That's the only thing they is to do in Atlantic City, is go up in the air. If you didn't do that, you didn't do nothing.

THOMPSON: I never been up.

HAINES: That's all they is to do down there, especially in August, when it's so hot.

THOMPSON: They was generally always a breeze.

HAINES: Yes, I know what that breeze is in August. It's like a blast out of a furnace. Did you go in any of them cabarets?

THOMPSON: Yes, I was in the Mecca and the Garden.

HAINES: Wasn't you in the La Marne?

THOMPSON: No.

HAINES: If you wasn't in the La Marne, you didn't see nothing.

THOMPSON: I had some real beer in the Mecca.

HAINES: Say, that stuff they give you in the Mecca is dishwater. They's only one place in Atlantic City to get real beer. That's the Wonderland. Didn't you make the Wonderland?

THOMPSON: No.

HAINES: Then you didn't have no real beer. Did you meet many dames?

THOMPSON: Only a couple of them. But they was pips!

HAINES: Pips! You don't see no real pips down there in August. The time to catch the pips down there is—well, June, July, September, May, or any time in the fall or winter or spring. You don't see them there in August. Did you go fishing?

THOMPSON: No.

HAINES: Oh, they's great fishing around there! If you didn't go fishing, you didn't do nothing.

THOMPSON (*rising*): Well, here we are.

HAINES: I think you're a sucker to pick out August for a vacation. May or June or September, that's the time for a vacation.

THOMPSON: Well, see you again.

Act II

Four minutes later. A downtown subway express. THOMPSON *is hanging on a strap.* DILLON *enters and hangs on the next strap.*

DILLON: Hello there, Thompson.

THOMPSON: Hello.

DILLON: How's everything?

THOMPSON: All right, I guess.

DILLON: Ain't you been on a vacation?

THOMPSON: Yeah.

DILLON: What kind of a time did you have?

THOMPSON: Rotten.

DILLON: Where was you?

THOMPSON: Nowhere.

Curtain

Robert Benchley was drama editor of *The New Yorker*
from 1929 till 1940. He was also in films, on the radio, and on the stage.
Stephen Leacock, who is often credited with founding the modern school
of nonsense humor, once said of Benchley: "As a writer of nonsense
for nonsense's sake, he is unsurpassed."

Sporting Life in America: Dozing

ROBERT BENCHLEY

We Americans are a hardy race, and hardy races need a lot of sleep. "Sleep, that knits up the ravell'd sleave of care,"[1] Shakespeare has called it, and, except for the fact that it doesn't mean much, it is a pretty good simile. I often think of it myself just as I am dropping off into a light doze: "Sleep, that sleeves up the raveled care of . . . knit, that sleeps up the shaveled neeve of pfor—pff—prpf—orpffff" (*trailing off into a low whistle*).

One of the most charming manifestations of sleep which we, as a nation, indulge in as a pastime is the Doze. By the Doze I mean those little snatches of sleep which are caught now and then during the day, usually with the collar on and choking slightly, with the head inclined coyly to one side, during which there is a semiconscious attempt to appear as if we were really awake. It is in this department of sleep that we are really at our best.

Of course, there is one form of doze which, to the casual observer or tourist, gives the appearance of legitimate sleep. This is the short doze, or "quickie," which is taken just after the main awakening in the morning. The alarm rings, or the Lord High Chamberlain taps us on the shoulder (in the absence of a chamberlain a relative will do. And right here I would like to offer for examination that type of sadistic relative who takes actual delight in awakening people. They hover about with ghoulish anticipation until the minute arrives when they may legitimately begin their dirty work, and then, leering unpleasantly, they shake the sleeper roughly with a "Come, come! Time to get up!" and wait right there until he is actually out on the cold floor in his bare feet. There is something radically wrong with such people, and the sooner they are exposed as pathological cases the better it will be for the world). I'm sorry. I didn't mean to be nasty about it.

At any rate, we are awakened and look at the clock. There are five minutes before it is absolutely necessary to get out of bed. If we leave shaving until night, there might even be fifteen minutes. If we leave dressing until we get to the office, snatching our clothes from the chair and carrying them downtown on our arm, there might even be half an hour more for a good, health-giving nap. Who knows? Perhaps those few minutes of extra sleep might make us just ten times as efficient during the day! That is what we must think of—efficiency. We must sacrifice our petty opinions on the matter and think of the rest of the day and our efficiency. There is no doubt that fifteen minutes' more sleep would do wonders for us, no matter how little we really want to take it.

"Sporting Life in America: Dozing" from *Benchley Beside Himself* by Robert Benchley. Copyright 1930 by Robert C. Benchley. Reprinted by permission of Harper & Row, Publishers.

1. **Sleep . . . care,** Shakespeare, *Macbeth*, Act II, Sc. 2, l. 36.

By the time we have finished this line of argument we are out pretty fairly cold again, but not so cold that we are not conscious of anyone entering the room. We feel that they are going to say: "Come, come, don't go back to sleep again!" and we forestall this warning with a brisk "I know! I know! I'm just thinking!" This is said with one eye partially open and one tiny corner of the brain functioning. The rest of our powers add up to a total loss.

It is one of Nature's wonders how a man can carry on an argument with someone standing beside his bed and still be asleep to all intents and purposes. Not a very good argument, perhaps, and one in which many important words are missing or indistinct, but still an argument. It is an argument, however, which seldom wins, the state of justice in the world being what it is today.

Dozing before arising does not really come within the range of this treatise. What we are concerned with are those little lapses when we are fully dressed, when we fondly believe that no one notices. Riding on a train, for example.

There is the short-distance doze in a day coach, probably the most humiliating form of train sleeping. In this the elbow is rested on the window sill and the head placed in the hand in an attitude of thought. The glass feels very cool on the forehead and we rest it there, more to cool off than anything else. The next thing we know the forehead (carrying the entire head with it) has slid down the length of the slippery pane and we have received a rather nasty bang against the woodwork. They shouldn't keep their glass so slippery. A person is likely to get badly hurt that way.

However, back again goes the forehead against the pane in its original position, with the hand serving more or less as a buffer, until another skid occurs, this time resulting in an angry determination to give the whole thing up entirely and sit up straight in the seat. Some dozers will take four or five slides without whimpering, going back each time for more with apparently undiminished confidence in their ability to see the thing through.

It is a game that you can't beat, however, and the sooner you sit up straight in your seat, the sooner you will stop banging your head.

Dozing in a Pullman chair is not so dangerous, as one does not have the risk of the sliding glass to cope with, but it is even less lovely in its appearance. Here the head is allowed to sink back against the antimacassar—just for a minute to see if the headrest is really as comfortable as it seems. It is then but the work of a minute for the mouth to open slightly and the head to tip roguishly to the right, and there you are—as pretty a picture as one would care to see. You are very lucky if, when you come to and look about, you do not find your neighbors smiling indulgently at some little vagaries of breathing or eccentricities of facial expression which you have been permitting yourself.

The game in all this public dozing is to act, on awakening, as if you had known all along what you were doing. If your neighbors are smiling, you should smile back, as if to say: "Fooled you that time! You thought I was asleep, didn't you?"

If they are not quite so rude as to smile, but look quickly back at their reading on seeing your eyes open, you should assume a brisk, businesslike expression indicating that you have been thinking out some weighty business problem with your eyes closed, and, now that you have at last come on its solution, that it is snap-snap! back to work for you! If, after a furtive look around, you discover that no one has caught you at it, then it will do no harm to give it another try, this time until your collar chokes you into awakening with a strangling gasp.

The collar, however, is not always an impediment to public dozing. In the theater, for example, a good, stiff dress collar and shirt bosom have been known to hold the sleeper in an upright position when otherwise he might have plunged forward and banged his head on the back of the seat in front.

In my professional capacity as play reviewer I have had occasion to experiment in the various ways of sitting up straight and still snatching a few winks of health-giving sleep. I have found that by far the safest is to keep one's heavy overcoat on, especially if it is made of some good, substantial material which will hold a sagging torso erect within its folds. With a good overcoat, reënforced by a stiff dress shirt and a high collar, one may even go beyond the dozing stage and sink into a deep, refreshing slumber, and still not be made conspicuous by continual lurchings and plungings. Of course, if you are an uneasy sleeper and given to thrashing about, you will find that even a heavy overcoat will let you down once in a while. But for the average man, who holds approximately the same position after he has gone to sleep, I don't think that this method can go wrong. Its only drawback is that you are likely to get a little warm along about the middle of the second act.

If you don't want to wear your overcoat in the theater, the next best method is to fold the arms across the chest and brace the chin against the dress collar, exerting a slight upward pressure with the arms against the shirt front. This, however, can be used only for the lightest of dozes, as, once unconsciousness has set in, the pressure relaxes and over you go.

Dozing at a play, however refreshing, makes it a bit difficult to follow the argument on the stage, as occasionally the nap drags itself out into a couple of minutes and you awake to find a wholly fresh set of characters on the scene, or even a wholly fresh scene. This is confusing. It is therefore wise to have someone along with you who will alternate watches with you, dozing when you are awake and keeping more or less alert while you are dozing. In this way you can keep abreast of what has been happening.

This, unfortunately, is impossible in personal conversations. If you slip off into a quick coma late some evening when your *vis-à-vis*[2] is telling you about South America or a new solvent process, it is usually pretty difficult to pick up the thread where you dropped it. You may remember that the last words he was saying were "—which is situated at the mouth of the Amazon," but that isn't going to help you much if you come to just as he is asking you: "What would *you* say are?" As in the personal-conversation doze the eyes very seldom completely close (it is more of a turning back of the eyeballs than a closing of the lids), you may escape detection if you have a ready answer for the emergency. I find that "Well, I don't know," said very slowly and deliberately, will fit almost any question that has been asked you. "Yes" and "No" should never be offered, as they might make you sound even sillier than you look. If you say: "Well, I—don't—know," it will give you a chance to collect your wits (what few there are left) and may lead your questioner into answering the thing himself.

At any rate, it will serve as a stall. If there are other people present, some one of them is quite likely to come to your rescue and say something which will tip you off as to the general subject under discussion. From then on, you will have to fight your own battle. I can't help you.

The whole problem is one which calls for a great deal of thought. If we can develop some way in which a man can doze and still keep from making a monkey of himself, we have removed one of the big obstacles to human happiness in modern civilization. It goes without saying that we don't get enough sleep while we are in bed; so we have got to get a little now and then while we are at work or at play. If we can find some way to keep the head up straight, the mouth closed, and just enough of the brain working to answer questions, we have got the thing solved right there.

I am working on it right now, as a matter of fact, but I find it a little difficult to keep awake.

---

2. **vis-à-vis**\'vē•zě 'vē\ person sitting opposite, face to face.

I
NONSENSE

In the form of comedy known as nonsense, there is no intention to criticize seriously or sympathize deeply with any particular person or group. The laughter that nonsense evokes is usually described as harmless. We laugh primarily at ridiculous or absurd ideas or situations, such as Haines's assertion that the best time to see girls in Atlantic City is any month *except* August, or at Benchley's comment that dozing before arising does not really come within the range of his essay, after he has spent nearly a third of his space on that topic.

II
IMPLICATIONS

Discuss each of the following propositions.

1. "Thompson's Vacation" is an implicit criticism of the human tendency to judge oneself (or see oneself) in the light of the opinions of others.

2. Lardner intends to show the susceptibility of the average person to advertisers, politicians, and other molders of opinion.

3. Benchley's chief target is the idea that Americans are a hardy and supremely efficient people.

4. One of the underlying reasons for Benchley's appeal is that he champions the cause of the average person against those whose tastes are sophisticated and intellectual.

5. Since nonsense involves neither healthy criticism nor sympathetic understanding, it has little, if any, reason for existence.

III
TECHNIQUES

Comedy

List as many ridiculous or absurd ideas or situations as you can from the two selections. Do you agree or disagree that the laughter that these provoke is accurately described as harmless?

Sympathy and Detachment

In pure humor the readers are involved and normally sympathize with one or more characters being portrayed. In the form of comedy known as *wit*, there is involvement of the reader's mind and a tendency to identify with superior characters or with the author. What is the pattern, so far as sympathy and detachment are concerned, in nonsense?

PROFESSOR BUTTS CHOKES ON A PRUNE PIT AND COUGHS UP AN IDEA FOR AN AUTOMATIC TYPEWRITER ERASER. RING FOR OFFICE BOY (A), WHO COMES RUNNING IN AND STUMBLES OVER FEET OF WINDOW CLEANER (B). HE GRABS FOR HAT-RACK (C) TO SAVE HIMSELF. HAT-RACK FALLS AGAINST BOOKS (D) WHICH DROP ON RULER (E), CAUSING PEN (F) TO FLY UP AND PUNCTURE BALLOON (G) WHICH EXPLODES WITH A LOUD REPORT. TRAINED MONKEY (H) MISTAKES REPORT FOR GUN THAT IS THE SIGNAL TO BEGIN HIS VAUDEVILLE ACT AND HE STARTS PEDALLING LIKE MAD. THE RUBBER TIRE (I) PASSES OVER PAPER (J) AND ERASES MISTAKE MADE BY SLEEPY STENOGRAPHER WHO IS TOO TIRED TO DO IT HERSELF BECAUSE SHE HAD SUCH A LONG WALK HOME FROM AN AUTOMOBILE RIDE THE NIGHT BEFORE.
IT IS ADVISABLE TO HAVE YOUR OFFICE OVER A GARAGE SO YOU CAN GET QUICK SERVICE IN CASE OF A PUNCTURE.

PROFESSOR BUTTS INVENTS A TYPEWRITER ERASER *Rube Goldberg*

Reuben Lucius Goldberg had actually been an engineer, and out of his industrial experience came the motivation for the zany inventions. His observations on things mechanical convulsed millions of Americans, even when they were deeply committed to a mechanically run society. This strip is "Another nightmare for the Patent Office . . . an attempt to make life easier for the working girl."

It is not often that a writer creates a character so real and lively
that the character becomes almost as famous as the author.
Yet this is what happened with Jesse B. Semple—"Simple," for short—
of Harlem, a superlative comic creation of the most prolific and probably best-known
modern black American writer, Langston Hughes. Published between
1950 and 1965, Hughes' Simple stories fill four volumes.
The following are a small but representative sample of this large output.

Four "Simple" Tales

LANGSTON HUGHES

CENSUS

"I have had so many hardships in this life," said Simple, "that it is a wonder I'll live until I die. I was born young, black, voteless, poor, and hungry, in a state where white folks did not even put Negroes on the census. My daddy said he were never counted in his life by the United States government. And nobody could find a birth certificate for me nowhere. It were not until I come to Harlem that one day a census taker dropped around to my house and asked me where were I born and why, also my age and if I was still living. I said, 'Yes, I am here, in spite of all.'

" 'All of what?' asked the census taker. 'Give me the data.'

" 'All my corns and bunions, for one,' I said. 'I were borned with corns. Most colored peoples get corns so young, they must be inherited. As for bunions, they seem to come natural, we stands on our feet so much. These feet of mine have stood in everything from soup lines to the draft board. They have supported everything from a packing trunk to a hongry woman. My feet have walked ten thousand miles running errands for white folks and another ten thousand trying to keep up with colored. My feet have stood before altars, at crap tables, bars, graves, kitchen doors, welfare windows, and social security railings. Be sure and include my feet on that census you are taking,' I told that man.

"Then I went on to tell him how my feet have helped to keep the American shoe industry going, due to the money I have spent on my feet. 'I have wore out seven hundred pairs of shoes, eight-nine tennis shoes, forty-four summer sandals, and two hundred and two loafers. The socks my feet have bought could build a knitting mill. The razor blades I have used cutting away my corns could pay for a razor plant. Oh, my feet have helped to make America rich, and I am still standing on them.

" 'I stepped on a rusty nail once, and mighty near had lockjaw. And from my feet up, so many other things have happened to me, since, it is a wonder I made it through this world. In my time, I have been cut, stabbed, run over, hit by a car, tromped by a horse, robbed, fooled, deceived, double-crossed, dealt

Reprinted with the permission of Hill and Wang (now a division of Farrar, Straus & Giroux, Inc.) from *Simple's Uncle Sam* by Langston Hughes. Copyright © 1965 by Langston Hughes.

259

seconds, and mighty near blackmailed—but I am still here! I have been laid off, fired and not rehired, Jim Crowed,[1] segregated, insulted, eliminated, locked in, locked out, locked up, left holding the bag, and denied relief. I have been caught in the rain, caught in jails, caught short with my rent, and caught with the wrong woman—but I am still here!

"'My mama should have named me Job[2] instead of Jesse B. Semple. I have been underfed, underpaid, undernourished, and everything but undertaken—yet I am still here. The only thing I am afraid of now—is that I will die before my time. So man, put me on your census now this year, because I may not be here when the next census comes around.'

"The census man said, 'What do you expect to die of—complaining?'

"'No,' I said, 'I expect to ugly away.' At which I thought the man would laugh. Instead you know he nodded his head, and wrote it down. He were white and did not know I was making a joke. Do you reckon that man really thought I am homely?"

TEMPTATION

"When the Lord said, 'Let there be light,' and there was light, what I want to know is where was us colored people?"

"What do you mean, 'Where were we colored people?'" I said.

"We must *not* of been there," said Simple, "because we are still dark. Either He did not include me or else I were not there."

"The Lord was not referring to people when He said, 'Let there be light.' He was referring to the elements, the atmosphere, the air."

"He must have included some people," said Simple, "because white people are light, in fact, *white*, whilst I am dark. How come? I say, we were not there."

"Then where do you think we were?"

"Late as usual," said Simple, "old C. P. Time. We must have been down the road a piece and did not get back on time."

"There was no C. P. Time in those days," I said. "In fact, no people were created—so there couldn't be any Colored People's Time. The Lord God had not yet breathed the breath of life into anyone."

"No?" said Simple.

"No," said I, "because it wasn't until Genesis 2 and 7 that God 'formed man of the dust of the earth and breathed into his nostrils the breath of life and man became a living soul.' His name was Adam. Then He took one of Adam's ribs and made a woman."

"Then trouble began," said Simple. "Thank God, they was both white."

"How do you know Adam and Eve were white?" I asked.

"When I was a kid I seen them on the Sunday school cards," said Simple. "Ever since I been seeing a Sunday school card, they was white. That is why I want to know where was us Negroes when the Lord said, 'Let there be light'?"

"Oh, man, you have a color complex so bad you want to trace it back to the Bible."

"No, I don't. I just want to know how come Adam and Eve was white. If they had started out black, this world might not be in the fix it is today. Eve might not of paid that serpent no attention. I never did know a Negro yet that liked a snake."

"That snake is a symbol," I said, "a symbol of temptation and sin. And that symbol would be the same, no matter what the race."

"I am not talking about no symbol," said Simple. "I am talking about the day when Eve took that apple and Adam et. From then on the human race has been in trouble. There ain't a colored woman living what would take no apple from a snake—and she better not give no snake-apples to her husband!"

"Adam and Eve are symbols, too," I said.

---

1. **Jim Crowed,** segregated.
2. **Job,** a man in the Bible who endured much suffering but did not lose his faith in God.

Reprinted with the permission of Hill and Wang (now a division of Farrar, Straus & Giroux, Inc.) from *The Best of Simple* by Langston Hughes. Copyright © 1961 by Langston Hughes.

"You are simple yourself," said Simple. "But I just wish we colored folks had been somewhere around at the start. I do not know where we was when Eden was a garden, but we sure didn't get in on none of the crops. If we had, we would not be so poor today. White folks started out ahead and they are still ahead. Look at me!"

"I am looking," I said.

"Made in the image of God," said Simple, "but I never did see anybody like me on a Sunday school card."

"Probably nobody looked like you in Biblical days," I said. "The American Negro did not exist in B.C. You're a product of Caucasia[1] and Africa, Harlem[2] and Dixie. You've been conditioned entirely by our environment, our modern times."

"Times have been hard," said Simple, "but still I am a child of God."

"In the cosmic sense, we are all children of God."

"I have been baptized," said Simple, "also anointed with oil. When I were a child I come through at the mourners' bench. I was converted. I have listened to Daddy Grace and et with Father Divine, moaned with Elder Lawson and prayed with Adam Powell.[3] Also I have been to the Episcopalians[4] with Joyce. But if a snake were to come up to me and offer *me* an apple, I would say, 'Varmint, be on your way! No fruit today! Bud, you got the wrong stud now, so get along somehow, be off down the road because you're lower than a toad!' Then that serpent would respect me as a wise man—and this world would not be where it is—all on account of an apple. That apple has turned into an atom now."

"To hear you talk, if you had been in the Garden of Eden, the world would still be a Paradise," I said. "Man would not have fallen into sin."

"Not *this* man," said Simple. "I would have stayed in that garden making grape wine, singing like Crosby,[5] and feeling fine! I would not be scuffling out in this rough world, neither would I be in Harlem. If I was Adam

I would just stay in Eden in that garden with no rent to pay, no landladies to dodge, no time clock to punch—and *my* picture on a Sunday school card. I'd be a *real gone guy* even if I didn't have but one name—Adam—and no initials."

"You would be *real gone* all right. But you were not there. So, my dear fellow, I trust you will not let your rather late arrival on our contemporary stage distort your perspective."

"No," said Simple.

COFFEE BREAK

"My boss is white," said Simple.

"Most bosses are," I said.

"And being white and curious, my boss keeps asking me just what does THE Negro want. Yesterday he tackled me during the coffee break, talking about THE Negro. He always says 'THE Negro,' as if there was not 50-11 different kinds of Negroes in the U.S.A.," complained Simple. "My boss says, 'Now that you-all have got the Civil Rights Bill and the Supreme Court, Adam Powell in Congress, Ralph Bunche[1] in the United Nations, and Leontyne Price[2] singing in the Metropolitan Opera, plus Dr. Martin Luther King[3] getting the Nobel Prize,[4] what more do you want? I am asking you, just what does THE Negro want?'

---

1. **Caucasia** \ˈkɔ'kā•zha\ a region of the U.S.S.R.
2. **Harlem,** area in New York City.
3. **Adam Powell** (1908–1972), black member of Congress, minister, and author.
4. **Episcopalian** \iˈpis•kɔˈpā•lē•ən\ member of the Protestant Episcopal Church.
5. **Crosby, Bing** (1904–1977), singer and actor.

---

1. **Ralph Bunche** (1904–1971), American diplomat and representative to the United Nations.
2. **Leontyne Price,** opera singer, soprano.
3. **Martin Luther King** (1929–1968), minister, civil-rights worker, Nobel Peace Prize winner.
4. **Nobel Prize,** in this case, money prize awarded for the promotion of peace.

Reprinted with the permission of Hill and Wang (now a division of Farrar, Straus & Giroux, Inc.) from *Simple's Uncle Sam* by Langston Hughes. Copyright © 1965 by Langston Hughes.

"'I am not THE Negro,' I says. 'I am *me*.'

"'Well,' says my boss, 'you represent THE Negro.'

"'I do not,' I says. 'I represent my own self.'

"'Ralph Bunche represents you, then,' says my boss, 'and Thurgood Marshall[5] and Martin Luther King. Do they not?'

"'I am proud to be represented by such men, if you say they represent me,' I said. 'But all them men you name are *way* up there, and they do not drink beer in my bar. I have never seen a single one of them mens on Lenox Avenue in my natural life. So far as I know, they do not even live in Harlem. I cannot find them in the telephone book. They all got private numbers. But since you say they represent THE Negro, why do you not ask them what THE Negro wants?'

"'I cannot get to them,' says my boss.

"'Neither can I,' I says, 'so we both is in the same boat.'

"'Well then, to come nearer home,' says my boss, 'Roy Wilkins fights your battles, also James Farmer.'

"'They do not drink in my bar, neither,' I said.

"'Don't Wilkins[6] and Farmer[7] live in Harlem?' he asked.

"'Not to my knowledge,' I said. 'And I bet they have not been to the Apollo since Jackie Mabley[8] cracked the first joke.'

"'I do not know him,' said my boss, 'but I see Nipsey Russell[9] and Bill Cosby[10] on TV.'

"'Jackie Mabley is no *him*,' I said. 'She is a *she*—better known as Moms.'

"'Oh,' said my boss.

"'And Moms Mabley has a story on one of her records about Little Cindy Ella and the magic slippers going to the Junior Prom at Ole Miss which tells all about what THE Negro wants.'

"'What's its conclusion?' asked my boss.

"'When the clock strikes midnight, Little Cindy Ella is dancing with the President of the Ku Klux Klan, says Moms, but at the stroke of twelve, Cindy Ella turns back to her natural self, black, and her blonde wig turns to a stocking cap—and her trial comes up next week.'

"'A symbolic tale,' says my boss, 'meaning, I take it, that THE Negro is in jail. But you are not in jail.'

"'That's what you think,' I said.

"'Anyhow, you claim you are not THE Negro,' said my boss.

"'I am not,' I said. 'I am *this* Negro.'

"'Then what do *you* want?' asked my boss.

"'To get out of jail,' I said.

"'What jail?'

"'The jail you got me in.'

"'Me?' yells my boss. 'I have not got you in jail. Why, boy, I like you. I am a liberal. I voted for Kennedy.[11] And this time for Johnson.[12] I believe in integration. Now that you got it, though, what more do you want?'

"'Reintegration,' I said.

"'Meaning by that, what?'

"'That you be integrated with *me*, not me with you.'

"'Do you mean that I come and live in Harlem?' asked my boss. 'Never!'

"'I live in Harlem,' I said.

"'You are adjusted to it,' said my boss. 'But there is so much crime in Harlem.'

"'There are no two-hundred-thousand-dollar bank robberies, though,' I said, 'of which there was three lately *elsewhere*—all done by white folks, and nary one in Harlem. The biggest and best crime is outside of Harlem. We never has no half-million-dollar jewelry robberies, no missing star sapphires. You better come uptown with me and reintegrate.'

---

5. **Thurgood Marshall**, American jurist; first black appointed to the U.S. Supreme Court (1967).
6. **Roy Wilkins**, American social reformer; executive secretary of the NAACP.
7. **James Farmer**, American civil-rights leader, national director of CORE (1961–1965).
8. **Jackie "Moms" Mabley** (1898–1975), black actress and comedian.
9. **Nipsey Russell**, black comedian.
10. **Bill Cosby**, black actor and comedian.
11. **Kennedy**, John F. (1917–1963), 35th President of the United States.
12. **Johnson**, Lyndon (1908–1973), 36th President of the United States.

"'Negroes are the ones who want to be integrated,' said my boss.

"'And white folks are the ones who do *not* want to be,' I said.

"'Up to a point, we do,' said my boss.

"'That is what THE Negro wants,' I said, 'to remove that *point*.'

"'The coffee break is over,' said my boss."

JAZZ, JIVE, AND JAM

"It being Negro History Week," said Simple, "Joyce took me to a pay lecture to hear some Negro hysterian——"

"Historian," I corrected.

"—hysterian speak," continued Simple, "and he laid our Negro race low. He said we was misbred, misread, and misled, also losing our time good-timing. Instead of time-taking and money-making, we are jazz-shaking. Oh, he enjoyed his self at the expense of the colored race—and him black as me. He really delivered a lecture—in which, no doubt, there is some truth."

"Constructive criticism, I gather—a sort of tearing down in order to build up."

"He tore us down good," said Simple. "Joyce come out saying to me, her husband, that he had really got my number. I said, 'Baby, he did not miss you, neither.' But Joyce did not consider herself included in the bad things he said.

"She come telling me on the way home by subway, 'Jess Semple, I have been pursuing culture since my childhood. But you, when I first met you, all you did was drape yourself over some beer bar and argue with the barflies.[1] The higher things of life do not come out of a licker trough.'

"I replied, 'But, Joyce, how come culture has got to be so dry?'

"She answers me back, 'How come your gullet[2] has got to be so wet? You are sitting in this subway right now looking like you would like to have a beer.'

"'Solid!' I said. 'I would. How did you guess it?'"

"'Married to you for three years, I can read your mind,' said Joyce. 'We'll buy a couple of cans to take home. I might even drink one myself.'

"'Joyce, baby,' I said, 'in that case, let's buy three cans.'

"Joyce says, 'Remember the budget, Jess.'

"I says, 'Honey, you done busted the budget going to that lecture program which cost One Dollar a head, also we put some small change in the collection to help Negroes get ahead.'

"'Small change?' says Joyce, 'I put a dollar.'

"'Then our budget is busted real good,' I said, 'so we might as well dent it some more. Let's get six cans of beer.'

"'All right,' says Joyce, 'go ahead, drink yourself to the dogs—instead of saving for that house we want to buy!'

"'Six cans of beer would not pay for even the bottom front step,' I said. 'But they would lift my spirits this evening. That Negro high-speaking doctor done tore my spirits down. I did not know before that the colored race was so misled, misread, and misbred. According to him there is hardly a pure black man left. But I was setting in the back, so I guess he did not see me.'

"'Had you not had to go to sleep in the big chair after dinner,' says Joyce, 'we would have been there on time and had seats up front.'

"'I were near enough to that joker,' I said. 'Loud as he could holler, we did not need to set no closer. And he certainly were nothing to look at!'

"'Very few educated men look like Harry Belafonte,'[3] said Joyce.

"'I am glad I am handsome instead of wise,' I said. But Joyce did not crack a smile. She had that lecture on her mind.

"'Dr. Conboy is smart,' says Joyce. 'Did you hear him quoting Aristotle?'

---

1. **barflies,** people who spend much time in barrooms.
2. **gullet**\ˈgül·ĭt\ throat.
3. **Harry Belafonte,** black singer and actor.

Reprinted with the permission of Hill and Wang (now a division of Farrar, Straus & Giroux, Inc.) from *The Best of Simple* by Langston Hughes. Copyright © 1961 by Langston Hughes.

" 'Who were Harry Stottle?' I asked.

" 'Some people are not even misread,' said Joyce. 'Aristotle was a Greek philosopher like Socrates, a great man of ancient times.'

" 'He must of been before Booker T. Washington[4] then,' I said, 'because, to tell the truth, I has not heard of him at all. But tonight being *Negro* History Week, how come Dr. Conboy has to quote some Greek?'

" 'There were black Greeks,' said Joyce. 'Did you not hear him say that Negroes have played a part in all history, throughout all time, from Eden to now?'

" 'Do you reckon Eve was brownskin?' I requested.

" 'I do not know about Eve,' said Joyce, 'but Cleopatra[5] was of the colored race, and the Bible says Sheba,[6] beloved of Solomon,[7] was black but comely.'

" 'I wonder would she come to me?' I says.

" 'Solomon also found Cleopatra comely. He was a king,' says Joyce.

" 'And I am Jesse B. Semple,' I said.

"But by that time the subway had got to our stop. At the store Joyce broke the budget again, opened up her pocket purse, and bought us six cans of beer. So it were a good evening. It ended well—except that I ain't for going to any more meetings—especially interracial meetings."

"Come now! Don't you want to improve race relations?"

"Sure," said Simple, "but in my opinion, jazz, jive, and jam[8] would be better for race relations than all this high-flown gab, gaff, and gas[9] the orators put out. All this talking that white folks do at meetings, and big Negroes, too, about how to get along together—just a little jam session would have everybody getting along fine without having to listen to so many speeches. Why, last month Joyce took me to a Race Relations Seminar which her club and twenty other clubs gave, and man, it lasted three days! It started on a Friday night and it were not over until Sunday afternoon. They had sessions' mammy! Joyce is a fiend for culture."

"And you sat through all that?"

"I did not set," said Simple. "I stood. I walked in and walked out. I smoked on the corner and snuck two drinks at the bar. But I had to wait for Joyce, and I thought them speeches would never get over! My wife were a delegate from her club, so she had to stay, although I think Joyce got tired her own self. But she would not admit it. Joyce said, 'Dr. Hillary Thingabod was certainly brilliant, were he not?'

"I said, 'He were not.'

"Joyce said, 'What did you want the man to say?'

"I said, 'I wish he had sung, instead of *said*. That program needed some music to keep folks awake.'

"Joyce said, 'Our forum was not intended for a musical. It was intended to see how we can work out integration.'

"I said, 'With a jazz band, they could work out integration in ten minutes. Everybody would have been dancing together like they all did at the Savoy[10]—colored and white—or down on the East Side[11] at them Casinos on a Friday night where jam holds forth—and we would have been integrated.'

"Joyce said, 'This was a serious seminar, aiming at facts, not fun.'

" 'Baby,' I said, 'what is more facts than acts? Jazz makes people get into action, move! Didn't nobody move in that hall where you were—except to jerk their head up when they went to sleep, to keep anybody from seeing

---

4. **Booker T. Washington** (1856–1885), American black educator and author.
5. **Cleopatra** \\'klē·ə ▲păt·rə\\ (69–30 B.C.), Queen of Eygpt.
6. **Sheba** \\ ▲shē·bə\\ in the Bible, the Queen who visited King Solomon to investigate his reputed wisdom and greatness.
7. **Solomon** \\ ▲sŏl·ə·mən\\ King of Israel in the nineteenth century B.C.
8. **jazz, jive, and jam**, spirited music; jazz jargon; and improvisation.
9. **gab, gaff, and gas**, chatter and idle talk.
10. **Savoy** \\sə ▲voi\\ a nightclub in Harlem.
11. **East Side**, of New York City.

that they was nodding. Why, that chairman, Mrs. Maxwell-Reeves, almost lost her glasses off her nose, she jerked her head up so quick one time when that man you say was so brilliant were speaking!'

" 'Jess Semple, that is not so!' yelled Joyce. 'Mrs. Maxwell-Reeves were just lost in thought. And if you think you saw *me* sleeping——'

" 'You was too busy trying to look around and see where I was,' I said. 'Thank God, I did not have to set up there like you with the delegation. I would not be a delegate to no such gabfest[12] for nothing on earth.'

" 'I thought you was so interested in saving the race!' said Joyce. 'Next time I will not ask you to accompany me to no cultural events, Jesse B., because I can see you do not appreciate them. That were a discussion of ways and means. And you are talking about jazz bands!'

" 'There's more ways than one to skin a cat,' I said. 'A jazz band like Duke's or Hamp's or Basie's[13] sure would of helped that meeting. At least on Saturday afternoon, they could have used a little music to put some pep into the proceedings. Now, just say for instant, baby, they was to open with jazz and close with jam—and do the talking in between. Start out, for example, with "The St. Louis Blues," which is a kind of colored national anthem. That would put every human in a good humor. Then play "Why Don't You Do Right?" which could be addressed to white folks. They could pat their feet to that. Then for a third number before introducing the speaker, let some guest star like Pearl Bailey[14] sing "There'll Be Some Changes Made"—which, as I understand it, were the theme of the meeting, anyhow—and all the Negroes could say *Amen!*

" 'Joyce, I wish you would let me plan them interracial seminaries next time. After the music, let the speechmaking roll for a while—with maybe a calypso[15] between speeches. Then, along about five o'clock, bring on the jam session, extra-special. Start serving tea to "Tea For Two," played real cool. Whilst drink-ing tea and dancing, the race relationers could relate, the integrators could integrate, and the desegregators desegregate. Joyce, you would not have to beg for a crowd to come out and support your efforts then. Jam—and the hall would be jammed! Even I would stick around, and not be outside sneaking a smoke, or trying to figure how I can get to the bar before the resolutions are voted on. *Resolved:* that we solve the race problem! Strike up the band! Hit it, men! Aw, play that thing! "How High the Moon!" How high! Wheee-ee-e!' "

"What did Joyce say to that?" I demanded.

"Joyce just thought I was high," said Simple.

I

SIMPLE'S ANCESTRY

Jesse B. Semple is not well educated. He does not use "big" words, and he often misunderstands them when they are used by others. He uses the language and practices the life-style of the average person or ordinary citizen.

In spite of this, Simple takes on all comers in argument; and he usually beats them—as he out-argues, in the selections you have just read, his friend at the bar, his boss, his wife, and Dr. Conboy, all of whom are better educated than he.

Jesse might be called a barroom philosopher. As such, his ancestry goes all the way back to the beginnings of American history, to the famed cracker-barrel philosopher of New England. The pre-Revolutionary New England general store may seem widely separated from the Harlem bar of today, but there is no mistaking the resemblance of Simple to his "ancestor." The cracker-barrel philosopher, like Simple, usually had little formal schooling but a great deal of common sense, the kind of natural intelligence that is also found in American heroes like Franklin and Lincoln. These, too, in their way, may be thought of as forerunners of Jesse B. Semple.

---

12. **gabfest**\\ ˄găb ˈfest\\ an occasion of much idle talk.
13. **Duke's, Hamp's and Basie's,** Duke Ellington, Lionel Hampton, and Count Basie, all famous black musicians.
14. **Pearl Bailey,** black singer and actress.
15. **calypso**\\kə ˄lĭp·sō\\ lively ballad of Trinidad.

IMPLICATIONS

A good subject to write about or discuss in connection with these stories is "How Simple Is Simple?" In discussing it, you will want to look very closely at the selections in an effort to see the *whole* picture.

For example, Simple's belief that Adam and Eve were white because he saw their pictures on a Sunday school card is simple—simpleminded. On the other hand, Simple's belief is also based on the evidence that "white folks started out ahead," which is certainly true enough, at least in the United States, and Simple knows that this sort of advantage is very powerful. It is this kind of advantage, in fact, that caused Adam and Eve to be represented as white in American Sunday schools. Thus there is a kind of truth in Simple's simple belief.

Be prepared to discuss other examples of simpleminded thinking that turn out to be not so simple after all.

III
TECHNIQUES

Comedy

Like many humorists, Hughes often uses the device of misunderstanding of words to produce amusing effects. Consider the following example from "Jazz, Jive, and Jam":

" '. . . the Bible says Sheba . . . was black but comely.' "

" 'I wonder would she come to me?' I says."

Simple relates the adjective "comely" ("attractive") to the verb "come" and provides us with a laugh. Now, keeping Simple's definition in mind, look at the next line:

" 'Solomon also found Cleopatra comely. . . .' says Joyce."

Though Joyce does not intend to use the word "comely" in Simple's sense, we may read it that way and have a laugh at her expense.

Look for other examples of this comic device in the selections you have just read.

Sympathy and Detachment

It is sometimes said that readers do not sympathize strongly with characters in comedies because the characters are types rather than individuals. In other words, comic characters tend to be "flat" rather than "round." A test for flat characters is that they may be summed up in a very brief statement; a round character is much more complex. Can you sum up Simple in a sentence or less? What about some of the other characters used by Hughes? Would you agree or disagree with the notion that flat characters tend to discourage readers from feeling deep sympathy?

IV
WORDS

A. Black idiom is uniquely rhythmical—often poetic. And Jesse B. Semple handles the idiom well. Consider the following statements by Semple; determine what, if any, poetic qualities they possess.

"But if a snake were to come up to me and offer *me* an apple, I would say, 'Varmint, be on your way! No fruit today! Bud, you got the wrong stud now, so get along somehow, be off down the road because you're lower than a toad!' "

"I would have stayed in that garden making grape wine, singing like Crosby, and feeling fine!"

"Then along about five o'clock, bring on the jam session, extra-special. Start serving tea to 'Tea For Two,' played real cool. Whilst drinking tea and dancing, the race relationers could relate, the integrators could integrate, and the desegregators desegregate."

"—hysterian speak," continued Simple, "and he laid our Negro race low. He said we was misbred, misread, and misled, also losing our time good-timing. Instead of time-taking and money-making, we are jazz-shaking. Oh, he enjoyed his self at the expense of the colored race—and him black as me."

B. Determine from context the meaning of the italicized words and phrases. Consult a dictionary when necessary.

1. "There's more ways than one to *skin a cat*," I said.

2. "I would not be a delegate to no such *gabfest* for nothing on earth."

3. "Everybody would have been dancing together like they all did at the Savoy—colored and white—or down on the East Side at them Casinos on a Friday night where *jam holds forth*."

4. "I have been underfed, underpaid, undernourished, and everything but *undertaken*—yet I am still here."

The Cutting Edge

All the poems in the next several pages criticize
failings of individuals or groups. Some of them might be classified as "light verse"
because of their rather playful manner of expression. Others adopt a more serious tone.
Whether they are "light" or "heavy," you will find that
all of them have a cutting edge.

The Politician

Behold the politician.
Self-preservation is his ambition.
He thrives in the D. of C.,[1]
Where he was sent by you and me.

Whether elected or appointed   5
He considers himself the Lord's anointed,
And indeed the ointment lingers on him
So thick you can't get your fingers on him.

He has developed a sixth sense
About living at the public expense,   10
Because in private competition
He would encounter malnutrition.

He has many profitable hobbies
Not the least of which is lobbies.
He would not sell his grandmother for a quarter   15
If he suspected the presence of a reporter.

He gains votes ever and anew
By taking money from everybody and giving it to a few,
While explaining that every penny
Was extracted from the few to be given to the many.   20

---

1. **D. of C.**, District of Columbia.

Copyright 1938 by Ogden Nash. From *I'm a Stranger Here Myself* by Ogden Nash, by
permission of Little, Brown and Company.

Some politicians are Republican, some Democratic,
And their feud is dramatic,
But except for the name
They are identically the same.

When a politician talks the foolishest,   25
And obstructs everything the mulishest,
And bellows the loudest,
Why his constituents are the proudest.

Wherever decent intelligent people get together
They talk about politicians as about bad weather,   30
But they are always too decent to go into politics themselves
    and too intelligent even to go to the polls,
So I hope the kind of politicians they get will have no
    mercy on their pocketbooks or souls.

OGDEN NASH

In laying bare the foolishness and foibles
of the twentieth century in America, Dorothy Parker had few rivals—
in verse or in prose. She was a master of the pithy epigram,
as the following sardonic poem attests.

Résumé

Razors pain you;
Rivers are damp;
Acids stain you;
And drugs cause cramp.
Guns aren't lawful;
Nooses give;
Gas smells awful;
You might as well live.

DOROTHY PARKER

From *The Portable Dorothy Parker.* Copyright 1926, renewed
1954 by Dorothy Parker. All rights reserved. Reprinted by
permission of The Viking Press, Inc.

e. e. cummings is one of the best-known
and most original American poets of the twentieth century.
The unorthodox typography of "old age sticks" is characteristic of his style.
See if it offers you any clues as to the best way
to read the following ironic comment
on the conservatism of old age
versus the radicalism of youth.

old age sticks

old age sticks
up Keep
Off
signs)&

youth yanks them   5
down(old
age
cries No

Tres)&(pas)
youth laughs   10
(sing
old age

scolds Forbid
den Stop
Must   15
n't Don't

&) youth goes
right on
gr
owing old   20

E. E. CUMMINGS

From *95 Poems,* copyright
1953, by E. E. Cummings.
Reprinted by permission of
Harcourt Brace Jovanovich,
Inc.

◈ Every year our superhighways multiply. Ask yourself whether
the following poem offers any hints as to how such highways may have affected
the quality of our living. The Merritt Parkway of Connecticut
is one of the older superhighways in this country.

*Merritt
Parkway*

As if it were
forever that they move, that we
keep moving—

Under a wan sky where
as the lights went on a star   5
pierced the haze & now
follows steadily
a constant
above our six lanes
the dreamlike continuum . . .   10

And the people—ourselves!
the humans from inside the
cars, apparent
only at gasoline stops
unsure,   15
eyeing each other

drink coffee hastily at the
slot machines & hurry
back to the cars
vanish   20
into them forever, to
keep moving—

Houses now & then beyond the
sealed road, the trees / trees, bushes
passing by, passing   25
the cars that
keep moving ahead of
us, past us, pressing behind us
and
over left, those that come   30
toward us shining too brightly
moving relentlessly

in six lanes, gliding
north & south, speeding with
a slurred sound—   35

DENISE LEVERTOV

From *The Jacob's Ladder.* Copyright © 1958 by
Denise Levertov Goodman. Reprinted by permission of New Directions Publishing Corporation.

At its mouth, the Hudson River flows
between a heavily industrialized section of New Jersey
and the island of Manhattan. In other words,
it is a center of environmental pollution. Notice how Robert Lowell,
the acknowledged dean of modern American poets, appeals to all our senses
with his description of this environmental horror.

The Mouth of the Hudson

A single man stands like a bird-watcher,
and scuffles the pepper and salt snow
from a discarded, gray
Westinghouse Electric cable drum.
He cannot discover America by counting   5
the chains of condemned freight-trains
from thirty states. They jolt and jar
and junk in the siding below him.
He has trouble with his balance.
His eyes drop,   10
and he drifts with the wild ice
ticking seaward down the Hudson,
like the blank sides of a jig-saw puzzle.

The ice ticks seaward like a clock.
A negro toasts   15
wheat-seeds over the coke-fumes[1]
in a punctured barrel.
Chemical air
sweeps in from New Jersey,
and smells of coffee.   20

Across the river,
ledges of suburban factories tan
in the sulphur-yellow sun
of the unforgivable landscape.

ROBERT LOWELL

---

1. **coke-fumes,** gases of a fuel that is made by the distillation of coal.

Reprinted with the permission of Farrar, Straus & Giroux, Inc., from *For the Union Dead* by Robert Lowell, copyright © 1964 by Robert Lowell.

I

EXPLORING YOUR PREFERENCES

The poems in this section have in common the intent to criticize a human failing. Apart from that, however, there may be more differences than similarities among some of them. For example, there is quite a large difference between a rather playful poem like Nash's "The Politician" and a highly serious one, such as "The Mouth of the Hudson." Try to rank these poems and those from "Light Verse" from the least to the most serious.

Which of the poems did you like the best? Are your preferences toward the lighter or the more serious poems? Assuming that your preferences run in one direction or the other, does this reveal something about your personality? How much of your liking of the poems is accounted for by your personality, and how much has to do with the poems themselves?

The questions above open up a very interesting issue that you might care to discuss or write about: How can you judge a poem (or a movie or a television show, for that matter) with some assurance that you are talking about *it* rather than about yourself?

II

IMPLICATIONS

Explain as specifically as you can what the poet is suggesting about life and the world in the following quotations.

1. . . . they [decent and intelligent people] are always too decent to go into politics themselves / and too intelligent even to go to the polls. . . .

2. You might as well live.

3. &) youth goes / right on / gr / owing old

4. And the people—ourselves! / the humans from inside the / cars, apparent / only at gasoline stops / unsure, / eyeing each other . . .

5. Across the river, / ledges of suburban factories tan / in the sulphur-yellow sun / of the unforgivable landscape.

III

TECHNIQUES

The Cutting Edge

All of the poems in this section have a critical intent. Nash is critical of politicians and of apathetic voters, Parker of would-be suicides, cummings of older people, Levertov and Lowell of a debasement in the quality of life brought on by the technology of our society. All of these poets, by implication at least, would like to see changes in persons or institutions in America today.

Given, however, the natural defensiveness of human beings in the face of criticism, how is such change likely to come about as a result of the poet's work? For example, isn't the politician likely to say, "Nash is referring to others, not to me"?

Would you say, therefore, that is it pointless for authors to make such criticisms? Or is there some way that poets manage to break down the defenses of their "targets"? In answering this question be sure to consider carefully the *full* meaning of each of the poems.

Although this selection is a fantasy, it also levels some serious criticism.
As you read it, see if you can determine what those criticisms are.
In particular, see if you can tell why Beaumont chose the title that he did.

The Vanishing American

CHARLES BEAUMONT

He got the notion shortly after five o'clock; at least, a part of him did, a small part hidden down beneath all the conscious cells—*he* didn't get the notion until some time later. At exactly 5 P.M. the bell rang. At two minutes after, the chairs began to empty. There was the vast slamming of drawers, the straightening of rulers, the sound of bones snapping and mouths yawning and feet shuffling tiredly.

Mr. Minchell relaxed. He rubbed his hands together and relaxed and thought how nice it would be to get up and go home, like the others. But of course there was the tape, only three-quarters finished. He would have to stay.

He stretched and said good night to the people who filed past him. As usual, no one answered. When they had gone, he set his fingers pecking again over the keyboard. The click-clicking grew loud in the suddenly still office, but Mr. Minchell did not notice. He was lost in the work. Soon, he knew, it would be time for the totaling, and his pulse quickened at the thought of this.

He lit a cigarette. Heart tapping, he drew in smoke and released it.

He extended his right hand and rested his index and middle fingers on the metal bar marked TOTAL. A mile-long ribbon of paper lay gathered on the desk, strangely festive. He glanced at it, then at the manifest sheet. The

Reprinted by permission of G. P. Putnam's Sons, Inc. from *The Hunger and Other Stories* by Charles Beaumont. Copyright 1957 by Charles Beaumont.

figure 18037448 was circled in red. He pulled breath into his lungs, locked it there; then he closed his eyes and pressed the TOTAL bar.

There was a smooth low metallic grinding, followed by absolute silence.

Mr. Minchell opened one eye, dragged it from the ceiling on down to the adding machine.

He groaned, slightly.

The total read: 18037447.

He stared at the figure and thought of the fifty-three pages of manifest, the three thousand separate rows of figures that would have to be checked again.

The day was lost, now. Irretrievably. It was too late to do anything. Madge would have supper waiting, and F.J. didn't approve of overtime; also——

He looked at the total again. At the last two digits.

He sighed. Forty-seven. And thought, startled: Today is my birthday! Today I am forty—what? forty-seven. And that explains the mistake, I suppose. Subconscious kind of thing . . .

Slowly he got up and looked around the deserted office.

Then he went to the dressing room and got his hat and his coat and put them on, carefully.

"Pushing fifty now . . ."

The outside hall was dark. Mr. Minchell walked softly to the elevator and punched the *down* button. "Forty-seven," he said, aloud;

then, almost immediately, the light turned red and the thick door slid back noisily. The elevator operator, a bird-thin, tan-fleshed girl, swiveled her head, looking up and down the hall. "Going down," she said.

"Yes," Mr. Minchell said, stepping forward.

"Going down." The girl clicked her tongue and muttered, "Lousy kids." She gave the lattice gate a tired push and moved the smooth wooden-handled lever in its slot.

Odd, Mr. Minchell decided, was the word for this particular girl. He wished now that he had taken the stairs. Being alone with only one other person in an elevator had always made him nervous: now it made him very nervous. He felt the tension growing. When it became unbearable, he cleared his throat and said, "Long day."

The girl said nothing. She had a surly look, and she seemed to be humming something deep in her throat.

Mr. Minchell closed his eyes. In less than a minute—during which time he dreamed of the cable snarling, of the car being caught between floors, of himself trying to make small talk with the odd girl for six straight hours—he opened his eyes again and walked into the lobby, briskly.

The gate slammed.

He turned and started for the doorway. Then he paused, feeling a sharp increase in his heartbeat. A large, red-faced, magnificently groomed man of middle years stood directly beyond the glass, talking with another man.

Mr. Minchell pushed through the door, with effort. He's seen me now, he thought. If he asks any questions, though, or anything, I'll just say I didn't put it on the time card; that ought to make it all right. . . .

He nodded and smiled at the large man. "Good night, Mr. Diemel."

The man looked up briefly, blinked, and returned to his conversation.

Mr. Minchell felt a burning come into his face. He hurried on down the street. Now the notion—though it was not even that yet, strictly: it was more a vague feeling—swam up

"You're all fired!"

from the bottom of his brain. He remembered that he had not spoken directly to F.J. Diemel for over ten years, beyond a good morning. . . .

Ice-cold shadows fell off the tall buildings, staining the streets, now. Crowds of shoppers moved along the pavement like juggernauts, exhaustedly, but with great determination. Mr. Minchell looked at them. They all had furtive appearances, it seemed to him, suddenly, even the children, as if each was fleeing from some hideous crime. They hurried along, staring.

But not, Mr. Minchell noticed, at him. Through him, yes. Past him. As the elevator operator had done, and now F.J. And had anyone said good night?

He pulled up his coat collar and walked toward the drugstore, thinking. He was forty-seven years old. At the current life-expectancy rate, he might have another seventeen or eighteen years left. And then death.

If you're not dead already.

He paused and for some reason remembered a story he'd once read in a magazine. Something about a man who dies and whose ghost takes up his duties, or something; anyway, the man didn't know he was dead—that was it. And at the end of the story, he runs into his own corpse.

Which is pretty absurd: he glanced down at his body. Ghosts don't wear $136 suits, nor do they have trouble pushing doors open, nor do their corns ache like blazes, and what the devil is wrong with me today?

He shook his head.

It was the tape, of course, and the fact that it was his birthday. That was why his mind was behaving so foolishly.

He went into the drugstore. It was an immense place, packed with people. He walked to the cigar counter, trying not to feel intimidated, and reached into his pocket. A small man elbowed in front of him and called loudly: "Gimme coupla nickels, will you, Jack?" The clerk scowled and scooped the change out of his cash register. The small man scurried off. Others took his place. Mr. Minchell thrust his arm forward. "A pack of Luckies, please," he said. The clerk whipped his fingers around a pile of cellophaned packages and, looking elsewhere, droned: "Fifty-three." Mr. Minchell put his fifty-three cents exactly on the glass shelf. The clerk shoved the cigarettes toward the edge and picked up the money, deftly. Not once did he lift his eyes.

Mr. Minchell pocketed the Luckies and went back out of the store. He was perspiring now, slightly, despite the chill wind. The word "ridiculous" lodged in his mind and stayed there. Ridiculous, yes, for heaven's sake. Still, he thought—now just answer the question—isn't it true? Can you honestly say that that clerk saw you?

Or that anyone saw you today?

Swallowing dryly, he walked another two blocks, always in the direction of the subway, and went into a bar called the Chez When. One

drink would not hurt, one small, stiff, steadying shot.

The bar was a gloomy place, and not very warm, but there was a good crowd. Mr. Minchell sat down on a stool and folded his hands. The bartender was talking animatedly with an old woman, laughing with boisterous good humor from time to time. Mr. Minchell waited. Minutes passed. The bartender looked up several times, but never made a move to indicate that he had seen a customer.

Mr. Minchell looked at his old gray overcoat, the humbly floraled tie, the cheap sharkskin suit-cloth, and became aware of the extent to which he detested this ensemble. He sat there and detested his clothes for a long time. Then he glanced around. The bartender was wiping a glass, slowly.

All right. I'll take my business somewhere else.

He slid off the stool. Just as he was about to turn he saw the mirrored wall, pink-tinted and curved. He stopped, peering. Then he almost ran out of the bar.

Cold wind went into his head.

Ridiculous. The mirror was curved. How do you expect to see yourself in curved mirrors?

He walked past high buildings, and now past the library and the stone lion he had once, long ago, named King Richard; and he did not look at the lion, because he'd always wanted to ride the lion, ever since he was a child, and he'd promised himself he would do that, but he never did.

He hurried on to the subway, took the stairs by twos, and clattered across the platform in time to board the express.

It roared and thundered. Mr. Minchell held onto the strap and kept himself from staring. No one watched him. No one even glanced at him when he pushed his way to the door and went out onto the empty platform.

He waited. Then the train was gone, and he was alone.

He walked up the stairs. It was fully night now, a soft, unshadowed darkness. He thought about the day and the strange things that were gouging into his mind and thought about all this as he turned down a familiar street which led to his familiar apartment.

The door opened.

His wife was in the kitchen, he could see. Her apron flashed across the arch, and back, and across. He called: "Madge, I'm home."

Madge did not answer. Her movements were regular. Jimmy was sitting at the table, drooling over a glass of pop, whispering to himself.

"I said——" Mr. Minchell began.

"Jimmy, get up and go to the bathroom, you hear? I've got your water drawn."

Jimmy promptly broke into tears. He jumped off the chair and ran past Mr. Minchell into the bedroom. The door slammed viciously.

"Madge."

Madge Minchell came into the room, tired and lined and heavy. Her eyes did not waver. She went into the bedroom, and there was a silence; then a sharp slapping noise, and a yelling.

Mr. Minchell walked to the bathroom, fighting down the small terror. He closed the door and locked it and wiped his forehead with a handkerchief. Ridiculous, he thought, and ridiculous and ridiculous. I am making something utterly foolish out of nothing. All I have to do is look in the mirror, and——

He held the handkerchief to his lips. It was difficult to breathe.

Then he knew that he was afraid, more so than ever before in a lifetime of being afraid.

Look at it this way, Minchell: why shouldn't *you vanish?*

"Young man, just you wait until your father gets here!"

He pushed the handkerchief against his mouth and leaned on the door and gasped.

"What do you mean, vanish?"

Go on, take a look. You'll see what I mean.

He tried to swallow, couldn't. Tried to wet his lips, they stayed dry.

"Good grief——"

He slitted his eyes and walked to the shaving mirror and looked in.

His mouth fell open.

The mirror reflected nothing. It held nothing. It was dull and gray and empty.

Mr. Minchell stared at the glass, put out his hand, drew it back hastily.

He squinted. Inches away. There was a form now: vague, indistinct, featureless: but a form.

Now he understood why the elevator girl hadn't seen him, and why F.J. hadn't answered him, and why the clerk at the drugstore and the bartender and Madge . . .

"I'm not dead."

Of course you're not dead—not that way.

"—tan your hide, Jimmy Minchell, when he gets home."

Mr. Minchell suddenly wheeled and clicked the lock. He rushed out of the steam-filled bathroom, across the room, down the stairs, into the street, into the cool night.

A block from home he slowed to a walk.

Invisible! He said the word over and over, in a half-voice. He said it and tried to control the panic that pulled at his legs, and at his brain, and filled him.

Why?

A fat woman and a little girl passed by. Neither of them looked up. He started to call out and checked himself. No. That wouldn't do any good. There was no question about it now. He was invisible.

He walked on. As he did, forgotten things returned; they came and they left, too fast. He couldn't hold onto them. He could only watch, and remember. Himself as a youngster, reading: the Oz books, and Tarzan, and Mr. Wells. Himself, going to the University, wanting to teach, and meeting Madge; then not planning any more, and Madge changing, and all the dreams put away. For later. For the right time. And then Jimmy—little strange Jimmy, who ate filth and picked his nose and watched television, who never read books, never; Jimmy, his son, whom he would never understand . . .

He walked by the edge of the park now. Then on past the park, through a maze of familiar and unfamiliar neighborhoods. Walking, remembering, looking at the people and feeling pain because he knew that they could not see him, not now or ever again, because he had vanished. He walked and remembered and felt pain.

All the stagnant dreams came back. Fully. The trip to Italy he'd planned. The open sports car. The first-hand knowledge that would tell him whether he did or did not approve of bullfighting. The book . . .

Then something occurred to him. It occurred to Mr. Minchell that he had not just suddenly vanished, like that, after all. No; he had been vanishing gradually for a long while. Every time he said good morning to that Diemel he got a little harder to see. Every time he put on this horrible suit he faded. The process of disappearing was set into action every time he brought his pay check home and turned it over to Madge, every time he kissed her, or listened to her vicious unending complaints, or decided against buying that novel, or punched the adding machine he hated so, or . . .

Certainly.

He had vanished for Diemel and the others in the office years ago. And for strangers right afterwards. Now even Madge and Jimmy couldn't see him. And he could barely see himself, even in a mirror.

It made terrible sense to him. *Why* shouldn't *you disappear?* Well, why, indeed? There wasn't any very good reason, actually. None. And this, in a nightmarish sort of a way, made it as brutally logical as a perfect tape.

Then he thought about going back to work tomorrow and the next day and the day after that. He'd have to, of course. He couldn't let Madge and Jimmy starve; and, besides, what else would he do? It wasn't as if anything important had changed. He'd go on punching the clock and saying good morning to people who didn't see him, and he'd run the tapes and come home beat, nothing altered, and someday he'd die and that would be that.

All at once he felt tired.

He sat down on a cement step and sighed. Distantly he realized that he had come to the library. He sat there, watching the people, feeling the tiredness seep through him, thickly.

Then he looked up.

Above him, black and regal against the sky, stood the huge stone lion. Its mouth was open, and the great head was raised proudly.

Mr. Minchell smiled. King Richard. Memories scattered in his mind: old King Richard, well, here we are.

He got to his feet. Fifty thousand times, at least, he had passed this spot, and every time he had experienced that instant of wild craving. Less so of late, but still, had it ever completely gone? He was amazed to find that now the childish desire was welling up again, stronger than ever before. Urgently.

He rubbed his cheek and stood there for several minutes. It's the most ridiculous thing in the world, he thought, and I must be going out of my mind, and that must explain everything. But, he inquired of himself, even so, why not?

After all, I'm invisible. No one can see me. Of course, it didn't have to be this way, not really. I don't know, he went on, I mean, I believed that I was doing the right thing. Would it have been right to go back to the University and forget Madge? I couldn't change that, could I? Could I have done anything about that, even if I'd known?

He nodded sadly.

All right, but don't make it any worse. Don't *dwell* on it!

To his surprise, Mr. Minchell found that he was climbing up the concrete base of the statue. It ripped the breath from his lungs—and he saw that he could much more easily have gone up a few extra steps and simply stepped on— but there didn't seem anything else to do but just this, what he was doing. Once upright, he passed his hand over the statue's flank. The surface was incredibly sleek and cold, hard as a lion's muscles ought to be, and tawny.

He took a step backwards. Had there ever been such power? Such marvelous downright power and . . . majesty, as was here? From stone—no, indeed. It fooled a good many people, but it did not fool Mr. Minchell. He knew. This lion was no mere library decoration. It was an animal, of deadly cunning and fantastic strength and unbelievable ferocity. And it didn't move for the simple reason that it did not care to move. It was waiting. Someday it would see what it was waiting for, its enemy, coming down the street. Then look out, people!

He remembered the whole yarn now. Of everyone on Earth, only he, Henry Minchell, knew the secret of the lion. And only he was allowed to sit astride this mighty back.

He stepped onto the tail, experimentally. He hesitated, gulped, and swung forward, swiftly, on up to the curved rump.

Trembling, he slid forward, until finally he was over the shoulders of the lion, just behind the raised head.

His breath came very fast.

He closed his eyes.

It was not long before he was breathing regularly again. Only now it was the hot, fetid air of the jungle that went into his nostrils. He felt the great muscles ripple beneath him and he listened to the fast crackle of crushed foliage, and he whispered:

"Easy, fellow."

The flying spears did not frighten him. He sat straight, smiling, with his fingers buried in the rich, tawny mane of King Richard, while the wind tore at his hair. . . .

Then, abruptly, he opened his eyes.

The city stretched before him, and the people, and the lights. He tried quite hard not to cry, because he knew that forty-seven-year-old men never cried, not even when they had vanished, but he couldn't help it. So he sat on the stone lion and lowered his head and cried.

He didn't hear the laughter at first.

When he did hear it, he thought that he was dreaming. But it was true: somebody was laughing.

He grasped one of the statue's ears for balance and leaned forward. He blinked. Below, some fifteen feet, there were people. Young people. Some of them with books. They were looking up and smiling and laughing.

Mr. Minchell wiped his eyes.

A slight horror came over him, and fell away. He leaned farther out.

One of the boys waved and shouted: "Ride him, Pop!"

Mr. Minchell almost toppled. Then, without understanding, without even trying to understand—merely knowing—he grinned, widely, showing his teeth, which were his own and very white.

"You . . . see me?" he called.

The young people roared.

"You do!" Mr. Minchell's face seemed to melt upwards. He let out a yell and gave King Richard's shaggy stone mane an enormous hug.

Below, other people stopped in their walking and a small crowd began to form. Dozens of eyes peered sharply, quizzically.

A woman in gray furs giggled.

A thin man in a blue suit grunted something about these crazy exhibitionists.

"You pipe down," another man said. "Guy wants to ride the lion it's his own business."

There were murmurings. The man who had said pipe down was small and he wore black-rimmed glasses. "I used to do it all the time." He turned to Mr. Minchell and cried: "How is it?"

Mr. Minchell grinned. Somehow, he realized, in some mysterious way, he had been given a second chance. And this time he knew what he would do with it. "Fine!" he shouted, and stood up on King Richard's back and sent his derby spinning out over the heads of the people. "Come on up!"

"Can't do it," the man said. "Got a date." There was a look of profound admiration in his eyes as he strode off. Away from the crowd he stopped and cupped his hands and cried: "I'll be seeing you!"

"That's right," Mr. Minchell said, feeling the cold new wind on his face. "You'll be seeing me."

Later, when he was good and ready, he got down off the lion.

I
SOME NOT SO FANTASTIC SYMBOLS

Although "The Vanishing American" seems quite fantastic on the surface, one does not have to go very far beneath its surface to find a great deal of realism. The key elements in the fantasy are Mr. Minchell's invisibility and his ride on the lion.

All of us—the psychology books say—seek recognition. Mr. Minchell, though he has nearly forgotten this human need, does in fact want to be recognized as a successful human being on some level. By making him turn invisible Beaumont hits upon a perfect and highly humorous way of symbolizing the fact that his "hero" has failed to achieve any success that would bring him recognition.

And then there's the ride on the library lion. Somehow that ride is a beginning for Minchell. Just as the invisibility symbolizes the fact that he has deserved no recognition, the lion ride is an excellent symbol for. . . What? Try to express in your own words what Minchell's ride means. Also try to explain why lion-riding is an especially appropriate symbol for the meaning the author wants to convey.

II
IMPLICATIONS

Discuss each of the following items.

1. Analyze the meaning of the title of the story. It has meaning on more than one level.

2. Recall what Mr. Minchell had wanted to do with his life. In what ways do you think this path would have led him to greater recognition and self-satisfaction?

3. As you no doubt realize, this story has some important implications for modern American life. We live in a technological society in which buttons, keyboards, tapes, and the machines they con-trol become increasingly important each year. Each year, therefore, we need more Mr. Minchells. Aside from taking rides on library lions, how are such individuals going to achieve a significant measure of self-respect and recognition?

4. Work involving little mental or emotional satisfaction is of course nothing new. What is new is the fact that today we have much more leisure time than our predecessors. What do you think are some of the most satisfying ways to spend this leisure time? How do you suppose Mr. Minchell spent his leisure time?

III
TECHNIQUES

Comedy

A satirist may be defined as one who uses laughter to criticize human institutions and humanity. Satirists, however, may use a great number of different weapons to make their criticisms. Which of the following would you say are Charles Beaumont's chief weapons?

1. humor
2. symbolism
3. invective
4. nonsense
5. exaggeration
6. understatement
7. wit

Sympathy and Detachment

Most readers are not likely to identify very closely with a forty-seven-year-old man who has wasted his life; yet it is important for Beaumont's purposes that readers not be too detached from the hero. What are some of the factors that cause readers to sympathize with Mr. Minchell and that keep them from being excessively detached from his problems?

THE
COMIC
IMAGINATION

The American culture has been rich in humor
from its beginning. American cartoonists
and comic-strip creators have been a kind
of thermometer indicating our health and vitality.
Our humorists have taken us to task
for shortsighted behavior.
Look at the cartoons and comics of the modern nations;
the creations of their comic imagination
hold many clues to understanding the heart
of a people. What is the point
of the humor? How fully can the nation look
at its ridiculous aspects
and still laugh?

An early American, David Claypool Johnson was born about twenty
years after the United States won independence. Much of his humor
was satirical—comic but not very kindly. THE MILITIA MUSTER
caricatures some very unmilitary maneuvers.

THE MILITIA MUSTER
David Claypool Johnson
Courtesy of the American
Antiquarian Society

While still very young,
another American went to war
and came home a famous cartoonist.
All Americans laughed
at the weary dog-faced soldiers
Mauldin recorded in the
battlefronts of World War II.
But back home they choked a little
on their laughter. It was
the troops themselves
who howled loudest as the absurdity
of their situation touched them.
A Pulitzer Prize was given
to Mauldin in 1945 for one cartoon
that is now a classic piece
of American humor.
Irony is one of Bill Mauldin's
greatest resources.

MAULDIN CARTOON
Bill Mauldin

*"Joe, yestiddy ya saved my life an' I swore I'd pay ya back.
Here's my last pair of dry socks."*

GRIN AND BEAR IT
George Maurice Lichtenstein

A cartoonist of the ludicrous situations
on the homefront
is George Maurice Lichtenstein—Lichty.
His characters are utterly nutty
in their straight-faced statements.
His target is society and human nature
in its most pointless inadequacy.

*". . . and it's gratifying to note that public co-
operation in the test evacuation of this city was
100%. . . . They had traffic hopelessly snarled
within minutes!"*

"Touché!"

Copyright © 1945 James Thurber.
From The Thurber Carnival,
published by Harper & Row.
Originally printed in The New Yorker.

Copyright © 1950 by Saul
Steinberg from The Passport
(Harper). Originally in The
New Yorker.

Writer, artist, managing editor of *The New Yorker* magazine, the quiet Thurber is one of the giants among recent American humorists. His one-frame domestic scenes help us realize our own absurdity. Masterpieces of brevity and punch are the pair of Thurber and Steinberg cartoons. The latter doesn't even need a caption.

George Price's sneaky punch at our exploitative world is more telling today than when it was first published in 1938.

Drawing by George Price;
copyright © 1938, 1966. The
New Yorker Magazine Inc.

"A magnificent fowl, Madam. Notice how he
looks you straight in the eye."

BRONTOSAURUS
Alexander Calder
Collection of Mrs. Hope B. Perlberg

Probably the purest form of humor is that which is unrelated to time or place. Alexander Calder's BRONTOSAURUS provokes both laughter and delight in the child that lives within us all.

In a playful vein is Johnson's SOUND ASLEEP AND WIDE AWAKE. Sheer slapstick on the surface, it can also be read as a social comment even more cynical than THE MILITIA MUSTER.

SOUND ASLEEP AND WIDE AWAKE
David Claypool Johnson
Courtesy of Kennedy Galleries, Inc.

For many years *Skippy* was probably
the most popular comic strip in America.
Marked by a scratchily drawn figure, an ample cap set
at a rakish angle, and always in motion,
Skippy conducted a constant warfare
between himself and society.

SKIPPY
Percy Crosby

© 1968 United Feature Syndicate, Inc.

© 1971 Walt Kelly. Courtesy of Publishers—Hall Syndicate.

Two contemporary classics in strip cartooning are *Pogo* and *Peanuts*, both
full of gentle humor. *Pogo* often takes out after dramatic issues on the
political scene. *Peanuts* confines itself to human interplay and our fragile
egos.

285

In 1940, James Thurber published
Fables for Our Time, drawings and texts
so wisely critical of human behavior
and so pertinent that they are likely
to become classics of their kind.
These four, only a sample
of the collection, need no commentary.

Four Fables

JAMES THURBER

The Very Proper Gander

Not so very long ago there was a very fine gander. He was strong and smooth and beautiful and he spent most of his time singing to his wife and children. One day somebody who saw him strutting up and down in his yard and singing remarked, "There is a very proper gander." An old hen overheard this and told her husband about it that night in the roost. "They said something about propaganda," she said. "I have always suspected that," said the rooster, and he went around the barnyard next day telling everybody that the very fine gander was a dangerous bird, more than likely a hawk in gander's clothing. A small brown hen remembered a time when at a great distance she had seen the gander talking with some hawks in the forest. "They were up to no good," she said. A duck remembered that the gander had once told him he did not believe in anything. "He said to heck with the flag, too," said the duck. A guinea hen recalled that she had once seen somebody who looked very much like the gander throw something that looked a great deal like a bomb. Finally everybody snatched up sticks and stones and descended on the gander's house. He was strutting in his front yard, singing to his children and his wife. "There he is!" everybody cried. "Hawk-lover! Unbeliever! Flag-hater! Bomb-thrower!" So they set upon him and drove him out of the country.

Moral: Anyone who you or your wife thinks is going to overthrow the government by violence must be driven out of the country.

Copyright 1940 James Thurber. Copyright © 1968 Helen Thurber. From *Fables for Our Time,* published by Harper & Row. Originally printed in *The New Yorker.*

The Shrike
and the Chipmunks

Once upon a time there were two chipmunks, a male and a female. The male chipmunk thought that arranging nuts in artistic patterns was more fun than just piling them up to see how many you could pile up. The female was all for piling up as many as you could. She told her husband that if he gave up making designs with the nuts there would be room in their large cave for a great many more and he would soon become the wealthiest chipmunk in the woods. But he would not let her interfere with his designs, so she flew into a rage and left him. "The shrike will get you," she said, "because you are helpless and cannot look after yourself." To be sure, the female chipmunk had not been gone three nights before the male had to dress for a banquet and could not find his studs or shirt or suspenders. So he couldn't go to the banquet, but that was just as well, because all the chipmunks who did go were attacked and killed by a weasel.

The next day the shrike began hanging around outside the chipmunk's cave, waiting to catch him. The shrike couldn't get in because the doorway was clogged up with soiled laundry and dirty dishes. "He will come out for a walk after breakfast and I will get him then," thought the shrike. But the chipmunk slept all day and did not get up and have breakfast until after dark. Then he came out for a breath of air before beginning work on a new design. The shrike swooped down to snatch up the chipmunk, but could not see very well on account of the dark, so he batted his head against an alder branch and was killed.

A few days later the female chipmunk returned and saw the awful mess the house was in. She went to the bed and shook her husband.

"What would you do without me?" she demanded. "Just go on living, I guess," he said. "You wouldn't last five days," she told him. She swept the house and did the dishes and sent out the laundry, and then she made the chipmunk get up and wash and dress. "You can't be healthy if you lie in bed all day and never get any exercise," she told him. So she took him for a walk in the bright sunlight and they were both caught and killed by the shrike's brother, a shrike named Stoop.

Moral: Early to rise and early to bed makes a male healthy and wealthy and dead.

The Glass in the Field

A short time ago some builders, working on a studio in Connecticut, left a huge square of plate glass standing upright in a field one day. A goldfinch flying swiftly across the field struck the glass and was knocked cold. When he came to he hastened to his club, where an attendant bandaged his head and gave him a stiff drink. "What happened?" asked a sea gull. "I was flying across a meadow when all of a sudden the air crystallized on me," said the goldfinch. The sea gull and a hawk and an eagle all laughed heartily. A swallow listened gravely. "For fifteen years, fledgling and bird, I've flown this country," said the eagle, "and I assure you there is no such thing as air crystallizing. Water, yes; air, no." "You were probably struck by a hailstone," the hawk told the goldfinch. "Or he may have had a stroke," said the sea gull. "What do you think, swallow?" "Why, I—I think maybe the air crystallized on him," said the swallow. The large birds laughed so loudly that the goldfinch became annoyed and bet them each a dozen worms that they couldn't follow the course he had flown across the field without encountering the hardened atmosphere. They all took his bet; the swallow went along to watch. The sea gull, the eagle, and the hawk decided to fly together over the route the goldfinch indicated. "You come, too," they said to the swallow. "I—I— well, no," said the swallow. "I don't think I will." So the three large birds took off together and they hit the glass together and they were all knocked cold.

Moral: He who hesitates is sometimes saved.

The Owl
Who Was God

Once upon a starless midnight there was an owl who sat on the branch of an oak tree. Two ground moles tried to slip quietly by, unnoticed. "You!" said the owl. "Who?" they quavered, in fear and astonishment, for they could not believe it was possible for anyone to see them in that thick darkness. "You two!" said the owl. The moles hurried away and told the other creatures of the field and forest that the owl was the greatest and wisest of all animals because he could see in the dark and because he could answer any question. "I'll see about that," said a secretary bird, and he called on the owl one night when it was again very dark. "How many claws am I holding up?" said the secretary bird. "Two," said the owl, and that was right. "Can you give me another expression for 'that is to say' or 'namely'?" asked the secretary bird. "To wit," said the owl. "Why does a lover call on his love?" asked the secretary bird. "To woo," said the owl.

The secretary bird hastened back to the other creatures and reported that the owl was indeed the greatest and wisest animal in the world because he could see in the dark and because he could answer any question. "Can he see in the daytime, too?" asked a red fox. "Yes," echoed a dormouse and a French poodle. "Can he see in the daytime, too?" All the other creatures laughed loudly at this silly question, and they set upon the red fox and his friends and drove them out of the region. Then they sent a messenger to the owl and asked him to be their leader.

When the owl appeared among the animals it was high noon and the sun was shining brightly. He walked very slowly, which gave him an appearance of great dignity, and he peered about him with large, staring eyes, which gave him an air of tremendous importance. "He's God!" screamed a Plymouth Rock hen. And the others took up the cry "He's God!" So they followed him wherever he went and when he began to bump into things they began to bump into things, too. Finally he came to a concrete highway and he started up the middle of it and all the other creatures followed him. Presently a hawk, who was acting as outrider, observed a truck coming toward them at fifty miles an hour, and he reported to the secretary bird and the secretary bird reported to the owl. "There's danger ahead," said the secretary bird. "To wit?" said the owl. The secretary bird told him. "Aren't you afraid?" he asked. "Who?" said the owl calmly, for he could not see the truck. "He's God!" cried all the creatures again, and they were still crying "He's God!" when the truck hit them and ran them down. Some of the animals were merely injured, but most of them, including the owl, were killed.

Moral: You can fool too many of the people too much of the time.

I
CRITICISM CLOSE TO HOME

Those who know James Thurber primarily through such made-up stories as "The Night the Ghost Got In" are often startled by the acid, almost cynical, comments of some of the satires in *Fables for Our Time*. Of course the characters are all disguised as animals, but there can be no question that Thurber's target is human nature; note, for example, that the morals to "The Owl Who Was God" and "The Very Proper Gander" refer directly to human beings and not to the animals who illustrate the point. Indeed, one of the chief characteristics of the morals of Thurber's fables is that they can be applied so frequently to ourselves and to those we know best.

II
IMPLICATIONS

Identify the fable or fables that bear upon the following statements and discuss both Thurber's and your own attitude toward each proposition.

1. Human beings are far too ready to follow; far to slow to lead.

2. Those who would live quiet lives and escape criticism had best be conformists.

3. Faith should never be so blind as to be completely out of touch with Reason.

4. Self-confidence should have narrow boundaries—It is far better to be too unsure of yourself than to be too sure.

5. Human beings readily react to the improbable by dismissing it rather than by seeking to discover its causes.

III
TECHNIQUES

Comedy

Mark Twain once observed that a humorist had to preach to "live forever." (He also added, "By forever, I mean thirty years.") Do you believe that a humorist must preach in order to have a lasting reputation? In answering, compare "The Night the Ghost Got In," in which Thurber does not "preach," with the fables, in which he does. Is either one more likely to endure than the other? If you think that the fables are likely to endure longer, would you say it is because they preach, or for some other reason?

Sympathy and Detachment

If you are familiar with the literary form known as the fable, you know that the characters in fables are most frequently animals. What does this fact have to do with the sympathy or detachment of the reader and with the fabulist's attempt to get a message across?

"It'll be an adventure," Mr. Leonard says to his eight-year-old son, Paul, as
he and his wife prepare to leave their boy alone for the first time while they go
to a movie. And what an adventure it turns out to be—with the entertainment
provided not by Paul's microscope and slides but by a radio DJ named
All-Night Sam and by the lively couple who live next door. The story will be
an adventure for you, too, thanks especially to several unexpected twists in
Vonnegut's plot.

Next Door

KURT VONNEGUT, JR.

The old house was divided into two dwellings by a thin wall that passed on, with high
fidelity, sounds on either side. On the north
side were the Leonards. On the south side
were the Hargers.

The Leonards—husband, wife, and eight-
year-old son—had just moved in. And, aware
of the wall, they kept their voices down as they
argued in a friendly way as to whether or not
the boy, Paul, was old enough to be left alone
for the evening.

"Shhhhh!" said Paul's father.

"Was I shouting?" said his mother. "I was
talking in a perfectly normal tone."

"If I could hear Harger pulling a cork, he can
certainly hear you," said his father.

"I didn't say anything I'd be ashamed to have
anybody hear," said Mrs. Leonard.

"You called Paul a baby," said Mr. Leonard.
"That certainly embarrasses Paul—and it embarrasses me."

"It's just a way of talking," she said.

"It's a way we've got to stop," he said. "And
we can stop treating him like a baby, too—
tonight. We simply shake his hand, walk out,
and go to the movie." He turned to Paul.

"Next Door" excerpted from the book *Welcome to the Monkey House* by Kurt
Vonnegut, Jr. Copyright © 1955 by Kurt Vonnegut, Jr. Originally published in
Cosmopolitan. Reprinted by permission of Delacorte Press/Seymour
Lawrence.

"You're not afraid—are you, boy?"

"I'll be all right," said Paul. He was very tall
for his age, and thin, and had a soft, sleepy,
radiant sweetness engendered by his mother.
"I'm fine."

"Darn right!" said his father, clouting him on
the back. "It'll be an adventure."

"I'd feel better about this adventure, if we
could get a sitter," said his mother.

"If it's going to spoil the picture for you,"
said the father, "let's take him with us."

Mrs. Leonard was shocked. "Oh—it isn't for
children."

"I don't care," said Paul amiably. The why of
their not wanting him to see certain movies,
certain magazines, certain books, certain television shows was a mystery he respected—
even relished a little.

"It wouldn't kill him to see it," said his
father.

"You *know* what it's about," she said.

"What *is* it about?" said Paul innocently.

Mrs. Leonard looked to her husband for
help, and got none. "It's about a girl who
chooses her friends unwisely," she said.

"Oh," said Paul. "That doesn't sound very
interesting."

"Are we going, or aren't we?" said Mr.
Leonard impatiently. "The show starts in ten
minutes."

Mrs. Leonard bit her lip. "All right!" she
said bravely. "You lock the windows and the
back door, and I'll write down the telephone
numbers for the police and the fire department
and the theater and Dr. Failey." She turned to
Paul. "You *can* dial, can't you, dear?"

"He's been dialing for years!" cried Mr.
Leonard.

291

"Sssssssh!" said Mrs. Leonard.

"Sorry," Mr. Leonard bowed to the wall. "My apologies."

"Paul, dear," said Mrs. Leonard, "what are you going to do while we're gone?"

"Oh—look through my microscope, I guess," said Paul.

"You're not going to be looking at germs, are you?" she said.

"Nope—just hair, sugar, pepper, stuff like that," said Paul.

His mother frowned judiciously. "I think that would be all right, don't you?" she said to Mr. Leonard.

"Fine!" said Mr. Leonard. "Just as long as the pepper doesn't make him sneeze!"

"I'll be careful," said Paul.

Mr. Leonard winced. "Shhhhh!" he said.

Soon after Paul's parents left, the radio in the Harger apartment went on. It was on softly at first—so softly that Paul, looking through his microscope on the living room coffee table, couldn't make out the announcer's words. The music was frail and dissonant—unidentifiable.

Gamely, Paul tried to listen to the music rather than to the man and woman who were fighting.

Paul squinted through the eyepiece of his microscope at a bit of his hair far below, and he turned a knob to bring the hair into focus. It looked like a glistening brown eel, flecked here and there with tiny spectra where the light struck the hair just so.

There—the voices of the man and woman were getting louder again, drowning out the radio. Paul twisted the microscope knob nervously, and the objective lens ground into the glass slide on which the hair rested.

The woman was shouting now.

Paul unscrewed the lens, and examined it for damage.

Now the man shouted back—shouted something awful, unbelievable.

Paul got a sheet of lens tissue from his bedroom, and dusted at the frosted dot on the lens, where the lens had bitten into the slide. He screwed the lens back in place.

All was quiet again next door—except for the radio.

Paul looked down into the microscope, down into the milky mist of the damaged lens.

Now the fight was beginning again—louder and louder, cruel and crazy.

Trembling, Paul sprinkled grains of salt on a fresh slide, and put it under the microscope.

The woman shouted again, a high, ragged, poisonous shout.

Paul turned the knob too hard, and the fresh slide cracked and fell in triangles to the floor. Paul stood, shaking, wanting to shout, too—to shout in terror and bewilderment. It had to stop. Whatever it was, it *had* to stop!

"If you're going to yell, turn up the radio!" the man cried.

Paul heard the clicking of the woman's heels across the floor. The radio volume swelled until the boom of the bass made Paul feel like he was trapped in a drum.

"And now!" bellowed the radio, "for Katy from Fred! For Nancy from Bob, who thinks she's swell! For Arthur, from one who's worshipped him from afar for six weeks! Here's *Stardust!* Remember! If you have a dedication, call Milton nine-three-thousand! Ask for All-Night

Sam, the record man!"

The music picked up the house and shook it.

A door slammed next door. Now someone hammered on a door.

Paul looked down into his microscope once more, looked at nothing—while a prickling sensation spread over his skin. He faced the truth: The man and woman would kill each other, if he didn't stop them.

He beat on the wall with his fist. "Mr. Harger! Stop it!" he cried. "Mrs. Harger! Stop it!"

"For Ollie from Lavinia!" All-Night Sam cried back at him. "For Ruth from Carl, who'll never forget last Tuesday! For Wilber from Mary, who's lonesome tonight! Here's the Sauter-Finnegan Band asking, *Love, What Are You Doing to My Heart?*"

Next door, crockery smashed, filling a split second of radio silence. And then the tidal wave of music drowned everything again.

Paul stood by the wall, trembling in his helplessness. "Mr. Harger! Mrs. Harger! Please!"

"Remember the number!" said All-Night Sam. "Milton nine-three-thousand!"

Dazed. Paul went to the phone and dialed the number.

"WJCD," said the switchboard operator.

"Would you kindly connect me with All-Night Sam?" said Paul.

"Hello!" said All-Night Sam. He was eating, talking with a full mouth. In the background, Paul could hear sweet, bleating music, the original of what was rending the radio next door.

"I wonder if I might make a dedication," said Paul.

"Dunno why not," said Sam. "Ever belong to any organization listed as subversive by the Attorney General's office?"

Paul thought a moment. "Nossir—I don't think so, sir," he said.

"Shoot," said Sam.

"From Mr. Lemuel K. Harger to Mrs. Harger," said Paul.

"What's the message?" said Sam.

"I love you," said Paul. "Let's make up and start all over again."

The woman's voice was so shrill with passion that it cut through the din of the radio, and even Sam heard it.

"Kid—are you in trouble?" said Sam. "Your folks fighting?"

Paul was afraid that Sam would hang up on him if he found out that Paul wasn't a blood relative of the Hargers. "Yessir," he said.

"And you're trying to pull 'em back together again with this dedication?" said Sam.

"Yessir," said Paul.

Sam became very emotional. "O.K., kid," he said hoarsely, "I'll give it everything I've got. Maybe it'll work. I once saved a guy from shooting himself the same way."

"How did you do that?" said Paul, fascinated.

"He called up and said he was gonna blow his brains out," said Sam, "and I played *The Bluebird of Happiness.*" He hung up.

Paul dropped the telephone into its cradle. The music stopped, and Paul's hair stood on end. For the first time, the fantastic speed of modern communications was real to him, and he was appalled.

"Folks!" said Sam, "I guess everybody stops and wonders sometimes what the heck he thinks he's doin' with the life the good Lord gave him! It may seem funny to you folks, because I always keep a cheerful front, no matter how I feel inside, that I wonder sometimes, too! And then, just like some angel was trying to tell me, 'Keep going, Sam, keep going,' something like this comes along.

"Folks!" said Sam, "I've been asked to bring a man and his wife back together again through the miracle of radio! I guess there's no sense in kidding ourselves about marriage! It isn't any bowl of cherries! There's ups and downs, and sometimes folks don't see how they can go on!"

Paul was impressed with the wisdom and authority of Sam. Having the radio turned up high made sense now, for Sam was speaking like the right-hand man of God.

When Sam paused for effect, all was still next door. Already the miracle was working.

"Now," said Sam, "a guy in my business has to be half musician, half philosopher, half psychiatrist, and half electrical engineer! And! If I've learned one thing from working with all you wonderful people out there, it's this: if folks would swallow their self-respect and pride, there wouldn't be any more divorces!"

There were affectionate cooings from next door. A lump grew in Paul's throat as he thought about the beautiful thing he and Sam were bringing to pass.

"Folks!" said Sam, "that's all I'm gonna say about love and marriage! That's all anybody needs to know! And now, for Mrs. Lemuel K. Harger, from Mr. Harger—I love you! Let's make up and start all over again!" Sam choked up. "Here's Eartha Kitt, and *Somebody Bad Stole De Wedding Bell!*"

The radio next door went off.

The world lay still.

A purple emotion flooded Paul's being. Childhood dropped away, and he hung, dizzy, on the brink of life, rich, violent, rewarding.

There was movement next door—slow, foot-dragging movement.

"So," said the woman.

"Charlotte—" said the man uneasily. "Honey—I swear."

"'I love you,'" she said bitterly. "'Let's make up and start all over again.'"

"Baby," said the man desperately, "it's another Lemuel K. Harger. It's got to be!"

"You want your wife back?" she said. "All right—I won't get in her way. She can have you, Lemuel—you jewel beyond price, you."

"*She* must have called the station," said the man.

"She can have you, you philandering, two-timing, two-bit Lochinvar,[1] she said. "But you won't be in very good condition."

---

1. Lochinvar, a romantic knight in Sir Walter Scott's poem *Marmion*. The term now carries connotations of a philandering lover.

"Charlotte—put down that gun," said the man. "Don't do anything you'll be sorry for."

"That's all behind me, you worm," she said.

There were three shots.

Paul ran out into the hall, and bumped into the woman as she burst from the Harger apartment. She was a big, blonde woman, all soft and awry, like an unmade bed.

She and Paul screamed at the same time, and then she grabbed him as he started to run.

"You want candy?" she said wildly. "Bicycle?"

"No, thank you," said Paul shrilly. "Not at this time."

"You haven't seen or heard a thing!" she said. "You know what happens to squealers?"

"Yes!" said Paul.

She dug into her purse, and brought out a perfumed mulch of face tissues, bobbypins and cash. "Here!" she panted. "It's yours! And there's more where that came from, if you keep your mouth shut." She stuffed it into his trousers pocket.

She looked at him fiercely, then fled into the street.

Paul ran back into his apartment, jumped into bed, and pulled the covers up over his head. In the hot, dark cave of the bed, he cried because he and All-Night Sam had helped to kill a man.

A policeman came clumping into the house very soon, and he knocked on both apartment doors with his billyclub.

Numb, Paul crept out of the hot, dark cave, and answered the door. Just as he did, the door across the hall opened, and there stood Mr. Harger, haggard but whole.

"Yes, sir?" said Harger. He was a small, balding man, with a hairline mustache. "Can I help you?"

"The neighbors heard some shots," said the policeman.

"Really?" said Harger urbanely. He dampened his mustache with the tip of his little finger. "How bizarre. I heard nothing." He looked at Paul sharply. "Have you been playing with your father's guns again, young man?"

"Oh, nossir!" said Paul, horrified.

"Where are your folks?" said the policeman to Paul.

"At the movies," said Paul.

"You're all alone?" said the policeman.

"Yessir," said Paul. "It's an adventure."

"I'm sorry I said that about the guns," said Harger. "I certainly would have heard any shots in this house. The walls are thin as paper, and I heard nothing."

Paul looked at him gratefully.

"And you didn't hear any shots, either, kid?" said the policeman.

Before Paul could find an answer, there was a disturbance out on the street. A big, motherly woman was getting out of a taxicab and wailing at the top of her lungs. "Lem! Lem, baby."

She barged into the foyer, a suitcase bumping against her leg and tearing her stocking to shreds. She dropped the suitcase, and ran to Harger, throwing her arms around him.

"I got your message, darling," she said, "and I did just what All-Night Sam told me to do. I swallowed my self-respect, and here I am!"

"Rose, Rose, Rose—my little Rose," said Harger. "Don't ever leave me again." They grappled with each other affectionately, and staggered into their apartment.

"Just look at this apartment!" said Mrs. Harger. "Men are just lost without women!" As she closed the door, Paul could see that she was awfully pleased with the mess.

"You *sure* you didn't hear any shots?" said the policeman to Paul.

The ball of money in Paul's pocket seemed to swell to the size of a watermelon. "Yessir," he croaked.

The policeman left.

Paul shut his apartment door, shuffled into his bedroom, and collapsed on the bed.

The next voices Paul heard came from his own side of the wall. The voices were sunny—

the voices of his mother and father. His mother was singing a nursery rhyme and his father was undressing him.

"Diddle-diddle-dumpling, my son John," piped his mother, "Went to bed with his stockings on. One shoe off, and one shoe on—diddle-diddle-dumpling, my son John."

Paul opened his eyes.

"Hi, big boy," said his father, "you went to sleep with all your clothes on."

"How's my little adventurer?" said his mother.

"O.K.," said Paul sleepily. "How was the show?"

"It wasn't for children, honey," said his mother. "You would have liked the short subject, though. It was all about bears—cunning little cubs."

Paul's father handed her Paul's trousers, and she shook them out, and hung them neatly on the back of a chair by the bed. She patted them smooth, and felt the ball of money in the pocket. "Little boys' pockets!" she said, delighted. "Full of childhood's mysteries. An enchanted frog? A magic pocketknife from a fairy princess?" She caressed the lump.

"He's not a little boy—he's a big boy," said Paul's father. "And he's too old to be thinking about fairy princesses."

Paul's mother held up her hands. "Don't rush it, don't rush it. When I saw him asleep there, I realized all over again how dreadfully short childhood is." She reached into the pocket and sighed wistfully. "Little boys are so hard on clothes—especially pockets."

She brought out the ball and held it under Paul's nose. "Now, would you mind telling Mommy what we have here?" she said gaily.

The ball bloomed like a frowzy chrysanthemum, with ones, fives, tens, twenties, and lipstick-stained Kleenex for petals. And rising from it, befuddling Paul's young mind, was the pungent musk of perfume.

Paul's father sniffed the air. "What's that smell?" he said.

Paul's mother rolled her eyes. "*Tabu*," she said.

I
THE ABSURDITY OF LIFE

Nothing, absolutely nothing in this story turns out the way one would logically expect. The Leonards leave Paul at home to protect him from a corrupting "adult" film, but the boy has a far more adult experience at home and winds up accepting a bribe. Paul and Sam expect to stop a fight but intensify one instead. Paul thinks he has caused a wife to shoot her husband, but in reality he has brought a husband and wife together.

By the end of the story, some readers may wonder whether all this really happened or whether it was just a fantasy of Paul's. They surmise this, in part, because Mr. Harger, at the end of the story, is obviously very much alive and not even wounded. But the world created here by Vonnegut is one in which reason has little place. The more likely explanation for Mr. Harger's good health is that Charlotte *missed*—like everyone else in the story; and it is life that is absurd, not Paul's imagination.

II
IMPLICATIONS

Those who have read other stories or novels by Kurt Vonnegut know that in spite of the humor that pervades much of his work he is an extremely serious writer. See if you can find support in this story for the following serious implications.

1. Our opinions about other people are based as much or even more on our own needs as on objective or accurate perceptions of others. (Consider especially the Leonards' perception of their son.)

2. Though modern communications are faster than they have ever been before, true communication between persons is virtually impossible.

3. We can never foresee the results of our actions. Thus, even good intentions may lead to evil.

III
TECHNIQUES

Comedy

Try to say why these quotations are funny.

1. About Rose: She barged into the foyer, a suitcase bumping against her leg and tearing her stocking to shreds.

2. Rose: "I swallowed my self-respect, and here I am!"

3. Mrs. Leonard: "Little boys' pockets! Full of childhood's mysteries. An enchanted frog? A magic pocketknife from a fairy princess?" She caressed the lump.

FINAL REFLECTIONS

The Comic Imagination

The writers represented in this unit have exposed some of the failings of American individuals and of American society. But they have done so, for the most part, by playing up sympathy and playing down cruelty. American comic writers have tended to be essentially optimistic rather than pessimistic. In this respect, American comedy tends to reflect the basically optimistic outlook that has characterized American society as a whole.

The optimism, the sympathetic emphasis of American comedy, is not, however, a loose and lazy optimism which binds us to do nothing because all things are for the best in this best of all possible societies. Although the prevailing spirit of American comedy has been sympathetic, we should not overlook the fact that it has criticized real faults. Although the writers in this section have often invited their readers to laugh at human failings, they have not invited us to forget them.

IMPLICATIONS

Recall the selections in this unit and use illustrations from them to support your evaluation of each of the following statements. You may also call upon your own experience, where applicable.

1. Americans resist rules and regulations of all kinds and enjoy "cutting up" authorities.

2. American comedy tends to be of the harmless variety; our writers invite us to laugh at human foibles but avoid more serious criticisms.

3. A major failing of the American character is our desire for material things like wealth, comforts, and bigger, better, and faster everythings.

4. Americans have an unusually strong sympathy for the underdog.

5. The hero-figure in much American humor is an ordinary sort of person, with more than an ordinary share of wit or intelligence.

6. Americans tend to identify with common folk and to be suspicious of all those who for one reason or another stand above the average.

7. Most Americans are rather insensitive both to their surroundings and to others.

TECHNIQUES
Comedy

Each of the following quotations makes some statement about comedy. Study each statement to determine what it means, and then be prepared to point out two or three selections that show the statement to be either true or false.

1. ". . . *too much* of anything, if plausibly brought in and playfully received, is comic."

2. "Humor is meant to blow up evil and make fun of the follies of life."

3. "Why we laugh is generally because we have seen or heard something that is at variance with custom."

4. "The true humorist must be an optimist."

5. ". . . humor is the best that lies closest to the familiar, to that part of the familiar which is humiliating, distressing, even tragic."

Sympathy and Detachment

Pick two or three of the selections in this section that you liked the most and two or three that you liked the least. Then try to determine how much of your enjoyment, or the lack of it, was due to the author's gaining or failing to gain your sympathy for either characters or situation. If in some cases you felt too detached from the characters or situation, was the fault the author's or your own?

BIOGRAPHICAL NOTES
O. Henry

O. Henry (1862–1910), a pseudonym for William Sydney Porter, has become synonymous with the surprise-ending short story. Born in North Carolina, he left school early and went first to Austin and then to Houston, Texas, working at various jobs, including teller at a bank, until he became editor of a weekly, *Rolling Stone,* which soon after went out of business. Fleeing from charges of embezzlement at the Austin bank, O. Henry went first to New Orleans, then to Honduras. In 1897 he returned to Austin and was sentenced to five years in a federal prison at Columbus, Ohio. In prison he wrote stories under a variety of names, but finally settled upon O. Henry as a pseudonym. When he was released, O. Henry first moved to Pittsburgh and then to New York where he settled down to writing stories for magazines, later collected under such titles as *Cabbages and Kings, The Four Million,* and *The Gentle Grafter.*

Ellis Parker Butler

Ellis Parker Butler (1869–1937) grew up on a farm in Muscatine, Iowa. Influenced by Mark Twain, who lived for a time in Butler's hometown, the Iowa humorist was a popular writer for over forty years, turning out great numbers of essays, sketches, and stories.

James Thurber

James Thurber (1894–1961) was born in Columbus, Ohio, and worked for a number of years as a journalist and magazine editor. He then became a free-lance contributor of stories and drawings to *The New Yorker* and published almost twenty volumes of magazine pieces in the next twenty years while earning for himself a reputation as one of the greatest American humorists of all time. Among his best-known works are *My Life and Hard Times, Let Your Mind Alone, Fables for Our Time, My World—and Welcome to It,* and *Alarms and Diversions.*

Richard Armour

Richard Armour (1906–   ) has made a career out of poking fun at the world and its foibles. His writings, serious and funny, and his humorous verse have dealt with such diverse subjects as Coleridge, Shakespeare, parents, the classics. His series, "It All Started with . . ." has included Columbus, Europe, Eve, and Karl Marx. He has written thousands of verses, some of them collected in such volumes as *Light Armour* and *Nights with Armour.* Armour has taught English at many colleges and universities, most recently at Scripps College. His latest books include *Going Like Sixty: A Lighthearted Look at the Later Years* and *It All Would Have Startled Columbus.*

David McCord

David McCord (1897–   ), a New Yorker by birth, earned his bachelor's and master's degrees at Harvard. He once served on the staff of the Boston *Evening Transcript.* He has written prose and poetry and published a number of volumes. His work has also appeared in *The New Yorker, Saturday Review, Atlantic,* and *Harper's.*

Phyllis McGinley

Phyllis McGinley (1905–1978) was born in Oregon and grew up in the West. She attended the Universities of Utah and California and then taught one year in Utah. Bent on a writing career, she moved to New York and held a succession of jobs, including writing for *Town and Country.* Her first children's book, *The Horse Who Lived Upstairs,* was published in 1944 and since that time she wrote many others. She was known chiefly for her verse, much of which was published in *The New Yorker.*

Conrad Aiken

Conrad Aiken (1889–1973), who was born in Savannah, Georgia, and educated in New England private schools and at Harvard, devoted his life to writing. In 1930 his *Selected Poems* was awarded the Pulitzer Prize for Poetry and in 1954 *Collected Poems* received the National Book Award. In addition, Aiken wrote short stories for *The New Yorker, Scribner's,* and *Esquire.*

Ring Lardner

Although Ring Lardner (1885–1933) studied engineering, he became a reporter instead—first in South Bend, Indiana, later in Chicago and New York. He wrote a sports column for the Chicago *Tribune* and printed there his first "You know me, Al" sketches, published later in a collection under that title. His favorite subjects were baseball players and boxers, and his style was a racy vernacular, humorous, sometimes cynical.

Robert Benchley

A versatile humorist, Robert Benchley (1889–1945) achieved fame as an essayist, editor, and motion picture actor. Benchley, born in Massachusetts, took an A.B. at Harvard in 1912. He worked for the advertising department in the Curtis Publishing Co. for two years and then did a stint in personnel work in Boston. Later he became editor of various newspapers in New York and Washington. After World War I, he served briefly as editor of the magazine *Vanity Fair* and then for almost a decade as drama editor for the old *Life.* His many books include two which were posthumously published, *Benchley—or Else* and *Chips Off the Old Benchley.*

Langston Hughes

Langston Hughes (1902–1967) was a man of many accomplishments. He was a sailor, dishwasher, and beachcomber as well as a novelist, poet, playwright, columnist, and translator. During his lifetime he was unofficially known as "the Poet Laureate of the Negro People," for he articulated the concept of black pride. Yet for all of his ability and in spite of all the professional honors he earned, Hughes will be best remembered for the creation of one great, comic character, Jesse B. Semple, who was born when Hughes overheard a conversation in a Harlem bar.

Ogden Nash

Ogden Nash (1902–1971) was a master of humorous verse—visual and auditory. He taught at Newport, Rhode Island, for one year and then worked several years in a publishing company. Somewhat sophisticated in style, often published in *The New Yorker*, Nash pushed, struggled, triumphed in the eventual rhyme. Occasionally bitter, Nash's verses are usually humorous. Among his best-known collections of verse are *I'm a Stranger Here Myself, Parents Keep Out, You Can't Get There from Here.*

Dorothy Parker

Dorothy Parker (1893–1967), New Jersey-born satiric poet and short-story writer, worked as drama critic and book critic for New York magazines. In 1927 her first book of verse, *Enough Rope*, was a best-seller. As a free-lance writer, she continued to write sardonic, satiric verse and a great many short stories, marked by their diversity, many revealing a strong social consciousness.

e. e. cummings

Edward Estlin Cummings (1894–1962) was born in Massachusetts and educated at Harvard University. During World War I, he went to France as an ambulance driver and later joined the American forces as a private. After a brief imprisonment in France, cummings wrote *The Enormous Room*, a full-length story which gained him a small but substantial reputation. It is, however, through his poetry—and his unconventionalities—that most readers today know him. Cummings' poetry was marked by experimentation with technique and typography.

Denise Levertov

Denise Levertov (1923–   ) lives in New York City and, during the summer, in Maine. Ms. Levertov's father was a Russian emigré who became an Anglican priest. Her mother was Welsh. She came to the United States in 1948 and is an American citizen. Among her many volumes of poetry are *The Jacob's Ladder, The Sorrow Dance,* and *Footprint.*

Robert Lowell

Robert Lowell (1917–1977) was from a famous literary family, which includes Amy Lowell and James Russell Lowell, and therefore was introduced to poetry at an early age. He also studied under John Crowe Ransom at Kenyon College. During World War II, he refused to register for the draft and was imprisoned as a conscientious objector, an important incident in the development of his poetry. In addition to writing such volumes as *Lord Weary's Castle, Life Studies,* and *For the Union Dead,* Lowell taught at the university level.

Charles Beaumont

Charles Beaumont (1929–   ), a prolific writer of short stories and articles, has also written scores of television plays and scripts for motion pictures. Among his recent books are *Remember? Remember?, When Engines Roar,* and *The Magic Man, and Other Science-Fantasy Stories.*

Kurt Vonnegut, Jr.

Born in Indianapolis, Indiana, Kurt Vonnegut, Jr., (1922–   ) was educated at Cornell University and the University of Chicago. He served in the U.S. infantry from 1942 to 1945, was captured by the Germans during the Battle of the Bulge, and was assigned to a prisoner-of-war work group in Dresden, Germany, which was bombed by the Allies while he was there. This experience served as the background for his best-selling novel, *Slaughterhouse Five*, which was also made into a movie. Among his other well-known novels are *The Sirens of Titan, Cat's Cradle,* and *Breakfast of Champions.*

AMERICAN LITERATURE

THE REALISTIC PERIOD

1865-1900

The year 1865, which marked the end of the Civil War, has also been used to mark an important shift in the direction of American literature. It was a shift from romanticism to realism. Realism grew gradually at first, but by the 1880s it was quite strong, and in the 1890s it clearly dominated prose fiction.

The terms *romanticism* and *realism* have been used so loosely that some authorities have despaired over their definition. Yet writers have called themselves romanticists or realists, and so the terms must have some meaning. As long as we try not to be too rigid, we can define these words meaningfully and use them to make some important distinctions.

ROMANTICISM VERSUS REALISM

Perhaps the chief tendency of romanticists is that they dwell on personal passions, on the subjective side of experience, on their own unique feelings and attitudes. Romantic writers also value highly the creative function of the imagination, often claiming that this faculty helps one arrive at greater truths than those revealed by facts or logic. By transcending the actual, romantics sometimes hope to discover an absolute or ideal.

The term *romanticism* is also associated with a concern for, or a return to, the past and sometimes with an escape from the day-to-day problems of the present. Romantic writers often make use of exotic settings, and Nature—frequently spelled with the capital letter—may figure prominently in their work. To varying degrees you can probably find most or all of these tendencies in the writing of Poe and Whitman, Emerson and Thoreau, Haw-thorne and Melville, as well as in Irving, Bryant, and Cooper.

Realists, in contrast, are less concerned with their own subjective responses and more concerned with the objective world outside their psyches. Usually, they portray with relish the very facts that the romanticist ignores or pushes to the background. Realists, too, are generally not concerned with absolutes or ideals and may even deny their existence. Realist writers often deal with the social problems of real persons in real places in the present. Their settings are ordinary, their characters are ordinary, their nature has flies. These qualities describe on the whole the writers of this period, from Mark Twain and William Dean Howells to Hamlin Garland and Stephen Crane.

LOCAL-COLOR OR REGIONAL WRITERS

Before we discuss the major realistic writers of this half century, a few words must be said about one of the most significant trends of the period under discussion. Because of the intense curiosity of readers to learn about other sections of the country, many writers specialized in describing places, events, manners, and even the speech of specific places. This is known as *regionalism* or local-color writing.

Although regionalism predates the Civil War, those local colorists who became best known began publishing about 1870. That was the year in which the short-story writer Bret Harte published *The Luck of Roaring Camp and Other Stories*. (The title story had first appeared in 1868.) Harte's region was the Far West. So hungry were other

Americans to learn about this new territory that the *Atlantic Monthly* magazine offered Harte the unheard-of sum of $10,000 for twelve short contributions. Only a handful of Harte's stories are read today, and even those few are sometimes criticized as being melodramatic. But in his own time he could barely keep up with the demand for his work.

Shortly after Harte's early success, Edward Eggleston published *The Hoosier School-Master* (1871), a local-color novel dealing with Decatur County, Indiana. It was an immediate best-seller and remained a minor classic for a generation. Although Eggleston is little read today, he influenced many later Midwestern realists, such as Hamlin Garland, Theodore Dreiser, and Willa Cather.

In the South the best-known regionalists were George Washington Cable, who wrote tales of life among the Creoles of Louisiana; the Georgian, Joel Chandler Harris, who created the famous Uncle Remus stories; and Thomas Nelson Page, who colored Virginia in magnolias and moonlight.

Two female writers were the best-known regionalists of the Northeast: Sarah Orne Jewett and Mary Wilkins Freeman. The former celebrated Maine in many stories and in *The Country of the Pointed Firs* (1896), which is considered the best regional work of the nineteenth century. Ms. Freeman wrote short stories about rural Massachusetts, some of which have survived into our own time.

Although some regional writing—especially in the seventies—was romantic in the sense that its authors tended to idealize their pictures, the movement as a whole has been described as fundamentally realistic. These writers strove to write dialogue that sounded the way persons actually spoke; they generally described places with great fidelity of detail; and they were basically interested in portraying and analyzing ordinary people and ordinary events. That is exactly what the dean of nineteenth-century realists, Mr. Howells, thought good writing should do.

THE MAJOR REALISTS

The major realistic writers whose important work was published in the nineteenth century were Mark Twain, William Dean Howells, Henry James, Hamlin Garland, Ambrose Bierce, and Stephen Crane. Since the first and last of these are discussed in detail elsewhere, we will focus here on the middle four.

The novelist and critic, William Dean Howells, was the main exponent of American realism; indeed, he has been called "in himself almost an entire literary movement." He assumed this position partly because he held influential positions on two of the major literary magazines of the time—first the *Atlantic Monthly* and then *Harper's*. He also knew and aided virtually every major American writer of his time.

Howells vigorously defended realism as "the truthful treatment of material." And for that material he wanted the writer to use what he called "poor Real Life." He felt that men and women should be portrayed as they actually were, even in their "habitual modes of vacancy and tiresomeness," in their "unaffected dullness."

A believer in democracy and the common people could hardly quarrel with Howells's basic impulses, but his own novels show that he had a narrow view of what real life was. Writing about "the more smiling aspects of life" because they were "the more American," he placed himself in what has been called the "genteel tradition"; and he became the target of hard-nosed realists like Ambrose Bierce, who called him "Miss Nancy Howells." Whatever we may think of his own work, however (*The Rise of Silas Lapham* [1885] is just about the only novel of his that is still read), no American did more to encourage realistic writing in the United States.

An artist who remained within the genteel tradition and yet made an enduring name for himself on two continents was Henry James. An early psychological novelist, James was most interested in what people thought and felt; and he portrayed those thoughts and feelings with a subtlety, an insightfulness, and a scrupulous honesty that has not been surpassed. James's main themes deal with what Europe does to Americans or the reverse, and this fact along with his high degree of sophistication, and his absorption with problems of technique probably precludes his ever becoming a novelist of the popular press.

Howells's realism was too tame for the Midwesterner, Hamlin Garland, who used the term *veritism* to denote a realism that would deal with the unpleasant as well as the pleasant facts of life. His early stories emphasize the poverty and hopelessness of farm life. We may see a nice contrast between realism and romanticism in Garland's insistence that environment, rather than some innate depravity or "power of blackness," is at the root of human misery.

Ambrose Bierce provides us with another excellent contrast between realism and romanticism when we compare him with Poe, for his stories are very much like Poe's in theme and structure. The difference between them lies in the fact that Bierce's settings and the motivations of his characters are far more realistic than those of Poe.

POETS OF THE PERIOD

Walt Whitman published poetry throughout this period, and Emily Dickinson's poems were first published in 1890, but we have discussed both elsewhere. Apart from them, two Southern poets —Henry Timrod and Sidney Lanier—have survived into our time with solid reputations. Timrod wrote some excellent war poems and might have developed into one of our best poets, but he died very young.

Lanier likewise died before his fortieth year. He nevertheless became the most famous of the post-war Southern poets and is still remembered for masterful musical performances such as "The Marshes of Glynn" and "The Symphony."

Several other poets of the time are remembered for special reasons. James Whitcomb Riley wrote poems in the dialect of the Indiana country and was a national favorite for a long period of time. Perhaps his most famous poem is "When the Frost Is on the Punkin." Eugene Field was best known as a newspaper humorist in his time, but in our time he is remembered as the author of such childhood poems as "Wynken, Blynken, and Nod" and "Little Boy Blue." Finally, we must mention a black writer, Paul Laurence Dunbar, who earned a national reputation in 1896 at the age of 22. Dunbar is best known today for his poems, but he also published several collections of short stories and four novels during his very short life.

LITERARY FIGURES

1829–1867	Henry Timrod	1848–1908	Joel Chandler Harris
1835–1910	Mark Twain	1849–1909	Sarah Orne Jewett
1836–1902	Bret Harte	1849–1916	James Whitcomb Riley
1837–1902	Edward Eggleston	1850–1895	Eugene Field
1837–1920	William Dean Howells	1852–1930	Mary Wilkins Freeman
1838–c. 1914	Ambrose Bierce	1853–1922	Thomas Nelson Page
1842–1881	Sidney Lanier	1860–1940	Hamlin Garland
1843–1916	Henry James	1871–1900	Stephen Crane
1844–1925	George Washington Cable	1872–1906	Paul Laurence Dunbar

1866 **Time Line** 1899

Historical Events	Literary Events

1860

1866 John Greenleaf Whittier, *Snowbound*

1867 Alaskan purchase

1868 Louisa May Alcott, *Little Women*

1869 Transcontinental railroad completed

1869 Mark Twain, *The Innocents Abroad*

1870

1870 Fifteenth Amendment ratified

1870 Bret Harte, *The Luck of Roaring Camp and Other Stories*

1871 Edward Eggleston, *The Hoosier School-Master*

1872 Twain, *Roughing It*

1873 Henry Timrod, *Collected Poems*

1876 Invention of the telephone

1876 Sidney Lanier, *Poems*
Twain, *The Adventures of Tom Sawyer*

1877 Invention of the phonograph

1877 Henry James, *The American*

1879 Invention of the incandescent light

1879 George Washington Cable, *Old Creole Days*

1880

1880 Joel Chandler Harris, *Uncle Remus*

1881 James, *Portrait of a Lady*

1883 James Whitcomb Riley, *The Ole Swimmin' Hole*
Twain, *Life on the Mississippi*

1884 Twain, *The Adventures of Huckleberry Finn*

1885 William Dean Howells, *The Rise of Silas Lapham*

1887 Thomas Nelson Page, *In Ole Virginia*

1888 Department of Labor established

1889 Department of Agriculture established

1890

1890 Emily Dickinson, *Poems*

1891 Ambrose Bierce, *In the Midst of Life*
Mary Wilkins Freeman, *A New England Nun*
Hamlin Garland, *Main-Travelled Roads*

1892 Walt Whitman, *Leaves of Grass* (final edition)

1893 First automobile

1893 Bierce, *Can Such Things Be?*
Stephen Crane, *Maggie: A Girl of the Streets*

1895 Crane, *The Red Badge of Courage*

1896 First motion picture
Invention of the wireless telegraph

1896 Paul Laurence Dunbar, *Lyrics of a Lowly Life*
Sarah Orne Jewett, *The Country of the Pointed Firs*

1898 Spanish-American War

MARK TWAIN

SAMUEL LANGHORNE CLEMENS

1835-1910

Courtesy of the Chicago Historical Society.

The evolution of Sam Clemens of Hannibal, Missouri, into Mark Twain, the internationally known literary artist, was a gradual process and, in some respects, accidental. When Clemens at the age of fourteen went to work as an apprentice to the publisher of the *Missouri Courier,* he had little thought of a career; his father had died and the sons had no choice but to support the family. Yet many years later Clemens wrote: "I became a printer and began to add one link after another to the chain which was to lead me into the literary profession." These "links" took him from Missouri to the East, then to Nevada and California, to Hawaii, to Europe, back to Buffalo, to Hartford, nine more years in Europe, and finally two lonely years in Redding, Connecticut—a crowded, busy, boisterous lifetime that brought him riches and fame. When Oxford University granted him an honorary degree in 1907, no one, looking back at his achievement, could have been more surprised than Sam Clemens himself at the distance he had come from that Mississippi River town.

Before personal unhappiness and financial disaster robbed Twain of his youthful enthusiasm, he produced two novels which alone would have made him a classic in American literature. They are built on the loose frame of his autobiographical volumes: a disjointed plot sprinkled with tall tales, extravagant excursions, sharp satire, and moral instruction. The Adventures of Tom Sawyer captured the imagination of most of America when it appeared in 1876. The Adventures of Huckleberry Finn, published in 1884, has become quite literally a world favorite.

Hannibal in the 1830s was a paradise for a young boy. "I can call back the solemn twilight and mystery of the deep woods, the earthy smells, the faint odors of the wild flowers, the sheen of rain-washed foliage," he wrote in his *Autobiography*. Nor did the hectic life on the waterfront ever quite leave his memory. It infected him with restlessness and the sweet smell of romantic journeys. At the age of seventeen, Sam left his brother's newspaper to discover for himself what the world had to offer. As a journeyman printer he wandered along the East coast and through the Middle West, never in want of work, occasionally contributing letters and humorous sketches to various papers, signing them "Grumbler" or "Rumbler" or "Thomas Jefferson Snodgrass."

After reading travel books on South America, he set out for the Amazon and the Orinoco. But once again the great Mississippi entered his life. On the boat to New Orleans he met Horace Bixby, the river pilot, and in a short time the young Sam Clemens was apprenticed to him as a "cub," eager to "learn the river" and eventually to earn his own exalted place on a magnificent steamboat. "After a year and a half of hard study," he recalled later, "the United States Inspectors rigorously examined me through a couple of long sittings and decided that I knew every inch of the Mississippi—thirteen hundred miles in the dark and in the day." For three years Clemens was a licensed pilot, watching more closely than perhaps he realized the motley crowds aboard—gamblers, prospectors, Southern planters, slave traders, harlots. His ear for local speech and his eye for melodramatic detail were given the best training they could have had.

But like the rest of America he was on the move. His brother Orion had been appointed Secretary to the Territory of Nevada and urged Sam to join him there. After a few weeks of Civil War service as a hopelessly bad Confederate soldier, Clemens turned westward, as prospector and miner. The lure of sudden wealth in the Nevada mountains was irresistible. Within a year he was back in Virginia City

as a reporter on the *Territorial Enterprise,* wiser but no richer. Now twenty-five, he realized he was happier in journalism than anywhere else, and his talent for writing humorous and satiric sketches had a chance to bloom. Sam Clemens signed his contributions with the pseudonym Mark Twain, a name he said he stole from a Captain Isaiah Sellers who used to write for the New Orleans *Picayune* and who had recently died. More likely it was a recollection from his river days, since "mark twain" was the leadsman's call telling the pilot that his ship was in two fathoms of water and therefore safe. As Mark Twain, Sam Clemens began a third and wildly successful career, but in 1862 he was still not a literary artist nor trying to be.

From Virginia City to San Francisco to Sacramento as journalist, and then to the Sandwich Islands (now called Hawaii) as travel correspondent, the talented Mark Twain was gaining a reputation as one of the wittiest writers on the West coast. He had always been a natural storyteller, a performer who genuinely enjoyed entertaining an audience with tall tales and whimsical anecdotes. It was natural for him to try the lecture platform after his travels to Hawaii. His success was instantaneous. He gave his first lecture in San Francisco at the age of thirty and continued to delight audiences all over the world well past his seventieth year, earning as much as $1,600 in one night. Before he left for the East, Mark Twain was hailed as "The Humorist of the Pacific Slope," a reputation built in part on his newspaper column but chiefly on his hilarious public lectures. One printed story, however, preceded him in the East and prepared the way for his arrival. Artemus Ward had persuaded him to write a tale about a jumping frog which Twain had heard in an Angel Camp tavern in Calaveras County. The New York *Saturday Press* published "The Celebrated Jumping Frog" in 1865; it was the beginning of literary fame, though Twain refused to call it that. He was, he said, a successful lecturer at best, a roving journalist at worst.

This roving spirit next took him eastward, to New York and Europe. He boarded the *Quaker City* in 1867 for a five-month tour of France, Italy, and the Holy Land. To meet expenses he accepted a commission to write letters periodically to the *Alta California* and the New York *Tribune*. In them Twain poured out a seemingly endless series of critical opinions based on American superiority to all things European. He knew well how to entertain the American reader. French manners, Italian guides, Greek ruins, Near Eastern monuments struck him as equally ridiculous. On his return he was besieged with offers. "I have 18 invitations to lecture, at $100 each, in various parts of the Union," he wrote his mother. "Have declined them all. I am for business now. Belong on the *Tribune* staff, and shall write occasionally." Business, little did he know at the time, meant literature, not journalism. New York publishers insisted the *Quaker City* letters cried out for republication, and they offered Twain an irresistible contract. "I had made my mind up to *one* thing," he told his friends. "I wasn't going to touch a book unless there was *money* in it, and a good deal of it. I told them so." Money there was; too much of it. *The Innocents Abroad* appeared in 1869, an immediate bestseller. Twain had been persuaded, moreover, to edit his letters, to rewrite some and destroy others. What began as journalism was soon shaped into literature. His newest career was launched.

To make money making people laugh, however, struck some of Twain's friends as an "unliterary" ambition, so he continued to call his work journalism. He bought a third interest in the Buffalo *Express* and married Olivia Langdon on the strength of *The Innocents Abroad* sales, hoping to settle down to a more sedate domestic life and to contribute nothing more than occasional satiric letters or humorous sketches to New York papers. Then he moved his family to Hartford, Connecticut. Harriet Beecher Stowe, of *Uncle Tom's Cabin* fame, was a near neighbor; William Dean Howells, editor of the *Atlantic Monthly*, became an inti-

mate friend, as did the Reverend Joseph Twichell of Hartford. Twain was surrounded by helpful critics. Howells asked for contributions to his magazine and Twain wrote him: "Twichell and I have had a long walk in the woods and I got to telling him about old Mississippi days of steamboating glory and grandeur as I saw them (during 5 years) from the pilot-house. He said 'What a virgin subject to hurl into a magazine!' I hadn't thought of that before. Would you like a series of papers to run . . . about 4 months, say?" Howells knew where Twain's strength lay and he urged him to begin his reminiscences. The appearance of these papers in the *Atlantic Monthly* in 1875 brought such instant praise and so many demands for more of his vivid prose that Twain was ready to admit that he had become a literary figure, almost against his will. The West had nourished the ambitious Sam Clemens. Mark Twain the artist was born in New England.

A newspaper friend of Twain's drew this
impression of the 1865 San Francisco earthquake.
It was one of Mark Twain's favorite drawings.

What of that West had he captured in his pages—its brash, overconfident youthfulness, its growing pains, its glorious abandon? His recipe for autobiographical writing smacks of the lawless frontier attitudes: "Start at no particular time of your life; wander at your free will all over your life; talk only about the thing which interests you for the moment; drop it the minute its interest threatens to pale, and turn your talk upon the new and more interesting thing that has intruded itself into your mind meantime." *Roughing It* (1872) was assembled in this way, a series of tall tales, brilliant descriptions, humorous anecdotes, and character studies, held together loosely by a first-person narrator, Twain himself. *Life on the Mississippi,* published ten years later, and his *Autobiography,* published after his death, continue the pattern. But reminiscence alone is not enough to make a great writer. Sam Clemens loved the Western brand of humor: the prac-

tical joke, the extravagant, improbable tale, the Native American legends, the coarse and ribald story. He not only preserved these for posterity but he also learned to preserve Western dialect speech, so easy to mimic on the lecture platform but so difficult to record. What is more, Twain as he matured let his satiric bent develop freely. *The Innocents Abroad* is full of healthy criticism of European culture. When he came to recall his early life in Missouri, Nevada, and California, he did not spare his native subjects: reckless speculators, brash politicians, brutal desperados, hypocritical ministers. He loved the life he lived in the West, but he could also look at it realistically. Indeed, by the time he died, in 1910, Twain had produced at least a half-dozen sharply satiric, even bitter, fictional studies of his society, beginning with *The Gilded Age* and ending with one of the most pessimistic stories written in the twentieth century, *The Mysterious Stranger.*

The reasons for this pessimism are numerous. Financial success came so easily that he squandered his money. The failure of the Paige typesetter and the bankruptcy of his publishing company sent him into enormous debt which only a grueling round-the-world lecture tour could erase. His daughter Susan died while he was living in England. A few years after his return, his wife died and then his daughter Jean. He faced the loneliness of old age with a firm conviction that "the damned human race" deserved all the misery it had brought on itself. No wonder that he could give one of his characters, Pudd'nhead Wilson, these black thoughts: "Whoever has lived long enough to find out what life is, knows how deep a debt of gratitude we owe to Adam, the first great benefactor of our age. He brought death into the world."

Before personal unhappiness and financial disaster robbed Twain of his youthful enthusiasm, however, he produced two novels which alone would have made him a classic in American literature. They are built on the loose frame of his autobiographical volumes: a disjointed plot sprinkled with tall tales, extravagant excursions, sharp satire, and moral instruction. *The Adventures of Tom Sawyer* captured the imagination of most of America when it appeared in 1876. *The Adventures of Huckleberry Finn,* published in 1884, has become quite literally a world favorite. They are children's books seemingly, melodramatic adventure stories told by a master storyteller. But beneath the surface lies more serious criticism of human foibles than some readers suspect. Twain had written plenty of social history and moral criticism. Now he tried to embody his feelings in imaginative characters, to shape a story around them, to disentangle his own life from Tom and Huck so that they could stand as free of their creator as Hamlet or Silas Marner. Twain did not wholly succeed; it is not difficult to trace characters and plot to specific incidents in Sam Clemens' life. But these parallels are unimportant. What is more essential is the universality Twain gives his story, the intense honesty with which he describes young boys growing into adulthood, the depth of feeling he is able to give to the moral crises all youths have to cope with sometime in their lives.

Tom Sawyer may well have been intended to entertain and to do little more. It entertains supremely well, being packed with midnight incantations, a cruel murder, blackmail, witchery, a court trial, and the expected happy ending. The mastermind is Tom himself, mischievous, clever, romantically imaginative. *Huckleberry Finn,* intended as a sequel, is infinitely more complex a story, and Twain almost abandoned the manuscript in despair several times during its creation. Huck's moral awareness is the heart of the novel, the center of the action. The greatest difficulty Twain faced was to untangle Huck and his friend Jim, the runaway slave, from a plot that threatened to swamp the hero and the story's moral at the same time. The plot suffers; some critics feel the ending is grotesquely mismanaged. But Huck emerges nevertheless a believable adolescent who is confronted by the moral decisions which test most of us. His decisions run counter to the society in which he lived and they were both a challenge to and a commentary on the values of that society.

Twain describes life on the raft in brutal contrast to life ashore. Huck is quick to see that each time he becomes entangled in "civilized" life in the riverbank towns he confronts violence or hypocrisy and has to flee to the raft and his friend Jim for safety. Twain lavishes his creative powers on the black, faithful Jim, the inherently good man who loves Huck no matter how the young boy treats him. In time, Huck comes to understand what friendship means, not through Sunday school texts but through the blunt realities of frontier life. And after his baptism on the river, he fears what civilized life can bring. "I reckon," he concludes, "I got to light out for the Territory ahead of the rest, because Aunt Sally she's going to adopt me and sivilize me, and I can't stand it. I been there before." Huck's cry is Sam Clemens' cry, for the freedom of childhood, for the romantic dream of the open road that somehow, in our growing up, has escaped us. It is our good fortune that a Mark Twain came into being to recollect that childhood.

This story is not original
with Twain. We are told that he first
heard it from a man named Ben Coon in a western
mining camp and that he probably read
Henry Leland's "Frogs Shot without Powder"
in the New York journal, *Spirit of the Times.*
But this version, at least, is his own,
particularly the leisurely way in which he moves
into the story and the manner in which he builds
suspense. When it appeared in the New York
Saturday Press on November 18, 1865,
Mark Twain's name became literary news.
Even so eminent a New Englander
as James Russell Lowell was ready to call it
"the finest piece of humorous literature
yet produced in America." With Bret Harte,
Twain became a spokesman for Western culture,
almost, one could say, against his will.
"The Jumping Frog" was, after all, only
a tall tale written down, oral history
now made "literary."

The Celebrated
Jumping Frog
of Calaveras County

In compliance with the request of a friend of mine who wrote me from the East, I called on good-natured, garrulous old Simon Wheeler and inquired after my friend's friend, Leonidas W. Smiley, as requested to do, and I hereunto append the result. I have a lurking suspicion that *Leonidas W.* Smiley is a myth, that my friend never knew such a personage, and that he only conjectured that if I asked old Wheeler

about him, it would remind him of his infamous *Jim* Smiley and he would go to work and bore me to death with some exasperating reminiscence of him as long and as tedious as it should be useless to me. If that was the design, it succeeded.

I found Simon Wheeler dozing comfortably by the barroom stove of the dilapidated tavern in the decayed mining camp of Angel's, and I noticed that he was fat and bald-headed and had an expression of winning gentleness and simplicity upon his tranquil countenance. He roused up and gave me good day. I told him that a friend of mine had commissioned me to make some inquiries about a cherished companion of his boyhood named *Leonidas W.* Smiley—*Rev. Leonidas W.* Smiley, a young minister of the Gospel, who he had heard was at one time a resident of Angel's Camp. I added that if Mr. Wheeler could tell me anything about this Rev. Leonidas W. Smiley, I would feel under many obligations to him.

Simon Wheeler backed me into a corner and blockaded me there with his chair, and then sat down and reeled off the monotonous narrative which follows this paragraph. He never smiled, he never frowned, he never changed his voice from the gentle-flowing key to which he tuned his initial sentence, he never betrayed the slightest suspicion of enthusiasm, but all through the interminable narrative there ran a vein of impressive earnestness and sincerity which showed me plainly that, so far from his imagining that there was anything ridiculous or funny about his story, he regarded it as a really important matter and admired its two heroes as men of transcendent genius in *finesse.*[1] I let him go on in his own way and never interrupted him once.

"Rev. Leonidas W. H'm, Reverend Le—— Well, there was a feller here once by the name of *Jim* Smiley, in the winter of '49—or maybe it was the spring of '50—I don't recollect exactly, somehow, though what makes me think it was one or the other is because I remember

From *In Defense of Harriet Shelley and Other Stories.* Reprinted with the permisison of Harper & Row, Publishers, Inc.

1. **finesse**\fĭ ▲nĕs\ clever maneuvering.

the big flume[2] warn't finished when he first come to the camp; but anyway, he was the curiousest man about always betting on anything that turned up you ever see, if he could get anybody to bet on the other side, and if he couldn't he'd change sides. Any way that suited the other man would suit *him*—any way just so's he got a bet, *he* was satisfied. But still he was lucky, uncommon lucky; he most always come out winner. He was always ready and laying for a chance; there couldn't be no solit'ry thing mentioned but that feller'd offer to bet on it and take ary side you please, as I was just telling you. If there was a horse-race, you'd find him flush or you'd find him busted at the end of it; if there was a dog-fight, he'd bet on it; if there was a cat-fight, he'd bet on it; if there was a chicken-fight, he'd bet on it; why, if there was two birds setting on a fence, he would bet you which one would fly first; or if there was a camp-meeting, he would be there reg'lar to bet on Parson Walker, which he judged to be the best exhorter about here, and so he was too, and a good man. If he even see a straddle-bug[3] start to go anywheres, he would bet you how long it would take him to get to—to wherever he was going to, and if you took him up, he would foller that straddle-bug to Mexico but what he would find out where he was bound for and how long he was on the road. Lots of the boys here has seen that Smiley and can tell you about him. Why, it never made no difference to *him*—he'd bet on *any* thing—the dangdest feller. Parson Walker's wife laid very sick once for a good while, and it seemed as if they warn't going to save her; but one morning he come in and Smiley up and asked him how she was, and he said she was considerable better—thank the Lord for his inf'nite mercy—and coming on so smart that with the blessing of Prov'dence she'd get well yet; and Smiley, before he thought, says, 'Well, I'll resk two-and-a-half she don't anyway.'

"Thish-yer Smiley had a mare—the boys called her the fifteen-minute nag but that was only in fun, you know, because of course she was faster than that—and he used to win money

on that horse, for all she was so slow and always had the asthma, or the distemper, or the consumption, or something of that kind. They used to give her two or three hundred yards' start and then pass her under way, but always at the fag end of the race she'd get excited and desperate like, and come cavorting and straddling up and scattering her legs around limber, sometimes in the air and sometimes out to one side among the fences, and kicking up m-o-r-e dust and raising m-o-r-e racket with her coughing and sneezing and blowing her nose—and *always* fetch up at the stand just about a neck ahead, as near as you could cipher[4] it down.

"And he had a little small bull-pup, that to look at him you'd think he warn't worth a cent but to set around and look ornery and lay for a chance to steal something. But as soon as money was up on him he was a different dog; his under-jaw'd begin to stick out like the fo'castle[5] of a steamboat and his teeth would uncover and shine like the furnaces. And a dog might tackle him and bully-rag[6] him, and bite him and throw him over his shoulder two or three times, and Andrew Jackson—which was the name of the pup—Andrew Jackson would never let on but what *he* was satisfied and hadn't expected nothing else—and the bets being doubled and doubled on the other side all the time, till the money was all up; and then all of a sudden he would grab that other dog jest by the j'int of his hind leg and freeze to it —not chaw, you understand, but only just grip and hang on till they throwed up the sponge, if it was a year. Smiley always come out winner on that pup till he harnessed a dog once that didn't have no hind legs, because they'd been sawed off in a circular saw, and when the thing had gone along far enough and the money was all up and he come to make a snatch for his pet holt, he see in a minute how he'd been imposed

---

2. **flume**\flūm\ channel for conveying water used for power, transportation, or irrigation.
3. **straddle-bug,** long-legged insect.
4. **cipher,** write.
5. **fo'castle** (forecastle)\fōk•səl\ upper deck of a ship.
6. **bully-rag,** to torment or harass.

Poster used by Mark Twain for a Brooklyn lecture, about 1869.

on and how the other dog had him in the door, so to speak, and he 'peared suprised, and then he looked sorter discouraged-like and didn't try no more to win the fight, and so he got shucked[7] out bad. He gave Smiley a look, as much as to say his heart was broke, and it was *his* fault for putting up a dog that hadn't no hind legs for him to take holt of, which was his main dependence in a fight, and then he limped off a piece and laid down and died. It was a good pup, was that Andrew Jackson, and would have made a name for hisself if he'd lived, for the stuff was in him and he had genius—I know it, because he hadn't no opportunities to speak of, and it don't stand to reason that a dog could make such a fight as he could under them circumstances if he hadn't no talent. It always makes me feel sorry when I think of that last fight of his'n and the way it turned out.

"Well, thish-yer Smiley had rat-tarriers, and chicken cocks, and tomcats and all them kind of things till you couldn't rest, and you couldn't fetch nothing for him to bet on but he'd match you. He ketched a frog one day and took him home, and said he cal'lated to educate him; and so he never done nothing for three months but set in his back yard and learn that frog to jump. And you bet you he *did* learn him, too. He'd give him a little punch behind, and the next minute you'd see that frog whirling in the air like a doughnut—see him turn one summerset, or maybe a couple if he got a good start, and come down flat-footed and all right, like a cat. He got him up so in the matter of ketching flies, and kep' him in practice so constant, that he'd nail a fly every time as fur as he could see him. Smiley said all a frog wanted was education and he could do 'most anything—and I believe him. Why, I've seen him set Dan'l Webster down here on this floor—Dan'l Webster was the name of the frog—and sing out, 'Flies, Dan'l, flies!' and quicker'n you could wink he'd spring straight up and snake a fly off'n the counter there, and flop down on the floor ag'in as solid as a gob of mud, and fall to scratching the side of his head with his hind foot as indifferent as if he hadn't no idea he'd been doin' any more'n any frog might do. You never see a frog so modest and straight-for'ard as he was, for all he was so gifted. And when it come to fair and square jumping on a dead level, he could get over more ground at one straddle than any animal of his breed you ever see. Jumping on a dead level was his strong suit, you understand; and when it come to that, Smiley would ante up money on him as long as he had a red. Smiley was monstrous proud of his frog, and well he might be for fellers that had traveled and been everywheres all said he laid over any frog that ever *they* see.

"Well, Smiley kep' the beast in a little lattice box, and he used to fetch him down-town sometimes and lay for a bet. One day a feller—a

---

7. **shucked**\shəkt\ stripped, cast off.

stranger in the camp, he was—come acrost him with his box and says:

" 'What might it be that you've got in the box?'

"And Smiley says, sorter indifferent-like, 'It might be a parrot, or it might be a canary, maybe, but it ain't—it's only just a frog.'

"And the feller took it and looked at it careful, and turned it round this way and that, and says, 'H'm—so 'tis. Well, what's *he* good for?'

" 'Well,' Smiley says, easy and careless, 'he's good enough for *one* thing, I should judge—he can outjump any frog in Calaveras County.'

"The feller took the box again and took another long, particular look, and give it back to Smiley and says, very deliberate, 'Well,' he says, 'I don't see no p'ints about that frog that's any better'n any other frog.'

" 'Maybe you don't,' Smiley says. 'Maybe you understand frogs and maybe you don't understand 'em; maybe you've had experience and maybe you ain't only a amature, as it were. Anyways, I've got *my* opinion, and I'll resk forty dollars that he can outjump any frog in Calaveras County.'

"And the feller studied a minute and then says, kinder sad-like, 'Well, I'm only a stranger here and I ain't got no frog; but if I had a frog, I'd bet you.'

"And then Smiley says, 'That's all right—that's all right—if you'll hold my box a minute, I'll go and get you a frog.' And so the feller took the box and put up his forty dollars along with Smiley's, and set down to wait.

"So he set there a good while thinking and thinking to himself, and then he got the frog out and prized his mouth open and took a teaspoon and filled him full of quail-shot—filled him pretty near up to his chin—and set him on the floor. Smiley he went to the swamp and slopped around in the mud for a long time, and finally he ketched a frog and fetched him in and give him to this feller, and says:

" 'Now, if you're ready, set him alongside of Dan'l, with his forepaws just even with Dan'l's, and I'll give the word.' Then he says, 'One—two—three—*git!*' and him and the feller

touched up the frogs from behind, and the new frog hopped off lively, but Dan'l give a heave and hysted up his shoulders—so—like a Frenchman, but it warn't no use—he couldn't budge; he was planted as solid as a church, and he couldn't no more stir than if he was anchored out. Smiley was a good deal surprised, and he was disgusted too, but he didn't have no idea what the matter was, of course.

"The feller took the money and started away, and when he was going out at the door, he sorter jerked his thumb over his shoulder—so—at Dan'l and says again, very deliberate, 'Well,' he says, '*I* don't see no p'ints about that frog that's any better'n any other frog.'

"Smiley he stood scratching his head and looking down at Dan'l a long time, and at last he says, 'I do wonder what in the nation that frog throw'd off for—I wonder if there ain't something the matter with him—he 'pears to look mighty baggy, somehow.' And he ketched Dan'l by the nap of the neck and hefted him, and says, 'Why, blame my cats if he don't weigh five pound!' and turned him upside down and he belched out a double handful of shot. And then he see how it was, and he was the maddest man—he set the frog down and took out after that feller, but he never ketched him. And—"

[Here Simon Wheeler heard his name called from the front yard and got up to see what was wanted.] And turning to me as he moved away, he said: "Just set where you are, stranger, and rest easy—I ain't going to be gone a second."

But, by your leave, I did not think that a continuation of the history of the enterprising vagabond *Jim* Smiley would be likely to afford me much information concerning the Rev. *Leonidas W.* Smiley and so I started away.

At the door I met the sociable Wheeler returning, and he buttonholed me and recommenced:

"Well, thish-yer Smiley had a yaller one-eyed cow that didn't have no tail, only just a short stump like a bannanner, and—"

However, lacking both time and inclination, I did not wait to hear about the afflicted cow but took my leave.

Twain began his autobiography in 1897
and kept working on it from time to time
until his death in 1910. As one would expect,
the manuscript he left was a grab bag
of reminiscences, portraits of friends, business
ventures, visits to Europe, his uncle's farm,
and much else, written in Vienna and Florence
and several American cities. In 1924,
Albert Bigelow Paine published about half
of the surviving pages, calling it *Mark Twain's
Autobiography.* In 1940, Bernard De Voto used
about half of the remainder to publish what is
really a third volume of the autobiography,
though he calls it *Mark Twain in Eruption.*
Finally, Charles Neider put the unwieldy
manuscript into proper sequence and published,
in 1959, *The Autobiography of Mark Twain:
Including Chapters Now Published for the First
Time.* Chapter 30 of this edition recalls a visit
Twain made in 1867 to Washington, immediately
after his return from Europe on the *Quaker City.*
The book he refers to in the first sentence
is *The Innocents Abroad.*

I Sell a Dog

I was out of money and I went down to Washington to see if I could earn enough there to keep me in bread and butter while I should write the book. I came across William Swinton, brother of the historian, and together we invented a scheme for our mutual sustenance; we became the fathers and originators of what is a common feature in the newspaper world now, the syndicate. We became the old original first Newspaper Syndicate on the planet; it was on a small scale but that is usual with untried new enterprises. We had twelve journals on our list; they were all weeklies, all obscure and poor and all scattered far away among the back settlements. It was a proud thing for those little newspapers to have a Washington correspondent and a fortunate thing for us that they felt in that way about it. Each of the twelve took two letters a week from us, at a dollar per letter; each of us wrote one letter per week and sent off six duplicates of it to these benefactors, thus acquiring twenty-four dollars a week to live on, which was all we needed in our cheap and humble quarters.

Swinton was one of the dearest and loveliest human beings I have ever known, and we led a charmed existence together, in a contentment which knew no bounds. Swinton was refined by nature and breeding; he was a gentle man by nature and breeding; he was highly educated; he was of a beautiful spirit; he was pure in heart and speech. He was a Scotchman and a Presbyterian; a Presbyterian of the old and genuine school, being honest and sincere in his religion and loving it and finding serenity and peace in it. He hadn't a vice, unless a large and grateful sympathy with Scotch whiskey may be called by that name. I didn't regard it as a vice, because he was a Scotchman, and Scotch whiskey to a Scotchman is as innocent as milk is to the rest of the human race. In Swinton's case it was a virtue and not an economical one. Twenty-four dollars a week would really have been riches to us if we hadn't had to support that jug; because of the jug we were always sailing pretty close to the wind, and any tardiness in the arrival of any part of our income was sure to cause some inconvenience.

I remember a time when a shortage occurred; we had to have three dollars and we had to have it before the close of the day. I don't know now how we happened to want all that money at one time; I only know we had to have it. Swinton told me to go out and find it and he said he would also go out and see what he could do. He didn't seem to have any doubt that we would succeed but I knew that that was his religion working in him; I hadn't the same confidence; I hadn't any idea where to

From *The Autobiography of Mark Twain,* edited by Charles Neider. Copyright 1959 by The Mark Twain Company. Reprinted by permission of Harper & Row, Publishers, Inc.

turn to raise all that bullion and I said so. I think he was ashamed of me, privately, because of my weak faith. He told me to give myself no uneasiness, no concern; and said in a simple, confident, and unquestioning way, "The Lord will provide." I saw that he fully believed the Lord would provide but it seemed to me that if he had had my experience—But never mind that; before he was done with me his strong faith had had its influence and I went forth from the place almost convinced that the Lord really would provide.

I wandered around the streets for an hour, trying to think up some way to get that money, but nothing suggested itself. At last I lounged into the big lobby of the Ebbitt House, which was then a new hotel, and sat down. Presently a dog came loafing along. He paused, glanced up at me and said with his eyes, "Are you friendly?" I answered with my eyes that I was. He gave his tail a grateful wag and came forward and rested his jaw on my knee and lifted his brown eyes to my face in a winningly affectionate way. He was a lovely creature, as beautiful as a girl, and he was made all of silk and velvet. I stroked his smooth brown head and fondled his drooping ears and we were a pair of lovers right away. Pretty soon Brig.-Gen. Miles, the hero of the land, came strolling by in his blue and gold splendors, with everybody's admiring gaze upon him. He saw the dog and stopped, and there was a light in his eye which showed that he had a warm place in his heart for dogs like this gracious creature; then he came forward and patted the dog and said,

"He is very fine—he is a wonder; would you sell him?"

I was greatly moved; it seemed a marvelous thing to me, the way Swinton's prediction had come true.

I said, "Yes."

The General said, "What do you ask for him?"

"Three dollars."

The General was manifestly surprised. He said, "Three dollars? Only three dollars? Why that dog is a most uncommon dog; he can't possibly be worth less than fifty. If he were mine, I wouldn't take a hundred for him. I'm afraid you are not aware of his value. Reconsider your price if you like, I don't wish to wrong you."

But if he had known me he would have known that I was no more capable of wronging him that he was of wronging me. I responded with the same quiet decision as before.

"No, three dollars. That is his price."

"Very well, since you insist upon it," said the General, and he gave me three dollars and led the dog away and disappeared upstairs.

In about ten minutes a gentle-faced, middle-aged gentleman came along and began to look around here and there and under tables and everywhere, and I said to him, "Is it a dog you are looking for?"

His face had been sad before and troubled; but it lit up gladly now and he answered, "Yes —have you seen him?"

"Yes," I said, "he was here a minute ago and I saw him follow a gentleman away. I think I could find him for you if you would like me to try."

I have seldom seen a person look so grateful, and there was gratitude in his voice too when he conceded that he would like me to try. I said I would do it with great pleasure but that as it might take a little time I hoped he would not mind paying me something for my trouble. He said he would do it most gladly—repeating that phrase "most gladly"—and asked me how much.

I said, "Three dollars."

He looked surprised, and said, "Dear me, it is nothing! I will pay you ten, quite willingly."

But I said, "No, three is the price," and I started for the stairs without waiting for any further argument, for Swinton had said that that was the amount that the Lord would provide and it seemed to me that it would be sacrilegious to take a penny more than was promised.

I got the number of the General's room from the office clerk as I passed by his wicket, and when I reached the room I found the General there caressing his dog and quite happy. I said, "I am sorry, but I have to take the dog again."

He seemed very much surprised and said, "Take him again? Why, he is my dog; you sold him to me and at your own price."

"Yes," I said, "it is true—but I have to have him, because the man wants him again."

"What man?"

"The man that owns him; he wasn't my dog."

The General looked even more surprised than before, and for a moment he couldn't seem to find his voice; then he said, "Do you mean to tell me that you were selling another man's dog—and knew it?"

"Yes, I knew it wasn't my dog."

"Then why did you sell him?"

I said, "Well, that is a curious question to ask. I sold him because you wanted him. You offered to buy the dog; you can't deny that. I was not anxious to sell him—I had not even thought of selling him—but it seemed to me that if it could be any accommodation to you—"

He broke me off in the middle, and said, "*Accommodation* to me? It is the most extraordinary spirit of accommodation I have ever heard of—the idea of your selling a dog that didn't belong to you—"

I broke him off there and said, "There is no relevance about this kind of argument; you said yourself that the dog was probably worth a hundred dollars. I only asked you three; was there anything unfair about that? You offered to pay more, you know you did. I only asked you three; you can't deny it."

"Oh, what in the world has that to do with it! The crux of the matter is that you didn't own the dog—can't you see that? You seem to think that there is no impropriety in selling property that isn't yours provided you sell it cheap. Now then—"

I said, "Please don't argue about it any more. You can't get around the fact that the price was perfectly fair, perfectly reasonable—considering that I didn't own the dog—and so arguing about it is only a waste of words. I have to have him back again because the man wants him;

don't you see that I haven't any choice in the matter? Put yourself in my place. Suppose you had sold a dog that didn't belong to you; suppose you—"

"Oh," he said, "don't muddle my brains any more with your idiotic reasoning! Take him along and give me a rest."

So I paid back the three dollars and led the dog downstairs and passed him over to his owner and collected three for my trouble.

I went away then with a good conscience, because I had acted honorably; I never could have used the three that I sold the dog for, because it was not rightly my own, but the three I got for restoring him to his rightful owner was righteously and properly mine, because I had earned it. That man might never have gotten that dog back at all, if it hadn't been for me. My principles have remained to this day what they were then. I was always honest; I know I can never be otherwise. It is as I said in the beginning—I was never able to persuade myself to use money which I had acquired in questionable ways.

Now then, that is the tale. Some of it is true.

I
THE ART OF FINESSE

Simon Wheeler admires the two heroes of the "Jumping Frog" tale as "men of transcendent genius in *finesse*." We may perhaps not agree that they deserve to be called "transcendent geniuses," but we can agree that each is engaged in the art of trying to outsmart the other. What Twain called *finesse*, we today might call "one-upmanship."

In the passage from *Autobiography*, we see that Twain himself was a master of the art of finesse.

II
IMPLICATIONS

Discuss the following statements.

1. Twain's heroes of the art of finesse have much in common with the Yankee peddler, as seen in O. Henry's "Jeff Peters as a Personal Magnet."

2. Finesse is most entertaining and humorous when it is practiced against persons like Jim Smiley and Brig.-Gen. Miles.

This excerpt from the first volume
of Twain's first best-seller can hardly do
more than suggest the pleasures he and his
friends derived from playing the "innocents"
across Europe and in the Near East. Twain was
ready, in his breezy Western manner,
to criticize everything from his fellow
passengers and the sights of Europe to the food,
the lodging, and the guides. Especially
the guides. He and the doctor baited them
cruelly, calling all of them Ferguson
because they could not remember their names.
The enthusiasm of the Italian guides for their
country's landmarks lent itself easily
to Twain's broad humor.

FROM

The Innocents Abroad

In this place I may as well jot down a chapter concerning those necessary nuisances, European guides. Many a man has wished in his heart he could do without his guide; but knowing he could not, has wished he could get some amusement out of him as a remuneration for the affliction of his society. We accomplished this latter matter, and if our experience can be made useful to others they are welcome to it.

Guides know about enough English to tangle everything up so that a man can make neither head nor tail of it. They know their story by heart—the history of every statue, painting, cathedral, or other wonder they show you. They know it and tell it as a parrot would—and if you interrupt, and throw them off the track, they have to go back and begin over again. All their lives long, they are employed in show-ing strange things to foreigners and listening to their bursts of admiration. It is human nature to take delight in exciting admiration. It is what prompts children to say "smart" things, and do absurd ones, and in other ways "show off" when company is present. It is what makes gossips turn out in rain and storm to go and be the first to tell a startling bit of news. Think, then, what a passion it becomes with a guide, whose privilege it is, every day, to show to strangers wonders that throw them into perfect ecstasies of admiration! He gets so that he could not by any possibility live in a soberer atmosphere. After we discovered this, we *never* went into ecstasies any more—we never admired anything—we never showed any but impassible faces and stupid indifference in the presence of the sublimest wonders a guide had to display. We had found their weak point. We have made good use of it ever since. We have made some of those people savage, at times, but we have never lost our own serenity.

The doctor asks the questions, generally, because he can keep his countenance, and look more like an inspired idiot, and throw more imbecility into the tone of his voice than any man that lives. It comes natural to him.

The guides in Genoa are delighted to secure an American party, because Americans so much wonder, and deal so much in sentiment and emotion before any relic of Columbus. Our guide there fidgeted about as if he had swallowed a spring mattress. He was full of animation—full of impatience. He said:

"Come wis me, genteelmen!—come! I show you ze letterwriting by Christopher Colombo! —write it himself!—write it wis his own hand! —come!"

He took us to the municipal palace. After much impressive fumbling of keys and opening of locks, the stained and aged document was spread before us. The guide's eyes sparkled. He danced about us and tapped the parchment with his finger:

"What I tell you, genteelmen! Is it not so? See! handwriting Christopher Colombo!— write it himself!"

From *The Innocents Abroad*, Vol. I. Reprinted with the permission of Harper & Row, Publishers, Inc.

We looked indifferent—unconcerned. The doctor examined the document very deliberately, during a painful pause. Then he said, without any show of interest:

"Ah—Ferguson—what—what did you say was the name of the party who wrote this?"

"Christopher Colombo! ze great Christopher Colombo!"

Another deliberate examination.

"Ah—did he write it himself, or—or how?"

"He write it himself!—Christopher Colombo! he's own handwriting, write by himself!"

Then the doctor laid the document down and said:

"Why, I have seen boys in America only fourteen years old that could write better than that."

"But zis is ze great Christo—"

"I don't care who it is! It's the worst writing I ever saw. Now you mustn't think you can impose on us because we are strangers. We are not fools, by a good deal. If you have got any specimens of penmanship of real merit, trot them out!—and if you haven't, drive on!"

We drove on. The guide was considerably shaken up, but he made one more venture. He had something which he thought would overcome us. He said:

"Ah, genteelmen, you come wis me! I show you beautiful, oh, magnificent bust Christopher Colombo!—splendid, grand, magnificent!"

He brought us before the beautiful bust—for it *was* beautiful—and sprang back and struck an attitude:

"Ah, look, genteelmen!—beautiful, grand,—bust Christopher Colombo!—beautiful bust, beautiful pedestal!"

The doctor put up his eyeglass—procured for such occasions:

"Ah—what did you say this gentleman's name was?"

"Christopher Colombo!—ze great Christopher Colombo!"

"'Christopher Colombo! ze great Christopher Colombo!' Well, what did *he* do?"

"Discover America!—discover America, oh, ze devil!"

"Discover America. No—that statement will hardly wash. We are just from America ourselves. We heard nothing about it. Christopher Colombo—pleasant name—is—is he dead?"

"Oh, *corpo di Baccho!*[1]—three hundred years!"

"What did he die of?"

"I do not know!—I cannot tell."

"Smallpox, think?"

"I do not know, genteelmen!—I do not know *what* he die of!"

"Measles, likely?"

"Maybe—maybe—I do *not* know—I think he die of somethings."

"Parents living?"

"Im-posseeble!"

"Ah—which is the bust and which is the pedestal?"

"Santa Maria!—zis ze bust!—zis ze pedestal!"

"Ah, I see, I see—happy combination—very happy combination, indeed. Is—is this the first time this gentleman was ever on a bust?"

That joke was lost on the foreigner—guides cannot master the subtleties of the American joke.

We have made it interesting for this Roman guide. Yesterday we spent three or four hours in the Vatican again, that wonderful world of curiosities. We came very near expressing interest, sometimes—even admiration—it was very hard to keep from it. We succeeded though. Nobody else ever did, in the Vatican museums. The guide was bewildered—nonplussed. He walked his legs off, nearly, hunting up extraordinary things, and exhausted all his ingenuity on us, but it was a failure; we never showed any interest in anything. He had reserved what he considered to be his greatest wonder till the last—a royal Egyptian mummy, the best-preserved in the world, perhaps. He took us there. He felt so sure, this time, that some of his old enthusiasm came back to him:

---

1. **corpo di Baccho**\ᴧkor·pō dē ᴧbak·kō\ mild curse, lit. body of Bacchus, mythical god of wine and revelry.

"See, genteelmen!—Mummy! Mummy!"

The eyeglasses came up as calmly, as deliberately as ever.

"Ah,—Ferguson—what did I understand you to say the gentleman's name was?"

"Name?—he got no name!—Mummy!—'Gyptian mummy!"

"Yes, yes. Born here?"

"No! 'Gyptian mummy!"

"Ah, just so. Frenchman, I presume?"

"No!—*not* Frenchman, not Roman!—born in Egypta!"

"Born in Egypta. Never heard of Egypta before. Foreign locality, likely. Mummy—mummy. How calm he is—how self-possessed. Is, ah—is he dead?"

"Oh, *sacré bleu,*[2] been dead three thousan' year!"

The doctor turned on him savagely:

"Here, now, what do you mean by such conduct as this? Playing us for Chinamen because we are strangers and trying to learn! Trying to impose your vile second-hand carcasses on *us!* —thunder and lightning, I've a notion to—to— if you've got a nice *fresh* corpse, fetch him out! —or, by George, we'll brain you!"

We make it exceedingly interesting for this Frenchman. However, he has paid us back, partly, without knowing it. He came to the hotel this morning to ask if we were up, and he endeavored as well as he could to describe us, so that the landlord would know which persons he meant. He finished with the casual remark that we were lunatics. The observation was so innocent and so honest that it amounted to a very good thing for a guide to say.

There is one remark (already mentioned) which never yet has failed to disgust these guides. We use it always, when we can think of nothing else to say. After they have exhausted their enthusiasm pointing out to us and praising the beauties of some ancient bronze image or broken-legged statue, we look at it stupidly and in silence for five, ten, fifteen minutes—as long as we can hold out, in fact— and then ask:

"Is—is he dead?"

That conquers the serenest of them. It is not what they are looking for—especially a new guide. Our Roman Ferguson is the most patient, unsuspecting, long-suffering subject we have had yet. We shall be sorry to part with him. We have enjoyed his society very much. We trust he has enjoyed ours, but we are harassed with doubts. . . .

---

2. **sacré bleu**\▲sa·krā 'blŭ\ literally "sacred blue," a reference to the Blessed Mother and hence a mild curse.

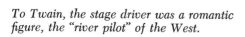

To Twain, the stage driver was a romantic figure, the "river pilot" of the West.

CALIFORNIA STAGE-DRIVER.

So slight a sketch as this
would hardly be worth reprinting
were it not so memorable an example
of the burlesque humor that delighted
Twain's newspaper audience in the 1860s.
On his way east, via Panama, he wrote
a series of letters for the San Francisco
Alta California; and in one of them
he incorporated this satire of the Little Rollo
books, stories about a boy named Rollo
devised by Jacob Abbott to teach honesty
and self-improvement. Twain loathed
the goody-goody characters in Abbott's work
and so tried, here, to turn the familiar
pattern upside down.

The Story of the Bad Little Boy Who Didn't Come to Grief

Once there was a bad little boy whose name was Jim—though, if you will notice, you will find that bad little boys are nearly always called James in your Sunday-school books. It was strange, but still it was true, that this one was called Jim.

He didn't have any sick mother, either—a sick mother who was pious and had the consumption, and would be glad to lie down in the grave and be at rest but for the strong love she bore her boy, and the anxiety she felt that the world might be harsh and cold toward him when she was gone. Most bad boys in the Sunday books are named James, and have sick mothers, who teach them to say, "Now, I lay me down," etc., and sing them to sleep with sweet, plaintive voices, and then kiss them good night, and kneel down by the bedside and weep. But it was different with this fellow. He was named Jim, and there wasn't anything the matter with his mother—no consumption, nor anything of that kind. She was stout rather than otherwise, and she was not pious; moreover, she was not anxious on Jim's account. She said if he were to break his neck it wouldn't be much loss. She always spanked Jim to sleep, and she never kissed him good night; on the contrary, she boxed his ears when she was ready to leave him.

Once this little bad boy stole the key of the pantry, and slipped in there and helped himself to some jam, and filled up the vessel with tar, so that his mother would never know the difference; but all at once a terrible feeling didn't come over him, and something didn't seem to whisper to him, "Is it right to disobey my mother? Isn't it sinful to do this? Where do bad little boys go who gobble up their kind good mother's jam?" and then he didn't kneel down all alone and promise never to be wicked any more, and rise up with a light, happy heart, and go and tell his mother all about it, and beg her forgiveness, and be blessed by her with tears of pride and thankfulness in her eyes. No; that is the way with all other bad boys in the books; but it happened otherwise with this Jim, strangely enough. He ate that jam, and said it was bully, in his sinful vulgar way; and he put in the tar, and said that was bully also, and laughed, and observed "that the old woman would get up and snort" when she found it out; and when she did find it out, he denied knowing anything about it, and she whipped him severely, and he did the crying himself. Everything about this boy was curious—everything turned out differently with him from the way it does to the bad Jameses in the books.

Once he climbed up in Farmer Acorn's apple tree to steal apples, and the limb didn't break,

Reprinted with the permission of Harper & Row, Publishers, Inc.

and he didn't fall and break his arm, and get torn by the farmer's great dog, and then languish on a sickbed for weeks, and repent and become good. Oh, no; he stole as many apples as he wanted and came down all right; and he was all ready for the dog, too, and knocked him endways with a brick when he came to tear him. It was very strange—nothing like it ever happened in those mild little books with marbled backs, and with pictures in them of men with swallow-tailed coats and bell-crowned hats, and pantaloons that are short in the legs, and women with the waists of their dresses under their arms, and no hoops on. Nothing like it in any of the Sunday-school books.

Once he stole the teacher's penknife, and, when he was afraid it would be found out and he would get whipped, he slipped it into George Wilson's cap—poor Widow Wilson's son, the moral boy, the good little boy of the village, who always obeyed his mother, and never told an untruth, and was fond of his lessons, and infatuated with Sunday-school. And when the knife dropped from the cap, and poor George hung his head and blushed, as if in conscious guilt, and the grieved teacher charged the theft upon him, and was just in the very act of bringing the switch down upon his trembling shoulders, a white-haired improbable justice of the peace did not suddenly appear in their midst, and strike an attitude and say, "Spare this noble boy—there stands the cowering culprit! I was passing the school at recess, and, unseen myself, I saw the theft committed!" And then Jim didn't get whaled, and the venerable justice didn't read the tearful school a homily, and take George by the hand and say such a boy deserved to be exalted, and then tell him to come and make his home with him, and sweep out the office, and make fires, and run errands, and chop wood, and study law, and help his wife do household labors, and have all the balance of the time to play, and get forty cents a month, and be happy. No; it would have happened that way in the books, but it didn't happen that way to Jim. No

meddling old clam of a justice dropped in to make trouble, and so the model boy got thrashed, and Jim was glad of it because, you know, Jim hated moral boys. Jim said he was "down on them milksops."[1] Such was the coarse language of this bad, neglected boy.

But the strangest thing that ever happened to Jim was the time he went boating on Sunday, and didn't get drowned, and that other time that he got caught out in the storm when he was fishing on Sunday, and didn't get struck by lightning. Why, you might look, and look, all through the Sunday-school books from now till next Christmas, and you would never come across anything like this. Oh, no; you would find that all the bad boys who get caught in storms when they are fishing on Sunday infallibly get struck by lightning. Boats with bad boys in them always upset on Sunday, and it always storms when bad boys go fishing on the Sabbath. How this Jim ever escaped is a mystery to me.

This Jim bore a charmed life—that must have been the way of it. Nothing could hurt him. He even gave the elephant in the menagerie a plug of tobacco, and the elephant didn't knock the top of his head off with his trunk. He browsed around the cupboard after essence of peppermint, and didn't make a mistake and drink *aqua fortis*.[2] He stole his father's gun and went hunting on the Sabbath, and didn't shoot three or four of his fingers off. He struck his little sister on the temple with his fist when he was angry, and she didn't linger in pain through long summer days, and die with sweet words of forgiveness upon her lips that redoubled the anguish of his breaking heart. No; she got over it. He ran off and went to sea at last, and didn't come back and find himself sad and alone in the world, his loved ones sleeping in the quiet churchyard, and the vine-embowered home of his boyhood tumbled down and gone to decay. Ah, no; he came home drunk

---

1. milksops, weaklings.
2. aqua fortis, literally "strong water"; a vile medicine or an acid.

as a piper, and got into the station-house the first thing.

And he grew up and married, and raised a large family, and brained them all with an ax one night, and got wealthy by all manner of cheating and rascality; and now he is the infernalest wickedest scoundrel in his native village, and is universally respected, and belongs to the legislature.

So you see there never was a bad James in the Sunday-school books that had such a streak of luck as this sinful Jim with the charmed life.

I
THE TASK OF THE SATIRIST

Certain classes of Americans in Twain's time thought that European products and institutions were greatly superior to their American counterparts; apparently most Americans of his time also loved to read about paragons of virtue, for Abbott's Rollo books (of which there were twenty-eight volumes!) had enormous circulations. Both in the admiration of the Rollo-type and in the adulation of things European, Twain saw something that was *uncritical* and *excessive* on the part of his fellow Americans. He felt it was his task as a satirist to cut such tendencies down to size. Of course, on another level Twain is directly criticizing certain aspects of Europe and good little boys, but his indirect criticism of Americans is equally if not more important.

II
IMPLICATIONS

Discuss the following propositions.

1. In both selections Twain adopts the values of the American pioneer as opposed to those of the cultured, metropolitan "Easterner."

2. There seems to be a natural human tendency to criticize those who carry things to excess, even if it is virtue that is excessive.

3. One of the chief functions of the satirist is to restore *balance* to our view of things.

4. A satire will strike readers as funny only if they share in the first place the same point of view as the author.

5. The danger of a satire like *The Innocents Abroad* is that it might lead to self-complacency on the part of Americans who shared Twain's point of view.

III
TECHNIQUES
Comedy and Sympathy and Detachment

The comedy in the four Twain selections you have just read might readily be called a comedy of irreverence; that is to say, Twain consistently cuts up things that many persons respect. Note, for example, that the names of the bull-pup and of the frog in "The Jumping Frog" are Andrew Jackson and Dan'l Webster, respectively. Similarly, at the end of the "Bad Little Boy" Jim "brains" his whole family with an ax. For most of Twain's readers, Jackson and Webster were revered men, and presumably most of his readers loved and respected their own spouses and children. What other venerated persons or things does Twain treat irreverently? How can such irreverence be funny?

In trying to answer the last question, consider carefully what you have learned from the previous unit regarding sympathy and detachment. Note whom you stand with in each of the four selections and how this affects your enjoyment.

321

Tom Sawyer and Huck Finn are,
without question, Twain's most famous
characters, and rightly so. They are the epitome
of youthful rebellion and lighthearted
independence, the kind of youth
Twain enjoyed in Hannibal. In *The Adventures
of Huckleberry Finn*, the main action is centered
on Huck's escape from his father's clutches
and the slave Jim's escape from his owner, Miss
Watson. Together they float down the Mississippi
on a raft, hoping to leave it at Cairo and take
a steamboat up the Ohio into free territory.
But one night the raft capsizes, and they
are separated. Huck swims ashore and, assuming
the name George Jackson, he seeks shelter
with a family called Grangerford who happen
to be feuding with their neighbors,
the Shepherdsons. The temporary separation
of Huck and Jim allows Twain to focus
on a second major element of the novel—
the social satire of the towns
and people along the river.

FROM

The Adventures
of Huckleberry Finn

CHAPTER XVII

In about half a minute somebody spoke out of a window, without putting his head out, and says:

"Be done, boys! Who's there?"

I says:

"It's me."

"Who's me?"

"George Jackson, sir."

Reprinted from *The Adventures of Huckleberry Finn*, by Mark Twain, with the permission of Harper & Row, Publishers, Inc.

"What do you want?"

"I don't want nothing, sir. I only want to go along by, but the dogs won't let me."

"What are you prowling around here this time of night, for—hey?"

"I warn't prowling around, sir; I fell overboard off of the steamboat."

"Oh, you did, did you? Strike a light there, somebody. What did you say your name was?"

"George Jackson, sir. I'm only a boy."

"Look here; if you're telling the truth, you needn't be afraid—nobody'll hurt you. But don't try to budge; stand right where you are. Rouse out Bob and Tom, some of you, and fetch the guns. George Jackson, is there anybody with you?"

"No, sir, nobody."

I heard the people stirring around in the house, now, and see a light. The man sung out:

"Snatch that light away, Betsy, you old fool—ain't you got any sense? Put it on the floor behind the front door. Bob, if you and Tom are ready, take your places."

"All ready."

"Now, George Jackson, do you know the Shepherdsons?"

"No, sir—I never heard of them."

"Well, that may be so, and it mayn't. Now, all ready. Step forward, George Jackson. And mind, don't you hurry—come mighty slow. If there's anybody with you, let him keep back—if he shows himself he'll be shot. Come along, now. Come slow; push the door open, yourself—just enough to squeeze in, d' you hear?"

I didn't hurry, I couldn't if I'd a wanted to. I took one slow step at a time, and there warn't a sound, only I thought I could hear my heart. The dogs were as still as the humans, but they followed a little behind me. When I got to the three log doorsteps, I heard them unlocking and unbarring and unbolting. I put my hand on the door and pushed it a little and a little more, till somebody said, "There, that's enough—put your head in." I done it, but I judged they would take it off.

The candle was on the floor, and there they all was, looking at me, and me at them, for about a quarter of a minute. Three big men with guns pointed at me, which made me wince, I tell you; the oldest, gray and about sixty, the other two thirty or more—all of them fine and handsome—and the sweetest old gray-headed lady, and back of her two young women which I couldn't see right well. The old gentleman says:

"There—I reckon it's all right. Come in."

As soon as I was in, the old gentleman he locked the door and barred it and bolted it, and told the young men to come in with their guns, and they all went in a big parlor that had a new rag carpet on the floor, and got together in a corner that was out of range of the front windows—there warn't none on the side. They held the candle, and took a good look at me, and all said, "Why *he* ain't a Shepherdson—no, there ain't any Shepherdson about him." Then the old man said he hoped I wouldn't mind being searched for arms, because he didn't mean no harm by it—it was only to make sure. So he didn't pry into my pockets, but only felt outside with his hands, and said it was all right. He told me to make myself easy and at home, and tell all about myself; but the old lady says:

"Why bless you, Saul, the poor thing's as wet as he can be; and don't you reckon it may be he's hungry?"

"True for you, Rachel—I forgot."

So the old lady says to the Negro woman:

"Betsy, you fly around and get him something to eat, as quick as you can, poor thing; and one of you girls go and wake up Buck and tell him—Oh, here he is himself. Buck, take this little stranger and get the wet clothes off from him and dress him up in some of yours that's dry."

Buck looked about as old as me—thirteen or fourteen or along there, though he was a little bigger than me. He hadn't on anything but a shirt, and he was very frowsy-headed.[1] He come in gaping and digging one fist into his eyes, and he was dragging a gun along with the other one. He says:

"Ain't they no Shepherdsons around?"

They said, no, 'twas a false alarm.

"Well," he says, "if they'd a ben some, I reckon I'd a got one."

They all laughed, and Bob says:

"Why, Buck, they might have scalped us all, you've been so slow in coming."

"Well, nobody come after me, and it ain't right. I'm always kep' down; I don't get no show."

"Never mind, Buck, my boy," says the old man, "you'll have show enough, all in good time, don't you fret about that. Go 'long with you now, and do as your mother told you."

When we got up stairs to his room, he got me a coarse shirt and a roundabout and pants of his, and I put them on. While I was at it he asked me what my name was, but before I could tell him, he started to telling me about a blue jay and a young rabbit he had catched in the woods day before yesterday, and he asked me where Moses was when the candle went out. I said I didn't know; I hadn't heard about it before, no way.

"Well, guess," he says.

"How'm I going to guess," says I, "when I never heard tell about it before?"

"But you can guess, can't you? It's just as easy."

"*Which* candle?" I says.

"Why, any candle," he says.

"I don't know where he was," says I; "where was he?"

"Why he was in the *dark!* That's where he was!"

"Well, if you knowed where he was, what did you ask me for?"

"Why, blame it, it's a riddle, don't you see? Say, how long are you going to stay here? You got to stay always. We can just have booming times—they don't have no school now. Do you own a dog? I've got a dog—and he'll go in the river and bring out chips that you throw in. Do you like to comb up, Sundays, and all that kind of foolishness? You bet I don't, but ma she makes me. Confound these ole britches, I

---

1. **frowsy-headed,** having unkempt hair.

reckon I'd better put 'em on, but I'd ruther not, it's so warm. Are you all ready? All right— come along, old hoss."

Cold corn-pone,[2] cold corn-beef, butter and butter-milk—that is what they had for me down there, and there ain't nothing better that ever I've come across yet. Buck and his ma and all of them smoked cob pipes, except the Negro woman, which was gone, and the two young women. They all smoked and talked, and I eat and talked. The young women had quilts around them, and their hair down their backs. They all asked me questions, and I told them how pap and me and all the family was living on a little farm down at the bottom of Arkansaw, and my sister Mary Ann run off and got married and never was heard of no more, and Bill went to hunt them and he warn't heard of no more, and Tom and Mort died, and then there warn't nobody but just me and pap left, and he was just trimmed down to nothing, on account of his troubles; so when he died I took what there was left, because the farm didn't belong to us, and started up the river, deck passage, and fell overboard; and that was how I come to be here. So they said I could have a home there as long as I wanted it. Then it was most daylight, and everybody went to bed, and I went to bed with Buck, and when I waked up in the morning, drat it all, I had forgot what my name was. So I laid there about an hour trying to think, and when Buck waked up, I says:

"Can you spell, Buck?"

"Yes," he says.

"I bet you can't spell my name," says I.

"I bet you what you dare I can," says he.

"All right," says I, "go ahead."

"G-o-r-g-e J-a-x-o-n—there now," he says.

"Well," says I, "you done it, but I didn't think you could. It ain't no slouch of a name to spell—right off without studying."

I set it down, private, because somebody might want *me* to spell it, next, and so I wanted to be handy with it and rattle it off like I was used to it.

It was a mighty nice family, and a mighty nice house, too. I hadn't seen no house out in the country before that was so nice and had so much style. It didn't have an iron latch on the front door, nor a wooden one with a buck-skin string, but a brass knob to turn, the same as houses in a town. There warn't no bed in the parlor, not a sign of a bed; but heaps of parlors in towns has beds in them. There was a big fireplace that was bricked on the bottom, and the bricks was kept clean and red by pouring water on them and scrubbing them with another brick; sometimes they washed them over with red water-paint that they call Span-ish-brown, same as they do in town. They had big brass dog-irons that could hold up a saw-log. There was a clock on the middle of the mantel-piece, with a picture of a town painted on the bottom half of the glass front, and a round place in the middle of it for the sun, and you could see the pendulum swing behind it. It was beautiful to hear that clock tick; and sometimes when one of these peddlers had been along and scoured her up and got her in good shape, she would start in and strike a hundred and fifty before she got tuckered out. They wouldn't took any money for her.

Well, there was a big outlandish parrot on each side of the clock, made out of something like chalk, and painted up gaudy. By one of the parrots was a cat made of crockery, and a crockery dog by the other; and when you pressed down on them they squeaked, but didn't open their mouths nor look different nor in-terested. They squeaked through underneath. There was a couple of big wild-turkey-wing fans spread out behind those things. On a table in the middle of the room was a kind of a lovely crockery basket that had apples and oranges and peaches and grapes piled up in it which was much redder and yellower and pret-tier than real ones is, but they warn't real be-cause you could see where pieces had got chipped off and showed the white chalk or whatever it was, underneath.

---

2. **corn-pone**, corn bread often made without milk or eggs.

This table had a cover made out of beautiful oil-cloth, with a red and blue spread-eagle painted on it, and a painted border all around. It come all the way from Philadelphia, they said. There was some books too, piled up perfectly exact, on each corner of the table. One was a big family Bible, full of pictures. One was "Pilgrim's Progress," about a man that left his family it didn't say why. I read considerable in it now and then. The statements was interesting, but tough. Another was "Friendship's Offering," full of beautiful stuff and poetry; but I didn't read the poetry. Another was Henry Clay's Speeches, and another was Dr. Gunn's Family Medicine, which told you all about what to do if a body was sick or dead. There was a Hymn Book, and a lot of other books. And there was nice split-bottom chairs, and perfectly sound, too—not bagged down in the middle and busted, like an old basket.

They had pictures hung on the walls—mainly Washingtons and Lafayettes, and battles, and Highland Marys, and one called "Signing the Declaration." There was some that they called crayons, which one of the daughters which was dead made her own self when she was only fifteen years old. They was different from any pictures I ever see before; blacker, mostly, than is common. One was a woman in a slim black dress, belted small under the arm-pits, with bulges like a cabbage in the middle of the sleeves, and a large black scoop-shovel bonnet with a black veil, and white slim ankles crossed about with black tape, and very wee black slippers, like a chisel, and she was leaning pensive on a tombstone on her right elbow, under a weeping willow, and her other hand hanging down her side holding a white handkerchief and a reticule, and underneath the picture it said "Shall I Never See Thee More Alas." Another one was a young lady with her hair all combed up straight to the top of her head, and knotted there in front of a comb like a chair-back, and she was crying into a handkerchief and had a dead bird laying on its back in her other hand with its heels up, and underneath the picture it said "I Shall Never Hear Thy Sweet Chirrup More Alas." There was one where a young lady was at a window looking up at the moon, and tears running down her cheeks; and she had an open letter in one hand with black sealing-wax showing on one edge of it, and she was mashing a locket with a chain to it against her mouth, and underneath the picture it said "And Art Thou Gone Yes Thou Art Gone Alas." These was all nice pictures, I reckon, but I didn't somehow seem to take to them, because if ever I was down a little, they always give me the fan-tods. Everybody was sorry she died, because she had laid out a lot more of these pictures to do, and a body could see by what she had done what they had lost. But I reckoned, that with her disposition, she was having a better time in the graveyard. She was at work on what they said was her greatest picture when she took sick, and every day and every night it was her prayer to be allowed to live till she got it done, but she never got the chance. It was a picture of a young woman in a long white gown, standing on the rail of a bridge all ready to jump off, with her hair all down her back, and looking up to the moon, with the tears running down her face, and she had two arms folded across her breast, and two arms stretched out in front, and two more reaching up towards the moon—and the idea was, to see which pair would look best and then scratch out all the other arms; but, as I was saying, she died before she got her mind made up, and now they kept this picture over the head of the bed in her room, and every time her birthday come they hung flowers on it. Other times it was hid with a little curtain. The young woman in the picture had a kind of a nice sweet face, but there was so many arms it made her look too spidery, seemed to me.

This young girl kept a scrap-book when she was alive, and used to paste obituaries and accidents and cases of patient suffering in it out of the *Presbyterian Observer*, and write poetry after them out of her own head. It was very good poetry. This is what she wrote about a boy by the name of Stephen Dowling Bots that fell down a well and was drownded:

ODE TO STEPHEN DOWLING BOTS, DEC'D.

And did young Stephen sicken,
    And did young Stephen die?
And did the sad hearts thicken,
    And did the mourners cry?

No; such was not the fate of
    Young Stephen Dowling Bots;
Though sad hearts round him thickened,
    'Twas not from sickness' shots.

No whooping-cough did rack his frame,
    Nor measles drear, with spots;
Not these impaired the sacred name
    Of Stephen Dowling Bots.

Despised love struck not with woe
    That head of curly knots,
Nor stomach troubles laid him low,
    Young Stephen Dowling Bots.

O no. Then list with tearful eye,
    Whilst I his fate do tell.
His soul did from this cold world fly,
    By falling down a well.

They got him out and emptied him;
    Alas it was too late;
His spirit was gone for to sport aloft
    In the realms of the good and great.

If Emmeline Grangerford could make poetry like that before she was fourteen, there ain't no telling what she could a done by-and-by. Buck said she could rattle off poetry like nothing. She didn't ever have to stop to think. He said she would slap down a line, and if she couldn't find anything to rhyme with it she would just scratch it out and slap down another one, and go ahead. She warn't particular, she could write about anything you choose to give her to write about, just so it was sadful. Every time a man died, or a woman died, or a child died, she would be on hand with her "tribute" before he was cold. She called them tributes. The neighbors said it was the doctor first, then Emmeline, then the undertaker—the undertaker never got in ahead of Emmeline but once, and then she hung fire on a rhyme for the dead person's name, which was Whistler. She warn't ever the same, after that; she never complained, but she kind of pined away and did not live long. Poor thing, many's the time I made myself go up to the little room that used to be hers and get out her poor old scrap-book and read in it when her pictures had been aggravating me and I had soured on her a little. I liked all that family, dead ones and all, and warn't going to let anything come between us. Poor Emmeline made poetry about all the dead people when she was alive, and it didn't seem right that there warn't nobody to make some about her, now she was gone; so I tried to sweat out a verse or two myself, but I couldn't seem to make it go, somehow. They kept Emmeline's room trim and nice and all the things fixed in it just the way she liked to have them when she was alive, and nobody ever slept there. The old lady took care of the room herself, and she sewed there a good deal and read her Bible there, mostly.

Well, as I was saying about the parlor, there was beautiful curtains on the windows: white, with pictures painted on them, of castles with vines all down the walls, and cattle coming down to drink. There was a little old piano, too, that had tin pans in it, I reckon, and nothing was ever so lovely as to hear the young ladies sing, "The Last Link is Broken" and play "The Battle of Prague" on it. The walls of all the rooms was plastered, and most had carpets on the floors, and the whole house was whitewashed on the outside.

It was a double house, and the big open place betwixt them was roofed and floored, and sometimes the table was set there in the middle of the day, and it was a cool, comfortable place. Nothing couldn't be better. And warn't the cooking good, and just bushels of it too!

CHAPTER XVIII

Col. Grangerford was a gentleman, you see. He was a gentleman all over; and so was his family. He was well born, as the saying is, and that's worth as much in a man as it is in a horse, so the Widow Douglas said, and nobody

*Hannibal, Missouri, Twain's childhood home and
the setting for many of Tom Sawyer's and Huck
Finn's adventures.*

ever denied that she was of the first aristocracy
in our town; and pap he always said it, too,
though he warn't no more quality than a mud-
cat, himself. Col. Grangerford was very tall and
very slim, and had a darkish-paly complexion,
not a sign of red in it anywheres; he was clean-
shaved every morning, all over his thin face,
and he had the thinnest kind of lips, and the
thinnest kind of nostrils, and a high nose, and
heavy eyebrows, and the blackest kind of eyes,
sunk so deep back that they seemed like they
was looking out of caverns at you, as you may
say. His forehead was high, and his hair was
black and straight, and hung to his shoulders.
His hands was long and thin, and every day of
his life he put on a clean shirt and a full suit
from head to foot made out of linen so white it
hurt your eyes to look at it; and on Sundays he
wore a blue tail-coat with brass buttons on it.
He carried a mahogany cane with a silver head
to it. There warn't no frivolishness about him,
not a bit, and he warn't ever loud. He was as
kind as he could be—you could feel that, you
know, and so you had confidence. Sometimes
he smiled, and it was good to see; but when he
straightened himself up like a liberty-pole, and
the lightning begun to flicker out from under
his eyebrows you wanted to climb a tree first,
and find out what the matter was afterwards.
He didn't ever have to tell anybody to mind
their manners—everybody was always good
mannered where he was. Everybody loved to
have him around, too; he was sunshine most
always—I mean he made it seem like good
weather. When he turned into a cloud-bank it
was awful dark for a half a minute and that
was enough; there wouldn't nothing go wrong
again for a week.

327

When him and the old lady come down in the morning, all the family got up out of their chairs and give them good-day, and didn't set down again till they had set down. Then Tom and Bob went to the sideboard where the decanters was, and mixed a glass of bitters and handed it to him, and he held it in his hand and waited till Tom's and Bob's was mixed, and then they bowed and said "Our duty to you, sir, and madam;" and *they* bowed the least bit in the world and said thank you, and so they drank, all three, and Bob and Tom poured a spoonful of water on the sugar and the mite of whisky or apple brandy in the bottom of their tumblers, and give it to me and Buck, and we drank to the old people too.

Bob was the oldest, and Tom next. Tall, beautiful men with very broad shoulders and brown faces, and long black hair and black eyes. They dressed in white linen from head to foot, like the old gentleman, and wore broad Panama hats.

Then there was Miss Charlotte, she was twenty-five, and tall and proud and grand, but as good as she could be, when she warn't stirred up; but when she was, she had a look that would make you wilt in your tracks, like her father. She was beautiful.

So was her sister, Miss Sophia, but it was a different kind. She was gentle and sweet, like a dove, and she was only twenty.

Each person had their own servant to wait on them—Buck, too. My servant had a monstrous easy time, because I warn't used to having anybody do anything for me, but Buck's was on the jump most of the time.

This was all there was of the family, now; but there used to be more—three sons; they got killed; and Emmeline that died.

The old gentleman owned a lot of farms, and over a hundred Negroes. Sometimes a stack of people would come there, horseback, from ten or fifteen mile around, and stay five or six days, and have such junketings round about and on the river, and dances and picnics in the woods, day-times, and balls at the house, nights. These people was mostly kin-folks of the family. The men brought their guns with them. It was a handsome lot of quality, I tell you.

There was another clan of aristocracy around there—five or six families—mostly of the name of Shepherdson. They was as high-toned, and well born, and rich and grand, as the tribe of Grangerfords. The Shepherdsons and the Grangerfords used the same steamboat landing, which was about two mile above our house; so sometimes when I went up there with a lot of our folks I used to see a lot of the Shepherdsons there, on their fine horses.

One day Buck and me was away out in the woods, hunting, and heard a horse coming. We was crossing the road. Buck says:

"Quick! Jump for the woods!"

We done it, and then peeped down the woods through the leaves. Pretty soon a splendid young man come galloping down the road, setting his horse easy and looking like a soldier. He had his gun across his pommel. I had seen him before. It was young Harney Shepherdson. I heard Buck's gun go off at my ear, and Harney's hat tumbled off from his head. He grabbed his gun and rode straight to the place where we was hid. But we didn't wait. We started through the woods on a run. The woods warn't thick, so I looked over my shoulder, to dodge the bullet, and twice I seen Harney cover Buck with his gun; and then he rode away the way he come—to get his hat, I reckon, but I couldn't see. We never stopped running till we got home. The old gentleman's eyes blazed a minute—'twas pleasure, mainly, I judged—then his face sort of smoothed down, and he says, kind of gentle:

"I don't like that shooting from behind a bush. Why didn't you step into the road, my boy?"

"The Shepherdsons don't, father. They always take advantage."

Miss Charlotte she held her head up like a queen while Buck was telling his tale, and her nostrils spread and her eyes snapped. The two young men looked dark, but never said nothing. Miss Sophia she turned pale, but the color come back when she found the man warn't hurt.

Soon as I could get Buck down by the corn-cribs under the trees by ourselves, I says:

"Did you want to kill him, Buck?"

"Well, I bet I did."

"What did he do to you?"

"Him? He never done nothing to me."

"Well, then, what did you want to kill him for?"

"Why nothing—only it's on account of the feud."

"What's a feud?"

"Why, where was you raised? Don't you know what a feud is?"

"Never heard of it before—tell me about it."

"Well," says Buck, "a feud is this way. A man has a quarrel with another man, and kills him; then that other man's brother kills *him;* then the other brothers, on both sides, goes for one another; then the *cousins* chip in—and by-and-by everybody's killed off, and there ain't no more feud. But it's kind of slow, and takes a long time."

"Has this one been going on long, Buck?"

"Well I should *reckon!* it started thirty year ago, or som'ers along there. There was trouble 'bout something and then a lawsuit to settle it; and the suit went agin one of the men, and so he up and shot the man that won the suit—which he would naturally do, of course. Anybody would."

"What was the trouble about, Buck?—land?"

"I reckon maybe—I don't know."

"Well, who done the shooting?—was it a Grangerford or a Shepherdson?"

"Laws, how do *I* know? it was so long ago."

"Don't anybody know?"

"Oh, yes, pa knows, I reckon, and some of the other old folks; but they don't know, now, what the row was about in the first place."

"Has there been many killed, Buck?"

"Yes—right smart chance of funerals. But they don't always kill. Pa's got a few buck-shot in him; but he don't mind it 'cuz he don't weigh much anyway. Bob's been carved up some with a bowie, and Tom's been hurt once or twice."

"Has anybody been killed this year, Buck?"

"Yes, we got one and they got one. 'Bout three months ago, my cousin Bud, fourteen year old, was riding through the woods, on t'other side of the river, and didn't have no weapon with him, which was blame' foolishness, and in a lonesome place he hears a horse a-coming behind him, and sees old Baldy Shepherdson a-linkin' after him with his gun in his hand and his white hair a-flying in the wind; and 'stead of jumping off and taking to the brush, Bud 'lowed he could outrun him; so they had it, nip and tuck, for five mile or more, the old man a-gaining all the time; so at last Bud seen it warn't any use, so he stopped and faced around so as to have the bullet holes in front, you know, and the old man he rode up and shot him down. But he didn't git much chance to enjoy his luck, for inside of a week our folks laid *him* out."

"I reckon that old man was a coward, Buck."

"I reckon he *warn't* a coward. Not by a blame' sight. There ain't a coward amongst them Shepherdsons—not a one. And there ain't no cowards amongst the Grangerfords, either. Why, that old man kep' up his end in a fight one day, for a half an hour, against three Grangerfords, and come out winner. They was all a-horseback; he lit off of his horse and got behind a little wood-pile, and kep' his horse before him to stop the bullets; but the Grangerfords staid on their horses and capered around the old man, and peppered away at him, and he peppered away at them. Him and his horse both went home pretty leaky and crippled, but the Grangerfords had to be *fetched* home—and one of 'em was dead, and another died the next day. No, sir, if a body's out hunting for cowards, he don't want to fool away any time amongst them Shepherdsons, becuz they don't breed any of that *kind.*"

Next Sunday we all went to church, about three mile, everybody a-horseback. The men took their guns along, so did Buck, and kept them between their knees or stood them handy against the wall. The Shepherdsons done the same. It was pretty ornery preaching—all about brotherly love, and such-like tiresomeness; but everybody said it was a good sermon, and they all talked it over going home, and had such a powerful lot to say about faith, and good works, and free grace, and prefore-ordestination, and I don't know what all, that it did seem to me to be one of the roughest Sundays I had run across yet.

About an hour after dinner everybody was dozing around, some in their chairs and some in their rooms, and it got to be pretty dull. Buck and a dog was stretched out on the grass in the sun, sound asleep. I went up to our room, and judged I would take a nap myself. I found that sweet Miss Sophia standing in her door, which was next to ours, and she took me in her room and shut the door very soft, and asked me if I liked her, and I said I did; and she asked me if I would do something for her and not tell anybody, and I said I would. Then she said she'd forgot her Testament, and left it in the seat at church, between two other books and would I slip out quiet and go there and fetch it to her, and not say nothing to nobody. I said I would. So I slid out and slipped off up the road, and there warn't anybody at the church, except maybe a hog or two, for there warn't any lock on the door, and hogs likes a puncheon floor in summer-time because it's cool. If you notice, most folks don't go to church only when they've got to; but a hog is different.

Says I to myself something's up—it ain't natural for a girl to be in such a sweat about a Testament; so I give it a shake, and out drops a little piece of paper with "*Half-past two*" wrote on it with a pencil. I ransacked it, but couldn't find anything else. I couldn't make anything out of that, so I put the paper in the book again, and when I got home and up stairs, there was Miss Sophia in her door waiting for me. She pulled me in and shut the door; then she looked in the Testament till she found the paper, and as soon as she read it she looked glad; and before a body could think, she grabbed me and give me a squeeze, and said I was the best boy in the world, and not to tell anybody. She was mighty red in the face, for a minute, and her eyes lighted up and it made her powerful pretty. I was a good deal aston-

ished, but when I got my breath I asked her what the paper was about, and she asked me if I had read it, and I said no, and she asked me if I could read writing, and I told her "no, only coarse-hand," and then she said the paper warn't anything but a book-mark to keep her place, and I might go and play now. . . .

I don't want to talk much about the next day. I reckon I'll cut it pretty short. I waked up about dawn, and was agoing to turn over and go to sleep again, when I noticed how still it was—didn't seem to be anybody stirring. That warn't usual. Next I noticed that Buck was up and gone. Well, I gets up, a-wondering, and goes down stairs—nobody around; everything as still as a mouse. Just the same outside; thinks I, what does it mean? Down by the wood-pile I comes across my Jack, and says:

"What's it all about?"

Says he:

"Don't you know, Mars Jawge?"

"No," says I, "I don't."

"Well, den, Miss Sophia's run off! 'deed she has. She run off in de night, sometime—nobody don't know jis' when—run off to git married to dat young Harney Shepherdson, you know—leastways, so dey 'spec. De fambly foun' it out, 'bout half an hour ago—maybe a little mo'—en' I *tell* you dey warn't no time los'. Sich another hurryin' up guns en hosses *you* never see! De women folks has gone for to stir up de relations, en ole Mars Saul en de boys tuck dey guns en rode up de river road for to try to ketch dat young man en kill him 'fo' he kin git acrost de river wid Miss Sophia. I reck'n dey's gwyne to be mighty rough times."

"Buck went off 'thout waking me up."

"Well I reck'n he *did!* Dey warn't gwyne to mix you up in it. Mars Buck he loaded up his gun en 'lowed he's gwyne to fetch home a Shepherdson or bust. Well, dey'll be plenty un 'm dah, I reck'n, en you bet you he'll fetch one ef he gits a chanst."

I took up the river road as hard as I could put. By-and-by I begin to hear guns a good ways off. When I come in sight of the log store and the wood-pile where the steamboats lands,

I worked along under the trees and brush till I got to a good place, and then I clumb up into the forks of a cotton-wood that was out of reach, and watched. There was a wood-rank four foot high, a little ways in front of the tree, and first I was going to hide behind that; but maybe it was luckier I didn't.

There was four or five men cavorting around on their horses in the open place before the log store, cussing and yelling, and trying to get at a couple of young chaps that was behind the wood-rank alongside of the steamboat landing —but they couldn't come it. Every time one of them showed himself on the river side of the wood-pile he got shot at. The two boys was squatting back to back behind the pile, so they could watch both ways.

By-and-by the men stopped cavorting around and yelling. They started riding towards the store; then up gets one of the boys, draws a steady bead over the wood-rank, and drops one of them out of his saddle. All the men jumped off of their horses and grabbed the hurt one and started to carry him to the store; and that minute the two boys started on the run. They go half-way to the tree I was in before the men noticed. Then the men see them, and jumped on their horses and took out after them. They gained on the boys, but it didn't do no good, the boys had too good a start; they got to the wood-pile that was in front of my tree, and slipped in behind it, and so they had the bulge on the men again. One of the boys was Buck, and the other was a slim young chap about nineteen years old.

The men ripped around awhile, and then rode away. As soon as they was out of sight, I sung out to Buck and told him. He didn't know what to make of my voice coming out of the tree, at first. He was awful surprised. He told me to watch out sharp and let him know when the men come in sight again; said they was up to some devilment or other—wouldn't be gone long. I wished I was out of that tree, but I dasn't come down. Buck begun to cry and rip, and 'lowed that him and his cousin Joe (that was the other young chap) would

make up for this day, yet. He said his father and his two brothers was killed, and two or three of the enemy. Said the Shepherdsons laid for them, in ambush. Buck said his father and brothers ought to waited for their relations— the Shepherdsons was too strong for them. I asked him what was become of young Harney and Miss Sophia. He said they'd got across the river and was safe. I was glad of that; but the way Buck did take on because he didn't manage to kill Harney that day he shot at him—I hain't ever heard anything like it.

All of a sudden, bang! bang! bang! goes three or four guns—the men had slipped around through the woods and come in from behind without their horses! The boys jumped for the river—both of them hurt—and as they swum down the current the men run along the bank shooting at them and singing out, "Kill them, kill them!" It made me so sick I most fell out of the tree. I ain't agoing to tell *all* that happened—it would make me sick again if I was to do that. I wished I hadn't ever come ashore that night, to see such things. I ain't ever going to get shut of them—lots of times I dream about them.

I staid in the tree till it begun to get dark, afraid to come down. Sometimes I heard guns away off in the woods; and twice I seen little gangs of men gallop past the log store with guns; so I reckoned the trouble was still agoing on. I was mighty down-hearted; so I made up my mind I wouldn't ever go anear that house again, because I reckoned I was to blame, somehow. I judged that that piece of paper meant that Miss Sophia was to meet Harney somewheres at half-past two and run off; and I judged I ought to told her father about that paper and the curious way she acted, and then maybe he would a locked her up and this awful mess wouldn't ever happened.

When I got down out of the tree, I crept along down the river bank a piece, and found the two bodies laying in the edge of the water, and tugged at them till I got them ashore; then I covered up their faces, and got away as quick as I could. I cried a little when I was covering up Buck's face, for he was mighty good to me.

It was just dark, now. I never went near the house, but struck through the woods and made for the swamp. Jim warn't on his island, so I tramped off in a hurry for the crick, and crowded through the willows, red-hot to jump aboard and get out of that awful country—the raft was gone! My souls, but I was scared! I couldn't get my breath for most a minute. Then I raised a yell. A voice not twenty-five foot from me, says—

"Good lan'! is dat you, honey? Doan' make no noise."

It was Jim's voice—nothing ever sounded so good before. I run along the bank a piece and got aboard, and Jim he grabbed me and hugged me, he was so glad to see me. He says—

"Laws bless you, chile, I 'uz right down sho' you's dead agin. Jack's been heah, he say he reck'n you's ben shot, kase you didn' come home no mo'; so I's jes' dis minute a startin' de raf' down towards de mouf er de crick, so's to be all ready for to shove out en leave soon as Jack comes agin en tells me for certain you *is* dead. Lawsy, I's mighty glad to git you back agin, honey."

I says—

"All right—that's mighty good; they won't find me, and they'll think I've been killed, and floated down the river—there's something up there that'll help them to think so—so don't you lose no time, Jim, but just shove off for the big water as fast as ever you can."

I never felt easy till the raft was two mile below there and out in the middle of the Mississippi. Then we hung up our signal lantern, and judged that we was free and safe once more. I hadn't had a bite to eat since yesterday; so Jim he got out some corn-dodgers and butter-milk, and pork and cabbage, and greens—there ain't nothing in the world so good, when it's cooked right—and whilst I eat my supper we talked, and had a good time. I was powerful glad to get away from the feuds, and so was Jim to get away from the swamp. We said there warn't no home like a raft, after all. Other places do seem so cramped up and smothery, but a raft don't. You feel mighty free and easy and comfortable on a raft.

I
FREEDOM AND SLAVERY

Although the main emphasis in this selection is on social criticism of the riverbank society, there is clearly a connection between this criticism and what may be the major theme of the novel as a whole, freedom. An important contrast between Huck and the Grangerford family is that Huck is essentially free whereas the lives of the Grangerfords are enmeshed in restrictions. Virtually everything they do *must* be done, and must be done in certain prescribed ways. In short, they have become slaves to a tradition which they follow unquestioningly, even when it is irrational. Thus Buck, for instance, dies in a tradition called a feud, without even knowing the source of the quarrel or why he is fighting.

II
IMPLICATIONS

Twain's social criticism in this selection is largely *indirect;* that is, his narrator, Huck, says one thing but the reader understands Twain to mean something else. Below are four statements made by Huck. For each statement discuss both Huck's attitude and the contrasting attitude of Twain.

1. Everybody was sorry she [Emmeline Grangerford] died. . . . But I reckoned, that with her disposition, she was having a better time in the graveyard.

2. Buck said she [Emmeline] could rattle off poetry like nothing. She didn't ever have to stop to think.

3. Next Sunday we all went to church. . . . The men took their guns along. . . . It was pretty ornery preaching—all about brotherly love, and such-like tiresomeness; but everybody said it was a good sermon, and they all talked it over going home, and had such a powerful lot to say about faith, and good works. . . .

4. . . . there warn't anybody at the church, except maybe a hog or two. . . . If you notice, most folks don't go to church only when they've got to; but a hog is different.

III
TECHNIQUES
Comedy and Sympathy and Detachment

Twain's comic technique in this selection rests heavily on a device called *irony of statement.* Huck, the narrator, makes statements usually showing either approval or neutrality toward a given thing, but these attitudes are in marked contrast with those of Twain. Thus there is a contrast in the statements between what is said and what is meant. This is irony of statement. (See p. 572.)

In his description of the parlor furnishings, for example, Huck says that the clock is "beautiful" and that the fruits in the crockery basket are "prettier than real ones is." Huck, in short, approves of both. But how does Twain feel about them? The fact is that Twain thinks both the clock and the fruits are pretentious and useless, tokens of the kind of life the Grangerfords live, a life in which appearances are more important than realities, in which the importance is placed on the shadow rather than the substance.

But how do readers know what Twain thinks, how do they know that there is a contrast between the feelings of the author and the feelings of the narrator?

It is true that Twain never reveals his attitudes directly; nevertheless it is possible for readers to infer the author's attitude from what Huck says and from the things he chooses to notice. Concerning the "pretty" fruits, for example, Huck notices not only that they are "prettier than real ones" but also that "they warn't real because you could see where pieces had got chipped off and showed the white chalk or whatever it was, underneath." Why should Huck mention this detail? The best answer seems to be because the detail gives readers a key to the author's attitude.

Ironies such as these demand a good deal from readers, especially with regard to their nearness to or distance from the characters in the work of fiction. In this case, for instance, readers must sympathize with Huck and yet at the same time remain sufficiently detached from him to see the contrast between his attitudes and the attitudes of his creator.

IV
WORDS

A. 1. The first paragraph of "The Celebrated Jumping Frog of Calaveras County" contains such literary words as *garrulous, append, personage, conjectured, infamous, reminiscence, tedious.* Find several synonyms for each word. Rewrite the paragraph using more conversational words, and then rewrite the paragraph using colloquial and slang terms. Explain how your revisions differ from and change the original.

2. Find a simple synonym for each word below. *sustenance, remuneration, dogmatic, savant, venerable, thesaurus.*

3. Many of our more literary words are borrowed words—words that came into the language directly from Latin or Greek or by way of French. Look up the origin of the words in number two above. Find a more learned or literary synonym for the following native words.

dark, forgive, greed, kind (adj.), *start* (v.), *sharp, angry, deep.*

B. Dialects attracted American writers from almost the beginning of American literature. Mark Twain, breaking away from the rhetorical flourish of contemporary English writers, wrote American colloquial speech, attempting to represent the speech of the far Westerner in "The Jumping Frog of Calaveras County," *Roughing It,* and the varieties of speech found in Pike County, Mississippi, in *The Adventures of Huckleberry Finn.* In the beginning of this novel, Twain explains to his readers that he used several dialects: the Missouri Negro dialect, the backwoods speech, and varieties of Pike County dialects.

1. Study the selections carefully. Make a list of pronunciation items, such as: use of "r" after vowels as in *idear;* "thish-yer" for "this here"; "jest" for "just" and so on. If you wish to make your description more accurate, use the pronunciation symbols found in your dictionary or the International Phonetic Alphabet system.

2. Make another list of vocabulary items, for example: *carry* for "escort," *cipher* for "write." What is a "straddle-bug"? Do you find any other regional names for objects, such as "corn-pone"?

3. Look for examples of meanings now obsolete, as in "I judged they would take it off." Using context as a guide, define the various vocabulary terms.

333

STEPHEN CRANE

1871-1900

To the day of his death, Crane had not forsaken the creed he lived by: "You can never do anything good aesthetically . . . unless it has at one time meant something important to you." That is not to say that Crane believed an artist must experience every event in order to describe it realistically. Much of Crane's best work was imagined. He was, however, talking of his own formula for fiction: taking a germ of an experience and then letting it grow in the mind, writing from the truth of the experience but always expressing that truth with acute feelings, acutely expressed.

Edgar Allan Poe and Stephen Crane had much in common. Both men were erratic writers: they experimented in prose and poetry with new styles and subjects; they attempted to live by their writing and frequently knew poverty because of it; they died young, having in a sense burned themselves out. What is more, the lives of both men started sentimental legends of wasted talent. It is an image too many readers enjoy perpetuating, even though the facts of honest biographies have exposed these myths. What we know now of Poe's personal life, his fragile health, his enormous powers of concentration even on hackwork helps to correct the popular belief that he wrote only under the influence of dope or alcohol. Crane's biography explains even more clearly what forces shaped his literary work, where he found his subjects, and how he developed his style.

Crane was a writer of such remarkable natural talent that he sprang at once into literary prominence. Before he was twenty-three, he had written two novels of major importance in the development of American fiction, yet his adolescence was much like that of other young people of his day. He was born in 1871 in Newark, New Jersey, but the family finally settled in Port Jervis, New York. It was a large family and the father, a Methodist minister, died when Crane was nine years old. Stephen, the youngest, had more schooling than the rest of the fourteen children but even that was limited. Two years at a military academy in Claverack, New York, preceded a fall term at Lafayette College, a spring term at Syracuse University. He cared little for reading and preferred baseball to the lecture room, so after one year of college he was eager to leave for the active life of the world. Since both parents were writers and two of his brothers newspaper reporters, he, too, wanted to get on with his writing, as a free-lance reporter for various newspapers in New York City and, when time allowed, as a novelist.

Crane came to know New York through its slums and street life, particularly in the Bowery. He thought that "one could train one's mind to observe and a man should be able to say something worthwhile about any event." His first Bowery tales were just that: honest recording of brutal poverty. When he came to write *Maggie: A Girl of the Streets* (1893), he went even further, for this short novel records slum life with the realistic accuracy of a camera. Although *Maggie* is an immature work in conception and execution, it marks a significant step in the development of American fiction. It is a plain story of Maggie Johnson and her brother Jimmie in Rum Alley, a tenement district of New York City. The young girl is driven out of her home by a drunken mother; she falls in love with a bartender named Pete, a friend of Jimmie, who leaves her to make a living as best she can. Eventually she ends her short life by drowning herself, the helpless victim of her sordid surroundings. Crane tells her story without softening its harshness and without judging his characters. The dialogue reflects as closely as possible this world of unrelieved depression. "It is inevitable that you will be greatly shocked by the book," Crane wrote his friend Hamlin Garland, "but continue please with all possible courage to the end. For it tries to show that environment is a tremendous thing in the world and frequently shapes lives regardless."

The word "environment" is the key to Crane's attitude. *Maggie* could easily have been reduced to a pious moral: "Poverty is the source of sin," but that was scarcely why Crane wanted to tell the story. Pete and Jimmie and the drunken mother are to blame for Maggie's death, but the real villain is the Bowery. Crane had learned from Garland that honest realism is the only right method for fiction, and the closer novelists approach the method of science —observation, analysis, careful judgment—the more faithful, so they believed, they are to life. What his observations of tenement life had shown to Crane depressed him utterly, and he wanted his readers to "feel" the weight of this environment in his story of a helpless girl. *Maggie* remained generally unread, however, until his second novel, *The Red Badge of Courage* (1895), made him an overnight success.

The American Civil War had long interested Crane. Obviously unable to observe his material at first hand, he immersed himself in Mathew Brady's remarkable photographs, in such books as *Battles and Leaders of the Civil War* and Colonel Wilbur F. Hinman's *Corporal Si Klegg and His "Pards,"* and in the war reminiscences of his brother William. Just three months after *Maggie* had been printed, he wrote a first draft of *The Red Badge of Courage.* He told a friend that "I have spent ten nights writing a story of the war on my own responsibility but I am not sure my facts are real and the books won't tell me what I want to know so I must do it all over again, I guess." A second draft followed several months later, and he continued to polish it for over a year before selling it to the Philadelphia *Press* for serializing. Just before his twenty-fourth birthday, in 1895, D. Appleton and Company published *The Red Badge* as a book.

His reputation was made. Though it was a war novel by a man who had never been to war, it was praised in England as well as in America for its unvarnished realism, its unheroic hero, and its smell of gunpowder. Crane had dared to be truthful. He had wiped away the glamor of combat and replaced it with a simple story of one confused soldier, trying to be brave but frightened to near hysteria during his baptism of fire. The battle is Chancellorsville; the soldier is Henry Fleming. But names and places are less important than the details of the action. As realist, Crane was adding another dimension to his fiction.

We call it impressionism. Joseph Conrad, the English novelist, was to define it several years after *The Red Badge* had appeared: "By the power of the written word, to make you hear, to make you feel—it is, before all, to make you *see*." Crane had tried to make us see the Bowery through Maggie's weary eyes. His readers were not ready for the truth. Or perhaps Crane was not ready for the supreme effort, to make us feel as well as see Maggie's suicide. Though her death takes place in a real world, one we can believe in, her suicide is still remote to us as readers because we do not enter Maggie's mind and heart. *The Red Badge,* by contrast, succeeds because it focuses on Henry's psychological problems as well as his physical discomforts. Crane never tries to paint the whole battlefield. We see only what Henry sees, and we soon come to realize that the hero is fighting himself as well as the enemy, that he is assailed with doubts about his own bravery. War can be presented realistically; that is no problem. What the impressionistic method adds to realism is the feeling of being there, of discovering and mastering fear *along with* Henry Fleming. Call it identification, if you wish, or rapport or empathy. The labels do not matter.

What matters is the success of Crane's simple plot, his accurate descriptions, and his determination to write nothing but what could have happened to his most unheroic hero. The style is disjointed because Henry's impressions are disjointed. The images are sometimes blurred, at other times as hard and flashing as swords. The action itself is so slight as to be

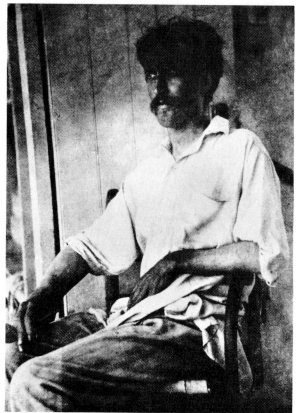

Rare informal photograph of Crane.

lost in the sense impressions, but all the time Crane is piling up these impressions to reinforce his theme; and his main theme is neither the miseries of war nor the nature of fear but spiritual growth, self-recognition, development of conscience as well as courage.

The remaining five years of Crane's life were crowded with activity. In 1895 he also published *The Black Riders,* a volume of poems. His reputation was reinforced in 1896 with a new novel, *George's Mother,* and a collection of tales, *The Little Regiment and Other Episodes of the American Civil War.* Two more novels, four collections of sketches and tales, and a second volume of poems appeared before he succumbed to tuberculosis in 1900. His premature death was the cause of much grief among American critics, but fellow writers who knew Crane in England during his last years had sensed a certain self-destructiveness in this young American and saw clearly that he was writing too much too fast. Much of this writing was done to earn a living, on assignments as roving correspondent. Bacheller's Syndicate sent him in 1895 to Nebraska, Arizona, Texas, and Mexico. In 1897 he was on his way from Florida to Cuba when his ship, the *Commodore*, sank and he spent thirty hours at sea in a dinghy. Later the same year he was sent to Athens to report the Greco-Turkish war for the New York *Journal*. In 1898, another war, the Spanish-American, took his energy and, ultimately, his health.

To the day of his death, Crane had not forsaken the creed he lived by: "You can never do anything good aesthetically . . . unless it has at one time meant something important to you." That is not to say that Crane believed an artist must experience every event in order to describe it realistically; if he had believed that, he would have been denying the imagination. Much of Crane's best work was imagined. He was, however, talking of his own formula for fiction: taking a germ of an experience and then letting it grow in the mind, writing from the truth of experience but always expressing that truth with acute feelings, acutely expressed. After the shipwreck off the coast of Florida, he transmuted his experiences into one of his best short stories, "The Open Boat." After seeing a Nebraska hotel painted a screaming blue, he used the image as the focus of his violent story "The Blue Hotel." Had he done no more, he would have remained a reporter, a roving journalist, who also wrote fiction. Crane's artistry lies in the immediacy of these descriptions, in the intensity of these feelings and of the imagination.

When Crane describes Scratchy Wilson in "The Bride Comes to Yellow Sky," he calls on his memories of the West. We not only see Scratchy, we hear him:

The man's face flamed in a rage begot of whisky. His eyes, rolling, and yet keen for ambush, hunted the still doorways and windows. He walked with the creeping movement of the midnight cat. As it occurred to him, he roared menacing information. The long revolvers in his hands moved with an electric swiftness. The little fingers of each hand played sometimes in a musician's way. . . . The only sounds were his terrible invitations. The calm adobes preserved their demeanour at the passing of this small thing in the middle of the street.

When he tells us, in "A Mystery of Heroism," what artillery fire does to men and houses, we can almost smell the burning powder:

A shell struck the grey ruins of the house, and as, after the roar, the shattered wall fell in fragments, there was a noise which resembled the flapping of shutters during a wild gale of winter. Indeed, the infantry paused in the shelter of the bank appeared as men standing upon a shore contemplating a madness of the sea . . . and after the flare, the smoke, the dust, the wrath of this blow were gone, it was possible to see white legs stretched horizontally upon the ground.

This is what is meant by transmutation: observation filtered through the imagination. A conscious artist like Crane worked valiantly to achieve the realistic, honest picture described in such accurate language as to make the impression indelible. With his work, modern American fiction was established.

In a volume called
*The Little Regiment and Other Episodes
of the American Civil War* (1896),
Crane published six stories,
of which this is one of the best. All of them
were imagined, written before he had a chance
to witness actual warfare. One critic
has called this story "pure, concentrated
Crane." He probably had in mind
the intensity of the description, especially
the sounds and smells of battle; the simple
but accurate dialogue; the irony of the title;
and the brutal anticlimax of the last paragraph.
Crane makes us feel that we are there,
in the midst of it all, and he lets us
fathom for ourselves the "mystery"
of Fred Collins' "heroism."

A Mystery of Heroism

The dark uniforms of the men were so coated with dust from the incessant wrestling of the two armies that the regiment almost seemed a part of the clay bank which shielded them from the shells. On the top of the hill a battery was arguing in tremendous roars with some other guns, and to the eye of the infantry the artillerymen, the guns, the caissons, the horses, were distinctly outlined upon the blue sky. When a piece was fired, a red streak as round as a log flashed low in the heavens, like a monstrous bolt of lightning. The men of the battery wore white duck trousers, which somehow emphasized their legs; and when they ran and crowded in little groups at the bidding of the shouting officers, it was more impressive than usual to the infantry.

Fred Collins, of A Company, was saying: "Thunder! I wisht I had a drink. Ain't there any water round here?" Then somebody yelled: "There goes th' bugler!"

As the eyes of half the regiment swept in one machine-like movement, there was an instant's picture of a horse in a great convulsive leap of a death-wound and a rider leaning back with a crooked arm and spread fingers before his face. On the ground was the crimson terror of an exploding shell, with fibres of flame that seemed like lances. A glittering bugle swung clear of the rider's back as fell headlong the horse and the man. In the air was an odour as from a conflagration.

Sometimes they of the infantry looked down at a fair little meadow which spread at their feet. Its long green grass was rippling gently in a breeze. Beyond it was the grey form of a house half torn to pieces by shells and by the busy axes of soldiers who had pursued firewood. The line of an old fence was now dimly marked by long weeds and by an occasional post. A shell had blown the well-house to fragments. Little lines of grey smoke ribboning upward from some embers indicated the place where had stood the barn.

From beyond a curtain of green woods there came the sound of some stupendous scuffle, as if two animals of the size of islands were fighting. At a distance there were occasional appearances of swift-moving men, horses, batteries, flags, and with the crashing of infantry volleys were heard, often, wild and frenzied cheers. In the midst of it all Smith and Ferguson, two privates of A Company, were engaged in a heated discussion which involved the greatest questions of the national existence.

The battery on the hill presently engaged in a frightful duel. The white legs of the gunners scampered this way and that way, and the officers redoubled their shouts. The guns, with their demeanours of stolidity and courage, were typical of something infinitely self-possessed in this clamour of death that swirled around the hill.

One of a "swing" team was suddenly smitten quivering to the ground, and his maddened brethren dragged his torn body in their struggle to escape from this turmoil and danger. A young soldier astride one of the leaders swore

The Battle of Antietam, Maryland. The only known photograph of a Civil War battle in progress.

and fumed in his saddle and furiously jerked at the bridle. An officer screamed out an order so violently that his voice broke and ended the sentence in a falsetto[1] shriek.

The leading company of the infantry regiment was somewhat exposed, and the colonel ordered it moved more fully under the shelter of the hill. There was the clank of steel against steel.

A lieutenant of the battery rode down and passed them, holding his right arm carefully in his left hand. And it was as if this arm was not at all a part of him, but belonged to another man. His sober and reflective charger went slowly. The officer's face was grimy and perspiring, and his uniform was tousled as if he had been in direct grapple with an enemy. He smiled grimly when the men stared at him. He turned his horse toward the meadow.

Collins, of A Company, said: "I wisht I had a drink. I bet there's water in that there ol' well yonder!"

"Yes; but how you goin' to git it?"

For the little meadow which intervened was now suffering a terrible onslaught of shells. Its green and beautiful calm had vanished utterly.

Brown earth was being flung in monstrous handfuls. And there was a massacre of the young blades of grass. They were being torn, burned, obliterated. Some curious fortune of the battle had made this gentle little meadow the object of the red hate of the shells, and each one as it exploded seemed like an imprecation in the face of a maiden.

The wounded officer who was riding across this expanse said to himself: "Why, they couldn't shoot any harder if the whole army was massed here!"

A shell struck the grey ruins of the house, and as, after the roar, the shattered wall fell in fragments, there was a noise which resembled the flapping of shutters during a wild gale of winter. Indeed, the infantry paused in the shelter of the bank appeared as men standing upon a shore contemplating a madness of the sea. The angel of calamity had under its glance the battery upon the hill. Fewer white-legged men laboured about the guns. A shell had smitten one of the pieces, and after the flare, the

---

1. **falsetto**, high, artificial tone of voice.

smoke, the dust, the wrath of this blow were gone, it was possible to see white legs stretched horizontally upon the ground. And at the interval to the rear where it is the business of battery horses to stand with their noses to the fight, awaiting the command to drag their guns out of the destruction, or into it, or wheresoever these incomprehensible humans demanded with whip and spur—in this line of passive and dumb spectators, whose fluttering hearts yet would not let them forget the iron laws of man's control of them—in this rank of brute-soldiers there had been relentless and hideous carnage. From the ruck of bleeding and prostrate horses, the men of the infantry could see one animal raising its stricken body with its forelegs and turning its nose with mystic and profound eloquence toward the sky.

Some comrades joked Collins about his thirst. "Well, if yeh want a drink so bad, why don't yeh go git it?"

"Well, I will in a minnet, if yeh don't shut up!"

A lieutenant of artillery floundered[2] his horse straight down the hill with as little concern as if it were level ground. As he galloped past the colonel of the infantry, he threw up his hand in swift salute. "We've got to get out of that," he roared angrily. He was a black-bearded officer, and his eyes, which resembled beads, sparkled like those of an insane man. His jumping horse sped along the column of infantry.

The fat major, standing carelessly with his sword held horizontally behind him and with his legs far apart, looked after the receding horseman and laughed. "He wants to get back with orders pretty quick, or there'll be no batt'ry left," he observed.

The wise young captain of the second company hazarded to the lieutenant-colonel that the enemy's infantry would probably soon attack the hill, and the lieutenant-colonel snubbed him.

A private in one of the rear companies looked out over the meadow, and then turned to a com-

panion and said, "Look there, Jim!" It was the wounded officer from the battery, who some time before had started to ride across the meadow, supporting his right arm carefully with his left hand. This man had encountered a shell, apparently, at a time when no one perceived him, and he could now be seen lying face downward with a stirruped foot stretched across the body of his dead horse. A leg of the charger extended slantingly upward, precisely as stiff as a stake. Around this motionless pair the shells still howled.

There was a quarrel in A Company. Collins was shaking his fist in the faces of some laughing comrades. "Dern yeh! I ain't afraid t' go. If yeh say much, I will go!"

"Of course, yeh will! You'll run through that there medder, won't yeh?"

Collins said, in a terrible voice: "You see now!"

At this ominous threat his comrades broke into renewed jeers.

Collins gave them a dark scowl, and went to find his captain. The latter was conversing with the colonel of the regiment.

"Captain," said Collins, saluting and standing at attention—in those days all trousers bagged at the knees—"Captain, I want t' get permission to go git some water from that there well over yonder!"

The colonel and the captain swung about simultaneously and stared across the meadow. The captain laughed. "You must be pretty thirsty, Collins?"

"Yes, sir, I am."

"Well—ah," said the captain. After a moment, he asked, "Can't you wait?"

"No, sir."

The colonel was watching Collins's face. "Look here, my lad," he said, in a pious sort of voice—"Look here, my lad"—Collins was not a lad—"don't you think that's taking pretty big risks for a little drink of water?"

"I dunno," said Collins uncomfortably. Some of the resentment toward his companions, which perhaps had forced him into this affair, was beginning to fade. "I dunno w'ether 'tis."

---

2. **floundered,** moved in awkward, struggling motion.

Battlefield, Missionary Ridge, near Chattanooga, Tennessee.

The colonel and the captain contemplated him for a time.

"Well," said the captain finally.

"Well," said the colonel, "if you want to go, why, go."

Collins saluted. "Much obliged t' yeh."

As he moved away the colonel called after him. "Take some of the other boys' canteens with you, an' hurry back, now."

"Yes, sir, I will."

The colonel and the captain looked at each other then, for it had suddenly occurred that they could not for the life of them tell whether Collins wanted to go or whether he did not.

They turned to regard Collins, and as they perceived him surrounded by gesticulating comrades, the colonel said: "Well, by thunder! I guess he's going."

Collins appeared as a man dreaming. In the midst of the questions, the advice, the

warnings, all the excited talk of his company mates, he maintained a curious silence.

They were very busy in preparing him for his ordeal. When they inspected him carefully, it was somewhat like the examination that grooms give a horse before a race; and they were amazed, staggered, by the whole affair. Their astonishment found vent in strange repetitions.

"Are yeh sure a-goin'?" they demanded again and again.

"Certainly I am," cried Collins at last, furiously.

He strode sullenly away from them. He was swinging five or six canteens by their cords. It seemed that his cap would not remain firmly on his head, and often he reached and pulled it down over his brow.

There was a general movement in the compact column. The long animal-like thing moved slightly. Its four hundred eyes were turned upon the figure of Collins.

"Well, sir, if that ain't th' derndest thing! I never thought Fred Collins had the blood in him for that kind of business."

"What's he goin' to do, anyhow?"

"He's goin' to that well there after water."

"We ain't dyin' of thirst, are we? That's foolishness."

"Well, somebody put him up to it, an' he's doin' it."

"Say, he must be a desperate cuss."

When Collins faced the meadow and walked away from the regiment, he was vaguely conscious that a chasm, the deep valley of all prides, was suddenly between him and his comrades. It was provisional, but the provision was that he return as a victor. He had blindly been led by quaint emotions, and laid himself under an obligation to walk squarely up to the face of death.

But he was not sure that he wished to make a retraction, even if he could do so without shame. As a matter of truth, he was sure of very little. He was mainly surprised.

It seemed to him supernaturally strange that he had allowed his mind to manœuvre his body into such a situation. He understood that it might be called dramatically great.

However, he had no full appreciation of anything, excepting that he was actually conscious of being dazed. He could feel his dulled mind groping after the form and colour of this incident. He wondered why he did not feel some keen agony of fear cutting his sense like a knife. He wondered at this, because human expression had said loudly for centuries that men should feel afraid of certain things, and that all men who did not feel this fear were phenomena—heroes.

He was, then, a hero. He suffered that disappointment which we would all have if we discovered that we were ourselves capable of those deeds which we most admire in history and legend. This, then, was a hero. After all, heroes were not much.

No, it could not be true. He was not a hero.

Heroes had no shames in their lives, and, as for him, he remembered borrowing fifteen dollars from a friend and promising to pay it back the next day, and then avoiding that friend for ten months. When, at home, his mother had aroused him for the early labour of his life on the farm, it had often been his fashion to be irritable, childish, diabolical; and his mother had died since he had come to the war.

He saw that, in this matter of the well, the canteens, the shells, he was an intruder in the land of fine deeds.

He was now about thirty paces from his comrades. The regiment had just turned its many faces toward him.

From the forest of terrific noises there suddenly emerged a little uneven line of men. They fired fiercely and rapidly at distant foliage on which appeared little puffs of white smoke. The spatter of skirmish firing was added to the thunder of the guns on the hill. The little line of men ran forward. A colour-sergeant fell flat with his flag as if he had slipped on ice. There was hoarse cheering from this distant field.

Collins suddenly felt that two demon fingers were pressed into his ears. He could see nothing but flying arrows, flaming red. He lurched from the shock of this explosion, but he made a mad rush for the house, which he viewed as a man submerged to the neck in a boiling surf might view the shore. In the air little pieces of shell howled, and the earthquake explosions drove him insane with the menace of their roar. As he ran the canteens knocked together with a rhythmical tinkling.

As he neared the house, each detail of the scene became vivid to him. He was aware of some bricks of the vanished chimney lying on the sod. There was a door which hung by one hinge.

Rifle bullets called forth by the insistent skirmishers came from the far-off bank of foliage. They mingled with the shells and the pieces of shells until the air was torn in all directions by hootings, yells, howls. The sky was full of fiends who directed all their wild rage at his head.

When he came to the well, he flung himself face downward and peered into its darkness. There were furtive silver glintings some feet from the surface. He grabbed one of the canteens and, unfastening its cap, swung it down by the cord. The water flowed slowly in with an indolent gurgle.

And now, as he lay with his face turned away, he was suddenly smitten with the terror. It came upon his heart like the grasp of claws. All the power faded from his muscles. For an instant he was no more than a dead man.

The canteen filled with a maddening slowness, in the manner of all bottles. Presently he recovered his strength and addressed a screaming oath to it. He leaned over until it seemed as if he intended to try to push water into it with his hands. His eyes as he gazed down into the well shone like two pieces of metal, and in their expression was a great appeal and a great curse. The stupid water derided him.

There was the blaring thunder of a shell. Crimson light shone through the swift-boiling smoke and made a pink reflection on part of the wall of the well. Collins jerked out his arm and canteen with the same motion that a man would use in withdrawing his head from a furnace.

He scrambled erect and glared and hesitated. On the ground near him lay the old well bucket, with a length of rusty chain. He lowered it swiftly into the well. The bucket struck the water and then, turning lazily over, sank. When, with hand reaching tremblingly over hand, he hauled it out, it knocked often against the walls of the well and spilled some of its contents.

In running with a filled bucket, a man can adopt but one kind of gait. So, through this terrible field over which screamed practical angels of death, Collins ran in the manner of a farmer chased out of a dairy by a bull.

His face went staring white with anticipation—anticipation of a blow that would whirl him around and down. He would fall as he had seen other men fall, the life knocked out of them so suddenly that their knees were no more quick to touch the ground than their heads. He saw the long blue line of the regiment, but his comrades were standing looking at him from the edge of an impossible star. He was aware of some deep wheel-ruts and hoofprints in the sod beneath his feet.

The artillery officer who had fallen in this meadow had been making groans in the teeth of the tempest of sound. These futile cries, wrenched from him by his agony, were heard only by shells, bullets. When wild-eyed Collins came running, this officer raised himself. His face contorted and blanched from pain, he was about to utter some great beseeching cry. But suddenly his face straightened, and he called: "Say, young man, give me a drink of water, will you?"

Collins had no room amid his emotions for surprise. He was mad from the threats of destruction.

"I can't!" he screamed, and in his reply was a full description of his quaking apprehension. His cap was gone and his hair was riotous. His clothes made it appear that he had been dragged over the ground by the heels. He ran on.

The officer's head sank down, and one elbow crooked. His foot in its brass-bound stirrup still stretched over the body of his horse, and the other leg was under the steed.

But Collins turned. He came dashing back. His face had now turned grey, and in his eyes was all terror. "Here it is! Here it is!"

The officer was as a man gone in drink. His arm bent like a twig. His head drooped as if his neck were of willow. He was sinking to the ground, to lie face downward.

Collins grabbed him by the shoulder. "Here it is. Here's your drink. Turn over. Turn over, man, for God's sake!"

With Collins hauling at his shoulder, the officer twisted his body and fell with his face turned toward that region where lived the unspeakable noises of the swirling missiles. There was the faintest shadow of a smile on his lips as he looked at Collins. He gave a sigh, a little primitive breath like that from a child.

Collins tried to hold the bucket steadily, but his shaking hands caused the water to splash all over the face of the dying man. Then he jerked it away and ran on.

The regiment gave him a welcoming roar. The grimed faces were wrinkled in laughter.

His captain waved the bucket away. "Give it to the men!"

The two genial, skylarking young lieutenants were the first to gain possession of it. They played over it in their fashion.

When one tried to drink, the other teasingly knocked his elbow. "Don't Billie! You'll make me spill it," said the one. The other laughed.

Suddenly there was an oath, the thud of wood on the ground, and a swift murmur of astonishment among the ranks. The two lieutenants glared at each other. The bucket lay on the ground, empty.

I
SOLDIERS AT WAR

Every paragraph of this story of Fred Collins drenches us with the sights, sounds, and smells of the battlefield. Crane intensifies his descriptions with phrases like "fibres of flame that seemed like lances," "the ruck of bleeding and prostrate horses," and "earthquake explosions drove him insane with the menace of their roar." He wants us to contemplate the senseless slaughter in the most vivid language he can manage.

But we, like the author, are only observers. Fred Collins is the participant. He and his fellow soldiers talk in the simplest kind of language. In the midst of the agony and carnage around him, Collins wants—of all things—a drink of water. Crane's problem is to make us see that this ordinary gesture—taking empty canteens to the well—is connected directly with the romantic idea of "a mystery of heroism."

II
IMPLICATIONS

Discuss the following propositions as we move from the first page to the last of this story.

1. Collins' thirst is literally of more concern to him than the death of the bugler.

2. Collins' heroism is merely a foolish dare triggered by a joke.

3. It is only as he begins to *think* about his action, that Collins contemplates "heroism" but rejects it.

4. Collins performs heroically almost without knowing it.

5. The trip back is for Collins the heroic gesture because he masters his fear, especially when he stops to give a dying man water rather than rush on to safety.

6. The essence of Collins' heroism is not to be without fears but rather to conquer them.

III
TECHNIQUES
Intention and Theme

Without the last four paragraphs, this story would lose much of its bite. When the captain "waved the bucket away" and the lieutenant spills the precious water on the ground, what is Crane saying about life? Could he be saying that life is often brutal in its treatment of heroic gestures, either out of ignorance (the lieutenants could not have known what the victory "cost" Collins) or out of vindictiveness (life is determined to "defeat" us no matter how we try to rise above it)? If this is the point of the story, then heroism is indeed a mystery, because Collins must be saying that his risking his life was futile after all, not worth the victory over fear.

Or could a wholly different intention have been in Crane's mind as he wrote these last paragraphs? Could he have felt that since Collins chose to make a foolish, even a stupid, gesture in running to the well for water, he deserved exactly what happens: a waste of effort? Is the story far more pessimistic—even fatalistic—than we realize at first?

Which way do you read it: Collins achieves heroic stature by facing death and his own fears; Collins acts stupidly and the ironic spilling of his prize is all he deserves; life will diminish our heroic acts no matter what we do to protect them? What would Crane have risked by giving Collins additional dialogue after the last sentence: "The bucket lay on the ground empty." Could the word *empty* be the clue to the author's intention?

Although this story
was written while Crane lived in England,
its beginnings lay in his tour of the Southwest
in 1895. Always alert to local color,
he had visited San Antonio and the Rio Grande,
hoping to collect short-story material.
The central dramatic incident is invented,
but the frontier code, the atmosphere,
the language the characters speak
ring true to what history records
of these days in the West. As with "A Mystery
of Heroism," the whole story hinges
on the last paragraphs; but here Crane
works harder at creating two sharply different
points of view: those of Jack Potter,
the marshal of Yellow Sky, and Scratchy Wilson,
the town drunk. As he brings them together,
these viewpoints inevitably clash,
yet not as we expected.

The Bride Comes to Yellow Sky

I

The great Pullman was whirling onward with such dignity of motion that a glance from the window seemed simply to prove that the plains of Texas were pouring eastward. Vast flats of green grass, dull-hued spaces of mesquit[1] and cactus, little groups of frame houses, woods of light and tender trees, all were sweeping into the east, sweeping over the horizon, a precipice.

A newly married pair had boarded this coach at San Antonio. The man's face was reddened from many days in the wind and sun, and a direct result of his new black clothes was that his brick-coloured hands were constantly performing in a most conscious fashion. From time to time he looked down respectfully at his attire. He sat with a hand on each knee, like a man waiting in a barber's shop. The glances he devoted to other passengers were furtive and shy.

The bride was not pretty, nor was she very young. She wore a dress of blue cashmere, with small reservations of velvet here and there, and with steel buttons abounding. She continually twisted her head to regard her puff sleeves, very stiff, straight, and high. They embarrassed her. It was quite apparent that she had cooked, and that she expected to cook, dutifully. The blushes caused by the careless scrutiny of some passengers as she had entered the car were strange to see upon this plain, under-class countenance, which was drawn in placid, almost emotionless lines.

They were evidently very happy. "Ever been in a parlour-car before?" he asked, smiling with delight.

"No," she answered; "I never was. It's fine, ain't it?"

"Great! And then after a while we'll go forward to the diner, and get a big lay-out. Finest meal in the world. Charge a dollar."

"Oh, do they?" cried the bride. "Charge a dollar? Why, that's too much—for us—ain't it, Jack?"

"Not this trip, anyhow," he answered bravely. "We're going to go the whole thing."

Later he explained to her about the trains. "You see, it's a thousand miles from one end of Texas to the other; and this train runs right across it, and never stops but four times." He had the pride of an owner. He pointed out to her the dazzling fittings of the coach; and in truth her eyes opened wider as she contemplated the sea-green figured velvet, the shining brass, silver, and glass, the wood that gleamed as darkly brilliant as the surface of a pool of oil. At one end a bronze figure sturdily held a support for a separated chamber, and at convenient places on the ceiling were frescos in olive and silver.

---

1. **mesquit**\měs▲kēt\ small shrub that yields sweet pods.

To the minds of the pair, their surroundings reflected the glory of their marriage that morning in San Antonio; this was the environment of their new estate; and the man's face in particular beamed with an elation that made him appear ridiculous to the Negro porter. This individual at times surveyed them from afar with an amused and superior grin. On other occasions he bullied them with skill in ways that did not make it exactly plain to them that they were being bullied. He subtly used all the manners of the most unconquerable kind of snobbery. He oppressed them; but of this oppression they had small knowledge, and they speedily forgot that infrequently a number of travellers covered them with stares of derisive enjoyment. Historically there was supposed to be something infinitely humorous in their situation.

"We are due in Yellow Sky at 3:42," he said, looking tenderly into her eyes.

"Oh, are we?" she said, as if she had not been aware of it. To evince surprise at her husband's statement was part of her wifely amiability. She took from a pocket a little silver watch; and as she held it before her, and stared at it with a frown of attention, the new husband's face shone.

"I bought it in San Anton' from a friend of mine," he told her gleefully.

"It's seventeen minutes past twelve," she said, looking up at him with a kind of shy and clumsy coquetry. A passenger, noting this play, grew excessively sardonic, and winked at himself in one of the numerous mirrors.

At last they went to the dining-car. Two rows of Negro waiters, in glowing white suits, surveyed their entrance with the interest, and also the equanimity, of men who had been forewarned. The pair fell to the lot of a waiter who happened to feel pleasure in steering them through their meal. He viewed them with the manner of a fatherly pilot, his countenance radiant with benevolence. The patronage, entwined with the ordinary deference, was not plain to them. And yet, as they returned to their coach, they showed in their faces a sense of escape.

To the left, miles down a long purple slope, was a little ribbon of mist where moved the keening Rio Grande. The train was approaching it at an angle, and the apex was Yellow Sky. Presently it was apparent that, as the distance from Yellow Sky grew shorter, the husband became commensurately restless. His brick-red hands were more insistent in their prominence. Occasionally he was even rather absent-minded and far-away when the bride leaned forward and addressed him.

As a matter of truth, Jack Potter was beginning to find the shadow of a deed weigh upon him like a leaden slab. He, the town marshal of Yellow Sky, a man known, liked, and feared in his corner, a prominent person, had gone to San Antonio to meet a girl he believed he loved, and there, after the usual prayers, had actually induced her to marry him, without consulting Yellow Sky for any part of the transaction. He was now bringing his bride before an innocent and unsuspecting community.

Of course people in Yellow Sky married as it pleased them, in accordance with a general custom; but such was Potter's thought of his duty to his friends, or of their idea of his duty, or of an unspoken form which does not control men in these matters, that he felt he was heinous. He had committed an extraordinary crime. Face to face with this girl in San Antonio, and spurred by his sharp impulse, he had gone headlong over all the social hedges. At San Antonio he was like a man hidden in the dark. A knife to sever any friendly duty, any form, was easy to his hand in that remote city. But the hour of Yellow Sky—the hour of daylight—was approaching.

He knew full well that his marriage was an important thing to his town. It could only be exceeded by the burning of the new hotel. His friends could not forgive him. Frequently he had reflected on the advisability of telling them by telegraph, but a new cowardice had been upon him. He feared to do it. And now the train was hurrying him toward a scene of amazement, glee, and reproach. He glanced out of the window at the line of haze swinging slowly in toward the train.

Yellow Sky had a kind of brass band, which played painfully, to the delight of the populace. He laughed without heart as he thought of it. If the citizens could dream of his prospective arrival with his bride, they would parade the band at the station and escort them, amid cheers and laughing congratulations, to his adobe home.

He resolved that he would use all the devices of speed and plainscraft in making the journey from the station to his house. Once within that safe citadel, he could issue some sort of vocal bulletin, and then not go among the citizens until they had time to wear off a little of their enthusiasm.

The bride looked anxiously at him. "What's worrying you, Jack?"

He laughed again. "I'm not worrying, girl; I'm only thinking of Yellow Sky."

She flushed in comprehension.

A sense of mutual guilt invaded their minds and developed a finer tenderness. They looked at each other with eyes softly aglow. But Potter often laughed the same nervous laugh; the flush upon the bride's face seemed quite permanent.

The traitor to the feelings of Yellow Sky narrowly watched the speeding landscape. "We're nearly there," he said.

Presently the porter came and announced the proximity of Potter's home. He held a brush in his hand, and, with all his airy superiority gone, he brushed Potter's new clothes as the latter slowly turned this way and that way. Potter fumbled out a coin and gave it to the porter, as he had seen others do. It was a heavy and muscle-bound business, as that of a man shoeing his first horse.

The porter took their bag, and as the train began to slow they moved forward to the hooded platform of the car. Presently the two engines and their long string of coaches rushed into the station of Yellow Sky.

"They have to take water here," said Potter, from a constricted throat and in mournful

cadence, as one announcing death. Before the train stopped his eye had swept the length of the platform, and he was glad and astonished to see there was none upon it but the station-agent, who, with a slightly hurried and anxious air, was walking toward the water-tanks. When the train had halted, the porter alighted first, and placed in position a little temporary step.

"Come on, girl," said Potter, hoarsely. As he helped her down they each laughed on a false note. He took the bag from the Negro, and bade his wife cling to his arm. As they slunk rapidly away, his hang-dog glance perceived that they were unloading the two trunks, and also that the station-agent, far ahead near the baggage-car, had turned and was running toward him, making gestures. He laughed, and groaned as he laughed, when he noted the first effect of his marital bliss upon Yellow Sky. He gripped his wife's arm firmly to his side, and they fled. Behind them the porter stood, chuckling fatuously.

II

The California express on the Southern Railway was due at Yellow Sky in twenty-one minutes. There were six men at the bar of the Weary Gentleman saloon. One was a drummer[2] who talked a great deal and rapidly; three were Texans who did not care to talk at that time; and two were Mexican sheep-herders, who did not talk as a general practice in the Weary Gentleman saloon. The barkeeper's dog lay on the board walk that crossed in front of the door. His head was on his paws, and he glanced drowsily here and there with the constant vigilance of a dog that is kicked on occasion. Across the sandy street were some vivid green grass-plots, so wonderful in appearance, amid the sands that burned near them in a blazing sun, that they caused a doubt in the mind. They exactly resembled the grass mats used to represent lawns on the stage. At the

---

2. **drummer,** traveling sales agent.

cooler end of the railway station, a man without a coat sat in a tilted chair and smoked his pipe. The fresh-cut bank of the Rio Grande circled near the town, and there could be seen beyond it a great plum-coloured plain of mesquit.

Save for the busy drummer and his companions in the saloon, Yellow Sky was dozing. The new-comer leaned gracefully upon the bar, and recited many tales with the confidence of a bard who has come upon a new field.

"—and at the moment that the old man fell downstairs with the bureau in his arms, the old woman was coming up with two scuttles[3] of coal, and of course—"

The drummer's tale was interrupted by a young man who suddenly appeared in the open door. He cried: "Scratchy Wilson's drunk, and has turned loose with both hands." The two Mexicans at once set down their glasses and faded out of the rear entrance of the saloon.

The drummer, innocent and jocular, answered: "All right, old man. S'pose he has? Come in and have a drink, anyhow."

But the information had made such an obvious cleft in every skull in the room that the drummer was obliged to see its importance. All had become instantly solemn. "Say," said he, mystified, "what is this?" His three companions made the introductory gesture of eloquent speech; but the young man at the door forestalled them.

"It means, my friend," he answered, as he came into the saloon, "that for the next two hours this town won't be a health resort."

The barkeeper went to the door, and locked and barred it; reaching out of the window, he pulled in heavy wooden shutters, and barred them. Immediately a solemn, chapel-like gloom was upon the place. The drummer was looking from one to another.

"But say," he cried, "what is this, anyhow? You don't mean there is going to be a gunfight?"

"Don't know whether there'll be a fight or not," answered one man, grimly; "but there'll be some shootin'—some good shootin'."

The young man who had warned them waved his hand. "Oh, there'll be a fight fast enough, if any one wants it. Anybody can get a fight out there in the street. There's a fight just waiting."

The drummer seemed to be swayed between the interest of a foreigner and a perception of personal danger.

"What did you say his name was?" he asked.

"Scratchy Wilson," they answered in chorus.

"And will he kill anybody? What are you going to do? Does this happen often? Does he rampage around like this once a week or so? Can he break in that door?"

"No; he can't break down that door," replied the barkeeper. "He's tried it three times. But when he comes you'd better lay down on the floor, stranger. He's dead sure to shoot at it, and a bullet may come through."

Thereafter the drummer kept a strict eye upon the door. The time had not yet been called for him to hug the floor, but, as a minor precaution, he sidled near to the wall. "Will he kill anybody?" he said again.

The men laughed low and scornfully at the question.

"He's out to shoot, and he's out for trouble. Don't see any good in experimentin' with him."

"But what do you do in a case like this? What do you do?"

A man responded: "Why, he and Jack Potter—"

"But," in chorus the other men interrupted, "Jack Potter's in San Anton'."

"Well, who is he? What's he got to do with it?"

"Oh, he's the town marshal. He goes out and fights Scratchy when he gets on one of these tears."

"Wow!" said the drummer, mopping his brow. "Nice job he's got."

The voices had toned away to mere whisperings. The drummer wished to ask further questions, which were born of an increasing anxiety and bewilderment; but when he attempted

---

3. **scuttles**\ˈskət·əlz\ metal pails for carrying coal.

them, the men merely looked at him in irritation and motioned him to remain silent. A tense waiting hush was upon them. In the deep shadows of the room their eyes shone as they listened for sounds from the street. One man made three gestures at the barkeeper; and the latter, moving like a ghost, handed him a glass and a bottle. The man poured a full glass of whisky, and set down the bottle noiselessly. He gulped the whisky in a swallow, and turned again toward the door in immovable silence. The drummer saw that the barkeeper, without a sound, had taken a Winchester from beneath the bar. Later he saw this individual beckoning to him, so he tiptoed across the room.

"You better come with me back of the bar."

"No, thanks," said the drummer, perspiring; "I'd rather be where I can make a break for the back door."

Whereupon the man of bottles made a kindly but peremptory gesture. The drummer obeyed it, and, finding himself seated on a box with his head below the level of the bar, balm was laid upon his soul at sight of various zinc and copper fittings that bore a resemblance to armour-plate. The barkeeper took a seat comfortably upon an adjacent box.

"You see," he whispered, "this here Scratchy Wilson is a wonder with a gun—a perfect wonder; and when he goes on the war-trail, we hunt our holes—naturally. He's about the last one of the old gang that used to hang out along the river here. He's a terror when he's drunk. When he's sober he's all right—kind of simple—wouldn't hurt a fly—nicest fellow in town. But when he's drunk—whoo!"

There were periods of stillness. "I wish Jack Potter was back from San Anton'," said the barkeeper. "He shot Wilson up once—in the leg—and he would sail in and pull out the kinks in this thing."

Presently they heard from a distance the sound of a shot, followed by three wild yowls. It instantly removed a bond from the men in the darkened saloon. There was a shuffling of feet. They looked at each other. "Here he comes," they said.

III

A man in a maroon-coloured flannel shirt, which had been purchased for purposes of decoration, and made principally by some Jewish women on the East Side of New York, rounded a corner and walked into the middle of the main street of Yellow Sky. In either hand the man held a long, heavy, blue-black revolver. Often he yelled, and these cries rang through a semblance of a deserted village, shrilly flying over the roofs in a volume that seemed to have no relation to the ordinary vocal strength of a man. It was as if the surrounding stillness formed the arch of a tomb over him. These cries of ferocious challenge rang against walls of silence. And his boots had red tops with gilded imprints, of the kind beloved in winter by little sledding boys on the hillsides of New England.

The man's face flamed in a rage begot of whisky. His eyes, rolling, and yet keen for ambush, hunted the still doorways and windows. He walked with the creeping movement of the midnight cat. As it occurred to him, he roared menacing information. The long revolvers in his hands were as easy as straws; they were moved with an electric swiftness. The little fingers of each hand played sometimes in a musician's way. Plain from the low collar of the shirt, the cords of his neck straightened and sank, straightened and sank, as passion moved him. The only sounds were his terrible invitations. The calm adobes preserved their demeanour at the passing of this small thing in the middle of the street.

There was no offer of fight—no offer of fight. The man called to the sky. There were no attractions. He bellowed and fumed and swayed his revolvers here and everywhere.

The dog of the barkeeper of the Weary Gentleman saloon had not appreciated the advance of events. He yet lay dozing in front of his master's door. At sight of the dog, the man paused and raised his revolver humorously. At sight of the man, the dog sprang up and walked diagonally away, with a sullen head, and growling. The man yelled, and the dog broke into a gallop. As it was about to enter an alley, there was a loud noise, a whistling, and something spat the ground directly before it. The dog screamed, and, wheeling in terror, galloped headlong in a new direction. Again there was a noise, a whistling, and sand was kicked viciously before it. Fear-stricken, the dog turned and flurried like an animal in a pen. The man stood laughing, his weapons at his hips.

Ultimately the man was attracted by the closed door of the Weary Gentleman saloon. He went to it and, hammering with a revolver, demanded drink.

The door remaining imperturbable, he picked a bit of paper from the walk, and nailed it to the framework with a knife. He then turned his back contemptuously upon this popular resort and, walking to the opposite side of the street and spinning there on his heel quickly and lithely, fired at the bit of paper. He missed it by a half-inch. He swore at himself, and went away. Later he comfortably fusilladed[4] the windows of his most intimate friend. The man was playing with this town; it was a toy for him.

But still there was no offer of fight. The name of Jack Potter, his ancient antagonist, entered his mind, and he concluded that it would be a glad thing if he should go to Potter's house, and by bombardment induce him to come out and fight. He moved in the direction of his desire, chanting Apache scalp-music.

When he arrived at it, Potter's house presented the same still front as had the other adobes. Taking up a strategic position, the man howled a challenge. But this house regarded him as might a great stone god. It gave no sign. After a decent wait, the man howled further challenges, mingling with them wonderful epithets.

Presently there came the spectacle of a man churning himself into deepest rage over the immobility of a house. He fumed at it as the winter wind attacks a prairie cabin in the North. To the distance there should have gone the sound of a tumult like the fighting of two hundred Mexicans. As necessity bade him, he paused for breath or to reload his revolvers.

IV

Potter and his bride walked sheepishly and with speed. Sometimes they laughed together shamefacedly and low.

"Next corner, dear," he said finally.

They put forth the efforts of a pair walking bowed against a strong wind. Potter was about to raise a finger to point the first appearance of the new home when, as they circled the corner, they came face to face with a man in a maroon-coloured shirt, who was feverishly pushing cartridges into a large revolver. Upon the instant the man dropped his revolver to the ground and, like lightning, whipped another from its holster. The second weapon was aimed at the bridegroom's chest.

There was a silence. Potter's mouth seemed to be merely a grave for his tongue. He exhibited an instinct to at once loosen his arm from the woman's grip, and he dropped the bag to the sand. As for the bride, her face had gone as yellow as old cloth. She was a slave to hideous rites, gazing at the apparitional snake.

The two men faced each other at a distance of three paces. He of the revolver smiled with a new and quiet ferocity.

"Tried to sneak up on me," he said. "Tried to sneak up on me!" His eyes grew more baleful. As Potter made a slight movement, the man thrust his revolver venomously forward. "No; don't you do it, Jack Potter. Don't you move a finger toward a gun just yet. Don't you move an eyelash. The time has come for me to settle with you, and I'm goin' to do it my own way, and loaf along with no interferin'. So if you don't want a gun bent on you, just mind what I tell you."

---

4. **fusilladed**\ˈfyū·sə ˈlād·əd\ fired a number of shots in rapid succession.

Potter looked at his enemy. "I ain't got a gun on me Scratchy," he said. "Honest, I ain't." He was stiffening and steadying, but yet somewhere at the back of his mind a vision of the Pullman floated: the sea-green figured velvet, the shining brass, silver, and glass, the wood that gleamed as darkly brilliant as the surface of a pool of oil—all the glory of the marriage, the environment of the new estate. "You know I fight when it comes to fighting, Scratchy Wilson; but I ain't got a gun on me. You'll have to do all the shootin' yourself."

His enemy's face went livid. He stepped forward, and lashed his weapon to and fro before Potter's chest. "Don't you tell me you ain't got no gun on you, you whelp.[5] Don't tell me no lie like that. There ain't a man in Texas ever seen you without no gun. Don't take me for no kid." His eyes blazed with light, and his throat worked like a pump.

"I ain't takin' you for no kid," answered Potter. His heels had not moved an inch backward. "I'm takin' you for a damn fool. I tell you I ain't got a gun, and I ain't. If you're goin' to shoot me up, you better begin now; you'll never get a chance like this again."

So much enforced reasoning had told on Wilson's rage; he was calmer. "If you ain't got a gun, why ain't you got a gun?" he sneered. "Been to Sunday-school?"

"I ain't got a gun because I've just come from San Anton' with my wife. I'm married," said Potter. "And if I'd thought there was going to be any galoots like you prowling around when I brought my wife home, I'd had a gun, and don't you forget it."

"Married!" said Scratchy, not at all comprehending.

"Yes, married. I'm married," said Potter, distinctly.

"Married?" said Scratchy. Seemingly for the first time, he saw the drooping, drowning woman at the other man's side. "No!" he said. He was like a creature allowed a glimpse of another world. He moved a pace backward, and his arm, with the revolver, dropped to his side. "Is this the lady?" he asked.

"Yes; this is the lady," answered Potter.

There was another period of silence.

"Well," said Wilson at last, slowly, "I s'pose it's all off now."

"It's all off if you say so, Scratchy. You know I didn't make the trouble." Potter lifted his valise.

"Well, I 'low it's off, Jack," said Wilson. He was looking at the ground. "Married!" He was not a student of chivalry; it was merely that in the presence of this foreign condition he was a simple child of the earlier plains. He picked up his starboard revolver, and, placing both weapons in their holsters, he went away. His feet made funnel-shaped tracks in the heavy sand.

I

STORY IN FOUR ACTS

Crane breaks this story into four distinct parts, and he handles them as deftly as though they were four acts of a drama. The first sets the scene: the timid newlyweds, still strangers to each other, wonder how to confront the hometown after their "daring" decision to get married. The second section sets another kind of scene, this time from the hometown's point of view, only the local rowdy is the main character and a more serious confrontation is at hand. In the third section, Crane shifts his focus to Scratchy Wilson himself. Crane is still the narrator, even though we now see Yellow Sky through Scratchy's eyes. As his rage mounts, Scratchy comes face to face not with Potter himself but with Potter's house. The fourth section is inevitable: the two adversaries must meet, and naturally they must meet unequally armed if Crane wishes to avoid bloodshed. The brandished pistols are menacing, without doubt, but Potter has a secret weapon, a single word: married. Now we see and feel the impact of the title as the retreating Scratchy Wilson makes "funnel-shaped

---

5. **whelp,** young person, usually used with unfavorable connotation.

tracks in the heavy sand." Has Crane cheated us of the rousing climax we might expect, or is he striving for more subtle effects, thus risking an anticlimax without fear of diminishing his story?

II
IMPLICATIONS

Crane often suggests more than he says. What do the following statements from the story reveal about the characters and the situation?

1. She continually twisted her head to regard her puff sleeves, very stiff, straight, and high.

2. He had committed an extraordinary crime. Face to face with this girl in San Antonio, and spurred by his sharp impulse, he had gone headlong over all the social hedges.

3. He gripped his wife's arm firmly to his side, and they fled. Behind them the porter stood, chuckling fatuously.

4. "Don't know whether there'll be a fight or not, but there'll be some shootin'—some good shootin'."

5. "Oh, he's the town marshal. He goes out and fights Scratchy when he gets on one of these tears."

6. The drummer saw that the barkeeper, without a sound, had taken a Winchester from beneath the bar.

7. Presently there came the spectacle of a man churning himself into deepest rage over the immobility of a house.

8. Potter's mouth seemed to be merely a grave for his tongue.

9. As for the bride, her face had gone as yellow as old cloth.

10. Seemingly for the first time, he saw the drooping, drowning woman at the other man's side.

III
TECHNIQUES

Intention and Theme

Like "A Mystery of Heroism," this story turns on the irony of the last paragraphs. The threatening man, gun in hand, is defeated by his unarmed enemy, and defeated not physically but spiritually, which is worse. Scratchy expected to encounter gunfire (he was ready for that; the whole town was ready), but he meets instead a marshal more resolute than ever. Potter is a new man. Marriage

has transformed him, not only in his own eyes but in Scratchy's eyes as well. Marriage, to Scratchy Wilson, is "another world," a "foreign condition." The one word—"married"—is like a blow aimed squarely at Scratchy's jaw. All he can say is "I s'pose it's all off now" and slump away through "the heavy sand."

What reaction do you think Crane expects from his reader: surprise, relief, laughter? What other endings could he have given this story? If "The Bride Comes to Yellow Sky" sets out to illustrate "what innocence can do if it has the opportunity," as one critic believes, could Crane have chosen any other ending?

IV
WORDS

A. Using what you have learned about context clues, determine the meaning of the following italicized words.

1. . . . he was vaguely conscious that a *chasm*, the deep valley of all prides, was suddenly between him and his comrades.

2. To *evince* surprise at her husband's statement was part of her wifely *amiability*.

3. . . . as the distance from Yellow Sky grew shorter, the husband became *commensurately* restless.

4. The train was approaching it at an angle, and the *apex* was Yellow Sky.

5. . . . spinning there on his heel quickly and *lithely*, fired at the bit of paper.

B. 1. Many antonyms are derived forms with one of the negative affixes: *in-, non-, dis-, mis-, un-, -less*. The antonym of subversive might be "nonsubversive"; *adequate*, inadequate; *exalted*, unexalted. Yet not all words have a clear-cut negative affix. For example, antonyms for *moral* might be *unmoral, immoral, amoral*; for *American, non-American* and *un-American*. Do these words carry the same implications?

2. For the words listed below, form negative words. Define negative forms that differ in meaning.

(a) the guns were *typical*; (b) guilty of *human* feelings; (c) the last *divisible* parts; (d) *similar* reaction; (e) *impassioned* plea; (f) *respectful* answer.

C. The function of language, written and spoken, is to communicate. Good English is English which communicates most completely and accurately in a specific situation. Speakers and writers adjust their language to their subject, to their audience, and to themselves. Yet in the social and in the business worlds success depends largely on how well you speak "good English." Survey your use of the spoken language. What do you say?

1. *waked up* or *woke up*; he *has proved, has proven* his case; he *couldn't help but feel* as he did, he *couldn't help feeling* as he did.

2. the girl *has got, has gotten* herself a boy-friend; he went no *farther, further* than the next town; neither of the moves *justify, justifies* the end result.

3. he was *enthused, enthusiastic* about the trip; the crowd *derided, ridiculed* him; inside that safe *citadel, fort.*

Again, good English is that which is most appropriate to the situation, to the listener, and to the speaker. Nonstandard usage is inappropriate most of the time. Use of standard usage, on the other hand, is appropriate most of the time. From a daily newspaper, find examples of each level of usage. What was the purpose of each writer?

Five Poems

When first published Crane's poems did not please
many readers, because the lines were not like the popular poetry of the day. Yet Crane
thought of them as a more ambitious effort than his famous novel *The Red Badge of Courage*,
because they gave his ideas of life as a whole. These ideas were frequently
bitter, always antiheroic, not unlike some of his short stories. The form
of these remarkable poems owes much to Crane's knowledge of the Bible
and to his admiration for Walt Whitman and Emily Dickinson.

A Man Saw a Ball of Gold in the Sky

A man saw a ball of gold in the sky.
He climbed for it,
And eventually he achieved it—
It was clay.

Now this is the strange part: 5
When the man went to earth
And looked again,
Lo, there was the ball of gold.
Now this is the strange part:
It was a ball of gold.   10
Ay, by the heavens it was a ball of gold.

God Fashioned
the Ship of the World

God fashioned the ship of the world carefully.
With the infinite skill of an All-Master
Made He the hull and the sails,
Held He the rudder
Ready for adjustment.   5
Erect stood He, scanning His work proudly.
Then—at fateful time—a wrong called,
And God turned, heeding.
Lo, the ship, at this opportunity, slipped slyly,
Making cunning noiseless travel down the ways.   10
So that, for ever rudderless, it went upon the seas
Going ridiculous voyages,
Making quaint progress,
Turning as with serious purpose
Before stupid winds.   15
And there were many in the sky
Who laughed at this thing.

The Wayfarer

The wayfarer,
Perceiving the pathway to truth,
Was struck with astonishment.
It was thickly grown with weeds.
"Ha," he said,   5
"I see that no one has passed here
In a long time."
Later he saw that each weed
Was a singular knife.
"Well," he mumbled at last,   10
"Doubtless there are other roads."

The Book of Wisdom

I met a seer.
He held in his hands
The book of wisdom.
"Sir," I addressed him,
"Let me read."   5
"Child—" he began.
"Sir," I said.
"Think not that I am a child,
For already I know much
Of that which you hold;   10
Aye, much."

He smiled.
Then he opened the book
And held it before me.
Strange that I should have grown so suddenly blind. 15

A Man Said to the Universe

A man said to the universe:
"Sir, I exist!"
"However," replied the universe,
"The fact has not created in me
A sense of obligation."

I
LINES ON LIFE

Reviewers used harsh language to damn these poems when they first appeared. But Crane ignored critical opinions about his poems; in fact, he called them "lines" rather than poetry. His poems are closely connected with his novels and short stories. They use the familiar reversals, the ironic conclusions, and the flat, direct language of his dialogue. What is more, they are sincere and honest statements that reflect Crane's constant concern over the bitter realities of our lives.

IMPLICATIONS

Discuss the interpretations or questions below.

*A Man Saw a Ball of Gold
in the Sky*

1. Beauty is in the eye of the beholder.

2. There is more joy in expectation than in fulfillment.

3. Even in the face of facts humans cling to illusion.

*God Fashioned
the Ship of the World*

1. Human lives are meaningless and without direction.

2. Human beings are absurd creatures, the laughingstock of the universe.

The Wayfarer

1. We are all wayfarers and this poem is a universal indictment. Crane was not the first to suggest that the path to truth is difficult, but what is he trying to suggest by "thickly grown with weeds" and then "each weed/ Was a singular knife"? Why "singular"?

2. The wayfarer "mumbles" a weak assurance, but the poet is skeptical. What would you tell the wayfarer: there is only one road to truth? All roads to truth are overgrown with weeds? Each person must kill the weeds alone?

The Book of Wisdom

1. Why are we told nothing about this "seer" and his "book of wisdom"?

2. How does the last line of the poem connect with the word "child"? How does it connect with the word "seer"?

3. What does the word "blind" suggest here in addition to "unable to see"?

A Man Said to the Universe

1. Shall we read "God" for universe, or is the whole point of the poem that the universe is God-less?

2. If we substitute "nature" for universe, what does this do to our idea of "Mother Nature" as a kindly benefactor?

THE INNER STRUGGLE

ALONE
Henri Linton
This painting graphically
illustrates the torment of
the inner struggle.

From the shrewd Yankee trader and the wealthy Southern aristocrat through the captains of industry to the modern corporate executive, Americans have frequently been characterized as persons concerned with material things, with getting and spending. These material involvements, some have said, have made us a people overconcerned with "show," with the outer rather than with the inner world.

America does have a high standard of living, a standard that probably could not have been achieved unless we had put great value on material things. On the other hand, there is much in American life to prove that we have had and have now an intense concern with the inner as well as with the outer reality.

Even a very brief study of major American writers would reveal this quite clearly. Writers like Edgar Allan Poe, Nathaniel Hawthorne, Herman Melville, Stephen Crane, and William Faulkner have become internationally famous for their explorations of the moral, spiritual, and psychological nature of the human spirit. They—and others—have written of our struggles with our own nature, with our conscience; they have been intensely concerned with the causes and consequences of human choices.

More than a century ago, Alexis de Tocqueville, the famous French critic of American culture, predicted that American writers would focus on "man himself, taken aloof from his age and his country and standing in the presence of nature and God, with his passions, his doubts, his rare propensities and inconceivable wretchedness."

THE INNER STRUGGLE focuses on human nature, on the drama of decision, and on the role conscience plays in this drama. The characters in these selections are, for the most part, ordinary people, but we meet them at critical moments in their lives. Because they are ordinary people, it is easy to identify with them and thus to share in their trials of conscience. As we share their tests and decisions, we gain a deeper insight into the inner nature of humanity, into the inner nature of ourselves.

In its simplest form, the inner struggle
involves an evil side of human nature on the one hand and a good side,
usually represented as the voice of conscience, on the other.
In modern times, psychologists have told us a good deal
about both of these forces, but long before the advent of modern psychology
Edgar Allan Poe showed, in his *Tales of the Grotesque and Arabesque*,
that he had a deep knowledge of the inner self, especially of the darker side
of human nature. "The Black Cat," one of the stories
in that collection, illustrates how the evil forces within one man
came to prevail completely over his conscience.

The Black Cat

EDGAR ALLAN POE

For the most wild yet most homely narrative which I am about to pen, I neither expect nor solicit belief. Mad indeed would I be to expect it, in a case where my very senses reject their own evidence. Yet, mad am I not —and very surely do I not dream. But tomorrow I die, and to-day I would unburden my soul. My immediate purpose is to place before the world, plainly, succinctly, and without comment, a series of mere household events. In their consequences, these events have terrified—have tortured—have destroyed me. Yet I will not attempt to expound them. To me, they have presented little but horror —to many they will seem less terrible than *baroques*.[1] Hereafter, perhaps, some intellect may be found which will reduce my phantasm to the commonplace—some intellect more calm, more logical, and far less excitable than my own, which will perceive, in the circumstances I detail with awe, nothing more than an ordinary succession of very natural causes and effects.

From my infancy I was noted for the docility and humanity of my disposition. My tenderness of heart was even so conspicuous as to make me the jest of my companions. I was especially fond of animals, and was indulged by my parents with a great variety of pets. With these I spent most of my time, and never was so happy as when feeding and caressing them. This peculiarity of character grew with my growth, and, in my manhood, I derived from it one of my principal sources of pleasure. To those who have cherished an affection for a faithful and sagacious dog, I need hardly be at the trouble of explaining the nature or the intensity of the gratification thus derivable. There is something in the unselfish and self-sacrificing love of a brute, which goes directly to the heart of him who has had frequent occasion to test the paltry friendship and gossamer[2] fidelity of mere *Man*.

I married early, and was happy to find in my wife a disposition not uncongenial with my own. Observing my partiality for domestic pets, she lost no opportunity of procuring

---

1. **baroques**\bə ⁀rōk\ fantastic; grotesque.
2. **gossamer**\⁀gŏs·ə·mər\ very light and thin; filmy.

those of the most agreeable kind. We had birds, gold-fish, a fine dog, rabbits, a small monkey, and a *cat*.

This latter was a remarkably large and beautiful animal, entirely black, and sagacious to an astonishing degree. In speaking of his intelligence, my wife, who at heart was not a little tinctured with superstition, made frequent allusion to the ancient popular notion, which regarded all black cats as witches in disguise. Not that she was ever *serious* upon this point—and I mention the matter at all for no better reason than that it happens, just now, to be remembered.

Pluto—this was the cat's name—was my favorite pet and playmate. I alone fed him, and he attended me wherever I went about the house. It was even with difficulty that I could prevent him from following me through the streets.

Our friendship lasted, in this manner, for several years, during which my general temperament and character—through the instrumentality of the Fiend Intemperance[3]—had (I blush to confess it) experienced a radical alteration for the worse. I grew, day by day, more moody, more irritable, more regardless of the feelings of others. I suffered myself to use intemperate language to my wife. At length, I even offered her personal violence. My pets, of course, were made to feel the change in my disposition. I not only neglected, but ill-used them. For Pluto, however, I still retained sufficient regard to restrain me from maltreating him, as I made no scruple of maltreating the rabbits, the monkey, or even the dog, when, by accident, or through affection, they came in my way. But my disease grew upon me—for what disease is like Alcohol!— and at length even Pluto, who was now becoming old, and consequently somewhat peevish—even Pluto began to experience the effects of my ill temper.

One night, returning home, much intoxicated, from one of my haunts about town, I fancied that the cat avoided my presence. I seized him; when, in his fright at my violence,

he inflicted a slight wound upon my hand with his teeth. The fury of a demon instantly possessed me. I knew myself no longer. My original soul seemed, at once, to take its flight from my body; and a more than fiendish malevolence, gin-nurtured, thrilled every fibre of my frame. I took from my waistcoat-pocket[4] a penknife, opened it, grasped the poor beast by the throat, and deliberately cut one of its eyes from the socket! I blush, I burn, I shudder, while I pen the damnable atrocity.

When reason returned with the morning— when I had slept off the fumes of the night's debauch—I experienced a sentiment half of horror, half of remorse, for the crime of which I had been guilty; but it was, at best, a feeble and equivocal feeling, and the soul remained untouched. I again plunged into excess, and soon drowned in wine all memory of the deed.

In the meantime the cat slowly recovered. The socket of the lost eye presented, it is true, a frightful appearance, but he no longer appeared to suffer any pain. He went about the house as usual, but, as might be expected, fled in extreme terror at my approach. I had so much of my old heart left, as to be at first grieved by this evident dislike on the part of a creature which had once so loved me. But this feeling soon gave place to irritation. And then came, as if to my final and irrevocable overthrow, the spirit of PERVERSENESS. Of this spirit philosophy takes no account. Yet I am not more sure that my soul lives, than I am that perverseness is one of the primitive impulses of the human heart—one of the indivisible primary faculties, or sentiments, which give direction to the character of Man. Who has not, a hundred times, found himself committing a vile or a stupid action, for no other reason than because he knows he should *not*? Have we not a perpetual inclination, in the teeth of our best judgment, to violate that which is *Law*, merely because we understand it to be such? This spirit of perverseness, I

---

3. **Fiend Intemperence**, alcoholism.
4. **waistcoat** \\▲wāst'kōt\\ a vest.

say, came to my final overthrow. It was this unfathomable longing of the soul *to vex itself* —to offer violence to its own nature—to do wrong for the wrong's sake only—that urged me to continue and finally to consummate the injury I had inflicted upon the unoffending brute. One morning, in cold blood, I slipped a noose about its neck and hung it to the limb of a tree;—hung it with the tears streaming from my eyes, and with the bitterest remorse at my heart;—hung it *because* I knew that it had loved me, and *because* I felt it had given me no reason of offence;—hung it *because* I knew that in so doing I was committing a sin—a deadly sin that would so jeopardize my immortal soul as to place it—if such a thing were possible—even beyond the reach of the infinite mercy of the Most Merciful and Most Terrible God.

On the night of the day on which this most cruel deed was done, I was aroused from sleep by the cry of fire. The curtains of my bed were in flames. The whole house was blazing. It was with great difficulty that my wife, a servant, and myself, made our escape from the conflagration. The destruction was complete. My entire worldly wealth was swallowed up, and I resigned myself thenceforward to despair.

I am above the weakness of seeking to establish a sequence of cause and effect, between the disaster and the atrocity. But I am detailing a chain of facts—and wish not to leave even a possible link imperfect. On the day succeeding the fire, I visited the ruins. The walls, with one exception, had fallen in. This exception was found in a compartment wall, not very thick, which stood about the middle of the house, and against which had rested the head of my bed. The plastering had here, in great measure, resisted the action of the fire—a fact which I attributed to its having been recently spread. About this wall a dense crowd were collected, and many persons seemed to be examining a particular portion of it with very minute and eager attention. The words "strange!" "singular!" and other similar expressions, excited my curiosity. I approached and saw, as if graven in *bas-relief* upon the white surface, the figure of a gigantic *cat*. The impression was given with an accuracy truly marvelous. There was a rope about the animal's neck.

When I first beheld this apparition[5]—for I could scarcely regard it as less—my wonder and my terror were extreme. But at length reflection came to my aid. The cat, I remembered, had been hung in a garden adjacent to the house. Upon the alarm of fire, this garden had been immediately filled by the crowd— by some one of whom the animal must have been cut from the tree and thrown, through an open window, into my chamber. This had probably been done with the view of arousing me from sleep. The falling of other walls had compressed the victim of my cruelty into the substance of the freshly-spread plaster; the lime of which, with the flames, and the *ammonia* from the carcass, had then accomplished the portraiture[6] as I saw it.

Although I thus readily accounted to my reason, if not altogether to my conscience, for the startling fact just detailed, it did not the less fail to make a deep impression upon my fancy. For months I could not rid myself of the phantasm of the cat; and, during this period, there came back into my spirit a half-sentiment that seemed, but was not, remorse. I went so far as to regret the loss of the animal, and to look about me, among the vile haunts which I now habitually frequented, for another pet of the same species, and of somewhat similar appearance, with which to supply its place.

One night as I sat, half stupefied, in a den of more than infamy, my attention was suddenly drawn to some black object, reposing upon the head of one of the immense hogsheads of gin, or of rum, which constituted the chief furniture of the apartment. I had been looking steadily at the top of this hogshead[7] for some minutes, and what now caused me surprise was the fact that I had not sooner perceived the object thereupon. I approached it, and touched it with my hand. It was a black cat—a very large one—fully as large as Pluto, and closely resembling him in every

respect but one. Pluto had not a white hair upon any portion of his body; but this cat had a large, although indefinite splotch of white, covering nearly the whole region of the breast.

Upon my touching him, he immediately arose, purred loudly, rubbed against my hand, and appeared delighted with my notice. This, then, was the very creature of which I was in search. I at once offered to purchase it of the landlord; but this person made no claim to it —knew nothing of it—had never seen it before.

I continued my caresses, and when I prepared to go home, the animal evinced a disposition to accompany me. I permitted it to do so; occasionally stooping and patting it as I proceeded. When it reached the house it domesticated itself at once, and became immediately a great favorite with my wife.

For my own part, I soon found a dislike to it arising within me. This was just the reverse of what I had anticipated; but—I knew not how or why it was—its evident fondness for myself rather disgusted and annoyed me. By slow degrees these feelings of disgust and annoyance rose into the bitterness of hatred. I avoided the creature; a certain sense of shame, and the remembrance of my former deed of cruelty, preventing me from physically abusing it. I did not, for some weeks, strike, or otherwise violently ill use it; but gradually—very gradually—I came to look upon it with unutterable loathing, and to flee silently from its odious presence, as from the breath of a pestilence.

What added, no doubt, to my hatred of the beast, was the discovery, on the morning after I brought it home, that, like Pluto, it also had been deprived of one of its eyes. This circumstance, however, only endeared it to my wife, who, as I have already said, possessed, in a high degree, that humanity of feeling which had once been my distinguishing trait,

---

5. **apparition**\\\'ăp•ə ⁁rĭsh•ən\\ ghost.
6. **portraiture**\⁁pōr•trĭ 'chur\\ picture of a person.
7. **hogshead**\⁁hŏgz 'hĕd\\ a large barrel.

and the source of many of my simplest and purest pleasures.

With my aversion to this cat, however, its partiality for myself seemed to increase. It followed my footsteps with a pertinacity which it would be difficult to make the reader comprehend. Whenever I sat, it would crouch beneath my chair, or spring upon my knees, covering me with its loathsome caresses. If I arose to walk it would get between my feet and thus nearly throw me down, or, fastening its long and sharp claws in my dress, clamber, in this manner, to my breast. At such times, although I longed to destroy it with a blow, I was yet withheld from so doing, partly by a memory of my former crime, but chiefly—let me confess it at once—by absolute *dread* of the beast.

This dread was not exactly a dread of physical evil—and yet I should be at a loss how otherwise to define it. I am almost ashamed to own—yes, even in this felon's cell, I am almost ashamed to own—that the terror and horror with which the animal inspired me, had been heightened by one of the merest chimeras it would be possible to conceive. My wife had called my attention, more than once, to the character of the mark of white hair, of which I have spoken, and which constituted the sole visible difference between the strange beast and the one I had destroyed. The reader will remember that this mark, although large, had been originally very indefinite; but, by slow degrees—degrees nearly imperceptible, and which for a long time my reason struggled to reject as fanciful—it had, at length, assumed a rigorous distinctness of outline. It was now the representation of an object that I shudder to name—and for this, above all, I loathed, and dreaded, and would have rid myself of the monster *had I dared*— it was now, I say, the image of a hideous—of a ghastly thing—of the GALLOWS!—oh, mournful and terrible engine of Horror and of Crime—of Agony and of Death!

And now was I indeed wretched beyond the wretchedness of mere Humanity. And *a brute beast*—whose fellow I had contemptuously destroyed—*a brute beast* to work out for *me*—for me, a man fashioned in the image of the High God—so much of insufferable woe! Alas! neither by day nor by night knew I the blessing of rest any more! During the former the creature left me no moment alone, and in the latter I started hourly from dreams of unutterable fear to find the hot breath of *the thing* upon my face, and its vast weight—an incarnate nightmare that I had no power to shake off—incumbent eternally upon my *heart!*

Beneath the pressure of torments such as these the feeble remnant of the good within me succumbed. Evil thoughts became my sole intimates—the darkest and most evil of thoughts. The moodiness of my usual temper increased to hatred of all things and of all mankind; while from the sudden, frequent, and ungovernable outbursts of a fury to which I now blindly abandoned myself, my uncomplaining wife, alas, was the most usual and the most patient of sufferers.

One day she accompanied me, upon some household errand, into the cellar of the old building which our poverty compelled us to inhabit. The cat followed me down the steep stairs, and, nearly throwing me headlong, exasperated me to madness. Uplifting an axe, and forgetting in my wrath the childish dread which had hitherto stayed my hand, I aimed a blow at the animal, which, of course, would have proved instantly fatal had it descended as I wished. But this blow was arrested by the hand of my wife. Goaded by the interference into a rage more than demoniacal, I withdrew my arm from her grasp and buried the axe in her brain. She fell dead upon the spot without a groan.

This hideous murder accomplished, I set myself forthwith, and with entire deliberation, to the task of concealing the body. I knew that I could not remove it from the house, either by day or by night, without the risk of being observed by the neighbors. Many projects entered my mind. At one period I thought of cutting the corpse into minute fragments, and destroying them by fire. At another, I resolved to dig a grave for it in the floor of the cellar. Again, I deliberated about casting it in the well in the yard—about packing it in a box, as if merchandise, with the usual arrangements, and so getting a porter to take it from the house. Finally I hit upon what I considered a far better expedient than either of these. I determined to wall it up in the cellar, as the monks of the Middle Ages are recorded to have walled up their victims.

For a purpose such as this the cellar was well adapted. Its walls were loosely constructed, and had lately been plastered throughout with a rough plaster, which the dampness of the atmosphere had prevented from hardening. Moreover, in one of the walls was a projection, caused by a false chimney, or fireplace, that had been filled up and made to resemble the rest of the cellar. I made no doubt that I could readily displace the bricks at this point, insert the corpse, and wall the whole up as before, so that no eye could detect any thing suspicious.

And in this calculation I was not deceived. By means of a crowbar I easily dislodged the bricks, and, having carefully deposited the body against the inner wall, I propped it in that position, while with little trouble I relaid the whole structure as it originally stood. Having procured mortar, sand, and hair, with every possible precaution, I prepared a plaster which could not be distinguished from the old, and with this I very carefully went over the new brick-work. When I had finished, I felt satisfied that all was right. The wall did not present the slightest appearance of having been disturbed. The rubbish on the floor was picked up with the minutest care. I looked around triumphantly, and said to myself: "Here at least, then, my labor has not been in vain."

My next step was to look for the beast which had been the cause of so much wretchedness; for I had, at length, firmly resolved to put it to death. Had I been able to

meet with it at the moment, there could have been no doubt of its fate; but it appeared that the crafty animal had been alarmed at the violence of my previous anger, and forbore to present itself in my present mood. It is impossible to describe or to imagine the deep, the blissful sense of relief which the absence of the detested creature occasioned in my bosom. It did not make its appearance during the night; and thus for one night, at least, since its introduction into the house, I soundly and tranquilly slept; aye, *slept* even with the burden of murder upon my soul.

The second and the third day passed, and still my tormentor came not. Once again I breathed as a freeman. The monster, in terror, had fled the premises for ever! I should behold it no more! My happiness was supreme! The guilt of my dark deed disturbed me but little. Some few inquiries had been made, but these had been readily answered. Even a search had been instituted—but of course nothing was to be discovered. I looked upon my future felicity as secured.

Upon the fourth day of the assassination, a party of the police came, very unexpectedly, into the house, and proceeded again to make rigorous investigation of the premises. Secure, however, in the inscrutability of my place of concealment, I felt no embarrassment whatever. The officers bade me accompany them in their search. They left no nook or corner unexplored. At length, for the third or fourth time, they descended into the cellar. I quivered not in a muscle. My heart beat calmly as that of one who slumbers in innocence. I walked the cellar from end to end. I folded my arms upon my bosom, and roamed easily to and fro. The police were thoroughly satisfied and prepared to depart. The glee at my heart was too strong to be restrained. I burned to say if but one word, by way of triumph, and to render doubly sure their assurance of my guiltlessness.

"Gentlemen," I said at last, as the party ascended the steps, "I delight to have allayed your suspicions. I wish you all health and a little more courtesy. By the bye, gentlemen, this—this is a very well-constructed house," (in the rabid desire to say something easily, I scarcely knew what I uttered at all),—"I may say an *excellently* well-constructed house. These walls—are you going, gentlemen?—these walls are solidly put together"; and here, through the mere frenzy of bravado, I rapped heavily with a cane which I held in my hand, upon that very portion of the brickwork behind which stood the corpse of the wife of my bosom.

But may God shield and deliver me from the fangs of the Arch-Fiend! No sooner had the reverberation of my blows sunk into silence, than I was answered by a voice from within the tomb!—by a cry, at first muffled and broken, like the sobbing of a child, and then quickly swelling into one long, loud, and continuous scream, utterly anomalous and inhuman—a howl—a wailing shriek, half of horror and half of triumph, such as might have arisen only out of hell, conjointly from the throats of the damned in their agony and of the demons that exult in the damnation.

Of my own thoughts it is folly to speak. Swooning, I staggered to the opposite wall. For one instant the party on the stairs remained motionless, through extermity of terror and awe. In the next a dozen stout arms were toiling at the wall. It fell bodily. The corpse, already greatly decayed and clotted with gore, stood erect before the eyes of the spectators. Upon its head, with red extended mouth and solitary eye of fire, sat the hideous beast whose craft had seduced me into murder, and whose informing voice had consigned me to the hangman. I had walled the monster up within the tomb.

I
THE INNER SELF

A serious discussion of the inner struggle must consider the conflicting forces within human nature. On the positive side, many thinkers believe that we have an inner spiritual nature, or soul, and nearly everyone believes in an inner moral voice, or conscience. To what are these inner positive forces opposed? Is there not also some inner *negative* force?

The famous psychiatrist Sigmund Freud claimed that there was within all of us a "death instinct," which stood opposed to the "life (or love) instinct." Poe wrote before Freud's time, but he too believed in an inner negative force. His "spirit of perverseness," which he calls a primitive inner impulse, is similar to Freud's death instinct, in that it seeks to do violence to the human soul. One of the chief reasons for Poe's reputation is his understanding of the darker side of human nature. This understanding is clearly evident in "The Black Cat."

II
IMPLICATIONS

What are your own opinions about the darker side of human nature? The following questions will help you to compare your own ideas with those expressed by Poe in "The Black Cat."

1. Do you believe that there is such a thing as a death instinct, or a spirit of perverseness? If not, how do you account for the various ways in which persons harm themselves, ranging from cigarette smoking to suicide? What other examples of self-injury can you cite? How do you account for them?

2. Another example of perverseness cited by Poe is the impulse to break the law simply for the sake of breaking it. Have you ever felt such an impulse? Do you know others who have? How would you argue for or against a person who insisted that laws are broken only by persons who hope to gain something by breaking them?

3. Children are supposed to enjoy such things as pulling the wings off flies; college students are known for tendencies to go on destructive "sprees." Does Poe's notion of the spirit of perverseness account for these things? Also, are such acts merely "passing phases" that persons go through, or are they more permanently rooted in human nature?

4. Studies of adults who go berserk often reveal that these same persons were very quiet, even very moral, in their youth. Similarly, the narrator of this story in his youth was tender of heart, fond of animals, and known for the "docility and humanity" of his disposition. Can you discover any connection between such a model childhood and such a destructive adulthood?

5. Some thinkers believe that we are good by nature. Assuming that you share, or would like to share, this belief, how do you account for evil acts toward the self or toward others? How do you square your belief in innate moral goodness with the belief that we have a conscience that helps us tell good from evil? In other words, if we are naturally good, why do we need a conscience?

III

TECHNIQUES

Conflict

Short stories have a *plot*. The simplest definition of the term "plot" is *action*. Now, a narrative telling everything that happened to a person from morning till night would certainly involve some action, but the chances are that such a narrative would not have the same sort of action that a short story has. The fact is that the action in a short story is centered on a *conflict*, a struggle between two opposed forces.

Because the plot of a short story is based upon conflict, it is best to define "plot" not simply as action, but rather as *structured* or *patterned* action. Clearly, if the person writing the narrative of a day has lived a typical twenty-four hours, the account would lack two of the important elements of a plot: a main conflict and a single point at which it reaches its climax.

Although you can usually expect one main conflict in a short story, there will often be one or more minor conflicts as well. The following are several conflicts in "The Black Cat." Can you decide which one is the main conflict and which ones are minor?

1. The narrator vs. his wife
2. The good vs. the evil side of the narrator's character
3. The narrator vs. the cats
4. The narrator vs. the police

Of these conflicts, the last is probably the least important. We can say this because that conflict does not arise until the story is nearly over. Even then, it is given only brief mention.

The conflict between the narrator and his wife is perhaps next in order of importance. We may assume that it is less important than the remaining two conflicts for two reasons. First of all, it is a conflict only in the middle portion of the story. Secondly, Poe does not play it up. If Poe had wanted this to be the major conflict, he would have given much greater attention to the character of the wife and to the relationship between her and her husband.

In the conflict between the good and evil side of the narrator's character, the good is represented by the narrator's childhood and by his conscience. The evil side is represented by his drinking and by his perverse and immoral actions. It is true that the good side is developed largely in the beginning of the story and the evil is brought out in the middle and the end. Nevertheless, the conflict extends throughout the story. Note, for example, that just before the narrator kills his wife, we are told that he has retained a feeble remnant of "the good within." And perhaps it is a remnant of this "good within" that causes the narrator to talk about the construction of the walls, which in turn brings on his retribution. At any rate, we may certainly refer to this conflict as the main *internal* conflict of the story.

The main *external* conflict, and probably the main conflict of the story, is the conflict between the narrator and the cats. How does one know that Poe intended this to be the main conflict?

In general, you should expect that the main conflict will be introduced quite early in the story. You may also expect that it will appear throughout the whole story and that it will not be fully resolved until the end. In this story, the conflict between the narrator and the cats is introduced when Poe italicizes the word "cat," thus indicating its importance. In a sense, the importance of this conflict is signaled even earlier—in Poe's choice of his title. It is obvious that this conflict recurs throughout the story and that it is not fully resolved until the final paragraph. At this point we learn that the second cat is going to hang the narrator, just as surely as the latter had previously hanged "Pluto," the lord of the dead.

Climax

A climax may be defined as the episode or moment when the action of the story reaches its peak, or when the reader's emotional response is greatest. In short stories the main climax typically occurs near the end of the story. The action of "The Black Cat" reaches its peak when the narrator (and the reader) discovers the black cat alive within the tomb.

Climax and conflict are closely related. If you can find the main climax, you can usually discover from it the main forces in conflict. Similarly, if you know the main forces in conflict, it is usually easy to locate the episode or moment when the action between these forces is at its peak.

When there are several conflicts within a story, there may also be several climaxes. Can you locate a climax for each of the conflicts mentioned above? Keep in mind that one climax may relate to more than one conflict.

Moment of Illumination

The climax of a story is related to its plot; the moment of illumination is related to its meaning or theme. It may be defined as the moment in which the full meaning of the story becomes clear. This moment may come at the climax, but it often occurs after the climax.

In this story, the moment of illumination comes when the narrator notes "the hideous beast whose craft had seduced me into murder." The word "craft" is especially significant here, suggesting, as it does, "witchcraft." With this suggestion, we are led back to the beginning of the story, where we were told that "an ancient popular notion" regards all black cats as "witches in disguise."

IV
WORDS

From the choices given, select an appropriate synonym for the italicized word in each sentence.

1. This latter was a remarkably large and beautiful animal, entirely black, and *sagacious* to an astonishing degree.

vicious　　　　shrewd　　　　loathsome

2. In speaking of his intelligence, my wife, who at heart was not a little *tinctured* with superstition, made frequent allusion to the ancient popular notion, which regarded all black cats as witches in disguise.

tinged　　　　jaded　　　　immured

3. I suffered myself to use *intemperate* language to my wife.

obscene　　　　harsh　　　　vague

4. I looked upon my future *felicity* as secured.

madness　　　　leisure　　　　happiness

5. Having *procured* mortar, sand, and hair, with every possible precaution, I prepared a plaster which could not be distinguished from the old, and with this I very carefully went over the new brick-work.

acquired　　　　stolen　　　　concealed

ULYSSES GRANT
Harold Von Schmidt

One way of picturing
the inner struggle is
to portray an individual
whose familiar life story
brings this conflict
immediately to mind.
Ulysses Grant was such a person,
and this pensive
wartime study
is full of his solitary debate.

TORMENTED MAN
Leonard Baskin
1956, Ink, 39½ x 26½" over all
Living Arts Foundation
Fund, Collection
Whitney Museum of
American Art, New York

Gallery

THE INNER STRUGGLE

The contradictions within a human being
challenge the writer to heights of poetry and drama,
but by their very nature the resulting
inner struggles would seem outside the province
of painters and sculptors. This gallery,
however, proves the fascination the theme
has held for artists and suggests the success
they have had in visualizing the conflict
inside our minds and hearts.

The intense, symbol-laden styles
of much modern painting
lend themselves especially well to portraying
the tormented individual. Distorted
and in obvious pain, the man is pictured
below the harpies of Greek legend.
Those dreadful hags have been an enduring symbol
of the conflicts springing
from conscience and tradition.

Torment is readily apparent in the twisted reaching
figure of Wyeth's crippled friend Christina. The
inner struggles of her lonely unhappiness are
unresolved.

CHRISTINA'S WORLD
Andrew Wyeth
1948, tempera on gesso panel, 32¼ x 47¾"
Collection, The Museum of Modern Art, New York. Purchase

EL PENITENTE
Lu Duble

The penitent writhes in guilt and remorse,
the struggle unmistakable
in this terracotta sculpture
by Lu Duble.
   And at the other end of the continuum,
the wood carving THE OBSESSED
shows a man immobilized, bound,
and rigid in response to
the battle within.

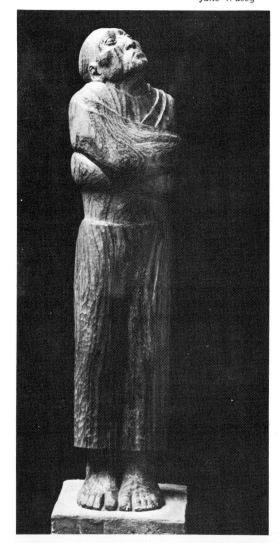

THE OBSESSED
Jane Wasey

Superficially,
an individual conflict
is shown by the wooden
carving entitled MINORITY
MAN NO. 1. Yet, while
the isolated individual
must struggle for the
strength to carry on,
it is possible to
look without
for comfort and aid.

MINORITY MAN NO. 1
Ed Wilson
1938, 38" H.
Collection—State University
of New York at Binghamton

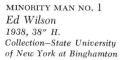

All of us from time to time experience
the night illusions of our inner
struggles as we see in the tangled
impressions of Beckmann's
THE DREAM.

THE DREAM
Max Beckmann
From the collection of Morton D. May

In most decisions there is moral value in
at least one of the options. What do we do, however,
when we must choose between two alternatives, *both* of which
may be wrong morally? This is the question raised in the following story
of a terrible moment of decision in the life of a Civil War soldier.

A Horseman in the Sky

AMBROSE BIERCE

I

One sunny afternoon in the autumn of the year 1861 a soldier lay in a clump of laurel by the side of a road in western Virginia. He lay at full length upon his stomach, his feet resting upon the toes, his head upon the left forearm. His extended right hand loosely grasped his rifle. But for the somewhat methodical disposition of his limbs and a slight rhythmic movement of the cartridge-box at the back of his belt he might have been thought to be dead. He was asleep at his post of duty. But if detected he would be dead shortly afterward, death being the just and legal penalty of his crime.

The clump of laurel in which the criminal lay was in the angle of a road which after ascending southward a steep acclivity to that point turned sharply to the west, running along the summit for perhaps one hundred yards. There it turned southward again and went zig-zagging downward through the forest. At the salient of that second angle was a large flat rock, jutting out northward, overlooking the deep valley from which the road ascended. The rock capped a high cliff; a stone dropped from its outer edge would have fallen sheer downward one thousand feet to the tops of the pines. The angle where the soldier lay was on another spur of the same cliff. Had he been awake he would have commanded a view, not only of the short arm of the road and the jutting rock, but of the entire profile of the cliff below it. It might well have made him giddy to look.

The country was wooded everywhere except at the bottom of the valley to the northward, where there was a small natural meadow, through which flowed a stream scarcely visible from the valley's rim. This open ground looked hardly larger than an ordinary door-yard, but was really several acres in extent. Its green was more vivid than that of the inclosing forest. Away beyond it rose a line of giant cliffs similar to those upon which we are supposed to stand in our survey of the savage scene, and through which the road had somehow made its climb to the summit. The configuration of the valley, indeed, was such that from this point of observation it seemed entirely shut in, and one could but have wondered how the road which found a way out of it had found a way into it, and whence came and whither went the waters of the stream that parted the meadow more than a thousand feet below.

No country is so wild and difficult but men will make it a theatre of war; concealed in the forest at the bottom of that military rat-trap, in which half a hundred men in possession of the exits might have starved an army to submission, lay five regiments of Federal infantry. They had marched all the previous day and night and were resting. At nightfall they would take to the road again, climb to the place where their unfaithful sentinel now slept, and descending the other slope of the ridge fall upon a camp of the enemy at about midnight. Their hope was to surprise it, for the road led to the rear of it. In case of failure, their position would be perilous in the extreme; and fail they surely would should accident or vigilance apprise the enemy of the movement.

II

The sleeping sentinel in the clump of laurel was a young Virginian named Carter Druse. He was the son of wealthy parents, an only child, and had known such ease and cultivation and high living as wealth and taste were able to command in the mountain country of western Virginia. His home was but a few miles from where he now lay. One morning he had risen from the breakfast-table and said, quietly but gravely: "Father, a Union regiment has arrived at Grafton.[1] I am going to join it."

The father lifted his leonine head, looked at the son a moment in silence, and replied: "Well, go, sir, and whatever may occur do what you conceive to be your duty. Virginia, to which you are a traitor, must get on without you. Should we both live to the end of the war, we will speak further of the matter. Your mother, as the physician has informed you, is in a most critical condition; at the best she cannot be with us longer than a few weeks, but that time is precious. It would be better not to disturb her."

So Carter Druse, bowing reverently to his father, who returned the salute with a stately courtesy that masked a breaking heart, left the home of his childhood to go soldiering. By conscience and courage, by deeds of devotion and daring, he soon commended himself to his fellows and his officers; and it was to these qualities and to some knowledge of the country that he owed his selection for his present perilous duty at the extreme outpost. Nevertheless, fatigue had been stronger than resolution and he had fallen asleep. What good or bad angel came in a dream to rouse him from his state of crime, who shall say? Without a movement,

without a sound, in the profound silence and the languor of the late afternoon, some invisible messenger of fate touched with unsealing finger the eyes of his consciousness—whispered into the ear of his spirit the mysterious awakening word which no human lips ever have spoken, no human memory ever has recalled. He quietly raised his forehead from his arm and looked between the masking stems of the laurels, instinctively closing his right hand about the stock of his rifle.

His first feeling was a keen artistic delight. On a colossal pedestal, the cliff,—motionless at the extreme edge of the capping rock and sharply outlined against the sky,—was an equestrian statue of impressive dignity. The figure of the man sat the figure of the horse, straight and soldierly, but with the repose of a Grecian god carved in the marble which limits the suggestion of activity. The gray costume harmonized with its aërial background; the metal of accoutrement[2] and caparison[3] was softened and subdued by the shadow; the animal's skin had no points of high light. A carbine strikingly foreshortened lay across the pommel of the saddle, kept in place by the right hand grasping it at the "grip"; the left hand, holding the bridle rein, was invisible. In silhouette against the sky the profile of the horse was cut with the sharpness of a cameo; it looked across the heights of air to the confronting cliffs beyond. The face of the rider, turned slightly away, showed only an outline of temple and beard; he was looking downward to the bottom of the valley. Magnified by its lift against the sky and by the soldier's testifying sense of the formidableness of a near enemy the group appeared of heroic, almost colossal, size.

For an instant Druse had a strange, half-defined feeling that he had slept to the end of the war and was looking upon a noble work of art

---

1. **Grafton,** county seat of Taylor County, northwest Virginia, on Tygart River.
2. **accoutrement**\ə ˈkū·tĕr·mənt\ soldiers' equipment except clothes and weapons.
3. **caparison**\kə ˈpă·rə·sən\ covering of the horse.

"Young Soldier," Winslow Homer

body slightly backward from the verge; the man remained immobile as before. Broad awake and keenly alive to the significance of the situation, Druse now brought the butt of his rifle against his cheek by cautiously pushing the barrel forward through the bushes, cocked the piece, and glancing through the sights covered a vital spot of the horseman's breast. A touch upon the trigger and all would have been well with Carter Druse. At that instant the horseman turned his head and looked in the direction of his concealed foeman—seemed to look into his very face, into his eyes, into his brave, compassionate heart.

Is it then so terrible to kill an enemy in war —an enemy who has surprised a secret vital to the safety of one's self and comrades—an enemy more formidable for his knowledge than all his army for its numbers? Carter Druse grew pale; he shook in every limb, turned faint, and saw the statuesque group before him as black figures, rising, falling, moving unsteadily in arcs of circles in a fiery sky. His hand fell away from his weapon, his head slowly dropped until his face rested on the leaves in which he lay. This courageous gentleman and hardy soldier was near swooning from intensity of emotion.

It was not for long; in another moment his face was raised from earth, his hands resumed their places on the rifle, his forefinger sought the trigger; mind, heart, and eyes were clear, conscience and reason sound. He could not hope to capture that enemy; to alarm him would but send him dashing to his camp with his fatal news. The duty of the soldier was plain: the man must be shot dead from ambush —without warning, without a moment's spiritual preparation, with never so much as an unspoken prayer, he must be sent to his account. But no—there is a hope; he may have discovered nothing—perhaps he is but admiring the sublimity of the landscape. If permitted, he may turn and ride carelessly away in the direction whence he came. Surely it will be possible to judge at the instant of his withdrawing whether he knows. It may well be that his fixity of attention—Druse turned his head and looked

reared upon that eminence to commemorate the deeds of an heroic past of which he had been an inglorious part. The feeling was dispelled by a slight movement of the group: the horse, without moving its feet, had drawn its

through the deeps of air downward, as from the surface to the bottom of a translucent sea. He saw creeping across the green meadow a sinuous line of figures of men and horses— some foolish commander was permitting the soldiers of his escort to water their beasts in the open, in plain view from a dozen summits!

Druse withdrew his eyes from the valley and fixed them again upon the group of man and horse in the sky, and again it was through the sights of his rifle. But this time his aim was at the horse. In his memory, as if they were a divine mandate, rang the words of his father at their parting: "Whatever may occur, do what you conceive to be your duty." He was calm now. His teeth were firmly but not rigidly closed; his nerves were as tranquil as a sleeping babe's—not a tremor affected any muscle of his body; his breathing, until suspended in the act of taking aim, was regular and slow. Duty had conquered; the spirit had said to the body: "Peace, be still." He fired.

III

An officer of the Federal force, who in a spirit of adventure or in quest of knowledge had left the hidden *bivouac* in the valley, and with aimless feet had made his way to the lower edge of a small open space near the foot of the cliff, was considering what he had to gain by pushing his exploration further. At a distance of a quarter-mile before him, but apparently at a stone's throw, rose from its fringe of pines the gigantic face of rock, towering to so great a height above him that it made him giddy to look up to where its edge cut a sharp, rugged line against the sky. It presented a clean, vertical profile against a background of blue sky to a point half the way down, and of distant hills, hardly less blue, thence to the tops of the trees at its base. Lifting his eyes to the dizzy altitude of its summit the officer saw an astonishing sight—a man on horseback riding down into the valley through the air!

Straight upright sat the rider, in military fashion, with a firm seat in the saddle, a strong clutch upon the rein to hold his charger from too impetuous a plunge. From his bare head his long hair streamed upward, waving like a plume. His hands were concealed in the cloud of the horse's lifted mane. The animal's body was as level as if every hoofstroke encountered the resistant earth. Its motions were those of a wild gallop, but even as the officer looked they ceased, with all the legs thrown sharply forward as in the act of alighting from a leap. But this was a flight!

Filled with amazement and terror by this apparition of a horseman in the sky—half believing himself the chosen scribe of some new Apocalypse,[4] the officer was overcome by the intensity of his emotions; his legs failed him and he fell. Almost at the same instant he heard a crashing sound in the trees—a sound that died without an echo—and all was still.

The officer rose to his feet, trembling. The familiar sensation of an abraded shin[5] recalled his dazed faculties. Pulling himself together he ran rapidly obliquely away from the cliff to a point distant from its foot; thereabout he expected to find his man; and thereabout he naturally failed. In the fleeting instant of his vision his imagination had been so wrought upon by the apparent grace and ease and intention of the marvelous performance that it did not occur to him that the line of march of aërial cavalry is directly downward, and that he could find the objects of his search at the very foot of the cliff. A half-hour later he returned to camp.

This officer was a wise man; he knew better than to tell an incredible truth. He said nothing of what he had seen. But when the commander asked him if in his scout he had learned anything of advantage to the expedition he answered:

---

4. **Apocalypse**\ə ˈpŏ·kə ˈlĭps\ Book of Revelation.
5. **abraded**\ə ˈbrād·əd\ **shin,** scraped shin.

"Yes, sir; there is no road leading down into this valley from the southward."

The commander, knowing better, smiled.

IV

After firing his shot, Private Carter Druse reloaded his rifle and resumed his watch. Ten minutes had hardly passed when a Federal sergeant crept cautiously to him on hands and knees. Druse neither turned his head nor looked at him, but lay without motion or sign of recognition.

"Did you fire?" the sergeant whispered.

"Yes."

"At what?"

"A horse. It was standing on yonder rock—pretty far out. You see it is no longer there. It went over the cliff."

The man's face was white, but he showed no other sign of emotion. Having answered, he turned away his eyes and said no more. The sergeant did not understand.

"See here, Druse," he said, after a moment's silence, "it's no use making a mystery. I order you to report. Was there anybody on the horse?"

"Yes."

"Well?"

"My father."

The sergeant rose to his feet and walked away. "Good God!" he said.

I
A CONFLICT OF LOYALTIES

When Carter Druse decides that he is obliged to join the Union army, this decision thrusts upon him a whole new set of responsibilities: As a soldier, he must obey his commander; he must destroy the enemy; he has a duty to protect his comrades in arms. These duties seem clear enough, but the army code does not say how one's military obligations affect one's other responsibilities—duties to God or to one's parents. Thus Carter Druse is forced into a situation in which either decision he may make seems morally wrong. How can you justify the choice he finally makes?

II
IMPLICATIONS

Consider the following statements and discuss those that you feel best reflect *the author's basic attitude and meaning* in this story. Justify your choice by citing details from the story.

1. Duty to country is more important than one's feelings for family.

2. The good of the individual must be sacrificed for the good of the many.

3. The desire for personal survival is stronger than the instinct of family love.

4. In moments of crisis the average person may rise to noble heights.

5. Carter Druse arrived at his decision by logical thought rather than by instinctive action.

6. War is a horrible institution.

III
TECHNIQUES

Conflict

It is often argued that the best conflicts are those in which both sides are evenly balanced; this increases suspense, for the reader cannot be sure which side will prevail. In this story the young man has to weigh the safety of himself and his regiments against the life of his father. Would you say that this is an evenly balanced conflict? How would the story be changed if the man on the horse had not been his father?

Two things help young Druse to make up his mind: (1) The fact that he could shoot the horse, and (2) his father's advice about duty. Why did Bierce bring in these details? To answer this question consider what your reaction might have been if these factors had not been brought in.

Climax and Moment of Illumination

As tense as the climax of this story is, you will probably agree that it would have been even more exciting if Bierce had revealed beforehand that

Carter was aiming at his father. Why, therefore, do you think he chose to withhold this information and use it as his moment of illumination?

IV
WORDS

A. Everyone who reads or listens confronts unfamiliar words. One way to figure out the meaning of a word is through the use of context clues. Using context clues, determine, if possible, enough meaning of the italicized words to make sense of each phrase or clause.

1. . . . road which, after ascending, southward, a steep *acclivity* to that point, turned sharply to the west.

2. . . . in the profound silence and the *languor* of the late afternoon . . .

3. . . . through the deeps of air downward, as from the surface to the bottom of a *translucent* sea . . .

4. In his memory, as if they were a divine *mandate*, rang the words of his father . . .

5. His nerves were as *tranquil* as a sleeping babe's.

6. . . . a strong clutch upon the rein to hold his charge from too *impetuous* a plunge . . .

B. 1. Find synonyms for the words below. Use each word in a sentence and decide if its synonym is able to replace it.

apparition, tranquil, genial, abraded, intrinsic, taciturn, ominous.

2. Synonyms differ in expressing size, degree, specificity, and judgment. The word *enormous* suggests something that exceeds measurement in size as well as degree; *elephantine* carries a metaphorical suggestion of the elephant; *huge* suggests bulk, whereas *vast* suggests space or extent. The words *censure, condemn,* and *denounce* vary in degree: *censure* suggests fault-finding by some authority, such as a judge or government official; *condemn* adds the severity of a final decision by authority; *denounce* adds the notion of public condemnation. Explain the differences among these sets.

(a) flash, sparkle, scintillate; (b) moral, ethical, virtuous, righteous; (c) follower, partisan, satellite; (d) escalate, intensify, aggravate; (e) plot, intrigue, conspiracy.

It takes great courage to sacrifice one's personal happiness
and security for the sake of some unpopular ideal or cause, especially
when the issue is not a matter of deciding between an obvious good
and a clearly recognized evil. Yet if we do not live up
to our deepest inner convictions, in spite of popular opinion
and political pressures, how much security and happiness
can we really have? As he stared into his open grave—the decision
which would kill his political life—this is the sort of question
that confronted Edmund Ross, a little-known man who served briefly
as Senator from Kansas during the administration of President
Andrew Johnson. This real-life inner struggle is one of the chapters
from the late John F. Kennedy's Pulitzer Prize-winning book,
Profiles in Courage.

"I looked down into my open grave … ." Edmund G. Ross

JOHN F. KENNEDY

In a lonely grave, forgotten and unknown, lies "the man who saved a President," and who as a result may well have preserved for ourselves and posterity constitutional government in the United States—the man who performed in 1868 what one historian has called "the most heroic act in American history, incomparably more difficult than any deed of valor upon the field of battle"—but a United States Senator whose name no one recalls: Edmund G. Ross of Kansas.

The impeachment of President Andrew Johnson, the event in which the obscure Ross was to play such a dramatic role, was the sensational climax to the bitter struggle between the President, determined to carry out Abraham Lincoln's policies of reconciliation with the defeated South, and the more radical Republican leaders in Congress, who sought to administer the downtrodden Southern states as conquered provinces which had forfeited their rights under the Constitution. It was, moreover, a struggle between Executive and Legislative authority. Andrew Johnson, the courageous if untactful Tennessean who had been the only Southern Member of Congress to refuse to secede with his state, had committed himself to the policies of the Great Emancipator to whose high station he had succeeded only by the course of an assassin's bullet. He knew that Lincoln prior to his death had already clashed with the extremists in Congress, who had opposed his approach to reconstruction in a constitutional and charitable manner and sought to make the Legislative Branch of the government supreme. And his own belligerent temperament soon destroyed any hope that Congress might now join hands in carrying out Lincoln's policies of permitting the South to resume its place in the Union with as little delay and controversy as possible.

By 1866, when Edmund Ross first came to the Senate, the two branches of the government

"I Looked down into my open grave . . ." from *Profiles in Courage* by John F. Kennedy. Copyright © 1955 by John F. Kennedy. Reprinted with the permission of Harper & Row, Publishers, Incorporated.

were already at each other's throats, snarling and bristling with anger. Bill after bill was vetoed by the President on the grounds that they were unconstitutional, too harsh in their treatment of the South, an unnecessary prolongation of military rule in peacetime or undue interference with the authority of the Executive Branch. And for the first time in our nation's history, important public measures were passed over a President's veto and became law without his support.

But not all of Andrew Johnson's vetoes were overturned; and the "Radical" Republicans of the Congress promptly realized that one final step was necessary before they could crush their despised foe (and in the heat of political battle their vengeance was turned upon their President far more than their former military enemies of the South). That one remaining step was the assurance of a two-thirds majority in the Senate—for under the Constitution, such a majority was necessary to override a Presidential veto. And more important, such a majority was constitutionally required to accomplish their major ambition, now an ill-kept secret, conviction of the President under an impeachment and his dismissal from office!

The temporary and unstable two-thirds majority which had enabled the Senate Radical Republicans on several occasions to enact legislation over the President's veto was, they knew, insufficiently reliable for an impeachment conviction. To solidify this bloc became the paramount goal of Congress, expressly or impliedly governing its decisions on other issues—particularly the admission of new states, the readmission of Southern states and the determination of senatorial credentials. By extremely dubious methods a pro-Johnson Senator was denied his seat. Over the President's veto Nebraska was admitted to the Union, seating two more anti-administration Senators. Although last minute maneuvers failed to admit Colorado over the President's veto (sparsely populated Colorado had rejected statehood in a referendum), an unexpected tragedy brought false tears and fresh hopes for a new vote, in Kansas.

Senator Jim Lane of Kansas had been a "conservative" Republican sympathetic to Johnson's plans to carry out Lincoln's reconstruction policies. But his frontier state was one of the most "radical" in the Union. When Lane voted to uphold Johnson's veto of the Civil Rights Bill of 1866 and introduced the administration's bill for recognition of the new state government of Arkansas, Kansas had arisen in outraged heat. A mass meeting at Lawrence had vilified the Senator and speedily reported resolutions sharply condemning his position. Humiliated, mentally ailing, broken in health and laboring under charges of financial irregularities, Jim Lane took his own life on July 1, 1866.

With this thorn in their side removed, the Radical Republicans in Washington looked anxiously toward Kansas and the selection of Lane's successor. Their fondest hopes were realized, for the new Senator from Kansas turned out to be Edmund G. Ross, the very man who had introduced the resolutions attacking Lane at Lawrence.

There could be no doubt as to where Ross's sympathies lay, for his entire career was one of determined opposition to the slave states of the South, their practices and their friends. In 1854, when only twenty-eight, he had taken part in the mob rescue of a fugitive slave in Milwaukee. In 1856, he had joined that flood of antislavery immigrants to "bleeding" Kansas who intended to keep it a free territory. Disgusted with the Democratic party of his youth, he had left that party, and volunteered in the Kansas Free State Army to drive back a force of proslavery men invading the territory. In 1862, he had given up his newspaper work to enlist in the Union Army, from which he emerged a Major. His leading role in the condemnation of Lane at Lawrence convinced the Radical Republican leaders in Congress that in Edmund G. Ross they had a solid member of that vital two-thirds.

The stage was now set for the final scene— the removal of Johnson. Early in 1867, Congress enacted over the President's veto the Tenure-of-Office Bill which prevented the

President from removing without the consent of the Senate all new officeholders whose appointment required confirmation by that body. At the time nothing more than the cry for more patronage was involved, Cabinet Members having originally been specifically exempt.

Edmund Ross

On August 5, 1867, President Johnson—convinced that the Secretary of War, whom he had inherited from Lincoln, Edwin M. Stanton, was the surreptitious tool of the Radical Republicans and was seeking to become the almighty dictator of the conquered South—asked for his immediate resignation; and Stanton arrogantly fired back the reply that he declined to resign before the next meeting of Congress. Not one to cower before this kind of effrontery, the President one week later suspended Stanton, and appointed in his place the one man whom Stanton did not dare resist, General Grant. On January 13, 1868, an angry Senate notified the President and Grant that it did not concur in the suspension of Stanton, and Grant vacated the office upon Stanton's return. But the situation was intolerable. The Secretary of War was unable to attend Cabinet meetings or associate with his colleagues in the administration; and

on February 21, President Johnson, anxious to obtain a court test of the act he believed obviously unconstitutional, again notified Stanton that he had been summarily removed from the office of Secretary of War.

While Stanton, refusing to yield possession, barricaded himself in his office, public opinion in the nation ran heavily against the President. He had intentionally broken the law and dictatorially thwarted the will of Congress! Although previous resolutions of impeachment had been defeated in the House, both in committee and on the floor, a new resolution was swiftly reported and adopted on February 24 by a tremendous vote. Every single Republican voted in the affirmative, and Thaddeus Stevens of Pennsylvania—the crippled, fanatical personification of the extremes of the Radical Republican movement, master of the House of Representatives, with a mouth like the thin edge of an ax—warned both Houses of the Congress coldly: "Let me see the recreant who would vote to let such a criminal escape. Point me to one who will dare do it and I will show you one who will dare the infamy of posterity."

With the President impeached—in effect, indicted—by the House, the frenzied trial for his conviction or acquittal under the Articles of Impeachment began on March 5 in the Senate, presided over by the Chief Justice. It was a trial to rank with all the great trials in history—Charles I before the High Court of Justice, Louis XVI before the French Convention, and Warren Hastings before the House of Lords.[1] Two great elements of drama were missing: the actual cause for which the President was being tried was not fundamental to the welfare of the nation; and the defendant himself was at all times absent.

---

1. **Charles I**, King of England (1625–1694); beheaded at Whitehall after being condemned by 67 judges to be a tyrant and enemy of England. **Louis XVI**, King of France (1774–1792); tried for treason, found guilty and condemned to guillotine. **Warren Hastings** (1732–1818), English diplomat and administrator in India; impeached for corruption (1788) but acquitted (1795).

But every other element of the highest court-room drama was present. To each Senator the Chief Justice administered an oath "to do impartial justice" (including even the hot-headed Radical Senator from Ohio, Benjamin Wade, who as President Pro Tempore of the Senate was next in line for the Presidency). The chief prosecutor for the House was General Benjamin F. Butler, the "butcher of New Orleans," a talented but coarse and demagogic Congressman from Massachusetts. (When he lost his seat in 1874, he was so hated by his own party as well as his opponents that one Republican wired concerning the Democratic sweep, "Butler defeated, everything else lost.") Some one thousand tickets were printed for admission to the Senate galleries during the trial, and every conceivable device was used to obtain one of the four tickets allotted each Senator.

From the fifth of March to the sixteenth of May, the drama continued. Of the eleven Articles of Impeachment adopted by the House, the first eight were based upon the removal of Stanton and the appointment of a new Secretary of War in violation of the Tenure-of-Office Act; the ninth related to Johnson's conversation with a general which was said to induce violations of the Army Appropriations Act; the tenth recited that Johnson had delivered "intemperate, inflammatory and scandalous harangues . . . as well against Congress as the laws of the United States"; and the eleventh was a deliberately obscure conglomeration of all the charges in the preceding articles, which had been designed by Thaddeus Stevens to furnish a common ground for those who favored conviction but were unwilling to identify themselves on basic issues. In opposition to Butler's inflammatory arguments in support of this hastily drawn indictment, Johnson's able and learned counsel replied with considerable effectiveness. They insisted that the Tenure-of-Office Act was null and void as a clear violation of the Constitution; that even if it were valid, it would not apply to Stanton, for the reasons previously mentioned; and that the only way that a judicial test of the law could be obtained

was for Stanton to be dismissed and sue for his rights in the courts.

But as the trial progressed, it became increasingly apparent that the impatient Republicans did not intend to give the President a fair trial on the formal issues upon which the impeachment was drawn, but intended instead to depose him from the White House on any grounds, real or imagined, for refusing to accept their policies. Telling evidence in the President's favor was arbitrarily excluded. Prejudgment on the part of most Senators was brazenly announced. Attempted bribery and other forms of pressure were rampant. The chief interest was not in the trial or the evidence, but in the tallying of votes necessary for conviction.

Twenty-seven states (excluding the unrecognized Southern states) in the Union meant fifty-four members of the Senate, and thirty-six votes were required to constitute the two-thirds majority necessary for conviction. All twelve Democratic votes were obviously lost, and the forty-two Republicans knew that they could afford to lose only six of their own members if Johnson were to be ousted. To their dismay, at a preliminary Republican caucus, six courageous Republicans indicated that the evidence so far introduced was not in their opinion sufficient to convict Johnson under the Articles of Impeachment. "Infamy!" cried the Philadelphia *Press.* The Republic has "been betrayed in the house of its friends!"

But if the remaining thirty-six Republicans would hold, there would be no doubt as to the outcome. All must stand together! But one Republican Senator would not announce his verdict in the preliminary poll—Edmund G. Ross of Kansas. The Radicals were outraged that a Senator from such an anti-Johnson stronghold as Kansas could be doubtful. "It was a very clear case," Senator Sumner of Massachusetts fumed, "especially for a Kansas man. I did not think that a Kansas man could quibble against his country."

From the very time Ross had taken his seat, the Radical leaders had been confident of his vote. His entire background, as already indicated, was one of firm support of their cause. One of his first acts in the Senate had been to read a declaration of his adherence to Radical Republican policy, and he had silently voted for all of their measures. He had made it clear that he was not in sympathy with Andrew Johnson personally or politically; and after the removal of Stanton, he had voted with the majority in adopting a resolution declaring such removal unlawful. His colleague from Kansas, Senator Pomeroy, was one of the most Radical leaders of the anti-Johnson group. The Republicans insisted that Ross's crucial vote was rightfully theirs, and they were determined to get it by whatever means available. As stated by DeWitt in his memorable *Impeachment of Andrew Johnson,* "The full brunt of the struggle turned at last on the one remaining doubtful Senator, Edmund G. Ross."

When the impeachment resolution had passed the House, Senator Ross had casually remarked to Senator Sprague of Rhode Island, "Well, Sprague, the thing is here; and, so far as I am concerned, though a Republican and opposed to Mr. Johnson and his policy, he shall have as fair a trial as an accused man ever had on this earth." Immediately the word spread that "Ross was shaky." "From that hour," he later wrote, "not a day passed that did not bring me, by mail and telegraph and in personal intercourse, appeals to stand fast for impeachment and not a few were the admonitions of condign visitations upon any indication even of lukewarmness."

Throughout the country, and in all walks of life, as indicated by the correspondence of Members of the Senate, the condition of the public mind was not unlike that preceding a great battle. The dominant party of the nation seemed to occupy the position of public prosecutor, and it was scarcely in the mood to brook delay for trial or to hear defense. Washington had become during the trial the central point of the politically dissatisfied and swarmed with representatives of every state of the Union, demanding in a practically united voice the deposition of the President. The footsteps of the anti-impeaching Republicans were dogged from the day's beginning to its end and far into the night, with entreaties, considerations, and threats. The newspapers came daily filled with not a few threats of violence upon their return to their constituents.

Ross and his fellow doubtful Republicans were daily pestered, spied upon and subjected to every form of pressure. Their residences were carefully watched, their social circles suspiciously scrutinized, and their every move and companions secretly marked in special notebooks. They were warned in the party press, harangued by their constituents, and sent dire warnings threatening political ostracism and even assassination. Stanton himself, from his barricaded headquarters in the War Department, worked day and night to bring to bear upon the doubtful Senators all the weight of his impressive military associations. The Philadelphia *Press* reported "a fearful avalanche of telegrams from every section of the country," a great surge of public opinion from the "common people" who had given their money and lives to the country and would not "willingly or unavenged see their great sacrifice made naught."

The New York *Tribune* reported that Edmund Ross in particular was "mercilessly dragged this way and that by both sides, hunted like a fox night and day and badgered by his own colleague, like the bridge at Arcola[2] now trod upon by one Army and now trampled by the other." His background and life were investigated from top to bottom, and his constituents and colleagues pursued him throughout Washington to gain some inkling of his opinion. He was the target of every eye, his name was on every mouth and his intentions were discussed in every newspaper. Although there is evidence that he gave some hint of agreement to each side, and each attempted to

---

2. Arcola\ˈȯr·kō·la\ a village in northern Italy where for three days (November 15–17, 1796) Napoleon fought a critical battle with Austria.

claim him publicly, he actually kept both sides in a state of complete suspense by his judicial silence.

But with no experience in political turmoil, no reputation in the Senate, no independent income and the most radical state in the Union to deal with, Ross was judged to be the most sensitive to criticism and the most certain to be swayed by expert tactics. A committee of Congressmen and Senators sent to Kansas, and to the states of the other doubtful Republicans, this telegram: "Great danger to the peace of the country and the Republican cause if impeachment fails. Send to your Senators public opinion by resolutions, letters, and delegations." A member of the Kansas legislature called upon Ross at the Capitol. A general urged on by Stanton remained at his lodge until four o'clock in the morning determined to see him. His brother received a letter offering $20,000 for revelation of the Senator's intentions. Gruff Ben Butler exclaimed of Ross, "There is a bushel of money! How much does the scoundrel want?" The night before the Senate was to take its first vote for the conviction or acquittal of Johnson, Ross received this telegram from home:

Kansas has heard the evidence and demands the conviction of the President.

[*signed*] D. R. ANTHONY AND 1,000 OTHERS

And on that fateful morning of May 16 Ross replied:

To D. R. Anthony and 1,000 Others: I do not recognize your right to demand that I vote either for or against conviction. I have taken an oath to do impartial justice according to the Constitution and laws, and trust that I shall have the courage to vote according to the dictates of my judgment and for the highest good of the country.

[signed]—E. G. Ross

That morning spies traced Ross to his breakfast; and ten minutes before the vote was taken his Kansas colleague warned him in the presence of Thaddeus Stevens that a vote for acquittal would mean trumped up charges and his political death.

But now the fateful hour was at hand. Neither escape, delay nor indecision was possible. As Ross himself later described it: "The galleries were packed. Tickets of admission were at an enormous premium. The House had adjourned and all of its members were in the Senate chamber. Every chair on the Senate floor was filled with a Senator, a Cabinet Officer, a member of the President's counsel or a member of the House." Every Senator was in his seat, the desperately ill Grimes of Iowa being literally carried in.

It had been decided to take the first vote under that broad Eleventh Article of Impeachment, believed to command the widest support. As the Chief Justice announced the voting would begin, he reminded "the citizens and strangers in the galleries that absolute silence and perfect order are required." But already a deathlike stillness enveloped the Senate chamber. A Congressman later recalled that "Some of the members of the House near me grew pale and sick under the burden of suspense"; and Ross noted that there was even "a subsidence of the shuffling of feet, the rustling of silks, the fluttering of fans, and of conversation."

The voting tensely commenced. By the time the Chief Justice reached the name of Edmund Ross twenty-four "guilties" had been pronounced. Ten more were certain and one other practically certain. Only Ross's vote was needed to obtain the thirty-six votes necessary to convict the President. But not a single person in the room knew how this young Kansan would vote. Unable to conceal the suspense and emotion in his voice, the Chief Justice put the question to him: "Mr. Senator Ross, how say you? Is the respondent Andrew Johnson guilty or not guilty of a high misdemeanor as charged in this Article?" Every voice was still; every eye was upon the freshman Senator from Kansas. The hopes and fears, the hatred and bitterness of past decades were centered upon this one man.

As Ross himself later described it, his "powers of hearing and seeing seemed developed in an abnormal degree."

Every individual in that great audience seemed distinctly visible, some with lips apart and bending forward in anxious expectancy, others with hand uplifted as if to ward off an apprehended blow . . . and each peering with an intensity that was almost tragic upon the face of him who was about to cast the fateful vote. . . . Every fan was folded, not a foot moved, not the rustle of a garment, not a whisper was heard. . . . Hope and fear seemed blended in every face, instantaneously alternating, some with revengeful hate . . . others lighted with hope. . . . The Senators in their seats leaned over their desks, many with hand to ear. . . . It was a tremendous responsibility, and it was not strange that he upon whom it had been imposed by a fateful combination of conditions should have sought to avoid it, to put it away from him as one shuns, or tries to fight off, a nightmare. . . . I almost literally looked down into my open grave. Friendships, position, fortune, everything that makes life desirable to an ambitious man were about to be swept away by the breath of my mouth, perhaps forever. It is not strange that my answer was carried waveringly over the air and failed to reach the limits of the audience, or that repetition was called for by distant Senators on the opposite side of the Chamber.

Then came the answer again in a voice that could not be misunderstood—full, final, definite, unhesitating and unmistakable: "Not guilty." The deed was done, the President saved, the trial as good as over and the conviction lost. The remainder of the roll call was unimportant, conviction had failed by the margin of a single vote and a general rumbling filled the chamber until the Chief Justice proclaimed that "on this Article thirty-five Senators having voted guilty and nineteen not guilty, a two-thirds majority not having voted for conviction, the President is, therefore, acquitted under this Article."

A ten-day recess followed, ten turbulent days to change votes on the remaining Articles. An attempt was made to rush through bills to re-admit six Southern states, whose twelve Senators were guaranteed to vote for conviction. But this could not be accomplished in time. Again Ross was the only one uncommitted on the

other Articles, the only one whose vote could not be predicted in advance. And again he was subjected to terrible pressure. From "D. R. Anthony and others," he received a wire informing him that "Kansas repudiates you as she does all perjurers and skunks." Every incident in his life was examined and distorted. Professional witnesses were found by Senator Pomeroy to testify before a special House committee that Ross had indicated a willingness to change his vote for a consideration. (Unfortunately this witness was so delighted in his exciting role that he also swore that Senator Pomeroy had made an offer to produce three votes for acquittal for $40,000.) When Ross, in his capacity as a Committee Chairman, took several bills to the President, James G. Blaine remarked: "There goes the rascal to get his pay." (Long afterward Blaine was to admit: "In the exaggerated denunciation caused by the anger and chagrin of the moment, great injustice was done to statesmen of spotless character.")

Again the wild rumors spread that Ross had been won over on the remaining Articles of Impeachment. As the Senate reassembled, he was the only one of the seven "renegade" Republicans to vote with the majority on preliminary procedural matters. But when the second and third Articles of Impeachment were read, and the name of Ross was reached again with the same intense suspense of ten days earlier, again came the calm answer "Not guilty."

Why did Ross, whose dislike for Johnson continued, vote "Not guilty"? His motives appear clearly from his own writings on the subject years later in articles contributed to *Scribner's* and *Forum* magazines:

In a large sense, the independence of the executive office as a coordinate branch of the government was on trial. . . . If . . . the President must step down . . . a disgraced man and a political outcast . . . upon insufficient proofs and from partisan considerations, the office of President would be degraded, cease to be a coordinate branch of the government, and ever after subordinated to the legislative will. It would practically have revolutionized our splendid political fabric into a partisan Congressional autocracy. . . . This government had never faced so insidious a danger . . . control by the worst element of American politics. . . . If Andrew Johnson were acquitted by a nonpartisan vote . . . America would pass the danger point of partisan rule and that intolerance which so often characterizes the sway of great majorities and makes them dangerous.

The "open grave" which Edmund Ross had foreseen was hardly an exaggeration. A Justice of the Kansas Supreme Court telegraphed him that "the rope with which Judas Iscariot hanged himself is lost, but Jim Lane's pistol is at your service." An editorial in a Kansas newspaper screamed:

On Saturday last Edmund G. Ross, United States Senator from Kansas, sold himself, and betrayed his constituents; stultified his own record, basely lied to his friends, shamefully violated his solemn pledge . . . and to the utmost of his poor ability signed the death warrant of his country's liberty. This act was done deliberately, because the traitor, like Benedict Arnold, loved money better than he did principle, friends, honor and his country, all combined. Poor, pitiful, shriveled wretch, with a soul so small that a little pelf[3] would outweigh all things else that dignify or ennoble manhood.

Ross's political career was ended. To the New York *Tribune,* he was nothing but "a miserable poltroon and traitor." The Philadelphia *Press* said that in Ross "littleness" had "simply borne its legitimate fruit," and that he and his fellow recalcitrant Republicans had "plunged from a precipice of fame into the groveling depths of infamy and death." The Philadelphia *Inquirer* said that "They had tried, convicted and sentenced themselves." For them there could be "no allowance, no clemency."

Comparative peace returned to Washington as Stanton relinquished his office and Johnson served out the rest of his term, later—unlike his Republican defenders—to return triumphantly to the Senate as Senator from Tennessee. But no one paid attention when Ross tried unsuc-

cessfully to explain his vote, and denounced the falsehoods of Ben Butler's investigating committee, recalling that the General's "well known grovelling instincts and proneness to slime and uncleanness" had led "the public to insult the brute creation by dubbing him 'the beast.'" He clung unhappily to his seat in the Senate until the expiration of his term, frequently referred to as "the traitor Ross," and complaining that his fellow Congressmen, as well as citizens on the street, considered association with him "disreputable and scandalous," and passed him by as if he were "a leper, with averted face and every indication of hatred and disgust."

Neither Ross nor any other Republican who had voted for the acquittal of Johnson was ever re-elected to the Senate, not a one of them retaining the support of their party's organization. When he returned to Kansas in 1871, he and his family suffered social ostracism, physical attack, and near poverty.

Who was Edmund G. Ross? Practically nobody. Not a single public law bears his name, not a single history book includes his picture, not a single list of Senate "greats" mentions his service. His one heroic deed has been all but forgotten. But who might Edmund G. Ross have been? That is the question—for Ross, a man with an excellent command of words, an excellent background for politics and an excellent future in the Senate, might well have outstripped his colleagues in prestige and power throughout a long Senate career. Instead, he chose to throw all of this away for one act of conscience.

But the twisting course of human events eventually upheld the faith he expressed to his wife shortly after the trial: "Millions of men cursing me today will bless me tomorrow for having saved the country from the greatest peril through which it has ever passed, though none but God can ever know the struggle it has cost me." For twenty years later Congress

---

3. **pelf,** money, riches.

repealed the Tenure-of-Office Act, to which every President after Johnson, regardless of party, had objected; and still later the Supreme Court, referring to "the extremes of that episode in our government," held it to be unconstitutional. Ross moved to New Mexico, where in his later years he was to be appointed Territorial Governor. Just prior to his death when he was awarded a special pension by Congress for his service in the Civil War, the press and the country took the opportunity to pay tribute to his fidelity to principle in a trying hour and his courage in saving his government from a devastating reign of terror. They now agreed with Ross's earlier judgment that his vote had "saved the country from . . . a strain that would have wrecked any other form of government." Those Kansas newspapers and political leaders who had bitterly denounced him in earlier years praised Ross for his stand against legislative mob rule: "By the firmness and courage of Senator Ross," it was said, "the country was saved from calamity greater than war, while it consigned him to a political martyrdom, the most cruel in our history. . . . Ross was the victim of a wild flame of intolerance which swept everything before it. He did his duty knowing that it meant his political death. . . . It was a brave thing for Ross to do, but Ross did it. He acted for his conscience and with a lofty patriotism, regardless of what he knew must be the ruinous consequences to himself. He acted right."

peachment would be to vote for the future welfare of the country as a whole. It takes enormous courage to follow "a different drummer" when doing so means one's personal ruin.

II
IMPLICATIONS

On the basis of this selection and of your own experience, discuss the justification or lack of justification for each of the following statements.

1. As President Kennedy points out, Ross would probably have become an exceptional legislator if he had been able to remain in the Senate. It was, therefore, foolish and even morally wrong for him to risk such a brilliant future for the sake of a single vote of principle.

2. Considering everything, Senator Ross would have been a much happier and a more satisfied person if he had voted with the majority of his colleagues.

3. It is morally wrong for Senators to vote according to their consciences when they know that the great majority of their constituents would not approve of such a vote.

4. When our conscience demands that we do something that will entail a loss of power, respect, wealth, and friends, we will usually not follow our conscience.

III
TECHNIQUES

Conflict

Although this selection is nonfiction, President Kennedy has so arranged his details that it reads almost like a short story. Especially evident here is the matter of conflict. How does the author manage to dramatize the conflict, especially at the moment of decision?

Climax

Locate the climaxes in this story. Would it have been better if only one climax had been used? If so, why did the author use more than one?

Moment of Illumination

Is there a moment of illumination in this story? If so, what is it? Judging from this and other nonfiction you have read, explain why you think that nonfiction typically has or has not a moment of illumination.

I
"A DIFFERENT DRUMMER"

Henry David Thoreau once wrote, "If a man does not keep pace with his companions, perhaps it is because he hears a different drummer." Senator Ross certainly did not "keep pace with his companions"—his decision was opposed both to the majority in his political party and to the desires of his constituents. He listened instead to his conscience, which told him that to vote against im-

Inner Conflicts in Love

◊

In "Parting, Without a Sequel,"
John Crowe Ransom renders a moving portrait of a lady
who has formally and "officially" broken with her sweetheart
by letter. As you read the poem, note the contrast
between the lady's emotional state at the end of the poem
and her sureness in the first stanza.
What might have caused this shift?

Parting, Without a Sequel

She has finished and sealed the letter
At last, which he so richly has deserved,
With characters venomous and hatefully curved,
And nothing could be better.

But even as she gave it   5
Saying to the blue-capped functioner of doom,
"Into his hands," she hoped the leering groom
Might somewhere lose and leave it.

Then all the blood
Forsook the face. She was too pale for tears,   10
Observing the ruin of her younger years.
She went and stood

Under her father's vaunting oak
Who kept his peace in wind and sun, and glistened
Stoical in the rain; to whom she listened   15
If he spoke.

And now the agitation of the rain
Rasped his sere[1] leaves, and he talked low and gentle
Reproaching the wan[2] daughter by the lintel;[3]
Ceasing and beginning again.   20

Away went the messenger's bicycle,
His serpent's track went up the hill forever,
And all the time she stood there hot as fever
And cold as any icicle.

JOHN CROWE RANSOM

Copyright 1927 by Alfred A. Knopf, Inc.,
and renewed 1955 by John Crowe Ransom.
Reprinted from *Selected Poems*, 3rd revised
edition, by permission of the publisher.

1. sere\ˈsi·ər\ parched, withered.
2. wan\wɔn\ pale, sickly.
3. lintel\ˈlin·təl\ crosspiece over a door
supporting the weight of the structure.

Like Ransom's poem,
"After Hours" deals with a conflict stimulated by a lost love.
There is a major difference between the poems, however,
as you will see when you reach the ending of Robert Mezey's poem.
Note how the author uses the setting of this poem—
winter, after the activity of the day is over—
to establish a mood for his speaker,
"lost in thought."

After Hours

Not yet five, and the light
is going fast. Milky and veined
a thin frost covers the flooded
ruts of the driveway, the grass
bends to the winter night. Her face   5
is before me now; I see it

in the misted glass, the same
impenetrable smile and I can feel
again on my bare shoulder
the dew of her breath. We made   10
a life in two years, a sky
and the very trees, lost in thought.

I know what it is, to be
alone, to have asked for everything
and to do without, to search   15
the mind for a face already dim,
to wait, and what it exacts.
I don't fear it, I say,

but I do, and this night
the wind against my window   20
and the top branches thrashing about
enter my life and I see
the coming time loose and dark
above me, with new strength.

ROBERT MEZEY

From *White Blossoms* by Robert Mezey. By permission
of Robert Mezey.

◇Love implies emotional involvement and sacrifice.
It may lead to sorrow, unhappiness, and inner stress as seen in Ransom's and Mezey's poems.
The inner conflict in "You Do Not Have to Love Me" is really within oneself:
whether to love another with all that such an act means
or to love the idea of love without the risk of involvement.
Lovers often hurt the ones they love; ideas seldom do.

You Do Not Have to Love Me

You do not have to love me
just because
you are all the women
I have ever wanted
I was born to follow you   5
every night
while I am still
the many men who love you

I meet you at a table
I take your fist between my hands   10
in a solemn taxi
I wake up alone
my hand on your absence
in Hotel Discipline

I wrote all these songs for you   15
I burned red and black candles
shaped like a man and a woman
I married the smoke
of two pyramids of sandalwood
I prayed for you   20
I prayed that you would love me
and that you would not love me

LEONARD COHEN

From *Selected Poems: 1956–1968* by Leonard Cohen.
Copyright © 1968 by Leonard Cohen. All rights reserved.
Reprinted by permission of The Viking Press, Inc.

◈ The inner struggle in this poem is well expressed
in the last stanza, where the speaker talks about the *pleasure*
of loneliness balanced against the *pain*
of loving. Her inner torment must be great
indeed if she can refer to loneliness as pleasure.

Balances

in life
one is always
balancing

like we juggle our mothers
against our fathers 5

or one teacher
against another
(only to balance our grade average)

3 grains salt
to one ounce truth 10

our sweet black essence
or the funky honkies down the street

and lately i've begun wondering
if you're trying to tell me something

we used to talk all night 15
and do things alone together

and i've begun

(as a reaction to a feeling)
to balance
the pleasure of loneliness 20
against the pain
of loving you

NIKKI GIOVANNI

"Balances" by Nikki Giovanni from *Black Judgement*. Copyright © 1968 by
Nikki Giovanni. Reprinted by permission of Broadside Press, Detroit, Michigan.

◇ One might imagine that if any love would be
uncomplicated and would not lead to a whirlpool of inner struggles,
it would be the love of a parent
for a child. Yet in the following poem by Anne Sexton to her daughter, Joy,
we find a deep conflict, provoked largely by the mother's guilt
at having left her Joy for three years while she (the mother) was in a mental institution.
It seems that—in love, at least—there are no "uncomplicated hymns."

A Little Uncomplicated Hymn
for Joy

Is what I wanted to write.
There *was* such a song!
A song for your kneebones,
a song for your ribs,
those delicate trees that bury your heart;   5
a song for your bookshelf
where twenty hand-blown ducks sit in a Venetian row;
a song for your dress-up high heels,
your fire-red skate board,
your twenty grubby fingers,   10
the pink knitting that you start
and never quite finish;
your poster-paint pictures,
all angels making a face,
a song for your laughter   15
that keeps wiggling a spoon in my sleep.

Even a song for your night
as during last summer's heat wave
where your fever stuck at 104 for two weeks,
where you slept, head on the window sill,   20
lips as dry as old erasers, your thirst
shimmering and heavy as I spooned water in,
your eyes shut on the thumping June bugs,
the lips moving, mumbling,
sending letters to the stars.   25
Dreaming, dreaming,
your body a boat,
rocked by your life and my death.
Your fists wound like a ball,
little fetus, little snail,   30
carrying a rage, a leftover rage
I cannot undo.

"A Little Uncomplicated Hymn" by Anne Sexton. Copyright © 1966 by Anne Sexton. Reprinted by permission of Houghton Mifflin Company.

391

Even a song for your flight
where you fell from the neighbor's tree hut,
where you thought you were walking onto solid blue air, 35
you thought, *why not?*
and then, you simply left the boards behind
and stepped out into the dust.

O little Icarus,
you chewed on a cloud, you bit the sun   40
and came tumbling down, head first,
not into the sea, but hard
on the hard packed gravel.
You fell on your eye. You fell on your chin.
What a shiner! What a faint you had   45
and then crawled home,
a knocked-out humpty dumpty
in my arms.

O humpty-dumpty girl,
I named you Joy,   50
That's someone's song all by itself.
In the naming of you I named
all things you are . . .
except the ditch
where I left you once,   55
like an old root that wouldn't take hold,
that ditch where I left you
while I sailed off in madness
over the buildings and under my umbrella,
sailed off for three years   60
so that the first candle
and the second candle
and the third candle
burned down alone on your birthday cake.
That ditch I want so much to forget   65
and that you try each day to forget.

Even here in your school portrait
where you repeat third grade,
caught in the need not to grow—
that little prison—   70

even here you keep up the barrier
with a smile that dies afraid
as it hides your crooked front tooth.
Joy, I call you
and yet your eyes just here   75
with their shades half-drawn over the gunsights,
over your gigantic knowledge,
over the little blue fish who dart back and forth,
over different streets, the strange rooms,
other people's chairs, other people's food,   80
ask, "Why was I shut in the cellar?"

And I've got words,
words that dog my heels,
words for sale you might say,
and multiplication cards and cursive writing   85
that you ignore to teach my fingers
the *cat's cradle* and the *witch's broom.*
Yes! I have instructions before dinner
and hugs after dinner and still those eyes—
away, away,   90
asking for hymns . . .
without guilt.

And I can only say
a little uncomplicated hymn
is what I wanted to write   95
and yet I find only your name.
There *was* such a song,
but it's bruised.
It's not mine.

You will jump to it someday   100
as you will jump out of the pitch of this house.
It will be a holiday, a parade, a fiesta!
Then you'll fly.
You'll really fly.
After that you'll, quite simply, quite calmly   105
make your own stones, your own floor plan,
your own sound.

I wanted to write such a poem
with such musics, such guitars going;
I tried at the teeth of sound   110
to draw up such legions of noise;
I tried at the breakwater
to catch the star off each ship;
and at the closing of hands
I looked for their houses   115
and silences.
I found just one.

    you were mine
    and I lent you out.

I look for uncomplicated hymns   120
but love has none.

ANNE SEXTON

Love does not occur only between persons.
Frequently, one of the deepest loves of childhood is the love of a youngster for a pet.
Often, too, it is in such a love that one first experiences the loss of love
and through that loss comes to a larger recognition of all that love involves.
The struggle in Richard Wilbur's "The Pardon"
is between a ten-year-old boy's love of his dog and his fear of death—
a conflict that is not fully resolved until the boy becomes an adult.

The Pardon

My dog lay dead five days without a grave
In the thick of summer, hid in a clump of pine
And a jungle of grass and honeysuckle-vine.
I who had loved him while he kept alive

Went only close enough to where he was   5
To sniff the heavy honeysuckle-smell
Twined with another odor heavier still
And hear the flies' intolerable buzz.

Well, I was ten and very much afraid.
In my kind world the dead were out of range   10
And I could not forgive the sad or strange
In beast or man. My father took the spade

And buried him. Last night I saw the grass
Slowly divide (it was the same scene
But now it glowed a fierce and mortal green)   15
And saw the dog emerging. I confess

I felt afraid again, but still he came
In the carnal sun, clothed in a hymn of flies,
And death was breeding in his lively eyes.
I started in to cry and call his name,   20

Asking forgiveness of his tongueless head.
. . . I dreamt the past was never past redeeming:
But whether this was false or honest dreaming
I beg death's pardon now. And mourn the dead.

RICHARD WILBUR

From *Ceremony and Other Poems*, copyright, 1948, 1949, 1950, by
Richard Wilbur. Reprinted by permission of Harcourt Brace Jovanovich, Inc.

THE LYRIC POET
AS A COMMUNICATOR OF FEELING

Though some poems are written largely to communicate ideas and others are written largely to tell stories, the lyric poem is one whose primary concern is the communication of feelings and emotions. This central purpose is apt to have certain side effects. For example, in each of the lyric poems above, you will find that the story elements are very slight. In the Ransom poem, for example, the reader never learns what happened to cause the lady to write the letter. Someone interested in the story element of this poem might well be curious about this omitted detail and might even reject the poem because it did not satisfy that curiosity. Such a reaction, however, would be inappropriate, for one should always judge a poem in terms of its intended effect. If Ransom had told why the lady wrote the letter, it is probable that the details would have distracted the reader from the woman's intense inner struggle while at the same time detracting from the wholeness of the poem, and, presumably, it was the woman's emotional reaction the author wanted to communicate.

Although there may be few story elements in lyric poetry, there is usually no lack of concrete detail. In Wilbur's poem, for example, we do not know how the dog died, but we are given a vivid impression of the dead animal. This is done through the contrast between the dog's odor and the sweet smell of the honeysuckle as well as through the sound of the flies buzzing as they feed on the corpse. Such concrete details are used to make the reader feel the emotions the poet wishes to communicate. The poet knows that the mature reader is not going to feel an emotion merely because the poet insists on it.

Emotions in life come in response to specific situations—a strange noise heard in the middle of the night causes the heart to pound with fear; the particular person one loves enters a room and one's pulse beats faster. Through concrete details —an odor heavier than the heavy odor of honeysuckle, "a smile that dies afraid/as it hides your crooked front tooth," an oak rasping its sere leaves—the poet tries to create a context parallel to, yet somehow more intense than, real life that will give rise to the desired emotions in readers. Such concrete details meant to appeal to the reader's senses of sight, smell, touch, taste, and hearing are commonly referred to as *images*.

In the following quotations, what is being described, and what feeling does it give you? To which of your senses does each image appeal primarily?

1. vaunting oak . . . glistened/Stoical in the rain.

2. His serpent's track went up the hill forever.

3. . . . on my bare shoulder/the dew of her breath.

4. the wind against my window/and the top branches thrashing about

5. I burned red and black candles/shaped like a man and a woman

6. I married the smoke/of two pyramids of sandalwood

7. our sweet black essence

8. and came tumbling down, head first,/not into the sea, but hard/on the hard packed gravel.

9. I wanted to write such a poem/with such musics, such guitars going

10. To sniff the heavy honeysuckle-smell/ Twined with another odor heavier still/And hear the flies' intolerable buzz.

11. And death was breeding in his lively eyes.

Have you ever been told by a person you loved that he or she loves someone else more than you? If you have, you should be able to sympathize with the main character in the following story. The rage, the self-doubt, and the impotence that a person in this situation may feel are powerfully expressed in this remarkable rendering of the inner struggle.

Solo on the Drums

ANN PETRY

The orchestra had a week's engagement at the Randlert Theater at Broadway and Forty-second Street. His name was picked out in lights on the marquee. The name of the orchestra and then his name underneath by itself.

There had been a time when he would have been excited by it. And stopped to let his mind and his eyes linger over it lovingly. Kid Jones. The name—his name—up there in lights that danced and winked in the brassy sunlight. And at night his name glittered up there on the marquee as though it had been sprinkled with diamonds. The people who pushed their way through the crowded street looked up at it and recognized it and smiled.

He used to eat it up. But not today. Not after what happened this morning. He just looked at the sign with his name on it. There it was. Then he noticed that the sun had come out, and he shrugged, and went on inside the theater to put on one of the cream-colored suits and get his music together.

After he finished changing his clothes, he glanced in the long mirror in his dressing room. He hadn't changed any. Same face. No fatter and no thinner. No gray hair. Nothing. He frowned. Because he felt that the things that were eating him up inside ought to show. But they didn't.

"Solo on the Drums" by Ann Petry. Reprinted from *Miss Muriel and Other Stories*. Copyright © 1971 by Ann Petry. Reprinted by permission of Houghton Mifflin Company.

When it was time to go out on the stage, he took his place behind the drums, not talking, just sitting there. The orchestra started playing softly. He made a mental note of the fact that the boys were working together as smoothly as though each one had been oiled.

The long gray curtains parted. One moment they were closed. And then they were open. Silently. Almost like magic. The high-powered spots flooded the stage with light. He could see specks of dust gliding down the wide beams of light. Under the bands of light the great space out front was all shadow. Faces slowly emerged out of it—disembodied heads and shoulders that slanted up and back, almost to the roof.

He hit the drums lightly. Regularly. A soft, barely discernible rhythm. A background. A repeated emphasis for the horns and the piano and the violin. The man with the trumpet stood up, and the first notes came out sweet and clear and high.

Kid Jones kept up the drum accompaniment. Slow. Careful. Soft. And he felt his left eyebrow lift itself and start to twitch as the man played the trumpet. It happened whenever he heard the trumpet. The notes crept up, higher, higher, higher. So high that his stomach sucked in against itself. Then a little lower and stronger. A sound sustained. The rhythm of it beating against his ears until he was filled with it and sighing with it.

He wanted to cover his ears with his hands because he kept hearing a voice that whispered the same thing over and over again. The voice was trapped somewhere under the roof—caught and held there by the trumpet. "I'm leaving I'm leaving I'm leaving."

The sound took him straight back to the rain, the rain that had come with the morning. He could see the beginning of the day—raw and cold. He was at home. But he was warm because he was close to her, holding her in his arms. The rain and the wind cried softly outside the window.

And now—well, he felt as though he were floating up and up and up on that long blue note of the trumpet. He half closed his eyes and rode up on it. It had stopped being music. It was that whispering voice, making him shiver. Hating it and not being able to do anything about it. "I'm leaving it's the guy who plays the piano I'm in love with him and I'm leaving now today." Rain in the streets. Heat gone. Food gone. Everything gone because a woman's gone. It's everything you ever wanted, he thought. It's everything you never got. Everything you ever had, everything you ever lost. It's all there in the trumpet—pain and hate and trouble and peace and quiet and love.

The last note stayed up in the ceiling. Hanging on and on. The man with the trumpet had stopped playing but Kid Jones could still hear that last note. In his ears. In his mind.

The spotlight shifted and landed on Kid Jones—the man behind the drums. The long beam of white light struck the top of his head and turned him into a pattern of light and shadow. Because of the cream-colored suit and shirt, his body seemed to be encased in light. But there was a shadow over his face, so that his features blended and disappeared. His hairline receding so far back that he looked like a man with a face that never ended. A man with a high, long face and dark, dark skin.

He caressed the drums with the brushes in his hands. They responded with a whisper of sound. The rhythm came over but it had to be listened for. It stayed that way for a long time. Low, insidious, repeated. Then he made the big bass drum growl and pick up the same rhythm.

The Marquis of Brund, pianist with the band, turned to the piano. The drums and the piano talked the same rhythm. The piano high. A little more insistent than the drums. The Marquis was turned sideways on the piano bench. His left foot tapped out the rhythm. His cream-colored suit sharply outlined the bulkiness of his body against the dark gleam of the piano. The drummer and the pianist were silhouetted in two separate brilliant shafts of light. The drums slowly dominated the piano.

The rhythm changed. It was faster. Kid Jones looked out over the crowded theater as he hit the drums. He began to feel as though he were the drums and the drums were he.

The theater throbbed with the excitement of the drums. A man sitting near the front shivered, and his head jerked to the rhythm. A sailor put his arm around the girl sitting beside him, took his hand and held her face still and pressed his mouth close over hers. Close. Close. Close. Until their faces seemed to melt together. Her hat fell off and neither of them moved. His hand dug deep into her shoulder and still they didn't move.

A kid sneaked in through a side door and slid into an aisle seat. His mouth was wide open, and he clutched his cap with both hands, tight and hard against his chest as he listened.

The drummer forgot he was in the theater. There was only he and the drums and they were far away. Long gone. He was holding Lulu, Helen, Susie, Mamie close in his arms. And all of them—all those girls blended into that one girl who was his wife. The one who said, "I'm leaving." She had said it over and over again, this morning, while rain dripped down the window panes.

When he hit the drums again it was with the thought that he was fighting with the piano player. He was choking the Marquis of Brund. He was putting a knife in clean between his ribs. He was slitting his throat with a long straight blade. Take my woman. Take your life.

The drums leaped with the fury that was in him. The men in the band turned their heads toward him—a faint astonishment showed in their faces.

He ignored them. The drums took him away

from them, took him back, and back, and back, in time and space. He built up an illusion. He was sending out the news. Grandma died. The foreigner in the litter has an old disease and will not recover. The man from across the big water is sleeping with the chief's daughter. Kill. Kill. Kill. The war goes well with the men with the bad smell and the loud laugh. It goes badly with the chiefs with the round heads and the peacock's walk.

It is cool in the deep track in the forest. Cool and quiet. The trees talk softly. They speak of the dance tonight. The young girl from across the lake will be there. Her waist is slender and her thighs are rounded. Then the words he wanted to forget were all around Kid Jones again. "I'm leaving I'm leaving I'm leaving."

He couldn't help himself. He stopped hitting the drums and stared at the Marquis of Brund—a long, malevolent look, filled with hate.

There was a restless, uneasy movement in the theater. He remembered where he was. He started playing again. The horn played a phrase. Soft and short. The drums answered. The horn said the same thing all over again. The drums repeated it. The next time it was more intricate. The phrase was turned around, it went back and forth and up and down. And the drums said it over, exactly the same.

He knew a moment of panic. This was where he had to solo again and he wasn't sure he could do it. He touched the drums lightly. They quivered and answered him.

And then it was almost as though the drums were talking about his own life. The woman in Chicago who hated him. The girl with the round, soft body who had been his wife and who had walked out on him, this morning, in the rain. The old woman who was his mother, the same woman who lived in Chicago, and who hated him because he looked like his father, his father who had seduced her and left her, years ago.

He forgot the theater, forgot everything but the drums. He was welded to the drums, sucked inside them. All of him. His pulse beat.

His heart beat. He had become part of the drums. They had become part of him.

He made the big bass rumble and reverberate. He went a little mad on the big bass. Again and again he filled the theater with a sound like thunder. The sound seemed to come not from the drums but from deep inside himself; it was a sound that was being wrenched out of him—a violent, raging, roaring sound. As it issued from him he thought, this is the story of my love, this is the story of my hate, this is all there is left of me. And the sound echoed and re-echoed far up under the roof of the theater.

When he finally stopped playing, he was trembling; his body was wet with sweat. He was surprised to see that the drums were sitting there in front of him. He hadn't become part of them. He was still himself. Kid Jones. Master of the drums. Greatest drummer in the world. Selling himself a little piece at a time. Every afternoon. Twice every evening. Only this time he had topped all his other performances. This time, playing like this after what had happened in the morning, he had sold all of himself—not just a little piece.

Someone kicked his foot. "Bow, you ape. Whassamatter with you?"

He bowed from the waist, and the spotlight slid away from him, down his pants legs. The light landed on the Marquis of Brund, the piano player. The Marquis' skin glistened like a piece of black seaweed. Then the light was back on Kid Jones.

He felt hot and he thought, I stink of sweat. The talcum he had dabbed on his face after he shaved felt like a constricting layer of cement. A thin layer but definitely cement. No air could get through to his skin. He reached for his handkerchief and felt the powder and the sweat mix as he mopped his face.

Then he bowed again. And again. Like a—like one of those things you pull the string and it jerks, goes through the motion of dancing. Pull it again and it kicks. Yeah, he thought, you were hot all right. The jitterbugs ate you up and you haven't any place to go. Since this morning you haven't had any place to go. "I'm leaving it's the guy who plays the piano I'm in love with the Marquis of Brund he plays such sweet piano I'm leaving leaving leaving ————"

He stared at the Marquis of Brund for a long moment.

Then he stood up and bowed again. And again.

I
FAME WITHOUT LOVE

Because his name is in lights at the beginning of the story and his face in a spotlight at the end, it is clear that Kid Jones is a huge success, a star. Yet success in the eyes of the world counts for very little if we do not feel successful in our own eyes. Whether we are successful or not depends primarily on whether or not we can satisfy our inner needs.

Probably because of the fact that his own mother did not love him, Kid Jones's greatest need seems to be for the love and acceptance of a woman. When he loses this, he is miserable in spite of his brilliant career as a musician. It is ironic that a person who appears to be drumming on top of the world is in reality down in the dumps.

II
IMPLICATIONS

A. The irony just pointed up is not the only one in the story. What is ironic about the following facts?

1. Kid Jones's name—and not the Marquis of Brund's—appears on the marquee.

2. Kid Jones's playing moves the sailor and his girl to kiss.

3. Kid Jones plays better after his wife leaves him than he has ever played before.

B. On the basis of articles, biographies, or autobiographies of famous persons that you have read, argue for or against the notion that those who have had great success in their careers are often personally unhappy. If you argue for this proposition, be sure to offer reasons to account for your opinion.

III
TECHNIQUES

Plot

We have defined *plot* as action structured around a conflict, leading to a climax. Modern short stories are sometimes described as plotless. It is said that they present character studies or "slices of life." What is your opinion of "Solo on the Drums"? If you think it has a plot, describe the conflict and identify the climax. If you think it is plotless, discuss how the story holds together, how it is unified.

Moment of Illumination

If you were looking for a fight between Kid Jones and the Marquis of Brund, this story may have left you unsatisfied; for all that happens at the end is that one stares at the other "for a long moment." When a reader feels displeased with the ending of a story, one of two things has usually happened: either the story was unsuccessful or the reader didn't fully grasp the author's intention.

How would you argue that Petry's main intention was *not* to develop the conflict between the two rivals? How does the moment of illumination—the author's comparison of Jones to a marionette—help to advance that argument?

Not all inner struggles involve significant, far-reaching,
dramatic choices between good and evil. More often the quiet plane
of our lives is daily rippled by almost countless little
nonmoral inner struggles. Should I get up five minutes early this morning?
Should I go to the show or to the ball game? Why don't I do my homework
before I watch television? In the following story George Stoyonovich
discovers that such little struggles can grow until suddenly they threaten
to affect one's very being and shape one's whole future.

A Summer's Reading

BERNARD MALAMUD

George Stoyonovich was a neighborhood boy who had quit high school on an impulse when he was sixteen, run out of patience, and though he was ashamed everytime he went looking for a job, when people asked him if he had finished and he had to say no, he never went back to school. This summer was a hard time for jobs and he had none. Having so much time on his hands, George thought of going to summer school, but the kids in his classes would be too young. He also considered registering in a night high school, only he didn't like the idea of the teachers always telling him what to do. He felt they had not respected him. The result was he stayed off the streets and in his room most of the day. He was close to twenty and had needs with the neighborhood girls, but no money to spend, and he couldn't get more than an occasional few cents because his father was poor, and his sister Sophie, who resembled George, a tall bony girl of twenty-three, earned very little and what she had she kept for herself. Their mother was dead, and Sophie had to take care of the house.

Very early in the morning George's father got up to go to work in a fish market. Sophie left about eight for her long ride in the subway to a cafeteria in the Bronx. George had his coffee by himself, then hung around in the house. When the house, a five-room railroad flat above a butcher store, got on his nerves he cleaned it up—mopped the floors with a wet mop and put things away. But most of the time he sat in his room. In the afternoons he listened to the ball game. Otherwise he had a couple of old copies of the *World Almanac* he had bought long ago, and he liked to read in them and also the magazines and newspapers that Sophie brought home, that had been left on the tables in the cafeteria. They were mostly picture magazines about movie stars and sports figures, also usually the *News* and *Mirror*. Sophie herself read whatever fell into her hands, although she sometimes read good books.

She once asked George what he did in his room all day and he said he read a lot too.

"Of what besides what I bring home? Do you ever read any worthwhile books?"

"Some," George answered, although he really didn't. He had tried to read a book or two that Sophie had in the house but found he was in no mood for them. Lately he couldn't stand made-up stories, they got on his nerves. He wished he had some hobby to work at—as a kid he was good in carpentry, but where could he work at it? Sometimes during the day he went for walks, but mostly he did his walking

From *The Magic Barrel* by Bernard Malamud, copyright © 1956, 1958 by Bernard Malamud. Reprinted with the permission of Farrar, Straus & Giroux, Inc.

after the hot sun had gone down and it was cooler in the streets.

In the evening after supper George left the house and wandered in the neighborhood. During the sultry days some of the storekeepers and their wives sat in chairs on the thick, broken sidewalks in front of their shops, fanning themselves, and George walked past them and the guys hanging out on the candy store corner. A couple of them he had known his whole life, but nobody recognized each other. He had no place special to go, but generally, saving it till the last, he left the neighborhood and walked for blocks till he came to a darkly lit little park with benches and trees and an iron railing, giving it a feeling of privacy. He sat on a bench here, watching the leafy trees and the flowers blooming on the inside of the railing, thinking of a better life for himself. He thought of the jobs he had had since he had quit school—delivery boy, stock clerk, runner, lately working in a factory—and he was dissatisfied with all of them. He felt he would someday like to have a good job and live in a private house with a porch, on a street with trees. He wanted to have some dough in his pocket to buy things with, and a girl to go with, so as not to be so lonely, especially on Saturday nights. He wanted people to like and respect him. He thought about these things often but mostly when he was alone at night. Around midnight he got up and drifted back to his hot and stony neighborhood.

One time while on his walk George met Mr. Cattanzara coming home very late from work. He wondered if he was drunk but then could tell he wasn't. Mr. Cattanzara, a stocky, bald-headed man who worked in a change booth on an IRT station, lived on the next block after George's, above a shoe repair store. Nights, during the hot weather, he sat on his stoop in an undershirt, reading the *New York Times* in the light of the shoemaker's window. He read it from the first page to the last, then went up to sleep. And all the time he was reading the paper, his wife, a fat woman with a white face, leaned out of the window, gazing into the street, her thick white arms folded under her loose breast, on the window ledge.

Once in a while Mr. Cattanzara came home drunk, but it was a quiet drunk. He never made any trouble, only walked stiffly up the street and slowly climbed the stairs into the hall. Though drunk, he looked the same as always, except for his tight walk, the quietness, and that his eyes were wet. George liked Mr. Cattanzara because he remembered him giving him nickels to buy lemon ice with when he was a squirt. Mr. Cattanzara was a different type than those in the neighborhood. He asked different questions than the others when he met you, and he seemed to know what went on in all the newspapers. He read them, as his fat sick wife watched from the window.

"What are you doing with yourself this summer, George?" Mr. Cattanzara asked. "I see you walkin' around at nights."

George felt embarrassed. "I like to walk."

"What are you doin' in the day now?"

"Nothing much just right now. I'm waiting for a job." Since it shamed him to admit he wasn't working, George said, "I'm staying home—but I'm reading a lot to pick up my education."

Mr. Cattanzara looked interested. He mopped his hot face with a red handkerchief.

"What are you readin'?"

George hesitated, then said, "I got a list of books in the library once, and now I'm gonna read them this summer." He felt strange and a little unhappy saying this, but he wanted Mr. Cattanzara to respect him.

"How many books are there on it?"

"I never counted them. Maybe around a hundred."

Mr. Cattanzara whistled through his teeth.

"I figure if I did that," George went on earnestly, "it would help me in my education. I don't mean the kind they give you in high school. I want to know different things than they learn there, if you know what I mean."

The change maker nodded. "Still and all, one hundred books is a pretty big load for one summer."

"It might take longer."

"After you're finished with some, maybe you and I can shoot the breeze about them?" said Mr. Cattanzara.

"When I'm finished," George answered.

Mr. Cattanzara went home and George continued on his walk. After that, though he had the urge to, George did nothing different from usual. He still took his walks at night, ending up in the little park. But one evening the shoemaker on the next block stopped George to say he was a good boy, and George figured that Mr. Cattanzara had told him all about the books he was reading. From the shoemaker it must have gone down the street, because George saw a couple of people smiling kindly at him, though nobody spoke to him personally. He felt a little better around the neighborhood and liked it more, though not so much he would want to live in it forever. He had never exactly disliked the people in it, yet he had never liked them very much either. It was the fault of the neighborhood. To his surprise, George found out that his father and Sophie knew about his reading too. His father was too shy to say anything about it—he was never much of a talker in his whole life—but Sophie was softer to George, and she showed him in other ways she was proud of him.

As the summer went on George felt in a good mood about things. He cleaned the house every day, as a favor to Sophie, and he enjoyed the ball games more. Sophie gave him a buck a week allowance, and though it still wasn't enough and he had to use it carefully, it was a helluva lot better than just having two bits now and then. What he bought with the money— cigarettes mostly, an occasional beer or movie ticket—he got a big kick out of. Life wasn't so bad if you knew how to appreciate it. Occasionally he bought a paperback book from the news-stand, but he never got around to reading it, though he was glad to have a couple of books in his room. But he read thoroughly Sophie's magazines and newspapers. And at night was the most enjoyable time, because when he passed the storekeepers sitting outside their stores, he could tell they regarded him highly. He walked erect, and though he did not say much to them, or they to him, he could feel approval on all sides. A couple of nights he felt so good that he skipped the park at the end of the evening. He just wandered in the neighborhood, where people had known him from the time he was a kid playing punchball whenever there was a game of it going; he wandered there, then came home and got undressed for bed, feeling fine.

For a few weeks he had talked only once with Mr. Cattanzara, and though the change maker had said nothing more about the books, asked no questions, his silence made George a little uneasy. For a while George didn't pass in front of Mr. Cattanzara's house anymore, until one night, forgetting himself, he approached it from a different direction than he usually did when he did. It was already past midnight. The street, except for one or two people, was deserted, and George was surprised when he saw Mr. Cattanzara still reading his newspaper by the light of the street lamp overhead. His impulse was to stop at the stoop and talk to him. He wasn't sure what he wanted to say, though he felt the words would come when he began to talk; but the more he thought about it, the more the idea scared him, and he decided he'd better not. He even considered beating it home by another street, but he was too near Mr. Cattanzara, and the change maker might see him as he ran, and get annoyed. So George unobtrusively crossed the street, trying to make it seem as if he had to look in a store window on the other side, which he did, and then went on, uncomfortable at what he was doing. He feared Mr. Cattanzara would glance up from his paper and call him a dirty rat for walking on the other side of the street, but all he did was sit there, sweating through his undershirt, his bald head shining in the dim light as he read his *Times,* and upstairs his fat wife leaned out of the window, seeming to read the paper along with him. George thought she would spy him and yell out to Mr. Cattanzara, but she never moved her eyes off her husband.

George made up his mind to stay away from the change maker until he had got some of his softback books read, but when he started them and saw they were mostly story books, he lost his interest and didn't bother to finish them. He lost his interest in reading other things too. Sophie's magazines and newspapers went unread. She saw them piling up on a chair in his room and asked why he was no longer looking at them, and George told her it was because of all the other reading he had to do. Sophie said she had guessed that was it. So for most of the day, George had the radio on, turning to music when he was sick of the human voice. He kept the house fairly neat, and Sophie said nothing on the days when he neglected it. She was still kind and gave him his extra buck, though things weren't so good for him as they had been before.

But they were good enough, considering. Also his night walks invariably picked him up, no matter how bad the day was. Then one night George saw Mr. Cattanzara coming down the street toward him. George was about to turn and run but he recognized from Mr. Cattanzara's walk that he was drunk, and if so, probably he would not even bother to notice him. So George kept on walking straight ahead until he came abreast of Mr. Cattanzara and though he felt wound up enough to pop into the sky, he was not surprised when Mr. Cattanzara passed him without a word, walking slowly, his face and body stiff. George drew a breath in relief at his narrow escape, when he heard his name called, and there stood Mr. Cattanzara at his elbow, smelling like the inside of a beer barrel. His eyes were sad as he gazed at George, and George felt so intensely uncomfortable he was tempted to shove the drunk aside and continue on his walk.

But he couldn't act that way to him, and, besides, Mr. Cattanzara took a nickel out of his pants pocket and handed it to him.

"Go buy yourself a lemon ice, Georgie."

"It's not that time anymore, Mr. Cattanzara," George said, "I am a big guy now."

"No, you ain't," said Mr. Cattanzara, to which George made no reply he could think of.

"How are all your books comin' along now?" Mr. Cattanzara asked. Though he tried to stand steady, he swayed a little.

"Fine, I guess," said George, feeling the red crawling up his face.

"You ain't sure?" The change maker smiled slyly, a way George had never seen him smile.

"Sure I'm sure. They're fine."

Though his head swayed in little arcs, Mr. Cattanzara's eyes were steady. He had small blue eyes which could hurt if you looked at them too long.

"George," he said, "name me one book on that list that you read this summer, and I will drink to your health."

"I don't want anybody drinking to me."

"Name me one so I can ask you a question on it. Who can tell, if it's a good book maybe I might wanna read it myself."

George knew he looked passable on the outside, but inside he was crumbling apart.

Unable to reply, he shut his eyes, but when—years later—he opened them, he saw that Mr. Cattanzara had, out of pity, gone away, but in his ears he still heard the words he had said when he left: "George, don't do what I did."

The next night he was afraid to leave his room, and though Sophie argued with him he wouldn't open the door.

"What are you doing in there?" she asked.

"Nothing."

"Aren't you reading?"

"No."

She was silent a minute, then asked, "Where do you keep the books you read? I never see any in your room outside of a few cheap trashy ones."

He wouldn't tell her.

"In that case you're not worth a buck of my hard-earned money. Why should I break my back for you? Go on out, you bum, and get a job."

He stayed in his room for almost a week, except to sneak into the kitchen when nobody was home. Sophie railed at him, then begged him to come out, and his old father wept, but George wouldn't budge, though the weather was terrible and his small room stifling. He found it very hard to breathe, each breath was like drawing a flame into his lungs.

One night, unable to stand the heat anymore, he burst into the street at one A.M., a shadow of himself. He hoped to sneak to the park without being seen, but there were people all over the block, wilted and listless, waiting for a breeze. George lowered his eyes and walked, in disgrace, away from them, but before long he discovered they were still friendly to him. He figured Mr. Cattanzara hadn't told on him. Maybe when he woke up out of his drunk the next morning, he had forgotten all about meeting George. George felt his confidence slowly come back to him.

That same night a man on a street corner asked him if it was true that he had finished reading so many books, and George admitted he had. The man said it was a wonderful thing for a boy his age to read so much.

"Yeah," George said, but he felt relieved. He hoped nobody would mention the books anymore, and when, after a couple of days, he accidentally met Mr. Cattanzara again, *he* didn't, though George had the idea he was the one who had started the rumor that he had finished all the books.

One evening in the fall, George ran out of his house to the library, where he hadn't been in years. There were books all over the place, wherever he looked, and though he was struggling to control an inward trembling, he easily counted off a hundred, then sat down at a table to read.

I
DUTY TO ONESELF

On the surface, George's inner struggle differs from those in most of our earlier stories in that no important moral issue seems to be involved in his case. Yet he suffers a great deal because of his indecision. One of the important questions for the reader to ask is how much of this suffering comes from a sense of guilt—guilt which arises from George's failure to meet the moral obligation to develop himself as fully as he can. To what extent do you think Mr. Cattanzara had this obligation in mind when he said to George, "Don't do what I did"?

II
IMPLICATIONS

Examine the following assumptions and discuss them in the light of this selection and of your own experience.

1. The chief factor standing in the way of George's self-realization is his unwholesome environment.

2. The chief factor causing George to move toward self-realization is his need for love and respect.

3. If George had managed to get a job, his conscience would have stopped bothering him.

4. In order to succeed in life people need to have models of success to stimulate them.

5. To develop oneself fully, one must have an education.

6. Before we can have any real success in life, we must accept as our duty the principle that we are obliged to strive for excellence.

III
TECHNIQUES

Conflict

What are the forces that move George in a positive direction and what are those that influence him negatively? What forces *within* George might be listed on the one side and on the other? Do the inner or the outer forces seem to be the more powerful? Does the conflict seem to be evenly or unevenly balanced?

Climax

A turning point and minor climax occur when George tells Mr. Cattanzara that he is reading good books. After this, George's fortunes definitely improve in the sense that his neighbors and family gain greater respect for him. At the same time, however, the reader is well aware that this moment is not the true climax of the story. How does the reader know this? When does the true climax occur?

IV
WORDS

A. The phrases and clauses below contain modifiers, connectors, appositives, or definitions that act as clues to the meaning of the italicized words. What does each italicized word mean? How does the context help you determine meaning?

1. A mass meeting at Lawrence had *vilified* the Senator and speedily reported resolutions sharply condemning his position.

2. . . . warned in the party press, *harangued* by their constituents. . . .

3. . . . "plunged from a *precipice* of fame into the *groveling* depths of infamy and death."

4. . . . the press and the country took the opportunity to pay tribute to his *fidelity* to principle in a trying hour. . . .

5. Also his night walks *invariably* picked him up, no matter how bad the day was.

6. . . . George wouldn't budge, though the weather was terrible and his small room *stifling*.

B. 1. The editors of most dictionaries give diction labels that help describe the various levels of usage words suggest. Look up *wan* and *sere*. What diction or usage labels do you find?

2. A term or word used regularly in a certain region is generally labeled *dialect*. Look up *peanuts* and *goobers*, *tawpie* and *simpleton*, *bet* and *punt*.

3. A word or sense used by most people in conversation and informal writing is generally marked *colloquial*. Colloquialisms have no particular connection with a certain region, social standing, or education. *Slang* is a label attached to terms used in very informal situations and generally within a small group. Slang may be shortened words, such as *mob, kook, bunk;* newly invented words, such as *snide, to goof;* old words with new meaning, such as *square* (conventional), *eye* (detective); or unusual figures of speech, such as "he *dimed* on me" (he called the police). Look up the italicized words below and note the diction labels given.

(a) put the check on my *cuff;* (b) everyone was there, *even* Tom; (c) he was *ever so polite;* (d) he gives me the *heebie jeebies;* (e) *enthused* about the project; (f) she stopped at the *hostel;* (g) *perchance* our paths shall cross again; (h) a rather *snide* remark; (i) she pointed to the *chesterfield;* (j) he is a *mule* about changing his mind; (k) you better *hump* to it.

This story is about one of the strangest characters in American fiction: Bartleby, a copier of legal documents, who chooses not to work. The inner struggle, however, focuses on the narrator, the head of a small law office, who must decide what to do with Bartleby, his employee. As an employer, the narrator knows that he must not retain a worker that won't produce; yet as a human being, he feels a responsibility toward a fellow mortal who appears unable to care for himself. A further complication is that Bartleby never says that he *will not* work, only that he "prefers" not to.

Herman Melville wrote this famous story at the height of his creative powers, just two years after the publication of *Moby Dick*.

Bartleby the Scrivener

A Story of Wall Street

HERMAN MELVILLE

I am a rather elderly man. The nature of my avocations for the last thirty years has brought me into more than ordinary contact with what would seem an interesting and somewhat singular set of men, of whom as yet nothing that I know of has ever been written—I mean, the law copyists, or scriveners.[1] I have known very many of them, professionally and privately, and if I pleased, could relate divers histories, at which good-natured gentlemen might smile, and sentimental souls might weep. But I waive the biographies of all other scriveners for a few passages in the life of Bartleby, who was a scrivener, the strangest I ever saw or heard of. While of other law copyists I might write the complete life, of Bartleby nothing of that sort can be done. I believe that no materials exist for a full and satisfactory biography of this man. It is an irreparable loss to literature. Bartleby was one of those beings of whom nothing is ascertainable except from the original sources, and in his case those are very small. What my own astonished eyes saw of Bartleby, *that* is all I know of him except, indeed, one vague report, which will appear in the sequel.

Ere introducing the scrivener, as he first appeared to me, it is fit I make some mention of myself, my employees, my business, my chambers, and general surroundings; because some such description is indispensable to an adequate understanding of the chief character about to be presented.

Imprimis:[2] I am a man who from his youth upwards has been filled with a profound conviction that the easiest way of life is the best. Hence, though I belong to a profession proverbially energetic and nervous, even to turbulence at times, yet nothing of that sort have I ever suffered to invade my peace. I am one of those unambitious lawyers who never addresses a jury or in any way draws down public applause; but in the cool tranquility of a snug retreat do a snug business among rich men's bonds and mortgages and title deeds. All who know me consider me an eminently *safe* man. The late John Jacob Astor, a personage little given to poetic enthusiasm, had no hesitation in pronouncing my first grand point to be prudence; my next, method. I do not speak it in vanity but simply record the fact that I was not unemployed in my profession by the late John Jacob Astor; a name which, I admit, I love

---

1. **scriveners,** copyists who duplicated legal documents.
2. **imprimis,** Latin word meaning "in the first place."

to repeat; for it hath a rounded and orbicular sound to it and rings like unto bullion. I will freely add that I was not insensible to the late John Jacob Astor's good opinion.

Some time prior to the period at which this little history begins, my avocations had been largely increased. The good old office, now extinct in the State of New York, of a master in chancery,[3] had been conferred upon me. It was not a very arduous office, but very pleasantly remunerative. I seldom lose my temper; much more seldom indulge in dangerous indignation at wrongs and outrages; but I must be permitted to be rash here and declare that I consider the sudden and violent abrogation of the office of master in chancery by the new constitution as a———premature act; inasmuch as I had counted upon a life-lease of the profits, whereas I only received those of a few short years. But this is by the way.

My chambers were upstairs at No.—Wall Street. At one end, they looked upon the white wall of the interior of a spacious skylight shaft, penetrating the building from top to bottom.

This view might have been considered rather tame than otherwise, deficient in what landscape painters call "life." But, if so, the view from the other end of my chambers offered, at least, a contrast, if nothing more. In that direction, my windows commanded an unobstructed view of a lofty brick wall, black by age and everlasting shade; which wall required no spyglass to bring out its lurking beauties, but for the benefit of all nearsighted spectators was pushed up to within ten feet of my window panes. Owing to the great height of the surrounding buildings, and my chambers being on the second floor, the interval between this wall and mine not a little resembled a huge square cistern.

At the period just preceding the advent of Bartleby, I had two persons as copyists in my employment, and a promising lad as an office boy. First, Turkey; second, Nippers; third,

Ginger Nut. These may seem names the like of which are not usually found in the Directory. In truth, they were nicknames, mutually conferred upon each other by my three clerks, and were deemed expressive of their respective persons or characters. Turkey was a short, pursy[4] Englishman of about my own age—that is, somewhere not far from sixty. In the morning, one might say, his face was of a fine, florid hue, but after twelve o'clock, meridian—his dinner hour—it blazed like a grate full of Christmas coals and continued blazing—but as it were with a gradual wane—till 6 o'clock, P.M., or thereabouts; after which, I saw no more of the proprietor of the face, which, gaining its meridian with the sun, seemed to set with it, to rise, culminate, and decline the following day, with the like regularity and undiminished glory. There are many singular coincidences I have known in the course of my life, not the least among which was the fact that exactly when Turkey displayed his fullest beams from his red and radiant countenance, just then, too, at that critical moment began the daily period when I considered his business capacities as seriously disturbed for the remainder of the twenty-four hours. Not that he was absolutely idle or averse to business then, far from it. The difficulty was, he was apt to be altogether too energetic. There was a strange, inflamed, flurried recklessness of activity about him. He would be incautious in dipping his pen into his inkstand. All his blots upon my documents were dropped there after twelve o'clock, meridian. Indeed, not only would he be reckless and sadly given to making blots in the afternoon, but some days he went further and was rather noisy. At such times, too, his face flamed with augmented blazonry, as if cannel coal had been heaped on anthracite.[5] He made an unpleasant racket with his chair; spilled his sandbox; in mending his pens impatiently split them all to pieces and threw them on the floor in a sudden passion; stood up

---

3. **master in chancery,** a judge in an equity court that handles contract adjustments, etc.

4. **pursy,** short of breath due to overweight.
5. **cannel coal . . . on anthracite,** a brightly burning coal heaped on a slow, long-burning one.

and leaned over his table, boxing his papers about in a most indecorous manner very sad to behold in an elderly man like him. Nevertheless, as he was in many ways a most valuable person to me, and all the time before twelve o'clock meridian, was the quickest, steadiest creature, too, accomplishing a great deal of work in a style not easily to be matched—for these reasons, I was willing to overlook his eccentricities, though, indeed, occasionally, I remonstrated with him. I did this very gently, however, because though the civilest, nay, the blandest and most reverential of men in the morning, yet in the afternoon he was disposed, upon provocation, to be slightly rash with his tongue—in fact, insolent. Now, valuing his morning services as I did, and resolved not to lose them—yet at the same time made uncomfortable by his inflamed ways after twelve o'clock—and being a man of peace, unwilling by my admonitions to call forth unseemly retorts from him, I took upon me one Saturday noon (he was always worse on Saturdays) to hint to him, very kindly, that perhaps now that he was growing old, it might be well to abridge his labors; in short, he need not come to my chambers after twelve o'clock, but dinner over, had best go home to his lodgings and rest himself till teatime. But no; he insisted upon his afternoon devotions. His countenance became intolerably fervid as he oratorically assured me—gesticulating with a long ruler at the other side of the room—that if his services in the morning were useful, how indispensable then in the afternoon?

"With submission, sir," said Turkey, on this occasion, "I consider myself your right-hand man. In the morning I but marshal and deploy my columns; but in the afternoon I put myself at their head, and gallantly charge the foe, thus"—and he made a violent thrust with the ruler.

"But the blots, Turkey," intimated I.

"True; but with submission, sir, behold these hairs! I am getting old. Surely, sir, a blot or two of a warm afternoon is not to be severely urged against gray hairs. Old age—even if it

blot the page—is honorable. With submission, sir, we *both* are getting old."

This appeal to my fellow feeling was hardly to be resisted. At all events, I saw that go he would not. So I made up my mind to let him stay, resolving, nevertheless, to see to it that during the afternoon he had to do with my less important papers.

Nippers, the second on my list, was a whiskered, sallow, and upon the whole, practical-looking young man, of above five and twenty. I always deemed him the victim of two evil powers—ambition and indigestion. The ambition was evinced by a certain impatience of the duties of a mere copyist, an unwarrantable usurpation of strictly professional affairs, such as the original drawing up of legal documents. The indigestion seemed betokened in an occasional nervous testiness and grinning irritability, causing the teeth to audibly grind together over mistakes committed in copying; unnecessary maledictions, hissed rather than spoken, in the heat of business; and especially by a continual discontent with the height of the table where he worked. Though of a very ingenious mechanical turn, Nippers could never get this table to suit him. He put chips under it, blocks of various sorts, bits of pasteboard, and at last went so far as to attempt an exquisite adjustment by final pieces of folded blotting paper. But no invention would answer. If for the sake of easing his back, he brought the table lid at a sharp angle well up towards his chin and wrote there like a man using the steep roof of a Dutch house for his desk, then he declared that it stopped the circulation in his arms. If now he lowered the table to his waistbands and stooped over it in writing, then there was a sore aching in his back. In short, the truth of the matter was, Nippers knew not what he wanted. Or if he wanted anything, it was to be rid of a scrivener's table altogether. Among the manifestations of his diseased ambition was a fondness he had for receiving visits from certain ambiguous-looking fellows in seedy coats, whom he called his clients. Indeed, I was aware that not only was he, at times, considerable of a ward politician, but he occasionally did a little business at the Justices' courts and was not unknown on the steps of the Tombs.[6] I have good reason to believe, however, that one individual who called upon him at my chambers, and who, with a grand air, he insisted was his client, was no other than a dun,[7] and the alleged title deed, a bill. But with all his failings, and the annoyances he caused me, Nippers, like his compatriot Turkey, was a very useful man to me; wrote a neat, swift hand; and when he chose, was not deficient in a gentlemanly sort of deportment. Added to this, he always dressed in a gentlemanly sort of way; and so, incidentally, reflected credit upon my chambers. Whereas, with respect to Turkey, I had much ado to keep him from being a reproach to me. His clothes were apt to look oily and smell of eating houses. He wore his pantaloons very loose and baggy in summer. His coats were execrable; his hat not to be handled. But while the hat was a thing of indifference to me, inasmuch as his natural civility and deference as a dependent Englishman always led him to doff it the moment he entered the room, yet his coat was another matter. Concerning his coats, I reasoned with him; but with no effect. The truth was, I suppose, that man with so small an income could not afford to sport such a lustrous face and a lustrous coat at one and the same time. As Nippers once observed, Turkey's money went chiefly for red ink. One winter day, I presented Turkey with a highly respectable-looking coat of my own—a padded gray coat, of a most comfortable warmth, and which buttoned straight up from the knee to the neck. I thought Turkey would appreciate the favor and abate his rashness and obstreperousness of afternoons. But no; I verily believe that buttoning himself up in so downy and blanketlike a coat had a pernicious effect upon him—upon the same principle that too much oats are bad for horses. In fact, precisely

as a rash, restive horse is said to feel his oats, so Turkey felt his coat. It made him insolent. He was a man whom prosperity harmed.

Though concerning the self-indulgent habits of Turkey, I had my own private surmises, yet touching Nippers, I was well persuaded that whatever might be his faults in other respects he was, at least, a temperate young man. But, indeed, nature herself seemed to have been his vintner, and at his birth charged him so thoroughly with an irritable brandylike disposition that all subsequent potations[8] were needless. When I consider how, amid the stillness of my chambers, Nippers would sometimes impatiently rise from his seat, and stooping over his table, spread his arms wide apart, seize the whole desk, and move it, and jerk it, with a grim, grinding motion on the floor, as if the table were a perverse voluntary agent intent on thwarting and vexing him, I plainly perceive that, for Nippers, brandy and water were altogether superfluous.

It was fortunate for me that owing to its peculiar cause—indigestion—the irritability and consequent nervousness of Nippers were mainly observable in the morning, while in the afternoon he was comparatively mild. So that, Turkey's paroxysms only coming on about twelve o'clock, I never had to do with their eccentricities at one time. Their fits relieved each other like guards. When Nipper's was on, Turkey's was off; and vice versa. This was a good natural arrangement, under the circumstances.

Ginger Nut, the third on my list, was a lad, some twelve years old. His father was a carman, ambitious of seeing his son on the bench, instead of a cart, before he died. So he sent him to my office as student at law, errand boy, cleaner and sweeper, at the rate of one dollar a week. He had a little desk to himself, but he did not use it much. Upon inspection, the drawer exhibited a great array of the shells of various sorts of nuts. Indeed, to this quick-witted youth the whole noble science of the

---

6. **the Tombs,** a jail in New York City.
7. **a dun,** a bill collector.

---

8. **potations,** alcoholic drinks or brews.

law was contained in a nutshell. Not the least among the employments of Ginger Nut, as well as one which he discharged with the most alacrity, was his duty as cake and apple purveyor for Turkey and Nippers. Copying law papers being proverbially a dry, husky sort of business, my two scriveners were fain to moisten their mouths very often with Spitzenbergs,[9] to be had at numerous stalls nigh the customhouse and post office. Also, they sent Ginger Nut very frequently for that peculiar cake—small, flat, round, and very spicy—after which he had been named by them. Of a cold morning when business was but dull, Turkey would gobble up scores of these cakes as if they were mere wafers—indeed, they sell them at the rate of six or eight for a penny—the scrape of his pen blending with the crunching of the crisp particles in his mouth. Of all the fiery afternoon blunders and flurried rashnesses of Turkey, was his once moistening a ginger cake between his lips and clapping it on to a mortgage for a seal. I came within an ace of dismissing him then. But he mollified me by making an oriental bow and saying—"With submission, sir, it was generous of me to find you in stationery on my own account."

Now to my original business—that of a conveyancer[10] and title hunter, and drawer-up of recondite documents of all sorts—was considerably increased by receiving the master's office. There was now great work for scriveners. Not only must I push the clerks already with me, but I must have additional help.

In answer to my advertisement, a motionless young man one morning stood upon my office threshold, the door being open, for it was summer. I can see that figure now—pallidly neat, pitiably respectable, incurably forlorn! It was Bartleby.

After a few words touching his qualifications, I engaged him, glad to have among my corps of copyists a man of so singularly sedate an aspect, which I thought might operate beneficially upon the flighty temper of Turkey and the fiery one of Nippers.

I should have stated before that ground-glass folding doors divided my premises into two parts, one of which was occupied by my scriveners, the other by myself. According to my humor I threw open these doors or closed them. I resolved to assign Bartleby a corner by the folding doors, but on my side of them, so as to have this quiet man within easy call in case any trifling thing was to be done. I placed his desk close up to a small side window in that part of the room, a window which originally had afforded a lateral view of certain grimy back yards and bricks, but which, owing to subsequent erections, commanded at present no view at all, though it gave some light. Within three feet of the panes was a wall, and the light came down from far above, between two lofty buildings, as from a very small opening in a dome. Still further to a satisfactory arrangement, I procured a high green folding screen, which might entirely isolate Bartleby from my sight, though not remove him from my voice. And thus, in a manner, privacy and society were conjoined.

At first Bartleby did an extraordinary quantity of writing. As if long famishing for something to copy, he seemed to gorge himself on my documents. There was no pause for digestion. He ran a day and night line, copying by sunlight and by candlelight. I should have been quite delighted with his application had he been cheerfully industrious. But he wrote on silently, palely, mechanically.

It is, of course, an indispensable part of a scrivener's business to verify the accuracy of his copy, word by word. Where there are two or more scriveners in an office, they assist each other in this examination, one reading from the copy, the other holding the original. It is a very dull, wearisome, and lethargic affair. I can readily imagine that to some sanguine temperaments it would be altogether intolerable. For example, I cannot credit that the mettlesome poet Byron would have contentedly sat

9. **Spitzenbergs,** a type of apple.
10. **conveyancer,** a lawyer who draws up deeds to transfer property titles.

down with Bartleby to examine a law document of, say, five hundred pages, closely written in a crimpy hand.

Now and then, in the haste of business, it had been my habit to assist in comparing some brief document myself, calling Turkey or Nippers for this purpose. One object I had in placing Bartleby so handy to me behind the screen was to avail myself of his services on such trivial occasions. It was on the third day, I think, of his being with me, and before any necessity had arisen for having his own writing examined, that being hurried to complete a small affair I had in hand, I abruptly called to Bartleby. In my haste and natural expectancy of instant compliance, I sat with my head bent over the original on my desk, and my right hand sideways, and somewhat nervously extended with the copy, so that immediately upon emerging from his retreat Bartleby might snatch it and proceed to business without the least delay.

In this very attitude did I sit when I called to him, rapidly stating what it was I wanted him to do—namely, to examine a small paper with me. Imagine my surprise, nay, my consternation, when, without moving from his privacy, Bartleby, in a singularly mild, firm voice, replied, "I would prefer not to."

I sat awhile in perfect silence, rallying my stunned facilities. Immediately it occurred to me that my ears had deceived me, or Bartleby had entirely misunderstood my meaning. I repeated my request in the clearest tone I could assume. But in quite as clear a tone came the previous reply, "I would prefer not to."

"Prefer not to," echoed I, rising in high excitement, and crossing the room with a stride. "What do you mean? Are you moonstruck? I want you to help me compare this sheet here—take it," and I thrust it towards him.

"I would prefer not to," said he.

I looked at him steadfastly. His face was leanly composed; his gray eye dimly calm. Not a wrinkle of agitation rippled him. Had there been the least uneasiness, anger, impatience, or impertinence in his manner; in other words, had there been anything ordinarily human about him, doubtless I should have violently dismissed him from the premises. But as it was, I should have as soon thought of turning my pale plaster-of-Paris bust of Cicero out of doors. I stood gazing at him awhile as he went on with his own writing, and then reseated myself at my desk. This is very strange, thought I. What had one best do? But my business hurried me. I concluded to forget the matter for the present, reserving it for my future leisure. So calling Nippers from the other room, the paper was speedily examined.

A few days after this, Bartleby concluded four lengthy documents, being quadruplicates of a week's testimony taken before me in my High Court of Chancery. It became necessary to examine them. It was an important suit, and great accuracy was imperative. Having all things arranged, I called Turkey, Nippers, and Ginger Nut from the next room, meaning to place the four copies in the hands of my four clerks, while I should read from the original. Accordingly, Turkey, Nippers, and Ginger Nut had taken their seats in a row, each with his document in his hand, when I called to Bartleby to join this interesting group.

"Bartleby! quick, I am waiting."

I heard a slow scrape of his chair legs on the uncarpeted floor, and soon he appeared standing at the entrance of his hermitage.

"What is wanted?" said he, mildly.

"The copies, the copies," said I, hurriedly. "We are going to examine them. There"—and I held toward him the fourth quadruplicate.

"I would prefer not to," he said, and gently disappeared behind the screen.

For a few moments I was turned into a pillar of salt,[11] standing at the head of my seated column of clerks. Recovering myself, I advanced towards the screen and demanded the reason for such extraordinary conduct.

---

11. **a pillar of salt,** an allusion to the Biblical story of Lot's wife, who disobeyed God's order and was consequently turned into a pillar of salt (Genesis 19).

"*Why* do you refuse?"

"I would prefer not to."

With any other man I should have flown outright into a dreadful passion, scorned all further words, and thrust him ignominiously from my presence. But there was something about Bartleby that not only strangely disarmed me, but in a wonderful manner touched and disconcerted me. I began to reason with him.

These are your own copies we are about to examine. It is labor saving for you, because one examination will answer for your four papers. It is common usage. Every copyist is bound to help examine his copy. Is it not so? Will you not speak? Answer!"

"I prefer not to," he replied in a flutelike tone. It seemed to me that while I had been addressing him, he carefully revolved every statement that I made; fully comprehended the meaning; could not gainsay the irresistible conclusion; but at the same time some paramount consideration prevailed with him to reply as he did.

"You are decided, then, not to comply with my request—a request made according to *common* usage and common sense?"

He briefly gave me to understand that on that point my judgment was sound. Yes: his decision was irreversible.

It is not seldom the case that when a man is browbeaten in some unprecedented and violently unreasonable way, he begins to stagger in his own plainest faith. He begins, as it were, vaguely to surmise that, wonderful as it may be, all the justice and all the reason is on the other side. Accordingly, if any disinterested persons are present, he turns to them for some reinforcement for his own faltering mind.

"Turkey," said I, "what do you think of this? Am I not right?"

"With submission, sir," said Turkey, in his blandest tone, "I think that you are."

"Nippers," said I, "what do *you* think of it?"

"I think I should kick him out of the office."

(The reader of nice[12] perceptions will have perceived that it being morning, Turkey's answer is couched in polite and tranquil terms, but Nippers replies in ill-tempered ones. Or to repeat a previous sentence, Nipper's ugly mood was on duty, and Turkey's off.)

"Ginger Nut," said I, willing to enlist the smallest suffrage in my behalf, "what do *you* think of it?"

"I think, sir, he's a little *luny*," replied Ginger Nut, with a grin.

"You hear what they say," said I, turning towards the screen, "come forth and do your duty."

But he vouchsafed no reply. I pondered a moment in sore perplexity. But once more business hurried me. I determined again to postpone the consideration of this dilemma to my future leisure. With a little trouble we made out to examine the papers without Bartleby, though at every page or two, Turkey deferentially dropped his opinion that this proceeding was quite out of the common; while Nippers, twitching in his chair with a dyspeptic nervousness, ground out between his set teeth occasional hissing maledictions against the stubborn oaf behind the screen. And for his (Nipper's) part, this was the first and the last time he would do another man's business without pay.

Meanwhile Bartleby sat in his hermitage, oblivious to everything but his own peculiar business there.

Some days passed, the scrivener being employed upon another lengthy work. His late remarkable conduct led me to regard his ways narrowly. I observed that he never went to dinner; indeed, that he never went anywhere. As yet I had never, of my personal knowledge, known him to be outside of my office. He was a perpetual sentry in the corner. At about eleven o'clock though, in the morning, I noticed that Ginger Nut would advance towards the opening in Bartleby's screen as if silently beckoned thither by a gesture invisible to me where I sat. The boy would then leave the office, jingling a few pence, and reappear with a

---

12. **nice,** sensitive.

handful of ginger nuts, which he delivered in the hermitage, receiving two of the cakes for his trouble.

He lives, then, on ginger nuts, thought I; never eats a dinner, properly speaking; he must be a vegetarian, then; but no, he never eats even vegetables, he eats nothing but ginger nuts. My mind then ran on in reveries concerning the probable effects upon the human constitution of living entirely on ginger nuts. Ginger nuts are so called because they contain ginger as one of their peculiar constituents and the final flavoring one. Now, what was ginger? A hot, spicy thing. Was Bartleby hot and spicy? Not at all. Ginger, then, had no effect upon Bartleby. Probably he preferred it should have none.

Nothing so aggravates an earnest person as a passive resistance. If the individual so resisted be of a not inhumane temper, and the resisting one perfectly harmless in his passivity, then in the better moods of the former, he will endeavor charitably to construe to his imagination what proves impossible to be solved by his judgment. Even so, for the most part, I regarded Bartleby and his ways. Poor fellow! thought I, he means no mischief; it is plain he intends no insolence; his aspect sufficiently evinces that his eccentricities are involuntary. He is useful to me. I can get along with him. If I turn him away, the chances are he will fall in with some less indulgent employer, and then he will be rudely treated and perhaps driven forth miserably to starve. Yes. Here I can cheaply purchase a delicious self-approval. To befriend Bartleby, to humor him in his strange willfulness, will cost me little or nothing, while I lay up in my soul what will eventually prove a sweet morsel for my conscience. But this mood was not invariable with me. The passiveness of Bartleby sometimes irritated me. I felt strangely goaded on to encounter him in new opposition—to elicit some angry spark from him answerable to my own. But, indeed, I might as well have essayed to strike fire with my knuckles against a bit of Windsor soap. But

one afternoon the evil impulse in me mastered me, and the following little scene ensued:

"Bartleby," said I, "when those papers are all copied, I will compare them with you."

"I would prefer not to."

"How? Surely you do not mean to persist in that mulish vagary?"

No answer.

I threw open the folding doors near by, and turning upon Turkey and Nippers, exclaimed:

"Bartleby a second time says he won't examine his papers. What do you think of it, Turkey?"

It was afternoon, be it remembered. Turkey sat glowing like a brass boiler; his bald head steaming; his hands reeling among his blotted papers.

"Think of it?" roared Turkey; "I think I'll just step behind his screen and black his eyes for him!"

So saying, Turkey rose to his feet and threw his arms into a pugilistic[13] position. He was hurrying away to make good his promise when I detained him, alarmed at the effect of incautiously rousing Turkey's combativeness after dinner.

"Sit down, Turkey," said I, "and hear what Nippers has to say. What do you think of it, Nippers? Would I not be justified in immediately dismissing Bartleby?"

"Excuse me, that is for you to decide, sir. I think his conduct quite unusual and, indeed, unjust, as regards Turkey and myself. But it may only be a passing whim."

"Ah," exclaimed I, "you have strangely changed your mind, then—you speak very gently of him now."

"All beer," cried Turkey; "gentleness is effects of beer—Nippers and I dined together today. You see how gentle *I* am, sir. Shall I go and black his eyes?"

"You refer to Bartleby, I suppose. No, not today, Turkey," I replied; "pray, put up your fists."

I closed the doors, and again advanced to-

_____
13. **pugilistic,** fighting, boxing.

wards Bartleby. I felt additional incentives tempting me to my fate. I burned to be rebelled against again. I remembered that Bartleby never left the office.

"Bartleby," said I, "Ginger Nut is away; just step round to the post office, won't you? (it was but a three minutes' walk), and see if there is anything for me."

"I would prefer not to."

"You *will* not?"

"I *prefer* not."

I staggered to my desk and sat there in a deep study. My blind inveteracy[14] returned. Was there any other thing in which I could procure myself to be ignominiously repulsed by this lean, penniless wight?[15] my hired clerk? What added thing is there, perfectly reasonable, that he will be sure to refuse to do?

"Bartleby!"

No answer.

"Bartleby," in a louder tone.

No answer.

"Bartleby," I roared.

Like a very ghost, agreeably to the laws of magical invocation, at the third summons he appeared at the entrance of his hermitage.

"Go to the next room and tell Nippers to come to me."

"I prefer not to," he respectfully and slowly said, and mildly disappeared.

"Very good, Bartleby," said I, in a quiet sort of serenely severe self-possessed tone, intimating the unalterable purpose of some terrible retribution very close at hand. At the moment I half intended something of the kind. But upon the whole, as it was drawing towards my dinner hour, I thought it best to put on my hat and walk home for the day, suffering much from perplexity and distress of mind.

Shall I acknowledge it? The conclusion of this whole business was that it soon became a fixed fact of my chambers that a pale young scrivener by the name of Bartleby had a desk

there; that he copied for me at the usual rate of four cents a folio (one hundred words); but he was permanently exempt from examining the work done by him, that duty being transferred to Turkey and Nippers, out of compliment, doubtless, to their superior acuteness; moreover, said Bartleby was never, on any account, to be despatched on the most trivial errand of any sort; and that even if entreated to take upon him such a matter, it was generally understood that he would "prefer not to"—in other words, that he would refuse pointblank.

As days passed on, I became considerably reconciled to Bartleby. His steadiness, his freedom from all dissipation, his incessant industry (except when he chose to throw himself into a standing revery behind his screen), his great stillness, his unalterableness of demeanor under all circumstances, made him a valuable acquisition. One prime thing was this—*he was always there*—first in the morning, continually through the day, and the last at night. I had a singular confidence in his honesty. I felt my most precious papers perfectly safe in his hands. Sometimes, to be sure, I could not, for the very soul of me, avoid falling into sudden spasmodic passions with him. For it was exceeding difficult to bear in mind all the time those strange peculiarities, privileges, and unheard of exemptions forming the tacit stipulations on Bartleby's part under which he remained in my office. Now and then, in the eagerness of despatching pressing business, I would inadvertently summon Bartleby, in a short, rapid tone, to put his finger, say, on the incipient tie of a bit of red tape with which I was about compressing some papers. Of course, from behind the screen the usual answer, "I prefer not to," was sure to come; and then, how could a human creature, with the common infirmities of our nature, refrain from bitterly exclaiming upon such perverseness—such unreasonableness. However, every added repulse of this sort which I received only tended to lessen the probability of my repeating the inadvertence.

Here it must be said that according to the

14. **inveteracy,** deeply rooted habit.
15. **wight,** creature.

custom of most legal gentlemen occupying chambers in densely populated law buildings, there were several keys to my door. One was kept by a woman residing in the attic, which person weekly scrubbed and daily swept and dusted my apartments. Another was kept by Turkey for convenience sake. The third I sometimes carried in my own pocket. The fourth I knew not who had.

Now one Sunday morning I happened to go to Trinity Church to hear a celebrated preacher, and finding myself rather early on the ground I thought I would walk round to my chambers for awhile. Luckily I had my key with me; but upon applying it to the lock, I found it resisted by something inserted from the inside. Quite surprised, I called out; when to my consternation a key was turned from within; and thrusting his lean visage at me, and holding the door ajar, the apparition of Bartleby appeared, in his shirt sleeves and otherwise in a strangely tattered dishabille,[16] saying quietly that he was sorry, but he was deeply engaged just then and—preferred not admitting me at present. In a brief word or two, he moreover added that perhaps I had better walk round the block two or three times, and by that time he would probably have concluded his affairs.

Now the utterly unsurmised appearance of Bartleby tenanting my law chambers of a Sunday morning, with his cadaverously gentlemanly nonchalance, yet withal firm and self-possessed, had such a strange effect upon me that incontinently I slunk away from my own door and did as desired. But not without sundry twinges of impotent rebellion against the mild effrontery of this unaccountable scrivener. Indeed, it was his wonderful mildness chiefly, which not only disarmed me but unmanned me as it were. For I consider that one, for the time, is of a sort unmanned when he tranquilly permits his hired clerk to dictate to him and order him away from his own prem-

ises. Furthermore, I was full of uneasiness as to what Bartleby could possibly be doing in my office in his shirt sleeves and in an otherwise dismantled condition of a Sunday morning. Was anything amiss going on? Nay, that was out of the question. It was not to be thought of for a moment that Bartleby was an immoral person. But what could he be doing there?— copying? Nay again, whatever might be his eccentricities, Bartleby was an eminently decorous person. He would be the last man to sit down to his desk in any state approaching to nudity. Besides, it was Sunday; and there was something about Bartleby that forbade the supposition that he would by any secular occupation violate the proprieties of the day.

Nevertheless, my mind was not pacified; and full of a restless curiosity, at last I returned to the door. Without hindrance I inserted my key, opened it, and entered. Bartleby was not to be seen. I looked round anxiously, peeped behind his screen; but it was very plain that he was gone. Upon more closely examining the place, I surmised that for an indefinite period Bartleby must have ate, dressed, and slept in my office, and that, too, without plate, mirror, or bed. The cushioned seat of a rickety old sofa in one corner bore the faint impress of a lean, reclining form. Rolled away under his desk, I found a blanket; under the empty grate, a blacking box and brush; on a chair, a tin basin with soap and a ragged towel; in a newspaper a few crumbs of ginger nuts and a morsel of cheese. Yes, thought I, it is evident enough that Bartleby has been making his home here, keeping bachelor's hall all by himself. Immediately then the thought came sweeping across me, what miserable friendlessness and loneliness are here revealed! His poverty is great; but his solitude, how horrible! Think of it. Of a Sunday, Wall Street is deserted as Petra;[17] and every night of every day it is an emptiness. This building, too, which of weekdays hums with industry and life, at nightfall echoes with sheer vacancy, and all through Sunday is for-

---

16. **dishabille**, French word meaning "casually or partially dressed."

17. **Petra**, the ruins of an ancient city in Jordan.

lorn. And here Bartleby makes his home; sole spectator of a solitude which he has seen all populous—a sort of innocent and transformed Marius[18] brooding among the ruins of Carthage.

For the first time in my life a feeling of overpowering stinging melancholy seized me. Before, I had never experienced aught but a not unpleasing sadness. The bond of a common humanity now drew me irresistibly to gloom. A fraternal melancholy! For both I and Bartleby were sons of Adam. I remembered the bright silks and sparkling faces I had seen that day in gala trim, swanlike sailing down the Mississippi of Broadway; and I contrasted them with the pallid copyist and thought to myself, Ah, happiness courts the light, so we deem the world is gay; but misery hides aloof, so we deem that misery there is none. These sad fancyings—chimeras, doubtless, of a sick and silly brain—led on to other and more special thoughts concerning the eccentricities of Bartleby. Presentiments of strange discoveries hovered round me. The scrivener's pale form appeared to me laid out, among uncaring strangers, in its shivering winding sheet.

Suddenly I was attracted by Bartleby's closed desk, the key in open sight left in the lock.

I mean no mischief, seek the gratification of no heartless curiosity, thought I; besides, the desk is mine, and its contents, too, so I will make bold to look within. Everything was methodically arranged, the papers smoothly placed. The pigeon holes were deep, and removing the files of documents, I groped into their recesses. Presently I felt something there and dragged it out. It was an old bandanna handkerchief, heavy and knotted. I opened it and saw it was a savings bank.

I now recalled all the quiet mysteries which I had noted in the man. I remembered that he never spoke but to answer; that though at

intervals he had considerable time to himself, yet I had never seen him reading—no, not even a newspaper; that for long periods he would stand looking out, at his pale window behind the screen, upon the dead brick wall; I was quite sure he never visited any refectory or eating house; while his pale face clearly indicated that he never drank beer like Turkey, or tea and coffee even, like other men; that he never went anywhere in particular that I could learn; never went out for a walk, unless, indeed, that was the case at present; that he had declined telling who he was, or whence he came, or whether he had any relatives in the world; that though so thin and pale, he never complained of ill health. And more than all, I remembered a certain unconscious air of pallid—how shall I call it?—of pallid haughtiness, say, or rather an austere reserve about him, which had positively awed me into my tame compliance with his eccentricities, when I had feared to ask him to do the slightest incidental thing for me, even though I might know from his long-continued motionlessness that behind his screen he must be standing in one of those dead-wall reveries of his.

Revolving all these things, and coupling them with the recently discovered fact that he made my office his constant abiding place and home, and not forgetful of his morbid moodiness; revolving all these things, a prudential feeling began to steal over me. My first emotions had been those of pure melancholy and sincerest pity; but just in proportion as the forlornness of Bartleby grew and grew to my imagination, did that same melancholy merge into fear, that pity into repulsion. So true it is, and so terrible, too, that up to a certain point the thought or sight of misery enlists our best affections; but in certain special cases, beyond that point it does not. They err who would assert that invariably this is owing to the inherent selfishness of the human heart. It rather proceeds from a certain hopelessness of remedying excessive and organic ill. To a sensitive being, pity is not seldom pain. And when at last it is perceived that such pity cannot lead

18. **Marius,** (c 155–86 B.C.), a Roman general who triumphed over Carthage, a city in North Africa, but who was banished from Rome by political enemies.

to effectual succor, common sense bids the soul be rid of it. What I saw that morning persuaded me that the scrivener was the victim of innate and incurable disorder. I might give alms to his body; but his body did not pain him; it was his soul that suffered, and his soul I could not reach.

I did not accomplish the purpose of going to Trinity Church that morning. Somehow, the things I had seen disqualified me for the time from churchgoing. I walked homeward, thinking what I would do with Bartleby. Finally, I resolved upon this—I would put certain calm questions to him the next morning touching his history, etc., and if he declined to answer them openly and unreservedly (and I supposed he would prefer not), then to give him a twenty-dollar bill over and above whatever I might owe him, and tell him his services were no longer required; but that if in any other way I could assist him, I would be happy to do so, especially if he desired to return to his native place, wherever that might be, I would willingly help to defray the expenses. Moreover, if after reaching home, he found himself at any time in want of aid, a letter from him would be sure of a reply.

The next morning came.

"Bartleby," said I, gently calling to him behind his screen.

No reply.

"Bartleby," said I, in a still gentler tone, "Come here; I am not going to ask you to do anything you would prefer not to do—I simply wish to speak to you."

Upon this he noiselessly slid into view.

"Will you tell me, Bartleby, where you were born?"

"I would prefer not to."

"Will you tell me *anything* about yourself?"

"I would prefer not to."

"But what reasonable objection can you have to speak to me? I feel friendly towards you."

He did not look at me while I spoke, but kept his glance fixed upon my bust of Cicero, which, as I then sat, was directly behind me, some six inches above my head.

"What is your answer, Bartleby," said I, after waiting a considerable time for a reply, during which his countenance remained immovable, only there was the faintest conceivable tremor of the white attenuated mouth.

"At present I prefer to give no answer," he said, and retired into his hermitage.

It was rather weak in me I confess, but his manner on this occasion nettled me. Not only did there seem to lurk in it a certain calm disdain, but his perverseness seemed ungrateful considering the undeniable good usage and indulgence he had received from me.

Again I sat ruminating what I should do. Mortified as I was at his behavior, and resolved as I had been to dismiss him when I entered my office, nevertheless I strangely felt something superstitious knocking at my heart, and forbidding me to carry out my purpose, and denouncing me for a villain if I dared to breathe one bitter word against this forlornest of mankind. At last, familiarly drawing my chair behind his screen, I sat down and said: "Bartleby, never mind, then, about revealing your history; but let me entreat you, as a friend, to comply as far as may be with the usages of this office. Say now, you will help to examine papers tomorrow or next day: in short, say now, that in a day or two you will begin to be a little reasonable:—say so, Bartleby."

"At present I would prefer not to be a little reasonable," was his mildly cadaverous reply.

Just then the folding doors opened, and Nippers approached. He seemed suffering from an unusually bad night's rest, induced by severer indigestion than common. He overheard those final words of Bartleby.

"*Prefer not*, eh?" gritted Nippers—"I'd *prefer* him if I were you, sir," addressing me—"I'd *prefer* him; I'd give him preferences, the stubborn mule! What is it, sir, pray, that he *prefers* not to do now?"

"Mr. Nippers," said I, "I'd prefer that you would withdraw for the present."

Somehow of late I had got into the way of involuntarily using this word "prefer" upon all sorts of not exactly suitable occasions. And I trembled to think that my contact with the scrivener had already and seriously affected me in a mental way. And what further and deeper aberration might it not yet produce? This apprehension had not been without efficacy in determining me to summary measures.

As Nippers, looking very sour and sulky, was departing, Turkey blandly and deferentially approached.

"With submission, sir," said he, "yesterday I was thinking about Bartleby here, and I think that if he would but prefer to take a quart of good ale every day, it would do much towards mending him and enabling him to assist in examining his papers."

"So you have got the word, too," said I, slightly excited.

"With submission, what word, sir?" asked Turkey, respectfully crowding himself into the contracted space behind the screen, and by so doing, making me jostle the scrivener. "What word, sir?"

"I would prefer to be left alone here," said Bartleby, as if offended at being mobbed in his privacy.

"*That's* the word, Turkey," said I—"*that's* it."

"Oh, *prefer?* oh, yes—queer word. I never use it myself. But, sir, as I was saying, if he would but prefer—"

"Turkey," interrupted I, "you will please withdraw."

"Oh certainly, sir, if you prefer that I should."

As he opened the folding door to retire, Nippers at his desk caught a glimpse of me and asked whether I would prefer to have a certain paper copied on blue paper or white. He did not in the least roguishly accent the word *prefer*. It was plain that it involuntarily rolled from his tongue. I thought to myself, surely I must get rid of a demented man who already has in some degree turned the tongues, if not the heads, of myself and clerks. But I thought it prudent not to break the dismission at once.

The next day I noticed that Bartleby did nothing but stand at his window in his dead-wall revery. Upon asking him why he did not write, he said that he had decided upon doing no more writing.

"Why, how now? what next?" exclaimed I, "do no more writing?"

"No more."

"And what is the reason?"

"Do you not see the reason for yourself?" he indifferently replied.

I looked steadfastly at him and perceived that his eyes looked dull and glazed. Instantly it occurred to me that his unexampled diligence in copying by his dim window for the first few weeks of his stay with me might have temporarily impaired his vision.

I was touched. I said something in condolence with him. I hinted that of course he did wisely in abstaining from writing for a while; and urged him to embrace that opportunity of taking wholesome exercise in the open air. This, however, he did not do. A few days after this, my other clerks being absent, and being in a great hurry to despatch certain letters by the mail, I thought that having nothing else earthly to do, Bartleby would surely be less inflexible than usual and carry these letters to the post office. But he blankly declined. So much to my inconvenience, I went myself.

Still added days went by. Whether Bartleby's eyes improved or not, I could not say. To all appearance, I thought they did. But when I asked him if they did, he vouchsafed no answer. At all events, he would do no copying. At last, in reply to my urgings, he informed me that he had permanently given up copying.

"What!" exclaimed I; "suppose your eyes should get entirely well—better than ever before—would you not copy then?"

"I have given up copying," he answered, and slid aside.

He remained as ever, a fixture in my chamber. Nay—if that were possible—he became still more of a fixture than before. What was to be done? He would do nothing in the office; why should he stay there? In plain fact, he had now become a millstone to me, not only useless as a necklace, but afflictive to bear. Yet I was sorry for him. I speak less than truth when I say that on his own account he occasioned me uneasiness. If he would but have named a single relative or friend, I would instantly have written and urged their taking the poor fellow away to some convenient retreat. But he seemed alone, absolutely alone in the universe. A bit of wreck in the mid Atlantic. At length, necessities connected with my business tyrannized over all other considerations. Decently as I could, I told Bartleby that in six days time he must unconditionally leave the office. I warned him to take measures, in the interval, for procuring some other abode. I offered to assist him in this endeavor if he himself would but take the first step towards a removal. "And when you finally quit me, Bartleby," added I, "I shall see that you go not away entirely unprovided. Six days from this hour, remember."

At the expiration of that period, I peeped behind the screen, and lo! Bartleby was there.

I buttoned up my coat, balanced myself; advanced slowly towards him, touched his shoulder, and said, "The time has come; you must quit this place; I am sorry for you; here is money; but you must go."

"I would prefer not," he replied, with his back still towards me.

"You *must*."

He remained silent.

Now I had an unbounded confidence in this man's common honesty. He had frequently restored to me sixpences and shillings carelessly dropped upon the floor, for I am apt to be very reckless in such shirt button affairs. The proceeding, then, which followed will not be deemed extraordinary.

"Bartleby," said I, "I owe you twelve dollars on account; here are thirty-two; the odd twenty are yours—Will you take it?" and I handed the bills towards him.

But he made no motion.

"I will leave them here, then," putting them under a weight on the table. Then taking my hat and cane and going to the door, I tranquilly turned and added—"After you have removed your things from these offices, Bartleby, you will of course lock the door—since every one is now gone for the day but you—and if you please, slip your key underneath the mat, so that I may have it in the morning. I shall not see you again; so good-bye to you. If, hereafter, in your new place of abode, I can be of any service to you, do not fail to advise me by letter. Good-bye Bartleby, and fare you well."

But he answered not a word; like the last column of some ruined temple, he remained standing mute and solitary in the middle of the otherwise deserted room.

As I walked home in a pensive mood, my vanity got the better of my pity. I could not but highly plume myself on my masterly management in getting rid of Bartleby. Masterly I call it, and such it must appear to any dispassionate thinker. The beauty of my procedure seemed to consist in its perfect quietness. There was no vulgar bullying, no bravado of any sort, no choleric hectoring, and striding to and fro across the apartment, jerking out vehement commands for Bartleby to bundle himself off with his beggarly traps. Nothing of the kind. Without loudly bidding Bartleby depart—as an inferior genius might have done—I *assumed* the ground that depart he must; and upon that assumption built all I had to say. The more I thought over my procedure, the more I was charmed with it. Nevertheless, next morning upon awakening I had my doubts—I had somehow slept off the fumes of vanity. One of the coolest and wisest hours a man has is just after he awakes in the morning. My procedure seemed as sagacious as ever— but only in theory. How it would prove in practice—there was the rub. It was truly a beautiful thought to have assumed Bartleby's departure; but after all, that assumption was simply my own, and none of Bartleby's. The great point was not whether I had assumed that he would quit me, but whether he would prefer so to do. He was more a man of preferences than assumptions.

After breakfast, I walked downtown, arguing the probabilities pro and con. One moment I thought it would prove a miserable failure, and Bartleby would be found all alive at my office as usual; the next moment it seemed certain that I should find his chair empty. And so I kept veering about. At the corner of Broadway and Canal Street, I saw quite an excited group of people standing in earnest conversation.

"I'll take odds he doesn't," said a voice as I passed.

"Doesn't go?—done!" said I, "put up your money."

I was instinctively putting my hand in my pocket to produce my own when I remembered that this was an election day. The words I had overheard bore no reference to Bartleby, but to the success or nonsuccess of some candidate for the mayoralty. In my intent frame of mind, I had, as it were, imagined that all Broadway shared in my excitement and were debating the same question with me. I passed on, very thankful that the uproar of the street screened my momentary absent-mindedness.

As I had intended, I was earlier than usual at my office door. I stood listening for a moment. All was still. He must be gone. I tried the knob. The door was locked. Yes, my procedure had worked to a charm; he indeed must be vanished. Yet a certain melancholy mixed with this: I was almost sorry for my brilliant success. I was fumbling under the door mat for the key, which Bartleby was to have left there for me, when accidentally my knee knocked against a panel, producing a summoning sound, and in response a voice came to me from within—"Not yet; I am occupied."

It was Bartleby.

I was thunderstruck. For an instant I stood like the man who, pipe in mouth, was killed one cloudless afternoon long ago in Virginia by summer lightning; at his own warm open window he was killed and remained leaning out there upon the dreamy afternoon till some one touched him, when he fell.

"Not gone!" I murmured at last. But again obeying that wondrous ascendancy which the inscrutable scrivener had over me, and from which ascendancy, for all my chafing, I could not completely escape, I slowly went downstairs and out into the street, and while walking round the block, considered what I should next do in this unheard-of perplexity. Turn the man out by an actual thrusting I could not; to drive him away by calling him hard names would not do; calling in the police was an unpleasant idea; and yet, permit him to enjoy his cadaverous triumph over me—this, too, I could not think of. What was to be done? or if nothing could be done, was there anything further that I could *assume* in the matter? Yes, as before I had prospectively assumed that Bartleby would depart, so now I might retrospectively assume that departed he was. In the legitimate carrying out of this assumption, I might enter my office in a great hurry, and pretending not to see Bartleby at all, walk straight against him as if he were air. Such a proceeding would in a singular degree have the appearance of a home thrust. It was hardly possible that Bartleby could withstand such an application of the doctrine of assumptions. But upon second thoughts the success of the plan seemed rather dubious. I resolved to argue the matter over with him, again.

"Bartleby," said I, entering the office, with a quietly severe expression, "I am seriously displeased. I am pained, Bartleby. I had thought better of you. I had imagined you of such a gentlemanly organization that in any delicate dilemma a slight hint would suffice—in short, an assumption. But it appears I am deceived. Why," I added, unaffectedly starting, "you have not even touched that money yet," pointing to it, just where I had left it the evening previous.

He answered nothing.

"Will you, or will you not, quit me?" I now demanded in a sudden passion, advancing close to him.

"I would prefer *not* to quit you," he replied, gently emphasizing the *not*.

"What earthly right have you to stay here?

Do you pay any rent? Do you pay my taxes? Or is this property yours?"

He answered nothing.

"Are you ready to go on and write now? Are your eyes recovered? Could you copy a small paper for me this morning? or help examine a few lines? or step round to the post office? In a word, will you do anything at all to give a coloring to your refusal to depart the premises?"

He silently retired into his hermitage.

I was now in such a state of nervous resentment that I thought it but prudent to check myself at present from further demonstrations. Bartleby and I were alone. I remembered the tragedy of the unfortunate Adams and the still more unfortunate Colt in the solitary office of the latter; and how poor Colt, being dreadfully incensed by Adams, and imprudently permitting himself to get wildly excited, was at unawares hurried into his fatal act—an act which certainly no man could possibly deplore more than the actor himself. Often it had occurred to me in my ponderings upon the subject that had that altercation taken place in the public street, or at a private residence, it would not have terminated as it did. It was the circumstance of being alone in a solitary office, upstairs, of a building entirely unhallowed by humanizing domestic associations—an uncarpeted office, doubtless, of a dusty, haggard sort of appearance—this it must have been which greatly helped to enhance the irritable desperation of the hapless Colt.

But when this old Adam of resentment rose in me and tempted me concerning Bartleby, I grappled him and threw him. How? Why, simply by recalling the divine injunction: "A new commandment give I unto you, that ye love one another." Yes, this it was that saved me. Aside from higher considerations, charity often operates as a vastly wise and prudent principle—a great safeguard to its possessor. Men have committed murder for jealousy's sake, and anger's sake, and hatred's sake, and selfishness' sake, and spiritual pride's sake; but no man, that ever I heard of, ever committed a diabolical murder for sweet charity's sake. Mere self-interest, then, if no better motive can be enlisted, should, especially with high-tempered men, prompt all beings to charity and philanthropy. At any rate, upon the occasion in question, I strove to drown my exasperated feelings towards the scrivener by benevolently construing his conduct. Poor fellow, poor fellow! thought I, he don't mean anything; and besides, he has seen hard times and ought to be indulged.

I endeavored, also, immediately to occupy myself, and at the same time to comfort my despondency. I tried to fancy that in the course of the morning, at such time as might prove agreeable to him, Bartleby of his own free accord would emerge from his hermitage and take up some decided line of march in the direction of the door. But no. Half-past twelve o'clock came; Turkey began to glow in the face, overturn his inkstand, and become generally obstreperous; Nippers abated down into quietude and courtesy; Ginger Nut munched his noon apple; and Bartleby remained standing at his window in one of his profoundest dead-wall reveries. Will it be credited? Ought I to acknowledge it? That afternoon I left the office without saying one further word to him.

Some days now passed, during which at leisure intervals I looked a little into "Edwards on the Will,"[19] and "Priestley on Necessity."[20] Under the circumstances, those books induced a salutary feeling. Gradually I slid into the persuasion that these troubles of mine, touching the scrivener, had been all predestinated from eternity, and Bartleby was billeted upon me for some mysterious purpose of an all-wise Providence, which it was not for a mere mortal like me to fathom. Yes, Bartleby, stay there behind your screen, thought I; I shall persecute you no more; you are harmless and

19. **"Edwards on the Will,"** Jonathan Edwards (1703–1758), a famous Puritan minister, wrote *Freedom of the Will.*
20. **"Priestley on Necessity,"** Joseph Priestley (1733–1804), the British chemist who discovered oxygen, wrote books on philosophy.

noiseless as any of these old chairs; in short, I never feel so private as when I know you are here. At last I see it, I feel it; I penetrate to the predestinated purpose of my life. I am content. Others may have loftier parts to enact; but my mission in this world, Bartleby, is to furnish you with office room for such period as you may see fit to remain.

I believe that this wise and blessed frame of mind would have continued with me had it not been for the unsolicited and uncharitable remarks obtruded upon me by my professional friends who visited the rooms. But thus if often is, that the constant friction of illiberal minds wears out at last the best resolves of the more generous. Though to be sure, when I reflected upon it, it was not strange that people entering my office should be struck by the peculiar aspect of the unaccountable Bartleby, and so be tempted to throw out some sinister observations concerning him. Sometimes an attorney, having business with me and calling at my office and finding no one but the scrivener there, would undertake to obtain some sort of precise information from him touching my whereabouts; but without heeding his idle talk, Bartleby would remain standing immovable in the middle of the room. So after contemplating him in that position, for a time, the attorney would depart, no wiser than he came.

Also, when a reference[21] was going on, and the room full of lawyers and witnesses, and business driving fast, some deeply occupied legal gentleman present, seeing Bartleby wholly unemployed, would request him to run round to his (the legal gentleman's) office and fetch some papers for him. Thereupon, Bartleby would tranquilly decline and yet remain idle as before. Then the lawyer would give a great stare and turn to me. And what could I say? At last I was made aware that all through the circle of my professional acquaintance a whisper of wonder was running round, having reference to the strange creature I kept at my office. This worried me very much. And as the

idea came upon me of his possibly turning out a long-lived man, and keep occupying my chambers, and denying my authority; and perplexing my visitors; and scandalizing my professional reputation; and casting a general gloom over the premises; keeping soul and body together to the last upon his savings (for doubtless he spent but half a dime a day), and in the end perhaps outlive me, and claim possession of my office by right of his perpetual occupancy: as all these dark anticipations crowded upon me more and more, and my friends continually intruded their relentless remarks upon the apparition in my room; a great change was wrought in me. I resolved to gather all my faculties together and forever rid me of this intolerable incubus.

Ere revolving any complicated project, however, adapted to this end, I first simply suggested to Bartleby the propriety of his permanent departure. In a calm and serious tone, I commended the idea to his careful and mature consideration. But having taken three days to meditate upon it, he apprised me that his original determination remained the same; in short, that he still preferred to abide with me.

What shall I do? I now said to myself, buttoning up my coat to the last button. What shall I do? what ought I to do? what does conscience say I *should* do with this man, or, rather, ghost? Rid myself of him, I must; go, he shall. But how? You will not thrust him, the poor, pale, passive mortal—you will not thrust such a helpless creature out of your door? you will not dishonor yourself by such cruelty? No, I will not, I cannot do that. Rather would I let him live and die here, and then mason up his remains in the wall. What, then, will you do? For all your coaxing, he will not budge. Bribes he leaves under your own paperweight on your table; in short, it is quite plain that he prefers to cling to you.

Then something severe, something unusual must be done. What! surely you will not have him collared by a constable and commit his innocent pallor to the common jail? And upon

---

21. **a reference**, a meeting between lawyers.

what ground could you procure such a thing to be done?—a vagrant, a wanderer, who refuses to budge? It is because he will *not* be a vagrant, then, that you seek to count him *as* a vagrant. That is too absurd. No visible means of support: there I have him. Wrong again: for indubitably he *does* support himself, and that is the only unanswerable proof that any man can show of his possessing the means so to do. No more, then. Since he will not quit me, I must quit him. I will change my offices; I will move elsewhere and give him fair notice that if I find him on my new premises I will then proceed against him as a common trespasser.

Acting accordingly, next day I thus addressed him: "I find these chambers too far from the city hall; the air is unwholesome. In a word, I propose to remove my offices next week and shall no longer require your services. I tell you this now, in order that you may seek another place."

He made no reply, and nothing more was said.

On the appointed day I engaged carts and men, proceeded to my chambers, and having but little furniture, everything was removed in a few hours. Throughout, the scrivener remained standing behind the screen, which I directed to be removed the last thing. It was withdrawn; and being folded up like a huge folio,[22] left him the motionless occupant of a naked room. I stood in the entry watching him a moment, while something from within me upbraided me.

I re-entered, with my hand in my pocket—and—and my heart in my mouth.

"Good-bye, Bartleby; I am going—good-bye, and God some way bless you; and take that," slipping something in his hand. But it dropped upon the floor, and then—strange to say—I tore myself from him whom I had so longed to be rid of.

Established in my new quarters, for a day or two I kept the door locked and started at every footfall in the passages. When I returned to my rooms after any little absence, I would pause at the threshold for an instant and attentively listen ere applying my key. But these fears were needless. Bartleby never came nigh me.

I thought all was going well, when a perturbed-looking stranger visited me, inquiring whether I was the person who had recently occupied rooms at No. — Wall Street.

Full of forebodings, I replied that I was.

"Then, sir," said the stranger, who proved a lawyer, "you are responsible for the man you left there. He refuses to do any copying; he refuses to do anything; and he says he prefers not to; and he refuses to quit the premises."

"I am very sorry, sir," said I, with assumed tranquility, but an inward tremor, "but really, the man you allude to is nothing to me—he is no relation or apprentice of mine, that you should hold me responsible for him."

"In mercy's name, who is he?"

"I certainly cannot inform you. I know nothing about him. Formerly I employed him as a copyist; but he has done nothing for me now for some time past."

"I shall settle him, then—good morning, sir."

Several days passed, and I heard nothing more; and though I often felt a charitable prompting to call at the place and see poor Bartleby, yet a certain squeamishness of I know not what, withheld me.

All is over with him by this time, thought I at last, when through another week, no further intelligence reached me. But coming to my room the day after, I found several persons waiting at my door in a high state of nervous excitement.

"That's the man—here he comes," cried the foremost one, whom I recognized as the lawyer who had previously called upon me alone.

"You must take him away, sir, at once," cried a portly person among them, advancing upon me, and whom I knew to be the landlord of No. — Wall Street. "These gentlemen, my tenants, cannot stand it any longer; Mr. B———," pointing to the lawyer, "has turned

___
22. a **folio**, a large book.

*A visiting artist's view of Wall Street,
New York, in the late nineteenth century.*

him out of his room, and he now persists in haunting the building generally, sitting upon the banisters of the stairs by day, and sleeping in the entry by night. Everybody is concerned; clients are leaving the offices; some fears are entertained of a mob; something you must do, and that without delay."

Aghast at this torrent, I fell back before it and would fain have locked myself in my new quarters. In vain I persisted that Bartleby was nothing to me—no more than to any one else. In vain—I was the last person known to have anything to do with him, and they held me to the terrible account. Fearful, then, of being exposed in the papers (as one person present obscurely threatened), I considered the matter, and at length said that if the lawyer would give me a confidential interview with the scrivener in his (the lawyer's) own room, I would, that afternoon, strive my best to rid them of the nuisance they complained of.

Going upstairs to my old haunt, there was Bartleby silently sitting upon the banister at the landing.

"What are you doing here, Bartleby?" said I.

"Sitting upon the banister," he mildly replied.

I motioned him into the lawyer's room, who then left us.

"Bartleby," said I, "are you aware that you are the cause of great tribulation to me by persisting in occupying the entry after being dismissed from the office?"

No answer.

"Now one of two things must take place. Either you must do something, or something must be done to you. Now what sort of business would you like to engage in? Would you like to re-engage in copying for some one?"

"No; I would prefer not to make any change."

"Would you like a clerkship in a dry goods store?"

"There is too much confinement about that. No, I would not like a clerkship; but I am not particular."

"Too much confinement," I cried, "why you keep yourself confined all the time!"

"I would prefer not to take a clerkship," he rejoined, as if to settle that little item at once.

"How would a bartender's business suit you? There is no trying of the eyesight in that."

"I would not like it at all; though as I said before, I am not particular."

His unwonted wordiness inspirited me. I returned to the charge.

"Well, then, would you like to travel through the country collecting bills for the merchants? That would improve your health."

"No, I would prefer to be doing something else."

"How, then, would going as a companion to Europe, to entertain some young gentleman with your conversation—how would that suit you?"

"Not at all. It does not strike me that there is anything definite about that. I like to be stationary. But I am not particular."

"Stationary you shall be, then," I cried, now losing all patience, and for the first time in all my exasperating connection with him, fairly flying into a passion. "If you do not go away from these premises before night I shall feel bound—indeed, I *am* bound—to—to—to quit the premises myself!" I rather absurdly concluded, knowing not with what possible threat to try to frighten his immobility into compliance. Despairing of all further efforts, I was precipitately leaving him, when a final thought occurred to me—one which had not been wholly unindulged before.

"Bartleby," said I, in the kindest tone I could assume under such exciting circumstances, "will you go home with me now—not to my office, but to my dwelling—and remain there till we can conclude upon some convenient arrangement for you at our leisure? Come, let us start now, right away."

"No: at present I would prefer not to make any change at all."

I answered nothing; but effectually dodging every one by the suddenness and rapidity of my flight, rushed from the building, ran up

Wall Street toward Broadway, and jumping into the first omnibus, was soon removed from pursuit. As soon as tranquility returned, I distinctly perceived that I had now done all that I possibly could, both in respect to the demands of the landlord and his tenants and with regard to my own desire and sense of duty, to benefit Bartleby and shield him from rude persecution. I now strove to be entirely carefree and quiescent; and my conscience justified me in the attempt; though, indeed, it was not so successful as I could have wished. So fearful was I of being again hunted out by the incensed landlord and his exasperated tenants that, surrendering my business to Nippers for a few days, I drove about the upper part of the town and through the suburbs in my rockaway;[23] crossed over to Jersey City and Hoboken and paid fugitive visits to Manhattanville and Astoria. In fact, I almost lived in my rockaway for the time.

When again I entered my office, lo, a note from the landlord lay upon the desk. I opened it with trembling hands. It informed me that the writer had sent to the police and had Bartleby removed to the Tombs as a vagrant. Moreover, since I knew more about him than any one else, he wished me to appear at that place and make a suitable statement of the facts. These tidings had a conflicting effect upon me. At first I was indignant; but at last almost approved. The landlord's energetic, summary disposition had led him to adopt a procedure which I do not think I would have decided upon myself, and yet, as a last resort, under such peculiar circumstances, it seemed the only plan.

As I afterwards learned, the poor scrivener, when told that he must be conducted to the Tombs, offered not the slightest obstacle, but in his pale, unmoving way, silently acquiesced.

Some of the compassionate and curious bystanders joined the party; and headed by one of the constables, arm in arm with Bartleby, the silent procession filed its way through all the noise, and heat, and joy of the roaring thoroughfares at noon.

The same day I received the note I went to the Tombs, or to speak more properly, the Halls of Justice. Seeking the right officer, I stated the purpose of my call and was informed that the individual I described was, indeed, within. I then assured the functionary that Bartleby was a perfectly honest man, and greatly to be compassionated, however unaccountably eccentric. I narrated all I knew, and closed by suggesting the idea of letting him remain in as indulgent confinement as possible till something less harsh might be done— though, indeed, I hardly knew what. At all events, if nothing else could be decided upon, the almshouse must receive him. I then begged to have an interview.

Being under no disgraceful charge, and quite serene and harmless in all his ways, they had permitted him freely to wander about the prison and especially in the enclosed grass-platted yards thereof. And so I found him there, standing all alone in the quietest of the yards, his face toward a high wall, while all around, from the narrow slits of the jail windows, I thought I saw peering out upon him the eyes of murderers and thieves.

"Bartleby!"

"I know you," he said, without looking round—"and I want nothing to say to you."

"It was not I that brought you here, Bartleby," said I, keenly pained at his implied suspicion. "And to you, this should not be so vile a place. Nothing reproachful attaches to you by being here. And see, it is not so sad a place as one might think. Look, there is the sky, and here is the grass."

"I know where I am," he replied, but would say nothing more, and so I left him.

As I entered the corridor again, a broad, meatlike man in an apron accosted me, and jerking his thumb over his shoulder said—"Is that your friend?"

"Yes."

---

23. **a rockaway,** a four-wheeled carriage seating two.

"Does he want to starve? If he does, let him live on the prison fare, that's all."

"Who are you?" asked I, not knowing what to make of such an unofficially speaking person in such a place.

"I am the grub-man. Such gentleman as have friends here, hire me to provide them with something good to eat."

"Is this so?" said I, turning to the turnkey.

He said it was.

"Well, then," said I, slipping some silver into the grub-man's hands (for so they called him), "I want you to give particular attention to my friend there; let him have the best dinner you can get. And you must be as polite to him as possible."

"Introduce me, will you?" said the grub-man, looking at me with an expression which seemed to say he was all impatience for an opportunity to give a specimen of his breeding.

Thinking it would prove of benefit to the scrivener, I acquiesced; and asking the grub-man his name, went up with him to Bartleby.

"Bartleby, this is a friend; you will find him very useful to you."

"Your sarvant, sir, your sarvant," said the grub-man, making a low salutation behind his apron. "Hope you find it pleasant here, sir; nice grounds—cool apartments—hope you'll stay with us some time—try to make it agreeable. What will you have for dinner today?"

"I prefer not to dine today," said Bartleby, turning away. "It would disagree with me; I am unused to dinners." So saying, he slowly moved to the other side of the enclosure and took up a position fronting the dead wall.

"How's this?" said the grub-man, addressing me with a stare of astonishment. "He's odd, ain't he?"

"I think he is a little deranged," said I, sadly.

"Deranged? deranged is it? Well, now, upon my word, I thought that friend of yourn was a gentleman forger; they are always pale and genteel-like, them forgers. I can't help pity 'em—can't help it, sir. Did you know Monroe Edwards?" he added touchingly and paused. Then, laying his hand piteously on my shoulder, sighed, "He died of consumption at Sing Sing. So you weren't acquainted with Monroe?"

"No, I was never socially acquainted with any forgers. But I cannot stop longer. Look to my friend yonder. You will not lose by it. I will see you again."

Some few days after this, I again obtained admission to the Tombs and went through the corridors in quest of Bartleby; but without finding him.

"I saw him coming from his cell not long ago," said a turnkey, "maybe he's gone to loiter in the yards."

So I went in that direction.

"Are you looking for the silent man?" said another turnkey, passing me. "Yonder he lies—sleeping in the yard there. 'Tis not twenty minutes since I saw him lie down."

The yard was entirely quiet. It was not accessible to the common prisoners. The surrounding walls, of amazing thickness, kept off all sounds behind them. The Egyptian character of the masonry weighed upon me with its gloom. But a soft imprisoned turf grew under foot. The heart of the eternal pyramids, it seemed, wherein by some strange magic, through the clefts, grass seed dropped by birds had sprung.

Strangely huddled at the base of the wall, his knees drawn up and lying on his side, his head touching the cold stones, I saw the wasted Bartleby. But nothing stirred. I paused; then went close up to him; stooped over and saw that his dim eyes were open; otherwise he seemed profoundly sleeping. Something prompted me to touch him. I felt his hand, when a tingling shiver ran up my arm and down my spine to my feet.

The round face of the grub-man peered upon me now. "His dinner is ready. Won't he dine today, either? Or does he live without dining?"

"Lives without dining," said I, and closed the eyes.

"Eh!—He's asleep, ain't he?"

"With kings and counselors,"[24] murmured I.

There would seem little need for proceeding further in this history. Imagination will readily supply the meager recital of poor Bartleby's interment. But ere parting with the reader, let me say that if this little narrative has sufficiently interested him to awaken curiosity as to who Bartleby was and what manner of life he led prior to the present narrator's making his acquaintance, I can only reply that in such curiosity I fully share, but am wholly unable to gratify it. Yet here I hardly know whether I should divulge one little item of rumor, which came to my ear a few months after the scrivener's decease. Upon what basis it rested, I could never ascertain; and hence, how true it is I cannot now tell. But inasmuch as this vague report has not been without a certain suggestive interest to me, however sad, it may prove the same with some others; and so I will briefly mention it. The report was this: that Bartleby had been a subordinate clerk in the Dead Letter Office at Washington, from which he had been suddenly removed by a change in the administration. When I think over this rumor, hardly can I express the emotions which seize me. Dead Letters! does it not sound like dead men? Conceive a man by nature and misfortune prone to a pallid hopelessness, can any business seem more fitted to heighten it than that of continually handling these dead letters and assorting them for the flames? For by the cartload they are annually burned. Sometimes from out the folded paper the pale clerk takes a ring—the finger it was meant for, perhaps, molders in the grave; a bank note sent in swiftest charity—he whom it would relieve, nor eats nor hungers any more; pardon for those who died despairing; hope for those who died unhoping; good tidings for those who died stifled by unrelieved calamities. On errands of life, these letters speed to death.

Ah, Bartleby! Ah, humanity!

I

ASSUMPTIONS VERSUS PREFERENCES

At one point in the story the narrator notes that Bartleby is "more a man of preferences than assumptions." Consider some of the implications stemming from Bartleby's preferences and the narrator's "doctrine of assumptions." It is generally *assumed* that persons will do what is expected of them. Indeed, it would seem as if society functions on the basis of such assumptions. Police officers are supposed to pursue lawbreakers; nurses are expected to care for the sick; it is assumed that business people will try to satisfy their customers and make profits; and we could go on and on. Normally human beings act according to such assumptions, and society runs smoothly.

But where do such assumptions leave the individual? Are we nothing more than the sum of the expectations of others? Are we bound by others' assumptions and not free to act on the basis of our preferences? Notice precisely what it is assumed that Bartleby will do (and cheerfully, yet!): he will spend the greater part of his waking hours, six days a week, slavishly copying words and then go through them all a second time to make sure he has not miscopied any. During those hours he will "live" in a little cubicle, isolated from everyone, his only view of the outside world being a "dead" wall. In short, walled in on Wall Street, Bartleby is being dehumanized by a system of assumptions that leaves no room for human preference. In his "I would prefer not to," he is reaffirming his independence against the very warp and woof of the social fabric.

II

IMPLICATIONS

A. Orally or in writing, answer one or more of the following questions, as your teacher directs.

1. Why does Melville use the subtitle, "A Story of Wall Street"?

2. Since the basic conflict of the story revolves around Bartleby and the narrator, why does Melville spend so much time in the opening discussing Turkey and Nippers?

---

24. **With kings and counselors,** a reference to Job 3:13–14 meaning that Bartleby is dead.

3. In what sense is Bartleby not "ordinarily human"?

4. What is the "paramount consideration" (p. 413) that forms the basis of Bartleby's actions?

5. What do you make of the narrator's description of Bartleby as a "valuable acquisition"? Why did Melville choose those words to put in the narrator's mouth?

B. Be prepared to state and justify your opinions, pro or con, of the following statements:

1. Melville's sympathies are basically with the narrator rather than with Bartleby.

2. It is the narrator's fault that Bartleby is sent to the Tombs and dies there.

3. Bartleby is actually a strong person, for it takes courage to buck the system.

4. If everyone lived by preferences, society as we know it would collapse.

5. The injunction "love one another" is generally ignored in the world of business and finance.

6. The scrivener's story is largely irrelevant today, for modern business no longer dehumanizes the worker.

III
TECHNIQUES

Conflict

The initial moment of the conflict between the narrator and Bartleby is the latter's assertion, "I would prefer not to." This statement shocks the narrator at first, for he is a person of assumptions, and he assumes, as an employer, that he will be obeyed. Nevertheless, for some period of time it appears that Bartleby will gain the upper hand and prevail. For example, others, including the narrator, begin using the word, *prefer;* and at one point, the narrator even decides to accept Bartleby on his own terms. What happens to turn the situation in the opposite direction?

Although Bartleby and the narrator are the chief characters in the conflict, each seems to represent a force larger than himself. What are those two forces?

Climax

One climax occurs when the narrator leaves Bartleby in the bare room. How do you know that this is not to be the final climax? A second climax, which is the major one, is Bartleby's death. Of what significance, at that time, is the narrator's comment that his scrivener is asleep "with kings and counselors"? Can you connect this phrase with the fact that Bartleby is in the Tombs?

Moment of Illumination

The story finally ends with the words, "Ah Bartleby! Ah humanity!" These words in the story are not in quotation marks; thus it is almost as if they were spoken by Melville himself rather than by the narrator. How does this great sighing statement illuminate the meaning of the story?

In connection with this closing, we might observe that, at the time Melville wrote this story, he was in desperate financial and emotional straits. His readers had assumed that he would continue to write the kind of popular adventure stories—like *Typee* and *Omoo*—that had made him well-known. But Melville preferred to pour his energies into profoundly probing books like *Moby Dick* and *Pierre*, both of which were dismal failures from a financial point of view.

Can you relate this biographical detail to the full meaning of the story? What does it tell you about those famous, final words—Ah Bartleby! Ah humanity!

FINAL REFLECTIONS

The Inner Struggle

FOCUS ON THE INNER SELF

As writers look to the inner self, they find complexities. There seems to be in us a strong "animal" side, a primitive urge for security and survival. This force may even urge us to kill, as it urged Kid Jones in Ann Petry's story. But there is also a moral side in us, the voice of conscience, which bids us to break neither the world's nor God's laws in our attempts to preserve and fulfill ourselves. In the struggles between these forces, our true worth is often tested. If our decisions go against our conscience, we may perhaps suffer no ill effects outwardly, but the inner effects and the loss of self-respect may be deeply felt and lasting. No matter how we may define the self that stands between our animal and moral nature, it can never find the highest fulfillment unless we live by moral principles and practice integrity.

Beyond the individual struggles that you have read about and discussed, there is another and a wider issue: When de Tocqueville predicted that American writers would focus on "man himself," he was especially mindful of the democratic nature of our society. He knew that the welfare of a democracy depended upon the moral strength of its citizens, that in a government of the people the moral fiber of the nation can only be as strong as the moral fiber of the Edmund Rosses and George Stoyonoviches who make it up. Thus, by focusing upon the inner struggle, American writers have frequently served as the living voices of the American conscience.

IMPLICATIONS

Below are seven statements dealing with themes brought up in selections in this unit. After each statement is a list of some of the works you have read. Discuss each statement in the light of *each* of the selections listed.

1. When an individual is faced with the need to make an important decision, the pressures exerted by family members are generally not very influential.
"A Horseman in the Sky"
"Parting, Without a Sequel"
"A Summer's Reading"
2. The need for a sense of integrity, of self-respect, is one of the most powerful impulses influencing human beings.
"I Looked Down into My Open Grave"
"A Little Uncomplicated Hymn"
"The Pardon"
"A Summer's Reading"
"Bartleby the Scrivener"
3. Fear freezes individuals and makes them incapable of arriving at intelligent decisions.
"A Horseman in the Sky"
"I Looked Down into My Open Grave"
"The Pardon"
4. When we are rejected by those we love, we typically face an inner struggle in which we seek to redefine ourselves.
"After Hours"
"Balances"
"Solo on the Drums"
"Bartleby the Scrivener"
5. Regardless of strength or uniqueness, every individual has a powerful need to share with, and be understood by, others.
"I Looked Down into My Open Grave"
"Parting, Without a Sequel"
"After Hours"
"You Do Not Have to Love Me"
"Solo on the Drums"
6. Our conscience will direct us to do those things that are approved in our particular society. Thus, conscience is essentially a social phenomenon.
"The Black Cat"
"A Summer's Reading"
"Bartleby the Scrivener"
7. The strength of our conscience, of our moral side, varies greatly from individual to individual; some persons seem to have no conscience at all.
"The Black Cat"
"A Summer's Reading"

TECHNIQUES

Conflict

Conflicts in literature—as well as conflicts in life—may be broadly divided into external and internal conflicts. Sometimes a conflict may be purely external: a family fighting against a flood, two boxers in a ring, two or more political candidates contesting an election. If we have some stake in the outcome and if there is at least a chance of either side winning, external conflicts may be quite gripping. Detective stories, for example, are good instances of fiction usually based primarily on external conflicts between the pursuer and the pursued.

A great deal of serious literature involves both an external and an internal conflict, and of course there is no reason why an internal conflict can't be just as exciting as an external one. Look over the selections in this unit, and consider the following points in the light of the three or four selections you most enjoyed reading.

1. Describe the external conflict.

2. Describe the internal conflict.

3. Which of the two conflicts held your interest more strongly and why?

4. Which conflict was the more suspenseful?

5. What "extra dimension" (if any) was added by the internal conflict?

Climax

We have defined the climax of a story as the moment when the action reaches its peak, the moment of greatest intensity. Intense moments, both real and fictional, are apt to change people. One of the main outcomes in a fictional crisis, in fact, may be the change in the character of the hero.

Locate the peak of the action in three or four of the selections you have read, and be prepared to discuss the following: (1) Did the climax lead naturally to a change in the fortunes of the main character? (2) Did the climax lead to a change in the character of the hero? Try to describe the change in some detail.

Moment of Illumination

As the point at which the meaning of a story becomes fully clear, the moment of illumination often has rather broad implications; that is, it may not only deal with the final fate of the main character but also with some more general ideas, which can be applied to people in general.

Locate the moment of illumination in two or three of the selections you have read and be prepared to discuss some of their broader implications.

BIOGRAPHICAL NOTES

Edgar Allan Poe

Edgar Allan Poe (1809–1849), one of the most colorful of American writers, was father of the detective story and master of the supernatural tale. Left an orphan at the age of two, he was adopted by the Allans of Richmond, Virginia. He studied abroad for five years and then returned to Virginia, first to study at Richmond Academy and then at the University of Virginia. Withdrawn from school by his foster father for drinking and gambling, he spent a short time in the Army before he received an appointment to West Point. The discipline of military life, however, was not to Poe's liking, and he was shortly expelled. During this period he was writing poetry and he published two volumes. In 1831 he published a third, *Poems by Edgar Allan Poe*, but it received little notice. Settling in Baltimore, he wrote a prizewinning short story for a newspaper contest: "MS Found in a Bottle." In 1835 he married his young cousin, Virginia Clemm. While editing various magazines, his stories of supernatural horror began appearing, and in 1840 he published *Tales of the Grotesque and Arabesque*. His short story "The Gold Bug" won a newspaper prize in 1843. When his poem "The Raven" appeared in the *Evening Mirror* and then in the *American Review,* his name became known the country over. His verse and short stories continued to appear up until his death in 1849. Poe won considerable fame in Europe, especially in France. His poems and short stories are widely reprinted today, and his works, particularly the writings of horror and mystery, have been a continuing source of radio and television plays and motion pictures.

Ambrose Bierce

Ambrose Bierce (1842–1914?), born in Ohio, fought in the Civil War and then moved west to become a successful journalist in San Francisco. He also lived several years in England and there published three books. In California he was the dominant literary figure in the 1890s, but a series of unhappy personal experiences made him an increasingly bitter man. Primarily a short-story writer, his best collections are *Tales of Soldiers and Civilians* and *Can Such Things Be?* both published in the nineties. In 1913 he went to Mexico to join the civil war there and disappeared.

John F. Kennedy

The 35th President of the United States, John F. Kennedy (1917–1963) was born in Brookline,

Massachusetts. A graduate of Harvard University, he wrote a senior honors thesis about England's lack of preparation for war with Germany, published as *Why England Slept*. His father was then U.S. Ambassador to Great Britain. In World War II, Kennedy's role in the dramatic rescue of his PT boat crew won him medals for his leadership and heroism. In 1946 he went to Congress as a Representative from Massachusetts. In 1952 he was elected U.S. Senator. During a long period of hospitalization for back injuries, Kennedy wrote *Profiles in Courage*, a Pulitzer Prize-winner in 1957. In 1960, at the age of 43, Kennedy was elected President of the United States, the youngest person to be elected. His assassination in November of 1963 stunned the world. Portions of the four-day television coverage of the tragedy served as the first broadcast of "Profiles in Courage," a television series based upon the book.

John Crowe Ransom

After graduation from Vanderbilt University in Tennessee, John Crowe Ransom (1888–1974) spent three years at Oxford as a Rhodes scholar. In 1914 he returned to teach at Vanderbilt, where he founded *The Fugitive*, a "little magazine" devoted to poetry and criticism. In 1937 he was made Carnegie Professor of Poetry at Kenyon College where, two years later, he established and became editor of the *Kenyon Review*, a quarterly literary journal. Poet, editor, professor, Ransom was also a widely read critic, one of the leaders of the so-called New Critics.

Robert Mezey

Born in Philadelphia (1935–   ), Robert Mezey worked at various factories and mental hospitals and served in the U.S. Army as a psychology technician. He taught at several colleges and universities and has lived with his wife and children in the Sierra Nevada. A volume of his selected poems, *The Door Standing Open*, was published in 1970.

Leonard Cohen

Leonard Cohen (1934–   ) combines the talents of a popular songwriter and singer with those of a serious short-story writer and poet. Many of his lyrics and poems, such as "Suzanne,"

his most popular song to date, are dreamlike private visions. His *Selected Poems, 1956–1968* was published in the latter year.

Nikki Giovanni

Nikki Giovanni, who has been called the "Princess of Black Poetry," was born in Knoxville, Tennessee (1943–   ). She was educated at Fisk University, the University of Pennsylvania, and Columbia. She received an honorary doctorate of humanities from Wilberforce University. She has published many volumes of poetry and an autobiography, *Gemini*.

Anne Sexton

Anne Sexton (1928–1974) lived most of her life in or near Newton, Massachusetts, where she was born. She was almost thirty before she first started to write—during a recovery from a nervous breakdown. She was a poet of the "confessional" school; many of her early poems dealt with the depression, despair, and suffering of her years of emotional illness. She won the Pulitzer Prize for Poetry in 1967 for *Live or Die*. Anne Sexton was a superlative public reader of her own works.

Richard Wilbur

Born in New York, Richard Wilbur (1921–   ) was educated at Amherst and Harvard and went on to teach at Harvard, Wellesley, Wesleyan, and, most recently, Smith College. The winner of many awards, including the National Book Award and the Pulitzer Prize (for *Things of This World* in 1957), Wilbur is one of the few distinguished modern poets who has continued to adhere to traditional verse forms. In addition to being known for his poetry, he is known for his translations of several French literary classics.

Ann Petry

Born in Old Saybrook, Connecticut, Ann Petry (1912–   ) worked as a journalist in New York from 1938 to 1944. She is currently practicing pharmacy in Old Saybrook, where she also enjoys gardening. Petry has written novels, short stories, and books for children. The underlying theme of much of her work deals with race relations in the United States.

Bernard Malamud

Born in Brooklyn, Bernard Malamud (1914–   ) grew up there; it is the scene of most of his stories and novels. He began writing in high school but turned to factory jobs to earn a living during the Depression. Educated at the College of the City of New York and Columbia University, Malamud was an English professor at Oregon State College from 1949 to 1961. Since then he has been at Bennington College. He has written several novels, including *The Fixer*, which won the National Book Award and the Pulitzer Prize in 1967. He has also published several volumes of short stories, the most recent being *Rembrandt's Hat* (1973).

Herman Melville

The author of *Moby Dick*, which is often called one of the two greatest American novels, is Herman Melville (1819–1898), who went to sea at the age of twenty. Eighteen months later he shipped aboard the *Acushnet*, bound for the southern waters of the Pacific. These voyages were to provide him the material and the locale for most of his novels. His experiences in the South Seas, especially during his captivity by cannibals, became the substance of *Typee* (1846) and *Omoo*. Other novels about the sea and sailors include *Mardi, Redburn,* and *White-Jacket.* His first two novels were especially successful with the reading public, and Melville became a popular writer. The reaction of the public and the critics to *Moby Dick*, however, was not only cool but in some instances hostile. His next novel, *Pierre*, was even more unpopular. These reactions and a fire at his publisher's that destroyed the plates of his books led to oblivion for Melville. He later wrote a number of significant long stories and the short novel *Billy Budd*, but to the end of his life he was virtually overlooked by readers and critics. Not until three decades after his death did anyone give Melville the attention he deserved. Then, in a rising tide of literary scholarship and critical acclaim, he emerged as a significant figure in the literature of the United States.

AMERICAN LITERATURE

THE PREMODERN PERIOD

1900-1930

The first three or four decades of the twentieth century were so fruitful in American literature that they have sometimes been called our second literary renaissance (the first having been the Classical period). Our first Nobel Prize winners—Sinclair Lewis, Pearl Buck, William Faulkner, Ernest Hemingway, and John Steinbeck—were all at work; and the great naturalists—Frank Norris, Jack London, and Theodore Dreiser—published their best novels during the period. In the years between 1925 and 1929 alone, one can count almost a dozen great novels by almost as many novelists, including F. Scott Fitzgerald's *The Great Gatsby*, Sinclair Lewis's *Arrowsmith*, Theodore Dreiser's *An American Tragedy*, and Ernest Hemingway's *The Sun Also Rises* and *A Farewell to Arms*.

Poets, too, abounded, from the fine black poets of the Harlem Renaissance—Langston Hughes, Claude McKay, Countee Cullen, and others—through symbolists and imagists such as Ezra Pound, Hilda Doolittle, and Amy Lowell; to such famous and enduring figures as Edwin Arlington Robinson, T. S. Eliot, and Robert Frost.

Finally, in the middle of the period, that giant of American drama, Eugene O'Neill, brought serious American drama to birth. Let us now look more closely at the novelists, poets, and dramatists of the early twentieth century.

THE AMERICAN NOVEL COMES OF AGE

The Scarlet Letter, Moby Dick, The Adventures of Huckleberry Finn, Portrait of a Lady, The Red Badge of Courage—great American novels had been written before the twentieth century. But nothing had been done to match the outpouring of major works by important novelists that crowd the first three decades of this century. In trying to account for that flood of great fiction, literary scholars often point to naturalism as its source.

Naturalism could be defined as realism carried to an extreme. Its fundamental idea is that people, like everything else in the universe, are subject to natural laws. Often, naturalists believe that humans do not have free will, that we are driven by powerful, blind biological urges, that we are slaves of our heredity and environment. The naturalists commonly used great masses of detail in rendering human experience, and they faced squarely the uglier sides of life. Once naturalism touched American fiction, it influenced almost all writers. You will find strong naturalistic elements, for example, in the works of John Steinbeck and Richard Wright, though the major work of both was published after this period.

The first great naturalist of the twentieth century was Frank Norris, who published two forceful novels—*McTeague* (1899) and *The Octopus* (1901) —just as the century turned. Following close upon him was Jack London, who stressed the helplessness of human beings and animals before all-powerful natural laws in such works as *The Call of the Wild* (1903), *The Sea Wolf* (1904), and the semi-autobiographical *Martin Eden* (1909). But the man who really brought naturalism into focus was Theodore Dreiser. In novels like *Sister Carrie* (first published in 1900 but suppressed until 1912), *Jennie Gerhardt* (1911), and *An American Tragedy* (1925), Dreiser emphasized the idea that we are the creatures of economic and biological necessities far beyond our power to control. Dreiser's first two novels set off long-lasting controversies because people did not want to hear what he had to say. By 1925, however, the climate had changed and *An American Tragedy* was a popular success.

Powerful as these early twentieth-century novelists are, style is not their forte. (One critic compared Dreiser's style to an elephant backing into an outhouse.) For literary talent in the early decades, we turn to three women—Willa Cather (who is discussed elsewhere), Ellen Glasgow, and Edith Wharton. Glasgow was the finest Southern novelist of her day—a social critic and a realist, but a defender of what her fellow-Southerner William Faulkner was later to call the "old verities and truths of the heart." Edith Wharton was more of a pessimist than either Glasgow or Cather, and she could be an abrasive satirist. Her most famous novel, *The Age of Innocence* (1920), focuses on New York society in the 1870s, a society for which she had a nostalgic attraction yet a sharp eye for its foibles.

A satirist with a much broader range (and a far heavier hand) was Sinclair Lewis, who was awarded America's first Nobel Prize for Literature for his uncompromising satire of the materialism of his time. Among the objects of his criticism were a typical Midwestern town (*Main Street*, 1920), American business (*Babbitt*, 1922), science and medicine (*Arrowsmith*, 1925), and the insincere clergy (*Elmer Gantry*, 1927).

Lewis was America's best-known writer during the 1920s, but a writer we associate more with the "jazz age" was F. Scott Fitzgerald. Of his several novels, the best is *The Great Gatsby* (1925), a satire on Fitzgerald's own Roaring Twenties, a commentary on the American success myth, and an analysis of several appearance-reality contrasts.

Many of the above writers also wrote excellent short stories, but we will close with references to three authors who were exclusively or almost exclusively short-story writers. The most popular short-story writer of the time was William Sydney Porter, known familiarly as O. Henry. He perfected a type of sentimental but well-plotted story with a surprise ending. Ring Lardner was largely a humorist. He added to the short story an emphasis on first-person narratives with a fine ear for speech rhythms and a fine eye for spellings. (One of his baseball characters refers to the World Series as "the World Serious.") Finally, Sherwood Anderson opened up the form of the short story for later writers by shifting emphasis from plot to theme and character.

THE BLOSSOMING OF POETRY

In the introduction of the midcentury edition of *The Oxford Book of American Poetry*, F. O. Matthiessen wrote that "The most notable fact about American literature . . . is the number and variety of our poets." There are so many good twentieth-century poets that we cannot mention all of them in our short treatment, and there is such a variety that grouping them is a trying task.

Among our greatest poets, for example, is Edwin Arlington Robinson, who was a loner all his life. Perhaps the most significant fact about Robinson is that while he was modern in his outlook—he was a naturalist, for example—he always used the poetic forms of the past. His greatest long poem is *Tristram* (1927), a modern rendering of the Arthurian Tristan and Iseult love story; but most of his readers know him through such portraits as "Miniver Cheevy" and "Richard Cory."

Another verbal portrait painter was Edgar Lee Masters, whose *Spoon River Anthology* (1915)—a gallery of epitaphs spoken by the dead of the fictional Spoon River, Illinois—was an extraordinary popular success. Masters is often linked with Carl Sandburg and Vachel Lindsay as a member of the Chicago school, but in fact the three do not have a great deal in common. Stylistically, Sandburg is a descendant of Walt Whitman and shares Whitman's and Lincoln's faith in the people. Lindsay is best known for rhythmic poems like "General William Booth Enters into Heaven" and "The Congo."

The imagists were a group that included, at one time or another, Hilda Doolittle, Ezra Pound, Amy Lowell, and William Carlos Williams, among others. (Williams later said that imagistic poetry lacked structure, and Pound, a somewhat irascible genius, left the group after Amy Lowell arrived, declaring that the movement had become "Amygism.") The name of the group comes from their belief that poets must present a firm, concrete image, not vague generalities. They rose to prominence between 1909 and 1918 and have left their mark on a good deal of modern poetry.

Two other important poets of the time were Edna St. Vincent Millay and Robinson Jeffers. Millay's "Renascence," originally published in 1912, has been a favorite ever since. Although she has been criticized by some who prefer a more intellectual style of poetry, at her best she has a fine feel for nature and has written some excellent lyrics. Jeffers considered himself a recorder of social decay. His most frequently anthologized poem, "Shine, Perishing Republic," comments on the decadence of American society as he saw it from his hilltop retreat in Carmel, California.

The central figures of the premodern period and of the modern period as well, perhaps, are Robert

Frost and T. S. Eliot. Of Frost we have spoken at length elsewhere. Suffice to say here that through his long career, he published many of the best and most popular poems ever written by an American.

Eliot, in contrast, has never been a broadly popular poet, but there is no question of his deep influence on American poets and critics. (One great modern critic once suggested that Eliot had invented a great deal of his [the critic's] own mind!) Eliot's essays on literature and on specific writers are among the best of our time—or of any time.

The poetry of T. S. Eliot is admittedly difficult, but it is difficult not because he was trying to be difficult or to put off readers but rather because his themes are so large and so complex. He was trying to express not just himself but our civilization—or at least important aspects of our civilization. The fact that "The Love Song of J. Alfred Prufrock" (1915), *The Waste Land* (1922), "The Hollow Men" (1925), and "Ash Wednesday" (1930) remain four of the great literary landmarks of the twentieth century is testimony that he achieved his aim.

EUGENE O'NEILL: THE BIRTH OF AMERICAN DRAMA

If we have said little about American drama in our history thus far, it has been because there has been very little to say. By and large, American theater audiences wanted sentimental melodramas, rollicking good humor, or revivals of old masterpieces rather than fresh contemporary work, and until the middle of the second decade of this century, that is what they were given.

But beginning with the opening of the Provincetown Theatre in Greenwich Village, New York, in 1915, they began to get much more. Between that time and 1927 Eugene O'Neill wrote *Beyond the Horizon, The Emperor Jones, The Hairy Ape, Anna Christie, Desire under the Elms, The Great God Brown,* and *Marco Millions.* In that torrent of brilliance serious American drama was born, and since then our dramatists have achieved a level of excellence comparable to that of our novelists and poets.

LITERARY FIGURES

1862–1910	O. Henry
1862–1937	Edith Wharton
1869–1935	Edwin Arlington Robinson
1869–1950	Edgar Lee Masters
1870–1902	Frank Norris
1871–1945	Theodore Dreiser
1873–1947	Willa Cather
1874–1925	Amy Lowell
1874–1945	Ellen Glasgow
1874–1963	Robert Frost
1876–1916	Jack London
1876–1941	Sherwood Anderson
1878–1967	Carl Sandburg
1879–1931	Vachel Lindsay
1883–1963	William Carlos Williams
1885–1933	Ring Lardner
1885–1951	Sinclair Lewis
1885–1972	Ezra Pound
1886–1961	Hilda Doolittle
1887–1962	Robinson Jeffers
1888–1953	Eugene O'Neill
1888–1965	T. S. Eliot
1890–1948	Claude McKay
1892–1950	Edna St. Vincent Millay
1896–1940	F. Scott Fitzgerald
1902–1967	Langston Hughes
1903–1946	Countee Cullen

1900 Time Line 1930

Historical Events

1900

1902 President McKinley shot; Theodore Roosevelt becomes President

1903 First flight of the Wright brothers

1909 Admiral Peary discovers the North Pole

1910

1912 First number of *Poetry: A Magazine of Verse* published (Chicago)

1914 Opening of the Panama Canal

1915 *Lusitania* ocean liner sunk by German submarine

1917 United States declares war on Germany

1918 World War I armistice signed

Theatre Guild established

1920

1920 Nineteenth Amendment gives women the right to vote

1925 *The New Yorker* magazine founded

1927 Charles Lindbergh makes first solo flight over Atlantic

1929 Stock market crash

1930

1930 Sinclair Lewis awarded the Nobel Prize for Literature

Literary Events

1900

1900 Theodore Dreiser, *Sister Carrie*

1901 Frank Norris, *The Octopus*

1903 Jack London, *The Call of the Wild*

1904 London, *The Sea Wolf*

1906 O. Henry, *The Four Million*

1909 London, *Martin Eden*

1910

1911 Edith Wharton, *Ethan Frome*

1912 Edna St. Vincent Millay, "Renascence"

1913 Willa Cather, *O, Pioneers!*

1914 Robert Frost, *North of Boston*
Vachel Lindsay, *The Congo and Other Poems*
Amy Lowell, *Sword Blades and Poppy Seeds*

1915 Edgar Lee Masters, *Spoon River Anthology*

1916 Carl Sandburg, *Chicago Poems*

1918 Cather, *My Ántonia*

1919 Sherwood Anderson, *Winesburg, Ohio*

1920

1920 T. S. Eliot, *Poems*
F. Scott Fitzgerald, *This Side of Paradise*
Sinclair Lewis, *Main Street*
Wharton, *The Age of Innocence*

1921 E. A. Robinson, *Collected Poems*

1922 Eliot, *The Waste Land*
Lewis, *Babbitt*
Claude McKay, *Harlem Shadows*

1923 Cather, *A Lost Lady*
Lindsay, *Collected Poems*

1924 Robinson Jeffers, *Tamar and Other Poems*

1925 H. D. (Hilda Doolittle), *Collected Poems*
Dreiser, *An American Tragedy*
Fitzgerald, *The Great Gatsby*
Ellen Glasgow, *Barren Ground*
Eugene O'Neill, *Desire under the Elms*

1926 Ernest Hemingway, *The Sun Also Rises*
Langston Hughes, *Weary Blues*
Ring Lardner, *The Love Nest*

1927 Cather, *Death Comes for the Archbishop*
Countee Cullen, *Copper Sun*
Robinson, *Tristram*
Thornton Wilder, *The Bridge of San Luis Rey*

1928 Frost, *West-Running Brook*
Ezra Pound, *Selected Poems*

1929 William Faulkner, *The Sound and the Fury*
Hemingway, *A Farewell to Arms*
Thomas Wolfe, *Look Homeward, Angel*

1930

WILLA CATHER

1873-1947

Willa Cather poured out her feelings about the rugged settlers of the West, their codes of behavior and their love for the earth. All of her major work comes out of her youthful impressions of the West, her wide reading in histories of its development, and frequent revisits to her relatives and her favorite towns. What she sought was the spiritual truths that are illuminated by a discriminating choice of fact and detail.

When Willa Cather began writing she had little intention of becoming a speaker for the Middle West. Born in the Virginia hills around Winchester, Virginia, she was nine years old before her father moved the family to a ranch near Red Cloud, Nebraska, and then to the little frontier village itself. Here she began her schooling, having been tutored previously by her grandmother. The young girl's love for foreign languages was evident at once. She spoke French and German with her neighbors and read the classics with "Uncle Billy" Ducker, a local amateur scholar. But she loved just as much the explorations with her brothers, Roscoe and Douglass, of the Republican River country south of Red Cloud and the high plains region—"The Divide"—where she revisited the Swedish, German, and Bohemian friends of her first days in Nebraska.

After a year at a preparatory school in Lincoln, Willa Cather entered the University of Nebraska thinking she wanted to study medicine and classics. After helping to found a college paper, she spent more and more of her time on English compositions and journalism, particularly dramatic criticism for the *Nebraska State Journal* at one dollar a column. The experience was fruitful. Her first job after graduation was editorial work on *The Home Monthly* in Pittsburgh and then dramatic criticism for the Pittsburgh *Daily Leader,* her hardest years financially and emotionally. In order to have more time to write the poetry and stories she was selling occasionally to New York magazines, she spent five years, 1901–1906, teaching Latin and English in Pittsburgh high schools. A volume of verse, *April Twilights,* appeared in 1903, and in 1905 the critics praised her first collection of short stories, *The Troll Garden,* especially "Paul's Case" and "The Sculptor's Funeral." The next year she made the break from apprenticeship to professional status with an appointment as associate and then managing editor of *McClure's Magazine* in New York City.

Working for S. S. McClure was something like living in a whirlwind, but Willa Cather thrived on it. She spent almost a year in Boston on a special assignment and part of another traveling in New England and to London. In a Boston drawing room she first met Sarah Orne Jewett, then widely known as the author of the splendid Maine sketches *The Country of the Pointed Firs.* Miss Jewett urged her to give over her whole life to fiction, no matter what the cost. "It is impossible for you to work so hard," she wrote, "and yet have your gifts mature as they should. . . . To work in silence and with all one's heart, that is the writer's lot; he is the only artist who must be solitary, and yet needs the widest outlook upon the world." After six years as an editor, Willa Cather took Miss Jewett's advice and left the McClure offices. She had published "The Enchanted Bluff" in *Harper's Magazine,* a short story in which for the first time she used the Southwest as a locale, and *Alexander's Bridge,* her first novel. She was ready to risk her future on her pen.

A visit to her brother in Winslow, Arizona, early in 1912, introduced her to the ancient cliff-dwellings of nearby canyons. On the way back to New York, she spent two months renewing her memories of the sights and sounds of Red Cloud. Though she continued to live in Greenwich Village, she was fully aware that nothing inspired her as much as the windy plains of Nebraska and the deserts of the Southwest. *Alexander's Bridge* had been a contrived novel, a "studio picture," as she later called it. Now she was ready to pour out her feelings about the rugged settlers of the West, their codes of behavior and their love for the earth. Except for *Shadows on the Rock* (1931; set in colonial Quebec) and *Sapphira and the Slave Girl* (1940; set in Virginia), all of Willa Cather's major work comes out of her youthful impressions of the West, her wide reading in histories of its development, and frequent revisits to her relatives and her favorite towns. In no sense was she exploiting her material, as might be said of some nineteenth-century humorists, nor did she feel compelled to paint the dismal, pessimistic portraits our naturalist novelists were painting. That was sensationalism, she said, and what she sought was the spiritual

Willa Cather's childhood home described in The Song of the Lark, *"Old Mrs. Harris," and "The Best Years."*

Red Cloud, Nebraska, 1885. Town of Willa Cather's childhood.

truths that are illuminated by a discriminating choice of fact and detail. Her characters are ordinary men and women; her plots are not in the least melodramatic or artificially heightened; and her style, though always concise, is steady and quiet rather than dazzling.

O Pioneers! (1913), the first of three novels concerned with the Nebraska frontier, begins: "One January day, thirty years ago, the little town of Hanover, anchored on a windy Nebraska tableland, was trying not to be blown away. A mist of fine snowflakes was curling and eddying about the cluster of low drab buildings huddled on the gray prairie, under a gray sky. The dwelling-houses were set about haphazard on the tough prairie sod; some of them looked as if they had been moved in overnight, and others as if they were straying off by themselves, headed straight for the open plain. None of them had any appearance of permanence, and the howling wind blew under them as well as over them." Readers know at once that they are in good hands because the novelist, with a shrewd eye for descriptive details, writes as though she were reliving, not just imagining, winter on *tough* sod in *drab* buildings under a *gray* sky. There is a sureness of touch in Willa Cather's style; she merely tells us how it really

was. In the same relaxed way she builds her plot around Alexandra Bergson, the first of many strong-willed heroines, unfolding her life after her father's untimely death. She makes of this novel not so much a hymn to the pioneer virtues—perseverance, courage, hard work—as a history of what one girl with vision could do with the stubborn land. "*O Pioneers!* interested me tremendously," she recalled later, "because it had to do with a kind of country I loved, because it was about old neighbors, once very dear, whom I had almost forgotten in the hurry and excitement of growing up and finding out what the world was like and trying to get on in it."

She recalled her old neighbors even more vividly when she plotted her third novel of the Nebraska frontier, *My Ántonia* (1918). In the Miners' house, next door to the Cathers in Red Cloud, had lived a young Bohemian hired girl, Annie Sadílek, an industrious and lively newcomer to Nebraska. Willa Cather turned her into Ántonia Shimerda, and though her life in Black Hawk is described by young Jim Burden, a native of the town, she is still the focus of the novel. It is a disarmingly simple story, a welding of earthy characters with the stubborn land. Again the young girl has to shoulder the family's burden after the father's suicide, but here we come to know the valiant heroine far better than Willa Cather's earlier heroines. When she moves to town we share her fears and frustrations at adjusting to "city" ways and being a "hired girl"; we sympathize with her in her unhappy love affairs; and we sense the relief she feels when she returns to till the land with Cusak, her husband, and their swarming brood of healthy children. *My Ántonia* has always been, for good reasons, one of Willa Cather's most popular novels. It has vitality and honesty in its telling. Its central character is no Earth Goddess, no epic heroine, but an adolescent who grows up in a land that demands perseverance and offers in return, at least in Ántonia's case, the joy of self-discovery.

After the first World War, Willa Cather published two collections of short stories and eight more novels. They are not all, understandably, of equal quality but all bear her particular mark. The war left her more disillusioned than she wished to admit; and as a growing materialism evidenced itself in America in the 1920s, she lost some of the glow of the optimism of her earlier work. In its place appeared a concern with moral failures. *A Lost Lady* (1923) is an unforgettable portrait of the young wife of a railroad engineer who succumbs to the town upstart, Ivy Peters. *My Mortal Enemy* (1926) is a depressing study of a marriage in slow collapse and the degeneration of the heroine. *Lucy Gayheart* (1935) chronicles the life of a Nebraska girl in Chicago who falls in love with a singer much older than she and who comes to grief after he dies in a boating accident.

With *Death Comes for the Archbishop* (1927), however, Willa Cather achieved lasting fame. It is her most ambitious work, a re-creation of history rather than a study of the contemporary Midwest. The lure of Arizona and New Mexico had increased in the years after the war and, though not a Catholic, she became enthralled with the history of the Church in the Southwest and of two eminent French missionary clerics, Archbishop Lamy and Bishop Machebeuf who became Archbishop Latour and Father Vaillant of the novel. The title is unfortunate; there are no murders in the book and the death of Latour is hardly the climax of the story. But climaxes never preoccupied Willa Cather. From the opening sentence—"One afternoon in the autumn of 1851 a solitary horseman, followed by a pack-mule, was pushing through an arid stretch of country somewhere in central New Mexico"—to the burial of the Archbishop in the great Santa Fé cathedral, the story proceeds with assurance and inevitability. There may be emotional scenes which a more ruthless narrator would have cut from the book, but no reader questions her religious devotion; her love for the brilliant landscape; her knowledge of native customs, corrupt Spanish priests, and the simple folk virtues of this last frontier. *Death Comes for the Archbishop* and *My Ántonia*, two quite different novels, must be experienced, not merely described, if one is to understand what Willa Cather meant by pioneer vision and courage.

The Troll Garden (1905)
was Willa Cather's first book in prose.
It is composed of three stories about artists
and their audiences, three stories
about artistic temperaments in conflict
with prairie town citizens, and a long,
widely popular story set in Pittsburgh, called
"Paul's Case." In "The Sculptor's Funeral,"
Cather tells the story of Harvey Merrick,
a sculptor of rare ability, and his return
to Sand City, Kansas, where he was
neither understood nor appreciated. Sand City
resembles Red Cloud and the hostility
of its inhabitants is not unlike
the hostility Cather met
in her own career.

The Sculptor's Funeral

A group of the townspeople stood on the station siding of a little Kansas town, awaiting the coming of the night train, which was already twenty minutes overdue. The snow had fallen thick over everything; in the pale starlight the line of bluffs across the wide, white meadows south of the town made soft, smoke-coloured curves against the clear sky. The men on the siding stood first on one foot and then on the other, their hands thrust deep into their trousers pockets, their overcoats open, their shoulders screwed up with the cold; and they glanced from time to time toward the southeast, where the railroad track wound along the river shore. They conversed in low tones and moved about restlessly, seeming uncertain as to what was expected of them. There was but one of the company who looked as if he knew exactly why he was there, and he kept con-

spicuously apart; walking to the far end of the platform, returning to the station door, then pacing up the track again, his chin sunk in the high collar of his overcoat, his burly shoulders drooping forward, his gait heavy and dogged. Presently he was approached by a tall, spare, grizzled man clad in a faded Grand Army suit, who shuffled out from the group and advanced with a certain deference, craning his neck forward until his back made the angle of a jack-knife three-quarters open.

"I reckon she's a-goin' to be pretty late agin tonight, Jim," he remarked in a squeaky falsetto. "S'pose it's the snow?"

"I don't know," responded the other man with a shade of annoyance, speaking from out an astonishing cataract of red beard that grew fiercely and thickly in all directions.

The spare man shifted the quill toothpick he was chewing to the other side of his mouth. "It ain't likely that anybody from the East will come with the corpse, I s'pose," he went on reflectively.

"I don't know," responded the other, more curtly than before.

"It's too bad he didn't belong to some lodge or other. I like an order funeral myself. They seem more appropriate for people of some reputation," the spare man continued, with an ingratiating concession in his shrill voice, as he carefully placed his toothpick in his vest pocket. He always carried the flag at the G. A. R.[1] funerals in the town.

The heavy man turned on his heel, without replying, and walked up the siding. The spare man rejoined the uneasy group. "Jim's ez full ez a tick, ez ushel," he commented commiseratingly.

Just then a distant whistle sounded, and there was a shuffling of feet on the platform. A number of lanky boys, of all ages, appeared as suddenly and slimily as eels wakened by the crack of thunder; some came from the waiting-room, where they had been warming them-

---

1. **G.A.R.** (Grand Army of the Republic), soldiers who served with the Union Army during the Civil War.

selves by the red stove, or half asleep on the slat benches; others uncoiled themselves from baggage trucks or slid out of express wagons. Two clambered down from the driver's seat of a hearse that stood backed up against the siding. They straightened their stooping shoulders and lifted their heads, and a flash of momentary animation kindled their dull eyes at that cold, vibrant scream, the worldwide call for men. It stirred them like the note of a trumpet; just as it had often stirred the man who was coming home tonight, in his boyhood.

The night express shot, red as a rocket, from out the eastward marsh lands and wound along the river shore under the long lines of shivering poplars that sentinelled the meadows, the escaping steam hanging in grey masses against the pale sky and blotting out the Milky Way. In a moment the red glare from the headlight streamed up the snow-covered track before the siding and glittered on the wet, black rails. The burly man with the dishevelled red beard walked swiftly up the platform toward the approaching train, uncovering his head as he went. The group of men behind him hesitated, glanced questioningly at one another, and awkwardly followed his example. The train stopped, and the crowd shuffled up to the express car just as the door was thrown open, the man in the G. A. R. suit thrusting his head forward with curiosity. The express messenger appeared in the doorway, accompanied by a young man in a long ulster[2] and travelling cap.

"Are Mr. Merrick's friends here?" inquired the young man.

The group on the platform swayed uneasily. Philip Phelps, the banker, responded with dignity: "We have come to take charge of the body. Mr. Merrick's father is very feeble and can't be about."

"Send the agent out here," growled the express messenger, "and tell the operator to lend a hand."

The coffin was got out of its rough-box and down on the snowy platform. The townspeople drew back enough to make room for it and then formed a close semicircle about it, looking curiously at the palm leaf which lay across the black cover. No one said anything. The baggage man stood by his truck, waiting to get at the trunks. The engine panted heavily, and the fireman dodged in and out among the wheels with his yellow torch and long oil-can, snapping the spindle boxes. The young Bostonian, one of the dead sculptor's pupils who had come with the body, looked about him helplessly. He turned to the banker, the only one of that black, uneasy, stoop-shouldered group who seemed enough of an individual to be addressed.

"None of Mr. Merrick's brothers are here?" he asked uncertainly.

The man with the red beard for the first time stepped up and joined the others. "No, they have not come yet; the family is scattered. The body will be taken directly to the house." He stooped and took hold of one of the handles of the coffin.

"Take the long hill road up, Thompson, it will be easier on the horses," called the liveryman as the undertaker snapped the door of the hearse and prepared to mount to the driver's seat.

Laird, the red-bearded lawyer, turned again to the stranger: "We didn't know whether there would be any one with him or not," he explained. "It's a long walk, so you'd better go up in the hack."[3] He pointed to a single battered conveyance, but the young man replied stiffly: "Thank you, but I think I will go up with the hearse. If you don't object," turning to the undertaker, "I'll ride with you."

They clambered up over the wheels and drove off in the starlight up the long, white hill toward the town. The lamps in the still village were shining from under the low, snow-burdened roofs; and beyond, on every side, the plains reached out into emptiness, peaceful and wide as the soft sky itself, and wrapped in a tangible, white silence.

---

2. **ulster**\ˈəls·tər\ a long, loose overcoat, of Irish origin.
3. **hack,** vernacular for taxicab.

When the hearse backed up to a wooden sidewalk before a naked, weather-beaten frame house, the same composite, ill-defined group that had stood upon the station siding was huddled about the gate. The front yard was an icy swamp, and a couple of warped planks, extending from the sidewalk to the door, made a sort of rickety footbridge. The gate hung on one hinge, and was opened wide with difficulty. Steavens, the young stranger, noticed that something black was tied to the knob of the front door.

The grating sound made by the casket, as it was drawn from the hearse, was answered by a scream from the house; the front door was wrenched open, and a tall, corpulent woman rushed out bareheaded into the snow and flung herself upon the coffin, shrieking: "My boy, my boy! And this is how you've come home to me!"

As Steavens turned away and closed his eyes with a shudder of unutterable repulsion, another woman, also tall, but flat and angular, dressed entirely in black, darted out of the house and caught Mrs. Merrick by the shoulders, crying sharply: "Come, come, mother; you mustn't go on like this!" Her tone changed to one of obsequious solemnity as she turned to the banker: "The parlour is ready, Mr. Phelps."

The bearers carried the coffin along the narrow boards, while the undertaker ran ahead with the coffin-rests. They bore it into a large, unheated room that smelled of dampness and disuse and furniture polish, and set it down under a hanging lamp ornamented with jingling glass prisms and before a "Rogers group" of John Alden and Priscilla, wreathed with smilax.[4] Henry Steavens stared about him with the sickening conviction that there had been a mistake, and that he had somehow arrived at the wrong destination. He looked at the clover-green Brussels, the fat plush upholstery, among the hand-painted china placques and panels and vases, for some mark of identification,—for something that might once conceivably have belonged to Harvey Merrick. It was not until he recognized his friend in the crayon portrait of a little boy in kilts and curls, hanging above

the piano, that he felt willing to let any of these people approach the coffin.

"Take the lid off, Mr. Thompson; let me see my boy's face," wailed the elder woman between her sobs. This time Steavens looked fearfully, almost beseechingly into her face, red and swollen under its masses of strong, black, shiny hair. He flushed, dropped his eyes, and then, almost incredulously, looked again. There was a kind of power about her face—a kind of brutal handsomeness, even; but it was scarred and furrowed by violence, and so coloured and coarsened by fiercer passions that grief seemed never to have laid a gentle finger there. The long nose was distended and knobbed at the end, and there were deep lines on either side of it; her heavy, black brows almost met across her forehead, her teeth were large and square, and set far apart—teeth that could tear. She filled the room; the men were obliterated, seemed tossed about like twigs in an angry water, and even Steavens felt himself being drawn into the whirlpool.

The daughter—the tall, raw-boned woman in crêpe, with a mourning comb in her hair which curiously lengthened her long face—sat stiffly upon the sofa, her hands, conspicuous for their large knuckles, folded in her lap, her mouth and eyes drawn down, solemnly awaiting the opening of the coffin. Near the door stood a mulatto woman, evidently a servant in the house, with a timid bearing and an emaciated face pitifully sad and gentle. She was weeping silently, the corner of her calico apron lifted to her eyes, occasionally suppressing a long, quivering sob. Steavens walked over and stood beside her.

Feeble steps were heard on the stairs, and an old man, tall and frail, odorous of pipe smoke, with shaggy, unkept grey hair and a dingy beard, tobacco stained about the mouth, entered uncertainly. He went slowly up to the coffin and stood rolling a blue cotton handkerchief between his hands, seeming so pained

---

4. **smilax**\ˈsmai·lăks\ woody vine, usually prickly, with bright-green leaves.

and embarrassed by his wife's orgy of grief that he had no consciousness of anything else.

"There, there, Annie, dear, don't take on so," he quavered timidly, putting out a shaking hand and awkwardly patting her elbow. She turned and sank upon his shoulder with such violence that he tottered a little. He did not even glance toward the coffin, but continued to look at her with a dull, frightened, appealing expression, as a spaniel looks at the whip. His sunken cheeks slowly reddened and burned with miserable shame. When his wife rushed from the room, her daughter strode after her with set lips. The servant stole up to the coffin, bent over it for a moment, and then slipped away to the kitchen, leaving Steavens, the lawyer, and the father to themselves. The old man stood looking down at his dead son's face. The sculptor's splendid head seemed even more noble in its rigid stillness than in life. The dark hair had crept down upon the wide fore-head; the face seemed strangely long, but in it there was not that repose we expect to find in the faces of the dead. The brows were so drawn that there were two deep lines above the beaked nose, and the chin was thrust forward defiantly. It was as though the strain of life had been so sharp and bitter that death could not at once relax the tension and smooth the countenance into perfect peace—as though he were still guarding something precious, which might even yet be wrested from him.

The old man's lips were working under his stained beard. He turned to the lawyer with timid deference: "Phelps and the rest are comin' back to set up with Harve, ain't they?" he asked. "Thank 'ee, Jim, thank 'ee." He brushed the hair back gently from his son's forehead. "He was a good boy, Jim; always a good boy. He was ez gentle ez a child and the kindest of 'em all—only we didn't none of us ever onderstand him." The tears trickled slowly down his beard and dropped upon the sculptor's coat.

"Martin, Martin! Oh, Martin! come here," his wife wailed from the top of the stairs. The old man started timorously: "Yes, Annie, I'm com-

ing." He turned away, hesitated, stood for a moment in miserable indecision; then reached back and patted the dead man's hair softly, and stumbled from the room.

"Poor old man, I didn't think he had any tears left. Seems as if his eyes would have gone dry long ago. At his age nothing cuts very deep," remarked the lawyer.

Something in his tone made Steavens glance up. While the mother had been in the room, the young man had scarcely seen any one else; but now, from the moment he first glanced into Jim Laird's florid face and blood-shot eyes, he knew that he had found what he had been heartsick at not finding before—the feeling, the understanding, that must exist in some one, even here.

The man was red as his beard, with features swollen and blurred by dissipation, and a hot, blazing blue eye. His face was strained—that of a man who is controlling himself with difficulty—and he kept plucking at his beard with a sort of fierce resentment. Steavens, sitting by the window, watched him turn down the glaring lamp, still its jangling pendants with an angry gesture, and then stand with his hands locked behind him, staring down into the master's face. He could not help wondering what link there had been between the porcelain vessel and so sooty a lump of potter's clay.

From the kitchen an uproar was sounding; when the dining-room door opened, the import of it was clear. The mother was abusing the maid for having forgotten to make the dressing for the chicken salad which had been prepared for the watchers. Steavens had never heard anything in the least like it; it was injured, emotional, dramatic abuse, unique and masterly in its excruciating cruelty, as violent and unrestrained as had been her grief of twenty minutes before. With a shudder of disgust the lawyer went into the dining-room and closed the door into the kitchen.

"Poor Roxy's getting it now," he remarked when he came back. "The Merricks took her out of the poor-house years ago; and if her loyalty would let her, I guess the poor old thing could tell tales that would curdle your blood. She's the mulatto woman who was standing in here a while ago, with her apron to her eyes. The old woman is a fury; there never was anybody like her. She made Harvey's life a hell for him when he lived at home; he was so sick ashamed of it. I never could see how he kept himself sweet."

"He was wonderful," said Steavens slowly, "wonderful; but until tonight I have never known how wonderful."

"That is the eternal wonder of it, anyway; that it can come even from such a dung heap as this," the lawyer cried, with a sweeping gesture which seemed to indicate much more than the four walls within which they stood.

"I think I'll see whether I can get a little air. The room is so close I am beginning to feel rather faint," murmured Steavens, struggling with one of the windows. The sash was stuck, however, and would not yield, so he sat down dejectedly and began pulling at his collar. The lawyer came over, loosened the sash with one blow of his red fist and sent the window up a few inches. Steavens thanked him, but the nausea which had been gradually climbing into his throat for the last half hour left him with but one desire—a desperate feeling that he must get away from this place with what was left of Harvey Merrick. Oh, he comprehended well enough now the quiet bitterness of the smile that he had seen so often on his master's lips!

Once when Merrick returned from a visit home, he brought with him a singularly feeling and suggestive bas-relief[5] of a thin, faded old woman, sitting and sewing something pinned to her knee; while a full-lipped, full-blooded little urchin, his trousers held up by a single gallows, stood beside her, impatiently twitching her gown to call her attention to a butterfly he had caught. Steavens, impressed by the tender and delicate modelling of the thin, tired face, had asked him if it were his mother. He remembered the dull flush that had burned up in the sculptor's face.

The lawyer was sitting in a rocking-chair beside the coffin, his head thrown back and his eyes closed. Steavens looked at him earnestly, puzzled at the line of the chin, and wondering why a man should conceal a feature of such distinction under that disfiguring shock of beard. Suddenly, as though he felt the young sculptor's keen glance, Jim Laird opened his eyes.

"Was he always a good deal of an oyster?" he asked abruptly. "He was terribly shy as a boy."

"Yes, he was an oyster, since you put it so," rejoined Steavens. "Although he could be very fond of people, he always gave one the impression of being detached. He disliked violent emotion; he was reflective, and rather distrustful of himself—except, of course, as regarded his work. He was sure enough there. He distrusted men pretty thoroughly and women even more, yet somehow without believing ill of them. He was determined, indeed, to believe the best; but he seemed afraid to investigate."

"A burnt dog dreads the fire," said the lawyer grimly, and closed his eyes.

Steavens went on and on, reconstructing that whole miserable boyhood. All this raw, biting ugliness had been the portion of the man whose mind was to become an exhaustless gallery of beautiful impressions—so sensitive that the mere shadow of a poplar leaf flickering against a sunny wall would be etched and held there for ever. Surely, if ever a man had the magic word in his finger tips, it was Merrick. Whatever he touched, he revealed its holiest secret; liberated it from enchantment and restored it to its pristine loveliness. Upon whatever he had come in contact with, he had left a beautiful record of the experience—a sort of ethereal signature; a scent, a sound, a colour that was his own.

Steavens understood now the real tragedy of his master's life; neither love nor wine, as many had conjectured; but a blow which had fallen earlier and cut deeper than anything else could have done—a shame not his, and yet so un-

---

5. **bas-relief**\ˈbä·rĭˈlēf, ˈbăs-\ piece of sculpture in which the figure stands out only slightly from the background.

escapably his, to hide in his heart from his very boyhood. And without—the frontier warfare; the yearning of a boy, cast ashore upon a desert of newness and ugliness and sordidness, for all that is chastened and old, and noble with traditions.

At eleven o'clock the tall, flat woman in black announced that the watchers were arriving, and asked them to "step into the dining-room." As Steavens rose, the lawyer said dryly: "You go on—it'll be a good experience for you. I'm not equal to that crowd tonight; I've had twenty years of them."

As Steavens closed the door after him he glanced back at the lawyer, sitting by the coffin in the dim light, with his chin resting on his hand.

The same misty group that had stood before the door of the express car shuffled into the dining-room. In the light of the kerosene lamp they separated and became individuals. The minister, a pale, feeble-looking man with white hair and blond chin-whiskers, took his seat beside a small side table and placed his Bible upon it. The Grand Army man sat down behind the stove and tilted his chair back comfortably against the wall, fishing his quill toothpick from his waistcoat pocket. The two bankers, Phelps and Elder, sat off in a corner behind the dinner-table, where they could finish their discussion of the new usury law and its effect on chattel security loans. The real estate agent, an old man with a smiling, hypocritical face, soon joined them. The coal and lumber dealer and the cattle shipper sat on opposite sides of the hard coal-burner, their feet on the nickel-work. Steavens took a book from his pocket and began to read. The talk around him ranged through various topics of local interest while the house was quieting down. When it was clear that the members of the family were in bed, the Grand Army man hitched his shoulders and, untangling his long legs, caught his heels on the rounds of his chair.

"S'pose there'll be a will, Phelps?" he queried in his weak falsetto.

The banker laughed disagreeably, and began trimming his nails with a pearl-handled pocket-knife.

"There'll scarcely be any need for one, will there?" he queried in his turn.

The restless Grand Army man shifted his position again, getting his knees still nearer his chin. "Why, the old man says Harve's done right well lately," he chirped.

The other banker spoke up. "I reckon he means by that Harve ain't asked him to mortgage any more farms lately, so as he could go on with his education."

"Seems like my mind don't reach back to a time when Harve wasn't bein' edycated," tittered the Grand Army man.

There was a general chuckle. The minister took out his handkerchief and blew his nose sonorously. Banker Phelps closed his knife with a snap. "It's too bad the old man's sons didn't turn out better," he remarked with reflective authority. "They never hung together. He spent money enough on Harve to stock a dozen cattle-farms, and he might as well have poured it into Sand Creek. If Harve had stayed at home and helped nurse what little they had, and gone into stock on the old man's bottom farm, they might all have been well fixed. But the old man had to trust everything to tenants and was cheated right and left."

"Harve never could have handled stock none," interposed the cattleman. "He hadn't it in him to be sharp. Do you remember when he bought Sander's mules for eight-year olds, when everybody in town knew that Sander's father-in-law give 'em to his wife for a wedding present eighteen years before, an' they was full-grown mules then?"

The company laughed discreetly, and the Grand Army man rubbed his knees with a spasm of childish delight.

"Harve never was much account for anything practical, and he shore was never fond of work," began the coal and lumber dealer. "I mind the last time he was home; the day he left, when the old man was out to the barn helpin' his hand hitch up to take Harve to the train, and Cal Moots was patchin' up the fence; Harve, he come out on the step and sings out, in his lady-like voice: 'Cal Moots, Cal Moots! please come cord my trunk.'"

"That's Harve for you," approved the Grand Army man. "I kin hear him howlin' yet, when he was a big feller in long pants and his mother used to whale him with a rawhide in the barn for lettin' the cows git foundered in the corn-field when he was drivin' 'em home from pasture. He killed a cow of mine that-a-way onct—a pure Jersey and the best milker I had, an' the ole man had to put up for her. Harve, he was watchin' the sun set acrost the marshes when the anamile got away."

"Where the old man made his mistake was in sending the boy East to school," said Phelps, stroking his goatee and speaking in a deliberate, judicial tone. "There was where he got his head full of nonsense. What Harve needed, of all people, was a course in some first-class Kansas City business college."

The letters were swimming before Steaven's eyes. Was it possible that these men did not understand, that the palm on the coffin meant nothing to them? The very name of their town would have remained for ever buried in the postal guide had it not been now and again mentioned in the world in connection with Harvey Merrick's. He remembered what his master had said to him on the day of his death, after the congestion of both lungs had shut off any probability of recovery, and the sculptor had asked his pupil to send his body home. "It's not a pleasant place to be lying while the world is moving and doing and bettering," he had said with a feeble smile, "but it rather seems as though we ought to go back to the place we came from, in the end. The townspeople will come in for a look at me; and after they have had their say, I shan't have much to fear from the judgment of God!"

The cattleman took up the comment. "Forty's young for a Merrick to cash in; they usually hang on pretty well. Probably he helped it along with whisky."

"His mother's people were not long lived, and Harvey never had a robust constitution," said the minister mildly. He would have liked to say more. He had been the boy's Sunday-school teacher, and had been fond of him; but he felt that he was not in a position to speak. His own sons had turned out badly, and it was not a year since one of them had made his last trip home in the express car, shot in a gambling-house in the Black Hills.

"Nevertheless, there is no disputin' that Harve frequently looked upon the wine when it was red, also variegated, and it shore made an oncommon fool of him," moralized the cattleman.

Just then the door leading into the parlour rattled loudly and every one started involuntarily, looking relieved when only Jim Laird came out. The Grand Army man ducked his head when he saw the spark in his blue, blood-shot eye. They were all afraid of Jim; he was a drunkard, but he could twist the law to suit his client's needs as no other man in all western Kansas could do, and there were many who tried. The lawyer closed the door behind him, leaned back against it and folded his arms, cocking his head a little to one side. When he assumed this attitude in the court-room, ears were always pricked up, as it usually foretold a flood of withering sarcasm.

"I've been with you gentlemen before," he began in a dry, even tone, "when you've sat by the coffins of boys born and raised in this town; and, if I remember rightly, you were never any too well satisfied when you checked them up. What's the matter, anyhow? Why is it that reputable young men are as scarce as millionaires in Sand City? It might almost seem to a stranger that there was some way something the matter with your progressive town. Why did Ruben Sayer, the brightest young lawyer you ever turned out, after he had come home from the university as straight as a die, take to drinking and forge a check and shoot himself? Why did Bill Merrit's son die of the shakes in a saloon in Omaha? Why was Mr. Thomas's son, here, shot in a gambling-house? Why did young Adams burn his mill to beat the insurance companies and go to the pen?"

The lawyer paused and unfolded his arms, laying one clenched fist quietly on the table. "I'll tell you why. Because you drummed nothing but money and knavery into their ears from the time they wore knickerbockers; because you carped away at them as you've been carping here tonight, holding our friends Phelps and Elder up to them for their models, as our grandfathers held up George Washington and John Adams. But the boys were young, and raw at the business you put them to, and how could they match coppers with such artists as Phelps and Elder? You wanted them to be successful rascals; they were only unsuccessful ones—that's all the difference. There was only one boy ever raised in this borderland between ruffianism and civilization who didn't come to grief, and you hated Harvey Merrick more for winning out than you hated all the other boys who got under the wheels. Yes indeed, how you did hate him! Phelps, here, is fond of saying that he could buy and sell us all out any time he's a mind to; but he knew Harve wouldn't have given a farthing for his bank and all his cattle-farms put together; and a lack of appreciation, that way, goes hard with Phelps.

"Old Nimrod thinks Harve drank too much; and this from such as Nimrod and me!

"Brother Elder says Harve was too free with the old man's money—fell short in filial consideration, maybe. Well, we can all remember the very tone in which brother Elder swore his own father was a liar, in the county court; and we all know that the old man came out of that partnership with his son as bare as a sheared lamb. But maybe I'm getting personal, and I'd better be driving ahead at what I want to say."

The lawyer paused a moment, squared his heavy shoulders, and went on: "Harvey Merrick and I went to school together, back East. We were dead in earnest, and we wanted you all to be proud of us some day. We meant to be great men. Even I, and I haven't lost my sense of humour, gentlemen, I meant to be a great man. I came back here to practise, and I found

you didn't in the least want me to be a great man. You wanted me to be a shrewd lawyer—oh, yes! Our veteran here wanted me to get him an increase of pension, because he had dyspepsia;[6] Phelps wanted a new county survey that would put the widow Wilson's little bottom farm inside his south line; Elder wanted to lend money at 5 per cent a month, and get it collected; and Stark here wanted to wheedle old women up in Vermont into investing their annuities in real-estate mortgages that are not worth the paper they are written on. Oh, you needed me hard enough, and you'll go on needing me!

"Well, I came back here and became the crooked shyster you wanted me to be. You pretend to have some sort of respect for me; and yet you'll stand up and throw mud at Harvey Merrick, whose soul you couldn't dirty and whose hands you couldn't tie. Oh, you're a discriminating lot of Christians! There have been times when the sight of Harvey's name in some Eastern paper has made me hang my head like a whipped dog; and, again, times when I liked to think of him off there in the world, away from all this hog-wallow, climbing the big, clean up-grade he'd set for himself.

"And we? Now that we've fought and lied and sweated and stolen, and hated as only the disappointed strugglers in a bitter, dead little Western town know how to do, what have we got to show for it? Harvey Merrick wouldn't have given one sunset over your marshes for all you've got put together, and you know it. It's not for me to say why, in the inscrutable wisdom of God, a genius should ever have been called from this place of hatred and bitter waters; but I want this Boston man to know that the drivel he's been hearing here tonight is the only tribute any truly great man could have from such a lot of sick, side-tracked, burnt-dog, land-poor sharks as the here-present financiers of Sand City—upon which town may God have mercy!"

---

6. dyspepsia\dĭs ˄pĕp·shə\ indigestion.

The lawyer thrust out his hand to Steavens as he passed him, caught up his overcoat in the hall, and had left the house before the Grand Army man had had time to lift his ducked head and crane his long neck about at his fellows.

Next day Jim Laird was drunk and unable to attend the funeral services. Steavens called twice at his office, but was compelled to start East without seeing him. He had a presentiment that he would hear from him again, and left his address on the lawyer's table; but if Laird found it, he never acknowledged it. The thing in him that Harvey Merrick had loved must have gone under ground with Harvey Merrick's coffin; for it never spoke again, and Jim got the cold he died of driving across the Colorado mountains to defend one of Phelps's sons who had got into trouble out there by cutting government timber.

I
FRONTIER WARFARE

In the popular imagination, warfare in a Western town means two tall Texans squared off in a dusty street in front of the local saloon. In this story, however, Willa Cather portrays a conflict, perhaps less violent, but far more serious in its implications for society. In this borderland "between ruffianism and civilization" where the rawness and bitterness of primitive struggle for physical survival sometimes fosters soul-crushing materialism, how, she asks, can the sensitive, refined, civilizing spirit find root, grow, and flourish. It is the latter, the creative mind filled with "an exhaustive gallery of beautiful impressions," that lifts life above the savage. Yet the conflict between the civilizing and the savage spirits is a warfare never wholly resolved; each age—indeed, each individual—must make the choice anew.

II
IMPLICATIONS

A. What does each of the following quotations reveal about the speaker, the person spoken about, or both?

1. Mrs. Merrick: "My boy, my boy! And this is how you've come home to me!"

2. Mr. Merrick: "He was a good boy, Jim; always a good boy. He was ez gentle ez a child and the kindest of 'em all—only we didn't none of us ever onderstand him."

3. Steavens: "He was wonderful . . . ; but until tonight I have never known how wonderful."

4. Banker Phelps: "It's too bad the old man's sons didn't turn out better. . . . He spent money enough on Harve to stock a dozen cattle-farms, and he might as well have poured it into Sand Creek."

5. The coal and lumber dealer: "Harve never was much account for anything practical, and he shore was never fond of work."

6. Jim Laird: "Harvey Merrick wouldn't have given one sunset over your marshes for all you've got put together, and you know it."

B. On the basis of this story and your own experience, discuss the following propositions:

1. Beauty and art have no place in the business world.

2. Great persons are great precisely because they overcome great obstacles.

3. People usually find fault with those ideas and individuals they don't understand.

4. Prophets are never honored in their own town.

III
TECHNIQUES

Conflict and Climax

Reread the beginning of the story to discover how soon Cather establishes the conflict between the lawyer, Jim Laird, and his fellow townspeople. Where does the climax of this conflict occur?

Moment of Illumination

Laird's final speech illuminates the nature of the conflict between Harvey Merrick and the citizens of Sand City; yet there is a later moment of illumination as well. What is that moment? How does it help modify your perception of the chief conflict of the story? What does it reveal about the story's fullest meaning?

In 1932, Willa Cather collected
three more stories based on her years
in Red Cloud and published them in a volume
called *Obscure Destinies*. "Neighbour Rosicky"
is drawn from the Cather family, but the hero
is a blending of Cather's father
with the husband of a childhood friend.
This simply told story was written early
in 1928, during the months in which Charles
Cather was dying from angina.
Having recently returned from a visit
with her father, Willa Cather was filled
with memories of the family home
in Red Cloud and the hidden strength
in these people who lived close to the land.
She finished the story a few months
after her father's death.

Neighbour Rosicky

I

When Doctor Burleigh told neighbour Rosicky he had a bad heart, Rosicky protested.

"So? No, I guess my heart was always pretty good. I got a little asthma, maybe. Just a awful short breath when I was pitchin' hay last summer, dat's all."

"Well now, Rosicky, if you know more about it than I do, what did you come to me for? It's your heart that makes you short of breath, I tell you. You're sixty-five years old, and you've always worked hard, and your heart's tired. You've got to be careful from now on, and you can't do heavy work any more. You've got five boys at home to do it for you."

The old farmer looked up at the Doctor with

Copyright 1932 by The Crowell Publishing Company, renewed 1960 by the executors of the estate of Willa Cather. Reprinted from *Obscure Destinies* by Willa Cather, by permission of Alfred A. Knopf, Inc.

a gleam of amusement in his queer triangular-shaped eyes. His eyes were large and lively, but the lids were caught up in the middle in a curious way, so that they formed a triangle. He did not look like a sick man. His brown face was creased but not wrinkled, he had a ruddy colour in his smooth-shaven cheeks and in his lips, under his long brown moustache. His hair was thin and ragged around his ears, but very little grey. His forehead, naturally high and crossed by deep parallel lines, now ran all the way up to his pointed crown. Rosicky's face had the habit of looking interested,—suggested a contented disposition and a reflective quality that was gay rather than grave. This gave him a certain detachment, the easy manner of an onlooker and observer.

"Well, I guess you ain't got no pills fur a bad heart, Doctor Ed. I guess the only thing is fur me to git me a new one."

Doctor Burleigh swung round in his desk-chair and frowned at the old farmer. "I think if I were you I'd take a little care of the old one, Rosicky."

Rosicky shrugged. "Maybe I don't know how. I expect you mean fur me not to drink my coffee no more."

"I wouldn't, in your place. But you'll do as you choose about that. I've never yet been able to separate a Bohemian from his coffee or his pipe. I've quit trying. But the sure thing is you've got to cut out farm work. You can feed the stock and do chores about the barn, but you can't do anything in the fields that makes you short of breath."

"How about shelling corn?"

"Of course not!"

Rosicky considered with puckered brows.

"I can't make my heart go no longer'n it wants to, can I, Doctor Ed?"

"I think it's good for five or six years yet, maybe more, if you'll take the strain off it. Sit around the house and help Mary. If I had a good wife like yours, I'd want to stay around the house."

His patient chuckled. "It ain't no place fur a man. I don't like no old man hanging round the kitchen too much. An' my wife, she's a awful hard worker her own self."

"That's it; you can help her a little. My word, Rosicky, you are one of the few men I know who has a family he can get some comfort out of; happy dispositions, never quarrel among themselves, and they treat you right. I want to see you live a few years and enjoy them."

"Oh, they're good kids, all right," Rosicky assented.

The Doctor wrote him a prescription and asked him how his oldest son, Rudolph, who had married in the spring, was getting on. Rudolph had struck out for himself, on rented land. "And how's Polly? I was afraid Mary mightn't like an American daughter-in-law, but it seems to be working out all right."

"Yes, she's a fine girl. Dat widder woman bring her daughters up very nice. Polly got lots of spunk, an' she got some style, too. Da's nice, for young folks to have some style." Rosicky inclined his head gallantly. His voice and his twinkly smile were an affectionate compliment to his daughter-in-law.

"It looks like a storm, and you'd better be getting home before it comes. In town in the car?" Doctor Burleigh rose.

"No, I'm in de wagon. When you got five boys, you ain't got much chance to ride round in de Ford. I ain't much for cars, noway."

"Well, it's a good road out to your place; but I don't want you bumping around in a wagon much. And never again on a hay-rake, remember!"

Rosicky placed the Doctor's fee delicately behind the desk-telephone, looking the other way, as if this were an absent-minded gesture. He put on his plush cap and his corduroy jacket with a sheepskin collar, and went out.

The Doctor picked up his stethoscope and frowned at it as if he were seriously annoyed with the instrument. He wished it had been telling tales about some other man's heart, some old man who didn't look the Doctor in the eye so knowingly, or hold out such a warm brown hand when he said good-bye. Doctor Burleigh had been a poor boy in the country before he went away to medical school; he had known Rosicky almost ever since he could remember, and he had a deep affection for Mrs. Rosicky.

Only last winter he had had such a good breakfast at Rosicky's, and that when he needed it. He had been out all night on a long, hard confinement case at Tom Marshall's,—a big rich farm where there was plenty of stock and plenty of feed and a great deal of expensive farm machinery of the newest model, and no comfort whatever. The woman had too many children and too much work, and she was no manager. When the baby was born at last, and handed over to the assisting neighbour woman, and the mother was properly attended to, Burleigh refused any breakfast in that slovenly house, and drove his buggy—the snow was too deep for a car—eight miles to Anton Rosicky's place. He didn't know another farm-house where a man could get such a warm welcome, and such good strong coffee with rich cream. No wonder the old chap didn't want to give up his coffee!

He had driven in just when the boys had come back from the barn and were washing up for breakfast. The long table, covered with a bright oilcloth, was set out with dishes waiting for them, and the warm kitchen was full of the smell of coffee and hot biscuit and sausage. Five big handsome boys, running from twenty to twelve, all with what Burleigh called natural good manners,—they hadn't a bit of the painful self-consciousness he himself had to struggle with when he was a lad. One ran to put his horse away, another helped him off with his fur coat and hung it up, and Josephine, the youngest child and the only daughter, quickly set another place under her mother's direction.

With Mary, to feed creatures was the natural expression of affection,—her chickens, the calves, her big hungry boys. It was a rare pleasure to feed a young man whom she seldom saw and of whom she was as proud as if he belonged to her. Some country housekeepers would have stopped to spread a white cloth over the oilcloth, to change the thick cups and plates for their best china, and the wooden-handled knives for plated ones. But not Mary.

"You must take us as you find us, Doctor Ed. I'd be glad to put out my good things for you if you was expected, but I'm glad to get you any way at all."

He knew she was glad,—she threw back her head and spoke out as if she were announcing him to the whole prairie. Rosicky hadn't said anything at all; he merely smiled his twinkling smile, put some more coal on the fire, and went into his own room to pour the Doctor a little drink in a medicine glass. When they were all seated, he watched his wife's face from his end of the table and spoke to her in Czech. Then, with the instinct of politeness which seldom failed him, he turned to the Doctor and said slyly: "I was just tellin' her not to ask you no questions about Mrs. Marshall till you eat some breakfast. My wife, she's terrible fur to ask questions."

The boys laughed, and so did Mary. She watched the Doctor devour her biscuit and sausage, too much excited to eat anything herself. She drank her coffee and sat taking in everything about her visitor. She had known him when he was a poor country boy, and was boastfully proud of his success, always saying: "What do people go to Omaha for, to see a doctor, when we got the best one in the State right here?" If Mary liked people at all, she felt physical pleasure in the sight of them, personal exultation in any good fortune that came to them. Burleigh didn't know many women like that, but he knew she was like that.

When his hunger was satisfied, he did, of course, have to tell them about Mrs. Marshall, and he noticed what a friendly interest the boys took in the matter.

Rudolph, the oldest one (he was still living at home then), said: "The last time I was over there, she was lifting them big heavy milkcans, and I knew she oughtn't to be doing it."

"Yes, Rudolph told me about that when he come home, and I said it wasn't right," Mary put in warmly. "It was all right for me to do them things up to the last, for I was terrible strong, but that woman's weakly. And do you think she'll be able to nurse it, Ed?" She sometimes forgot to give him the title she was so proud of. "And to think of your being up all night and then not able to get a decent breakfast! I don't know what's the matter with such people."

"Why, Mother," said one of the boys, "if Doctor Ed had got breakfast there, we wouldn't have him here. So you ought to be glad."

"He knows I'm glad to have him, John, any time. But I'm sorry for that poor woman, how bad she'll feel the Doctor had to go away in the cold without his breakfast."

"I wish I'd been in practice when these were getting born." The doctor looked down the row of close-clipped heads. "I missed some good breakfasts by not being."

The boys began to laugh at their mother because she flushed so red, but she stood her ground and threw up her head. "I don't care, you wouldn't have got away from this house without breakfast. No doctor ever did. I'd have had something ready fixed that Anton could warm up for you."

The boys laughed harder than ever, and exclaimed at her: "I'll bet you would!" "She would, that!"

"Father, did you get breakfast for the doctor when we were born?"

"Yes, and he used to bring me my breakfast, too, mighty nice. I was always awful hungry!" Mary admitted with a guilty laugh.

While the boys were getting the Doctor's horse, he went to the window to examine the house plants. "What do you do to your geraniums to keep them blooming all winter, Mary? I never pass this house that from the road I don't see your windows full of flowers."

She snapped off a dark red one, and a ruffled new green leaf, and put them in his buttonhole. "There, that looks better. You look too solemn for a young man, Ed. Why don't you git married? I'm worried about you. Settin' at breakfast, I looked at you real hard, and I seen you've got some grey hairs already."

"Oh, yes! They're coming. Maybe they'd come faster if I married."

"Don't talk so. You'll ruin your health eating at the hotel. I could send your wife a nice loaf of nut bread, if you only had one. I don't like to see a young man getting grey. I'll tell you something, Ed; you make some strong black tea and keep it handy in a bowl, and every morning just brush it into your hair, an' it'll keep the grey from showin' much. That's the way I do!"

Sometimes the Doctor heard the gossipers in the drug-store wondering why Rosicky didn't get on faster. He was industrious, and so were his boys, but they were rather free and easy, weren't pushers, and they didn't always show good judgment. They were comfortable, they were out of debt, but they didn't get much ahead. Maybe, Doctor Burleigh reflected, people as generous and warm-hearted and affectionate as the Rosickys never got ahead much; maybe you couldn't enjoy your life and put it into the bank, too.

II

When Rosicky left Doctor Burleigh's office he went into the farm-implement store to light his pipe and put on his glasses and read over the list Mary had given him. Then he went into the general merchandise place next door and stood about until the pretty girl with the plucked eyebrows, who always waited on him, was free. Those eyebrows, two thin India-ink strokes, amused him, because he remembered how they used to be. Rosicky always prolonged his shopping by a little joking; the girl knew the old fellow admired her, and she liked to chaff with him.

"Seems to me about every other week you buy ticking, Mr. Rosicky, and always the best quality," she remarked as she measured off the heavy bolt with red stripes.

"You see, my wife is always makin' goose-fedder pillows, an' de thin stuff don't hold in dem little down-fedders."

"You must have lots of pillows at your house."

"Sure. She makes quilts of dem, too. We sleeps easy. Now she's makin' a fedder quilt for my son's wife. You know Polly, that married my Rudolph. How much my bill, Miss Pearl?"

"Eight eighty-five."

"Chust make it nine, and put in some candy fur de women."

"As usual. I never did see a man buy so much candy for his wife. First thing you know, she'll be getting too fat."

"I'd like dat. I ain't much fur all dem slim women like what de style is now."

"That's one for me, I suppose, Mr. Bohunk!" Pearl sniffed and elevated her India-ink strokes.

When Rosicky went out to his wagon, it was beginning to snow,—the first snow of the season, and he was glad to see it. He rattled out of town and along the highway through a wonderfully rich stretch of country, the finest farms in the county. He admired this High Prairie, as it was called, and always liked to drive through it. His own place lay in a rougher territory, where there was some clay in the soil and it was not so productive. When he bought his land, he hadn't the money to buy on High Prairie; so he told his boys, when they grumbled, that if their land hadn't some clay in it, they wouldn't own it at all. All the same, he enjoyed looking at these fine farms, as he enjoyed looking at a prize bull.

After he had gone eight miles, he came to the graveyard, which lay just at the edge of his own hay-land. There he stopped his horses and sat still on his wagon seat, looking about at the snowfall. Over yonder on the hill he could see his own house, crouching low, with the clump of orchard behind and the windmill before, and all down the gentle hill-slope the rows of pale gold cornstalks stood out against the white field. The snow was falling over the cornfield and the pasture and the hay-land, steadily, with very little wind,—a nice dry snow. The graveyard had only a light wire fence about it and was all overgrown with long red grass. The fine snow, settling into this red grass and upon the few little evergreens and the headstones, looked very pretty.

It was a nice graveyard, Rosicky reflected, sort of snug and homelike, not cramped or mournful,—a big sweep all round it. A man could lie down in the long grass and see the complete arch of the sky over him, hear the wagons go by; in summer the mowing-machine rattled right up to the wire fence. And it was so near home. Over there across the cornstalks his own roof and windmill looked so good to him that he promised himself to mind the Doctor and take care of himself. He was awful fond of his place, he admitted. He wasn't anxious to leave it. And it was a comfort to think that he would never have to go farther than the edge of his own hayfield. The snow, falling over his barnyard and the graveyard, seemed to draw things together like. And they were all old neighbours in the graveyard, most of them friends; there was nothing to feel awkward or embarrassed about. Embarrassment was the most disagreeable feeling Rosicky knew. He didn't often have it,—only with certain people whom he didn't understand at all.

Well, it was a nice snowstorm; a fine sight to see the snow falling so quietly and graciously over so much open country. On his cap and shoulders, on the horses' back and manes, light, delicate, mysterious it fell; and with it a dry cool fragrance was released into the air. It meant rest for vegetation and men and beasts, for the ground itself; a season of long nights for sleep, leisurely breakfasts, peace by the fire. This and much more went through Rosicky's mind, but he merely told himself that winter was coming, clucked to his horses, and drove on.

When he reached home, John, the youngest boy, ran out to put away his team for him, and he met Mary coming up from the outside cellar with her apron full of carrots. They went into the house together. On the table, covered with oilcloth figured with clusters of blue grapes, a place was set, and he smelled hot coffee-cake of some kind. Anton never lunched in town; he thought that extravagant, and anyhow he didn't like the food. So Mary always had something ready for him when he got home.

After he was settled in his chair, stirring his coffee in a big cup, Mary took out of the oven a pan of *kolache*[1] stuffed with apricots, examined them anxiously to see whether they had got too dry, put them beside his plate, and then sat down opposite him.

Rosicky asked her in Czech if she wasn't going to have any coffee.

She replied in English, as being somehow the right language for transacting business: "Now what did Doctor Ed say, Anton? You tell me just what."

"He said I was to tell you some compliments, but I forgot 'em." Rosicky's eyes twinkled.

"About you, I mean. What did he say about your asthma?"

"He says I an't got no asthma." Rosicky took one of the little rolls in his broad brown fingers. The thickened nail of his right thumb told the story of his past.

"Well, what is the matter? And don't try to put me off."

"He don't say nothing much, only I'm a little older, and my heart ain't so good like it used to be."

Mary started and brushed her hair back from her temples with both hands as if she were a little out of her mind. From the way she glared, she might have been in a rage with him.

"He says there's something the matter with your heart? Doctor Ed says so?"

"Now don't yell at me like I was a hog in de garden, Mary. You know I always did like to hear a woman talk soft. He didn't say anything de matter wid my heart, only it ain't so young like it used to be, an' he tell me not to pitch hay or run de corn-sheller."

Mary wanted to jump up, but she sat still. She admired the way he never under any circumstances raised his voice or spoke roughly. He was city-bred, and she was country-bred; she often said she wanted her boys to have their papa's nice ways.

---

1. **kolache**\ˈkō ˈlach\ a sweet bun filled with jam or fruit pulp.

"You never have no pain there, do you? It's your breathing and your stomach that's been wrong. I wouldn't believe nobody but Doctor Ed about it. I guess I'll go see him myself. Didn't he give you no advice?"

"Chust to take it easy like, an' stay round de house dis winter. I guess you got some carpenter work for me to do. I kin make some new shelves for you, and I want dis long time to build a closet in de boys' room and make dem two little fellers keep dere clo'es hung up."

Rosicky drank his coffee from time to time, while he considered. His moustache was of the soft long variety and came down over his mouth like the teeth of a buggy-rake over a bundle of hay. Each time he put down his cup, he ran his blue handkerchief over his lips. When he took a drink of water, he managed very neatly with the back of his hand.

Mary sat watching him intently, trying to find any change in his face. It is hard to see anyone who has become like your own body to you. Yes, his hair had got thin, and his high forehead had deep lines running from left to right. But his neck, always clean shaved except in the busiest seasons, was not loose or baggy. It was burned a dark reddish brown, and there were deep creases in it, but it looked firm and full of blood. His cheeks had a good colour. On either side of his mouth there was a half-moon down the length of his cheek, not wrinkles, but two lines that had come there from his habitual expression. He was shorter and broader than when she married him; his back had grown broad and curved, a good deal like the shell of an old turtle, and his arms and legs were short.

He was fifteen years older than Mary, but she had hardly ever thought about it before. He was her man, and the kind of man she liked. She was rough, and he was gentle,—city-bred, as she always said. They had been shipmates on a rough voyage and had stood by each other in trying times. Life had gone well with them because, at bottom, they had the same ideas about life. They agreed, without discussion, as to what was most important and what was secondary. They didn't often exchange opinions, even in Czech,—it was as if they had thought the same thought together. A good deal had to be sacrificed and thrown overboard in a hard life like theirs, and they had never disagreed as to the things that could go. It had been a hard life, and a soft life, too. There wasn't anything brutal in the short, broad-backed man with the three-cornered eyes and the forehead that went on to the top of his skull. He was a city man, a gentle man, and though he had married a rough farm girl, he had never touched her without gentleness.

They had been at one accord not to hurry through life, not to be always skimping and saving. They saw their neighbours buy more land and feed more stock than they did, without discontent. Once when the creamery agent came to the Rosickys to persuade them to sell him their cream, he told them how much money the Fasslers, their nearest neighbours, had made on their cream last year.

"Yes," said Mary, "and look at them Fassler children! Pale, pinched little things, they look like skimmed milk. I'd rather put some colour into my children's faces than put money into the bank."

The agent shrugged and turned to Anton.

"I guess we'll do like she says," said Rosicky.

III

Mary very soon got into town to see Doctor Ed, and then she had a talk with her boys and set a guard over Rosicky. Even John, the youngest, had his father on his mind. If Rosicky went to throw hay down from the loft, one of the boys ran up the ladder and took the fork from him. He sometimes complained that though he was getting to be an old man, he wasn't an old woman yet.

That winter he stayed in the house in the afternoons and carpentered, or sat in the chair between the window full of plants and the wooden bench where the two pails of drinking-water stood. This spot was called "Father's corner," though it was not a corner at all. He had a shelf there, where he kept his Bohemian papers and his pipes and tobacco, and his shears and needles and thread and tailor's thimble. Having been a tailor in his youth, he couldn't bear to see a woman patching at his clothes, or at the boys'. He liked tailoring, and always patched all the overalls and jackets and work shirts. Occasionally he made over a pair of pants one of the older boys had outgrown, for the little fellow.

While he sewed, he let his mind run back over his life. He had a good deal to remember, really; life in three countries. The only part of his youth he didn't like to remember was the two years he had spent in London, in Cheapside, working for a German tailor who was wretchedly poor. Those days, when he was nearly always hungry, when his clothes were dropping off him for dirt, and the sound of a strange language kept him in continual bewilderment, had left a sore spot in his mind that wouldn't bear touching.

He was twenty when he landed at Castle Garden in New York, and he had a protector who got him work in a tailor shop in Vesey Street, down near the Washington Market. He looked upon that part of his life as very happy. He became a good workman, he was industrious, and his wages were increased from time to time. He minded his own business and envied nobody's good fortune. He went to night school and learned to read English. He often did overtime work and was well paid for it, but somehow he never saved anything. He couldn't refuse a loan to a friend, and he was self-indulgent. He liked a good dinner, and a little went for beer, a little for tobacco; a good deal went to the girls. He often stood through an opera on Saturday nights; he could get standing-room for a dollar. Those were the great days of opera in New York, and it gave a fellow something to think about for the rest of the week. Rosicky had a quick ear, and a childish love of all the stage splendour; the scenery, the costumes, the ballet. He usually went with a chum, and after the performance they had beer and maybe some oysters somewhere. It was a fine life; for the first five years or so it satisfied him

completely. He was never hungry or cold or dirty, and everything amused him: a fire, a dog fight, a parade, a storm, a ferry ride. He thought New York the finest, richest, friendliest city in the world.

Moreover, he had what he called a happy home life. Very near the tailor shop was a small furniture-factory, where an old Austrian, Loeffler, employed a few skilled men and made unusual furniture, most of it to order, for the rich German housewives up-town. The top floor of Loeffler's five-storey factory was a loft, where he kept his choice lumber and stored the odd pieces of furniture left on his hands. One of the young workmen he employed was a Czech, and he and Rosicky became fast friends. They persuaded Loeffler to let them have a sleeping-room in one corner of the loft. They bought good beds and bedding and had their pick of the furniture kept up there. The loft was low-pitched, but light and airy, full of windows, and good-smelling by reason of the fine lumber put up there to season. Old Loeffler used to go down to the docks and buy wood from South America and the East from the sea captains. The young men were as foolish about their house as a bridal pair. Zichec, the young cabinet-maker, devised every sort of convenience, and Rosicky kept their clothes in order. At night and on Sundays, when the quiver of machinery underneath was still, it was the quietest place in the world, and on summer nights all the sea winds blew in. Zichec often practised on his flute in the evening. They were both fond of music and went to the opera together. Rosicky thought he wanted to live like that for ever.

But as the years passed, all alike, he began to get a little restless. When spring came round, he would begin to feel fretted, and he got to drinking. He was likely to drink too much of a Saturday night. On Sunday he was languid and heavy, getting over his spree. On Monday he plunged into work again. So he never had time to figure out what ailed him, though he knew something did. When the grass turned green in Park Place, and the lilac hedge at the back of Trinity churchyard put out its blossoms, he was tormented by a longing to run away. That was why he drank too much; to get a temporary illusion of freedom and wide horizons.

Rosicky, the old Rosicky, could remember as if it were yesterday the day when the young Rosicky found out what was the matter with him. It was on a Fourth of July afternoon, and he was sitting in Park Place in the sun. The lower part of New York was empty. Wall Street, Liberty Street, Broadway, all empty. So much stone and asphalt with nothing going on, so many empty windows. The emptiness was intense, like the stillness in a great factory when the machinery stops and the belts and bands cease running. It was too great a change, it took all the strength out of one. Those blank buildings, without the stream of life pouring through them, were like empty jails. It struck young Rosicky that this was the trouble with big cities; they built you in from the earth itself, cemented you away from any contact with the ground. You lived in an unnatural world, like the fish in an aquarium, who were probably much more comfortable than they ever were in the sea.

On that very day he began to think seriously about the articles he had read in the Bohemian papers, describing prosperous Czech farming communities in the West. He believed he would like to go out there as a farm hand; it was hardly possible that he could ever have land of his own. His people had always been workmen; his father and grandfather had worked in shops. His mother's parents had lived in the country, but they rented their farm and had a hard time to get along. Nobody in his family had ever owned any land,—that belonged to a different station of life altogether. Anton's mother died when he was little, and he was sent into the country to her parents. He stayed with them until he was twelve, and formed those ties with the earth and the farm animals and growing things which are never made at all unless they are made early. After his grandfather died, he went back to live with his father and stepmother, but she was very

hard on him, and his father helped him to get passage to London.

After that Fourth of July day in Park Place, the desire to return to the country never left him. To work on another man's farm would be all he asked; to see the sun rise and set and to plant things and watch them grow. He was a very simple man. He was like a tree that has not many roots, but one tap-root that goes down deep. He subscribed for a Bohemian paper printed in Chicago, then for one printed in Omaha. His mind got farther and farther west. He began to save a little money to buy his liberty. When he was thirty-five, there was a great meeting in New York of Bohemian athletic societies, and Rosicky left the tailor shop and went home with the Omaha delegates to try his fortune in another part of the world.

IV

Perhaps the fact that his own youth was well over before he began to have a family was one reason why Rosicky was so fond of his boys. He had almost a grandfather's indulgence for them. He had never had to worry about any of them—except, just now, a little about Rudolph.

On Saturday night the boys always piled into the Ford, took little Josephine, and went to town to the moving-picture show. One Saturday morning they were talking at the breakfast table about starting early that evening, so that they would have an hour or so to see the Christmas things in the stores before the show began. Rosicky looked down the table.

"I hope you boys ain't disappointed, but I want you to let me have de car tonight. Maybe some of you can go in with de neighbours."

Their faces fell. They worked hard all week, and they were still like children. A new jack-knife or a box of candy pleased the older ones as much as the little fellow.

"If you and Mother are going to town," Frank said, "maybe you could take a couple of us along with you, anyway."

"No, I want to take de car down to Rudolph's, and let him an' Polly go in to de show.

She don't git into town enough, an' I'm afraid she's gettin' lonesome, an' he can't afford no car yet."

That settled it. The boys were a good deal dashed. Their father took another piece of apple-cake and went on: "Maybe next Saturday night de two little fellers can go along wid dem."

"Oh, is Rudolph going to have the car every Saturday night?"

Rosicky did not reply at once; then he began to speak seriously: "Listen, boys; Polly ain't lookin' so good. I don't like to see nobody lookin' sad. It comes hard fur a town girl to be a farmer's wife. I don't want no trouble to start in Rudolph's family. When it starts, it ain't so easy to stop. An American girl don't git used to our ways all at once. I like to tell Polly she and Rudolph can have the car every Saturday night till after New Year's, if it's all right with you boys."

"Sure it's all right, Papa," Mary cut in. "And it's good you thought about that. Town girls is used to more than country girls. I lay awake nights, scared she'll make Rudolph discontented with the farm."

The boys put as good a face on it as they could. They surely looked forward to their Saturday nights in town. That evening Rosicky drove the car the half-mile down to Rudolph's new, bare little house.

Polly was in a short-sleeved gingham dress, clearing away the supper dishes. She was a trim, slim little thing, with blue eyes and shingled yellow hair, and her eyebrows were reduced to a mere brush-stroke, like Miss Pearl's.

"Good evening, Mr. Rosicky. Rudolph's at the barn, I guess." She never called him father, or Mary mother. She was sensitive about having married a foreigner. She never in the world would have done it if Rudolph hadn't been such a handsome, persuasive fellow and such a gallant lover. He had graduated in her class in the high school in town, and their friendship began in the ninth grade.

Rosicky went in, though he wasn't exactly asked. "My boys ain't goin' to town tonight, an'

I brought de car over fur you two to go in to de picture show."

Polly, carrying dishes to the sink, looked over her shoulder at him. "Thank you. But I'm late with my work tonight, and pretty tired. Maybe Rudolph would like to go in with you."

"Oh, I don't go to de shows! I'm too old-fashioned. You won't feel so tired after you ride in de air a ways. It's a nice clear night, an' it ain't cold. You go an' fix yourself up, Polly, an' I'll wash de dishes an' leave everything nice fur you."

Polly blushed and tossed her bob. "I couldn't let you do that, Mr. Rosicky. I wouldn't think of it."

Rosicky said nothing. He found a bib apron on a nail behind the kitchen door. He slipped it over his head and then took Polly by her two elbows and pushed her gently toward the door of her own room. "I washed up de kitchen many times for my wife, when de babies was sick or somethin'. You go an' make yourself look nice. I like you to look prettier'n any of dem town girls when you go in. De young folks must have some fun, an' I'm goin' to look out fur you, Polly."

That kind, reassuring grip on her elbows, the old man's funny bright eyes, made Polly want to drop her head on his shoulder for a second. She restrained herself, but she lingered in his grasp at the door of her room, murmuring tearfully: "You always lived in the city when you were young, didn't you? Don't you ever get lonesome out here?"

As she turned round to him, her hand fell naturally into his, and he stood holding it and smiling into her face with his peculiar, knowing, indulgent smile without a shadow of reproach in it. "Dem big cities is all right fur de rich, but dey is terrible hard fur de poor."

"I don't know. Sometimes I think I'd like to take a chance. You lived in New York, didn't you?"

"An' London. Da's bigger still. I learned my trade dere. Here's Rudolph comin', you better hurry."

"Will you tell me about London some time?"

"Maybe. Only I ain't no talker, Polly. Run an' dress yourself up."

The bedroom door closed behind her, and Rudolph came in from the outside, looking anxious. He had seen the car and was sorry any of his family should come just then. Supper hadn't been a very pleasant occasion. Halting in the doorway, he saw his father in a kitchen apron, carrying dishes to the sink. He flushed crimson and something flashed in his eye. Rosicky held up a warning finger.

"I brought de car over fur you an' Polly to go to de picture show, an' I made her let me finish here so you won't be late. You go put on a clean shirt, quick!"

"But don't the boys want the car, Father?"

"Not tonight dey don't." Rosicky fumbled under his apron and found his pants pocket. He took out a silver dollar and said in a hurried whisper: "You go an' buy dat girl some ice cream an' candy tonight, like you was courtin'. She's awful good friends wid me."

Rudolph was very short of cash, but he took the money as if it hurt him. There had been a crop failure all over the county. He had more than once been sorry he'd married this year.

In a few minutes the young people came out, looking clean and a little stiff. Rosicky hurried them off, and then he took his own time with the dishes. He scoured the pots and pans and put away the milk and swept the kitchen. He put some coal in the stove and shut off the draughts, so the place would be warm for them when they got home late at night. Then he sat down and had a pipe and listened to the clock tick.

Generally speaking, marrying an American girl was certainly a risk. A Czech should marry a Czech. It was lucky that Polly was the daughter of a poor widow woman; Rudolph was proud, and if she had a prosperous family to throw up at him, they could never make it go. Polly was one of four sisters, and they all worked; one was book-keeper in the bank, one taught music, and Polly and her younger sister had been clerks, like Miss Pearl. All four of them were musical, had pretty voices, and sang in the Methodist choir, which the eldest sister directed.

Polly missed the sociability of a store position. She missed the choir, and the company of her sisters. She didn't dislike housework, but she disliked so much of it. Rosicky was a little anxious about this pair. He was afraid Polly would grow so discontented that Rudy would quit the farm and take a factory job in Omaha. He had worked for a winter up there, two years ago, to get money to marry on. He had done very well, and they would always take him back at the stockyards. But to Rosicky that meant the end of everything for his son. To be a landless man was to be a wage-earner, a slave, all your life; to have nothing, to be nothing.

Rosicky thought he would come over and do a little carpentering for Polly after the New Year. He guessed she needed jollying. Rudolph was a serious sort of chap, serious in love and serious about his work.

Rosicky shook out his pipe and walked home across the fields. Ahead of him the lamplight shone from his kitchen windows. Suppose he were still in a tailor shop on Vesey Street, with a bunch of pale, narrow-chested sons working on machines, all coming home tired and sullen to eat supper in a kitchen that was a parlour also; with another crowded, angry family quarrelling just across the dumb-waiter shaft, and squeaking pulleys at the windows where dirty washings hung on dirty lines above a court full of old brooms and mops and ash-cans. . . .

He stopped by the windmill to look up at the frosty winter stars and draw a long breath before he went inside. That kitchen with the shining windows was dear to him; but the sleeping fields and bright stars and the noble darkness were dearer still.

V

On the day before Christmas the weather set in very cold; no snow, but a bitter, biting wind that whistled and sang over the flat land and lashed one's face like fine wires. There was baking going on in the Rosicky kitchen all day, and Rosicky sat inside, making over a coat that Albert had outgrown into an overcoat for John. Mary had a big red geranium in bloom for Christmas, and a row of Jerusalem cherry trees, full of berries. It was the first year she had ever grown these; Doctor Ed brought her the seeds from Omaha when he went to some medical convention. They reminded Rosicky of plants he had seen in England; and all afternoon, as he stitched, he sat thinking about those two years in London, which his mind usually shrank from even after all this while.

He was a lad of eighteen when he dropped down into London, with no money and no connexions except the address of a cousin who was supposed to be working at confectioner's. When he went to the pastry shop, however, he found that the cousin had gone to America. Anton tramped the streets for several days, sleeping in doorways and on the Embankment, until he was in utter despair. He knew no English, and the sound of the strange language all about him confused him. By chance he met a poor German tailor who had learned his trade in Vienna, and could speak a little Czech. This tailor, Lifschnitz, kept a repair shop in a Cheapside basement, underneath a cobbler. He didn't much need an apprentice, but he was sorry for the boy and took him in for no wages but his keep and what he could pick up. The pickings were supposed to be coppers given you when you took work home to a customer. But most of the customers called for their clothes themselves, and the coppers that came Anton's way were very few. He had, however, a place to sleep. The tailor's family lived upstairs in three rooms; a kitchen, a bedroom, where Lifschnitz and his wife and five children slept, and a living-room. Two corners of this living-room were curtained off for lodgers; in one Rosicky slept on an old horsehair sofa, with a feather quilt to wrap himself in. The other corner was rented to a wretched, dirty boy, who was studying the violin. He actually practised there. Rosicky was dirty, too. There was no way to be anything else. Mrs. Lifschnitz got the water she cooked and washed with from a pump in a brick court, four flights down. There were bugs in the place, and multitudes of fleas, though the poor woman did the best she could. Rosicky knew she often went empty to give another potato or a spoonful of dripping to the two hungry, sad-eyed boys who lodged with her. He used to think he would never get out of there, never get a clean shirt to his back again. What would he do, he wondered, when his clothes actually dropped to pieces and the worn cloth wouldn't hold patches any longer?

It was still early when the old farmer put aside his sewing and his recollections. The sky had been a dark grey all day, with not a gleam of sun, and the light failed at four o'clock. He went to shave and change his shirt while the turkey was roasting. Rudolph and Polly were coming over for supper.

After supper they sat round in the kitchen, and the younger boys were saying how sorry they were it hadn't snowed. Everybody was sorry. They wanted a deep snow that would lie long and keep the wheat warm, and leave the ground soaked when it melted.

"Yes, sir!" Rudolph broke out fiercely; "if we have another dry year like last year, there's going to be hard times in this country."

Rosicky filled his pipe. "You boys don't know what hard times is. You don't owe nobody, you got plenty to eat an' keep warm, an' plenty water to keep clean. When you got them, you can't have it very hard."

Rudolph frowned, opened and shut his big right hand, and dropped it clenched upon his knee. "I've got to have a good deal more than that, Father, or I'll quit this farming gamble. I can always make good wages railroading, or at the packing house, and be sure of my money."

"Maybe so," his father answered dryly.

Mary, who had just come in from the pantry and was wiping her hands on the roller towel, thought Rudy and his father were getting too serious. She brought her darning-basket and sat down in the middle of the group.

"I ain't much afraid of hard times, Rudy," she said heartily. "We've had a plenty, but we've always come through. Your father wouldn't never take nothing very hard, not even hard times. I got a mind to tell you a story on him. Maybe you boys can't hardly remember the year we had that terrible hot wind, that burned everything up on the Fourth of July? All the corn an' the gardens. An' that was in the days when we didn't have alfalfa yet,—I guess it wasn't invented.

"Well, that very day your father was out cultivatin' corn, and I was here in the kitchen makin' plum preserves. We had bushels of plums that year. I noticed it was terrible hot, but it's always hot in the kitchen when you're preservin', an' I was too busy with my plums to mind. Anton come in from the field about three o'clock, an' I asked him what was the matter.

"'Nothin',' he says, 'but it's pretty hot, an' I think I won't work no more today.' He stood round for a few minutes, an' then he says: 'Ain't you near through? I want you should git up a nice supper for us tonight. It's Fourth of July.'

"I told him to git along, that I was right in the middle of preservin', but the plums would taste good on hot biscuit. 'I'm goin' to have fried chicken, too,' he says, and he went off an' killed a couple. You three oldest boys was little fellers, playin' round outside, real hot an' sweaty, an' your father took you to the horse tank down by the windmill an' took off your clothes an' put you in. Them two box-elder trees was little then, but they made shade over the tank. Then he took off all his own clothes, an' got in with you. While he was playin' in the water with you, the Methodist preacher drove into our place to say how all the neighbours was goin' to meet at the schoolhouse that night, to pray for rain. He drove right to the windmill, of course, and there was your father and you three with no clothes on. I was in the kitchen door, an' I had to laugh, for the preacher acted like he ain't never seen a naked man before. He surely was embarrassed, an'

your father couldn't git to his clothes; they was all hangin' up on the windmill to let the sweat dry out of 'em. So he laid in the tank where he was, an' put one of you boys on top of him to cover him up a little, an' talked to the preacher.

"When you got through playin' in the water, he put clean clothes on you and a clean shirt on himself, an' by that time I'd begun to get supper. He says: 'It's too hot in here to eat comfortable. Let's have a picnic in the orchard. We'll eat our supper behind the mulberry hedge, under them linden trees.'

"So he carried our supper down, an' a bottle of my wild-grape wine, an' everything tasted good, I can tell you. The wind got cooler as the sun was goin' down, and it turned out pleasant, only I noticed how the leaves was curled up on the linden trees. That made me think, an' I asked your father if that hot wind all day hadn't been terrible hard on the gardens an' the corn.

"'Corn,' he says, 'there ain't no corn.'

"'What you talkin' about?' I said. 'Ain't we got forty acres?'

"'We ain't got an ear,' he says, 'nor nobody else ain't got none. All the corn in this country was cooked by three o'clock today, like you'd roasted it in an oven.'

"'You mean you won't get no crop at all?' I asked him. I couldn't believe it, after he'd worked so hard.

"'No crop this year,' he says. 'That's why we're havin' a picnic. We might as well enjoy what we got.'

"An' that's how your father behaved, when all the neighbours was so discouraged they couldn't look you in the face. An' we enjoyed ourselves that year, poor as we was, an' our neighbours wasn't a bit better off for bein' miserable. Some of 'em grieved till they got poor digestions and couldn't relish what they did have.

The younger boys said they thought their father had the best of it. But Rudolph was thinking that, all the same, the neighbours had managed to get ahead more, in the fifteen years since that time. There must be something wrong about his father's way of doing things. He wished he knew what was going on in the back of Polly's mind. He knew she liked his father, but he knew, too, that she was afraid of something. When his mother sent over coffee-cake or prune tarts or a loaf of fresh bread, Polly seemed to regard them with a certain suspicion. When she observed to him that his brothers had nice manners, her tone implied that it was remarkable they should have. With his mother she was stiff and on her guard. Mary's hearty frankness and gusts of good humour irritated her. Polly was afraid of being unusual or conspicuous in any way, of being "ordinary," as she said!

When Mary had finished her story, Rosicky laid aside his pipe.

"You boys like me to tell you about some of dem hard times I been through in London?" Warmly encouraged, he sat rubbing his forehead along the deep creases. It was bothersome to tell a long story in English (he nearly always talked to the boys in Czech), but he wanted Polly to hear this one.

"Well, you know about dat tailor shop I worked in in London? I had one Christmas dere I ain't never forgot. Times was awful bad before Christmas; de boss ain't got much work, an' have it awful hard to pay his rent. It ain't so much fun, bein' poor in a big city like London, I'll say! All de windows is full of good t'ings to eat, an' all de pushcarts in de streets is full, an' you smell 'em all de time, an' you ain't got no money,—not a darn bit. I din't mind de cold so much, though I didn't have no overcoat, chust a short jacket I'd outgrowed so it wouldn't meet on me, an' my hands was chapped raw. But I always had a good appetite, like you all know, an' de sight of dem pork pies in de windows was awful fur me!

"Day before Christmas was terrible foggy dat year, an' dat fog gits into your bones and makes you all damp like. Mrs. Lifschnitz didn't give us nothin' but a little bread an' drippin' for supper, because she was savin' to try for to give us a good dinner on Christmas Day. After

supper de boss say I can go an' enjoy myself, so I went into de streets to listen to de Christmas singers. Dey sing old songs an' make very nice music, an' I run round after dem a good ways, till I got awful hungry. I t'ink maybe if I go home, I can sleep till morning an' forget my belly.

"I went into my corner real quiet, and roll up in my fedder quilt. But I ain't got my head down, till I smell somet'ing good. Seem like it git stronger an' stronger, an' I can't git to sleep noway. I can't understand dat smell. Dere was a gas light in a hall across de court, dat always shine in at my window a little. I got up an' look round. I got a little wooden box in my corner fur a stool, 'cause I ain't got no chair. I picks up dat box, and under it dere is a roast goose on a platter! I can't believe my eyes. I carry it to de window where de light comes in, an' touch it and smell it to find out, an' den I taste it to be sure. I say, I will eat chust one little bite of dat goose, so I can go to sleep, and tomorrow I won't eat none at all. But I tell you, boys, when I stop, one half of dat goose was gone!"

The narrator bowed his head, and the boys shouted. But little Josephine slipped behind his chair and kissed him on the neck beneath his ear.

"Poor little Papa, I don't want him to be hungry!"

"Da's long ago, child. I ain't never been hungry since I had your mudder to cook fur me."

"Go on and tell us the rest, please," said Polly.

"Well, when I come to realize what I done, of course, I felt terrible. I felt better in de stomach, but very bad in de heart. I set on my bed wid dat platter on my knees, an' it all come to me; how hard dat poor woman save to buy dat goose, and how she got some neighbour to cook it dat got more fire, an' how she put it in my corner to keep it away from dem hungry children. Dey was an old carpet hung up to shut my corner off, an' de children wasn't allowed to go in dere. An' I know she put it in my corner because she trust me more'n she did de violin boy. I can't stand it to face her after I spoil de Christmas. So I put on my shoes and go out into de city. I tell myself I better throw myself in de river; but I guess I ain't dat kind of a boy.

"It was after twelve o'clock, an' terrible cold, an' I start out to walk about London all night. I walk along de river awhile, but dey was lots of drunks all along; men, and women too. I chust move along to keep away from de police. I git onto de Strand, an' den over to New Oxford Street, where dere was a big German restaurant on de ground floor, wid big windows all fixed up fine, an' I could see de people havin' parties inside. While I was lookin' in, two men and two ladies come out, laughin' and talkin' and feelin' happy about all dey been eatin' an' drinkin', and dey was speakin' Czech, —not like de Austrians, but like de home folks talk it.

"I guess I went crazy, an' I done what I ain't never done before nor since. I went right up to dem gay people an' begun to beg dem: 'Fellow-countrymen, please give me money enough to buy a goose!'

"Dey laugh, of course, but de ladies speak awful kind to me, an' dey take me back into de restaurant and give me hot coffee and cakes, an' make me tell all about how I happened to come to London, an' what I was doin' dere. Dey take my name and where I work down on paper, an' both of dem ladies give me ten shillings.

"De big market at Covent Garden ain't very far away, an' by dat time it was open. I go dere an' buy a big goose an' some pork pies, an' potatoes and onions, an' cakes an' oranges fur de children,—all I could carry! When I git home, everybody is still asleep. I pile all I bought on de kitchen table, an' go in an' lay down on my bed, an' I ain't waken up till I hear dat woman scream when she come out into her kitchen. My goodness, but she was surprise! She laugh an' cry at de same time, an' hug me and waken all de children. She ain't stop fur no breakfast; she git de Christmas dinner ready dat morning, and we all sit down an' eat all we can hold. I ain't never seen dat violin boy have all he can hold before.

"Two three days after dat, de two men come to hunt me up, an' dey ask my boss, and he give me a good report an' tell dem I was a steady boy all right. One of dem Bohemians was very smart an' run a Bohemian newspaper in New York, an' de odder was a rich man, in de importing business, an' dey been travelling togedder. Dey told me how t'ings was easier in New York, an' offered to pay my passage when dey was goin' home soon on a boat. My boss say to me: 'You go. You ain't got no chance here, an' I like to see you git ahead, fur you always been a good boy to my woman, and fur dat fine Christmas dinner you give us all.' An' da's how I got to New York."

That night when Rudolph and Polly, arm in arm, were running home across the fields with the bitter wind at their backs, his heart leaped for joy when she said she thought they might have his family come over for supper on New Year's Eve. "Let's get up a nice supper, and not let your mother help at all; make her be company for once."

"That would be lovely of you, Polly," he said humbly. He was a very simple, modest boy, and he, too, felt vaguely that Polly and her sisters were more experienced and worldly than his people.

VI

The winter turned out badly for farmers. It was bitterly cold, and after the first light snows before Christmas there was no snow at all,— and no rain. March was as bitter as February. On those days when the wind fairly punished the country, Rosicky sat by his window. In the fall he and the boys had put in a big wheat planting, and now the seed had frozen in the ground. All that land would have to be ploughed up and planted over again, planted in corn. It had happened before, but he was younger then, and he never worried about what had to be. He was sure of himself and of Mary; he knew they could bear what they had to bear, that they would always pull through somehow. But he was not so sure about the young ones, and he felt troubled because Rudolph and Polly were having such a hard start.

Sitting beside his flowering window while the panes rattled and the wind blew in under the door, Rosicky gave himself to reflection as he had not done since those Sundays in the loft of the furniture-factory in New York, long ago. Then he was trying to find what he wanted in life for himself; now he was trying to find what he wanted for his boys, and why it was he so hungered to feel sure they would be here, working this very land, after he was gone.

They would have to work hard on the farm, and probably they would never do much more than make a living. But if he could think of them as staying here on the land, he wouldn't have to fear any great unkindness for them. Hardships, certainly; it was a hardship to have the wheat freeze in the ground when seed was so high; and to have to sell your stock because you had no feed. But there would be other years when everything came along right, and you caught up. And what you had was your own. You didn't have to choose between bosses and strikers, and go wrong either way. You didn't have to do with dishonest and cruel people. They were the only things in his experience he had found terrifying and horrible; the look in the eyes of a dishonest and crafty man, of a scheming and rapacious woman.

In the country, if you had a mean neighbour, you could keep off his land and make him keep off yours. But in the city, all the foulness and misery and brutality of your neighbours was part of your life. The worst things he had come upon in his journey through the world were human,—depraved and poisonous specimens of man. To this day he could recall certain terrible faces in the London streets. There were mean people everywhere, to be sure, even in their own country town here. But they weren't tempered, hardened, sharpened, like the treacherous people in cities who live by grinding or cheating or poisoning their fellow-men. He had helped to bury two of his fellow-workmen in the tailoring trade, and he was distrustful of the organized industries that see one

out of the world in big cities. Here, if you were sick, you had Doctor Ed to look after you; and if you died, fat Mr. Haycock, the kindest man in the world, buried you.

It seemed to Rosicky that for good, honest boys like his, the worst they could do on the farm was better than the best they would be likely to do in the city. If he'd had a mean boy, now, one who was crooked and sharp and tried to put anything over on his brothers, then town would be the place for him. But he had no such boy. As for Rudolph, the discontented one, he would give the shirt off his back to anyone who touched his heart. What Rosicky really hoped for his boys was that they could get through the world without ever knowing much about the cruelty of human beings. "Their mother and me ain't prepared them for that," he sometimes said to himself.

These thoughts brought him back to a grateful consideration of his own case. What an escape he had had, to be sure! He, too, in his time, had had to take money for repair work from the hand of a hungry child who let it go so wistfully; because it was money due his boss. And now, in all these years, he had never had to take a cent from anyone in bitter need,—never had to look at the face of a woman become like a wolf's from struggle and famine. When he thought of these things, Rosicky would put on his cap and jacket and slip down to the barn and give his work-horses a little extra oats, letting them eat it out of his hand in their slobbery fashion. It was his way of expressing what he felt, and made him chuckle with pleasure.

The spring came warm, with blue skies,— but dry, dry as a bone. The boys began ploughing up the wheat-fields to plant them over in corn. Rosicky would stand at the fence corner and watch them, and the earth was so dry it blew up in clouds of brown dust that hid the horses and the sulky plough and the driver. It was a bad outlook.

The big alfalfa-field that lay between the home place and Rudolph's came up green, but Rosicky was worried because during that open windy winter a great many Russian thistle plants had blown in there and lodged. He kept asking the boys to rake them out; he was afraid their seed would root and "take the alfalfa." Rudolph said that was nonsense. The boys were working so hard planting corn, their father felt he couldn't insist about the thistles, but he set great store by that big alfalfa field. It was a feed you could depend on,—and there was some deeper reason, vague, but strong. The peculiar green of that clover woke early memories in old Rosicky, went back to something in his childhood in the old world. When he was a little boy, he had played in fields of that strong blue-green colour.

One morning, when Rudolph had gone to town in the car, leaving a work-team idle in his barn, Rosicky went over to his son's place, put the horses to the buggy-rake, and set about quietly raking up those thistles. He behaved with guilty caution, and rather enjoyed stealing a march on Doctor Ed, who was just then taking his first vacation in seven years of practice and was attending a clinic in Chicago. Rosicky got the thistles raked up, but did not stop to burn them. That would take some time, and his breath was pretty short, so he thought he had better get the horses back to the barn.

He got them into the barn and to their stalls, but the pain had come on so sharp in his chest that he didn't try to take the harness off. He started for the house, bending lower with every step. The cramp in his chest was shutting him up like a jack-knife. When he reached the windmill, he swayed and caught at the ladder. He saw Polly coming down the hill, running with the swiftness of a slim greyhound. In a flash she had her shoulder under his armpit.

"Lean on me, Father, hard! Don't be afraid. We can get to the house all right."

Somehow they did, though Rosicky became blind with pain; he could keep on his legs, but he couldn't steer his course. The next thing he was conscious of was lying on Polly's bed, and Polly bending over him wringing out bath towels in hot water and putting them on his chest. She stopped only to throw coal into the stove, and she kept the tea-kettle and the black pot going. She put these hot applications on him for nearly an hour, she told him afterwards, and all that time he was drawn up stiff and blue, with the sweat pouring off him.

As the pain gradually loosed its grip, the stiffness went out of his jaws, the black circles round his eyes disappeared, and a little of his natural colour came back. When his daughter-in-law buttoned his shirt over his chest at last, he sighed.

"Da's fine, de way I feel now, Polly. It was a awful bad spell, an' I was so sorry it all come on you like it did."

Polly was flushed and excited. "Is the pain really gone? Can I leave you long enough to telephone over to your place?"

Rosicky's eyelids fluttered. "Don't telephone, Polly. It ain't no use to scare my wife. It's nice and quiet here, an' if I ain't too much trouble to you, just let me lay still till I feel like myself. I ain't got no pain now. It's nice here."

Polly bent over him and wiped the moisture from his face. "Oh, I'm so glad it's over!" she broke out impulsively. "It just broke my heart to see you suffer so, Father."

Rosicky motioned her to sit down on the chair where the tea-kettle had been, and looked up at her with that lively affectionate gleam in his eyes. "You was awful good to me, I won't never forget dat. I hate it to be sick on you like dis. Down at de barn I say to myself, dat young girl ain't had much experience in sickness, I don't want to scare her, an' maybe she's got a baby comin' or somet'ing."

Polly took his hand. He was looking at her so intently and affectionately and confidingly; his eyes seemed to caress her face, to regard it with pleasure. She frowned with her funny streaks of eyebrows, and then smiled back at him.

"I guess maybe there is something of that kind going to happen. But I haven't told anyone yet, not my mother or Rudolph. You'll be the first to know."

His hand pressed hers. She noticed that it was warm again. The twinkle in his yellow-brown eyes seemed to come nearer.

"I like mighty well to see dat little child,

467

Polly," was all he said. Then he closed his eyes and lay half-smiling. But Polly sat still thinking hard. She had a sudden feeling that nobody in the world, not her mother, not Rudolph, or anyone, really loved her as much as old Rosicky did. It perplexed her. She sat frowning and trying to puzzle it out. It was as if Rosicky had a special gift for loving people, something that was like an ear for music or an eye for colour. It was quiet, unobtrusive; it was merely there. You saw it in his eyes,—perhaps that was why they were merry. You felt it in his hands, too. After he dropped off to sleep, she sat holding his warm, broad, flexible brown hand. She had never seen another in the least like it. She wondered if it wasn't a kind of gypsy hand, it was so alive and quick and light in its communications,—very strange in a farmer. Nearly all the farmers she knew had huge lumps of fists, like mauls, or they were knotty and bony and uncomfortable-looking, with stiff fingers. But Rosicky's was like quicksilver, flexible, muscular, about the colour of a pale cigar, with deep, deep creases across the palm. It wasn't nervous, it wasn't a stupid lump; it was a warm brown human hand, with some cleverness in it, a great deal of generosity, and something else which Polly could only call "gypsy-like,"—something nimble and lively and sure, in the way that animals are.

Polly remembered that hour long afterwards; it had been like an awakening to her. It seemed to her that she had never learned so much about life from anything as from old Rosicky's hand. It brought her to herself; it communicated some direct and untranslatable message.

When she heard Rudolph coming in the car, she ran out to meet him.

"Oh, Rudy, your father's been awful sick! He raked up those thistles he's been worrying about, and afterwards he could hardly get to the house. He suffered so I was afraid he was going to die."

Rudolph jumped to the ground. "Where is he now?"

"On the bed. He's asleep. I was terribly scared, because, you know, I'm so fond of your father." She slipped her arm through his and they went into the house. That afternoon they took Rosicky home and put him to bed, though he protested that he was quite well again.

The next morning he got up and dressed and sat down to breakfast with his family. He told Mary that his coffee tasted better than usual to him, and he warned the boys not to bear any tales to Doctor Ed when he got home. After breakfast he sat down by his window to do some patching and asked Mary to thread several needles for him before she went to feed her chickens,—her eyes were better than his, and her hands steadier. He lit his pipe and took up John's overalls. Mary had been watching him anxiously all morning, and as she went out of the door with her bucket of scraps, she saw that he was smiling. He was thinking, indeed, about Polly, and how he might never have known what a tender heart she had if he hadn't got sick over there. Girls nowadays didn't wear their heart on their sleeve. But now he knew Polly would make a fine woman after the foolishness wore off. Either a woman had that sweetness at her heart or she hadn't. You couldn't always tell by the look of them; but if they had that, everything came out right in the end.

After he had taken a few stitches, the cramp began in his chest, like yesterday. He put his pipe cautiously down on the window-sill and bent over to ease the pull. No use,—he had better try to get to his bed if he could. He rose and groped his way across the familiar floor, which was rising and falling like the deck of a ship. At the door he fell. When Mary came in, she found him lying there, and the moment she touched him she knew that he was gone.

Doctor Ed was away when Rosicky died, and for the first few weeks after he got home he was hard driven. Every day he said to himself that he must get out to see that family that had lost their father. One soft, warm moonlight night in early summer he started for the farm. His mind was on other things, and not until his road ran by the graveyard did he realize that Rosicky wasn't over there on the hill where the red lamplight shone, but here, in the moonlight. He stopped his car, shut off the engine, and sat there for a while.

A sudden hush had fallen on his soul. Everything here seemed strangely moving and significant, though signifying what, he did not know. Close by the wire fence stood Rosicky's mowing-machine, where one of the boys had been cutting hay that afternoon; his own workhorses had been going up and down there. The new-cut hay perfumed all the night air. The moonlight silvered the long, billowy grass that grew over the graves and hid the fence; the few little evergreens stood out black in it, like shadows in a pool. The sky was very blue and soft, the stars rather faint because the moon was full.

For the first time it struck Doctor Ed that this was really a beautiful graveyard. He thought of city cemeteries; acres of shrubbery and heavy stone, so arranged and lonely and unlike anything in the living world. Cities of the dead, indeed; cities of the forgotten, of the "put away." But this was open and free, this little square of long grass which the wind forever stirred. Nothing but the sky overhead, and the many-coloured fields running on until they met that sky. The horses worked here in summer; the neighbours passed on their way to town; and over yonder, in the cornfield, Rosick's own cattle would be eating fodder as winter came on. Nothing could be more undeathlike than this place; nothing could be more right for a man who had helped to do the work of great cities and had always longed for the open country and had got to it at last. Rosicky's life seemed to him complete and beautiful.

I
THE GOOD HEART

Although the story of Anton Rosicky opens ironically with the news that he has a "bad" heart, the reader soon comes to realize that his physical affliction in no way impairs his "special gift for loving people"—his good heart. Contrary to Harvey Merrick who fled the prairies to find truth, culture, and freedom, Rosicky, after searching long, sought the prairies because they were open and free. Here, close to nature, his Old World sensitivity and gentleness find their fullest expressions in the simple folk virtues of this last frontier. If Anton Rosicky's sincerity, compassion, and charity differ from the savagery of Sand City, it is not only because his life in the cities helps him appreciate the cleanness and beauty of the countryside but especially because he comes to it and life with the "good heart"—eager to love, to give of himself.

II
IMPLICATIONS

In your opinion, how true are the following statements from the story:

1. Maybe, Doctor Burleigh reflected, people as generous and warm-hearted and affectionate as the Rosickys never got ahead much; maybe you couldn't enjoy your life and put it into the bank, too.

2. To be a landless man was to be a wage-earner, a slave, all your life; to have nothing, to be nothing.

3. Rosicky: "No crop this year. . . . We might as well enjoy what we got."

III
TECHNIQUES

Conflict and Climax

Like Rosicky and his wife, this story is resolved "not to hurry through life." Nor does it have a strong central conflict that runs from beginning to end. It is basically, as its title shows, another kind of story—a character sketch. It would be unreasonable to require that such a story be action-packed.

Yet the story does begin with a tension, an instability; and it does not end until that tension is relaxed. Can you describe that tension and follow it from inception to climax? Can you also find a subplot with a conflict and climax of its own?

Moment of Illumination

Why is the perception that Rosicky's life was "complete and beautiful" more appropriately given to the doctor than to Rosicky himself or a member of his family?

ROBERT FROST

1874–1963

For Frost, poetry was very much a game he played with the world and his readers. The seriousness of the game did not detract from its fun nor from his joy in performance. He had, as he said, "a lover's quarrel with the world," and it was the peculiar nature of his genius that he could combine traditional forms, homely subjects, and serious insights with a perceptive sense of humor and wit.

When President Kennedy in 1961 decided to include a poet in his Inaugural Day ceremonies, it was natural for him to choose Robert Frost, a fellow-New Englander and the dean of American poets. Frost published his first volume, *A Boy's Will,* in 1913, his last, *In the Clearing,* in 1962. Four times he won the Pulitzer Prize. His verse was known wherever English poetry was read. Yet Robert Frost was never one to forget that he was forty years old before his genius was recognized, that his early life was filled with hardship and disappointment.

Although Frost will always be celebrated as a New England poet, he was actually born in San Francisco, in 1874. His father had left Maine and hastened to the West Coast because he hated New England. The poet and his younger sister, Jeanie, might have spent their whole lives on the Pacific Coast had their father not died early of tuberculosis, leaving the strange request that he be buried in the New England he had loathed. After the trip east, the widow and her children settled in Salem, New

Hampshire, and later in Lawrence, Massachusetts. Following graduation from Lawrence High School, Frost enrolled in Dartmouth College, but he stayed less than a year.

Until his marriage to Elinor White in 1895, Frost drifted from one job to another: mill work in Lawrence, school teaching, newspaper reporting. After marriage he spent two years teaching in his mother's small private school, then two years at Harvard College, hoping to prepare for a career as a college instructor. Although he enjoyed the classics and philosophy, he revolted against academic discipline. Because of his poor health, he had to live in the country; so he and his growing family tried farming and chicken raising in Derry, New Hampshire. Five years of near failure as a farmer sent him back to school teaching in Derry, and then in Plymouth; but he disliked teaching as much as tilling the stubborn New Hampshire soil. Since the day he sold his first poem, in 1894, he knew poetry should be his profession, indeed his whole life. In 1912, he took the gamble. Unable to find a publisher for his poetry, he sold his farm and packed off his wife and four children to Buckinghamshire, England, where living was cheaper and poetry had a larger audience. The decision was one of the wisest he ever made. *A Boy's Will* was issued by an English publisher in 1913 and was followed the next year by *North of Boston*. When Frost returned to the United States in 1915, his reputation was made; both books had been republished here. He bought a farm in Franconia, New Hampshire, with the hope of settling down to write the best poetry he could and to avoid the literary marketplace.

He succeeded in doing both. The National Institute of Arts and Letters elected him to membership in 1916. Amherst College offered him a professorship in English. Invitations to lecture and to give public readings came from all parts of the country. For the next forty-five years he was to become, almost against his will, a teacher-at-large. Though he was a splendid teacher and held audiences entranced by reading his own poetry, he also wished to remain close to the land. After his wife's death in 1938, he moved to the hills of Ripton, Vermont. To see Frost at home in Ripton was to see the poet next to his source, finally free from the enervating labor of cultivating the land for a living but still lovingly tied to the woodlands of Vermont where he could know "the line where man leaves off and nature starts."

There is a risk, of course, in thinking of Frost as only a New England poet and periodic visitor to college campuses. His friend and fellow-poet John Ciardi has warned us not to think of Frost as "a kindly, vague, white-haired great-grandfather" who just tells pleasant little stories in verse. Frost was a New Englander but not a mere recorder of regional folkways. He wrote of Vermont because he knew it best, but his subject was always the perils of the human condition. "It is the man we lose," Ciardi wrote after Frost's death, "a man salty and rough with the earth trace, and though towering above it, never removed from it, a man above all who could tower precisely because he was rooted in real earth." Naturally he put his characters in rural settings: small boys in deep woods, young married couples, transient farm workers, lumberjacks, gum-gatherers, just as John Steinbeck chose to write of his native California and William Faulkner of Oxford, Mississippi. But like the good teacher he was, Frost was always intent on expanding his subject or, rather, on urging his reader to expand his subject along with him, to discover that essentially New England mirrored the world.

If on occasion Frost's poems seem to be about little things in simple words—a burned house, apple-picking, birch trees, ax handles, a west-running brook, stone walls, a drumlin woodchuck—it takes only a second reading to catch the hints Frost drops along the way that there is a deceptively simple surface poem here and a vital below-the-surface meaning. Frost quite clearly used the objects of the farm world as symbols of a deeper meaning, as a way of moving from the concrete world to abstract ideas.

471

For him a poem "begins in delight and ends in wisdom."

The delights of "Nothing Gold Can Stay" are obvious at first reading. Seven of its eight lines are clear and direct observation of nature:

> Nature's first green is gold,
> Her hardest hue to hold.
> Her earthly leaf's a flower;
> But only so an hour.
> Then leaf subsides to leaf.
> So Eden sank to grief.
> So dawn goes down to day.
> Nothing gold can stay.

The opening line may sound like a paradox, a self-contradictory statement, but our own memory of spring reinforces the poet's image: the yellow weeping willows, the first trees to bud. And he reminds us that as yellow turns to green, so flower turns to leaf, and leaves will fall. Growth and decay are natural. No one can hold that "ecstasy should be static and stand still in one place," as Frost says on another occasion. Even the golden sunrise must turn to the harsher light of day.

But the chief pleasure of poetry, as the careful reader will discover, is moving from the surface delight of local details to the wisdom of suggested meanings. Frost need plant only two words in this poem to suggest ulterior, or hidden, latent meanings: Eden and grief. With line six, the poem expands to include human nature. *Our* hardest hue to hold is innocence; our paradise, once golden, turned to grief. And as we reread the last line of the poem, our imagination seizes the word gold. In terms of the visual images—dawn's light and earth's first green—Frost is suggesting the abstract idea of loss. The verbs—subsides, sank, goes down—lead toward a double or triple meaning of gold,

but the poet stops short of equating. The art is the implication. He is not telling us; he is only suggesting. "Poems can be pressed too hard for meaning," he warns us, yet at the same time our imagination plays with the hints he has given. In human terms, does gold mean innocence, or love, or perhaps life? Or all three? Delight will lead to wisdom if we allow it.

One of the reasons for Frost's popularity as a poet was that he stayed close to traditional forms: the sonnet, blank verse, the dramatic monologue, the simple lyric. He was not afraid of rhyme; he found the couplet and the quatrain a challenge, not a confinement. And like Shakespeare, he knew how to contain natural speech rhythms in blank verse. Writing free verse—poetry with rhythm but without meter and regular rhyme scheme—he likened to playing tennis with the net down. "To the right person," he wrote, "it must seem naive to distort form as such. The very words of the dictionary are a restriction to make the best of or stay out of and be silent. Coining new words isn't encouraged. We play the words as we find them. We make them do."

For Frost, poetry was very much a game he played both with the world and with his readers. The seriousness of the game did not detract from its fun nor from his joy in performance. He had, as he said, "a lover's quarrel with the world," and it was the peculiar nature of his genius that he could combine traditional forms, homely subjects, and serious insights with a perceptive sense of humor and wit. He once offered this sly warning to those about to read his verse:

> It takes all kinds of in and outdoor schooling
> To get adapted to my kind of fooling.

From THE POETRY OF ROBERT FROST, edited by Edward Connery Lathem. Copyright 1916, 1923, 1930, 1939, © 1969 by Holt, Rinehart and Winston, Inc. Copyright 1936, 1940, 1942, 1944, 1951, © 1958 by Robert Frost. Copyright © 1964, 1967, 1968, 1970 by Lesley Frost Ballantine. Reprinted by permission of Holt, Rinehart and Winston, Inc.

The World of Nature

One of Frost's perennial subjects is rural New England,
the land he knew so well and loved. Although these three poems
are widely separated in time of composition ("Birches" appeared in 1916,
"Our Hold on the Planet" in 1942), they attest to the continuing attraction
nature's laws held for him. Frost always remains cautious,
or at least modest, in talking of the relationship of humans to the natural forces,
but that does not keep him from being forever curious.

Dust of Snow

The way a crow
Shook down on me
The dust of snow
From a hemlock tree

Has given my heart
A change of mood
And saved some part
Of a day I had rued.

Our Hold on the Planet

We asked for rain. It didn't flash and roar.
It didn't lose its temper at our demand
And blow a gale. It didn't misunderstand
And give us more than our spokesman bargained for;
And just because we owned to a wish for rain,   5
Send us a flood and bid us be damned and drown.
It gently threw us a glittering shower down.
And when we had taken that into the roots of grain,
It threw us another and then another still
Till the spongy soil again was natal[1] wet.   10
We may doubt the just proportion of good to ill.
There is much in nature against us. But we forget:
Take nature altogether since time began,
Including human nature, in peace and war,
And it must be a little more in favor of man,   15
Say a fraction of one per cent at the very least,
Or our number living wouldn't be steadily more,
Our hold on the planet wouldn't have so increased.

From THE POETRY OF ROBERT FROST,
edited by Edward Connery Lathem. Copyright
1916, 1923, 1930, 1939, © 1969 by Holt, Rinehart and Winston, Inc. Copyright 1936, 1940,
1942, 1944, 1951, © 1958 by Robert Frost.
Copyright © 1964, 1967, 1968, 1970 by Lesley
Frost Ballantine. Reprinted by permission of Holt,
Rinehart and Winston, Inc.

1. **natal**\ˈnā·təl\ **wet**, as at birth; here, wet as on the
third day of Creation when the waters were gathered
together in one place and dry land appeared. Genesis
1:9.

Birches

When I see birches bend to left and right
Across the lines of straighter darker trees,
I like to think some boy's been swinging them.
But swinging doesn't bend them down to stay
As ice storms do. Often you must have seen them   5
Loaded with ice a sunny winter morning
After a rain. They click upon themselves
As the breeze rises, and turn many-colored
As the stir cracks and crazes[1] their enamel.
Soon the sun's warmth makes them shed crystal shells   10
Shattering and avalanching on the snow crust—
Such heaps of broken glass to sweep away
You'd think the inner dome of heaven had fallen.
They are dragged to the withered bracken[2] by the load,
And they seem not to break; though once they are bowed   15
So low for long, they never right themselves:
You may see their trunks arching in the woods
Years afterwards, trailing their leaves on the ground
Like girls on hands and knees that throw their hair
Before them over their heads to dry in the sun.   20
But I was going to say when Truth broke in
With all her matter of fact about the ice storm,
I should prefer to have some boy bend them
As he went out and in to fetch the cows—
Some boy too far from town to learn baseball,   25
Whose only play was what he found himself,
Summer or winter, and could play alone.
One by one he subdued his father's trees
By riding them down over and over again
Until he took the stiffness out of them,   30
And not one but hung limp, not one was left
For him to conquer. He learned all there was
To learn about not launching out too soon
And so not carrying the tree away
Clear to the ground. He always kept his poise   35
To the top branches, climbing carefully
With the same pains you use to fill a cup
Up to the brim, and even above the brim.
Then he flung outward, feet first, with a swish,
Kicking his way down through the air to the ground.   40
So was I once myself a swinger of birches.
And so I dream of going back to be.
It's when I'm weary of considerations,

From THE POETRY OF ROBERT FROST, edited by Edward Connery Lathem. Copyright 1916, 1923, 1930, 1939, © 1968 by Holt, Rinehart and Winston, Inc. Copyright 1936, 1940, 1942, 1944, 1951, © 1958 by Robert Frost. Copyright © 1964, 1967, 1968, 1970 by Lesley Frost Ballantine. Reprinted by permission of Holt, Rinehart and Winston, Inc.

1. **crazes**\ˈkrā·zəz\ makes small cracks in the surface of "enamel."
2. **bracken**\ˈbră·kən\ large ferns.

And life is too much like a pathless wood
Where your face burns and tickles with the cobwebs   45
Broken across it, and one eye is weeping
From a twig's having lashed across it open.
I'd like to get away from earth awhile
And then come back to it and begin over.
May no fate willfully misunderstand me   50
And half grant what I wish and snatch me away
Not to return. Earth's the right place for love:
I don't know where it's likely to go better.
I'd like to go by climbing a birch tree,
And climb black branches up a snow-white trunk   55
Toward heaven, till the tree could bear no more,
But dipped its top and and set me down again.
That would be good both going and coming back.
One could do worse than be a swinger of birches.

I
NEW ENGLAND ROOTS

Though Frost's poetry is made up of observations on his New England countryside—snow, birches, rain—his real subject is human nature. His poems talk of simple things in simple words, but these simple objects become symbols leading to deeper meanings. Neither a nature poet nor a lyricist, he sees in the birch trees and hemlocks of New England something that belongs to each person everywhere: joy, doubts, horror. Frost uses New England as a means of revealing what is universal, not merely local. He accomplishes this so well because he accepts the premise that human nature is purest and most understandable when closest to nature. Here, above all, he realizes how narrowly limited is his capacity for changing the world.

Dust of Snow

1. Frost originally titled this poem "A Favor." What relation between nature and humanity does this indicate?

2. This simple one-sentence poem leaves many things unsaid. The poet does not tell us what made him rue the day. He leads us to consider why he changed his mood. Why do you think he did?

Our Hold on the Planet

1. To whom is Frost referring by the pronoun "it" in the first line of this poem? How does this first line set up the basic contrast in the poem?

2. Granting that the poem deals with "our hold on the planet" and is rather philosophical in nature, how does the asking for rain which opens the poem relate to the broader, philosophical consideration?

Birches

1. How does the poet make the birch tree an appropriate symbol for a human dilemma: the desire both to escape the earth and to return to it?

2. Why does Frost describe the digression (lines 5–16) by saying "when Truth broke in with all her matter-of-fact"? What is Truth opposed to here?

3. How is life a "pathless wood" as Frost suggests? What further meaning can you read into "cobwebs" and "twigs that lash the eye"?

II
IMPLICATIONS

Discuss the following statements.

1. Nature helps us to come to grips with ultimate problems of choice.

2. We should not complacently accept only what nature is willing to give.

3. Every person must basically be either an optimist or a pessimist.

The World of Work

Because he lived so close to the soil, Frost understood early
in life that the farmer's code is not the city worker's code. Whether Frost is
splitting wood, picking apples, or sharpening knives, he speaks
"from within," from a deep understanding of how country living affects
human behavior. But in each of these poems, the poet sees beyond the job
at hand. At the same time he is talking about tramps and grindstones,
he is enlarging his subject to a consideration of friendship,
independence, cooperation, and other universal, abstract ideas.

Two Tramps in Mud Time

Out of the mud two strangers came
And caught me splitting wood in the yard.
And one of them put me off my aim
By hailing cheerily "Hit them hard!"
I knew pretty well why he dropped behind   5
And let the other go on a way.
I knew pretty well what he had in mind:
He wanted to take my job for pay.

Good blocks of oak it was I split,
As large around as the chopping block;   10
And every piece I squarely hit
Fell splinterless as a cloven rock.
The blows that a life of self-control
Spares to strike for the common good,
That day, giving a loose to my soul,   15
I spent on the unimportant wood.

The sun was warm but the wind was chill.
You know how it is with an April day
When the sun is out and the wind is still,
You're one month on in the middle of May.   20
But if you so much as dare to speak,
A cloud comes over the sunlit arch,
A wind comes off a frozen peak,
And you're two months back in the middle of March.

A bluebird comes tenderly up to alight   25
And turns to the wind to unruffle a plume,
His song so pitched as not to excite
A single flower as yet to bloom.
It is snowing a flake: and he half knew
Winter was only playing possum.   30

From THE POETRY OF ROBERT FROST,
edited by Edward Connery Lathem. Copyright 1916, 1923, 1930, 1939, © 1969 by
Holt, Rinehart and Winston, Inc. Copyright
1936, 1940, 1942, 1944, 1951, © 1958 by
Robert Frost. Copyright © 1964, 1967, 1968,
1970 by Lesley Frost Ballantine. Reprinted
by permission of Holt, Rinehart and Winston,
Inc.

Except in color he isn't blue,
But he wouldn't advise a thing to blossom.

The water for which we may have to look
In summertime with a witching-wand,[1]
In every wheelrut's now a brook,   35
In every print of a hoof a pond.
Be glad of water, but don't forget
The lurking frost in the earth beneath
That will steal forth after the sun is set
And show on the water its crystal teeth.   40

The time when most I loved my task
These two must make me love it more
By coming with what they came to ask.
You'd think I never had felt before
The weight of an ax-head poised aloft,   45
The grip on earth of outspread feet,
The life of muscles rocking soft
And smooth and moist in vernal[2] heat.

Out of the woods two hulking tramps
(From sleeping God knows where last night,   50
But not long since in the lumber camps).
They thought all chopping was theirs of right.
Men of the woods and lumberjacks,
They judged me by their appropriate tool.
Except as a fellow handled an ax   55
They had no way of knowing a fool.

Nothing on either side was said.
They knew they had but to stay their stay
And all their logic would fill my head:
As that I had no right to play   60
With what was another man's work for gain.
My right might be love but theirs was need.
And where the two exist in twain
Theirs was the better right—agreed.

But yield who will to their separation,   65
My object in living is to unite
My avocation and my vocation
As my two eyes make one in sight.
Only where love and need are one,
And the work is play for mortal stakes,   70
Is the deed ever really done
For Heaven and the future's sakes.

1. **witching-wand,** a forked hazel branch which it is believed will in the hands of certain persons turn downward when an underground water course is crossed.
2. **vernal**\ˈvər·nəl\ springtime.

After
Apple-Picking

My long two-pointed ladder's sticking through a tree
Toward heaven still,
And there's a barrel that I didn't fill
Beside it, and there may be two or three
Apples I didn't pick upon some bough.   5
But I am done with apple-picking now.
Essence of winter sleep is on the night,
The scent of apples: I am drowsing off.
I cannot rub the strangeness from my sight
I got from looking through a pane of glass   10
I skimmed this morning from the drinking trough
And held against the world of hoary grass.
It melted, and I let it fall and break.
But I was well
Upon my way to sleep before it fell,   15
And I could tell
What form my dreaming was about to take.
Magnified apples appear and disappear,
Stem end and blossom end,
And every fleck of russet[1] showing clear.   20
My instep arch not only keeps the ache,
It keeps the pressure of a ladder-round.
I feel the ladder sway as the boughs bend.
And I keep hearing from the cellar bin
The rumbling sound   25
Of load on load of apples coming in.
For I have had too much
Of apple-picking: I am overtired
Of the great harvest I myself desired.
There were ten thousand thousand fruit to touch,   30
Cherish in hand, lift down, and not let fall.
For all
That struck the earth,
No matter if not bruised or spiked with stubble,
Went surely to the cider-apple heap   35
As of no worth.
One can see what will trouble
This sleep of mine, whatever sleep it is.
Were he not gone,
The woodchuck[2] could say whether it's like his   40
Long sleep, as I describe its coming on,
Or just some human sleep.

From THE POETRY OF ROBERT FROST,
edited by Edward Connery Lathem. Copyright
1916, 1923, 1930, 1939, © 1969 by Holt,
Rinehart and Winston, Inc. Copyright 1936,
1940, 1942, 1944, 1951, © 1958 by Robert
Frost. Copyright © 1964, 1967, 1968, 1970 by
Lesley Frost Ballantine. Reprinted by permission of Holt, Rinehart and Winston, Inc.

1. **russet**\ˈrə·sət\ reddish brown.
2. **woodchuck**\ˈwʊd·chək\ the ground hog, a marmot
or rodent with a stout body. It burrows in the ground
and hibernates in the winter.

The Grindstone

Having a wheel and four legs of its own
Has never availed the cumbersome grindstone
To get it anywhere that I can see.
These hands have helped it go, and even race;
Not all the motion, though, they ever lent,   5
Not all the miles it may have thought it went,
Have got it one step from the starting place.
It stands beside the same old apple tree.
The shadow of the apple tree is thin
Upon it now, its feet are fast in snow.   10
All other farm machinery's gone in,
And some of it on no more legs and wheel
Than the grindstone can boast to stand or go.
(I'm thinking chiefly of the wheelbarrow.)
For months it hasn't known the taste of steel   15
Washed down with rusty water in a tin.
But standing outdoors hungry, in the cold,
Except in towns at night, is not a sin.
And, anyway, its standing in the yard
Under a ruinous live apple tree   20
Has nothing any more to do with me,
Except that I remember how of old
One summer day, all day I drove it hard,
And someone mounted on it rode it hard,
And he and I between us ground a blade.   25

I gave it the preliminary spin,
And poured on water (tears it might have been);
And when it almost gayly jumped and flowed,
A Father-Time-like man got on and rode,
Armed with a scythe and spectacles that glowed.   30
He turned on will-power to increase the load
And slow me down—and I abruptly slowed,
Like coming to a sudden railroad station.
I changed from hand to hand in desperation.
I wondered what machine of ages gone   35
This represented an improvement on.
For all I knew it may have sharpened spears

From THE POETRY OF ROBERT FROST, edited by Edward Connery Lathem. Copyright 1916, 1923, 1930, 1939, © 1969 by Holt,
Rinehart and Winston, Inc. Copyright 1936, 1940, 1942, 1944,
1951, © 1958 by Robert Frost. Copyright © 1964, 1967, 1968,
1970 by Lesley Frost Ballantine. Reprinted by permission of
Holt, Rinehart and Winston, Inc.

And arrowheads itself. Much use for years
Had gradually worn it an oblate
Spheroid[1] that kicked and struggled in its gait,   40
Appearing to return me hate for hate
(But I forgive it now as easily
As any other boyhood enemy
Whose pride has failed to get him anywhere).
I wondered who it was the man thought ground—   45
The one who held the wheel back or the one
Who gave his life to keep it going round?
I wondered if he really thought it fair
For him to have the say when we were done.
Such were the bitter thoughts to which I turned.   50

Not for myself was I so much concerned.
Oh no!—although, of course, I could have found
A better way to pass the afternoon
Than grinding discord out of a grindstone,
And beating insects at their gritty tune.   55
Nor was I for the man so much concerned.
Once when the grindstone almost jumped its bearing
It looked as if he might be badly thrown
And wounded on his blade. So far from caring,
I laughed inside, and only cranked the faster   60
(It ran as if it wasn't greased but glued);
I'd welcome any moderate disaster
That might be calculated to postpone
What evidently nothing could conclude.
The thing that made me more and more afraid   65
Was that we'd ground it sharp and hadn't known,
And now were only wasting precious blade.
And when he raised it dripping once and tried
The creepy edge of it with wary touch,
And viewed it over his glasses funny-eyed,   70
Only disinterestedly to decide
It needed a turn more, I could have cried
Wasn't there danger of a turn too much?
Mightn't we make it worse instead of better?
I was for leaving something to the whetter.[2]   75
What if it wasn't all it should be? I'd
Be satisfied if he'd be satisfied.

---

1. **oblate** \ˈŏb·lāt\ **spheroid** \ˈsfĭ·roid\ a sphere flattened by rotation; here, a circle so flattened.
2. **whetter** \ˈhwĕ·tər\ the person who sharpened the
scythe by turning the wheel of the grindstone.

I

THE DIGNITY OF LABOR

One of Frost's major themes is the sheer joy of work. We fulfill ourselves in labor. Frost's preference for rural New England comes from a deep-rooted sense of the refreshment we gain from working close to the earth. The city shields us from nature and from the sense of creating with our own hands. Frost's poetry represents a return to a pastoral life, a revival of the dignity of manual labor. His rural viewpoint helps us see all the virtues we have lost in a mechanized, "departmental" world. His poetry gives us experiences that renew our conviction that in the aching strain of labor, done with love, we fulfill our being.

Two Tramps in Mud Time

1. Is this poem about the two anonymous tramps or about the poet who is speaking?

2. Lines 9 to 40 deal with the experience of spring on an April day. How does this fit into the poem? Why is mud time the appropriate season?

3. Why are the tramps never given work? When is work "play for mortal stakes"?

4. We must always make difficult choices. Why does the poet here make his choice?

After Apple-Picking

1. What are the most striking images or sensations that the poet uses to convey to us the dream world his drowsy laborer is entering?

2. How do lines 9 to 17, in which the "pane of glass" is a metaphor for ice, give the first impressions of drowsiness? Judging by your own experience, why are the strange and illogical details a precise and accurate description of the first entry into the world of dreams?

3. What can you tell about the character of the speaker? What is his present attitude toward his work? Does he have a sense of humor? Why would he like to discuss sleep with the woodchuck?

4. What different meanings does Frost use for the word "sleep" in this poem? If at times it means death, what are the virtues in not "speaking straight out," as Frost calls it?

5. "After Apple-Picking" is a poem about obligations unmet, tasks left unfinished, and duties forsaken. How is this meaning carried through the poem?

6. Why is the rhyme scheme of this poem irregular?

The Grindstone

1. Frost called "The Grindstone" one of his favorite poems and a symbol of the world. What kind of personality does Frost ascribe to the grindstone? Is it proud, indifferent, menacing? How does Frost make the grindstone a symbol of something ancient and evil?

2. What different aspects of creativity does each worker represent? What is Frost saying about the world of work through the relationship of these two people?

3. What do the last lines tell us of the speaker's fears of perfection? Why is he for "leaving something to the whetter"?

4. Could the blade be either an instrument of good or of evil, just like the act of creation? Why is this point left deliberately vague?

5. The speaker is a person of both good humor and scorn, resignation and protest. How does the poet show us this?

II

IMPLICATIONS

Discuss the following statements.

1. In Frost's poetry, the life of the imagination and the humble business of earning a living come together to the enrichment of both.

2. We must protect the right to choose our own work and our own play because they tie together our loves and needs.

3. The dream world in "After Apple-Picking" carries over both the fatigue and the satisfactions of the day. It is not a nightmare world, but one in which work brings fulfillment.

4. Reward and labor should not be separate, but the reward should come from labor well-performed.

5. "The Grindstone" gives us the historic sense of the aching strain we must exert to make nature subject to our own demands.

6. Human beings cannot create except in terms of some unattainable ideal.

The World of Society

The nature of human behaviour and human society
are two subjects Frost pursued all his life. In the first poem,
Frost's delightful sense of humor urges him to talk about human life in relation
to the insect world. How do we compare to the lesser animals?
Are our codes of behavior naturally superior?
The second of these poems raises issues which touch every one of us:
private property and common property, rights and responsibilities.

Departmental

An ant on the tablecloth
Ran into a dormant[1] moth
Of many times his size.
He showed not the least surprise.
His business wasn't with such.   5
He gave it scarcely a touch,
And was off on his duty run.
Yet if he encountered one
Of the hive's enquiry squad
Whose work is to find out God   10
And the nature of time and space,
He would put him onto the case.
Ants are a curious race;
One crossing with hurried tread
The body of one of their dead   15
Isn't given a moment's arrest—
Seems not even impressed.
But he no doubt reports to any
With whom he crosses antennae,
And they no doubt report   20
To the higher up at court.
Then word goes forth in Formic:[2]
"Death's come to Jerry McCormic,
Our selfless forager[3] Jerry.
Will the special Janizary[4]   25

Whose office it is to bury
The dead of the commissary[5]
Go bring him home to his people.
Lay him in state on a sepal.[6]
Wrap him for shroud in a petal.   30
Embalm him with ichor[7] of nettle.
This is the word of your Queen,"
And presently on the scene
Appears a solemn mortician;
And taking formal position   35
With feelers calmly atwiddle,
Seizes the dead by the middle,
And heaving him high in air,
Carries him out of there.
No one stands round to stare.   40
It is nobody else's affair.

It couldn't be called ungentle.
But how thoroughly departmental.

---

1. **dormant**\ˈdȯr·mənt\ sleeping.
2. **Formic**\ˈfȯr·mĭk\ here, the language of ants. Ants secrete formic acid used in dyeing and finishing textiles.
3. **selfless forager,** an unselfish seeker of provisions for all.
4. **Janizary**\ˈjă·nə·zĕ·rē\ also spelled Janissary. Here, the special service ant who buries the dead. The Janizary was an elite corps of Turkish troops organized in the fourteenth century.
5. **commissary,** a store for equipment and provisions.
6. **sepal**\ˈsē·pəl\ one of the modified leaves of a flower which surround the lower part of a blossom.
7. **ichor**\ˈī·kər\ in Greek myth, the fluid that flowed through the veins of the gods.

From THE POETRY OF ROBERT FROST, edited by Edward Connery Lathem. Copyright 1916, 1923, 1930, 1939, © 1969 by Holt, Rinehart and Winston, Inc. Copyright 1936, 1940, 1942, 1944, 1951, © 1958 by Robert Frost. Copyright © 1964, 1967, 1968, 1970 by Lesley Frost Ballantine. Reprinted by permission of Holt, Rinehart and Winston, Inc.

Mending Wall

Something there is that doesn't love a wall,
That sends the frozen-ground-swell under it
And spills the upper boulders in the sun,
And makes gaps even two can pass abreast.
The work of hunters is another thing: 5
I have come after them and made repair
Where they have left not one stone on a stone,
But they would have the rabbit out of hiding,
To please the yelping dogs. The gaps I mean,
No one has seen them made or heard them made,   10
But at spring mending-time we find them there.
I let my neighbor know beyond the hill;
And on a day we meet to walk the line
And set the wall between us once again.
We keep the wall between us as we go.   15
To each the boulders that have fallen to each.
And some are loaves and some so nearly balls
We have to use a spell to make them balance:
"Stay where you are until our backs are turned!"
We wear our fingers rough with handling them.   20
Oh, just another kind of outdoor game,
One on a side. It comes to little more:
There where it is we do not need the wall:
He is all pine and I am apple orchard.
My apple trees will never get across   25
And eat the cones under his pines, I tell him.
He only says, "Good fences make good neighbors."
Spring is the mischief in me, and I wonder
If I could put a notion in his head:
"*Why* do they make good neighbors? Isn't it   30
Where there are cows? But here there are no cows.
Before I built a wall I'd ask to know
What I was walling in or walling out,
And to whom I was like to give offense.
Something there is that doesn't love a wall,   35
That wants it down." I could say "Elves" to him,
But it's not elves exactly, and I'd rather
He said it for himself. I see him there

From THE POETRY OF ROBERT FROST, edited by Edward Connery Lathem. Copyright 1916, 1923, 1930, 1939, © 1969 by Holt, Rinehart and Winston, Inc. Copyright 1936, 1940, 1942, 1944, 1951, © 1958 by Robert Frost. Copyright © 1964, 1967, 1968, 1970 by Lesley Frost Ballantine. Reprinted by permission of Holt, Rinehart and Winston, Inc.

Bringing a stone grasped firmly by the top
In each hand, like an old-stone savage armed.   40
He moves in darkness as it seems to me,
Not of woods only and the shade of trees.
He will not go behind his father's saying,
And he likes having thought of it so well
He says again, "Good fences make good neighbors."   45

I

THE HUMAN COMMUNITY

Most of Frost's poetry centers on the family, the home, the individual. In these two poems, though, he looks at the world of human relationships: the human community. In each case, Frost's rich sense of humor enables him to strike gentle but well-aimed blows at the blind effects of custom and human indifference. Such indifference strikes at the roots of life, but the poet shows us, in his words, "a way of grappling with life." His poems, in fact, are strategies for overcoming that cold dehumanizing indifference that comes from living in too much isolation.

Departmental

1. Like all good animal fables, this one is funny because it explores the resemblances between ants and people so thoroughly. Explain the resemblances you see in the poem. What rhymes and what images add to the humor of the poem?

2. If you read this poem as a satire on bureaucracy or specialization, just what defects are being ridiculed?

3. Apply these lines to our own lives: "No one stands round to stare./ It is nobody else's affair." What comment is Frost making on human society? Is he saying that we should learn from the ants?

4. Why does the poet separate the last two lines from the rest of the poem? In what sense is this

the moral of the fable? Is this the way the poet says: "Look out—I'm spoofing"?

Mending Wall

1. The meaning of this poem can be summed up in the problem it raises: Should we tear down the barriers that isolate us from one another, or are these boundaries and limits necessary to human life? What is the view of the speaker in the poem?

2. What is the "something" that doesn't love a wall?

3. Does the neighbor in this poem look on wall-mending as "just another kind of outdoor game"?

II

IMPLICATIONS

Discuss the following statements.

1. As human life becomes more specialized and mechanical, its cold efficiency comes closer to the blind instincts of the ant colony.

2. "Mending Wall" stands for all artificial barriers.

3. We change people's attitudes only by putting notions in their heads, by having them see things for themselves.

4. Those who unthinkingly inherit the opinions of their parents live forever in the mental darkness of childhood.

Life and Death

All poets, in time, face the major question: What is death?
Frost sees it not as an absolute, but as perpetually involved with life
and the living. These four poems will need several readings. The first is
intentionally simple but baffling, like a riddle; its meanings, however,
are multiple. The last two poems are narratives, unforgettable in their
local details but also universal in their contemplation of death.

Fire and Ice

Some say the world will end in fire,
Some say in ice.
From what I've tasted of desire
I hold with those who favor fire.
But if it had to perish twice,
I think I know enough of hate
To say that for destruction ice
Is also great
And would suffice.

Stopping by Woods on a Snowy Evening

Whose woods these are I think I know.
His house is in the village though;
He will not see me stopping here
To watch his woods fill up with snow.

My little horse must think it queer   5
To stop without a farmhouse near
Between the woods and frozen lake
The darkest evening of the year.

He gives his harness bells a shake
To ask if there is some mistake.   10
The only other sound's the sweep
Of easy wind and downy flake.

The woods are lovely, dark and deep,
But I have promises to keep,
And miles to go before I sleep,   15
And miles to go before I sleep.

From THE POETRY OF ROBERT FROST, edited by Edward Connery Lathem. Copyright 1916, 1923, 1930, 1939, © 1969 by
Holt, Rinehart and Winston, Inc. Copyright 1936, 1940, 1942, 1944, 1951, © 1958 by Robert Frost. Copyright © 1964, 1967,
1968, 1970 by Lesley Frost Ballantine. Reprinted by permission of Holt, Rinehart and Winston, Inc.

"Out, Out—"

The buzz saw snarled and rattled in the yard
And made dust and dropped stove-length sticks of wood,
Sweet-scented stuff when the breeze drew across it.
And from there those that lifted eyes could count
Five mountain ranges one behind the other   5
Under the sunset far into Vermont.
And the saw snarled and rattled, snarled and rattled,
As it ran light, or had to bear a load.
And nothing happened: day was all but done.
Call it a day, I wish they might have said   10
To please the boy by giving him the half hour
That a boy counts so much when saved from work.
His sister stood beside them in her apron
To tell them "Supper." At the word, the saw,
As if to prove saws knew what supper meant,   15
Leaped out at the boy's hand, or seemed to leap—
He must have given the hand. However it was,
Neither refused the meeting. But the hand!
The boy's first outcry was a rueful laugh,
As he swung toward them holding up the hand,   20
Half in appeal, but half as if to keep
The life from spilling. Then the boy saw all—
Since he was old enough to know, big boy
Doing a man's work, though a child at heart—
He saw all spoiled. "Don't let them cut my hand off—   25
The doctor, when he comes. Don't let them, sister!"
So. But the hand was gone already.
The doctor put him in the dark of ether.
He lay and puffed his lips out with his breath.
And then—the watcher at his pulse took fright.   30
No one believed. They listened at his heart.
Little—less—nothing!—and that ended it.
No more to build on there. And they, since they
Were not the one dead, turned to their affairs.

From THE POETRY OF ROBERT FROST, edited by Edward Connery Lathem.
Copyright 1916, 1923, 1930, 1939, © 1969 by Holt, Rinehart, and Winston,
Inc. Copyright 1936, 1940, 1942, 1944, 1951, © 1958 by Robert Frost.
Copyright © 1964, 1967, 1968, 1970 by Lesley Frost Ballantine. Reprinted
by permission of Holt, Rinehart and Winston, Inc.

The Death of the Hired Man

Mary sat musing on the lamp-flame at the table,
Waiting for Warren. When she heard his step,
She ran on tip-toe down the darkened passage
To meet him in the doorway with the news
And put him on his guard. "Silas is back."   5
She pushed him outward with her through the door
And shut it after her. "Be kind," she said.
She took the market things from Warren's arms
And set them on the porch, then drew him down
To sit beside her on the wooden steps.   10

"When was I ever anything but kind to him?
But I'll not have the fellow back," he said.
"I told him so last haying, didn't I?
If he left then, I said, that ended it.
What good is he? Who else will harbor him   15
At his age for the little he can do?
What help he is there's no depending on.
Off he goes always when I need him most.
He thinks he ought to earn a little pay,
Enough at least to buy tobacco with,   20
So he won't have to beg and be beholden.[1]
'All right,' I say, 'I can't afford to pay
Any fixed wages, though I wish I could.'
'Someone else can.' 'Then someone else will have to.'
I shouldn't mind his bettering himself   25
If that was what it was. You can be certain,
When he begins like that, there's someone at him
Trying to coax him off with pocket money,—
In haying time, when any help is scarce.
In winter he comes back to us. I'm done."   30

"Sh! not so loud: he'll hear you," Mary said.

"I want him to: he'll have to soon or late."

"He's worn out. He's asleep beside the stove.
When I came up from Rowe's I found him here,

---

1. **be beholden**\bē ᵊhōl·dən\ be under obligation for a
favor or a gift.

From THE POETRY OF ROBERT FROST, edited by Edward Connery
Lathem. Copyright 1916, 1923, 1930, 1939, © 1969 by Holt, Rinehart
and Winston, Inc. Copyright 1936, 1940, 1942, 1944, 1951, © 1958 by
Robert Frost. Copyright © 1964, 1967, 1968, 1970 by Lesley Frost Ballantine. Reprinted by permission of Holt, Rinehart and Winston, Inc.

Huddled against the barn door fast asleep,   35
A miserable sight, and frightening, too—
You needn't smile—I didn't recognize him—
I wasn't looking for him—and he's changed.
Wait till you see."

                    "Where did you say he'd been?"   40

"He didn't say. I dragged him to the house,
And gave him tea and tried to make him smoke.
I tried to make him talk about his travels.
Nothing would do: he just kept nodding off."

"What did he say? Did he say anything?"   45

"But little."

                    "Anything? Mary, confess
He said he'd come to ditch the meadow[2] for me."

"Warren!"

                    "But did he? I just want to know."   50

"Of course he did. What would you have him say?
Surely you wouldn't grudge the poor old man
Some humble way to save his self-respect.
He added, if you really care to know,
He meant to clear the upper pasture, too.   55
That sounds like something you have heard before?
Warren, I wish you could have heard the way
He jumbled everything. I stopped to look
Two or three times—he made me feel so queer—
To see if he was talking in his sleep.   60
He ran on[3] Harold Wilson—you remember—
The boy you had in haying four years since.
He's finished school, and teaching in his college.
Silas declares you'll have to get him back.
He says they two will make a team for work: 65
Between them they will lay this farm as smooth!
The way he mixed that in with other things.
He thinks young Wilson a likely lad, though daft
On education—you know how they fought
All through July under the blazing sun,   70
Silas up on the cart to build the load,
Harold along beside to pitch it on."

————————

2. **to ditch the meadow,** to dig ditches to drain the
meadow.
3. **He ran on,** he talked of.

"Yes, I took care to keep well out of earshot."

"Well, those days trouble Silas like a dream.
You wouldn't think they would. How some things linger!   75
Harold's young college-boy's assurance piqued[4] him.
After so many years he still keeps finding
Good arguments he sees he might have used.
I sympathize. I know just how it feels
To think of the right thing to say too late.   80
Harold's associated in his mind with Latin.
He asked me what I thought of Harold's saying
He studied Latin like the violin
Because he liked it—that an argument!
He said he couldn't make the boy believe   85
He could find water with a hazel prong—
Which showed how much good school had ever done him.
He wanted to go over that. But most of all
He thinks if he could have another chance
To teach him how to build a load of hay—"   90

"I know, that's Silas' one accomplishment.
He bundles every forkful in its place,
And tags and numbers it for future reference,
So he can find and easily dislodge it
In the unloading. Silas does that well.   95
He takes it out in bunches like big birds' nests.
You never see him standing on the hay
He's trying to lift, straining to lift himself."

"He thinks if he could teach him that, he'd be
Some good perhaps to someone in the world.   100
He hates to see a boy the fool of books.
Poor Silas, so concerned for other folk,
And nothing to look backward to with pride,
And nothing to look forward to with hope,
So now and never any different."   105

Part of a moon was falling down the west,
Dragging the whole sky with it to the hills.
Its light poured softly in her lap. She saw it
And spread her apron to it. She put out her hand
Among the harp like morning-glory strings,   110
Taut with the dew from garden bed to eaves,
As if she played unheard some tenderness

---

4. **piqued**\pēkd\ irritated, provoked.

That wrought on him beside her in the night.
"Warren," she said, "he has come home to die:
You needn't be afraid he'll leave you this time."   115

"Home," he mocked gently.

                              "Yes, what else but home?
It all depends on what you mean by home.
Of course he's nothing to us, any more
Than was the hound that came a stranger to us   120
Out of the woods, worn out upon the trail."

"Home is the place where, when you have to go there,
They have to take you in."

                        "I should have called it
Something you somehow haven't to deserve."   125

Warren leaned out and took a step or two,
Picked up a little stick, and brought it back
And broke it in his hand and tossed it by.
"Silas has better claim on us you think
Than on his brother? Thirteen little miles   130
As the road winds would bring him to his door.
Silas has walked that far no doubt today.
Why doesn't he go there? His brother's rich,
A somebody—director in the bank."

"He never told us that."   135

                    "We know it though."

"I think his brother ought to help, of course.
I'll see to that if there is need. He ought of right
To take him in, and might be willing to—
He may be better than appearances.   140
But have some pity on Silas. Do you think
If he had any pride in claiming kin
Or anything he looked for from his brother,
He'd keep so still about him all this time?"

"I wonder what's between them."   145

                          "I can tell you.
Silas is what he is—we wouldn't mind him—
But just the kind that kinsfolk can't abide.
He never did a thing so very bad.

He don't know why he isn't quite as good   150
As anybody. Worthless though he is,
He won't be made ashamed to please his brother."

"I can't think Si ever hurt anyone."

"No, but he hurt my heart the way he lay
And rolled his old head on that sharp-edged chair-back.   155
He wouldn't let me put him on the lounge.
You must go in and see what you can do.
I made the bed up for him there tonight.
You'll be surprised at him—how much he's broken.
His working days are done; I'm sure of it."   160

"I'd not be in a hurry to say that."

"I haven't been. Go, look, see for yourself.
But Warren, please remember how it is:
He's come to help you ditch the meadow.
He has a plan. You mustn't laugh at him.   165
He may not speak of it, and then he may.
I'll sit and see if that small sailing cloud
Will hit or miss the moon."

                    It hit the moon.
Then there were three there, making a dim row,   170
The moon, the little silver cloud, and she.

Warren returned—too soon, it seemed to her,
Slipped to her side, caught up her hand and waited.

"Warren?" she questioned.

                  "Dead," was all he answered.   175

I
THE ULTIMATE QUESTIONS

It is one of the jobs of the poet to ask the ultimate questions and to suggest some partial yet penetrating answers. They may not be the only answers or ours, but they are comments that reveal something about human nature. The poet extends our horizons and our experiences by allowing us to see and to judge human passions, obligations, and death through new eyes. Through the honesty of this vision, the poet reminds us of the strength of human passions and creates a sympathy for human frailties. By identifying values that make us human, the poet serves as a great teacher to the world.

Fire and Ice

1. Frost's Yankee manner is not just a way of speaking, but a mode of thought, a way of facing the world. Find in this poem evidence of these characteristics of the Yankee manner:

   a. a harsh, tight-lipped, yet humorous manner.

   b. a recurrent understatement.

   c. a homey, informal, and dryly factual speech.

d. a restraint of one's strongest feelings.

2. Why are fire and ice such appropriate symbols for desire and hatred?

Stopping by Woods on a Snowy Evening

1. Why does the traveler stop at the woods? Why should his horse think this queer?

2. What similarity does the rural traveler's journey have with that of anyone journeying through life? How does the poet make a personal experience the image of experiences common to us all?

3. Why does the traveler leave with reluctance?

4. Why does the poet repeat the last line?

"Out, Out—"

1. The title, "Out, Out—" comes from a famous soliloquy in Shakespeare's *Macbeth*, in which life "is a tale/Told by an idiot, full of sound and fury/Signifying nothing." How does the same meaningless view of life fit into this poem?

2. The contrast between the boy and the machine is central to this poem. How does Frost suggest this contrast?

3. The hand is the symbol of power and creativity. Here it is not merely the symbol, but the instrument. In this rural world, for this "boy, doing a man's work," what does the loss of his hand mean?

4. Some critics feel Frost is heartless when he writes "and that ended it./No more to build on there." What is your opinion?

5. In the last two lines, do those who "turn to their affairs" do so out of shock, indifference, or a frank acceptance of realities?

The Death of the Hired Man

1. This poem is a dramatic narrative. Like all good drama, it is essentially psychological. What is the psychological conflict in the poem?

2. We never see or hear Silas. What does the poet gain by keeping Silas offstage?

3. Warren's gradual conversion to pity and mercy through his wife's deliberate and gentle persuasiveness is the real subject of this poem. Trace the stages in Warren's transformation and the strategies by which Mary achieves this.

4. Why is Warren's discovery of Silas' death an ironic but not surprising fulfillment and end of the dramatic conflict?

II
IMPLICATIONS

Discuss the following statements:

1. The intensity of our deepest passions, love and hate, creates the greatest forces for destruction.

2. People wish to make permanent their moments of honest pleasure and discovery. Why?

3. In life, the shock of the truth and all its implications is often more fatal than mere physical loss or impairment.

4. It is not the death of Silas, but Mary's intuitive sympathy for Silas and Warren's slow searching for justice that are the subject of "The Death of the Hired Man."

III
TECHNIQUES

Blank Verse

Shakespeare and Milton first popularized *blank verse*. It is based on five stresses or beats to each line and it is unrhymed. "Mending Wall," "Birches," and "The Death of the Hired Man" are particularly fine examples of the ease with which Frost handles this traditional form. The first lines of "Birches" are built around a wholly regular beat: ten syllables, alternately unaccented and accented. We call this regular line *iambic pentameter*. But note that by line 5 Frost is ready to vary this beat, in order to avoid monotony. He still keeps five accents to each line, but their order varies. To suggest even greater naturalness, even closer approximation to ordinary speech, in "The Death of the Hired Man," Frost breaks the sentences in the middle of the line, lets sentences run on for three or four lines, splits a line between two speakers; yet the beat is always five to the line.

Frost on Poetry

Frost often discussed the art of poetry. The following quotations from Robert Frost should be studied and discussed in terms of the poems you have just read.

1. And were an epitaph to be my story
I'd have a short one ready for my own.
I would have written of me on my stone
I had a lover's quarrel with the world.

2. A poem is a reaching-out toward expression: an effort to find fulfillment. A complete poem is one where an emotion has found its thought, and the thought has found the words.

THE STRUGGLE
FOR JUSTICE

"With liberty and justice for all." Every time we Americans recite the Pledge of Allegiance, we use the word "justice." What, precisely, do we mean by this word? How do we discriminate between what is just and what is unjust?

In trying to answer these questions, it is natural to think of the judicial department of the government and of the courts. It is true—in America, at least—that juries and judges are charged with the duty of deciding what is just and unjust in a given case. Consequently, we may feel that people are given justice when they are treated according to laws and certain legal procedures. In part, justice may be defined as equal treatment under the law.

But the word "law" itself raises several problems. Where does the law come from? Are laws always just? Do they, for example, always protect the rights of minority groups? On the other hand, do they always protect the rights of the majority against a minority that has power and influence?

It is obvious that legal codes are formed to some extent both by majority and minority pressures. It is equally obvious that there have always been laws which some persons have considered unjust. Before 1920, for example, women were not guaranteed the right to vote in the United States. Today, we would agree that women were treated unjustly by the laws which denied them voting privileges.

The fact that some laws have been considered unjust raises a fundamental question: How do we determine whether or not any given law is "just?" If we say, for instance, that the laws that prohibited women from voting were not "just" laws, upon what standard are we basing our idea of justice? Certainly, we are using some standard other than the law itself.

In the Declaration of Independence, Thomas Jefferson named some of these extralegal standards when he spoke of "the laws of nature and of nature's God." According to Jefferson's view, justice is based not upon human laws only, but especially upon what we might call natural and supernatural "laws." These standards, he affirmed, are the standards upon which legal codes should be based; and if human laws are not based upon such standards, people have the right to revolt against them. That, of course, is exactly what Jefferson and many of his fellow-Americans did; our country was born partly because certain colonists believed that English laws of the time were unjust.

Our history has been and continues to be characterized by struggles led by individuals who have felt themselves and their groups unjustly treated. The struggle for justice is a theme that runs throughout American history and it is natural that American writers have made it the theme of many stories, essays, and poems. The selections in the following unit deal with this struggle. Some are concerned with historical struggles of groups of people; others with the struggles of individuals against other individuals or against "the tyranny of the majority." As you read these selections you may find opinions or points of view with which you may disagree, but try to remember—as James Madison pointed out—that justice is secured neither by destroying liberty nor by giving every citizen the same opinions.

One of the earliest and most horrible acts of injustice in America
was the hanging of a number of citizens as witches in Salem, Massachusetts,
in 1692. Though this episode occurred over two centuries ago,
mob reactions and suspicions of one's neighbors have produced incidents
in modern history that closely parallel the events in Salem.

Trials at Salem

STEPHEN VINCENT BENÉT

Salem Village had got a new minister—the Reverend Samuel Parris, ex-merchant in the West Indies. The most important thing about Samuel Parris was the fact that he brought with him to Salem Village two West Indian servants —a man known as John Indian and a woman named Tituba. And when he bought those two or their services in the West Indies, he was buying a rope that was to hang nineteen men and women of New England—so odd are the links in the circumstantial chain.

Perhaps the nine-year-old Elizabeth Parris, the daughter of the parsonage, boasted to her new friends of the odd stories Tituba told and the queer things she could do. Perhaps Tituba herself let the report of her magic powers be spread about the village. She must have been as odd and imagination-stirring a figure as a parrot or a tame monkey in the small New England town. And the winters were long and white—and any diversion a godsend.

In any case, during the winter of 1691–92 a group of girls and women began to meet nightly at the parsonage, with Tituba and her fortune telling as the chief attraction. Elizabeth Parris, at nine, was the youngest; then came Abigail Williams, eleven, and Ann Putnam, twelve. The rest were older—Mercy Lewis, Mary Wolcott, and Elizabeth Hubbard were seventeen; Elizabeth Booth and Susan Sheldon,

eighteen; and Mary Warren and Sarah Churchill, twenty. Three were servants—Mercy Lewis had been employed by the Reverend George Burroughs, a previous minister of Salem Village, and now worked for the Putnams; Mary Warren was a maid at the John Procters'; Sarah Churchill, at the George Jacobs'. All, except for Elizabeth Parris, were adolescent or just leaving adolescence.

The elder women included a pair of gossipy, superstitious busybodies—Mrs. Pope and Mrs. Bibber; and young Ann Putnam's mother, Ann Putnam, Sr., who deserves a sentence to herself.

For the Putnams were a powerful family in the neighborhood and Ann Putnam, married at seventeen and now only thirty, is described as handsome, arrogant, temperamental, and high-strung. She was also one of those people who can cherish a grudge and revenge it.

The circle met—the circle continued to meet —no doubt with the usual giggling, whispering, and gossip. From mere fortune telling it proceeded to other and more serious matters— table rapping, perhaps, and a little West Indian voodoo—weird stories told by Tituba and weird things shown, while the wind blew outside and the big shadows flickered on the wall. Adolescent girls, credulous servants, superstitious old women—and the two enigmatic figures of Tituba, the West Indian, and Ann Putnam, Sr.

From *We Aren't Superstitious* by Stephen Vincent Benét. Copyright, 1937, by Esquire, Inc. Reprinted by permission of Brandt & Brandt.

But soon the members of the circle began to show hysterical symptoms. They crawled under tables and chairs; they made strange sounds; they shook and trembled with nightmare fears. The thing became a village celebrity—and more. Something strange and out of nature was happening—who had ever seen normal young girls behave like these young girls? And no one—certainly not the Reverend Samuel Parris—even suggested that a mixed diet of fortune telling, ghost stories, and voodoo is hardly the thing for impressionable minds during a long New England winter. Hysteria was possession by an evil spirit; pathological lying, the devil putting words into one's mouth. The Reverend Samuel became very busy. Grave ministers were called in to look at the afflicted children. A Dr. Gregg gave his opinion. It was almost too terrible to believe, and yet what else could be believed? Witchcraft!

Meanwhile, one may suppose, the "afflicted children," like most hysterical subjects, enjoyed the awed stares, the horrified looks, the respectful questions that greeted them, with girlish zest. They had been unimportant girls of a little hamlet;[1] now they were, in every sense of the word, spot news. And any reporter knows what that does to certain kinds of people. They continued to writhe and demonstrate—and be the center of attention. There was only one catch about it. If they were really bewitched, somebody must be doing the bewitching.

On the twenty-ninth of February, 1692, in the midst of an appropriate storm of thunder and lightning, three women—Sarah Good, Sarah Osburn, and Tituba—were arrested on the deadly charge of bewitching the children.

The next day, March 1, two magistrates, Justice Hawthorne[2] and Justice Corwin, arrived with appropriate pomp and ceremony. The first hearing was held in the crowded meetinghouse of the village; and all Salem swarmed to it, as crowds in our time have swarmed to other sleepy little villages suddenly notorious.

The children—or the children and Tituba—had picked their first victims well. Sarah Good

and Sarah Osburn were old women of no particular standing in the community.

We can imagine that meetinghouse—and the country crowd within it—on that chill March day. At one end was the majesty of the law—and the "afflicted children," where all might see them and observe. Dressed in their best, very likely, and with solicitous relatives near at hand. Do you see Mercy Lewis? Do you see Ann Putnam? And then the whole crowd turned to one vast, horrified eye. For there was the accused—the old woman—the witch!

The justices—grim Justice Hawthorne in particular—had, evidently, arrived with their minds made up. For the first question addressed to Sarah Good was, bluntly:

"What evil spirit have you familiarity with?"

"None," said the piping old voice. But everybody in the village knew worthless Sarah Good. And the eye of the audience went from her to the deadly row of "afflicted children" and back again.

"Have you made no contracts with the devil?" proceeded the Justice.

"No."

The Justice went to the root of the matter at once.

"Why do you hurt these children?"

A rustle must have gone through the meetinghouse at that. Aye, that's it; the Justice speaks shrewdly; hark to the Justice! Aye, but look too! Look at the children! Poor things, poor things!

"I do not hurt them. I scorn it," said Sarah Good defiantly. But the Justice had her now; he was not to be brushed aside.

"Who, then, do you employ to do it?"

"I employ nobody."

"What creature do you employ then?" For all witches had familiars.

"No creature, but I am falsely accused." But the sweat must have been on the old woman's palms by now.

---

1. hamlet, a small village.
2. **Justice Hawthorne,** distant relative of Nathaniel Hawthorne. The Justice actually spelled his name Hathorne; the *w* was added by Nathaniel.

The Justice considered. There was another point, minor but illuminating.

"Why did you go away muttering from Mr. Parris, his house?"

"I did not mutter, but I thanked him for what he gave my child."

The Justice returned to the main charge, like any prosecuting attorney.

"Have you made no contract with the devil?"

"No."

It was time for Exhibit A. The Justice turned to the children. Was Sarah Good one of the persons who tormented them? Yes, yes!—and a horrified murmur running through the crowd. And then, before the awe-stricken eyes of all, they began to be tormented. They writhed; they grew stiff; they contorted; they were stricken moaning or speechless. Yet, when they were brought to Sarah Good and allowed to touch her, they grew quite quiet and calm. For, as everyone knew, a witch's physical body was like an electric conductor—it reabsorbed, on touch, the malefic force discharged by witchcraft into the bodies of the tormented. Everybody could see what happened—and everybody saw. When the meetinghouse was quiet, the Justice spoke again.

"Sarah Good, do you not see now what you have done? Why do you not tell us the truth? Why do you torment these poor children?"

And with these words Sarah Good was already hanged. For all that she could say was, "I do not torment them." And yet everyone had seen her, with their own eyes.

Sarah Osburn's examination followed the same course, the same prosecutor's first question, the same useless denial, the same epileptic feats of the "afflicted children," the same end.

Then Tituba was examined and gave them their fill of marvels, prodigies, and horrors.

The West Indian woman, a slave in a strange land, was fighting for her life, and she did it shrewdly, and desperately. She admitted, repentantly, that she had tormented the children. But she had been forced to do so. By whom? By Goody Good and Goody Osburn and two other witches whom she hadn't yet been able to

TRIAL OF GEORGE JACOBS,
T. H. Matterson

recognize. Her voodoo knowledge aided her—she filled the open ears of Justices and crowd with tales of hairy familiars and black dogs, red cats and black cats and yellow birds, the phantasm of a woman with legs and wings. And everybody could see that she spoke the truth. For, when she was first brought in, the children were tormented at her presence; but as soon as she had confessed and turned King's evidence, she was tormented herself, and fearfully. To Boston Jail with her—but she had saved her neck.

The hearing was over; the men and women of Salem and its outlying farms went broodingly or excitedly back to their homes to discuss the fearful workings of God's providence. Here and there a common sense voice murmured a doubt or two—Sarah Good and Sarah Osburn were no great losses to the community; but still, to convict two old women of heinous crime on the testimony of greensick girls and a West Indian slave! But, on the whole, the villagers of Salem felt relieved. The cause of the plague had been found; it would be stamped out and the afflicted children recover. The Justices, no doubt, congratulated themselves on their prompt and intelligent action. The "afflicted children" slept, after a tiring day—they were not quite so used to such performances as they were to become.

As for the accused women, they went to Boston Jail—to be chained there while waiting trial and gallows.

Meanwhile, on an outlying farm, Giles Corey, a turbulent, salty old fellow of eighty-one, began to argue the case with his wife, Martha. He believed, fanatically, in the "afflicted children." She did not, and said so—even going so far as to say that the magistrates were blinded and she could open their eyes. It was one of those marital disputes that occur between strong-willed people. And it was to bring Martha Corey to the gallows and Giles Corey to an even stranger doom.

Yet now there was a lull, through which people whispered.

As for what went on in the minds of the "afflicted children," during that lull we may not say. But this much is evident. They had seen and felt their power. The hearing had been the greatest and most exciting event of their narrow lives. And it was so easy to do; they grew more and more ingenious with each rehearsal. You twisted your body and groaned —and grown people were afraid.

Add to this the three girl-servants, with the usual servants' grudges against present or former masters. Add to this that high-strung, dominant woman Ann Putnam, Sr., who could hold a grudge and remember it. Such a grudge as there might be against the Towne sisters, for instance—they were all married women of the highest standing, particularly Rebecca Nurse. So suppose—just suppose—that one of them were found out to be a witch? And hadn't Tituba deposed that there were other women, besides Good and Osburn, who made her torment the children?

On March 19 Martha Corey and Rebecca Nurse were arrested on the charge of witchcraft. On March 21 they were examined and committed. And with that the real reign of terror began.

Salem Village, as a community, was no longer sane.

Let us get it over quickly. The Salem witches ceased to be Salem's affair—they became a matter affecting the whole colony. Sir William Phips, the new governor, appointed a special court of oyer and terminer[3] to try the cases. And the hangings began.

On January 1, 1692, no one, except possibly the "circle children," had heard of Salem witches. On June 10 Bridget Bishop was hanged. She had not been one of the first accused, but she was the first to suffer. She had been married three times, kept a roadhouse on the road to Beverly where people drank rum and played shovelboard, and dressed, distinctively for the period, in a "black cap and black hat and red paragon bodice broidered and looped with diverse colors." But those seem to have been her chief offenses. When questioned, she said, "I never saw the devil in my life."

All through the summer the accusations, the arrests, the trials, came thick and fast till the jails were crowded. Nor were those now accused friendless old beldames like Sarah Good. They included Captain John Alden (son of Miles Standish's friend[4]), who saved himself by breaking jail, and the wealthy and prominent Englishes, who saved themselves by flight. The most disgraceful scenes occurred at the trial of the saintly Rebecca Nurse. Thirty-nine citizens of Salem were brave enough to sign a petition for her, and the jury brought in a verdict of "not guilty." The mob in the sweating courtroom immediately began to cry out, and the presiding judge as much as told the jury to reverse their verdict. They did so, to the mob's delight. Then the governor pardoned her. And "certain gentlemen of Salem"—and perhaps the mob—persuaded him into reversing his pardon. She was hanged on Gallows Hill on July 19 with Sarah Good, Sarah Wilds, Elizabeth How, and Susanna Martin.

Susanna Martin's only witchcraft seems to have been that she was an unusually tidy woman and had once walked a muddy road

---

3. **court of oyer and terminer**\\'ōy•ər . . . ▲tĕr•mə•nər\\ a high court which hears and determines criminal cases.
4. **Miles Standish's friend,** John Alden, Sr., who with Standish founded Duxbury.

without getting her dress bedraggled. No, I am quoting from testimony, not inventing. As for Elizabeth How, a neighbor testified, "I have been acquainted with Goodwife How as a naybor for nine or ten years and I never saw any harm in her but found her just in her dealings and faithful to her promises . . . I never heard her revile any person but she always pitied them and said, 'I pray God forgive them now.'" But the children cried, "I am stuck with a pin. I am pinched," when they saw her—and she hanged.

It took a little more to hang the Reverend George Burroughs. He had been Salem Village's second minister—then gone on to a parish in Maine. And the cloth had great sanctity. But Ann Putnam and Mercy Lewis managed to doom him between them, with the able assistance of the rest of the troupe. Mr. Burroughs was unfortunate enough to be a man of unusual physical strength—anyone who could lift a gun by putting four fingers in its barrel must do so by magic arts. Also, he had been married three times. So when the ghosts of his first two wives, dressed in winding sheets, appeared in a sort of magic lantern show to Ann Putnam and cried out that Mr. Burroughs had murdered them—the cloth could not save him then.

Here and there in the records gleams a flash of frantic common sense. Susanna Martin laughs when Ann Putnam and her daughter go into convulsions at her appearance. When asked why, she says, "Well I may, at such folly. I never hurt this woman or her child in my life." John Procter, the prosperous farmer who employed Mary Warren, said sensibly, before his arrest, "If these girls are left alone, we will all be devils and witches. They ought all to be sent to the whipping post." He was right enough about it—but his servant helped hang him.

Judge, jury, and colony preferred to believe the writhings of the children; the stammerings of those whose sows had died inexplicably; the testimony of such as Bernard Peach, who swore that Susanna Martin had flown in through his window, bent his body into the shape of a "Whoope," and sat upon him for an hour and a half.

One hanging on June 10, five on July 19, five on August 19, eight on September 22, including Mary Easty and Martha Corey. And of these the Reverend Noyes remarked, with unction, "What a sad thing it is to see eight firebrands of hell hanging there!" But for stubborn Giles Corey a different fate was reserved.

The old man had begun by believing in the whole hocus-pocus. He had quarreled with his wife about it. He had seen her arrested as a witch, insulted by the magistrates, condemned to die. Two of his sons-in-law had testified against her; he himself had been closely questioned as to her actions and had made the deposition of a badgered and simple man. Yes, she prayed a good deal; sometimes he couldn't hear what she said—that sort of thing. The memory must have risen to haunt him when she was condemned. Now he himself was in danger.

Well, he could die as his wife would. But there was the property—his goods, his prospering lands. By law, the goods and property of those convicted of witchcraft were confiscated by the state and the name attainted. With a curious, grim heroism, Giles Corey drew up a will leaving that property to the two sons-in-law who had not joined in the prevailing madness. And then at his trial, he said, "I will not plead. If I deny, I am condemned already in courts where ghosts appear as witnesses and swear men's lives away."

A curious, grim heroism? It was so. For those who refused to plead either guilty or not guilty in such a suit were liable to the old English punishment called *peine forte et dure*.[5] It consisted in heaping weights or stones upon the unhappy victim till he accepted a plea—or until his chest was crushed. And exactly that happened to old Giles Corey. They heaped the stones upon him until they killed him—and two

---

5. **peine forte et dure**\pĕn fȯr·tĕ dūr\ lit. severe and strong punishment; a form of punishment by pressing under heavy weights.

days before his wife was hanged, he died. But his property went to the two loyal sons-in-law, without confiscation—and his name was not attainted. So died Giles Corey, New England to the bone.

And then, suddenly and fantastically as the madness had come, it was gone.

The "afflicted children," at long last, had gone too far. They had accused the governor's lady. They had accused Mrs. Hall, the wife of the minister at Beverly and a woman known throughout the colony for her virtues. And there comes a point when driven men and women revolt against blood and horror. It was that which ended Robespierre's[6] terror—it was that which ended the terror of the "afflicted children." The thing had become a *reductio ad absurdum*.[7] If it went on, logically, no one but the "afflicted children" and their protégées would be left alive.

In 1706 Ann Putnam made public confession that she had been deluded by the devil in testifying as she had. She had testified in every case but one. And in 1711 the colony of Massachusetts paid fifty pounds to the heirs of George Burroughs, twenty-one pounds to the heirs of Giles Corey—five hundred and seventy-eight pounds in all to the heirs of various victims. An expensive business for the colony, on the whole.

What happened to the survivors? Well, the Reverend Samuel Parris quit Salem Village to go into business in Boston and died at Sudbury in 1720. And Ann Putnam died in 1716 and from the stock of the Putnams sprang Israel Putnam, the Revolutionary hero. And from the stock of the "Witches," the Nurses and the others, sprang excellent and distinguished people of service to state and nation. And hanging Judge Hawthorne's descendant was Nathaniel Hawthorne.

We have no reason to hold Salem up to obloquy. It was a town, like another, and a strange madness took hold of it. But it is not a stranger thing to hang a man for witchcraft than to hang him for the shape of his nose or the color of his skin. We are not superstitious, no. Well, let us be a little sure we are not. For persecution follows superstition and intolerance as fire follows the fuse. And once we light that fire we cannot foresee where it will end or what it will consume—any more than they could in Salem two hundred and sixty-seven years ago.

I

INSANITY AND JUSTICE

Laws in themselves never guarantee justice; there must also be fair and sane administration of the laws. If judges and juries are irrational, no amount of law can protect the individual citizen. Injustice was done at Salem largely because the community, the citizens themselves, had temporarily lost their sanity, their ability to distinguish between the real and the unreal.

In communities and even in nations mass madness is not nearly as uncommon as most of us would like to believe. Especially in a nation where extremes of opinion are allowed, there is always likely to be some "community," some group, which stands upon beliefs that are not grounded in reality. Benét puts his finger on two of the causes leading to irrational belief and conduct—superstition and intolerance. What modern instances of group insanity can you point to and to what extent are they rooted in either superstition or intolerance?

II

IMPLICATIONS

Resolved: "When a group or a community within our nation shows that it cannot distinguish between what is real and what is unreal (as in Salem in 1692), some force outside of that group or community should step in and take charge until sanity has been restored."

Debate this proposition on either the affirmative or the negative side. As you think about your case, consider the following questions.

1. What standard or standards can one use to determine whether or not a given group is "sane"?

---

6. **Robespierre**\ro ˈbĕs ˈpyär\ French revolutionist responsible for much of the reign of terror.
7. **reductio ad absurdum**\rē ˈdŭk·shē·ō ăd ăb ˈsər·dəm\ proof of the falsity of a conclusion by reducing it to absurdity.

2. Who can be entrusted with making this kind of a decision?

3. Will the control of a group by outside pressure destroy freedom of opinion?

4. Can true democracy flourish only when extremes of opinion are tolerated?

5. If certain types of groups are not controlled, might they destroy democracy entirely?

III
TECHNIQUES

This unit examines *intention* and *theme* in literature. These two elements are sometimes very closely related; in an essay, for example, the author's intention may be to define and express a theme. Our discussions of intention, however, will generally explore how the reader can learn what the author's intention is. When we discuss theme, we will be concerned with the author's methods of stating and developing a theme.

Intention

We often feel that we have grasped the "true" meaning of a work of literature when the meaning we infer and the meaning the writer intended are identical. This feeling, however, may raise a vexing question: "How do we know what a writer's intention is?"

First of all, it is usually impractical and often impossible to get at the writer's intention by asking about it in person or by reading what may have been said about it in some other work.

It is usually best, then—or at least most convenient—to judge a writer's intentions by looking at the work itself rather than at some source outside the work. There are usually many clues to intention within the work itself. In Benét's article, let us observe one of the simplest—*the writer's choice of words.*

In his third, fourth, and fifth paragraphs Benét names the girls and women who met with Tituba. His description of the younger members of the circle is relatively neutral; he does little but mention their names and ages. In the fourth paragraph, however, where he takes up the older members, he calls Mrs. Pope and Mrs. Bibber "a pair of gossipy, superstitious busybodies." His description of Ann Putnam, Sr., in the next paragraph is even stronger; among other things, he notes that she is "arrogant" and that she "can cherish a grudge and revenge it."

From words like "arrogant," "busybody," and "gossipy," we can judge that Benét's intention is certainly not to treat these women sympathetically.

The contrast between Benét's neutral description of the younger members and his criticism of the older ones does not necessarily mean that he considers the former group blameless; it does, however, show effectively that he believes the older women should have known better. He has placed the primary responsibility on their shoulders.

But there is one other important caution concerning a writer's choice of words as a means of grasping intention: We must be sure that the author means what is said and is not speaking ironically. When in Shakespeare's *Julius Caesar* Antony calls Brutus, "an honorable man," we know that Antony does not mean what he says. How do you know that Benét means what he says when he calls the older women "gossipy, superstitious busybodies"?

Benét's intention of creating an unsympathetic picture of the older women is only a minor aspect of his overall intention. What was his major intention in "Trials at Salem"? What evidence from the essay supports your opinion?

Theme

Theme may be defined as the *central idea* in a work of literature. In nonfiction theme often takes the form of a *thesis;* that is, a position or proposition to be proved or supported by evidence.

How may an author's theme be expressed by a reader? A popular way of expressing theme is choosing a single word or phrase to describe the central idea. However, it may be difficult to decide what single word to use. Consider "Trials at Salem." Which of the following words most adequately describes its theme: "superstition," "injustice," "persecution," "community insanity," or "intolerance"? Even assuming that you can choose one of these words as somehow more appropriate than the others, you will probably agree that you haven't given a very clear indication of Benét's central idea.

The adequate expression of a theme almost always requires more than a single word. Indeed especially in nonfiction, it usually must be expressed in a complete sentence. Hence, Benét's theme might be stated as follows: "Community insanity, which grows out of superstition and intolerance, leads to injustice and persecution."

THE STRUGGLE FOR JUSTICE

It has been said, "All that is necessary for evil to succeed in the world is that enough good men do nothing." Like all great goods, justice rarely comes without a struggle, and the resulting drama becomes the natural concern of the aware and sensitive recorders among us—notably, the writers and the artists. This gallery displays something of the pictorial range of painters' concern for justice.

LAW VERSUS MOB RULE
John Steuart Curry

The vigor of the young nation was not a steadfast blessing. Faced with an affront to their young societies, citizens intense in their efforts to carve out a life in a new land, became, all too easily, a mob bent on destroying whatever threatened them. From the halls of the United States Department of Justice comes the fresco depicting the mastery of reason over the mob.

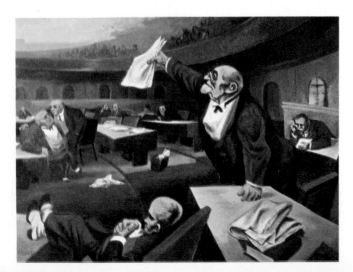

Angry over social injustices, the contemporary humorist William Gropper laces the legislature with a searing comment about the character and purpose of its members.

THE OPPOSITION
William Gropper

Even within the courts, justice has many sides. In the 1920s, the trial of two Italian immigrants accused of robbery and murder stirred passions throughout the country. Because the accused men held what were considered dangerous political beliefs, there were many Americans who felt that the trial was a cover for political persecution. After the men were convicted and executed, Ben Shahn's forceful painting was one of many protests.

THE PASSION OF
SACCO AND VANZETTI
Ben Shahn
*From the Sacco-Vanzetti series of
23 paintings. Tempera on canvas,
84½ x 48. Gift of Edith and
Milton Lowenthal in memory
of Juliana Force. Collection
Whitney Museum of American
Art, New York.*

BATTLE OF BUNKER'S HILL
John Trumbull
Yale University Art Gallery

What gallery of this theme in America could be complete
without a spirited scene from the Revolutionary War?
The painter, John Trumbull, a schoolteacher
in Connecticut before the war, had hoped
to become the acclaimed chronicler
of the struggle for justice
that began in 1776.

The contemporary American painter Jacob Lawrence
has created a stark, semiabstract painting
based on a famous incident in the Revolutionary War.
Notice how the bayonets
and sharp triangular shapes add tension
and an air of conflict to the scene.

GEORGE WASHINGTON CROSSING THE DELAWARE, NO. 46
Jacob Lawrence

Not without cynical humor
are the many election scenes painted
by that recorder of Young America, George Caleb Bingham.
The rough and tumble excesses of COUNTY ELECTION
may not have been all order and reason
but they were part of the pattern of political justice
for which the new nation was struggling.

COUNTY ELECTION
George Caleb Bingham

THE WOUNDED DRUMMER BOY
Eastman Johnson

Grace under pressure,"
was the novelist Hemingway's definition
for courage. It might seem
that during the Civil War,
Eastman Johnson said something similar
in his painting of THE WOUNDED DRUMMER
BOY. The youth saw the battle as a fight
for justice, and he was not easily put off.

The pilgrims seeking their place
in the sun are a poignant observation
that the struggle for justice
is never over.

MINORITIES 1939
William Gropper

Hamlin Garland, who was himself raised on a Midwestern farm, speaks with authority of the life of prairie farmers in the late 1800s. As you read the following story, consider how its title serves to point up the author's intention and theme.

Under the Lion's Paw

HAMLIN GARLAND

I

It was the last of autumn and first day of winter coming together. All day long the ploughmen on their prairie farms had moved to and fro in their wide level fields through the falling snow, which melted as it fell, wetting them to the skin—all day, notwithstanding the frequent squalls of snow, the dripping, desolate clouds, and the muck of the furrows, black and tenacious as tar.

Under their dripping harness the horses swung to and fro silently, with that marvellous uncomplaining patience which marks the horse. All day the wild geese, honking wildly, as they sprawled sidewise down the wind, seemed to be fleeing from an enemy behind, and with neck outthrust and wings extended, sailed down the wind, soon lost to sight.

Yet the ploughman behind his plough, though the snow lay on his ragged great-coat, and the cold clinging mud rose on his heavy boots, fettering him like gyves,[1] whistled in the very beard of the gale. As day passed, the snow, ceasing to melt, lay along the ploughed land, and lodged in the depth of the stubble, till on each slow round the last furrow stood out black and shining as jet between the ploughed land and the gray stubble.

When night began to fall, and the geese, flying low, began to alight invisibly in the near corn-field, Stephen Council was still at work "finishing a land." He rode on his sulky plough when going with the wind, but walked when facing it. Sitting bent and cold but cheery under his slouch hat, he talked encouragingly to his four-in-hand.

"Come round there, boys!—Round agin! We got t' finish this land. Come in there, Dan! *Stiddy*, Kate,—stiddy! None o' y'r tantrums, Kittie. It's purty tuff, but got a be did. *Tchk! tchk!* Step along, Pete! Don't let Kate git y'r single-tree on the wheel. *Once* more!"

They seemed to know what he meant, and that this was the last round, for they worked with greater vigor than before.

"Once more, boys, an' then, sez I, oats an' a nice warm stall, an' sleep f'r all."

By the time the last furrow was turned on the land it was too dark to see the house, and the snow was changing to rain again. The tired and hungry man could see the light from the kitchen shining through the leafless hedge, and he lifted a great shout, "Supper f'r a half a dozen!"

It was nearly eight o'clock by the time he had finished his chores and started for supper. He was picking his way carefully through the mud, when the tall form of a man loomed up before him with a premonitory cough.

"Waddy ye want?" was the rather startled question of the farmer.

---

1. **fettering,** binding or shackling the feet. **gyves**\jaivz\ another word for fetter or chain.

Reprinted by permission of Mrs. Constance Garland Doyle.

"Well, ye see," began the stranger, in a deprecating tone, "we'd like t' git in f'r the night. We've tried every house f'r the last two miles, but they hadn't any room f'r us. My wife's jest about sick, 'n' the children are cold and hungry —"

"Oh, y' want 'o stay all night, eh?"

"Yes, sir; it 'ud be a great accom—"

"Waal, I don't make it a practice t' turn anybuddy way hungry, not on sech nights as this. Drive right in. We ain't got much, but sech as it is—"

But the stranger had disappeared. And soon his steaming, weary team, with drooping heads and swinging single-trees, moved past the well to the block beside the path. Council stood at the side of the "schooner"[2] and helped the children out—two little half-sleeping children—and then a small woman with a babe in her arms.

"There ye go!" he shouted jovially, to the children. "*Now* we're all right! Run right along to the house there, an' tell Mam' Council you wants sumphin' t' eat. Right this way, Mis'—keep right off t' the right there. I'll go an' git a lantern. Come," he said to the dazed and silent group at his side.

"Mother," he shouted, as he neared the fragrant and warmly lighted kitchen, "here are some wayfarers an' folks who need sumphin' t' eat an' a place t' snooze." He ended by pushing them all in.

Mrs. Council, a large, jolly, rather coarse-looking woman, took the children in her arms. "Come right in, you little rabbits. 'Most asleep, hey? Now here's a drink o' milk f'r each o' ye. I'll have s'm tea in a minute. Take off y'r things and set up t' the fire."

While she set the children to drinking milk, Council got out his lantern and went out to the barn to help the stranger about his team, where his loud, hearty voice could be heard as it came and went between the haymow[3] and the stalls.

The woman came to light as a small, timid, and discouraged-looking woman, but still pretty, in a thin and sorrowful way.

"Land sakes! An' you've travelled all the way from Clear Lake t'-day in this mud! Waal! waal! No wonder you're all tired out. Don't wait f'r the men, Mis'—" She hesitated, waiting for the name.

"Haskins."

"Mis' Haskins, set right up to the table an' take a good swig o' tea whilst I make y' s'm toast. It's green tea, an' it's good. I tell Council as I git older I don't seem to enjoy Young Hyson n'r Gunpowder.[4] I want the reel green tea, jest as it comes off'n the vines. Seems t' have more heart in it, some way. Don't s'pose it has. Council says it's all in m' eye."

Going on in this easy way, she soon had the children filled with bread and milk and the woman thoroughly at home, eating some toast and sweet-melon pickles, and sipping the tea.

"See the little rats!" she laughed at the children. "They're full as they can stick now, and they want to go to bed. Now, don't git up, Mis' Haskins; set right where you are an' let me look after 'em. I know all about young ones, though I'm all alone now. Jane went an' married last fall. But, as I tell Council, it's lucky we keep our health. Set right there, Mis' Haskins; I won't have you stir a finger."

It was an unmeasured pleasure to sit there in the warm, homely kitchen, the jovial chatter of the housewife driving out and holding at bay the growl of the impotent, cheated wind.

The little woman's eyes filled with tears which fell down upon the sleeping baby in her arms. The world was not so desolate and cold and hopeless, after all.

"Now I hope Council won't stop out there and talk politics all night. He's the greatest man to talk politics an' read the *Tribune*—How old is it?"

She broke off and peered down at the face of the babe.

"Two months 'n' five days," said the mother, with a mother's exactness.

---

2. **schooner**, covered wagon.
3. **haymow**, a part of the barn where the hay is stored.
4. **Young Hyson . . . Gunpowder**, kinds of tea.

"Ye don't say! I want 'o know! The dear little pudzy-wudzy!" she went on, stirring it up in the neighborhood of the ribs with her fat fore-finger.

"Pooty tough on 'oo to go gallivant'n' 'cross lots this way—"

"Yes, that's so; a man can't lift a mountain," said Council, entering the door. "Mother, this is Mr. Haskins, from Kansas. He's been eat up 'n' drove out by grasshoppers."

"Glad t' see yeh!—Pa, empty that wash-basin 'n' give him a chance t' wash."

Haskins was a tall man, with a thin, gloomy face. His hair was a reddish brown, like his coat, and seemed equally faded by the wind and sun, and his sallow face, though hard and set, was pathetic somehow. You would have felt that he had suffered much by the line of his mouth showing under his thin, yellow mustache.

"Hain't Ike got home yet, Sairy?"

"Hain't seen 'im."

"W-a-a-l, set right up, Mr. Haskins; wade right into what we've got; 'tain't much, but we manage to live on it—she gits fat on it," laughed Council, pointing his thumb at his wife.

After supper, while the women put the children to bed, Haskins and Council talked on, seated near the huge cooking-stove, the steam rising from their wet clothing. In the Western fashion Council told as much of his own life as he drew from his guest. He asked but few questions, but by and by the story of Haskins' struggles and defeat came out. The story was a terrible one, but he told it quietly, seated with his elbows on his knees, gazing most of the time at the hearth.

"I didn't like the looks of the country, any-how," Haskins said, partly rising and glancing at his wife. "I was ust t' northern Ingyannie,[5] where we have lots o' timber 'n' lots o' rain, 'n' I didn't like the looks o' that dry prairie. What galled me the worst was goin' s' far away acrosst so much fine land layin' all through here vacant."

"And the 'hoppers eat ye four years, hand runnin', did they?"

"Eat! They wiped us out. They chawed everything that was green. They jest set around waitin' f'r us to die t' eat us, too. I swear! I ust t' dream of 'em sittin' 'round on the bedpost, six feet long, workin' their jaws. They eet the fork-handles. They got worse 'n' worse till they jest rolled on one another, piled up like snow in winter. Well, it ain't no use. If I was t' talk all winter I couldn't tell nawthin'. But all the while I couldn't help thinkin' of all that land back here that nobuddy was usin' that I ought 'o had 'stead o' bein' out there in that cussed country."

"Waal, why didn't ye stop an' settle here?" asked Ike, who had come in and was eating his supper.

"Fer the simple reason that you fellers wantid ten 'r fifteen dollars an acre fer the bare land, and I hadn't no money fer that kind o' thing."

"Yes, I do my own work," Mrs. Council was heard to say in the pause which followed. "I'm a gettin' purty heavy t' be on m' laigs all day, but we can't afford t' hire, so I keep rackin'[6] around somehow, like a foundered horse.[7] S' lame—I tell Council he can't tell how lame I am, f'r I'm jest as lame in one laig as t'other." And the good soul laughed at the joke on her-self as she took a handful of flour and dusted the biscuit-board to keep the dough from sticking.

"Well, I hain't *never* been very strong," said Mrs. Haskins. "Our folks was Canadians an' small-boned, and then since my last child I hain't got up again fairly. I don't like t' com-plain. Tim has about all he can bear now—but they was days this week when I jest wanted to lay right down an' die."

"Waal, now, I'll tell ye," said Council, from his side of the stove, silencing everybody with his good-natured roar, "I'd go down and *see* Butler, *anyway*, if I was you. I guess he'd let you have his place purty cheap; the farm's all run down. He's ben anxious t' let t' somebuddy next year. It 'ud be a good chance fer you. Any-

---

5. **Ingyannie**, Indiana.
6. **rackin'**, stretching and straining.
7. **foundered horse**, horse disabled or gone lame.

how, you go to bed and sleep like a babe. I've got some ploughin' t' do, anyhow, an' we'll see if somethin' can't be done about your case. Ike, you go out an' see if the horses is all right, an' I'll show the folks t' bed."

When the tired husband and wife were lying under the generous quilts of the spare bed, Haskins listened a moment to the wind in the eaves, and then said, with a slow and solemn tone,

"There are people in this world who are good enough t' be angels, an' only haff t' die to *be* angels."

II

Jim Butler was one of those men called in the West "land poor." Early in the history of Rock River he had come into the town and started in the grocery business in a small way, occupying a small building in a mean part of the town. At this period of his life he earned all he got, and was up early and late sorting beans, working over butter, and carting his goods to and from the station. But a change came over him at the end of the second year, when he sold a lot of land for four times what he paid for it. From that time forward he believed in land speculation as the surest way of getting rich. Every cent he could save or spare from his trade he put into land at forced sale, or mortgages on land, which were "just as good as the wheat," he was accustomed to say.

Farm after farm fell into his hands, until he was recognized as one of the leading landowners of the county. His mortgages were scattered all over Cedar County, and as they slowly but surely fell in he sought usually to retain the former owner as tenant.

He was not ready to foreclose; indeed, he had the name of being one of the "easiest" men in the town. He let the debtor off again and again, extending the time whenever possible.

"I don't want y'r land," he said. "All I'm after is the int'rest on my money—that's all. Now, if y' want o' stay on the farm, why, I'll give y' a good chance. I can't have the land layin' va-

cant." And in many cases the owner remained as tenant.

In the meantime he had sold his store; he couldn't spend time in it; he was mainly occupied now with sitting around town on rainy days smoking and "gassin' with the boys," or in riding to and from his farms. In fishing-time he fished a good deal. Doc Grimes, Ben Ashley, and Cal Cheatham were his cronies on these fishing excursions or hunting trips in the time of chickens or partridges. In winter they went to Northern Wisconsin to shoot deer.

In spite of all these signs of easy life Butler persisted in saying he "hadn't enough money to pay taxes on his land," and was careful to convey the impression that he was poor in spite of his twenty farms. At one time he was said to be worth fifty thousand dollars, but land had been a little slow of sale of late, so that he was not worth so much.

A fine farm, known as the Higley place, had fallen into his hands in the usual way the previous year, and he had not been able to find a tenant for it. Poor Higley, after working himself nearly to death on it in the attempt to lift the mortgage, had gone off to Dakota, leaving the farm and his curse to Butler.

This was the farm which Council advised Haskins to apply for; and the next day Council hitched up his team and drove down town to see Butler.

"You jest let *me* do the talkin'," he said. "We'll find him wearin' out his pants on some salt barrel somew'ers; and if he thought you *wanted* a place he'd sock it to you hot and heavy. You jest keep quiet; I'll fix 'im."

Butler was seated in Ben Ashley's store telling fish yarns when Council sauntered in casually.

"Hello, But; lyin' agin, hey?"

"Hello, Steve! how goes it?"

"Oh, so-so. Too dang much rain these days. I thought it was goin' t' freeze up fr good last night. Tight squeak if I get m' ploughin' done. How's farmin' with *you* these days?"

"Bad. Ploughin' ain't half done."

"It 'ud be a religious idee f'r you t' go out an' take a hand y'rself."

"I don't haff to," said Butler, with a wink.

"Got anybody on the Higley place?"

"No. Know of anybody?"

"Waal, no; not eggsackly. I've got a relation back t' Michigan who's ben hot an' cold on the idee o' comin' West f'r some time. *Might* come if he could get a good lay-out. What do you talk on the farm?"

"Well, I d' know. I'll rent it on shares or I'll rent it money rent."

"Waal, how much money, say?"

"Well, say ten per cent, on the price—two-fifty."

"Waal, that ain't bad. Wait on 'im till 'e thrashes?"

Haskins listened eagerly to his important question, but Council was coolly eating a dried apple which he had speared out of a barrel with his knife. Butler studied him carefully.

"Well, knocks me out of twenty-five dollars interest."

"My relation'll need all he's got t' git his crops in," said Council, in the safe, indifferent way.

"Well, all right; *say* wait," concluded Butler.

"All right; this is the man. Haskins, this is Mr. Butler—no relation to Ben—the hardest-working man in Cedar County."

On the way home Haskins said: "I ain't much better off. I'd like that farm; it's a good farm, but it's all run down, an' so 'm I. I could make a good farm of it if I had half a show. But I can't stock it n'r seed it."

"Waal, now, don't you worry," roared Council in his ear. "We'll pull y' through somehow till next harvest. He's agreed t' hire it ploughed, an' you can earn a hundred dollars ploughin' an' y' c'n git the seed o' me, an' pay me back when y' can."

Haskins was silent with emotion, but at last he said, "I ain't got nothin' t' live on."

"Now, don't you worry 'bout that. You jest make your headquarters at ol' Steve Council's. Mother'll take a pile o' comfort in havin' y'r wife an' children 'round. Y' see, Jane's married off latey, an' Ike's away a good 'eal, so we'll be darn glad t' have y' stop with us this winter. Nex' spring we'll see if y' can't git a start agin." And he chirruped to the team, which sprang forward with the rumbling, clattering wagon.

"Say, looky here, Council, you can't do this. I never saw—" shouted Haskins in his neighbor's ear.

Council moved about uneasily in his seat and stopped his stammering gratitude by saying: "Hold on, now; don't make such a fuss over a little thing. When I see a man down, an' things all on top of 'm, I jest like t' kick 'em off an' help 'm up. That's the kind of religion I got, an' it's about the *only* kind."

They rode the rest of the way home in silence. And when the red light of the lamp shone out into the darkness of the cold and windy night, and he thought of this refuge for his children and wife, Haskins could have put his arm around the neck of his burly companion and squeezed him like a lover. But he contented himself with saying, "Steve Council, you'll git y'r pay f'r this some day."

"Don't want any pay. My religion ain't run on such business principles."

The wind was growing colder, and the ground was covered with a white frost, as they turned into the gate of the Council farm, and the children came rushing out, shouting, "Papa's come!" They hardly looked like the same children who had sat at the table the night before. Their torpidity, under the influence of sunshine and Mother Council, had given way to a sort of spasmodic cheerfulness, as insects in winter revive when laid on the hearth.

III

Haskins worked like a fiend, and his wife, like the heroic woman that she was, bore also uncomplainingly the most terrible burdens. They rose early and toiled without intermission till the darkness fell on the plain, then tumbled into bed, every bone and muscle aching with fatigue, to rise with the sun next morning to the same round of the same ferocity of labor.

The eldest boy drove a team all through the spring, ploughing and seeding, milked the cows, and did chores innumerable, in most ways taking the place of a man.

An infinitely pathetic but common figure—this boy on the American farm, where there is no law against child labor. To see him in his coarse clothing, his huge boots, and his ragged cap, as he staggered with a pail of water from the well, or trudged in the cold and cheerless dawn out into the frosty field behind his team, gave the city-bred visitor a sharp pang of sympathetic pain. Yet Haskins loved his boy, and would have saved him from this if he could, but he could not.

By June the first year the result of such Herculean[8] toil began to show on the farm. The yard was cleaned up and sown to grass, the garden ploughed and planted, and the house mended.

Council had given them four of his cows.

"Take 'em an' run 'em on shares. I don't want 'o milk s' many. Ike's away s' much now, Sat'd'ys an' Sund'ys, I can't stand the bother anyhow."

Other men, seeing the confidence of Council in the newcomer, had sold him tools on time; and as he was really an able farmer, he soon had round him many evidences of his care and thrift. At the advice of Council he had taken the farm for three years, with the privilege of re-renting or buying at the end of the term.

"It's a good bargain, an' y' want 'o nail it," said Council. "If you have any kind ov a crop, you c'n pay y'r debts, an' keep seed an' bread."

The new hope which now sprang up in the heart of Haskins and his wife grew great almost as a pain by the time the wide field of wheat began to wave and rustle and swirl in the winds of July. Day after day he would snatch a few moments after supper to go and look at it.

"Have ye seen the wheat t'-day, Nettie?" he asked one night as he rose from supper.

"No, Tim, I ain't had time."

"Well, take time now. Le's go look at it."

She threw an old hat on her head—Tommy's hat—and looking almost pretty in her thin, sad way, went out with her husband to the hedge.

"Ain't it grand, Nettie? Just look at it."

It was grand. Level, russet here and there, heavy-headed, wide as a lake, and full of multitudinous whispers and gleams of wealth, it stretched away before the gazers like the fabled field of the cloth of gold.[9]

"Oh, I think—I *hope* we'll have a good crop, Tim; and oh, how good the people have been to us!"

"Yes; I don't know where we'd be t'-day if it hadn't ben f'r Council and his wife."

"They're the best people in the world," said the little woman, with a great sob of gratitude.

"We'll be in the field on Monday, sure," said Haskins, gripping the rail on the fence as if already at the work of the harvest.

The harvest came, bounteous, glorious, but the winds came and blew it into tangles, and the rain matted it here and there close to the ground, increasing the work of gathering it threefold.

Oh, how they toiled in those glorious days! Clothing dripping with sweat, arms aching, filled with briers, fingers raw and bleeding, backs broken with the weight of heavy bundles, Haskins and his man toiled on. Tommy drove the harvester, while his father and a hired man bound on the machine. In this way they cut ten acres every day, and almost every night after supper, when the hand went to bed, Haskins returned to the field shocking the bound grain in the light of the moon. Many a night he worked till his anxious wife came out at ten o'clock to call him in to rest and lunch.

At the same time she cooked for the men, took care of the children, washed and ironed, milked the cows at night, made the butter, and sometimes fed the horses and watered them while her husband kept at the shocking.

No slave in the Roman galleys could have toiled so frightfully and lived, for this man thought himself a free man, and that he was working for his wife and babes.

---

8. **Herculean**\ˈhər·kyə ᴧlē·ən\ work requiring superhuman strength like that of Hercules.
9. **cloth of gold,** Golden Fleece rescued by Jason.

When he sank into his bed with a deep groan of relief, too tired to change his grimy, dripping clothing, he felt that he was getting nearer and nearer to a home of his own, and pushing the wolf of want a little farther from his door.

There is no despair so deep as the despair of a homeless man or woman. To roam the roads of the country or the streets of the city, to feel there is no rood of ground on which the feet can rest, to halt weary and hungry outside lighted windows and hear laughter and song within,—these are the hungers and rebellions that drive men to crime and women to shame.

It was the memory of this homelessness, and the fear of its coming again, that spurred Timothy Haskins and Nettie, his wife, to such ferocious labor during that first year.

IV

"'M, yes; 'm, yes; first-rate," said Butler, as his eye took in the neat garden, the pig-pen, and the well-filled barnyard. "You're gitt'n' quite a stock around yeh. Done well, eh?"

Haskins was showing Butler around the place. He had not seen it for a year, having spent the year in Washington and Boston with Ashley, his brother-in-law, who had been elected to Congress.

"Yes, I've laid out a good deal of money durin' the last three years. I've paid out three hundred dollars f'r fencin'."

"Um—h'm! I see, I see," said Butler, while Haskins went on:

"The kitchen there cost two hundred; the barn ain't cost much in money, but I've put a lot o' time on it. I've dug a new well, and I—"

"Yes, yes, I see. You've done well. Stock worth a thousand dollars," said Butler, picking his teeth with a straw.

"About that," said Haskins, modestly. "We begin to feel's if we was gitt'n' a home f'r ourselves; but we've worked hard. I tell you we begin to feel it, Mr. Butler, and we're goin' t' begin to ease up purty soon. We've been kind o' plannin' a trip back t' *her* folks after the fall ploughin's done."

"*Eggs*-actly!" said Butler, who was evidently thinking of something else. "I suppose you've kind o' calc'lated on stayin' here three years more?"

"Well, yes. Fact is, I think I c'n buy the farm this fall, if you'll give me a reasonable show."

"Um—m! What do you call a reasonable show?"

"Well, say a quarter down and three years' time."

Butler looked at the huge stacks of wheat, which filled the yard, over which the chickens were fluttering and crawling, catching grasshoppers, and out of which the crickets were singing innumerably. He smiled in a peculiar way as he said, "Oh, I won't be hard on yeh. But what did you expect to pay f'r the place?"

"Why, about what you offered it for before, two thousand five hundred, or *possibly* three thousand dollars," he added quickly, as he saw the owner shake his head.

"This farm is worth five thousand and five hundred dollars," said Butler, in a careless and decided voice.

"*What!*" almost shrieked the astounded Haskins. "What's that? Five thousand? Why, that's double what you offered it for three years ago."

"Of course, and it's worth it. It was all run down then; now it's in good shape. You've laid out fifteen hundred dollars in improvements, according to your own story."

"But *you* had nothin' t' do about that. It's my work an' my money."

"You bet it was; but it's my land."

"But what's to pay me for all my—"

"Ain't you had the use of 'em?" replied Butler, smiling calmly into his face.

Haskins was like a man struck on the head with a sandbag; he couldn't think; he stammered as he tried to say: "But—I never'd git the use—You'd rob me! More'n that: you agreed—you promised that I could buy or rent at the end of three years at—"

"That's all right. But I didn't say I'd let you carry off the improvements, nor that I'd go on renting the farm at two-fifty. The land is doubled in value, it don't matter how; it don't enter into the question; an' now you can pay me five hundred dollars a year rent, or take it on your own terms at fifty-five hundred, or—git out."

He was turning away when Haskins, the sweat pouring from his face, fronted him, saying again:

"But *you've* done nothing to make it so. You hain't added a cent. I put it all there myself, expectin' to buy. I worked an' sweat to improve it. I was workin' for myself an' babes—"

"Well, why didn't you buy when I offered to sell? What y' kickin' about?"

"I'm kickin' about payin' you twice fr my own things,—my own fences, my own kitchen, my own garden."

Butler laughed. "You're too green t' eat, young feller. *Your* improvements! The law will sing another tune."

"But I trusted your word."

"Never trust anybody, my friend. Besides, I didn't promise not to do this thing. Why, man, don't look at me like that. Don't take me for a thief. It's the law. The reg'lar thing. Everybody does it."

"I don't care if they do. It's stealin' jest the same. You take three thousand dollars of my money—the work o' my hands and my wife's." He broke down at this point. He was not a strong man mentally. He could face hardship, ceaseless toil, but he could not face the cold and sneering face of Butler.

"But I don't take it," said Butler, coolly. "All you've got to do is to go on jest as you've been a-doin', or give me a thousand dollars down, and a mortgage at ten per cent on the rest."

Haskins sat down blindly on a bundle of oats near by, and with staring eyes and drooping head went over the situation. He was under the lion's paw. He felt a horrible numbness in his heart and limbs. He was hid in a mist, and there was no path out.

Butler walked about, looking at the huge stacks of grain, and pulling now and again a few handfuls out, shelling the heads in his hands and blowing the chaff away. He hummed a little tune as he did so. He had an accommodating air of waiting.

Haskins was in the midst of the terrible toil of the last year. He was walking again in the rain and the mud behind his plough; he felt the dust and dirt of the threshing. The ferocious husking-time, with its cutting wind and biting, clinging snows, lay hard upon him. Then he thought of his wife, how she had cheerfully cooked and baked, without holiday and without rest.

"Well, what do you think of it?" inquired the cool, mocking, insinuating voice of Butler.

"I think you're a thief and a liar!" shouted Haskins, leaping up. "A black-hearted houn'!" Butler's smile maddened him; with a sudden leap he caught a fork in his hands, and whirled it in the air. "You'll never rob another man, I swear!" he grated through his teeth, a look of pitiless ferocity in his accusing eyes.

Butler shrank and quivered, expecting the blow; stood, held hypnotized by the eyes of the man he had a moment before despised—a man transformed into an avenging demon. But in the deadly hush between the lift of the weapon and its fall there came a gush of faint, childish laughter and then across the range of his vision, far away and dim, he saw the sun-bright head of his baby girl, as, with the pretty, tottering run of a two-year-old, she moved across the grass of the dooryard. His hands relaxed; the fork fell to the ground; his head lowered.

"Make out y'd deed an' mor'gage, an git off'n my land, an' don't ye never cross my line agin; if y' do, I'll kill ye."

Butler backed away from the man in wild haste, and climbing into his buggy with trembling limbs drove off down the road, leaving Haskins seated dumbly on the sunny pile of sheaves, his head sunk into his hands.

I

LOCAL-COLOR WRITING
AND REGIONALISM

Previous to the Civil War, New York and New England were the dominant centers of American literature. Soon after the War, however, a tendency toward decentralization was marked. Many writers tried to capture the local color of the region in which they lived by reporting its speech, customs, and geographical details. Such writers are often called "local colorists" or "regionalists."

Today, the term "local colorist" is chiefly used to denote those writers who capitalize on the oddities of setting with little or no attention to deeper and more universal values. The term "regionalist," by contrast, is reserved for writers who, though they concentrate on a given geographical area, do so with an eye to revealing deeper and larger aspects of human nature.

Using these definitions, classify "Under the Lion's Paw" as local color or as regionalist literature. Specifically, are Garland's characters solid individuals, or merely Midwestern "types"?

II
IMPLICATIONS

The following represent possible reactions to the story. Compare each reaction with your own, and discuss why you agree or disagree with them.

1. Haskins "got what he deserved." He should have been intelligent enough to protect himself against a man like Butler.

2. The story should have ended with Haskins killing Butler.

3. The appearance of the child at the end of the story is a "trick"; it cheapens the story because the only motive for the child's appearance is the author's desire not to have Haskins become a murderer.

4. The whole story was unrealistic; it was impossible to believe that Butler would actually have had the law on his side.

III
TECHNIQUES

Intention

Writers reveal their intentions not only by choice of words but also by *choice of incidents.* Try to determine how the following incidents reveal Garland's intentions.

1. Council plowing his field.

2. The appearance of the Haskins family and the conversations between the Haskinses and the Councils.

3. The appearance of Butler and the conversation between him and the other two men.

4. The conversation between Haskins and Council that follows the above incident.

5. The details and conversation concerning the result of the first year's work on the farm.

6. The final conversation between Haskins and Butler.

Theme

The nature and relative importance of a theme in a short story may be highlighted by a reference to it or to some aspect of it in the title of the story. Considering the story itself and its title, state the theme of "Under the Lion's Paw."

Do you agree or disagree with the notion that Garland was primarily interested in getting across the theme, as opposed to such other things as (1) drawing a vivid portrait of farm life in the Midwest, (2) telling an exciting story, or (3) creating a number of convincing and interesting characters?

IV
WORDS

A. In each of the following phrases, substitute the word in the parentheses for the italicized word. Explain the difference in meaning between the italicized word and the possible synonym.

(1) *credulous* (superstitious) servants; (2) *enigmatic* (obscure) figure; (3) *circumstantial* (presumptive) chain; (4) *revile* (scold) any person; (5) *badgering* (riding) of the regulars; (6) *infuriated* (enraged) masses; (7) *tenacious* (sturdy) as tar.

B. Usage depends on the situation. Such a statement as "we haven't much" would be acceptable in most situations but "we ain't got much" would not. A speaker who habitually uses such structures "see if the horses is all right," "I likes to do that," "ain't seen them people," we consider uneducated. Which of the following statements would be acceptable in most situations? Which would not? Which are ungrammatical?

(a) I'm all whipped out; (b) I'm so very tired; (c) I ain't got no energy; (d) I haven't any energy left; (e) I am extremely exhausted; (f) My energy state is presently at a depressed level.

The following selection, by the contemporary author Jesse Stuart,
is a chapter from a biography entitled *Clearing in the Sky*. As you read it
you will find that it has many parallels with Garland's
"Under the Lion's Paw," but it also differs in a number of ways
from the Garland story. Look especially for the contrast in the styles
of the two authors and for the contrast in the reactions
of the protagonists.

Testimony of Trees

JESSE STUART

We had just moved onto the first farm we had ever owned when Jake Timmins walked down the path to the barn where Pa and I were nailing planks on a barn stall. Pa stood with a nail in one hand and his hatchet in the other while I stood holding the plank. We watched this small man with a beardy face walk toward us. He took short steps and jabbed his sharpened sourwood cane into the ground as he hurried down the path.

"Wonder what he's after?" Pa asked as Jake Timmins came near the barn.

"Don't know," I said.

"Howdy, Mick," Jake said as he leaned on his cane and looked over the new barn that we had built.

"Howdy, Jake," Pa grunted. We had heard how Jake Timmins had taken men's farms. Pa was nervous when he spoke, for I watched the hatchet shake in his hand.

"I see ye're a-putting improvements on yer barn," Jake said.

"A-tryin' to get it fixed for winter," Pa told him.

"I'd advise ye to stop now, Mick," he said. "Jist want to be fair with ye so ye won't go ahead and do a lot of work fer me fer nothing."

"How's that, Jake?" Pa asked.

"Ye've built yer barn on my land, Mick," he said with a little laugh.

"Ain't you a-joking, Jake?" Pa asked him.

"Nope, this is my land by rights," he told Pa as he looked our new barn over. "I hate to take this land with this fine barn on it, but it's mine and I'll haf to take it."

"I'm afraid not, Jake," Pa said. "I've been around here since I was a boy. I know where the lines run. I know that ledge of rocks with that row of oak trees a-growing on it is the line!"

"No it hain't, Mick," Jake said. "If it goes to court, ye'll find out. The line runs from that big dead chestnut up there on the knoll, straight across this holler to the top of the knoll up there where the twin hickories grow."

"But that takes my barn, my meadow, my garden," Pa said. "That takes ten acres of the best land I have. It almost gets my house!"

The hatchet quivered in Pa's hand and his lips trembled when he spoke.

"Tim Mennix sold ye land that belonged to me," Jake said.

"But you ought to a-said something about it before I built my house and barn on it," Pa told Jake fast as the words would leave his mouth.

"Sorry, Mick," Jake said, "but I must be a-going. I've given ye fair warning that ye air a-building on my land!"

From *Clearing in the Sky* by Jesse Stuart. Copyright 1950 McGraw-Hill Book Company. Used by permission.

"But I bought this land," Pa told him. "I'm a-goin' to keep it."

"I can't hep that," Jake told Pa as he turned to walk away. "Don't tear this barn down fer it's on my property!"

"Don't worry, Jake," Pa said. "I'm not a-tearing this barn down. I'll be a-feeding my cattle in it this winter!"

Jake Timmins walked slowly up the path the way he had come. Pa and I stood watching him as he stopped and looked our barn over; then he looked at our garden that we had fenced and he looked at the new house that we had built.

"I guess he'll be a-claiming the house too," Pa said.

And just as soon as Jake Timmins crossed the ledge of rocks that separated our farms Pa threw his hatchet to the ground and hurried from the barn.

"Where are you a-going, Pa?" I asked.

"To see Tim Mennix."

"Can I go too?"

"Come along," he said.

We hurried over the mountain path toward Tim Mennix's shack. He lived two miles from us. Pa's brogan shoes[1] rustled the fallen leaves that covered the path. October wind moaned among the leafless treetops. Soon as we reached the shack we found Tim cutting wood near his woodshed.

"What's the hurry, Mick?" Tim asked Pa who stood wiping sweat from his October-leaf-colored face with his blue bandanna.

"Jake Timmins is a-tryin' to take my land," Pa told Tim.

"Ye don't mean it?"

"I do mean it," Pa said. "He's just been to see me and he said the land where my barn, garden, and meadow were belonged to him. Claims about ten acres of the best land I got. I told him I bought it from you and he said it didn't belong to you to sell."

"That ledge of rocks and the big oak trees that grow along the backbone of the ledge has been the line fer seventy years," Tim said. "But

lissen, Mick, when Jake Timmins wants a piece of land, he takes it."

"People told me he's like that," Pa said. "I was warned against buying my farm because he's like that. People said he'd steal all my land if I lived beside him ten years."

"He'll have it before then, Mick," Tim Mennix told Pa in a trembling voice. "He didn't have but an acre to start from. That acre was a bluff where three farms jined and no one fenced it in because it was worthless and they didn't want it. He had a deed made fer this acre and he's had forty lawsuits when he set his fence over on other people's farms and took their land, but he goes to court and wins every time."

"I'll have the County Surveyor, Finn Madden, to survey my lines," Pa said.

"That won't hep any," Tim told Pa. "There's been more people kilt over the line fences that he's surveyed than has been kilt over any other one thing in this county. Surveyor Finn Madden's a good friend to Jake."

"But he's the County Surveyor," Pa said. "I'll haf to have him."

"Jake Timmins is a dangerous man," Tim Mennix warned Pa. "He's dangerous as a loaded double-barrel shotgun with both hammers cocked."

"I've heard that," Pa said. "I don't want any trouble. I'm a married man with a family."

When we reached home, we saw Jake upon the knoll at the big chestnut tree sighting across the hollow to the twin hickories on the knoll above our house. And as he sighted across the hollow, he walked along and drove stakes into the ground. He set one stake in our front yard, about five feet from the corner of our house. Pa started out on him once but Mom wouldn't let him go. Mom said let the law settle the dispute over the land.

And that night Pa couldn't go to sleep. I was awake and heard him a-walking the floor when the clock struck twelve. I knew that Pa was worried, for Jake was the most feared man

---

1. **brogan shoes,** coarse leather work shoes.

among our hills. He had started with one acre and now had over four hundred acres that he had taken from other people.

Next day Surveyor Finn Madden and Jake ran a line across the hollow just about on the same line that Jake had surveyed with his own eyes. And while Surveyor Finn Madden looked through the instrument, he had Jake set the stakes and drive them into the ground with a poleax. They worked at the line all day. And when they had finished surveying the line, Pa went up on the knoll at the twin hickories behind our house and asked Surveyor Finn Madden if his line was right.

"Surveyed it right with the deed," he told Pa. "Tim Mennix sold you land that didn't belong to him."

"Looks like this line would've been surveyed before I built my barn," Pa said.

"Can't see why it wasn't," he told Pa. "Looks like you're a-losing the best part of your farm, Mick."

Then Surveyor Finn Madden, a tall man with a white beard, and Jake Timmins went down the hill together.

"I'm not so sure that I'm a-losing the best part of my farm," Pa said. "I'm not a-goin' to sit down and take it! I know Jake's a land thief and it's time his stealing land is stopped."

"What are you a-goin' to do, Pa?" I asked.

"Don't know," he said.

"You're not a-goin' to hurt Jake over the land, are you?"

He didn't say anything but he looked at the two men as they turned over the ledge of rocks and out of sight.

"You know Mom said the land wasn't worth hurting anybody over," I said.

"But it's my land," Pa said.

And that night Pa walked the floor. And Mom got out of bed and talked to him and made him go to bed. And that day Sheriff Eif Whiteapple served a notice on Pa to keep his cattle out of the barn that we had built. The notice said that the barn belonged to Jake Timmins. Jake ordered us to put our chickens up, to keep them off his garden when it was our

garden. He told us not to let anything trespass on his land and his land was on the other side of the stakes. We couldn't even walk in part of our yard.

"He'll have the house next if we don't do something about it," Pa said.

Pa walked around our house in a deep study. He was trying to think of something to do about it. Mom talked to him. She told him to get a lawyer and fight the case in court. But Pa said something had to be done to prove that the land belonged to us, though we had a deed for our land in our trunk. And before Sunday came, Pa dressed in his best clothes.

"Where're you a-going, Mick?" Mom asked.

"A-goin' to see Uncle Mel," he said. "He's been in a lot of line-fence fights and he could give me some good advice!"

"We hate to stay here and you gone, Mick," Mom said.

"Just don't step on property Jake laid claim to until I get back," Pa said. "I'll be back soon as I can. Some time next week you can look for me."

Pa went to West Virginia to get Uncle Mel. And while he was gone, Jake Timmins hauled wagonloads of hay and corn to the barn that we had built. He had taken over as if it were his own and as if he would always have it. We didn't step beyond the stakes where Surveyor Finn Madden had surveyed. We waited for Pa to come. And when Pa came, Uncle Mel came with him carrying a long-handled double-bitted ax and a turkey of clothes across his shoulder. Before they reached the house, Pa showed Uncle Mel the land Jake Timmins had taken.

"Land hogs air pizen as copperhead snakes," Uncle Mel said, then he fondled his long white beard in his hand. Uncle Mel was eighty-two years old, but his eyes were keen as sharp-pointed briers and his shoulders were broad and his hands were big and rough. He had been a timber cutter all his days and he was still a-cuttin' timber in West Virginia at the age of eighty-two. "He can't do this to ye, Mick!"

Uncle Mel was madder than Pa when he looked over the new line that they had surveyed from the dead chestnut on one knoll to the twin hickories on the other knoll.

"Anybody would know the line wouldn't go like that," Uncle Mel said. "The line would follow the ridge."

"Looks that way to me too," Pa said.

"He's a-stealin' yer land, Mick," Uncle Mel said. "I'll hep ye get yer land back. He'll never beat me. I've had to fight too many squatters a-tryin' to take my land. I know how to fight 'em with the law."

That night Pa and Uncle Mel sat before the fire and Uncle Mel looked over Pa's deed. Uncle Mel couldn't read very well and when he came to a word he couldn't read, I told him what it was.

"We'll haf to have a court order first, Mick," Uncle Mel said. "When we get the court order, I'll find the line."

I didn't know what Uncle Mel wanted with a court order, but I found out after he got it. He couldn't chop on a line tree until he got an order from the court. And soon as Pa got the court order and gathered a group of men for witnesses, Uncle Mel started work on the line fence.

"Sixteen rods from the dead chestnut due north," Uncle Mel said, and we started measuring sixteen rods due north.

"That's the oak tree, there," Uncle Mel said. It measured exactly sixteen rods from the dead chestnut to the black oak tree.

"Deed said the oak was blazed," Uncle Mel said, for he'd gone over the deed until he'd memorized it.

"See the scar, men," Uncle Mel said.

"But that was done seventy years ago," Pa said.

"Funny about the testimony of trees," Uncle Mel told Pa, Tim Mennix, Orbie Dorton, and Dave Sperry. "The scar will allus stay on the outside of a tree well as on the inside. The silent trees will keep their secrets."

Uncle Mel started chopping into the tree. He swung his ax over his shoulder and bit out a slice of wood every time he struck. He cut a neat block into the tree until he found a dark place deep inside the tree.

"Come, men, and look," Uncle Mel said. "Look at that scar. It's as pretty a scar as I ever seen in the heart of a tree!"

And while Uncle Mel wiped sweat with his blue bandanna from his white beard, we looked at the scar.

"It's a scar, all right," Tim Mennix said, since he had been a timber cutter most of his life and knew a scar on a tree.

"Think that was cut seventy years ago," Orbie Dorton said. "That's when the deed was made and the old survey was run."

"We'll see if it's been seventy years ago," Uncle Mel said as he started counting the rings in the tree. "Each ring is a year's growth."

We watched Uncle Mel pull his knife from his pocket, open the blade, and touch each ring with his knife-blade point as he counted the rings across the square he had chopped into the tree. Uncle Mel counted exactly seventy rings from the bark to the scar.

"Ain't it the line tree, boys?" Uncle Mel asked.

"Can't be anything else," Dave Sperry said.

And then Uncle Mel read the deed, which called for a mulberry thirteen rods due north from the black oak. We measured to the mulberry and Uncle Mel cut his notch to the scar and counted the rings. It was seventy rings from the bark to the scar. Ten more rods we came to the poplar the deed called for, and he found the scar on the outer bark and inside the tree. We found every tree the deed called for but one, and we found its stump. We surveyed the land from the dead chestnut to the twin hickories. We followed it around the ledge.

"We have the evidence to take to court," Uncle Mel said. "I'd like to bring the jurymen right here to this line fence to show 'em."

"I'll go right to town and put this thing in court," Pa said.

"I'll go around and see the men that have lost land to Jake Timmins," Uncle Mel said. "I want 'em to be at the trial."

Before our case got to court, Uncle Mel had shown seven of our neighbors how to trace their lines and get their land back from Jake Timmins. And when our trial was called, the courthouse was filled with people who had lost land and who had disputes with their neighbors over line fences, attending the trial to see if we won. Jake Timmins, Surveyor Finn Madden, and their lawyer, Henson Stapleton, had produced their side of the question before the jurors and we had lawyer Sherman Stone and our witnesses to present our side, while all the landowners Jake Timmins had stolen land from listened to the trial. The foreman of the jury asked that the members of the jury be taken to the line fence.

"Now here's the way to tell where a line was blazed on saplings seventy years ago," Uncle Mel said, as he showed them the inner mark on the line oak; then he showed them the outward scar. Uncle Mel took them along the line fence and showed them each tree that the deed called for all but the one that had fallen.

"It's plain as the nose on your face," Uncle Mel would say every time he explained each line tree. "Too many land thieves in this county and a county surveyor the devil won't have in hell."

After Uncle Mel had explained the line fence to the jurors, they followed Sheriff Whiteapple and his deputies back to the courtroom. Pa went with them to get the decision. Uncle Mel waited at our house for Pa to return.

"That land will belong to Mick," Uncle Mel told us. "And the hay and corn in that barn will belong to him."

When Pa came home, there was a smile on his face.

"It's yer land, ain't it, Mick?" Uncle Mel asked.

"It's still my land," Pa said, "and sixteen men are now filing suits to recover their land. Jake Timmins won't have but an acre left."

"Remember the hay and corn he put in yer barn is yourn," Uncle Mel said.

Uncle Mel got up from his chair, stretched his arms. Then he said, "I must be back on my way to West Virginia."

"Can't you stay longer with us, Uncle Mel?" Pa said.

"I must be a-gettin' back to cut timber," he said. "If ye have any more land troubles, write me."

We tried to get Uncle Mel to stay longer. But he wouldn't stay. He left with his turkey of clothes and his long-handled, double-bitted ax across his shoulder. We waved good-by to him as he walked slowly down the path and out of sight on his way to West Virginia.

I
"THE PURSUIT OF HAPPINESS"

America was founded on the belief that people are entitled to certain "unalienable rights," among which are "life, liberty, and the pursuit of happiness." When we say that a government ought to guarantee individuals the right to pursue happiness, what do we mean? What rights must a person have in order to be able to "pursue happiness"?

Because each of us tends to define "happiness" a little differently, we may also disagree to some extent on the rights needed to pursue it. In early America, however, one of the guarantees thought essential to secure happiness was the right to obtain and hold one's own property. You have just read two selections in which this right was threatened by unscrupulous men, both of whom claimed to have the law on their side. Assuming that the law should protect the rights of individuals, how did it happen in these two cases that this purpose of the law was perverted?

II
IMPLICATIONS

Discuss the following questions in terms of "Under the Lion's Paw" and "Testimony of Trees."

1. In which selection does the setting and the dialogue seem more convincing to you? Can you tell why?

2. Compare and contrast Timothy Haskins with Mick Stuart. What is the essential difference between them?

3. Compare the motives of the "villains" in each selection. Would you describe them as "natural" human motives?

4. Which character seemed more realistic—Butler or Jake Timmins?

5. What roles do Mrs. Haskins and Mrs. Stuart play in the tales? Do you think they are essential characters? If not, why did the authors use them?

III
TECHNIQUES

Intention

In a story like "Under the Lion's Paw," told in part by the author himself, we usually feel confident that we can take his comments on the action at face value. In "Testimony of Trees," however, we get the action through the report of a young boy, the son of Mick Stuart. Since he is likely to favor his own father, how do we know that he is giving us a "straight" story, that he truly reflects the author's intention? To what extent do we actually have to depend upon him?

IV
WORDS

Usage levels fall into two broad classifications: standard and nonstandard. Standard usage includes *formal* or *literary* (spoken and written communication for a select educated group) and *informal* (speech and writing used in personal, casual situations, including regionalisms and slang words, as well as more liberal grammar). Generally we classify written work according to the appropriateness of usage, diction, and types of sentences. But when we come to informal speech, we are confronted with numerous dialects.

Study carefully "Under the Lion's Paw" and "Testimony of Trees," listing variants in pronunciation, vocabulary, and grammar. Again, be careful about judging a pronunciation such as "git" for the word *get*, or "jist" for the word *just* as nonstandard. Both occur in the speech of educated people. Britishers, for example, pronounce ate "et." Review your lists for examples of nonstandard usages and then for standard but regional variants.

That justice must often be fought for is clear from the history
of the women's rights movement, and that such a struggle can succeed
is shown in the life story of Susan B. Anthony.
You may be surprised to learn of the contrast between the rights
that women had in the mid-nineteenth century and the rights they have today.
That the situation could alter so dramatically is testimony that change
can occur within a democratic society without serious damage
to social stability. "Susan B. Anthony" is one of ninety-two biographies
presented in Louis Untermeyer's *Makers of the Modern World*.

Susan B. Anthony

LOUIS UNTERMEYER

*That women might own
and possess their own souls.*

What is perhaps the most radical alteration of social relationships in the last century is already so taken for granted that its newness is generally overlooked. Yet less than one hundred years ago women had no rights. The first organized demand occurred as late as 1848 and asked for such essentials as the right "to have personal freedom, to acquire an education, to earn a living, to claim her wages, to own property, to make contracts, to bring suit, to testify in court, to obtain a divorce for just cause, to possess her children, to claim a fair share of the accumulations during marriage." Only one college in the United States admitted women; there were no women doctors or lawyers in the country. Married women literally "belonged" to their husbands as slaves or chattels. If they earned money or inherited it, legally it was not theirs but their husbands'. Single women had to be represented by male guardians. Obviously, no woman was entitled to vote. Except in ancient Egypt and under Roman law, this approximately had been the status of women from the beginnings of time.

The dogged seventy-five-year campaign of prodding, petitioning, and pleading that emancipated modern woman owed its strength and its strategy to Susan Brownell Anthony, sometimes called "the Napoleon of Feminism." She was born February 15, 1820, in Adams, Massachusetts, the second child in a family of eight. Her father, Daniel Anthony, was a man of strong intellect and liberal inclinations. Though a Quaker, he was not a conformist. For his wife he picked Lucy Read, who was not only a Baptist but a young woman of lively disposition. However, when she became Mrs. Anthony she observed all the Quaker customs. Susan was brought up in a household that, in her childhood, wore Quaker clothes, spoke in Quaker terms, and proscribed frivolity. Though Daniel was a prosperous mill owner, it was incumbent on his wife to do all her own work, including farm chores, as well as board and serve the mill hands who lived with them from time to time. The children, particularly the older girls, were trained early in household accomplishments. But their education was far from neglected. Before she was five, precocious Susan could read and write. As her schooling progressed, whenever she came to a subject in which she was interested (such as more and more advanced arithmetic) she insisted on being taught it—even though it was nothing that girls were supposed to know. The early learning was ob-

Copyright © 1955, by Louis Untermeyer. Reprinted by permission of Simon & Schuster, Inc.

tained at home from a governess. In her teens, Susan was sent to an inexpensive finishing school near Philadelphia, Miss Deborah Moulson's Select Seminary for Females. Miss Moulson's task, as she saw it, was to mold her pupils in the prevailing forms, rather than direct an inquisitive spirit, and Susan's inquiring mind was bound to rebel.

Daniel Anthony went bankrupt in the panic of 1838. He was forced to move his family from Battenville, New York, where they had been living for more than ten years, to the aptly named town of Hardscrabble, where he had a farm. All other means of surviving failed; Daniel found employment with the New York Life Insurance Company and was a salaried worker for them for the rest of his life.

Susan was not unhappy to be taken out of Miss Moulson's Seminary; her main concern was to help in the financial emergency. Due to the depression, probably for the first time numbers of young women from formerly well-to-do homes were thinking the same thing, and the more courageous—or more desperate—were moving into the world of men's concerns. Susan's first step, however, was in a field where women had been tolerated for some time: the teaching profession. She served as assistant

principal of a boarding school, succeeding a man who had been paid $10 a week. Not being a man, Susan was given a salary of $2.50 a week.

Better teaching posts followed, culminating in a position as the principal of the girls' department in the Canajoharie Academy.[1] Living away from home, in a free environment, with money of her own to spend on a few indulgences, Susan broke away from her Quaker ways and repressions. Tall, broad-shouldered, vigorous, she attracted suitors, but none suited her. She was conceded to be "the smartest woman in Canajoharie"; her sympathies were with the extreme Abolitionists; she had become interested in the temperance movement, a genuine social problem during that hard-drinking period. For some time she had questioned the inequalities in employment of women, not only in the teaching field but from what she had seen in her own father's mills. She waited only for the opportunity to help right the prevailing wrongs.

It was through her own family that in 1848 she heard about the Seneca Falls Convention, derided as "The Hen Convention," called by Elizabeth Cady Stanton and Lucretia Mott to discuss the social, civil, and religious rights of women. Preferring to throw her now impatient energy into the temperance fight, Susan joined the Daughters of Temperance, sparked her local Canajoharie branch, spread out as an organizer up to state level, finally gave up her teaching position and devoted herself to the Woman's State Temperance Society. Not an eloquent speaker, she became a convincing one. Her main gift was for organization. It was dismaying to find that her work was being blocked, not by an indifferent public, but by the opposition of the men's temperance society. The men would not allow the women to work with them—at that time women might be seen but not heard at a public meeting—and were afraid they would do disservice to the whole

---

1. **Canajoharie**\kă•na•jo ⁴hă•rĭ\ **Academy**, located in Montgomery County, east New York, on the Mohawk River.

temperature cause by raising the diverting question of women's rights. Susan, who had embarked on her fifty-year friendship with Elizabeth Stanton, was beginning to be swayed by her friend's reiteration that the fight for women's rights was really the main fight. She shifted her focus of attention for the last time. Susan carried one of her earliest bids for recognition into the New York State Teachers' Association and succeeded in forcing through a vote that permitted female teachers to "share in all the privileges and deliberations" of the organization.

By 1853, the women's rights cause had become her main absorbing interest. At first she was junior to Elizabeth Stanton in age and leadership; gradually she became the guiding mind of the crusade. Much of the time Susan lived with Elizabeth and her lawyer husband, so that the two friends could write speeches, organize groups, draft petitions, and agitate the country between household chores. Susan was already termed an old maid, but Mrs. Stanton mothered seven children. Since Mrs. Stanton was the better speaker, Susan frequently minded the home so that Elizabeth could campaign.

For several years, the leaders in the movement dramatized their protest against the stifling constraint of corsets and other oppressive clothing by appearing in public in "bloomers," loose trousers that were gathered at the ankles. Susan cut off her lustrous brown hair for further effect. Soon it became evident that the sensationalism of the costumes drew attention away from basic issues, and the feminists, more publicized than they had ever been, went back to layers and layers of floor-sweeping skirts.

Still the work lagged, mainly through lack of funds. The root of the difficulty, Susan saw, was that few women had money to call their own. A radical remedy was needed: a campaign to force the New York State legislature to alter the status of women. Susan threatened to bring the matter up again year after year until the laws were changed. It took ten years, ten years wearing the same old clothes, slogging away at

Susan B. Anthony photographed near the end of her life.

tedious details, traveling about in all weathers under adverse conditions, in all kinds of conveyances, carrying arguments into other states where word about her had spread. In 1860, the first great change was accomplished. By New York State law, a married woman thenceforward could control her own property, her own earnings, would have joint guardianship over her children, and be granted many of the economic demands raised by Susan and her co-workers. Several other states were forced by strong women's rights groups to take similar action.

In between victories were many defeats and bitter, merciless opposition. The onslaughts were vicious: a typical volume, written by a noted minister, was entitled *Woman's Suffrage: the Reform Against Nature.* Many of the attacks were spiteful and personally wounding. The *New York World* reported gleefully that "Susan is lean, cadaverous, and intellectual, with the proportions of a file, and the voice of a hurdy-gurdy."[2]

Meanwhile, the Civil War was embroiling the nation. Immediately upon Lincoln's election the extreme Abolitionists, with whom Susan had always identified herself, had campaigned—at first against Lincoln who was trying to prevent the war—for immediate emancipation. During the war the women's rights fight was suspended. The New York State legislature took advantage of the situation by repealing that part of the law they had passed two years earlier covering women's rights over children. Susan was immobilized on her father's farm. In her journal she noted: "Tried to interest myself in a sewing society; but little intelligence among them." Besides the farm work, she passed the time reading Elizabeth Barrett Browning and George Eliot, storing up energy towards the next battle. The call for it sounded in the clanging notes of the Emancipation Proclamation. Free the women as well as the slaves, Susan demanded. Let this be a government of the people, by the people, including women, she insisted—assuming that women are people.

Arguing that women's rights could be tied in with Negro rights, Elizabeth Stanton and Susan organized large numbers of women to campaign for a constitutional amendment abolishing slavery; the signatures they succeeded in getting to a petition helped effect the passage of the Thirteenth Amendment. It was with dismay, then, that they read the proposed Fourteenth Amendment and learned that civil rights were reserved for previously disenfranchised *male* citizens only. If they could have that one word struck out of the amendment, then all women, white as well as Negro, would win the vote at one stroke. The amendment, however, was passed as written.

Susan retired to home ground, concentrating on the votes-for-women issue in Albany. It was at this time that the famous exchange of discourtesies took place between her and Horace Greeley.

"Miss Anthony," said Greeley with deadly suavity, "you are aware that the ballot and the bullet go together. If you vote, are you also prepared to fight?"

"Certainly, Mr. Greeley," Susan retorted. "Just as you fought in the last war—at the point of a goose-quill."

Greeley and other opponents blocked the drive for votes for women in the New York State legislature. Discouraging years followed. Susan briefly edited a newspaper, called *Revolution.* Its motto was: "Men, their rights, and nothing more; Women, their rights, and nothing less." The paper was finally forced to suspend, and although it took years for her to do it, Susan personally paid off the newspaper's debt of ten thousand dollars. During all this time, she lived on a bit of money left her by her father and on lecture earnings. She often spent her last cent to enable women with no money at all to attend conventions and participate in the work. She was a party to a suit in 1872 to test the Fourteenth and Fifteenth Amendments. She cast a vote in the Presidential election of that year, was tried for violating the constitution, was fined $100 and costs. She refused to pay. On and off she worked on the monumental *History of Woman Suffrage,* the first three volumes with the collaboration of Mrs. Stanton and Matilda Joslyn Gage, the last two with Ida Husted Harper.

By now, the organization which she headed was called the National American Woman Suffrage Association. As Mrs. Rheta Childe Dorr explained in *Susan B. Anthony: The Woman Who Changed the Mind of a Nation,* "To her the whole object of the woman suffrage movement was sex equality, the wiping out of every arbitrary distinction in law and custom, that women, as she phrased it, might own and possess their own souls." In 1883, she took the first vacation she ever had, went to Europe, and found herself famous, particularly in England, where the feminist movement was just gaining momentum.

---

2. **hurdy-gurdy**\\'hər·dē ˄gər·dē\\ a musical instrument played by turning a crank.

When she was seventy, her sister Mary, retiring as a school teacher, urged her to make a home with her in Rochester. Neither had enough money to furnish the house they had inherited there. As a tribute to her, the Political Equality League of Rochester furnished the house. But Susan was too busy to stay in it. Not before she was eighty did she retire as president of the Woman Suffrage Association. Completing the *History of Woman Suffrage*, she emphasized her final demand that American women must get the vote through an amendment to the federal constitution, not through state laws.

In 1904, when the International Woman Suffrage Alliance was formed, she was automatically acknowledged by the women of the world as their undisputed leader. Early in 1906, she attended what she suspected would be her last convention and told the delegates: "The fight must not stop. You must see it does not stop!" On her eighty-sixth birthday, she insisted on going to Washington to attend a dinner in her honor and ended her remarks by insisting, "Failure is impossible."

It was success, however, that seemed impossible. When, as the result of a cold caught on the trip to Washington, she died on March 13, 1906, though the country flew its flags at half-mast in grief at her passing, she was eulogized as "The Champion of a Lost Cause."

Thirteen years later, on May 21, 1919, the lost cause was won; an amendment giving women the full rights of citizenship was added to the United States Constitution. It was called the Susan B. Anthony Amendment.

I
TOLERATION OF EXTREME OPINIONS

It is probably natural in a stable society that we should hold in suspicion those who have extreme opinions. In her day Susan Anthony was a member of a small minority. People everywhere—including women—dismissed her opinions without granting her a fair hearing. Today, we wonder at the intolerance of her contemporaries, and we can see that yesterday's "radicalism" sometimes becomes tomorrow's "common sense." Thus, Susan B. Anthony's story illustrates the importance of tolerating views that differ from widely accepted opinions.

II
IMPLICATIONS

The history of women's rights has implications for many present-day struggles for justice, including the women's rights movement. Select some contemporary group that claims to be seeking a greater measure of justice and discuss its similarities to and differences from the women's rights movement. What lessons might this group learn from the story of Susan B. Anthony and her fellow-workers.

III
TECHNIQUES

Intention

Untermeyer set out to write a brief biography. Thus, he had to select with great care the incidents that would carry out his intentions. How do the following incidents reveal Untermeyer's intentions particularly well?

1. Susan's job as teacher.
2. Susan's interests in temperance and slavery.
3. Susan's exchange with Horace Greeley.
4. The last few years of her life.
5. Her early home life.

Theme

Untermeyer's subject is Susan B. Anthony, but it would be awkward to say that she is his "theme." If "theme" is defined as the central idea, what in your opinion is the theme of this work?

Edwin Markham was inspired to write his famous poem,
"The Man with the Hoe," after seeing Jean François Millet's
world-famous painting of a French peasant standing in a field, leaning
on his hoe. It has been said that no poem ever published in America
has had the instant and lasting popularity of "The Man with the Hoe."
See if you can tell why this poem should have such broad
and enduring appeal.

The Man with the Hoe

WRITTEN AFTER SEEING MILLET'S WORLD-FAMOUS PAINTING

God made man in His own image;
in the image of God made He him.—Genesis.

Bowed by the weight of centuries he leans
Upon his hoe and gazes on the ground,
The emptiness of ages in his face,
And on his back the burden of the world.
Who made him dead to rapture and despair,   5
A thing that grieves not and that never hopes,
Stolid and stunned, a brother to the ox?
Who loosened and let down this brutal jaw?
Whose was the hand that slanted back this brow?
Whose breath blew out the light within this brain?   10

Is this the thing the Lord God made and gave
To have dominion over sea and land;
To trace the stars and search the heavens for power;
To feel the passion of eternity?
Is this the Dream He dreamed who shaped the suns   15
And pillared the blue firmament with light?
Down all the stretch of hell to its last gulf
There is no shape more terrible than this—
More tongued with cries against the world's blind greed—
More filled with signs and portents for the soul—   20
More fraught with menace to the universe.

What gulfs between him and the seraphim![1]
Slave of the wheel of labor, what to him
Are Plato and the swing of Pleiades?[2]

---

1. **seraphim**\ˈsĕr·ə·fĭm\ the highest order of angels.
2. **Pleiades**\ˈplē·ə·dēz\ in Greek mythology the seven daughters of Atlas
transformed by Zeus into a group of stars near the constellation Orion.

What the long reaches of the peaks of song,   25
The rift of dawn, the reddening of the rose?
Through this dread shape the suffering ages look;
Time's tragedy is in that aching stoop;
Through this dread shape humanity betrayed,
Plundered, profaned, and disinherited,   30
Cries protest to the Powers that made the world,
A protest that is also prophecy.

O masters, lords and rulers in all lands,
Is this the handiwork you give to God,
This monstrous thing distorted and soul-quenched?   35
How will you ever straighten up this shape;
Touch it again with immortality;
Give back the upward looking and the light;
Rebuild in it the music and the dream;
Make right the immemorial infamies,   40
Perfidious wrongs, immedicable woes?

O masters, lords and rulers in all lands,
How will the future reckon with this Man?
How answer his brute question in that hour
When whirlwinds of rebellion shake the world?   45
How will it be with kindoms and with kings—
With those who shaped him to the thing he is—
When this dumb Terror shall reply to God,
After the silence of the centuries?

EDWIN MARKHAM

IMPLICATIONS

1. What mental picture of the hoer does the reader get from the first stanza? Which of the following does the picture make you feel: despair, anger, indifference, sadness?

2. What is the answer to the questions asked in the first stanza of the poem? What is the relationship between those questions and the questions in the second stanza?

3. In the second stanza the poet says that the enslaved hoer is "fraught with menace to the universe." What does this mean? Can you cite any evidence to support or deny the idea?

4. What is your own opinion of Markham's belief that the "masters, lords and rulers" are responsible for the condition of the hoer? Are there other things or persons that might also be responsible? If so, name them.

5. Describe the prophecy the author makes in the final stanza. Is the prophecy justified by what the author has said previously or is he, perhaps, only playing on the human wish to see wrongs righted?

A little over a generation after the appearance
of "The Man with the Hoe," Carl Sandburg published a book of poems
about the average citizen, entitled *The People, Yes* (1936). Having worked
as a porter in a barbershop, a sceneshifter,
a truck handler, a dishwasher, a harvest hand, a janitor, and a sales clerk,
Carl Sandburg is well qualified to speak about "the people."
"The People Will Live On" is the last poem in *The People, Yes*.
As you read it, pay close attention to the comparisons and contrasts
between Markham's and Sandburg's views on the common person.

The People Will Live On

107

The people will live on.
The learning and blundering people will live on.
They will be tricked and sold and again sold
And go back to the nourishing earth for rootholds,
The people so peculiar in renewal and comeback,   5
You can't laugh off their capacity to take it.
The mammoth rests between his cyclonic[1] dramas.

The people so often sleepy, weary, enigmatic,
is a vast huddle with many units saying:
"I earn my living.   10
I make enough to get by
and it takes all my time.
If I had more time
I could do more for myself
and maybe for others.   15
I could read and study
and talk things over
and find out about things.
It takes time.
I wish I had the time."   20

The people is a tragic and comic two-face:
hero and hoodlum: phantom and gorilla twisting to moan with a gargoyle[2] mouth: "They
buy me and sell me . . . it's a game . . .
sometime I'll break loose . . ."   25

---

1. **cyclonic**\sai ᴧklɔ•nĭk\ having the nature of a cyclone.
2. **gargoyle**\ᴧgɔr 'goil\ a grotesquely carved figure.

From *The People, Yes*, by Carl Sandburg, copyright 1936, by Harcourt Brace
Jovanovich, Inc.; renewed © 1964, by Carl Sandburg, and reprinted by permission of the publishers.

                Once having marched
Over the margins of animal necessity,
Over the grim line of sheer subsistence
        Then man came
To the deeper rituals of his bones,   30
To the lights lighter than any bones,
To the time for thinking things over,
To the dance, the song, the story,
Or the hours given over to dreaming,
            Once having so marched.   35

Between the finite limitations of the five senses
and the endless yearnings of man for the beyond
the people hold to the humdrum bidding of work and food
while reaching out when it comes their way
for lights beyond the prison of the five senses,   40
for keepsakes lasting beyond any hunger or death.
    This reaching is alive.
The panderers and liars have violated and smutted it.
        Yet this reaching is alive yet
        for lights and keepsakes.   45

        The people know the salt of the sea
        and the strength of the winds
        lashing the corners of the earth.
        The people take the earth
        as a tomb of rest and a cradle of hope.   50
        Who else speaks for the Family of Man?
        They are in tune and step
        with constellations of universal law.

        The people is a polychrome,[3]
        a spectrum and a prism   55
        held in a moving monolith,[4]
        a console organ of changing themes,
        a clavilux[5] of color poems
        wherein the sea offers fog
        and the fog moves off in rain   60
        and the labrador sunset shortens
        to a nocturne of clear stars
        serene over the shot spray
        of northern lights.

---

3. **polychrome,** many colored.
4. **monolith,** a great stone in the form of a column.
5. **clavilux**\ˈklä·və ˈləks\ an instrument which throws patterns of light and color upon a screen.

The steel mill sky is alive.   65
The fire breaks white and zigzag
shot on a gun-metal gloaming.
Man is a long time coming.
Man will yet win.
Brother may yet line up with brother: 70

This old anvil laughs at many broken hammers.
There are men who can't be bought.
The fireborn are at home in fire.
The stars make no noise.
You can't hinder the wind from blowing.   75
Time is a great teacher.
Who can live without hope?

In the darkness with a great bundle of grief
the people march.
In the night, and overhead a shovel of stars for   80
keeps, the people march:
"Where to? what next?"

CARL SANDBURG

I
"CONSTELLATIONS OF UNIVERSAL LAW"

Sandburg sees the people marching "In the darkness with a great bundle of grief," yet he also sees them ". . . in tune and step with constellations of universal law." Markham does not speak directly of "universal law," yet it is obvious that he, too, believes in some such concept. He presumably condemns the "lords and rulers of all lands" for not obeying universal laws.

How would you describe the "universal law" to which these poets appeal? What signs—if any—in each poem point to the possibility that a spiritual force is the arbiter of such law? Finally, if there is such a thing as universal law, why is it that it is so readily ignored, and why aren't our laws modeled more closely to it?

II
IMPLICATIONS

Discuss the truth or falsity of the following propositions.

1. The poor and the ignorant are always exploited by the wealthy and the more intelligent.

2. The difficulty of earning a living is no excuse for ignoring the finer things in life.

3. Life without hope isn't worth living.

4. The ability to endure almost any hardship is the chief virtue of the people.

5. We will someday build a near-perfect world marked by justice for all.

Before you begin to read Shirley Jackson's "The Lottery,"
be sure you have enough time to finish the story in a single sitting
and allow yourself some time afterward to think about it before you read
the editorial comment. The emotional impact of "The Lottery"
is immediate, but it may be some time before you become aware
of its full meaning.

The Lottery

SHIRLEY JACKSON

The morning of June 27th was clear and sunny, with the fresh warmth of a full-summer day; the flowers were blossoming profusely and the grass was richly green. The people of the village began to gather in the square, between the post office and the bank, around ten o'clock; in some towns there were so many people that the lottery took two days and had to be started on June 26th, but in this village, where there were only about three hundred people, the whole lottery took less than two hours, so it could begin at ten o'clock in the morning and still be through in time to allow the villagers to get home for noon dinner.

The children assembled first, of course. School was recently over for the summer, and the feeling of liberty sat uneasily on most of them; they tended to gather together quietly for a while before they broke into boisterous play, and their talk was still of the classroom and the teacher, of books and reprimands. Bobby Martin had already stuffed his pockets full of stones, and the other boys soon followed his example, selecting the smoothest and roundest stones; Bobby and Harry Jones and Dickie Delacroix[1]—the villagers pronounced this name "Dellacroy"—eventually made a great pile of stones in one corner of the square and guarded it against the raids of the other boys.

The girls stood aside, talking among themselves, looking over their shoulders at the boys, and the very small children rolled in the dust or clung to the hands of their older brothers or sisters.

Soon the men began to gather, surveying their own children, speaking of planting and rain, tractors and taxes. They stood together, away from the pile of stones in the corner, and their jokes were quiet and they smiled rather than laughed. The women, wearing faded house dresses and sweaters, came shortly after their menfolk. They greeted one another and exchanged bits of gossip as they went to join their husbands. Soon the women, standing by their husbands, began to call to their children, and the children came reluctantly, having to be called four or five times. Bobby Martin ducked under his mother's grasping hand and ran, laughing, back to the pile of stones. His father spoke up sharply, and Bobby came quickly and took his place between his father and his oldest brother.

The lottery was conducted—as were the square dances, the teen-age club, the Halloween program—by Mr. Summers, who had time and energy to devote to civic activities. He was a round-faced, jovial man and he ran the coal business, and people were sorry for him, because he had no children and his wife was a

---

Reprinted from *The Lottery* by Shirley Jackson, by permission of Farrar, Strauss & Giroux, Inc. Copyright 1948 by New Yorker Magazine Inc. Copyright 1949 by Shirley Jackson.

1. **Delacroix**\dĕ 'la ▲krwa\.

scold. When he arrived in the square, carrying the black wooden box, there was a murmur of conversation among the villagers, and he waved and called, "Little late today, folks." The postmaster, Mr. Graves, followed him, carrying a three-legged stool, and the stool was put in the center of the square and Mr. Summers set the black box down on it. The villagers kept their distance, leaving a space between themselves and the stool, and when Mr. Summers said, "Some of you fellows want to give me a hand?" there was a hesitation before two men, Mr. Martin and his oldest son, Baxter, came forward to hold the box steady on the stool while Mr. Summers stirred up the papers inside it.

The original paraphernalia[2] for the lottery had been lost long ago, and the black box now resting on the stool had been put into use even before Old Man Warner, the oldest man in town, was born. Mr. Summers spoke frequently to the villagers about making a new box, but no one liked to upset even as much tradition as was represented by the black box. There was a story that the present box had been made with some pieces of the box that had preceded it, the one that had been constructed when the first people settled down to make a village here. Every year, after the lottery, Mr. Summers began talking again about a new box, but every year the subject was allowed to fade off without anything's being done. The black box grew shabbier each year; by now it was no longer completely black but splintered badly along one side to show the original wood color, and in some places faded or stained.

Mr. Martin and his oldest son, Baxter, held the black box securely on the stool until Mr. Summers had stirred the papers thoroughly with his hand. Because so much of the ritual had been forgotten or discarded, Mr. Summers had been successful in having slips of paper substituted for the chips of wood that had been used for generations. Chips of wood, Mr. Summers had argued, had been all very well when the village was tiny, but now that the population was more than three hundred and likely to keep on growing, it was necessary to use something that would fit more easily into the black box. The night before the lottery, Mr. Summers and Mr. Graves made up the slips of paper and put them in the box, and it was then taken to the safe of Mr. Summers' coal company and locked up until Mr. Summers was ready to take it to the square next morning. The rest of the year, the box was put away, sometimes one place, sometimes another; it had spent one year in Mr. Graves's barn and another year underfoot in the post office, and sometimes it was set on a shelf in the Martin grocery and left there.

There was a great deal of fussing to be done before Mr. Summers declared the lottery open. There were the lists to make up—of heads of families, heads of households in each family, members of each household in each family. There was the proper swearing-in of Mr. Summers by the postmaster, as the official of the lottery; at one time, some people remembered, there had been a recital of some sort, performed by the official of the lottery, a perfunctory, tuneless chant that had been rattled off duly each year; some people believed that the official of the lottery used to stand just so when he said or sang it, others believed that he was supposed to walk among the people, but years and years ago this part of the ritual had been allowed to lapse. There had been, also, a ritual salute, which the official of the lottery had had to use in addressing each person who came up to draw from the box, but this also had changed with time, until now it was felt necessary only for the official to speak to each person approaching. Mr. Summers was very good at all this; in his clean white shirt and blue jeans, with one hand resting carelessly on the black box, he seemed very proper and important as he talked interminably to Mr. Graves and the Martins.

Just as Mr. Summers finally left off talking and turned to the assembled villagers, Mrs. Hutchinson came hurriedly along the path to

---

2. **paraphernalia**\ˌpăr·ə·fə(r) ˈnāl·yə\ furnishings, apparatus, equipment.

the square, her sweater thrown over her shoulders, and slid into place in the back of the crowd. "Clean forgot what day it was," she said to Mrs. Delacroix, who stood next to her, and they both laughed softly. "Thought my old man was out back stacking wood," Mrs. Hutchinson went on, "and then I looked out the window and the kids were gone, and then I remembered it was the twenty-seventh and came a-running." She dried her hands on her apron, and Mrs. Delacroix said, "You're in time, though. They're still talking away up there."

Mrs. Hutchinson craned her neck to see through the crowd and found her husband and children standing near the front. She tapped Mrs. Delacroix on the arm as a farewell and began to make her way through the crowd. The people separated good-humoredly to let her through; two or three people said, in voices just loud enough to be heard across the crowd, "Here comes your Missus, Hutchinson," and "Bill, she made it after all." Mrs. Hutchinson reached her husband, and Mr. Summers, who had been waiting, said cheerfully, "Thought we were going to have to get on without you, Tessie." Mrs. Hutchinson said, grinning, "Wouldn't have me leave m'dishes in the sink, now, would you, Joe?," and soft laughter ran through the crowd as the people stirred back into position after Mrs. Hutchinson's arrival.

"Well, now," Mr. Summers said soberly, "guess we better get started, get this over with, so's we can go back to work. Anybody ain't here?"

"Dunbar," several people said. "Dunbar, Dunbar."

Mr. Summers consulted his list. "Clyde Dunbar," he said. "That's right. He's broke his leg, hasn't he? Who's drawing for him?"

"Me, I guess," a woman said, and Mr. Summers turned to look at her. "Wife draws for her husband," Mr. Summers said. "Don't you have a grown boy to do it for you, Janey?" Although Mr. Summers and everyone else in the village knew the answer perfectly well, it was the business of the official of the lottery to ask such questions formally. Mr. Summers waited with

an expression of polite interest while Mrs. Dunbar answered.

"Horace's not but sixteen yet," Mrs. Dunbar said regretfully. "Guess I gotta fill in for the old man this year."

"Right," Mr. Summers said. He made a note on the list he was holding. Then he asked, "Watson boy drawing this year?"

A tall boy in the crowd raised his hand. "Here," he said. "I'm drawing for m'mother and me." He blinked his eyes nervously and ducked his head as several voices in the crowd said things like "Good fellow, Jack," and "Glad to see your mother's got a man to do it."

"Well," Mr. Summers said, "guess that's everyone. Old Man Warner make it?"

"Here," a voice said, and Mr. Summers nodded.

A sudden hush fell on the crowd as Mr. Summers cleared his throat and looked at the list. "All ready?" he called. "Now, I'll read the names—heads of families first—and the men come up and take a paper out of the box. Keep the paper folded in your hand without looking at it until everyone has had a turn. Everything clear?"

The people had done it so many times that they only half listened to the directions; most of them were quiet, wetting their lips, not looking around. Then Mr. Summers raised one hand high and said, "Adams." A man disengaged himself from the crowd and came forward. "Hi, Steve," Mr. Summers said, and Mr. Adams said, "Hi, Joe." They grinned at one another humorlessly and nervously. Then Mr. Adams reached into the black box and took out a folded paper. He held it firmly by one corner as he turned and went hastily back to his place in the crowd, where he stood a little apart from his family, not looking down at his hand.

"Allen," Mr. Summers said. "Anderson. . . . Bentham."

"Seems like there's no time at all between lotteries any more," Mrs. Delacroix said to Mrs. Graves in the back row. "Seems like we got through with the last one only last week."

"Time sure goes fast," Mrs. Graves said.

"Clark. . . . Delacroix."

"There goes my old man," Mrs. Delacroix said. She held her breath while her husband went forward.

"Dunbar," Mr. Summers said, and Mrs. Dunbar went steadily to the box while one of the women said, "Go on, Janey," and another said, "There she goes."

"We're next," Mrs. Graves said. She watched while Mr. Graves came around from the side of the box, greeted Mr. Summers gravely, and selected a slip of paper from the box. By now, all through the crowd there were men holding the small folded papers in their large hands, turning them over and over nervously. Mrs. Dunbar and her two sons stood together, Mrs. Dunbar holding the slip of paper.

"Harburt. . . . Hutchinson."

"Get up there, Bill," Mrs. Hutchinson said, and the people near her laughed.

"Jones."

"They do say," Mr. Adams said to Old Man Warner, who stood next to him, "that over in the north village they're talking of giving up the lottery."

Old Man Warner snorted. "Pack of crazy fools," he said. "Listening to the young folks, nothin's good enough for *them*. Next thing you know, they'll be wanting to go back to living in caves, nobody work any more, live *that* way for a while. Used to be a saying about 'Lottery in June, corn be heavy soon.' First thing you know, we'd all be eating stewed chickweed and acorns. There's *always* been a lottery," he added petulantly. "Bad enough to see young Joe Summers up there joking with everybody."

"Some places have already quit lotteries," Mrs. Adams said.

"Nothing but trouble in *that*," Old Man Warner said stoutly. "Pack of young fools."

"Martin." And Bobby Martin watched his father go forward. "Overdyke. . . . Percy."

"I wish they'd hurry," Mrs. Dunbar said to her older son. "I wish they'd hurry."

"They're almost through," her son said.

"You get ready to run tell Dad," Mrs. Dunbar said.

Mr. Summers called his own name and then stepped forward precisely and selected a slip from the box. Then he called, "Warner."

"Seventy-seventh year I been in the lottery," Old Man Warner said as he went through the crowd. "Seventy-seventh time."

"Watson." The tall boy came awkwardly through the crowd. Someone said, "Don't be nervous, Jack," and Mr. Summers said, "Take your time, son."

"Zanini."

After that, there was a long pause, a breathless pause, until Mr. Summers, holding his slip of paper in the air, said, "All right, fellows." For a minute, no one moved, and then all the slips of paper were opened. Suddenly, all the women began to speak at once, saying, "Who is it?," "Who's got it?," "Is it the Dunbars?," "Is it the Watsons?" Then the voices began to say, "It's Hutchinson. It's Bill." "Bill Hutchinson's got it."

"Go tell your father," Mrs. Dunbar said to her older son.

People began to look around to see the Hutchinsons. Bill Hutchinson was standing quiet, staring down at the paper in his hand. Suddenly, Tessie Hutchinson shouted to Mr. Summers, "You didn't give him time enough to take any paper he wanted. I saw you. It wasn't fair."

"Be a good sport, Tessie," Mrs. Delacroix called, and Mrs. Graves said, "All of us took the same chance."

"Shut up, Tessie," Bill Hutchinson said.

"Well, everyone," Mr. Summers said, "that was done pretty fast, and now we've got to be hurrying a little more to get done in time." He consulted his next list. "Bill," he said, "you draw for the Hutchinson family. You got any other households in the Hutchinsons?"

"There's Don and Eva," Mrs. Hutchinson yelled. "Make *them* take their chance!"

"Daughters draw with their husbands' families, Tessie," Mr. Summers said gently. "You know that as well as anyone else."

"It wasn't *fair*," Tessie said.

"I guess not, Joe," Bill Hutchinson said regretfully. "My daughter draws with her husband's family, that's only fair. And I've got no other family except the kids."

"Then, as far as drawing for families is concerned, it's you," Mr. Summers said in explanation, "and as far as drawing for households is concerned, that's you, too. Right?"

"Right," Bill Hutchinson said.

"How many kids, Bill?" Mr. Summers asked formally.

"Three," Bill Hutchinson said. "There's Bill, Jr., and Nancy, and little Dave. And Tessie and me."

"All right, then," Mr. Summers said. "Harry, you got their tickets back?"

Mr. Graves nodded and held up the slips of paper. "Put them in the box, then," Mr. Summers directed. "Take Bill's and put it in."

"I think we ought to start over," Mrs. Hutchinson said, as quietly as she could. "I tell you it wasn't *fair*. You didn't give him time enough to choose. *Every*body saw that."

Mr. Graves had selected the five slips and put them in the box, and he dropped all the papers but those onto the ground, where the breeze caught them and lifted them off.

"Listen, everybody," Mrs. Hutchinson was saying to the people around her.

"Ready, Bill?" Mr. Summers asked, and Bill Hutchinson, with one quick glance around at his wife and children, nodded.

"Remember," Mr. Summers said, "take the slips and keep them folded until each person has taken one. Harry, you help little Dave." Mr. Graves took the hand of the little boy, who came willingly with him up to the box. "Take a paper out of the box, Davy," Mr. Summers said. Davy put his hand into the box and laughed. "Take just one paper," Mr. Summers said. "Harry, you hold it for him." Mr. Graves took the child's hand and removed the folded paper from the tight fist and held it while little Dave stood next to him and looked up at him wonderingly.

"Nancy next," Mr. Summers said. Nancy was twelve, and her school friends breathed heavily as she went forward, switching her skirt, and took a slip daintily from the box. "Bill, Jr.," Mr. Summers said, and Billy, his face red and his feet over-large, nearly knocked the box over as he got a paper out. "Tessie," Mr. Summers said. She hesitated for a minute, looking around defiantly, and then set her lips and went up to the box. She snatched a paper out and held it behind her.

"Bill," Mr. Summers said, and Bill Hutchinson reached into the box and felt around, bringing his hand out at last with the slip of paper in it.

The crowd was quiet. A girl whispered, "I hope it's not Nancy," and the sound of the whisper reached the edges of the crowd.

"It's not the way it used to be," Old Man Warner said clearly. "People ain't the way they used to be."

"All right," Mr. Summers said. "Open the papers. Harry, you open little Dave's."

Mr. Graves opened the slip of paper and there was a general sigh through the crowd as he held it up and everyone could see that it was blank. Nancy and Bill, Jr., opened theirs at the same time, and both beamed and laughed, turning around to the crowd and holding their slips of paper above their heads.

"Tessie," Mr. Summers said. There was a pause, and then Mr. Summers looked at Bill Hutchinson, and Bill unfolded his paper and showed it. It was blank.

"It's Tessie," Mr. Summers said, and his voice was hushed. "Show us her paper, Bill."

Bill Hutchinson went over to his wife and forced the slip of paper out of her hand. It had a black spot on it, the black spot Mr. Summers had made the night before with the heavy pencil in the coal-company office. Bill Hutchinson held it up, and there was a stir in the crowd.

"All right, folks," Mr. Summers said. "Let's finish quickly."

Although the villagers had forgotten the ritual and lost the original black box, they still remembered to use stones. The pile of stones the boys had made earlier was ready; there were stones on the ground with the blowing scraps of paper that had come out of the box.

Mrs. Delacroix selected a stone so large she had to pick it up with both hands and turned to Mrs. Dunbar. "Come on," she said. "Hurry up."

Mrs. Dunbar had small stones in both hands, and she said, gasping for breath, "I can't run at all. You'll have to go ahead and I'll catch up with you."

The children had stones already, and someone gave little Davy Hutchinson a few pebbles.

Tessie Hutchinson was in the center of a cleared space by now, and she held her hands out desperately as the villagers moved in on her. "It isn't fair," she said. A stone hit her on the side of the head.

Old Man Warner was saying, "Come on, come on, everyone." Steve Adams was in the front of the crowd of villagers, with Mrs. Graves beside him.

"It isn't fair, it isn't right," Mrs. Hutchinson screamed, and then they were upon her.

I
TRADITIONS—
BLIND, FROZEN AND UNJUST

At one point in the story Old Man Warner recalls an old saying, "Lottery in June, corn be heavy soon." The proverb seems to imply some causal connection between the holding of the lottery and the growth of the corn. We would say that any such connection was purely superstitious. But we *know* what makes corn grow.

Perhaps in the distant past your primitive ancestors, knowing nothing about science, soil, fertilization, or the effect of rain upon crops, attributed the growth of corn to spirits. When the spirits were pleased, they made corn grow; when they were displeased, they caused corn to die. When the corn didn't grow, your ancestors probably believed that some member of the community had displeased the spirits. To appease them, the guilty member (or someone else) had to be sacrificed.

Soon someone had to be sacrificed every year in order to ensure good crops.

Eventually your ancestors learn what really causes corn to grow, but by that time the ceremonial sacrifice has been going on for generations. They still believe in the spirits and are fearful of disturbing them. The sacrifice goes on.

As time passes your people forget the original purpose of the sacrifice. All they know is "There's *always* been a sacrifice." And so the tradition goes on—with perhaps some modifications—even though it is totally senseless and horrible. Year after year after year the blind, frozen, unjust tradition goes on.

Shirley Jackson is not suggesting that there is a civilized community in which a lottery of the sort she describes is actually practiced; but she is implying that traditions similar to lotteries are practiced and that they can produce tragic consequences.

II
IMPLICATIONS

All of the following statements have some relation to the story you have just read. Discuss their meaning and implications.

1. Traditions are good because they tend to bind people together.

2. Self-preservation is the most powerful human instinct.

3. People enjoy being part of terrible events, as long as they can remain only spectators.

4. No traditional belief or custom should be accepted until one has examined it and its possible consequences thoroughly

5. Traditions crush individuality and make human beings slaves to society.

6. Every time a test is given, somebody will be chosen to fail. This is similar to the situation in "The Lottery."

III
TECHNIQUES

Intention

Shirley Jackson does not intrude in her story to let the reader know her opinion of the custom she depicts. Nevertheless, we feel quite certain that her attitude is one of condemnation. *How* has she managed to communicate this part of her intention?

Theme

It is not uncommon for a person to read "The Lottery" and not realize its theme. By not giving us more clues to the meaning of her story, Shirley Jackson took the risk of baffling some of her readers. Why do you suppose she was willing to take this risk? Did she gain anything by not entering into her story herself to make her theme more explicit?

IV
WORDS

A. Using what you know about context clues, work out the meaning of the italicized words below.

1. . . . then he *fondled* his long white beard in his hand.

2. The dogged seventy-five-year campaign of prodding, petitioning, and pleading that *emancipated* modern woman.

3. Her father was a man of strong intellect and liberal *inclinations*.

4. Though Daniel was a prosperous mill owner, it was *incumbent* on his wife to do all her own work. . . .

5. Before she was five, *precocious* Susan could read and write.

6. Living away from home, in a free environment, with money of her own to spend on a few *indulgences*. . . .

7. Civil rights were reserved for previously *disenfranchised* male citizens only.

8. She was *eulogized* as "The champion of a lost cause."

9. The original *paraphernalia* for the lottery had been lost long ago.

10. There had been a recital of some sort . . . a *perfunctory* tuneless chant that had been rattled off duly each year.

B. If synonyms had exactly the same meaning, writers would have no need of them. Good writers select the right synonym. But writers must strive for even greater accuracy in their choice of antonyms. An antonym is a word that means the opposite of another word; for example, *good* is the antonym of *bad*, *wet* of *dry*, *poor* of *rich*. The proper selection of an antonym shows precise thought. For example, *wild* and *savage* are sometimes used as synonyms, yet the antonym of *wild* in "a wild shot" is *controlled* and that of *savage* is *civilized*. Common words have acquired more than one meaning and an additional set of synonyms and antonyms for each meaning. Give one synonym and one antonym for each meaning. For example:

	synonym	antonym
a *clear* day	cloudless	cloudy
a *clear* style	lucid	obscure

1. *fast* living   hard and *fast* rules
fast-acting medicine   *fast*-thinking person

2. a *clean* miss   a *clean* copy
a *clean* shirt   a *clean* edge

3. *hard* work   *hard* agreement
hard heart   *hard* water

4. *bright* light   *bright* idea   *bright* child

5. *dead* faint   *dead* center   *dead* ball

6. *high* note   *high* winds   *high* and dry

C. Linguists have found three main dialect areas in the United States: Northern, Midland, and Southern. These dialects reveal differences in pronunciation, vocabulary, and grammar. A dialect does not mean a foreign accent or refer to a nonstandard level. Each speaker, educated or uneducated, has a dialect. Survey your own dialect for regionalisms, or names for certain objects. Which do you use?

1. garment traditionally worn by men in the 1800s: trousers, pants, breeches.

2. a fixture that controls flow of water: tap, hydrant, faucet, spigot, cock.

3. a variety of beans: green beans, snap beans, beans.

4. piece of furniture with drawers for storing clothes: chest of drawers, dresser, bureau, chifferobe.

5. strong cold wind from the north: norther, blue norther, nor'easter.

6. a pan for frying: skillet, spider, fry pan.

7. a nutlike seed: goobers, grubies, peanuts, pinders.

8. which of these phrases do you use?

a. He *caught, took, take, ketched* cold.

b. They are *fixing, making, getting* supper.

c. Please *cook, boil, steep, make* some tea.

d. Will you *look after, tend, mind, take care of, see after* the baby?

e. The police are going to *escort, take, carry, drag, accompany* her.

f. It is a quarter *of, to, till* ten.

Nine War Poems

How does the topic of war fit into the theme
of the struggle for justice? Some wars, of course, are fought to gain justice or to secure it.
We refer to them as "just" wars. There is, however, another way of looking at war,
particularly modern war: It often seems to involve a kind of cosmic injustice—
the mass slaughter of millions of innocent men, women, and children.
Even if the cause is "just," therefore, the results may be unjust. As a person
more sensitive than most, the poet cries out against the
mutilation and destruction of innocent people.

The Arsenal at Springfield

This is the Arsenal. From floor to ceiling,
   Like a huge organ, rise the burnished arms;
But from their silent pipes no anthem pealing
   Startles the villages with strange alarms.

Ah! what a sound will rise, how wild and dreary,   5
   When the death-angel touches those swift keys!
What loud lament and dismal Miserere[1]
   Will mingle with their awful symphonies!

I hear even now the infinite fierce chorus,
   The cries of agony, the endless groan,   10
Which, through the ages that have gone before us,
   In long reverberations reach our own.

On helm and harness rings the Saxon hammer,
   Through Cimbric[2] forest roars the Norseman's song,
And loud, amid the universal clamor,   15
   O'er distant deserts sounds the Tartar[3] gong.

---

1. **Miserere**\mĭ·zə ˈrar·ē\ the 51st Psalm in the Vulgate, the 50th in
the Douay Bible: the first word of the Latin Version; "Have mercy!"
This psalm is frequently recited in services for the dead.
2. **Cimbric**\ˈsĭm·brĭk\ pertaining to Germanic people of central Europe
who were defeated in northern Italy, 101 B.C.
3. **Tartar**, refers to the Tartars who ruled Tartar, a region of Asia and
eastern Europe, in the thirteenth and fourteenth centuries and who
reached greatest power under Genghis Khan.

I hear the Florentine, who from his palace
    Wheels out his battle-bell with dreadful din,
And Aztec priests upon their teocallis[4]
    Beat the wild war-drums made of serpent's skin;   20

The tumult of each sacked and burning village;
    The shout that every prayer for mercy drowns;
The soldiers' revels in the midst of pillage;
    The wail of famine in beleaguered towns;

The bursting shell, the gateway wrenched asunder,   25
    The rattling musketry, the clashing blade;
And ever and anon, in tones of thunder,
    The diapason[5] of the cannonade.

Is it, O man, with such discordant noises,
    With such accursed instruments as these,   30
Thou drownest Nature's sweet and kindly voices,
    And jarrest the celestial harmonies?

Were half the power, that fills the world with terror,
    Were half the wealth bestowed on camps and courts,
Given to redeem the human mind from error,   35
    There were no need of arsenals or forts:

The warrior's name would be a name abhorred!
    And every nation, that should lift again
Its hand against a brother, on its forehead
    Would wear forevermore the curse of Cain!   40

Down the dark future, through long generations,
    The echoing sounds grow fainter and then cease;
And like a bell, with solemn, sweet vibrations,
    I hear once more the voice of Christ say, "Peace!"

Peace! and no longer from its brazen portals   45
    The blast of War's great organ shakes the skies!
But beautiful as songs of the immortals,
    The holy melodies of love arise.

HENRY WADSWORTH LONGFELLOW

---

4. **teocallis**\\'tē·ə ᴧkă·lēz\\ temples erected by ancient Mexicans and Central Americans.
5. **diapason**\\'dai·ə ᴧpā·sən\\ in general, a vast, majestic production of sound. Specifically, on an organ a principal flue stop extending through the instrument's complete scale.

Drypoint by Kerr Eby

I Have a Rendezvous with Death

I have a rendezvous with Death
At some disputed barricade,
When Spring comes back with rustling shade
And apple-blossoms fill the air—
I have a rendezvous with Death   5
When Spring brings back blue days and fair.

It may be he shall take my hand
And lead me into his dark land
And close my eyes and quench my breath—
It may be I shall pass him still.   10
I have a rendezvous with Death

On some scarred slope of battered hill,
When Spring comes round again this year
And the first meadow-flowers appear.

God knows 'twere better to be deep   15
Pillowed in silk and scented down,
Where Love throbs out in blissful sleep,
Pulse nigh to pulse, and breath to breath,
Where hushed awakenings are dear . . .
But I've a rendezvous with Death   20
At midnight in some flaming town,
When Spring trips north again this year,
And I to my pledged word am true,
I shall not fail that rendezvous.

ALAN SEEGER

I Have a Rendezvous with Death is reprinted by permission of Charles Scribner's Sons from *Poems* by Alan Seeger. Copyright 1916 Charles Scribner's Sons; renewal copyright 1944 Elsie Adams Seeger.

Eleven o' Clock News Summary

Fold up the papers now. It is hushed, it is late;
Now the quick day unwinds.
Yawning, empty the ashtrays into the grate.
Close the Venetian blinds.
Then turn, by custom, the dial a wave length lower.   5
This is the hour (directly upon the hour)
Briefly to hear
With half-attentive and habitual ear
Important news bulletins.
                        Our armies are valiant.   10
They have taken another ridge,
Another town, a fort, a strip, a salient.
They have held a bridge
(With heavy casualties). Our planes today,
According to a recent communique,   15
Struck (though the loss was high) at a vital border.
Remember to leave a note for the dairy order
And to set the thermostat at sixty-two.
We have captured an island at merely a moderate cost.
One of our submarines is overdue   20
And must be presumed lost.

In forests, in muddy fields, while winter fades,
Our troops are smashing through the Barricades,
They Push, they Storm, they Forge Ahead, they die
And lie on litters or unburied lie.   25
Static is bad tonight.
There—twiddle the knob a little to the right.

Here in the nation
Obedient curfews sound their midnight wails.
This is America's leading independent station.   30
Read the paper tomorrow for further details—
Details of death on the beaches, in the heat, in the cold,
Of death in gliders, in tanks, at a city's gate,
Death of young men who fancied they might grow old
But could not wait   35
(Being given, of course, no choice).

Well, snap the switch, turn off the announcer's voice,
Plump up the pillows on the green divan,
For day unwinds like a thread
And it is time now for a punctual man,   40
Drowsy, a little absent, warmed and fed,
To dim the light, turn down the blanketed bed,
And sleep, if he can.

PHYLLIS MCGINLEY

From *Stones from a Glass House* by Phyllis McGinley. Originally appeared in *The New Yorker*. Copyright 1945 by Phyllis McGinley. Reprinted by permission of The Viking Press, Inc.

Lines for an Interment

Now it is fifteen years you have lain in the meadow:
The boards at your face have gone through: the earth is
Packed down and the sound of the rain is fainter:
The roots of the first grass are dead.
It's a long time to lie in the earth with your honor: 5
The world, Soldier, the world has been moving on.
The girls wouldn't look at you twice in the cloth cap:
Six years old they were when it happened:
It bores them even in books: "Soissons[1] besieged!"
As for the gents they have joined the American Legion: 10
Belts and a brass band and the ladies' auxiliaries:
The Californians march in the OD silk.[2]
We are all acting again like civilized beings:
People mention it at tea . . .
The Facts of Life we have learned are Economic: 15
You were deceived by the detonations of bombs:
You thought of courage and death when you thought of warfare.
Hadn't they taught you the fine words were unfortunate?
Now that we understand we judge without bias:
We feel of course for those who had to die: 20
Women have written us novels of great passion
Proving the useless death of the dead was a tragedy.
Nevertheless it is foolish to chew gall:
The foremost writers on both sides have apologized:
The Germans are back in the Midi with cropped hair: 25
The English are drinking the better beer in Bavaria.
You can rest now in the rain in the Belgian meadow—
Now that it's all explained away and forgotten:
Now that the earth is hard and the wood rots:
Now you are dead . . .   30

ARCHIBALD MACLEISH

---

1. **Soissons**\swa ˈson\ a city in northeast France.
2. **OD silk,** olive drab.

From *Collected Poems 1917–1952* by Archibald MacLeish. Copyright 1952 by Archibald MacLeish. Reprinted by permission of the publisher, Houghton Mifflin Company.

The Dead in Europe

After the planes unloaded, we fell down
Buried together, unmarried men and women;
Not crown of thorns, not iron, not Lombard[1] crown,
Not grilled and spindle spires pointing to heaven
Could save us. Raise us, Mother, we fell down   5
Here hugger-mugger[2] in the jellied fire:
Our sacred earth in our day was our curse.

Our Mother, shall we rise on Mary's day
In Maryland, wherever corpses married
Under the rubble, bundled together? Pray   10
For us whom the blockbusters[3] marred and buried;
When Satan scatters us on Rising-day,
O Mother, snatch our bodies from the fire:
Our sacred earth in our day was our curse.

Mother, my bones are trembling and I hear   15
The earth's reverberations and the trumpet
Bleating into my shambles. Shall I bear,
(O Mary!) unmarried man and powder-puppet,
Witness to the Devil? Mary, hear,
O Mary, marry earth, sea, air and fire;   20
Our sacred earth in our day is our curse.

ROBERT LOWELL

---

1. **Lombard,** Germanic people that invaded northern
Italy in 568 A.D., settling in the Po valley and establishing a kingdom.
2. **hugger-mugger,** jumbled, confused.
3. **blockbuster**\\ˈblŏk ˈbŭs·tər\\ a large bomb.

From *Lord Weary's Castle*. Copyright 1946 by Robert
Lowell. Reprinted by permission of Harcourt Brace Jovanovich, Inc.

Lunch on Omaha Beach

The killers are killed, their violent rinds
Conveyed, and the beach is back to summer.
I eat sausage with bread. Full of ease, the sea
Makes the sound of cows chewing through high grass.

They're deposited in government lawn   5
Set with nine thousand decencies of stone
To wet the eye, shake the heart, and lose
Each name in a catalog of graven names.

They are wasted in the blank of herohood.
They are dead to fondness and paradox.   10
They're all the same. In the field of lawn
Above the beach, they're put away the same.

They should be left exactly here below where
Death's great bronze mares shook earth and bloodied them,
Where violence of noise isolated each boy   15
In the body of his scream, and dropped him.

No worn Norman hill should be scarred and smoothed
To suit officials' tidy thoughts for graveyards
But the wreckage left, shrinking in rust and rags
And carrion to dust or tumuli.   20

To honor my thoughts against shrines, to find
The beast who naked wakes in us and walks
In flags, to watch the color of his day
I spill my last Bordeaux[1] into the sand.

Watching, I wonder at the white quiet,   25
The fields of butter cows, my countrymen
Come to study battle maps, blue peasants
Still moving back and forth, the day's soft sea.

BINK NOLL

---

1. **Bordeaux**\bɔr ▲dō\ a French red or white wine.

From *The Center of the Circle.* Copyright © 1962 by Bink Noll. Reprinted by permission of Harcourt Brace Jovanovich, Inc.

for Ichiro Kawamoto,
humanitarian, electrician,
survivor of Hiroshima

The Horse

They spoke of the horse alive
without skin, naked, hairless,
without eyes and ears, searching
for the stableboy's caress.
Shoot it, someone said, but they   5
let it go on colliding with
tattered walls, butting his long
skull to pulp, finding no path
where iron fences corkscrewed in
the street and bicycles turned   10
like question marks.
                    Some fled and
some sat down. The river burned
all that day and into the
night, the stones sighed a moment   15
and were still, and the shadow
of a man's hand entered
a leaf.
          The white horse never
returned, and later they found   20
the stableboy, his back crushed
by a hoof, his mouth opened
around a cry that no one heard.
They spoke of the horse again
and again; their mouths opened   25
like the gills of a fish caught
above water.
                    Mountain flowers
burst from the red clay walls, and
they said a new life was here.   30
Raw grass sprouted from the cobbles
like hair from a deafened ear.

The horse would never return.

There had been no horse. I could
tell from the way they walked   35
testing the ground for some cold
that the rage had gone out of
their bones in one mad dance.

PHILIP LEVINE

Copyright 1963 by Philip Levine from *On the*
Edge, Stone Wall Press, 1963.

The Death of the Ball Turret Gunner

From my mother's sleep I fell into the State,
And I hunched in its belly till my wet fur froze.
Six miles from earth, loosed from its dream of life,
I woke to black flak[1] and the nightmare fighters.
When I died they washed me out of the turret with a hose.

RANDALL JARRELL

---

1. **flak**\flăk\ antiaircraft fire.

Reprinted with the permission of Farrar, Straus, and Giroux,
Inc., from *The Complete Poems* by Randall Jarrell. Copyright
© 1945, 1969 by Mrs. Randall Jarrell.

Looking

You have no word for soldiers to enjoy
The feel of, as an apple, and to chew
With masculine satisfaction. Not "good-by!"
"Come back!" or "careful!" Look, and let him go.
"Good-by!" is brutal, and "come back!" the raw   5
Insistence of an idle desperation
Since could he favor he would favor now.
He will be "careful!" if he has permission.
Looking is better. At the dissolution
Grab greatly with the eye, crush in a steel   10
Of study—Even that is vain. Expression,
The touch or look or word, will little avail.
The brawniest will not beat back the storm
Nor the heaviest haul your little boy from harm.

GWENDOLYN BROOKS

Copyright © 1945 by Gwendolyn Brooks Blakely, from *The World of Gwendolyn Brooks* (1971). Reprinted by permission of Harper & Row, Publishers, Incorporated.

FOR DISCUSSION

The Arsenal at Springfield

The theme of Longfellow's poem might be summed up in a few words: "War is terrifying and morally wrong; it can be avoided through understanding and love." This thematic statement might then be broken down into four separate propositions, as follows: (1) War is terrifying. (2) War is morally wrong. (3) War can be avoided by increasing human understanding. (4) War can be avoided by increasing human love.

What is your opinion of the truth or falsity of each of these propositions? How might you expand or qualify some of them? Finally, what is your opinion of the *practicality* of propositions three and four?

I Have a Rendezvous with Death

If you liked this poem, perhaps one source of your enjoyment was the poem's structure. Of course, it is not necessary for a reader to be consciously aware of structure in order to respond to it. Observe how Seeger has structured the poem to convey his theme.

1. Extract for a moment lines 7 to 10 and lines 15 to 19. Observe that the remaining lines alternate between references to Death and to Spring: lines 1 and 2 deal with Death, lines 3 and 4 deal with Spring; line 5 deals with Death, line 6 with Spring, and so on. What is the result, emotionally, of the poet's having intimately linked Death and Spring?

2. Now consider lines 7 to 10 and lines 15 to 19. Do you see any relationship between them and the rest of the poem? Note particularly the possible comparisons between the latter section and Spring. How are these two sections linked by rhyme to each other and to the rest of the poem?

Structure in poetry—in all art—is not incidental; it is essential. It is essential because what art does is precisely to order and arrange, to impose a structure (and hence, a meaning) upon raw experience.

Eleven o'Clock News Summary

1. This poem is divided about equally between italicized and nonitalicized lines. The italicized portions represent a person thinking or speaking to himself, but it is obvious that his thoughts are being screened by the poet. Where is it most obvi-

ous that the poet has intruded her own thought rather than given the thought of the man?

2. The nonitalicized lines in this poem for the most part represent the voice of the news commentator, but again his words are being given to the reader through the poet. Where are you most conscious that you are being given the poet's thoughts rather than the newscaster's?

3. From your answers to the above questions you should see clearly that McGinley intends to criticize the man listening to the news summary. Less obvious, and more interesting, however, is the question of what the man represents. Does the poet criticize a single individual, or is her intention a broader one?

Lines for an Interment

1. In the sixth line, MacLeish—addressing the dead soldier—says that "the world has been moving on." How does he prove his point?

2. Note especially the last instance of "progressive" movement—lines 25 and 26. Is MacLeish really trying to prove that the world has been moving on in a progressive sense? If not, in what sense was it "moving on"? in what direction?

3. In the last line of the poem MacLeish omits the word "that" (which he had used in the two previous lines). Is this a significant omission? Does it help you to see something about the direction of events since the war?

The Dead in Europe

Beginning with a reference to planes unloading their blockbuster bombs, this poem focuses on the extensive bombing that took place virtually everywhere in Europe during World War II. Lowell was concerned with what he saw as an unnecessary destruction of civilians. In the poem, he expresses his concern in the form of a prayer to Mary, the mother of Jesus.

1. What are the several things the speaker asks Mary to do?

2. Repetition, which makes for unity and emphasis, is an important element in this poem. Can you answer the following questions about it?

a. Note the extensive use of a marriage metaphor. Why does the poet use this image so extensively?

b. Note the repetition of the final line in each stanza. Why is that line so important? Do you find any special significance in the word shift in the last line?

c. Note the repeated use of the word "fire" in the same position in each stanza. Is it the same or a different fire that the poet refers to in each case?

3. To "bear witness to the Devil" would be to speak in his behalf. Why might the speaker of the poem feel he should speak *for* the Devil on "Rising-day" (Judgment Day)?

Lunch on Omaha Beach

"Omaha Beach" was a code name for one of the beaches in Normandy, France, attacked by American forces on D day (June 6, 1944). The beachhead was established but at the cost of a great number of American lives. The speaker of the poem is visiting the beach where the battle was fought.

1. Divide the poem into the following parts: The Scene, The Suggestion, The Gesture, and The Reaction. Discuss the appropriateness of these divisions and of the progression of the poem.

2. What is meant by "the beast who naked wakes in us and walks in flags"? Why does the speaker refer to this inner force as a beast? Why does he have it walk (dressed) in flags?

The Horse

Hiroshima, which had been a Japanese military center for three-quarters of a century, was struck by the first American atomic bomb on August 6, 1945. The blast destroyed about two-thirds of the city and accounted for the deaths of about 75,000 people. Today, the city is a peace center.

1. The greater part of the poem vividly portrays the effects of the atomic blast. What is the emotional effect of this description on you? Which images did you find most effective?

2. What does the poet gain by focusing the poem on a horse? Does the horse have any symbolic significance?

3. Because of its isolation, the line "The horse would never return" gets tremendous emphasis. Why should the poet want this line to have so much emphasis?

4. Who "speaks" the line "There had been no horse"? Precisely what does it mean?

5. In spite of the focus on the horse, the poem ends with a reference to the people. In what sense have they been the main subject all along? What is the meaning of the last sentence of the poem?

The Death of the Ball Turret Gunner

This poem is a good complement to the Lowell poem; it tells the story of the bombing in Europe from the point of view of one of the air corps. Jarrell knew them well, for he trained B-29 bomber crews.

1. Whom or what does the poem identify as the chief villain and the chief victim of modern war?

2. What is the meaning of the phrase, "fell into the State"?

3. What is the effect on your own emotions of the deliberate brutality of expression of the last line of the poem?

Looking

1. Modern poets may use traditional verse forms, but often in an experimental way, shaping them to their own ends. The sonnet form seems to be so used here. This form is defined as a fourteen-line poem with five stresses to a line (usually iambic) and a fixed rhyme scheme. One of these fixed rhyme schemes is called the "Spenserian" (after the English poet, Edmund Spenser); it connects the quatrains—four line units—by interlacing the rhymes: *abab bcbc cdcd ee.* This type of sonnet usually deals with a single idea or emotion, and its final couplet is frequently used as a sort of summary of or conclusion for what has gone before.

Discuss "Looking" as a variation of the Spenserian sonnet form. What are its chief similarities to and differences from the "pure" Spenserian sonnet?

2. "Looking" expresses a distinctly feminine viewpoint on war. In what way or ways is it different from the viewpoint of Seeger's or Jarrell's poems?

Though lawyers, lawmakers, and judges have a powerful influence on justice, the ultimate decisions regarding guilt and innocence are made in American society by the people themselves in their roles as jurors. Reginald Rose's television drama, *Twelve Angry Men*, focuses on a group of citizens who are charged with the duty of determining the fate of a nineteen-year-old boy accused of the murder of his father. You will find that the characters are identified only by a number. This is not a drawback on the television screen, of course, but in reading the play you will need to take extra care to keep the characters separate. To help you, a brief description of each juror is given in the table at the beginning of the play. While you read the play, refer to it as often as necessary. The chief characters are Juror Number 8, who is the protagonist, and Juror Number 3, who is the antagonist. Juror Number 10 also plays an important role as an antagonist.

Twelve Angry Men

REGINALD ROSE

Cast

JUDGE
CLERK
JURORS (Numbers 2–12)
GUARD
FOREMAN

Description of Jurors

FOREMAN. *A small, petty man who is impressed with the authority he has and handles himself quite formally. Not overly bright, but dogged.*

JUROR NO. 2. *A meek, hesitant man who finds it difficult to maintain any opinions of his own. Easily swayed and usually adopts the opinion of the last person to whom he has spoken.*

JUROR NO. 3. *A very strong, very forceful, extremely opinionated man within whom can be detected a streak of sadism. A humorless man who is intolerant of opinions other than his own and accustomed to forcing his wishes and views upon others.*

JUROR NO. 4. *Seems to be a man of wealth and position. A practiced speaker who presents himself well at all times. Seems to feel a little bit above the rest of the jurors. His only concern is with the facts in this case, and he is appalled at the behavior of the others.*

JUROR NO. 5. *A naive, very frightened young man who takes his obligations in this case very seriously, but who finds it difficult to speak up when his elders have the floor.*

JUROR NO. 6. *An honest but dull-witted man who comes upon his decisions slowly and carefully. A man who finds it difficult to create positive opinions, but who must listen to and digest and accept those opinions offered by others which appeal to him most.*

JUROR NO. 7. *A loud, flashy, gladhanded salesman type who has more important things to do than to sit on a jury. He is quick to show temper, quick to form opinions on things about which he knows nothing. Is a bully and, of course, a coward.*

JUROR NO. 8. *A quiet, thoughtful, gentle man. A man who sees all sides of every question and constantly seeks the truth. A man of*

Reprinted by permission of International Famous Agency. Copyright © 1956 by Reginald Rose.

strength tempered with compassion. Above all, a man who wants justice to be done and will fight to see that it is.

JUROR NO. 9. *A mild, gentle old man, long since defeated by life and now merely waiting to die. A man who recognizes himself for what he is and mourns the days when it would have been possible to be courageous without shielding himself behind his many years.*

JUROR NO. 10. *An angry, bitter man. A man who antagonizes almost at sight. A bigot who places no values on any human life save his own. A man who has been nowhere and is going nowhere and knows it deep within him.*

JUROR NO. 11. *A refugee from Europe who has come to this country in 1941. A man who speaks with an accent and who is ashamed, humble, almost subservient to the people around him, but who will honestly seek justice because he has suffered through so much injustice.*

JUROR NO. 12. *A slick, bright advertising man who thinks of human beings in terms of percentages, graphs and polls and has no real understanding of people. A superficial snob, but trying to be a good fellow.*

Act I

Fade in on a jury box. Twelve men are seated in it, listening intently to the voice of the JUDGE *as he charges them. We do not see the* JUDGE. *He speaks in slow, measured tones and his voice is grave. The camera drifts over the faces of the jurymen as the* JUDGE *speaks and we see that most of their heads are turned to camera's left.* NO. 7 *looks down at his hands.* NO. 3 *looks off in another direction, the direction in which the defendant would be sitting.* NO. 10 *keeps moving his head back and forth nervously. The* JUDGE *drones on.*

JUDGE. Murder in the first degree—premeditated homicide—is the most serious charge

tried in our criminal courts. You've heard a long and complex case, gentlemen, and it is now your duty to sit down to try and separate the facts from the fancy. One man is dead. The life of another is at stake. If there is a reasonable doubt in your minds as to the guilt of the accused . . . then you must declare him not guilty. If, however, there is no reasonable doubt, then he must be found guilty. Whichever way you decide, the verdict must be unanimous. I urge you to deliberate honestly and thoughtfully. You are faced with a grave responsibility. Thank you, gentlemen.

There is a long pause.

CLERK (*Droning*). The jury will retire.

And now, slowly, almost hesitantly, the members of the jury begin to rise. Awkwardly, they file out of the jury box and off camera to the left. Camera holds on jury box, then fades out.

Fade in on a large, bare, unpleasant-looking room. This is the jury room in the county criminal court of a large Eastern city. It is about 4:00 P.M. The room is furnished with a long conference table and a dozen chairs. The walls are bare, drab and badly in need of a fresh coat of paint. Along one wall is a row of windows which look out on the skyline of the city's financial district. High on another wall is an electric clock. A washroom opens off the jury room. In one corner of the room is a water fountain. On the table are pads, pencils, ashtrays. One of the windows is open. Papers blow across the table and onto the floor as the door opens. Lettered on the outside of the door are the words "Jury Room." A uniformed GUARD *holds the door open. Slowly, almost self-consciously, the twelve jurors file in. The* GUARD *counts them as they enter the door, his lips moving, but no sound coming forth. Four or five of the jurors light cigarettes as they enter the room.* JUROR NO. 5 *lights his pipe, which he smokes constantly throughout the play.* JURORS NO.

2 and 12 go to the water fountain. NO. *9 goes into the washroom, the door of which is lettered "Men." Several of the jurors take seats at the table. Others stand awkwardly around the room. Several look out the windows. These are men who are ill at ease, who do not really know each other to talk to and who wish they were anywhere but here.* NO. *7, standing at window, takes out a pack of gum, takes a piece and offers it around. There are no takers. He mops his brow.*

NO. 7 *(To* NO. *6).* Y'know something? It's hot. *(*NO. *6 nods)* You'd think they'd at least air-condition the place. I almost dropped dead in court.

NO. 7 *opens the window a bit wider. The* GUARD *looks them over and checks his count. Then, satisfied, he makes ready to leave.*

GUARD. Okay, gentlemen. Everybody's here. If there's anything you want, I'm right outside. Just knock.

He exits, closing the door. Silently they all look at the door. We hear the lock clicking.

NO. 5. I never knew they locked the door.

NO. 10 *(Blowing nose).* Sure, they lock the door. What did you think?

NO. 5. I don't know. It just never occurred to me.

Some of the jurors are taking off their jackets. Others are sitting down at the table. They still are reluctant to talk to each other. FORE-MAN *is at head of table, tearing slips of paper for ballots. Now we get a close shot of* NO. *8. He looks out the window. We hear* NO. *3 talking to* NO. *2.*

NO. 3. Six days. They should have finished it in two. Talk, talk, talk. Did you ever hear so much talk about nothing?

NO. 2 *(Nervously laughing).* Well . . . I guess . . . they're entitled.

NO. 3. Everybody gets a fair trial. *(He shakes his head)* That's the system. Well, I suppose you can't say anything against it.

NO. 2 *looks at him nervously, nods and goes*

over to water cooler. Cut to shot of NO. *8 staring out window. Cut to table.* NO. *7 stands at the table, putting out a cigarette.*

NO. 7 *(To* NO. *10).* How did you like that business about the knife? Did you ever hear a phonier story?

NO. 10 *(Wisely).* Well, look, you've gotta expect that. You know what you're dealing with.

NO. 7. Yeah, I suppose. What's the matter, you got a cold?

NO. 10 *(Blowing).* A lulu. These hot-weather colds can kill you.

NO. 7 *nods sympathetically.*

FOREMAN *(Briskly).* All right, gentlemen. Let's take seats.

NO. 7. Right. This better be fast. I've got tickets to *The Seven Year Itch* tonight. I must be the only guy in the whole world who hasn't seen it yet. *(He laughs and sits down)* Okay, your honor, start the show.

They all begin to sit down. The FOREMAN *is seated at the head of the table.* NO. *8 continues to look out the window.*

FOREMAN *(To* NO. *8).* How about sitting down? *(*NO. *8 doesn't hear him)* The gentleman at the window.

NO. 8 *turns, startled.*

FOREMAN. How about sitting down?

NO. 8. Oh. I'm sorry.

He heads for a seat.

NO. 10 *(To* NO. *6).* It's tough to figure, isn't it? A kid kills his father. Bing! Just like that. Well, it's the element. They let the kids run wild. Maybe it serves 'em right.

FOREMAN. Is everybody here?

NO. 12. The old man's inside.

The FOREMAN *turns to the washroom just as the door opens.* NO. *9 comes out, embarrassed.*

FOREMAN. We'd like to get started.

NO. 9. Forgive me, gentlemen. I didn't mean to keep you waiting.

FOREMAN. It's all right. Find a seat.

NO. 9 *heads for a seat and sits down. They look at the* FOREMAN *expectantly.*

FOREMAN. All right. Now, you gentlemen can handle this any way you want to. I mean, I'm not going to make any rules. If we want to discuss it first and then vote, that's one way. Or we can vote right now to see how we stand.

NO. 7. Let's vote now. Who knows, maybe we can all go home.

NO. 10. Yeah. Let's see who's where.

NO. 3. Right. Let's vote now.

FOREMAN. Anybody doesn't want to vote? *(He looks around the table. There is no answer)* Okay, all those voting guilty raise your hands.

Seven or eight hands go up immediately. Several others go up more slowly. Everyone looks around the table. There are two hands not raised, NO. 9*'s and* NO. 8*'s.* NO. 9*'s hand goes up slowly now as the foreman counts.*

FOREMAN. . . . Nine . . . ten . . . eleven . . . That's eleven for guilty. Okay. Not guilty? *(*NO. 8*'s hand is raised)* One. Right. Okay. Eleven to one, guilty. Now we know where we are.

NO. 3. Somebody's in left field. *(To* NO. 8*)* You think he's not guilty?

NO. 8 *(Quietly)*. I don't know.

NO. 3. I never saw a guiltier man in my life. You sat right in court and heard the same thing I did. The man's a dangerous killer. You could see it.

NO. 8. He's nineteen years old.

NO. 3. That's old enough. He knifed his own father. Four inches into the chest. An innocent little nineteen-year-old kid. They proved it a dozen different ways. Do you want me to list them?

NO. 8. No.

NO. 10 (To NO. 8). Well, do you believe his story?

NO. 8. I don't know whether I believe it or not. Maybe I don't.

NO. 7. So what'd you vote not guilty for?

NO. 8. There were eleven votes for guilty. It's not so easy for me to raise my hand and send a boy off to die without talking about it first.

NO. 7. Who says it's easy for me?

NO. 8. No one.

NO. 7. What, just because I voted fast? I think the guy's guilty. You couldn't change my mind if you talked for a hundred years.

NO. 8. I don't want to change your mind. I just want to talk for a while. Look, this boy's been kicked around all his life. You know, living in a slum, his mother dead since he was nine. That's not a very good head start. He's a tough, angry kid. You know why slum kids get that way? Because we knock 'em on the head once a day, every day. I think maybe we owe him a few words. That's all.

He looks around the table. Some of them look back coldly. Some cannot look at him. Only NO. *9 nods slowly.* NO. *12 doodles steadily.* NO. *4 begins to comb his hair.*

NO. 10. I don't mind telling you this, mister. We don't owe him a thing. He got a fair trial, didn't he? You know what that trial cost? He's lucky he got it. Look, we're all grown-ups here. You're not going to tell us that we're supposed to believe him, knowing what he is. I've lived among 'em all my life. You can't believe a word they say. You know that.

NO. 9 (To NO. 10 very slowly). I don't know that. What a terrible thing for a man to believe! Since when is dishonesty a group characteristic? You have no monopoly on the truth——

NO. 3 (Interrupting). All right. It's not Sunday. We don't need a sermon.

NO. 9. What this man says is very dangerous. . . .

NO. *8 puts his hand on* NO. *9's arm and stops*

him. Somehow his touch and his gentle expression calm the old man. He draws a deep breath and relaxes.

NO. 4. I don't see any need for arguing like this. I think we ought to be able to behave like gentlemen.

NO. 7. Right!

NO. 4. If we're going to discuss this case, let's discuss the facts.

FOREMAN. I think that's a good point. We have a job to do. Let's do it.

NO. 11 (With accent). If you gentlemen don't mind, I'm going to close the window. (He gets up and does so) (Apologetically). It was blowing on my neck.

NO. *10 blows his nose fiercely.*

NO. 12. I may have an idea here. I'm just thinking out loud now, but it seems to me that it's up to us to convince this gentleman (Indicating NO. 8) that we're right and he's wrong. Maybe if we each took a minute or two, you know, if we sort of try it on for size . . .

FOREMAN. That sounds fair enough. Supposing we go once around the table.

NO. 7. Okay, let's start it off.

FOREMAN. Right. (To NO. 2) I guess you're first.

NO. 2 (Timidly). Oh. Well . . . (Long pause) I just think he's guilty. I thought it was obvious. I mean nobody proved otherwise.

NO. 8 (Quietly). Nobody has to prove otherwise. The burden of proof is on the prosecution. The defendant doesn't have to open his mouth. That's in the Constitution. The Fifth Amendment. You've heard of it.

NO. 2 (Flustered). Well, sure, I've heard of it. I know what it is. I . . . what I meant . . . well, anyway, I think he was guilty.

NO. 3. Okay, let's get to the facts. Number one, let's take the old man who lived on the second floor right underneath the room where the murder took place. At ten minutes after twelve on the night of the killing he heard loud noises in the upstairs apartment. He said it sounded like a fight. Then he heard the kid say to his father, "I'm gonna kill you." A second later he heard a body falling, and he ran to the door of his apartment, looked out, and saw the kid running down the stairs and out of the house. Then he called the police. They found the father with a knife in his chest.

FOREMAN. And the coroner fixed the time of death at around midnight.

NO. 3. Right. Now what else do you want?

NO. 4. The boy's entire story is flimsy. He claimed he was at the movies. That's a little ridiculous, isn't it? He couldn't even remember what pictures he saw.

NO. 3. That's right. Did you hear that? (*To* NO. *4)* You're absolutely right.

NO. 10. Look, what about the woman across the street? If her testimony don't prove it, then nothing does.

NO. 12. That's right. She saw the killing, didn't she?

FOREMAN. Let's go in order.

NO. 10 (*Loud*). Just a minute. Here's a woman who's lying in bed and can't sleep. It's hot, you know. (*He gets up and begins to walk around, blowing his nose and talking)* Anyway, she looks out the window, and right across the street she sees the kid stick the knife into his father. She's known the kid all his life. His window is right opposite hers, across the el tracks,[1] and she swore she saw him do it.

NO. 8. Through the windows of a passing elevated train.

NO. 10. Okay. And they proved in court that you can look through the windows of a passing el train at night and see what's happening on the other side. They proved it.

NO. 8. I'd like to ask you something. How come you believed her? She's one of "them" too, isn't she?

NO. *10 walks over to* NO. *8.*

NO. 10. You're a pretty smart fellow, aren't you?

FOREMAN (*Rising*). Now take it easy.

NO. *3 gets up and goes to* NO. *10.*

NO. 3. Come on. Sit down. (*He leads* NO. *10 back to his seat*) What're you letting him get

you all upset for? Relax.

NO. *10 and* NO. *3 sit down.*

FOREMAN. Let's calm down now. (*To* NO. *5)* It's your turn.

NO. 5. I'll pass it.

FOREMAN. That's your privilege. (*To* NO. *6)* How about you?

NO. 6 (*Slowly*). I don't know. I started to be convinced, you know, with the testimony from those people across the hall. Didn't they say something about an argument between the father and the boy around seven o'clock that night? I mean, I can be wrong.

NO. 11. I think it was eight o'clock. Not seven.

NO. 8. That's right. Eight o'clock. They heard the father hit the boy twice and then saw the boy walk angrily out of the house. What does that prove?

NO. 6. Well, it doesn't exactly prove anything. It's just part of the picture. I didn't say it proved anything.

FOREMAN. Anything else?

NO. 6. No.

NO. *6 goes to the water fountain.*

FOREMAN (*To* NO. *7*). All right. How about you?

NO. 7. I don't know, most of it's been said already. We can talk all day about this thing, but I think we're wasting our time. Look at the kid's record. At fifteen he was in reform school. He stole a car. He's been arrested for mugging.[2] He was picked up for knife-fighting. I think they said he stabbed somebody in the arm. This is a very fine boy.

NO. 8. Ever since he was five years old his father beat him up regularly. He used his fists.

NO. 7. So would I! A kid like that.

NO. 3. You're right. It's the kids. The way they are—you know? They don't listen. (*Bitter*) I've got a kid. When he was eight years old he ran away from a fight. I saw him. I was so ashamed, I told him right out, "I'm gonna make a man out of you or I'm gonna bust you

---

1. **el tracks,** elevated railroad.
2. **mugging,** assaulting and robbing someone.

up into little pieces trying." When he was fifteen he hit me in the face. He's big, you know. I haven't seen him in three years. Rotten kid! You work your heart out. . . . *(Pause)* All right. Let's get on with it.

Looks away embarrassed.

NO. 4. We're missing the point here. This boy —let's say he's a product of a filthy neighborhood and a broken home. We can't help that. We're not here to go into the reasons why slums are breeding grounds for criminals. They are. I know it. So do you. The children who come out of slum backgrounds are potential menaces to society.

NO. 10. You said it there. I don't want any part of them, believe me.

There is a dead silence for a moment, and then NO. *5 speaks haltingly.*

NO. 5. I've lived in a slum all my life—

NO. 10. Oh, now wait a second!

NO. 5. I used to play in a back yard that was filled with garbage. Maybe it still smells on me.

FOREMAN. Now let's be reasonable. There's nothing personal—

NO. *5 stands up.*

NO. 5. There is something personal!

Then he catches himself and, seeing everyone looking at him, sits down, fists clenched.

NO. 3 *(Persuasively)*. Come on, now. He didn't mean you, feller. Let's not be so sensitive. . . .

There is a long pause.

NO. 11. I can understand this sensitivity.

FOREMAN. Now let's stop the bickering. We're wasting time. *(To* NO. *8)* It's your turn.

NO. 8. All right. I had a peculiar feeling about this trial. Somehow I felt that the defense counsel never really conducted a thorough cross-examination. I mean, he was appointed by the court to defend the boy. He hardly seemed interested. Too many questions were left unasked.

NO. 3 *(Annoyed)*. What about the ones that

were asked? For instance, let's talk about that cute little switch-knife. You know, the one that fine, upright kid admitted buying.

NO. 8. All right. Let's talk about it. Let's get it in here and look at it. I'd like to see it again, Mr. Foreman.

The FOREMAN *looks at him questioningly and then gets up and goes to the door. During the following dialogue the* FOREMAN *knocks, the* GUARD *comes in, the* FOREMAN *whispers to him, the* GUARD *nods and leaves, locking the door.*

NO. 3. We all know what it looks like. I don't see why we have to look at it again. *(To* NO. *4)* What do you think?

NO. 4. The gentleman has a right to see exhibits in evidence.

NO. 3 *(Shrugging)*. Okay with me.

NO. 4 *(To* NO. *8)*. This knife is a pretty strong piece of evidence, don't you agree?

NO. 8. I do.

NO. 4. The boy admits going out of his house at eight o'clock after being slapped by his father.

NO. 8. Or punched.

NO. 4. Or punched. He went to a neighborhood store and bought a switch-knife. The storekeeper was arrested the following day when he admitted selling it to the boy. It's a very unusual knife. The storekeeper identified it and said it was the only one of its kind he had in stock. Why did the boy get it? *(Sarcastically)* As a present for a friend of his, he says. Am I right so far?

NO. 8. Right.

NO. 3. You bet he's right. *(To all)* Now listen to this man. He knows what he's talking about.

NO. 4. Next, the boy claims that on the way home the knife must have fallen through a hole in his coat pocket, that he never saw it again. Now there's a story, gentlemen. You know what actually happened. The boy took the knife home and a few hours later stabbed his father with it and even remembered to wipe off the fingerprints.

The door opens and the GUARD *walks in with*

an oddly designed knife with a tag on it. NO. *4 gets up and takes it from him. The* GUARD *exits.*

NO. 4. Everyone connected with the case identified this knife. Now are you trying to tell me that someone picked it up off the street and went up to the boy's house and stabbed his father with it just to be amusing?

NO. 8. No, I'm saying that it's possible that the boy lost the knife and that someone else stabbed his father with a similar knife. It's possible.

NO. *4 flips open the knife and jams it into the table.*

NO. 4. Take a look at that knife. It's a very strange knife. I've never seen one like it before in my life. Neither had the storekeeper who sold it to him.

NO. *8 reaches casually into his pocket and withdraws an object. No one notices this. He stands up quietly.*

NO. 4. Aren't you trying to make us accept a pretty incredible coincidence?

NO. 8. I'm not trying to make anyone accept it. I'm just saying it's possible.

NO. 3 (*Shouting*). And I'm saying it's not possible.

NO. *8 swiftly flicks open the blade of a switchknife and jams it into the table next to the first one. They are exactly alike. There are several gasps and everyone stares at the knife. There is a long silence.*

NO. 3 (*Slowly amazed*). What are you trying to do?

NO. 10 (*Loud*). Yeah, what is this? Who do you think you are?

NO. 5. Look at it! It's the same knife!

FOREMAN. Quiet! Let's be quiet.

They quiet down.

NO. 4. Where did you get it?

NO. 8. I got it last night in a little junk shop around the corner from the boy's house. It cost two dollars.

NO. 3. Now listen to me! You pulled a real smart

trick here, but you proved absolutely zero. Maybe there are ten knives like that, so what?

NO. 8. Maybe there are.

NO. 3. The boy lied and you know it.

NO. 8. He may have lied. (*To* NO. *10*) Do you think he lied?

NO. 10 (*Violently*). Now that's a stupid question. Sure he lied!

NO. 8 (*To* NO. *4*). Do you?

NO. 4. You don't have to ask me that. You know my answer. He lied.

NO. 8 (*To* NO. *5*). Do you think he lied?

NO. *5 can't answer immediately. He looks around nervously.*

NO. 5. I . . . I don't know.

NO. 7. Now wait a second. What are you, the guy's lawyer? Listen, there are still eleven of us who think he's guilty. You're alone. What do you think you're gonna accomplish? If you want to be stubborn and hang this jury, he'll be tried again and found guilty, sure as he's born.

NO. 8. You're probably right.

NO. 7. So what are you gonna do about it? We can be here all night.

NO. 9. It's only one night. A man may die.

NO. *7 glares at* NO. *9 for a long while, but has no answer.* NO. *8 looks closely at* NO. *9 and we can begin to sense a rapport between them. There is a long silence. Then suddenly everyone begins to talk at once.*

NO. 3. Well, whose fault is that?

NO. 6. Do you think maybe if we went over it again? What I mean is . . .

NO. 10. Did anyone force him to kill his father? (*To* NO. *3*) How do you like him? Like someone forced him!

NO. 11. Perhaps this is not the point.

NO. 5. No one forced anyone. But listen . . .

NO. 12. Look, gentlemen, we can spitball all night here.

NO. 2. Well, I was going to say—

NO. 7. Just a minute. Some of us've got better things to do than sit around a jury room.

NO. 4. I can't understand a word in here. Why do we all have to talk at once?

FOREMAN. He's right. I think we ought to get on with it.

NO. 8 has been listening to this exchange closely.

NO. 3 (*To* NO. 8). Well, what do you say? You're the one holding up the show.

NO. 8 (*Standing*). I've got a proposition to make.

We catch a close shot of NO. 5, *looking steadily at him as he talks.* NO. 5, *seemingly puzzled, listens closely.*

NO. 8. I want to call for a vote. I want you eleven men to vote by secret ballot. I'll abstain. If there are still eleven votes for guilty, I won't stand alone. We'll take in a guilty verdict right now.

NO. 7. Okay. Let's do it.

FOREMAN. That sounds fair. Is everyone agreed?

They all nod their heads. NO. 8 *walks over to the window, looks out for a moment and then faces them.*

FOREMAN. Pass these along.

The FOREMAN *passes ballot slips to all of them, and now* NO. 8 *watches them tensely as they begin to write. Fade out.*

Act II

Fade in on same scene, no time lapse. NO. 8 *stands tensely watching as the jurors write on their ballots. He stays perfectly still as one by one they fold the ballots and pass them along to the* FOREMAN. *The* FOREMAN *takes them, riffles through the folded ballots, counts eleven and now begins to open them. He reads each one out loud and lays it aside. They watch him quietly, and all we hear is his voice and the sound of* NO. 2 *sucking on a cough drop.*

FOREMAN. Guilty. Guilty. Guilty. Guilty. Guilty. Guilty. Guilty. Guilty. Guilty. (*He pauses at the tenth ballot and then reads it*) Not Guilty. (NO. 3 *slams down hard on the table. The* FOREMAN *opens the last ballot*) Guilty.

NO. 10 (*Angry*). How do you like that!

NO. 7. Who was it? I think we have a right to know.

NO. 11. Excuse me. This was a secret ballot. We agreed on this point, no? If the gentleman wants it to remain secret—

NO. 3 (*Standing up angrily*). What do you mean? There are no secrets in here! I know who it was. (*He turns to* NO. 5) What's the matter with you? You come in here and you vote guilty and then this slick preacher starts to tear your heart out with stories about a poor little kid who just couldn't help becoming a murderer. So you change your vote. If that isn't the most sickening—

NO. 5 *stares at* NO. 3, *frightened at this outburst.*

FOREMAN. Now hold it.

NO. 3. Hold it? We're trying to put a guilty man into the chair where he belongs—and all of a sudden we're paying attention to fairy tales.

NO. 5. Now just a minute . . .

NO. 11. Please. I would like to say something here. I have always thought that a man was entitled to have unpopular opinions in this country. This is the reason I came here. I wanted to have the right to disagree. In my own country, I am ashamed to say—

NO. 10. What do we have to listen to now—the whole history of your country?

NO. 7. Yeah, let's stick to the subject. (*To* NO. 5) I want to ask you what made you change your vote.

There is a long pause as NO. 7 *and* NO. 5 *eye each other angrily.*

NO. 9 (*Quietly*). There's nothing for him to tell you. He didn't change his vote. I did. (*There is a pause*) Maybe you'd like to know why.

NO. 3. No, we wouldn't like to know why.

FOREMAN. The man wants to talk.

NO. 9. Thank you. (*Pointing at* NO. 8) This gentleman chose to stand alone against us. That's his right. It takes a great deal of courage to stand alone even if you believe in something very strongly. He left the verdict up to us. He gambled for support and I gave it to him. I want to hear more. The vote is ten to two.

NO. 10. That's fine. If the speech is over, let's go on.

FOREMAN *gets up, goes to door, knocks, hands* GUARD *the tagged switch-knife and sits down again.*

NO. 3 (*To* NO. 5). Look, buddy, I was a little excited. Well, you know how it is. I . . . I didn't mean to get nasty. Nothing personal.

NO. *5 looks at him.*

NO. 7 (*To* NO. 8). Look, supposing you answer me this. If the kid didn't kill him, who did?

NO. 8. As far as I know, we're supposed to decide whether or not the boy on trial is guilty. We're not concerned with anyone else's motives here.

NO. 9. Guilty beyond a reasonable doubt. This is an important thing to remember.

NO. 3 (*To* NO. *10*). Everyone's a lawyer. (*To* NO. *9*) Supposing you explain what your reasonable doubts are.

NO. 9. This is not easy. So far, it's only a feeling I have. A feeling. Perhaps you don't understand.

NO. 10. A feeling! What are we gonna do, spend the night talking about your feelings? What about the facts?

NO. 3. You said a mouthful. (*To* NO. *9*) Look, the old man heard the kid yell, "I'm gonna kill you." A second later he heard the father's body falling, and he saw the boy running out of the house fifteen seconds after that.

NO. 12. That's right. And let's not forget the woman across the street. She looked into the open window and saw the boy stab his father. She saw it. Now if that's not enough for you . . .

NO. 8. It's not enough for me.

NO. 7. How do you like him? It's like talking into a dead phone.

NO. 4. The woman saw the killing through the windows of a moving elevated train. The train had five cars, and she saw it through the windows of the last two. She remembers the most insignificant details.

Cut to close shot of NO. *12 who doodles a picture of an el train on a scrap of paper.*

NO. 3. Well, what have you got to say about that?

NO. 8. I don't know. It doesn't sound right to me.

NO. 3. Well, supposing you think about it. (*To* NO. *12*) Lend me your pencil.

NO. *12 gives it to him. He draws a tic-tac-toe square on the same sheet of paper on which* NO. *12 has drawn the train. He fills in an X, hands the pencil to* NO. *12.*

NO. 3. Your turn. We might as well pass the time.

NO. *12 takes the pencil.* NO. 8 *stands up and snatches the paper away.* NO. 3 *leaps up.*

NO. 3. Wait a minute!

NO. 8 (*Hard*). This isn't a game.

NO. 3 (*Angry*). Who do you think you are?

NO. 7 (*Rising*). All right, let's take it easy.

NO. 3. I've got a good mind to walk around this table and belt him one!

FOREMAN. Now, please. I don't want any fights in here.

NO. 3. Did ya see him? The nerve! The absolute nerve!

NO. 10. All right. Forget it. It don't mean anything.

NO. 6. How about sitting down.

NO. 3. This isn't a game. Who does he think he is?

He lets them sit him down. NO. 8 *remains standing, holding the scrap of paper. He looks at it closely now and seems to be suddenly interested in it. Then he throws it back toward* NO. 3. *It lands in center of table.* NO. 3 *is angered again at this, but* NO. 4 *puts his hand on his arm.* NO. 8 *speaks now and his voice is more intense.*

NO. 8 (*To* NO. *4*). Take a look at that sketch. How long does it take an elevated train going at top speed to pass a given point?

NO. 4. What has that got to do with anything?

NO. 8. How long? Guess.

NO. 4. I wouldn't have the slightest idea.

NO. 8 (*To* NO. *5*). What do you think?

NO. 5. About ten or twelve seconds, maybe.

NO. 8. I'd say that was a fair guess. Anyone else?

NO. 11. I would think about ten seconds, perhaps.

NO. 2. About ten seconds.

NO. 4. All right. Say ten seconds. What are you getting at?

NO. 8. This. An el train passes a given point in ten seconds. That given point is the window of the room in which the killing took place. You can almost reach out of the window of that room and touch the el. Right? (*Several of them nod*) All right. Now let me ask you this. Did anyone here ever live right next to the el tracks? I have. When your window is open and the train goes by, the noise is almost unbearable. You can't hear yourself think.

NO. 10. Okay. You can't hear yourself think. Will you get to the point?

NO. 8. The old man heard the boy say, "I'm going to kill you," and one second later he heard a body fall. One second. That's the testimony, right?

NO. 2. Right.

NO. 8. The woman across the street looked through the windows of the last two cars of the el and saw the body fall. Right? The *last two* cars.

NO. 10. What are you giving us here?

NO. 8. An el takes ten seconds to pass a given point or two seconds per car. That el had been going by the old man's window for at least six seconds, and maybe more, *before the body fell*, according to the woman. The old man would have had to hear the boy say, "I'm going to kill you," while the front of the el was roaring past his nose. It's not possible that he could have heard it.

NO. 3. What d'ya mean! Sure he could have heard it.

NO. 8. Could he?

NO. 3. He said the boy yelled it out. That's enough for me.

NO. 9. I don't think he could have heard it.

NO. 2. Maybe he didn't hear it. I mean with the el noise . . .

NO. 3. What are you people talking about? Are you calling the old man a liar?

NO. 5. Well, it stands to reason.

NO. 3. You're crazy. Why would he lie? What's he got to gain?

NO. 9. Attention, maybe.

NO. 3. You keep coming up with these bright sayings. Why don't you send one in to a newspaper? They pay two dollars.

NO. *8 looks hard at* NO. *3 and then turns to* NO. *9.*

NO. 8 (*Softly*). Why might the old man have lied? You have a right to be heard.

NO. 9. It's just that I looked at him for a very long time. The seam of his jacket was split under the arm. Did you notice that? He was a very old man with a torn jacket, and he carried two canes. I think I know him better than anyone here. This is a quiet, frightened, insignificant man who has been nothing all his life, who has never had recognition—his name in the newspapers. Nobody knows him after seventy-five years. That's a very sad thing. A man like this needs to be recognized. To be questioned, and listened to and quoted just once. This is very important.

NO. 12. And you're trying to tell us he lied about a thing like this just so that he could be important?

NO. 9. No. He wouldn't really lie. But perhaps he'd make himself believe that he heard those words and recognized the boy's face.

NO. 3 (*Loud*). Well, that's the most fantastic story I've ever heard. How can you make up a thing like that? What do you know about it?

NO. 9 (*Low*). I speak from experience.

There is a long pause. Then the FOREMAN *clears his throat.*

FOREMAN (*To* NO. 8). All right. Is there anything else?

NO. 8 *is looking at* NO. 9. NO. 2 *offers the* FOREMAN *a box of cough drops. The* FOREMAN *pushes it away.*

NO. 2 (*Hesitantly*). Anybody . . . want a cough . . . drop?

FOREMAN (*Sharply*). Come on. Let's get on with it.

NO. 8. I'll take one. (NO. 2 *almost gratefully slides him one along the table*) Thanks.

NO. 2 *nods and* NO. 8 *puts the cough drop into his mouth.*

NO. 8. Now. There's something else I'd like to point out here. I think we proved that the old man couldn't have heard the boy say, "I'm going to kill you," but supposing he really did hear it? This phrase: how many times has each of you used it? Probably hundreds. "If you do that once more, Junior, I'm going to murder you." "Come on, Rocky, kill him!" We say it every day. This doesn't mean that we're going to kill someone.

NO. 3. Wait a minute. The phrase was "I'm going to kill you," and the kid screamed it out at the top of his lungs. Don't try and tell me he didn't mean it. Anybody says a thing like that the way he said it—they mean it.

NO. 10. And how they mean it!

NO. 8. Well, let me ask you this. Do you really think the boy would shout out a thing like that so the whole neighborhood would hear it? I don't think so. He's much too bright for that.

NO. 10 (*Exploding*). Bright! He's a common, ignorant slob. He don't even speak good English!

NO. 11 (*Slowly*). He *doesn't* even speak good English.

NO. 10 *stares angrily at* NO. 11, *and there is silence for a moment. Then* NO. 5 *looks around the table nervously.*

NO. 5. I'd like to change my vote to not guilty.

NO. 3 *gets up and walks to the window, furious, but trying to control himself.*

FOREMAN. Are you sure?

NO. 5. Yes. I'm sure.

FOREMAN. The vote is nine to three in favor of guilty.

NO. 7. Well, if that isn't the end. (*To* NO. 5) What are you basing it on? Stories this guy (*Indicating* NO. 8) made up! He oughta write for *Amazing Detective Monthly*. He'd make a fortune. Listen, the kid had a lawyer, didn't he? Why didn't his lawyer bring up all these points?

NO. 5. Lawyers can't think of everything.

NO. 7. Oh, brother! (*To* NO. 8) You sit in here and pull stories out of thin air. Now we're supposed to believe that the old man didn't get up out of bed, run to the door and see the kid beat it downstairs fifteen seconds after the killing. He's only saying he did to be important.

NO. 5. Did the old man say he *ran* to the door?

NO. 7. Ran. Walked. What's the difference? He got there.

NO. 5. I don't remember what he said. But I don't see how he could run.

NO. 4. He said he *went* from his bedroom to the front door. That's enough, isn't it?

NO. 8. Where was his bedroom again?

NO. 10. Down the hall somewhere. I thought you remembered everything. Don't you remember that?

NO. 8. No. Mr. Foreman, I'd like to take a look at the diagram of the apartment.

NO. 7. Why don't we have them run the trial over just so you can get everything straight?

NO. 8. Mr. Foreman . . .

FOREMAN (*Rising*). I heard you.

The FOREMAN *gets up, goes to door during following dialogue. He knocks on door,* GUARD *opens it, he whispers to* GUARD, GUARD *nods and closes door.*

NO. 3 (*To* NO. 8). All right. What's this for? How come you're the only one in the room who wants to see exhibits all the time.

NO. 5. I want to see this one, too.

NO. 3. And I want to stop wasting time.

NO. 4. If we're going to start wading through

all that nonsense about where the body was found . . .

NO. 8. We're not. We're going to find out how a man who's had two strokes in the past three years, and who walks with a pair of canes, could get to his front door in fifteen seconds.

NO. 3. He said twenty seconds.

NO. 2. He said fifteen.

NO. 3. How does he know how long fifteen seconds is? You can't judge that kind of a thing.

NO. 9. He said fifteen. He was very positive about it.

NO. 3 (*Angry*). He's an old man. You saw him. Half the time he was confused. How could he be positive about . . . anything?

NO. 3 looks around sheepishly, unable to cover up his blunder. The door opens and the GUARD walks in, carrying a large pen-and-ink diagram of the apartment. It is a railroad flat. A bedroom faces the el tracks. Behind it is a series of rooms off a long hall. In the front bedroom is a diagram of the spot where the body was found. At the back of the apartment we see the entrance into the apartment hall from the building hall. We see a flight of stairs in the building hall. The diagram is clearly labeled and included in the information on it are the dimensions of the various rooms. The GUARD gives the diagram to the FOREMAN.

GUARD. This what you wanted?

FOREMAN. That's right. Thank you.

The GUARD nods and exits. NO. 8 goes to FOREMAN and reaches for it.

NO. 8. May I?

The FOREMAN nods. NO. 8 takes the diagram and sets it up on a chair so that all can see it. NO. 8 looks it over. Several of the jurors get up to see it better. NO. 3, NO. 10 and NO. 7, however, barely bother to look at it.

NO. 7 (*To NO. 10*). Do me a favor. Wake me up when this is over.

NO. 8 (*Ignoring him*). All right. This is the apartment in which the killing took place. The old man's apartment is directly beneath

it and exactly the same. (*Pointing*) Here are the el tracks. The bedroom. Another bedroom. Living room. Bathroom. Kitchen. And this is the hall. Here's the front door to the apartment. And here are the steps. (*Pointing to front bedroom and then front door*) Now, the old man was in bed in this room. He says he got up, went out into the hall, down the hall to the front door, opened it and looked out just in time to see the boy racing down the stairs. Am I right?

NO. 3. That's the story.

NO. 8. Fifteen seconds after he heard the body fall.

NO. 11. Correct.

NO. 8. His bed was at the window. It's (*Looking closer*) twelve feet from his bed to the bedroom door. The length of the hall is forty-three feet, six inches. He had to get up out of bed, get his canes, walk twelve feet, open the bedroom door, walk forty-three feet and open the front door—all in fifteen seconds. Do you think this possible?

NO. 10. You know it's possible.

NO. 11. He can only walk very slowly. They had to help him into the witness chair.

NO. 3. You make it sound like a long walk. It's not.

NO. 8 gets up, goes to the end of the room and takes two chairs. He puts them together to indicate a bed.

NO. 9. For an old man who uses canes, it's a long walk.

NO. 3 (*To NO. 8*). What are you doing?

NO. 8. I want to try this thing. Let's see how long it took him. I'm going to pace off twelve feet —the length of the bedroom.

He begins to do so.

NO. 3. You're crazy. You can't recreate a thing like that.

NO. 11. Perhaps if we could see it . . . this is an important point.

NO. 3 (*Mad*). It's a ridiculous waste of time.

NO. 6. Let him do it.

NO. 8. Hand me a chair. (*Someone pushes a*

chair to him) All right. This is the bedroom door. Now how far would you say it is from here to the door of this room?

NO. 6. I'd say it was twenty feet.

NO. 2. Just about.

NO. 8. Twenty feet is close enough. All right, from here to the door and back is about forty feet. It's shorter than the length of the hall, wouldn't you say that?

NO. 9. A few feet, maybe.

NO. 10. Look, this is absolutely insane. What makes you think you can—

NO. 8. Do you mind if I try it? According to you, it'll only take fifteen seconds. We can spare that. *(He walks over to the two chairs now and lies down on them)* Who's got a watch with a second hand?

NO. 2. I have.

NO. 8. When you want me to start, stamp your foot. That'll be the body falling. Time me from there. *(He lies down on the chairs)* Let's say he keeps his canes right at his bedside. Right?

NO. 2. Right!

NO. 8. Okay. I'm ready.

They all watch carefully. NO. *2 stares at his watch, waiting for the second hand to reach 60. Then, as it does, he stamps his foot loudly.* NO. *8 begins to get up. Slowly he swings his legs over the edges of the chairs, reaches for imaginary canes and struggles to his feet.* NO. *2 stares at the watch.* NO. *8 walks as a crippled old man would walk, toward the chair which is serving as the bedroom door. He gets to it and pretends to open it.*

NO. 10 *(Shouting).* Speed it up. He walked twice as fast as that.

NO. *8, not having stopped for this outburst, begins to walk the simulated forty-foot hallway.*

NO. 11. This is, I think, even more quickly than the old man walked in the courtroom.

NO. 8. If you think I should go faster, I will.

He speeds up his pace slightly. He reaches the door and turns now, heading back, hob-bling as an old man would hobble, bent over his imaginary canes. They watch him tensely. He hobbles back to the chair, which also serves as the front door. He stops there and pretends to unlock the door. Then he pretends to push it open.

NO. 8 *(Loud).* Stop.

NO. 2. Right.

NO. 8. What's the time?

NO. 2. Fifteen . . . twenty . . . thirty . . . thirty-one seconds exactly.

NO. 11. Thirty-one seconds.

Some of the jurors ad-lib their surprise to each other.

NO. 8. It's my guess that the old man was trying to get to the door, heard someone racing down the stairs and *assumed* that it was the boy.

NO. 6. I think that's possible.

NO. 3 *(Infuriated).* Assumed? Now, listen to me, you people. I've seen all kinds of dishonesty in my day . . . but this little display takes the cake. *(To NO. 4)* Tell him, will you?

NO. *4 sits silently.* NO. *3 looks at him and then he strides over to* NO. 8.

NO. 3. You come in here with your heart bleeding all over the floor about slum kids and injustice and you make up these wild stories, and you've got some softhearted old ladies listening to you. Well I'm not. I'm getting real sick of it. *(To all)* What's the matter with you people? This kid is guilty! He's got to burn! We're letting him slip through our fingers here.

NO. 8 *(Calmly).* Our fingers. Are you his executioner?

NO. 3 *(Raging).* I'm one of 'em.

NO. 8. Perhaps you'd like to pull the switch.

NO. 3 *(Shouting).* For this kid? You bet I'd like to pull the switch!

NO. 8. I'm sorry for you.

NO. 3 *(Shouting).* Don't start with me.

NO. 8. What it must feel like to want to pull the switch!

NO. 3. Shut up!

NO. 8. You're a sadist.

NO. 3 (*Louder*). Shut up!

NO. 8 (*Strong*). You want to see this boy die because you personally want it—not because of the facts.

NO. 3 (*Shouting*). Shut up!

He lunges at NO. 8, *but is caught by two of the jurors and held. He struggles as* NO. 8 *watches calmly.*

NO. 3 (*Screaming*). Let me go! I'll kill him. I'll kill him!

NO. 8 (*Softly*). You don't really mean you'll kill me, do you?

NO. 3 stops struggling now and stares at NO. 8. *All the jurors watch in silence as we fade out.*

Act III

Fade in on same scene. No time lapse. NO. 3 *glares angrily at* NO. 8. *He is still held by two jurors. After a long pause, he shakes himself loose and turns away. He walks to the windows. The other jurors stand around the room now, shocked by this display of anger. There is silence. Then the door opens and the* GUARD *enters. He looks around the room.*

GUARD. Is there anything wrong, gentlemen? I heard some noise.

FOREMAN. No. There's nothing wrong. (*He points to the large diagram of the apartment*) You can take that back. We're finished with it.

The GUARD *nods and takes the diagram. He looks curiously at some of the jurors and exits. The jurors still are silent. Some of them slowly begin to sit down.* NO. 3 *still stands at the window. He turns around now. The jurors look at him.*

NO. 3 (*Loud*). Well, what are you looking at?

They turn away. He goes back to his seat now. Silently the rest of the jurors take their seats. NO. 12 *begins to doodle.* NO. 10 *blows his nose, but no one speaks. Then, finally—*

NO. 4. I don't see why we have to behave like children here.

NO. 11. Nor do I. We have a responsibility. This is a remarkable thing about democracy. That we are . . . what is the word? . . . Ah, notified! That we are notified by mail to come down to this place and decide on the guilt or innocence of a man we have not known before. We have nothing to gain or lose by our verdict. This is one of the reasons why we are strong. We should not make it a personal thing.

There is a long, awkward pause.

NO. 12. Well—we're still nowhere. Who's got an idea?

NO. 6. I think maybe we should try another vote. Mr. Foreman?

FOREMAN. It's all right with me. Anybody doesn't want to vote?

He looks around the table.

NO. 7. All right, let's do it.

NO. 3. I want an open ballot. Let's call out our votes. I want to know who stands where.

FOREMAN. That sounds fair. Anyone object? (*No one does*) All right. I'll call off your jury numbers.

He takes a pencil and paper and makes marks now in one of two columns after each vote.

FOREMAN. I vote guilty. No. 2?

NO. 2. Not guilty.

FOREMAN. No. 3?

NO. 3. Guilty.

FOREMAN. No. 4?

NO. 4. Guilty.

FOREMAN. No. 5?

NO. 5. Not guilty.

FOREMAN. No. 6?

NO. 6. Not guilty.

FOREMAN. No. 7?

NO. 7. Guilty.

FOREMAN. No. 8?

NO. 8. Not guilty.

FOREMAN. No. 9?

NO. 9. Not guilty.

FOREMAN. No. 10?

NO. 10. Guilty.

FOREMAN. No. 11?

NO. 11. Not guilty.

FOREMAN. No. 12?

NO. 12. Guilty.

NO. 4. Six to six.

NO. 10 (*Mad*). I'll tell you something. The crime is being committed right in this room.

FOREMAN. The vote is six to six.

NO. 3. I'm ready to walk into court right now and declare a hung jury. There's no point in this going on any more.

NO. 7. I go for that, too. Let's take it in to the judge and let the kid take his chances with twelve other guys.

NO. 5 (*To* NO. 7). You mean you still don't think there's room for reasonable doubt?

NO. 7. No, I don't.

NO. 11. I beg your pardon. Maybe you don't understand the term "reasonable doubt."

NO. 7 (*Angry*). What do you mean I don't understand it? Who do you think you are to talk to me like that? (*To all*) How do you like this guy? He comes over here running for his life, and before he can even take a big breath he's telling us how to run the show. The arrogance of him!

NO. 5 (*To* NO. 7). Wait a second. Nobody around here's asking where you came from.

NO. 7. I was born right here.

NO. 5. Or where your father came from. . . . (*He looks at* NO. 7, *who doesn't answer but looks away*) Maybe it wouldn't hurt us to take a few tips from people who come running here! Maybe they learned something we don't know. We're not so perfect!

NO. 11. Please—I am used to this. It's all right. Thank you.

NO. 5. It's not all right!

NO. 7. Okay, okay, I apologize. Is that what you want?

NO. 5. That's what I want.

FOREMAN. All right. Let's stop the arguing. Who's got something constructive to say?

NO. 2 (*Hesitantly*). Well, something's been bothering me a little . . . this whole business about

the stab wound and how it was made, the downward angle of it, you know?

NO. 3. Don't tell me we're gonna start that. They went over it and over it in court.

NO. 2. I know they did—but I don't go along with it. The boy is five feet eight inches tall. His father was six two. That's a difference of six inches. It's a very awkward thing to stab *down* into the chest of someone who's half a foot taller than you are.

NO. *3 jumps up, holding the knife.*

NO. 3. Look, you're not going to be satisfied till you see it again. I'm going to give you a demonstration. Somebody get up.

He looks around the table. NO. *8 stands up and walks toward him.* NO. *3 closes the knife and puts it in his pocket. They stand face to face and look at each other for a moment.*

NO. 3. Okay. (*To* NO. 2) Now watch this. I don't want to have to do it again. (*He crouches down now until he is quite a bit shorter than* NO. 8) Is that six inches?

NO. 12. That's more than six inches.

NO. 3. Okay, let it be more.

He reaches into his pocket and takes out the knife. He flicks it open, changes its position in his hand and holds the knife aloft, ready to stab. He and NO. *8 look steadily into each other's eyes. Then he stabs downward, hard.*

NO. 2 (*Shouting*). Look out!

He stops short just as the blade reaches NO. *8's chest.* NO. *3 laughs.*

NO. 6. That's not funny.

NO. 5. What's the matter with you?

NO. 3. Now just calm down. Nobody's hurt, are they?

NO. 8 (*Low*). No. Nobody's hurt.

NO. 3. All right. There's your angle. Take a look at it. Down and in. That's how I'd stab a taller man in the chest, and that's how it was done. Take a look at it and tell me I'm wrong.

NO. *2 doesn't answer.* NO. *3 looks at him for*

a moment, then jams the knife into the table and sits down. They all look at the knife.

NO. 6. Down and in. I guess there's no argument.

NO. 8 *picks the knife out of the table and closes it. He flicks it open and, changing its position in his hand, stabs downward with it.*

NO. 8 (*To* NO. 6). Did you ever stab a man?

NO. 6. Of course not.

NO. 8 (*To* NO. 3). Did you?

NO. 3. All right, let's not be silly.

NO. 8. Did you?

NO. 3 (*Loud*). No, I didn't!

NO. 8. Where do you get all your information about how it's done?

NO. 3. What do you mean? It's just common sense.

NO. 8. Have you ever seen a man stabbed?

NO. 3 (*Pauses and looks around the room nervously*). No.

NO. 8. All right. I want to ask you something. The boy was an experienced knife fighter. He was even sent to reform school for knifing someone, isn't that so?

NO. 12. That's right.

NO. 8. Look at this. (NO. 8 *closes the knife, flicks it open and changes the position of the knife so that he can stab overhanded*) Doesn't it seem like an awkward way to handle a knife?

NO. 3. What are you asking me for?

NO. 8 *closes the blade and flicks it open, holds it ready to slash underhanded.*

NO. 5. Wait a minute! What's the matter with me? Give me that.

He reaches out for the knife.

NO. 8. Have you ever seen a knife fight?

NO. 5. Yes, I have.

NO. 8. In the movies?

NO. 5. In my back yard. On my stoop. In the vacant lot across the street. Too many of them. Switch-knives came with the neighborhood where I lived. Funny I didn't think of it before. I guess you try to forget those things. (*Flicking the knife open*) Anyone who's ever used a switch-knife would never have stabbed downward. You don't handle a switch-knife that way. You use it underhanded.

NO. 8. Then he couldn't have made the kind of wound which killed his father.

NO. 5. No. He couldn't have. Not if he'd ever had any experience with switch-knives.

NO. 3. I don't believe it.

NO. 10. Neither do I. You're giving us a lot of mumbo jumbo.

NO. 8 (*To* NO. 12). What do you think?

NO. 12 (*Hesitantly*). Well . . . I don't know.

NO. 8 (*To* NO. 7). What about you?

NO. 7. Listen, I'll tell you something. I'm a little sick of this whole thing already. We're getting nowhere fast. Let's break it up and go home. I'm changing my vote to not guilty.

NO. 3. You're what?

NO. 7. You heard me. I've had enough.

NO. 3. What do you mean, you've had enough? That's no answer.

NO. 11 (*Angry*). I think perhaps you're right. This is not an answer. (*To* NO. 7) What kind of a man are you? You have sat here and voted guilty with everyone else because there are some theater tickets burning a hole in your pocket. Now you have changed your vote for the same reason. I do not think you have the right to play like this with a man's life. This is an ugly and terrible thing to do.

NO. 7. Now wait a minute . . . you can't talk like that to me.

NO. 11 (*Strong*). I can talk like that to you! If you want to vote not guilty, then do it because you are convinced the man is not guilty. If you believe he is guilty, then vote that way. Or don't you have the . . . the . . . guts—the guts to do what you think is right?

NO. 7. Now listen . . .

NO. 11. Is it guilty or not guilty?

NO. 7 (*Hesitantly*). I told you. Not . . . guilty.

NO. 11 (*Hard*). Why?

NO. 7. I don't have to—

NO. 11. You have to! Say it! Why?

They stare at each other for a long while.

NO. 7 (*Low*). I . . . don't know . . . he's guilty.

NO. 8 (*Fast*). I want another vote.

FOREMAN. Okay, there's another vote called for. I guess the quickest way is a show of hands. Anybody object? (*No one does*) All right. All those voting not guilty, raise your hands.

NUMBERS *2, 5, 6, 7, 8, 9 and 11 raise their hands immediately. Then, slowly, NO. 12 raises his hand. The FOREMAN looks around the table carefully and then he too raises his hand. He looks around the table, counting silently.*

FOREMAN. Nine. (*The hands go down*) All those voting guilty.

NUMBERS *3, 4 and 10 raise their hands.*

FOREMAN. Three. (*They lower their hands*) The vote is nine to three in favor of acquittal.

NO. 10. I don't understand you people. How can you believe this kid is innocent? Look, you know how those people lie. I don't have to tell you. They don't know what the truth is. And lemme tell you, they—(NO. *5 gets up from table, turns his back to it and goes to window*)—don't need any real big reason to kill someone either. You know, they get drunk, and *bang*, someone's lying in the gutter. Nobody's blaming them. That's how they are. You know what I mean? Violent!

NO. *9 gets up and does the same. He is followed by NO. 11.*

NO. 10. Human life don't mean as much to them as it does to us. Hey, where are you going? Look, these people are drinking and fighting all the time, and if somebody gets killed, so somebody gets killed. They don't care. Oh, sure, there are some good things about them, too. Look, I'm the first to say that.

NO. *8 gets up, and then NO. 2 and NO. 6 follow him to the window.*

NO. 10. I've known a few who were pretty decent, but that's the exception. Most of them, it's like they have no feelings. They can do anything. What's going on here?

The FOREMAN gets up and goes to the windows, followed by NO. 7 and NO. 12.

NO. 10. I'm speaking my piece, and you—Listen to me! They're no good. There's not a one of 'em who's any good. We better watch out. Take it from me. This kid on trial . . .

NO. *3 sits at table toying with the knife and NO. 4 gets up and starts for the window. All have their backs to NO. 10.*

NO. 10. Well, don't you know about them? Listen to me! What are you doing? I'm trying to tell you something. . . .

NO. *4 stands over him as he trails off. There is a dead silence. Then NO. 4 speaks softly.*

NO. 4. I've had enough. If you open your mouth again, I'm going to split your skull.

NO. *4 stands there and looks at him. No one moves or speaks. NO. 10 looks at him, then looks down at the table.*

NO. 10 (*Softly*). I'm only trying to tell you . . .

There is a long pause as NO. 4 stares down at NO. 10.

NO. 4 (*To all*). All right. Sit down everybody.

They all move back to their seats. When they are all seated, NO. 4 then sits down.

NO. 4 (*Quietly*). I still believe the boy is guilty of murder. I'll tell you why. To me, the most damning evidence was given by the woman across the street who claimed she actually saw the murder committed.

NO. 3. That's right. As far as I'm concerned, that's the most important testimony.

NO. 8. All right. Let's go over her testimony. What exactly did she say?

NO. 4. I believe I can recount it accurately. She said that she went to bed at about eleven o'clock that night. Her bed was next to the open window, and she could look out of the window while lying down and see directly into the window across the street. She tossed and turned for over an hour, unable to fall asleep. Finally she turned toward the window at about twelve-ten and, as she looked out, she saw the boy stab his father. As far as I can see, this is unshakable testimony.

NO. 3. That's what I mean. That's the whole case.

NO. *4 takes off his eyeglasses and begins to polish them, as they all sit silently watching him.*

NO. 4 (*To the jury*). Frankly, I don't see how you can vote for acquittal. (*To* NO. *12*) What do you think about it?

NO. 12. Well . . . maybe . . . there's so much evidence to sift.

NO. 3. What do you mean, maybe? He's absolutely right. You can throw out all the other evidence.

NO. 4. That was my feeling.

NO. *2, polishing his glasses, squints at clock, can't see it.* NO. *6 watches him closely.*

NO. 2. What time is it?

NO. 11. Ten minutes of six.

NO. 2. It's late. You don't suppose they'd let us go home and finish it in the morning. I've got a kid with mumps.

NO. 5. Not a chance.

NO. 6 (*To* NO. *2*). Pardon me. Can't you see the clock without your glasses?

NO. 2. Not clearly. Why?

NO. 6. Oh, I don't know. Look, this may be a dumb thought, but what do you do when you wake up at night and want to know what time it is?

NO. 2. What do you mean? I put on my glasses and look at the clock.

NO. 6. You don't wear them to bed.

NO. 2. Of course not. No one wears eyeglasses to bed.

NO. 12. What's all this for?

NO. 6. Well, I was thinking. You know the woman who testified that she saw the killing wears glasses.

NO. 3. So does my grandmother. So what?

NO. 8. Your grandmother isn't a murder witness.

NO. 6. Look, stop me if I'm wrong. This woman wouldn't wear her eyeglasses to bed, would she?

FOREMAN. Wait a minute! Did she wear glasses at all? I don't remember.

NO. 11 (*Excited*). Of course she did! The woman wore bifocals. I remember this very clearly. They looked quite strong.

NO. 9. That's right. Bifocals. She never took them off.

NO. 4. She did wear glasses. Funny. I never thought of it.

NO. 8. Listen, she wasn't wearing them in bed. That's for sure. She testified that in the midst of her tossing and turning she rolled over and looked casually out the window. The murder was taking place as she looked out, and the lights went out a split second later. She couldn't have had time to put on her glasses. Now maybe she honestly thought she saw the boy kill his father. I say that she saw only a blur.

NO. 3. How do you know what she saw? Maybe she's far-sighted.

He looks around. No one answers.

NO. 3 (*Loud*). How does he know all these things?

There is silence.

NO. 8. Does anyone think there still is not a reasonable doubt?

He looks around the room, then squarely at NO. *10.* NO. *10 looks down and shakes his head no.*

NO. 3 (*Loud*). I think he's guilty!

NO. 8 (*Calmly*). Does anyone else?

NO. 4 (*Quietly*). No. I'm convinced.

NO. 8 (*To* NO. *3*). You're alone.

NO. 3. I don't care whether I'm alone or not! I have a right.

NO. 8. You have a right.

There is a pause. They all look at NO. *3.*

NO. 3. Well, I told you I think the kid's guilty. What else do you want?

NO. 8. Your arguments.

They all look at NO. *3.*

NO. 3. I gave you my arguments.

NO. 8. We're not convinced. We're waiting to hear them again. We have time.

NO. *3 runs to* NO. *4 and grabs his arm.*

NO. 3 (*Pleading*). Listen. What's the matter with you? You're the guy. You made all the arguments. You can't turn now. A guilty man's gonna be walking the streets. A murderer. He's got to die! Stay with me.

NO. 4. I'm sorry. There's a reasonable doubt in my mind.

NO. 8. We're waiting.

NO. *3 turns violently on him.*

NO. 3 (*Shouting*). Well, you're not going to intimidate me! (*They all look at* NO. 3) I'm entitled to my opinion! (*No one answers him*) It's gonna be a hung jury! That's it!

NO. 8. There's nothing we can do about that, except hope that some night, maybe in a few months, you'll get some sleep.

NO. 5. You're all alone.

NO. 9. It takes a great deal of courage to stand alone.

NO. *3 looks around at all of them for a long time. They sit silently, waiting for him to speak, and all of them despise him for his stubbornness. Then, suddenly, his face contorts as if he is about to cry, and he slams his fist down on the table.*

NO. 3 (*Thundering*). All right!

NO. *3 turns his back on them. There is silence for a moment and then the* FOREMAN *goes to the door and knocks on it. It opens. The* GUARD *looks in and sees them all standing. The* GUARD *holds the door for them as they begin slowly to file out.* NO. *8 waits at the door as the others file past him. Finally he and* NO. *3 are the only ones left.* NO. *3 turns around and sees that they are alone. Slowly he moves toward the door. Then he stops at the table. He pulls the switch-knife out of the table and walks over to* NO. *8 with it. He holds it in the approved knife-fighter fashion and looks long and hard at* NO. *8, pointing the knife at his belly.* NO. *8 stares back. Then* NO.

3 turns the knife around. NO. *8 takes it by the handle.* NO. *3 exits.* NO. *8 closes the knife, puts it away and, taking a last look around the room, exits, closing the door. The camera moves in close on the littered table in the empty room, and we clearly see a slip of crumpled paper on which are scribbled the words "Not guilty."*

Fade out.

I

A CORNERSTONE OF JUSTICE

Of all our attempts to find some way to determine justice fairly, the jury system is perhaps the best. It is based upon the idea of a jury of one's peers, a jury of one's equals; thus it is essentially a democratic institution. It is believed that such a jury is likely to be the most impartial way of determining justice.

As you saw in this play, however, the ideal of the impartial jury is not always reached in practice. Which of the jurors are not impartial? What causes their partiality in each case? How did these men get on the jury in the first place?

II

IMPLICATIONS

The following statements are generalities that might or might not be based on this play. In discussing them, draw on your own experience as well as your understanding of the play.

1. In reality, the decisions of juries are determined by two or three strong jurors, not by all twelve.

2. When people are publicly committed to a belief or an opinion, it is extremely difficult to get them to change their minds.

3. In practice, a member of a minority group is much less likely to get a fair trial by jury than a member of a majority group.

4. One's first impressions and opinions are far more likely to be ruled by emotion than by reason.

5. It is easy to stand alone when one is emotionally convinced of the rightness of one's beliefs.

TECHNIQUES

Intention

Just as authors might have more than one theme in a given work, so, too, might they have more than one intention. Below is a list of intentions that Reginald Rose *might* have had. What evidence can you offer to show that each of these was or was not one of his intentions? Which—if any—might you classify as *major* intentions, and which—if any—might you classify as *minor* intentions? Be prepared to defend your opinions.

1. To create a gallery of psychological character studies.

2. To show how reason triumphs over the irrational.

3. To examine and criticize the institution of trial by jury.

4. To create a dramatically intense and unstable situation and to bring it through a series of complications to a relatively stable situation.

5. To illustrate how emotions and prejudices affect the decisions of juries.

Irony

On a number of occasions in the play Rose makes use of *irony*. For example, when No. 3 says, "I'll kill him. I'll kill him!" his statement is ironic in that it contrasts with his earlier statement that those who say, "I'll kill you," mean it and will follow through with the threat.

A somewhat different sort of irony occurs when No. 10 says, "The crime is being committed right in this room." In this case the contrast is between what 10 intends his statement to mean—that the jurors are committing a crime by moving toward the verdict of "not guilty"—and what it *does* mean for the reader—that 10 is committing a crime by declaring the boy guilty purely on the basis of prejudice.

In both of these examples the essential element is a *contrast*. In fact, irony arises when there is a contrast between what is expected or intended and what is actual or real. On the basis of this definition and of the two examples given, try to detect the irony in the following statements:

1. NO. 3: Everybody gets a fair trial. . . . That's the system.

2. NO. 3: He's an old man. You saw him. Half the time he was confused. How could he be positive about . . . anything?

3. NO. 11: We have nothing to gain or lose by our verdict. This is one of the reasons why we are strong.

4. NO. 10: Human life don't mean as much to them as it does to us.

5. NO. 10: Bright! He's a common, ignorant slob. He don't even speak good English!

Why might an author wish to use irony? What specifically does Rose gain by using it?

FINAL REFLECTIONS

The Struggle for Justice

As one looks back on the American past, one cannot help feeling that the struggle for justice has had positive results: Women have achieved a much higher status than they had in the nineteenth century; the worker and the farmer are in a much better position than their ancestors; slavery has been abolished; and, in fact, our laws and Constitution guarantee a much greater measure of freedom to every individual than was known 200 years ago. Yet we know that the struggle for justice remains a lively one at the present time and promises to continue in the future.

The writers you have read have tended to focus on some of the social and psychological factors that have prevented the realization of "liberty and justice *for all.*" Some of these factors have been listed below. Choose one or more of them and be prepared to discuss at least one concrete instance of how it (or they) has resulted in an injustice done to some specific individual or group.

1. Black-and-white thinking.

2. Perversion of the law.

3. Prejudice.

4. Traditionalism or conformity resulting from insecurity.

5. Inertia—the failure of an individual or a group to press for its rights.

6. Pressure groups working against justice.

7. Insensitivity toward others.

You have also seen that it is pointless to define justice as "equal treatment under the law," when the laws themselves are unjust. This fact raises some fundamental questions: (1) By what standard may one judge whether or not a law is just? (2) How can a reasonable agreement on such a standard be reached? (3) How does one go about changing a law that one considers unjust? Select one, two, or all three of these questions and be prepared to discuss it (them). Be sure to bring your reading to bear on your discussion.

IMPLICATIONS

Below are five statements dealing with justice. After each statement is a list of some of the selections you have read. Be prepared to discuss each statement in the light of *each* of the selections listed.

1. So far as justice is concerned, the individual is very much at the mercy of society.
"Trials at Salem"
"Under the Lion's Paw"
"Testimony of Trees"
"Susan B. Anthony"
"The Man with the Hoe"
Twelve Angry Men

2. There would be a great deal more justice in the world if human beings were more charitable to or more sensitive toward each other.
"Arsenal at Springfield"
"Eleven o'Clock News Summary"
"Lines for an Interment"
Twelve Angry Men

3. Guilty, insecure people tend to band together and to seek scapegoats on whom they can inflict unjust punishments.
"Trials at Salem"
"Susan B. Anthony"
"The Lottery"
Twelve Angry Men

4. In general, common people are reluctant to fight for justice; too often they tend merely to accept their lot without protest.
"Under the Lion's Paw"
"Testimony of Trees"

"The Man with the Hoe"
"The People Will Live On"
"The Lottery"
"Looking"

5. "Universal law" has generally been on the side of the common people and minority groups, but this fact has not helped them very much in their struggle to achieve identity and justice.
"Susan B. Anthony"
"The Man with the Hoe"
"The People Will Live On"
"The Arsenal at Springfield"
"I Have a Rendezvous with Death"
"Lines for an Interment"

TECHNIQUES

Intention

We have seen that a reader can best grasp a writer's intention by focusing on the work itself and by paying close attention to such matters as word choice, choice of incidents and details, and the amount of attention or development given to incidents and details. We have also touched from time to time on how readers know whether or not writers mean what they say. At this time let us take up this matter in some detail.

Consider the following situation: Three boys are discussing a fourth boy, Jack. The first boy says, "Jack's a giant." The second says, "Jack is 6 feet tall." The third says, "Jack's a shrimp." Suppose you know Jack and, in fact, he *is* 6 feet tall. You could then classify the statements of the boys as follows:

Exaggeration (Overstatement): "Jack's a giant."
Objective Statement: "Jack is 6 feet tall."
Understatement: "Jack's a shrimp."

Although our example is a crude one, the fact is that there is nothing unusual about such uses of language, and there are some very good reasons why writers use both exaggeration and understatement as well as objective statement. Exaggeration may often produce a strong and immediate effect on a reader, and it is commonly found in satire and in propagandist literature. Objective statement is the characteristic mode of expression of the reporter, the scientist, the historian, the philosopher, and of some literary essayists, all of whose main intention usually is to communicate information simply and clearly. Finally, understatement is used in much poetry and in most forms of serious modern fiction. It often helps to get readers *inside* a poem or a story; it forces them to *participate* by placing on them the task of determining what the writer really means.

Of course, writers on occasion may use any of these forms of statement in any literary work—a poet may exaggerate, a satirist may use understatement, both may use objective statement, and so on. The type of statement writers actually use depends more upon their major purpose, upon the immediate context, and upon their style than upon the type of writing they are doing. By paying close attention to these points as well as to word choice, selection and importance of incidents and details, readers will develop the ability to grasp a writer's intention.

Try to pick from the works in this unit at least one selection that employs a fair amount of exaggeration, one that uses objective statement, mainly, and one that makes extensive use of understatement. Discuss how you know which method each writer is using and why each may have chosen to use that method.

Theme

We have defined "theme" as the central idea in a literary work. We have also discovered that many literary works contain a number of themes and that if the work is to have unity, the final expression of the central idea should take account of subordinate themes. In Benét's "Trials at Salem," we noted that no single word expressed its theme adequately; we needed at least a full sentence to express the central idea fully. To put it in another way, an adequate expression of theme requires a certain amount of *modification and qualification*.

In fiction the task of expressing theme is likely to be still more complicated. The reader has to consider not only subordinate ideas but also elements such as character, setting, incident; indeed, the total pattern or organization. These elements modify and qualify fictional themes to such an extent that it has been said that the precise theme of most fictional works can be found only by reading the work itself.

The essential point is that *theme* is not merely something that is "tacked on" to a piece of fiction; it is something integral, something woven into the total pattern. And it cannot be extracted from that total pattern as if it were one of several teeth.

In spite of this, however, shorthand expressions of theme do have value. They may help readers tell someone else what a given work of fiction is about in a general way. Expressions of theme also help readers unify their impressions and test their understanding of a story or poem.

Below are given five simple statements about human nature. After each statement are listed at least two selections for which the statement might be considered *a* theme. Discuss in each case why you consider the statement to be an inadequate expression of the central idea of the works involved.

1. Superstitions and blind traditions make individuals commit unjust acts ("Trials at Salem" and "The Lottery").

2. Common people will allow themselves to be pushed around a good deal without fighting back ("The Man with the Hoe" and "The People Will Live On").

3. People usually show very little concern for matters that do not affect them directly ("Eleven o'Clock News Summary" and "Lines for an Interment").

4. Laws alone do not guarantee that human beings will show respect for the rights of others ("Under the Lion's Paw" and "Testimony of Trees").

5. People in general are very ready to make judgments against others on the basis of emotions alone ("The Lottery" and *Twelve Angry Men*).

6. War is the ultimate injustice, the ultimate expression of our own inhumanity ("The Dead in Europe," "Lunch on Omaha Beach," "The Horse," and "The Death of the Ball Turret Gunner").

BIOGRAPHICAL NOTES

Stephen Vincent Benét

Stephen Vincent Benét (1898–1943), born in Bethlehem, Pennsylvania, lived in many parts of the country and, as he grew older, developed a deep interest in America's past. His first writings were ballads, such as "William Sycamore," combining American folklore and humor. He then turned to the writing of epic poems, notably the

Pulitzer Prize-winning *John Brown's Body*, the story of men and women in both the North and South during the Civil War, and *Western Star*, in which he captured the flavor, excitement, and color of a robust young country. Benét also wrote five novels, two one-act operas, and many short stories.

Hamlin Garland

Hamlin Garland (1860–1940), born in Wisconsin and reared in Iowa and the Dakotas, was himself a child of the middle border—the prairie lands of the Midwest of which he wrote. Except for three propaganda novels which appeared in the 1890s, the farms and people of the prairies were the themes for Garland's realistic, yet romantic writings. Among his early books were collections of short stories, *Main-Travelled Roads* (1891), *Prairie Folks* (1893), and *Wayside Courtships* (1897). Probably his best books are two autobiographical works: *A Son of the Middle Border* (1917) and *A Daughter of the Middle Border* (1921), which was awarded a Pulitzer Prize.

Jesse Stuart

Jesse Stuart (1907–   ), living today on the hill farm where he was born, continues writing about the Kentucky people and places he loves. Though he could attend school only irregularly as a boy, because he was needed to help with the farm chores, he finally finished high school and saved enough money to go to college. Returning home, he taught first in a rural school, then in a high school, and later served as a principal and county superintendent. He recounts these experiences in *The Thread That Runs So True*. A prolific short-story writer, Stuart has also written such novels as *Trees of Heaven, Taps for Private Tussie,* and *Hie to the Hunter.*

Louis Untermeyer

Louis Untermeyer (1885–1977) was a poet in his own right, although most famous for his editing of many volumes of verse. In addition, he wrote many brief biographies and extensive critical essays. Untermeyer was born and grew up in the East. He left school at seventeen to enter his father's jewelry manufacturing firm. Twenty

years later, as vice-president, he resigned to devote himself to writing and lecturing. His productivity in the years since was extremely high; he edited more than a dozen anthologies and wrote more than twenty-five volumes of verse.

Edwin Markham

Edwin Markham's (1852–1940) fame rests largely on the single poem, "The Man with the Hoe." First published in the San Francisco *Examiner*, the poem brought an immediate response from the American people who at that time were very much concerned about the living and working conditions of the common worker. Two years after the publication of *The Man with the Hoe and Other Poems* in 1899, Markham gave up his teaching career in California and moved to New York. He published four more volumes of poetry, the last, *New Poems,* on his eightieth birthday.

Carl Sandburg

Carl Sandburg (1878–1967), son of Swedish emigrants, was born in Galesburg, Illinois. He left school at thirteen and worked at a variety of odd jobs until he enlisted in the infantry in the Spanish-American War. Afterwards he attended Lombard College, where his writing was encouraged by one of the professors who paid for the publication of Sandburg's first volume of verse. After four years he went to Milwaukee as a news reporter and later became secretary to the mayor. In 1912 he moved to Chicago and there his poems were printed in the new *Poetry: A Magazine of Verse*. He wrote many volumes of verse, including poems such as "Chicago" that became world famous. Long an admirer of Lincoln, Sandburg wrote the magnificent biography, *The Prairie Years,* two volumes, and *The War Years,* four volumes. He also wrote several children's books and collected a number of folktales and folk songs.

Shirley Jackson

Shirley Jackson (1919–1965) was born in California and attended Syracuse University in the East. Mother of four lively children, she has described their hectic and hilarious life in *Life*

Among the Savages and *Raising Demons.* In quite another vein are other novels, *The Bird's Nest* and *The Haunting of Hill House.* Of all her writings, "The Lottery" is among the best known. When it first appeared in *The New Yorker,* the reaction was immediate and widespread.

Henry Wadsworth Longfellow

Henry Wadsworth Longfellow (1807–1882), one of the "Cambridge Poets" (with James Russell Lowell and Oliver Wendell Holmes), enjoyed great popularity as a poet during his lifetime. After he was graduated from Bowdoin College, where he had been a classmate of Nathaniel Hawthorne, Longfellow traveled widely in Europe, studying languages and literature. Returning to Bowdoin, he became one of America's first professors of modern languages. After a few years at Bowdoin, Longfellow again traveled in Europe and then joined the faculty at Harvard, where he remained for eighteen years, resigning his position then to devote his full attention to writing. His best-loved poems today are those on American themes.

Alan Seeger

Alan Seeger (1888–1916), born and reared in New York, attended Harvard College and, in his senior year, edited the *Harvard Monthly.* Always a nonconformist, Seeger rebelled against the conventions of the time and finally moved to Paris in 1912. He enlisted in the Foreign Legion at the beginning of World War I and was killed in 1916. *Collected Poems,* published in 1916, includes his only famous poem, "I Have a Rendezvous with Death."

Phyllis McGinley

Phyllis McGinley (1905–1978) was born in Oregon and grew up in the West. She attended the Universities of Utah and California and then taught one year in Utah. Bent on a writing career, she moved to New York and held a succession of jobs, including writing for *Town and Country.* Her first children's book, *The Horse Who Lived Upstairs,* was published in 1944, and since that time she wrote many others. She was known chiefly for her verse, much of which was published in *The New Yorker.* Among her collections of verse, two of the best-known volumes are *A Short Walk from the Station* and *The Love Letters of Phyllis McGinley.* In 1961 she became the first writer of light verse to win the Pulitzer Prize.

Archibald MacLeish

Archibald MacLeish, who was born in Glencoe, Illinois, in 1892, was educated at Yale and at Harvard Law School. After serving with the American Army in France during World War I, he returned to Boston to practice law. Soon, however, he gave up his practice to devote full time to traveling and to writing. His travels included retracing the route of Cortez through Mexico, which led to his writing *Conquistador.* Caught up in America's mood of social protest in the thirties, he wrote *Frescoes for Mr. Rockefeller's City* and *America Was Promises.* Twice winner of the Pulitzer Prize for Poetry, versatile MacLeish also wrote prose, a ballet, and radio and stage plays. From 1939 to 1944 he was Librarian of Congress. In 1972 he published a book of selected poems, *The Human Season.*

Robert Lowell

For biographical note see page 299.

Bink Noll

Bink Noll (1927–   ) was born in Orange, New Jersey and educated at Princeton, Johns Hopkins, and the University of Colorado. Since 1953 he has been teaching at colleges and universities. Mr. Noll is married, the father of three children, and claims a single obsessive hobby—gourmet cooking. His poems have been widely published in magazines. His volumes include *The Center of the Circle* and *The Feast.*

Philip Levine

Originally from Detroit, Philip Levine (1928–   ) lived in various places in the United States and abroad before settling in Fresno, California. Married and the father of three, he teaches English at the university level. He has published three volumes of poetry: *On the Edge, Not This Pig,* and *They Feed the Lion.*

Randall Jarrell

Randall Jarrell (1914–1965), poet, critic, and teacher, was born in Nashville and grew up to earn two degrees at Vanderbilt University in Nashville. He went on to teach at Kenyon College and the University of Tennessee. His first book of poetry, *Blood for a Stranger*, was published in 1942. His experiences in the Air Corps were recounted in *Little Friend, Little Friend*, published in 1945. After the war he was briefly the editor of *The Nation* and a professor at Sarah Lawrence College. In 1947 he moved to the University of North Carolina and a year later his volume of verse entitled *Losses* was published. While continuing to teach and to write poetry, Jarrell turned to the novel and to literary criticism.

Gwendolyn Brooks

Gwendolyn Brooks (1917–   ), in 1950, became the first black woman to win a Pulitzer Prize. She won the award for her second volume of verse, *Annie Allen*. Her first book of poems, *A Street in Bronzeville*, had appeared in 1945. One critic has characterized Brooks' style as an "individual staccato manner—the partial statement, the deliberately broken scansion, the startling, particularized image." She has recently published an autobiography, *Report from Part One* (1972).

Reginald Rose

Reginald Rose (1921–   ) is one of the most sought-after writers of television scripts in recent years. Camp counselor, public relations worker for a motion picture company, advertising account executive, and copy chief—these were his jobs before he turned to television. *The Bus to Nowhere* was his first television play (1951). In addition to many adaptations, he has written a number of original scripts. Two, *Crime in the Streets* and *Twelve Angry Men*, were made into motion pictures. A collection of his best work appears in *Six Television Plays* (1956). He has won several Emmy awards for his work.

AMERICAN LITERATURE

THE MODERN PERIOD

1930-1966

If writers can truly be said to reflect their times, we can expect little optimism from American writers of the middle decades of the twentieth century. Our society was first upset by a long and devastating depression, beginning with the stock market crash of 1929. It had barely righted itself when it was rocked by World War II. After this hot war came the cold war, with its overhanging threat of imminent and catastrophic nuclear destruction. Then the wars in Korea and Vietnam drained American material and spiritual energies, and the latter nearly tore the country apart. In addition, writers could hardly escape the pervasive influence of the psychoanalyst Sigmund Freud, who, even more than Charles Darwin a half-century earlier, seemed to reduce the stature of humankind.

In the period up to about 1950, many writers continued in the naturalistic tradition, often with strong regional overtones. After 1950, American writers tended to look increasingly into the self in what seemed to be an attempt to redefine and perhaps redeem the modern world.

THE NOVELISTS AND SHORT-STORY WRITERS

We may speak first of Ernest Hemingway, for two of his best novels were published before this period began, *The Sun Also Rises* in 1926 and *A Farewell to Arms* in 1929. Both of these, as well as the later *For Whom the Bell Tolls* (1940), deal either with war itself or with a society shattered by war; and Hemingway's last novel, *The Old Man and the Sea* (1952), deals with a kind of private war. Violence, in short, is a principal part of Hemingway's world, as it was of the world of his time. The heroes of that world illustrate that life is a solitary struggle more likely to end in failure or defeat than in victory. But we may be reminded here of Melville's words in *Moby Dick*, "The truest of all men was the Man of Sorrow." And though many of Hemingway's characters face sorrow, they face it courageously, remaining true to the code by which they have lived—like the old fisherman Santiago in *The Old Man and the Sea*, who is clearly marked by his creator as a Christ figure.

If Hemingway made use of his naturalistic license to write about wars on battlefields, in bullrings, in trout streams, and on oceans, William Faulkner made use of the same license even more extensively to write about a 2,400-square-mile piece of land, which he called Yoknapatawpha County, Mississippi. In the novels for which he is best remembered—*The Sound and the Fury* (1929), *As I Lay Dying* (1930), *Light in August* (1932), and *Absalom, Absalom!* (1936)—there is so much sin, so much guilt, so much violence, so many crimes and perversions that it is as if the unconscious mind had gone on a rampage. Yet when Faulkner went to Stockholm in 1950 to receive the Nobel Prize for Literature, he delivered an optimistic and idealistic speech defending traditional values (see p. 704).

Many of his readers were surprised, and some even accused Faulkner of insincerity. Yet as one looks back over the novels, it is not difficult to find precisely those values that Faulkner defended in his speech. Of the black woman Dilsey in *The Sound and the Fury*, he had written the terse, eloquent biographical note, "They endured." The Bundrens in *As I Lay Dying* were examplars of pride and self-sacrifice. *Light in August* contains as much compassion as one could find in a novel, and it ends on a note of innocence and hope. Indeed, Faulkner's endings, generally, like the endings of Shakespeare's tragedies, usually point in the direction of renewal and redemption.

There were several other distinguished Southern regionalists during this period, including Thomas Wolfe, Carson McCullers, Flannery O'Connor, and Robert Penn Warren (who was also one of our best poets and critics). Wolfe, whom Faulkner once identified as the best writer of the mid-twentieth century, was more of a romantic than a naturalist, though attention has been called to many naturalistic elements in his first novel, *Look Homeward, Angel* (1929). That work and his second, *Of Time and the River* (1935), tell the story of himself (as Eugene Gant) and his attempts to escape his family and the narrowness of his environment in order to find himself. Though Wolfe has been criticized for the shapelessness of his work and a sometimes-awkward style, he writes with an energy and passion that have been matched by few.

Both Carson McCullers and Flannery O'Connor also move away from naturalism toward a romantic fiction that is preoccupied with the grotesque. There is a kind of brooding terror in their novels and stories that places them in the tradition of their fellow-Southerner, Edgar Allan Poe. McCullers is best known for her novel, *The Heart Is a Lonely Hunter* (1940); her novella, *The Ballad of the Sad Café* (1951); and the novel *The Member of the Wedding* (1946), which she rewrote as a play in 1950. O'Connor wrote two novels but is probably best known for her finely crafted short stories, collected under the titles *A Good Man Is Hard to Find* (1955) and *Everything That Rises Must Converge* (1965).

Although Robert Penn Warren has written over half a dozen novels, beginning with *Night Rider* in 1939, it is probably *All the King's Men* (1946) that remains his most widely read work. Ostensibly the story of the rise and fall of Willie Stark, a Louisiana political figure, the deeper theme of the novel is self-knowledge and the pain that may be entailed in achieving it.

Self-knowledge and the nature of the self— these are the themes that increasingly occupy the attention of writers as we move closer to our own time. The authors who treat the theme have in common the fact that they move away from naturalism and regionalism to make extensive use of symbolism, fantasy, myth, surrealism, and ironic or antic comedy.

One of the earliest novelists in this tradition is Ralph Ellison, whose *Invisible Man* was published in 1952. Though the nameless hero, who winds up in a coal cellar, is black, he clearly typifies the individual of the twentieth century when at the end of the novel he says, "Who knows but that, on the lower frequencies, I speak for you?"

If all people are black (and white), then perhaps it is also true that "all men are Jews," as Bernard Malamud has said. The statement seems to mean—at least in the novel *The Assistant* (1957)—that all people suffer. Or perhaps we should say that we are all victims, as is the hero of *The Fixer* (1966), who ironically is condemned to death for being a Jew, even though he rejects Jewish religious beliefs.

Saul Bellow, who won the Nobel Prize in 1976, specializes in creating comic heroes who also are victims: of the modern world, of others, even of themselves. His most famous victim-heroes are Augie March of *The Adventures of Augie March* (1953) and Henderson of *Henderson the Rain King* (1959). Augie's adventures consist chiefly in his escapes from the influence of others who try to dominate him, until he comes finally to accept himself. Henderson is on a quest for a self to accept. He ultimately decides not to be a "being person" but to accept himself as a "becoming person," even though, to use his own language, such persons are "very unlucky, always in a tizzy."

With the novels of John Barth we seem to reach an impasse insofar as the theme of self-knowledge is concerned. In books like *The End of the Road* (1958) and *The Sot-Weed Factor* (1960), the self is seen as nothing more than a series of roles or masks. And as the "Founder's Scroll" reads in *Giles Goat-Boy* (1966), "Self-knowledge is always bad news."

THE MAJOR DRAMATISTS

In the thirties—apart from Eugene O'Neill, who continued to be a major influence through the fifties— a number of serious American dramatists produced important plays, the most significant names being Maxwell Anderson, Clifford Odets, Robert Sherwood, Lillian Hellman, and Thornton Wilder. But it is in the forties that the best known of our modern playwrights (apart from Wilder, who is discussed elsewhere)— Tennessee Williams and Arthur Miller—produced their first big successes: Williams's *The Glass Menagerie* in 1945 and *A Streetcar Named Desire* in 1947, and Miller's *Death of a Salesman* in 1949. One could hardly imagine two more different dramatists: Williams, a romantic, exploring the unconscious mind through exotic characters; and Miller, fundamentally a realist, dealing with the moral and social problems of his time. Yet together they dominated the American stage for two decades.

A FEW MAJOR MODERN POETS

One cannot say when modern poetry begins. It is also difficult to isolate trends or schools that include more than a handful of poets. Modern poets are notoriously individualistic. Let us look at a few of them, individually.

So, in me, come flinging
Forms, flames, and the flakes of flames.

These lines are typical of the lush verbal texture of the poetry of Wallace Stevens. If you enjoy saying them, enjoy hearing them, you would probably like many of his poems, even though he is in the symbolist tradition and much of his work, like T. S. Eliot's, is difficult. Stevens, a lawyer and vice-president of an insurance company, does not fit the typical image of a poet. Yet among critics and his fellow poets, he is invariably placed at or near the top of any list of America's greatest modern poets.

Probably the best-known lines of Archibald MacLeish are "A poem should not mean/ But be." They express an art-for-art's-sake attitude, which is characteristic of his early work. In the thirties and forties, however, MacLeish plunged into public life and held several important positions in government. Much of his poetry of this period is frankly propaganda on behalf of one cause or another. In the fifties he shifted again, this time to personal themes and a subtler style. MacLeish also wrote essays, screen and radio scripts, and verse plays, such as *J. B.*, which is based on the Book of Job. Archibald MacLeish illustrates another reason why it is difficult to categorize modern poets: they will not stay still long enough.

As he said in one of his introductions, e. e. cummings did not much care for "mostpeople." Instead he identified with flesh and trees, stars and stones, flowers and Spring, "anyone" and "noone." A thoroughgoing nonconformist and critic of the establishment, he also wrote some of the greatest love lyrics of all time, of which the following ending is but a small example:

lady through whose profound and fragile lips
the sweet small clumsy feet of April came
into the ragged meadow of my soul.

Like MacLeish, Robert Lowell has shifted both style and content through the years. In his early poetry there is much religious symbolism connected with his conversion to Catholicism. In *Life Studies*, however, psychoanalysis is the dominant influence, and Lowell becomes a confessional poet; that is, a poet who uses material from his private, innermost life as subject matter. (Other noteworthy confessional poets include W. D. Snodgrass, Anne Sexton, and Sylvia Plath.) Regardless of what he wrote about, Lowell was probably the most highly regarded poet of his time.

LITERARY FIGURES

1879–1955	Wallace Stevens	1911–	Tennessee Williams
1892–	Archibald MacLeish	1914–	Ralph Ellison
1894–1962	e. e. cummings	1914–	Bernard Malamud
1897–1962	William Faulkner	1915–	Saul Bellow
1897–1975	Thornton Wilder	1915–	Arthur Miller
1899–1961	Ernest Hemingway	1917–1967	Carson McCullers
1900–1938	Thomas Wolfe	1917–1977	Robert Lowell
1902–1968	John Steinbeck	1925–1964	Flannery O'Connor
1905–	Robert Penn Warren	1930–	John Barth
1908–1960	Richard Wright		

1930 **Time Line** 1966
Literary Events

1930

1930 T. S. Eliot, "Ash Wednesday"
Robert Frost, *Collected Poems*

1931 Eugene O'Neill, *Mourning Becomes Electra*

1932 William Faulkner, *Light in August*

1935 John Steinbeck, *Tortilla Flat*
Thomas Wolfe, *Of Time and the River*

1936 Faulkner, *Absolom, Absolom!*

1937 Steinbeck, *Of Mice and Men*

1938 e.e. cummings, *Collected Poems*
Thornton Wilder, *Our Town*

1939 Steinbeck, *The Grapes of Wrath*
Robert Penn Warren, *Night Rider*

1940

1940 Ernest Hemingway, *For Whom the Bell Tolls*
Carson McCullers, *The Heart Is a Lonely Hunter*
Richard Wright, *Native Son*

1944 Robert Lowell, *Land of Unlikeness*

1945 Tennessee Williams, *The Glass Menagerie*
Wright, *Black Boy*

1946 McCullers, *The Member of the Wedding*
Warren, *All the King's Men*

1947 Williams, *A Streetcar Named Desire*

1949 Arthur Miller, *The Death of a Salesman*

1950

1952 Ralph Ellison, *The Invisible Man*
Hemingway, *The Old Man and the Sea*
Archibald MacLeish, *Collected Poems*
O'Neill, *A Moon for the Misbegotten*
Steinbeck, *East of Eden*

1953 Saul Bellow, *The Adventures of Augie March*
Miller, *The Crucible*

1954 Wallace Stevens, *Collected Poems*

1955 cummings, *Poems, 1923–1954*
Flannery O'Connor, *A Good Man Is Hard to Find*
Williams, *Cat on a Hot Tin Roof*

1956 O'Neill, *A Long Day's Journey into Night*
MacLeish, *J. B.*

1957 Bernard Malamud, *The Assistant*

1958 John Barth, *The End of the Road*

1959 Bellow, *Henderson the Rain King*
Lowell, *Life Studies*

1960

1962 Steinbeck, *Travels with Charley*

1965 O'Connor, *Everything That Rises
Must Converge*

1966 Barth, *Giles Goat-Boy*
Malamud, *The Fixer*

JOHN STEINBECK

1902–1968

In 1962 John Ernst Steinbeck became the sixth American to receive the Nobel Prize for Literature. The award was given not for any particular book but for a career of "realistic and imaginative writings" spanning more than a generation. At the time, Steinbeck had published no less than sixteen novels, beginning with *Cup of Gold* in 1929 and ending with the last novel he was to publish, *The Winter of Our Discontent,* in 1961.

Steinbeck was not only prolific, he also had as wide a range of talent as any writer America had produced. The novels themselves varied widely in theme and style. But there was much more than the novels. Steinbeck had also written some excellent short stories, especially those that make up *The Long Valley,* and there were a number of nonfiction books, like *The Sea of Cortez,* which tells of a scientific expedition to the Gulf of California, and *Travels with Charley,* which describes a trip made with a poodle in a camping truck to the four corners of the United States, "in search of America."

Steinbeck also did an extensive amount of writing for newspapers and magazines, and he wrote plays and films as well. The plays were all more or less adapted from novels (*The Moon Is Down* and *Of Mice and Men* were two of the most successful). Many of the films were adaptations too, but in this media there were also original works such as *The Forgotten Village; Lifeboat,* which was directed by Alfred Hitchcock; and *Viva Zapata,* which starred Marlon Brando.

It will obviously not be easy to make many generalizations on a career as long and varied as Steinbeck's, but it is certainly safe to say that much of that career was deeply affected and colored by the author's early life in and around Salinas, California. Not only did the area provide him with a setting for much of his best work, but it also gave him a deep respect for nature, for simple living, and for natural people.

After graduating from Salinas High School, where he was senior class president and a member of the track and basketball teams, Steinbeck enrolled as an English major at Stanford University. He took many writing courses and also electives in science, but he did not graduate. Having already decided that he wanted to be a writer, he left the college in 1925 for New York, where the publishers were. His first job, however, left him no time for seeking publishers, no time for anything but eating and sleeping. He wheeled cement, seven days a week, for the construction of Madison Square Garden. His next job, as a reporter for the *New York American,* was somewhat less consuming of his physical energies, but he was even less well prepared for it than he had been for wheeling cement, and he was soon fired. None of his fiction sold either, and he returned to California as a deck hand on a ship, a very disappointed young man.

But he wanted to be a writer, and for the next several years he remained in California, living on from $35 to $50 a month and pouring all the energy he could into his fiction. Even the commercial failure of his first three novels—*Cup of Gold* (1929), *The Pastures of Heaven* (1932), and *To a God Unknown*

(1933)—did not turn him away from his goal.

The fourth novel was *Tortilla Flat* (1935). It is the story of Danny and his friends, a group of *paisanos* (mixtures of Spanish, Indian, Mexican, and assorted Caucasian bloods, as Steinbeck describes them) from the uphill district above the town of Monterey, California. A humorous celebration of poor but spirited everyday folk, the book had great appeal to a reading public still suffering the effects of the Great Depression. It appeared on best-seller lists for months and won an award for the best novel by a Californian. With *Tortilla Flat*, Steinbeck's career as a popular writer had begun.

But unlike many writers who follow up their successes with more books in the same vein, Steinbeck refused to be typed. He wrote to his publisher that he wanted "no tag of humorist on me, nor any other kind," and he published next *In Dubious Battle*, a serious novel about the role of Communist agitators in an agricultural laborers' strike. In theme, in style, in tone, it is markedly different from anything Steinbeck had previously written. It is a good novel, however, in which to see some of the author's most characteristic attitudes.

For one thing, we may see Steinbeck's sympathy for those who have been wronged, specifically here for the worker, whom he knew so well from the many jobs he himself had held from his high school years onward. Secondly, we can see an emphasis on thinking concerned with what *is* rather than with what might be or should be or could be. It seeks out the relations among things, but it does not deceive itself into a belief that it can discover a final answer to the question *why*.

Doc Burton is the character in the novel who practices this kind of thinking. He is clearly modeled on Steinbeck's great friend, the marine biologist, Ed Ricketts, and we find similar heroes in many other Steinbeck novels, such as *The Grapes of Wrath, The Moon Is Down, Cannery Row,* and *East of Eden*. Doc

Burton tries to be objective about the strike, and although he helps the strikers, he does not join the Communist Party. He shares one of Steinbeck's deepest beliefs—that subordination of the individual to a cause is an affront to human dignity.

The next two Steinbeck novels represent the author at the height of both his power and his popularity. The first of them, *Of Mice and Men* (1937), was an immediate success, and in its play version won the Drama Critics' Circle Award (beating out Thornton Wilder's *Our Town* for that honor). The second novel, which won the Pulitzer Prize, was *The Grapes of Wrath* (1939). It has been aptly described as nothing less than a national event. It was banned, it was burned, it was debated over national radio and criticized on the floor of Congress. And it was the number one best-seller in 1939 and remained among the top ten books in the following year.

Both books may be classified as social protest literature, for both are concerned with the exploitation of migrant workers. (Steinback actually traveled with a group of migrant workers and worked with them in California for a time while he was writing *The Grapes of Wrath.*) But looking at the novels today, we can see that they are much more than criticisms of social conditions of their day.

The title *Of Mice and Men* comes from the Robert Burns poem "To a Mouse," whose theme is that the best-made plans of mice and men often go awry. The novel describes how the dream of two migrant workers, George and Lennie, for a house and a little plot of ground is destroyed. The social structure can be blamed, in part, for the tragedy, for it should not be as difficult as it is for the workers to raise the money they need. But the tragedy is even more directly brought on by the strong but mindless Lennie, who unintentionally kills the things he loves. The relationship between Lennie, the animal side of human nature, and George, the mental side, is forcefully portrayed in this novel, which the Nobel Prize Committee called a "masterpiece."

As for *The Grapes of Wrath,* it is impossible, even today, to read it without feeling great sympathy for the plight of the Joad family and for other "Okies," who fled the Oklahoma "dust bowl" for the promise of paradise in California. Nevertheless, this novel, too, strongly invites interpretation on more than one level. The initials of the preacher-leader, Jim Casy, are J. C., and there are a number of parallels between him and Jesus Christ. Even more clearly, the structure of the novel is based upon the Biblical migration of the Israelites from Egypt. It has been convincingly analyzed as "conscious and consistent Christian allegory."

We tend to be suspicious, these days, of "overinterpretation," of finding symbols where none exist. With Steinbeck, however, a marked tendency to write allegory and a preoccupation with archetypal figures may be clearly observed from the beginning to the end of his career. For all his concern with human biology and with the objectivity of the scientist, Steinbeck has also been consistently concerned with myth and with our spiritual heritage. Frequently, in fact, he has made specific reference to parallels between his works and books that influenced him—to Malory's *Arthur* in *Tortilla Flat,* to the morality play *Everyman* in *The Wayward Bus,* and to the Biblical Cain and Abel story in *East of Eden,* to name a few.

Not long after the publication of *The Grapes of Wrath,* it became apparent that a much larger cause than the exploitation of migrant workers was going to have to occupy the center of Steinbeck's attention, as well as the attention of all other Americans who cared about democracy. Steinbeck participated in World War II in several ways.

Perhaps the most direct contribution was the book–movie *Bombs Away,* which told the story of "the kind and quality of our Air Force, of the caliber of its men and of the excellence of its equipment." In addition, Steinbeck gained some firsthand experience of the war. Becoming a correspondent for the New York *Herald Tribune,* he spent a good part of 1943 abroad, writing articles from England and North Africa. In September of that year, Steinbeck went on the beaches of Italy with the invading American army. Years later, his war dispatches were published in a book, *Once There Was a War* (1958).

Finally, there was the "war novel" *The Moon Is Down* (1942), written as a result of conversations Steinbeck had with a colonel in the Office of Strategic Services. The novel is said to have been very popular among those involved in resistance movements in Nazi-occupied countries, and the King of Norway decorated Steinbeck for its contribution to the resistance.

Like many sensitive persons, Steinbeck detested most of what he saw when he was directly involved in the war, and that feeling perhaps played a major role in his next three novels. Though none of them is directly about the war, all show a strong distaste for what might be regarded as typical persons or practices of our civilization. In *Cannery Row* (1944), Steinbeck positively affirms the values of *paisanos,* who may appear as "bums" in the eyes of more "civilized" persons. In the beautiful short novel, *The Pearl* (1945), the Mexican hero, Kino, and his wife must throw away the pearl of *the world* in order that they may survive. And in *The Wayward Bus* (1947) Steinbeck makes a strong and direct attack on many of the morally repulsive persons that populate our society while making a hero out of a "natural man," the Mexican bus driver, Juan Chicoy.

Of the five novels that Steinbeck was to publish in the fifties and sixties, the most important by far is his philosophic epic, *East of Eden* (1952). Some five years in the making, it was clearly intended by its author to be a crown of his career. Some critics have found it to be a crown of thorns rather than a jeweled crown, but although there may be some question of its artistic success, there is no question that it is a major work. This is guaranteed by its scope and the grandeur and power of its theme. What it says may be summed up in the words "Thou mayest rule," the translation that the key character, the Chinese servant, Lee, accepts for the Hebrew word, *timshel.* What this means is that we may rule our passions, that we have freedom of will, that we have a real choice between right and wrong, and that by choosing right we affirm our human dignity.

Optimists and lovers of happy endings as most of us Americans are, it would no doubt have pleased us if the affirmative *East of Eden* had been Steinbeck's last work of fiction. Instead, that place is occupied by *The Winter of Our Discontent,* a study of the corrupt moral climate of modern America and a novel that is neither optimistic nor very successful. Anyone wishing for a happier conclusion to John Steinbeck's long and distinguished career, however, would be untrue to the spirit of the author himself. He was a man who insisted that one should see not what one wishes or what one expects, but what is. And though he always tried to write good books, he also saw that

A book is like a man—clever and dull, brave and cowardly, beautiful and ugly. For every flowering thought there will be a page like a wet and mangy mongrel, and for every looping flight a tap on the wing and a reminder that wax cannot hold the feathers too near the sun.[1]

---

1. Steinbeck to his editor, Pascal Covici. *Journal of a Novel: The "East of Eden" Letters,* p. 180.

The Pastures of Heaven (1932), Steinbeck's second book, consisted of ten short stories—"each one complete in itself," as their author said—united by their common setting and the "evil cloud" that followed the Munroe family. The common location was a California valley near Monterey, Corral de Tierra, which Steinbeck renamed the Pastures of Heaven. You will see the evil cloud when Bert Munroe enters the scene. But the chief character here is the nineteen-year-old rural schoolteacher, Molly Morgan, for whom this eighth story from *The Pastures of Heaven* is named.

Molly Morgan

Molly Morgan got off the train in Salinas and waited three quarters of an hour for the bus. The big automobile was empty except for the driver and Molly.

"I've never been to the Pastures of Heaven, you know," she said. "Is it far from the main road?"

"About three miles," said the driver.

"Will there be a car to take me into the valley?"

"No, not unless you're met."

"But how do people get in there?"

The driver ran over the flattened body of a jack rabbit with apparent satisfaction. "I only hit 'em when they're dead," he apologized. "In the dark, when they get caught in the lights, I try to miss 'em."

"Yes, but how am I going to get into the Pastures of Heaven?"

"I dunno. Walk, I guess. Most people walk if they ain't met."

When he set her down at the entrance to the dirt side-road, Molly Morgan grimly picked up her suitcase and marched toward the draw in the hills. An old Ford truck squeaked up beside her.

From *The Pastures of Heaven* by John Steinbeck. Copyright 1932, © 1960 by John Steinbeck. Reprinted by permission of The Viking Press.

"Goin' into the valley, ma'am?"

"Oh—yes, yes, I am."

"Well, get in, then. Needn't be scared. I'm Pat Humbert. I got a place in the Pastures."

Molly surveyed the grimy man and acknowledged his introduction. "I'm the new schoolteacher, I mean, I think I am. Do you know where Mr. Whiteside lives?"

"Sure, I go right by there. He's clerk of the board. I'm on the school board myself, you know. We wondered what you'd look like." Then he grew embarrassed at what he had said, and flushed under his coating of dirt.

"Course I mean what you'd *be* like. Last teacher we had gave a good deal of trouble. She was all right, but she was sick—I mean, sick and nervous. Finally quit because she was sick."

Molly picked at the fingertips of her gloves. "My letter says I'm to call on Mr. Whiteside. Is he all right? I don't mean that. I mean—is he—what kind of a man is he?"

"Oh, you'll get along with him all right. He's a fine old man. Born in that house he lives in. Been to college, too. He's a good man. Been clerk of the board for over twenty years."

When he put her down in front of the big old house of John Whiteside, she was really frightened. "Now it's coming," she said to herself. "But there's nothing to be afraid of. He can't do anything to me." Molly was only nineteen. She felt that this moment of interview for her first job was a tremendous inch in her whole existence.

The walk up to the door did not reassure her, for the path lay between tight little flower beds hedged in with clipped box, seemingly planted with the admonition, "Now grow and multiply, but don't grow too high, nor multiply too greatly, and above all things, keep out of this path!" There was a hand on those flowers, a guiding and a correcting hand. The large white house was very dignified. Venetian blinds of yellow wood were tilted down to keep out the noon sun. Halfway up the path she came in sight of the entrance. There was a veranda as broad and warm and welcoming as an embrace. Through her mind flew the thought, "Surely you can tell the hospitality of a house by its entrance. Suppose it had a little door and no porch." But in spite of the welcoming of the wide steps and the big doorway, her timidities clung to her when she rang the bell. The big door opened, and a large, comfortable woman stood smiling at Molly.

"I hope you're not selling something," said Mrs. Whiteside. "I never want to buy anything and I always do, and then I'm mad."

Molly laughed. She felt suddenly very happy. Until that moment she hadn't known how frightened she really was. "Oh, no," she cried. "I'm the new schoolteacher. My letter says I'm to interview Mr. Whiteside. Can I see him?"

"Well, it's noon, and he's just finishing his dinner. Did you have dinner?"

"Oh, of course. I mean, no."

Mrs. Whiteside chuckled and stood aside for her to enter. "Well, I'm glad you're sure." She led Molly into a large dining room, lined with mahogany, glass-fronted dish closets. The square table was littered with the dishes of a meal. "Why, John must have finished and gone. Sit down, young woman. I'll bring back the roast."

"Oh, no. Really, thank you, no, I'll just talk to Mr. Whiteside and then go along."

"Sit down. You'll need nourishment to face John."

"Is—is he very stern, with new teachers, I mean?"

"Well," said Mrs. Whiteside. "That depends. If they haven't had their dinner, he's a regular bear. He shouts at them. But when they've just got up from the table, he's only just fierce."

Molly laughed happily. "You have children," she said. "Oh, you've raised lots of children—and you like them."

Mrs. Whiteside scowled. "One child raised me. Raised me right through the roof. It was too hard on me. He's out raising cows now, poor devils. I don't think I raised him very high."

When Molly had finished eating, Mrs. Whiteside threw open a side door and called, "John, here's someone to see you." She pushed Molly through the doorway into a room that was a kind of a library, for big bookcases were loaded with thick, old, comfortable books, all filigreed in gold. And it was a kind of a sitting room. There was a fireplace of brick with a mantel of little red tile bricks and the most extraordinary vases on the mantel. Hung on a nail over the mantel, slung really, like a rifle on a shoulder strap, was a huge meerschaum pipe in the Jaeger fashion. Big leather chairs with leather tassels hanging to them, stood about the fireplace, all of them patent rocking chairs with the kind of springs that chant when you rock them. And lastly, the room was a kind of an office, for there was an old-fashioned roll-top desk, and behind it sat John Whiteside. When he looked up, Molly saw that he had at once the kindest and the sternest eyes she had ever seen, and the whitest hair, too. Real blue-white, silky hair, a great duster of it.

"I am Mary Morgan," she began formally.

"Oh, yes, Miss Morgan, I've been expecting you. Won't you sit down?"

She sat in one of the big rockers, and the springs cried with sweet pain. "I love these chairs," she said. "We used to have one when I was a little girl." Then she felt silly. "I've come to interview you about this position. My letter said to do that."

"Don't be so tense, Miss Morgan. I've interviewed every teacher we've had for years. And," he said, smiling, "I still don't know how to go about it."

"Oh—I'm glad, Mr. Whiteside. I never asked for a job before. I was really afraid of it."

"Well, Miss Mary Morgan, as near as I can figure, the purpose of this interview is to give me a little knowledge of your past and of the kind of person you are. I'm supposed to know something about you when you've finished. And now that you know my purpose, I suppose you'll be self-conscious and anxious to give a good impression. Maybe if you just tell me a little about yourself, everything'll be all right. Just a few words about the kind of girl you are, and where you came from."

Molly nodded quickly. "Yes, I'll try to do that, Mr. Whiteside," and she dropped her mind back into the past.

There was the old, squalid, unpainted house with its wide back porch and the round washtubs leaning against the rail. High in the great willow tree her two brothers, Joe and Tom, crashed about crying, "Now I'm an eagle." "I'm a parrot." "Now I'm an old chicken." "Watch me!"

The screen door on the back porch opened, and their mother leaned tiredly out. Her hair would not lie smoothly no matter how much she combed it. Thick strings of it hung down beside her face. Her eyes were always a little red, and her hands and wrists painfully cracked. "Tom, Joe," she called. "You'll get hurt up there. Don't worry me so, boys! Don't you love your mother at all?" The voices in the tree were hushed. The shrieking spirits of the eagle and the old chicken were drenched in self-reproach. Molly sat in the dust, wrapping a rag around a stick and doing her best to imagine it a tall lady in a dress. "Molly, come in and stay with your mother. I'm so tired today."

Molly stood up the stick in the deep dust. "You, miss," she whispered fiercely. "You'll get whipped on your bare bottom when I come back." Then she obediently went into the house.

Her mother sat in a straight chair in the kitchen. "Draw up, Molly. Just sit with me a little while. Love me, Molly! Love your mother a little bit. You are mother's good little girl, aren't you?" Molly squirmed on her chair. "Don't you love your mother, Molly?"

The little girl was very miserable. She knew her mother would cry in a moment, and then she would be compelled to stroke the stringy hair. Both she and her brothers knew they should love their mother. She did everything for them. They were ashamed that they hated to be near her, but they couldn't help it. When she called to them and they were not in sight, they pretended not to hear, and crept away, talking in whispers.

"Well, to begin with, we were very poor," Molly said to John Whiteside. "I guess we were really poverty-stricken. I had two brothers a little older than I. My father was a traveling salesman, but even so, my mother had to work. She worked terribly hard for us."

About once in every six months a great event occurred. In the morning the mother crept silently out of the bedroom. Her hair was brushed as smoothly as it could be; her eyes sparkled, and she looked happy and almost pretty. She whispered, "Quiet, children! Your father's home."

Molly and her brothers sneaked out of the house, but even in the yard they talked in excited whispers. The news traveled quickly about the neighborhood. Soon the yard was filled with whispering children. "They say their father's home." "Is your father really home?" "Where's he been this time?" By noon there were a dozen children in the yard, standing in expectant little groups, cautioning one another to be quiet.

About noon the screen door on the porch sprang open and whacked against the wall. Their father leaped out. "Hi," he yelled. "Hi, kids!" Molly and her brothers flung themselves upon him and hugged his legs, while he plucked them off and hurled them into the air like kittens.

Mrs. Morgan fluttered about, clucking with excitement, "Children, children. Don't muss your father's clothes."

The neighbor children threw handsprings and wrestled and shrieked with joy. It was better than any holiday.

"Wait till you see," their father cried. "Wait till you see what I brought you. It's a secret now." And when the hysteria had quieted a little he carried his suitcase out on the porch and opened it. There were presents such as no one had ever seen, mechanical toys unknown before—tin bugs that crawled, dancing wooden figures and astounding steam shovels that worked in sand. There were superb glass marbles with bears and dogs right in their centres. He had something for everyone, several things for everyone. It was all the great holidays packed into one.

Usually it was midafternoon before the children became calm enough not to shriek occasionally. But eventually George Morgan sat on the steps, and they all gathered about while he told his adventures. This time he had been to Mexico while there was a revolution. Again he had gone to Honolulu, had seen the volcano and had himself ridden on a surfboard. Always there were cities and people, strange people; always adventures and a hundred funny incidents, funnier than anything they had ever heard. It couldn't all be told at one time. After school they had to gather to hear more and more. Throughout the world George Morgan tramped, collecting glorious adventures.

"As far as my home life went," Miss Morgan said, "I guess I almost didn't have any father. He was able to get home very seldom from his business trips."

John Whiteside nodded gravely.

Molly's hands rustled in her lap and her eyes were dim.

One time he brought a dumpy, woolly puppy in a box, and it wet on the floor immediately.

"What kind of a dog is it?" Tom asked in his most sophisticated manner.

Their father laughed loudly. He was so young! He looked twenty years younger than their mother. "It's a dollar and a half dog," he explained. "You get an awful lot of kinds of dog for a dollar and a half. It's like this. . . . Suppose you go into a candy store and say, 'I want a nickel's worth of peppermints and gumdrops and licorice and raspberry chews.' Well, I went in and said, 'Give me a dollar and a half's worth of mixed dog.' That's the kind it is. It's Molly's dog, and she has to name it."

"I'm going to name it George," said Molly.

Her father bowed strangely to her, and said, "Thank you, Molly." They all noticed that he wasn't laughing at her, either.

Molly got up very early the next morning and took George about the yard to show him the secrets. She opened the hoard where two pennies and a gold policeman's button were buried. She hooked his little front paws over the back fence so he could look down the street at the schoolhouse. Lastly she climbed into the willow tree, carrying George under one arm. Tom came out of the house and sauntered under the tree. "Look out you don't drop him," Tom called, and just at that moment the puppy squirmed out of her arms and fell. He landed on the hard ground with a disgusting little thump. One leg bent out at a crazy angle, and the puppy screamed long, horrible screams, with sobs between breaths. Molly scrambled out of the tree, dull and stunned by the accident. Tom was standing over the puppy, his face white and twisted with pain, and George, the puppy, screamed on and on.

"We can't let him," Tom cried. "We can't let him." He ran to the woodpile and brought back a hatchet. Molly was too stupefied to look away, but Tom closed his eyes and struck. The screams stopped suddenly. Tom threw the hatchet from him and leaped over the back fence. Molly saw him running away as though he were being chased.

At that moment Joe and her father came out of the back door. Molly remembered how haggard and thin and gray her father's face was when he looked at the puppy. It was something in her father's face that started Molly to crying. "I dropped him out of the tree, and he hurt himself, and Tom hit him, and then Tom ran away." Her voice sounded sulky. Her father hugged Molly's head against his hip.

"Poor Tom!" he said. "Molly, you must remember never to say anything to Tom about it, and never to look at him as though you remembered." He threw a gunny sack over the puppy. "We must have a funeral," he said. "Did I ever tell you about the Chinese funeral I went to, about the colored paper they throw in the air, and the little fat roast pigs on the grave?" Joe edged in closer, and even Molly's eyes took on a gleam of interest. "Well, it was this way. . . ."

Molly looked up at John Whiteside and saw that he seemed to be studying a piece of paper on his desk. "When I was twelve years old, my father was killed in an accident," she said.

The great visits usually lasted about two weeks. Always there came an afternoon when George Morgan walked out into the town and did not come back until late at night. The mother made the children go to bed early, but they could hear him come home, stumbling a little against the furniture, and they could hear his voice through the wall. These were the only times when his voice was sad and discouraged. Lying with held breaths, in their beds, the children knew what that meant. In the morning he would be gone, and their hearts would be gone with him.

They had endless discussions about what he was doing. Their father was a glad argonaut, a silver knight. Virtue and Courage and Beauty—he wore a coat of them. "Sometime," the boys said, "sometime when we're big, we'll go with him and see all those things."

"I'll go, too," Molly insisted.

"Oh, you're a girl. You couldn't go, you know."

"But he'd let me go, you know he would. Sometime he'll take me with him. You see if he doesn't."

When he was gone their mother grew plaintive again, and her eyes reddened. Querulously she demanded their love, as though it were a package they could put in her hand.

One time their father went away, and he never came back. He had never sent any money, nor had he ever written to them, but this time he just disappeared for good. For two years they waited, and then their mother said he must be dead. The children shuddered at the thought, but they refused to believe it, because no one so beautiful and fine as their father could be dead. Some place in the world he was having adventures. There was some good reason why he couldn't come back to them. Some day when the reason was gone, he would come. Some morning he would be there with finer presents and better stories than ever before. But their mother said he must have had an accident. He must be dead. Their mother was distracted. She read those advertisements which offered to help her make money at home. The children made paper flowers and shamefacedly tried to sell them. The boys tried to develop magazine routes, and the whole family nearly starved. Finally, when they couldn't stand it any longer, the boys ran away and joined the navy. After that Molly saw them as seldom as she had seen her father, and they were so changed, so hard and boisterous, that she didn't even care, for her brothers were strangers to her.

"I went through high school, and then I went to San Jose and entered Teachers' College. I worked for my board and room at the home of Mrs. Allen Morit. Before I finished school my mother died, so I guess I'm a kind of an orphan, you see."

"I'm sorry," John Whiteside murmured gently.

Molly flushed. "That wasn't a bid for sympathy, Mr. Whiteside. You said you wanted to know about me. Everyone has to be an orphan some time."

Molly worked for her board and room. She did the work of a full time servant, only she received no pay. Money for clothes had to be accumulated by working in a store during summer vacation. Mrs. Morit trained her girls. "I can take a green girl, not worth a cent," she often said, "and when that girl's worked for me six months, she can get fifty dollars a month. Lots of women know it, and they just snap up my girls. This is the first schoolgirl I've tried, but even she shows a lot of improvement. She reads too much though. I always say a servant should be asleep by ten o'clock, or else she can't do her work right."

Mrs. Morit's method was one of constant criticism and nagging, carried on in a just, firm tone. "Now, Molly, I don't want to find fault, but if you don't wipe the silver drier than that, it'll have streaks."—"The butter knife goes this way, Molly. Then you can put the tumbler here."

"I always give a reason for everything," she told her friends.

In the evening, after the dishes were washed, Molly sat on her bed and studied, and when the light was off, she lay on her bed and thought of her father. It was ridiculous to do it, she knew. It was a waste of time. Her father came up to the door, wearing a cutaway coat, and striped trousers and a top hat. He carried a huge bouquet of red roses in his hand. "I couldn't come before, Molly. Get on your coat quickly. First we're going down to get that evening dress in the window of Prussia's, but we'll have to hurry. I have tickets for the train to New

York tonight. Hurry up, Molly! Don't stand there gawping." It was silly. Her father was dead. No, she didn't really believe he was dead. Somewhere in the world he lived beautifully, and sometime he would come back.

Molly told one of her friends at school, "I don't really believe it, you see, but I don't disbelieve it. If I ever knew he was dead, why it would be awful. I don't know what I'd do then. I don't want to think about *knowing* he's dead."

When her mother died, she felt little besides shame. Her mother had wanted so much to be loved, and she hadn't known how to draw love. Her importunities had bothered the children and driven them away.

"Well, that's about all," Molly finished. "I got my diploma, and then I was sent down here."

"It was about the easiest interview I ever had," John Whiteside said.

"Do you think I'll get the position, then?"

The old man gave a quick, twinkly glance at the big meerschaum hanging over the mantel.

"That's his friend," Molly thought. "He has secrets with that pipe."

"Yes, I think you'll get the job. I think you have it already. Now, Miss Morgan, where are you going to live? You must find board and room some place."

Before she knew she was going to say it, she had blurted, "I want to live here."

John Whiteside opened his eyes in astonishment. "But we never take boarders, Miss Morgan."

"Oh, I'm sorry I said that. I just like it so much here, you see."

He called, "Willa," and when his wife stood in the half-open door, "This young lady wants to board with us. She's the new teacher."

Mrs. Whiteside frowned. "Couldn't think of it. We never take boarders. She's too pretty to be around that fool of a Bill. What would happen to those cows of his? It'd be a lot of trouble. You can sleep in the third bedroom upstairs," she said to Molly. "It doesn't catch much sun anyway."

Life changed its face. All of a sudden Molly found she was a queen. From the first day the children of the school adored her, for she understood them, and what was more, she let them understand her. It took her some time to realize that she had become an important person. If two men got to arguing at the store about a point of history or literature or mathematics, and the argument deadlocked, it ended up, "Take it to the teacher! If she doesn't know, she'll find it." Molly was very proud to be able to decide such questions. At parties she had to help with the decorations and to plan refreshments.

"I think we'll put pine boughs around everywhere. They're pretty, and they smell so good. They smell like a party." She was supposed to know everything and to help with everything, and she loved it.

At the Whiteside home she slaved in the kitchen under the mutterings of Willa. At the end of six months, Mrs. Whiteside grumbled to her husband, "Now if Bill only had any sense. But then," she continued, "if *she* has any sense—" and there she left it.

At night Molly wrote letters to the few friends she had made in Teachers' College, letters full of little stories about her neighbors, and full of joy. She must attend every party because of the social prestige of her position. On Saturdays she ran about the hills and brought back ferns and wild flowers to plant about the house.

Bill Whiteside took one look at Molly and scuttled back to his cows. It was a long time before he found the courage to talk to her very much. He was a big, simple young man who had neither his father's balance nor his mother's humor. Eventually, however, he trailed after Molly and looked after her from distances.

One evening, with a kind of feeling of thanksgiving for her happiness, Molly told Bill about her father. They were sitting in canvas chairs on the wide veranda, waiting for the moon. She told him about the visits, and then about the disappearance. "Do you see what I have, Bill?" she cried. "My lovely father is some place. He's mine. You think he's living, don't you, Bill?"

"Might be," said Bill. "From what you say, he was a kind of an irresponsible cuss, though. Excuse me, Molly. Still, if he's alive, it's funny he never wrote."

Molly felt cold. It was just the kind of reasoning she had successfully avoided for so long. "Of course," she said stiffly, "I know that. I have to do some work now, Bill."

High up on a hill that edged the valley of the Pastures of Heaven, there was an old cabin which commanded a view of the whole country and of all the roads in the vicinity. It was said that the bandit Vasquez had built the cabin and lived in it for a year while the posses went crashing through the country looking for him. It was a landmark. All the people of the valley had been to see it at one time or another. Nearly everyone asked Molly whether she had been there yet. "No," she said, "but I will go up some day. I'll go some Saturday. I know where the trail to it is." One morning she dressed in her new hiking boots and corduroy skirt. Bill sidled up and offered to accompany her. "No," she said. "You have work to do. I can't take you away from it."

"Work be hanged!" said Bill.

"Well, I'd rather go alone. I don't want to hurt your feelings, but I just want to go alone, Bill." She was sorry not to let him accompany her, but his remark about her father had frightened her. "I want to have an adventure," she said to herself. "If Bill comes along, it won't be an adventure at all. It'll just be a trip." It took her an hour and a half to climb up the steep trail under the oaks. The leaves on the ground were as slippery as glass, and the sun was hot. The good smell of ferns and dank moss and yerba buena filled the air. When Molly came at last to the ridge crest, she was damp and winded. The cabin stood in a small clearing in the brush, a little square wooden room with no windows. Its doorless entrance was a black shadow. The place was quiet, the kind of humming quiet that flies and bees and crickets make. The whole hillside sang softly in

the sun. Molly approached on tiptoe. Her heart was beating violently.

"Now I'm having an adventure," she whispered. "Now I'm right in the middle of an adventure at Vasquez' cabin. She peered in at the doorway and saw a lizard scuttle out of sight. A cobweb fell across her forehead and seemed to try to restrain her. There was nothing at all in the cabin, nothing but the dirt floor and the rotting wooden walls, and the dry, deserted smell of the earth that has long been covered from the sun. Molly was filled with excitement. "At night he sat in there. Sometimes when he heard noises like men creeping up on him, he went out of the door like the ghost of a shadow, and just melted into the darkness." She looked down on the valley of the Pastures of Heaven. The orchards lay in dark green squares; the grain was yellow, and the hills behind, a light brown washed with lavender. Among the farms the roads twisted and curled, avoiding a field, looping around a huge tree, half circling a hill flank. Over the whole valley was stretched a veil of heat shimmer. "Unreal," Molly whispered, "fantastic. It's a story, a real story, and I'm having an adventure." A breeze rose out of the valley like the sigh of a sleeper, and then subsided.

"In the daytime that young Vasquez looked down on the valley just as I'm looking. He stood right here, and looked at the roads down there. He wore a purple vest braided with gold, and the trousers on his slim legs widened at the bottom like the mouths of trumpets. His spur rowels were wrapped with silk ribbons to keep them from clinking. Sometimes he saw the posses riding by on the road below. Lucky for him the men bent over their horses' necks, and didn't look up at the hilltops. Vasquez laughed, but he was afraid, too. Sometimes he sang. His songs were soft and sad because he knew he couldn't live very long."

Molly sat down on the slope and rested her chin in her cupped hands. Young Vasquez was standing beside her, and Vasquez had her father's gay face, his shining eyes as he came on the porch shouting, "Hi, kids!" This was the kind of adventure her father had. Molly shook herself and stood up. "Now I want to go back to the first and think it all over again."

In the late afternoon Mrs. Whiteside sent Bill out to look for Molly. "She might have turned an ankle, you know." But Molly emerged from the trail just as Bill approached it from the road.

"We were beginning to wonder if you'd got lost," he said. "Did you go up to the cabin?"

"Yes."

"Funny old box, isn't it? Just an old woodshed. There are a dozen just like it down here. You'd be surprised, though, how many people go up there to look at it. The funny part is, nobody's sure Vasquez was ever there."

"Oh, I think he must have been there."

"What makes you think that?"

"I don't know."

Bill became serious. "Everybody thinks Vasquez was a kind of hero, when really he was just a thief. He started in stealing sheep and horses and ended up robbing stages. He had to kill a few people to do it. It seems to me, Molly, we ought to teach people to hate robbers, not worship them."

"Of course, Bill," she said wearily. "You're perfectly right. Would you mind not talking for a little while, Bill? I guess I'm a little tired, and nervous, too."

The year wheeled around. Pussywillows had their kittens, and wild flowers covered the hills. Molly found herself wanted and needed in the valley. She even attended school board meetings. There had been a time when those secret and august conferences were held behind closed doors, a mystery and a terror to everyone. Now that Molly was asked to step into John Whiteside's sitting room, she found that the board discussed crops, told stories, and circulated mild gossip.

Bert Munroe had been elected early in the fall, and by the springtime he was the most energetic member. He it was who planned dances at the schoolhouse, who insisted upon having plays and picnics. He even offered prizes for the best report cards in the school.

The board was coming to rely pretty much on Bert Munroe.

One evening Molly came down late from her room. As always, when the board was meeting, Mrs. Whiteside sat in the dining room. "I don't think I'll go in to the meeting," Molly said. "Let them have one time to themselves. Sometimes I feel that they would tell other kinds of stories if I weren't there."

"You go on in, Molly! They can't hold a board meeting without you. They're so used to you, they'd be lost. Besides, I'm not at all sure I want them to tell those other stories."

Obediently Molly knocked on the door and went into the sitting room. Bert Munroe paused politely in the story he was narrating. "I was just telling about my new farm hand, Miss Morgan. I'll start over again, 'cause it's kind of funny. You see, I needed a hay hand, and I picked this fellow up under the Salinas River bridge. He was pretty drunk, but he wanted a job. Now I've got him, I find he isn't worth a cent as a hand, but I can't get rid of him. That son of a gun has been every place. You ought to hear him tell about the places he's been. My kids wouldn't let me get rid of him if I wanted to. Why he can take the littlest thing he's seen and make a fine story out of it. My kids just sit around with their ears spread, listening to him. Well, about twice a month he walks into Salinas and goes on a bust. He's one of those dirty, periodic drunks. The Salinas cops always call me up when they find him in a gutter, and I have to drive in to get him. And you know, when he comes out of it, he's always got some kind of present in his pocket for my kid Manny. There's nothing you can do with a man like that. He disarms you. I don't get a dollar's worth of work a month out of him."

Molly felt a sick dread rising in her. The men were laughing at the story. "You're too soft, Bert. You can't afford to keep an entertainer on the place. I'd sure get rid of him quick."

Molly stood up. She was dreadfully afraid someone would ask the man's name. "I'm not feeling very well tonight," she said. "If you gentlemen will excuse me, I think I'll go to bed." The men stood up while she left the room. In her bed she buried her head in the pillow. "It's crazy," she said to herself. "There isn't a chance in the world. I'm forgetting all about it right now." But she found to her dismay that she was crying.

The next few weeks were agonizing to Molly. She was reluctant to leave the house. Walking to and from school she watched the road ahead of her. "If I see any kind of a stranger I'll run away. But that's foolish. I'm being a fool." Only in her own room did she feel safe. Her terror was making her lose color, was taking the glint out of her eyes.

"Molly, you ought to go to bed," Mrs. Whiteside insisted. "Don't be a little idiot. Do I have to smack you the way I do Bill to make you go to bed?" But Molly would not go to bed. She thought too many things when she was in bed.

The next time the board met, Bert Munroe did not appear. Molly felt reassured and almost happy at his absence.

"You're feeling better, aren't you, Miss Morgan?"

"Oh, yes. It was only a little thing, a kind of a cold. If I'd gone to bed I might have been really sick."

The meeting was an hour gone before Bert Munroe came in. "Sorry to be late," he apologized. "The same old thing happened. My so-called hay hand was asleep in the street in Salinas. What a mess! He's out in the car sleeping if off now. I'll have to hose the car out tomorrow."

Molly's throat closed with terror. For a second she thought she was going to faint. "Excuse me, I must go," she cried, and ran out of the room. She walked into the dark hallway and steadied herself against the wall. Then slowly and automatically she marched out of the front door and down the steps. The night was filled with whispers. Out in the road she could see the black mass that was Bert Munroe's car. She was surprised at the way her footsteps plodded down the path of their own

volition. "Now I'm killing myself," she said. "Now I'm throwing everything away. I wonder why." The gate was under her hand, and her hand flexed to open it. Then a tiny breeze sprang up and brought to her nose the sharp foulness of vomit. She heard a blubbering, drunken snore. Instantly something whirled in her head. Molly spun around and ran frantically back to the house. In her room she locked the door and sat stiffly down, panting with the effort of her run. It seemed hours before she heard the men go out of the house, calling their good-nights. Then Bert's motor started, and the sound of it died away down the road. Now that she was ready to go she felt paralyzed.

John Whiteside was writing at his desk when Molly entered the sitting room. He looked up questioningly at her. "You aren't well, Miss Morgan. You need a doctor."

She planted herself woodenly beside the desk. "Could you get a substitute teacher for me?" she asked.

"Of course I could. You pile right into bed and I'll call a doctor."

"It isn't that, Mr. Whiteside. I want to go away tonight."

"What are you talking about? You aren't well."

"I told you my father was dead. I don't know whether he's dead or not. I'm afraid—I want to go away tonight."

He stared intently at her. "Tell me what you mean," he said softly.

"If I should see that drunken man of Mr. Munroe's—" she paused, suddenly terrified at what she was about to say.

John Whiteside nodded very slowly.

"No," she cried. "I don't think that. I'm sure I don't."

"I'd like to do something, Molly."

"I don't want to go, I love it here——— But I'm afraid. It's so important to me."

John Whiteside stood up and came close to her and put his arm about her shoulders. "I don't think I understand, quite," he said. "I don't think I want to understand. That isn't necessary." He seemed to be talking to himself. "It wouldn't be quite courteous—to understand."

"Once I'm away I'll be able not to believe it," Molly whimpered.

He gave her shoulders one quick squeeze with his encircling arm. "You run upstairs and pack your things, Molly," he said. "I'll get out the car and drive you right in to Salinas now."

I
GROWING UP

Psychologists say that one important aspect of growing up is learning to accept realities. Molly seems to have coped with most realities quite well. Indeed, she seems unusually mature for nineteen. She supports herself; she does her job competently; she is even a leader in her community. Moreover, she seems to have accepted the harsh fact that both her parents are dead. When Mr. Whiteside expresses sorrow at her being an orphan, she says, "That wasn't a bid for sympathy, Mr. Whiteside. You said you wanted to know about me. Everyone has to be an orphan some time."

In spite of all her mature accomplishments, Molly abruptly leaves her happy life. Does her running away show that she is not as mature—able to accept reality—as we had thought? Why or why not? And precisely what is it that she is trying to escape?

II
IMPLICATIONS

Be prepared to discuss the implications of the following:

1. Steinbeck's choice of the name *Morgan*. (If you do not know who Sir Henry Morgan was, look him up.)

2. "Throughout the world George Morgan tramped collecting glorious adventures." (p. 589)

3. "'I want to have an adventure,' she [Molly] said to herself." (p. 592)

4. "There was nothing at all in the cabin, nothing but the dirt floor and the rotting wooden walls." (p. 592)

5. Bill Whitehead's revelation that Vasquez was a thief and a murderer. (p. 593)

III
TECHNIQUES

Intention

As we noted in the headnote of this story, Steinbeck's declared intention in writing *The Pastures of Heaven*, from which "Molly Morgan" is taken, was to show how the Munroe family puts a curse on everything and everyone it touches. Cite the evidence of that intention in this story. How much can you tell from this story alone about the nature of that curse? That is, why might Bert Munroe be the kind of person who would be followed by an evil cloud?

In discussing this issue, keep in mind that Steinbeck was a naturalist and was trained in science. He did not believe in evil spirits.

Theme

If we assume that the curse theme was the only one that Steinbeck consciously intended, does it follow that it is the only theme present in the story? Why or why not?

Below are some other themes that critics have found in this or other stories from *The Pastures of Heaven*. Which would *you* say are themes in "Molly Morgan"? How would you demonstrate that they are?

1. The contrast between dreams and reality

2. The realization of life through illusion

3. The suppression of the individual by society

Steinbeck's novel *The Grapes of Wrath* (1939) tells the story of the pilgrimage of the Joad family from the Oklahoma dust bowl to the promise of a fertile Eden in California. The following selection is the third chapter of that book. As you read it, see if you can determine for yourself why Steinbeck would interrupt the flow of his novel to include this chapter.

The Turtle

The concrete highway was edged with a mat of tangled, broken, dry grass, and the grass heads were heavy with oat beards to catch on a dog's coat, and foxtails to tangle in a horse's fetlocks, and clover burrs to fasten in sheep's wool; sleeping life waiting to be spread and dispersed, every seed armed with an appliance of dispersal: twisting darts and parachutes for the wind, little spears and balls of tiny thorns, and all waiting for animals and for the wind, for a man's trouser cuff or the hem of a woman's skirt, all passive but armed with appliances of activity, still, but each possessed of the anlage of movement.

The sun lay on the grass and warmed it, and in the shade under the grass the insects moved, ants and ant lions to set traps for them, grasshoppers to jump into the air and flick their yellow wings for a second, sow bugs like little armadillos, plodding restlessly on many tender feet. And over the grass at the roadside a land turtle crawled, turning aside for nothing, dragging his high-domed shell over the grass. His hard legs and yellow-nailed feet threshed slowly through the grass, not really walking, but boosting and dragging his shell along. The barley beards slid off his shell, and the clover burrs fell on him and rolled to the ground. His horny beak was partly open, and his fierce,

humorous eyes, under brows like fingernails, stared straight ahead. He came over the grass leaving a beaten trail behind him, and the hill, which was the highway embankment, reared up ahead of him. For a moment he stopped, his head held high. He blinked and looked up and down. At last he started to climb the embankment. Front clawed feet reached forward but did not touch. The hind feet kicked his shell along, and it scraped on the grass, and on the gravel. As the embankment grew steeper and steeper, the more frantic were the efforts of the land turtle. Pushing hind legs strained and slipped, boosting the shell along, and the horny head protruded as far as the neck could stretch. Little by little the shell slid up the embankment until at last a parapet cut straight across its line of march, the shoulder of the road, a concrete wall four inches high. As though they worked independently the hind legs pushed the shell against the wall. The head upraised and peered over the wall to the broad smooth plain of cement. Now the hands, braced on top of the wall, strained and lifted, and the shell came slowly up and rested its front end on the wall. For a moment the turtle rested. A red ant ran into the shell, into the soft skin inside the shell, and suddenly head and legs snapped in, and the armored tail clamped in sideways. The red ant was crushed between body and legs. And one head of wild oats was clamped into the shell by a front leg.

From *The Grapes of Wrath* by John Steinbeck. Copyright 1939, © 1967 by John Steinbeck. Reprinted by permission of The Viking Press.

For a long moment the turtle lay still, and then the neck crept out and the old humorous frowning eyes looked about and the legs and tail came out. The back legs went to work, straining like elephant legs, and the shell tipped to an angle so that the front legs could not reach the level cement plain. But higher and higher the hind legs boosted it, until at last the center of balance was reached, the front tipped down, the front legs scratched at the pavement, and it was up. But the head of wild oats was held by its stem around the front legs.

Now the going was easy, and all the legs worked, and the shell boosted along, waggling from side to side. A sedan driven by a forty-year old woman approached. She saw the turtle and swung to the right, off the highway, the wheels screamed and a cloud of dust boiled up. Two wheels lifted for a moment and then settled. The car skidded back onto the road, and went on, but more slowly. The turtle had jerked into its shell, but now it hurried on, for the highway was burning hot.

And now a light truck approached, and as it came near, the driver saw the turtle and swerved to hit it. His front wheel struck the edge of the shell, flipped the turtle like a tiddly-wink, spun it like a coin, and rolled it off the highway. The truck went back to its course along the right side. Lying on its back, the turtle was tight in its shell for a long time. But at last its legs waved in the air, reaching for something to pull it over. Its front foot caught a piece of quartz and little by little the shell pulled over and flopped upright. The wild oat head fell out and three of the spearhead seeds stuck in the ground. And as the turtle crawled on down the embankment, its shell dragged dirt over the seeds. The turtle entered a dust road and jerked itself along, drawing a wavy shallow trench in the dust with its shell. The old humorous eyes looked ahead, and the horny beak opened a little. His yellow toe nails slipped a fraction in the dust.

I
THE WRITER AS OBSERVER

One can hardly read this selection without being impressed by Steinbeck's powers of observation and his ability to convey such observations to the reader. Steinbeck clearly knew what turtles looked like and how they behaved.

But a novelist is not a scientist. Steinbeck's description of the turtle is accurate, but it is also selective, less complete than a scientist's might be. In addition, Steinbeck uses some descriptive adjectives for his turtle that a scientist would not use. What are some of these adjectives? How do they help you see the symbolic import of the turtle?

II
IMPLICATIONS

What the turtle does also helps us see what it symbolizes. Fundamentally, what it does is go on a journey. In the course of that journey the following events occur. How do they reinforce or modify your impression of what the turtle symbolizes?

1. It stares straight ahead and turns aside for nothing.

2. It overcomes insuperable obstacles.

3. A force (the truck) tries to kill it.

4. It crosses a highway.

5. It "plants" seeds on the other side.

III
TECHNIQUES

Intention

When a writer intends the reader to interpret something symbolically, why doesn't the writer simply come out and tell the reader what the meaning of the symbol is? What would have been lost if Steinbeck had directly said what the turtle symbolized?

In his travels with Charley, a large French poodle, Steinbeck drove through
almost forty states, going from Long Island, New York, to Maine; across
the northern tier of states; down the West Coast to Salinas, California, his
birthplace; then eastward through New Mexico and Arizona and the
Deep South; finally turning north from Alabama through Virginia, West
Virginia, Pennsylvania, and New Jersey. We have gathered here chapters or
parts of chapters from the East, the North, the West, and the South
so that you will be able to share with Steinbeck and Charley an appreciation of
the immensity of our land.

Travels with Charley was first published in 1962, the same year in which
Steinbeck won the Nobel Prize for Literature.

FROM # Travels with Charley

Introduction

When I was very young and the urge to
be someplace else was on me, I was assured by
mature people that maturity would cure this
itch. When years described me as mature, the
remedy prescribed was middle age. In middle
age I was assured that greater age would calm
my fever and now that I am fifty-eight perhaps
senility will do the job. Nothing has worked.
Four hoarse blasts of a ship's whistle still raise
the hair on my neck and set my feet to tapping.
The sound of a jet, an engine warming up,
even the clopping of shod hooves on pavement
brings on the ancient shudder, the dry mouth
and vacant eye, the hot palms and the churn of
stomach high up under the rib cage. In other
words, I don't improve; in further words, once
a bum always a bum. I fear the disease is
incurable. I set this matter down not to instruct
others but to inform myself.

When the virus of restlessness begins to take
possession of a wayward man, and the road
away from Here seems broad and straight and
sweet, the victim must first find in himself a
good and sufficient reason for going. This to the
practical bum is not difficult. He has a built-in
garden of reasons to choose from. Next he must
plan his trip in time and space, choose a
direction and a destination. And last he must
implement the journey. How to go, what to
take, how long to stay. This part of the process
is invariable and immortal. I set it down only
so that newcomers to bumdom, like teen-agers
in new-hatched sin, will not think they invented it.

Once a journey is designed, equipped, and
put in process, a new factor enters and takes
over. A trip, a safari, an exploration, is an
entity, different from all other journeys. It
has personality, temperament, individuality,
uniqueness. A journey is a person in itself; no
two are alike. And all plans, safeguards, polic-
ing, and coercion are fruitless. We find after
years of struggle that we do not take a trip; a
trip takes us. Tour masters, schedules, reservations, brass-bound and inevitable, dash themselves to wreckage on the personality of the
trip. Only when this is recognized can the
blown-in-the-glass bum relax and go along with
it. Only then do the frustrations fall away. In
this a journey is like marriage. The certain way

From *Travels with Charley* by John Steinbeck. Copyright © 1961, 1962 by
The Curtis Publishing Company, Inc. Copyright © 1962 by John Steinbeck.
Reprinted by permission of The Viking Press.

to be wrong is to think you control it. I feel better now, having said this, although only those who have experienced it will understand it.

Starting Out

My plan was clear, concise, and reasonable, I think. For many years I have traveled in many parts of the world. In America I live in New York, or dip into Chicago or San Francisco. But New York is no more America than Paris is France or London is England. Thus I discovered that I did not know my own country. I, an American writer, writing about America, was working from memory, and the memory is at best a faulty, warpy reservoir. I had not heard the speech of America, smelled the grass and trees and sewage, seen its hills and water, its color and quality of light. I knew the changes only from books and newspapers. But more than this, I had not felt the country for twenty-five years. In short, I was writing of something I did not know about, and it seems to me that in a so-called writer this is criminal. My memories were distorted by twenty-five intervening years.

Once I traveled about in an old bakery wagon, double-doored rattler with a mattress on its floor. I stopped where people stopped or gathered, I listened and looked and felt, and in the process had a picture of my country the accuracy of which was impaired only by my own shortcomings.

So it was that I determined to look again, to try to rediscover this monster land. Otherwise, in writing, I could not tell the small diagnostic truths which are the foundations of the larger truth. One sharp difficulty presented itself. In the intervening twenty-five years my name had become reasonably well known. And it has been my experience that when people have heard of you, favorably or not, they change; they become, through shyness or the other qualities that publicity inspires, something

they are not under ordinary circumstances. This being so, my trip demanded that I leave my name and my identity at home. I had to be peripatetic eyes and ears, a kind of moving gelatin plate. I could not sign hotel registers, meet people I knew, interview others, or even ask searching questions. Furthermore, two or more people disturb the ecologic complex of an area. I had to go alone and I had to be self-contained, a kind of casual turtle carrying his house on his back.

With all this in mind I wrote to the head office of a great corporation which manufactures trucks. I specified my purpose and my needs. I wanted a three-quarter-ton pick-up truck, capable of going anywhere under possible rigorous conditions, and on this truck I wanted a little house built like the cabin of a small boat. A trailer is difficult to maneuver on mountain roads, is impossible and often illegal to park, and is subject to many restrictions. In due time, specifications came through, for a tough, fast, comfortable vehicle, mounting a camper top—a little house with double bed, a four-burner stove, a heater, refrigerator and lights operating on butane, a chemical toilet, closet space, storage space, windows screened against insects—exactly what I wanted. It was delivered in the summer to my little fishing place at Sag Harbor near the end of Long Island. Although I didn't want to start before Labor Day, when the nation settles back to normal living, I did want to get used to my turtle shell, to equip it and learn it. It arrived in August, a beautiful thing, powerful and yet lithe. It was almost as easy to handle as a passenger car. And because my planned trip had aroused some satiric remarks among my friends, I named it Rocinante, which you will remember was the name of Don Quixote's horse.

Since I made no secret of my project, a number of controversies arose among my friends and advisers. (A projected journey spawns advisers in schools.) I was told that since my photograph was as widely distributed as my publisher could make it, I would find it impossible to move about without being recognized. Let me say in advance that in over ten thousand miles, in thirty-four states, I was not recognized even once. I believe that people identify things only in context. Even those people who might have known me against a background I am supposed to have, in no case identified me in Rocinante.

I was advised that the name Rocinante painted on the side of my truck in sixteenth-century Spanish script would cause curiosity and inquiry in some places. I do not know how many people recognized the name, but surely no one ever asked about it.

Next, I was told that a stranger's purpose in moving about the country might cause inquiry or even suspicion. For this reason I racked a shotgun, two rifles, and a couple of fishing rods in my truck, for it is my experience that if a man is going hunting or fishing his purpose is understood and even applauded. Actually, my hunting days are over. I no longer kill or catch anything I cannot get into a frying pan; I am too old for sport killing. This stage setting turned out to be unnecessary.

It was said that my New York license plates would arouse interest and perhaps questions, since they were the only outward identifying marks I had. And so they did—perhaps twenty or thirty times in the whole trip. But such contacts followed an invariable pattern, somewhat as follows:

Local man: "New York, huh?"

Me: "Yep."

Local man: "I was there in nineteen thirty-eight—or was it thirty-nine? Alice, was it thirty-eight or thirty-nine we went to New York?"

Alice: "It was thirty-six. I remember because it was the year Alfred died."

Local man: "Anyway, I hated it. Wouldn't live there if you paid me."

There was some genuine worry about my traveling alone, open to attack, robbery, assault. It is well known that our roads are dangerous. And here I admit I had senseless qualms. It is some years since I have been

alone, nameless, friendless, without any of the safety one gets from family, friends, and accomplices. There is no reality in the danger. It's just a very lonely, helpless feeling at first— a kind of desolate feeling. For this reason I took one companion on my journey—an old French gentleman poodle known as Charley. Actually his name is Charles le Chien. He was born in Bercy on the outskirts of Paris and trained in France, and while he knows a little poodle-English, he responds quickly only to commands in French. Otherwise he has to translate, and that slows him down. He is a very big poodle, of a color called *bleu*, and he is blue when he is clean. Charley is a born diplomat. He prefers negotiation to fighting, and properly so, since he is very bad at fighting. Only once in his ten years has he been in trouble—when he met a dog who refused to negotiate. Charley lost a piece of his right ear that time. But he is a good watch dog—has a roar like a lion, designed to conceal from night-wandering strangers the fact that he couldn't bite his way out of a *cornet de papier*. He is a good friend and traveling companion, and would rather travel about than anything he can imagine. If he occurs at length in this account, it is because he contributed much to the trip. A dog, particularly an exotic like Charley, is a bond between strangers. Many conversations en route began with "What degree of a dog is that?"

The techniques of opening conversation are universal. I knew long ago and rediscovered that the best way to attract attention, help, and conversation is to be lost. A man who seeing his mother starving to death on a path kicks her in the stomach to clear the way, will cheerfully devote several hours of his time giving wrong directions to a total stranger who claims to be lost.

Maine

Maine seemed to stretch on endlessly. I felt as Peary must have when he approached what he thought was the North Pole. But I wanted to see Aroostook County, the big northern county of Maine. There are three great potato-raising sections—Idaho, Suffolk County on Long Island, and Aroostook, Maine. Lots of people had talked of Aroostook County, but I had never met anyone who had actually been there. I had been told that the crop is harvested by Canucks from Canada who flood over the border at harvest time. My way went endlessly through forest country and past many lakes, not yet frozen. As often as I could I chose the small wood roads, and they are not conducive to speed. The temperature lifted and it rained endlessly and the forests wept. Charley never got dry, and smelled as though he were mildewed. The sky was the color of wet gray aluminum and there was no indication on the translucent shield where the sun might be, so I couldn't tell direction. On a curving road I might have been traveling east or south or west instead of the north I wanted. That old fake about the moss growing on the north sides of trees lied to me when I was a Boy Scout. Moss grows on the shady side, and that may be any side. I determined to buy a compass in the next town, but there wasn't any next town on the road I was traveling. The darkness crept down and the rain drummed on the steel roof of the cab and the windshield wipers sobbed their arcs. Tall dark trees lined the road, crowding the gravel. It seemed hours since I had passed a car or a house or a store, for this was the country gone back to forest. A desolate loneliness settled on me—almost a frightening loneliness. Charley, wet and shivering, curled up in his corner of the seat and offered no companionship. I pulled in behind the approach to a concrete bridge, but couldn't find a level place on the sloping roadside.

Even the cabin was dismal and damp. I turned the gas mantle high, lit the kerosene lamp, and lighted two burners of my stove to drive the loneliness away. The rain drummed on the metal roof. Nothing in my stock of foods looked edible. The darkness fell and the trees moved closer. Over the rain drums I seemed to hear voices, as though a crowd of people

muttered and mumbled offstage. Charley was restless. He didn't bark an alarm, but he growled and whined uneasily, which is very unlike him, and he didn't eat his supper and he left his water dish untouched—and that by a dog who drinks his weight in water every day and needs to because of the outgo. I succumbed utterly to my desolation, made two peanut-butter sandwiches, and went to bed and wrote letters home, passing my loneliness around. Then the rain stopped falling and the trees dripped and I helped to spawn a school of secret dangers. Oh, we can populate the dark with horrors, even we who think ourselves informed and sure, believing nothing we cannot measure or weigh. I knew beyond all doubt that the dark things crowding in on me either did not exist or were not dangerous to me, and still I was afraid. I thought how terrible the nights must have been in a time when men knew the things were there and were deadly. But no, that's wrong. If I knew they were there, I would have weapons against them, charms, prayers, some kind of alliance with forces equally strong but on my side. Knowing they were not there made me defenseless against them and perhaps more afraid.

Long ago I owned a little ranch in the Santa Cruz mountains in California. In one place a forest of giant madrone trees joined their tops over a true tarn, a black, spring-fed lake. If there is such a thing as a haunted place, that one was haunted, made so by dim light strained through the leaves and various tricks of perspective. I had working for me a Filipino man, a hill man, short and dark and silent, of the Maori people perhaps. Once, thinking he must have come from a tribal system which recognizes the unseen as a part of reality, I asked this man if he was not afraid of the haunted place, particularly at night. He said he was not afraid because years before a witch doctor gave him a charm against evil spirits.

"Let me see that charm," I asked.

"It's words," he said. "It's a word charm."

"Can you say them to me?"

"Sure," he said and he droned, "*In nomine*

Patris et Fillii et Spiritus Sancti."

"What does it mean?" I asked.

He raised his shoulders. "I don't know," he said. "It's a charm against evil spirits so I am not afraid of them."

I've dredged this conversation out of a strange-sounding Spanish but there is no doubt of his charm, and it worked for him.

Lying in my bed under the weeping night I did my best to read to take my mind out of misery, but while my eyes moved on the lines I listened to the night. On the edge of sleep a new sound jerked me awake, the sound of footsteps, I thought, moving stealthily on gravel. On the bed beside me I had a flashlight two feet long, made for coon hunters. It throws a powerful beam at least a mile. I got up from bed and lifted my 30/30 carbine from the wall and listened again near the door of Rocinante—and I heard the steps come closer. Then Charley roared his warning and I opened the door and sprayed the road with light. It was a man in boots and a yellow oilskin. The light pinned him still.

"What do you want?" I called.

He must have been startled. It took him a moment to answer. "I want to go home. I live up the road."

And now I felt the whole silly thing, the ridiculous pattern that had piled up layer on layer. "Would you like a cup of coffee, or a drink?"

"No, it's late. If you'll take that light out of my face I'll get along."

I snapped off the light and he disappeared but his voice in passing said, "Come to think of it, what are you doing here?"

"Camping," I said, "just camped for the night." And I went to sleep the moment I hit the bed.

The sun was up when I awakened and the world was remade and shining. There are as many worlds as there are kinds of days, and as an opal changes its colors and its fire to match the nature of a day, so do I. The night fears and loneliness were so far gone that I could hardly remember them.

Crossing the Border

Niagara Falls is very nice. It's like a large version of the old Bond sign on Times Square. I'm very glad I saw it, because from now on if I am asked whether I have seen Niagara Falls I can say yes, and be telling the truth for once.

When I told my adviser that I was going to Erie, Pennsylvania, I had no idea of going there, but as it turned out, I was. My intention was to creep across the neck of Ontario, bypassing not only Erie but Cleveland and Toledo.

I find out of long experience that I admire all nations and hate all governments, and nowhere is my natural anarchism more aroused than at national borders where patient and efficient public servants carry out their duties in matters of immigration and customs. I have never smuggled anything in my life. Why, then, do I feel an uneasy sense of guilt on approaching a customs barrier? I crossed a high toll bridge and negotiated a no man's land and came to the place where the Stars and Stripes stood shoulder to shoulder with the Union Jack. The Canadians were very kind. They asked where I was going and for how long, gave Rocinante a cursory inspection, and came at last to Charley.

"Do you have a certificate of rabies vaccination on the dog?"

"No, I haven't. You see he's an old dog. He was vaccinated long ago."

Another official came out. "We advise you not to cross the border with him, then."

"But I'm just crossing a small part of Canada and reentering the U.S."

"We understand," they said kindly. "You can take him into Canada but the U.S. won't let him back."

"But technically I am still in the U.S. and there's no complaint."

"There will be if he crosses the line and tries to get back."

"Well, where can I get him vaccinated?"

They didn't know. I would have to retrace

my way at least twenty miles, find a vet, have Charley vaccinated, and then return. I was crossing only to save a little time, and this would wipe out the time saved and much more.

"Please understand, it is your own government, not ours. We are simply advising you. It's the rule."

I guess this is why I hate governments, all governments. It is always the rule, the fine print, carried out by fine-print men. There's nothing to fight, no wall to hammer with frustrated fists. I highly approve of vaccination, feel it should be compulsory; rabies is a dreadful thing. And yet I found myself hating the rule and all governments that made rules. It was not the shots but the certificate that was important. And it is usually so with governments—not a fact but a small slip of paper. These were such nice men, friendly and helpful. It was a slow time at the border. They gave me a cup of tea and Charley half a dozen cookies. And they seemed genuinely sorry that I had to go to Erie, Pennsylvania, for the lack of a paper. And so I turned about and proceeded toward the Stars and Stripes and another government. Exiting I had not been required to stop, but now the barrier was down.

"Are you an American citizen?"

"Yes, sir, here's my passport."

"Do you have anything to declare?"

"I haven't been away."

"Have you a rabies vaccination certificate for your dog?"

"He hasn't been away either."

"But you are coming from Canada."

"I have not been in Canada."

I saw the steel come into eyes, the brows lower to a level of suspicion. Far from saving time, it looked as though I might lose much more than even Erie, Pennsylvania.

"Will you step into the office?"

This request had the effect on me a Gestapo knock on the door might have. It raises panic, anger, and guilty feelings whether or not I have done wrong. My voice took on the stri-

dent tone of virtuous outrage which automatically arouses suspicion.

"Please step into the office."

"I tell you I have not been in Canada. If you were watching, you would have seen that I turned back."

"Step this way, please, sir."

Then into the telephone: "New York license so-and-so. Yes. Pick-up truck with camper top. Yes—a dog." And to me: "What kind of dog is it?"

"Poodle."

"Poodle—I said poodle. Light brown."

"Blue," I said.

"Light brown. Okay. Thanks."

I do hope I did not sense a certain sadness at my innocence.

"They say you didn't cross the line."

"That's what I told you."

"May I see your passport?"

"Why? I haven't left the country. I'm not about to leave the country." But I handed over my passport just the same. He leafed through it, pausing at the entry-and-exit stamps of other journeys. He inspected my photograph, opened the yellow smallpox vaccination certificate stapled to the back cover. At the bottom of the last page he saw pencilled in a faint set of letters and figures. "What is this?"

"I don't know. Let me see. Oh, that! Why, it's a telephone number."

"What's it doing in your passport?"

"I guess I didn't have a slip of paper. I don't even remember whose number it is."

By now he had me on the run and he knew it. "Don't you know it is against the law to deface a passport?"

"I'll erase it."

"You should not write anything in your passport. That's the regulation."

"I won't ever do it again. I promise." And I wanted to promise him I wouldn't lie or steal or associate with persons of loose morals, or covet my neighbor's wife, or anything. He closed my passport firmly and handed it back to me. I'm sure he felt better having found that telephone number. Suppose after all his trouble he hadn't found me guilty of anything, and on a slow day.

"Thank you, sir," I said. "May I proceed now?"

He waved his hand kindly. "Go ahead," he said.

And that's why I went toward Erie, Pennsylvania, and it was Charley's fault. I crossed the high iron bridge and stopped to pay toll. The man leaned out the window. "Go on," he said, "it's on the house."

"How do you mean?"

"I seen you go through the other way a little while ago. I seen the dog. I knew you'd be back."

"Why didn't you tell me?"

"Nobody believes it. Go ahead. You get a free ride one way."

He wasn't government, you see. But government can make you feel so small and mean that it takes some doing to build back a sense of self-importance. Charley and I stayed at the grandest auto court we could find that night, a place only the rich could afford, a pleasure dome of ivory and apes and peacocks and moreover with a restaurant, and room service. I ordered ice and soda and made a scotch and soda and then another. Then I had a waiter in and bespoke soup and a steak and a pound of raw hamburger for Charley, and I overtipped mercilessly. Before I went to sleep I went over all the things I wished I had said to that immigration man, and some of them were incredibly clever and cutting.

Yellowstone

I must confess to a laxness in the matter of National Parks. I haven't visited many of them. Perhaps this is because they enclose the unique, the spectacular, the astounding—the greatest waterfall, the deepest canyon, the highest cliff, the most stupendous works of man or nature. And I would rather see a good Brady photograph than Mount Rushmore. For it is my opinion that we enclose and celebrate the freaks of our nation and of our civilization. Yellowstone National Park is no more representative of America than is Disneyland.

This being my natural attitude, I don't know what made me turn sharply south and cross a state line to take a look at Yellowstone. Perhaps it was a fear of my neighbors. I could hear them say, "You mean you were that near to Yellowstone and didn't go? You must be crazy." Again it might have been the American tendency in travel. One goes, not so much to see but to tell afterward. Whatever my purpose in going to Yellowstone, I'm glad I went because I discovered something about Charley I might never have known.

A pleasant-looking National Park man checked me in and then he said, "How about that dog? They aren't permitted in except on leash."

"Why?" I asked.

"Because of the bears."

"Sir," I said, "this is an unique dog. He does not live by tooth or fang. He respects the right of cats to be cats although he doesn't admire them. He turns his steps rather than disturb an earnest caterpillar. His greatest fear is that someone will point out a rabbit and suggest that he chase it. This is a dog of peace and tranquility. I suggest that the greatest danger to your bears will be pique at being ignored by Charley."

The young man laughed. "I wasn't so much worried about the bears," he said. "But our bears have developed an intolerance for dogs. One of them might demonstrate his prejudice with a clip on the chin, and then—no dog."

"I'll lock him in the back, sir. I promise you Charley will cause no ripple in the bear world, and as an old bear-looker, neither will I."

"I just have to warn you," he said. "I have no doubt your dog has the best of intentions. On the other hand, our bears have the worst. Don't leave food about. Not only do they steal but they are critical of anyone who tries to reform them. In a word, don't believe their sweet faces or you might get clobbered. And don't let the dog wander. Bears don't argue."

We went on our way into the wonderland of nature gone nuts, and you will have to believe what happened. The only way I can prove it would be to get a bear.

Less than a mile from the entrance I saw a bear beside the road, and it ambled out as though to flag me down. Instantly a change came over Charley. He shrieked with rage. His lips flared, showing wicked teeth that have some trouble with a dog biscuit. He screeched insults at the bear, which hearing, the bear reared up and seemed to me to overtop Rocinante. Frantically I rolled the windows shut and, swinging quickly to the left, grazed the animal, then scuttled on while Charley raved and ranted beside me, describing in detail what he would do to that bear if he could get at him. I was never so astonished in my life. To the best of my knowledge Charley had never seen a bear, and in his whole history had showed great tolerance for every living thing. Besides all this, Charley is a coward, so deep-seated a coward that he has developed a technique for concealing it. And yet he showed every evidence of wanting to get out and murder a bear that outweighed him a thousand to one. I don't understand it.

A little farther along two bears showed up, and the effect was doubled. Charley became a maniac. He leaped all over me, he cursed and growled, snarled and screamed. I didn't know he had the ability to snarl. Where did he learn it? Bears were in good supply, and the road became a nightmare. For the first time in his life Charley resisted reason, even resisted a cuff on the ear. He became a primitive killer lusting for the blood of his enemy, and up to this moment he had had no enemies. In a bearless stretch, I opened the cab, took Charley by the collar, and locked him in the house. But that did no good. When we passed other bears he leaped on the table and scratched at the windows trying to get out at them. I could hear canned goods crashing as he struggled in his mania. Bears simply brought out the Hyde in my Jekyll-headed dog. What could have caused it? Was it a pre-breed memory of a time when the wolf was in him? I know him well. Once in a while he tries a bluff, but it is a palpable lie. I swear that this was no lie. I am certain that if he were released he would have charged every bear we passed and found victory or death.

It was too nerve-wracking, a shocking spectacle, like seeing an old, calm friend go insane. No amount of natural wonders, of rigid cliffs and belching waters, of smoking springs could even engage my attention while that pandemonium went on. After about the fifth encounter I gave up, turned Rocinante about, and retraced my way. If I had stopped the night and bears had gathered to my cooking, I dare not think what would have happened.

At the gate the park guard checked me out. "You didn't stay long. Where's the dog?"

"Locked up back there. And I owe you an apology. That dog has the heart and soul of a bear-killer and I didn't know it. Heretofore he has been a little tender-hearted toward an underdone steak."

"Yeah!" he said. "That happens sometimes. That's why I warned you. A bear dog would know his chances, but I've seen a Pomeranian go up like a puff of smoke. You know, a well-favored bear can bat a dog like a tennis ball."

I moved fast, back the way I had come, and I was reluctant to camp for fear there might be some unofficial non-government bears about. That night I spent in a pretty auto court near Livingston. I had my dinner in a restaurant, and when I had settled in with a drink and a comfortable chair and my bathed bare feet on a carpet with red roses, I inspected Charley. He was dazed. His eyes held a faraway look and he was totally exhausted, emotionally no doubt. Mostly he reminded me of a man coming out of a long, hard drunk—worn out, depleted, collapsed. He couldn't eat his dinner, he refused the evening walk, and once we were in he collapsed on the floor and went to sleep. In the night I heard him whining and yapping, and when I turned on the light his feet were making running gestures and his body jerked and his eyes were wide open, but it was only a night bear. I awakened him and gave him some water. This time he went to sleep and didn't stir all night. In the morning he was still tired. I wonder why we think the thoughts and emotions of animals are simple.

The Redwoods

I stayed two days close to the bodies of the giants, and there were no trippers, no chattering troupes with cameras. There's a cathedral hush here. Perhaps the thick soft bark absorbs sound and creates a silence. The trees rise straight up to zenith; there is no horizon. The dawn comes early and remains dawn until the sun is high. Then the green fernlike foliage so far up strains the sunlight to a green gold and distributes it in shafts or rather in stripes of light and shade. After the sun passes zenith, it is afternoon and quickly evening with a whispering dusk as long as was the morning.

Thus time and the ordinary divisions of the day are changed. To me dawn and dusk are quiet times, and here in the redwoods nearly the whole of daylight is a quiet time. Birds move in the dim light or flash like sparks through the stripes of sun, but they make little sound. Underfoot is a mattress of needles deposited for over two thousand years. No sound of footsteps can be heard on this thick blanket. To me there's a remote and cloistered feeling here. One holds back speech for fear of disturbing something—what? From my earliest childhood I've felt that something was going on in the groves, something of which I was not a part. And if I had forgotten the feeling, I soon got it back.

At night, the darkness is black—only straight up a patch of gray and an occasional star. And there's a breathing in the black, for these huge things that control the day and inhabit the night are living things and have presence, and perhaps feeling, and, somewhere in deep-down

ning memory of what the world was like once long ago. Can it be that we do not love to be reminded that we are very young and callow in a world that was old when we came into it? And could there be a strong resistance to the certainty that a living world will continue its stately way when we no longer inhabit it?

The Salinas Valley

In my flurry of nostalgic spite, I have done the Monterey Peninsula a disservice. It is a beautiful place, clean, well run, and progressive. The beaches are clean where once they festered with fish guts and flies. The canneries which once put up a sickening stench are gone, their places filled with restaurants, antique shops, and the like. They fish for tourists now, not pilchards, and that species they are not likely to wipe out. And Carmel, begun by starveling writers and unwanted painters, is now, a community of the well-to-do and the retired. If Carmel's founders should return, they could not afford to live there, but it wouldn't go that far. They would be instantly picked up as suspicious characters and deported over the city line.

The place of my origin had changed, and having gone away I had not changed with it. In my memory it stood as it once did and its outward appearance confused and angered me.

What I am about to tell must be the experience of very many in this nation where so many wander and come back. I called on old and valued friends. I thought their hair had receded a little more than mine. The greetings were enthusiastic. The memories flooded up. Old crimes and old triumphs were brought out and dusted. And suddenly my attention wandered, and looking at my ancient friend, I saw that his wandered also. And it was true what I had said to Johnny Garcia—I was the ghost. My town had grown and changed and my friend along with it. Now returning, as changed to my friend as my town was to me, I distorted

perception, perhaps communication. I have had lifelong association with these things. (Odd that the word "trees" does not apply.) I can accept them and their power and their age because I was early exposed to them. On the other hand, people lacking such experience begin to have a feeling of uneasiness here, of danger, of being shut in, enclosed and overwhelmed. It is not only the size of these redwoods but their strangeness that frightens them. And why not? For these are the last remaining members of a race that flourished over four continents as far back in geologic time as the upper Jurassic period. Fossils of these ancients have been found dating from the Cretaceous era while in the Eocene and Miocene they were spread over England and Europe and America. And then the glaciers moved down and wiped the Titans out beyond recovery. And only these few are left—a stun-

his picture, muddied his memory. When I went away I had died, and so became fixed and unchangeable. My return caused only confusion and uneasiness. Although they could not say it, my old friends wanted me gone so that I could take my proper place in the pattern of remembrance—and I wanted to go for the same reason. Tom Wolfe was right. You can't go home again because home has ceased to exist except in the mothballs of memory.

My departure was flight. But I did do one formal and sentimental thing before I turned my back. I drove up to Fremont's Peak, the highest point for many miles around. I climbed the last spiky rocks to the top. Here among these blackened granite outcrops General Frémont made his stand against a Mexican army, and defeated it. When I was a boy we occasionally found cannon balls and rusted bayonets in the area. This solitary stone peak overlooks the whole of my childhood and youth, the great Salinas Valley stretching south for nearly a hundred miles, the town of Salinas where I was born now spreading like crab grass toward the foothills. Mount Toro, on the brother range to the west, was a rounded benign mountain, and to the north Monterey Bay shone like a blue platter. I felt and smelled and heard the wind blow up from the long valley. It smelled of the brown hills of wild oats.

I remembered how once, in that part of youth that is deeply concerned with death, I wanted to be buried on this peak where without eyes I could see everything I knew and loved, for in those days there was no world beyond the mountains. And I remembered how intensely I felt about my interment. It is strange and perhaps fortunate that when one's time grows nearer one's interest in it flags as death becomes a fact rather than a pageantry. Here on these high rocks my memory myth repaired itself. Charley, having explored the area, sat at my feet, his fringed ears blowing like laundry on a line. His nose, moist with curiosity, sniffed the wind-borne pattern of a hundred miles.

"You wouldn't know, my Charley, that right down there, in that little valley, I fished for trout with your namesake, my Uncle Charley. And over there—see where I'm pointing—my mother shot a wildcat. Straight down there, forty miles away, our family ranch was—old starvation ranch. Can you see that darker place there? Well, that's a tiny canyon with a clear and lovely stream bordered with wild azaleas and fringed with big oaks. And on one of those oaks my father burned his name with a hot iron together with the name of the girl he loved. In the long years the bark grew over the burn and covered it. And just a little while ago, a man cut that oak for firewood and his splitting wedge uncovered my father's name and the man sent it to me. In the spring, Charley, when the valley is carpeted with blue lupines like a flowery sea, there's the smell of heaven up here, the smell of heaven."

I printed it once more on my eyes, south, west, and north, and then we hurried away from the permanent and changeless past where my mother is always shooting a wildcat and my father is always burning his name with his love.

Texas

When I started this narrative, I knew that sooner or later I would have to have a go at Texas, and I dreaded it. I could have bypassed Texas about as easily as a space traveler can avoid the Milky Way. It sticks its big old Panhandle up north and it slops and slouches along the Rio Grande. Once you are in Texas it seems to take forever to get out, and some people never make it.

Let me say in the beginning that even if I wanted to avoid Texas I could not, for I am wived in Texas and mother-in-lawed and uncled and aunted and cousined within an inch of my life. Staying away from Texas geographically is no help whatever, for Texas moves through our house in New York, our fishing cottage at Sag Harbor, and when we had a flat in Paris, Texas was there too. It permeates the world to a ridiculous degree. Once, in Florence, on seeing a lovely little Italian princess, I said to her father, "But she doesn't look Italian. It may seem strange, but she looks like an American Indian." To which her father replied, "Why shouldn't she? Her grandfather married a Cherokee in Texas."

Writers facing the problem of Texas find themselves floundering in generalities, and I am no exception. Texas is a state of mind. Texas is an obsession. Above all, Texas is a nation in every sense of the word. And there's an opening covey of generalities. A Texan outside of Texas is a foreigner. My wife refers to herself as the Texan that got away, but that is only partly true. She has virtually no accent until she talks to a Texan, when she instantly reverts. You would not have to scratch deep to find her origin. She says such words as yes, air, hair, guess, with two syllables—yayus, ayer, hayer, gayus. And sometimes in a weary moment the word ink becomes ank. Our daughter, after a stretch in Austin, was visiting New York friends. She said, "Do you have a pin?"

"Certainly, dear," said her host, "Do you want a straight pin or a safety pin?"

"Aont a fountain pin," she said.

I've studied the Texas problem from many angles and for many years. And of course one of my truths is inevitably canceled by another. Outside their state I think Texans are a little frightened and very tender in their feelings, and these qualities cause boasting, arrogance, and noisy complacency—the outlets of shy children. At home Texans are none of these things. The ones I know are gracious, friendly, generous, and quiet. In New York we hear them so often bring up their treasured uniqueness. Texas is the only state that came into the Union by treaty. It retains the right to secede at will. We have heard them threaten to secede so often that I formed an enthusiatic organization—The American Friends for Texas Secession. This stops the subject cold. They want to be able to secede but they don't want anyone to want them to.

Like most passionate nations Texas has its own private history based on, but not limited by, facts. The tradition of the tough and versatile frontiersman is true but not exclusive. It is for the few to know that in the great old days of Virginia there were three punishments for high crimes—death, exile to Texas, and imprisonment, in that order. And some of the deportees must have descendants.

Again—the glorious defense to the death of the Alamo against the hordes of Santa Anna is a fact. The brave bands of Texans did indeed wrest their liberty from Mexico, and freedom, liberty, are holy words. One must go to contemporary observers in Europe for a non-Texan opinion as to the nature of the tyranny that raised need for revolt. Outside observers say the pressure was twofold. The Texans, they say, didn't want to pay taxes and, second, Mexico had abolished slavery in 1829, and Texas, being part of Mexico, was required to free its slaves. Of course there were other causes of revolt, but these two are spectacular to a European, and rarely mentioned here.

I have said that Texas is a state of mind, but I think it is more than that. It is a mystique closely approximating a religion. And this is true to the extent that people either passionately love Texas or passionately hate it and, as in other religions, few people dare to inspect it for fear of losing their bearings in mystery and paradox. Any observations of mine can be quickly cancelled by opinion or counter-observation. But I think there will be little quarrel with my feeling that Texas is one thing. For all its enormous range of space, climate, and physical appearance, and for all the internal squabbles, contentions, and strivings, Texas has a tight cohesiveness perhaps stronger than any other section of America. Rich, poor, Panhandle, Gulf, city, country, Texas is the obsession, the proper study and the passionate possession of all Texans. Some years ago, Edna Ferber wrote a book about a very tiny group of very rich Texans. Her description was accurate, so far as my knowledge extends, but the emphasis was one of disparagement. And instantly the book was attacked by Texans of all groups, classes, and possessions. To attack one Texas is to draw fire from all Texans. The Texas joke, on the other hand, is a revered institution, beloved and in many cases originating in Texas.

The tradition of the frontier cattleman is as tenderly nurtured in Texas as is the hint of Norman blood in England. And while it is true that many families are descended from contract colonists not unlike the present-day braceros, all hold to the dream of the longhorn steer and the unfenced horizon. When a man makes his fortune in oil or government contracts, in chemicals or wholesale groceries, his first act is to buy a ranch, the largest he can afford, and to run some cattle. A candidate for public office who does not own a ranch is said to have little chance of election. The tradition of the land is deep fixed in the Texas psyche. Businessmen wear heeled boots that never feel a stirrup, and men of great wealth who have houses in Paris and regularly shoot grouse in Scotland refer to themselves as little old country boys. It would be easy to make sport of their attitude if one did not know that in this way they try to keep their association with the strength and simplicity of the land. Instinctively they feel that this is the source not only of wealth but of energy. And the energy of Texans is boundless and explosive. The successful man with his traditional ranch, at least in my experience, is no absentee owner. He works at it, oversees his herd and adds to it. The energy, in a climate so hot as to be staggering, is also staggering. And the tradition of hard work is maintained whatever the fortune or lack of it.

The power of an attitude is amazing. Among other tendencies to be noted, Texas is a military nation. The armed forces of the United States are loaded with Texans and often dominated by Texans. Even the dearly loved spectacular sports are run almost like military operations. Nowhere are there larger bands or more marching organizations, with corps of costumed girls whirling glittering batons. Sec-

tional football games have the glory and the despair of war, and when a Texas team takes the field against a foreign state, it is an army with banners.

If I keep coming back to the energy of Texas, it is because I am so aware of it. It seems to me like that thrust of dynamism which caused and permitted whole peoples to migrate and to conquer in earlier ages. The land mass of Texas is rich in recoverable spoil. If this had not been so, I think I believe the relentless energy of Texans would have moved out and conquered new lands. This conviction is somewhat borne out in the restless movement of Texas capital. But now, so far, the conquest has been by purchase rather than by warfare. The oil deserts of the Near East, the opening lands of South America have felt the thrust. Then there are new islands of capital conquest: factories in the Middle West, food-processing plants, tool and die works, lumber and pulp. Even publishing houses have been added to the legitimate twentieth-century Texas spoil. There is no moral in these observations, nor any warning. Energy must have an outlet and will seek one.

In all ages, rich, energetic, and successful nations, when they have carved their place in the world, have felt hunger for art, for culture, even for learning and beauty. The Texas cities shoot upward and outward. The colleges are heavy with gifts and endowments. Theaters and symphony orchestras sprout overnight. In any huge and boisterous surge of energy and enthusiasm there must be errors and miscalculations, even breach of judgment and taste. And there is always the non-productive brotherhood of critics to disparage and to satirize, to view with horror and contempt. My own interest is attracted to the fact that these things are done at all. There will doubtless be thousands of ribald failures, but in the world's history artists have always been drawn where they are welcome and well treated.

By its nature and its size Texas invites generalities, and the generalities usually end up as paradox—the "little ol' country boy" at a symphony, the booted and blue-jeaned ranchman in Neiman-Marcus, buying Chinese jades.

Politically Texas continues its paradox. Traditionally and nostalgically it is Old South Democrat, but this does not prevent its voting conservative Republican in national elections while electing liberals to city and county posts. My opening statement still holds—everything in Texas is likely to be canceled by something else.

Most areas in the world may be placed in latitude and longitude, described chemically in their earth, sky and water, rooted and fuzzed over with identified flora and peopled with known fauna, and there's an end to it. Then there are others where fable, myth, preconception, love, longing, or prejudice step in and so distort a cool, clear appraisal that a kind of high-colored magical confusion takes permanent hold. Greece is such an area, and those parts of England where King Arthur walked. One quality of such places as I am trying to define is that a very large part of them is personal and subjective. And surely Texas is such a place.

I have moved over a great part of Texas and I know that within its borders I have seen just about as many kinds of country, contour, climate, and conformation as there are in the world saving only the Arctic, and a good north wind can even bring the icy breath down. The stern horizon-fenced plains of the Panhandle are foreign to the little wooded hills and sweet streams in the Davis Mountains. The rich citrus orchards of the Rio Grande valley do not relate to the sagebrush grazing of South Texas. The hot and humid air of the Gulf Coast has no likeness in the cool crystal in the northwest of the Panhandle. And Austin on its hills among the bordered lakes might be across the world from Dallas.

What I am trying to say is that there is no physical or geographical unity in Texas. Its unity lies in the mind. And this is not only in Texans. The word Texas becomes a symbol to everyone in the world. There's no question that this Texas-of-the-mind fable is often synthetic, sometimes untruthful, and frequently romantic, but that in no way diminishes its strength as a symbol.

The foregoing investigation into the nature of the idea of Texas is put down as a prelude to my journeying across Texas with Charley in Rocinante. It soon became apparent that this stretch had to be different from the rest of the trip. In the first place I knew the countryside, and in the second I had friends and relatives by marriage, and such a situation makes objectivity practically impossible, for I know no place where hospitality is practiced so fervently as in Texas.

But before that most pleasant and sometimes exhausting human trait took hold, I had three days of namelessness in a beautiful motor hotel in the middle of Amarillo. A passing car on a gravel road had thrown up pebbles and broken out the large front window of Rocinante and it had to be replaced. But, more important, Charley had been taken with his old ailment again, and this time he was in bad trouble and great pain. I remembered the poor incompetent veterinary in the Northwest, who did not know and did not care. And I remembered how Charley had looked at him with pained wonder and contempt.

In Amarillo the doctor I summoned turned out to be a young man. He drove up in a medium-priced convertible. He leaned over Charley. "What's his problem?" he asked. I explained Charley's difficulty. Then the young vet's hands went down and moved over hips and distended abdomen—trained and knowing hands. Charley sighed a great sigh and his tail wagged slowly up from the floor and down again. Charley put himself in this man's care, completely confident. I've seen this instant rapport before, and it is good to see.

The strong fingers probed and investigated and then the vet straightened up. "It can happen to any little old boy," he said.

"Is it what I think it is?"

"Yep. Prostatitis."

"Can you treat it?"

"Sure. I'll have to relax him first, and then I can give him medication for it. Can you leave him for maybe four days?"

"Whether I can or not, I will."

He lifted Charley in his arms and carried him out and laid him in the front seat of the convertible, and the tufted tail twittered against the leather. He was content and confident, and so was I. And that is how I happened to stay around Amarillo for a while. To complete the episode, I picked up Charley four days later, completely well. The doctor gave me pills to give at intervals while traveling so that the ailment never came back. There's absolutely nothing to take the place of a good man.

I
TRAVELS WITH STEINBECK

When *Travels with Charley* was published, Steinbeck was a world-famous writer. Certainly every American who read fiction knew who he was. And yet as we travel with him through America, we are likely to feel that we are in the company of a favorite uncle rather than a famous person. We discover that Steinbeck has the same needs, the same emotions, many of the same hopes and fears that we have. Even some of his ideas have probably occurred to you.

It is a pleasant thought that we are, in a way, on the same level as a famous and highly gifted person. But this should not really come as a surprise, for it is something we experience every time we read a work of literature with understanding.

II
IMPLICATIONS

Can you restate in your own words what Steinbeck is saying in each of the following quotations? (Locate the quote in the text if necessary.) Tell whether you agree or disagree with him and why.

1. We do not take a trip; a trip takes us. (p. 598)

2. Two or more people disturb the ecologic complex of an area. I had to go alone. . . . (p. 599)

3. Oh, we can populate the dark with horrors, even we who think ourselves informed and sure, believing nothing we cannot measure or weigh. (p. 601)

4. I find out of long experience that I admire all nations and hate all governments. (p. 602)

5. It is my opinion that we enclose and celebrate the freaks of our nation and of our civilization. (p. 604)

6. I wonder why we think the thoughts and emotions of animals are simple. (p. 606)

7. Can it be that we do not love to be reminded that we are very young and callow in a world that was old when we came into it? And could there be a strong resistance to the certainty that a living world will continue its stately way when we no longer inhabit it? (p. 607)

8. Tom Wolfe was right. You can't go home again because home has ceased to exist except in the mothballs of memory. (p. 609)

9. There's absolutely nothing to take the place of a good man. (p. 612)

III
TECHNIQUES

Intention and Theme

A. Writers of fiction rarely state directly in their works either their intention or their theme. Yet in nonfiction, writers often directly declare their intention and theme. Why should there be a difference between the two?

B. *Travels with Charley* bears the subtitle, "In Search of America," and at one point Steinbeck tells us that his intention is to try to "rediscover this monster land." From what you have read, why does it seem to you that he has either succeeded or failed to realize this intention?

C. In the final chapter of *Travels with Charley*, Steinbeck rushes from Abingdon, in southern Virginia, all the way to New York City, stopping only for necessities like food and gas. When he reaches New York, he gets lost. He laughs at the irony of the fact that he should get lost in his own town after traveling across the country. The book then ends with a single-sentence paragraph: "And that's how the traveler came home again." Why do you think this is or is not a fitting conclusion for the book?

RICHARD WRIGHT

1908-1960

Photographs taken of Richard Wright in his later years show him as a kindly, good-humored person. It is an impression that was also left on many of those who met him during this period. Yet readers of his fiction know that his trademark was violence. Rarely did he write a novel or story which did not contain a murder or a suicide.

The explanation of this paradox is not hard to find. Wright's adult life—at least from his midthirties on—was the kind of life that would make most people happy. He had a good wife, Ellen, and two fine daughters, Julia and Rachel. He had many friends, including some of the best-known writers and intellectuals of his time. He had achieved international fame while still in his thirties; and he was able to live fairly comfortably, considering the fact that he earned his living largely as a writer. Finally, in France, where he spent the last thirteen years of his life, he had experienced a freedom from racial prejudice that gave him peace and a sense of human dignity.

Yet in spite of such "wealth," Richard Wright could never forget the poverty of his childhood and youth. Among the titles he considered for the autobiographical *Black Boy* was *American Hunger*. It would have been an appropriate title, for as one critic has pointed out, hunger was the most important thing in his life. And alongside of hunger, no doubt, was fear, which Wright himself identified as the most dominant emotion in the life of the blacks of his time.

How does one react to hunger and fear? One possibility is to submit—and die in spirit, or body, or both. The other is to rebel,

to fight back and live. The violence in Richard Wright's fiction suggests which of the alternatives he chose.

All of us can learn from the life story of Richard Wright. It is, on the one hand, a success story, the story of a person who achieved greatness in the face of almost insuperable obstacles. But it is also a story that illustrates that the wounds of youth can never be fully healed.

Born on September 4, 1908, on a plantation near Natchez, Mississippi, Richard Wright was the first child of Ella Wilson Wright, a schoolteacher, and Nathaniel Wright, an illiterate sharecropper. The early years of the marriage were apparently happy ones, but in 1914 cotton prices fell, and sharecroppers from all over the South left their homes. Nathaniel Wright took his family to Memphis, where he worked for a time as a night porter in a drugstore on Beale Street. In the unfamiliar city, the uprooted farmer underwent a radical personality change and soon deserted his wife and children.

Ella Wright had to leave her young children, Richard and his brother Alan, and go to work. At one point her burden became so unbearable that she had to put her children into an orphanage. After six months, however, Richard's Aunt Maggie was able to send money for Ella and her children to come live with her and her husband in Arkansas.

After a visit with her mother, who had moved to Jackson, Mississippi, Mrs. Wright and her children moved in with Aunt Maggie and Uncle Fred Hoskins. The move would have provided the family with a good deal of security, for Richard's uncle was a prosperous owner of a popular saloon. But Hoskins had refused to sell his business to some whites, and not long after the Wright family arrived, their uncle was shot to death in retaliation.

The family moved to Jackson, then back to Arkansas, where another family disaster befell them: Mrs. Wright suffered a paralytic stroke. Richard was not yet twelve.

Although he was separated from his brother, who went to live with relatives in Detroit, and although his mother remained ill, Richard entered at about this time a period of relative stability. He entered a public school in Jackson in September, 1921, transferred to another two years later, and remained in school till he graduated—valedictorian of his class—in May, 1925.

This was to be the end of his formal education, ninth grade. It is not much as formal education goes these days; but Richard had already published a short story, and what is more important, he had acquired a love of reading. He had learned how to educate himself.

After his graduation, Richard held a few jobs briefly but kept leaving or getting fired for "not knowing his place." Then in November of 1925, he went to Memphis, where he worked briefly as a dishwasher and then as an employee of the American Optical Company. Finally, having saved enough money, he fled the South permanently in December, 1927. The important decision is described in the concluding paragraph of *Black Boy:*

With ever watchful eyes and bearing scars, visible and invisible, I headed North, full of a hazy notion that life could be lived with dignity, that the personalities of others should not be violated, that men should be able to confront other men without fear and shame, and that if men were lucky in their living on earth they might win some redeeming meaning for their having struggled and suffered here beneath the stars.

In the twenty years he was to spend in Chicago (1927–1937) and New York (1937–1947), Wright's hopes that he would find dig-

nity and a life free of fear and shame were only partially realized. But he did begin to find "some redeeming meaning" for his struggles and suffering through his art. He published a short story as early as 1931 and a good deal of poetry in left-wing magazines from 1934 to 1937.

Then, in 1938, in a competition with hundreds of other authors, Richard Wright won the Federal Writers' Project prize with *Uncle Tom's Children,* a collection of four long stories. (An autobiographical sketch, "The Ethics of Living Jim Crow," and another long story, "Bright and Morning Star," were added to the collection in 1940.) The reviews were almost all favorable, and Wright's career as a professional writer was launched.

The reference in the title to Uncle Tom is to Harriet Beecher Stowe's Uncle Tom of *Uncle Tom's Cabin,* the Negro who has become the stereotype of the submissive black. But Wright made it clear that Uncle Tom's children were *not* submissive.

In the first story of the volume, "Big Boy Leaves Home," Big Boy kills a white soldier who has shot two of his young friends and escapes before he can be caught. Brother Mann, in "Down by the Riverside," does not escape the wrath of the mob, but neither does he submit. Shot in the back while running, Mann has clearly cheated the mob of the "pleasure" of lynching him. The third story, "Long Black Song," ends similarly, when Silas kills as many of the mob as he can and then remains in his burning shack rather than allowing the mob to get him.

Finally, in the capstone story of the original volume, the hero, Reverend Dan Taylor, not only does not submit, he prevails. Experiencing "a baptism of clean joy" while leading a protest march of blacks and whites, he exults at the end of the story in his perception that *"Freedom belongs t the strong!"*

Not yet thirty years old, Wright must have been pleased with the fame he had won. Yet he was not entirely satisfied with his book, for he saw that too many of the whites that

read it wept and felt sorry but were not moved to *do* anything to change the conditions under which the members of his race were living.

It is much more difficult—perhaps impossible—to weep and feel sorry for Bigger Thomas, the hero of Wright's next book, *Native Son*, published in 1940. Bigger kills a white girl who had tried to be kind to him, cuts off her head, and burns her body in the furnace of her own home. He also bludgeons his own black girl friend with a brick and throws her body out of a window into the snow. Furthermore, we are asked to believe that Bigger *began to live* only after the first murder, and Bigger's attorney describes that murder as "an act of *creation.*"

It is not an easy novel to get down, yet the power of Wright's style is so great that one is virtually *driven* to read it through, just as the author himself was driven to write it: "In fact," Wright said in an article, "the novel . . . grew upon me to the extent that it became a necessity to write it; the writing of it turned into a way of living for me."

And people did read about Bigger Thomas, a native son not of the South only but also of the Chicago ghetto, where he had lived for five years before his crimes. In New York, the book sold out within three hours of its publication, and within a month, it had sold a quarter of a million copies. Whatever else we may say about *Native Son*, it is clear that it had touched a nerve of the American conscience. As Irving Howe has written, "The day *Native Son* appeared, American culture was changed forever. . . . Richard Wright's novel brought out into the open, as no one ever had before, the hatred, fear and violence that have crippled and may yet destroy our culture."

From *Native Son*, Richard Wright moved on five years later to a second best-seller, the autobiography of his first nineteen years, *Black Boy*. It is a remarkable book, probably among the best autobiographies ever written. Unlike *Native Son*, which is flawed artistically by the propagandistic flavor of the final third of the book, *Black Boy* makes no direct appeals to end racism nor any direct analysis of it. Yet in its quiet, indirect way, it remains one of the best analyses of the effects of racism and one of the most moving appeals to end it that has ever been written.

In *Black Boy*, Wright took the chance of letting the facts speak for themselves, and they speak very eloquently indeed. In reality, the eloquence stems from Wright's artistry; for in this book he succeeded brilliantly in doing what he set out to do—in making the words disappear, so that readers would be conscious only of their individual responses.

Responses will differ from reader to reader, certainly, yet most readers surely come away from the book with a deep admiration for the short, thin, courageous black boy who never bowed to anyone, black or white, peer or master.

Less than two years after the publication of *Black Boy*, Richard Wright chose to exile himself from his native land permanently. It was a move that he did not take lightly. He had foreseen, correctly, that in the third quarter of this century American blacks would look into themselves and develop self-consciousness and individuality, and Wright would have liked to have been on the scene. On the other hand, he was concerned with the health and safety of his family, particularly with what racism might do to his daughter Julia, then five years old. Moreover, he reasoned that a move to France would not be a retreat any more than the move to Chicago had been. Wright intended to continue to speak for his race and to make the question of race a human, rather than merely an American, matter.

In France, Wright produced eight books, equally divided between fiction and nonfiction. Three of the latter were travel books—*Black Power* (1954), *The Color Curtain* (1956), and *Pagan Spain* (1957)—detailing visits to the Gold Coast, Indonesia, and Spain, respectively. The fourth was *White Man, Listen!* (1957), a collection of lectures delivered between 1950 and 1956.

The fiction included three novels—*The Outsider* (1953), *Savage Holiday* (1954), and *The Long Dream* (1958)—and a collection of short stories, *Eight Men* (1961). Judgments of these books vary, though none of them met with the public or critical acclaim that Wright's earlier work had received. *Eight Men* does contain some of the author's best writing, but four of the eight stories were written and published while Wright was still in America.

It is sometimes alleged that Wright's creativity dried up when he left the United States. But this is a very dubious proposition at best. One could just as well argue that he would have written even better books than *Native Son* and *Black Boy* if he had not left the South. Moreover, though Richard Wright physically left the country of his birth, emotionally he never left it. The "scars, visible and invisible," were still on him, even to his death. As if in recognition of this fact, Ellen Wright lay next to the body of her husband a copy of *Black Boy* to replace the spray of flowers that some well-meaning but less perceptive person had placed in his hands.

Richard Wright's own father was a sharecropper, like the main character in the following story, and the Wright family lived in a cabin much like the one described here until Richard was almost six. Originally called "Silt" and published in 1937, this story was retitled "The Man Who Saw the Flood" and included in *Eight Men* (1961).

The Man Who Saw the Flood

When the flood waters recede, the poor folk along the river start from scratch.

At last the flood waters had receded. A black father, a black mother, and a black child tramped through muddy fields, leading a tired cow by a thin bit of rope. They stopped on a hilltop and shifted the bundles on their shoulders. As far as they could see the ground was covered with flood silt. The little girl lifted a skinny finger and pointed to a mud-caked cabin.

"Look, Pa! Ain tha our home?"

The man, round-shouldered, clad in blue, ragged overalls, looked with bewildered eyes. Without moving a muscle, scarcely moving his lips, he said: "Yeah."

For five minutes they did not speak or move. The flood waters had been more than eight feet high here. Every tree, blade of grass, and stray stick had its flood mark: caky, yellow mud. It clung to the ground, cracking thinly here and there in spider web fashion. Over the stark fields came a gusty spring wind. The sky was high, blue, full of white clouds and sunshine. Over all hung a first-day strangeness.

"The Man Who Saw the Flood" from *Eight Men* by Richard Wright. Copyright 1937 by Weekly Masses Company, Inc. Used by permission of Thomas Y. Crowell Company, Inc.

"The henhouse is gone," sighed the woman.

"N the pigpen," sighed the man.

They spoke without bitterness.

"Ah reckon them chickens is all done drowned."

"Yeah."

"Miz Flora's house is gone, too," said the little girl.

They looked at a clump of trees where their neighbor's house had stood.

"Lawd!"

"Yuh reckon anybody knows where they is?"

"Hard t tell."

The man walked down the slope and stood uncertainly.

"There wuz a road erlong here somewheres," he said.

But there was no road now. Just a wide sweep of yellow, scalloped silt.

"Look, Tom!" called the woman. "Here's a piece of our gate!"

The gatepost was half buried in the ground. A rusty hinge stood stiff, like a lonely finger. Tom pried it loose and caught it firmly in his hand. There was nothing particular he wanted to do with it; he just stood holding it firmly. Finally he dropped it, looked up, and said:

"C mon. Les go down n see whut we kin do."

Because it sat in a slight depression, the ground about the cabin was soft and slimy.

"Gimme tha bag o lime, May," he said.

With his shoes sucking in mud, he went slowly around the cabin, spreading the white lime with thick fingers. When he reached the front again he had a little left; he shook the bag out on the porch. The fine grains of floating lime flickered in the sunlight.

"Tha oughta hep some," he said.

"Now, yuh be careful, Sal!" said May. "Don yuh go n fall down in all this mud, yuh hear?"

"Yessum."

The steps were gone. Tom lifted May and Sally to the porch. They stood a moment looking at the half-opened door. He had shut it when he left, but somehow it seemed natural that he should find it open. The planks in the porch floor were swollen and warped. The cabin had two colors; near the bottom it was a solid yellow; at the top it was the familiar gray. It looked weird, as though its ghost were standing beside it.

The cow lowed.

"Tie Pat t the pos on the en of the porch, May."

May tied the rope slowly, listlessly. When they attempted to open the front door, it would not budge. It was not until Tom placed his shoulders against it and gave it a stout shove that it scraped back jerkily. The front room was dark and silent. The damp smell of flood silt came fresh and sharp to their nostrils. Only one-half of the upper window was clear, and through it fell a rectangle of dingy light. The floors swam in ooze. Like a mute warning, a wavering flood mark went high around the walls of the room. A dresser sat cater-cornered, its drawers and sides bulging like a bloated corpse. The bed, with the mattress still on it, was like a giant casket forged of mud. Two smashed chairs lay in a corner, as though huddled together for protection.

"Les see the kitchen," said Tom.

The stovepipe was gone. But the stove stood in the same place.

"The stove's still good. We kin clean it."

"Yeah."

"But where's the table?"

"Lawd knows."

"It must've washed erway wid the rest of the stuff, Ah reckon."

They opened the back door and looked out. They missed the barn, the henhouse, and the pigpen.

"Tom, yuh bettah try tha ol pump n see ef eny watah's there."

The pump was stiff. Tom threw his weight on the handle and carried it up and down. No water came. He pumped on. There was a dry, hollow cough. The yellow water trickled. He caught his breath and kept pumping. The water flowed white.

"Thank Gawd! We's got some watah."

"Yuh bettah boil it fo yuh use it," he said.

"Yeah. Ah know."

"Look, Pa! Here's yo ax," called Sally.

Tom took the ax from her. "Yeah. Ah'll need this."

"N here's somethin else," called Sally, digging spoons out of the mud.

"Waal, Ahma git a bucket n start cleanin," said May. "Ain no use in waitin, cause we's gotta sleep on them floors tonight."

When she was filling the bucket from the pump, Tom called from around the cabin. "May, look! Ah done foun mah plow!" Proudly he dragged the silt-caked plow to the pump. "Ah'll wash it n it'll be awright."

"Ahm hongry," said Sally.

"Now, yuh jus wait! Yuh et this mawnin," said May. She turned to Tom. "Now, whutcha gonna do, Tom?"

He stood looking at the mud filled fields.

"Yuh goin back t Burgess?"

"Ah reckon Ah have to."

"Whut else kin yuh do?"

"Nothin," he said. "Lawd, but Ah sho hate t start all over wid tha white man. Ah'd leave here ef Ah could. Ah owes im nigh eight hundred dollahs. N we needs a hoss, grub, seed, n a lot mo other things. Ef we keeps on like this tha white man'll own us body n soul."

"But, Tom, there ain nothin else t do," she said.

"Ef we try t run erway they'll put us in jail."

"It coulda been worse," she said.

Sally came running from the kitchen. "Pa!"

"Hunh?"

"There's a shelf in the kitchen the flood didn git!"

"Where?"

"Right up over the stove."

"But, chile, ain nothin up there," said May.

"But there's somethin on it," said Sally.

"C mon. Les see."

High and dry, untouched by the flood-water, was a box of matches. And beside it a half-full sack of Bull Durham tobacco. He took a match from the box and scratched it on his overalls. It burned to his fingers before he dropped it.

"May!"

"Hunh?"

"Look! Here's ma bacco n some matches!"

She stared unbelievingly. "Lawd!" she breathed.

Tom rolled a cigarette clumsily.

May washed the stove, gathered some sticks, and after some difficulty, made a fire. The kitchen stove smoked, and their eyes smarted. May put water on to heat and went into the front room. It was getting dark. From the bundles they took a kerosene lamp and lit it. Outside Pat lowed longingly into the thickening gloam and tinkled her cowbell.

"That old cow's hongry," said May.

"Ah reckon Ah'll have t be gittin erlong t Burgess."

They stood on the front porch.

"Yuh bettah git on, Tom, fo it gits too dark."

"Yeah."

The wind had stopped blowing. In the east a cluster of stars hung.

"Yuh goin, Tom?"

"Ah reckon Ah have t."

"Ma, Ah'm hongry," said Sally.

"Wait erwhile, honey. Ma knows yuh's hongry."

Tom threw his cigarette away and sighed.

"Look! Here comes somebody!"

"Thas Mistah Burgess now!"

A mud-caked buggy rolled up. The shaggy horse was plattered all over. Burgess leaned his white face out of the buggy and spat.

"Well, I see you're back."

"Yessuh."

"How things look?"

"They don look so good, Mistah."

"What seems to be the trouble?"

"Waal. Ah ain got no hoss, no grub, nothin. The only thing Ah got is that ol cow there . . ."

"You owe eight hundred dollahs down at the store, Tom."

"Yessuh, Ah know. But, Mistah Burgess, can't yuh knock somethin off of tha, seein as how Ahm down n out now?"

"You ate that grub, and I got to pay for it, Tom."

"Yessuh, Ah know."

"It's going to be a little tough, Tom. But you got to go through with it. Two of the boys tried to run away this morning and dodge their debts, and I had to have the sheriff pick em up. I wasn't looking for no trouble out of you, Tom . . . The rest of the families are going back."

Leaning out of the buggy, Burgess waited. In the surrounding stillness the cowbell tinkled again. Tom stood with his back against a post.

"Yuh got t go on, Tom. We ain't got nothin here," said May.

Tom looked at Burgess.

"Mistah Burgess, Ah don wanna make no trouble. But this is jus *too* hard. Ahm worse off now than befo. Ah got to start from scratch."

"Get in the buggy and come with me. I'll stake you with grub. We can talk over how you can pay it back." Tom said nothing. He rested his back against the post and looked at the mud-filled fields.

"Well," asked Burgess. "You coming?" Tom said nothing. He got slowly to the ground and pulled himself into the buggy. May watched them drive off.

"Hurry back, Tom!"

"Awright."

"Ma, tell Pa t bring me some 'lasses," begged Sally.

"Oh, Tom!"

Tom's head came out of the side of the buggy.

"Hunh?"

"Bring some 'lasses!"

"Hunh?"

"Bring some 'lasses for Sal!"

"Awright!"

She watched the buggy disappear over the crest of the muddy hill. Then she sighed, caught Sally's hand, and turned back into the cabin.

I
". . . THE POOR GET POORER"

A popular song of the twenties contains the line, "There is nothing surer—the rich get rich, and the poor get poorer." The song was not written about plantation owners and sharecroppers, but it might well have been.

A sharecropper was a farmer who shared a crop with a plantation owner, the owner being paid a percentage of the crop (Wright's father paid fifty percent) as a return for things furnished the sharecropper, such as a cabin, seeds, tools, and so on. The money from the rest of the crop belonged to the farmer.

What often happened, however, was that sharecroppers already owed the owner more than their share was worth because they had bought food and other supplies on credit while their crops were growing. The fact that the records of such dealings were kept by the plantation owner plus the fact that the sharecroppers were often illiterate made cheating a fairly common practice.

Even when they had a good crop, then, the sharecroppers often owed more than they earned. When the crop was poor or wiped out by a natural disaster, the poor really got poorer.

II
IMPLICATIONS

Be prepared to discuss your own reactions to the following statements.

1. In calling the main character of this story "Tom," Wright is implying that he is a submissive black, an "Uncle Tom."

2. One should keep in mind the fact that a natural disaster such as a flood hurt the plantation owner just as much as the sharecropper.

3. Too often, we forget that there were as many risks in the sharecropper arrangement for the plantation owners as there were for the farmers. The latter might be lazy workers, for example, or they might leave their farms before paying the owner back for the credit advanced them.

4. The arrangement between a sharecropper and a plantation owner was very similar to that between a customer with a credit card and a department store or other business.

5. Although the specific situation portrayed here may be rarer today than it was in Wright's

time, it is still very common for the rich to cheat the poor. The slum landlord is one good example.

III

TECHNIQUES

Intention and Theme

In judging the writer's intended theme for a story, it is often a good idea to look very closely at the end of the work. Something very curious happens at the end of this story, as you can see from the following quoted portion:

"Ma, tell Pa t bring me some 'lasses," begged Sally.

"Oh, Tom!"

Tom's head came out of the side of the buggy.

"Hunh?"

"Bring some 'lasses!"

"Hunh?"

"Bring some 'lasses for Sal!"

What reason or reasons might the author have had for repeating the word " 'lasses" (molasses) three times in seven lines in this important position in the story?

Another interesting fact is that the story ends with reference to the mother and daughter, thus giving a certain emphasis to them rather than to the sharecropper or the plantation owner. What effect does this have on your understanding of the theme of the story?

IV

WORDS

A. A writer chooses words carefully. Choose from the given synonyms the one which you feel is most effective. (One of the choices is the word used by the author.)

1. The bed, with the mattress still on it, was like a giant casket _____ of mud. (a) made (b) forged (c) constructed (b) fabricated

2. The fine grains of floating lime _____ in the sunlight. (a) flickered (b) flared (c) gleamed (d) sparkled

3. The planks in the porch floor were _____ and warped. (a) swollen (b) distended (c) bloated (d) bulgy

4. Like a mute warning, a(n) _____ flood mark went high around the walls of the room. (a) uneven (b) oscillating (c) wavering (d) fluctuating

5. Two smashed chairs lay in a corner, as though _____ together for protection. (a) bunched (b) grouped (c) arranged (d) huddled

B. The sounds of words, besides pleasing the ear, can also help to convey meaning. The clearest instance of this is the figure of speech known as *onomatopoeia*, which refers to a word whose sound resembles the thing or action denoted by words: *buzz, clang, jangle, rustling, bubbling,* and so on. For each of the following sentences, identify the onomatopoetic words; suggest other onomatopoetic words that could be substituted for that word you have identified.

1. He took a match from the box and scratched it on his overalls.

2. The yellow water trickled.

3. In the surrounding stillness the cowbell tinkled again.

4. With his shoes sucking in mud, he went slowly around the cabin, spreading the white lime with thick fingers.

5. It was not until Tom placed his shoulder against the door and gave it a stout shove that it scraped back jerkily.

Have you ever wanted something
so badly that it seemed as if
your whole life depended on getting it?
If so, you will find it easy to identify
with Dave Saunders, the hero
of this next selection. Wright used this
as the lead story of *Eight Men*, but it was
originally published in 1940, the same
year that *Native Son* appeared.

The Man Who Was Almost a Man

Dave struck out across the fields, looking homeward through paling light. Whut's the use talkin wid em niggers in the field? Anyhow, his mother was putting supper on the table. Them niggers can't understan nothing. One of these days he was going to get a gun and practice shooting, then they couldn't talk to him as though he were a little boy. He slowed, looking at the ground. Shucks, Ah ain scareda them even ef they are biggern me! Aw, Ah know whut Ahma do. Ahm going by ol Joe's sto n git that Sears Roebuck catlog n look at them guns. Mebbe Ma will lemme buy one when she gits mah pay from ol man Hawkins. Ahma beg her t gimme some money. Ahm ol ernough to hava gun. Ahm seventeen. Almost a man. He strode, feeling his long loose-jointed limbs. Shucks, a man oughta hava little gun aftah he done worked hard all day.

He came in sight of Joe's store. A yellow lantern glowed on the front porch. He mounted steps and went through the screen door, hearing it bang behind him. There was a strong smell of coal oil and mackerel fish. He felt very confident until he saw fat Joe walk in through the rear door, then his courage began to ooze.

"Howdy, Dave! Whutcha want?"

"How yuh, Mistah Joe? Aw, Ah don wanna buy nothing. Ah jus wanted t see ef yuhd lemme look at tha catlog erwhile."

"Sure! You wanna see it here?"

"Nawsuh. Ah wants t take it home wid me. Ah'll bring it back termorrow when Ah come in from the fiels."

"You plannin on buying something?"

"Yessuh."

"Your ma lettin you have your own money now?"

"Shucks. Mistah Joe, Ahm gittin t be a man like anybody else!"

Joe laughed and wiped his greasy white face with a red bandanna.

"Whut you plannin on buyin?"

Dave looked at the floor, scratched his head, scratched his thigh, and smiled. Then he looked up shyly.

"Ah'll tell yuh, Mistah Joe, if yuh promise yuh won't tell."

"I promise."

"Waal, Ahma buy a gun."

"A gun? What you want with a gun?"

"Ah wanna keep it."

"You ain't nothing but a boy. You don't need a gun."

"Aw, lemme have the catlog, Mistah Joe. Ah'll bring it back."

Joe walked through the rear door. Dave was elated. He looked around at barrels of sugar and flour. He heard Joe coming back. He craned his neck to see if he were bringing the book. Yeah, he's got it. Gawddog, he's got it!

"Here, but be sure you bring it back. It's the only one I got."

"Sho, Mistah Joe."

"Say, if you wanna buy a gun, why don't you buy one from me? I gotta gun to sell."

"Will it shoot?"

"Sure it'll shoot."

"Whut kind is it?"

"Oh, it's kinda old . . . a left-hand Wheeler.

Reprinted by permission of The World Publishing Company from *Eight Men* by Richard Wright. Copyright © 1961, 1940 by Richard Wright.

A pistol. A big one."

"Is it got bullets in it?"

"It's loaded."

"Kin Ah see it?"

"Where's your money?"

"What yuh wan fer it?"

"I'll let you have it for two dollars."

"Just two dollahs? Shucks, Ah could buy tha when Ah git mah pay."

"I'll have it here when you want it."

"Awright, suh. Ah be in fer it."

He went through the door, hearing it slam again behind him. Ahma git some money from Ma n buy me a gun! Only two dollahs! He tucked the thick catalogue under his arm and hurried.

"Where yuh been, boy?" His mother held a steaming dish of black-eyed peas.

"Aw, Ma, Ah jus stopped down the road t talk wid the boys."

"Yuh know bettah t keep suppah waitin."

He sat down, resting the catalogue on the edge of the table.

"Yuh git up from there and git to the well n wash yosef! Ah ain feedin no hogs in mah house!"

She grabbed his shoulder and pushed him. He stumbled out of the room, then came back to get the catalogue.

"Whut this?"

"Aw, Ma, it's jusa catlog."

"Who yuh git it from?"

"From Joe, down at the sto."

"Waal, thas good. We kin use it in the outhouse."

"Naw, Ma." He grabbed for it. "Gimme ma catlog, Ma."

She held onto it and glared at him.

"Quit hollerin at me! Whut's wrong wid yuh? Yuh crazy?"

"But Ma, please. It ain mine! It's Joe's! He tol me t bring it back t im termorrow."

She gave up the book. He stumbled down the back steps, hugging the thick book under his arm. When he had splashed water on his face and hands, he groped back to the kitchen and fumbled in a corner for the towel. He bumped into a chair; it clattered to the floor. The catalogue sprawled at his feet. When he had dried his eyes he snatched up the book and held it again under his arm. His mother stood watching him.

"Now, ef yuh gonna act a fool over that ol book, Ah'll take it n burn it up."

"Naw, Ma, please."

"Waal, set down n be still!"

He sat down and drew the oil lamp close. He thumbed page after page, unaware of the food his mother set on the table. His father came in. Then his small brother.

"Whutcha got there, Dave?" his father asked.

"Jusa catlog," he answered, not looking up.

"Yeah, here they is!" His eyes glowed at blue-and-black revolvers. He glanced up, feeling sudden guilt. His father was watching him. He eased the book under the table and rested it on his knees. After the blessing was asked, he ate. He scooped up peas and swallowed fat meat without chewing. Buttermilk helped to wash it down. He did not want to mention money before his father. He would do much better by cornering his mother when she was alone. He looked at his father uneasily out of the edge of his eye.

"Boy, how come yuh don quit foolin wid tha book n eat yo suppah?"

"Yessuh."

"How you n ol man Hawkins gittin erlong?"

"Suh?"

"Can't yuh hear? Why don yuh lissen? Ah ast yu how wuz yuh n ol man Hawkins gittin erlong?"

"Oh, swell, Pa. Ah plows mo lan than anybody over there."

"Waal, yuh oughta keep you mind on whut yuh doin."

"Yessuh."

He poured his plate full of molasses and sopped it up slowly with a chunk of cornbread. When his father and brother had left the kitchen, he still sat and looked again at the guns in the catalogue, longing to muster courage enough to present his case to his mother.

Lawd, ef Ah only had tha pretty one! He could almost feel the slickness of the weapon with his fingers. If he had a gun like that he would polish it and keep it shining so it would never rust. N Ah'd keep it loaded, by Gawd!

"Ma?" His voice was hesitant.

"Hunh?"

"Ol man Hawkins give yuh mah money yit?"

"Yeah, but ain no usa yuh thinking bout throwin nona it erway. Ahm keepin tha money sos yuh kin have cloes t go to school this winter."

He rose and went to her side with the open catalogue in his palms. She was washing dishes, her head bent low over a pan. Shyly he raised the book. When he spoke, his voice was husky, faint.

"Ma, Gawd knows Ah wans one of these."

"One of whut?" she asked, not raising her eyes.

"One of these," he said again, not daring even to point. She glanced up at the page, then at him with wide eyes.

"Nigger, is yuh gone plumb crazy?"

"Aw, Ma——"

"Git outta here! Don yuh talk t me bout no gun! Yuh a fool!"

"Ma, Ah kin buy one fer two dollahs."

"Not ef Ah knows it, yuh ain!"

"But yuh promised me one——"

"Ah don care what Ah promised! Yuh ain nothing but a boy yit!"

"Ma, ef yuh lemme buy one Ah'll *never* ast yuh fer nothing no mo."

"Ah tol yuh t git outta here! Yuh ain gonna toucha penny of tha money fer no gun! Thas how come Ah has Mistah Hawkins t pay yo wages t me, cause Ah knows yuh ain got no sense."

"But, Ma, we needa gun. Pa ain got no gun. We needa gun in the house. Yuh kin never tell whut might happen."

"Now don yuh try to maka fool outta me, boy! Ef we did hava gun, yuh wouldn't have it!"

He laid the catalogue down and slipped his arm around her waist.

"Aw, Ma, Ah done worked hard alla summer n ain ast yuh fer nothing, is Ah, now?"

"Thas whut yuh spose t do!"

"But Ma, Ah wans a gun. Yuh kin lemme have two dollahs outta mah money. Please, Ma. I kin give it to Pa . . . Please, Ma! Ah loves yuh, Ma."

When she spoke her voice came soft and low.

"What yu wan wida gun, Dave? Yuh don need no gun. Yuh'll git in trouble. N ef yo pa jus thought Ah let yuh have money t buy a gun he'd hava fit."

"Ah'll hide it, Ma. It ain but two dollahs."

"Lawd, chil, whut's wrong wid yuh?"

"Ain nothin wrong. Ma. Ahm almos a man now. Ah wans a gun."

"Who gonna sell yuh a gun?"

"Ol Joe at the sto."

"N it don cos but two dollahs?"

"Thas all, Ma. Jus two dollahs. Please, Ma."

She was stacking the plates away; her hands moved slowly, reflectively. Dave kept an anxious silence. Finally, she turned to him.

"Ah'll let yuh git tha gun ef yuh promise me one thing."

"What's tha, Ma?"

"Yuh bring it straight back t me, yuh hear? It be fer Pa."

"Yessum! Lemme go now, Ma."

She stooped, turned slightly to one side, raised the hem of her dress, rolled down the top of her stocking, and came up with a slender wad of bills.

"Here," she said. "Lawd knows yuh don need no gun. But yer pa does. Yuh bring it right back t me, yuh hear? Ahma put it up. Now ef yuh don, Ahma have yuh pa lick yuh so hard yuh won fergit it."

"Yessum."

He took the money, ran down the steps, and across the yard.

"Dave! Yuuuuuh Daaaaave!"

He heard, but he was not going to stop now. "Naw, Lawd!"

The first movement he made the following

morning was to reach under his pillow for the gun. In the gray light of dawn he held it loosely, feeling a sense of power. Could kill a man with a gun like this. Kill anybody, black or white. And if he were holding his gun in his hand, nobody could run over him; they would have to respect him. It was a big gun, with a long barrel and a heavy handle. He raised and lowered it in his hand, marveling at its weight.

He had not come straight home with it as his mother had asked; instead he had stayed out in the fields, holding the weapon in his hand, aiming it now and then at some imaginary foe. But he had not fired it; he had been afraid that his father might hear. Also he was not sure he knew how to fire it.

To avoid surrendering the pistol he had not come into the house until he knew that they were all asleep. When his mother had tiptoed to his bedside late that night and demanded the gun, he had first played possum; then he had told her that the gun was hidden outdoors, that he would bring it to her in the morning. Now he lay turning it slowly in his hands. He broke it, took out the cartridges, felt them, and then put them back.

He slid out of bed, got a long strip of old flannel from a trunk, wrapped the gun in it, and tied it to his naked thigh while it was still loaded. He did not go in to breakfast. Even though it was not yet daylight, he started for Jim Hawkins' plantation. Just as the sun was rising he reached the barns where the mules and plows were kept.

"Hey! That you, Dave?"

He turned. Jim Hawkins stood eyeing him suspiciously.

"What're yuh doing here so early?"

"Ah didn't know Ah wuz gittin up so early, Mistah Hawkins. Ah was fixin t hitch up ol Jenny n take her t the fiels."

"Good. Since you're so early, how about plowing that stretch down by the woods?"

"Suits me, Mistah Hawkins."

"O.K. Go to it!"

He hitched Jenny to a plow and started across the fields. Hot dog! This was just what he wanted. If he could get down by the woods, he could shoot his gun and nobody would hear. He walked behind the plow, hearing the traces creaking, feeling the gun tied tight to his thigh.

When he reached the woods, he plowed two whole rows before he decided to take out the gun. Finally, he stopped, looked in all directions, then untied the gun and held it in his hand. He turned to the mule and smiled.

"Know whut this is, Jenny? Naw, yuh wouldn know! Yuhs jusa ol mule! Anyhow, this is a gun, n it kin shoot, by Gawd!"

He held the gun at arm's length. Whut t hell, Ahma shoot this thing! He looked at Jenny again.

"Lissen here, Jenny! When Ah pull this ol trigger, Ah don wan yuh t run n acka fool now!"

Jenny stood with head down, her short ears pricked straight. Dave walked off about twenty feet, held the gun far out from him at arm's length, and turned his head. He told himself, Ah ain afraid. The gun felt loose in his fingers; he waved it wildly for a moment. Then he shut his eyes and tightened his forefinger. Bloom! A report half deafened him and he thought his right hand was torn from his arm. He heard Jenny whinnying and galloping over the field, and he found himself on his knees, squeezing his fingers hard between his legs. His hand was numb; he jammed it into his mouth, trying to warm it, trying to stop the pain. The gun lay at his feet. He did not quite know what had happened. He stood up and stared at the gun as though it were a living thing. He gritted his teeth and kicked the gun. Yuh almos broke mah arm! He turned to look for Jenny; she was far over the fields, tossing her head and kicking wildly.

"Hol on there, ol mule!"

When he caught up with her she stood trembling, walling her big white eyes at him. The plow was far away; the traces had broken. Then Dave stopped short, looking, not believing. Jenny was bleeding. Her left side was red and wet with blood. He went closer. Lawd, have mercy! Wondah did Ah shoot this mule? He grabbed for Jenny's mane. She flinched, snorted, whirled, tossing her head.

"Hol on now! Hol on."

Then he saw the hole in Jenny's side, right between the ribs. It was round, wet, red. A crimson stream streaked down the front leg, flowing fast. Good Gawd! Ah wuzn't shootin at tha mule. He felt panic. He knew he had to stop that blood, or Jenny would bleed to death. He had never seen so much blood in all his life. He chased the mule for half a mile, trying to catch her. Finally she stopped, breathing hard, stumpy tail half arched. He caught her mane and led her back to where the plow and gun lay. Then he stooped and grabbed handfuls of damp black earth and tried to plug the bullet hole. Jenny shuddered, whinnied, and broke from him.

"Hol on! Hol on now!"

He tried to plug it again, but blood came anyhow. His fingers were hot and sticky. He rubbed dirt into his palms, trying to dry them. Then again he attempted to plug the bullet hole, but Jenny shied away, kicking her heels high. He stood helpless. He had to do something. He ran at Jenny; she dodged him. He watched a red stream of blood flow down Jenny's leg and form a bright pool at her feet.

"Jenny . . . Jenny," he called weakly.

His lips trembled. She's bleeding t death! He looked in the direction of home, wanting to go back, wanting to get help. But he saw the pistol lying in the damp black clay. He had a queer feeling that if he only did something, this would not be; Jenny would not be there bleeding to death.

When he went to her this time, she did not move. She stood with sleepy, dreamy eyes; and when he touched her she gave a low-pitched whinny and knelt to the ground, her front knees slopping in blood.

"Jenny . . . Jenny . . ." he whispered.

For a long time she held her neck erect; then her head sank, slowly. Her ribs swelled with a mighty heave and she went over.

Dave's stomach felt empty, very empty. He picked up the gun and held it gingerly between his thumb and forefinger. He buried it at the foot of a tree. He took a stick and tried to cover the pool of blood with dirt—but what was the use? There was Jenny lying with her mouth open and her eyes walled and glassy. He could not tell Jim Hawkins he had shot his mule. But he had to tell something. Yeah, Ah'll tell em Jenny started gittin wil n fell on the joint of the plow. . . . But that would hardly happen to a mule. He walked across the field slowly, head down.

It was sunset. Two of Jim Hawkins' men were over near the edge of the woods digging a hole in which to bury Jenny. Dave was surrounded by a knot of people, all of whom were looking down at the dead mule.

"I don't see how in the world it happened," said Jim Hawkins for the tenth time.

The crowd parted and Dave's mother, father, and small brother pushed into the center.

"Where Dave?" his mother called.

"There he is," said Jim Hawkins.

His mother grabbed him.

"Whut happened, Dave? Whut yuh done?"

"Nothin."

"C mon, boy, talk," his father said.

Dave took a deep breath and told the story he knew nobody believed.

"Waal," he drawled. "Ah brung ol Jenny down here sos Ah could do mah plowin. Ah plowed bout two rows, just like yuh see." He stopped and pointed at the long rows of upturned earth. "Then somethin musta been wrong wid ol Jenny. She wouldn ack right a-tall. She started snortin n kickin her heels. Ah tried t hol her, but she pulled erway, rearin n goin in. Then when the point of the plow was stickin up in the air, she swung erroun' n twisted herself back on it . . . She stuck herself n started t bleed. N fo Ah could do anything, she wuz dead."

"Did you ever hear of anything like that in

all your life?" asked Jim Hawkins.

There were white and black standing in the crowd. They murmured. Dave's mother came close to him and looked hard into his face. "Tell the truth, Dave," she said.

"Looks like a bullet hole to me," said one man.

"Dave, whut yuh do wid the gun?" his mother asked.

The crowd surged in, looking at him. He jammed his hands into his pockets, shook his head slowly from left to right, and backed away. His eyes were wide and painful.

"Did he hava gun?" asked Jim Hawkins.

"By Gawd, Ah tol yuh tha wuz a gun wound," said a man, slapping his thigh.

His father caught his shoulders and shook him till his teeth rattled.

"Tell whut happened, yuh rascal! Tell whut . . ."

Dave looked at Jenny's stiff legs and began to cry.

"Whut yuh do wid tha gun?" his mother asked.

"Whut wuz he doin wida gun?" his father asked.

"Come on and tell the truth," said Hawkins. "Ain't nobody going to hurt you . . ."

His mother crowded close to him.

"Did yuh shoot tha mule, Dave?"

Dave cried, seeing blurred white and black faces.

"Ahh ddinn gggo tt sshooot hher . . . Ah ssswear ffo Gawd Ahh ddin. . . . Ah wuz a-tryin t sssee ef the old gggun would sshoot—"

"Where yuh git the gun from?" his father asked.

"Ah got it from Joe, at the sto."

"Where yuh git the money?"

"Ma give it t me."

"He kept worryin me, Bob. Ah had t. Ah tol im t bring the gun right back t me . . . It was fer yuh, the gun."

"But how yuh happen to shoot that mule?" asked Jim Hawkins.

"Ah wuzn shootin at the mule, Mistah Haw-kins. The gun jumped when Ah pulled the trigger. . . . N fo Ah knowed anythin Jenny was there a-bleedin."

Somebody in the crowd laughed. Jim Hawkins walked close to Dave and looked into his face.

"Well, looks like you have bought you a mule, Dave."

"Ah swear fo Gawd, Ah didn go t kill the mule, Mistah Hawkins!"

"But you killed her!"

All the crowd was laughing now. They stood on tiptoe and poked heads over one another's shoulders.

"Well, boy, looks like yuh done bought a dead mule! Hahaha!"

"Ain that ershame."

"Hohohohoho."

Dave stood, head down, twisting his feet in the dirt.

"Well, you needn't worry about it, Bob," said Jim Hawkins to Dave's father. "Just let the boy keep on working and pay me two dollars a month."

"Whut yuh wan fer yo mule, Mistah Haw-kins?"

Jim Hawkins screwed up his eyes.

"Fifty dollars."

"Whut yuh do wid that gun?" Dave's father demanded.

Dave said nothing.

"Yuh wan me t take a tree n beat yuh till yuh talk!"

"Nawsuh!"

"Whut yuh do wid it?"

"Ah throwed it erway."

"Where?"

"Ah . . . Ah throwed it in the creek."

"Waal, c mon home. N firs thing in the mawnin git to tha creek n fin tha gun."

"Yessuh."

"Whut yuh pay fer it?"

"Two dollahs."

"Take tha gun n git yo money back n carry it t Mistah Hawkins, yuh hear? N don fergit Ahma lam you black bottom good fer this! Now march yosef on home, suh!"

Dave turned and walked slowly. He heard people laughing. Dave glared, his eyes welling with tears. Hot anger bubbled in him. Then he swallowed and stumbled on.

That night Dave did not sleep. He was glad that he had gotten out of killing the mule so easily, but he was hurt. Something hot seemed to turn over inside him each time he remembered how they had laughed. He tossed on his bed, feeling his hard pillow. N Pa says he's gonna beat me . . . He remembered other beatings, and his back quivered. Naw, naw, Ah sho don wan im t beat me tha way no mo. Nobody ever gave him anything. All he did was work. They treat me like a mule, n then they beat me. He gritted his teeth. N Ma had t tell on me.

Well, if he had to, he would take old man Hawkins that two dollars. But that meant selling the gun. And he wanted to keep that gun. Fifty dollars for a dead mule.

He turned over, thinking how he had fired the gun. He had an itch to fire it again. Ef other men kin shoota gun, by Gawd, Ah kin! He was still, listening. Mebbe they all sleepin now. The house was still. He heard the soft breathing of his brother. Yes, now! He would go down and get that gun and see if he could fire it! He eased out of bed and slipped into overalls.

The moon was bright. He ran almost all the way to the edge of the woods. He stumbled over the ground, looking for the spot where he had buried the gun. Yeah, here it is. Like a hungry dog scratching for a bone, he pawed it up. He puffed his black cheeks and blew dirt from the trigger and barrel. He broke it and found four cartridges unshot. He looked around; the fields were filled with silence and moonlight. He clutched the gun stiff and hard in his fingers. But, as soon as he wanted to pull the trigger, he shut his eyes and turned his head. Naw, Ah can't shoot wid mah eyes closed n mah head turned. With effort he held his eyes open; then he squeezed. *Blooooom!* He was stiff, not breathing. The gun was still in his hands. He'd done it!

He fired again. *Blooooom!* He smiled. *Blooooom! Blooooom! Click, click.* There! It was empty. If anybody could shoot a gun, he could. He put the gun into his hip pocket and started across the fields.

When he reached the top of a ridge he stood straight and proud in the moonlight, looking at Jim Hawkins' big white house, feeling the gun sagging in his pocket. Lawd, ef Ah had just one mo bullet Ah'd taka shot at tha house. Ah'd like t scare ol man Hawkins jusa little . . . Jusa enough t let im know Dave Saunders is a man.

To his left the road curved, running to the tracks of the Illinois Central. He jerked his head, listening. From far off came a faint *hoooof-hooooof; hooooof-hooooof.* . . . He stood rigid. Two dollahs a mont. Les see now . . . Tha means it'll take about two years. Shucks!

He started down the road, toward the tracks. Yeah, here she comes! He stood beside the track and held himself stiffly. Here she comes, erroun the ben . . . C mon, yuh slow poke! C mon! He had his hand on his gun; something quivered in his stomach. Then the train thundered past, the gray and brown box cars rumbling and clinking. He gripped the gun tightly; then he jerked his hand out of his pocket. Ah betcha Bill wouldn't do it! Ah betcha . . . The cars slid past, steel grinding upon steel. Ahm ridin yuh ternight, so hep me Gawd! He was hot all over. He hesitated just a moment; then he grabbed, pulled atop of a car, and lay flat. He felt his pocket; the gun was still there. Ahead the long rails were glinting in the moonlight, stretching away, away to somewhere, somewhere where he could be a man . . .

I

TO BECOME A MAN

When a desire is as strong as Dave's desire for a gun, it is often a sign that the object desired is, in a sense, more than an object. Dave does not seem to want the gun for the sake of recreation—target practice or hunting, for example. Nor does he seem to need it to defend himself or to kill others. It is not, therefore, what the gun is or what it can do that directly matters to Dave, but what it stands for or symbolizes—his becoming a man.

II
IMPLICATIONS

What symbols of manhood other than a gun can you think of? Which one do you value the most? Why might a gun be an especially appropriate symbol of manhood for Dave?

Do you know of any symbols of manhood from other cultures or from times previous to your own? (For example, one's first pair of long pants used to be a symbol of manhood. Why is this no longer a manhood symbol?)

Why is the achievement of manhood so important to Dave Saunders? To people in general?

III
TECHNIQUES

Intention

Did Richard Wright intend his readers to think that Dave had become a man?

To answer this question, you might begin by considering what becoming a man involves. Then look closely at the details of the story. For instance, what is the significance of each of the following:

1. The title of the story
2. Dave's initial inability to shoot the gun properly
3. Dave's refusal to accept the responsibility for having shot the mule
4. Dave's desire to scare old man Hawkins by shooting at his house
5. Dave's running away at the end of the story

Theme

If you concluded that Wright intended for Dave to become a man, would you say that this is the theme of the story? Why or why not? If, in contrast, you concluded that Wright did not in-

tend for Dave to become a man, would you say that that is the theme? This would be a sort of *negative* theme. Why might an author write a story with a negative theme?

IV
WORDS

A. Wright uses many unorthodox spellings and constructions in transcribing the Southern dialect. Instead of saying "I can buy one for two dollars," one of Wright's characters would say, "Ah kin buy one fer two dollahs." Write each of the following sentences in Southern dialect.

1. I told you to get out of here.
2. Now don't you try to make a fool out of me.
3. I will let you get that gun if you promise me one thing.
4. Oh, mother, I just stopped down the road to talk with the boys.
5. I wasn't shooting at the mule, Mr. Hawkins.
6. When I pull this old trigger, I don't want you to run and act like a fool now.

B. Writers choose their words carefully. Determine whether each sentence is weakened or improved by the substitution of the given synonym for the italicized word.

1. Like a hungry dog scratching for a bone, he *pawed* it up.   dug
2. Then the train thundered past, the gray and brown box cars rumbling and *clinking*.   tinkling
3. He poured his plate full of molasses and *sopped* it up slowly with a chunk of cornbread. mopped
4. He laid the catalogue down and *slipped* his arm around her waist.   put
5. Joe laughed and *wiped* his greasy white face with a red bandanna.   swabbed
6. When he reached the top of a ridge he stood straight and proud in the moonlight, looking at Jim Hawkins' big white house, feeling the gun *sagging* in his pocket.   resting
7. He *slid* out of bed, got a long strip of old flannel from a trunk, wrapped the gun in it, and tied it to his naked thigh.   slithered

Rarely does a writer of fiction
begin an autobiography while still
in his early thirties, and Richard Wright
at first did not respond very positively
when his literary agent suggested that he
think about writing one. But the idea
grew upon him, often interfering with the
novel on which he was working.
Finally, seeing that he could use his own youth
as a symbol of what white America
had done to the black, he decided
to do the book. Surprisingly, there are no
white villains in *Black Boy*. As you will see
in this first chapter, blacks, and even
Wright himself, are as much responsible for
the horrors of his early years as whites are.

FROM

Black Boy

CHAPTER I

One winter morning in the long-ago, four-year-old days of my life I found myself standing before a fireplace, warming my hands over a mound of glowing coals, listening to the wind whistle past the house outside. All morning my mother had been scolding me, telling me to keep still, warning me that I must make no noise. And I was angry, fretful, and impatient. In the next room Granny lay ill and under the day and night care of a doctor and I knew that I would be punished if I did not obey. I crossed restlessly to the window and pushed back the long fluffy white curtains—

From Chapter 1, *Black Boy* by Richard Wright (Perennial Edition). Copyright 1937, 1942, 1944, 1945 by Richard Wright. Reprinted by permission of Harper & Row, Publishers, Incorporated.

which I had been forbidden to touch—and looked yearningly out into the empty street. I was dreaming of running and playing and shouting, but the vivid image of Granny's old, white, wrinkled, grim face, framed by a halo of tumbling black hair, lying upon a huge feather pillow, made me afraid.

The house was quiet. Behind me my brother—a year younger than I—was playing placidly upon the floor with a toy. A bird wheeled past the window and I greeted it with a glad shout.

"You better hush," my brother said.

"You shut up," I said.

My mother stepped briskly into the room and closed the door behind her. She came to me and shook her finger in my face.

"You stop that yelling, you hear?" she whispered. "You know Granny's sick and you better keep quiet!"

I hung my head and sulked. She left and I ached with boredom.

"I told you so," my brother gloated.

"You shut up," I told him again.

I wandered listlessly about the room, trying to think of something to do, dreading the return of my mother, resentful of being neglected. The room held nothing of interest except the fire and finally I stood before the shimmering embers, fascinated by the quivering coals. An idea of a new kind of game grew and took root in my mind. Why not throw something into the fire and watch it burn? I looked about. There was only my picture book and my mother would beat me if I burned that. Then what? I hunted around until I saw the broom leaning in a closet. That's it . . . Who would bother about a few straws if I burned them? I pulled out the broom and tore out a batch of straws and tossed them into the fire and watched them smoke, turn black, blaze, and finally become white wisps of ghosts that vanished. Burning straws was a teasing kind of fun and I took more of them from the broom and cast them into the fire. My brother came to my side, his eyes drawn by the blazing straws.

"Don't do that," he said.

"How come?" I asked.

"You'll burn the whole broom," he said.

"You hush," I said.

"I'll tell," he said.

"And I'll hit you," I said.

My idea was growing, blooming. Now I was wondering just how the long fluffy white curtains would look if I lit a bunch of straws and held it under them. Would I try it? Sure. I pulled several straws from the broom and held them to the fire until they blazed; I rushed to the window and brought the flame in touch with the hems of the curtains. My brother shook his head.

"Naw," he said.

He spoke too late. Red circles were eating into the white cloth; then a flare of flames shot out. Startled, I backed away. The fire soared to the ceiling and I trembled with fright. Soon a sheet of yellow lit the room. I was terrified; I wanted to scream but was afraid. I looked around for my brother; he was gone. One half of the room was now ablaze. Smoke was choking me and the fire was licking at my face, making me gasp.

I made for the kitchen; smoke was surging there too. Soon my mother would smell that smoke and see the fire and come and beat me. I had done something wrong, something which I could not hide or deny. Yes, I would run away and never come back. I ran out of the kitchen and into the back yard. Where could I go? Yes, under the house! Nobody would find me there. I crawled under the house and crept into a dark hollow of a brick chimney and balled myself into a tight knot. My mother must not find me and whip me for what I had done. Anyway, it was all an accident; I had not really intended to set the house afire. I had just wanted to see how the curtains would look when they burned. And neither did it occur to me that I was hiding under a burning house.

Presently footsteps pounded on the floor above me. Then I heard screams. Later the gongs of fire wagons and the clopping hoofs of horses came from the direction of the street. Yes, there was really a fire, a fire like the one I had seen one day burn a house down to the ground, leaving only a chimney standing black. I was stiff with terror. The thunder of sound above me shook the chimney to which I clung. The screams came louder. I saw the image of my grandmother lying helplessly upon her bed and there were yellow flames in her black hair. Was my mother afire? Would my brother burn? Perhaps everybody in the house would burn! Why had I not thought of those things before I fired the curtains? I yearned to become invisible, to stop living. The commotion above me increased and I began to cry. It seemed that I had been hiding for ages, and when the stomping and screaming died down I felt lonely, cast forever out of life. Voices sounded near-by and I shivered.

"Richard!" my mother was calling frantically.

I saw her legs and the hem of her dress moving swiftly about the back yard. Her wails were full of an agony whose intensity told me that my punishment would be measured by its depth. Then I saw her taut face peering under the edge of the house. She had found me! I held my breath and waited to hear her command me to come to her. Her face went away; no, she had not seen me huddled in the dark nook of the chimney. I tucked my head into my arms and my teeth chattered.

"Richard!"

The distress I sensed in her voice was as sharp and painful as the lash of a whip on my flesh.

"Richard! The house is on fire. Oh, find my child!"

Yes, the house was afire, but I was determined not to leave my place of safety. Finally I saw another face peering under the edge of the house; it was my father's. His eyes must have become accustomed to the shadows, for he was now pointing at me.

"There he is!"

"Naw!" I screamed.

"Come here, boy!"

"Naw!"

"The house is on fire!"

"Leave me 'lone!"

He crawled to me and caught hold of one of my legs. I hugged the edge of the brick chimney with all of my strength. My father yanked my leg and I clawed at the chimney harder.

"Come outta there, you little fool!"

"Turn me loose!"

I could not withstand the tugging at my leg and my fingers relaxed. It was over. I would be beaten. I did not care any more. I knew what was coming. He dragged me into the back yard and the instant his hand left me I jumped to my feet and broke into a wild run, trying to elude the people who surrounded me, heading for the street. I was caught before I had gone ten paces.

From that moment on things became tangled for me. Out of the weeping and the shouting and the wild talk, I learned that no one had died in the fire. My brother, it seemed, had finally overcome enough of his panic to warn my mother, but not before more than half the house had been destroyed. Using the mattress as a stretcher, Grandpa and an uncle had lifted Granny from her bed and had rushed her to the safety of a neighbor's house. My long absence and silence had made everyone think, for a while, that I had perished in the blaze.

"You almost scared us to death," my mother muttered as she stripped the leaves from a tree limb to prepare it for my back.

I was lashed so hard and long that I lost consciousness. I was beaten out of my senses and later I found myself in bed, screaming, determined to run away, tussling with my mother and father who were trying to keep me still. I was lost in a fog of fear. A doctor was called—I was afterwards told—and he ordered that I be kept abed, that I be kept quiet, that my very life depended upon it. My body seemed on fire and I could not sleep. Packs of ice were put on my forehead to keep down the fever. Whenever I tried to sleep I would see huge wobbly white bags, like the full udders of cows, suspended from the ceiling above me. Later, as I grew worse, I could see the bags in the daytime with my eyes open and I was gripped by the fear that they were going to fall and drench me with some horrible liquid. Day and night I begged my mother and father to take the bags away, pointing to them, shaking with terror because no one saw them but me. Exhaustion would make me drift toward sleep and then I would scream until I was wide awake again; I was afraid to sleep. Time finally bore me away from the dangerous bags and I got well. But for a long time I was chastened whenever I remembered that my mother had come close to killing me.

Each event spoke with a cryptic tongue. And the moments of living slowly revealed their coded meanings. There was the wonder I felt when I first saw a brace of mountainlike, spotted, black-and-white horses clopping down a dusty road through clouds of powdered clay.

There was the delight I caught in seeing long straight rows of red and green vegetables stretching away in the sun to the bright horizon.

There was the faint, cool kiss of sensuality when dew came on to my cheeks and shins as I ran down the wet green garden paths in the early morning.

There was the vague sense of the infinite as I looked down upon the yellow, dreaming waters of the Mississippi River from the verdant bluffs of Natchez.[1]

There were the echoes of nostalgia I heard in the crying strings of wild geese winging south against a bleak, autumn sky.

There was the tantalizing melancholy in the tingling scent of burning hickory wood.

There was the teasing and impossible desire to imitate the petty pride of sparrows

1. **verdant bluffs of Natchez,** green cliffs of Natchez, Mississippi.

wallowing and flouncing in the red dust of country roads.

There was the yearning for identification loosed in me by the sight of a solitary ant carrying a burden upon a mysterious journey.

There was the disdain that filled me as I tortured a delicate, blue-pink crawfish[2] that huddled fearfully in the mudsill[3] of a rusty tin can.

There was the aching glory in masses of clouds burning gold and purple from an invisible sun.

There was the liquid alarm I saw in the blood-red glare of the sun's afterglow mirrored in the squared panes of whitewashed frame houses.

There was the languor I felt when I heard green leaves rustling with a rainlike sound.

There was the incomprehensible secret embodied in a whitish toadstool hiding in the dark shade of a rotting log.

There was the experience of feeling death without dying that came from watching a chicken leap about blindly after its neck had been snapped by a quick twist of my father's wrist.

There was the great joke that I felt God had played on cats and dogs by making them lap their milk and water with their tongues.

There was the thirst I had when I watched clear, sweet juice trickle from sugar cane being crushed.

There was the hot panic that welled up in my throat and swept through my blood when I first saw the lazy, limp coils of a blue-skinned snake sleeping in the sun.

There was the speechless astonishment of seeing a hog stabbed through the heart, dipped into boiling water, scraped, split open, gutted, and strung up gaping and bloody.

There was the love I had for the mute regality[4] of tall moss-clad oaks.

There was the hint of cosmic cruelty that I felt when I saw the curved timbers of a wooden shack that had been warped in the summer sun.

There was the saliva that formed in my mouth whenever I smelt clay dust potted with fresh rain.

There was the cloudy notion of hunger when I breathed the odor of new-cut, bleeding grass.

And there was the quiet terror that suffused my senses when vast hazes of gold washed earthward from star-heavy skies on silent nights . . .

One day my mother told me that we were going to Memphis on a boat, the *Kate Adams*, and my eagerness thereafter made the days seem endless. Each night I went to bed hoping that the next morning would be the day of departure.

"How big is the boat?" I asked my mother.

"As big as a mountain," she said.

"Has it got a whistle?"

"Yes."

"Does the whistle blow?"

"Yes."

"When?"

"When the captain wants it to blow."

"Why do they call it the *Kate Adams*?"

"Because that's the boat's name."

"What color is the boat?"

"White."

"How long will we be on the boat?"

"All day and all night."

"Will we sleep on the boat?"

"Yes, when we get sleepy, we'll sleep. Now, hush."

For days I had dreamed about a huge white boat floating on a vast body of water, but when my mother took me down to the levee[5] on the day of leaving, I saw a tiny, dirty boat that was not at all like the boat I had imagined. I was disappointed and when time came to go on board I cried and my mother thought that I did not want to go with her to Memphis,

---

2. crawfish\ˈkrɔ ˈfish\ a small, freshwater shellfish.
3. mudsill\ˈmŭd·sĭl\ the lowest timber in the foundation of a structure.
4. mute regality, silent authority.
5. levee\ˈlĕv·ē\ landing place along the bank of a river.

and I could not tell her what the trouble was. Solace came when I wandered about the boat and gazed at Negroes throwing dice, drinking whisky, playing cards, lolling on boxes, eating, talking, and singing. My father took me down into the engine room and the throbbing machines enthralled me for hours.

In Memphis we lived in a one-story brick tenement. The stone buildings and the concrete pavements looked bleak and hostile to me. The absence of green, growing things made the city seem dead. Living space for the four of us—my mother, my brother, my father, and me—was a kitchen and a bedroom. In the front and rear were paved areas in which my brother and I could play, but for days I was afraid to go into the strange city streets alone.

It was in this tenement that the personality of my father first came fully into the orbit of my concern. He worked as a night porter in a Beale Street drugstore and he became important and forbidding to me only when I learned that I could not make noise when he was asleep in the daytime. He was the law-giver in our family and I never laughed in his presence. I used to lurk timidly in the kitchen doorway and watch his huge body sitting slumped at the table. I stared at him with awe as he gulped his beer from a tin bucket, as he ate long and heavily, sighed, belched, closed his eyes to nod on a stuffed belly. He was quite fat and his bloated stomach always lapped over his belt. He was always a stranger to me, always somehow alien and remote.

One morning my brother and I, while playing in the rear of our flat, found a stray kitten that set up a loud, persistent meowing. We fed it some scraps of food and gave it water, but it still meowed. My father, clad in his underwear, stumbled sleepily to the back door and demanded that we keep quiet. We told him that it was the kitten that was making the noise and he ordered us to drive it away. We tried to make the kitten leave, but it would not budge. My father took a hand.

"Scat!" he shouted.

The scrawny kitten lingered, brushing itself

against our legs, and meowing plaintively.

"Kill that thing!" my father exploded. "Do anything, but get it away from here!"

He went inside, grumbling. I resented his shouting and it irked me that I could never make him feel my resentment. How could I hit back at him? Oh, yes ... He had said to kill the kitten and I would kill it! I knew that he had not really meant for me to kill the kitten, but my deep hate of him urged me toward a literal acceptance of his word.

"He said for us to kill the kitten," I told my brother.

"He didn't mean it," my brother said.

"He did, and I'm going to kill 'im."

"Then he *will* howl," my brother said.

"He can't howl if he's dead," I said.

"He didn't really say kill 'im," my brother protested.

"He did!" I said. "And you heard him!"

My brother ran away in fright. I found a piece of rope, made a noose, slipped it about the kitten's neck, pulled it over a nail, then jerked the animal clear of the ground. It gasped, slobbered, spun, doubled, clawed the air frantically; finally its mouth gaped and its pink-white tongue shot out stiffly. I tied the rope to a nail and went to find my brother. He was crouching behind a corner of the building.

"I killed 'im," I whispered.

"You did bad," my brother said.

"Now Papa can sleep," I said, deeply satisfied.

"He didn't mean for you to kill 'im," my brother said.

"Then why did he *tell* me to do it?" I demanded.

My brother could not answer; he stared fearfully at the dangling kitten.

"That kitten's going to get you," he warned me.

"That kitten can't even breathe now," I said.

"I'm going to tell," my brother said, running into the house.

I waited, resolving to defend myself with my father's rash words, anticipating my enjoyment in repeating them to him even though I knew that he had spoken them in anger. My mother hurried toward me, drying her hands upon her apron. She stopped and paled when she saw the kitten suspended from the rope.

"What in God's name have you done?" she asked.

"The kitten was making noise and Papa said to kill it," I explained.

"You little fool!" she said. "Your father's going to beat you for this!"

"But he told me to kill it," I said.

"You shut your mouth!"

She grabbed my hand and dragged me to my father's bedside and told him what I had done.

"You know better than that!" my father stormed.

"You told me to kill 'im," I said.

"I told you to drive him away," he said.

"You told me to kill 'im," I countered positively.

"You get out of my eyes before I smack you down!" my father bellowed in disgust, then turned over in bed.

I had had my first triumph over my father. I had made him believe that I had taken his words literally. He could not punish me now without risking his authority. I was happy because I had at last found a way to throw my criticism of him into his face. I had made him feel that, if he whipped me for killing the kitten, I would never give serious weight to his words again. I had made him know that I felt he was cruel and I had done it without his punishing me.

But my mother, being more imaginative, retaliated with an assault upon my sensibilities that crushed me with the moral horror involved in taking a life. All that afternoon she directed toward me calculated words that spawned in my mind a horde of invisible demons bent upon exacting vengeance for what I had done. As evening drew near, anxiety filled me and I was afraid to go into an empty room alone.

"You owe a debt you can never pay," my mother said.

"I'm sorry," I mumbled.

"Being sorry can't make that kitten live again," she said.

Then, just before I was to go to bed, she uttered a paralyzing injunction: she ordered me to go out into the dark, dig a grave, and bury the kitten.

"No!" I screamed, feeling that if I went out of doors some evil spirit would whisk me away.

"Get out there and bury that poor kitten," she ordered.

"I'm scared!"

"And wasn't that kitten scared when you put that rope around its neck?" she asked.

"But it was only a kitten," I explained.

"But it was alive," she said. "Can you make it live again?"

"But Papa said to kill it," I said, trying to shift the moral blame upon my father.

My mother whacked me across my mouth with the flat palm of her hand.

"You stop that lying! You knew what he meant!"

"I didn't!" I bawled.

She shoved a tiny spade into my hands.

"Go out there and dig a hole and bury that kitten!"

I stumbled out into the black night, sobbing, my legs wobbly from fear. Though I knew that I had killed the kitten, my mother's words had made it live again in my mind. What would that kitten do to me when I touched it? Would it claw at my eyes? As I groped toward the dead kitten, my mother lingered behind me, unseen in the dark, her disembodied voice egging me on.

"Mama, come and stand by me," I begged.

"You didn't stand by that kitten, so why should I stand by you?" she asked tauntingly from the menacing darkness.

"I can't touch it," I whimpered, feeling that the kitten was staring at me with reproachful eyes.

"Untie it!" she ordered.

Shuddering, I fumbled at the rope and the kitten dropped to the pavement with a thud that echoed in my mind for many days and nights. Then, obeying my mother's floating voice, I hunted for a spot of earth, dug a shallow hole, and buried the stiff kitten; as I handled its cold body my skin prickled. When I had completed the burial, I sighed and started back to the flat, but my mother caught hold of my hand and led me again to the kitten's grave.

"Shut your eyes and repeat after me," she said.

I closed my eyes tightly, my hand clinging to hers.

"Dear God, our Father, forgive me, for I knew not what I was doing..."

"Dear God, our Father, forgive me, for I knew not what I was doing," I repeated.

"And spare my poor life, even though I did not spare the life of the kitten..."

"And spare my poor life, even though I did not spare the life of the kitten," I repeated.

"And while I sleep tonight, do not snatch the breath of life from me..."

I opened my mouth but no words came. My mind was frozen with horror. I pictured myself gasping for breath and dying in my sleep. I broke away from my mother and ran into the night, crying, shaking with dread.

"No," I sobbed.

My mother called to me many times, but I would not go to her.

"Well, I suppose you've learned your lesson," she said at last.

Contrite, I went to bed, hoping that I would never see another kitten.

Hunger stole upon me so slowly that at first I was not aware of what hunger really meant. Hunger had always been more or less at my elbow when I played, but now I began to wake up at night to find hunger standing at my bedside, staring at me gauntly. The hunger I had known before this had been no grim, hostile stranger; it had been a normal hunger that had made me beg constantly for bread, and when I ate a crust or two I was satisfied. But this new hunger baffled me, scared me, made me angry and insistent. Whenever I begged for food now my mother would pour me a cup of tea which would still the clamor in my stomach for a moment or two; but a little later I would feel hunger nudging my ribs, twisting my empty guts until they ached. I would grow dizzy and my vision would dim. I became less active in my play, and for the first time in my life I had to pause and think of what was happening to me.

"Mama, I'm hungry," I complained one afternoon.

"Jump up and catch a kungry," she said, trying to make me laugh and forget.

"What's a *kungry*?"

"It's what little boys eat when they get hungry," she said.

"What does it taste like?"

"I don't know."

"Then why do you tell me to catch one?"

"Because you said that you were hungry," she said, smiling.

I sensed that she was teasing me and it made me angry.

"But I'm hungry. I want to eat."

"You'll have to wait."

"But I want to eat now."

"But there's nothing to eat," she told me.

"Why?"

"Just because there's none," she explained.

"But I want to eat," I said, beginning to cry.

"You'll just have to wait," she said again.

"But why?"

"For God to send some food."

"When is He going to send it?"

"I don't know."

"But I'm hungry!"

She was ironing and she paused and looked at me with tears in her eyes.

"Where's your father?" she asked me.

I stared in bewilderment. Yes, it was true that my father had not come home to sleep for many days now and I could make as much noise as I wanted. Though I had not known why he was absent, I had been glad that he was not there to shout his restrictions at me. But it had never occurred to me that his absence would mean that there would be no food.

"I don't know," I said.

"Who brings food into the house?" my mother asked me.

"Papa," I said. "He always brought food."

"Well, your father isn't here now," she said.

"Where is he?"

"I don't know," she said.

"But I'm hungry," I whimpered, stomping my feet.

"You'll have to wait until I get a job and buy food," she said.

As the days slid past the image of my father became associated with my pangs of hunger, and whenever I felt hunger I thought of him with a deep biological bitterness.

My mother finally went to work as a cook and left me and my brother alone in the flat each day with a loaf of bread and a pot of tea. When she returned at evening she would be tired and dispirited and would cry a lot. Sometimes, when she was in despair, she would call us to her and talk to us for hours, telling us that we now had no father, that our lives would be different from those of other children, that we must learn as soon as possible to take care of ourselves, to dress ourselves, to prepare our own food; that we must take upon ourselves the responsibility of the flat while she worked. Half frightened, we would promise solemnly. We did not understand what had happened between our father and our mother and the most that these long talks did to us was to make us feel a vague dread. Whenever we asked why father had left, she would tell us that we were too young to know.

One evening my mother told me that thereafter I would have to do the shopping for food. She took me to the corner store to show me the way. I was proud; I felt like a grownup. The next afternoon I looped the basket over my arm and went down the pavement toward the store. When I reached the corner, a gang of boys grabbed me, knocked me down, snatched the basket, took the money, and sent me running home in panic. That evening I told my mother what had happened, but she made no comment; she sat down at once, wrote another note, gave me more money, and sent me out to the grocery again. I crept down the steps and saw the same gang of boys playing down the street. I ran back into the house.

"What's the matter?" my mother asked.

"It's those same boys," I said. "They'll beat me."

"You've got to get over that," she said. "Now, go on."

"I'm scared," I said.

"Go on and don't pay any attention to them," she said.

I went out of the door and walked briskly down the sidewalk, praying that the gang would not molest me. But when I came abreast of them someone shouted.

"There he is!"

They came toward me and I broke into a wild run toward home. They overtook me and flung me to the pavement. I yelled, pleaded, kicked, but they wrenched the money out of my hand. They yanked me to my feet, gave me a few slaps, and sent me home sobbing. My mother met me at the door.

"They b-beat m-me," I gasped. "They t-t-took the m-money."

I started up the steps, seeking the shelter of the house.

"Don't you come in here," my mother warned me.

I froze in my tracks and stared at her.

"But they're coming after me," I said.

"You just stay right where you are," she said in a deadly tone. "I'm going to teach you this night to stand up and fight for yourself."

She went into the house and I waited, terrified, wondering what she was about. Presently she returned with more money and another note; she also had a long heavy stick.

"Take this money, this note, and this stick," she said. "Go to the store and buy those groceries. If those boys bother you, then fight."

I was baffled. My mother was telling me to fight, a thing that she had never done before.

"But I'm scared," I said.

"Don't you come into this house until you've gotten those groceries," she said.

"They'll beat me; they'll beat me," I said.

"Then stay in the streets; don't come back here!"

I ran up the steps and tried to force my way past her into the house. A stinging slap came on my jaw. I stood on the sidewalk, crying.

"Please, let me wait until tomorrow," I begged.

"No," she said. "Go now! If you come back into this house without those groceries, I'll whip you!"

She slammed the door and I heard the key turn in the lock. I shook with fright. I was alone upon the dark, hostile streets and gangs were after me. I had the choice of being beaten at home or away from home. I clutched the stick, crying, trying to reason. If I were beaten at home, there was absolutely nothing that I could do about it; but if I were beaten in the streets, I had a chance to fight and defend myself. I walked slowly down the sidewalk, coming closer to the gang of boys, holding the stick tightly. I was so full of fear that I could scarcely breathe. I was almost upon them now.

"There he is again!" the cry went up.

They surrounded me quickly and began to grab for my hand.

"I'll kill you!" I threatened.

They closed in. In blind fear I let the stick fly, feeling it crack against a boy's skull. I swung again, lamming another skull, then another. Realizing that they would retaliate if I let up for but a second, I fought to lay them low, to knock them cold, to kill them so that they could not strike back at me. I flayed with tears in my eyes, teeth clenched, stark fear making me throw every ounce of my strength behind each blow. I hit again and again, dropping the money and the grocery list. The boys scattered, yelling, nursing their heads, staring at me in utter disbelief. They had never seen such frenzy. I stood panting, egging them on, taunting them to come on and fight. When they refused, I ran after them and they tore out for their homes, screaming. The parents of the boys rushed into the streets and threatened me, and for the first time in my life I shouted at grownups, telling them that I would give them the same if they bothered me. I finally found my grocery list and the money and went to the store. On my way back I kept my stick poised for instant use, but there was not a single boy in sight. That night I won the right to the streets of Memphis. . . .

To keep us out of mischief, my mother often took my brother and me with her to her cooking job. Standing hungrily and silently in a corner of the kitchen, we would watch her go from the stove to the sink, from the cabinet to the table. I always loved to stand in the white folks' kitchen when my mother cooked, for it meant that I got occasional scraps of bread and meat; but many times I regretted having come, for my nostrils would be assailed with the scent of food that did not belong to me and which I was forbidden to eat. Toward evening my mother would take the hot dishes into the dining room where the white people were seated, and I would stand as near the dining-room door as possible to get a quick glimpse of the white faces gathered around the loaded table, eating, laughing, talking. If the white people left anything, my brother and I would eat well; but if they did not, we would have our usual bread and tea.

Watching the white people eat would make my empty stomach churn and I would grow vaguely angry. Why could I not eat when I was hungry? Why did I always have to wait until others were through? I could not understand why some people had enough food and others did not.

I now found it irresistible to roam during the day while my mother was cooking in the kitchens of the white folks. A block away from our flat was a saloon in front of which I used to loiter all day long. Its interior was an enchanting place that both lured and frightened me. I would beg for pennies, then peer under the swinging doors to watch the men and women drink. When some neighbor would chase me away from the door, I would follow the drunks about the streets, trying to understand their mysterious mumblings, pointing at them, teasing them, laughing at them, imitating them, jeering, mocking, and taunting them about their lurching antics. For me the most amusing spectacle was a drunken woman stumbling and urinating, the dampness seeping down her stockinged legs. Or I would stare in horror at a man retching. Somebody informed my mother about my fondness for the saloon and she beat me, but it did not keep me from peering under the swinging doors and listening to the wild talk of drunks when she was at work.

One summer afternoon—in my sixth year— while peering under the swinging doors of the neighborhood saloon, a black man caught hold of my arm and dragged me into its smoky and noisy depths. The odor of alcohol stung my nostrils. I yelled and struggled, trying to break free of him, afraid of the staring crowd of men and women, but he would not let me go. He lifted me and set me upon the counter, put his hat upon my head and ordered a drink for me. The tipsy men and women yelled with delight. Somebody tried to jam a cigar into my mouth, but I twisted out of the way.

"How do you feel, setting there like a man, boy?" a man asked.

"Make 'im drunk and he'll stop peeping in here," somebody said.

"Let's buy 'im drinks," somebody said.

Some of my fright left as I stared about. Whisky was set before me.

"Drink it, boy," somebody said.

I shook my head. The man who had dragged me in urged me to drink it, telling me that it would not hurt me. I refused.

"Drink it! it'll make you feel good," he said.

I took a sip and coughed. The men and women laughed. The entire crowd in the saloon gathered about me now, urging me to drink. I took another sip. Then another. My head spun and I laughed. I was put on the floor and I ran giggling and shouting among the yelling crowd. As I would pass each man, I would take a sip from an offered glass. Soon I was drunk. . . .

Toward early evening they let me go. I staggered along the pavements, drunk, repeating obscenities to the horror of the women I passed and to the amusement of the men en route to their homes from work.

To beg drinks in the saloon became an obsession. Many evenings my mother would find me wandering in a daze and take me home and beat me; but the next morning, no sooner had she gone to her job than I would run to the saloon and wait for someone to take me in and buy me a drink. My mother protested tearfully to the proprietor of the saloon, who ordered me to keep out of his place. But the men—reluctant to surrender their sport—would buy me drinks anyway, letting me drink out of their flasks on the streets, urging me to repeat obscenities.

I was a drunkard in my sixth year, before I had begun school. With a gang of children, I roamed the streets, begging pennies from passers-by, haunting the doors of saloons, wandering farther and farther away from home each day. I saw more than I could understand and heard more than I could remember. The point of life became for me the times when I could beg drinks. My mother was in despair. She beat me; then she prayed and wept over me, imploring me to be good, telling me that she had to work, all of which carried no weight to my wayward mind. Finally she placed me and my brother in the keeping of an old black woman who watched me every moment to keep me from running to the doors of the saloons to beg for whisky. The craving for alcohol finally left me and I forgot the taste of it.

In the immediate neighborhood there were many school children who, in the afternoons, would stop and play en route to their homes; they would leave their books upon the sidewalk and I would thumb through the pages and question them about the baffling black print. When I had learned to recognize certain words, I told my mother that I wanted to learn to read and she encouraged me. Soon I was able to pick my way through most of the children's books I ran across. There grew in me a consuming curiosity about what was happening around me and, when my mother came home from a hard day's work, I would question her so relentlessly about what I had heard in the streets that she refused to talk to me.

One cold morning my mother awakened me and told me that, because there was no coal in the house, she was taking my brother to the job with her and that I must remain in bed until the coal she had ordered was delivered. For the payment of the coal, she left a note together with some money under the dresser scarf. I went back to sleep and was awakened by the ringing of the doorbell. I opened the door, let in the coal man, and gave him the money and the note. He brought in a few bushels of coal, then lingered, asking me if I were cold.

"Yes," I said, shivering.

He made a fire, then sat and smoked.

"How much change do I owe you?" he asked me.

"I don't know," I said.

"Shame on you," he said. "Don't you know how to count?"

"No, sir," I said.

"Listen and repeat after me," he said.

He counted to ten and I listened carefully; then he asked me to count alone and I did. He then made me memorize the words twenty, thirty, forty, etc., then told me to add one, two, three, and so on. In about an hour's time I had learned to count to a hundred and I was overjoyed. Long after the coal man had gone I danced up and down on the bed in my nightclothes, counting again and again to a hundred, afraid that if I did not keep repeating the numbers I would forget them. When my mother returned from her job that night I insisted that she stand still and listen while I counted to one hundred. She was dumbfounded. After that she taught me to read, told me stories. On Sundays I would read the newspapers with my mother guiding me and spelling out the words.

'I soon made myself a nuisance by asking far too many questions of everybody. Every happening in the neighborhood, no matter how trivial, became my business. It was in this manner that I first stumbled upon the relations between whites and blacks, and what I learned frightened me. Though I had long known that there were people called "white" people, it had never meant anything to me emotionally. I had seen white men and women upon the streets a thousand times, but they had never looked particularly "white." To me they were merely people like other people, yet somehow strangely different because I had never come in close touch with any of them. For the most part I never thought of them; they simply existed somewhere in the background of the city as a whole. It might have been that my tardiness in learning to sense white people as "white" people came from the fact that many of my relatives were "white"-looking people. My grandmother, who was white as any "white" person, had never looked "white" to me. And when word circulated among the black people of the neighborhood that a "black" boy had been severely beaten by a "white" man, I felt that the "white" man had had a right to beat the "black" boy, for I naïvely assumed that the "white" man must have been the "black" boy's father. And did not all fathers, like my father, have the right to beat their children? A

paternal right was the only right, to my understanding, that a man had to beat a child. But when my mother told me that the "white" man was not the father of the "black" boy, was no kin to him at all, I was puzzled.

"Then why did the 'white' man whip the 'black' boy?" I asked my mother.

"The 'white' man did not *whip* the 'black' boy," my mother told me. "He *beat* the 'black' boy."

"But why?"

"You're too young to understand."

"I'm not going to let anybody beat me," I said stoutly.

"Then stop running wild in the streets," my mother said.

I brooded for a long time about the seemingly causeless beating of the "black" boy by the "white" man and the more questions I asked the more bewildering it all became. Whenever I saw "white" people now I stared at them, wondering what they were really like. . . .

After my father's desertion, my mother's ardently religious disposition dominated the household and I was often taken to Sunday school where I met God's representative in the guise of a tall, black preacher. One Sunday my mother invited the tall, black preacher to a dinner of fried chicken. I was happy, not because the preacher was coming but because of the chicken. One or two neighbors also were invited. But no sooner had the preacher arrived than I began to resent him, for I learned at once that he, like my father, was used to having his own way. The hour for dinner came and I was wedged at the table between talking and laughing adults. In the center of the table was a huge platter of golden-brown fried chicken. I compared the bowl of soup that sat before me with the crispy chicken and decided in favor of the chicken. The others began to eat their soup, but I could not touch mine.

"Eat your soup," my mother said.

"I don't want any," I said.

"You won't get anything else until you've eaten your soup," she said.

The preacher had finished his soup and had asked that the platter of chicken be passed to him. It galled me. He smiled, cocked his head this way and that, picking out choice pieces. I forced a spoonful of soup down my throat and looked to see if my speed matched that of the preacher. It did not. There were already bare chicken bones on his plate, and he was reaching for more. I tried eating my soup faster, but it was no use; the other people were now serving themselves chicken and the platter was more than half empty. I gave up and sat staring in despair at the vanishing pieces of fried chicken.

"Eat your soup or you won't get anything," my mother warned.

I looked at her appealingly and could not answer. As piece after piece of chicken was eaten, I was unable to eat my soup at all. I grew hot with anger. The preacher was laughing and joking and the grownups were hanging on his words. My growing hate of the preacher finally became more important than God or religion and I could no longer contain myself. I leaped up from the table, knowing that I should be ashamed of what I was doing, but unable to stop, and screamed, running blindly from the room.

"That preacher's going to eat *all* the chicken!" I bawled.

The preacher tossed back his head and roared with laughter, but my mother was angry and told me that I was to have no dinner because of my bad manners.

When I awakened one morning my mother told me that we were going to see a judge who would make my father support me and my brother. An hour later all three of us were sitting in a huge crowded room. I was overwhelmed by the many faces and the voices which I could not understand. High above me was a white face which my mother told me was the face of the judge. Across the huge room sat my father, smiling confidently, look-

ing at us. My mother warned me not to be fooled by my father's friendly manner; she told me that the judge might ask me questions, and if he did I must tell him the truth. I agreed, yet I hoped that the judge would not ask me anything.

For some reason the entire thing struck me as being useless; I felt that if my father were going to feed me, then he would have done so regardless of what a judge said to him. And I did not want my father to feed me; I was hungry, but my thoughts of food did not now center about him. I waited, growing restless, hungry. My mother gave me a dry sandwich and I munched and stared, longing to go home. Finally I heard my mother's name called; she rose and began weeping so copiously that she could not talk for a few moments; at last she managed to say that her husband had deserted her and two children, that her children were hungry, that they stayed hungry, that she worked, that she was trying to raise them alone. Then my father was called; he came forward jauntily, smiling. He tried to kiss my mother, but she turned away from him. I only heard one sentence of what he said.

"I'm doing all I can, Your Honor," he mumbled, grinning.

It had been painful to sit and watch my mother crying and my father laughing and I was glad when we were outside in the sunny streets. Back at home my mother wept again and talked complainingly about the unfairness of the judge who had accepted my father's word. After the court scene, I tried to forget my father; I did not hate him; I simply did not want to think of him. Often when we were hungry my mother would beg me to go to my father's job and ask him for a dollar, a dime, a nickel... But I would never consent to go. I did not want to see him.

My mother fell ill and the problem of food became an acute, daily agony. Hunger was with us always. Sometimes the neighbors would feed us or a dollar bill would come in the mail from my grandmother. It was winter and I would buy a dime's worth of coal each morning from the corner coalyard and lug it home in paper bags. For a time I remained out of school to wait upon my mother, then Granny came to visit us and I returned to school.

At night there were long, halting discussions about our going to live with Granny, but nothing came of it. Perhaps there was not enough money for railroad fare. Angered by having been hauled into court, my father now spurned us completely. I heard long, angrily whispered conversations between my mother and grandmother to the effect that "that woman ought to be killed for breaking up a home." What irked me was the ceaseless talk and no action. If someone had suggested that my father be killed, I would perhaps have become interested; if someone had suggested that his name never be mentioned, I would no doubt have agreed; if someone had suggested that we move to another city, I would have been glad. But there was only endless talk that led nowhere and I began to keep away from home as much as possible, preferring the simplicity of the streets to the worried, futile talk at home.

Finally we could no longer pay the rent for our dingy flat; the few dollars that Granny had left us before she went home were gone. Half sick and in despair, my mother made the rounds of the charitable institutions, seeking help. She found an orphan home that agreed to assume the guidance of me and my brother provided my mother worked and made small payments. My mother hated to be separated from us, but she had no choice.

The orphan home was a two-story frame building set amid trees in a wide, green field. My mother ushered me and my brother one morning into the building and into the presence of a tall, gaunt, mulatto woman who called herself Miss Simon. At once she took a fancy to me and I was frightened speechless; I was afraid of her the moment I saw her and my fear lasted during my entire stay in the home.

The house was crowded with children and there was always a storm of noise. The daily routine was blurred to me and I never quite grasped it. The most abiding feeling I had each day was hunger and fear. The meals were skimpy and there were only two of them. Just before we went to bed each night we were given a slice of bread smeared with molasses. The children were silent, hostile, vindictive, continuously complaining of hunger. There was an over-all atmosphere of nervousness and intrigue, of children telling tales upon others, of children being deprived of food to punish them.

The home did not have the money to check the growth of the wide stretches of grass by having it mown, so it had to be pulled by hand. Each morning after we had eaten a breakfast that seemed like no breakfast at all, an older child would lead a herd of us to the vast lawn and we would get to our knees and wrench the grass loose from the dirt with our fingers. At intervals Miss Simon would make a tour of inspection, examining the pile of pulled grass beside each child, scolding or praising according to the size of the pile. Many mornings I was too weak from hunger to pull the grass; I would grow dizzy and my mind would become blank and I would find myself, after an interval of unconsciousness, upon my hands and knees, my head whirling, my eyes staring in bleak astonishment at the green grass, wondering where I was, feeling that I was emerging from a dream . . .

During the first days my mother came each night to visit me and my brother, then her visits stopped. I began to wonder if she, too, like my father, had disappeared into the unknown. I was rapidly learning to distrust everything and everybody. When my mother did come, I asked her why had she remained away so long and she told me that Miss Simon had forbidden her to visit us, that Miss Simon had said that she was spoiling us with too much attention. I begged my mother to take me away; she wept and told me to wait, that soon she would take us to Arkansas. She left and my heart sank.

Miss Simon tried to win my confidence; she asked me if I would like to be adopted by her if my mother consented and I said no. She would take me into her apartment and talk to me, but her words had no effect. Dread and distrust had already become a daily part of my being and my memory grew sharp, my senses more impressionable; I began to be aware of myself as a distinct personality striving against others. I held myself in, afraid to act or speak until I was sure of my surroundings, feeling most of the time that I was suspended over a void. My imagination soared; I dreamed of running away. Each morning I vowed that I would leave the next morning, but the next morning always found me afraid.

One day Miss Simon told me that thereafter I was to help her in the office. I ate lunch with her and, strangely, when I sat facing her at the table, my hunger vanished. The woman killed something in me. Next she called me to her desk where she sat addressing envelopes.

"Step up close to the desk," she said. "Don't be afraid."

I went and stood at her elbow. There was a wart on her chin and I stared at it.

"Now, take a blotter from over there and blot each envelope after I'm through writing on it," she instructed me, pointing to a blotter that stood about a foot from my hand.

I stared and did not move or answer.

"Take the blotter," she said.

I wanted to reach for the blotter and succeeded only in twitching my arm.

"Here," she said sharply, reaching for the blotter and shoving it into my fingers.

She wrote in ink on an envelope and pushed it toward me. Holding the blotter in my hand, I stared at the envelope and could not move.

"Blot it," she said.

I could not lift my hand. I knew what she had said; I knew what she wanted me to do; and I had heard her correctly. I wanted to look at her and say something, tell her why I could not move; but my eyes were fixed upon the floor. I could not summon enough courage while she sat there looking at me to reach over the yawning space of twelve inches and blot the wet ink on the envelope.

"Blot it!" she spoke sharply.

Still I could not move or answer.

"Look at me!"

I could not lift my eyes. She reached her hand to my face and I twisted away.

"What's wrong with you?" she demanded.

I began to cry and she drove me from the room. I decided that as soon as night came I would run away. The dinner bell rang and I did not go to the table, but hid in a corner of the hallway. When I heard the dishes rattling at the table, I opened the door and ran down the walk to the street. Dusk was falling. Doubt made me stop. Ought I go back? No; hunger was back there, and fear. I went on, coming to concrete sidewalks. People passed me. Where was I going? I did not know. The farther I walked the more frantic I became. In a confused and vague way I knew that I was doing more running *away* from than running *toward* something. I stopped. The streets seemed dangerous. The buildings were massive and dark. The moon shone and the trees loomed frighteningly. No, I could not go on. I would go back. But I had walked so far and had turned too many corners and had not kept track of the direction. Which way led back to the orphan home? I did not know. I was lost.

I stood in the middle of the sidewalk and cried. A "white" policeman came to me and I wondered if he was going to beat me. He asked me what was the matter and I told him that I was trying to find my mother. His "white" face created a new fear in me. I was remembering the tale of the "white" man who had beaten the "black" boy. A crowd gathered and I was urged to tell where I lived. Curiously, I was too full of fear to cry now. I wanted to tell the "white" face that I had run off from an orphan home and that Miss Simon ran it, but I was afraid. Finally I was taken to the police station where I was fed. I felt better. I sat in a big chair where I was surrounded by "white" policemen, but they seemed to ignore me. Through the window I could see that night had completely fallen and that lights now gleamed in the streets. I grew sleepy and dozed. My shoulder was shaken gently and I opened my eyes and looked into a "white" face of another policeman who was sitting beside me. He asked me questions in a quiet, confidential tone, and quite before I knew it he was not "white" any more. I told him that I had run away from an orphan home and that Miss Simon ran it.

It was but a matter of minutes before I was walking alongside a policeman, heading toward the home. The policeman led me to the front gate and I saw Miss Simon waiting for me on the steps. She identified me and I was left in her charge. I begged her not to beat me, but she yanked me upstairs into an empty room and lashed me thoroughly. Sobbing, I slunk off to bed, resolved to run away again. But I was watched closely after that.

My mother was informed upon her next visit that I had tried to run away and she was terribly upset.

"Why did you do it?" she asked.

"I don't want to stay here," I told her.

"But you must," she said. "How can I work if I'm to worry about you? You must remember that you have no father. I'm doing all I can."

"I don't want to stay here," I repeated.

"Then, if I take you to your father . . ."

"I don't want to stay with him either," I said.

"But I want you to ask him for enough money for us to go to my sister's in Arkansas," she said.

Again I was faced with choices I did not like, but I finally agreed. After all, my hate for my father was not so great and urgent as my hate for the orphan home. My mother held to her idea and one night a week or so later I found myself standing in a room in a frame house. My father and a strange woman were sitting before a bright fire that blazed in a grate. My mother and I were standing about six feet away, as though we were afraid to approach them any closer.

"It's not for me," my mother was saying. "It's for your children that I'm asking you for money."

"I ain't got nothing," my father said, laughing.

"Come here, boy," the strange woman called to me.

I looked at her and did not move.

"Give him a nickel," the woman said. "He's cute."

"Come here, Richard," my father said, stretching out his hand.

I backed away, shaking my head, keeping my eyes on the fire.

"He is a cute child," the strange woman said.

"You ought to be ashamed," my mother said to the strange woman. "You're starving my children."

"Now, don't you-all fight," my father said, laughing.

"I'll take that poker and hit you!" I blurted at my father.

He looked at my mother and laughed louder.

"You told him to say that," he said.

"Don't say such things, Richard," my mother said.

"You ought to be dead," I said to the strange woman.

The woman laughed and threw her arms about my father's neck. I grew ashamed and wanted to leave.

"How can you starve your children?" my mother asked.

"Let Richard stay with me," my father said.

"Do you want to stay with your father, Richard?" my mother asked.

"No," I said.

"You'll get plenty to eat," he said.

"I'm hungry now," I told him. "But I won't stay with you."

"Aw, give the boy a nickel," the woman said.

My father ran his hand into his pocket and pulled out a nickel.

"Here, Richard," he said.

"Don't take it," my mother said.

"Don't teach him to be a fool," my father said. "Here, Richard, take it."

I looked at my mother, at the strange woman, at my father, then into the fire. I wanted to take the nickel, but I did not want to take it from my father.

"You ought to be ashamed," my mother said, weeping. "Giving your son a nickel when he's hungry. If there's a God, He'll pay you back."

"That's all I got," my father said, laughing again and returning the nickel to his pocket.

We left. I had the feeling that I had had to do with something unclean. Many times in the years after that the image of my father and the strange woman, their faces lit by the dancing flames, would surge up in my imagination so vivid and strong that I felt I could reach out and touch it; I would stare at it, feeling that it possessed some vital meaning which always eluded me.

A quarter of a century was to elapse between the time when I saw my father sitting with the strange woman and the time when I was to see him again, standing alone upon the red clay of a Mississippi plantation, a sharecropper, clad in ragged overalls, holding a muddy hoe in his gnarled, veined hands— a quarter of a century during which my mind and consciousness had become so greatly and violently altered that when I tried to talk to him I realized that, though ties of blood made us kin, though I could see a shadow of my face in his face, though there was an echo of my voice in his voice, we were forever strangers, speaking a different language, living on vastly distant planes of reality. That day a quarter of a century later when I visited him on the plantation—he was standing against the sky, smiling toothlessly, his hair whitened, his body bent, his eyes glazed with dim recollection, his fearsome aspect of twenty-five years ago gone forever from him—I was overwhelmed to realize that he could never understand me or the scalding experiences that had

swept me beyond his life and into an area of living that he could never know. I stood before him, poised, my mind aching as it embraced the simple nakedness of his life, feeling how completely his soul was imprisoned by the slow flow of the seasons, by wind and rain and sun, how fastened were his memories to a crude and raw past, how chained were his actions and emotions to the direct, animalistic impulses of his withering body . . .

From the white landowners above him there had not been handed to him a chance to learn the meaning of loyalty, of sentiment, of tradition. Joy was as unknown to him as was despair. As a creature of the earth, he endured, hearty, whole, seemingly indestructible, with no regrets and no hope. He asked easy, drawling questions about me, his other son, his wife, and he laughed, amused, when I informed him of their destinies. I forgave him and pitied him as my eyes looked past him to the unpainted wooden shack. From far beyond the horizons that bound this bleak plantation there had come to me through my living the knowledge that my father was a black peasant who had gone to the city seeking life, but who had failed in the city; a black peasant whose life had been hopelessly snarled in the city, and who had at last fled the city—that same city which had lifted me in its burning arms and borne me toward alien and undreamed-of shores of knowing.

I

WHO IS TO BLAME

Wright's autobiography is a complex book. Nowhere in it does the author make simple judgments about who is to blame for the life he lived. Thus the book opens with an episode in which he himself is largely responsible for the beating his mother gives him; and he makes it clear that apart from himself, it was often members of his own race who were responsible for his sufferings, including centrally his own mother and father.

One especially noteworthy detail is Wright's sympathetic sketch of the white police officer near the end of the first chapter. It would have been easy for a black writer to have played down or ignored this detail. But Wright had the courage to be fully honest.

In spite of all this, one should not be unaware of the full implications of Wright's work. In the last paragraph of Chapter 1, he makes it quite clear that "white landowners above him" were heavily responsible for the condition of his father. And if we ask not who is to blame but what is to blame for the hunger, the fear, the ignorance and poverty—even for the boredom that partially motivated Richard to set his home on fire—we can see that "the environment" is a good answer. And the character of that environment was shaped mainly not by people like Ella and Nathaniel Wright, but by those "above them."

II
IMPLICATIONS

Be prepared to discuss the following:

1. It has been observed that violence is one of the major themes in Richard Wright's work. Judging from the opening chapter of *Black Boy*, would you say that his concern with violence stems mainly from something within himself or from something in his early environment? Explain.

2. One of Wright's beliefs was that fear was the dominant emotion among blacks in America. What does the opening of *Black Boy* reveal about the origins of Wright's own fears? Explain why you think he might have held (or not held) a different belief if he had had a different background.

3. What was the role of hunger in Wright's early development? Why would you agree or disagree with the critic who claimed that hunger was the most important thing in Wright's life?

4. Discuss Richard Wright's attitude toward his father—both in his childhood and when he visited him again in 1940. What role—positive or negative—would you say that the father played in shaping the identity of his son?

5. The early years of Richard Wright were marked by fears and hardships. Yet there are many others whose experiences have been just as bad, or even worse. What makes Wright's case interesting is that he overcame his background. What positive elements can you find in Wright's early years, what experiences or what qualities did he have that might have helped him to prevail over his many disadvantages?

III
TECHNIQUES

Intention

One of Wright's intentions in *Black Boy* was to expose the evils of racism. (Wright was not concerned only with racism in the South, by the way. The original manuscript of *Black Boy* was a third longer than the published version; it dealt with many of Wright's experiences in Chicago and New York. This part of the book was cut by the publishers and was only recently released under the title *American Hunger*.) What evidences, direct or indirect, of this intention can you find?

Theme

One of the characteristics of a longer work is that it may have themes rather than a theme. Often, most of these themes are at least introduced in the first chapter. Apart from the racism theme, what other themes can you find in the initial chapter of *Black Boy*?

IV
WORDS

Personification is a variety of metaphor in which inanimate objects are endowed with life and personality. For example, when Emily Dickinson, the American poet, says that "Shadows hold their breath. . . . ," she causes us to see these shadows as people, living and breathing and in motion. Determine whether each of the following sentences does or does not contain a personified image. For those that do, describe the comparison that is made.

1. Hunger had always been more or less at my elbow when I played, but now I began to wake up at night to find hunger standing at my bedside, staring at me gauntly.

2. I pictured myself gasping for breath and dying in my sleep.

3. My father was a black peasant who had gone to the city seeking life, but who had failed in the city; a black peasant whose life had been hopelessly snarled in the city, and who had at last fled the city—that same city which had lifted me in its burning arms and borne me toward alien and undreamed-of shores of knowing.

4. When I heard the dishes rattling at the table, I opened the door and ran down the walk to the street.

5. Each event spoke with a cryptic tongue.

THE SEARCH FOR VALUES

For all of us, much of life is routine. We get up in the morning. We dress and have breakfast. We go to school or to work. We relax in the evening. We go to bed. It is much the same round, day after day. There are a few accents—a trip, a special party, an occasional big event like a birth, a marriage, or a death. Now and then we may be especially happy or especially sad. But most of the time our feelings do not run to extremes.

From a tradition fast disappearing
come the memory paintings of a rural childhood.
Simple, childlike, bright, and full of joy,
the pictures of Grandma Moses contain a set of values
hard to hold onto in today's world.

OUT FOR THE CHRISTMAS TREES
Grandma Moses

647

A popular song of another generation asked, "Why was I born? Why am I living?" These are nagging questions, kept usually just below the surface of our minds. But they point to the real, human need for finding ways to tie the fragments of our lives together, to form patterns that will give our lives day-by-day significance, to give meaning to our lives by directing all our actions toward something which we value above all else.

This need to find meaning and values may well be more acute for Americans than for others because of certain factors in our background. Americans came from many parts of the world to find a new way of life, and each second generation found itself cut off—at least in part—from the customs, the beliefs, the patterns of life that were shared by its ancestors, who had perhaps lived for centuries in one place. The new Americans often gained more freedom, but they lost a great deal of security.

In time, the rich resources of America provided for many the opportunity to achieve material possessions and material security. But as this type of security became relatively commonplace, more and more people grew to realize that they had to find something more in order to achieve a real sense of fulfillment. Emerson wrote, "Things are in the saddle and ride mankind." Thoughtful Americans wanted mankind in the saddle, riding things; they knew that materialism was not the key to happiness.

By the twentieth century, materialism was only one of many concerns of thinking Americans. Large-scale wars at first, and later the harrowing, ever-present possibility of a nuclear holocaust, seemed to reduce human stature; to some, we seemed no more than a pebble at the mercy of chance. The age of anxiety was born; it is still very much alive today.

Though most people certainly suffer anxiety and are aware of nagging doubts about life and its direction, it has been writers, with their talent for observation and expression, who have made vivid for us the search for values, who have put into words our feeling that we must seek fundamental values and live by them. Sometimes writers have painted extremely gloomy and pessimistic pictures; yet even the most pessimistic portraits can bring knowledge and self-awareness and thus can lead to change rather than despair. More often, however, writers have questioned and probed for positive answers to common human problems; they have sought values that will help humans not only endure but prevail.

Many American writers of the 1920s and 1930s
were pessimistic, giving negative answers to such questions as whether
happiness is possible or life has meaning. One of the best-known postwar poets
was T. S. Eliot. In the following poem he pictures people of the midtwenties
as empty of animal, intellectual, and spiritual values; he sees them
as essentially hollow, living in "death's dream kingdom." Note, too,
how his poetic method—sudden shifts, violent contrasts, apparent disunity—
tends to underscore the chaos of modern life.

The Hollow Men

Mistah Kurtz—he dead.[1]

A penny for the Old Guy[2]

I

We are the hollow men
We are the stuffed men
Leaning together
Headpiece filled with straw. Alas!
Our dried voices, when   5
We whisper together
Are quiet and meaningless
As wind in dry grass
Or rats' feet over broken glass
In our dry cellar   10

Shape without form, shade without color,
Paralyzed force, gesture without motion

Those who have crossed
With direct eyes, to death's other Kingdom
Remember us—if at all—not as lost   15
Violent souls, but only
As the hollow men
The stuffed men.

II

Eyes I dare not meet in dreams
In death's dream kingdom   20
These do not appear;
There, the eyes are
Sunlight on a broken column
There, is a tree swinging
And voices are   25
In the wind's singing
More distant and more solemn
Than a fading star.

Let me be no nearer
In death's dream kingdom   30
Let me also wear
Such deliberate disguises
Rat's coat, crowskin, crossed staves
In a field
Behaving as the wind behaves   35
No nearer—

Not that final meeting
In the twilight kingdom

From COLLECTED POEMS 1909–1962 by T. S. Eliot, copyright, 1936, by Harcourt Brace Jovanovich, Inc. © 1963, 1964, by T. S. Eliot. Reprinted by permission of Harcourt Brace Jovanovich, Inc.

1. **Mistah Kurtz,** a character in Joseph Conrad's *Heart of Darkness* who is destroyed by his own base instincts.
2. **A . . . Guy,** English children say this on Guy Fawkes Day—the anniversary of his abortive plot to blow up Parliament.

III

This is the dead land
This is cactus land   40
Here the stone images[1]
Are raised, here they receive
The supplication of a dead man's hand
Under the twinkle of a fading star.

Is it like this   45
In death's other kingdom
Waking alone
At the hour when we are
Trembling with tenderness
Lips that would kiss   50
Form prayers to broken stone.

IV

The eyes are not here
There are no eyes here
In this valley of dying stars
In this hollow valley   55
This broken jaw of our lost kingdoms

In this last of meeting places
We grope together
And avoid speech
Gathered on this beach of the tumid[2] river   60

Sightless, unless
The eyes reappear
As the perpetual star
Multifoliate rose[3]
Of death's twilight kingdom   65
The hope only
Of empty men.

V

Here we go round the prickly pear
Prickly pear prickly pear
Here we go round the prickly pear   70
At five o'clock in the morning.

Between the idea
And the reality

T. S. ELIOT   *Wyndham Lewis*

Between the motion
And the act   75
Falls the Shadow
                    For Thine is the Kingdom

Between the conception
And the creation
Between the emotion   80
And the response
Falls the Shadow
                            Life is very long

Between the desire
And the spasm   85
Between the potency

---

1. **stone images,** the idols, Wealth and Power, before
which the poet felt America, after World War I, was
bowing down.
2. **tumid**\ˈtū·məd\ **river,** the swollen river.
3. **Multifoliate**\məl·tĭ ˈfō·lē·ət\ **rose,** literally, the many
leafed rose, perhaps many petaled. In religious symbolism a rose with many petals is the symbol of a soul unfolding spiritually. In Dante's *Paradise,* the multifoliate
rose is his great metaphor for his vision of God.

And the existence
Between the essence
And the descent
Falls the Shadow   90
> *For Thine is the Kingdom*
For Thine is[4]
Life is
For Thine is the

This is the way the world ends   95
This is the way the world ends
This is the way the world ends
Not with a bang but a whimper.

T. S. ELIOT

I

THE PLIGHT OF HUMANITY

Perhaps the two most significant characteristics of "the hollow men" are fear and impotence; and note that they are fearful and powerless with respect to *all* aspects of life. They are afraid to love, afraid to think, afraid to worship or face the afterlife. These fears are symbolized in Part V by the "Shadow" that falls between ideas and realities, emotions and responses, and so on. The shadow breaks the chain before fulfillment in much the same way as the Lord's Prayer is broken off just before it reaches the words, "the Power and the Glory."

II

IMPLICATIONS

Answer the following questions:

1. "A penny for the Old Guy" is what English children say when they go from door to door soliciting money for fireworks on Guy Fawkes Day (November 5). Look up Guy Fawkes or the Gunpowder Plot in a reference book and report your findings. How does knowledge of Fawkes help you to better understand the poem?

2. What is meant by a "lost violent soul"? Why are the hollow men not in this category?

3. Note as many instances as you can of the hollow men's inability to communicate effectively. How is this inability related to their fate?

4. Could a person with sincere religious convictions be a hollow man in Eliot's sense?

III

TECHNIQUES

Symbolism

A symbol is an object or condition used to suggest something else. The moon, for example, may suggest romance, mystery, purity, imagination, and other things. The particular meaning or group of meanings that the symbol calls forth will depend upon how the writer handles the symbol, upon the contexts in which it occurs.

In the last stanza of Part IV, Eliot says that the hollow men are "Sightless, unless/ The eyes reappear/ As the perpetual star/ Multifoliate rose/ Of death's twilight kingdom. . . ." The condition of sightlessness is a symbol of the lack of vision of the hollow men—they do not "see" with imagination or spirit as a poet or a saint or prophet does. The lines say, however, that they might have such a vision if the eyes should reappear as "the perpetual star."

In trying to determine the symbolic meaning of this star readers must call up those characteristics of stars that fit the present context. They might note that stars give light; they are in the heavens; and this star at least is "perpetual." Now especially in the context of this poem a perpetual light in the heavens can hardly fail to suggest God, or at least some aspect of divinity.

Since "Multifoliate rose" is an appositive to the perpetual star, it must suggest much the same meanings. Roses, of course, suggest brightness and beauty; and further support for thinking of the multifoliate rose as a symbol of divinity comes from the fact that this is what it symbolizes in the final portion of Dante's *Divine Comedy*, a famous poem of which Eliot was deeply fond.

1. Briefly, then, the lines suggest that the hollow men would cease to be hollow if they had spiritual vision. What are some of the advantages and disadvantages of the fact that the poet has chosen to communicate this idea symbolically rather than literally?

2. Discuss the symbolism of the earlier lines in Part IV, paying special attention to the meaning of "eyes" and to the physical setting.

---

4. **For Thine is,** note that the poem falters as from weariness. The hollow men cannot pray.

Gallery

THE SEARCH FOR VALUES

Artists, like writers, are deeply sensitive
to the values of their society. They tend either to accept
and support them or to reject them with contempt and satire.
In either case, by their vivid responses to the values
upon which we operate, they dramatize what is or what should be
and so play a vital part in our search for values.
This gallery is divided among those who protest inadequate values,
those who suggest larger life goals,
and those who point poignantly to the search itself.

RED STAIRWAY   *Ben Shahn*   *The St. Louis Art Museum*

Ben Shahn often explores the tragic situations people create by blindly living
on short-term values. Yet in RED STAIRWAY, he is strangely optimistic about the
human spirit. Hopper, in ROOMS BY THE SEA, states that there is a starkness
in solitude, but there is a beauty, too. Early in the last century self-taught
Edward Hicks chose the passage of Isaiah 11:6–9 as the basis for THE PEACEABLE
KINGDOM. He filled his painting with his values, real and symbolic. In the
background William Penn makes his treaty with the Native Americans.

ROOMS BY THE SEA
Edward Hopper
Yale University Art Gallery
Bequest of Stephen C. Clark

THE
PEACEABLE
KINGDOM
Edward Hicks

653

CHURCH OF THE MINORITIES (II), 1926
Lyonel Feininger

The two paintings on this page are both trying
to make us appreciate our lives
on a higher plane. In the Feininger,
the bold vertical lines and shafts of light
draw our eyes and souls upward.
In SAVE OUR PLANET by the revered
New Mexican painter Georgia O'Keeffe,
gentle, geometric pools suggest clouds whose
beauty, in itself, argues for the preservation
of nature in the face of today's pollution.
O'Keeffe may be saying that to lose the
beauty of nature for the sake of industry
is to lose our sense of proportion,
our sense of loveliness.

SAVE OUR PLANET
Georgia O'Keeffe

Consider the elements within LIGHT OF THE WORLD: the church to the left, the distant factory and fields, the dead tree, the hypnotized people on the checkered deck, and the bizarre structure holding the flashing globe. Where have we been, and where are we headed? Have we passed up beauty for a light that could go out? This is a picture which you must interpret for yourself.

LIGHT OF THE WORLD
Peter Blume
1932, oil on composition board,
18 x 20¼". Collection,
Whitney Museum of American Art,
New York

Driftwood, emptiness, decay, and a shabby string of colored lights. What is it John Atherton would have us realize? What brings us here, and where should we be headed?

CHRISTMAS EVE
John Atherton
1941, oil on canvas, 30¼ x 35"
Collection, The Museum
of Modern Art, New York
Purchase

655

These are the people who have nowhere to go but up. The artist has given us a portrait gallery of human types characterized by famous paintings which tell us of their several goals.

From right to left the paintings are Boucher's MADAME DE POMPADOUR, romantic and feminine and much more; a Daumier cartoon of social satire; Picasso's GIRL IN A MIRROR, boldly abstract, defiant and searching; an old and realistic portrait of a man like the merchants of the sixteenth-century Dutch painters, traditional and prosperous; Grant Wood's AMERICAN GOTHIC, classic commentary on tightly held values but with a serenity not to be mistaken; Millet's THE SOWER with its agricultural values; and a modern piece of social, industrial protest.

Even the children hold their own painted hopes for life.

The paintings become metaphors to express the traditions and goals of the people who have selected them.

WORKERS AND PAINTINGS   *Honoré Sharrer*
1943, oil on composition board, 11⅜ x 37"
Collection, The Museum of Modern Art, New York. Gift of Lincoln Kirstein.

A general
is welcomed home;
a group
has been gathered
for a formal banquet,
but the artist
has no mercy
in his satire.
In his own search
for values
he has found
these people
and their way
of life inadequate.

WELCOME HOME   *Jack Levine*
Courtesy of the Brooklyn Museum, J.B. Woodward Memorial Fund

The American writers of the generation that fought
World War I have been called "the lost generation." The term
refers to the fact that they felt they could no longer maintain
the traditional values of the past. Ernest Hemingway was
one of the chief speakers for this lost generation, and in this story
he gives the reader a glimpse of the effects of the First World War
on the soldiers who fought it.

In Another Country

ERNEST HEMINGWAY

In the fall the war was always there, but we did not go to it any more. It was cold in the fall in Milan[1] and the dark came very early. Then the electric lights came on, and it was pleasant along the streets looking in the windows. There was much game hanging outside the shops, and the snow powdered in the fur of the foxes and the wind blew their tails. The deer hung stiff and heavy and empty, and small birds blew in the wind and the wind turned their feathers. It was a cold fall and the wind came down from the mountains.

We were all at the hospital every afternoon, and there were different ways of walking across the town through the dusk to the hospital. Two of the ways were alongside canals, but they were long. Always, though, you crossed a bridge across a canal to enter the hospital. There was a choice of three bridges. On one of them a woman sold roasted chestnuts. It was warm, standing in front of her charcoal fire, and the chestnuts were warm afterward in your pocket. The hospital was very old and very beautiful, and you entered through a gate and walked across a courtyard and out a gate on the other side. There were usually funerals starting from the courtyard. Beyond the old hospital were the new brick pavilions, and there we met every afternoon and were all very polite and interested in what was the matter, and sat in the machines[2] that were to make so much difference.

The doctor came up to the machine where I was sitting and said: "What did you like best to do before the war? Did you practice a sport?"

I said: "Yes, football."

"Good," he said. "You will be able to play football again better than ever."

My knee did not bend and the leg dropped straight from the knee to the ankle without a calf, and the machine was to bend the knee and make it move as in riding a tricycle. But it did not bend yet, and instead the machine lurched when it came to the bending part. The doctor said: "That will all pass. You are a fortunate young man. You will play football again like a champion."

In the next machine was a major who had a little hand like a baby's. He winked at me when the doctor examined his hand, which was between two leather straps that bounced up and down and flapped the stiff fingers, and said: "And will I too play football, captain-doctor?"

"In Another Country" (copyright 1927 Charles Scribner's Sons; renewal copyright © 1955) is reprinted with the permission of Charles Scribner's Sons from *Men Without Women* by Ernest Hemingway.

1. **Milan**\mĭ ▲lan\ a large industrial city in northern Italy.
2. **machines**, physical therapy machines for exercising the damaged muscles of the wounded.

He had been a very great fencer, and before the war the greatest fencer in Italy.

The doctor went to his office in the back room and brought a photograph which showed a hand that had been withered almost as small as the major's, before it had taken a machine course, and after was a little larger. The major held the photograph with his good hand and looked at it very carefully. "A wound?" he asked.

"An industrial accident," the doctor said.

"Very interesting, very interesting," the major said, and handed it back to the doctor.

"You have confidence?"

"No," said the major.

There were three boys who came each day who were about the same age I was. They were all three from Milan, and one of them was to be a lawyer, and one was to be a painter, and one had intended to be a soldier, and after we were finished with the machines, sometimes we walked back together to the Café Cova, which was next door to the Scala.[3] We walked the short way through the communist quarter because we were four together. The people hated us because we were officers, and from a wine shop some one called out, "A basso gli ufficiali!"[4] as we passed. Another boy who walked with us sometimes and made us five wore a black silk handkerchief across his face because he had no nose then and his face was to be rebuilt. He had gone out to the front from the military academy and had been wounded within an hour after he had gone into the front line for the first time. They rebuilt his face, but he came from a very old family and they could never get the nose exactly right. He went to South America and worked in a bank. But this was a long time ago, and then we did not any of us know how it was going to be afterward. We only knew then that there was always the war, but that we were not going to it any more.

We all had the same medals, except the boy with the black silk bandage across his face, and he had not been at the front long enough to get any medals. The tall boy with a very pale face who was to be a lawyer had been a lieutenant

of Arditi[5] and had three medals of the sort we each had only one of. He had lived a very long time with death and was a little detached. We were all a little detached, and there was nothing that held us together except that we met every afternoon at the hospital. Although, as we walked to the Cova through the tough part of town, walking in the dark, with light and singing coming out of the wine shops, and sometimes having to walk into the street when the men and women would crowd together on the sidewalk so that we would have had to jostle them to get by, we felt held together by there being something that happened that they, the people who disliked us, did not understand.

We ourselves all understood the Cova, where it was rich and warm and not too brightly lighted, and noisy and smoky at certain hours, and there were always girls at the tables and the illustrated papers on a rack on the wall. . . .

The boys at first were very polite about my medals and asked me what I had done to get them. I showed them the papers, which were written in very beautiful language and full of *fratellanza*[6] and *abnegazione*,[7] but which really said, with the adjectives removed, that I had been given the medals because I was an American. After that their manner changed a little toward me, although I was their friend against outsiders. I was a friend, but I was never really one of them after they had read the citations, because it had been different with them and they had done very different things to get their medals. I had been wounded, it was true; but we all knew that being wounded, after all, was really an accident. I was never ashamed of the ribbons, though, and sometimes, after the cocktail hour, I would imagine myself having done all the things they had done to get their medals; but walking home at night through the empty streets with the cold wind and all the shops

3. **Scala**\ˈskä·lä\ La Scala, a famous opera house in Milan.
4. **A basso gli ufficiali**, "Down with officers."
5. **Arditi**\är ˈdē·tē\ Italian storm troops.
6. **fratellanza**\frä·tə ˈlän·zə\ brotherhood.
7. **abnegazione**\äb·nəg·ə ˈzō·nē\ self-sacrifice.

closed, trying to keep near the street lights, I knew that I would never have done such things, and I was very much afraid to die, and often lay in bed at night by myself, afraid to die and wondering how I would be when I went back to the front again.

The three with the medals were like hunting hawks; and I was not a hawk, although I might seem a hawk to those who had never hunted; they, the three, knew better and so we drifted apart. But I stayed good friends with the boy who had been wounded his first day at the front, because he would never know now how he would have turned out; so he could never be accepted either, and I liked him because I thought perhaps he would not have turned out to be a hawk either.

The major, who had been the great fencer, did not believe in bravery, and spent much time while we sat in the machines correcting my grammar. He had complimented me on how I spoke Italian, and we talked together very easily. One day I had said that Italian seemed such an easy language to me that I could not take a great interest in it; everything was so easy to say. "Ah, yes," the major said. "Why, then, do you not take up the use of grammar?" So we took up the use of grammar, and soon Italian was such a difficult language that I was afraid to talk to him until I had the grammar straight in my mind.

The major came very regularly to the hospital. I do not think he ever missed a day, although I am sure he did not believe in the machines. There was a time when none of us believed in the machines, and one day the major said it was all nonsense. The machines were new then and it was we who were to prove them. It was an idiotic idea, he said, "a theory, like another." I had not learned my grammar, and he said I was a stupid impossible disgrace, and he was a fool to have bothered with me. He was a small man and he sat straight up in his chair with his right hand thrust into the machine and looked straight ahead at the wall while the straps thumped up and down with his fingers in them.

"What will you do when the war is over if it is over?" he asked me. "Speak grammatically!"

"I will go to the States."

"Are you married?"

"No, but I hope to be."

"The more of a fool you are," he said. He seemed very angry. "A man must not marry."

"Why, Signor Maggiore?"[8]

"Don't call me 'Signor Maggiore.'"

"Why must not a man marry?"

"He cannot marry. He cannot marry," he said angrily. "If he is to lose everything, he should not place himself in a position to lose that. He should not place himself in a position to lose. He should find things he cannot lose."

He spoke very angrily and bitterly, and looked straight ahead while he talked.

"But why should he necessarily lose it?"

"He'll lose it," the major said. He was looking at the wall. Then he looked down at the machine and jerked his little hand out from between the straps and slapped it hard against his thigh. "He'll lose it," he almost shouted. "Don't argue with me!" Then he called to the attendant who ran the machines. "Come and turn this thing off."

He went back into the other room for the light treatment and the massage. Then I heard him ask the doctor if he might use his telephone and he shut the door. When he came back into the room, I was sitting in another machine. He was wearing his cape and had his cap on, and he came directly toward my machine and put his arm on my shoulder.

"I am so sorry," he said, and patted me on the shoulder with his good hand. "I would not be rude. My wife has just died. You must forgive me."

"Oh——" I said, feeling sick for him. "I am *so* sorry."

He stood there biting his lower lip. "It is very difficult," he said. "I cannot resign myself."

He looked straight past me and out through the window. Then he began to cry. "I am utterly unable to resign myself," he said, and

---

8. **Signor Maggiore**\sē·nyōr ma ▴jō·rē\ Mister Major.

choked. And then crying, his head up looking at nothing, carrying himself straight and soldierly, with tears on both his cheeks and biting his lip, he walked past the machines and out the door.

The doctor told me that the major's wife, who was very young and whom he had not married until he was definitely invalided out of the war, had died of pneumonia. She had been sick only a few days. No one expected her to die. The major did not come to the hospital for three days. Then he came at the usual hour, wearing a black band on the sleeve of his uniform. When he came back, there were large framed photographs around the wall, of all sorts of wounds before and after they had been cured by the machines. In front of the machine the major used were three photographs of hands like his that were completely restored. I do not know where the doctor got them. I always understood we were the first to use the machines. The photographs did not make much difference to the major because he only looked out of the window.

I
THE LOST GENERATION AND THE WAR

There are at least three important effects of the war on the characters in this story: (1) It has caused them wounds; (2) it has given them a sense of detachment from life; and (3) it has made them pessimistic and unhappy. These may all be considered characteristics of the lost generation, but an interesting question is, To what extent are they due to the war?

Why does Hemingway bring in the death of the major's wife, an event that has virtually nothing to do with the war?

II
IMPLICATIONS

Discuss the following questions in some detail.

1. Is the First World War a symptom of the loss of traditional values or is it the cause of the loss?

2. What does the first sentence of the story mean? In particular, what does "there" mean and why does the narrator use the adverb "always"?

3. The first photograph the doctor shows the major is a picture of an industrial wound rather than a war wound. What does this fact suggest regarding the author's conception of "wounds" in the story?

4. What is ironic about the fact that the major did not marry until he was "definitely invalided out of the war"?

5. Who is the main character of this story—the major or the narrator?

6. What does the title of the story mean?

7. It is sometimes said that Hemingway was a believer in the philosophy known as "stoicism," one of whose basic ideas is stated below. Do you think that Hemingway would agree with this statement? Would any of his characters accept it, or might they be happier if they did?

"Ask not that events should happen as you will, but let your will be that events should happen as they do, and you shall have peace."

III
TECHNIQUES

Symbolism

Should such things as the dead animals, the hospital, and the machines be treated as symbols, or not? If readers do decide to interpret them symbolically, how do they know whether they have the right interpretation?

1. Suppose that one person (A) supports the opinion that the hospital suggests a zoo because the men who go there are like dumb animals in that they communicate very little and are concerned chiefly with the body rather than with the mind or soul. Why might you agree or disagree with this person?

2. Another person (B) might point out that the story is set in Italy, a country that contains many very old and very beautiful churches. He might then note that the hospital is described as "very old and very beautiful." In addition he might point out that the soldiers do not go to this hospital—they walk around it and go instead to the "new brick pavilions" where the machines are kept.

Accordingly, then, the soldiers would be passing up or rejecting traditional Christian values (symbolized by the hospital) in favor of the values of the machine age (symbolized by the brick pavilions).

On what grounds might B argue that his interpretation is better than A's?

Poems by Robinson

Although Edwin Arlington Robinson was born in 1869
and began writing poems at a very early age, he was largely unknown
until the end of the First World War. It may be partly because he shared
the pessimistic spirit of many writers of the 1920s and 1930s
that he became known about that time as America's greatest living poet.
As you read the following poems, ask yourself about the parallels
and contrasts between his subjects and Eliot's "hollow men."

Miniver Cheevy

Miniver Cheevy, child of scorn,
   Grew lean while he assailed the seasons;
He wept that he was ever born,
   And he had reasons.

Miniver loved the days of old   5
   When swords were bright and steeds were prancing;
The vision of a warrior bold
   Would set him dancing.

Miniver sighed for what was not,
   And dreamed, and rested from his labors;   10
He dreamed of Thebes[1] and Camelot,[2]
   And Priam's neighbors.[3]

---

1. **Thebes**\thēbz\ the poet may have had in mind either of two ancient cities named Thebes. The more ancient (2000 B.C.) was in Egypt, its site marked by the magnificent ruins of Karnak and Luxor. The other ancient city of Thebes was in Greece and is frequently mentioned in Greek legends. It was destroyed, 336 B.C., by Alexander the Great.
2. **Camelot**\ˈcă·mə·lŏt\ was the beautiful rose-red city built for King Arthur by the magician Merlin.
3. **Priam's neighbors,** the kings of those neighboring cities in Asia Minor who helped Priam, king of Troy, resist the invading Greeks in the Trojan War, of which Homer tells in the *Iliad*.

Miniver mourned the ripe renown
    That made so many a name so fragrant;
He mourned Romance, now on the town,   15
    And Art, a vagrant.

Miniver loved the Medici,[4]
    Albeit he had never seen one;
He would have sinned incessantly
    Could he have been one.   20

Miniver cursed the commonplace
    And eyed a khaki suit with loathing;
He missed the mediaeval grace
    Of iron clothing.

Miniver scorned the gold he sought,   25
    But sore annoyed was he without it;
Miniver thought, and thought, and thought,
    And thought about it.

Miniver Cheevy, born too late,
    Scratched his head and kept on thinking;   30
Miniver coughed, and called it fate,
    And kept on drinking.

EDWIN ARLINGTON ROBINSON

---

4. **Medici** \ˈmĕ·dɔ·chē\ a family of bankers and leaders under whose tolerant rule Florence, Italy, became
one of the most beautiful cities in the world. In power
from the fifteenth to the eighteenth century, they
were patrons and protectors of the scholars and artists
who made Florence the very center of the Italian
Renaissance.

Richard Cory

Whenever Richard Cory went down town,
    We people on the pavement looked at him:
He was a gentleman from sole to crown,
    Clean favored, and imperially slim.

And he was always quietly arrayed,   5
    And he was always human when he talked;
But still he fluttered pulses when he said,
    "Good-morning," and he glittered when he walked.

And he was rich—yes, richer than a king,
    And admirably schooled in every grace: 10
In fine, we thought that he was everything
    To make us wish that we were in his place.

So on we worked, and waited for the light,
    And went without the meat, and cursed the bread;
And Richard Cory, one calm summer night,   15
    Went home and put a bullet through his head.

EDWIN ARLINGTON ROBINSON

I
THE ALIENATED

Although Robinson's characters seem to share the fate of Eliot's hollow men, they differ from them in several ways. One important difference is that Robinson's characters have dreams, even ideals often, but they have been cheated of a chance to realize these by fate or by the society in which they live. Another important difference is that the hollow men exist in a group and Robinson's characters usually have no one to share their burdens. They are desperately, tragically alone, alienated from the community. Who is responsible for this alienation—the individual, the society, or both?

II
IMPLICATIONS

Discuss each of the following statements in the light of these poems and of your own experience.

1. A person must be able to live with other human beings in order to be happy.

2. Cheevy's life shows that the fact that one has a strong sense of values is not enough to secure happiness.

3. Great pain and personal tragedy cannot be shared; where such things are concerned we are all, always, alone.

4. Wealth and material possessions are probably the least important factors in human happiness.

5. In the long run, individuals have only themselves to blame if they are unhappy.

III
TECHNIQUES

Structure

A literary work is in certain ways like a building. Both the architect's office building or house and the writer's essay, story, or poem have a *planned framework* or *structure*, and the materials used—the wood or the words—are arranged according to this planned framework.

1. Robinson's poems tend to be highly structured. Scan at least two stanzas of each poem and describe its rhyme and rhythm scheme. What regularities do you find? Are there any irregularities?

2. Notice also Robinson's stanza divisions. Explain how they serve to frame the thought structure of the poem.

Symbolism

Not only words and phrases but also actions may have symbolic significance. Cory's suicide, for example, might be regarded as a symbolic act, for it suggests a meaning beyond the act itself. Discuss the meaning of this suicide and the meanings of some of the other symbolic acts in the Robinson poems.

IV
WORDS

A. 1. Having discussed synonyms and antonyms previously, we should also consider *homonyms,* words that are identical in spelling and sound, but different in meaning. For example, *base* in the "base of the column" and *base* in "base remark" are alike in sound and spelling but different in origins and meanings. *Bay* in "a bay mare" and *bay* in "bay window" are also homonyms. Find several other examples.

2. Words that are alike in spelling but different in origin, meaning, and pronunciation are *homographs.* The word *tear* in "a tear fell from his eye" and *tear* in "a tear in his shirt" are homographs, as are *wind* in "wind the clock" and *wind* in "the wind from the east." List other examples.

3. *Homophones* are words which sound alike but differ in origin, meaning, and spelling. For each word, find another word that sounds just like it: *fair, break, minor, male, tale, right, bare, wait, plain, site.*

4. Now, if possible, find an antonym for each member of the pairs of homophones you listed for number three. You will find that some members of the pairs do not have antonyms.

5. Each of the following words has a homonym. Look up the origins and meanings of *bear, list, guy, mean, halter, hide, last, launch, mole, nob, palatine, palm, pan, scale.*

B. Every person has not one vocabulary but three vocabularies: a speaking vocabulary, words used when speaking with friends and with the public; a reading vocabulary, words we recognize in print; and a writing vocabulary, words we use in writing. The vocabularies are not identical; but certain words, what we might call general vocabulary, are common to all three. The guiding principle in one's choice of words is appropriateness. Is the word or phrase appropriate to the audience and to the situation? In previous exercises, we divided usage into two broad, general classes: *standard* and *nonstandard.* The term *nonstandard* generally refers to grammatical constructions, expressions and pronunciations rejected by most educated speakers. Unfortunately there is no universally recognized system of identifying the varieties of standard English. The different varieties indicate different styles for different occasions and different audiences. One variety is no better than another if each is appropriate to the subject and to the situation.

The varieties of standard English refer more to word choice than to pronunciation, spelling, or grammar. The guiding principle of word choice is appropriateness to the subject and to the situation. For example, synonyms or near synonyms sometimes indicate degrees of refinement. Classify these words as formal, general and/or informal: *fear, terror, trepidation; goodness, virtue, probity.*

Study your own vocabulary. Make a list of the words you have learned from your readings in this book. Take an essay you have written recently and classify the nouns you have used. Try substituting nouns from your "other" vocabularies.

Traditionally, Americans have always looked to the future. Complete happiness, prosperity, and fulfillment are the promises of future progress, we earnestly believe. But will tomorrow be happier? Will it be free of hollow men and lost generations? Is it possible to escape the past and start a new life?

The Million-Year Picnic

RAY BRADBURY

Somehow the idea was brought up by Mom that perhaps the whole family would enjoy a fishing trip. But they weren't Mom's words; Timothy knew that. They were Dad's words, and Mom used them for him somehow.

Dad shuffled his feet in a clutter of Martian pebbles and agreed. So immediately there was a tumult and a shouting, and very quickly the camp was tucked into capsules and containers, Mom slipped into traveling jumpers and blouse, Dad stuffed his pipe full with trembling hands, his eyes on the Martian sky, and the three boys piled yelling into the motorboat, none of them really keeping an eye on Mom and Dad, except Timothy.

Dad pushed a stud.[1] The water boat sent a humming sound up into the sky. The water shook back and the boat nosed ahead, and the family cried, "Hurrah!"

Timothy sat in the back of the boat with Dad, his small fingers atop Dad's hairy ones, watching the canal twist, leaving the crumbled place behind where they had landed in their small family rocket all the way from Earth. He remembered the night before they left Earth, the hustling and hurrying, the rocket that Dad had found somewhere, somehow, and the talk of a vacation on Mars. A long way to go for a vacation, but Timothy said nothing because of his younger brothers. They came to Mars and now, first thing, or so they said, they were going fishing.

Dad had a funny look in his eyes as the boat went up-canal. A look that Timothy couldn't figure. It was made of strong light and maybe a sort of relief. It made the deep wrinkles laugh instead of worry or cry.

So there went the cooling rocket, around a bend, gone.

"How far are we going?" Robert splashed his hand. It looked like a small crab jumping in the violet water.

Dad exhaled. "A million years."

"Gee," said Robert.

"Look, kids." Mother pointed one soft long arm. "There's a dead city."

They looked with fervent anticipation, and the dead city lay dead for them alone, drowsing in a hot silence of summer made on Mars by a Martian weatherman.

And Dad looked as if he was pleased that it was dead.

It was a futile spread of pink rocks sleeping on a rise of sand, a few tumbled pillars, one lonely shrine, and then the sweep of sand again. Nothing else for miles. A white desert around the canal and a blue desert over it.

Just then a bird flew up. Like a stone thrown across a blue pond, hitting, falling deep, and vanishing.

Copyright 1946 by Ray Bradbury, renewal © 1974 by Ray Bradbury. Reprinted by permission of the Harold Matson Co., Inc.

1. stud\stəd\ here, a rod or pin projecting from the motor of the boat.

Dad got a frightened look when he saw it. "I thought it was a rocket."

Timothy looked at the deep ocean sky, trying to see Earth and the war and the ruined cities and the men killing each other since the day he was born. But he saw nothing. The war was as removed and far off as two flies battling to the death in the arch of a great high and silent cathedral. And just as senseless.

William Thomas wiped his forehead and felt the touch of his son's hand on his arm, like a young tarantula, thrilled. He beamed at his son. "How goes it, Timmy?"

"Fine, Dad."

Timothy hadn't quite figured out what was ticking inside the vast adult mechanism beside him. The man with the immense hawk nose, sunburnt, peeling—and the hot blue eyes like agate marbles you play with after school in summer back on Earth, and the long thick columnar legs in the loose riding breeches.

"What are you looking at so hard, Dad?"

"I was looking for Earthian logic, common sense, good government, peace, and responsibility."

"All that up there?"

"No. I didn't find it. It's not there any more. Maybe it'll never be there again. Maybe we fooled ourselves that it was ever there."

"Huh?"

"See the fish," said Dad, pointing.

There rose a soprano clamor from all three boys as they rocked the boat in arching their tender necks to see. They *oohed* and *ahed*. A silver ring fish floated by them, undulating, and closing like an iris, instantly, around food particles, to assimilate them.

Dad looked at it. His voice was deep and quiet.

"Just like war. War swims along, sees food, contracts. A moment later—Earth is gone."

"William," said Mom.

"Sorry," said Dad.

They sat still and felt the canal water rush cool, swift, and glassy. The only sound was the motor hum, the glide of water, the sun expanding the air.

"When do we see the Martians?" cried Michael.

"Quite soon, perhaps," said Father. "Maybe tonight."

"Oh, but the Martians are a dead race now," said Mom.

"No, they're not. I'll show you some Martians, all right," Dad said presently.

Timothy scowled at that but said nothing. Everything was odd now. Vacations and fishing and looks between people.

The other boys were already engaged making shelves of their small hands and peering under them toward the seven-foot stone banks of the canal, watching for Martians.

"What do they look like?" demanded Michael.

"You'll know them when you see them." Dad sort of laughed, and Timothy saw a pulse beating time in his cheek.

Mother was slender and soft, with a woven plait of spun-gold hair over her head in a tiara, and eyes the color of the deep cool canal water where it ran in shadow, almost purple, with flecks of amber caught in it. You could see her thoughts swimming around in her eyes, like fish—some bright, some dark, some fast, quick, some slow and easy, and sometimes, like when she looked up where Earth was, being nothing but color and nothing else. She sat in the boat's prow, one hand resting on the side lip, the other on the lap of her dark blue breeches, and a line of sunburnt soft neck showing where her blouse opened like a white flower.

She kept looking ahead to see what was there, and, not being able to see it clearly enough, she looked backward toward her husband, and through his eyes, reflected then, she saw what was ahead; and since he added part of himself to this reflection, a determined firmness, her face relaxed and she accepted it and she turned back, knowing suddenly what to look for.

Timothy looked too. But all he saw was a straight pencil line of canal going violet through a wide shallow valley penned by low, eroded hills, and on until it fell over the sky's

edge. And this canal went on and on, through cities that would have rattled like beetles in a dry skull if you shook them. A hundred or two hundred cities dreaming hot summer-day dreams and cool summer-night dreams . . .

They had come millions of miles for this outing—to fish. But there had been a gun on the rocket. This was a vacation. But why all the food, more than enough to last them years and years, left hidden back there near the rocket? Vacation. Just behind the veil of the vacation was not a soft face of laughter, but something hard and bony and perhaps terrifying. Timothy could not lift the veil, and the two other boys were busy being ten and eight years old, respectively.

"No Martians yet. Nuts." Robert put his V-shaped chin on his hands and glared at the canal.

Dad had brought an atomic radio along, strapped to his wrist. It functioned on an old-fashioned principle: you held it against the bones near your ear and it vibrated singing or talking to you. Dad listened to it now. His face looked like one of those fallen Martian cities, caved in, sucked dry, almost dead.

Then he gave it to Mom to listen. Her lips dropped open.

"What——" Timothy started to question, but never finished what he wished to say.

For at that moment there were two titanic, marrow-jolting explosions that grew upon themselves, followed by a half dozen minor concussions.

Jerking his head up, Dad notched the boat speed higher immediately. The boat leaped and jounced and spanked. This shook Robert out of his funk[2] and elicited yelps of frightened but ecstatic joy from Michael, who clung to Mom's legs and watched the water pour by his nose in a wet torrent.

Dad swerved the boat, cut speed, and ducked the craft into a little branch canal and under an ancient, crumbling stone wharf that smelled of crab flesh. The boat rammed the wharf hard enough to throw them all forward, but no one was hurt, and Dad was already twisted to see if the ripples on the canal were enough to map their route into hiding. Water lines went across, lapped the stones, and rippled back to meet each other, settling, to be dappled by the sun. It all went away.

Dad listened. So did everybody.

Dad's breathing echoed like fists beating against the cold wet wharf stones. In the shadow, Mom's cat eyes just watched Father for some clue to what next.

Dad relaxed and blew out a breath, laughing at himself.

"The rocket, of course. I'm getting jumpy. The rocket."

Michael said, "What happened, Dad, what happened?"

"Oh, we just blew up our rocket, is all," said Timothy, trying to sound matter-of-fact. "I've heard rockets blow up before. Ours just blew."

"Why did we blow up our rocket?" asked Michael. "Huh, Dad?"

"It's part of the game, silly!" said Timothy.

"A game!" Michael and Robert loved the word.

"Dad fixed it so it would blow up and no one'd know where we landed or went! In case they ever came looking, see?"

"Oh boy, a secret!"

"Scared by my own rocket," admitted Dad to Mom. "I am nervous. It's silly to think there'll ever be any more rockets. Except *one*, perhaps, if Edwards and his wife get through with *their* ship."

He put his tiny radio to his ear again. After two minutes he dropped his hand as you would drop a rag.

"It's over at last," he said to Mom. "The radio just went off the atomic beam. Every other world station's gone. They dwindled down to a couple in the last few years. Now the air's completely silent. It'll probably remain silent."

"For how long?" asked Robert.

"Maybe—your great-grandchildren will hear it again," said Dad. He just sat there, and the children were caught in the center of his awe and defeat and resignation and acceptance.

Finally he put the boat out into the canal again, and they continued in the direction in which they had originally started.

It was getting late. Already the sun was down the sky, and a series of dead cities lay ahead of them.

Dad talked very quietly and gently to his sons. Many times in the past he had been brisk, distant, removed from them, but now he patted them on the head with just a word and they felt it.

"Mike, pick a city."

"What, Dad?"

"Pick a city, Son. Any one of these cities we pass."

"All right," said Michael. "How do I pick?"

"Pick the one you like the most. You, too, Robert and Tim. Pick the city you like best."

"I want a city with Martians in it," said Michael.

"You'll have that," said Dad. "I promise." His lips were for the children, but his eyes were for Mom.

They passed six cities in twenty minutes. Dad didn't say anything more about the explosions; he seemed much more interested in having fun with his sons, keeping them happy, than anything else.

Michael liked the first city they passed, but this was vetoed because everyone doubted

---

2. funk\fəŋk\ depression.

quick first judgments. The second city nobody liked. It was an Earth Man's settlement, built of wood and already rotting into sawdust. Timothy liked the third city because it was large. The fourth and fifth were too small and the sixth brought acclaim from everyone, including Mother, who joined in the Gees, Goshes, and Look-at-thats!

There were fifty or sixty huge structures still standing, streets were dusty but paved, and you could see one or two old centrifugal fountains still pulsing wetly in the plazas. That was the only life—water leaping in the late sunlight.

"This is the city," said everybody.

Steering the boat to a wharf, Dad jumped out.

"Here we are. This is ours. This is where we live from now on!"

"From now on?" Michael was incredulous. He stood up, looking, and then turned to blink back at where the rocket used to be. "What about the rocket? What about Minnesota?"

"Here," said Dad.

He touched the small radio to Michael's blond head. "Listen."

Michael listened.

"Nothing," he said.

"That's right. Nothing. Nothing at all any more. No more Minneapolis, no more rockets, no more Earth."

Michael considered the lethal revelation and began to sob little dry sobs.

"Wait a moment," said Dad the next instant. "I'm giving you a lot more in exchange, Mike!"

"What?" Michael held off the tears, curious, but quite ready to continue in case Dad's further revelation was as disconcerting as the original.

"I'm giving you this city, Mike. It's yours."

"Mine?"

"For you and Robert and Timothy, all three of you, to own for yourselves."

Timothy bounded from the boat. "Look, guys, all for us! All of that!" He was playing the game with Dad, playing it large and playing it well. Later, after it was all over and

things had settled, he could go off by himself and cry for ten minutes. But now it was still a game, still a family outing, and the other kids must be kept playing.

Mike jumped out with Robert. They helped Mom.

"Be careful of your sister," said Dad, and nobody knew what he meant until later.

They hurried into the great pink-stoned city, whispering among themselves, because dead cities have a way of making you want to whisper, to watch the sun go down.

"In about five days," said Dad quietly, "I'll go back down to where our rocket was and collect the food hidden in the ruins there and bring it here; and I'll hunt for Bert Edwards and his wife and daughters there."

"Daughters?" asked Timothy. "How many?"

"Four."

"I can see that'll cause trouble later." Mom nodded slowly.

"Girls." Michael made a face like an ancient Martian stone image. "Girls."

"Are they coming in a rocket too?"

"Yes. If they make it. Family rockets are made for travel to the Moon, not Mars. We were lucky we got through."

"Where did you get the rocket?" whispered Timothy, for the other boys were running ahead.

"I saved it. I saved it for twenty years, Tim. I had it hidden away, hoping I'd never have to use it. I suppose I should have given it to the government for the war, but I kept thinking about Mars. . . ."

"And a picnic!"

"Right. This is between you and me. When I saw everything was finishing on Earth, after I'd waited until the last moment, I packed us up. Bert Edwards had a ship hidden, too, but we decided it would be safer to take off separately, in case anyone tried to shoot us down."

"Why'd you blow up the rocket, Dad?"

"So we can't go back, ever. And so if any of those evil men ever come to Mars they won't know we're here."

"Is that why you look up all the time?"

"Yes, it's silly. They won't follow us, ever. They haven't anything to follow with. I'm being too careful, is all."

Michael came running back. "Is this really our city, Dad?"

"The whole darn planet belongs to us, kids. The whole darn planet."

They stood there, King of the Hill, Top of the Heap, Ruler of All They Surveyed, Unimpeachable Monarchs and Presidents, trying to understand what it meant to own a world and how big a world really was.

Night came quickly in the thin atmosphere, and Dad left them in the square by the pulsing fountain, went down to the boat, and came walking back carrying a stack of paper in his big hands.

He laid the papers in a clutter in an old courtyard and set them afire. To keep warm, they crouched around the blaze and laughed, and Timothy saw the little letters leap like frightened animals when the flames touched and engulfed them. The papers crinkled like an old man's skin, and the cremation surrounded innumerable words:

"GOVERNMENT BONDS; Business Graph, 1999; Religious Prejudice: An Essay; The Science of Logistics; Problems of the Pan-American Unity; Stock Report for July 3, 1998; The War Digest . . ."

Dad had insisted on bringing these papers for this purpose. He sat there and fed them into the fire, one by one, with satisfaction, and told his children what it all meant.

"It's time I told you a few things. I don't suppose it was fair, keeping so much from you. I don't know if you'll understand, but I have to talk, even if only part of it gets over to you."

He dropped a leaf in the fire.

"I'm burning a way of life, just like that way of life is being burned clean of Earth right now. Forgive me if I talk like a politician. I am, after all, a former state governor, and I was honest and they hated me for it. Life on Earth never settled down to anything very good. Science ran too far ahead of us too quickly, and the people got lost in a mechanical wilderness, like children making over pretty things, gadgets, helicopters, rockets; emphasizing the wrong items, emphasizing machines instead of how to run the machines. Wars got bigger and bigger and finally killed Earth. That's what the silent radio means. That's what we ran away from.

"We were lucky. There aren't any more rockets left. It's time you knew this isn't a fishing trip at all. I put off telling you. Earth is gone. Interplanetary travel won't be back for centuries, maybe never. But that way of life proved itself wrong and strangled itself with its own hands. You're young. I'll tell you this again every day until it sinks in."

He paused to feed more papers to the fire.

"Now we're alone. We and a handful of others who'll land in a few days. Enough to start over. Enough to turn away from all that back on Earth and strike out on a new line——"

The fire leaped up to emphasize his talking. And then all the papers were gone except one. All the laws and beliefs of Earth were burnt into small hot ashes which soon would be carried off in a wind.

Timothy looked at the last thing that Dad tossed in the fire. It was a map of the World, and it wrinkled and distorted itself hotly and went—flimpf—and was gone like a warm, black butterfly. Timothy turned away.

"Now I'm going to show you the Martians," said Dad. "Come on, all of you. Here, Alice." He took her hand.

Michael was crying loudly, and Dad picked him up and carried him, and they walked down through the ruins toward the canal.

The canal. Where tomorrow or the next day their future wives would come up in a boat, small laughing girls now, with their father and mother.

The night came down around them, and there were stars. But Timothy couldn't find Earth. It had already set. That was something to think about.

A night bird called among the ruins as they walked. Dad said, "Your mother and I will try to teach you. Perhaps we'll fail. I hope not. We've had a good lot to see and learn from. We planned this trip years ago, before you were born. Even if there hadn't been a war we would have come to Mars, I think, to live and form our own standard of living. It would have been another century before Mars would have been really poisoned by the Earth civilization. Now, of course——"

They reached the canal. It was long and straight and cool and wet and reflective in the night.

"I've always wanted to see a Martian," said Michael. "Where are they, Dad? You promised."

"There they are," said Dad, and he shifted Michael on his shoulder and pointed straight down.

The Martians were there. Timothy began to shiver.

The Martians were there—in the canal—reflected in the water. Timothy and Michael and Robert and Mom and Dad.

The Martians stared back up at them for a long, long silent time from the rippling water. . . .

I
THE SEARCH
FOR A NEW TOMORROW

On the surface it may seem as if this is a thoroughly pessimistic story: Bradbury condemns our way of life and predicts that the consequence of that life is self-destruction. On the other hand, at least one family is allowed to escape disaster, and the comments of the head of that family reveal what was wrong with the old life and suggest by implication the values upon which a new life can be built. Thus, for example, when one of his sons asks Mr. Thomas why he is looking so hard at

Earth, he says he is looking for logic, common sense, good government, peace, and responsibility. Such values will presumably be cornerstones of the family's future life on Mars, but there is also the suggestion that the same things may help to avert the disaster Bradbury predicts. The story thus can be read as a protest against the values of today, but also as an affirmation of those values that may help us to create a new tomorrow before it is too late.

II
IMPLICATIONS

Below are listed several quotations and situations from this story. Discuss them in terms of their meaning and your reactions to them.

1. The war [on Earth] was as removed and far off as two flies battling to the death in the arch of a great high and silent cathedral. And just as senseless.

2. The ceremonial burning of "all the laws and beliefs of Earth."

3. "Life on earth never settled down to anything very good."

4. The shiver and the silence as the Martians stare up at them from the canal.

5. "Science ran too far ahead of us too quickly, and the people got lost in a mechanical wilderness. . . ."

III
TECHNIQUES

Structure

One of the important aspects of the structure in many short stories is *suspense*. This is a device used to awaken and maintain the reader's interest in the outcome of the work. It may center in one or more of a number of issues: (1) The question of *what* will happen, (2) the question of *how* it will happen, (3) the question of *to whom* it will happen, and (4) the question of *when* something will happen. In this story the author provokes suspense in several ways—he raises the issue of the reasons for the trip, the somewhat mysterious behavior of the father, and the matter of what the Martians look like. Using any one of these, point out the place where the author first introduces it, how he develops it to maintain reader interest, and which of the four points mentioned above is/are concerned.

Protest and Affirmation in Modern Poetry

One of the strongest directions in modern poetry has been the tendency toward social criticism. But the criticism of most poets has not been irresponsible and negative. For while poets have protested against certain modern values or the lack of any values, they have also tended to affirm new values or reaffirm tested values of the past.

On the morning of September 1, 1939,
the Nazi war machine moved into Poland. Two days later
England and France declared war on Germany,
and World War II had begun. What were some of the thoughts
that went through the mind of a poet at this fateful time? What values
did he feel were still worth cherishing in a chaotic world?
In the following poem the reader may glimpse into the mind of W. H. Auden
as he sat in a New York cafe on September 1, 1939.

September 1, 1939

I sit in one of the dives
On Fifty-second Street
Uncertain and afraid
As the clever hopes expire
Of a low dishonest decade:[1]   5
Waves of anger and fear
Circulate over the bright
And darkened lands of the earth,
Obsessing our private lives;
The unmentionable odour of death   10
Offends the September night.

Accurate scholarship can
Unearth the whole offence
From Luther until now
That has driven a culture mad,   15
Find what occurred at Linz,[2]
What huge imago made
A psychopathic god:[3]
I and the public know

---

1. **a low dishonest decade,** 1929–1939. These were the years of the Great Depression which began with the stock market crash of 1929.
2. **Linz**\lĭntz\ capital of upper Austria on the Danube river west of Vienna. Hitler invaded Austria March 11, 1938, and annexed it two days later.
3. **a psychopathic**\sī·kə ᴧpăth·ĭk\ **god,** here, a mentally ill or unstable dictator, for example, Adolf Hitler.

Copyright 1940 and renewed 1968 by W. H. Auden. Reprinted from THE COLLECTED POETRY OF W. H. AUDEN, by permission of Random House, Inc.

What all schoolchildren learn,   20
Those to whom evil is done[4]
Do evil in return.

Exiled Thucydides[5] knew
All that a speech can say
About Democracy,   25
And what dictators do,
The elderly rubbish they talk
To an apathetic grave;[6]
Analysed all in his book,
The enlightenment driven away,   30
The habit-forming pain,
Mismanagement and grief:
We must suffer them all again.

Into this neutral air
Where blind skyscrapers use   35
Their full height to proclaim
The strength of Collective Man,
Each language pours its vain
Competitive excuse:
But who can live for long   40
In an euphoric dream;[7]
Out of the mirror they stare,
Imperialism's face
And the international wrong.

Faces along the bar   45
Cling to their average day:
The lights must never go out,
The music must always play,
All the conventions conspire
To make this fort assume   50
The furniture of home;
Lest we should see where we are,
Lost in a haunted wood,
Children afraid of the night
Who have never been happy or good.   55

The windiest militant trash
Important Persons shout
Is not so crude as our wish:
What mad Nijinsky[8] wrote
About Diaghilev[9]   60
Is true of the normal heart;
For the error bred in the bone

Of each woman and each man
Craves what it cannot have,
Not universal love   65
But to be loved alone.

From the conservative dark
Into the ethical life
The dense commuters come,
Repeating their morning vow;   70
"I *will* be true to the wife,
I'll concentrate more on my work,"
And helpless governors wake
To resume their compulsory game:
Who can release them now,   75
Who can reach the deaf,
Who can speak for the dumb?

Defenceless under the night
Our world in stupor lies;
Yet, dotted everywhere,   80
Ironic points of light
Flash out wherever the Just
Exchange their messages:
May I, composed like them
Of Eros[10] and of dust,   85
Beleaguered by the same
Negation and despair,
Show an affirming flame.

W. H. AUDEN

---

4. **those to whom evil is done.** Here, the poet may be suggesting that the Treaty of Versailles, dealing harshly with the defeated Germans, set the stage for other wars.
5. **Exiled Thucydides**\thū ˄sĭ·də·dēz\ considered the greatest historian of ancient times. After commanding an unsuccessful expedition, he went into exile. He was noted for his speeches, among them, Pericles' funeral oration.
6. **an apathetic**\'ă·pə ˄thĕ·tĭk\ **grave.** Here, "grave" is a metonymy and stands for the soldier dead who lie in graves, indifferent now to the words of dictators.
7. **euphoric**\yū ˄fō·rĭk\ **dream,** a dream of unaccountable well-being and elation.
8. **Nijinsky**\nĭ ˄zhĭn·skē\ Waslaw (1890–1950), Russian dancer who appeared in Paris (1909) with Diaghilev's Ballet Russe but who later went insane.
9. **Diaghilev**\˄dya·gĭ·lĕf\ Sergei Pavlovich (1872–1929), Russian ballet producer and art critic who introduced ballets adapted to orchestral works.
10. **Eros**\˄ĕr·əs\ the Greek god of love whom the Romans called Cupid.

Although Karl Shapiro himself served as a sergeant
in the South Pacific during the Second World War, he was,
nevertheless, able to sympathize with and understand the conscientious
objector, the person who refused to serve in the Armed Forces
on religious or moral grounds. At the conclusion of the following poem,
what justification does he give for defending the conscientious?

The Conscientious Objector

The gates clanged and they walked you into jail
More tense than felons but relieved to find
The hostile world shut out, the flags that dripped
From every mother's windowpane, obscene
The bloodlust sweating from the public heart,   5
The dog authority slavering at your throat.
A sense of quiet, of pulling down the blind
Possessed you. Punishment you felt was clean.

The decks, the catwalks, and the narrow light
Composed a ship. This was a mutinous crew   10
Troubling the captains for plain decencies,
A *Mayflower* brim with pilgrims headed out
To establish new theocracies to west,
A Noah's ark coasting the topmost seas
Ten miles above the sodomites and fish.   15
These inmates loved the only living doves.

Like all men hunted from the world you made
A good community, voyaging the storm
To no safe Plymouth or green Ararat;[1]
Trouble or calm, the men with Bibles prayed,   20
The gaunt politicals construed our hate.
The opposite of all armies, you were best
Opposing uniformity and yourselves;
Prison and personality were your fate.

You suffered not so physically but knew   25
Maltreatment, hunger, ennui of the mind.
Well might the soldier kissing the hot beach
Erupting in his face d _ _ _ all your kind.

---

1. **Ararat**\\ǎr·ə·răt\\ a mountain in Turkey where
Noah's Ark supposedly came to rest.

Copyright 1947 by Karl Shapiro. Reprinted from SELECTED
POEMS, by permission of Random House, Inc.

Yet you who saved neither yourselves nor us
Are equally with those who shed the blood   30
The heroes of our cause. Your conscience is
What we come back to in the armistice.

KARL SHAPIRO

e. e. cummings has long been identified as a critic
of materialistic values and of "man's inhumanity to man." These are
the objects of his criticism in the following poem; but though the poem
is satiric in tone and seems to be a rather general condemnation
of humanity, a close reading will reveal that cummings is also
commending the positive values of "a world of born."

pity this busy monster, manunkind

pity this busy monster, manunkind,

not. Progress is a comfortable disease:
your victim (death and life safely beyond)

plays with the bigness of his littleness
—electrons deify one razorblade   5
into a mountainrange; lenses extend

unwish through curving wherewhen till unwish
returns on its unself.
                    A world of made
is not a world of born—pity poor flesh   10

and trees, poor stars and stones, but never this
fine specimen of hypermagical

ultraomnipotence. We doctors know

a hopeless case if—listen: there's a hell
of a good universe next door; let's go.   15

E. E. CUMMINGS

Copyright, 1944, by e. e. cummings. Reprinted from his
volume POEMS 1923–1954 by permission of Harcourt Brace
Jovanovich, Inc.

◆ As you might infer from lines seven and eight
in the following poem, Robinson Jeffers has been considered
one of the bitterest and most pessimistic of all modern poets. Yet even he—
who has called civilization a sickness and consciousness a disease—
is not without some measure of affirmation in his poetry.

To the Stone-Cutters

Stone-cutters fighting time with marble, you foredefeated
Challengers of oblivion
Eat cynical earnings, knowing rock splits, records fall down,
The square-limbed Roman letters
Scale in the thaws, wear in the rain. The poet as well   5
Builds his monument mockingly;
For man will be blotted out, the blithe earth die, the brave sun
Die blind and blacken to the heart:
Yet stones have stood for a thousand years, and pained thoughts found
The honey of peace in old poems.   10

ROBINSON JEFFERS

Copyright 1924 and renewed 1952 by Robinson Jeffers. Reprinted from THE SELECTED POETRY, by permission of Random House, Inc.

◆ To appreciate the following poem, you will have to see that there are three
distinct "characters" in it. The character who opens the poem and speaks the alternate
stanzas up to the last is the seventeenth-century philosopher Baruch Spinoza.
The words are from his essay "On the Improvement of the Understanding" and from
his *Ethics.* The second character speaks the indented stanzas up to the last; he is a
military officer telling his troops how they can save themselves from an enemy
if they are caught without any weapons. The third character, who speaks the final
stanza, has been listening to the other two and,
as a result, asks a question.

"After Experience Taught Me . . ."

After experience taught me that all the ordinary
Surroundings of social life are futile and vain;

From AFTER EXPERIENCE by W. D. Snodgrass. Copyright © 1964 by W. D. Snodgrass. Reprinted by permission of Harper & Row, Publishers, Inc.

I'm going to show you something very
Ugly: someday, it might save your life.

Seeing that none of the things I feared contain   5
In themselves anything either good or bad

What if you get caught without a knife;
Nothing—even a loop of piano wire;

Excepting only in the effect they had
Upon my mind, I resolved to inquire   10

Take the first two fingers of this hand;
Fork them out—kind of a "V for Victory"—

Whether there might be something whose discovery
Would grant me supreme, unending happiness.

And jam them into the eyes of your enemy.   15
You have to do this hard. Very hard. Then press

No virtue can be thought to have priority
Over this endeavor to preserve one's being.

Both fingers down around the cheekbone
And setting your foot high into the chest   20

No man can desire to act rightly, to be blessed,
To live rightly, without simultaneously

You must call up every strength you own
And you can rip off the whole facial mask.

Wishing to be, to act, to live. He must ask   25
First, in other words, to actually exist.

And you, whiner, who wastes your time
Dawdling over the remorseless earth,
What evil, what unspeakable crime
Have you made your life worth?   30

W. D. SNODGRASS

Most modern poets are not religious
in the narrow or sectarian sense of that word. Yet, many of them
would agree with a statement once made by the author
of the following poem: "Poetry, whether avowedly so or not,
is always religious; it is akin to prayer,
an act of love." Below, we have
a strongly affirmative poem, the expression of faith
in the belief that the world will one day
return to God.

Return

From what I am, to be what I am not,
To be what once I was, from plan and plot
To learn to take no thought,
I go, my God, to Thee.

With act of faith whose throes and throbs convulse   5
My heart as if all other acts were else
Than dyings, prayer than pulse,
I go, my God, to Thee.

On feet thread through by seams of blood and fire,
Dancing the narrow pathway, strictest wire,   10
As butterflies a briar,
I go, my God, to Thee.

To balance like a bird with wings aflare,
Pinned to the cross as though I merely were
Stenciled by light on air,   15
I go, my God, to Thee.

My spirit, trim, uncorseted from stress,
Stripping to wind and sunlight, to the grace
Of Eden's nakedness
Will go, my God, to Thee.   20

VASSAR MILLER

Copyright © 1960 by Vassar Miller. Reprinted from *Wage War on Silence,* by permission of Wesleyan University Press.

Perhaps more than any other group,
the black Americans have a right to protest. That protest
is strong at times, as we see in Claude McKay's sonnet "America."
But protest is not the only note
sung by the black. Observe the strongly affirmative
note on which Margaret Walker concludes "For My People,"
asking for a "race of men" to "rise and take control."

America

Although she feeds me bread of bitterness,
And sinks into my throat her tiger's tooth,
Stealing my breath of life, I will confess
I love this cultured hell that tests my youth!
Her vigor flows like tides into my blood,   5
Giving me strength erect against her hate.
Her bigness sweeps my being like a flood.
Yet as a rebel fronts a king in state,
I stand within her walls with not a shred
Of terror, malice, not a word of jeer.   10
Darkly I gaze into the days ahead,
And see her might and granite wonders there,
Beneath the touch of Time's unerring hand,
Like priceless treasures sinking in the sand.

CLAUDE MC KAY

Reprinted with the permission of Twayne Publishers, a division of G. K. Hall & Co., Boston.

For My People

For my people everywhere singing their slave songs repeatedly:
    their dirges and their ditties[1] and their blues and jub-
    ilees, praying their prayers nightly to an unknown god,
    bending their knees humble to an unseen power;

For my people lending their strength to the years, to the gone   5
    years and the now years and the maybe years, washing
    ironing cooking scrubbing sewing mending hoeing plowing
    digging planting pruning patching dragging along never
    gaining never reaping never knowing and never understanding;

For my playmates in the clay and dust and sand of Alabama   10
    backyards playing baptizing and preaching and doctor
    and jail and soldier and school and mama and cooking
    and playhouse and concert and store and hair and Miss
    Choomby and company;

For the cramped bewildered years we went to school to learn   15
    to know the reasons why and the answers to and the
    people who and the places where and the days when,
    in memory of the bitter hours when we discovered we
    were black and poor and small and different and nobody
    cared and nobody wondered and nobody understood;   20

For the boys and girls who grew in spite of these things to be
    man and woman, to laugh and dance and sing and play and
    drink their wine and religion and success, to marry
    their playmates and bear children and then die of consump-
    tion and anemia[2] and lynching;   25

For my people thronging 47th Street in Chicago and Lenox
    Avenue in New York and Rampart Street in New Orleans,
    lost disinherited dispossessed and happy people
    filling the cabarets[3] and taverns and other people's
    pockets needing bread and shoes and milk and land   30
    and money and something—something all our own;

---

1. **dirges . . . ditties,** funeral hymns . . . short simple songs.
2. **anemia**\ə ˈnē•mē•ə\ condition in the blood where there is a reduction of
red blood cells.
3. **cabarets**\kăb 'ə ˈrāz\ restaurants with entertainment.

Reprinted by permission of Margaret Walker Alexander.

For my people walking blindly spreading joy, losing time
   being lazy, sleeping when hungry, shouting when
   burdened, drinking when hopeless, tied and shackled
   and tangled among ourselves by the unseen creatures   35
   who tower over us omnisciently and laugh;

For my people blundering and groping and floundering in
   the dark of churches and schools and clubs and
   societies, associations and councils and committees
   and conventions, distressed and disturbed and de-   40
   ceived and devoured by money-hungry glory-craving
   leeches, preyed on by facile force of state and fad
   and novelty, by false prophet and holy believer;

For my people standing staring trying to fashion a better
   way from confusion, from hypocrisy and misunder-   45
   standing, trying to fashion a world that will hold
   all the people, all the faces, all the adams and eves
   and their countless generations;

Let a new earth rise. Let another world be born. Let a bloody
   peace be written in the sky. Let a second generation   50
   full of courage issue forth; let a people loving freedom come to growth. Let a beauty full of healing and
   a strength of final clenching be the pulsing in our
   spirits and our blood. Let the martial songs be
   written, let the dirges disappear. Let a race of men   55
   now rise and take control.

MARGARET WALKER

I
THE POET
AGAINST THE WORLD AS IT IS

Over eight hundred years ago the Persian poet
Omar Khayyám wrote the following lines:

Ah Love! could Thou and I with Fate conspire
To grasp this sorry Scheme of Things entire,
   Would we not shatter it to bits—and then
Remold it nearer to the Heart's Desire!

The feeling expressed here is a familiar one in
poetry. The poet has often protested against life
as it is ("this sorry Scheme of Things") and expressed the hope that he could make it better ("Remold it nearer to the Heart's Desire"). Khayyám
would begin by conspiring with Love and Fate to
shatter to bits the world as it is.

The protest against life as it is echoes through

the poems you have just read. Cummings, for example, protests against "a world of made," a world
in which progress is judged in materialistic terms;
McKay is protesting against racial hatred. Underlying all the protest, however, you can detect,
directly or indirectly, that the poet's concern is
basically positive.

II
IMPLICATIONS

Be prepared to discuss the meaning and full
implications of each of the following groups of
key lines from the poems.

1. May I, composed like them
   Of Eros and of dust,
   Beleaguered by the same
   Negation and despair,
   Show an affirming flame.   (W. H. Auden)

2.   Your conscience is
    What we come back to in the armistice.
                                   (Karl Shapiro)

3.   A world of made
    is not a world of born. . . . (e. e. cummings)

4. Yet stones have stood for a thousand years,
       and pained thoughts found
    The honey of peace in old poems.
                                (Robinson Jeffers)

5. And you, whiner, who wastes your time
       Dawdling over the remorseless earth,
    What evil, what unspeakable crime
       Have you made your life worth?
                                (W. D. Snodgrass)

6. With act of faith whose throes and throbs con-
       vulse
    My heart as if all other acts were else
    Than dying . . .   (Vassar Miller)

7.   . . . I will confess
    I love this cultured hell that tests my youth!
                                (Claude McKay)

8.   tied and shackled
    and tangled among ourselves by the unseen
    creatures who tower over us omnisciently and
    laugh;   (Margaret Walker)

III
TECHNIQUES

Figurative Language

The most common figures of speech are simile
and metaphor. The former is usually defined as a
stated comparison between two things, using *like*
or *as*; a metaphor is defined as an implied comparison between two things.

It is important to note that the two things are
never compared in all respects and important to
see in just which respects they are being compared.
Consider the following lines from the fifth stanza
of Auden's "September 1, 1939":

> All the conventions conspire
> To make this fort assume
> The furniture of home;

"This fort" is clearly a metaphor involving a
comparison between a fort and the cafe in which
the speaker is seated. But a fort has many aspects—
which should we compare with the cafe?

This is obviously a matter of the greatest importance. If readers were to select the wrong
aspect for comparison, they might completely
mistake the poet's meaning. If readers decide that
the fort and cafe should be compared on the basis
of physical appearance, for example, they will not
understand the poet's true intention, which is not
to call up a visual image at all but rather to call
up the similarities in the protective qualities of
the two things—just as a fort protects those within
it from hostile and destructive forces without, so
does the cafe protect those sitting in it from hostile
ideas and realities that would shatter their complacency.

There is no magic way in which one can be certain one is selecting the proper actions, qualities, or
sense appeals (or combinations of the three) for
comparison, but the basic key is context. In Auden's
poem, for example, the lines following those quoted
clearly tell the basis on which the author wants the
fort and cafe compared. Find other examples of
figurative language in the poems you have just
studied, and be prepared to discuss the bases for
each comparison.

We usually think of values as highly personal, differing widely
from individual to individual. But isn't it equally obvious
that all human beings have a great deal in common?
If so, what are the implications of
this fact for living? These are some of the
matters touched upon in the
following simple but
powerful short story.

The Traveler

WALLACE STEGNER

He was rolling in the first early dark down
a snowy road, his headlights pinched between
dark walls of trees, when the engine coughed,
recovered, coughed again, and died. Down a
slight hill he coasted in compression, working
the choke, but at the bottom he had to pull over
against the three-foot wall of plowed snow.
Snow creaked under the tires as the car eased
to a stop. The heater fan unwound with a final
tinny sigh.

Here in its middle age this hitherto depend-
able mechanism had betrayed him, but he
refused to admit immediately that he was betrayed. Some speck of dirt or bubble of water
in the gas line, some momentary short circuit,
some splash of snow on distributor points or
plug connections—something that would cure
itself before long. But turning off the lights and
pressing on the starter brought no result; he
held the choke out for several seconds, and got
only the hopeful stink of gasoline; he waited
and let the flooded carburetor rest and tried
again, and nothing. Eventually he opened the
door and stepped out onto the packed snow of
the road.

It was so cold that his first breath turned to
iron in his throat, the hairs in his nostrils

webbed into instant ice, his eyes stung and
watered. In the faint starlight and the bluish
luminescence of the snow everything beyond
a few yards away swam deceptive and without
depth, glimmering with things half seen or
imagined. Beside the dead car he stood with
his head bent, listening, and there was not a
sound. Everything on the planet might have
died in the cold.

Indecisively seeking help, he walked to the
top of the next rise, but the faintly-darker furrow of the road blurred and disappeared in
the murk, the shadows pressed inward, there
was no sign of a light. Back at the car he made
the efforts that the morality of self-reliance demanded: trying to see by the backward diffu-
sion of the headlamps, he groped over the
motor feeling for broken wires or loose connections, until he had satisfied himself that he was
helpless. He had known all along that he was.

His hands were already stung with cold, and
around his ankles between low shoes and
trouser cuffs he felt the chill like leg irons.
When he had last stopped, twenty miles back,
it had been near zero. It could be ten or fifteen
below now. So what did he do, stranded in
mid-journey fifty miles or more from his destination? He could hardly go in for help, leaving
the sample cases, because the right rear door
didn't lock properly. A little jiggling swung it

"The Traveler" from Stegner's CITY OF THE LIVING. Copyright © 1950, 1951, 1952, 1953, 1954 by Wallace Stegner.
Reprinted by permission of the publisher, Houghton Mifflin Co.

open. And all those drugs, some of them designed to cure anything—wonder drugs, sulphas, streptomycin, aureomycin, penicillin, pills and antitoxins and unguents—represented not only a value but a danger. They should not be left around loose. Someone might think they really *would* cure anything.

Not quite everything, he told the blue darkness. Not a fouled-up distributor or a cranky coil box. Absurdly, there came into his mind a fragment of an ancient hymn to mechanical transport:

> If she runs out of dope, just fill her up with soap
> And the little Ford will ramble right along.

He saw himself pouring a bottle of penicillin into the gas tank and driving off with the exhaust blowing happy smoke rings. A mock-heroic montage[1] of scientific discovery unreeled itself—white-coated scientists peering into microscopes, adjusting gauges, pipetting[2] precious liquids, weighing grains of powder on miniscule scales. Messenger boys sped with telegrams to the desks of busy executives. A group of observers stood beside an assembly line while the first tests were made. They broke a car's axle with sledges, gave it a drink of the wonder compound, and drove it off. They demolished the carburetor and cured it with one application. They yanked loose all the wires and watched the same magic set the motor purring.

But here he stood in light overcoat and thin leather gloves, without overshoes, and his car all but blocked the road, and the door could not be locked, and there was not a possibility that he could carry the heavy cases with him to the next farm or village. He switched on the headlights again and studied the roadside they revealed, and saw a rail fence, with cedars and spruces behind it. When more complex gadgets and more complex cures failed, there was always the lucifer match.

Ten minutes later he was sitting with the auto robe over his head and shoulders and his back against the plowed snowbank, digging the half melted snow from inside his shoes and gloating over the growing light and warmth of the fire. He had a supply of fence rails good for an hour. In that time, someone would come along and he could get a push or a tow. In this country, in winter, no one ever passed up a stranded motorist.

In the stillness the flames went straight upward; the heat was wonderfully pleasant on icy hands and numb ankles and stiffened face. He looked across the road, stained by horses, broken by wheel and runner tracks, and saw how the roadside acquired definition and sharp angles and shadows in the firelight. He saw too how he would look to anyone coming along: like a calendar picture.

But no one came along. Fifteen minutes stretched into a half hour, he had only two broken pieces of rail left, the fire sizzled half floating in the puddle of its melting. Restlessly he rose with the blanket around him and walked back up the road a hundred steps. Eastward, above jagged trees, he saw the sky where it lightened to moonrise, but here there was still only the blue glimmer of starlight on the snow. Something long-buried and forgotten tugged in him, and a shiver not entirely from cold prickled his whole body with goose flesh. There had been times in his childhood when he had walked home alone and been temporarily lost in nights like this. In many years he could not remember being out alone under such a sky. He felt spooked, his feet were chilled lumps, his nose leaked. Down the hill car and snow swam deceptively together; the red wink of the fire seemed inexpressibly far off.

Abruptly he did not want to wait in that lonely snow-banked ditch any longer. The sample cases could look after themselves, any motorist who passed could take his own chances. He would walk ahead to the nearest

---

1. **montage**\mŏn ⋆tazh\ a composite picture made by combining several separate pictures.
2. **pipetting**\⋆pai·pə·tĭŋ\ drawing into a glass tube by suction.

help, and if he found himself getting too cold on the way, he could always build another fire. The thought of action cheered him; he admitted to himself that he was all but terrified at the silence and the iron cold.

Locking the car doors, he dropped his key case in the snow, and panic stopped his pulse as he bent and frantically, with bare hand, brushed away the snow until he found it. The powdery snow ached and burned at his finger tips. He held them a last moment to the fire, and then, bundled like a squaw, with the blanket held across nose and mouth to ease the harshness of the cold in his lungs, he started up the road that looked as smooth as a table-cloth, but was deceptively rough and broken. He thought of what he had had every right to expect for this evening. By now, eight o'clock or so, he should have had a smoking supper, the luxury of a hot bath, the pleasure of a brandy in a comradely bar. By now he should be in pajamas making out sales reports by the bedlight, in a room where steam knocked com-fortingly in the radiators and the help of a hundred hands was available to him at a word into the telephone. For all of this to be torn away suddenly, for him to be stumbling up a deserted road in danger of freezing to death, just be-cause some simple mechanical part that had functioned for thirty thousand miles refused to function any longer, this was outrage, and he hated it. He thought of garage men and service station attendants he could blame. Ignoring the evidence of the flooded carburetor, he brooded about watered gas that could make ice in the gas line. A man was dependent on too many people; he was at everybody's mercy.

And then, on top of the second long rise, he met the moon.

Instantly the character of the night changed. The uncertain starlight was replaced at a step by an even flood of blue-white radiance. He looked across a snow meadow and saw how a rail fence had every stake and rider doubled in solid shadow, and how the edge of woods beyond was blackest India ink. The road ahead was drawn with a ruler, one bank smoothed by the flood of light, the other deeply shad-owed. As he looked into the eye of the moon he saw the air shiver and glint with falling particles of frost.

In this White-Christmas night, this Good-King-Wenceslaus night, he went warily, not to be caught in sentimentality, and to an invisible audience he deprecated it profanely as a night in which no one would believe. Yet here it was, and he in it. With the coming of the moon the night even seemed to warm; he found that he could drop the blanket from across his face and drink the still air.

Along the roadside as he passed the meadow and entered woods again the moon showed him things. In moonlight openings he saw the snow stitched with tiny perfect tracks, mouse or weasel or the three-toed crowding tracks of partridge. These too, an indigenous[3] part of the night, came back to him as things once known and long forgotten. In his boyhood he had trapped and hunted the animals that made such tracks as these; it was as if his mind were a snowfield where the marks of their secret little feet had been printed long ago. With a queer tightening of the throat, with an odd pride, he read the trail of a fox that had wallowed through the soft snow from the woods, angling into the packed road and along it for a little way and out again, still angling, across the plowed bank, and then left a pur-poseful trail of clearly punched tracks, the hind feet out of line with the front, across the clean snow and into the opposite woods, from shadow across moonlight and into shadow again, mysterious.

Turning with the road, he passed through the stretch of woods and came into the open to see the moon-white, shadow-black buildings of a farm, and the weak bloom of light in a window.

His feet whined on the snow, dry as metal powder, as he turned in the loop of drive the county plow had cleared. But as he approached

_____

3. indigenous\in ᴧdǐ·jə·nəs\ **part,** a natural part.

the house doubt touched him. In spite of the light, the place looked unused, somehow. No dog welcomed him. The sound of his feet in the snow was alien, the hammer of his knuckles on the door an intrusion. Looking upward for some trace of telephone wires, he saw none, and he could not tell whether the quivering of the air that he thought he saw above the chimney was heat or smoke or the phantasmal falling frost.

"Hello?" he said, and knocked again. "Anybody home?" No sound answered him. He saw the moon glint on the great icicles along the eaves. His numb hand ached with the pain of knocking; he pounded with the soft edge of his fist.

Answer finally came, not from the door before which he stood, but from the barn, down at the end of a staggered string of attached sheds. A door creaked open against a snowbank and a figure with a lantern appeared, stood for a moment, and came running. The traveler wondered at the way it came, lurching and stumbling in the uneven snow, until it arrived at the porch and he saw that it was a boy of eleven or twelve. The boy set his lantern on the porch; between the upturned collar of his mackinaw and the down-pulled stocking cap his face was a pinched whiteness, his eyes enormous. He stared at the traveler until the traveler became aware of the blanket he still held over head and shoulders, and began to laugh.

"My car stopped on me, a mile or so up the road," he said. "I was just hunting a telephone or some place where I could get help."

The boy swallowed, wiped the back of his mitt across his nose. "Grandpa's sick!" he blurted, and opened the door.

Warmth rushed in their faces, cold rushed in at their backs, warm and cold mingled in an eddy of air as the door closed. The traveler saw a cot bed pulled close to the kitchen range, and on the cot an old man covered with a quilt, who breathed heavily and whose closed eyes did not open when the two came near. The gray-whiskered cheeks were sunken, the mouth open to expose toothless gums in a parody look of ancient mischief.

"He must've had a shock," the boy said. "I came in from chores and he was on the floor." He stared at the mummy under the quilt, and he swallowed.

"Has he come to at all?"

"No."

"Only the two of you live here?"

"Yes."

"No telephone?"

"No."

"How long ago did you find him?"

"Chore time. About six?"

"Why didn't you go for help?"

The boy looked down, ashamed. "It's near two miles. I was afraid he'd. . . ."

"But you left him. You were out in the barn."

"I was hitching up to go," the boy said. "I'd made up my mind."

The traveler backed away from the stove, his face smarting with the heat, his fingers and feet beginning to ache. He looked at the old man and knew that here, as at the car, he was helpless. The boy's thin anxious face told him how thoroughly his own emergency had been swallowed up in this other one. He had been altered from a man in need of help to one who must give it. Salesman of wonder cures, he must now produce something to calm this over-worried boy, restore a dying man. Rebelliously, victimized by circumstances, he said, "Where were you going for help?"

"The Hill place. They've got a phone."

"How far are they from a town?"

"About five miles."

"Doctor there?"

"Yes."

"If I took your horse and—what is it, sleigh? —could someone at the Hills' bring them back, do you think?"

"Cutter. One of the Hill boys could, I should say."

"Or would you rather go, while I look after your Grandpa?"

"He don't know you," the boy said directly.

"If he should wake up he might . . . wonder . . . it might. . . ."

The traveler grudgingly gave up the prospect of staying in the warm kitchen while the boy did the work. And he granted that it was extraordinarily sensitive of the boy to know how it might disturb a man to wake from sickness in his own house and stare into the face of an utter stranger. "Yes," he said. "Well, I could call the doctor from the Hills'. Two miles, did you say?"

"About." The boy had pulled the stocking cap off so that his hair stood on end above his white forehead. He had odd eyes, very large and dark and intelligent, with an expectancy in them.

The traveler, watching him with interest, said, "How long have you lived with your grandfather?"

"Two years."

"Parents living?"

"No sir, that's why."

"Go to school?"

He got a queer sidling look. "Have to till you're sixteen."

"Is that the only reason you go?"

What he was trying to force out of the boy came out indirectly, with a shrugging of the shoulders. "Grandpa would take me out if he could."

"Would you be glad?"

"No sir," the boy said, but would not look at him. "I like school."

The traveler consciously corked his flow of questions. Once he himself had been an orphan living with his grandparents on a back farm; he wondered if this boy went as he had gone, knocking in imagination at all of life's closed doors.

The old man's harsh breathing filled the overwarm room. "Well," the traveler said, "maybe you'd better go finish hitching up. It's been thirty years since I harnessed a horse. I'll keep an eye on your Grandpa."

Pulling the stocking cap over his disheveled hair, the boy slid out the door. The traveler unbuttoned his overcoat and sat down beside the old man, felt the spurting, weak pulse, raised one eyelid with his thumb and looked without comprehension at the uprolled eye. He knew it was like feeling over a chilling motor for loose wires, and after two or three abortive motions he gave it up and sat contemplating the gray, sunken face, the unfamiliar face of an old man who would die, and thinking that the face was the only unfamiliar thing about the whole night. The kitchen smells, coffee and peanut butter and the mouldy, barky smell of wood from the woodbox, and the smell of the hot range and of paint baking in the heat, those were as familiar as light or dark. The spectacular night outside, the snowfields and the moon and the mysterious woods, the tracks venturing out across the snow from the protective eaves of firs and skunk spruce, the speculative, imagining expression of the boy's eyes, were just as familiar. He sat bemused, touching some brink as a man will walk along a cutbank trying to knock loose the crumbling overhang with an outstretched foot. The ways a man fitted in with himself and with other human beings were curious and complex.

And when he heard the jingle and creak outside, and buttoned himself into the overcoat again and wrapped his shoulders in the blanket and stepped out into the yard, there was a moment when the boy passed him the lines and they stood facing each other in the broken snow.

It was a moment like farewell, like a poignant parting. Touched by his pressing sense of familiarity and by a sort of compassion, the traveler reached out and laid his hand on the boy's shoulder. "Don't worry," he said. "I'll have someone back here right away. Your grandfather will be all right. Just keep him warm and don't worry."

He climbed into the cutter and pulled over his lap the balding buffalo robe he found there; the scallop of its felt edges was like a key that fitted a door. The horses breathed jets of steam in the moonlight, restlessly moving, jingling their harness bells, as the moment lengthened itself. The traveler saw how the boy, now that his anxiety was somewhat quieted, now that he had been able to unload part of his burden, watched him with a thousand questions in his face, and he remembered how he himself, thirty years ago, had searched the faces of passing strangers for something he could not name, how he had listened to their steps and seen their shadows lengthen ahead of them down roads that led to unimaginable places, and how he had ached with the desire to know them, who they were. But none of them had looked back at him as he tried now to look at this boy.

He was glad that no names had been spoken and no personal histories exchanged to obscure this meeting, for sitting in the sleigh above the boy's white upturned serious face he felt that some profound contact had unintentionally, almost casually, been made.

For half a breath he was utterly bewitched, frozen at the heart of some icy dream. Abruptly he slapped the reins across the backs of the horses; the cutter jerked and then slid smoothly out toward the road. The traveler looked back once, to fix forever the picture of himself standing silently watching himself go. As he slid into the road the horses broke into a trot. The icy flow of air locked his throat and made him let go the reins with one hand to pull the hairy, wool-smelling edge of the blanket all but shut across his face.

Along a road he had never driven he went swiftly toward an unknown farm and an unknown town, to distribute according to some wise law part of the burden of the boy's emergency and his own; but he bore in his mind, bright as moonlight over snow, a vivid wonder, almost an awe. For from that most chronic[4] and incurable of ills, identity, he had looked outward and for one unmistakable instant recognized himself.

---

4. **chronic**\ˈkrŏ•nĭk\ marked by long duration or frequent recurrence.

I
"NO MAN IS AN ISLAND"

In the last paragraph of this story—its moment of illumination—the narrator calls identity "that most chronic and incurable of ills." Offhand, you might wonder at such a statement—after all, isn't it good to have a sense of identity, a sense of who you are? As a matter of fact, isn't it precisely his identity that the traveler discovers?

Lost for thirty years, he searched in the wrong places. He looked inward for his identity—for those things that marked him off from others and made him unique. Identity, in this sense, could be called an illness, for it could lead to isolation from others and to the loss of such virtues as sympathy and compassion.

By looking outward, by loving—giving himself—the traveler discovers a deeper sense of his identity. He discovers not what separates him from others but what he has in common with them.

II
IMPLICATIONS

Discuss the following propositions.

1. The search for self-knowledge (or identity) is a lifelong one.

2. The stronger one's sense of identity is, the stronger one's sense of values.

3. We are dependent on too many people; we are at everybody's mercy.

4. The deeper one looks inward, the more one will find one has in common with others.

III
TECHNIQUES

Structure

This story may be divided in half almost perfectly. The first half is devoted to the traveler, his car problem, and his loneliness; the second half brings in the boy and his dilemma. The parallel between the man's and the boy's situation is thus forced on the reader's attention. In what ways does the division of the story into two parts relate to the no-man-is-an-island theme?

Symbolism

1. What are some of the symbolic implications of the story's title?

2. Note all references to the moon or moonlight. What might they symbolize?

Can a human soul—when it is once pinched by fear, sickened
by pain and sorrow, anguished by its own and the world's crimes—
can such a soul be removed, reborn to a fresh awareness of
and faith in the world's fundamental beauty and goodness? Be alert
for the poet's shifting moods as she searches successfully for purpose
and meaning in life and the world.

Renascence

All I could see from where I stood
Was three long mountains and a wood;
I turned and looked another way,
And saw three islands in a bay.
So with my eyes I traced the line   5
Of the horizon, thin and fine,
Straight around till I was come
Back to where I'd started from;
And all I saw from where I stood
Was three long mountains and a wood.   10
Over these things I could not see;
These were the things that bounded me;
And I could touch them with my hand,
Almost, I thought, from where I stand.

And all at once things seemed so small   15
My breath came short, and scarce at all.
But, sure, the sky is big, I said;
Miles and miles above my head;
So here upon my back I'll lie
And look my fill into the sky.   20
And so I looked, and, after all,
The sky was not so very tall.
The sky, I said, must somewhere stop,
And—sure enough!—I see the top!
The sky, I thought, is not so grand;   25
I 'most could touch it with my hand!
And, reaching up my hand to try,
I screamed to feel it touch the sky.

I screamed, and—lo!—Infinity[1]
Came down and settled over me;   30
Forced back my scream into my chest,
Bent back my arm upon my breast,
And, pressing of the Undefined
The definition on my mind,[2]
Held up before my eyes a glass   35
Through which my shrinking sight did pass
Until it seemed I must behold
Immensity made manifold;
Whispered to me a word whose sound
Deafened the air for worlds around,   40
And brought unmuffled to my ears
The gossiping of friendly spheres,
The creaking of the tented sky,
The ticking of Eternity.

I saw and heard, and knew at last   45
The How and Why of all things, past
And present, and forevermore.
The universe, cleft to the core,
Lay open to my probing sense
That, sick'ning, I would fain pluck thence 50
But could not—nay! But needs must suck
At the great wound, and could not pluck

Reprinted by permission of Norma Millay Ellis, literary
executor.

1. **Infinity,** when capitalized, as here, stands for God,
the One, the First Cause.
2. **pressing of the Undefined/The definition on my
mind,** revealing to my mind the meaning of that Being
who can not be defined in the usual sense of the word
because to define means to set limits (*Latin:* definire,
to limit) and limits cannot be set to the Infinite.

My lips away till I had drawn
All venom out.—Ah, fearful pawn![3]
For my omniscience paid I toll[4]   55
In infinite remorse of soul.
All sin was of my sinning, all
Atoning mine, and mine the gall
Of all regret. Mine was the weight
Of every brooded wrong, the hate   60
That stood behind each envious thrust,
Mine every greed, mine every lust.
And all the while for every grief,
Each suffering, I craved relief
With individual desire—   65
Craved all in vain! And felt fierce fire
About a thousand people crawl;
Perished with each—then mourned for all!
A man was starving in Capri;[5]
He moved his eyes and looked at me;   70
I felt his gaze, I heard his moan,
And knew his hunger as my own.
I saw at sea a great fog bank
Between two ships that struck and sank;
A thousand screams the heavens smote;   75
And every scream tore through my throat.
No hurt I did not feel, no death
That was not mine; mine each last breath
That, crying, met an answering cry
From the compassion that was I.   80
All suffering mine, and mine its rod;[6]
Mine, pity like the pity of God.
Ah, awful weight! Infinity
Pressed down upon the finite Me!
My anguished spirit, like a bird,   85
Beating against my lips I heard;
Yet lay the weight so close about
There was no room for it without.
And so beneath the weight lay I
And suffered death, but could not die.   90

Deep in the earth I rested now;
Cool is its hand upon the brow
And soft its breast beneath the head
Of one who is so gladly dead.
And all at once, and over all,   95
The pitying rain began to fall;
I lay and heard each pattering hoof
Upon my lowly, thatchèd roof,

And seemed to love the sound far more
Than ever I had done before.   100
For rain it hath a friendly sound
To one who's six feet underground;
And scarce[7] the friendly voice or face:
A grave is such a quiet place.

The rain, I said, is kind to come   105
And speak to me in my new home.
I would I were alive again
To kiss the fingers of the rain,
To drink into my eyes the shine
Of every slanting silver line,   110
To catch the freshened, fragrant breeze
From drenched and dripping apple trees.
For soon the shower will be done,
And then the broad face of the sun
Will laugh above the rain-soaked earth   115
Until the world with answering mirth
Shakes joyously, and each round drop
Rolls, twinkling, from its grass-blade top.
How can I bear it; buried here,
While overhead the sky grows clear   120
And blue again after the storm?

O, multicolored, multiform
Belovèd beauty over me,
That I shall never, never see
Again! Spring silver, autumn gold,   125
That I shall never more behold!
Sleeping your myriad magics through,
Close sepulchered away from you!
O God, I cried, give me new birth,
And put me back upon the earth!   130
Upset each cloud's gigantic gourd[8]

---

3. **fearful pawn**\pɒn\ *Latin:* pedo, foot soldier. One of the sixteen chessmen of least value and with greatest limitation of movement on the chessboard. Here, an insignificant person full of fear.
4. **For my omniscience paid I toll,** for my all-knowing I paid a price. I had become one with all; I suffered with all.
5. **Capri**\ka ˈprē\ an Italian island south of Naples.
6. **all suffering mine, and mine its rod.** In the moment of attunement with the Infinite, the poet was at one both with the sufferer and with that (the rod) which caused the suffering.
7. **scarce,** here, the word means *seldom met.*
8. **gourd**\gōrd\ a plant that bears fruit with a shell which is often dried and used to make dippers.

And let the heavy rain, down poured
In one big torrent, set me free,
Washing my grave away from me!

I ceased; and, through the breathless hush   135
That answered me, the far-off rush
Of herald wings came whispering
Like music down the vibrant string
Of my ascending prayer, and—crash!
Before the wild wind's whistling lash   140
The startled storm clouds reared on high
And plunged in terror down the sky,
And the big rain in one black wave
Fell from the sky and struck my grave.
I know not how such things can be   145
I only know there came to me
A fragrance such as never clings
To aught save happy living things;
A sound as of some joyous elf
Singing sweet songs to please himself,   150
And, through and over everything,
A sense of glad awakening.
The grass, a-tiptoe at my ear,
Whispering to me I could hear;
I felt the rain's cool finger tips   155
Brushed tenderly across my lips,
Laid gently on my sealèd sight,
And all at once the heavy night
Fell from my eyes and I could see—
A drenched and dripping apple tree,   160
A last long line of silver rain,
A sky grown clear and blue again.
And as I looked a quickening gust
Of wind blew up to me and thrust
Into my face a miracle   165
Of orchard breath, and with the smell—
I know not how such things can be!—
I breathed my soul back into me.

Ah! Up then from the ground sprang I
And hailed the earth with such a cry   170
As is not heard save from a man
Who has been dead, and lives again.
About the trees my arms I wound;
Like one gone mad I hugged the ground;
I raised my quivering arms on high;   175
I laughed and laughed into the sky,

Till at my throat a strangling sob
Caught fiercely, and a great heartthrob
Sent instant tears into my eyes;
O God, I cried, no dark disguise   180
Can e'er hereafter hide from me
Thy radiant identity!
Thou canst not move across the grass
But my quick eyes will see Thee pass,
Nor speak, however silently,   185
But my hushed voice will answer Thee.
I know the path that tells Thy way
Through the cool eve of every day;
God, I can push the grass apart
And lay my finger on Thy heart!   190

The world stands out on either side
No wider than the heart is wide;
Above the world is stretched the sky—
No higher than the soul is high.
The heart can push the sea and land   195
Farther away on either hand;
The soul can split the sky in two,
And let the face of God shine through.
But East and West will pinch the heart
That cannot keep them pushed apart;   200
And he whose soul is flat—the sky
Will cave in on him by and by.

EDNA ST. VINCENT MILLAY

I

THE REBIRTH OF THE SOUL

The feeling that one needs to be reborn spiritually often has its beginnings in the frustrations and
failings of one's personal life, as well as in one's
concern over the sufferings and crimes of humanity. And nearly always the rebirth involves some
sort of suffering or atonement by which the soul is
purged and washed clean.

1. What personal frustrations seem to beset the
narrator?

2. What sufferings and crimes of the world
trouble her? How do they affect her?

3. What does she suffer before she is reborn?

4. How does her rebirth change her?

II
IMPLICATIONS

Discuss the meaning of the following quotations and show how they relate to one another in telling the story of the narrator's rebirth.

1. And all I saw from where I stood
   Was three long mountains and a wood.
   Over these things I could not see;
   These were the things that bounded me;
   (lines 9–12)

2. I screamed, and—lo!—Infinity
   Came down and settled over me;
   (lines 29–30)

   . . . .

   Until it seemed I must behold
   Immensity made manifold;   (lines 37–38)

3. All suffering mine, and mine its rod;
   Mine, pity like the pity of God.
   Ah, awful weight! Infinity
   Pressed down upon the finite Me!
   (lines 81–84)

4. Before the wild wind's whistling lash
   The startled storm clouds reared on high
   And plunged in terror down the sky,
   And the big rain in one black wave
   Fell from the sky and struck my grave.
   (lines 140–144)

5. O God, I cried, no dark disguise
   Can e'er hereafter hide from me
   Thy radiant identity!   (lines 180–182)

   . . . .

   God, I can push the grass apart
   And lay my finger on Thy heart!
   (lines 189–190)

6. The world stands out on either side
   No wider than the heart is wide;
   Above the world is stretched the sky—
   No higher than the soul is high.
   (lines 191–194)

III
TECHNIQUES

Structure

Note the division of the poem into ten stanzas. Try to summarize the thought in each of them in a sentence or two in order to better see the planned framework of the poem. Also, compare the following: lines 1–16 with lines 151–160; lines 105–112 with lines 153–162; lines 1–28 with lines 187–202. Show how these comparisons argue for the idea that the poem was carefully planned.

Symbolism

1. What do the wind and the rain symbolize? Be prepared to argue for or against the notion that they are well-chosen symbols.

2. What does the poet's touching the sky symbolize?

3. What is the symbolic meaning of the "great wound"?

IV
WORDS

To develop large speaking, reading, and writing vocabularies, you must become interested in words, in how words acquire meanings, in how words change, and in how to add meanings to words you already know. The study of synonyms and antonyms helps sharpen your understanding of the distinctions that set words apart. Test your word knowledge by giving a synonym and antonym for the italicized words in each phrase.

stigma of a fiction *monger*
certain *alacrity* in his gait
all had *furtive* appearances
fervent explorations
inured to my high-handed raids
bogus refugees
filed *sullenly* aboard
languid with rest
precariously rooted shrub
salient characteristics

"Why was I born? Why am I living?" . . .
No other modern American writer has sought to answer
these haunting, universal questions so honestly and profoundly
as the Nobel Prize-winning author, William Faulkner. Ironically,
though he exposes human degradation and depravity in many of his stories,
Faulkner's works make a firm affirmation of his faith in the fundamental
nobility of humanity and the purposefulness of the universe. The following
two works, both by Faulkner, reflect this affirmation. "Race at Morning"
is a hunting story with a very unusual outcome, seen through the eyes
of a twelve-year-old boy. "Man Will Prevail" is Faulkner's Nobel Prize
Acceptance Speech. See what common elements you can find in the two.

Race at Morning

WILLIAM FAULKNER

I was in the boat when I seen him. It was jest dusk-dark; I had jest fed the horses and clumb back down the bank to the boat and shoved off to cross back to camp when I seen him, about half a quarter up the river, swimming; jest his head above the water, and it no more than a dot in that light. But I could see that rocking chair[1] he toted on it and I knowed it was him, going right back to that canebrake in the fork of the bayou[2] where he lived all year until the day before the season opened, like the game wardens had give him a calendar, when he would clear out and disappear, nobody knowed where, until the day after the season closed. But here he was, coming back a day ahead of time, like maybe he had got mixed up and was using last year's calendar by mistake. Which was jest too bad for him, because me and Mister Ernest would be setting on the horse right over him when the sun rose tomorrow morning.

So I told Mister Ernest and we et supper and fed the dogs, and then I help Mister Ernest in the poker game, standing behind his chair un-

til about ten o'clock, when Roth Edmonds said, "Why don't you go to bed, boy?"

"Or if you're going to set up," Willy Legate said, "why don't you take a spelling book to set up over? . . . He knows every cuss word in the dictionary, every poker hand in the deck and every whisky label in the distillery, but he can't even write his name . . . Can you?" he says to me.

"I don't need to write my name down," I said. "I can remember in my mind who I am."

"You're twelve years old," Walter Ewell said. "Man to man, now, how many days in your life did you ever spend in school?"

"He ain't got time to go to school," Willy Legate said. "What's the use in going to school from September to middle of November, when he'll have to quit then to come in here and do Ernest's hearing for him? And what's the use in going back to school in January, when in jest eleven months it will be November fifteenth

---

© Copyright 1955 by The Curtis Publishing Company. Reprinted from *Big Woods*, by William Faulkner, by permission of Random House, Inc.

1. **rocking chair**, the twelve-pointed antlers or horns of a great stag.
2. **canebrake in the fork of the bayou**\ᵇai·ō\ a thicket of reeds and woody grasses on an island at the fork of the marshy, sluggish little river.

again and he'll have to start all over telling Ernest which way the dogs went?"

"Well, stop looking into my hand, anyway," Roth Edmonds said.

"What's that? What's that?" Mister Ernest said. He wore his listening button in his ear all the time, but he never brought the battery to camp with him because the cord would bound to get snagged ever time we run through a thicket.

"Willy says for me to go to bed!" I hollered.

"Don't you never call nobody 'mister'?" Willy said.

"I call Mister Ernest 'mister,' " I said.

"All right," Mister Ernest said. "Go to bed then. I don't need you."

"That ain't no lie," Willy said. "Deaf or no deaf, he can hear a fifty-dollar raise if you don't even move your lips."

So I went to bed, and after a while Mister Ernest come in and I wanted to tell him again how big them horns looked even half a quarter away in the river. Only I would 'a' had to holler, and the only time Mister Ernest agreed he couldn't hear was when we would be setting on Dan, waiting for me to point which way the dogs was going. So we jest laid down, and it wasn't no time Simon was beating the bottom of the dishpan with the spoon, hollering, "Raise up and get your four-o'clock coffee!" and I crossed the river in the dark this time, with the lantern, and fed Dan and Roth Edmondziz horse. It was going to be a fine day, cold and bright; even in the dark I could see the white frost on the leaves and bushes—jest exactly the kind of day that big old son of a gun laying up there in that brake would like to run.

Then we et, and set the stand-holder[3] across for Uncle Ike McCaslin to put them on the stands where he thought they ought to be, because he was the oldest one in camp. He had been hunting deer in these woods for about a hundred years, I reckon, and if anybody would know where a buck would pass, it would be him. Maybe with a big old buck like this one, that had been running the woods for what would amount to a hundred years in a deer's

life, too, him and Uncle Ike would sholy manage to be at the same place at the same time this morning—provided, of course, he managed to git away from me and Mister Ernest on the jump. Because me and Mister Ernest was going to git him.

Then me and Mister Ernest and Roth Edmonds set the dogs over, with Simon holding Eagle and the other old dogs on leash because the young ones, the puppies, wasn't going nowhere until Eagle let them, nohow. Then me and Mister Ernest and Roth saddled up, and Mister Ernest got up and I handed him up his pump gun and let Dan's bridle go for him to git rid of the spell of bucking he had to git shut of ever morning until Mister Ernest hit him between the ears with the gun barrel. Then Mister Ernest loaded the gun and give me the stirrup, and I got up behind him and we taken the fire road[4] up toward the bayou, the five big dogs dragging Simon along in front with his single-barrel britchloader slung on a piece of plow line across his back, and the puppies moiling along in ever'body's way. It was light now and it was going to be jest fine; the east already yellow for the sun and our breaths smoking in the cold still bright air until the sun would come up and warm it, and a little skim of ice in the ruts, and ever leaf and twig and switch and even the frozen clods frosted over, waiting to sparkle like a rainbow when the sun finally come up and hit them. Until all my insides felt light and strong as a balloon, full of that light cold strong air, so that it seemed to me like I couldn't even feel the horse's back I was straddle of—jest the hot strong muscles moving under the hot strong skin, setting up there without no weight atall, so that when old Eagle struck and jumped, me and Dan and Mister Ernest would go jest like

---

3. **stand-holder,** a wooden platform with four legs which can be driven into soft earth or into the bottom of a bayou or marsh. On it hunters wait for the game to be driven toward them so that they may have a chance to shoot. Here, the stand-holder is floated across the bayou and set up on the far side.
4. **fire road,** a firebreak, a barrier of cleared land intended to stop a forest fire.

a bird, not even touching the ground. It was jest fine. When that big old buck got killed today, I knowed that even if he had put it off another ten years, he couldn't 'a' picked a better one.

And sho enough, as soon as we come to the bayou we seen his foot in the mud where he had come up out of the river last night, spread in the soft mud like a cow's foot, big as a cow's, big as a mule's, with Eagle and the other dogs laying into the leash rope now until Mister Ernest told me to jump down and help Simon hold them. Because me and Mister Ernest knowed exactly where he would be—a little canebrake island in the middle of the bayou, where he could lay up until whatever doe or little deer the dogs had happened to jump could go up or down the bayou in either direction and take the dogs on away, so he could steal out and creep back down the bayou to the river and swim it, and leave the country like he always done the day the season opened.

Which is jest what we never aimed for him to do this time. So we left Roth on his horse to cut him off and turn him over Uncle Ike's standers if he tried to slip back down the bayou, and me and Simon, with the leashed dogs, walked on up the bayou until Mister Ernest on the horse said it was fur enough; then turned up into the woods about half a quarter above the brake because the wind was going to be south this morning when it riz, and turned down toward the brake, and Mister Ernest give the word to cast them,[5] and we slipped the leash and Mister Ernest give me the stirrup again and I got up.

Old Eagle had done already took off because he knowed where that old son of a gun would be laying as good as we did, not making no racket atall yet, but jest boring on through the buck vines with the other dogs trailing along behind him, and even Dan seemed to know about that buck, too, beginning to souple up and jump a little through the vines, so that I taken my holt on Mister Ernest's belt already before the time had come for Mister Ernest to touch him. Because when we got strung out,

going fast behind a deer, I wasn't on Dan's back much of the time nohow, but mostly jest strung out from my holt on Mister Ernest's belt, so that Willy Legate said that when we was going through the wood fast, it looked like Mister Ernest had a boy-size pair of empty overhalls blowing out of his hind pocket.

So it wasn't even a strike, it was a jump. Eagle must 'a' walked right up behind him or maybe even stepped on him while he was laying there still thinking it was day after tomorrow. Eagle jest throwed his head back and up and said, "There he goes," and we even heard the buck crashing through the first of the cane. Then all the other dogs was hollering behind him, and Dan give a squat to jump, but it was against the curb[6] this time, not jest the snaffle,[7] and Mister Ernest let him down into the bayou and swung him around the brake and up the other bank. Only he never had to say, "Which way?" because I was already pointing past his shoulder, freshening my holt on the belt jest as Mister Ernest touched Dan with that big old rusty spur on his nigh heel, because when Dan felt it he would go off jest like a stick of dynamite, straight through whatever he could bust and over or under what he couldn't.

The dogs was already almost out of hearing. Eagle must 'a' been looking right up that big son of a gun's tail until he finally decided he better git on out of there. And now they must 'a' been getting pretty close to Uncle Ike's standers, and Mister Ernest reined Dan back and held him, squatting and bouncing and trembling like a mule having his tail roached,[8] while we listened for the shots. But never none come, and I hollered to Mister Ernest we better go on while I could still hear the dogs, and he let Dan off, but still there wasn't no shots, and now we knowed the race had done already

---

5. **to cast them,** to let the dogs run.
6. **curb,** a chain or strap on the upper part of the branches of a bit used to restrain a horse.
7. **snaffle,** a simple jointed bit.
8. **tail roached,** the removal of hair from the upper part of a mule's tail.

passed the standers; and we busted out of a thicket, and sho enough there was Uncle Ike and Willy standing beside his foot in a soft patch.

"He got through us all," Uncle Ike said. "I don't know how he done it. I just had a glimpse of him. He looked big as a elephant, with a rack[9] on his head you could cradle a yellin' calf in. He went right on down the ridge. You better get on, too; that Hog Bayou camp might not miss him."

So I freshened my holt and Mister Ernest touched Dan again. The ridge run due south; it was clear of vines and bushes so we could go fast, into the wind, too, because it had riz now, and now the sun was up too. So we would hear the dogs again any time now as the wind get up; we could make time now, but still holding Dan to a canter,[10] because it was either going to be quick, when he got down to the standers from that Hog Bayou camp eight miles below ourn, or a long time, in case he got by them too. And sho enough, after a while we heard the dogs; we was walking Dan now to let him blow a while, and we heard them, the sound coming faint up the wind, not running now, but trailing because the big son of a gun had decided a good piece back, probably, to put an end to this foolishness, and picked hisself up and soupled out and put about a mile between hisself and the dogs—until he run up on them other standers from that camp below. I could almost see him stopped behind a bush, peeping out and saying, "What's this? What's this? Is this whole durn country full of folks this morning?" Then looking back over his shoulder at where old Eagle and the others was hollering along after him while he decided how much time he had to decide what to do next.

Except he almost shaved it too fine. We heard the shots; it sounded like a war. Old Eagle must 'a' been looking right up his tail again and he had to bust on through the best way he could. "Pow, pow, pow, pow" and then "Pow, pow, pow, pow," like it must 'a' been three or four ganged right up on him before

he had time even to swerve, and me hollering, "No! No! No! No!" because he was ourn. It was our beans and oats he et and our brake he laid in; we had been watching him ever year, and it was like we had raised him, to be killed at last on our jump, in front of our dogs, by some strangers that would probably try to beat the dogs off and drag him away before we could even git a piece of the meat.

"Shut up and listen," Mister Ernest said. So I done it and we could hear the dogs; not just the others, but Eagle, too, not trailing no scent now and not baying no downed meat, neither, but running hot on sight long after the shooting was over. I jest had time to freshen my holt. Yes, sir, they was running on sight. Like Willy Legate would say, if Eagle jest had a drink of whisky he would ketch that deer; going on, done already gone when we broke out of the thicket and seen the fellers that had done the shooting, five or six of them, squatting and crawling around, looking at the ground and the bushes, like maybe if they looked hard enough, spots of blood would bloom out on the stalks and leaves like frogstools or hawberries.

"Have any luck, boys?" Mister Ernest said.

"I think I hit him," one of them said. "I know I did. We're hunting blood, now."

"Well, when you have found him, blow your horn and I'll come back and tote him in to camp for you," Mister Ernest said.

So we went on, going fast now because the race was almost out of hearing again, going fast, too, like not jest the buck, but the dogs, too, had took a new leash on life[11] from all the excitement and shooting.

We was in strange country now because we never had to run this fur before, we had always killed before now; now we had come to Hog Bayou that runs into the river a good fifteen miles below our camp. It had water in it, not to mention a mess of down trees and logs and

---

9. **rack,** antlers, horns.
10. **canter,** a three-beat trot, resembling but smoother and slower than a gallop.
11. **a new leash on life,** the boy means a new lease or hold on life.

such, and Mister Ernest checked Dan again, saying, "Which way?" I could just barely hear them, off to the east a little, like the old son of a gun had give up the idea Vicksburg or New Orleans, like he first seemed to have, and had decided to have a look at Alabama; so I pointed and we turned up the bayou hunting for a crossing, and maybe we could 'a' found one, except that I reckon Mister Ernest decided we never had time to wait.

We come to a place where the bayou had narrowed down to about twelve or fifteen feet, and Mister Ernest said, "Look out, I'm going to touch him," and done it.

I didn't even have time to freshen my holt when we was already in the air, and then I seen the vine—it was a loop of grapevine nigh as big as my wrist, looping down right across the middle of the bayou—and I thought he seen it, too, and was jest waiting to grab it and fling it up over our heads to go under it, and I know Dan seen it because he even ducked his head to jump under it. But Mister Ernest never seen it atall until it skun back along Dan's neck and hooked under the head of the saddle horn, us flying on through the air, the loop of the vine gitting tighter and tighter until something somewhere was going to have to give. It was the saddle girth.[12] It broke, and Dan going on and scrabbling up the other bank bare nekkid except for the bridle, and me and Mister Ernest and the saddle, Mister Ernest still setting in the saddle holding the gun, and me still holding onto Mister Ernest's belt, hanging in the air over the bayou in the tightened loop of that vine like in the drawed-back loop of a big rubber-banded slingshot, until it snapped back and shot us back across the bayou and flang us clear, me still holding onto Mister Ernest's belt and on the bottom now, so that when we lit I would 'a' had Mister Ernest and the saddle both on top of me if I hadn't clumb fast around the saddle and up Mister Ernest's side, so that when we landed, it was the saddle first, then Mister Ernest, and me on top, until I jumped up, and Mister Ernest

Copyright © 1963, Martin J. Dain

A hunter in the woods near Faulkner's home

still laying there with jest the white rim of his eyes showing.

"Mister Ernest!" I hollered, and then clumb down to the bayou and scopped my cap full of water and clumb back and throwed it in his face, and he opened his eyes and laid there on the saddle cussing me.

"Why didn't you stay behind where you started out?" he said.

---

12. **saddle girth,** the band or strap that encircles a horse's body to hold the saddle on its back.

"You was the biggest!" I said. "You would 'a' mashed me flat!"

"What do you think you done to me?" Mister Ernest said. "Next time, if you can't stay where you start out, jump clear. Don't climb up on top of me no more. You hear?"

"Yes, sir," I said.

So he got up then, still cussing and holding his back, and clumb down to the water and dipped some in his hand onto his face and neck and dipped some more up and drunk it, and I drunk some, too, and clumb back and got the saddle and the gun, and we crossed the bayou on the down logs. If we could jest ketch Dan; not that he would have went them fifteen miles back to camp, because, if anything, he would have went on by hisself to try to help Eagle ketch that buck. But he was about fifty yards away, eating buck vines, so I brought him back, and we taken Mister Ernest's galluses[13] and my belt and the whang leather[14] loop off Mister Ernest's horn and tied the saddle back on Dan. It didn't look like much, but maybe it would hold.

"Provided you don't let me jump him through no more grapevines without hollering first," Mister Ernest said.

"Yes, sir," I said. "I'll holler first next time—provided you'll holler a little quicker when you touch him next time too." But it was all right; we jest had to be a little easy getting up. "Now which-a-way?" I said. Because we couldn't hear nothing now, after wasting all this time. And this was new country, sho enough. It had been cut over and growed up in thickets we couldn't 'a' seen over even standing up on Dan.

But Mister Ernest never even answered. He jest turned Dan along the bank of the bayou where it was a little more open, and we could move faster again, soon as Dan and us got used to that homemade cinch strop and got a little confidence in it. Which jest happened to be east, or so I thought then, because I never paid no particular attention to east then because the sun—I don't know where the morning had went, but it was gone, the morning and the frost, too—was up high now.

And then we heard him. No, that's wrong; what we heard was shots. And that was when we realized how fur we had come, because the only camp we knowed about in that direction was the Hollyknowe camp, and Hollyknowe was exactly twenty-eight miles from Van Dorn, where me and Mister Ernest lived—just the shots, no dogs nor nothing. If old Eagle was still behind him and the buck was still alive, he was too wore out now to even say, "Here he comes."

"Don't touch him!" I hollered. But Mister Ernest remembered that cinch strop, too, and he jest let Dan off the snaffle. And Dan heard them shots, too, picking his way through the thickets, hopping the vines and logs when he could and going under them when he couldn't. And sho enough, it was jest like before—two or three men squatting and creeping among the bushes, looking for blood that Eagle had done already told them wasn't there. But we never stopped this time, jest trotting on by. Then Mister Ernest swung Dan until we was going due north.

"Wait!" I hollered. "Not this way."

But Mister Ernest jest turned his face back over his shoulder. It looked tired, too, and there was a smear of mud on it where that 'ere grapevine had snatched him off the horse.

"Don't you know where he's heading?" he said. "He's done done his part, give everybody a fair open shot at him, and now he's going home, back to that brake in our bayou. He ought to make it exactly at dark."

And that's what he was doing. We went on. It didn't matter to hurry now. There wasn't no sound nowhere; it was that time in the early afternoon in November when don't nothing move or cry, not even birds, the peckerwoods and yellowhammers and jays, and it seemed to me like I could see all three of us—me and Mister Ernest and Dan—and Eagle, and the other

---

13. **galluses**\ˈgăl·əs·əs\ suspenders.
14. **whang leather,** rawhide leather.

dogs, and that big old buck, moving through the quiet woods in the same direction, headed for the same place, not running now but walking, that had all run the fine race the best we knowed how, and all three of us now turned like on a agreement to walk back home, not together in a bunch because we didn't want to worry or tempt one another, because what we had all three spent this morning doing was no play-acting jest for fun, but was serious, and all three of us was still what we was—that old buck that had to run, not because he was skeered, but because running was what he done the best and was proudest at; and Eagle and the dogs that chased him, not because they hated or feared him, but because that was the thing they done the best and was proudest at; and me and Mister Ernest and Dan, that run him not because we wanted his meat, which would be too tough to eat anyhow, or his head to hang on a wall, but because now we could go back and work hard for eleven months making a crop, so we would have the right to come back here next November—all three of us going back home now, peaceful and separate, until next year, next time.

Then we seen him for the first time. We was out of the cutover now; we could even 'a' cantered, except that all three of us was long past that. So we was walking, too, when we come on the dogs—the puppies and one of the old ones—played out, laying in a little wet swag,[15] panting, jest looking up at us when we passed. Then we come to a long open glade, and we seen the three other old dogs and about a hundred yards ahead of them Eagle, all walking, not making no sound; and then suddenly, at the fur end of the glade, the buck hisself getting up from where he had been resting for the dogs to come up, getting up without no hurry, big, big as a mule, tall as a mule, and turned, and the white underside of his tail for a second or two more before the thicket taken him.

It might 'a' been a signal, a good-by, a farewell. Still walking, we passed the other three old dogs in the middle of the glade, laying down, too; and still that hundred yards ahead

of them, Eagle, too, not laying down, because he was still on his feet, but his legs was spraddled and his head was down; maybe jest waiting until we was out of sight of his shame, his eyes saying plain as talk when we passed, "I'm sorry, boys, but this here is all."

Mister Ernest stopped Dan. "Jump down and look at his feet," he said.

"Nothing wrong with his feet," I said. "It's his wind has done give out."

"Jump down and look at his feet," Mister Ernest said.

So I done it, and while I was stooping over Eagle I could hear the pump gun go, "Snick-cluck. Snick-cluck. Snick-cluck" three times, except that I never thought nothing then. Maybe he was jest running the shells through to be sho it would work when we seen him again or maybe to make sho they was all buck-shot. Then I got up again, and we went on, still walking; a little west of north now, because when we seen his white flag that second or two before the thicket hid it, it was on a beeline for that notch in the bayou. And it was evening, too, now. The wind had done dropped and there was a edge to the air and the sun jest touched the tops of the trees. And he was taking the easiest way, too, now, going straight as he could. When we seen his foot in the soft places he was running for a while at first after his rest. But soon he was walking, too, like he knowed, too, where Eagle and the dogs was.

And then we seen him again. It was the last time—a thicket, with the sun coming through a hole onto it like a searchlight. He crashed jest once; then he was standing there broadside to us, not twenty yards away, big as a statue and red as gold in the sun, and the sun sparking on the tips of his horns—they was twelve of them—so that he looked like he had twelve lighted candles branched around his head, standing there looking at us while Mister Ernest raised the gun and aimed at his neck, and the gun went, "Click. Snick-cluck. Click. Snick-cluck. Click. Snick-cluck" three times, and Mister

_____
15. **wet swag,** a little wet depression.

Ernest still holding the gun aimed while the buck turned and give one long bound, the white underside of his tail like a blaze of fire, too, until the thicket and the shadows put it out; and Mister Ernest laid the gun slow and gentle back across the saddle in front of him, saying quiet and peaceful, and not much louder than jest breathing, "Dawg."

Then he jogged me with his elbow and we got down, easy and careful because of that ere cinch strop, and he reached into his vest and taken out one of the cigars. It was busted where I had fell on it, I reckon, when we hit the ground. He throwed it away and taken out the other one. It was busted, too, so he bit off a hunk of it to chew and throwed the rest away. And now the sun was gone even from the tops of the trees and there wasn't nothing left but a big red glare in the west.

"Don't worry," I said. "I ain't going to tell them you forgot to load your gun. For that matter, they don't need to know we ever seed him."

"Much oblige," Mister Ernest said. There wasn't going to be no moon tonight neither, so he taken the compass off the whang leather loop in his buttonhole and handed me the gun and set the compass on a stump and stepped back and looked at it. "Jest about the way we're headed now," he said, and taken the gun from me and opened it and put one shell in the britch[16] and taken up the compass, and I taken Dan's reins and we started, with him in front with the compass in his hand.

And after a while it was full dark; Mister Ernest would have to strike a match ever now and then to read the compass, until the stars come out good and we could pick out one to follow, because I said, "How fur do you reckon it is?" and he said, "A little more than one box of matches." So we used a star when we could, only we couldn't see it all the time because the woods was too dense and we would git a little off until he would have to spend another match. And now it was good and late, and he stopped and said, "Get on the horse."

"I ain't tired," I said.

"Get on the horse," he said. "We don't want to spoil him."

Because he had been a good feller ever since I had knowed him, which was even before that day two years ago when maw went off with the Vicksburg roadhouse feller and the next day pap didn't come home neither, and on the third one Mister Ernest rid Dan up to the door of the cabin on the river he let us live in, so pap could work his piece of land and run his fish line, too, and said, "Put that gun down and come on here and climb up behind."

So I got in the saddle even if I couldn't reach the stirrups, and Mister Ernest taken the reins and I must 'a' went to sleep, because the next thing I knowed a buttonhole of my lumberjack was tied to the saddle horn with that ere whang cord off the compass, and it was good and late now and we wasn't fur, because Dan was already smelling water, the river. Or maybe it was the feed lot itself he smelled, because we struck the fire road not a quarter below it, and soon I could see the river, too, with the white mist laying on it soft and still as cotton. Then the lot, home; and up yonder in the dark, not no piece akchully, close enough to hear us unsaddling and shucking corn prob'ly, and sholy close enough to hear Mister Ernest blowing his horn at the dark camp for Simon to come in the boat and git us, that old buck in his brake in the bayou; home, too, resting, too, after the hard run, waking hisself now and then, dreaming of dogs behind him or maybe it was the racket we was making would wake him.

Then Mister Ernest stood on the bank blowing until Simon's lantern went bobbing down into the mist; then we clumb down to the landing and Mister Ernest blowed again now and then to guide Simon, until we seen the lantern in the mist, and then Simon and the boat; only it looked like ever time I set down and got still, I went back to sleep, because Mister Ernest

16. **britch,** breech, the part of the gun behind the barrel.

was shaking me again to git out and climb the bank into the dark camp, until I felt a bed against my knees and tumbled into it.

Then it was morning, tomorrow; it was all over now until next November, next year, and we could come back. Uncle Ike and Willy and Walter and Roth and the rest of them had come in yestiddy, soon as Eagle taken the buck out of hearing, and they knowed that deer was gone, to pack up and be ready to leave this morning for Yoknapatawpha,[17] where they lived, until it would be November again and they could come back again.

So, as soon as we et breakfast, Simon run them back up the river in the big boat to where they left their cars and pickups, and now it wasn't nobody but jest me and Mister Ernest setting on the bench against the kitchen wall in the sun; Mister Ernest smoking a cigar—a whole one this time that Dan hadn't had no chance to jump him through a grapevine and bust. He hadn't washed his face neither where that vine had throwed him into the mud. But that was all right, too; his face usually did have a smudge of mud or tractor grease or beard stubble on it, because he wasn't jest a planter; he was a farmer, he worked as hard as ara one of his hands and tenants—which is why I knowed from the very first that we would git along, that I wouldn't have no trouble with him and he wouldn't have no trouble with me, from that very first day when I woke up and maw had done gone off with that Vicksburg road-house feller without even waiting to cook breakfast, and the next morning pap was gone, too, and it was almost night the next day when I heard a horse coming up and I taken the gun that I had already throwed a shell into the britch when pap never come home last night, and stood in the door while Mister Ernest rid up and said, "Come on. Your paw ain't coming back neither."

"You mean he give me to you?" I said.

"Who cares?" he said. "Come on. I brought a lock for the door. We'll send the pickup back tomorrow for whatever you want."

So I come home with him and it was all right, it was jest fine—his wife had died about three years ago—without no women to worry us or take off in the middle of the night with a durn Vicksburg roadhouse jake without even waiting to cook breakfast. And we would go home this afternoon, too, but not jest yet; we always stayed one more day after the others left because Uncle Ike always left what grub they hadn't et, and the rest of the home-made corn whisky he drunk and that town whisky of Roth Edmondziz he called Scotch that smelled like it come out of a old bucket of roof paint; setting in the sun for one more day before we went back home to git ready to put in next year's crop of cotton and oats and beans and hay; and across the river yonder, behind the wall of trees where the big woods started, that old buck laying up today in the sun, too—resting today, too, without nobody to bother him until next November.

So at least one of us was glad it would be eleven months and two weeks before he would have to run that fur that fast again. So he was glad of the very same thing we was sorry of, and so all of a sudden I thought about how maybe planting and working and then harvesting oats and cotton and beans and hay wasn't jest something me and Mister Ernest done three hundred and fifty-one days to fill in the time until we could come back hunting again, but it was something we had to do, and do honest and good during the three hundred and fifty-one days, to have the right to come back into the big woods and hunt for the other fourteen; and the fourteen days that the old buck run in front of dogs wasn't jest something to fill his time until the three hundred and fifty-one when he didn't have to, but the running and the risking in front of guns and dogs was something he had to do for fourteen days to have the right not to be bothered for the other three hundred

17. **Yoknapatawpha**\ˈyɔk·nə·pə ˈtɔ·fə\ the fictitious county in northern Mississippi invented by William Faulkner as the scene of many of his stories.

and fifty-one. And so the hunting and the farming wasn't two different things atall—they was jest the other side of each other.

"Yes," I said. "All we got to do now is put in that next year's crop. Then November won't be no time away."

"You ain't going to put in the crop next year," Mister Ernest said. "You're going to school."

So at first I didn't even believe I had heard him. "What?" I said. "Me? Go to school?"

"Yes," Mister Ernest said. "You must make something out of yourself."

"I am," I said. "I'm doing it now. I'm going to be a hunter and a farmer like you."

"No," Mister Ernest said. "That ain't enough any more. Time was when all a man had to do was just farm eleven and a half months, and hunt the other half. But not now. Now just to belong to the farming business and the hunting business ain't enough. You got to belong to the business of mankind."

"Mankind?" I said.

"Yes," Mister Ernest said. "So you're going to school. Because you got to know why. You can belong to the farming and hunting business and you can learn the difference between what's right and what's wrong, and do right. And that used to be enough—just to do right. But not now. You got to know why it's right and why it's wrong, and be able to tell the folks that never had no chance to learn it; teach them how to do what's right, not just because they know it's right, but because they know now why it's right because you just showed them, told them, taught them why. So you're going to school."

"It's because you been listening to that durn Will Legate and Walter Ewell!" I said.

"No," Mister Ernest said.

"Yes!" I said. "No wonder you missed that buck yestiddy, taking ideas from the very fellers that let him git away, after me and you had run Dan and the dogs durn nigh clean to death! Because you never even missed him! You never forgot to load that gun! You had done already unloaded it a purpose! I heard you!"

"All right, all right," Mister Ernest said. "Which would you rather have? His bloody head and hide on the kitchen floor yonder and half his meat in a pickup truck on the way to Yoknapatawpha County, or him with his head and hide and meat still together over yonder in that brake, waiting for next November for us to run him again?"

"And git him, too," I said. "We won't even fool with no Willy Legate and Walter Ewell next time."

"Maybe," Mister Ernest said.

"Yes," I said.

"Maybe," Mister Ernest said. "The best word in our language, the best of all. That's what mankind keeps going on: Maybe. The best days of his life ain't the ones when he said 'Yes' beforehand: they're the ones when all he knew to say was 'Maybe.' He can't say 'Yes' until afterward because he not only don't know it until then, he don't want to know. 'Yes' until them. . . Step in the kitchen and make me a toddy. Then we'll see about dinner."

"All right," I said. I got up. "You want some of Uncle Ike's corn or that town whisky of Roth Edmondziz?"

"Can't you say Mister Roth or Mister Edmonds?" Mister Ernest said.

"Yes, sir," I said. "Well, which do you want? Uncle Ike's corn or that ere stuff of Roth Edmondziz?"

Man Will Prevail

WILLIAM FAULKNER

Nobel Prize Acceptance Speech,
Stockholm, December 10, 1950

I feel that this award was not made to me as a man, but to my work—a life's work in the agony and sweat of the human spirit, not for glory and least of all for profit, but to create out of the materials of the human spirit something which did not exist before. So this award is only mine in trust. It will not be difficult to find a dedica-

tion for the money part of it commensurate[1] with the purpose and significance of its origin. But I would like to do the same with the acclaim too, by using this moment as a pinnacle from which I might be listened to by the young men and women already dedicated to the same anguish and travail, among whom is already that one who will some day stand here where I am standing.

Our tragedy today is a general and universal physical fear so long sustained by now that we can even bear it. There are no longer problems of the spirit. There is only the question: When will I be blown up? Because of this, the young man or woman writing today has forgotten the problems of the human heart in conflict with itself which alone can make good writing because only that is worth writing about, worth the agony and the sweat.

He must learn them again. He must teach himself that the basest of all things is to be afraid; and, teaching himself that, forget it forever, leaving no room in his workshop for anything but the old verities and truths of the heart, the old universal truths lacking which any story is ephemeral[2] and doomed—love and honor and pity and pride and compassion and sacrifice. Until he does so, he labors under a curse. He writes not of love but of lust, of defeats in which nobody loses anything of value, of victories without hope and, worst of all, without pity or compassion. His griefs grieve on no

1. **commensurate**\kə ˈměn·shə·rĭt\ suitable in measure and importance.
2. **ephemeral**\ə ˈfěm·rəl\ lasting for only a day, or for only a short time.

universal bones, leaving no scars. He writes not of the heart but of the glands.

Until he relearns these things, he will write as though he stood among and watched the end of man. I decline to accept the end of man. It is easy enough to say that man is immortal simply because he will endure: that when the last ding-dong of doom has clanged and faded from the last worthless rock hanging tideless in the last red and dying evening, that even then there will still be one more sound: that of his puny inexhaustible voice, still talking. I refuse to accept this. I believe that man will not merely endure: he will prevail. He is immortal, not because he alone among creatures has an inexhaustible voice, but because he has a soul, a spirit capable of compassion and sacrifice and endurance. The poet's, the writer's, duty is to write about these things. It is his privilege to help man endure by lifting his heart, by reminding him of the courage and honor and hope and pride and compassion and pity and sacrifice which have been the glory of his past. The poet's voice need not merely be the record of man, it can be one of the props, the pillars to help him endure and prevail.

I
"THE BUSINESS OF MANKIND"

In his Acceptance Speech, Faulkner affirms "the old verities and truths of the heart, the old universal truths," some of which are courage, honor, hope, pride, compassion, pity, and sacrifice. In short, though he recognizes that the world has changed, he still maintains that our basic values do not have to change.

In "Race at Morning," however, Mr. Ernest tells the young boy that the life he has been living "ain't enough any more." What does he mean by this and by the related statement that the boy has to belong to "the business of mankind"? Also, be prepared to discuss how these statements relate to Faulkner's basic philosophy, as expressed in "Man Will Prevail."

II
IMPLICATIONS

Discuss the following statements in the light of these selections and your own experience.

1. In life everyone has a job, which, when performed faithfully and honestly, not only brings self-satisfaction but also earns public esteem for a person.

2. A person who knows why something is right or wrong is more likely to do right and avoid wrong than a person who does not know the "whys."

3. School is the best place for a young person to learn why some things are wrong and others are right.

4. Faulkner tremendously oversimplifies the matter of right and wrong.

5. Faulkner's optimism is sentimental and too easy.

6. Faulkner overrates the powers of the writer.

7. It is perfectly possible for a person to be completely happy in the modern world even though completely isolated from other human beings.

III
TECHNIQUES

Structure

How does the "philosophical" discussion at the end of "Race at Morning" grow out of the earlier focus on the buck hunt? If you decide that they are not very closely related, would you conclude that the story is poorly structured, or what?

Symbolism

What—if anything—might the buck symbolize? If you decide that the animal is a symbol, try to relate its symbolic meaning to various facts in the story, especially to the fact that Mister Ernest purposely shoots at the buck with an empty rifle.

IV
WORDS

A. Using what you know about word parts and context clues, determine the meaning of the italicized words.

1. A dedication for the money part of it *commensurate* with the purpose and significance of its origin.

2. . . . by using this *pinnacle* from which I might be listened to by young men and women.

3. . . . leaving no room in his workshop for anything but the old *verities* and truths of the heart.

B. The same thing may be said in many different ways. The vocabulary of English, so rich in synonyms, gives many choices among words. We generally choose our words to fit the occasions, but our choices should reflect a consistency. Below is part of a paragraph from Faulkner's "Man Will Prevail." Discuss how the alternate choices change the tone as well as variety of standard English.

> "It will not be (hard, difficult, arduous) to find a dedication for the (money, cash, legal tender) part of it (tantamount to, offsetting, commensurate with) the purpose and (significance, importance, meaning) of its (root, inception, origin). But I would like to do the same with the (acclaim, applause, hurrah) too, by using this moment as a (peak, apogee, pinnacle) from which I might be listened to by the young men and women already (devoted, dedicated, consecrated) to the same (heartache, agony, anguish) and (work, grind, travail), among whom is already that one who will some day stand here where I am standing.

C. It is no longer possible to draw precise lines about slang usage. We know that certain slang terms, such as *dig* (a curt remark), *put down* (deflate), *jittery* (nervous), *dirt* (gossip), may be appropriate to casual conversations and even to light, friendly writing. Much of the slang of yesterday has become part of our general vocabulary or at least appropriate to ordinary speech and writing. Words, such as *rascal, varsity, hot dog, jazz* (particular kind of music), once considered slang are now generally accepted.

Slang has levels of its own. Which of the following expressions do you consider appropriate to general, informal conversation? to friendly, informal writing? Which do you consider inappropriate, in poor taste?

nuts (insane)	drag out
new lease on life	hang loose
hit the sack	fink
get into	dig (appreciate)
cop out	jalopy
cram	louses (people)
up tight	fin (five dollars)

FINAL REFLECTIONS

The Search for Values

VALUES AND LITERATURE

Literature relates to the search for values in many ways. Poems and stories like "The Hollow Men," "Richard Cory," and "In Another Country" may awaken in us a sense of the *need* for values in order to avoid living an empty life. Essays such as "Man Will Prevail" may persuade us to adopt specific values, or they may help us to understand better the reasons for living by a particular value or set of values.

A story like "In Another Country" might serve to make us aware of human despair and failure of nerve. "The Traveler" shows us that we must look outside of ourselves in order to fully know ourselves.

It is important to note, however, that stories and poems are not simply devices for telling about someone else's experiences, they are experiences in themselves. Fully appreciated, they stir readers emotionally as well as intellectually. They may thereby have a deep and lasting effect on our own values—on how we live, on how we answer those persistent questions, "Why was I born? Why am I living?"

IMPLICATIONS

Discuss each of the following propositions. In your discussion you may call upon your experience, but be sure that you also make some reference to at least three of the selections in this unit for each of the propositions.

1. A person's values are determined by emotion rather than by intellect.

2. The search for values is a lifelong search, for you can never be sure you have the right or final answers.

3. Fear and inertia are far greater barriers to happiness than are lack of wealth and position.

4. The concentration upon one set of human needs to the exclusion of all the others is bound to cause unhappiness.

5. Skeptics and pessimists have little or nothing to contribute to the search for values.

6. Writers don't create values for a society; they merely reflect those that already exist.

7. Never before in history has it been more important to recognize "our common humanity" as a major social value.

TECHNIQUES

Structure

Over two thousand years ago the famous Greek philosopher Plato wrote a dialogue in which he portrayed the writer as a divinely inspired madman. This image of the writer as a person full of passion but with little intellectual control has persisted down to the present day in the minds of some persons.

If this were a true picture of writers, we would expect to find that their work would be structurally loose, that it would show little sign of careful control and planning. Analyze at least one prose selection and two poems in this unit and present the evidence (or lack of evidence) for thinking of writers as people who work chiefly from inspiration.

Symbolism

Select a poem and a prose selection that you think contain little or no symbolism and another poem and prose selection that you think are highly symbolic. Justify your choices by listing your reasons for thinking that one pair of selections is not symbolic and the other is.

BIOGRAPHICAL NOTES

T. S. Eliot

Regarded by many as the outstanding poet of contemporary English letters, T. S. Eliot (1888–1965) was born in St. Louis in 1888, lived there for 18 years, and then went to Harvard to take both a bachelor's and a master's degree in four years. Work at the Sorbonne and more graduate work at Harvard were followed by a period at Oxford and then a series of jobs in England. His poem "The Wasteland" (1922) brought him international recognition. Though a controversial poem, it had major influence on other twentieth-century writers. In 1948 he was awarded the Nobel Prize in Literature. Much of his popularity in later life in both England and the United States came from his

plays *Murder in the Cathedral* and *The Cocktail Party*. In 1927 he became a British subject in deed as he had been in spirit most of his life. However, he returned to the United States in the thirties to lecture at Harvard; and for the rest of his life he made periodic visits, usually lecture tours, to his native land.

Ernest Hemingway

Ernest Hemingway (1898–1962) was one of America's most widely read twentieth-century writers. During World War I, he served first with the French ambulance corps and then in the Italian army, where he was wounded and decorated. He stayed on in Europe as a correspondent, later joining the expatriates and coming under the influence of Gertrude Stein, Ezra Pound, and Sherwood Anderson. In the early 20s, his first work appeared in print: verse and short stories. His first novel, *The Sun Also Rises*, a story of the so-called lost generation, was published in 1926. His other major works include *Death in the Afternoon, A Farewell to Arms, For Whom the Bell Tolls*, and *The Old Man and the Sea*. Included in several collections are these significant short stories: "The Killers," "The Snows of Kilimanjaro," "The Big Two-Hearted River," and "The Short Happy Life of Francis Macomber." Several of Hemingway's works have appeared as motion pictures. In 1954 he was awarded the Nobel Prize in Literature. During his lifetime Hemingway became the prototype of the strong, virile deep-sea fisher, big-game hunter—hearty, tough, courageous. His stories reflect this strong, masculine approach to life.

Edwin Arlington Robinson

Plagued by poverty, illness, and poor eyesight, Edwin Arlington Robinson (1869–1935) worked against great odds in his determination to write poetry. During his two years at Harvard, a number of his poems, including "Richard Cory," were published by campus periodicals. His first books of poetry were privately underwritten and made little stir on the American literary scene. Theodore Roosevelt, however, was impressed by *The Children of the Night* and gave Robinson a post in the New York Customs House. Years passed without the sale of a single poem, but finally friends made it possible for Robinson to devote all his energies to writing. With the publication of *The Man Against the Sky* in 1915, critical success came to Robinson, and in the 1920s he became one of America's most widely read poets. During that decade, he won the Pulitzer Prize for Poetry three times.

Ray Bradbury

Probably America's best-known writer of science fiction and fantasy, Ray Bradbury (1920–   ) has seen many of his stories appear in collections of "best stories" of the year. Though his work is high in entertainment value, much of it also illustrates his serious interest in using the short story as a weapon against those who attempt to control freedom of thought and expression. Since 1947 he has written almost two dozen books. Some of his most popular works are: *Martian Chronicles* (1950), *Fahrenheit 451* (1953), *Switch on the Night* (1955), *A Medicine for Melancholy* (1959), *Something Wicked This Way Comes* (1962). Among his most recent works are *The Halloween Tree* (1972), a novel, and *The Small Assassin* (1973), a collection of short stories.

W. H. Auden

W. H. Auden (1907–1973), born in England, came to America in 1939 and became a United States citizen in 1946. A prolific writer of poetry and critical essays, he was awarded the Pulitzer Prize for Poetry in 1948 for *The Age of Anxiety.* In 1956 he won the National Book Award for *The Shield of Achilles.* A collection of his criticism, *Forewards and Afterwards,* was published in 1973. Auden taught at many colleges and universities throughout his long career.

Karl Shapiro

Karl Shapiro (1913–   ) served with the Army in the South Pacific from 1942 to 1945, and it was while he was there that some of his first books appeared. *Person, Place and Thing* appeared in 1942 and won him immediate recognition; just two years later he published *V-Letter and Other Poems,* which won the Pulitzer Prize in Poetry in 1945. Shapiro has also been Consultant in Poetry at the

Library of Congress, a teacher of English, and the editor of such well-established literary magazines as *The Prairie Schooner* and *Poetry.*

e. e. cummings

The biographical note for e. e. cummings can be found on page 299.

Robinson Jeffers

Robinson Jeffers (1887–1962) spent part of his childhood in Europe and moved with his family to California in 1903. After taking his bachelor's degree at Occidental College, he studied at various colleges for many years, attempting to find a suitable profession. In 1914 he fell heir to his uncle's fortune and was able to settle down to a life of writing. On Point Sur, near Carmel, California, he found a solitary existence which he prized for the rest of his life. Jeffers wrote many volumes of poetry, many of which were powerful and heavily symbolic. His best-known longer work was *Medea,* his adaptation of Euripides' drama.

W. D. Snodgrass

W. D. Snodgrass (1926–   ) was born in Wilkinsburg, Pennsylvania. He attended college for a year and then joined the Navy as an apprentice sailor. He later finished college and embarked upon a career as a teacher at the university level. His first book of poetry, *Heart's Needle,* was awarded the Pulitzer Prize in 1960. His second book of poems was *After Experience* (1968), and since then he has published a book of essays, *In Radical Pursuit* (1975).

Vassar Miller

Born in 1924 in Houston, Texas, Vassar Miller received her B.S. and M.A. at the University of Houston and lives in Houston. Afflicted with cerebral palsy from birth, she has dedicated herself singlemindedly to poetry and has demonstrated—if demonstration were needed—that talent, religious fervor, and personal joy and agony can produce major poetry. Her books include *Adam's Footprint* (1956), *Wage War on Silence* (1960), *My Bones Being Wiser* (1963), and *Onions and Roses* (1968).

Claude McKay

Claude McKay (1890–1948) was born in Sunny Ville, Jamaica, but came to the United States in 1912. His poetry has elements of Jamaican folklore, social protest, and the Harlem ghetto. Yet perhaps more than any other black poet he converts this mixture into poems of permanent value.

Margaret Walker

Margaret Walker (1915–   ), born in Birmingham, Alabama, has been a social worker, newspaper reporter, magazine editor, and teacher. However, she is best known for her poetry volume, *For My People* (1942), and her novel, *Jubilee* (1966). Her second volume of poetry, *Prophets for a New Day,* was published in 1970.

Wallace Stegner

Growing up in a family that moved from place to place in the western United States and Canada, Wallace Stegner (1909–   ) developed early an affinity for country life. He earned college degrees, including a Ph.D., and then settled down to a career of college teaching and writing. He has written many short stories and almost a dozen novels. Among the latter are the well-received *Big Rock Candy Mountain* and *Angle of Repose,* which won the Pulitzer Prize in 1972.

Edna St. Vincent Millay

The first verses of Edna St. Vincent Millay (1892–1952) were published in the *St. Nicholas* magazine while she was still a young girl. She attended Vassar College and continued to write poetry. One of her most famous poems appeared as the title poem of *Renascence and Other Poems* (1912). A prototype of the Greenwich Village poet, Edna Millay wrote continuously and published a number of volumes in the twenties and thirties. *The Harp Weaver and Other Poems* won the Pulitzer Prize in 1923. Her style ranged from exuberance to great bitterness. With each succeeding generation, she has found receptive listeners.

William Faulkner

Born and reared in Mississippi, William Faulkner (1897–1962) spent most of his life writing, for years unrecognized and little read. Privately he published a book of poems and then, in 1926, his first novel, *Soldier's Pay. Sartoris* (1929), a novel about the degeneration of a family, paralleled in large measure Faulkner's own family, a story that was to emerge in several later stories and novels. Faulkner's prose demands a close reading and rereading. In some stories he uses a stream-of-consciousness technique. Gradually critics began to pay more attention to him, and eventually he moved, as a literary figure, from obscurity to international fame. In 1950 he won the Nobel Prize in Literature. His *A Fable* (1954) won both a National Book Award for fiction and a Pulitzer Prize.

THORNTON WILDER

1897-1975

Thornton Wilder playing the Stage Manager in Our Town, *New York, 1938. He was convinced that the confining three walls, the curtain, and the proscenium arch of the modern theater "shut the play up into a museum showpiece." Instead of the universals he was witnessing only local happenings. "The novel," he argued, "is pre-eminently the vehicle of the unique occasion, the theatre of the generalized one. It is through the theatre's power to raise the exhibited individual action into the realm of idea and type and universal that it is able to evoke our belief."*

Thornton Wilder could always be counted on to try new forms, to avoid the obvious. Since 1915, he has been experimenting in prose fiction and drama, but it was 1927 before he achieved critical approval and a national reputation.

Born in Madison, Wisconsin, he moved to China at the age of nine when his father was appointed consul general at Hong Kong and Shanghai. He spent six months in a German School in Hong Kong. In the following years, he attended the public schools of Berkeley, California; an English Mission boarding school in Cheefoo, China; and the Thacker School in Ojai, California. He was graduated from high school in Berkeley and entered Oberlin College in 1915. Later he transferred to Yale. He interrupted his studies to serve in the Coast Artillery and, when World War I was over, completed his B.A. degree at Yale.

He spent the next year in residence at the American Academy in Rome. He returned to teach French for six years at the Lawrenceville School in New Jersey. During that time he finished his first novel, *The Cabala*, which was published in 1926. Also during that period he earned an M.A. at Princeton and wrote *The Bridge of San Luis Rey* (1927). Wilder did not, however, abandon teaching as he gained fame as a writer. He later taught at the University of Chicago for six years and held the Charles Eliot Norton Professorship at Harvard.

It was natural that a young scholar back from Rome should want to gather his impressions of the Eternal City into a romantic story with himself at the center. *The Cabala* is that kind of novel, but, as readers have come to expect from Wilder, it is fantasy with an ironic twist. The young American introduces us to the wealthy and eccentric aristocrats who make up a group known as the Cabala. He soon becomes intrigued with these people as people only to discover they are the pagan gods of Europe masquerading as citizens of Rome, 1920. Not all readers of the novel were as convinced as the narrator seemed to be, but Wilder was not deterred. He had had his first try at combining a realistic setting with a fantastic plot, and he had the satisfaction of shaping his novel from his own pattern. Originality was to play an important role in Wilder's development.

The Bridge of San Luis Rey not only won him a Pulitzer Prize, the first of three, but made him financially independent for several years following its publication. Like *The Cabala, The Bridge of San Luis Rey* is a philosophical novel, but it is set in eighteenth-century Peru, not Europe. Wilder was convinced that America had had enough stark realism in the novels of John Dos Passos, enough critical examination of our own society in the work of Sinclair Lewis. It was ready now for historical romance, and what he provided in *The Bridge of San Luis Rey* was made to the public's order: memorable characters, a remote and ornate setting, religious themes, a sense of mystery, and, above all, concise dialogue.

The central incident is simple: on a Friday in July, 1714, a bridge collapses on the road between Lima and Cuzco, sending five people to their deaths. The plot is more complex: Brother Juniper, who was present at the accident, sets out to discover why *these* five people should have died. He tells us the story of a lonely old marquesa and her lovely daughter, then of an actor-manager and his mistress, finally of twin brothers and a secret passion. Wilder's purpose in letting Brother Juniper tell the stories is made clear in the epilogue, called "Perhaps an Intention." Here Wilder enters the book, as the omniscient narrator, in order to underscore his dominant

theme: Love is a moral responsibility; the world we live in is purposeless without it. "There is a land of the living and a land of the dead," his last sentence reads, "and the bridge is love, the only survival, the only meaning."

Following his resignation from Lawrenceville, Wilder spent two years in Europe studying Continental drama. On his return he published his third novel, *The Woman of Andros,* a failure with both the public and the critics. Set in pre-Christian Greece, it tried to probe further into the hidden meanings of human life. With his next novel, however, Wilder recouped his reputation and if anything enlarged his audience. In *Heaven's My Destination* (1935) he shifted gears, adopted the conventional realistic method for this social satire, set the story of George Brush, a traveling sales agent, in the Middle West Bible Belt about 1930, and concentrated on pitting this humanitarian hero against a materialistic society. In his travels about the country, Brush moves from comedy to pathos and back again. At one moment we laugh at his naïveté, at another we wince at the grim truths he demonstrates. The novel quite rightly has been compared to Mark Twain's *Huckleberry Finn.* Wilder commenced work on his fifth novel, *The Ides of March* (1948), after serving three years with the Intelligence Corps of the Air Force in World War II. Another best-seller, it tells the familiar story of the last months of Julius Caesar's life with such originality that again Wilder turned history into perceptive character study. Using only letters and documents, some seventy, all of them imaginary, to retell the events leading up to the assassination, for the first time in his fiction Wilder stood wholly outside the main action, not commenting as omniscient narrator on the moral of his story. The letters, however, are of such variety and fascination that the reader needs no guide to discover their implications.

Had Wilder published only novels, he would have had a satisfying if modest reputation among American literary artists. When *Our Town* opened on Broadway in 1938, the critics knew a genuine theatrical talent had blossomed. *The Skin of Our Teeth* (1942) and *The Matchmaker* (1954) are the full flowering. "Toward the end of the twenties," Wilder tells us, "I began to lose pleasure in going to the theatre. I ceased to believe in the stories I saw presented there." He feared that the playwrights of his day were afraid to disturb their middle-class patrons with biting comedy or social satire and consequently soothed them with comfortable, tidy plays of little consequence. But chief among his reasons for disbelief was the box set. He was convinced that the confining three walls, the curtain, and the proscenium arch of the modern theater "shut the play up into a museum showcase." Instead of the universals he was witnessing only local happenings. "The novel," he argued, "is pre-eminently the vehicle of the unique occasion, the theatre of the generalized one. It is through the theatre's power to raise the exhibited individual action into the realm of idea and type and universal that it is able to evoke our belief."

Our Town breaks down the confinements of a box set in order to speak of universals. It was not Wilder's first attempt. As early as 1931 he had published *The Long Christmas Dinner and Other Plays*. These one-act experiments tried "to capture not versimilitude but reality," as he put it. In other words, he did not wish to hamper his audience with elaborate sets that looked like reproductions of our own dining rooms or the interior of actual pullman cars; he avoided placing the action in a specific year or a certain town; his characters were dressed in ordinary clothes, not costumes. *The Long Christmas Dinner,* for example, spans ninety years, yet the basic set never changes. In *Pullman Car Hiawatha* plain chairs serve as berths. In *The Happy Journey to Trenton and Camden* four kitchen chairs and a low platform represent an automobile; Pa's hands hold an imaginary steering wheel; and the family travels seventy miles in twenty minutes. The Stage Manager acts as interpreter and scene changer as well as various characters in the play. In *Our Town,* Wilder experiments even further.

Though set in Grover's Corners, the play is not offered, Wilder insists, "as a picture of life in a New Hampshire village; or as a speculation about the conditions of life after death." He is attempting here "to find a value above all price for the smallest events in our daily life." He makes the claim "as preposterous as possible," for he has "set the village against the largest dimensions of time and place."

To bring belief back into the theater, in other words, Wilder strives to embody universal meaning in specific incidents, actions, and characters. His primary concern is not with the individual lives of the Gibbs family or the Webbs but with life itself, with all its vain strivings, its petty concerns, its joys and sorrows. Small wonder that this play has been performed in the best theaters of the world; it translates easily because the audience identification is almost immediate. Grover's Corners could be Denmark or Italy, Brazil or Japan. The need for love is a theme of much of Wilder's fiction; the need for awareness, for savoring every minute of our brief lives is at the heart of his tragic play. Failing to realize life's potential, no matter how modestly life is lived, leads only to frustration and waste. Emily Webb comes to know this truth too late. Have *we* made this discovery in time, Wilder seems to ask his audience. He does not wait for our answer, for he knows how we have trapped ourselves in our getting and spending, our overweening pride, our ignorance of the value of time. To Simon Stimson, the town drunk, Wilder gives his most biting lines, but Simon ironically speaks from the grave: "Now you know! That's what it was to be alive. To move about in a cloud of ignorance; to go up and down trampling on the feelings of those . . . of those about you. To spend and waste time as though you had a million years. To be always at the mercy of one self-centered passion, or another . . . that's the happy existence you wanted to go back to. Ignorance and blindness." *The Bridge of San Luis Rey* taught this moral to a legion of readers. *Our Town* continues to speak this truth on stages everywhere.

When this play opened in New York
in February, 1938, the first-night audience was not quite prepared
for the bare and dimly lit stage as it entered the theater, a stage
without curtain and without scenery. Since that time,
audiences have grown accustomed to the easy informality of the Stage Manager
as he introduces each scene, interrupts the action with commentary,
takes the part of several minor characters, improvises scenery, and speaks the epilogue.
Playwrights of another age would have called him the Chorus. What he adds to this play
is invaluable: an affectionate understanding of the simple, ordinary life that goes on
day after day in Grover's Corners and an earnest desire to make us share
that understanding. He wants us to see ourselves in these people,
to laugh and cry with them, to enjoy life as they do. Because so many audiences
willingly respond, *Our Town* is one of the most successful plays
in the modern American theater.

OUR TOWN

a play in three acts

CHARACTERS

*(in the order
of their appearance)*

STAGE MANAGER	MR. WEBB
DR. GIBBS	WOMAN IN THE BALCONY
JOE CROWELL	MAN IN THE AUDITORIUM
HOWIE NEWSOME	LADY IN THE BOX
MRS. GIBBS	SIMON STIMSON
MRS. WEBB	MRS. SOAMES
GEORGE GIBBS	CONSTABLE WARREN
REBECCA GIBBS	SI CROWELL
WALLY WEBB	THREE BASEBALL PLAYERS
EMILY WEBB	SAM CRAIG
PROFESSOR WILLARD	JOE STODDARD

*The entire play takes place
in Grover's Corners,
New Hampshire.*

OUR TOWN by Thornton Wilder. Copyright © 1948, 1957 by Thornton Wilder. Reprinted by permission of Harper and Row, Publishers, Inc. No reprints are to be made from Coward-McCann or Samuel French acting editions of OUR TOWN or from Bantam paperback reprint of THREE PLAYS.

Act I

No curtain.

No scenery.

The audience, arriving, sees an empty stage in half-light.

Presently the STAGE MANAGER, *hat on and pipe in mouth, enters and begins placing a table and three chairs downstage left, and a table and three chairs downstage right. He also places a low bench at the corner of what will be the Webb house, left.*

"Left" and "right" are from the point of view of the actor facing the audience. "Up" is toward the back wall.

As the house lights go down he has finished setting the stage and leaning against the right proscenium pillar watches the late arrivals in the audience.

When the auditorium is in complete darkness he speaks:

STAGE MANAGER. This play is called "Our Town." It was written by Thornton Wilder; produced and directed by A. . . . [or: produced by A. . . . ; directed by B. . . .]. In it you will see Miss C. . . . ; Miss D. . . . ; Miss E. . . . ; and Mr. F. . . . ; Mr. G. . . . ; Mr. H. . . . ; and many others. The name of the town is Grover's Corners, New Hampshire—just across the Massachusetts line: latitude 42 degrees 40 minutes; longitude 70 degrees 37 minutes. The First Act shows a day in our town. The day is May 7, 1901. The time is just before dawn. (*A rooster crows.*)

The sky is beginning to show some streaks of light over in the East there, behind our mount'in.

The morning star always gets wonderful bright the minute before it has to go,—doesn't it? (*He stares at it for a moment, then goes upstage.*)

Well, I'd better show you how our town lies.

Up here—(*That is: parallel with the back wall.*) is Main Street. Way back there is the railway station; tracks go that way. Polish Town's across the tracks, and some Canuck[1] families.

(*Toward the left.*) Over there is the Congregational Church; across the street's the Presbyterian.

Methodist and Unitarian are over there.

Baptist is down in the holla' by the river.

Catholic Church is over beyond the tracks.

Here's the Town Hall and Post Office combined; jail's in the basement.

Bryan once made a speech from these very steps here.

Along here's a row of stores. Hitching posts and horse blocks in front of them. First automobile's going to come along in about five years—belonged to Banker Cartwright, our richest citizen . . . lives in the big white house up on the hill.

Here's the grocery store and here's Mr. Morgan's drugstore. Most everybody in town manages to look into those two stores once a day.

Public School's over yonder. High School's still farther over. Quarter of nine mornings, noontimes, and three o'clock afternoons, the hull town can hear the yelling and screaming from those schoolyards.

He approaches the table and chairs downstage right.

This is our doctor's house,—Doc Gibbs'. This is the back door. (*Two arched trellises, covered with vines and flowers, are pushed out, one by each proscenium pillar.*) There's some scenery for those who think they have to have scenery.

This is Mrs. Gibbs' garden. Corn . . . peas . . .

---

1. **Canuck**\kə ᷃nək\ slang for French Canadian, usually used disparagingly.

beans . . . hollyhocks . . . heliotrope[2] . . . and a lot of burdock.[3] (*Crosses the stage.*)

In those days our newspaper come out twice a week—the Grover's Corners *Sentinel*—and this is Editor Webb's house.

And this is Mrs. Webb's garden.

Just like Mrs. Gibbs', only it's got a lot of sunflowers, too.

He looks upward, center stage.

Right here . . . 's a big butternut tree. (*He returns to his place by the right proscenium[4] pillar and looks at the audience for a minute.*)

Nice town, y'know what I mean?

Nobody very remarkable ever come out of it, s'far as we know.

The earliest tombstones in the cemetery up there on the mountain say 1670–1680—they're Grovers and Cartwrights and Gibbses and Herseys—same names as are around here now.

Well, as I said: it's about dawn.

The only lights on in town are in a cottage over by the tracks where a Polish mother's just had twins. And in the Joe Crowell house, where Joe Junior's getting up so as to deliver the paper. And in the depot, where Shorty Hawkins is gettin' ready to flag the 5:45 for Boston. (*A train whistle is heard. The* STAGE MANAGER *takes out his watch and nods.*)

Naturally, out in the country—all around—there've been lights on for some time, what with milkin's and so on. But town people sleep late.

So—another day's begun.

There's Doc Gibbs comin' down Main Street now, comin' back from that baby case. And here's his wife comin' downstairs to get breakfast. (MRS. GIBBS, *a plump, pleasant woman in the middle thirties, comes "downstairs" right. She pulls up an imaginary window shade in her kitchen and starts to make a fire in her stove.*)

Doc Gibbs died in 1930. The new hospital's named after him.

Mrs. Gibbs died first—long time ago, in fact. She went out to visit her daughter, Rebecca, who married an insurance man in Canton, Ohio, and died there—pneumonia—but her body was brought back here. She's up in the cemetery there now—in with a whole mess of Gibbses and Herseys—she was Julia Hersey 'fore she married Doc Gibbs in the Congregational Church over there.

In our town we like to know the facts about everybody.

There's Mrs. Webb, coming downstairs to get her breakfast, too.

—That's Doc Gibbs. Got that call at half past one this morning. And there comes Joe Crowell, Jr., delivering Mr. Webb's *Sentinel*.

DR. GIBBS *has been coming along Main Street from the left. At the point where he would turn to approach his house, he stops, sets down his—imaginary—black bag, takes off his hat, and rubs his face with fatigue, using an enormous handkerchief.*

MRS. WEBB, *a thin, serious, crisp woman, has entered her kitchen, left, tying on an apron. She goes through the motions of putting wood into a stove, lighting it, and preparing breakfast.*

Suddenly, JOE CROWELL, JR., *eleven, starts down Main Street from the right, hurling imaginary newspapers into doorways.*

JOE CROWELL, JR. Morning, Doc Gibbs.
DR. GIBBS. Morning, Joe.
JOE CROWELL, JR. Somebody been sick, Doc?
DR. GIBBS. No. Just some twins born over in Polish Town.
JOE CROWELL, JR. Do you want your paper now?

2. **heliotrope**\ˈhē·lē·ə·trōp\ plant that turns toward the sun and usually bears fragrant white or purplish flowers.
3. **burdock,** coarse weed with a bur; also called cocklebur.
4. **proscenium**\prō ˈsē·nē·əm\ the part of the stage in front of the curtain.

715

DR. GIBBS. Yes, I'll take it.—Anything serious goin' on in the world since Wednesday?

JOE CROWELL, JR. Yessir. My schoolteacher, Miss Foster, 's getting married to a fella over in Concord.

DR. GIBBS. I declare.—How do you boys feel about that?

JOE CROWELL, JR. Well, of course, it's none of my business—but I think if a person starts out to be a teacher, she ought to stay one.

DR. GIBBS. How's your knee, Joe?

JOE CROWELL, JR. Fine, Doc, I never think about it at all. Only like you said, it always tells me when it's going to rain.

DR. GIBBS. What's it telling you today? Goin' to rain?

JOE CROWELL, JR. No, sir.

DR. GIBBS. Sure?

JOE CROWELL, JR. Yessir.

DR. GIBBS. Knee ever make a mistake?

JOE CROWELL, JR. No, sir. (JOE *goes off.* DR. GIBBS *stands reading his paper.*)

STAGE MANAGER. Want to tell you something about that boy Joe Crowell there. Joe was awful bright—graduated from high school here, head of his class. So he got a scholarship to Massachusetts Tech. Graduated head of his class there, too. It was all wrote up in the Boston paper at the time. Goin' to be a great engineer, Joe was. But the war broke out and he died in France.—All that education for nothing.

HOWIE NEWSOME (*off left*). Giddap, Bessie! What's the matter with you today?

STAGE MANAGER. Here comes Howie Newsome, deliverin' the milk. (HOWIE NEWSOME, *about thirty, in overalls, comes along Main Street from the left, walking beside an invisible horse and wagon and carrying an imaginary rack with milk bottles. The sound of clinking milk bottles is heard. He leaves some bottles at* MRS. WEBB's *trellis, then, crossing the stage to* MRS. GIBBS', *he stops center to talk to* DR. GIBBS.)

HOWIE NEWSOME. Morning, Doc.

DR. GIBBS. Morning, Howie.

HOWIE NEWSOME. Somebody sick?

DR. GIBBS. Pair of twins over to Mrs. Goruslawski's.

HOWIE NEWSOME. Twins, eh? This town's gettin' bigger every year.

DR. GIBBS. Goin' to rain, Howie?

HOWIE NEWSOME. No, no. Fine day—that'll burn through. Come on, Bessie.

DR. GIBBS. Hello, Bessie. (*He strokes the horse, which has remained up center.*) How old is she, Howie?

HOWIE NEWSOME. Going on seventeen. Bessie's all mixed up about the route ever since the Lockharts stopped takin' their quart of milk every day. She wants to leave 'em a quart just the same—keeps scolding me the hull trip. (*He reaches* MRS. GIBBS' *back door. She is waiting for him.*)

MRS. GIBBS. Good morning, Howie.

HOWIE NEWSOME. Morning, Mrs. Gibbs. Doc's just comin' down the street.

MRS. GIBBS. Is he? Seems like you're late today.

HOWIE NEWSOME. Yes. Somep'n went wrong with the separator. Don't know what 'twas. (*He passes* DR. GIBBS *up center.*) Doc!

DR. GIBBS. Howie!

MRS. GIBBS (*calling upstairs*). Children! Children! Time to get up.

HOWIE NEWSOME. Come on, Bessie! (*He goes off right.*)

MRS. GIBBS. George! Rebecca! (DR. GIBBS *arrives at his back door and passes through the trellis into his house.*)

MRS. GIBBS. Everything all right, Frank?

DR. GIBBS. Yes. I declare—easy as kittens.

MRS. GIBBS. Bacon'll be ready in a minute. Set down and drink your coffee. You can catch a couple hours' sleep this morning, can't you?

DR. GIBBS. Hm! . . . Mrs. Wentworth's coming at eleven. Guess I know what it's about, too. Her stummick ain't what it ought to be.

MRS. GIBBS. All told, you won't get more'n three hours' sleep. Frank Gibbs, I don't know what's goin' to become of you. I do wish I could get you to go away someplace and take a rest. I think it would do you good.

MRS. WEBB. Emileeee! Time to get up! Wally! Seven o'clock!

MRS. GIBBS. I declare, you got to speak to George. Seems like something's come over him lately. He's no help to me at all. I can't even get him to cut me some wood.

DR. GIBBS. (*Washing and drying his hands at the sink.* MRS. GIBBS *is busy at the stove.*) Is he sassy to you?

MRS. GIBBS. No. He just whines! All he thinks about is that baseball—George! Rebecca! You'll be late for school.

DR. GIBBS. M-m-m . . .

MRS. GIBBS. George!

DR. GIBBS. George, look sharp!

GEORGE'S VOICE. Yes, Pa!

DR. GIBBS (*as he goes off the stage*). Don't you hear your mother calling you? I guess I'll go upstairs and get forty winks.

MRS. WEBB. Walleee! Emileee! You'll be late for school! Walleee! You wash yourself good or I'll come up and do it myself.

REBECCA GIBBS' VOICE. Ma! What dress shall I wear?

MRS. GIBBS. Don't make a noise. Your father's been out all night and needs his sleep. I washed and ironed the blue gingham for you special.

REBECCA. Ma, I hate that dress.

MRS. GIBBS. Oh, hush-up-with-you.

REBECCA. Every day I go to school dressed like a sick turkey.

MRS. GIBBS. Now, Rebecca, you always look *very* nice.

REBECCA. Mama, George's throwing soap at me.

MRS. GIBBS. I'll come and slap the both of you,—that's what I'll do. (*A factory whistle sounds. The children dash in and take their places at the tables. Right,* GEORGE, *about sixteen, and* REBECCA, *eleven. Left,* EMILY *and* WALLY, *same ages. They carry strapped school-books.*)

STAGE MANAGER. We've got a factory in our town too—hear it? Makes blankets. Cartwrights own it and it brung 'em a fortune.

MRS. WEBB. Children! Now I won't have it. Breakfast is just as good as any other meal and I won't have you gobbling like wolves.

It'll stunt your growth,—that's a fact. Put away your book, Wally.

WALLY. Aw, Ma! By ten o'clock I got to know all about Canada.

MRS. WEBB. You know the rule's well as I do—no books at table. As for me, I'd rather have my children healthy than bright.

EMILY. I'm both, Mama: you know I am. I'm the brightest girl in school for my age. I have a wonderful memory.

MRS. WEBB. Eat your breakfast.

WALLY. I'm bright, too, when I'm looking at my stamp collection.

MRS. GIBBS. I'll speak to your father about it when he's rested. Seems to me twenty-five cents a week's enough for a boy your age. I declare I don't know how you spend it all.

GEORGE. Aw, Ma,—I gotta lotta things to buy.

MRS. GIBBS. Strawberry phosphates[5]—that's what you spend it on.

GEORGE. I don't see how Rebecca comes to have so much money. She has more'n a dollar.

REBECCA (*spoon in mouth, dreamily*). I've been saving it up gradual.

MRS. GIBBS. Well, dear, I think it's a good thing to spend some every now and then.

REBECCA. Mama, do you know what I love most in the world—do you?—Money.

MRS. GIBBS. Eat your breakfast.

THE CHILDREN. Mama, there's first bell.—I gotta hurry.—I don't want any more.—I gotta hurry. (*The children rise, seize their books and dash out through the trellises. They meet, down center, and chattering, walk to Main Street, then turn left. The* STAGE MANAGER *goes off, unobtrusively, right.*)

MRS. WEBB. Walk fast, but you don't have to run. Wally, pull up your pants at the knee. Stand up straight, Emily.

MRS. GIBBS. Tell Miss Foster I send her my best congratulations—can you remember that?

REBECCA. Yes, Ma.

MRS. GIBBS. You look real nice, Rebecca. Pick up your feet.

---

5. **strawberry phosphates,** beverage made of a mixture of soda water and strawberry flavoring.

ALL. Good-by. (MRS. GIBBS *fills her apron with food for the chickens and comes down to the footlights.*)

MRS. GIBBS. Here, chick, chick, chick.

No, go away, you. Go away.

Here, chick, chick, chick.

What's the matter with *you?* Fight, fight, fight,—that's all you do. Hm . . . *you* don't belong to me. Where'd you come from? (*She shakes her apron.*)

Oh, don't be so scared. Nobody's going to hurt you. (MRS. WEBB *is sitting on the bench by her trellis, stringing beans.*)

Good Morning, Myrtle. How's your cold?

MRS. WEBB. Well, I still get that tickling feeling in my throat. I told Charles I didn't know as I'd go to choir practice tonight. Wouldn't be any use.

MRS. GIBBS. Have you tried singing over your voice?

MRS. WEBB. Yes, but somehow I can't do that and stay on the key. While I'm resting myself I thought I'd string some of these beans.

MRS. GIBBS (*rolling up her sleeves as she crosses the stage for a chat*). Let me help you. Beans have been good this year.

MRS. WEBB. I've decided to put up forty quarts if it kills me. The children say they hate 'em, but I notice they're able to get 'em down all winter. (*Pause. Brief sound of chickens cackling.*)

MRS. GIBBS. Now, Myrtle. I've got to tell you something, because if I don't tell somebody I'll burst.

MRS. WEBB. Why, Julia Gibbs!

MRS. GIBBS. Here, give me some more of those beans. Myrtle, did one of those secondhand-furniture men from Boston come to see you last Friday?

MRS. WEBB. No-o.

MRS. GIBBS. Well, he called on me. First I thought he was a patient wantin' to see Dr. Gibbs. 'N he wormed his way into my parlor, and, Myrtle Webb, he offered me three hundred and fifty dollars for Grandmother Wentworth's highboy, as I'm sitting here!

MRS. WEBB. Why, Julia Gibbs!

MRS. GIBBS. He did! That old thing! Why, it was so big I didn't know where to put it and I almost give it to Cousin Hester Wilcox.

MRS. WEBB. Well, you're going to take it, aren't you?

MRS. GIBBS. I don't know.

MRS. WEBB. You don't know—three hundred and fifty dollars! What's come over you?

MRS. GIBBS. Well, if I could get the Doctor to take the money and go away someplace on a real trip, I'd sell it like that.—Y'know, Myrtle, it's been the dream of my life to see Paris, France.—Oh, I don't know. It sounds crazy, I suppose, but for years I've been promising myself that if we ever had the chance—

MRS. WEBB. How does the Doctor feel about it?

MRS. GIBBS. Well, I did beat about the bush a little and said that if I got a legacy—that's the way I put it—I'd make him take me somewhere.

MRS. WEBB. M-m-m . . . What did he say?

MRS. GIBBS. You know how he is. I haven't heard a serious word out of him since I've known him. No, he said, it might make him discontented with Grover's Corners to go traipsin' about Europe; better let well enough alone, he says. Every two years he makes a trip to the battlefields of the Civil War and that's enough treat for anybody, he says.

MRS. WEBB. Well, Mr. Webb just *admires* the way Dr. Gibbs knows everything about the Civil War. Mr. Webb's a good mind to give up Napoleon and move over to the Civil War, only Dr. Gibbs being one of the greatest experts in the country just makes him despair.

MRS. GIBBS. It's a fact! Dr. Gibbs is never so happy as when he's at Antietam or Gettysburg. The times I've walked over those hills, Myrtle, stopping at every bush and pacing it all out, like we were going to buy it.

MRS. WEBB. Well, if that secondhand man's really serious about buyin' it, Julia, you sell it. And then you'll get to see Paris, all right. Just keep droppin' hints from time to time—

that's how I got to see the Atlantic Ocean, y'know.

MRS. GIBBS. Oh, I'm sorry I mentioned it. Only it seems to me that once in your life before you die you ought to see a country where they don't talk in English and don't even want to. (*The* STAGE MANAGER *enters briskly from the right. He tips his hat to the ladies, who nod their heads.*)

STAGE MANAGER. Thank you, ladies. Thank you very much. (MRS. GIBBS *and* MRS. WEBB *gather up their things, return into their homes and disappear.*)

Now we're going to skip a few hours.

But first we want a little more information about the town, kind of a scientific account, you might say.

So I've asked Professor Willard of our State University to sketch in a few details of our past history here.

Is Professor Willard here? (PROFESSOR WILLARD, *a rural savant,*[6] *pince-nez*[7] *on a wide satin ribbon, enters from the right with some notes in his hand.*)

May I introduce Professor Willard of our State University. A few brief notes, thank you, Professor,—unfortunately our time is limited.

PROFESSOR WILLARD. Grover's Corners . . . let me see . . . Grover's Corners lies on the old Pleistocene[8] granite of the Appalachian range. I may say it's some of the oldest land in the world. We're very proud of that. A shelf of Devonian[9] basalt crosses it with vestiges of Mesozoic[10] shale, and some sandstone outcroppings; but that's all more recent: two hundred, three hundred million years old.

Some highly interesting fossils have been found . . . I may say: unique fossils . . . two miles out of town, in Silas Peckham's cow pasture. They can be seen at the museum in our University at any time—that is, at any reasonable time. Shall I read some of Professor Gruber's notes on the meteorological situation—mean precipitation, et cetera?

STAGE MANAGER. Afraid we won't have time for that, Professor. We might have a few words on the history of man here.

PROFESSOR WILLARD. Yes . . . anthropological data: Early Amerindian stock. Cotahatchee tribes . . . no evidence before the tenth century of this era . . . hm . . . now entirely disappeared . . . possible traces in three families. Migration toward the end of the seventeenth century of English brachiocephalic[11] blue-eyed stock . . . for the most part. Since then some Slav and Mediterranean—

STAGE MANAGER. And the population, Professor Willard?

PROFESSOR WILLARD. Within the town limits: 2,640.

STAGE MANAGER. Just a moment, Professor. (*He whispers into the* PROFESSOR'S *ear.*)

PROFESSOR WILLARD. Oh, yes, indeed?—The population, *at the moment,* is 2,642. The Postal District brings in 507 more, making a total of 3,149.—Mortality and birth rates: constant.—By MacPherson's gauge: 6.032.

STAGE MANAGER. Thank you very much, Professor. We're all very much obliged to you, I'm sure.

PROFESSOR WILLARD. Not at all, sir; not at all.

STAGE MANAGER. This way, Professor, and thank you again. (*Exit* PROFESSOR WILLARD.) Now the political and social report: Editor Webb. —Oh, Mr. Webb? (MRS. WEBB *appears at her back door.*)

---

6. savant \sa▲vant\ a learned person.
7. pince-nez\pĭns ▲nĕz\ eyeglasses held on the nose by a spring.
8. Pleistocene\plaī·stə·sēn\ the great ice age.
9. Devonian\dĭ ▲vō·nē·ən\ that period which began with the continents mainly dry. Later large areas were flooded and sediment forming old red sandstone was laid down. The sea was full of fish. Frogs and other amphibians appeared. The land was covered with great ferns and fern-like trees.
10. Mesozoic\mĕ·zə ▲zō·ĭk\ the era when the Appalachian Mts. were elevated. Reptiles and dinosaurs were numerous, but became extinct when violent disturbances brought the era to an end.
11. brachiocephalic\bră·kē·ō·sə ▲fa·lĭk\ (usually spelled brachycephalic) short-headed, with the breadth of the head at least four-fifths of its length.

MRS. WEBB. He'll be here in a minute. . . . He just cut his hand while he was eatin' an apple.

STAGE MANAGER. Thank you, Mrs. Webb.

MRS. WEBB. Charles! Everybody's waitin'. (*Exit* MRS. WEBB.)

STAGE MANAGER. Mr. Webb is Publisher and Editor of the Grover's Corners *Sentinel.* That's our local paper, y'know. (MR. WEBB *enters from his house, pulling on his coat. His finger is bound in a handkerchief.*)

MR. WEBB. Well . . . I don't have to tell you that we're run here by a Board of Selectmen.— All males vote at the age of twenty-one. Women vote indirect. We're lower middle 'class: sprinkling of professional men . . . ten per cent illiterate laborers. Politically, we're eighty-six per cent Republicans; six per cent Democrats; four per cent Socialists; rest, indifferent.

Religiously, we're eighty-five per cent Protestants; twelve per cent Catholics; rest, indifferent.

STAGE MANAGER. Have you any comments, Mr. Webb?

MR. WEBB. Very ordinary town, if you ask me. Little better behaved than most. Probably a lot duller.

But our young people here seem to like it well enough. Ninety per cent of 'em graduating from high school settle down right here to live—even when they've been away to college.

STAGE MANAGER. Now, is there anyone in the audience who would like to ask Editor Webb anything about the town?

WOMAN IN THE BALCONY. Is there much drinking in Grover's Corners?

MR. WEBB. Well, ma'am, I wouldn't know what you'd call *much.* Satiddy nights the farmhands meet down in Ellery Greenough's stable and holler some. We've got one or two town drunks, but they're always having remorses every time an evangelist comes to town. No, ma'am, I'd say likker ain't a regular thing in the home here, except in the

medicine chest. Right good for snake bite, y'know—always was.

BELLIGERENT MAN AT BACK OF AUDITORIUM. Is there no one in town aware of—

STAGE MANAGER. Come forward, will you, where we can all hear you—What were you saying?

BELLIGERENT MAN. Is there no one in town aware of social injustice and industrial inequality?

MR. WEBB. Oh, yes, everybody is—somethin' terrible. Seems like they spend most of their time talking about who's rich and who's poor.

BELLIGERENT MAN. Then why don't they do something about it? (*He withdraws without waiting for an answer.*)

MR. WEBB. Well, I dunno. . . . I guess we're all hunting like everybody else for a way the diligent and sensible can rise to the top and the lazy and quarrelsome can sink to the bottom. But it ain't easy to find. Meanwhile, we do all we can to help those that can't help themselves and those that can we leave alone. —Are there any other questions?

LADY IN A BOX. Oh, Mr. Webb? Mr. Webb, is there any culture or love of beauty in Grover's Corners?

MR. WEBB. Well, ma'am, there ain't much—not in the sense you mean. Come to think of it, there's some girls that play the piano at High School Commencement; but they ain't happy about it. No, ma'am, there isn't much culture; but maybe this is the place to tell you that we've got a lot of pleasures of a kind here: we like the sun comin' up over the mountain in the morning, and we all notice a good deal about the birds. We pay a lot of attention to them. And we watch the change of the seasons; yes, everybody knows about them. But those other things—you're right, ma'am,— there ain't much.—*Robinson Crusoe* and the Bible; and Handel's "Largo," we all know that; and Whistler's "Mother"—those are just about as far as we go.

LADY IN A BOX. So I thought. Thank you, Mr. Webb.

STAGE MANAGER. Thank you, Mr. Webb. (MR. WEBB *retires.*) Now, we'll go back to the town.

It's early afternoon. All 2,642 have had their dinners and all the dishes have been washed. (MR. WEBB, *having removed his coat, returns and starts pushing a lawn mower to and fro beside his house.*) There's an early-afternoon calm in our town: a buzzin' and a hummin' from the school buildings; only a few buggies on Main Street—the horses dozing at the hitching posts; you all remember what it's like. Doc Gibbs is in his office, tapping people and making them say "ah." Mr. Webb's cuttin' his lawn over there; one man in ten thinks it's a privilege to push his own lawn mower.

No, sir. It's later than I thought. There are the children coming home from school already. (*Shrill girls' voices are heard, off left.* EMILY *comes along Main Street, carrying some books. There are some signs that she is imagining herself to be a lady of startling elegance.*)

EMILY. I *can't,* Lois. I've got to go home and help my mother. I *promised.*

MR. WEBB. Emily, walk simply. Who do you think you are today?

EMILY. Papa, you're terrible. One minute you tell me to stand up straight and the next minute you call me names. I just don't listen to you. (*She gives him an abrupt kiss.*)

MR. WEBB. Golly, I never got a kiss from such a great lady before. (*He goes out of sight.* EMILY *leans over and picks some flowers by the gate of her house.* GEORGE GIBBS *comes careening down Main Street. He is throwing a ball up to dizzying heights, and waiting to catch it again. This sometimes requires his taking six steps backward. He bumps into an old lady invisible to us.*)

GEORGE. Excuse me, Mrs. Forrest.

STAGE MANAGER (*as Mrs. Forrest*). Go out and play in the fields, young man. You got no business playing baseball on Main Street.

GEORGE. Awfully sorry, Mrs. Forrest.—Hello, Emily.

EMILY. H'lo.

GEORGE. You made a fine speech in class.

EMILY. Well . . . I was really ready to make a speech about the Monroe Doctrine, but at the last minute Miss Corcoran made me talk about the Louisiana Purchase instead. I worked an awful long time on both of them.

GEORGE. Gee, it's funny, Emily. From my window up there I can just see your head nights when you're doing your homework over in your room.

EMILY. Why, can you?

GEORGE. You certainly do stick to it, Emily. I don't see how you can sit still that long. I guess you like school.

EMILY. Well, I always feel it's something you have to go through.

GEORGE. Yeah.

EMILY. I don't mind it really. It passes the time.

GEORGE. Yeah.—Emily, what do you think? We might work out a kinda telegraph from your window to mine; and once in a while you could give me a kinda hint or two about one of those algebra problems. I don't mean the answers, Emily, of course not . . . just some little hint . . .

EMILY. Oh, I think *hints* are allowed.—So—ah —if you get stuck, George, you whistle to me; and I'll give you some hints.

GEORGE. Emily, you're just naturally bright, I guess.

EMILY. I figure that it's just the way a person's born.

GEORGE. Yeah. But, you see, I want to be a farmer, and my Uncle Luke says whenever I'm ready I can come over and work on his farm and if I'm any good I can just gradually have it.

EMILY. You mean the house and everything? (*Enter* MRS. WEBB *with a large bowl and sits on the bench by her trellis.*)

GEORGE. Yeah. Well, thanks . . . I better be getting out to the baseball field. Thanks for the talk, Emily.—Good afternoon, Mrs. Webb.

MRS. WEBB. Good afternoon, George.

GEORGE. So long, Emily.

EMILY. So long, George.

MRS. WEBB. Emily, come and help me string these beans for the winter. George Gibbs let himself have a real conversation, didn't he? Why, he's growing up. How old would George be?

EMILY. I don't know.

MRS. WEBB. Let's see. He must be almost sixteen.

EMILY. Mama, I made a speech in class today and I was very good.

MRS. WEBB. You must recite it to your father at supper. What was it about?

EMILY. The Louisiana Purchase. It was like silk off a spool. I'm going to make speeches all my life.—Mama, are these big enough?

MRS. WEBB. Try and get them a little bigger if you can.

EMILY. Mama, will you answer me a question, serious?

MRS. WEBB. Seriously, dear—not serious.

EMILY. Seriously,—will you?

MRS. WEBB. Of course, I will.

EMILY. Mama, am I good looking?

MRS. WEBB. Yes, of course you are. All my children have got good features; I'd be ashamed if they hadn't.

EMILY. Oh, Mama, that's not what I mean. What I mean is: am I *pretty?*

MRS. WEBB. I've already told you, yes. Now that's enough of that. You have a nice young pretty face. I never heard of such foolishness.

EMILY. Oh, Mama, you never tell us the truth about anything.

MRS. WEBB. I *am* telling you the truth.

EMILY. Mama, were *you* pretty?

MRS. WEBB. Yes, I was, if I do say it. I was the prettiest girl in town next to Mamie Cartwright.

EMILY. But, Mama, you've got to say *something* about me. Am I pretty enough . . . to get anybody . . . to get people interested in me?

MRS. WEBB. Emily, you make me tired. Now stop it. You're pretty enough for all normal purposes.—Come along now and bring that bowl with you.

EMILY. Oh, Mama, you're no help at all.

STAGE MANAGER. Thank you. Thank you! That'll do. We'll have to interrupt again here. Thank you, Mrs. Webb; thank you, Emily. (MRS. WEBB *and* EMILY *withdraw.*) There are some more things we want to explore about this town. (*He comes to the center of the stage. During the following speech the lights gradually dim to darkness, leaving only a spot on him.*) I think this is a good time to tell you that the Cartwright interests have just begun building a new bank in Grover's Corners— had to go to Vermont for the marble, sorry to say. And they've asked a friend of mine what they should put in the cornerstone for people to dig up . . . a thousand years from now. . . . Of course, they've put in a copy of the *New York Times* and a copy of Mr. Webb's *Sentinel.* . . . We're kind of interested in this because some scientific fellas have found a way of painting all that reading matter with a glue—a silicate glue—that'll make it keep a thousand—two thousand years.

We're putting in a Bible . . . and the Constitution of the United States—and a copy of William Shakespeare's plays. What do you say, folks? What do you think?

Y'know—Babylon once had two million people in it, and all we know about 'em is the names of the kings and some copies of wheat contracts . . . and contracts for the sale of slaves. Yet every night all those families sat down to supper, and the father came home from his work, and the smoke went up the chimney,—same as here. And even in Greece and Rome, all we know about the *real* life of the people is what we can piece together out of the joking poems and the comedies they wrote for the theatre back then.

So I'm going to have a copy of this play put in the cornerstone and the people a thousand years from now'll know a few simple facts about us—more than the Treaty of Versailles[12] and the Lindbergh flight.[13]

---

12. **Treaty of Versailles**\věr ▲sai\ the treaty between the Allies and Germany at the end of World War I.
13. **Lindbergh flight,** first nonstop transatlantic flight from west to east. Charles A. Lindbergh flew alone from New York to Paris, 1927, in his monoplane, *The Spirit of St. Louis.*

See what I mean?

So—people a thousand years from now—this is the way we were in the provinces north of New York at the beginning of the twentieth century.—This is the way we were: in our growing up and in our marrying and in our living and in our dying. (*A choir partially concealed in the orchestra pit has begun singing "Blessed Be the Tie That Binds."* SIMON STIMSON *stands directing them. Two ladders have been pushed onto the stage; they serve as indication of the second story in the Gibbs and Webb houses.* GEORGE *and* EMILY *mount them, and apply themselves to their schoolwork.* DR. GIBBS *has entered and is seated in his kitchen reading.*)

Well!—good deal of time's gone by. It's evening.

You can hear choir practice going on in the Congregational Church.

The children are at home doing their schoolwork.

The day's running down like a tired clock.

SIMON STIMSON. Now look here, everybody. Music come into the world to give pleasure. —Softer! Softer! Get it out of your heads that music's only good when it's loud. You leave loudness to the Methodists. You couldn't beat 'em, even if you wanted to. Now again. Tenors!

GEORGE. Hssst! Emily!

EMILY. Hello.

GEORGE. Hello!

EMILY. I can't work at all. The moonlight's so *terrible*.

GEORGE. Emily, did you get the third problem?

EMILY. Which?

GEORGE. The *third?*

EMILY. Why, yes, George—that's the easiest of them all.

GEORGE. I don't see it. Emily, can you give me a hint?

EMILY. I'll tell you one thing: the answer's in yards.

GEORGE. ! ! ! In yards? How do you mean?

Emily: "You're welcome. My, isn't the moonlight terrible?"

EMILY. In *square* yards.

GEORGE. Oh . . . in square yards.

EMILY. Yes, George, don't you see?

GEORGE. Yeah.

EMILY. In square yards of *wallpaper*.

GEORGE. Wallpaper,—oh, I see. Thanks a lot, Emily.

EMILY. You're welcome. My, isn't the moonlight *terrible?* And choir practice going on.—I think if you hold your breath you can hear the train all the way to Contoocook. Hear it?

GEORGE. M-m-m—What do you know!

EMILY. Well, I guess I better go back and try to work.

GEORGE. Good night, Emily. And thanks.

EMILY. Good night, George.

SIMON STIMSON. Before I forget it: how many of you will be able to come in Tuesday afternoon and sing at Fred Hersey's wedding?— show your hands. That'll be fine; that'll be right nice. We'll do the same music we did for Jane Trowbridge's last month.

—Now we'll do: "Art Thou Weary; Art Thou Languid?" It's a question, ladies and gentlemen, make it talk. Ready.

DR. GIBBS. Oh, George, can you come down a minute?

GEORGE. Yes, Pa. (*He descends the ladder.*)

DR. GIBBS. Make yourself comfortable, George; I'll only keep you a minute. George, how old are you?

GEORGE. I? I'm sixteen, almost seventeen.

DR. GIBBS. What do you want to do after school's over?

GEORGE. Why, you know, Pa. I want to be a farmer on Uncle Luke's farm.

DR. GIBBS. You'll be willing, will you, to get up early and milk and feed the stock . . . and you'll be able to hoe and hay all day?

GEORGE. Sure, I will. What are you . . . what do you mean, Pa?

DR. GIBBS. Well, George, while I was in my office today I heard a funny sound . . . and what do you think it was? It was your mother chopping wood. There you see your mother—getting up early; cooking meals all day long; washing and ironing;—and still she has to go out in the back yard and chop wood. I suppose she just got tired of asking you. She just gave up and decided it was easier to do it herself. And you eat her meals, and put on the clothes she keeps nice for you, and you run off and play baseball,—like she's some hired girl we keep around the house but that we don't like very much. Well, I knew all I had to do was call your attention to it. Here's a handkerchief, son. George, I've decided to raise your spending money twenty-five cents a week. Not, of course, for chopping wood for your mother, because that's a present you give her, but because you're getting older—and I imagine there are lots of things you must find to do with it.

GEORGE. Thanks, Pa.

DR. GIBBS. Let's see—tomorrow's your payday. You can count on it—Hmm. Probably Rebecca'll feel she ought to have some more too. Wonder what could have happened to your mother. Choir practice never was as late as this before.

GEORGE. It's only half past eight, Pa.

DR. GIBBS. I don't know why she's in that old choir. She hasn't any more voice than an old crow. . . . Traipsin' around the streets at this hour of the night . . . Just about time you retired, don't you think?

GEORGE. Yes, Pa. (GEORGE *mounts to his place on the ladder. Laughter and good nights can be heard on stage left and presently* MRS. GIBBS, MRS. SOAMES *and* MRS. WEBB *come down Main Street. When they arrive at the corner of the stage they stop.*)

MRS. SOAMES. Good night, Martha. Good night, Mr. Foster.

MRS. WEBB. I'll tell Mr. Webb; I *know* he'll want to put in in the paper.

MRS. GIBBS. My, it's late!

MRS. SOAMES. Good night, Irma.

MRS. GIBBS. Real nice choir practice, wa'n't it? Myrtle Webb! Look at that moon, will you? Tsk-tsk-tsk. Potato weather, for sure. (*They are silent a moment, gazing up at the moon.*)

MRS. SOAMES. Naturally, I didn't want to say a word about it in front of those others, but now we're alone—really, it's the worst scandal that ever was in this town!

MRS. GIBBS. What?

MRS. SOAMES. Simon Stimson!

MRS. GIBBS. Now, Louella!

MRS. SOAMES. But, Julia! To have the organist of a church *drink* and *drunk* year after year. You know he was drunk tonight.

MRS. GIBBS. Now, Louella! We all know about Mr. Stimson, and we all know about the troubles he's been through, and Dr. Ferguson knows too, and if Dr. Ferguson keeps him on there in his job the only thing the rest of us can do is just not to notice it.

MRS. SOAMES. *Not to notice it!* But it's getting worse.

MRS. WEBB. No, it isn't, Louella. It's getting better. I've been in that choir twice as long as you have. It doesn't happen anywhere near so often. . . . My, I hate to go to bed on a night like this.—I better hurry. Those children'll be sitting up till all hours. Good night, Louella. (*They all exchange good nights. She hurries downstage, enters her house and disappears.*)

MRS. GIBBS. Can you get home safe, Louella?

MRS. SOAMES. It's as bright as day. I can see Mr. Soames scowling at the window now. You'd think we'd been to a dance the way the menfolk carry on. (*More good nights.* MRS. GIBBS *arrives at her home and passes through the trellis into the kitchen.*)

MRS. GIBBS. Well, we had a real good time.

DR. GIBBS. You're late enough.

MRS. GIBBS. Why, Frank, it ain't any later 'n usual.

DR. GIBBS. And you stopping at the corner to gossip with a lot of hens.

MRS. GIBBS. Now, Frank, don't be grouchy. Come out and smell the heliotrope in the moonlight. (*They stroll out arm in arm along the footlights.*) Isn't that wonderful? What did you do all the time I was away?

DR. GIBBS. Oh, I read—as usual. What were the girls gossiping about tonight?

MRS. GIBBS. Well, believe me, Frank—there is something to gossip about.

DR. GIBBS. Hmm! Simon Stimson far gone, was he?

MRS. GIBBS. Worst I've ever seen him. How'll that end, Frank? Dr. Ferguson can't forgive him forever.

DR. GIBBS. I guess I know more about Simon Stimson's affairs than anybody in this town. Some people ain't made for small-town life. I don't know how that'll end; but there's nothing we can do but just leave it alone. Come, get in.

MRS. GIBBS. No, not yet . . . Frank, I'm worried about you.

DR. GIBBS. What are you worried about?

MRS. GIBBS. I think it's my duty to make plans for you to get a real rest and change. And if I get that legacy, well, I'm going to insist on it.

DR. GIBBS. Now, Julia, there's no sense in going over that again.

MRS. GIBBS. Frank, you're just *unreasonable!*

DR. GIBBS (*starting into the house*). Come on, Julia, it's getting late. First thing you know you'll catch cold. I gave George a piece of my mind tonight. I reckon you'll have your wood chopped for a while anyway. No, no, start getting upstairs.

MRS. GIBBS. Oh, dear. There's always so many things to pick up, seems like. You know, Frank, Mrs. Fairchild always locks her front door every night. All those people up that part of town do.

DR. GIBBS (*blowing out the lamp*). They're all getting citified, that's the trouble with them. They haven't got nothing fit to burgle and everybody knows it. (*They disappear.* REBECCA *climbs up the ladder beside* GEORGE.)

GEORGE. Get out, Rebecca. There's only room for one at this window. You're always spoiling everything.

REBECCA. Well, let me look just a minute.

GEORGE. Use your own window.

REBECCA. I did, but there's no moon there. . . . George, do you know what I think, do you? I think maybe the moon's getting nearer and nearer and there'll be a big 'splosion.

GEORGE. Rebecca, you don't know anything. If the moon were getting nearer, the guys that sit up all night with telescopes would see it first and they'd tell about it, and it'd be in all the newspapers.

REBECCA. George, is the moon shining on South America, Canada and half the whole world?

GEORGE. Well—prob'ly is. (*The* STAGE MANAGER *strolls on. Pause. The sound of crickets is heard.*)

STAGE MANAGER. Nine thirty. Most of the lights are out. No, there's Constable Warren trying a few doors on Main Street. And here comes Editor Webb, after putting his newspaper to bed. (MR. WARREN, *an elderly policeman, comes along Main Street from the right,* MR. WEBB *from the left.*)

MR. WEBB. Good evening, Bill.

CONSTABLE WARREN. Evenin', Mr. Webb.

MR. WEBB. Quite a moon!

CONSTABLE WARREN. Yepp.

MR. WEBB. All quiet tonight?

CONSTABLE WARREN. Simon Stimson is rollin' around a little. Just saw his wife movin' out to hunt for him so I looked the other way—there he is now. (SIMON STIMSON *comes down Main Street from the left, only a trace of unsteadiness in his walk.*)

MR. WEBB. Good evening, Simon . . . Town seems to have settled down for the night pretty well. . . . (SIMON STIMSON *comes up to him and pauses a moment and stares at him, swaying slightly.*) Good evening . . . Yes, most of the town's settled down for the night, Simon. . . . I guess we better do the same. Can I walk along a ways with you? (SIMON STIMSON *continues on his way without a word and disappears at the right.*) Good night.

CONSTABLE WARREN. I don't know how that's goin' to end, Mr. Webb.

MR. WEBB. Well, he's seen a peck of trouble, one thing after another. . . . Oh, Bill . . . if you see my boy smoking cigarettes, just give him a word, will you? He thinks a lot of you, Bill.

CONSTABLE WARREN. I don't think he smokes no cigarettes, Mr. Webb. Leastways, not more'n two or three a year.

MR. WEBB. Hm . . . I hope not.—Well, good night, Bill.

CONSTABLE WARREN. Good night, Mr. Webb. (*Exit.*)

MR. WEBB. Who's that up there? Is that you, Myrtle?

EMILY. No, it's me, Papa.

MR. WEBB. Why aren't you in bed?

EMILY. I don't know. I just can't sleep yet, Papa. The moonlight's so *won*-derful. And the smell of Mrs. Gibbs' heliotrope. Can you smell it?

MR. WEBB. Hm . . . Yes. Haven't any troubles on your mind, have you, Emily?

EMILY. *Troubles,* Papa? *No.*

MR. WEBB. Well, enjoy yourself, but don't let your mother catch you. Good night, Emily.

EMILY. Good night, Papa. (MR. WEBB *crosses into the house, whistling "Blessed Be the Tie That Binds" and disappears.*)

REBECCA. I never told you about that letter Jane Crofut got from her minister when she was sick. He wrote Jane a letter and on the envelope the address was like this: It said: Jane Crofut; The Crofut Farm; Grover's Corners; Sutton County; New Hampshire; United States of America.

GEORGE. What's funny about that?

REBECCA. But listen, it's not finished: the United States of America; Continent of North America; Western Hemisphere; the Earth; the Solar System; the Universe; the Mind of God—that's what it said on the envelope.

GEORGE. What do you know!

REBECCA. And the postman brought it just the same.

GEORGE. What do you know!

STAGE MANAGER. That's the end of the First Act, friends. You can go and smoke now, those that smoke.

I

DAILY LIFE IN "OUR TOWN"

The announced purpose of the first act is to give a picture of a day in "our town." Most of the details contribute to that picture, but there are others which may function to suggest the brevity and insignificance of human life. Professor Willard's speech, for example, serves that purpose, as does the long speech of the Stage Manager, the one in which he tells us how all Joe Crowell, Jr.'s, education went for nothing. Finally, Jane Crofut's letter shows human life to be the smallest element in a widening arena that ends in the mind of God. Ironically, however, that same life is given dignity and importance precisely because it lies at the center of God's mind.

And what can be said about the daily life itself and the people who live it? Are they cheerful and warm-hearted, good illustrations of the joys of simple living? Or are they dull and ordinary, good illustrations of the tragedies brought on by conformity? Is "the tie that binds" really "blessed," or does it make people "weary" and "languid"?

II
IMPLICATIONS

Discuss your own attitudes toward the following *pairs* of facts regarding Grover's Corners and its people.

1a. There is little culture or "love of beauty" in Grover's Corners.

b. The people in Grover's Corners appreciate sunrise and moonlight and the odor of flowers.

2a. Mrs. Gibbs' strong desire to visit Paris before she dies.

b. Dr. Gibbs' lack of interest in travel for fear that it might make him discontent with Grover's Corners.

3a. The unthinking acceptance of the ordinary, dull, and routine of life in Grover's Corners.

b. Editor Webb's straightforward admission that life in Grover's Corners *is* dull and ordinary.

4a. Mrs. Soames' gossip about Simon Stimson.

b. Dr. Gibbs' statement (near the end of the act) about Simon Stimson.

III
TECHNIQUES

Structure: Tension-Raising

A play is generally designed in such a manner that all of the major characters and all the major tensions (or conflicts) are introduced by the end of the first act. It is, therefore, a good practice to pause at the end of that act and ask yourself what the major tensions of the drama are. If you can identify them, you will be in a good position to follow the action in the ensuing acts more effectively.

We have already noted one of the chief tensions above (Section I); another important tension centers upon Emily. When we last see her, she is staring at the moonlight and her father asks her if she has any troubles on her mind. She answers, *"Troubles,* Papa. *No."* Her emphatic tone (conveyed in print by italics) suggests that it would be virtually impossible for her to have any serious troubles. Although we may take her at her word, we also know from our own experience that people's lives do not run as smoothly as Emily's for very long. Thus, ironically, the very fact that she is so emphatically untroubled creates a tension for the reader and suggests that we may find a change in her life in the near future.

Act II

The tables and chairs of the two kitchens are still on the stage.

The ladders and the small bench have been withdrawn.

The STAGE MANAGER *has been at his accustomed place watching the audience return to its seats.*

STAGE MANAGER. Three years have gone by.

Yes, the sun's come up over a thousand times.

Summers and winters have cracked the mountains a little bit more and the rains have brought down some of the dirt.

Some babies that weren't even born before have begun talking regular sentences already; and a number of people who thought they were right young and spry have noticed that they can't bound up a flight of stairs like they used to, without their heart fluttering a little.

All that can happen in a thousand days.

Nature's been pushing and contriving in other ways, too; a number of young people fell in love and got married.

Yes, the mountain got bit away a few fractions of an inch; millions of gallons of water went by the mill; and here and there a new home was set up under a roof.

Almost everybody in the world gets married, —you know what I mean? In our town there aren't hardly any exceptions. Most everybody in the world climbs into their graves married.

The First Act was called the Daily Life. This act is called Love and Marriage. There's another act coming after this: I reckon you can guess what that's about.

So:

It's three years later. It's 1904.

It's July 7th, just after High School Commencement.

That's the time most of our young people jump up and get married.

Soon as they've passed their last examinations in solid geometry and Cicero's Orations, looks like they suddenly feel themselves fit to be married.

It's early morning. Only this time it's been raining. It's been pouring and thundering.

Mrs. Gibbs' garden, and Mrs. Webb's here: drenched.

All those bean poles and pea vines: drenched.

All yesterday over there on Main Street, the rain looked like curtains being blown along.

Hm . . . it may begin again any minute.

There! You can hear the 5:45 for Boston. (MRS. GIBBS *and* MRS. WEBB *enter their kitchen and start the day as in the First Act.*)

And there's Mrs. Gibbs and Mrs. Webb come down to make breakfast, just as though it were an ordinary day. I don't have to point out to the women in my audience that those ladies they see before them, both of those ladies cooked three meals a day—one of 'em for twenty years, the other for forty—and no summer vacation. They brought up two children apiece, washed, cleaned the house,—and *never a nervous breakdown.*

It's like what one of those Middle West poets said: You've got to love life to have life, and you've got to have life to love life. . . .

It's what they call a vicious circle.

HOWIE NEWSOME (*off stage left*). Giddap, Bessie!

STAGE MANAGER. Here comes Howie Newsome delivering the milk. And there's Si Crowell delivering the papers like his brother before him. (SI CROWELL *has entered hurling imaginary newspapers into doorways;* HOWIE NEWSOME *has come along Main Street with Bessie.*)

SI CROWELL. Morning, Howie.

HOWIE NEWSOME. Morning, Si.—Anything in the papers I ought to know?

SI CROWELL. Nothing much, except we're losing about the best baseball pitcher Grover's Corners ever had—George Gibbs.

HOWIE NEWSOME. Reckon he is.

SI CROWELL. He could hit and run bases, too.

HOWIE NEWSOME. Yep. Mighty fine ball player. —Whoa! Bessie! I guess I can stop and talk if I've a mind to!

SI CROWELL. I don't see how he could give up a thing like that just to get married. Would you, Howie?

HOWIE NEWSOME. Can't tell, Si. Never had no talent that way. (CONSTABLE WARREN *enters. They exchange good mornings.*) You're up early, Bill.

CONSTABLE WARREN. Seein' if there's anything I can do to prevent a flood. River's been risin' all night.

HOWIE NEWSOME. Si Crowell's all worked up here about George Gibbs' retiring from baseball.

CONSTABLE WARREN. Yes, sir; that's the way it goes. Back in '84 we had a player, Si—even George Gibbs couldn't touch him. Name of Hank Todd. Went down to Maine and became a parson. Wonderful ball player.— Howie, how does the weather look to you?

HOWIE NEWSOME. Oh, 'tain't bad. Think maybe it'll clear up for good. (CONSTABLE WARREN *and* SI CROWELL *continue on their way.* HOWIE NEWSOME *brings the milk first to* MRS. GIBBS' *house. She meets him by the trellis.*)

MRS. GIBBS. Good morning, Howie. Do you think it's going to rain again?

HOWIE NEWSOME. Morning, Mrs. Gibbs. It rained so heavy, I think maybe it'll clear up.

MRS. GIBBS. Certainly hope it will.

HOWIE NEWSOME. How much did you want today?

MRS. GIBBS. I'm going to have a houseful of relations, Howie. Looks to me like I'll need three-a-milk and two-a-cream.

HOWIE NEWSOME. My wife says to tell you we both hope they'll be very happy, Mrs. Gibbs. Know they *will.*

MRS. GIBBS. Thanks a lot, Howie. Tell your wife I hope she gits there to the wedding.

HOWIE NEWSOME. Yes, she'll be there; she'll be

there if she kin. (HOWIE NEWSOME *crosses to* MRS. WEBB's *house.*) Morning, Mrs. Webb.

MRS. WEBB. Oh, good morning, Mr. Newsome. I told you four quarts of milk, but I hope you can spare me another.

HOWIE NEWSOME. Yes'm . . . and the two of cream.

MRS. WEBB. Will it start raining again, Mr. Newsome?

HOWIE NEWSOME. Well. Just sayin' to Mrs. Gibbs as how it may lighten up. Mrs. Newsome told me to tell you as how we hope they'll both be very happy, Mrs. Webb. Know they *will*.

MRS. WEBB. Thank you, and thank Mrs. Newsome and we're counting on seeing you at the wedding.

HOWIE NEWSOME. Yes, Mrs. Webb. We hope to git there. Couldn't miss that. Come on, Bessie. (*Exit* HOWIE NEWSOME. DR. GIBBS *descends in shirt sleeves, and sits down at his breakfast table.*)

DR. GIBBS. Well, Ma, the day has come. You're losin' one of your chicks.

MRS. GIBBS. Frank Gibbs, don't you say another word. I feel like crying every minute. Sit down and drink your coffee.

DR. GIBBS. The groom's up shaving himself— only there ain't an awful lot to shave. Whistling and singing, like he's glad to leave us.— Every now and then he says "I do" to the mirror, but it don't sound convincing to me.

MRS. GIBBS. I declare, Frank, I don't know how he'll get along. I've arranged his clothes and seen to it he's put warm things on,—Frank! they're too *young*. Emily won't think of such things. He'll catch his death of cold within a week.

DR. GIBBS. I was remembering my wedding morning, Julia.

MRS. GIBBS. Now don't start that, Frank Gibbs.

DR. GIBBS. I was the scaredest young fella in the State of New Hampshire. I thought I'd make a mistake for sure. And when I saw you comin' down that aisle I thought you were the prettiest girl I'd ever seen, but the only trouble was that I'd never seen you before.

There I was in the Congregational Church marryin' a total stranger.

MRS. GIBBS. And how do you think I felt!— Frank, weddings are perfectly awful things. Farces,—that's what they are! (*She puts a plate before him.*) Here, I've made something for you.

DR. GIBBS. Why, Julia Hersey—French toast!

MRS. GIBBS. 'Tain't hard to make and I had to do something. (*Pause.* DR. GIBBS *pours on the syrup.*)

DR. GIBBS. How'd you sleep last night, Julia?

MRS. GIBBS. Well, I heard a lot of the hours struck off.

DR. GIBBS. Ye-e-s! I get a shock every time I think of George setting out to be a family man— that great gangling thing!—I tell you, Julia, there's nothing so terrifying in the world as a *son*. The relation of father and son is the darndest, awkwardest—

MRS. GIBBS. Well, mother and daughter's no picnic, let me tell you.

DR. GIBBS. They'll have a lot of troubles, I suppose, but that's none of our business. Everybody has a right to their own troubles.

MRS. GIBBS. (*at the table, drinking her coffee, meditatively*). Yes . . . people are meant to go through life two by two. 'Tain't natural to be lonesome. (*Pause.* DR. GIBBS *starts laughing.*)

DR. GIBBS. Julia, do you know one of the things I was scared of when I married you?

MRS. GIBBS. Oh, go along with you!

DR. GIBBS. I was afraid we wouldn't have material for conversation more'n'd last us a few weeks. (*Both laugh.*) I was afraid we'd run out and eat our meals in silence, that's a fact.—Well, you and I been conversing for twenty years now without any noticeable barren spells.

MRS. GIBBS. Well,—good weather, bad weather —'tain't very choice, but I always find something to say. (*She goes to the foot of the stairs.*) Did you hear Rebecca stirring around upstairs?

DR. GIBBS. No. Only day of the year Rebecca hasn't been managing everybody's business up there. She's hiding in her room.—I got the impression she's crying.

MRS. GIBBS. Lord's sakes!—This has got to stop.—Rebecca! Rebecca! Come and get your breakfast. (GEORGE *comes rattling down the stairs, very brisk.*)

GEORGE. Good morning, everybody. Only five more hours to live. (*Makes the gesture of cutting his throat, and a loud "k-k-k," and starts through the trellis.*)

MRS. GIBBS. George Gibbs, where are you going?

GEORGE. Just stepping across the grass to see my girl.

MRS. GIBBS. Now, George! You put on your overshoes. It's raining torrents. You don't go out of this house without you're prepared for it.

GEORGE. Aw, Ma. It's just a *step!*

MRS. GIBBS. George! You'll catch your death of cold and cough all through the service.

DR. GIBBS. George, do as your mother tells you!

(DR. GIBBS *goes upstairs.* GEORGE *returns reluctantly to the kitchen and pantomimes putting on overshoes.*)

MRS. GIBBS. From tomorrow on you can kill yourself in all weathers, but while you're in my house you'll live wisely, thank you.—Maybe Mrs. Webb isn't used to callers at seven in the morning.—Here, take a cup of coffee first.

GEORGE. Be back in a minute. (*He crosses the stage, leaping over the puddles.*) Good morning, Mother Webb.

MRS. WEBB. Goodness! You frightened me!—Now, George, you can come in a minute out of the wet, but you know I can't ask you in.

GEORGE. Why not—?

MRS. WEBB. George, you know's well as I do: the groom can't see his bride on his wedding day, not until he sees her in church.

GEORGE. Aw!—that's just a superstition.—Good morning, Mr. Webb. (*Enter* MR. WEBB.)

MR. WEBB. Good morning, George.

GEORGE. Mr. Webb, you don't believe in that superstition, do you?

MR. WEBB. There's a lot of common sense in some superstitions, George. (*He sits at the table, facing right.*)

MRS. WEBB. Millions have folla'd it, George, and you don't want to be the first to fly in the face of custom.

GEORGE. How is Emily?

MRS. WEBB. She hasn't waked up yet. I haven't heard a sound out of her.

GEORGE. Emily's *asleep! ! !*

MRS. WEBB. No wonder! We were up 'til all hours, sewing and packing. Now I'll tell you what I'll do; you set down here a minute with Mr. Webb and drink this cup of coffee; and I'll go upstairs and see she doesn't come down and surprise you. There's some bacon, too; but don't be long about it. (*Exit* MRS. WEBB. *Embarrassed silence.* MR. WEBB *dunks doughnuts in his coffee. More silence.*)

MR. WEBB (*suddenly and loudly*). Well, George, how are you?

GEORGE (*startled, choking over his coffee*). Oh, fine, I'm fine. (*Pause.*) Mr. Webb, what sense could there be in a superstition like that?

MR. WEBB. Well, you see,—on her wedding morning a girl's head's apt to be full of . . . clothes and one thing and another. Don't you think that's probably it?

GEORGE. Ye-e-s. I never thought of that.

MR. WEBB. A girl's apt to be a mite nervous on her wedding day. (*Pause.*)

GEORGE. I wish a fellow could get married without all that marching up and down.

MR. WEBB. Every man that's ever lived has felt that way about it, George; but it hasn't been any use. It's the womenfolk who've built up weddings, my boy. For a while now the women have it all their own. A man looks pretty small at a wedding, George. All those good women standing shoulder to shoulder making sure that the knot's tied in a mighty public way.

GEORGE. But . . . you *believe* in it, don't you, Mr. Webb?

MR. WEBB (*with alacrity*). Oh, yes; *oh, yes.* Don't you misunderstand me, my boy. Marriage is a wonderful thing,—wonderful thing. And don't you forget that, George.

GEORGE. No, sir.—Mr. Webb, how old were you when you got married?

MR. WEBB. Well, you see: I'd been to college and I'd taken a little time to get settled. But Mrs. Webb—she wasn't much older than what Emily is. Oh, age hasn't much to do with it, George,—not compared with . . . uh . . . other things.

GEORGE. What were you going to say, Mr. Webb?

MR. WEBB. Oh, I don't know.—Was I going to say something? (*Pause.*) George, I was thinking the other night of some advice my father gave me when I got married. Charles, he said, Charles, start out early showing who's boss, he said. Best thing to do is to give an order, even if it don't make sense; just so she'll learn to obey. And he said: if anything about your wife irritates you—her conversation, or anything—just get up and leave the house. That'll make it clear to her, he said. And, oh, yes! he said never, *never* let your wife know how much money you have, never.

GEORGE. Well, Mr. Webb . . . I don't think I could . . .

MR. WEBB. So I took the opposite of my father's advice and I've been happy ever since. And let that be a lesson to you, George, never to ask advice on personal matters.—George, are you going to raise chickens on your farm?

GEORGE. What?

MR. WEBB. Are you going to raise chickens on your farm?

GEORGE. Uncle Luke's never been much interested, but I thought—

MR. WEBB. A book came into my office the other day, George, on the Philo System of raising chickens. I want you to read it. I'm thinking of beginning in a small way in the back yard, and I'm going to put an incubator in the cellar—(*Enter* MRS. WEBB.)

MRS. WEBB. Charles, are you talking about that old incubator again? I thought you two'd be talking about things worth while.

MR. WEBB (*bitingly*). Well, Myrtle, if you want to give the boy some good advice, I'll go upstairs and leave you alone with him.

MRS. WEBB (*pulling* GEORGE *up*). George, Emily's got to come downstairs and eat her breakfast. She sends you her love but she doesn't want to lay eyes on you. Good-by.

GEORGE. Good-by. (GEORGE *cross the stage to his own home, bewildered and crestfallen. He slowly dodges a puddle and disappears into his house.*)

MR. WEBB. Myrtle, I guess you don't know about that older superstition.

MRS. WEBB. What do you mean, Charles?

MR. WEBB. Since the cave men: no bridegroom should see his father-in-law on the day of the wedding, or near it. Now remember that. (*Both leave the stage.*)

STAGE MANAGER. Thank you very much, Mr. and Mrs. Webb.—Now I have to interrupt again here. You see, we want to know how all this began—this wedding, this plan to spend a lifetime together. I'm awfully interested in how big things like that begin.

You know how it is: you're twenty-one or twenty-two and you make some decisions; then whisssh! you're seventy: you've been a lawyer for fifty years, and that white-haired lady at your side has eaten over fifty thousand meals with you.

How do such things begin?

George and Emily are going to show you now the conversation they had when they first knew that . . . that . . . as the saying goes . . . they were meant for one another.

But before they do it I want you to try and remember what it was like to have been very young.

And particularly the days when you were first in love; when you were like a person sleep-walking, and you didn't quite see the street you were in, and didn't quite hear everything that was said to you.

You're just a little bit crazy. Will you remember that, please?

Now they'll be coming out of high school at

three o'clock. George has just been elected President of the Junior Class, and as it's June, that means he'll be President of the Senior Class all next year. And Emily's just been elected Secretary and Treasurer. I don't have to tell you how important that is. (*He places a board across the backs of two chairs, which he takes from those at the Gibbs family's table. He brings two high stools from the wings and places them behind the board. Persons sitting on the stools will be facing the audience. This is the counter of Mr. Morgan's drugstore. The sounds of young people's voices are heard off left.*) Yepp,—there they are coming down Main Street now. (EMILY, *carrying an armful of—imaginary—schoolbooks, comes along Main Street from the left.*)

EMILY. I can't, Louise. I've got to go home. Good-by. Oh, Ernestine! Ernestine! Can you come over tonight and do Latin? Isn't that Cicero the worst thing—! Tell your mother you *have* to. G'by. G'by, Helen. G'by, Fred. (GEORGE, *also carrying books, catches up with her.*)

GEORGE. Can I carry your books home for you, Emily?

EMILY (*coolly*). Why . . . uh . . . Thank you. It isn't far. (*She gives them to him.*)

GEORGE. Excuse me a minute, Emily.—Say, Bob, if I'm a little late, start practice anyway. And give Herb some long high ones.

EMILY. Good-by, Lizzy.

GEORGE. Good-by, Lizzy.—I'm awfully glad you were elected, too, Emily.

EMILY. Thank you. (*They have been standing on Main Street, almost against the back wall. They take the first steps toward the audience when* GEORGE *stops and says:*)

GEORGE. Emily, why are you mad at me?

EMILY. I'm not mad at you.

GEORGE. You've been treating me so funny lately.

EMILY. Well, since you ask me, I might as well say it right out, George—(*She catches sight of a teacher passing.*) Good-by, Miss Corcoran.

GEORGE. Good-by, Miss Corcoran.—Wha—What is it?

EMILY (*not scoldingly; finding it difficult to say*). I don't like the whole change that's come over you in the last year. I'm sorry if that hurts your feelings, but I've got to—tell the truth and shame the devil.

GEORGE. A *change?*—Wha—what do you mean?

EMILY. Well, up to a year ago I used to like you a lot. And I used to watch you as you did everything . . . because we'd been friends so long . . . and then you began spending all your time at baseball . . . and you never stopped to speak to anybody any more. Not even to your own family you didn't . . . and, George, it's a fact, you've got awful conceited and stuck-up, and all the girls say so. They may not say so to your face, but that's what they say about you behind your back, and it hurts me to hear them say it, but I've got to agree with them a little. I'm sorry if it hurts your feelings . . . but I can't be sorry I said it.

GEORGE. I . . . I'm glad you said it, Emily. I never thought that such a thing was happening to me. I guess it's hard for a fella not to have faults creep into his character. (*They take a step or two in silence, then stand still in misery.*)

EMILY. I always expect a man to be perfect and I think he should be.

GEORGE. Oh . . . I don't think it's possible to be perfect, Emily.

EMILY. Well, my *father* is, and as far as I can see *your* father is. There's no reason on earth why you shouldn't be, too.

GEORGE. Well, I feel it's the other way round. That men aren't naturally good; but girls are.

EMILY. Well, you might as well know right now that I'm not perfect. It's not as easy for a girl to be perfect as a man, because we girls are more—more—nervous.—Now I'm sorry I said all that about you. I don't know what made me say it.

GEORGE. Emily,—

EMILY. Now I can see it's not the truth at all. And suddenly I feel that it isn't important, anyway.

GEORGE. Emily . . . would you like an ice-cream soda, or something, before you go home?

EMILY. Well, thank you. . . . I would. (*They advance toward the audience and make an abrupt right turn, opening the door of Morgan's drugstore. Under strong emotion, EMILY keeps her face down. GEORGE speaks to some passers-by.*)

GEORGE. Hello, Stew,—how are you?—Good afternoon, Mrs. Slocum. (*The STAGE MANAGER, wearing spectacles and assuming the role of Mr. Morgan, enters abruptly from the right and stands between the audience and the counter of his soda fountain.*)

STAGE MANAGER. Hello, George. Hello, Emily. What'll you have?—Why, Emily Webb, what have you been crying about?

GEORGE (*he gropes for an explanation*). She . . . she just got an awful scare, Mr. Morgan. She almost got run over by that hardware-store wagon. Everybody says that Tom Huckins drives like a crazy man.

STAGE MANAGER (*drawing a drink of water*). Well, now! You take a drink of water, Emily. You look all shook up. I tell you, you've got to look both ways before you cross Main Street these days. Gets worse every year.—What'll you have?

EMILY. I'll have a strawberry phosphate, thank you, Mr. Morgan.

GEORGE. No, no, Emily. Have an ice-cream soda with me. Two strawberry ice-cream sodas, Mr. Morgan.

STAGE MANAGER (*working the faucets*). Two strawberry ice-cream sodas, yes sir. Yes, sir. There are a hundred and twenty-five horses in Grover's Corners this minute I'm talking to you. State Inspector was in here yesterday. And now they're bringing in these auto-mobiles, the best thing to do is to just stay home. Why, I can remember when a dog could go to sleep all day in the middle of Main Street and nothing come along to disturb him. (*He sets the imaginary glasses before them.*) There they are. Enjoy 'em. (*He sees a customer, right.*) Yes, Mrs. Ellis. What can I do for you? (*He goes out right.*)

EMILY. They're so expensive.

GEORGE. No, no,—don't you think of that. We're celebrating our election. And then do you know what else I'm celebrating?

EMILY. N-no.

GEORGE. I'm celebrating because I've got a friend who tells me all the things that ought to be told me.

EMILY. George, *please* don't think of that. I don't know why I said it. It's not true. You're—

GEORGE. No, Emily, you stick to it. I'm glad you spoke to me like you did. But you'll *see:* I'm going to change so quick—you bet I'm going to change. And, Emily, I want to ask you a favor.

EMILY. What?

GEORGE. Emily, if I go away to State Agriculture College next year, will you write me a letter once in a while?

EMILY. I certainly will. I certainly will, George . . . (*Pause. They start sipping the sodas through the straws.*) It certainly seems like being away three years you'd get out of touch with things. Maybe letters from Grover's Corners wouldn't be so interesting after a while. Grover's Corners isn't a very important place when you think of all—New Hampshire; but I think it's a very nice town.

GEORGE. The day wouldn't come when I wouldn't want to know everything that's happening here. I know *that's* true, Emily.

EMILY. Well, I'll try to make my letters interesting. (*Pause.*)

GEORGE. Y'know. Emily, whenever I meet a farmer I ask him if he thinks it's important to go to Agriculture School to be a good farmer.

EMILY. Why, George—

GEORGE. Yeah, and some of them say that it's even a waste of time. You can get all those things, anyway, out of the pamphlets the government sends out. And Uncle Luke's getting old,—he's about ready for me to start taking over his farm tomorrow, if I could.

EMILY. My!

GEORGE. And, like you say, being gone all that time . . . in other places and meeting other people . . . Gosh, if anything like that can happen I don't want to go away. I guess new people aren't any better than old ones. I'll bet they almost never are. Emily . . . I feel that you're as good a friend as I've got. I don't need to go and meet the people in other towns.

EMILY. But, George, maybe it's very important for you to go and learn all that about—cattle judging and soils and those things. . . . Of course, I don't know.

GEORGE (*after a pause, very seriously*). Emily, I'm going to make up my mind right now. I won't go. I'll tell Pa about it tonight.

EMILY. Why, George, I don't see why you have to decide right now. It's a whole year away.

GEORGE. Emily, I'm glad you spoke to me about that . . . that fault in my character. What you said was right; but there was *one* thing wrong in it, and that was when you said that for a year I wasn't noticing people, and . . . you, for instance. Why, you say you were watching me when I did everything . . . I was doing the same about you all the time. Why, sure, —I always thought about you as one of the chief people I thought about. I always made

sure where you were sitting on the bleachers, and who you were with, and for three days now I've been trying to walk home with you; but something's always got in the way. Yesterday I was standing over against the wall waiting for you, and you walked home with *Miss Corcoran.*

EMILY. George! . . . Life's awful funny! How could I have known that? Why, I thought—

GEORGE. Listen, Emily, I'm going to tell you why I'm not going to Agriculture School. I think that once you've found a person that you're very fond of . . . I mean a person who's fond of you, too, and likes you enough to be interested in your character . . . Well, I think that's just as important as college is, and even more so. That's what I think.

EMILY. I think it's awfully important, too.

GEORGE. Emily.

EMILY. Y-yes, George.

GEORGE. Emily, if I do improve and make a big change . . . would you be . . . I mean: *could* you be . . .

EMILY. I . . . I am now; I always have been.

GEORGE (*pause*). So I guess this is an important talk we've been having.

EMILY. Yes . . . yes.

GEORGE (*takes a deep breath and straightens his back*). Wait just a minute and I'll walk you home. (*With mounting alarm he digs into his pockets for the money. The* STAGE MANAGER *enters, right.* GEORGE, *deeply embarrassed, but direct, says to him:*) Mr. Morgan, I'll have to go home and get the money to pay you for this. It'll only take me a minute.

STAGE MANAGER (*pretending to be affronted*). What's that? George Gibbs, do you mean to tell me—!

GEORGE. Yes, but I had reasons, Mr. Morgan.— Look, here's my gold watch to keep until I come back with the money.

STAGE MANAGER. That's all right. Keep your watch. I'll trust you.

GEORGE. I'll be back in five minutes.

STAGE MANAGER. I'll trust you ten years, George,

—not a day over.—Got all over your shock, Emily?

EMILY. Yes, thank you, Mr. Morgan. It was nothing.

GEORGE (*taking up the books from the counter*). I'm ready. (*They walk in grave silence across the stage and pass through the trellis at the Webbs' back door and disappear. The* STAGE MANAGER *watches them go out, then turns to the audience, removing his spectacles.*)

STAGE MANAGER. Well,—(*He claps his hand as a signal.*) Now we're ready to go on with the wedding. (*He stands waiting while the set is prepared for the next scene. Stagehands remove the chairs, tables and trellises from the Gibbs and Webb houses. They arrange the pews for the church in the center of the stage. The congregation will sit facing the back wall. The aisle of the church starts at the center of the back wall and comes toward the audience. A small platform is placed against the back wall on which the* STAGE MANAGER *will stand later, playing the minister. The image of a stained-glass window is cast from a lantern slide upon the back wall. When all is ready the* STAGE MANAGER *strolls to the center of the stage, down front, and, musingly, addresses the audience.*) There are a lot of things to be said about a wedding; there are a lot of thoughts that go on during a wedding.

We can't get them all into one wedding, naturally, and especially not into a wedding at Grover's Corners, where they're awfully plain and short.

In this wedding I play the minister. That gives me the right to say a few things more about it.

For a while now, the play gets pretty serious. Y'see, some churches say that marriage is a sacrament. I don't quite know what that means, but I can guess. Like Mrs. Gibbs said a few minutes ago: People were made to live two-by-two.

This is a good wedding, but people are so put together that even at a good wedding there's a lot of confusion way down deep in people's minds and we thought that that ought to be in our play, too.

The real hero of this scene isn't on the stage at all, and you know who that is. It's like what one of those European fellas said: every child born into the world is nature's attempt to make a perfect human being. Well, we've seen nature pushing and contriving for some time now. We all know that nature's interested in quantity; but I think she's interested in quality, too—that's why I'm in the ministry.

And don't forget all the other witnesses at this wedding,—the ancestors. Millions of them. Most of them set out to live two-by-two, also. Millions of them.

Well, that's all my sermon. 'Twan't very long, anyway. (*The organ starts playing Handel's "Largo." The congregation streams into the church and sits in silence. Church bells are heard.* MRS. GIBBS *sits in the front row, the first seat on the aisle, the right section; next to her are* REBECCA *and* DR. GIBBS. *Across the aisle are* MRS. WEBB, WALLY *and* MR. WEBB. *A small choir takes its place, facing the audience under the stained-glass window.* MRS. WEBB, *on the way to her place, turns back and speaks to the audience.*)

MRS. WEBB. I don't know why on earth I should be crying. I suppose there's nothing to cry about. It came over me at breakfast this morning; there was Emily eating her breakfast as she's done for seventeen years and now she's going off to eat it in someone else's house, I suppose that's it.

And Emily! She suddenly said: I can't eat another mouthful, and she put her head down on the table and *she* cried. (*She starts toward her seat in the church, but turns back and adds:*) Oh, I've got to say it: you know, there's something downright cruel about sending our girls out into marriage this way.

I hope some of her girl friends have told her a thing or two. It's cruel, I know, but I couldn't bring myself to say anything. I went into it blind as a bat myself. (*In half-amused exasperation.*) The whole world's wrong, that's what's the matter.

There they come. (*She hurries to her place in the pew.* GEORGE *starts to come down the right aisle of the theatre, through the audience. Suddenly three members of his baseball team appear by the right proscenium pillar and start whistling and catcalling to him. They are dressed for the ball field.*)

THE BASEBALL PLAYERS. Eh, George, George! Hast—yaow! Look at him, fellas—he looks scared to death. Yaow! George, don't look so innocent, you old geezer. We know what you're thinking. Don't disgrace the team, big boy. Whoo-oo-oo.

STAGE MANAGER. All right! All right! That'll do. That's enough of that. (*Smiling, he pushes them off the stage. They lean back to shout a few more catcalls.*) There used to be an awful lot of that kind of thing at weddings in the old days,—Rome, and later. We're more civilized now,—so they say. (*The choir starts singing "Love Divine, All Love Excelling—."* GEORGE *has reached the stage. He stares at the congregation a moment, then takes a few steps of withdrawal, toward the right proscenium pillar. His mother, from the front row, seems to have felt his confusion. She leaves her seat and comes down the aisle quickly to him.*)

MRS. GIBBS. George! George! What's the matter?

GEORGE. Ma, I don't want to grow old. Why's everybody pushing me so?

MRS. GIBBS. Why, George . . . you wanted it.

GEORGE. No, Ma, listen to me—

MRS. GIBBS. No, no, George,—you're a man now.

GEORGE. Listen, Ma,—for the last time I ask you . . . All I want to do is to be a fella—

MRS. GIBBS. George! If anyone should hear you! Now stop. Why, I'm ashamed of you!

GEORGE (*he comes to himself and looks over the scene*). What's the matter? I've been dreaming. Where's Emily?

MRS. GIBBS (*relieved*). George! You gave me such a turn.

GEORGE. Cheer up, Ma. I'm getting married.

MRS. GIBBS. Let me catch my breath a minute.

GEORGE (*comforting her*). Now, Ma, you save Thursday nights. Emily and I are coming over to dinner every Thursday night . . . you'll see. Ma, what are you crying for? Come on; we've got to get ready for this. (MRS. GIBBS, *mastering her emotion, fixes his tie and whispers to him. In the meantime,* EMILY, *in white and wearing her wedding veil, has come through the audience and mounted onto the stage. She too draws back, frightened, when she sees the congregation in the church. The choir begins: "Blessed Be the Tie That Binds."*)

EMILY. I never felt so alone in my whole life. And George over there, looking so . . .! I hate him. I wish I were dead. Papa! Papa!

MR. WEBB (*leaves his seat in the pews and comes toward her anxiously*). Emily! Emily! Now don't get upset. . . .

EMILY. But, Papa,—I don't want to get married . . .

MR. WEBB. Sh—sh—Emily. Everything's all right.

EMILY. Why can't I stay for a while just as I am? Let's go away,—

MR. WEBB. No, no, Emily. Now stop and think a minute.

EMILY. Don't you remember that you used to say,—all the time you used to say—all the time: that I was *your* girl! There must be lots of places we can go to. I'll work for you. I could keep house."

MR. WEBB. Sh . . . you mustn't think of such things. You're just nervous, Emily. (*He turns and calls:*) George! George! Will you come here a minute? (*He leads her toward* GEORGE.) Why you're marrying the best young fellow in the world. George is a fine fellow.

EMILY. But Papa,—(MRS. GIBBS *returns unobtrusively to her seat.* MR. WEBB *has one arm around his daughter. He places his hand on* GEORGE's *shoulder.*)

MR. WEBB. I'm giving away my daughter, George. Do you think you can take care of her?

GEORGE. Mr. Webb, I want to . . . I want to try. Emily, I'm going to do my best. I love you, Emily. I need you.

EMILY. Well, if you love me, help me. All I want is someone to love me.

GEORGE. I will, Emily. Emily, I'll try.

EMILY. And I mean for *ever*. Do you hear? For ever and ever. (*They fall into each other's arms. The March from* Lohengrin[1] *is heard. The* STAGE MANAGER, *as clergyman, stands on the box, up center.*)

MR. WEBB. Come, they're waiting for us. Now you know it'll be all right. Come, quick. (GEORGE *slips away and takes his place beside the* STAGE MANAGER-*clergyman.* EMILY *proceeds up the aisle on her father's arm.*)

STAGE MANAGER. Do you, George, take this woman, Emily, to be your wedded wife, to have . . . (MRS. SOAMES *has been sitting in the last row of the congregation. She now turns to her neighbors and speaks in a shrill voice. Her chatter drowns out the rest of the clergyman's words.*)

MRS. SOAMES. Perfectly lovely wedding! Loveliest wedding I ever saw. Oh, I do love a good wedding, don't you? Doesn't she make a lovely bride?

GEORGE. I do.

STAGE MANAGER. Do you, Emily, take this man, George, to be your wedded husband,— (*Again his further words are covered by those of* MRS. SOAMES.)

MRS. SOAMES. Don't know *when* I've seen such a lovely wedding. But I always cry. Don't know why it is, but I always cry. I just like to see young people happy, don't you? Oh, I think it's lovely. (*The ring. The kiss. The stage is suddenly arrested into silent tableau. The* STAGE MANAGER, *his eyes on the distance, as though to himself:*)

STAGE MANAGER. I've married over two hundred couples in my day.

Do I believe in it?

I don't know.

M. . . . marries N. . . . millions of them.

The cottage, the go-cart, the Sunday-afternoon drives in the Ford, the first rheumatism, the grandchildren, the second rheumatism, the deathbed, the reading of the will,—(*He now looks at the audience for the first time, with a warm smile that removes any sense of cynicism from the next line.*) Once in a thousand times it's interesting.

—Well, let's have Mendelssohn's "Wedding March!" (*The organ picks up the March. The bride and groom come down the aisle, radiant, but trying to be very dignified.*)

MRS. SOAMES. Aren't they a lovely couple? Oh, I've never been to such a nice wedding. I'm sure they'll be happy. I always say: *happiness*, that's the great thing! The important thing is to be happy. (*The bride and groom reach the steps leading into the audience. A bright light is thrown upon them. They descend into the auditorium and run up the aisle joyously.*)

STAGE MANAGER. That's all the Second Act, folks. Ten minutes' intermission.

I

MARRIAGE AND HAPPINESS

Just before the wedding, the Stage Manager says that even at a good wedding people are so put together that "there's a lot of confusion way down deep in people's minds." Judging from the action that follows his speech, it seems that the people of Grover's Corners are quite uncertain about marriage. The town minister (played by the Stage Manager) says flatly that he doesn't know whether he believes in marriage or not and that it is "interesting" only once in a thousand times. These statements are followed immediately by Mrs. Soames' last speech, in which she says, ". . . *happiness*, that's the great thing! The important thing is to be happy."

By placing these speeches side by side, Wilder forces the reader to question the relationship between marriage and happiness; it strongly suggests

---

1. **Lohengrin**\ˈlō·ən·grĭn\ opera by Richard Wagner based on the legend of the Holy Grail.

that there are no grounds for assuming that marriage in itself (even a "good" marriage) is any guarantee of happiness. This is not to suggest, however, that marriage is an evil institution—the act ends with the bride and groom running up the aisle "joyously." But will they be happy "forever after"?

II
IMPLICATIONS

In his introductory speech to Act II, the Stage Manager remarks, "Most everybody in the world climbs into their graves married." Does this strike you as a strange way of expressing the simple thought that most persons get married? At any rate, after a brief street scene, we enter the Gibbs' home on George's wedding day. The following are some quotations from that scene:

1. DR. GIBBS. Well, Ma, the day has come. You're losin' one of your chicks.

2. MRS. GIBBS. He'll catch his death of cold within a week.

3. GEORGE. Only five more hours to live. (*Makes the gesture of cutting his throat. . . .*)

4. MRS. GIBBS. From tomorrow on you can kill yourself in all weathers. . . .

Is this clustering of death images with George's impending marriage of no special significance, or is it related to incidents and dialogue later in the act, like Mrs. Webb's speech before the wedding and George and Emily's drawing back from the altar?

III
TECHNIQUES

Structure

1. Act II takes place three years after Act I, yet the two are tied together quite intimately. Note, for example, that Mrs. Soames appears very close to the end of both acts. Compare the first scene (after the Stage Manager's introductory speech) of Act I with the first scene of Act II and note the similarities. In addition to the fact that these scenes help to tie the two acts together, what other reason or reasons might Wilder have had for using such similar openings?

2. The chances are that you thought at the end of Act I that Simon Stimson was going to play an important role in this play, yet he does not appear in Act II. Does this necessarily mean that he is not going to play an important role?

Act III

During the intermission the audience has seen the stagehands arranging the stage. On the right-hand side, a little right of the center, ten or twelve ordinary chairs have been placed in three openly spaced rows facing the audience.

These are graves in the cemetery.

Toward the end of the intermission the actors enter and take their places. The front row contains: toward the center of the stage, an empty chair; then MRS. GIBBS; SIMON STIMSON.

The second row contains, among others, MRS. SOAMES.

The third row has WALLY WEBB.

The dead do not turn their heads or their eyes to right or left, but they sit in a quiet without stiffness. When they speak their tone is matter-of-fact, without sentimentality and, above all, without lugubriousness.

The STAGE MANAGER *takes his accustomed place and waits for the house lights to go down.*

STAGE MANAGER. This time nine years have gone by, friends—summer, 1913.

Gradual changes in Grover's Corners. Horses are getting rarer.

Farmers coming into town in Fords.

Everybody locks their house doors now at night. Ain't been any burglars in town yet, but everybody's heard about 'em.

You'd be surprised, though—on the whole, things don't change much around here.

This is certainly an important part of Grover's Corners. It's on a hilltop—a windy hilltop—lots of sky, lots of clouds,—often lots of sun and moon and stars.

You come up here, on a fine afternoon and you can see range on range of hills—awful blue they are—up there by Lake Sunapee and Lake Winnipesaukee[1] . . . and way up, if you've got a glass, you can see the White Mountains and Mt. Washington—where North Conway and Conway is. And, of course, our favorite mountain, Mt. Monadnock, 's right here—and all these towns that lie around it: Jaffrey, 'n East Jaffrey, 'n Peterborough, 'n Dublin; and (*Then pointing down in the audience.*) there, quite a ways down, is Grover's Corners.

Yes, beautiful spot up here. Mountain laurel and li-lacks. I often wonder why people like to be buried in Woodlawn and Brooklyn when they might pass the same time up here in New Hampshire. Over there—(*Pointing to stage left.*) are the old stones,—1670, 1680. Strong-minded people that come a long way to be independent. Summer people walk around there laughing at the funny words on the tombstones . . . it don't do any harm. And genealogists come up from Boston—get paid by city people for looking up their ancestors. They want to make sure they're Daughters of the American Revolution and of the *Mayflower*. . . . Well, I guess that don't do any harm, either. Wherever you come near the human race, there's layers and layers of nonsense. . . .

Over there are some Civil War veterans. Iron flags on their graves . . . New Hampshire boys . . . had a notion that the Union ought to be kept together, though they'd never seen more than fifty miles of it themselves. All they knew was the name, friends—the United States of America. The United States of America. And they went and died about it.

This here is the new part of the cemetery. Here's your friend Mrs. Gibbs. 'N let me see—Here's Mr. Stimson, organist at the Congregational Church. And Mrs. Soames who enjoyed the wedding so—you remember? Oh, and a lot of others. And Editor Webb's boy, Wallace, whose appendix burst while he was on a Boy Scout trip to Crawford Notch.

Yes, an awful lot of sorrow has sort of quieted down up here.

People just wild with grief have brought their relatives up to this hill. We all know how it is . . . and then time . . . and sunny days . . . and rainy days . . . 'n snow . . . We're all glad they're in a beautiful place and we're coming up here ourselves when our fit's over.

Now there are some things we all know, but we don't take'm out and look at'm very often. We all know that *something* is eternal. And it ain't houses and it ain't names, and it ain't earth, and it ain't even the stars . . . everybody knows in their bones that *something* is eternal, and that something has to do with human beings. All the greatest people ever lived have been telling us that for five thousand years and yet you'd be surprised how people are always losing hold of it. There's something way down deep that's eternal about every human being. (*Pause.*)

You know as well as I do that the dead don't stay interested in us living people for very long. Gradually, gradually, they lose hold of the earth . . . and the ambitions they had . . . and the pleasures they had . . . and the things they suffered . . . and the people they loved.

They get weaned away from earth—that's the way I put it,—weaned away.

And they stay here while the earth part of 'em burns away, burns out; and all that time they slowly get indifferent to what's goin' on in Grover's Corners.

They're waitin'. They're waitin' for something that they feel is comin'. Something important, and great. Aren't they waitin' for the eternal part in them to come out clear?

Some of the things they're going to say maybe'll hurt your feelings—but that's the way it is: mother'n daughter . . . husband 'n

---

1. **Lake Sunapee,** boundary between Sullivan and Merrimack counties in New Hampshire; summer resort. **Lake Winnipesaukee**\ˈwĭ·nĭ·pĕ ˈsŏ·kē\ largest lake in New Hampshire.

wife . . . enemy 'n enemy . . . money 'n miser
. . . all those terribly important things kind
of grow pale around here. And what's left
when memory's gone, and your identity,
Mrs. Smith? (*He looks at the audience a
minute, then turns to the stage.*)

Well! There are some *living* people. There's
Joe Stoddard, our undertaker, supervising a
new-made grave. And here comes a Grover's
Corners boy, that left town to go out West.
(JOE STODDARD *has hovered about in the
background.* SAM CRAIG *enters left, wiping
his forehead from the exertion. He carries an
umbrella and strolls front.*)

SAM CRAIG. Good afternoon, Joe Stoddard.

JOE STODDARD. Good afternoon, good afternoon.
Let me see now: do I know you?

SAM CRAIG. I'm Sam Craig.

JOE STODDARD. Gracious sakes' alive! Of all
people! I should'a knowed you'd be back for
the funeral. You've been away a long time,
Sam.

SAM CRAIG. Yes, I've been away over twelve
years. I'm in business out in Buffalo now, Joe.
But I was in the East when I got news of
my cousin's death, so I thought I'd combine
things a little and come and see the old
home. You look well.

JOE STODDARD. Yes, yes, can't complain. Very
sad, our journey today, Samuel.

SAM CRAIG. Yes.

JOE STODDARD. Yes, yes. I always say I hate to
supervise when a young person is taken.
They'll be here in a few minutes now. I had
to come here early today—my son's super-
visin' at the home.

SAM CRAIG (*reading stones*). Old Farmer Mc-
Carty, I used to do chores for him—after
school. He had the lumbago.

JOE STODDARD. Yes, we brought Farmer Mc-
Carty here a number of years ago now.

SAM CRAIG (*staring at* MRS. GIBBS' *knees*). Why,
this is my Aunt Julia . . . I'd forgotten that
she'd . . . of course, of course.

JOE STODDARD. Yes, Doc Gibbs lost his wife
two-three years ago . . . about this time. And
today's another pretty bad blow for him, too.

MRS. GIBBS (*to* SIMON STIMSON: *in an even
voice*). That's my sister Carey's boy, Sam
. . . Sam Craig.

SIMON STIMSON. I'm always uncomfortable
when *they're* around.

MRS. GIBBS. Simon.

SAM CRAIG. Do they choose their own verses
much, Joe?

JOE STODDARD. No . . . not usual. Mostly the
bereaved pick a verse.

SAM CRAIG. Doesn't sound like Aunt Julia.
There aren't many of those Hersey sisters left
now. Let me see: where are . . . I wanted to
look at my father's and mother's . . .

JOE STODDARD. Over there with the Craigs . . .
Avenue F.

SAM CRAIG (*reading* SIMON STIMSON'S *epitaph*).
He was organist at church, wasn't he?—Hm,
drank a lot, we used to say.

JOE STODDARD. Nobody was supposed to know
about it. He'd seen a peck of trouble. (*Behind his hand.*) Took his own life, y' know?

SAM CRAIG. Oh, did he?

JOE STODDARD. Hung himself in the attic. They
tried to hush it up, but of course it got
around. He chose his own epy-taph. You can
see it there. It ain't a verse exactly.

SAM CRAIG. Why, it's just some notes of music
—what is it?

JOE STODDARD. Oh, I wouldn't know. It was
wrote up in the Boston papers at the time.

SAM CRAIG. Joe, what did she die of?

JOE STODDARD. Who?

SAM CRAIG. My cousin.

JOE STODDARD. Oh, didn't you know? Had some
trouble bringing a baby into the world. 'Twas
her second, though. There's a little boy 'bout
four years old.

SAM CRAIG (*opening his umbrella*). The grave's
going to be over there?

JOE STODDARD. Yes, there ain't much more room
over here among the Gibbses, so they're
opening up a whole new Gibbs section over
by Avenue B. You'll excuse me now. I see
they're comin'. (*From left to center, at the
back of the stage, comes a procession. Four*

men carry a casket, invisible to us. All the rest are under umbrellas. One can vaguely see: DR. GIBBS, GEORGE, *the* WEBBS, *etc. They gather about a grave in the back center of the stage, a little to the left of center.*)

MRS. SOAMES. Who is it, Julia?

MRS. GIBBS (*without raising her eyes*). My daughter-in-law, Emily Webb.

MRS. SOAMES (*a little surprised, but no emotion*). Well, I declare! The road up here must have been awful muddy. What did she die of, Julia?

MRS. GIBBS. In childbirth.

MRS. SOAMES. Childbirth. (*Almost with a laugh.*) I'd forgotten all about that. My, wasn't life awful—(*With a sigh.*) and wonderful.

SIMON STIMSON (*with a sideways glance*). Wonderful, was it?

MRS. GIBBS. Simon! Now, remember!

MRS. SOAMES. I remember Emily's wedding. Wasn't it a lovely wedding! And I remember her reading the class poem at Graduation Exercises. Emily was one of the brightest girls ever graduated from High School. I've heard Principal Wilkins say so time after time. I called on them at their new farm, just before I died. Perfectly beautiful farm.

A WOMAN FROM AMONG THE DEAD. It's on the same road we lived on.

A MAN AMONG THE DEAD. Yepp, right smart farm. (*They subside. The group by the grave starts singing "Blessed Be the Tie That Binds."*)

A WOMAN AMONG THE DEAD. I always liked that hymn. I was hopin' they'd sing a hymn. (*Pause. Suddenly* EMILY *appears from among the umbrellas. She is wearing a white dress. Her hair is down her back and tied by a white ribbon like a little girl. She comes slowly, gazing wonderingly at the dead, a little dazed. She stops halfway and smiles faintly. After looking at the mourners for a moment, she walks slowly to the vacant chair beside* MRS. GIBBS *and sits down.*)

EMILY (*to them all, quietly, smiling*). Hello.

MRS. SOAMES. Hello, Emily.

A MAN AMONG THE DEAD. Hello, M's Gibbs.

EMILY (*warmly*). Hello, Mother Gibbs.

MRS. GIBBS. Emily.

EMILY. Hello. (*With surprise.*) It's raining. (*Her eyes drift back to the funeral company.*)

MRS. GIBBS. Yes . . . They'll be gone soon, dear. Just rest yourself.

EMILY. It seems thousands and thousands of years since I . . . Papa remembered that that was my favorite hymn.

Oh, I wish I'd been here a long time. I don't like being new here.—How do you do, Mr. Stimson?

SIMON STIMSON. How do you do, Emily. (EMILY *continues to look about her with a wondering smile; as though to shut out from her mind the thought of the funeral company she starts speaking to* MRS. GIBBS *with a touch of nervousness.*)

EMILY. Mother Gibbs, George and I have made that farm into just the best place you ever saw. We thought of you all the time. We wanted to show you the new barn and a great long ce-ment drinking fountain for the stock. We bought that out of the money you left us.

MRS. GIBBS. I did?

EMILY. Don't you remember, Mother Gibbs— the legacy you left us? Why, it was over three hundred and fifty dollars.

MRS. GIBBS. Yes, yes, Emily.

EMILY. Well, there's a patent device on the drinking fountain so that it never overflows, Mother Gibbs, and it never sinks below a certain mark they have there. It's fine. (*Her voice trails off and her eyes return to the funeral group.*) It won't be the same to George without me, but it's a lovely farm. (*Suddenly she look directly at* MRS. GIBBS.) Live people don't understand, do they?

MRS. GIBBS. No, dear—not very much.

EMILY. They're sort of shut up in little boxes, aren't they? I feel as though I knew them last a thousand years ago . . . My boy is spending the day at Mrs. Carter's. (*She sees* MR. CARTER *among the dead.*) Oh, Mr.

Carter, my little boy is spending the day at your house.

MR. CARTER. Is he?

EMILY. Yes, he loves it there.—Mother Gibbs, we have a Ford, too. Never gives any trouble. I don't drive, though. Mother Gibbs, when does this feeling go away?—Of being . . . one of *them*? How long does it . . . ?

MRS. GIBBS. Sh! dear. Just wait and be patient.

EMILY (*with a sigh*). I know.—Look, they're finished. They're going.

MRS. GIBBS. Sh—. (*The umbrellas leave the stage.* DR. GIBBS *has come over to his wife's grave and stands before it a moment.* EMILY *looks up at his face.* MRS. GIBBS *does not raise her eyes.*)

EMILY. Look! Father Gibbs is bringing some of my flowers to you. He looks just like George, doesn't he? Oh, Mother Gibbs, I never realized before how troubled and how . . . how in the dark live persons are. Look at him. I loved him so. From morning till night, that's all they are—troubled. (DR. GIBBS *goes off.*)

THE DEAD. Little cooler than it was.—Yes, that rain's cooled it off a little. Those northeast winds always do the same thing, don't they? If it isn't a rain, it's a three-day blow.—(*A patient calm falls on the stage. The* STAGE MANAGER *appears at his proscenium pillar, smoking.* EMILY *sits up abruptly with an idea.*)

EMILY. But, Mother Gibbs, one can go back; one can go back there again . . . into the living. I feel it. I know it. Why just then for a moment I was thinking about . . . about the farm . . . and for a minute I *was* there, and my baby was on my lap as plain as day.

MRS. GIBBS. Yes, of course you can.

EMILY. I can go back there and live all those days over again . . . why not?

MRS. GIBBS. All I can say is, Emily, don't.

EMILY (*she appeals urgently to the* STAGE MANAGER). But it's true, isn't it? I can go and live . . . back there . . . again.

STAGE MANAGER. Yes, some have tried—but they soon come back here.

MRS. GIBBS. Don't do it, Emily.

MRS. SOAMES. Emily, don't. It's not what you think it'd be.

EMILY. But I won't live over a sad day. I'll choose a happy one—I'll choose the day I first knew that I loved George. Why should that be painful? (*They are silent. Her question turns to the* STAGE MANAGER.)

STAGE MANAGER. You not only live it; but you watch yourself living it.

EMILY. Yes?

STAGE MANAGER. And as you watch it, you see the thing that they—down there—never know. You see the future. You know what's going to happen afterwards.

EMILY. But is that—painful? Why?

MRS. GIBBS. That's not the only reason why you shouldn't do it, Emily. When you've been here longer you'll see that our life here is to forget all that, and think only of what's ahead, and be ready for what's ahead. When you've been here longer you'll understand.

EMILY (*softly*). But Mother Gibbs, how can I *ever* forget that life? It's all I know. It's all I had.

MRS. SOAMES. Oh, Emily. It isn't wise. Really, it isn't.

EMILY. But it's a thing I must know for myself. I'll choose a happy day, anyway.

MRS. GIBBS. *No!*—At least, choose an unimportant day. Choose the least important day in your life. It will be important enough.

EMILY (*to herself*). Then it can't be since I was married; or since the baby was born. (*To the* STAGE MANAGER, *eagerly*.) I can choose a birthday at least, can't I?—I choose my twelfth birthday.

STAGE MANAGER. All right. February 11th, 1899. A Tuesday.—Do you want any special time of day?

EMILY. Oh, I want the whole day.

STAGE MANAGER. We'll begin at dawn. You remember it had been snowing for several days; but it had stopped the night before, and they had begun clearing the roads. The sun's coming up.

EMILY (*with a cry; rising*). There's Main Street . . . why, that's Mr. Morgan's drugstore before he changed it! . . . And there's the livery stable. (*The stage at no time in this act has been very dark; but now the left half of the stage gradually becomes very bright—the brightness of a crisp winter morning.* EMILY *walks toward Main Street.*)

STAGE MANAGER. Yes, it's 1899. This is fourteen years ago.

EMILY. Oh, that's the town I knew as a little girl. And, *look,* there's the old white fence that used to be around our house. Oh, I'd forgotten that! Oh, I love it so! Are they inside?

STAGE MANAGER. Yes, your mother'll be coming downstairs in a minute to make breakfast.

EMILY (*softly*). Will she?

STAGE MANAGER. And you remember: your father had been away for several days; he came back on the early-morning train.

EMILY. No . . . ?

STAGE MANAGER. He'd been back to his college to make a speech—in western New York, at Clinton.

EMILY. Look! There's Howie Newsome. There's our policeman. But he's *dead;* he *died.* (*The voices of* HOWIE NEWSOME, CONSTABLE WARREN *and* JOE CROWELL, JR., *are heard at the left of the stage.* EMILY *listens in delight.*)

HOWIE NEWSOME. Whoa, Bessie!—Bessie! 'Morning, Bill.

CONSTABLE WARREN. Morning, Howie.

HOWIE NEWSOME. You're up early.

CONSTABLE WARREN. Been rescuin' a party; darn near froze to death, down by Polish Town thar. Got drunk and lay out in the snowdrifts. Thought he was in bed when I shook'm.

EMILY. Why, there's Joe Crowell. . . .

JOE CROWELL. Good morning, Mr. Warren. 'Morning, Howie. (MRS. WEBB *has appeared in her kitchen, but* EMILY *does not see her until she calls.*)

MRS. WEBB. Chil-*dren!* Wally! Emily! . . . Time to get up.

EMILY. Mama, I'm here! Oh! how young Mama looks! I didn't know Mama was ever that young.

MRS. WEBB. You can come and dress by the kitchen fire, if you like; but hurry. (HOWIE NEWSOME *has entered along Main Street and brings the milk to* MRS. WEBB's *door.*) Good morning, Mr. Newsome. Whhhh—it's cold.

HOWIE NEWSOME. Ten below by my barn, Mrs. Webb.

MRS. WEBB. Think of it! Keep yourself wrapped up. (*She takes her bottles in, shuddering.*)

EMILY (*with an effort*). Mama, I can't find my blue hair ribbon anywhere.

MRS. WEBB. Just open your eyes, dear, that's all. I laid it out for you special—on the dresser, there. If it were a snake it would bite you.

EMILY. Yes, yes . . . (*She puts her hand on her heart.* MR. WEBB *comes along Main Street, where he meets* CONSTABLE WARREN. *Their movements and voices are increasingly lively in the sharp air.*)

MR. WEBB. Good morning, Bill.

CONSTABLE WARREN. Good morning, Mr. Webb. You're up early.

MR. WEBB. Yes, just been back to my old college in New York State. Been any trouble here?

CONSTABLE WARREN. Well, I was called up this mornin' to rescue a Polish fella—darn near froze to death he was.

MR. WEBB. We must get it in the paper.

CONSTABLE WARREN. 'Twan't much.

EMILY (*whispers*). Papa. (MR. WEBB *shakes the snow off his feet and enters his house.* CONSTABLE WARREN *goes off, right.*)

MR. WEBB. Good morning, Mother.

MRS. WEBB. How did it go, Charles?

MR. WEBB. Oh, fine, I guess. I told'm a few things.—Everything all right here?

MRS. WEBB. Yes—can't think of anything that's happened, special. Been right cold. Howie Newsome says it's ten below over to his barn.

MR. WEBB. Yes, well, it's colder than that at Hamilton College.[2] Students' ears are falling off. It ain't Christian.—Paper have any mistakes in it?

MRS. WEBB. None that I noticed. Coffee's ready

---

2. **Hamilton College,** private college in Clinton, New York.

when you want it. (*He starts upstairs.*) Charles! Don't forget; it's Emily's birthday. Did you remember to get her something?

MR. WEBB (*patting his pocket*). Yes, I've got something here. (*Calling up the stairs.*) Where's my girl? Where's my birthday girl? (*He goes off left.*)

MRS. WEBB. Don't interrupt her now, Charles. You can see her at breakfast. She's slow enough as it is. Hurry up, children! It's seven o'clock. Now, I don't want to call you again.

EMILY (*softly, more in wonder than in grief*). I can't bear it. They're so young and beautiful. Why did they ever have to get old? Mama, I'm here. I'm grown up. I love you all, everything.—I can't look at everything hard enough. (*She looks questioningly at the* STAGE MANAGER, *saying or suggesting: "Can I go in?" He nods briefly. She crosses to the inner door to the kitchen, left of her mother, and as though entering the room, says, suggesting the voice of a girl of twelve:*) Good morning, Mama.

MRS. WEBB (*crossing to embrace and kiss her; in her characteristic matter-of-fact manner*). Well, now, dear, a very happy birthday to my girl and many happy returns. There are some surprises waiting for you on the kitchen table.

EMILY. Oh, Mama, you *shouldn't* have. (*She throws an anguished glance at the* STAGE MANAGER.) I can't—I can't.

MRS. WEBB (*facing the audience, over her stove*). But birthday or no birthday, I want you to eat your breakfast good and slow. I want you to grow up and be a good strong girl.

That in the blue paper is from your Aunt Carrie; and I reckon you can guess who brought the post-card album. I found it on the doorstep when I brought in the milk—George Gibbs . . . must have come over in the cold pretty early . . . right nice of him.

EMILY (*to herself*). Oh, George! I'd forgotten that. . . .

MRS. WEBB. Chew that bacon good and slow. It'll help keep you warm on a cold day.

EMILY (*with mounting urgency*). Oh, Mama, just look at me one minute as though you really saw me. Mama, fourteen years have gone by. I'm dead. You're a grandmother, Mama. I married George Gibbs, Mama. Wally's dead, too. Mama, his appendix burst on a camping trip to North Conway. We felt just terrible about it—don't you remember? But, just for a moment now we're all together. Mama, just for a moment we're happy. *Let's look at one another.*

MRS. WEBB. That in the yellow paper is something I found in the attic among your grandmother's things. You're old enough to wear it now, and I thought you'd like it.

EMILY. And this is from you. Why, Mama, it's just lovely and it's just what I wanted. It's beautiful! (*She flings her arms around her mother's neck. Her mother goes on with her cooking, but is pleased.*)

MRS. WEBB. Well, I hoped you'd like it. Hunted all over. Your Aunt Norah couldn't find one in Concord, so I had to send all the way to Boston. (*Laughing.*)

Wally has something for you, too. He made it at manual-training class and he's very proud of it. Be sure you make a big fuss about it.—Your father has a surprise for you, too; don't know what it is myself. Sh—here he comes.

MR. WEBB (*off stage*). Where's my girl? Where's my birthday girl?

EMILY (*in a loud voice to the* STAGE MANAGER). I can't. I can't go on. It goes so fast. We don't have time to look at one another. (*She breaks down sobbing. The lights dim on the left half of the stage.* MRS. WEBB *disappears.*)

I didn't realize. So all that was going on and we never noticed. Take me back—up the hill—to my grave. But first: Wait! One more look.

Good-by, Good-by, world. Good-by, Grover's Corners . . . Mama and Papa. Good-by to clocks ticking . . . and Mama's sunflowers.

And food and coffee. And new-ironed dresses and hot baths . . . and sleeping and waking up. Oh, earth, you're too wonderful for anybody to realize you. (*She looks toward the* STAGE MANAGER *and asks abruptly, through her tears:*)

Do any human beings ever realize life while they live it?—every, every minute?

STAGE MANAGER. No. (*Pause.*) The saints and poets, maybe—they do some.

EMILY. I'm ready to go back. (*She returns to her chair beside* MRS. GIBBS. *Pause.*)

MRS. GIBBS. Were you happy?

EMILY. No . . . I should have listened to you. That's all human beings are! Just blind people.

MRS. GIBBS. Look, it's clearing up. The stars are coming out.

EMILY. Oh, Mr. Stimson, I should have listened to them.

SIMON STIMSON (*with mounting violence; bitingly*). Yes, now you know. Now you know! That's what it was to be alive. To move about in a cloud of ignorance; to go up and down trampling on the feelings of those . . . of those about you. To spend and waste time as though you had a million years. To be always at the mercy of one self-centered passion, or another. Now you know—that's the happy existence you wanted to go back to. Ignorance and blindness.

MRS. GIBBS (*spiritedly*). Simon Stimson, that ain't the whole truth and you know it. Emily, look at that star. I forget its name.

A MAN AMONG THE DEAD. My boy Joel was a sailor,—knew 'em all. He'd set on the porch evenings and tell 'em all by name. Yes, sir, wonderful!

ANOTHER MAN AMONG THE DEAD. A star's mighty good company.

A WOMAN AMONG THE DEAD. Yes. Yes, 'tis.

SIMON STIMSON. Here's one of them coming.

THE DEAD. That's funny. 'Tain't no time for one of them to be here.—Goodness sakes.

EMILY. Mother Gibbs, it's George.

MRS. GIBBS. Sh, dear. Just rest yourself.

EMILY. It's George. (GEORGE *enters from the left, and slowly comes toward them.*)

A MAN FROM AMONG THE DEAD. And my boy, Joel, who knew the stars—he used to say it took millions of years for that speck of light to git to the earth. Don't seem like a body could believe it, but that's what he used to say—millions of years. (GEORGE *sinks to his knees then falls full length at* EMILY's *feet.*)

A WOMAN AMONG THE DEAD. Goodness! That ain't no way to behave!

MRS. SOAMES. He ought to be home.

EMILY. Mother Gibbs?

MRS. GIBBS. Yes, Emily?

EMILY. They don't understand, do they?

MRS. GIBBS. No, dear. They don't understand. (*The* STAGE MANAGER *appears at the right, one hand on a dark curtain which he slowly draws across the scene. In the distance a clock is heard striking the hour very faintly.*)

STAGE MANAGER. Most everybody's asleep in Grover's Corners. There are a few lights on: Shorty Hawkins, down at the depot, has just watched the Albany train go by. And at the livery stable somebody's setting up late and talking.—Yes, it's clearing up. There are the stars—doing their old, old crisscross journeys in the sky. Scholars haven't settled the matter yet, but they seem to think there are no living beings up there. Just chalk . . . or fire. Only this one is straining away, straining away all the time to make something of itself. The strain's so bad that every sixteen hours everybody lies down and gets a rest. (*He winds his watch.*) Hm. . . . Eleven o'clock in Grover's Corners.—You get a good rest, too. Good night.

The End

I
"LIFE" AND "DEATH"

A title for the last act of *Our Town* might be " 'Life' and 'Death'," with the terms in quotes to emphasize the ironic handling of the theme. The first "living" person the Stage Manager notices at the end of his introductory speech is, ironically, the undertaker. Again, during the funeral scene Emily, who has just left her coffin, says of the "living" people that "They're sort of shut up in little boxes. . . ." Later, as she relives her twelfth birthday, she proves to be more alive than the living. Her mother's statement that Emily could find her blue hair ribbon if she would just open her eyes is heavily charged with irony since it is Mrs. Webb and not her daughter whose eyes are not alive to the full potential of life.

II
IMPLICATIONS

Discuss the following statements in the light of this play and of your own experience.

1. Life in Grover's Corners is very much the same as life in any community, large or small.

2. All change is superficial; there is really no significant difference between life in the past and life in the present decade.

3. "Wherever you come near the human race, there's layers and layers of nonsense."

4. Marriage demands a great deal of conformity and severely limits an individual's freedom.

5. A person who tried to live every minute fully would probably suffer a mental breakdown in a very short time.

III
TECHNIQUES
Structure: Tension and Resolution

Structurally speaking, in a three-act play, we expect the first act to be a "tension-raising" act and the third to be a "tension-resolving" act. One of the basic tensions in this play concerns its attitude toward life in Grover's Corners. Is *Our Town* a celebration of the simple joys of small-town life, or is it a condemnation of the dullness, conformity, and lack of awareness in that life?

Does the final act serve to resolve this question, and if so, how? In your discussion pay special attention to the following parts of the third act:

1. The talk between Mrs. Soames, Mrs. Gibbs, and Simon Stimson, as they watch Emily's funeral.

2. The final argument between Mrs. Gibbs and Simon.

3. The last conversation between Emily and Mrs. Gibbs.

NEW DIRECTIONS

All the prose and poetry in this section was recently published, and nearly all the authors represented were born after 1932. Just as writers of earlier decades helped to shape their time and were shaped by their time, so these men and women have influenced and been influenced by what has happened in your lifetime. Those influences may not always be immediately apparent, but they are there nonetheless.

Before commenting on some new directions in contemporary literature, we should note that while good writers always strive for freshness, they do not attempt to be novel for novelty's sake. That would be faddish, not independent or original. In recognition of these facts, we have included in NEW DIRECTIONS some selections that do not depart from the past in form or subject matter. They are new in the sense they are personally felt, intensely observed, and artistically wrought stories or poems.

To turn toward new directions, there does seem to be a tendency among contemporary prose writers to create shorter and more "poetic" types of fiction. Good illustrations of this new direction would be the "sketches" of such writers as Richard Brautigan, W. S. Merwin, and Donald Barthelme. At its best, the work of these writers exhibits a linguistic control and subtlety more frequently encountered in poetry than in prose.

Some of the best novels of recent years are also comparatively short and poetic. Several may be read in just a sitting or two, like Barthelme's *The Dead Father*, E. L. Doctorow's *Ragtime*, and Joan Didion's *Play It As It Lays* and *The Book of Common Prayer*. Even some novels that cover a comparatively long time span are relatively short. Toni Morrison's *Song of Solomon*, for example, which surveys nearly a century of a family's history, runs to little more than 300 pages.

In poetry, there is such a distinct (and continuing) preference for open forms that one is almost tempted to predict that poets will soon return to regular metrical patterns and rhyme just for the change. Yet there is truly no sign of that at the moment. Although one hears less today about "confessional" poetry as such, contemporary poets are continuing to write about themselves, often with a greater frankness and explicitness than ever before.

One direction that does seem new in recent poetry is a tendency to write poems dealing with inner realities or questions of being. We have represented that trend with a group of selections entitled "Journey into the Self" at the end of this section.

There are no doubt many other trends alive today that are too close to us to be seen. Discerning new directions in the great masses of printed matter that are being published today is like trying to see a pattern of snowflakes in a blizzard. Perhaps 100 years from now, critics will label our age as we have labeled periods of the past. But for us whom living writers are addressing now, it may be best simply to give each one that we wish to hear some small part of the energy and attention that she or he gave us in writing a poem or a story or a book.

After all, we do not read writers of the past, such as Whitman and Dickinson, primarily because they wrote work that was new in their time and established one trend or another. We read them because they are Whitman and Dickinson, and because we enjoy them, and because they speak to us.

The editors of this book hope that at least some of the writers in the pages that follow will speak to you.

In spite of the rise in popularity of the short prose sketch, good old-fashioned short stories continue to be written by contemporary writers, as the following selection proves. Ask yourself what the title of this story might mean before you start to read. Ask again when you have finished.

Average Waves in Unprotected Waters

ANNE TYLER

As soon as it got light, Bet woke him and dressed him, and then she walked him over to the table and tried to make him eat a little cereal. He wouldn't, though. He could tell something was up. She pressed the edge of the spoon against his lips till she heard it click on his teeth, but he just looked off at a corner of the ceiling—a knobby child with great glassy eyes and her own fair hair. Like any other nine-year-old, he wore a striped shirt and jeans, but the shirt was too neat and the jeans too blue, unpatched and unfaded, and would stay that way till he outgrew them. And his face was elderly—pinched, strained, tired—though it should have looked as unused as his jeans. He hardly ever changed his expression.

She left him in his chair and went to make the beds. Then she raised the yellowed shade, rinsed a few spoons in the bathroom sink, picked up some bits of magazines he'd torn the night before. This was a rented room in an ancient, crumbling house, and nothing you could do to it would lighten its cluttered look. There was always that feeling of too many lives layered over other lives, like the layers of brownish wallpaper her child had peeled away in the corner by his bed.

She slipped her feet into flat-heeled loafers

and absently patted the front of her dress, a worn beige knit she usually saved for Sundays. Maybe she should take it in a little; it hung from her shoulders like a sack. She felt too slight and frail, too wispy for all she had to do today. But she reached for her coat anyhow, and put it on and tied a blue kerchief under her chin. Then she went over to the table and slowly spun, modelling the coat. "See, Arnold?" she said. "We're going out."

Arnold went on looking at the ceiling, but his gaze turned wild and she knew he'd heard.

She fetched his jacket from the closet—brown corduroy, with a hood. It had set her back half a week's salary. But Arnold didn't like it; he always wanted his old one, a little red duffel coat he'd long ago outgrown. When she came toward him, he started moaning and rocking and shaking his head. She had to struggle to stuff his arms in the sleeves. Small though he was, he was strong, wiry; he was getting to be too much for her. He shook free of her hands and ran over to his bed. The jacket was on, though. It wasn't buttoned, the collar was askew, but never mind; that just made him look more real. She always felt bad at how he stood inside his clothes, separate from them, passive, unaware of all the buttons and snaps she'd fastened as carefully as she would a doll's.

She gave a last look around the room, checked to make sure the hot plate was off, and

Reprinted by permission of Russell & Volkening, Inc., as agents for the author. Copyright 1977 by Anne Tyler. Originally appeared in *The New Yorker*.

then picked up her purse and Arnold's suitcase. "Come along, Arnold," she said.

He came, dragging out every step. He looked at the suitcase suspiciously, but only because it was new. It didn't have any meaning for him. "See?" she said. "It's yours. It's Arnold's. It's going on the train with us."

But her voice was all wrong. He would pick it up, for sure. She paused in the middle of locking the door and glanced over at him fearfully. Anything could set him off nowadays. He hadn't noticed, though. He was too busy staring around the hallway, goggling at a freckled, walnut-framed mirror as if he'd never seen it before. She touched his shoulder. "Come, Arnold," she said.

They went down the stairs slowly, both of them clinging to the sticky mahogany railing. The suitcase banged against her shins. In the entrance hall, old Mrs. Puckett stood waiting outside her door—a huge, soft lady in a black crepe dress and orthopedic shoes. She was holding a plastic bag of peanut-butter cookies, Arnold's favorites. There were tears in her eyes. "Here, Arnold," she said, quavering. Maybe she felt to blame that he was going. But she'd done the best she could: baby-sat him all these years and only given up when he'd grown too strong and wild to manage. Bet wished Arnold would give the old lady some sign—hug her, make his little crowing noise, just take the cookies, even. But he was too excited. He raced on out the front door, and it was Bet who had to take them. "Well, thank you, Mrs. Puckett," she said. "I know he'll enjoy them later."

"Oh, no . . ." said Mrs. Puckett, and she flapped her large hands and gave up, sobbing.

They were lucky and caught a bus first thing. Arnold sat by the window. He must have thought he was going to work with her; when they passed the red-and-gold Kresge's sign, he jabbered and tried to stand up. "No, honey," she said, and took hold of his arm. He settled down then and let his hand stay curled in hers awhile. He had very small, cool fingers, and nails as smooth as thumbtack heads.

At the train station, she bought the tickets and then a pack of Wrigley's spearmint gum. Arnold stood gaping at the vaulted ceiling, with his head flopped back and his arms hanging limp at his sides. People stared at him. She would have liked to push their faces in. "Over here, honey," she said, and she nudged him toward the gate, straightening his collar as they walked.

He hadn't been on a train before and acted a little nervous, bouncing up and down in his seat and flipping the lid of his ashtray and craning forward to see the man ahead of them. When the train started moving, he crowed and pulled at her sleeve. "That's right, Arnold. Train. We're taking a trip," Bet said. She unwrapped a stick of chewing gum and gave it to him. He loved gum. If she didn't watch him closely, he sometimes swallowed it—which worried her a little because she'd heard it clogged your kidneys; but at least it would keep him busy. She looked down at the top of his head. Through the blond prickles of his hair, cut short for practical reasons, she could see his skull bones moving as he chewed. He was so thin-skinned, almost transparent; sometimes she imagined she could see the blood travelling in his veins.

When the train reached a steady speed, he grew calmer, and after a while he nodded over against her and let his hands sag on his knees. She watched his eyelashes slowly drooping—two colorless, fringed crescents, heavier and heavier, every now and then flying up as he tried to fight off sleep. He had never slept well, not ever, not even as a baby. Even before they'd noticed anything wrong, they'd wondered at his jittery, jerky catnaps, his tiny hands clutching tight and springing open, his strange single wail sailing out while he went right on sleeping. Avery said it gave him the chills. And after the doctor talked to them Avery wouldn't have anything to do with Arnold anymore—just walked in wide circles around the crib, looking stunned and sick. A few weeks later, he left. She wasn't surprised.

She even knew how he felt, more or less. Halfway, he blamed her; halfway, he blamed himself. You can't believe a thing like this will just fall on you out of nowhere.

She'd had moments herself of picturing some kind of evil gene in her husband's ordinary, stocky body—a dark little egg like a black jelly bean, she imagined it. All his fault. But other times she was sure the gene was hers. It seemed so natural; she never could do anything as well as most people. And then other times she blamed their marriage. They'd married too young, against her parents' wishes. All she'd wanted was to get away from home. Now she couldn't remember why. What was wrong with home? She thought of her parents' humped green trailer, perched on cinder blocks near a forest of masts in Salt Spray, Maryland. At this distance (parents dead, trailer rusted to bits, even Salt Spray changed past recognition), it seemed to her that her old life had been beautifully free and spacious. She closed her eyes and saw wide gray skies. Everything had been ruled by the sea. Her father (who'd run a fishing boat for tourists) couldn't arrange his day till he'd heard the marine forecast—the wind, the tides, the smallcraft warnings, the height of average waves in unprotected waters. He loved to fish, offshore and on, and he swam every chance he could get. He'd tried to teach her to bodysurf, but it hadn't worked out. There was something about the breakers: she just gritted her teeth and stood staunch and let them slam into her. As if standing staunch were a virtue, really. She couldn't explain it. Her father thought she was scared, but it wasn't that at all.

She'd married Avery against their wishes and been sorry ever since—sorry to move so far from home, sorrier when her parents died within a year of each other, sorriest of all when the marriage turned grim and cranky. But she never would have thought of leaving him. It was Avery who left; she would have stayed forever. In fact, she did stay on in their apartment for months after he'd gone, though the rent was far too high. It wasn't that she expected him back. She just took some comfort from enduring.

Arnold's head snapped up. He looked around him and made a gurgling sound. His chewing gum fell onto the front of his jacket. "Here, honey," she told him. She put the gum in her ashtray. "Look out the window. See the cows?"

He wouldn't look. He began bouncing in his seat, rubbing his hands together rapidly.

"Arnold? Want a cookie?"

If only she'd brought a picture book. She'd meant to and then forgot. She wondered if the train people sold magazines. If she let him get too bored, he'd go into one of his tantrums, and then she wouldn't be able to handle him. The doctor had given her pills just in case, but she was always afraid that while he was screaming he would choke on them. She looked around the car. "Arnold," she said, "see the . . . see the hat with feathers on? Isn't it pretty? See the red suitcase? See the, um . . ."

The car door opened with a rush of clattering wheels and the conductor burst in, singing "Girl of my dreams, I love you." He lurched down the aisle, plucking pink tickets from the back of each seat. Just across from Bet and Arnold, he stopped. He was looking down at a tiny black lady in a purple coat, with a fox fur piece biting its own tail around her neck. "You!" he said.

The lady stared straight ahead.

"You, I saw you. You're the one in the washroom."

A little muscle twitched in her cheek.

"You got on this train in Beulah, didn't you. Snuck in the washroom. Darted back like you thought you could put something over on me. I saw that bit of purple! Where's your ticket gone to?"

She started fumbling in a blue cloth purse. The fumbling went on and on. The conductor shifted his weight.

"Why!" she said finally. "I must've left it back in my other seat."

"What other seat?"

"Oh, the one back . . ." She waved a spidery hand.

The conductor sighed. "Lady," he said, "you owe me money."

"I do no such thing!" she said. "Viper! Monger! Hitler!" Her voice screeched up all at once; she sounded like a parrot. Bet winced and felt herself flushing, as if *she* were the one. But then at her shoulder she heard a sudden, rusty clang, and she turned and saw that Arnold was laughing. He had his mouth wide open and his tongue curled, the way he did when he watched "Sesame Street." Even after the scene had worn itself out, and the lady had paid and the conductor had moved on, Arnold went on chortling and la-la-ing, and Bet looked gratefully at the little black lady, who was settling her fur piece fussily and muttering under her breath.

From the Parkinsville Railroad Station, which they seemed to be tearing down or else remodelling—she couldn't tell which—they took a taxicab to Parkins State Hospital. "Oh, I been out there many and many a time," said the driver. "Went out there just the other ———"

But she couldn't stop herself; she had to tell him before she forgot. "Listen," she said, "I want you to wait for me right in the driveway. I don't want you to go on away."

"Well, fine," he said.

"Can you do that? I want you to be sitting right by the porch or the steps or whatever, right where I come out of, ready to take me back to the station. Don't just go off and ———"

"I *got* you, I got you," he said.

She sank back. She hoped he understood.

Arnold wanted a peanut-butter cookie. He was reaching and whimpering. She didn't know what to do. She wanted to give him anything he asked for, anything; but he'd get it all over his face and arrive not looking his best. She couldn't stand it if they thought he was just ordinary and unattractive. She wanted them to see how small and neat he was, how some-

body cherished him. But it would be awful if he went into one of his rages. She broke off a little piece of cookie from the bag. "Here," she told him, "Don't mess, now."

He flung himself back in the corner and ate it, keeping one hand flattened across his mouth while he chewed.

The hospital looked like someone's great, pillared mansion, with square brick buildings all around it. "Here we are," the driver said.

"Thank you," she said. "Now you wait here, please. Just wait till I get———"

"*Lady*," he said. "I'll wait."

She opened the door and nudged Arnold out ahead of her. Lugging the suitcase, she started toward the steps. "Come on, Arnold," she said.

He hung back.

"Arnold?"

Maybe he wouldn't allow it, and they would go on home and never think of this again.

But he came, finally, climbing the steps in his little hobbled way. His face was clean, but there were a few cookie crumbs on his jacket. She set down the suitcase to brush them off. Then she buttoned all his buttons and smoothed his shirt collar over his jacket collar before she pushed open the door.

In the admitting office, a lady behind a wooden counter showed her what papers to sign. Secretaries were clacketing typewriters all around. Bet thought Arnold might like that, but instead he got lost in the lights—chilly, hanging ice-cube tray lights with a little flicker to them. He gazed upward, looking astonished. Finally a flat-fronted nurse came in and touched his elbow. "Come along, Arnold. Come, Mommy. We'll show you where Arnold is staying," she said.

They walked back across the entrance hall, then up wide marble steps with hollows worn in them. Arnold clung to the bannister. There was a smell Bet hated, pine-oil disinfectant, but Arnold didn't seem to notice. You never knew; sometimes smells could just put him in a state.

The nurse unlocked a double door that had

chicken-wired windows. They walked through a corridor, passing several fat, ugly women in shapeless gray dresses and ankle socks. "Ha!" one of the women said, and fell giggling into the arms of a friend. The nurse said, "*Here* we are." She led them into an enormous hallway lined with little white cots. Nobody else was in it; there wasn't a sign that children lived here except for a tiny cardboard clown picture hanging on one vacant wall. "This one is your bed, Arnold," said the nurse. Bet laid the suitcase on it. It was made up so neatly, the sheets might have been painted on. A steely-gray blanket was folded across the foot. She looked over at Arnold, but he was pivoting back and forth to hear how his new sneakers squeaked on the linoleum.

"Usually," said the nurse, "we like to give new residents six months before the family visits. That way they settle in quicker, don't you see." She turned away and adjusted the clown picture, though as far as Bet could tell it was fine the way it was. Over her shoulder, the nurse said, "You can tell him goodbye now, if you like."

"Oh," Bet said. "All right." She set her hands on Arnold's shoulders. Then she laid her face against his hair, which felt warm and fuzzy. "Honey," she said. But he went on pivoting. She straightened and told the nurse, "I brought his special blanket."

"Oh, fine," said the nurse, turning toward her again. "We'll see that he gets it."

"He always likes to sleep with it; he has ever since he was little."

"All right."

"Don't wash it. He hates if you wash it."

"Yes. Say goodbye to Mommy now, Arnold."

"A lot of times he'll surprise you. I mean there's a whole lot to him. He's not just _____"

"We'll take very good care of him, Mrs. Blevins, don't worry."

"Well," she said. "'Bye, Arnold."

She left the ward with the nurse and went down the corridor. As the nurse was unlocking

the doors for her, she heard a single, terrible scream, but the nurse only patted her shoulder and pushed her gently on through.

In the taxi, Bet said, "Now, I've just got fifteen minutes to get to the station. I wonder if you could hurry?"

"Sure thing," the driver said.

She folded her hands and looked straight ahead. Tears seemed to be coming down her face in sheets.

Once she'd reached the station, she went to the ticket window. "Am I in time for the twelve-thirty-two?" she asked.

"Easily," said the man. "It's twenty minutes late."

"What?"

"Got held up in Norton somehow."

"But you can't!" she said. The man looked startled. She must be a sight, all swollen-eyed and wet-cheeked. "Look," she said, in a lower voice. "I figured this on purpose. I chose the one train from Beulah that would let me catch another one back without waiting. I do not want to sit and wait in this station."

"Twenty *minutes*, lady. That's all it is."

"What am I going to do?" she asked him.

He turned back to his ledgers.

She went over to a bench and sat down. Ladders and scaffolding towered above her, and only ten or twelve passengers were dotted through the rest of the station. The place looked bombed out—nothing but a shell. "Twenty minutes!" she said aloud. "What am I going to do?"

Through the double glass doors at the far end of the station, a procession of gray-suited men arrived with briefcases. More men came behind them, dressed in work clothes, carrying folding chairs, black trunklike boxes with silver hinges, microphones, a wooden lectern, and an armload of bunting. They set the lectern down in the center of the floor, not six feet from Bet. They draped the bunting across it—an arc of red, white, and blue. Wires were connected, floodlights were lit. A microphone screeched. One of the workmen said, "Try her, Mayor."

He held the microphone out to a fat man in a suit, who cleared his throat and said, "Ladies and gentlemen, on the occasion of the expansion of this fine old railway station _____"

"Sure do get an echo here," the workman said. "Keep on going."

The Mayor cleared his throat again. "If I may," he said, "I'd like to take about twenty minutes of your time, friends."

He straightened his tie. Bet blew her nose, and then she wiped her eyes and smiled. They had come just for her sake, you might think. They were putting on a sort of private play. From now on, all the world was going to be like that—just something on a stage, for her to sit back and watch.

I
FICTION AND LIFE

There is no denying the fact that this story is very sad. Bet, the mother of a severely retarded child, takes him to a state institution, where he will probably remain for the rest of his life. In addition, her marriage has failed, and her parents are dead. She seems very much alone at the end of the story. Furthermore, the author does not hold out much hope for Bet's future: in the last paragraph we read that "all the world" is going to be just "something on a stage, for her to sit back and watch."

One would think that such a story would leave readers profoundly depressed. Yet it does *not* have this effect on many. Assuming that you are one of these, why were you not depressed by the story? (If you were depressed, listen to and trade reactions with those who were not.) What might the disparity between your reaction to the story and the sad events in it teach you about the relationship between fiction and life?

II
IMPLICATIONS

Be prepared to discuss your opinions of the following statements and the extent to which the story does or does not bear them out.

1. If we truly love someone, we do what is best for her or him, regardless of our own feelings or desires.

2. Rational solutions to problems are not necessarily the best solutions.

3. Standing staunch is a virtue.

4. When we have something distasteful to do, it's best to do it without leaving ourselves any time to think.

5. No one can fully prepare for what life may bring.

6. People who see things through are always more admirable than those who run away.

III
TECHNIQUES

Symbolism

One of the most important tasks of a good short-story writer is to make everything hang together. Sometimes, it is a symbol that helps to crystallize a story in a writer's mind. Tyler probably knew early on that she wanted to write about Bet and Arnold, but what probably pulled everything into perspective for her was the symbol that ultimately became the title of the story. What does the title mean to you? Do you agree or disagree that it serves to crystallize the story, and why?

Structure: Foreshadowing and Flashback

Foreshadowing and *flashback* are aspects of structure that are more commonly seen in longer rather than shorter works, but there are instances of both in this short story. *Foreshadowing* is simply the hinting at something that will occur later in the story. How many examples of foreshadowing can you find in "Average Waves"? What purposes do they serve?

A *flashback* is a device by which the author presents scenes or incidents that occurred prior to the opening of the story. Notice that in this story Tyler uses as a flashback a recollection of Bet's in order to sketch in some details about her past life. Locate this flashback and note how smoothly the author moves into and out of it. How essential is this flashback to the design and meaning of the story?

Four Contemporary Poems

Because there are more people writing poems
today in America than ever before,
the following poem is a particularly good introduction
to contemporary poetry. Although the poems and the poets
are new, what people choose to write about
and even their manner of expression are not necessarily novel.
See if you can find similarities between the style of this poem
and that of Walt Whitman, who is sometimes called
the father of modern poetry.

I carried with me poems

I carried with me poems, poems which spewed out of
    everything; I saw poems hanging from the clotheslines,
    hanging from the streetlamps: I saw poems glowing in
    the bushes, pushing out of the earth as tulips do;
I felt poems breathe in the dark March night like ghosts
    which squared and wheeled through the air;
I felt poems brushing the tops of chimneys, brushing by in
    the dark; I felt poems being born in the city, Venuses
    breaking through a shattered sea of mirrors;
I felt all the poets of the city straining,
    isolated poets, knowing none of the others, straining;
I felt that some gazed into the March night, looking, and
    finding;   5
and others were running down the steep streets, seeking, and
    seeking to embrace;
and others stood in empty bookstores turning over pages
    of fellow poets whom they loved but didn't know;
and some pondered over coffee growing cold, in harshly lit
    cafeterias, and gazed at the reflections of the eaters in the
    wall-to-wall mirrors;
some dwelt on what it was to grow old;
some dwelled on love;   10
some had gone out of time;
some, going out of time, looked back into time, and started;

I felt all these lives and existences, all with poems at
    their center;

I knew none of these poets;
but I felt these intimations augured well, for me, and for
poetry;   15
and my steps grew big, giant steps, I bounded down Parker
Street,
a tall, taciturn, fast-walking poets' accomplice.

GAIL DUSENBERY

John Updike, the author of this poem,
is better known as a novelist and short-story writer
than as a poet, but it is not unusual
for a prose writer to compose poetry as well.
This poem—a tribute to the famous
American sculptor Alexander Calder—was probably prompted by
Calder's death. The movie referred to in the poem
shows Calder playing with human and animal figures from
his wire sculpture "Circus."

Calder's Hands

In the little movie
at the Whitney[1]
you can see them
at the center of the spell
of wire and metal: 5

a clumsy man's hands,
square and mitten-thick,
that do everything
without a pause:
unroll a tiny rug   10

with a flick,
tug a doll's arm up,
separate threads.
These hands now dead
never doubted, never rested.   15

JOHN UPDIKE

1. **Whitney,** a museum of American art in New York
City.

"Calder's Hands" by John Updike. From *Tossing and Turning* by John
Updike. Copyright © 1977 by John Updike. Reprinted by permission of
Alfred A. Knopf, Inc. This poem originally appeared in *The New Yorker*.

John Updike was moved to write a poem
by the death of a fellow artist,
but poets—like all of us—are touched by far more commonplace events,
such as the sight of an old horse in subzero weather.
This poem is not about the horse only, however;
look for the miracle at the end.

Ten Below

It is bad enough crying for children
suffering neglect and starvation in our world
without having on a day like this
to see an old cart-horse covered with foam,
quivering so hard that when he stops   5
the sheels[1] still rock slowly in place
like gears in an engine.
A man will do that, shiver where he stands,
frozen with false starts
before decisions, just staring,   10
but with a man you can take his arm,
talk him out of it, lead him away.

What do you do when both hands
and your voice are simply goads?
When the eyes you solace see space,   15
the wall behind you, the wisp of grass
pushing up through the curb at your feet?
I have thought that all the animals
we kill and maim, if they wanted to
could stare us down, wither us   20
and turn us into smoke with their glances—
they forbear because they pity us,
like angels, and love of something else
is why they suffer us and submit.

---

1. **sheels,** parts of the harness.

"Ten Below" by C. K. Williams from *Major Young Poets*.

But this is Pine Street, Philadelphia, 1965.　　25
You don't believe
in anything divine being here.
There is an old plug with a worn blanket
thrown over its haunches. There is a wagon
full of junk—pipes and rotted sinks,　　30
the grates from furnaces—and there
is a child walking beside the horse
with sugar, and the mammoth head lowering,
delicately nibbling from those vulnerable
fingers. You can't cut your heart out.　　35
Sometimes, just what is, is enough.

C. K. WILLIAMS

One of the characteristics of good poetry
is that it manages to say so much in so few words.
The following poem is an excellent example. It seems to present
a very simple situation: a woman will allow
a man to lift her down from a fence
but will not allow him to lift her back up. She says she has
an urge to keep her feet on the ground,
but see what deeper meanings you can discover by
reading between the lines.

Feet on the Ground

I climbed / up
the grey iron fence
myself,
only a few feet high
placed my feet between the spikes　　5
put my hands on your shoulders
let you
lift me / down

"Feet on the Ground" from *Smudging* by Diane Wakoski. Copyright ©
1972 by The Black Sparrow Press.

it seemed like a perfectly reasonable
act of trust   10
between a woman and a man

you could not understand
then
why I would not
let you   15
lift me / up

when we
were standing together
watching the yellow lights
stain the water   20
like iodine on a bruised knee
asked me
what else I was afraid of
beside being lifted /
up   25
I said I wasn't
afraid, just didn't like it
thought of
my urge to keep
my feet on the ground   30

the height
even of a three foot fence
being something to get down from
by any means

the ground not a thing   35
to leave
by any means.

DIANE WAKOSKI

I
"ALL WITH POEMS AT THEIR CENTER"

Referring to poets, which she seems to find everywhere, Gail Dusenbery says toward the end of her poem that she felt "these lives . . . all with poems at their center." Perhaps she is implying that *all* of us have poems at our center. Assuming that this is so, why do we not express those poems more frequently?

The notion of having poems at one's center suggests that the poems are already there. Possibly what is needed to bring them out is some special internal or external happening that will touch us at our center. What were the special things that touched the center of the people who wrote the poems you have just read? Why didn't they simply let those things touch them? Why did they *also* write poems?

II
IMPLICATIONS

Be prepared to discuss the following questions:

I carried with me poems

1. Dusenbery's poem uses familiar words, has no rhyme, and has no regular metrical pattern. For these reasons some people will consider it unpoetic. Is that a valid reaction? Why or why not?

2. Compare the lines below with the same lines in Dusenbery's poem. Which lines do you prefer? What reasons can you give for your preference?

I felt some looked into the March evening,
  seeking, and discovering;
and others were running down the hilly streets,
  looking, and hoping to embrace;

3. At the end of the poem, the speaker calls herself "taciturn." If you are not sure of the meaning of this word, look it up. Why is it ironic here?

Calder's Hands

1. To what does "them" refer in line 3? Why didn't Updike use a noun rather than the pronoun?

2. What is paradoxical in lines 7 to 8? It has been said that poets often use paradoxes. From this instance of paradox, can you suggest some reasons why this might be true?

3. The poem says that Calder's hands "never doubted." What does this mean?

Ten Below

1. In the opening stanza, Williams mentions children, the horse, and "a man." What connection or connections do you find in the stanza among these?

2. What is the "something else" referred to in line 22?

3. In the first line of the last stanza, the speaker mentions three specific things. Why does he choose to be so specific here?

4. What is the meaning of the last line of the poem? Why do you agree or disagree that it is a good final line for the poem?

Feet on the Ground

1. The woman has allowed the man to lift her down from the fence but will not allow him to lift her up. Why is this reasonable or unreasonable of her?

2. Although the woman says she has an urge to keep her feet on the ground, she herself climbed the fence initially. How do you account for this disparity between her statement and her action?

3. How is this poem a study of the difficulty of communication?

Three Contemporary Prose Sketches

Contemporary writers have turned the short prose sketch into an art form. Here are three such sketches, each one written by a writer known for his excellence in that form: Richard Brautigan, W. S. Merwin, and Donald Barthelme. Note that each offers a criticism of some aspect of modern American life or values. Does each also offer a solution or alternative values?

Corporal

RICHARD BRAUTIGAN

Once I had visions of being a general. This was in Tacoma[1] during the early years of World War II when I was a child going to grade school. They had a huge paper drive that was brilliantly put together like a military career.

It was very exciting and went something like this: If you brought in fifty pounds of paper you became a private and seventy-five pounds of paper were worth a corporal's stripes and a hundred pounds to be a sergeant, then spiralling pounds of paper leading upward until finally you arrive at being a general.

I think it took a ton of paper to be a general or maybe it was only a thousand pounds. I can't remember the exact amount but in the beginning it seemed so simple to gather enough paper to be a general.

I started out by gathering all the loose paper that was lying innocently around the house. That added up to three or four pounds. I'll have to admit that I was a little disappointed. I don't know where I got the idea that the house was just filled with paper. I actually thought there was paper all over the place. It's an interesting surprise that paper can be deceptive.

I didn't let it throw me, though. I marshalled my energies and went out and started going door to door asking people if they had any newspapers or magazines lying around that could be donated to the paper drive, so that we could win the war and destroy evil forever.

An old woman listened patiently to my spiel and then she gave me a copy of *Life* magazine that she had just finished reading. She closed the door while I was still standing there staring dumbfoundedly at the magazine in my hands. The magazine was warm.

At the next house, there wasn't any paper, not even a used envelope because another kid had already beaten me to it.

At the next house, nobody was home.

That's how it went for a week, door after door, house after house, block after block until finally I got enough paper together to become a private.

I took my stupid little private's stripe home in the absolute bottom of my pocket. There were already some paper officers, lieutenants and captains, on the block. I didn't even bother to have the stripe sewed on my coat. I just threw it in a drawer and covered it up with some socks.

I spent the next few days cynically looking for paper and lucked into a medium pile of *Collier's* from somebody's basement which was enough to get my corporal's stripes that immediately joined my private's stripe under the socks.

1. **Tacoma**, city in the state of Washington.

"Corporal" by Richard Brautigan from *Revenge of the Lawn*. Copyright © 1963, 1964, 1965, 1966, 1967, 1969, 1970, 1971 by Richard Brautigan. Reprinted by permission of Simon & Schuster, a division of Gulf & Western Corporation.

The kids who wore the best clothes and had a lot of spending money and got to eat hot lunch every day were already generals. They had known where there were a lot of magazines and their parents had cars. They strutted military airs around the playground and on their way home from school.

Shortly after that, like the next day, I brought a halt to my glorious military career and entered into the disenchanted paper shadows of America where failure is a bounced check or a bad report card or a letter ending a love affair and all the words that hurt people when they read them.

Make This Simple Test

W. S. MERWIN

Blindfold yourself with some suitable object. If time permits remain still for a moment. You may feel one or more of your senses begin to swim back toward you in the darkness, singly and without their names. Meanwhile have someone else arrange the products to be used in a row in front of you. It is preferable to have them in identical containers, though that is not necessary. Where possible, perform the test by having the other person feed you a portion—a spoonful—of each of the products in turn, without comment.

Guess what each one is, and have the other person write down what you say.

Then remove the blindfold. While arranging the products the other person should have detached part of the label or container from each and placed it in front of the product it belongs to, like a title.

This bit of legend must not contain the product's trade name nor its generic name, nor any suggestion of the product's taste or desirability. Or price. It should be limited to that part of the label or container which enumerates the actual components of the product in question.

Thus, for instance:

Contains dextrinized flours, cocoa processed with alkali, nonfat dry milk solids, yeast nutrients, vegetable proteins, agar, hydrogenated vegetable oil, dried egg yolk, GUAR, sodium cyclamate, soya lecithin, imitation lemon oil, acetyl tartaric esters of mono- and diglycerides as emulsifiers, polysorbate 60, 1/10 of 1% of sodium benzoate to retard spoilage.

Or:

Contains anhydrated potatoes, powdered whey, vegetable gum, emulsifier (gycerol monosterate), invert syrup, shortening with freshness preserver, lactose, sorbic acid to retard mold growth, caramel color, natural and artificial flavors, sodium acid pyrophosphate, sodium bisulfite.

Or:

Contains beef extract, wheat and soya derivatives, food starch—modified, dry sweet whey, calcium carageenan, vegetable oil, sodium phosphates to preserve freshness, BHA, BHT, prophylene glycol, pectin niacinamide, artificial flavor, U.S. certified color.

There should be not less than three separate products.

Taste again, without the blindfold. Guess again and have the other person record the answers. Replace the blindfold. Have the other person change the order of the products and again feed you a spoonful of each.

Guess again what you are eating or drinking in each case (if you can make the distinction). But this time do not stop there. Guess why you are eating or drinking it. Guess what it may do for you. Guess what it was meant to do for you. By whom. When. Where. Why. Guess where in the course of evolution you took the first step toward it. Guess which of your organs recognized it. Guess whether it is welcomed to their temples. Guess how it figures in their

"Make This Simple Test" by W. S. Merwin. From *The Miner's Pale Children*, copyright © 1969–1970 by W. S. Merwin. Reprinted by permission of Atheneum Publishers.

prayers. Guess how completely you become what you eat. Guess how soon. Guess at the taste of locusts and wild honey. Guess at the taste of water. Guess what the rivers see as they die. Guess why the babies are burning. Guess why there is silence in heaven. Guess why you were ever born.

The Police Band

DONALD BARTHELME

It was kind of the Department to think up the Police Band. The original impulse, I believe, was creative and humanitarian. A better way of doing things. Unpleasant, bloody things required by the line of duty. Even if it didn't work out.

The Commissioner (the old Commissioner, not the one they have now) brought us up the river from Detroit. Where our members had been, typically, working the Sho Bar two nights a week. Sometimes the Glass Crutch. Friday and Saturday. And the rest of the time wandering the streets disguised as postal employees. Bitten by dogs and burdened with third-class mail.

What are our duties? we asked at the interview. Your duties are to wail, the Commissioner said. That only. We admired our new dark-blue uniforms as we came up the river in canoes like Indians. We plan to use you in certain situations, certain tense situations, to alleviate tensions, the Commissioner said. I can visualize great success with this new method. And would you play "Entropy." He was pale, with a bad liver.

We are subtle, the Commissioner said, never forget that. Subtlety is what has previously been lacking in our line. Some of the old ones, the Commissioner said, all they know is the club. He took a little pill from a little box and swallowed it with his Scotch.

When we got to town we looked at those Steve Canyon[1] recruiting posters and wondered if we resembled them. Henry Wang, the bass man, looks like a Chinese Steve Canyon, right? The other cops were friendly in a suspicious way. They liked to hear us wail, however.

The Police Band is a very sensitive highly trained and ruggedly anti-Communist unit whose efficacy will be demonstrated in due time, the Commissioner said to the Mayor (the old Mayor). The Mayor took a little pill from a little box and said, We'll see. He could tell we were musicians because we were holding our instruments, right? Emptying spit valves, giving the horn that little shake. Or coming in at letter E with some sly emotion stolen from another life.

The old Commissioner's idea was essentially that if there was a disturbance on the city's streets—some ethnic group cutting up some other ethnic group on a warm August evening—the Police Band would be sent in. The handsome dark-green band bus arriving with sirens singing, red lights whirling. Hard-pressed men on the beat in their white hats raising a grateful cheer. We stream out of the vehicle holding our instruments at high port. A skirmish line fronting the angry crowd. And play "Perdido." The crowd washed with new and true emotion. Startled, they listen. Our emotion stronger than their emotion. A triumph of art over good sense.

That was the idea. The old Commissioner's *musical* ideas were not very interesting, because after all he was a cop, right? But his police ideas were interesting.

We had drills. Poured out of that mother-loving bus onto vacant lots holding our instruments at high port like John Wayne. Felt we were heroes already. Playing "Perdido,"

Reprinted with the permission of Farrar, Straus & Giroux, Inc. From *Unspeakable Practices, Unnatural Acts* by Donald Barthelme, copyright © 1964, 1966 by Donald Barthelme. These selections originally appeared in *The New Yorker*.

1. **Steve Canyon,** a famous pilot in the comic strip by the same name.

"Stumblin'," "Gin Song," "Feebles." Laving[2] the terrain with emotion stolen from old busted-up loves, broken marriages, the needle, economic deprivation. A few old ladies leaning out of high windows. Our emotion washing rusty Rheingold cans and parts of old doors.

This city is too much! We'd be walking down the street talking about our techniques and we'd see out of our eyes a woman standing in the gutter screaming to herself about what we could not imagine. A drunk trying to strangle a dog somebody'd left leashed to a parking meter. The drunk and the dog screaming at each other. This city is too much!

We had drills and drills. It is true that the best musicians come from Detroit but there is something here that you have to get in your playing and that is simply the scream. We got that. The Commissioner, a sixty-three-year-old hippie with no doubt many graft qualities and unpleasant qualities, nevertheless understood that. When we'd play "ugly," he understood that. He understood the rising expectations of the world's peoples also. That our black members didn't feel like toting junk mail around Detroit forever until the ends of their lives. For some strange reason.

He said one of our functions would be to be sent out to play in places where people were trembling with fear inside their houses, right? To inspirit them in difficult times. This was the plan. We set up in the street. Henry Wang grabs hold of his instrument. He has a four-bar lead-in all by himself. Then the whole group. The iron shutters raised a few inches. Shorty Alanio holding his horn at his characteristic angle (sideways). The reeds dropping lacy little fill-ins behind him. We're cooking. The crowd roars.

The Police Band was an idea of a very romantic kind. The Police Band was an idea that didn't work. When they retired the old Commissioner (our Commissioner), who it turned out had a little drug problem of his own, they didn't let us even drill anymore. We

have never been used. His idea was a romantic idea, they said (right?), which was not adequate to the rage currently around in the world. Rage must be met with rage, they said. (Not in so many words.) We sit around the precinct houses, under the filthy lights, talking about our techniques. But I thought it might be good if you knew that the Department still has us. We have a good group. We still have emotion to be used. We're still here.

I
THE WRITER AS CONSCIENCE

One respect in which contemporary writers do *not* differ from their literary predecessors is in playing the role of social conscience. America has always been considered the land of equality, yet Richard Brautigan clearly implies that he believes we have not lived up to that ideal. Merwin criticizes us for what we are doing to our bodies through the food we eat. Donald Barthelme is critical of the way we have dealt with violence in our cities. Are these special problems of contemporary American life only or have they been with us for some time? And why should writers feel that they need to speak as consciences? Why don't they assume that all of us have consciences?

II
IMPLICATIONS

Can you name the prose sketch in which each of the following propositions is implicitly or explicitly stated? What is the writer's opinion on the matter, and why do you agree or disagree?

1. There is virtually no limit to what America can do.

2. One has to fight fire with fire.

3. Artists are impractical people, never problem solvers.

4. American advertisers have "sold" us poor health.

5. Americans worship success and turn their back on failure.

6. The pace of American life is so fast that we do not have time to think about the consequences of what we do.

7. When there is a strong contrast between what a people or a nation says it believes in and what it does, youth may become cynical.

---

2. **laving** \ lāv·iŋ\ washing.

Journeys into the Self

In this section, four poets and one prose writer
invite us to share with them their explorations of
inner realities. The first journey
is by a native Midwesterner, David Young,
who was drawn back to explore what he saw
as the "spiritual emptiness" of his roots.

West of Omaha, Surprised by Fear

Driving into these plains
I tremble and squint, not
wanting to see the terrible white
grain elevators, fertilizer spheres,
the dry stone horizon.   5

Instead I imagine
bats flipping through aspen groves
in mountain twilight
or the lemon air of certain
harbors and beaches.   10

But it is no good. The urge
to return, to explore
this spiritual emptiness
invades the dawn gas
and the evening gas.   15

It means the time has come
to travel the level prairies
of Nebraska and Wyoming;
truck doors swing open inside me
revealing terrible loads.   20

Desperate I try to recall
pine slopes, red cliffs,
thickets, rockheaps, junkpiles, ravines,
the green teeth of the sea,
but I can't. . . .   25

Catamounts,[1] stepping delicately,
from the line of mountains
three hundred miles away,
walk with burning eyes
in the flat center of my life.   30
DAVID P. YOUNG

---

1. **catamount** \\ˈkat ə'maunt\\ cougar or lynx.

Reprinted from *Sweating Out the Winter* by David P. Young.
By permission of University of Pittsburgh Press. © 1969 by
University of Pittsburgh Press.

Possibly one reason why many people
resist the inward journey
is fear that they will discover that there is
nothing special about them.
Is that what this poet is saying?
Is it *all* that she is saying?

(the thirty eighth year)

the thirty eighth year
of my life,
plain as bread
round as a cake
an ordinary woman.   5

an ordinary woman.

i had expected to be
smaller than this,
more beautiful,
wiser in Afrikan ways,   10
more confident,
i had expected
more than this.

i will be forty soon.
my mother once was forty.   15

my mother died at forty four,
a woman of sad countenance
leaving behind a girl
awkward as a stork.
my mother was thick,   20
her hair was a jungle and
she was very wise
and beautiful
and sad.

i have dreamed dreams   25
for you mama
more than once.
i have wrapped me
in your skin

and made you live again   30
more than once.
i have taken the bones you hardened
and built daughters
and they blossom and promise fruit
like Afrikan trees.   35
i am a woman now.
an ordinary woman.

in the thirty eighth
year of my life,
surrounded by life,   40
a perfect picture of
blackness blessed,
i had not expected this
loneliness.

if it is western,   45
if it is the final
Europe of my mind,
if in the middle of my life
i am turning the final turn
into the shining dark   50
let me come to it whole
and holy
not afraid
not lonely
out of my mother's life   55
into my own.
into my own.

i had expected more than this.
i had not expected to be
an ordinary woman.   60

"the 38th year" by Lucille Clifton. From *An Ordinary Woman* by Lucille Clifton. Copyright © 1974 by Lucille Clifton. Reprinted by permission of Random House, Inc.

LUCILLE CLIFTON

Have you ever been told by someone else,
"That's not the *real* you"? If you have,
you should be interested in this poem about the inner self.
Note that Simic's treatment of
inner reality is partly humorous.

Inner Man

It isn't the body
That's a stranger.
It's someone else.

We poke the same
Ugly mug   5
At the world.
When I scratch
He scratches too.

There are women
Who claim to have held him.   10
A dog
Follows me about.
It might be his.

If I'm quiet, he's quieter.
So I forget him.   15
Yet, as I bend down
To tie my shoelaces,
He's standing up.

We cast a single shadow.
Whose shadow?   20

I'd like to say:
"He was in the beginning
And he'll be in the end,"
But one can't be sure.

At night   25
As I sit
Shuffling the cards of our silence,
I say to him:

"Though you utter
Every one of my words,   30
You are a stranger.
It's time you spoke."

CHARLES SIMIC

From *Somewhere Among Us a Stone Is Taking Notes* by Charles Simic, *Kayak Magazine.* Copyright 1969 by Charles Simic.

I

ON THE NATURE OF BEING

In their differing ways and manners, each of the poems you have just read is concerned with discovering or revealing a fundamental inner reality. Young believes that he cannot know himself fully unless he can face the territory of his origin, however terrifying that confrontation may be. Clifton suggests that part of her inner landscape is the recognition that she is an ordinary woman, related somehow to her mother. Simic feels that there is a reality within himself that he barely knows, and he bids it to speak. And Warren draws a portrait of a man on the edge of the silence between night and day, wondering where his true being lies.

Unlike philosophers, who attempt intellectual answers to questions about the nature of reality, and psychologists, who try to arrive at answers on the basis of experiments, poets dramatize their experiences in words and images. Which of the poems did you like best? Did you learn from it something about yourself of which you had not been aware?

If you have ever awakened before the birds,
just before dawn, you have been in that
undefined place between night and day.
It is a time that might well
provoke one to wonder which is more real:
the waking self or the dreaming self?

First Dawn Light

By lines fainter gray than the faintest geometry
Of chalk on a wall like a blackboard, first light
Defines the window edges. Last dream, last owl-cry
Now past, now is the true emptiness of night.

For not yet first bird-stir, first bird-note, only   5
Your breath as you wonder what daylight will bring—and you try
To recall what the last dream was, and think how lonely
In sun-blaze you have seen the buzzard hang black in the sky.

For day has its loneliness, too, you think, even as
First bird-stir does come, first twitter, faithless and fearful   10
That new night, in the deep leaves, may lurk. So silence has
Returned. Then, sudden, the glory, heart-full and ear-full,

For triggered now is the mysterious mechanism
Of the forest's joy, and yours, by temperature or beam,
And until a sludge-thumb smears the sunset's prism,   15
You must wait to resume, in night's black hood, the reality of dream.

ROBERT PENN WARREN

Originally appeared in *The New Yorker*, April 4, 1977.

II
IMPLICATION

Be prepared to comment on the following:

1. There is an inner urge toward self-knowledge that cannot successfully be denied.

2. People cannot know themselves without full awareness of their geographical roots.

3. Knowing one's parents is an important aspect of knowing oneself.

4. We are all ordinary women and men.

5. The self that dreams is a truer and more real self than the daytime self.

III
TECHNIQUES

Symbolism

Be prepared to comment on the symbolic significance of each of the following:

1. "Catamounts . . . walk with burning eyes/in the flat center of my life."

2. "if it is western,/if it is the final/Europe of my mind. . . ."

3. "As I sit/Shuffling the cards of our silence. . . ."

4. ". . . you have seen the buzzard hang black in the sky."

What do you do when you go on a journey? Do you plan everything in advance? Do you take along a map with the shortest route marked by a felt-tipped pen? Do you worry about getting lost? Most of us would probably answer "yes" to most of these questions. That may be why many readers find the following sketch a little unsettling, a little unnerving.

Journey

JOYCE CAROL OATES

You begin your journey on so high an elevation that your destination is already in sight—a city that you have visited many times and that, moreover, is indicated on a traveler's map you have carefully folded up to take along with you. You are a lover of maps, and you have already committed this map to memory, but you bring it with you just the same.

The highway down from the mountains is broad and handsome, constructed after many years of ingenious blasting and leveling and paving. Engineers from all over the country aided in the construction of this famous highway. Its cost is so excessive that many rumors have circulated about it—you take no interest in such things, sensing that you will never learn the true cost anyway, and that this will make no difference to your journey.

After several hours on this excellent highway, where the sun shines ceaselessly and where there is a moderate amount of traffic, cars like your own at a safe distance from you, as if to assure you that there are other people in the world, you become sleepy from the monotony and wonder if perhaps there is another, less perfect road parallel to this. You discover on the map a smaller road, not exactly parallel to the highway and not as direct, but one that leads to the same city.

You turn onto this road, which winds among foothills and forests and goes through several small villages. You sense by the attitude of the villagers that traffic on this road is infrequent but nothing to draw special attention. At some curves the road shrinks, but you are fortunate enough to meet no oncoming traffic.

The road leads deep into a forest, always descending in small cramped turns. Your turning from left to right and from right to left, in a slow hypnotic passage, makes it impossible for you to look out at the forest. You discover that for some time you have not been able to see the city you are headed for, though you know it is still somewhere ahead of you.

By mid-afternoon you are tired of this road, though it has served you well, and you come upon a smaller, unpaved road that evidently leads to your city, though in a convoluted way. After only a moment's pause you turn onto this road, and immediately your automobile registers the change—the chassis bounces, something begins to vibrate, something begins to rattle. This noise is disturbing, but after a while you forget about it in your interest in the beautiful countryside. Here the trees are enormous. There are no villages or houses. For a while the dirt road runs alongside a small river, dangerously close to the river's steep bank, and you begin to feel apprehension. It is necessary for you to drive very slowly. At times your speedometer registers less than five miles an hour. You will not get to the city before dark.

The road narrows until it is hardly more than

Reprinted from *The Poisoned Kiss* by Fernandes/Joyce Carol Oates by permission of the publisher, Vanguard Press, Inc. Copyright © 1975, 1974, 1972, 1971 by Joyce Carol Oates.

a lane. Grass has begun to grow in its center. As the river twists and turns, so does the road twist and turn, curving around hills that consist of enormous boulders, bare of all trees and plants, covered only in patches by a dull, brown lichen that is unfamiliar to you. Along one stretch rocks of varying sizes have fallen down onto the road, so that you are forced to drive around them with great caution.

Navigating these blind turns, you tap your horn to give warning in case someone should be approaching. But it is all unnecessary, since you come upon no other travelers.

Late in the afternoon, your foot numb from its constant pressure on the accelerator, your body jolted by the constant bumps and vibrations of the car, you decide to make the rest of your journey on foot, since you must be close to your destination by now.

A faint path leads through a tumble of rocks and bushes and trees, and you follow it enthusiastically. You descend a hill, slipping a little, so that a small rockslide is released; but you are able to keep your balance. At the back of your head is the precise location of your parked car, and behind that the curving dirt road, and behind that the other road, and then the magnificent highway itself: you understand that it would be no difficult feat to make your way back to any of these roads, should you decide that going by foot is unwise. But the path, though overgrown, is through a lovely forest, and then through a meadow in which yellow flowers are blooming, and you feel no inclination to turn back.

By evening you are still in the wilderness and you wonder if perhaps you have made a mistake. You are exhausted, your body aches, your eyes are seared by the need to stare so intently at everything around you. Now that the sun has nearly set, it is getting cold; evenings here in the mountains are always chilly.

You find yourself standing at the edge of a forest, staring ahead into the dark. Is that a field ahead, or a forest of small trees? Your path has long since given way to wild grass.

Clouds obscure the moon, which should give you some light by which to make your way, and you wonder if you dare continue without this light.

Suddenly you remember the map you left back in the car, but you remember it as a blank sheet of paper.

You resist telling yourself you are lost. In fact, though you are exhausted and it is almost night, you are not lost. You have begun to shiver, but it is only with cold, not with fear. You are really satisfied with yourself. You are not lost. Though you can remember your map only as a blank sheet of paper, which can tell you nothing, you are not really lost.

If you had the day to begin again, on that highway which was so wide and clear, you would not have varied your journey in any way: in this is your triumph.

I

EMOTIONS AND THE MIND

Although "Journey" mystifies many readers at first, few escape emotional involvement in the story. One might almost say that though the mind does not know what is happening in the story, the emotions do.

Sometimes it is enough that we have been entertained or emotionally involved by a story. We do not need to know—we may not even want to know—what it "means." But at other times we may feel unsatisfied with a story unless we can discover why it has moved us. In such cases, readers can ask such questions as, "When have I felt like this before?" and "What kinds of things or experiences in my past have led to the same or similar emotions?" If we can find answers to such questions, we can reread the story to gain intellectual insight as well as emotional enjoyment.

II

IMPLICATIONS

In a story as short as this, you can be fairly certain that each detail counts for something. Explain the significance of as many of the following details as you can.

1. You are a lover of maps.

2. On the big highway cars "like your own" travel "at a safe distance" from you.

3. The second road leads deep into a forest, but you cannot look at it.

4. On the third road there are no villages or houses.

5. You remember the map as a blank sheet of paper.

III
TECHNIQUES

Structure

Short as it is, this story is very highly structured, especially with respect to several progressions that flow through it. For example, the "you" in the story goes from a first-rate highway to a curving paved road, to an unpaved dirt road, to a faint path, to no path at all. Another progression is a movement from the familiar to the unfamiliar. Still another begins with "sleepy from the monotony." What are the other steps in this progression? How does it end? What other progressions, if any, can you trace?

Symbolism

How can you decide whether or not this story should be interpreted symbolically? For one thing you might observe that "you" has no name and no background. Notice that the mountain and the city are also nameless; in fact, there isn't a single proper name in the whole story. In short it is not the things and person that are important but what they stand for.

What, in your opinion, does the journey of "you" symbolize? What other details can be interpreted symbolically? How does your tracing of the progressions in the story help you to see its symbolic import?

BIOGRAPHICAL NOTES

Anne Tyler

Born in Minneapolis, Minnesota, Anne Tyler (1941–   ) studied Russian at Duke University and Columbia. She finished her first novel while she was still in her early twenties. Since then, she has written six others, including *Celestial Navigation, Searching for Caleb*, and her latest, *Earthly Possessions* (1977). Tyler has said that she writes because she wants to live other lives—"I've never quite believed that one chance is all I get."

Gail Dusenbery

Gail Dusenbery (1939–   ) was born in Albany, New York, and attended Cornell University and the University of California at Berkeley. Her first book of poetry, *The Mark*, was published in 1967.

John Updike

Originally, John Updike (1932–   ), who was born in Shillington, Pennsylvania, wanted to be a poet or a painter. But he turned mainly to the writing of prose fiction after the appearance of his first novel, *The Poorhouse Fair*, in 1959. Since then, he has published over half a dozen other novels plus collections of his short stories from *The New Yorker*.

C. K. Williams

C. K. Williams (1936–   ) was born in Newark, New Jersey, and educated at Bucknell and the University of Pennsylvania. He received a Guggenheim Fellowship in 1974 and has been a contributing editor for *American Poetry Review*. Among his books are *A Day for Anne Frank, Lie*, and *I Am the Bitter Name*.

Diane Wakoski

Born in Whittier, California, Diane Wakoski (1937–   ) received her degree from the University of California. She taught English in a junior high school in New York, was a lecturer at the New School for Social Research, and has been a poet-in-residence at various universities. Among her many volumes of poetry are *Inside the Blood Factory, Thanking My Mother for Piano Lessons*, and *Smudging*.

Richard Brautigan

Richard Brautigan (1933–   ) was born in the Pacific Northwest. Although he did not himself attend college, he is an extremely popular reader on American college campuses today. His most recent novels are *The Hawkline Monster: A Gothic Western* and *Willard and His Bowling Trophy: A Perverse Mystery*, both published in 1975. Some of his works have been recorded by Columbia Records.

W. S. Merwin

One of the most highly respected of all contemporary American poets, W. S. Merwin (1927–   ) is also well known as a translator and, more recently, as a writer of prose. Born in New York City, he grew up in Union City, New Jersey, and Scranton, Pennsylvania. After graduating from Princeton, he spent much of his life abroad. His first book of poems, *A Mask for Janus*, was the 1952 selection of the Yale Series of Younger Poets. In 1971 he won the Pulitzer Prize for Poetry for *The Carrier of Ladders*.

Donald Barthelme

Donald Barthelme (1931–   ) was born in Philadelphia, Pennsylvania, but grew up in Texas and studied at the University of Houston. He has written two novels, *Snow White* and *The Dead Father*, and a book for children, *The Slightly Irregular Fire Engine*. He is probably best known, however, for the sketches that he regularly contributes to *The New Yorker*, which he has collected and published under such titles as *Come Back, Dr. Caligari, City Life*, and *Sadness*.

David Young

Born in Davenport, Iowa, David Young (1936–   ) earned his Ph.D. at Yale University in 1965. He has taught at Oberlin College, Ohio, since 1961. He is an editor and has done translations and literary criticism in addition to his poetry. His two collections of poetry are *Sweating Out the Winter* (1968) and *Boxcars* (1973).

Lucille Clifton

Lucille Clifton (1936–   ) was born in Depew, New York, and was educated at Howard University and Fredonia State Teachers College. The author of several children's books, her volumes of poetry to date are *Good Times, Good News about the Earth*, and *An Ordinary Woman*.

Charles Simic

Born in Yugoslavia, Charles Simic (1938–   ) emigrated to the United States in 1949 and was educated at New York University. He now teaches at the college level. Known for numerous translations of French, Russian, and Yugoslav poetry, Simic has published five volumes of his own poetry since 1967. His most recent volume, published in 1974, is *Return to a Place Lit by a Glass of Milk*.

Robert Penn Warren

Robert Penn Warren (1905–   ), born in Guthrie, Kentucky, is one of the best-known literary figures of the twentieth century. He has written excellent literary criticism and (with Cleanth Brooks) two of the most influential textbooks of our time—*Understanding Poetry* and *Understanding Fiction*. In 1947 he won the Pulitzer Prize for Fiction for his novel, *All the King's Men*. Then, in 1958, he won the Pulitzer Prize for Poetry for *Promises*.

Joyce Carol Oates

Joyce Carol Oates (1938–   ) was born in Lockport, New York, and is an acknowledged master of the modern short story. She has also written many novels, including *Them*, which won the National Book Award in 1970. Her most recent collection of stories is *Night-Side* (1977).

Glossary of Literary Terms

Definitions given here refer only to the meaning of the word as related to works of literature.

Alliteration: The repetition of consonants, particularly initial consonants with the same sound, in a line of poetry. Here is an example from Millay's "Renascence": "The *s*oul can *s*plit the *s*ky in two."

Assonance: Identity of vowel sounds, as in dr*ea*m and t*ea*ch.

Atmosphere: The overall mood or emotional aura of a literary work. Atmosphere is created by the handling of such elements as setting, character, and theme. It is often described by the same adjectives we would use to describe the weather: "gloomy," "cheerful," "threatening," "tranquil," and the like. Also see the terms *setting* and *tone*.

Blank Verse: Unrhymed verse with five iambic feet to the line, as in Frost's "Birches": "Whĕn Í sĕe bír chĕs bĕnd tŏ léft ănd ríght." The accents may not always be quite as regular as this, but there will always be five per line.

Characterization: The means used by a writer to show what his or her characters are like. These means may include (1) direct description, (2) presentation of the character in action, (3) presentation of the thoughts of the character, (4) comparison of one character with another, and (5) reactions to or discussions of the character by other characters.

Climax: The point in a narrative at which the conflict reaches its highest intensity. The reader's emotional response is likely to be greatest at this point.

Comedy: A work of literature that (1) ends happily and (2) aims primarily to amuse.

Confessional Poetry: Poetry grounded in painful and relatively private areas of the author's own experience. A crisis of identity is often at its core. Among the best-known confessional poets are Robert Lowell, Allen Ginsberg, Sylvia Plath, Anne Sexton, and W. D. Snodgrass.

Conflict: A struggle between two opposed forces in a plot. One of the forces is the *protagonist*, or hero. He or she may be in conflict with another person (often referred to as the *antagonist*), with forces within him- or herself, with society, or with nature. Often, more than one of these conflicts may be present in the same plot.

Consonance: Identity of the pattern of consonants within words, as in *"loves"* and *"loaves."*

End-stopped Line: A line in a poem whose end coincides with a normal speech pause. Such lines typically conclude with a mark of punctuation. A line that does not end with a normal speech pause is called a *run-on line*.

Fable: A brief tale told to stress a moral. The characters in fables are most frequently animals, though they may speak and act like people.

Figurative Language: Any intentional departure from the everyday use of language in order to gain strength or freshness of expression, create a pictorial or other sense impression, or convey ideas through comparisons. (See *Metaphor* below.)

Flashback: A device used by an author to present scenes or incidents that occurred prior to the opening of a story or novel.

Foreshadowing: A hint or suggestion at something that will occur later on in a narrative.

Free Verse: Verse that does not conform to any fixed metrical pattern. Whitman wrote in free verse, and most of the poems in our New Directions section are also in free verse.

Hero: The chief character in a literary work. Since a hero need not be heroic, heroes are often referred to instead by the term *protagonist*.

Humor: A type of writing whose purpose is to make the reader laugh. Humor is sympathetic and tolerant, as opposed to *wit* (see below).

Image: The representation, usually in poetry, of a sensory experience, which evokes emotion in the reader.

Intention: The effect or the meaning that the writer wished the work to have. We typically discover intention, however, not from direct statements by the writer but rather from inferences we make from the work itself.

Irony: A contrast, usually between what is expected and what turns out or between what is said and what is meant. It is ironic, for instance, that in Crane's "The Bride Comes to Yellow Sky," the man with the gun loses the duel to the man who is unarmed.

Local Color: (See *Regionalism*.)

Lyric Poem: A poem with a single speaker who expresses her or his feelings about a subject.

Metaphor: An implied comparison between two unlike things. When Anne Sexton calls her child's ribs, "those delicate trees," she creates a metaphor. (See page 391.) Metaphor is closely allied to *simile*, which is a stated comparison—generally introduced by "like" or "as"—between two things. If Sexton had written, "Your ribs are like trees," she would have written a simile. Both metaphor and simile are figures of speech.

Meter: (See *Rhythm*.)

Moment of Illumination: The moment in a story at which its full meaning becomes clear. At such moments, all the parts of the story fit into place, and the reader sees the unity of the whole.

Narrative Poem: A poem that tells a story.

Naturalism: See "American Literature, 1900–1930: The Premodern Period," p. 435.

Onomatopoeia: A word that sounds like or imitates the thing to which it refers, such as *moo, buzz, snap.*

Personification: The endowment of inanimate objects or ideas with human qualities.

Plot: A planned series of actions based on a conflict moving from a beginning through a logically related sequence to a logical and natural outcome.

Point of View: The person through whose eyes and mind the reader sees the story. In first-person point of view, the teller will be "I," a character (major or minor) in the work. In third-person point of view, the teller will be the author. If the author allows him- or herself great freedom to reveal the thoughts, motives, etc., of many characters, we refer to an *omniscient* (all-knowing) point of view. In most modern fiction, the point of view in third person will be *limited.* See for example Anne Tyler's "Average Waves," where we enter the mind of the main character but of no one else.

Protagonist: (See *Hero.*)

Quatrain: A unit or stanza in poetry consisting of four lines.

Realism: See "American Literature, 1865–1900: The Realistic Period," p. 300.

Regionalism: A quality in literature of accurately portraying a particular geographical section. The term may be used interchangeably with *local-color* writing, but sometimes the latter term has a narrower and less favorable connotation, as though the local colorist were interested in the region mainly for its oddities. William Faulkner and Willa Cather were both regionalists.

Rhyme: Repetition of similar or identical accented vowels and all following consonants and vowels occurring at the end of lines of poetry. Rhyme that occurs elsewhere is usually called *internal rhyme.*

Rhyme scheme: The pattern, or sequence, in which the rhyme sounds occur in a stanza or poem. In the first stanza of Robinson's "Richard Cory," for example, the first and third and the second and fourth lines rhyme. This rhyme scheme would be represented as *abab.*

Rhythm: In poetry, the pattern of accented, or stressed, and unaccented, or unstressed, syllables. This is also referred to as *meter.* See *Blank Verse* above for a specific example of a line whose rhythm has been indicated.

Romanticism: See "American Literature, 1865–1900: The Realistic Period," p. 300.

Satire: A literary manner or a literary work which uses wit or humor to criticize humanity or human institutions with the hope of improving them.

Setting: The time and the place—and often the atmosphere—of a literary work.

Simile: (See *Metaphor.*)

Sonnet: A lyric poem of fourteen lines, usually also with subdivisions, following one or another of several set rhyme schemes.

Structure: In general, the planned framework of any work of literature. In the analysis of structure one looks for how the parts are related to one another and to the work as a whole.

Style: The selection and arrangement of words that best expresses the individuality of the author and the idea or intention in her or his mind.

Suspense: The anticipation of the reader regarding the outcome of the events in a work of literature. Suspense may focus on questions of who, what, how, or when.

Symbol: An object, character, or incident that suggests something else. In a given work, for example, the sun might symbolize clarity of vision, or a character might stand as a Christ symbol.

Sympathy and Detachment: The "distance" between character and author or character and reader. If we feel close to a character, we are sympathic; we identify with him or her. If we stand apart from a character, we speak of ourselves as "detached"; we tend to be observers of her or him.

Tall Tale: A simple, humorous narrative using realistic details and common speech to relate extravagant happenings. The main character of a tall tale is often a superhuman figure.

Tension: An unsettled state induced in the reader at or near the beginning of a literary work. Generally, a work of literature moves from tension to relaxation, from relative instability to relative stability.

Theme: The generalized "point" or meaning of a work of literature or its central idea. In nonfiction, the theme may be a particular *thesis*; that is, an attitude or position taken by the author with the intent of proving or supporting it.

Tone: A writer's attitude toward his or her subject and toward his or her audience. Tone is described by such adjectives as "dignified," "sarcastic," "informal," "jovial," and "condescending." To appreciate the difference between tone and atmosphere, compare these adjectives with those listed under *Atmosphere* above.

Transcendentalism: See "American Literature, 1830–1865: The Classical Period," p. 188.

Understatement: The saying of less than what one truly means or the representation of something as less than it is in fact. Understatement is a form of *irony*; it is the opposite of *exaggeration* or overstating one's meaning.

Wit: A type of writing whose purpose is to make the reader laugh. It is primarily intellectual and unsympathetic toward its subject. It is also rapid, sharp, and incisive. A good illustration would be Josh Billings's advice, "Remember the poor—it costs nothing."

Glossary

This glossary contains difficult words which are not in the vocabularies of average eleventh-grade students. The definitions apply to the uses of words in this text. For more complete study of the range of meanings for these words, the student must consult a dictionary.

Pronunciation Guide

A key to the pronunciation symbols is given at the bottom of every other page. By consulting the most recent dictionaries, the student may notice that the symbols here represent a series of compromises between current scholarly interpretations of sounds and less precise symbols which continue to have wide acceptance. A few minutes' study of the pronunciation key before using this glossary will make it possible for the student to use the pronunciation transcriptions with the greatest ease and efficiency.

The same key is used for pronunciations given here and in the footnotes. Foreign terms and names are transcribed so as to be acceptable in standard American speech rather than precise in terms of their original languages.

Accent marks precede the stressed syllables. The mark ◆ indicates the heaviest stress and the mark ' indicates an intermediate stress as needed.

Abbreviations indicate parts of speech and special spellings. The following are used:

n.	noun
v.	verb
adj.	adjective
adv.	adverb

a·bash\ ə ◆băsh\ v. To make ashamed and uneasy, embarrassed and confused.

abey·ance\ə ◆bā·əns\ n. Temporary inactivity.

ab·jure\ăb ◆jūr\ v. To reject solemnly.

ab·ste·mi·ous\ăb ◆stē·mē·əs\ adj. Sparing (especially in eating and drinking).

ac·cli·màte\◆ăk·lə·māt\ v. To adapt to a new temperature, altitude, climate, or situation.

ac·cliv·i·ty\ə ◆klĭv·ə·tē\ n. An upward slope.

ac·cou·ter·ment\ə ◆kū·tər·mənt\ n. Equipment or accessories of a soldier other than arms and uniform.

ac·qui·es·cent\'ăk·wē ◆es·ənt\ adj. Disposed to yield, accept, or comply passively.

ac·ri·mo·ni·ous·ly\'ăk·rə ◆mō·nē·əs·lē\ adv. In a sharp or bitter manner.

a·cute\ə ◆kyūt\ adj. Severe and sharp.

adren·a·line\ə ◆drē·nə·lən\ n. A secretion of the adrenal gland that acts as a stimulator.

ad·ven·ti·tious\'ăd·vən ◆tish·əs\ adj. Accidentally acquired.

ad·vert\ăd ◆vərt\ v. To direct attention, refer to.

af·front\ə ◆frənt\ v. To insult openly.

ag·gre·ga·tion\'ăg·rə ◆ga·shən\ n. A group or mass of distinct things or individuals.

ague\◆ā·gyū\ n. A fever (such as malaria) marked by fits of shivering and sweating that recur at regular intervals.

al·lay\ə ◆lā\ v. To put fears to rest, calm.

al·ter·ca·tion\'al·tər ◆kā·shən\ n. A noisy or angry dispute often ending in blows.

al·ve·o·lar\ăl ◆vē·ə·lər\ adj. Relating to the part of jaws where the teeth arise.

am·big·u·ous\ăm ◆bĭ·gū·əs\ adj. Having a double meaning.

a·mi·a·ble\◆ā·mē·ə·bəl\ adj. Having a pleasant disposition, friendly.

anath·e·ma\ə ◆nă·thə·mə\ n. One who is cursed and denounced by the church.

an·i·mos·i·ty\'ă·nə ◆mŏ·sə·tē\ n. Intense ill will that threatens to become hostility.

an·nu·i·ty\ə ◆nū·ə·tē\ n. An income paid yearly or at other regular intervals.

anom·a·lous\ə ◆nŏ·mə·ləs\ adj. Irregular, abnormal.

an·o·nym·i·ty\'ă·nə ◆nĭ·mə·tē\ n. The quality of lacking individuality or personality.

ap·o·gee\◆ăp·ə·jē\ n. The highest or farthest point.

ap·pel·la·tion\'ăp·ə ◆lā·shən\ n. An identifying name or title.

ap·pend\ə ◆pĕnd\ v. To add as a supplement.

ap·prise\ə ◆praiz\ v. To give notice to.

ar·bi·trary\◆ŏr·bə 'trĕ·rē\ adj. Selected at random and without reason, subject to individual will or judgment.

ar·du·ous\◆ar·jū·əs\ adj. Difficult, strenuous.

arid·i·ty\ə ◆rĭ·də·tē\ n. Insufficient rainfall, dryness.

ar·rears\ə ◆rĭrz\ n. *plural.* Unfinished duties, state of being behind in discharge of obligations.

ar·ti·fice\◆ŏr·tə·fəs\ n. Guile or clever trickery, ingenuity.

askance\ə ◆skăns\ adv. With disapproval or distrust.

as·sim·i·late\ə ◆sĭ·mə·lāt\ v. To take into body or mind as nourishment, absorb.

as·suage\ə ◆swāj\ v. To ease.

as·tral\◆ăs·trəl\ adj. Of or relating to the stars.

ă bad, ā bake, a father, ĕ sell, ē equal, ai mile, ĭ sit, ŏ cot, ō note, ɔ law, ū boom, ʊ wood, yū you, yʊ fury, aʊ cow, ɔi boy. The schwa is used for both stressed and unstressed sounds: ə mud, word, even; ch chase, itch; sh shell, wish; th path, thin; th the, either; ŋ wing; w wet, wheat; zh pleasure.

at·a·vism\ătə 'vĭzəm\ n. State of reversion to a primitive ancestral type, a throwback.

at·taint\ə ᵃtānt\ v. To infect, corrupt, disgrace.

au·re·o·la\ɔ ᵃrē·ə·lə\ n. Bright light seen through mist.

au·ro·ral\a ᵃrō·rəl\ adj. Pertaining to the dawn.

av·o·ca·tion\ᵃə·və ᵃkā·shən\ n. An occasional occupation or hobby.

bale·ful\bāl·fəl\ adj. Deadly, ominous, sinister.

bas·re·lief\'ba·rĭ ᵃlēf\ n. A type of sculpture in which figures project slightly from the background surface.

be·foul\bĭ ᵃfaul\ v. To make foul with dirt or filth.

be·gird\bĭ ᵃgərd\ v. To encompass with a band.

be·hold·en\bĭ ᵃhōl·dən\ adj. Indebted, obligated.

bel·dame\bĕl·dəm\ n. An ugly old woman, a hag.

be·night·ed\bĭ ᵃnai·təd\ adj. Overtaken by darkness.

be·nign\bĭ ᵃnain\ adj. Showing gentleness or kindness.

be·reft\bĭ ᵃrĕft\ v. Deprived of.

be·sot·ted\bĭ ᵃso·təd\ adj. Foolish, stupid, muddled.

bes·tial\bĕs·chəl\ adj. Resembling a beast.

be·to·ken\bĭ ᵃtō·kĕn\ v. To give evidence of, foreshadow.

bi·be·lot\bĭb·lō\ n. A small, decorative, and often rare trinket.

bib·u·lous\bĭ·byə·ləs\ adj. Inclined to drink.

bit·tern\bĭ·tərn\ n. A heron with a characteristic screaming cry.

blanch\blănch\ v. To turn pale in the face.

blas·phe·my\blăs·fə·mē\ n. Vulgar speaking of God or sacred persons or things.

bla·tant\blā·tənt\ adj. Offensively loud or noisy.

blithe\blīth\ adj. Gay, joyful, cheerful.

bo·he·mi·an\bō ᵃhē·mē·ən\ adj. Unconventional.

bought·en\bɔ·tən\ adj. *dialect.* Bought at a store.

brack·en\bră·kən\ n. A coarse, hardy fern (also called *brake*).

broach\brōch\ v. To open up a subject for discussion.

broil\brɔil\ n. An angry quarrel or struggle.

bouy·ant\bɔi·ənt *or* ᵃbū·ənt\ adj. Cheerful, gay.

bur·then\bər·thən\ n. *archaic.* Burden.

ca·dav·er·ous\kə ᵃdăv·rəs\ adj. Resembling a corpse.

cal·low\kă·lō\ adj. Inexperienced, immature.

can·ter\kăn·tər\ n. A moderate, easy gallop.

ca·price\kə ᵃprēs\ n. A sudden, impulsive change of mind without evident motivation.

cap·tious\kăp·shəs\ adj. Marked by a tendency to confuse or entangle in argument.

car·bun·cle\kɔr·bun·kəl\ n. A sore resembling a boil (only larger).

car·nal\kar·nəl\ adj. In or of the flesh, worldly, not spiritual.

carp\karp\ v. To find fault, complain unreasonably.

car·ri·on\kă·rē·ən\ n. Dead flesh.

cat·a·pult\kăt·ə 'pəlt\ n. An ancient weapon for propelling stones or arrows against an enemy or hostile fortifications.

cat·a·ract\kă·tə 'răkt\ n. 1. A clouding of the lens of the eye obstructing passage of light. 2. Figuratively, a growth that obstructs light.

cen·sure\sĕn·shər\ v. To blame, condemn as wrong.

cen·tri·fuge\sĕn·trə·fyūj\ n. A rotary machine that separates substances of different densities, a machine that simulates gravitational effects.

cer·ve·lat\sər·va 'lăt\ n. Smoked sausage made of pork and beef.

chat·tel\chăt·l\ n. An article of personal property, an item of movable property.

chi·me·ra\kai·mīr·ə\ n. An impossible or foolish fancy.

chit\chĭt\ n. A signed voucher of a small debt (as for food).

cinch\sĭnch\ n. A strong girth for a pack or saddle.

ci·pher\sai·fər\ v. To write in code in order to conceal meaning.

clav·i·cle\klă·vĭ·kəl\ n. A bone of the vertebrate shoulder.

clem·en·cy\klĕ·mən·sē\ n. Act of showing mercy.

clew\klū\ v. To haul a sail up or down by ropes through a metal loop attached to the lower corner of a sail.

clo·ven\klō·vən\ adj. Parted, split (alternative past participle of *cleave.* To split).

co·eval\kō ᵃē·vəl\ adj. Of the same age or time.

col·or·a·tu·ra\'kə·lə·rə ᵃtyu·rə\ n. Runs, trills, decoration (in vocal music).

com·mune\kə ᵃmyūn\ v. To talk intimately.

con·cil·i·ate\kən ᵃsĭ·lē·āt\ v. To gain goodwill by pleasing acts.

con·de·scend·ing\'kŏn·dĭ ᵃsĕn·dĭŋ\ adj. Gracious and patronizing to inferiors, lowering oneself.

con·fla·gra·tion\'kŏn·flə ᵃgrā·shən\ n. A large disastrous fire.

con·gre·ga·tion\'kŏŋ·grə ᵃgā·shən\ n. The membership of a particular place of worship.

con·jure\kŏn·jər\ v. To call on, appeal to solemnly.

con·nings\kŏn·iŋs\ n. Periods of learning and committing to memory.

con·sign·ment\kən ᵃsain·mənt\ n. Something transferred formally to another.

con·sort\kŏn ᵃsɔrt\ v. To keep company or associate with.

con·sum·mate\kən ᵃsu·mət *or* ᵃkən·su·mət\ adj. Of the highest degree or the greatest excellence.

con·sump·tion\kən ᵃsump·shən\ n. A progressive wasting away of the body (especially tuberculosis).

con·tem·pla·tion\'kŏn·təm ᵃplā·shən\ n. Thoughtful consideration or study.

con·tin·gent\kən ᵃtĭn·jənt\ n. A quota or share of persons representative of a group.

con·tort\kən ᵃtɔrt\ v. To twist violently.

con·tra·ri·ety\'kŏn·trə ᵃrai·ə·tē\ n. The quality of being opposed in purpose, incompatibility.

con·ven·ti·cle\kən ᵃvĕn·tĭ·kəl\ n. A meeting for religious worship (especially a secret one not sanctioned by law).

con·vo·lu·tion\'kŏn·və ᵃlū·shən\ n. One of the irregular ridges upon the surface of the brain.

co·quet·ry\kō·kə·trē\ n. Act of flirting or showing trifling attention.

cor·dial\kɔr·jəl\ adj. Warm and hearty.

cork·er\kɔr·kər\ n. *slang.* One that is excellent.

cor·nice\kɔr·nəs\ n. The molded projection at the top of a wall or building.

cor·po·re·al\kər ⁺pō·rē·əl\ adj. Relating to a physical body.

cos·mic\⁺kŏz·mĭk\ adj. Having to do with the whole universe.

cos·mog·ra·phy\kŏz ⁺mŏg·rə·fē\ n. Science that describes the order of the universe.

cov·ert\⁺kə·vərt or ⁺kō·vərt\ adj. Concealed, secret.

cox·comb\⁺kŏk·skōm\ n. A conceited, foolish person.

crux\krʊks or ⁺krəks\ n. 1. A vital point. 2. A baffling problem.

cryp·tic\⁺krĭp·tĭk\ adj. Having a hidden meaning.

cu·po·la\⁺kyū·pə·lə\ n. A rounded roof, dome.

cur·mudg·eon\kər ⁺mə·jən\ n. A gruff, irritable old man.

cur·ry\⁺kər·rē\ v. To arrange or dress the coat of a horse by combing and brushing.

cus·pid\⁺kəs·pəd\ n. A canine tooth.

cy·lin·dric\sə ⁺lĭn·drĭk\ adj. Having the shape of a cylinder.

dal·li·ance\⁺dă·lē·əns\ n. Romantic play, flirtation.

de·bauch\dĭ ⁺bŏch\ v. To lead astray morally, corrupt.

de·bouch\dĭ ⁺būsh\ v. To march out into open ground.

de·co·rum\dĭ ⁺kō·rəm\ n. Good taste in conduct and appearance.

def·er·ence\⁺def·rəns\ n. Respectful regard for another's wishes.

de·lin·ea·tion\dĭ 'lĭ·nē ⁺ā·shən\ n. The act of describing or tracing out graphically.

dem·a·gog·ic\'dĕ·mə ⁺gŏ·jĭk\ adj. Characteristic of a leader who makes false claims to gain power.

de·mo·ni·ac\dĭ ⁺mō·nē 'ăk\ n. A person regarded as possessed by a demon.

demur\dĭ ⁺mur\ v. To offer objections.

de·nun·ci·a·tion\dĭ 'nən·sē ⁺ā·shən\ n. An informing against someone to the authorities, accusation.

de·port·ment\dĭ ⁺pōrt·mənt\ n. The manner of conducting oneself.

dep·o·si·tion\'dĕ·pə 'zĭ·shən\ n. Written testimony of someone under oath.

dep·re·cate\⁺dĕp·rĭ 'kāt\ v. To express disapproval of.

dep·re·da·tion\'dĕp·rə ⁺dā·shən\ n. A plundering, a robbing.

dep·u·ta·tion\'dĕp·yū ⁺tā·shən\ n. A person or persons appointed to represent others.

des·e·crate\dĕ·sĭ 'krāt\ v. To treat irreverently or contemptuously.

des·ti·tute\⁺dĕs·tə 'tūt\ adj. Lacking something needed or desirable.

det·ri·ment\⁺dĕt·rə·mənt\ n. That which causes injury or danger.

di·a·bol·i·cal\'dai·ə ⁺bŏ·lĭ·kəl\ adj. Befitting the devil, fiendish.

di·a·dem\⁺dai·ə·dĕm\ n. A headband or crown worn as a symbol of royalty.

di·a·pa·son\'dai·ə ⁺pā·zən\ n. A full deep outburst of sound.

dif·fi·dence\⁺dĭ·fə·dənts\ n. Quality of being reserved, timid, or unassertive.

dif·fuse\dĭ ⁺fyūz\ v. To pour out and cause to spread freely.

di·lat·ed\dai ⁺lā·təd or ⁺dai·lā·təd\ adj. Expanded or made wider.

dil·et·tante\'dĭ·lə ⁺tan·tē\ n. One who interests himself in a subject merely for amusement, an amateur.

di·min·u·tive\dĭ ⁺mĭ·nyə·tĭv\ adj. Indicating small size.

dis·con·cert\dĭs·kən ⁺sərt\ v. To throw into confusion, disturb.

dis·en·fran·chise\'dĭ·sən ⁺frăn·chaiz\ v. To deprive of the right to vote.

dis·ha·bille\'dĭ·sə ⁺bĕl\ n. State of being loosely or carelessly dressed.

di·shev·eled\dĭ ⁺shĕ·vəld\ adj. Marked by disorder and loose arrangement (especially with hair disarranged).

dis·port\dĭs ⁺pōrt\ v. To frolic, amuse oneself.

dis·so·lute\⁺dĭ·sə 'lūt\ adj. Loose in morals or conduct.

dis·tend·ed\dĭs ⁺tĕnd·əd\ adj. Swollen, expanded.

dog·ged\dȯ·gəd\ adj. Stubbornly determined.

dot·age\⁺dō·tĭj\ n. A state of feeblemindedness (especially in old age).

droll\⁺drōl\ adj. Whimsical, humorous, odd.

duc·tile\⁺dək·təl\ adj. Easily fashioned into a new form, pliable.

ec·cen·tric·i·ty\'ĕk 'sĕn ⁺trĭ·sə·tē\ n. A deviation from established pattern, rule, or norm.

ef·fem·i·nate\ə ⁺fē·mə·nĭt\ adj. Having womanlike qualities.

ef·fete\ĕ ⁺fēt\ adj. Worn out with age.

ef·fron·tery\ĭ ⁺frən·tə·rē\ n. Shameless boldness.

e·gre·gious\ĭ ⁺grē·jəs\ adj. Outstanding for undesirable qualities, remarkably bad.

em·a·nate\⁺ĕm·ə 'nāt\ v. To come forth, issue.

en·fran·chised\in ⁺frăn 'chaizd\ adj. Admitted to political privileges or rights of a citizen.

enig·mat·ic\'ĕ·nĭg ⁺mă·tĭk\ adj. Puzzling.

en·nui\⁺ȯn 'wē\ n. A feeling of listless weariness or discontent resulting from lack of interest.

ep·i·taph\⁺ĕ·pə·tăf\ n. Short piece of writing or an inscription honoring someone dead.

ep·i·thet\⁺ĕ·pə·thĕt\ n. Descriptive word or phrase.

es·cu·lent\⁺ĕs·kyə·lənt\ adj. Edible.

e·the·re·al\ĭ ⁺thĭr·ē·əl\ adj. Not of earth, heavenly.

eu·lo·gize\⁺yū·lə·jaiz\ v. To speak or write in high praise of.

ev·a·nes·cent\'ĕ·və ⁺nē·sənt\ adj. Passing away, liable to pass away like vapor.

ev·i·ta·ble\⁺ĕ·və·tə·bəl\ adj. Avoidable.

ex·em·pla·ry\ĭg ⁺zĕm·plə·rē\ adj. Serving as an example worthy of imitation.

ă bad, ā bake, a father, ĕ sell, ē equal, ai mile, ĭ sit, ŏ cot, ō note, ȯ law, ū boom, ʊ wood, yū you, yʊ fury, aʊ cow, ȯi boy. The schwa is used for both stressed and unstressed sounds: ə mud, word, even; ch chase, itch; sh shell, wish; th path, thin; ᵺ the, either; ŋ wing; w wet, wheat; zh pleasure.

ex·ergue\ĕk 'sərg\ n. Space on a medal usually on the reverse below the central part of the design.

ex·hor·ta·tion\ĕk·sɔr 'tā·shən\ n. A warning plea or sermon, a cautioning.

ex·pe·di·ent\ĕk 'spē·dē·ənt\ adj. Advantageous or convenient to the circumstances or the occasion.

ex·pe·dite\ĕk·spə·dait\ v. To speed up a process.

ex·ten·u·a·tion\ik 'stĕ·nyū 'ā·shən\ n. That which partially excuses or makes something less serious.

ex·tol\ĕk 'stōl\ v. To praise highly.

fa·çade\fə 'sɔd\ n. The front of a building.

fac·ile\'făs·əl\ adj. Easy to influence or persuade.

fag end\'făg ĕnd\ n. The last part.

fain\'fān\ adj. Willing, content, inclined.

fal·set·to\fɔl 'sĕ·tō\ n. An artificially high voice (especially one that extends beyond full voice range).

fash\'făsh\ v. To worry, fret.

fat·u·ous·ly\'fă·chū·əs·lē\ adv. Foolishly, in a silly way.

fer·ret\'fĕ·rət\ v. To search out by careful investigation.

fer·ule\'fĕ·rəl\ n. A flat stick or ruler sometimes used for punishment.

fet·lock\'fĕt 'lŏk\ n. A growth surrounded by a tuft of hair on the back of the leg above the hoof of a horse.

fil·a·ment\'fil·ə·mənt\ n. A very fine thread.

fire·brand\'fair 'brănd\ n. One who stirs up trouble.

flail\'flāl\ v. To beat as if threshing grain by hand.

fledg·ling\'flĕj·liŋ\ n. A young bird.

flor·id\'flŏ·rĭd\ adj. Having a ruddy color, flushed with redness.

for·ay\'fŏ·rā\ n. A raid for plunder.

foun·der\'faun·dər\ v. To stumble and become lame.

fraught\'frɔt\ adj. Filled or loaded down.

frow·sy\'frau·zē\ adj. Having an unkempt or uncared-for appearance.

fru·gal·i·ty\frū 'gă·lə·tē\ n. Thriftiness, wise and sparing use.

funk\'fəŋk\ n. A state of fear.

fur·row\'fər·rō\ v. To make a trench in the earth.

fu·sil·lad\'fyū·zə 'lad\ v. To fire shots in rapid succession.

gall\'gɔl\ v. To vex, irritate.

gal·va·nize\'găl·və·naiz\ v. To rouse to action, startle, excite.

gan·gling\'găŋ·gliŋ\ adj. Awkwardly tall, lanky.

gan·gre·nous\'găŋ·grə·nəs\ adj. Given to rotting of tissue as a result of a failure in blood circulation.

gant\'gɔnt\ adj. *dialect* for *gaunt.* Thin and hollow-eyed (as from hunger or illness).

gar·goyle\'gar·gɔil\ n. A waterspout (usually in the form of a grotesque human or animal figure).

gaunt·let\'gɔnt·lət\ n. A glove with a long extension over the wrist.

ger·mi·nal\'jər·mə·nəl\ adj. In an embryonic stage.

ges·ta·tion\jĕ 'stā·shən\ n. The period of carrying young from conception to birth.

ges·tic·u·late\jĕ 'stĭk·yū 'lāt\ v. To use energetic gestures to help express a meaning.

glut\'glut\ v. To feed or supply to an excess.

green·horn\'grēn·hɔrn\ n. An inexperienced person.

grid·iron\'grĭd·airn\ n. Something covered with a network such as a football field.

grov·el·ing\'gru·və·liŋ\ adj. Hopelessly low condition, humble.

gull·ibil·i·ty\'gə·lə 'bĭ·lə·tē\ n. The quality of being easily deceived.

gy·rat·ing\jai·rā·tiŋ\ adj. Rotating, winding about, oscillating.

ha·bil·i·ment\hə 'bĭ·lə·mənt\ n. Clothing.

ham\'hăm\ n. The back part of the thigh and buttock.

ha·rangue\hə 'răŋ\ n. A lengthy, loud, and passionate speech.

har·row\'hă·rō\ v. To torment, painfully distress.

hoary\'hō·rē\ adj. Gray or white with age.

hock\'hŏk\ n. Joint of a hind leg of a horse (corresponding to the ankle of a man).

hom·i·ly\'hŏ·mə·lē\ n. A sermon, moral lecture.

hy·poth·e·sis\hai 'pŏ·thə·sis\ n. An unproven conclusion drawn from known facts and used as basis for reasoning.

ilk\ilk\ adj. Of that kind or sort.

im·med·i·ca·ble\ĭ 'mĕ·dĭ·kə·bəl\ adj. Incurable.

im·pal·pa·ble\ĭm 'păl·pə·bəl\ adj. Incapable of being perceived by the senses.

im·pe·ri·ous\ĭm 'pī·rē·əs\ adj. Commanding or domineering attitude.

im·per·ti·nent\ĭm 'pərt·n·ənt\ adj. Irrelevant, pointless, inappropriate.

im·per·vi·ous\ĭm 'pər·vē·əs\ adj. Incapable of being passed through, impenetrable.

im·pre·ca·tion\'ĭm·prə 'kā·shən\ n. A curse.

im·pu·ni·ty\ĭm 'pyū·nə·tē\ n. Freedom from punishment.

in·can·ta·tion\'ĭn 'kăn 'tā·shən\ n. The use of spells and words chanted as part of a ritual of magic.

in·con·gru·ous·ly\ĭn 'kŏŋ·grū·əs·lē\ adv. On a manner inconsistent with what is reasonable or proper.

in·cor·ri·gi·ble\ĭn 'kŏ·rə·jə·bəl\ n. Incapable of being changed or corrected.

in·cre·du·li·ty\'ĭn·krə 'dū·lə·tē\ n. State of disbelief, unwillingness to believe.

in·cum·bent\ĭn 'kŭm·bənt\ adj. Resting or pressing with its weight on something.

in·del·i·ble\ĭn 'dĕl·ə·bəl\ adj. Cannot be erased, permanent.

in·dem·ni·ty\ĭn 'dĕm·nə·tē\ n. That which is given as compensation for a loss or damage.

in·den·ture\ĭn 'dĕn·chər\ v. To bind by contract to the services of another.

in·dom·i·ta·ble\ĭn 'dŏ·mə·tə·bəl\ adj. Not easily defeated, unconquerable.

in·ex·o·ra·ble\ĭn 'ĕk·sər·ə·bəl\ adj. Cannot be influenced by persuasion, inflexible, relentless.

in·fal·li·bly\ĭn 'fă·lə·blē\ adv. Unfailingly.

in·gen·ious\ĭn ᵃjēn·yəs\ adj. Having inventive ability, cleverly skillful.

in·gen·u·ous\ĭn ᵃjēn·yū·əs\ adj. Straightforward, simple.

in·gres·sion\ĭn ᵃgrĕ·shən\ n. Act of going in.

in·im·i·ta·ble\ĭn ᵃĭm·ə·tə·bəl\ adj. Defying imitation, matchless.

in·noc·u·ous\ĭ ᵃnŏ·kyə·wəs\ adj. Not likely to give offense.

in·sa·tiate\ĭn ᵃsā·sh(ē)ət\ adj. Incapable of being satisfied.

in·scru·ta·ble\ĭn ᵃskrū·tə·bəl\ adj. Cannot readily be understood or searched.

in·sig·ni·a\ĭn ᵃsĭg·nē·ə\ n. Badges, emblems, or other distinguishing marks.

in·su·lar·i·ty\'ĭn·sə ᵃlər·ə·tē\ n. Narrow-mindedness, prejudice.

in·tan·gi·ble\ĭn ᵃtăn·jə·bəl\ adj. 1. Not touchable. 2. Realized by the mind in a vague and imprecise way.

in·ter·po·si·tion\'ĭn·tər·pə ᵃzĭsh·ən\ n. An interruption in a conversation or debate.

in·tran·si·gent\ĭn ᵃtrăn·sə·jənt\ n. Uncompromising.

in·un·da·tion\'ĭn·ən ᵃdā·shən\ n. State of being covered by overflowing, flood.

i·ras·ci·ble\ĭ ᵃrăs·ə·bəl\ adj. Easily angered, quick tempered.

ir·ra·di·a·tion\ĭr ᵃād·ē ᵃə·shən\ n. Giving off radiant energy (such as heat and light).

ir·rev·o·ca·ble\ĭ ᵃrĕv·ə·kə·bəl\ adj. Not to be recalled or withdrawn.

jack ᵃjăk\ n. 1. A man employed to do odd jobs, a servant. 2. Slang for money.

jal·ap\ᵃja·ləp\ n. Dried root of a plant used as a purgative.

jaun·dice\ᵃjŏn·dĭs\ v. To affect with a diseased condition of the liver, marked by yellowness of skin and eyeballs.

jet·ti·son\ᵃjĕ·tə·sən\ n. The act of dropping a cargo to lighten load in time of distress.

jug·ger·naut\ᵃjə·gər 'nŏt\ n. A massive, relentless force or object that crushes everything in its path.

lac·te·al\ᵃlăk·tē·əl\ adj. Pertaining to milk.

lan·guor\ᵃlăŋ·gər\ n. Lack of energy or enthusiasm.

leech\lēch\ n. A person who clings to another for gain, parasite.

leer·ing\ᵃlĭ·rĭŋ\ adj. Having a knowing, malicious expression.

leg·a·cy\ᵃlĕg·ə·sē\ n. Anything left to someone by request or by a will.

le·o·nine\ᵃlē·ə·nain\ adj. Characteristic of a lion.

leth·ar·gy\ᵃlĕ·thər·jē\ n. A state of sluggish inactivity, indifference.

le·vant\lə ᵃvănt\ n. A kind of Morocco leather with an irregularly grained surface.

lev·i·ty\ᵃlĕ·və·tē\ n. An act characterized by lack of seriousness, humor.

lief\lēf\ adv. Willingly, readily.

lin·tel\ᵃlĭn·təl\ n. A horizontal part spanning the opening of a door or window.

liv·id\ᵃlĭ·vĭd\ adj. 1. Black and blue as if bruised. 2. Pale, ashen.

lo·qua·cious\lō ᵃkwā·shəs\ adj. Given to excessive talking.

low\ᵃlō\ v. To call, summon, moo.

lu·gu·bri·ous\lu ᵃgū·brē·əs\ adj. Very mournful (especially in an exaggerated manner exciting ridicule).

lum·ber\ᵃlʊm·bər\ v. To move in a heavy or clumsy manner.

lu·mi·nes·cent\'lū·mə ᵃnĕ·sənt\ adj. Characterized by the giving off of light.

lus·tral\ᵃləs·trəl\ adj. Pertaining to something used in purification.

lus·trum\ᵃləs·trəm\ n. A period of five years.

mal·e·dic·tion\'măl·ə ᵃdĭk·shən\ n. A curse.

ma·lef·ic\mə ᵃlĕ·fĭk\ adj. Causing evil or disaster.

maned\ᵃmānd or poetical ᵃmān·əd\ adj. Having long heavy hair about the neck.

man·i·fold\ᵃmă·nə ᵃfōld\ adj. Having many and varied forms.

mar·tial\ᵃmar·shəl\ adj. Of or suitable for war.

maud·lin\ᵃmɔd·lən\ adj. Being emotionally silly.

mead\mēd\ n. Meadow.

meta·phys·i·cal\'mĕ·tə ᵃfĭ·zĭ·kəl\ adj. Marked by a highly complex subtlety of thought and expression.

me·tem·psy·cho·sis\mə 'tĕm·sĭ ᵃkō·səs\ n. The passing of the soul after death into another body (either human or animal).

mire\ᵃmair\ n. Wet, soggy earth; mud.

mit·i·gate\ᵃmĭt·ə·gāt\ v. To make or become milder or less severe.

mo·les·ta·tion\mō ᵃlĕs ᵃtā·shən\ n. An annoyance, state of being annoyed or disturbed.

mon·ger\ᵃməŋ·gər\ n. One engaged in dealing or trading.

mo·ni·tion\mō ᵃnĭ·shən\ n. A warning (possibly of impending danger).

mon·o·lith\ᵃmō·nə·lĭth\ n. A single block of stone (usually very large).

mo·no·po·ly\mə ᵃnŏ·pə·lē\ n. Exclusive ownership or possession of something by one person or one group.

mon·tage\mŏn ᵃtɔzh\ n. A rapid sequence of images to show a group of ideas.

mor·ti·fi·ca·tion\'mɔr·tə·fə ᵃkā·shən\ n. A feeling of humiliation or shame.

mor·tise\ᵃmɔr·təs\ v. To fasten securely.

muck\ᵃmək\ n. Moist dung mixed with decomposed vegetable matter.

mus·lin\ᵃmŭz·lĭn\ n. Fine cotton cloths of plain weave.

ă bad, ā bake, a father, ĕ sell, ē equal, ai mile, ĭ sit, ŏ cot, ō note, ɔ law, ū boom, ʊ wood, yū you, yʊ fury, aʊ cow, ɔi boy. The schwa is used for both stressed and unstressed sounds: ə mud, word, even; ch chase, itch; sh shell, wish; th path, thin; th the, either; ŋ wing; w wet, wheat; zh pleasure.

na·ive·té\nə ᵃē·və ᵃtā\ n. The state or quality of having a simple nature, lacking wordly experience.

na·tal\nāt·l\ adj. Pertaining to time of birth.

ne·phri·tis\nĭ ᵃfrai·tĭs\ n. Inflammation of the kidneys.

neu·ri·tis\nu ᵃrai·tĭs\ n. Inflammation of a nerve.

nig·gling\nĭg·liŋ\ adj. Spending too much effort on minor detail, finding fault in a petty way.

noc·turne\nŏk·tərn\ n. A night scene in painting.

nov·ice\nŏ·vəs\ n. A beginner.

nox·ious\nŏk·shəs\ adj. Tending to cause injury to health or morals.

oblate\ŏb ᵃlāt\ adj. The state of being flattened at the poles.

oblique·ly\ō ᵃblēk·lē or ə ᵃblēk·lē\ adv. Indirectly or without straightforwardness in meaning.

ob·lo·quy\ŏb·lə·kwē\ adj. Abusive language.

ob·trude\əb ᵃtrūd\ v. To force oneself upon another.

oc·u·lar\ŏ·kyə·lər\ adj. Of or related to the eye or sight.

or·a·cle\'ɔ·rə·kəl\ n. A person who gives wise opinions or reveals hidden knowledge.

os·ten·si·ble\ŏs ᵃtĕn·sə·bəl\ adj. Offered as real or genuine.

os·ten·ta·tion\'ɔ·stən ᵃtā·shən\ n. Excessive display.

os·tra·cism\ŏs·trə ᵃsĭ·zəm\ n. Temporary banishment.

pa·lav·er\pə ᵃlă·vər\ v. To talk idly.

pal·lid\ᵃpă·ləd\ adj. Lacking color, pale.

pan·der·er\păn·də·rər\ n. Someone who exploits the weaknesses of others.

pan·o·ply\pă·nə·plē\ n. The complete covering or armor of a warrior.

par·a·ble\ᵃpăr·ə·bəl\ n. A short simple story with a moral lesson.

par·a·dox\ᵃpăr·ə·dŏks\ n. A statement seemingly absurd or self-contradictory.

par·ox·ysm\ᵃpă·rək ᵃsĭ·zəm\ n. A sudden, violent emotion or action.

patho·log·i·cal\'pă·thə ᵃlŏ·jĭ·kəl\ adj. Caused by disease.

pa·tron·age\ᵃpă·trə·nĭj or ᵃpā·trə·nĭj\ n. Making a display of courtesy with an air of superiority toward inferiors.

pa·vil·ion\pə ᵃvĭl·yən\ n. A building or part of a building used for exhibits or entertainment.

pelf\ᵃpĕlf\ n. Money (especially if dishonestly acquired).

per·ad·ven·ture\ᵃpər·əd 'vĕn·chər\ adv. Perhaps, possibly.

per·am·bu·la·tion\pər 'ăm·byə ᵃlā·shən\ n. The act of walking about.

per·fid·i·ous\'pər ᵃfĭ·dē·əs\ adj. Characterized by disloyalty or faithlessness.

per·func·to·ry\pər ᵃfəŋ·tə·rē\ adj. Characterized by a routine or mechanical performance.

peri·he·lion\'pĕ·rə ᵃhēl·yən\ n. The point in the path of a planet that is nearest the sun.

pe·riph·er·al\pə ᵃrĭf·rəl\ adj. Relating to an area lying away from center.

per·ti·nac·i·ty\'pər·tə ᵃnă·sə·tē\ n. The quality of adhering without yielding to a purpose.

per·tur·ba·tion\'pər·tər ᵃbā·shən\ n. Disturbance, alarm, agitation.

phleg·mat·ic\flĕg ᵃmă·tĭk\ adj. Having a slow, stolid temperament.

phos·pho·res·cence\'fŏs·fə ᵃrĕ·səns\ n. Light that continues after possible source of energy has stopped.

phys·i·ol·o·gy\'fĭ·zē ᵃŏl·ə·jē\ n. The branch of biology that treats processes of living matter.

pi·pet\pai ᵃpĕt\ v. To draw liquid by suction through a glass tube and hold it by closing the upper end.

plau·si·bil·i·ty\'plɔ·zə ᵃbĭl·ə·tē\ n. An acceptable situation or quality.

ply\plai\ v. To go or travel regularly.

pol·troon\pŏl ᵃtrūn\ n. A mean, spiritless coward.

poly·chrome\'pŏ·lĭ ᵃkrōm\ adj. Made with several colors.

pom·mel\pə·məl\ n. The protruding portion at the front end and top of a saddle.

pre·co·cious\prĭ ᵃkō·shəs\ adj. Marked by exceptional development at an unusually early age.

pre·des·ti·na·tion\prē 'dĕs·tə ᵃnā·shən\ n. The belief that all things are decided beforehand by God.

pre·mo·ni·tion\'prē·mə ᵃnĭsh·ən or prē·mə ᵃnĭsh·ən\ n. A warning or feeling of something about to occur.

pre·mon·i·tory\prē ᵃmɔ·nə ᵃtō·rē\ adj. Giving previous warning.

pre·sen·ti·ment\prĭ ᵃzĕn·tə·mənt\ n. A feeling that something will happen or is about to take place.

prim·er\ᵃprĭm·ər\ n. A first book in reading.

prof·li·ga·cy\ᵃprŏf·lə·gə·cē\ n. The state of being insensible to principle, virtue, or decency.

prom·on·to·ry\ᵃprŏ·mən ᵃtō·rē\ n. A high point of land or rock projecting into a body of water.

pro·mul·ga·tion\'prŏ·məl ᵃgā·shən\ n. A proposed law, state of being made public, proclamation.

pro·pi·tia·to·ry\prō ᵃpĭsh·ə ᵃtō·rē\ adj. Relating to making favorable, appeasing.

pros·e·lyte\ᵃprŏ·sə·lait\ n. One who has been brought over to any belief, a convert.

prov·en·der\ᵃprŏ·vən·dər\ n. Dry food for domestic animals.

psy·cho·so·mat·ic\'sai·kō·sə ᵃmă·tĭk or 'sai·kə·sə ᵃmă·tĭk\ adj. Relating to the interrelationship of mind and body in causing disease.

pun·cheon\ᵃpən·chən\ n. A split or heavy log with a smoothed face.

pun·dit\ᵃpən·dət\ n. A learned man.

purl\pərl\ v. To move in ripples or with a murmuring sound.

quaff\ᵃkwŏf\ v. To drink deeply and with great relish.

quar·to\ᵃkwɔr·tō\ n. A book or pamphlet having pages the size of a fourth of a sheet.

rail·lery\ᵃrā·lə·rē\ n. Mocking, imitating in order to make fun of, good-natured ridicule.

ran·cor\ᵃrăŋ·kər\ n. Intense brooding over wrong, bitterness.

ra·pa·cious\rə ᵃpā·shəs\ adj. Grasping, greedy.

re·cal·ci·trant\rĭ ᵃkăl·sə·trənt\ adj. Stubbornly disobedient, rebellious.

rec·i·ta·tive\\'rĕ·sə·ta ˄tĭv\\ n. 1. A narrative of facts and details. 2. Language in rhythm of ordinary speech, but set to music.

re·doubt·a·ble\\rĭ ˄dau·tə·bəl\\ adj. Deserving of respect, fearsome, dreadful.

re·it·er·a·tion\\'rē·ĭ·tə ˄rā·shən\\ n. The act of repeating or doing something again.

re·ju·ve·nes·cent\\rĭ 'jū·və ˄nĕ·sənt\\ adj. Pertaining to the renewal of youth.

rem·i·nis·cence\\'rĕ·mə ˄nĭ·sənts\\ n. Recollection of some previous experience.

re·mon·strance\\rĭ ˄mŏn·strəns\\ n. The act of pleading in protest or opposition.

re·mu·ner·a·tion\\rĭ 'myū·nə ˄rā·shən\\ n. Equal payment for services rendered.

ren·dez·vous\\'ran·dā 'vū\\ n. A place for a meeting or gathering.

re·plete\\rĭ ˄plēt\\ adj. Abundantly supplied or provided for.

res·o·nance\\rĕ·zə·nəns\\ n. State or quality of sending back or prolonging sound.

re·spite\\rĕs·pĭt\\ n. A temporary suspension of labor or effort, a time for rest.

ret·i·nue\\'rĕ·tə 'nyū\\ n. Group of followers.

ret·ri·bu·tion\\'rĕt·rə ˄byū·shən\\ n. A deserved punishment.

re·vamp\\rē ˄vămp\\ v. To make over, reorganize, reconstruct.

re·vile\\rĭ ˄vail\\ v. To use abusive language, slander or curse someone.

roil\\˄rɔil\\ v. To make muddy or turbid.

ruck\\˄rək\\ n. A jumbled mass.

sa·ga·cious\\sə ˄gä·shəs\\ adj. Perceptive, shrewd.

sal·low\\˄să 'lō\\ adj. A grayish greenish yellow color.

sar·don·ic\\sŏr ˄dŏ·nĭk\\ adj. Marked by cynicism and bitterness.

scup·per·nong\\'skə·pər·nɔŋ\\ n. A variety of grapes cultivated in the United States.

scut\\˄skət\\ n. A short erect tail (as of a rabbit).

sec·tar·i·an\\sĕk ˄tĕr·ē·ən\\ adj. Characteristic of one sect only, strongly prejudiced.

sem·blance\\˄sĕm·bləns\\ n. The look or appearance of something else, resemblance.

se·pal\\˄sē·pəl\\ n. One of the leaves of the leafy part of a flower.

sere\\˄sĭr\\ adj. Withered, dried up.

ser·vi·tor\\˄sər·və·tər\\ n. A male servant.

sib·i·lant\\˄sĭ·bə·lənt\\ adj. Having or producing a hissing sound.

sil·i·cate\\˄sĭ·lə·kāt or ˄sĭ·lə·kĭt\\ n. A salt compound of silica and water.

skit·ter\\˄skĭ·tər\\ v. To glide lightly along, touching the surface at intervals.

smite\\˄smait\\ v. To attack or afflict suddenly and injuriously.

smut\\˄smət\\ v. To taint, blacken, stain.

snaf·fle\\˄snă·fəl\\ n. A simple jointed bit for a bridle.

sough·ing·ly\\˄sau·ŋ·lē\\ adv. With a rustling or murmuring sound.

spec·tre\\˄spĕk·tər\\ n. A ghost, apparition.

spit\\˄spĭt\\ n. A slender pointed rod for holding meat over a fire.

stip·u·la·tion\\'stĭp·yə ˄lā·shən\\ n. Point or condition agreed upon.

sto·lid·i·ty\\stŏ ˄lĭ·də·tē\\ n. The quality of having little or no sensibility.

strin·gen·cy\\˄strĭn·jən·sē\\ n. Strictness, severity.

strop\\strŏp\\ n. A strip of leather for sharpening a straight razor.

stub·ble\\˄stə·bəl\\ n. Grasses remaining growing after a harvest.

stul·ti·fy\\˄stul·tə·fai\\ v. To cause to appear absurd, allege to be of unsound mind.

sub·li·mate\\˄səb·lə·māt\\ v. To convert energy of something primitive in aim into something more socially and culturally acceptable.

sub·lu·na·ry\\˄səb·lū·nə·rē\\ adj. Situated beneath the moon.

suf·fu·sion\\sə ˄fyū·zhən\\ n. The act of overspreading as with color or light.

sul·ly\\˄sə·lē\\ v. To soil, tarnish.

su·per·cil·i·ous\\'sū·pər ˄sĭ·lē·əs\\ adj. Haughty, proud, arrogant.

su·per·erog·a·to·ry\\'sū·pə·rə ˄rŏ·gə·tō·rē\\ adj. Pertaining to excess of demands or requirements.

su·per·nal\\su ˄pər·nəl\\ adj. Being or coming from the heavens.

su·per·nu·mer·ar·y\\'sū·pər ˄nū·mə·rē·rē\\ n. A performer who appears in a scene (especially a mob scene) without a speaking part.

sur·feit\\˄sər·fət\\ v. To indulge in or partake of to an excess.

tab·leau\\˄tăb·lō\\ n. A striking dramatic scene done as if it were a picture or drawing.

tac·i·turn\\˄tă·sə·tərn\\ adj. Not inclined by temperament to talk.

tan·gent\\˄tăn·jənt\\ adj. Breaking off suddenly from a line of action or train of thought to pursue another course.

te·mer·i·ty\\tə ˄mĕr·ə·tē\\ n. Reckless boldness, rashness.

tem·per·ance\\˄tĕm·pə·rəns\\ n. The practice of not consuming alcohol.

ten·on\\˄tē·nən\\ v. To insert in a socket to form a joint.

te·o·cal·li\\'tē·ə ˄kə·lē\\ n. A mound upon which an ancient temple was built.

ter·ma·gant\\˄tər·mə·gənt\\ n. A nagging, overbearing woman.

the·oc·ra·cy\\thē ˄ŏk·rə·sē\\ n. A government of a state which recognizes a god or God as their ruler.

tor·por\\˄tɔr·pər\\ n. A temporary loss of all or part of the power of sensation or motion.

ă bad, ā bake, a father, ĕ sell, ē equal, ai mile, ĭ sit, ŏ cot, ō note, ɔ law, ū boom, ʊ wood, yū you, yʊ fury, aʊ cow, ɔi boy. The schwa is used for both stressed and unstressed sounds: ə mud, word, even; ch chase, itch; sh shell, wish; th path, thin; th the, either; ŋ wing; w wet, wheat; zh pleasure.

tra·jec·to·ry\trə ▴jĕk·tə·rē\ n. The curve that a rocket or other body follows in space after being fired.

tran·scen·dent\'trăn ▴sən·dənt\ adj. Extending beyond the limits of ordinary experience.

trem·u·lous\▴trĕ·myə·ləs\ adj. Affected by trembling.

truc·u·lent·ly\▴trŭk·yū·lənt·lē\ adv. In a fierce, cruel, or savage manner.

tu·mu·lus\▴tūm·yū·lus\ n. An artificial mound, a burial mound.

tur·pi·tude\▴tər·pə 'tyūd\ n. By nature lacking moral values, a depraved condition.

tu·te·lage\▴tū·tə·lĭj\ n. Instruction.

two-score\tū·skōr\ n. Forty people or objects.

um·bil·i·cal\'əm ▴bĭ·lĭ·kəl\ n. A servicing cable that is detached from a rocket at launching.

unc·tion\▴əŋk·shən\ n. A state of being affected by deep religious or spiritual fervor.

un·ob·tru·sive\ən·əb ▴trū·sĭv\ adj. Not forcing oneself or one's opinions upon another without a request, not aggressive.

un·or·tho·dox\ən ▴ōr·thə 'dŏks\ adj. Not conforming to established doctrine in religion.

un·wont·ed\ən ▴wɔn·tĭd\ adj. Pertaining to something unusual or out of the ordinary.

ur·chin\▴ər·chĭn\ n. A poor, ragged child.

util·i·tar·i·an\yū 'tĭ·lə ▴tĕ·rē·ən\ adj. Pertaining to something useful or designed to be used.

va·ga·ry\▴vā·gə·rē\ n. An eccentric, unpredictable action.

var·i·e·gat·ed\▴vă·rē·ə 'gā·təd\ adj. Varied in colors.

ve·ra·cious\və ▴rā·shəs\ adj. Truthful, habitually speaking the truth.

ver·dant\▴vər·dənt\ adj. Green in color.

ver·i·est\▴vĕ·rē·əst\ adj. Absolute, actual.

ver·nal\▴vər·nəl\ adj. Appearing in the spring.

ves·ti·gi·al\vĕs ▴tĭ·jē·əl\ adj. Of the nature of a visible trace of something gone.

vice·roy\▴vais·rɔi\ n. A representative, a governor who represents a king or sovereign.

vict·ual\▴vĭt·əl\ v. To supply with food.

vil·i·fy\▴vĭ·lə·fai\ v. To abuse with language, slander.

vit·ri·ol\▴vĭ·trē·əl\ n. Sulfuric acid.

vo·lup·tuous\və ▴lup·chū·əs\ adj. Relating to satisfaction of the physical desires and sensual pleasures.

vor·tex\▴vōr·tĕks\ n. State of affairs that is similar to a whirlwind or whirlpool.

vo·tive\▴vō·tĭv\ adj. Offered in devotion or in fulfillment of a vow.

wily\▴wai·lē\ adj. Crafty, sly.

wont\▴wɔnt\ adj. Doing habitually, accustomed to.

wot \▴wɔt\ v. To know.

wry\▴rai\ adj. 1. Cleverly or grimly humorous. 2. Twisted.

General Index

Literary Types Index

Autobiography

Dramas

Essays—Biographical and Historical

Essays—Formal

Essays—Informal

Novels

Poetry—Light Verse

Poetry—Lyric

Poetry—Narrative

Short Stories

Literary Terms Index

Fine Art Index

Illustration Sources

8 9 10 KPKP 87 86